New Complete Book of NEEDLECRAFT

Good Housekeeping

New Complete Book of NEEDLECRAFT

by Vera P. Guild

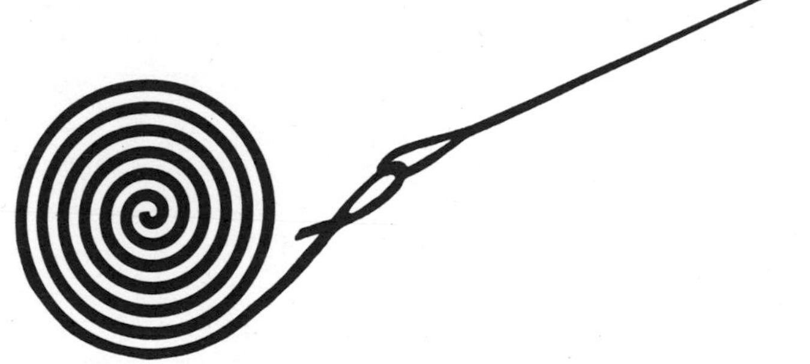

Good Housekeeping Books New York

GOOD HOUSEKEEPING BOOKS

Editor MINA WHITE MULVEY
Art Director WILLIAM LEFT
Senior Editor PATRICIA DEMPSEY
Copy Editor JUANITA G. CHAUDHRY
Art Editor for *Needlecraft* LYNN THOMPSON

FOR GOOD HOUSEKEEPING MAGAZINE

Editor WADE H. NICHOLS
Executive Editor JOHN B. DANBY
Managing Editor BENSON SRERE
Art Director BERNARD SPRINGSTEEL
Director, The Institute WILLIE MAE ROGERS
Publisher RAYMOND J. PETERSEN

PUBLISHED BY THE HEARST CORPORATION

President RICHARD E. BERLIN
President, Magazine Division RICHARD E. DEEMS
Executive Vice-President, Magazines JOHN R. MILLER
Vice-President, Magazines WILLIAM S. CAMPBELL
Vice-President-Director, Book Division JAMES B. FISHER
Production Manager, Book Division HENRY L. WENZ

 ISBN 0–87851–002–8. Library of Congress Catalog Card Number 76–137519.

Acknowledgments

For their gracious co-operation and assistance in the preparation of the technical material in this book, grateful acknowledgment is made to the following authorities in the sewing and allied fields: Coats and Clark, Inc.; Lily Mills; American Thread Co.; Simplicity Pattern Co.; Singer Sewing Machine Co.; Necchi Sewing Machine Sales Co.; Pfaff Sewing Machine Co.; Paragon Art and Linen Co.; Emile Bernat and Sons; Columbia-Minerva Corp.; Bernhard Ulmann Co.; Consolidated Trimming Corp.; Kate's Trade Shop; William E. Wright & Sons; Reynolds Yarn; Spinnerin Yarn Co., Inc.; Airloom Needlework Guild, Inc.

Special thanks are offered to Janette Householder, designer of the hooked rug pattern on page 229; to Berta Fry, weaving consultant, for editorial assistance; to Mildred Spaeth, weaving instructor, for the loan of handwoven articles; and to Ingrid Nygards-Kers, weaving consultant, for the loan of handwoven tapestries. Thanks are also due to Marcia Sarowitz for her careful attention to the physical appearance of the book.

V.P.G

Contents

COLOR PLATES

New Complete Book of NEEDLECRAFT

Chapter 1

Sewing

Almost all women do some kind of sewing. They sew for the most part because they like to. They have found that it is fun and that it satisfies the urge to create. Furthermore there are many advantages in making your own clothes: they fit better, they are styled for your figure, and you can use the fabric of your choice. And who can resist the lovely fabrics offered to the home sewer today? In addition to all of this you can save money, or for the same money you can have more clothes.

Even if you prefer buying your own and your children's clothes it is sometimes great fun to make something for someone else, an appropriate gift for a friend. And many women who have never sewed in their lives feel the urge to do so when the first grandchild comes along.

Sewing is a satisfying occupation and makes a wonderful hobby. The basic techniques are given here to start you on your way or to serve as a reference when you come up against a problem.

IN-A-WALL SEWING ROOM

You may be fortunate enough to have a room to devote exclusively to sewing. However, with today's limited living space you may have only a section of a wall you can utilize for it.

Actually a fully equipped sewing room can be planned in a rather small space as shown on Color Plate 1. This is an In-a-Wall Sewing Room built in the *Good Housekeeping* Sewing Center.

On the upper shelves you will see storage boxes for fabrics. These are, in reality, blanket boxes which come ready-covered in attractive glazed chintz. The front panels drop down, which makes it easy to get at the fabrics. One of the boxes can be reserved for work-in-process.

Shoe storage boxes and transparent plastic refrigerator boxes serve as containers for all kinds of notions, such as snaps, buttons, elastic, zippers, etc.

The sewing machine rests on a pull-out table which is on casters and slides in and out easily. A swivel lamp attached to the wall casts a direct light on your sewing.

The two drawers below can be used for storage of attachments, etc., or for extra thread. There is also a roomy storage cabinet beneath the sewing machine large enough to hold a mending basket or other sewing equipment.

A scissors-and-spool board pulls out at the right of the sewing machine. This can hold thread, scissors and pinking shears, bobbins, pin cushion, gauges, and all the small things needed as you work at the machine.

In the large space at the right there is room to hang partly finished garments on an adjustable rod.

The folding doors have two full-length

mirrors on the inside. When the mirrors are set at an angle they will give you front, side, and rear views of your garment. With the doors shut, the unit is closed off out of sight.

The plans for this unit are available. Send 35 cents for In-a-Wall Sewing Room, Good Housekeeping Bulletin Service, 959 Eighth Avenue, New York, New York 10019.

SEWING EQUIPMENT

Start with the Essentials

Sewing Machine. Improvements are continually being made on sewing machines. Investigate thoroughly a number of good machines before you buy, and purchase one that suits your needs.

You may want only a simple straight stitching model on which you will be able to make clothing, curtains, or any ordinary sewing project. Buttonhole and zigzag attachments are available for straight-stitching models. You may prefer a zigzag machine, which, in addition to straight stitching, will overcast seams, apply lace and appliqué, and so on. The third choice is a zigzag machine which also does decorative stitching. You will also want to choose between portable and cabinet machines, depending upon available space. But whatever type you buy, insist upon a thorough demonstration before purchasing. Study the instruction leaflet before using your machine, and then keep it clean and in good running order.

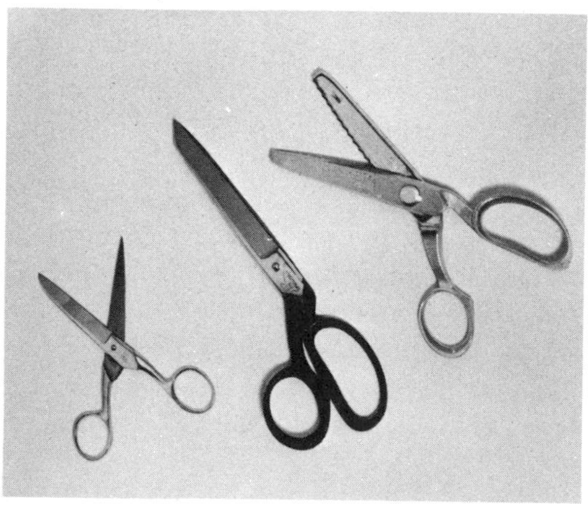

Scissors and Shears. Bent-handle dressmaking shears, 7″ to 8″ long, and of good quality steel for cutting out garments, are a necessity. Keep them for this purpose only. The bent handles let the blade rest flat on the table while cutting. Scissors, 4″ to 6″ long, with ring handles are needed for lighter work such as trimming and clipping. Pinking shears are useful for finishing seams. Buy all of high-grade steel, and give them good care. Apply a drop of oil at the screw occasionally, and wipe off the excess.

Needles. Save time by keeping assorted sizes of both hand and machine needles on hand. Hand needles come in several types: Sharps, Betweens, and Crewel. Sharps are of medium length and are most commonly used. Betweens are extra short and are especially good for doing fine stitching on heavy fabric. Crewel or embroidery needles have large eyes and can also be used for regular sewing.

Many other kinds of needles are available for various purposes: leather (a three-sided needle), curved upholstery and mattress, chenille (large eye and blunt point), darners, milliners, beading, canvas, tapestry, bodkins, and others sold at notions counters. Select a needle which will make an opening large enough for the thread to pass through easily. An emery bag for cleaning rusty needles is useful.

Thread. Have available an assortment of threads in colors and black and white. There is a thread for every purpose. For hand or machine sewing on fine or sheer fabric, use a fine needle and thread; for medium-weight fabrics, use a medium-sized needle, and so on.

Also for fine fabrics use more stitches to the inch in both hand and machine sewing. Use cotton thread (plain or mercerized) on cotton fabrics. Mercerized cotton may also be used on linen, silk, wool, and synthetics. Use silk thread on silk, wool, and possibly synthetics. Use silk buttonhole twist for buttons, buttonholes, and fastenings. There are new synthetic threads which are suitable for synthetic fabrics. Use care in pressing. Button-and-carpet thread is used for its special purposes. Since it works up lighter, use thread one shade darker than the fabric. A contrasting color is good for basting.

A single thread 18″ or 20″ in length is used for almost all kinds of hand sewing. For easier threading, cut the thread coming from the spool on a slant, and use this end to thread the needle. Pull it through and knot this end. See diagrams on page 16 for How to Make a Knot.

Iron and Ironing Board. An electric iron with heat control for various fibers and fabrics is best. Use the lowest setting for synthetics and the highest for linen. An iron should weigh from 3 to 4 pounds—heavier ones are for tailoring. When buying, try several to find the iron most suited to your hand.

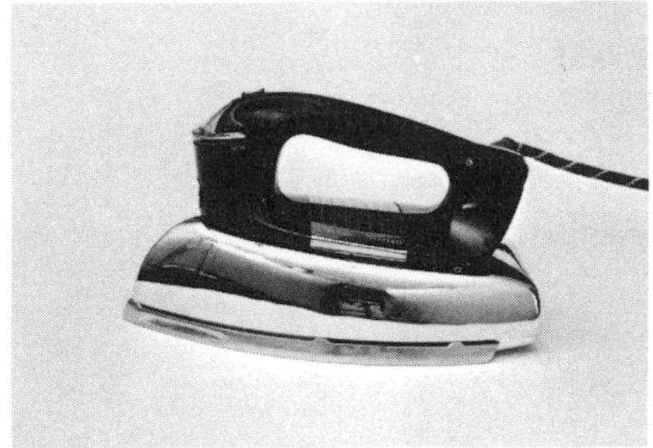

Steam irons may also fit your needs.

An ironing board should be adjustable so one can sit or stand while working. Padding and two lint-free covers (for changing) are needed.

Rulers and Yard Stick. A 6″ ruler, a 12″ or 18″ ruler, and a yard stick are all very much needed.

Tape Measure. Select a 60″ length of sturdy type. For the sake of accuracy, replace when worn.

Tailor's Chalk. Keep both light and dark non-greasy chalk for marking various colored fabrics.

Press Cloths. You can use an old sheet or a length of cotton drill. It should be free of starch and lint. Chemically treated cloths and a new see-through cloth are also available. You will need both heavy and light weight press cloths. Cheese cloth is very useful. It is lintless and can be folded into any thickness. Several layers dampened are good for steaming.

Pins. Use good quality nonrust dressmaker pins and a pin cushion.

Thimble. This should comfortably fit the middle finger. Never try to sew without a thimble.

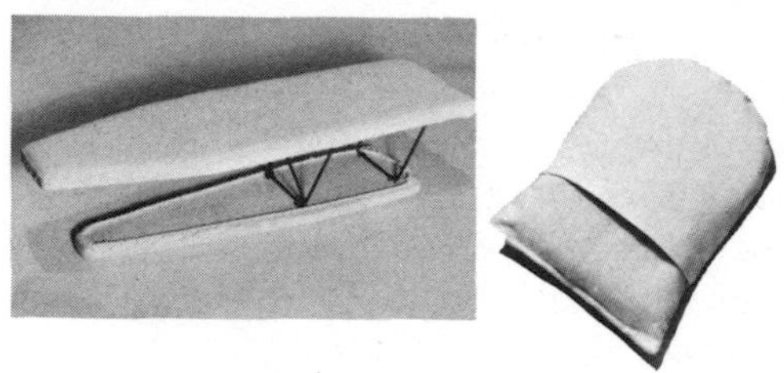

Additional Equipment to Aid You

Sleeve board, well padded, or a seam roll. This can be made by covering a tightly rolled magazine.
Tailor's ham, press mitt, wooden clapper, and point presser (see section on pressing)
Velvet board (a stiff but pliable "board" covered with needles over which velvet can be pressed) or a piece of plush 6″ by 12″
Dressmaker's carbon paper, light and dark colors
Tracing wheel
Loop turner
Small sharp awl
Bodkin
Ripper
Skirt marker
Cutting table
Full-length mirror
Dress form

Inquire at notions counters for the above, and look occasionally thereafter for new and useful sewing aids which appear from time to time.

IF YOU ARE A BEGINNER

It *is* possible to *jump right in* and make something to wear. If you have never done much sewing and would like to learn to make your own clothes, *then learn by doing.* For example you might try a simple dress or skirt. This is possible *if you can follow directions.* There are many industries in existence today because women like to sew, and they are doing everything in their power to help make sewing easy. This includes making available all kinds of sewing aids, such as sewing machines which do everything but talk, notions and gadgets to save time, thread, zippers, beautiful fabrics, and patterns for things to make for the whole family. Many of these same companies distribute instruction leaflets designed to teach even the least experienced; magazines do their share to assist and inspire; and the patterns themselves include easy to follow directions with step-by-step diagrams to show you the way.

Assuming that you have a *place to sew* and have assembled at least a minimum of equipment necessary for this fascinating craft, here is a list of suggestions offered to help you on your way.

Step-by-Step Procedure

1. Take these measurements of your figure, jot them down, and take them with you to the store.

a. Bust, over the fullest part—do not let tape measure drop at the back.

b. Hips, over the largest part, which is usually about 7″ below the waist.

c. Waist, around smallest part of the waistline.

d. Length of waist at center back.

2. Find out the width of the fabric you want, and select one that is easy to handle. Do not start with sheer, slippery or plaid fabrics, or ones with a nap or pile such as velvet or corduroy.

3. Select your pattern. Choose a simple design. To choose your correct pattern size you will first have to forget all about your ready-to-wear size. It has no meaning here—this is a different world. Study the measurement charts in the front (or back) of the pattern book and decide (according to your measurements) which *type* you are—misses, women's, junior (a size, not an age), half-size, etc. Then look for a pattern under that category. Buy a dress or blouse pattern by bust measurement, with this exception: when buying a dress pattern, if your hip measurement is unusually large and out of proportion to the bust, then buy according to hip measurement. Since this may necessitate a great deal of alteration on the blouse pattern, it might pay to buy two patterns, one for bust measurement and one for hip. Buy skirt patterns by waist measure. Always buy the pattern size nearest your actual measurements.

4. Look on the pattern envelope to determine how much fabric to buy for your size in the width fabric you have selected.

5. Ask if the fabric has been preshrunk. If not, buy a few inches more than the pattern calls for. Also learn the fiber content of the fabric. Is it all wool, silk, cotton, linen (natural fibers); or is it a synthetic or man-made fiber like rayon, nylon, polyester or acrylic. It may be a blend of two or more of any of these fibers or it may have a special finish. In any case, this knowledge is necessary for proper handling and care of the fabric. If there are any special instructions on care of the fabric, try to find this out when purchasing. Buy fabric and "findings" (thread, zipper, etc.).

6. If the fabric was not preshrunk, do this before cutting (see special instructions on shrinking fabrics).

7. Remove the instruction sheet from the pattern envelope and read it carefully. This will save time and errors.

8. If your pattern needs alterations, *make them now.* If this is properly done there will be little fitting to do. (See Pattern Alteration.)

9. Assemble your sewing equipment. Study cutting guide of pattern and circle proper one for your size and the width of fabric. Cut the garment watching the grain line and observing other precautions. (See section on Cutting.)

10. Mark, pin, and baste, following instructions as given on sheet. Fit garment and make adjustments.

11. Stitch and press as you go. (See section on Pressing.)

12. Fit again.

13. Finish details, hang skirt, and give final pressing.

This is the general procedure. The following pages give methods and techniques in more detail.

PUTTING A GARMENT TOGETHER

There are two general methods:

Custom Method

Compare your measurements with those of the pattern and alter the pattern carefully before cutting. (See section on Pattern Adjustment.) After cutting garment, mark all pieces at one time. Then remove pattern from blouse parts and stay-stitch all curved or slanted edges. If there are no center seams, baste a guide line down center front and back. Make a row of machine basting between notches at top of sleeve.

Sew darts on front, back, and sleeves. Press. Join blouse front and back at shoulder and underarm seams, leaving opening for placket. Press. Stitch sleeve seam and press. Baste sleeve in armhole, easing in fulness between notches by pulling one thread of machine basting. Underline if necessary. Press seam toward sleeve.

Remove pattern from skirt, stay-stitch curved edges, and baste guide line down center front and back. Pin and baste side seams starting from bottom or hem edge, leaving left side open for placket. Try on, adjust, stitch, and press.

Baste bodice and skirt together at waistline and fit garment.

Pin in shoulder pads if called for. Make necessary adjustments. Stitch waistline seam and put in zipper. Finish neckline. Press. Try on, mark, and put in hem.

Quick Construction Method

There are short cuts which can be taken when speed is important. Children's clothes and some types of house dresses and work clothes can be made in this way when time is limited. Proceed as follows: Alter pattern before cutting the garment. Stay-stitch all curved edges. Do all flat work, such as darts in bodice front and back and skirt front and back. Finish front of bodice if seamed or faced. Face back of neck (if no collar). Join shoulder seams of bodice and facings in one

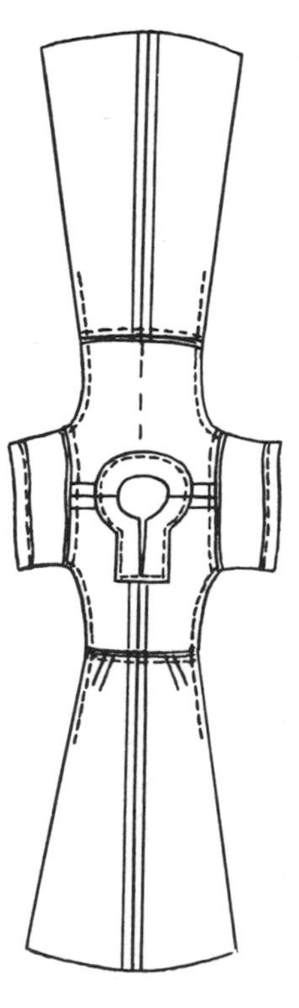

operation. Press and turn facing to inside. Adjust waist length if necessary. Join front and back seams of skirt if any. Press seams up. Make the sleeves but do not sew up underarm seam. Join front bodice to front skirt and back bodice to back skirt. Press seams open. Sew sleeves to armhole. The garment at this stage should still be flat. Try on and adjust at side seams if necessary. Now join side seams and underarm sleeve seam in one operation. Stitch, starting at bottom or hem edge and leave side seam open for placket. Press seams, finish placket, and put in hem.

Hints on Choosing and Using a Pattern

When choosing a pattern keep in mind: suitability to your figure, the season, where the garment will be worn, and the fabric you wish to use. Consideration of all these things is very important. When ready to use your pattern, study it thoroughly. It is filled with information to make your sewing project easier, more fun, and a complete success.

From the pattern envelope you can learn:

1. How the garment should look when finished, front and back views, and usually some variations.
2. Sizes and standard measurements for each.
3. Yardage requirements for each size, for various fabric widths, for linings, interlinings, etc., if any.
4. Suggestions for fabrics suitable to the design.
5. Necessary findings such as zipper, buttons, etc.

Inside the envelope you will find pattern and instruction leaflets, both of which are replete with more information. Read them carefully.

The instruction leaflet tells you:

1. How many pieces are in the pattern. (They are usually numbered in the order of their use.)
2. How to lay the pattern on the fabric (select the one that suits your width of fabric and circle it). Layouts for interfacing, lining, etc., are also given.
3. A quick listing of steps to take and an explanation of each.
4. Step-by-step diagrams and detailed instructions for making and finishing each part of the garment.

On the pattern itself, look for:

1. Lines for shortening and lengthening the pattern to suit your figure.
2. Grain lines for placing pattern correctly on the fabric.
3. Cutting lines and width-of-seam lines.
4. Darts, notches, and other markings to be used when setting the pieces together.
5. Marks for placing buttonholes, pockets, and other features of the pattern.

FABRICS

Fabric can be classified in several different ways: fiber content, type of weave, appearance, weight, use, etc.

Probably the most important thing to the woman who sews is the use to which the fabric is to be put. Under usage, several things come to mind: season or time of day to be worn, ease of care, suitability to pattern design, adult or children's wear and so on.

Some basic fabric types are illustrated in Color Plate 2.

Fabrics are available in a great variety of textures, weights, colors, etc. Even the old familiar ones undergo changes. For example: a piece of fabric may look like old-fashioned cotton gingham, but be woven of a synthetic fiber requiring special care in handling and pressing.

There is a steady flow of new fabrics. Fashion designers are continually looking for new and different effects, and fabric manufacturers respond with all kinds of innovations. Because of constant change it is not possible to cover the field adequately here. Therefore, it is well to learn the basic types of fabrics. Try to determine the fiber content and the special finish, if any, of the fabric you buy so as to work with and care for it better.

Fibers

The natural fibers are as follows:

Silk, which comes from the cocoon of the silk worm. Silk is very strong. It is lustrous, soft and absorbent, and drapes well. It takes dye well and beautiful rich colors can be obtained. These can be (but are not always) fast to light and washing.

Cotton, which is obtained from the seed pod of the cotton plant. Cotton is a versatile fiber, very absorbent, strong, and light weight. It can be dyed fast to light and washing and takes well to special finishes.

Linen, which comes from the stem of the flax plant. Linen is one of the strongest fibers and very absorbent. It creases easily unless treated. It is cool, has a high luster, and can be dyed color fast.

Wool, which comes from sheep. Wool is inherently warm, is absorbent, and wears well. It can be dyed fast to light and washing and is fairly strong.

And other fibers such as camel's-hair, cashmere, mohair, and vicuna, which come from various animals.

Man-made Fibers. The synthetic fibers are made from various materials and by many chemical processes. Their number is growing. Some of the better known ones are rayon, nylon, polyesters such as Dacron, Fortrel, Kodel, and Vycron and acrylics such as Acrilan, Creslan, and Orlon. Also Fiberglas.

These also have their own distinctive properties. Some of the qualities of the new fibers to look for are quick drying, wrinkle resistance, water repellence, moth and mildew resistance, and low absorption.

Blends. There are many blends of natural and synthetic fibers giving fabric some of the qualities of each. Many fabrics contain several fibers, and new combinations are continually being devised.

When buying fabric learn its fiber content, what can be expected of it, and the special care it will need.

Fabric Terms

An outside edge of any fabric is known as the *Selvage.* It is usually a woven edge and will not fray. Knit fabrics have no selvage; they may or may not be woven as a tube. The selvage is often woven more tightly than the rest of the fabric and therefore should either be trimmed off or clipped at intervals to prevent drawing.

The *Grain* of the fabric runs lengthwise and crosswise. Lengthwise threads are called warp and crosswise threads are called weft. The lengthwise grain is especially important when cutting a garment. *The grain line of the fabric must match the grain line on the pattern.*

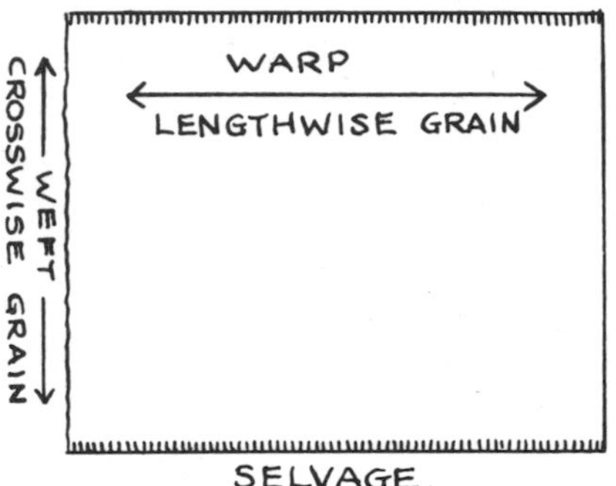

Fabric Preparation

The ends of the fabric may not have been cut exactly with the cross grain when purchased and will need to be straightened. If fabric can be torn, clip selvage and tear across. If not, pull a crosswise thread and cut along the line it leaves.

If the fabric has been rolled diagonally during the manufacturing process it should

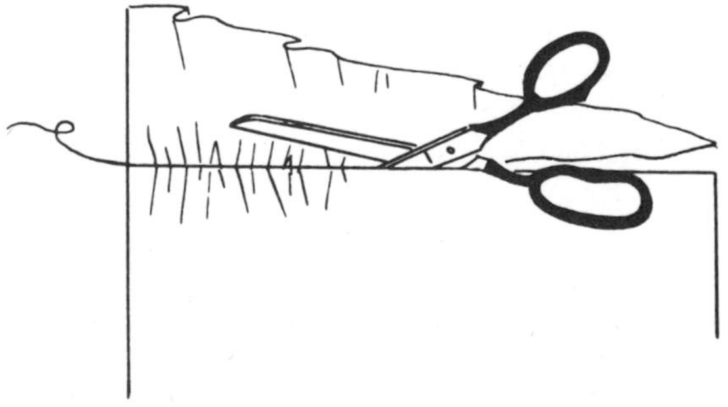

be brought back into shape. Pull it in the opposite direction, on the bias, until the cross grain is at right angles with the lengthwise grain. If the fabric has been treated to resist wrinkles it may not be possible to straighten it. Examine the fabric before purchasing.

Press out all wrinkles. Most woolens are now preshrunk.

Shrinking the Fabric. If this is needed, a tailor will shrink woolen fabric for you, but you can do it yourself. Start the day before you want to do the cutting. Wet a bed sheet and lay it on a flat surface. Snip the selvages of your fabric if they appear tightly woven. Leave the fabric folded lengthwise and lay it on the wet sheet. Roll up the sheet and fabric and leave overnight. Remove and smooth out to dry. The fabric may require some pressing and, if so, do this while slightly damp. Linen and cotton may be soaked in cold water several hours to shrink. Hang evenly, drip dry. Iron while slightly damp.

How to Handle Special Fabrics

The weave, design or texture of some fabrics require special care in sewing. Here are suggestions for working with them.

Plaids. Plaids present a problem in cutting because they must be matched. There are two kinds of plaids, even and uneven. An even plaid repeats itself in both directions at regular intervals. Uneven plaids do not. Matching an even plaid is not very difficult. The matching notches must be laid on corresponding stripes of the plaid. The pattern pieces can, however, be placed facing either way. If the fabric is folded, be sure the plaid lines are directly over one another. Pin in place.

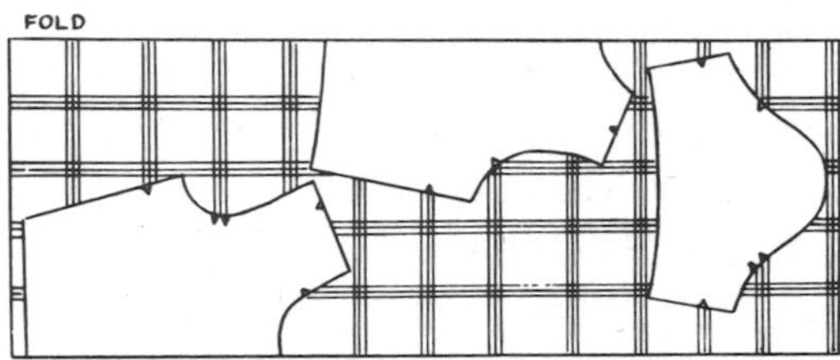

An uneven plaid is more difficult. It must be treated as a one-way fabric with all pattern pieces laid in the same direction. Here again, matching notches must be placed on corresponding horizontal and vertical stripes.

Stripes. The final appearance is the most important thing when working with stripes. Woven-in stripes run with the grain. Printed stripes may be slightly off grain. Choose a piece whose stripes run with the grain as closely as possible. When placing the pattern on printed stripes, follow the stripe and disregard the grain. It is preferable to have a

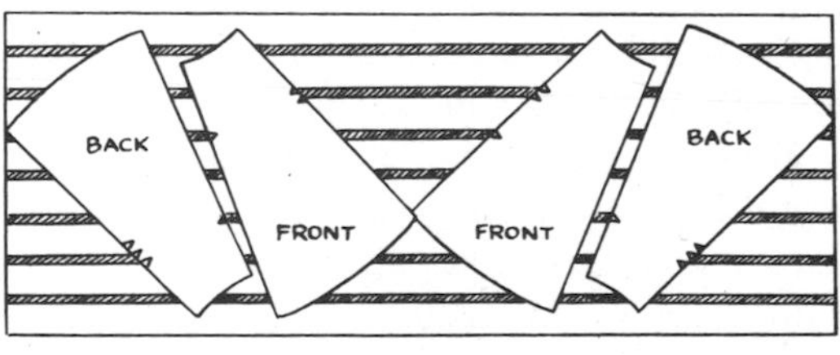

garment with the stripes running correctly than to have the fabric grain perfect.

Stripes can run lengthwise or crosswise. Try to choose a pattern with few pieces and simple lines. Buy a little extra fabric for matching stripes.

There are balanced and unbalanced stripes. Balanced stripes present no problem other than matching, but care must be used in cutting irregular or unbalanced stripes. The latter can be handled in two ways: They can be reversed starting at center back and center front (if the pattern is to be cut on the fold, add a center seam), or they can be run in their regular rotation around the figure by cutting each piece separately in opposite directions on the stripe.

MATCHING STRIPES. The key to matching crosswise stripes is watching the notches when laying on the pattern. Shift the pattern so the corresponding notches fall on the same stripe. Predetermine the length of the garment, then see that the hemline ends on a dominant stripe. Stripes are matched at side seams as far as the bust dart. For set-in sleeves, match the stripes at the front and back armhole notches. Match the stripes on collar facing to those on the collar. Pocket stripes may exactly match those on the dress, be cut diagonally, or be cut crosswise. Center the dominant stripe on cuffs. Make a center back seam on collar so points can be made to match.

Stripes must be perfectly matched on seams.

Pin and slip baste (see under Basic Sewing) carefully from the right side so they will not slip when machine stitched.

Diagonal Weaves. Fine and hard-to-distinguish diagonal weaves present no problems and are cut like other fabrics. Fabrics with a prominent twill weave, the result of heavy fiber or change in color, entail planning before cutting. Choose patterns with:

1. Set-in sleeves.

2. Slim skirts with few seams.

3. Simple lines without intricate seaming.

The diagonal line must be kept going in one direction around the garment. Patterns are usually so marked when "not suitable for diagonal fabrics." Watch carefully when placing pattern on the fabric.

Knitted Fabrics. Jerseys—both lightweight or double knit—rayon knits, Banlon, or any fabric with stretch, requires special handling. In cutting knits, watch the grain just as you would in any other fabric. The rib is the lengthwise grain but the side fold is not necessarily on grain. Jersey is sold both tubular and flat. When tubular, there is a crease on each side which is difficult to remove. Try not to use it where it will show.

Knitted fabrics may be lined but not underlined (see Interfacings, Linings, Interlinings). Use very sharp shears and try not to stretch when cutting. Stay-stitch all curved and slanted seam edges.

Use a medium tension and about 12 to 14 stitches per inch. Stretch the seam very slightly as you stitch to prevent seams breaking under strain. A zigzag stitch is often used since it gives under stress.

To prevent stretching, reinforce the shoulder and waistline seams (if any) with seam binding. Allow the garment to hang a day before marking and hemming, so as to take care of as much stretch as possible.

Sheer Fabrics. There are many types of sheers, and those with body (batiste, dimity, lawn, dotted swiss, voile, silk organdy, etc.) are easily handled. The softer ones such as chiffon are more difficult to work with. Straighten ends of fabric and clip selvages. To prevent slipping, lay the fabric over a sheet-covered cutting surface. Use sharp scissors and a generous amount of pins. Chiffon is often used in two or more layers for blouses and dresses. Cut all layers of each part at once. Pick up each layer and mark separately. Baste layers together down center on grain line. Baste every few inches over all to keep layers together. Treat layers as one piece of fabric, stitching seams with tissue paper underneath. When possible, use French seams and bind edges with double bias (see section on Seams). Wide hems or narrow rolled hand hems are used on chiffon.

Velvet and Other Napped Fabrics. Fabrics with a pile or nap such as velvet, velveteen, corduroy, broadcloth, etc., take some care in cutting and sewing. All pattern pieces must be laid in the same direction so the nap will run in the same direction throughout the garment and thus avoid a light and dark appearance. You will notice that when the nap runs up, the fabric looks darker and richer; when it runs down, it appears lighter and shiny. By running the hand over the fabric you can easily tell which way the nap lies.

The fabric may be folded lengthwise when cutting double thicknesses but never crosswise (the pile will run in the opposite direction). Use sharp scissors and cut in the direction of the pile—from the hem to the top of the garment. Baste (to prevent crawling), and stitch the same way. Mark with tailor's tacks, not a tracing wheel. To avoid bulk, use taffeta for neck, armhole, and other facings. To control shape, an underlining may be used. If the bottom layer goes through faster than the top, release the presser foot a little on your sewing machine. Use a medium-length stitch (about 10 to the inch), and a fine, sharp needle. Omit top stitching if possible. Press only where necessary and press over a needle board or a piece of velvet with pile side up. Insert zipper by hand.

The same general rules apply to fake fur fabrics. If the "hair" is long, cut on the wrong side with a razor blade as you would real fur.

Satin. Treat satin also as a one-way fabric. Because of the way it is woven there is an "up-and-down" which shows in differences of shading. To avoid markings, pin pattern to fabric inside the seam allowance. Use sharp shears when cutting and mark with tailor's tacks or non-greasy tailor's chalk. Use a sharp needle and silk thread for stitching. To avoid puckering, hold the fabric taut while stitching.

Press lightly to prevent seam allowances from showing through. To hold shape, use a lightweight underlining such as organza. Strips of lamb's wool are sometimes used to make softly rolled hems. Other elegant touches: insert zipper by hand, and be sure it is well covered, cover snaps with matching thin fabric, use corded bound buttonholes. Handle fabric as little as possible to keep it fresh-looking.

Stretch Fabrics. Be sure fabric is "relaxed" before cutting. To prevent stretching, avoid letting one end hang off the cutting table. Lengthwise stretch fabric (stretch runs parallel with selvages) is used on garments needing up-and-down stretch, such as pants. Crosswise stretch fabric is used for actionwear garments, where stretch is needed across shoulders, etc., to allow for "give" when fitting.

Use very sharp shears for cutting. Zigzag stitching, which gives under strain, is suitable for most seams; or use nylon thread, which has some stretch in it. Use 10 to 16 stitches per inch so seam will not pull open under stress.

Choose a lining with stretch. It defeats the purpose of expandable fabrics to use nonstretch linings and interfacings in areas where stretch is wanted.

For tight-fitting stretch garments it may be advisable to use a longer zipper than usual. Set in zippers by machine for added strength.

Lace. Lace, depending upon the pattern and the kind used, should be worn over its own slip or underlined with net, silk, organdy, tulle, or chiffon or a fabric of a weight suitable to the weight of the lace.

Use care in placing the pattern to take advantage of the design in the lace. Watch patterns at seams wherever possible. Bordered laces take special care in planning before cutting.

Do not face lace with lace, use net or other lining material. Very sheer lace should be basted to tissue paper before stitching.

Use a small needle and about 12 stitches to the inch when sewing lace. Avoid making buttonholes. Make invisible seams by stitching twice; the second stitching should be close to the first, but not on top of it. Then trim close to the last stitching. (See page 62 for other sewing techniques used on lace.)

Felt. Felt is made of wool and/or other fibers matted together. It is easy to cut and sew and, because it has no grain, patterns may be laid in any direction, thus saving fabric. Seams are usually lapped and sewed, and since felt will not ravel, edges can be left unfinished. Use about 10 to 12 stitches to the inch. Edges are sometimes pinked for a decorative effect.

Leather. Select skins as much alike as possible. They are usually about 24″ by 36″, which is not large enough for a full-length coat or dress. Therefore, a pattern with a seam across the back and front must be selected. About 5 or 6 skins (or more) will be needed for a coat or dress with sleeves. Choose a pattern with simple lines and with no fullness to be eased. Carefully make adjustments in the pattern before cutting into the leather. It is even a good idea to make a muslin first, since you cannot rip and restitch leather.

Cut one thickness at a time, using very sharp scissors. Tape the pattern to the skin or *pin within the seam allowance.*

The neck of the skin should be at the top (neckline or top of skirt) of the pattern.

Leather has a right and wrong side, so be sure to reverse pattern. Mark with chalk which can be removed.

Sew with about 10 to 12 stitches per inch and a smaller-than-average needle. Leather has a tendency to stretch. This can be prevented somewhat by sewing seam binding on top of the seams. Round all corners.

Place brown paper on top of leather and press with a warm iron. Use no moisture. Press seams open and hold flat with rubber cement. Apply it to the underside of the seam allowance, to the hem, and to the garment. Pound with a beater till dry. For hand finishing, there is a special three-sided needle (glover's needle) for use on leather. Use machine- or hand-worked buttonholes.

Vinyl. Vinyl cannot be "eased," so select a simple pattern with few pieces and without a set-in sleeve. Alter the pattern before cutting. Since pins make permanent holes, pin inside the seam allowance or use weights to hold the pattern in place while stitching. Hold the parts together with Scotch tape. Use sharp shears for cutting vinyl and a grease pencil for marking—it can be rubbed off later. Sew with long stitches (8 or 10 to the inch), a fine needle, and mercerized thread.

Vinyl cannot be pressed; therefore use lapped or welt seams. If, with the shiny side out, the fabric does not feed, place strips of tissue paper under the foot and over the throat plate. This will help ease the fabric through. Stitch slowly to avoid ripping and restitching.

Double-faced Fabrics. Double-faced fabrics are made of two layers of cloth either woven or bonded together. Either side is the right side.

Choose a pattern of simple design and with as few seams as possible. Kimono or raglan sleeves are best. Use loops instead of buttonholes. Since no facings are needed, you may require less fabric than called for on the pattern envelope.

DARTS. Pull the layers of fabric apart and make darts on the inside. Slit darts on the fold and press open. Sew together invisibly along the seam line through all thicknesses. Flat, felled seams are probably best and are made in the usual way—trimming one side very short before turning the second. Plain seams can also be made. Open the edges of the fabric. Make a plain seam on one with the right sides together, trim and press open. Trim edges of the second side, then turn one edge over the other and slip-stitch along seam line. Hems can be made by opening the edges, turning them in, and slip-stitching along fold. You can also open the edge and cut one side away at the seam line. Then fold the other side over it, miter the corners, and slip-stitch in place.

TO INSERT ZIPPER. Separate the layers of fabric to a depth of about 1½″ on either side of the seam opening. Fold seam allowance on each layer to the inside, and press. Center zipper under seam line and baste to the upper layer. Top stitch or sew by hand ¼″ from seam line. Hem second layer to the zipper by hand.

FITTING AND FINISHING HINTS

1. Buy the correct pattern for your type and size.

2. Alter your pattern before cutting.

Check your measurements with the pattern, allowing for "ease," and make necessary adjustments. (See section on Pattern Alteration.) This will save much fitting later.

3. Run a basting line the full length of center front and back of garment to show if lengthwise threads ("grain") are perfectly straight. Similarly, crosswise threads should be perfectly horizontal and should also be marked with basting.

4. Retain the lines of the design by keeping the picture before you when you fit. Since one hip or shoulder may be higher than the other, try dress on right side out.

5. Wear suitable undergarments when trying on dress. Also wear heels of proper height. Try on a suit jacket over a blouse and skirt and a coat over a dress. Stand in a natural manner before a long mirror.

6. Try on the belt if called for; this helps to locate the normal waistline. Pin in shoulder pads if called for; add a little more padding if one shoulder is low.

7. Do not fit too tightly. Ease is necessary for movement and for appearance. Avoid wrinkles. The customary allowance for ease at bust is about 4½", and 2½" at upper arm. Also avoid tightness across the back, as the sleeves will pull out. A skirt will slip up if too tight around the hips.

8. In plain set-in sleeves the seam at the armhole should be perfectly smooth.

9. Baggy shorts or slacks may need a shorter crotch.

10. Underarm bodice seams should be perfectly straight up and down, and shoulder seams should be directly on top of the shoulder.

11. Side and lower darts in blouse should point to the crown of the bust and end about an inch from it. In case of a low, heavy bust they may end further from the crown.

12. If collar stands away from the neck at the back, remove it and take darts at top of blouse back. Pin collar to blouse. If it is too long, trim shorter at front ends following the line of the pattern.

13. If there are wrinkles across top back of blouse it is probably too long in the center. Trim at neckline and top of shoulder.

14. If skirt wrinkles at top across the back, it may be either too tight around the hips or too long between waistline and hips. Adjust.

15. Waistline seam should not show above or below the belt.

16. Be sure the zipper is entirely covered with the lap.

17. There should be no ridge at top of hemline. If so, the stitches may be too tight or the pressing not done well.

18. Do not omit interfacings when called for; they make a big difference in the finished appearance of a garment. (See section on Interfacing.)

19. A well-finished garment is a well-pressed garment. Press as you go and again when completed.

CUTTING

General Rules

Allow yourself *plenty of space* for cutting. Use the floor if you have no table large enough. Accurate cutting is difficult in cramped quarters.

Look over your pattern carefully. Study especially the enclosed instruction sheet. A cutting diagram will be given. Select the one for your size and fabric width and circle it for easy reference.

Alter your pattern before cutting. Patterns have to be made in standard measurements but almost every figure varies somewhat from standard proportions. (See section on Pattern Alteration for altering the pattern to fit your figure.)

Grain line is so important that we mention it again, as it must be kept in mind while cutting. Most patterns have a long printed line which is to be laid parallel with the selvage. Check with ruler as you pin on the pattern. Pin carefully on seam line or at right angles to it, keeping pattern and fabric flat and smooth.

Cut each piece accurately. Notches may be cut in or out or marked later with chalk.

To Cut a True Bias. Fold fabric so the cross grain threads run parallel to the selvage or lengthwise grain. The diagonal line formed is the true bias. Cut on the fold; then measure and cut strips the width desired.

MARKING

There are several ways of marking the notches, darts, etc., which serve as guides when putting the garment together. Marking should be done on the wrong side of the garment.

With Chalk. Use light chalk on dark material, dark chalk on light colored material. Mark notches on edges. For inside markings, insert pins straight through pattern and fabric at intervals along lines. Fold pattern back to pins, mark both sides and remove pins.

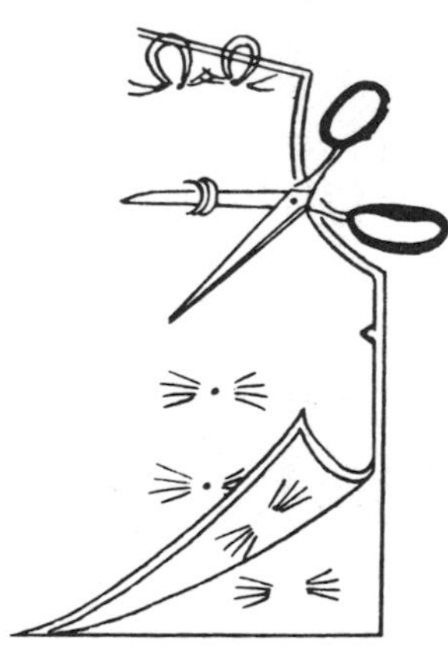

With Tailor's Tacks. Use an unknotted double thread in a contrasting color. Take two short stitches through pattern and the layers of fabric. Cut top loops and clip threads between layers leaving tufts on both pieces of fabric.

With Tracing Wheel. Use dressmaker's carbon paper in a color which will show on your fabric. This method is not practical for loosely woven or very sheer fabrics. It will also spot in pressing on certain fabrics, so it should be tested first. Cut paper in strips and lay one piece face up under fabric layers and another face down on top layer under pattern. (This method assumes that fabric has been laid wrong side out for cutting.) Trace straight lines with ruler and others free hand. Diagram shows one layer of fabric only.

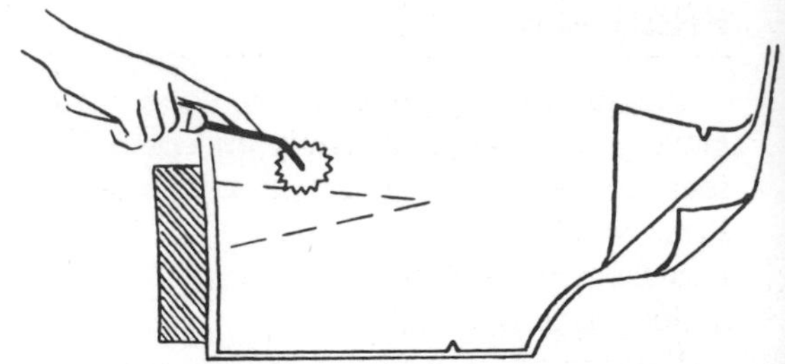

STITCHING

Machine Sewing Hints. Pull both the top- and bobbin-thread ends back of the presser foot before stitching. To prevent the machine from jamming, lower the needle into the fabric before beginning to stitch. After ending a seam and before removing fabric, be sure the take-up lever on the machine is at its highest point. This prevents the thread from slipping out of the needle.

Use the same kind of thread on upper and bobbin threading and be sure to wind bobbin evenly.

If the thread breaks while you are sewing, check the following: Is there a knot in the thread coming from the spool? Is the machine correctly threaded; does the thread go through the needle from the correct (grooved) side? Is the needle well into its socket and placed with flat side against the needle bar? Are you trying to sew with a blunt or bent needle? Is the needle too fine for the fabric you are using? Check the hole in the throat plate for roughness. An unevenly wound bobbin or thread that is too heavy, may cause bobbin thread to break. Puckered stitching can be caused by a blunt needle. Skipped stitches may be caused by a needle that is too short or one not suited to your machine.

PRESSING

Pressing is very important to good sewing. Have your equipment handy and press each seam or dart before joining to another seam. Press with the grain of the fabric. Lift the iron from place to place instead of pushing it along as in ironing.

Equipment. A well-padded ironing board and a good iron of suitable weight. Steam irons are preferred by many. (See Sewing Equipment.)

A sleeve board. If necessary a rolled magazine covered with a towel can be used.

Press mitt for armholes, etc. This can be made.

Press cloths: one heavy cotton drill and one of lighter weight muslin.

Tailor's cushion. This can be made.

Sponge.

Clapper.

Needle board or piece of plush.

Darts. Waistline and shoulder darts are pressed toward the center of the garment. Underarm and sleeve darts are pressed downward. If the fabric is heavy, slash darts and press open.

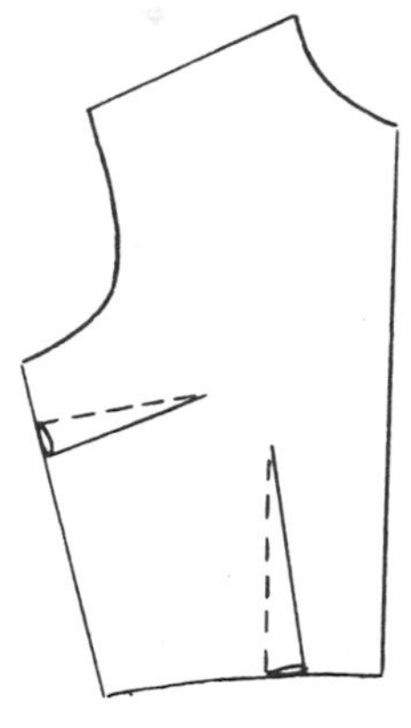

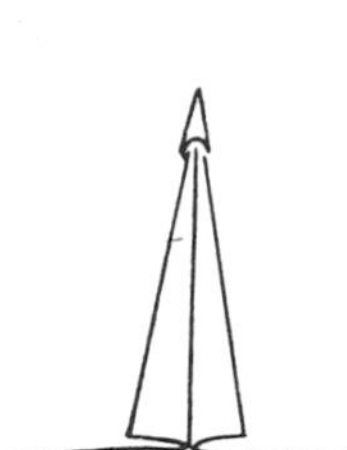

Seams. Plain seams are pressed open before being joined to the next section. Edge-stitched seams are pressed flat.

Use a tailor's cushion or press mitt when pressing curved seams to keep the rounded

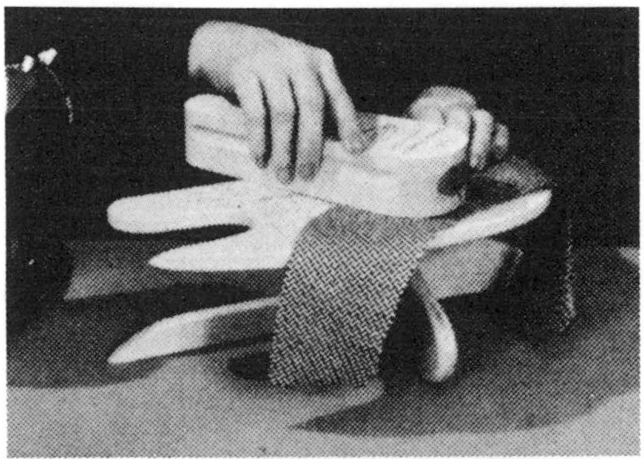

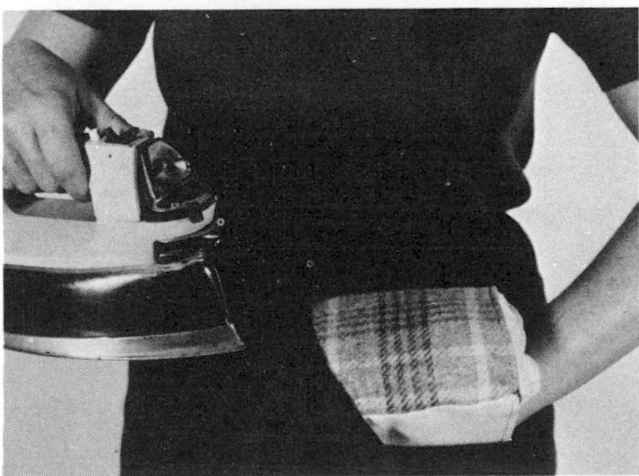

lines of the garment. A press mitt or tailor's ham is very useful for armhole seams. Finish off by turning right side out, using heavy cloth on top and press mitt inside.

Use a point presser for collar and lapel corners.

A tailor's wooden clapper is used on woolens to sharpen edges of the collar, lapels, etc. Beat during pressing while fabric is full of steam.

When pressing pleats, press only to within 5 or 6 inches of lower edge. After hemming, finish pressing.

Pressing Various Fabrics

Always use a press cloth over wool and press on the wrong side and with the grain to avoid stretching. It can be pressed from the right side if necessary (pockets, etc.) by placing a piece of the woolen fabric under the press cloth.

Rayon and silk should always be pressed on the wrong side using a warm iron only. All synthetics are very sensitive to heat. It is well to test a piece of the fabric to learn how warm the iron should be. If there is much sizing, use tissue paper as a press cloth.

Cotton can be pressed from the right side. Dampen to remove wrinkles.

Linen can be pressed from either side.

Embroidered fabrics should be pressed from the wrong side over a thick soft pad or towel.

A needle board is used for velvet, but a piece of plush or velveteen may answer. To steam velvet, place damp cloth over standing iron and hold velvet lightly over steam. To avoid press marks on seams use a strip of paper between seam allowance and body of garment. Also, use paper strips under pleats.

Never press over snaps. Use warm iron on nylon zippers.

BASIC SEWING

Stitches Done by Hand

How to Make a Knot. 1. Hold end of thread between thumb and forefinger of left hand and wind or roll together.

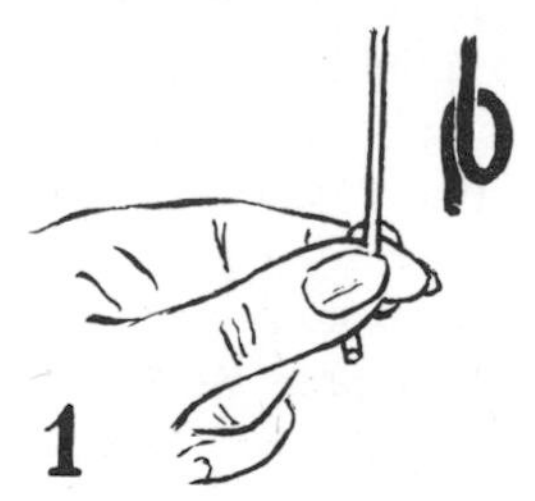

2. Wind or roll thread between these two fingers.

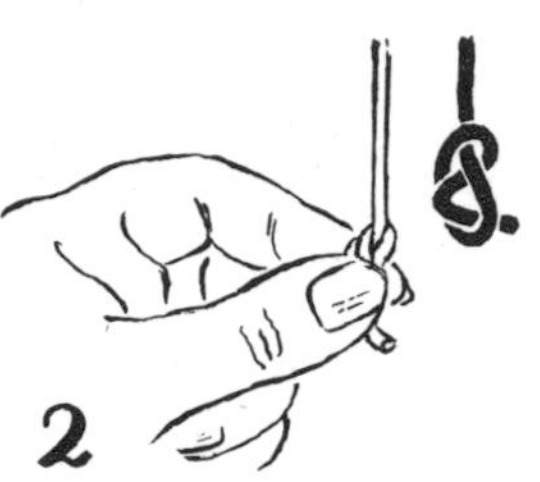

3. With nail of middle finger against loop formed on thumb, slide it to the end of the thread tightening it into a knot. With practice the knot will form near or at the end of the thread.

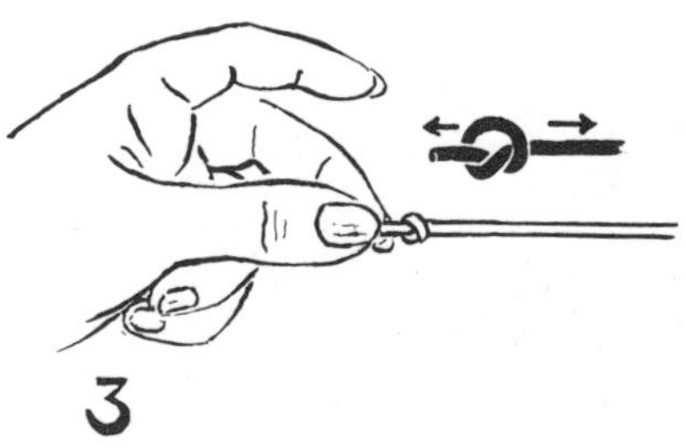

Basting. Basting is temporary and is used to hold the fabric in place until it is stitched. Basting may be even (all stitches the same length) or uneven (long and short stitches). Do not pull too tightly or stretch fabric as you work.

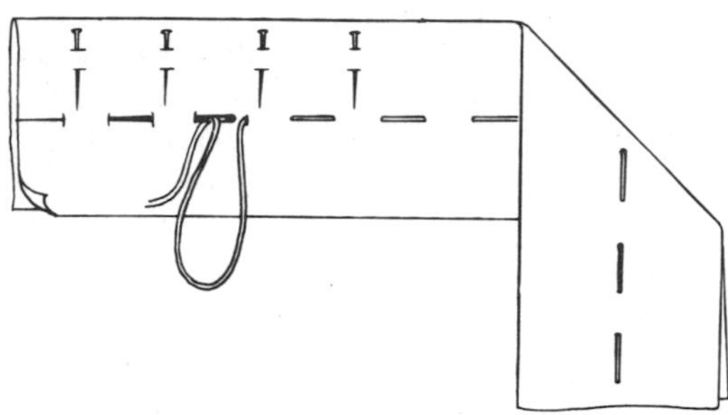

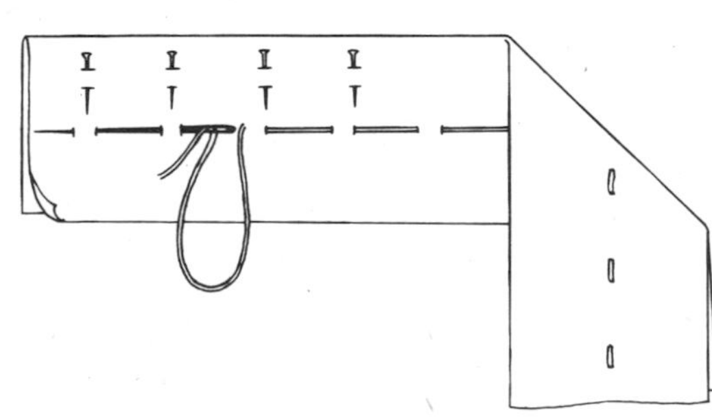

Diagonal Basting. Used for holding several thicknesses of fabric together on collars, front interfacings, etc. Keep the needle straight up and down; this makes a slanted stitch.

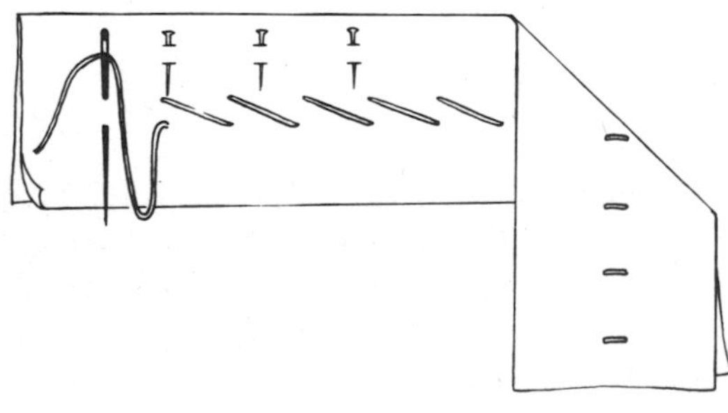

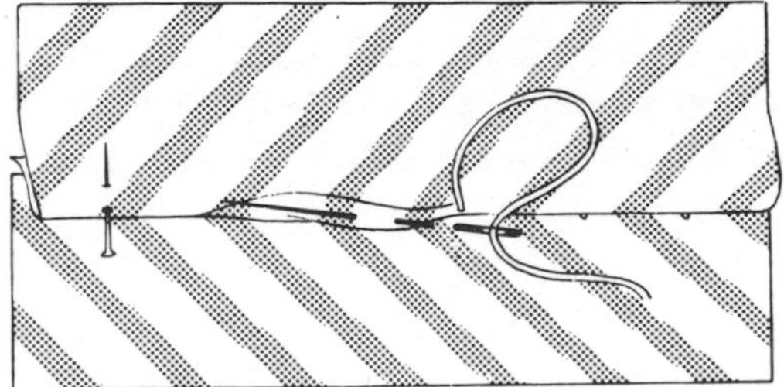

Slip Basting. Used for matching stripes or plaids from the right side and for alterations when fitting. Take a short stitch on lower layer, then take a stitch by slipping needle inside upper layer. Stitches should not show on outside.

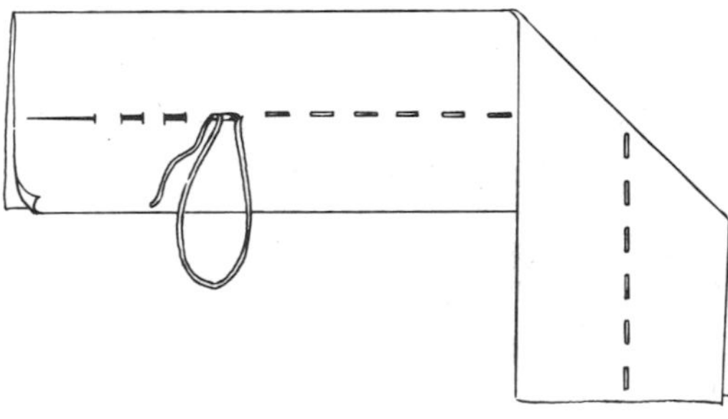

Running Stitch. Used for handsewn seams on delicate fabrics or where there is no strain. Hold fabric taut and take up smallest possible amount on the needle. Make all stitches an even length. With practice several stitches may be taken on the needle at one time.

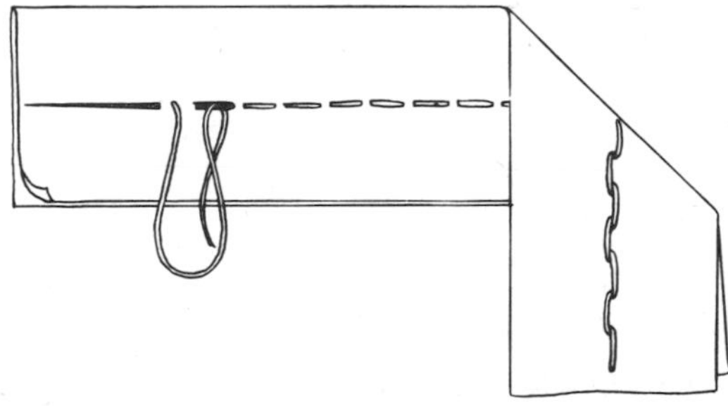

Back-Stitch. Bring needle out on the seam line and insert it one stitch back. Bring out one stitch ahead. Insert needle where it last came out and bring out one stitch ahead. Repeat. If done evenly this looks much like machine stitching and can take the place of it.

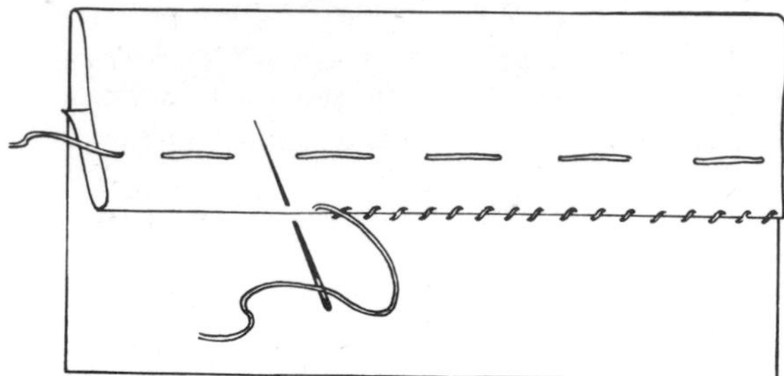

Hemming. Hide knot under hem edge. Take a small stitch picking up a thread or two of the fabric, then catching into very edge of hem as shown. Used for many types of hems but not on skirts, as it will show on the outside.

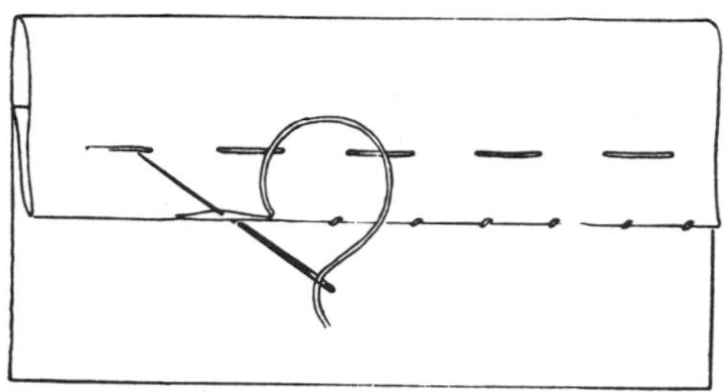

Blind-Hemming. This is done the same as plain hemming but the stitches are farther apart. The stitches should not show on the right side. It is sometimes used for hems of skirts.

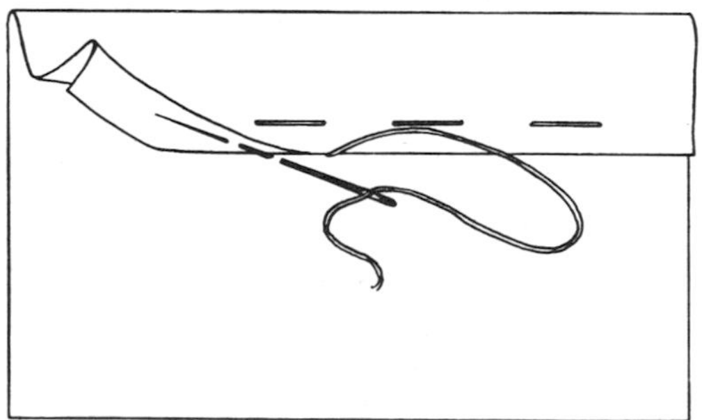

Slip-Stitch. This should be invisible on both sides. Pick up a thread or two of the fabric; then run needle inside hem edge about 1/4″. Often used for hemming skirts.

Note: Two folded edges can be slip-stitched together by catching into inside fold first on one side, then on the other. Do not let stitches show on outside.

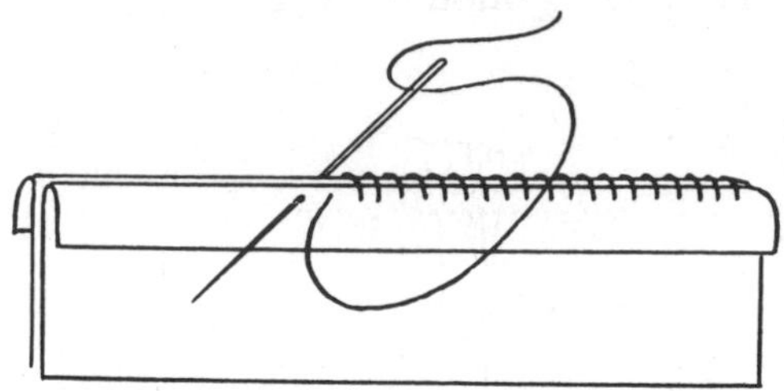

Whipping. Used to join two folded or hemmed edges. If needle is slanted as shown, stitches will be slanted. Work on very edge.

Note: Overhanding is done in the same way except needle is pointed toward you, which causes stitches to lie straight across.

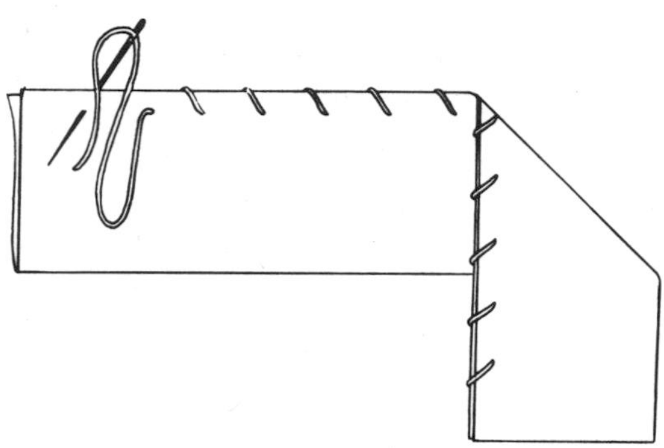

Overcasting. Usually done on raw edges and made deep enough to prevent fraying on single or double seams. Slant needle to make diagonal stitches.

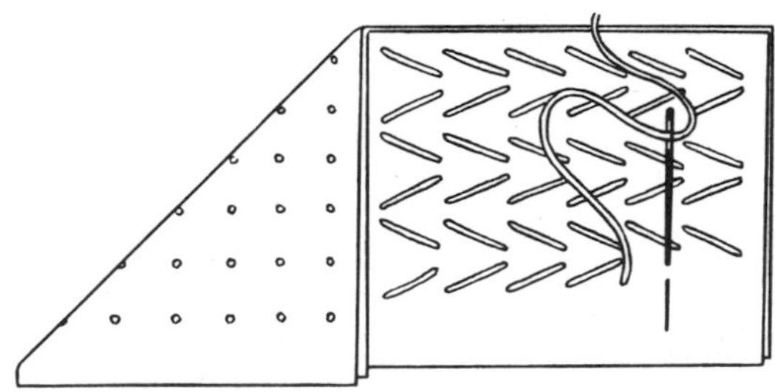

Padding Stitch. Work from left to right or right to left. It's similar to slanted basting. Take a short stitch holding needle in vertical position. Barely catch into lowest layer as stitch should be invisible on outside.

Stitches by Hand or by Machine

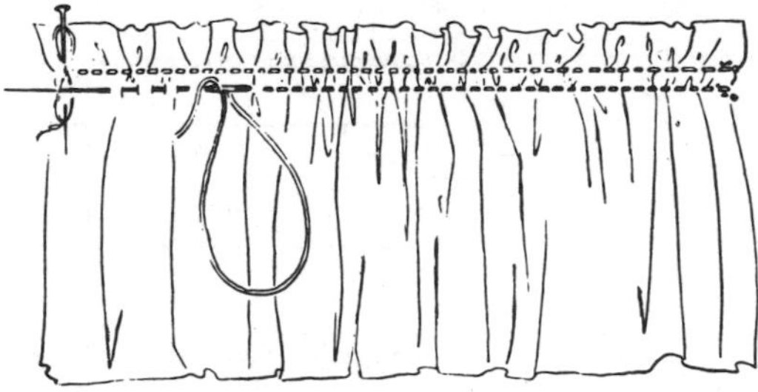

Gathering. This is running stitch drawn up to make gathers. (See Gathering, Shirring, Ruffles for machine gathering.)

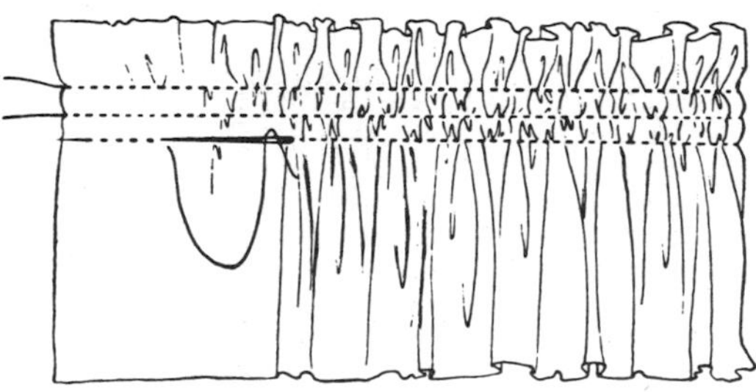

Shirring. This is several rows of gathers at even distances apart.

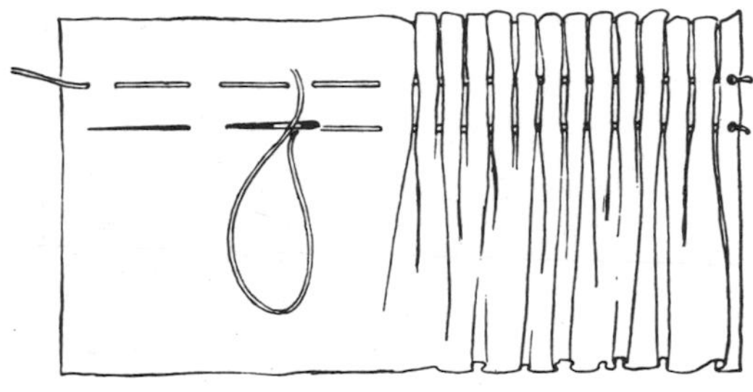

Gauging. This is the foundation for smocking. The stitch is a little longer on the right side than underneath but must be done evenly. The rows should be spaced evenly and the stitches directly under each other. When drawn up it will make even folds or pleats. Allow about three times the width for fulness.

Stay-Stitching. As the name implies, stay-stitching is done before sewing a garment together to prevent stretching and to preserve the lines of the pattern. It is a line of regular-length machine stitches and is done through a single thickness of material along curved and slanted edges. It is done outside of the seam line (within the seam allowance) so it will not show after the garment is constructed.

It is important to stitch in the correct direction. *Note:* Stitch from widest part to the narrowest arrows in the diagrams.

Seams and Seam Finishes

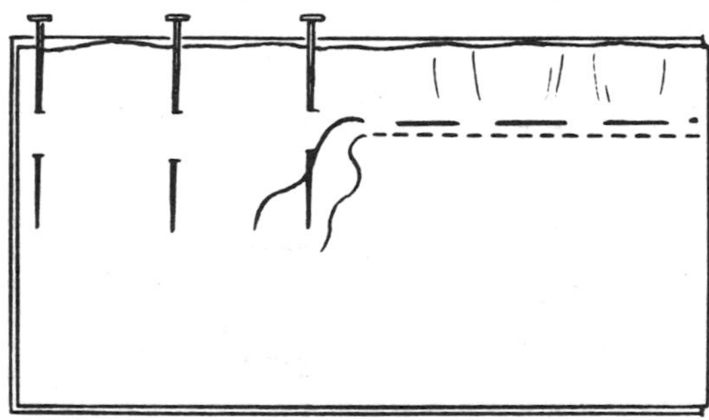

Easing Fulness. Keep full side toward you. Pin at close intervals, matching ends or notches. Baste and stitch. Allow no tiny pleats to form.

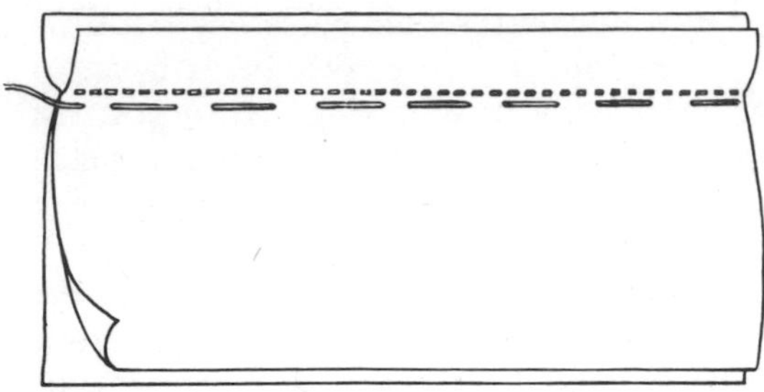

Plain Seam. With edges even, pin and baste right sides together. Stitch and press open. No finishing is needed when seam will be covered or the garment lined. On sheer fabrics stitch again just outside first stitching and trim close to the second stitching.

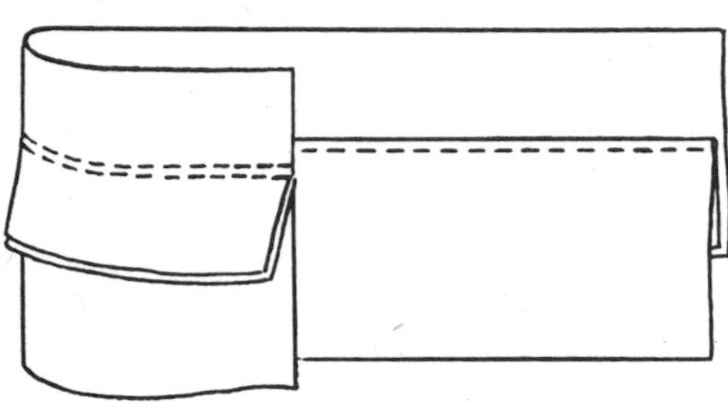

Top-stitched Plain Seam. Make a plain seam and press edges to one side. Top-stitch near seam line on right side.

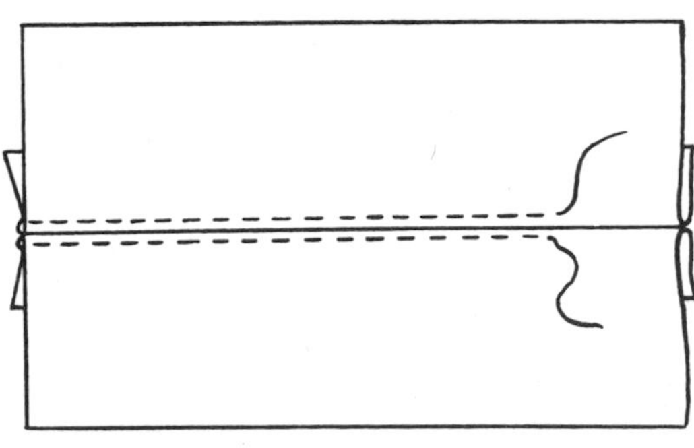

Double Top-stitched Seam. Make a plain seam and press open. On outside, stitch close to the seam line on both sides. This gives a tailored-looking finish.

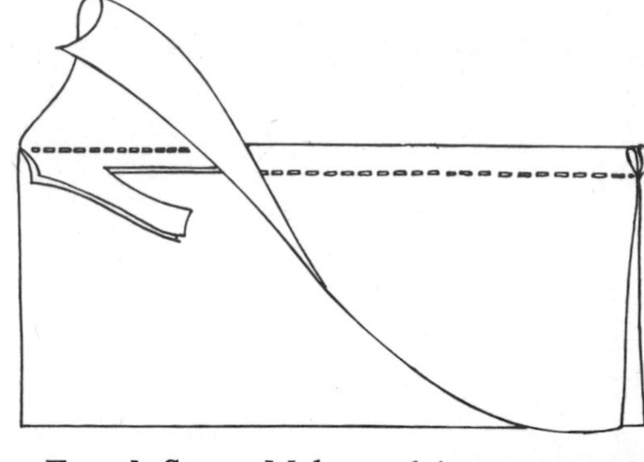

French Seam. Make a plain seam on the right side and trim close to the stitching. Turn, crease and stitch again deep enough to cover raw edges on inside. Used on fine fabrics and children's wear.

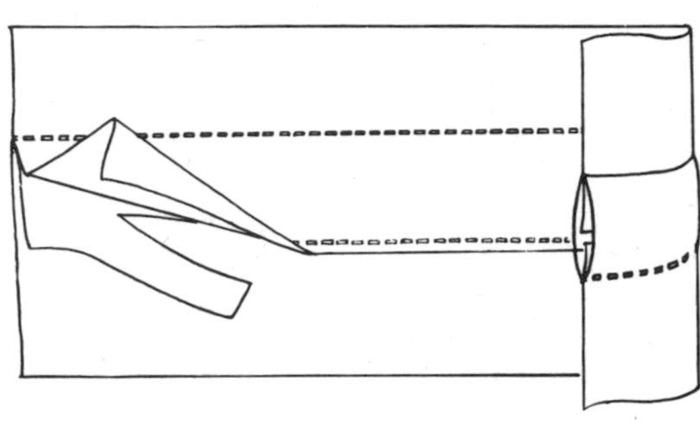

Flat Felled Seam. This may be done on the inside or outside of the garment. Stitch a plain seam and press to one side. Trim the under seam allowance. Turn under the raw edge of top seam allowance; baste and stitch close to edge. Used on tailored garments, pajamas, men's shirts, etc.

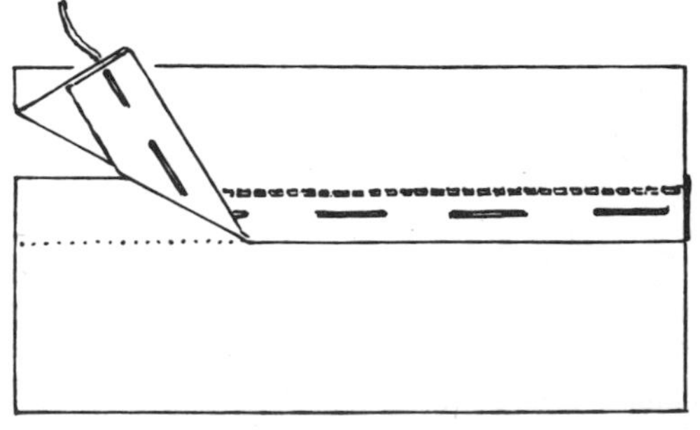

Lapped Seam. This is done on the right side of the garment. Turn under one seam allowance and lap over the other. Stitch along folded edge. If stitching is done about ¼″ from the edge, the seam will look like a tuck.

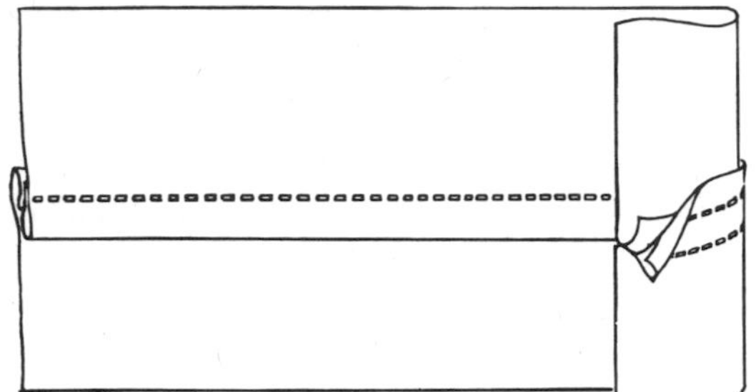

Welt Seam. Make a plain seam. Trim one edge. Press with wider seam allowance over narrow one. Stitch on outside ¼″ from seam line. A second stitching may be done near the seam line for a double-stitched welt seam. Very useful on heavy fabrics.

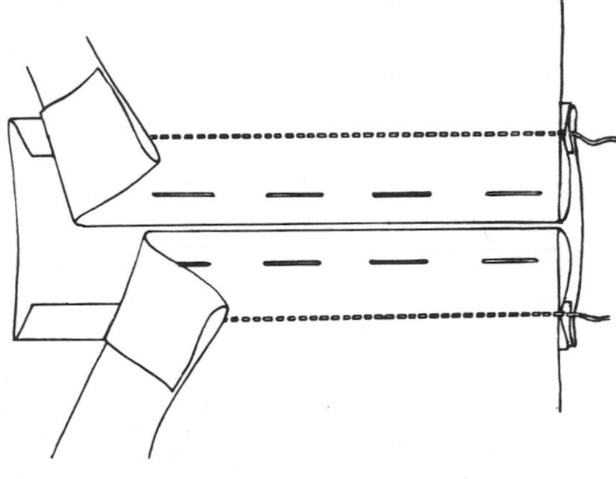

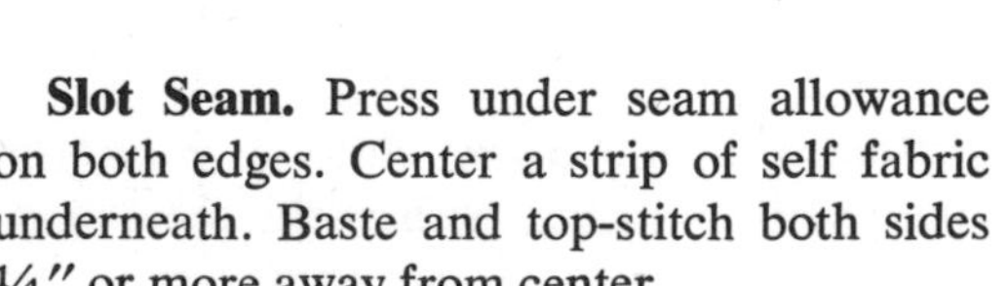

Slot Seam. Press under seam allowance on both edges. Center a strip of self fabric underneath. Baste and top-stitch both sides ¼″ or more away from center.

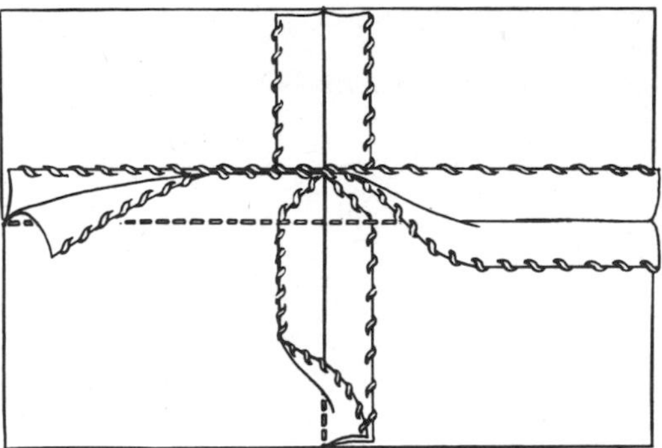

Crossed Seams. Stitch and press open first seam. Match and stitch crossing seam. Clip corners as shown.

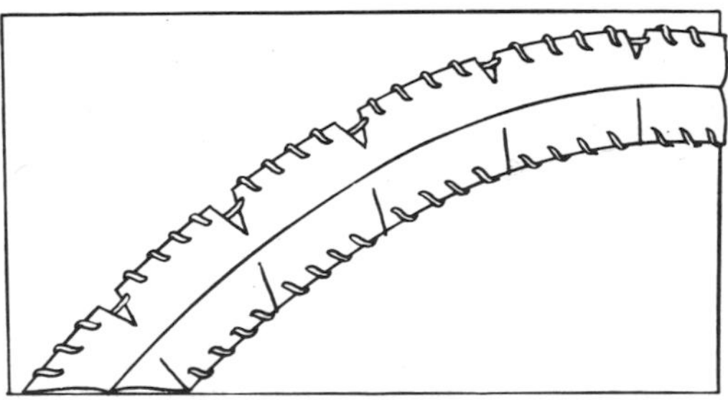

Curved Seam. Curved seams must be clipped in order to lie flat. They may be pressed open or to one side and edges overcast.

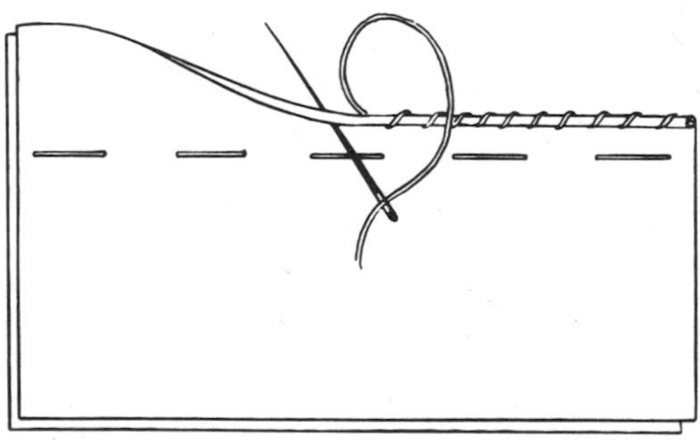

Rolled Seam. Suitable for sheer fabrics. Make a plain seam. Roll edges together and whip while rolling. Do not pull tight.

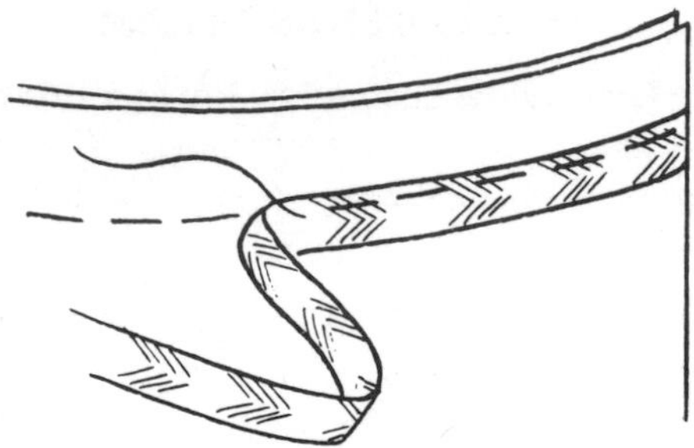

Stayed Seam. Certain places in tailored and knitted garments require taped seams. Apply the tape as the seam is basted. Stitch through all thicknesses, or whip tape on by hand after seam is stitched.

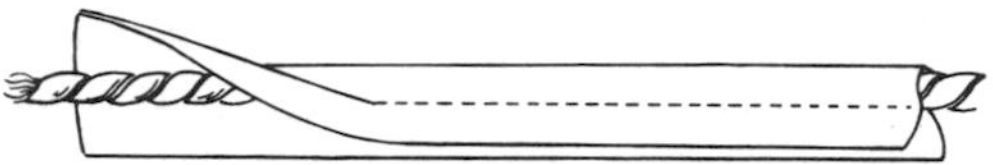

Piped and Corded Seam. For a piped seam, fold a strip of bias through the center. Place between edges of seam with the fold extending beyond the seam line on right side.

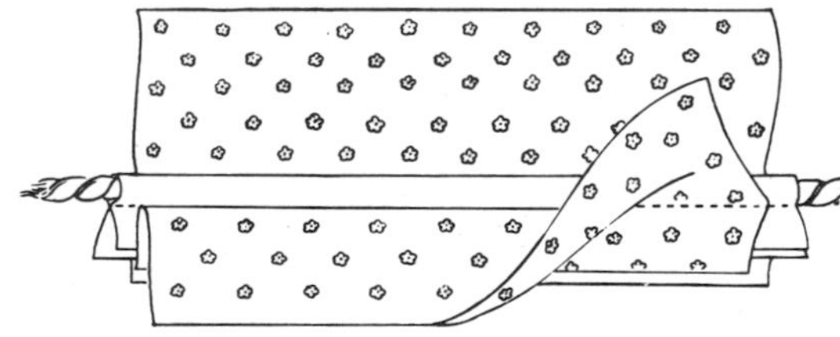

Baste and stitch. To make a corded seam insert cording inside bias fold, and baste before placing in seam. Pin or baste, then stitch close to cord using cording foot.

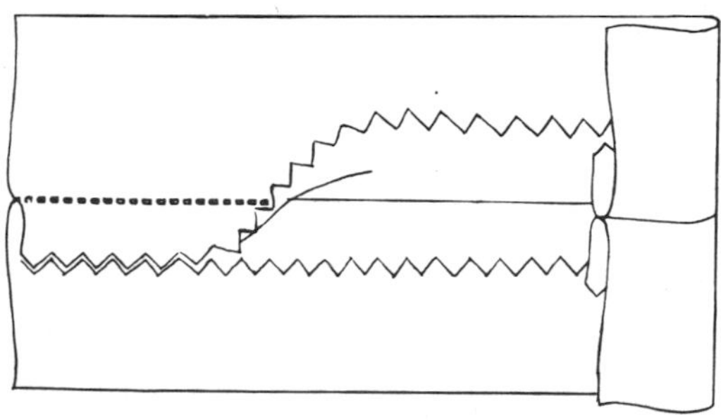

Pinked Seam. Use only on firmly woven fabrics. Stitch and press open or to one side and pink edges.

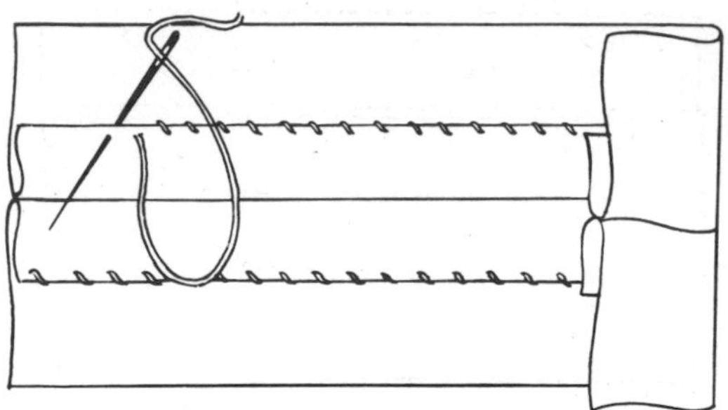

Overcast Seam. Edges of a plain seam may be overcast after pressing open. If edges are pressed to one side, overcast together.

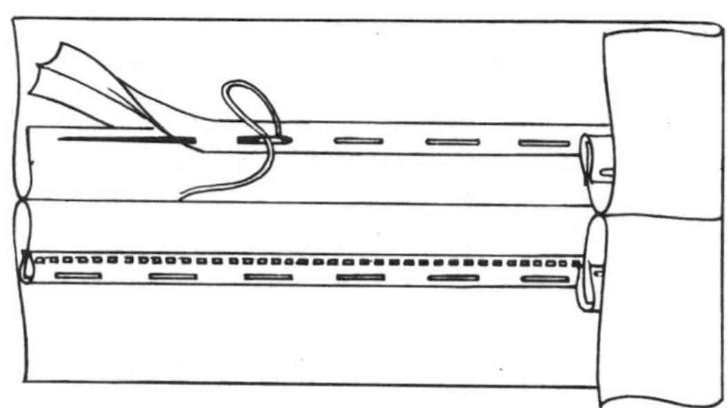

Bound Seam. Used on unlined jackets or coats. Stitch seam and press open. Bind edges with seam binding or bias fold.

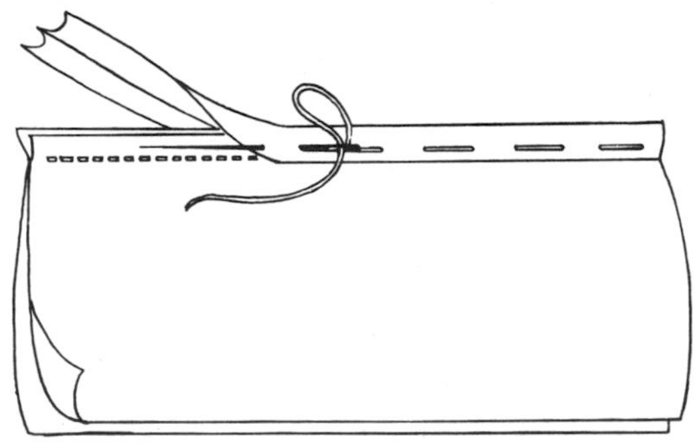

Double-bound Seam. Stitch seam, trim and bind both edges together with seam binding or bias fold.

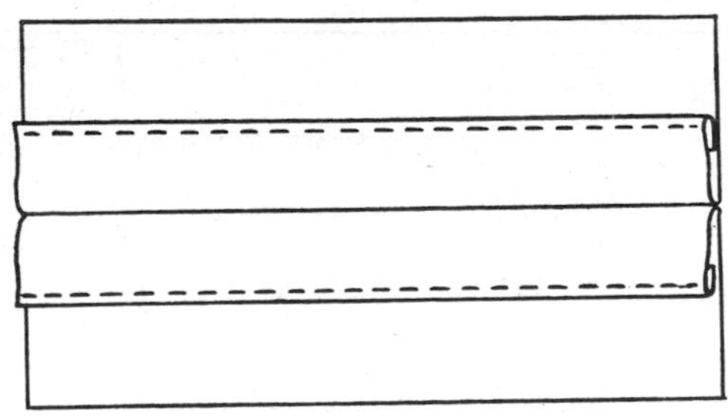

Seam with Stitched Edges. Make seams and press open. Turn edges under and stitch close to edge. They can be stitched before being pressed open.

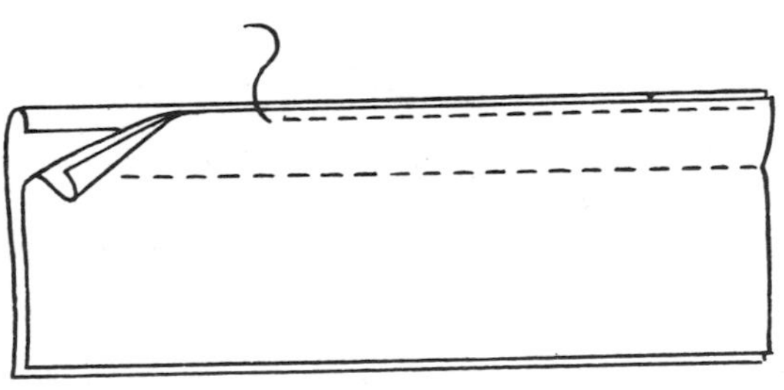

Seam with Edges Stitched Together. Make a plain seam. Turn edges toward each other and stitch together.

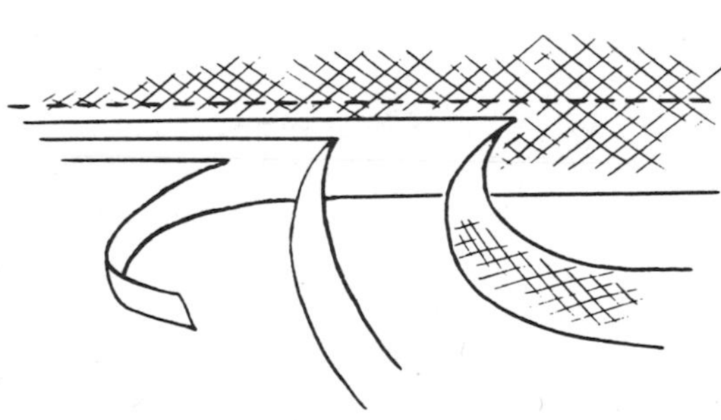

Beveled Seam. Used on seams with interfacing or on thick fabrics. After seam is stitched, the layers are trimmed to different widths. This avoids a ridge on edge of seam.

Hems and Hem Finishes

Hems can be decorative, but as a rule they are meant to be inconspicuous. For skirt hems, after marking, turn on the hem line

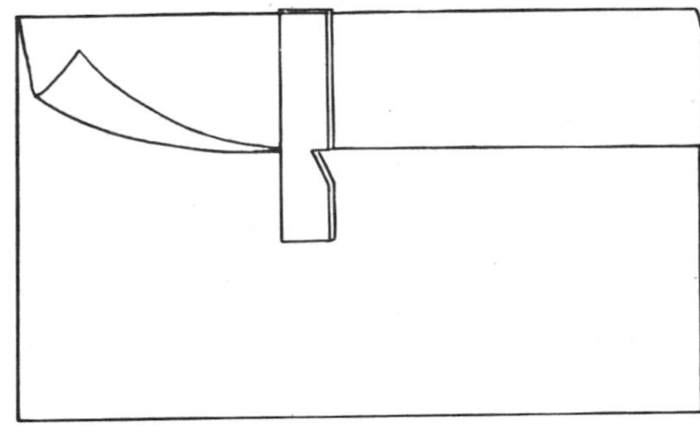

and pin and baste on the fold. Use a gauge to mark the width of hem and trim. Use the finish best suited to fabric and garment.

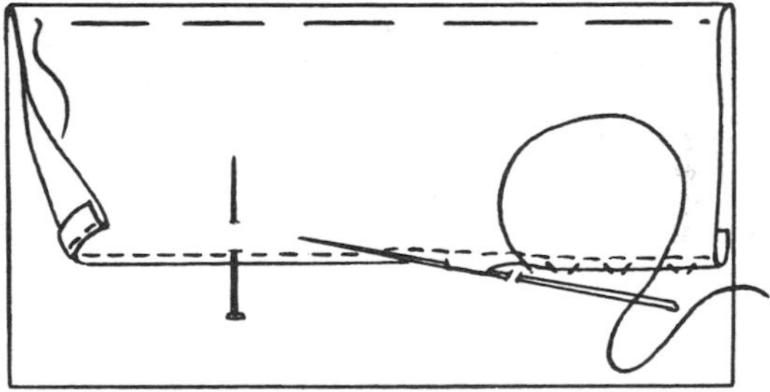

Hem with Stitched Edge. Use on cotton or firmly woven silk or synthetic fabrics. Turn under raw edge and stitch. Pin in place and slip-stitch. Do not use on thick fabrics.

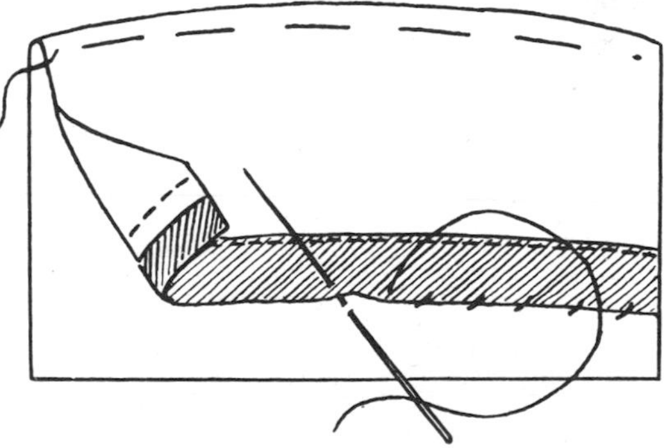

Taped Hem. Especially good for heavy fabrics and those which ravel easily. After turning and trimming, stitch seam binding to raw edge of hem, easing slightly. Pin and blind-hem edge of tape to skirt.

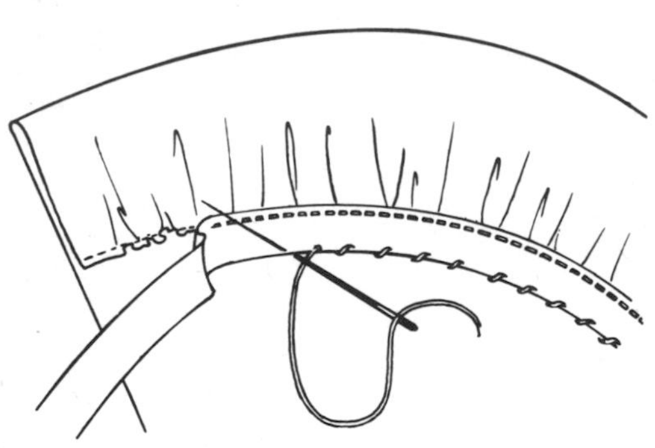

Circular Hem. To adjust fulness evenly at top of hem, run a row of machine-basting (long stitches) at top of hem. Pull up to fit and distribute fulness evenly. Using a damp cloth, press to shrink out fulness. Stitch seam binding to edge and blind-hem to position.

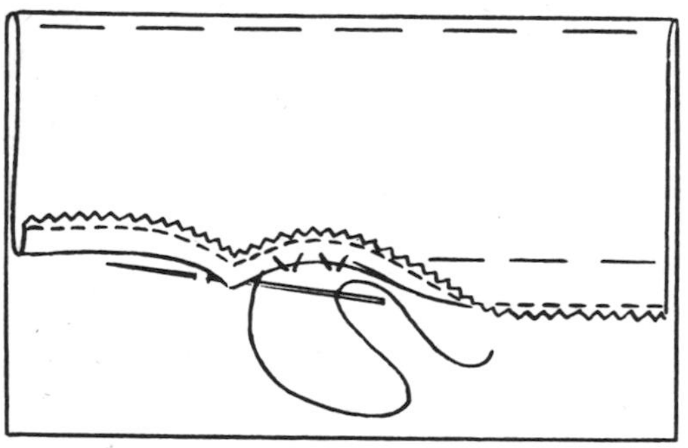

Tailor's Invisible Hem. Stitch and pink the raw edge. Baste hem ½″ away from stitching. Turn the pinked edge back and slip-stitch, catching into hem and then picking up only a thread or two of skirt fabric. Press edge flat. There is little pull on this type of hem and it is practically invisible on the outside.

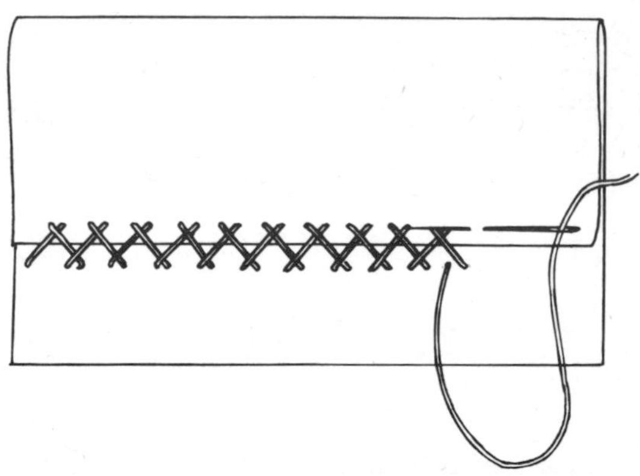

Catch-stitched Hem. Very good for heavy fabrics. Work from left to right. With backstitch, catch into edge of hem and then into the fabric above, working back and forth. This is the same as herringbone stitch in embroidery.

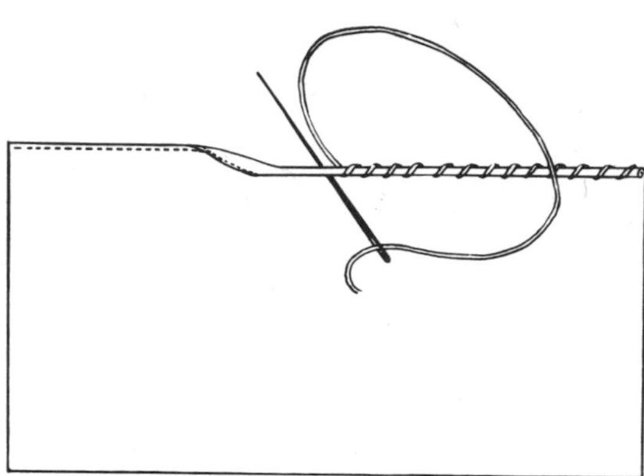

Rolled and Whipped Hem. Machine-stitch close to edge. Roll edge between thumb and forefinger and hold in place with whipping stitches. Instead of whipping, the roll can be caught with slip-stitching.

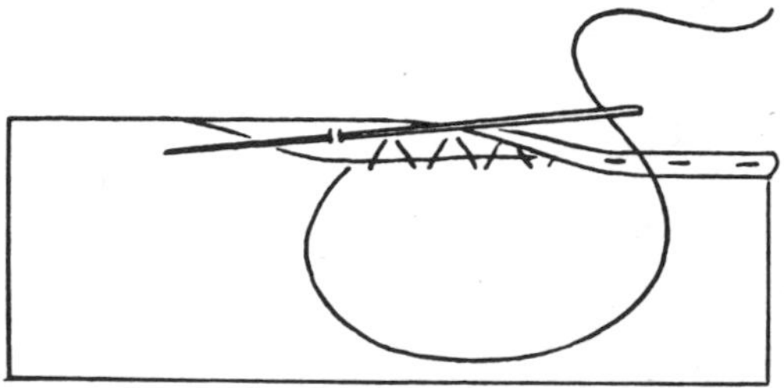

Jiffy Hand-rolled Hem. This is a quick way to make a narrow rolled hem. Fold the edge toward you ¼″ or less. Hide the knot under the fold and take a tiny stitch in the fabric slightly below the fold and a little forward. Take a tiny stitch in edge of fold and a little forward. Repeat for an inch or so. The effect will be zigzag stitches. Draw up and the hem will roll. Repeat.

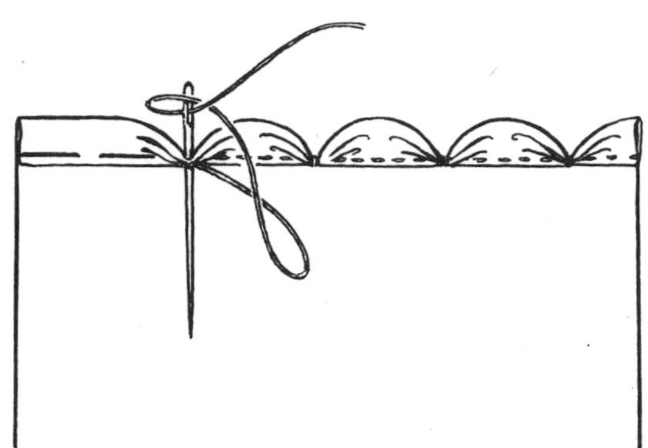

Shell Hem. This is a decorative finish. Baste a narrow hem (about ½″ or less). Make running stitches along turned edge of hem for ¼″ to ½″. Take 2 stitches over the edge, drawing up tightly. Repeat, spacing evenly. This can also be used on tucks.

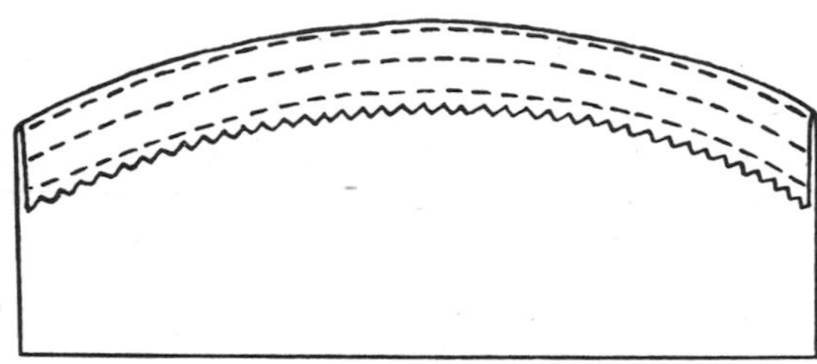

Machine-stitched Hem. After pinking edge, turn a narrow hem and press. Do several rows of machine-stitching, spacing evenly. Suitable for a circular hem.

Corners

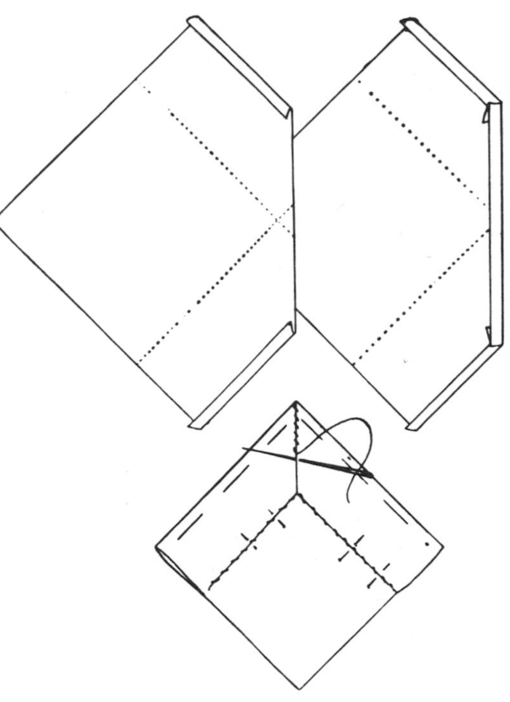

Trimmed Corner. Used on pockets, etc. Turn hems the desired width and crease. Turn edges on seam line and press. Fold corner diagonally exactly on creased corner point and trim to within ¼″ of corner. Turn hem on creased lines, baste edges, press, and hem by hand.

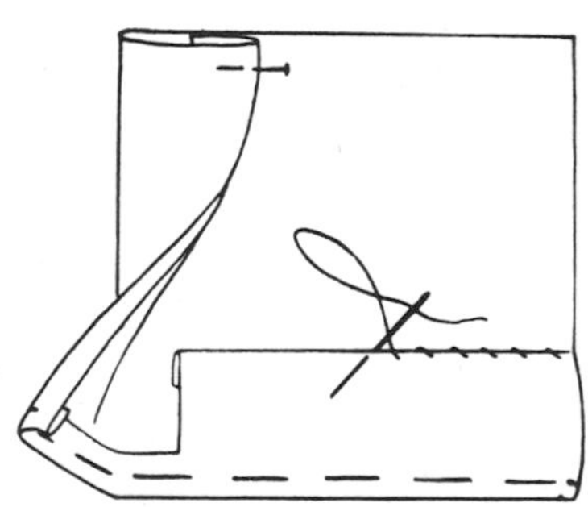

Overlapping Corner. Turn up hem on one side and baste. Before turning second hem, cut away fabric where it overlaps, leaving seam width. Put in hems and slip-stitch lower edge.

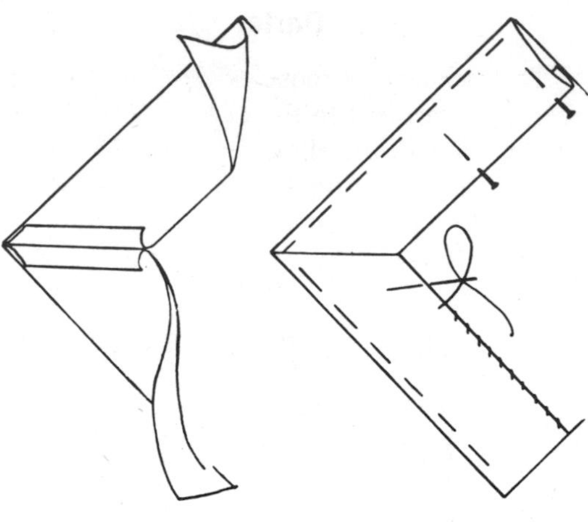

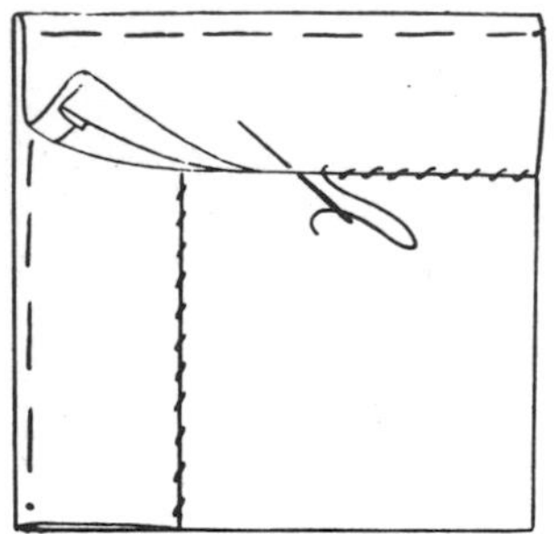

agonally on the folded line, ending exactly at the corner. Trim seam and press open. Turn to inside and finish hem.

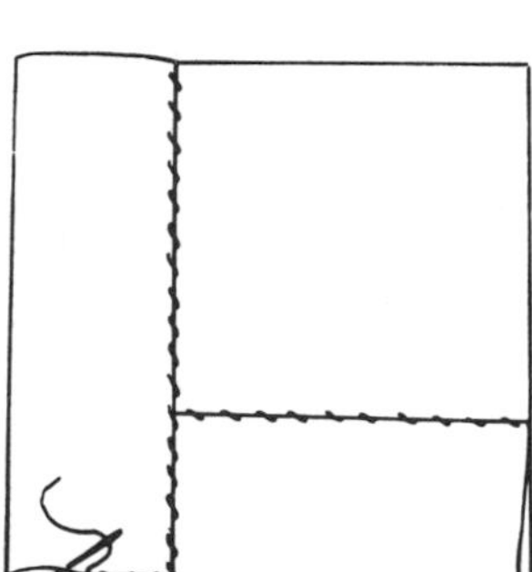

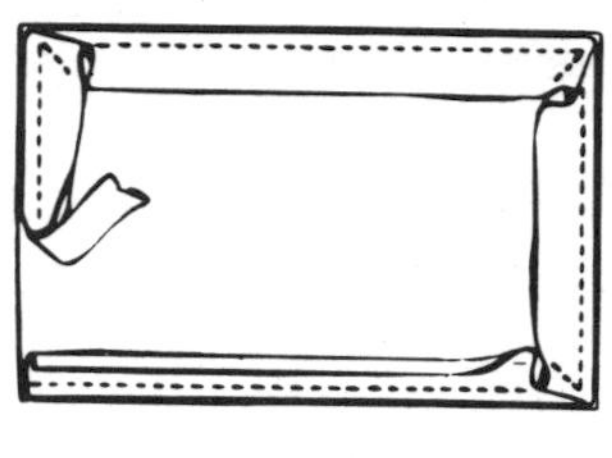

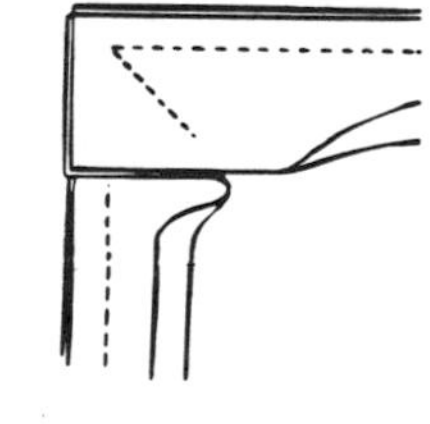

Mitered Corner. Turn hem to the outside and fold the corner so it lies flat. Stitch di-

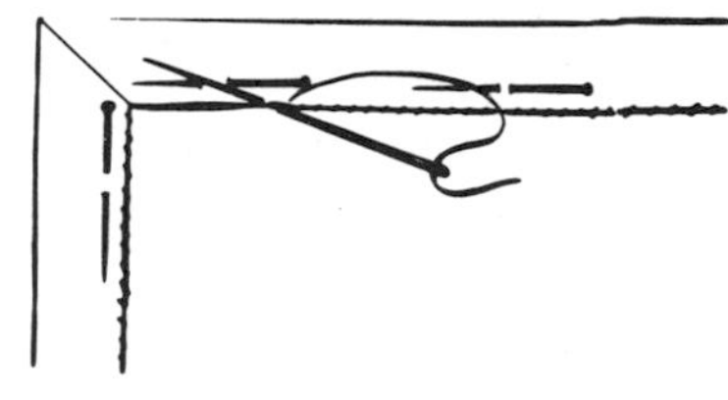

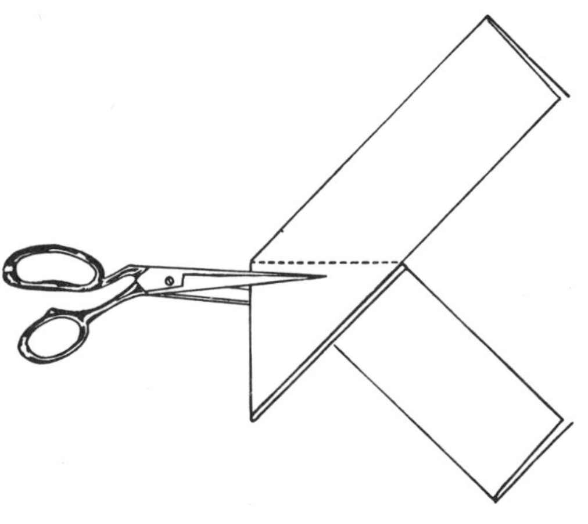

Turning Corner with Trimming Band. Right sides together, pin band to edge of fabric. Turn corner by making a fold in band to make it lie flat. Crease fold. Unpin and stitch on crease. Trim and press seam open. Turn band to reverse side of fabric, and hem by hand.

Darts

The primary purpose of darts is to fit or mold the garment to the curves of the figure at the bust, hips, shoulders, etc. They are usually done on the inside of the garment. Darts should be basted for a first fitting and adjusted if necessary.

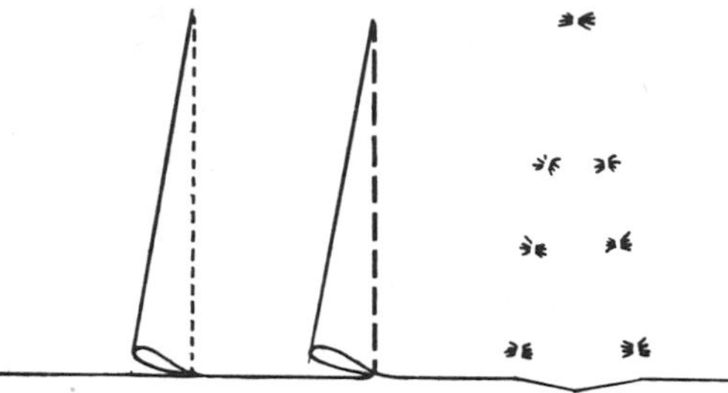

Simple Dart. After marking, fold fabric so markings match. Pin, baste, and stitch. Last few stitches at point should taper off very close to edge. In heavy fabrics, slash and press open.

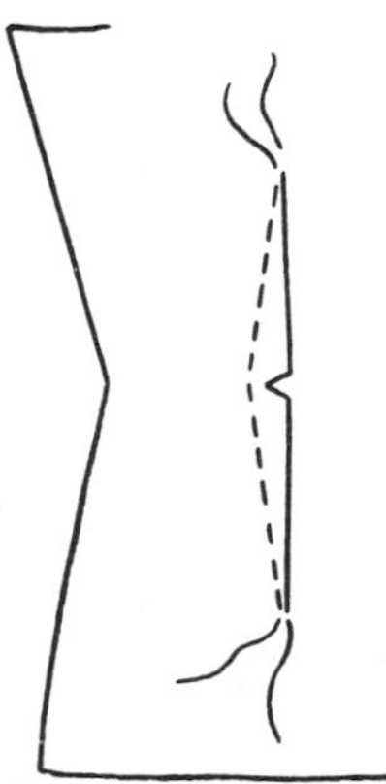

Waistline Dart. These darts come to a point at both ends and are clipped at the waistline to prevent drawing.

Edge-stitched Dart. Mark, pin, and baste. Stitch on the folded edge only. Turn dart and baste to garment across top. After seaming, remove basting.

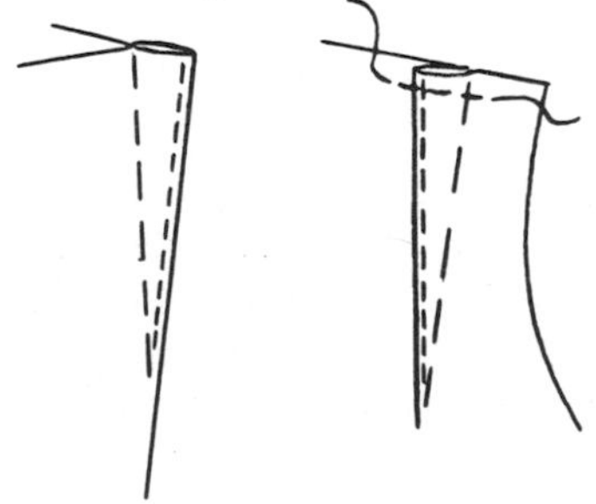

To Stitch a Dart with No Thread Ends. Darts are sometimes made on the outside as functional trimming. When used in this way, there is a method of stitching with one thread so there are no thread ends at the point of the dart. Thread machine as usual but leave needle unthreaded. Thread the needle with the bobbin thread but in reverse of the way it is usually threaded. Tie the bobbin thread to the spool thread and wind spool until the knot is up to the spool. Now start at the point of the dart and stitch the dart with this continuous thread.

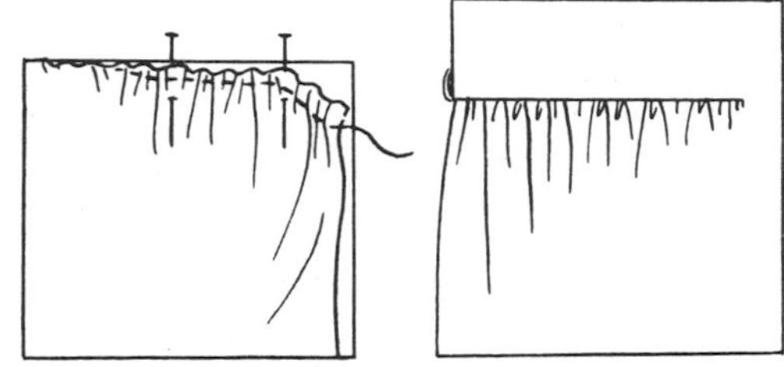

Gathered or Pleated Dart. The lower edge of the slash is wider than the top, as indicated by the pattern. Gather or pleat the lower edge to fit the upper. Seam together, tapering to the end of the slash. The slash may be stayed with a piece of fabric before stitching.

Tucks

Tucks are usually used for decoration and may be all of even width or graduated in

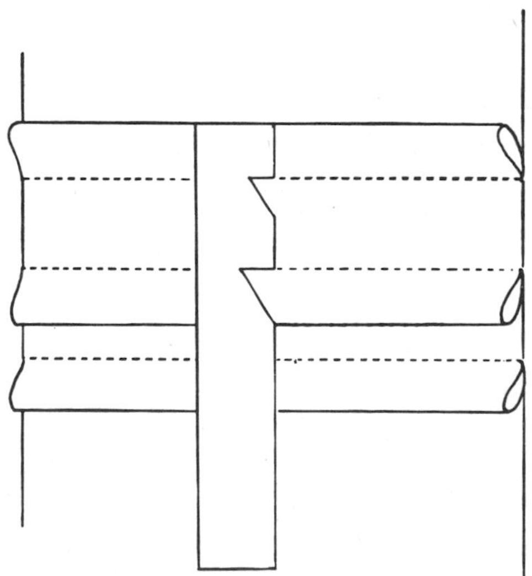

width. To insure even spacing, make a notched gauge to indicate width of tuck as well as the space between tucks.

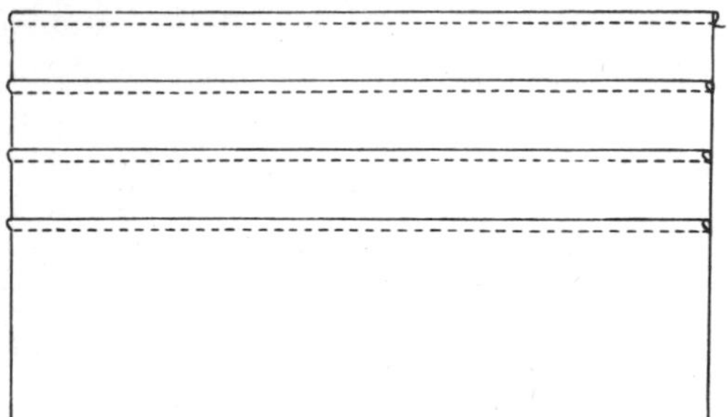

Pin Tucks. These can be run by hand or by machine. Measure and crease the fabric on the grain. Stitch close to the crease.

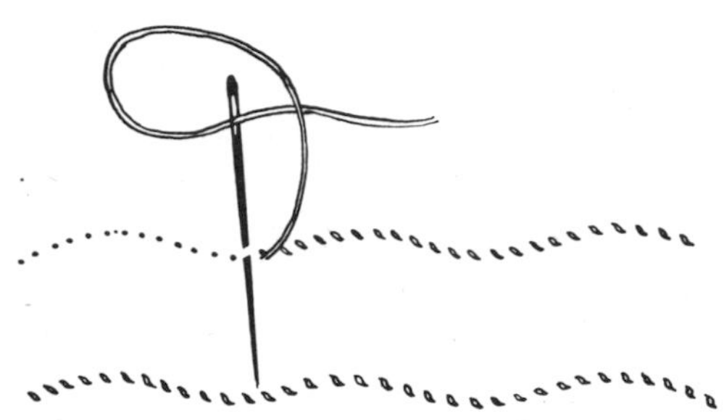

Decorative Trimming Tucks. Draw a wavy or scalloped line. Use tiny overhand stitches, following the line.

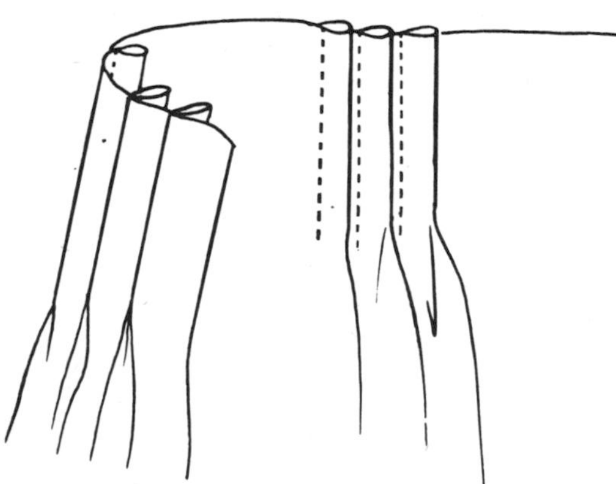

Grouped Tucks. Arrange tucks in groups, spacing as desired.

Cross Tucks. Measure, mark, and stitch tucks in one direction. Mark and stitch tucks in opposite direction, crossing the first group. Use on light weight fabrics only.

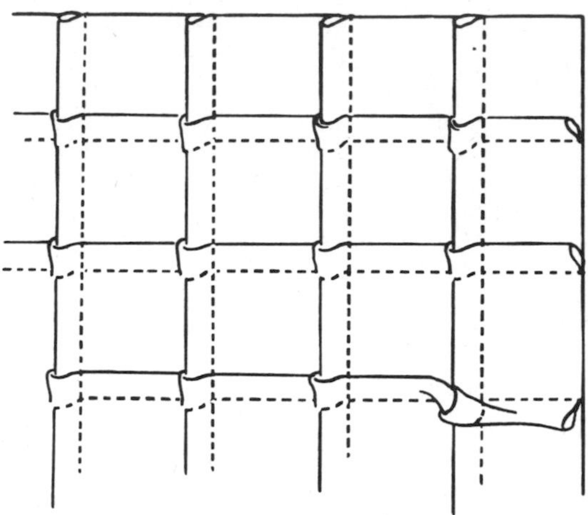

Corded Tucks. Measure for tucks. Encase cord at marking and stitch using cording foot.

Bias Bindings and Facings

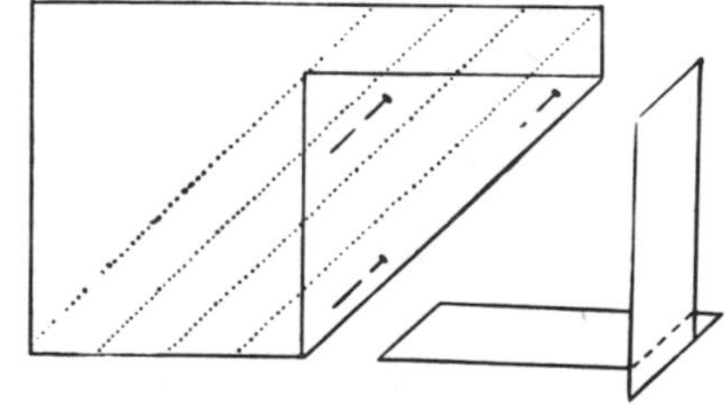

Cutting Bias Binding. Use a square or rectangular piece of fabric. Fold so the crosswise grain (weft) meets, or is parallel to the selvage edge or lengthwise grain. The diagonal edge is the true bias. Pin on fold and mark rows of bias the desired width. Cut.

To piece bias strips, lap ends of 2 strips so threads are parallel. Stitch, trim, and press open.

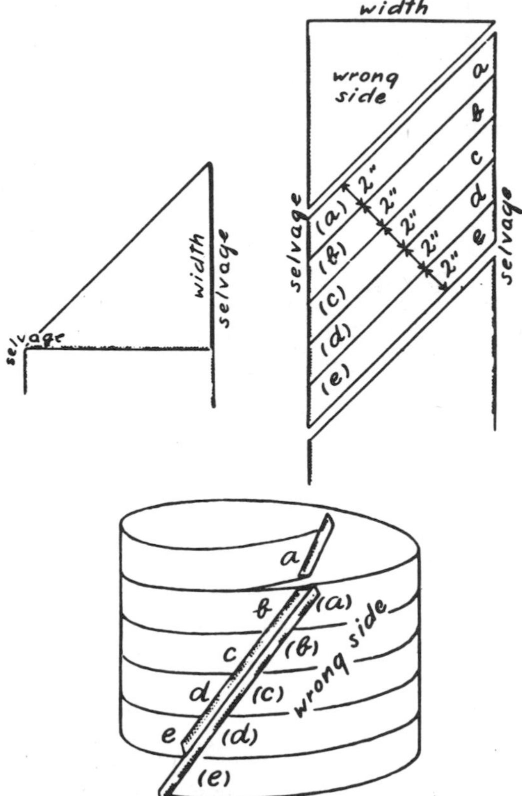

Cutting a Continuous Strip of Bias. Use a rectangular piece of fabric which has been cut on the grain.

On the wrong side of the fabric mark a true bias line from the upper corner to the opposite side. (The easiest way to do this is to crease and fold as explained above.)

Measure down the width of bias wanted and draw a second line. Measure and mark remaining space.

With right sides together, fold lengthwise (markings will be crosswise). Match the first line to the second line allowing for a 1/4" seam. The following lines will match. Stitch seam, press open, and cut a continuous strip.

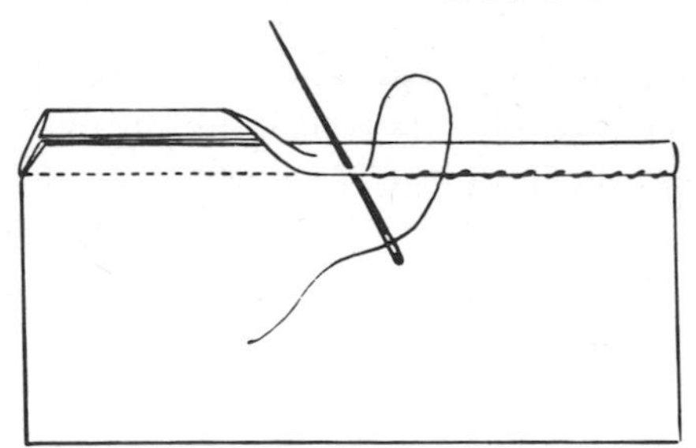

Using Single Binding. Use bias tape or cut a bias strip. With right sides together and edges even, stitch seam. Turn binding over seam to wrong side. Hem to seam. Edge may also be encased in bias fold tape in one operation. Baste and stitch catching all thicknesses.

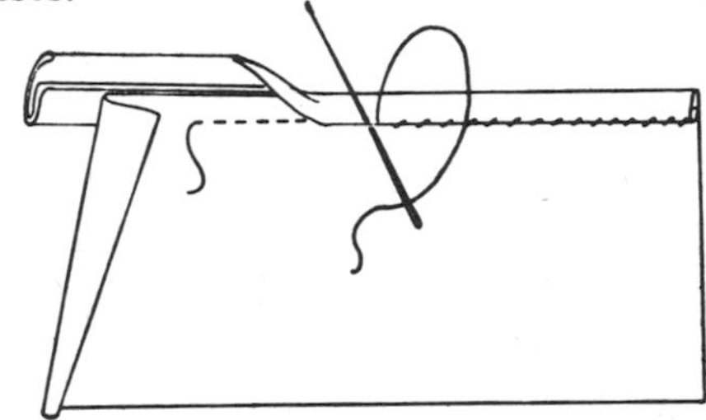

French Binding. Used on sheer fabrics. Cut binding 6 times the finished width and press double lengthwise. Raw edges together, stitch seam. Turn folded edge over and hem to seam line. Most attractive when very narrow.

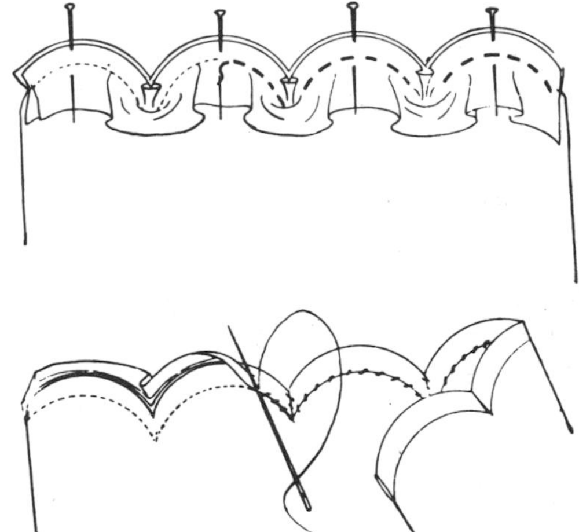

Binding Scallops. With bias toward you and edges even, pin, then baste binding to scalloped edge, easing it over curves and stretching at corners. Stitch and trim seam to 1/8 inch. Turn under on wrong side and hem to stitching, mitering corners.

Piped Facing. Press the edges on a true bias strip so the fold is twice as wide on one side as on the other. This will prevent raw edges on wrong side. Wrong sides together, place piping so it extends beyond fold. Baste and stitch on outside edge.

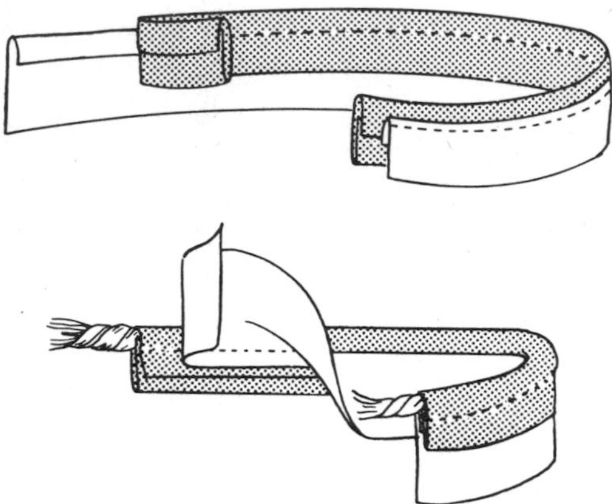

Note: Cording may be encased in bias before sewing to fabric.

Scallops with Piping. Turn and baste the edges of the scallops to the wrong side, clipping them so that the curves will be true and they will lie flat. Baste a folded bias piping under edges, clip at corners, letting a little extend beyond edge. Top-stitch on edge of scallops.

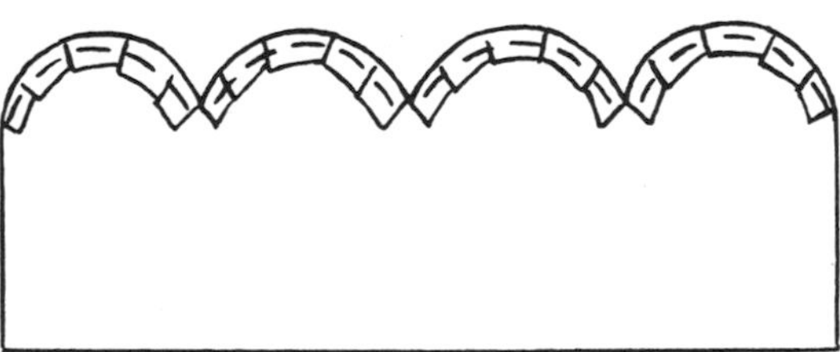

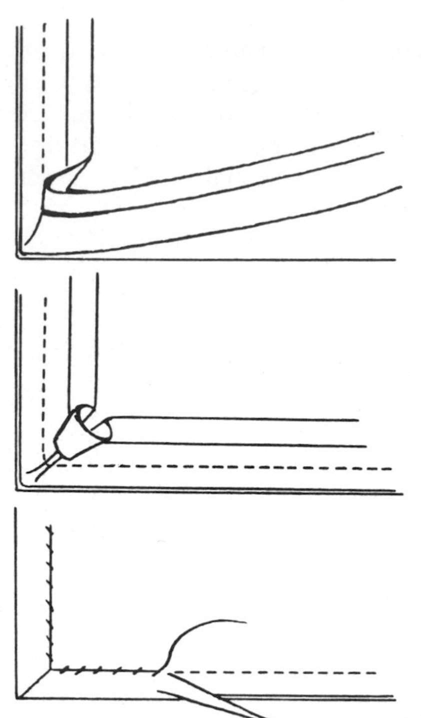

Binding an Outside Corner. With right sides together and edges even, pin and baste bias binding to corner. Allow fabric to make a perfect miter at corner. Stitch around, raising needle over fold at corner. Turn to wrong side and hem, mitering corner.

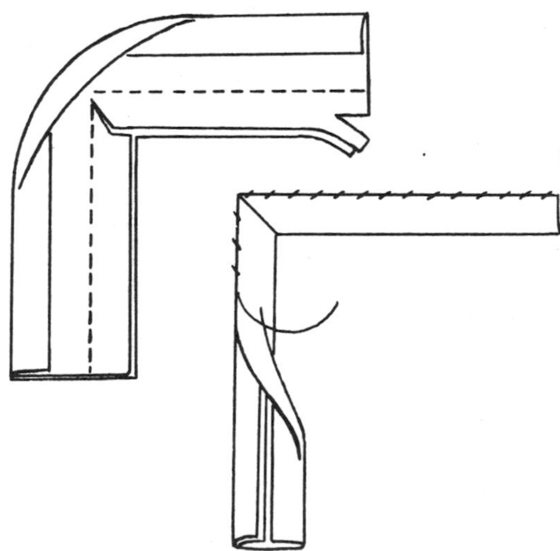

Binding Inside Corner. With right sides together and edges even, pin and baste bias binding to corner. Stretch binding at corner, and when stitching pivot the needle. Turn to wrong side and hem, mitering corner.

Facing a Hem. Cut a true bias about 2″ wide for facing or use ready-made facing in cotton or acetate. Lay right sides together with edges even and stitch. Press seam open. Turn to wrong side, making the fold a seam-width beyond the stitching, and baste. Turn under and stitch the raw edge of the facing. Hem to skirt.

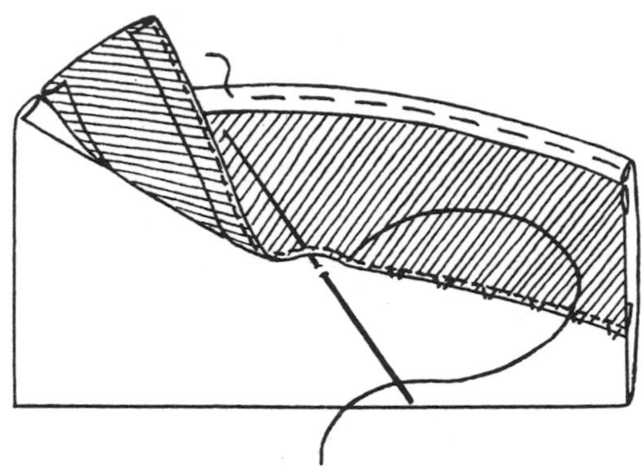

Facing Points or Scallops. With right sides together, baste and stitch facing to fabric. Trim seam, clip corner, and cut off points. Turn to right side and baste along fold.

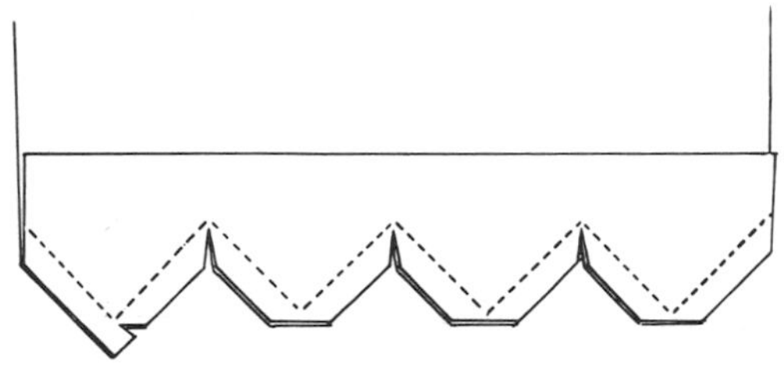

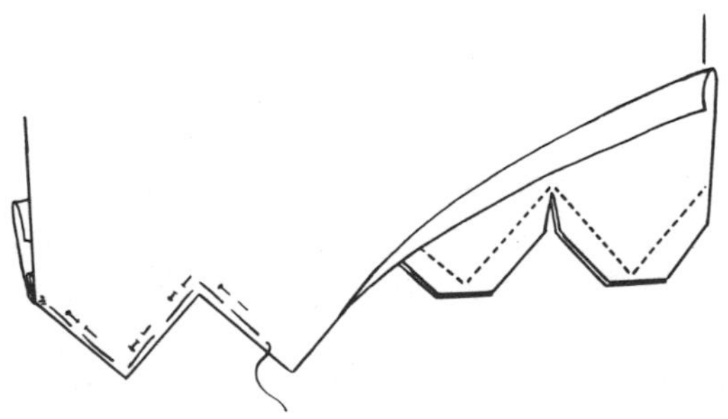

Gathering, Shirring, Ruffles

Gathering and shirring may be done by hand or machine. (See Stitches under Basic Sewing for gathering by hand.) To gather by machine, set for longest stitch. Pull up the bobbin thread. One or more rows may be made. Gathering or fine pleating may be done with a machine attachment.

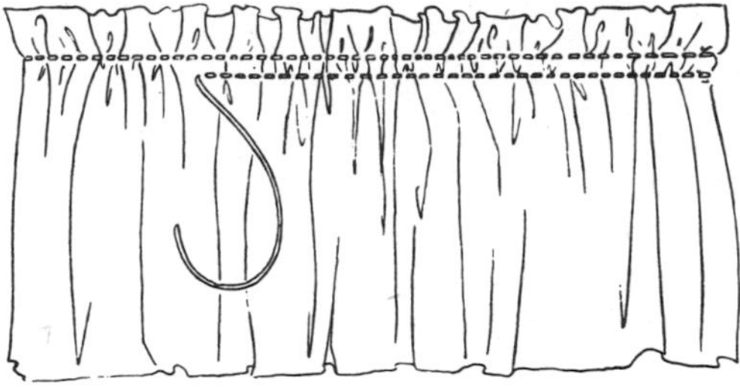

Stayed Shirring. Cut a piece of fabric for a stay the size of shirred area plus seam all around. Turn under edges of a stay so it is the width of the shirring. Pin and baste to wrong side and hem invisibly.

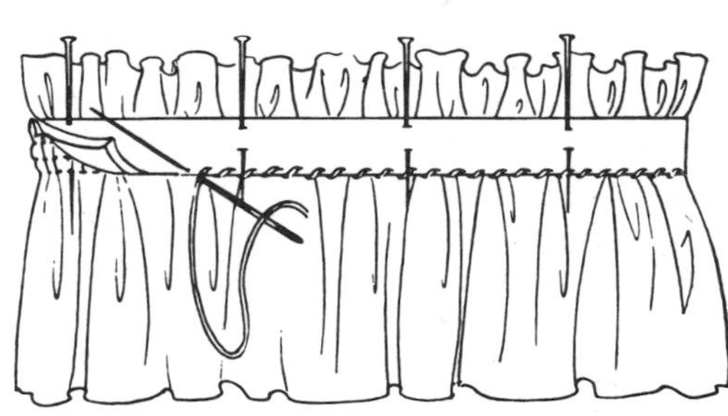

Circular Ruffle. Cut, using a pattern. Finish the edge of the ruffle. Stay-stitch near the seam line on inside curve and clip almost to the stitching. With right sides together, pin and stitch ruffle in position.

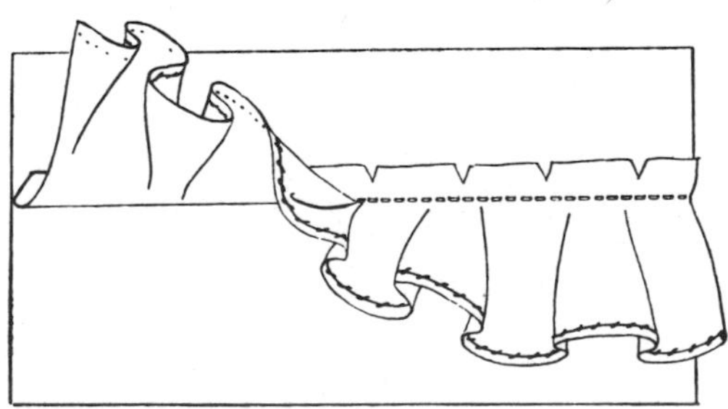

Adjusting Fulness. Measure and mark ruffle and the space it is to fit into 4 equal parts (or more if it is a long space). Draw up and match markings and adjust fulness evenly in the spaces. Fasten gathering threads. Baste and stitch.

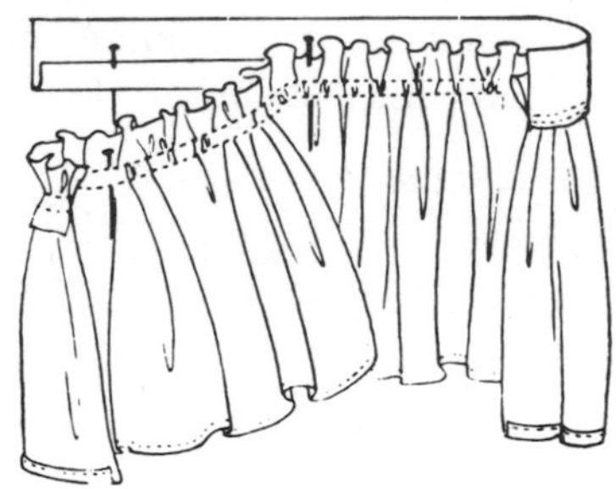

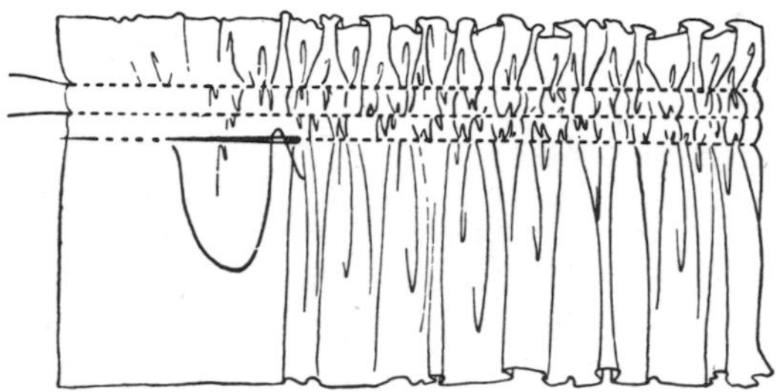

Ruffle with Heading. Turn edge the width of the heading plus seam allowance. Make 2 or 3 rows of gathers by hand or machine. Baste in place, adjusting fulness, and stitch.

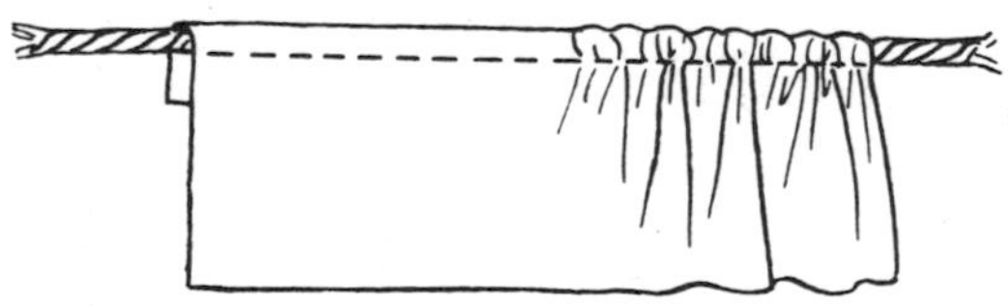

Corded Shirring. Turn fabric, encasing the cord, and stitch close to cord by hand or machine (use cording foot). Make as many rows as desired. Draw gathers up on the cord to the required fulness.

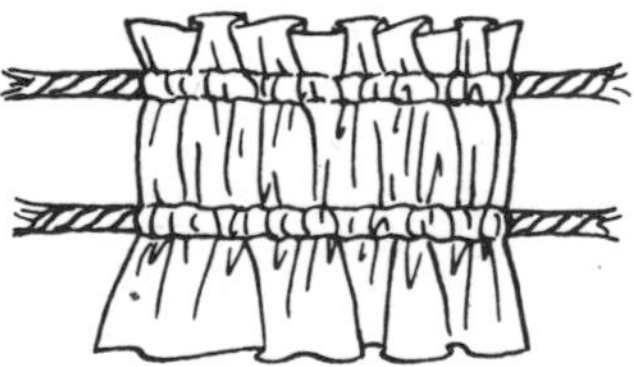

Pleating

Pleats may be pressed or, for a softer effect, be left unpressed. Careful marking is necessary if pleats are to look professional. This can be done with or without a pattern.

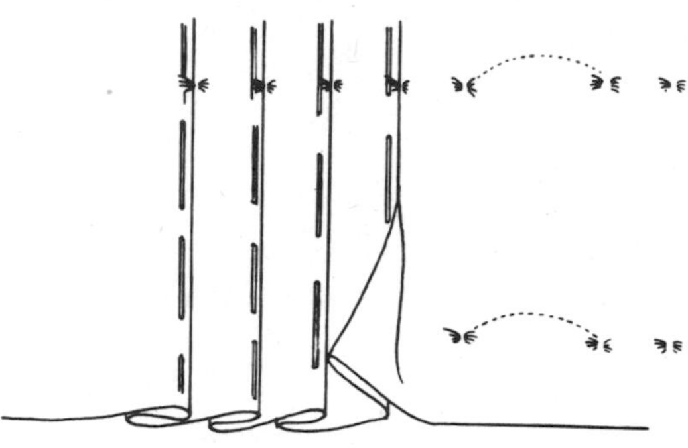

Pleating with a Pattern. Mark carefully the pattern indications given for pleats. Bring markings of a fold to the next line of markings. Pin, baste, and press. Repeat. In small areas it is possible to pin on pattern and pleat pattern and fabric together. Baste and press. Remove pattern, stitch, and press.

Pleating without a Pattern. For a full pleated skirt (edges of pleats meeting) the fabric allowance is 3 times the hip measurement at its widest part. Join seams leaving placket opening at top of one seam. Measure length and hem the skirt. Lay in the pleats, pin and baste, tapering and lapping to fit waistline. Keep pleats uniform. Try on. Press and stitch.

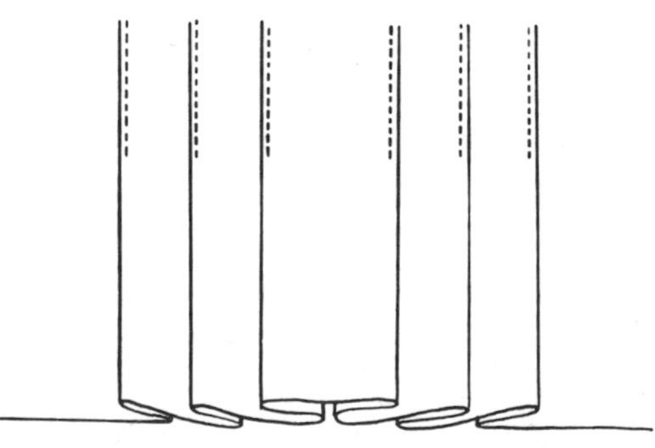

Stitching Pleats. To prevent stretching fabric, stitch yoke pleats in place from the bottom up.

One-way Knife Pleats. Lap pleat from right to left and arrange so a pleat will cover the placket.

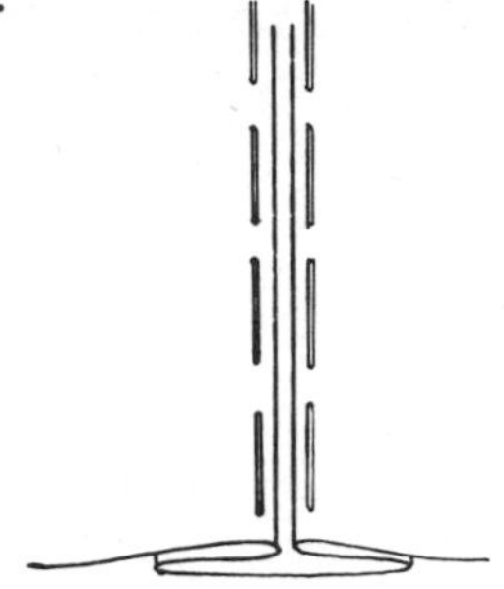

Inverted Pleat. An inverted pleat consists of two straight pleats turned toward each other and meeting.

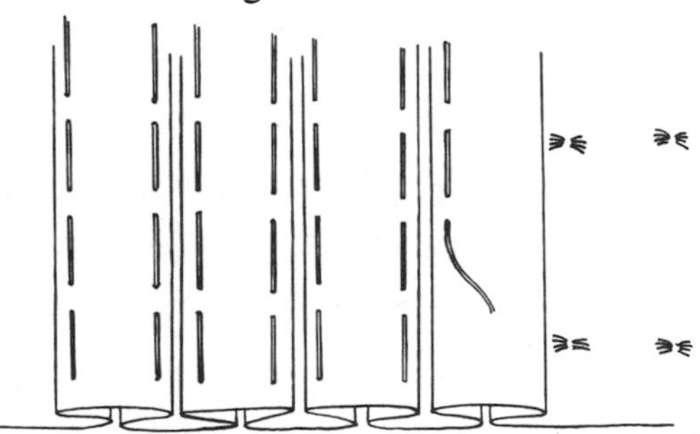

Box Pleats. A box pleat consists of two straight pleats turned in opposite directions. They may or may not meet underneath. Actually, box pleats are a series of inverted pleats placed close together.

Edge-stitching Pleats. Pleats may be edge-stitched (on the fold) if desired. This keeps the pleats in. After skirt is hemmed and pleats are basted, start at the bottom and stitch to waistline or to the point where the pleats are to be stitched in place. Edge-stitching is often used on sunburst pleats.

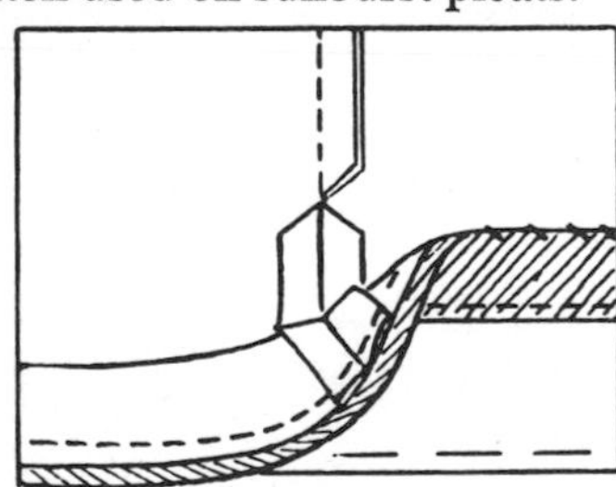

Hemming Pleat with a Seam. Press seam open inside of hem.

Turn up hem and clip seam at top if fabric is firmly woven. In thin fabrics turn the edge gradually. Finish hem and press pleat.

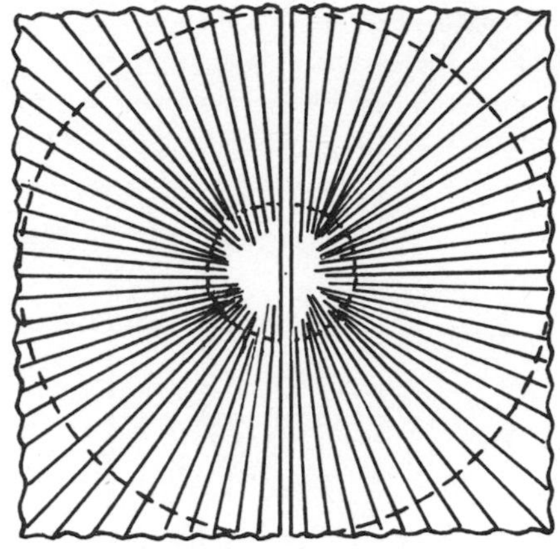

Sunburst Pleats. This kind of pleating is done by machine. Prepare fabric by sewing together pieces to form a large square. Have it pleated. Cut out center circle a little less than the waist measurement. Stay-stitch the cut edge. Make placket at seam and on line of a pleat. Attach waistband to the cut edge clipping curves. Edge-stitch pleats if desired. Try on and mark hem.

Machine Pleating. There are many kinds to choose from. If you are near a good pleating establishment, consult them to learn how much width to allow and how to prepare fabric. It will differ for various pleating designs. After pleating, baste around top edge catching each pleat.

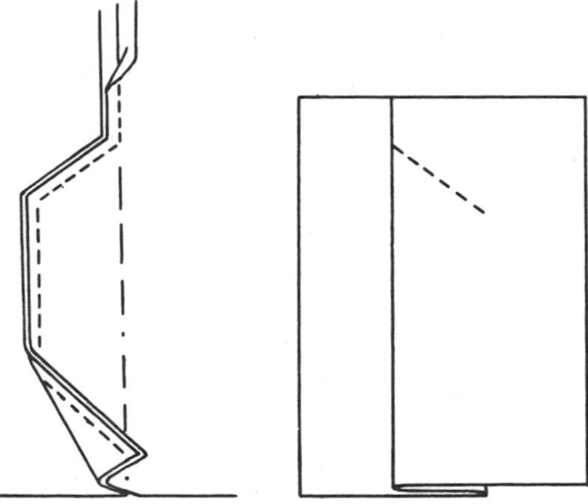

Extension Pleat. Stitch seam and extension seam. Fold pleat on seam line. Clip corner and press open the seam above pleat. On right side stitch top of extension to skirt to hold in place.

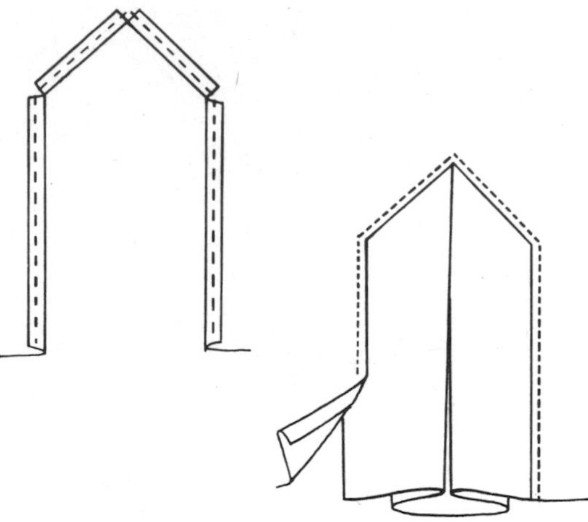

Inverted Box Pleat, Set In. Clip corners of opening the width of seam. Lay pleated section which has been cut to fit under opening, centers matching. Baste and stitch around opening.

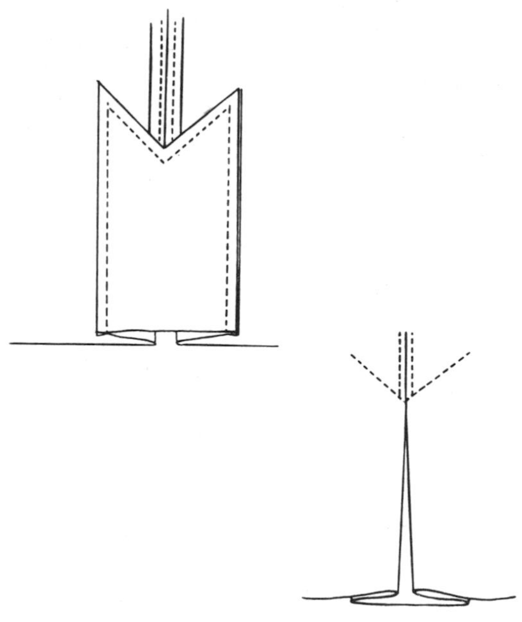

Set-in Pleat at Seam. Stitch seam above extension and press open. Fold extension to inside and press. Pin and stitch the underlay piece, matching sides and top edges. Stitch slant-wise on outside to hold in place.

Buttonholes

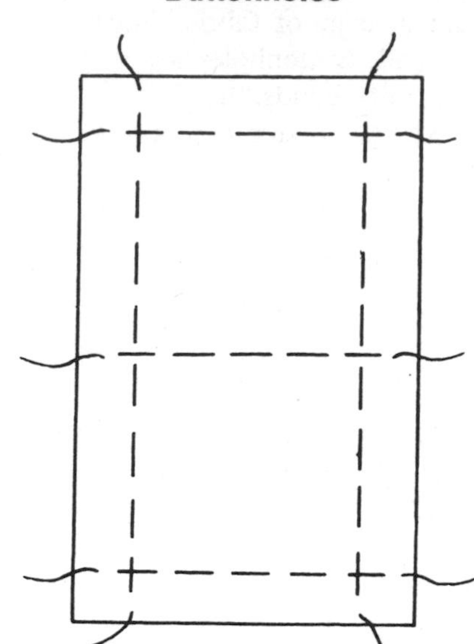

Marking for Buttonholes. Buttonholes should be ⅛″ longer than the buttons (larger for ball buttons). For one or more buttonholes, mark the width with vertical basting lines. Mark for each buttonhole with horizontal basting. Follow grain of fabric in both bastings.

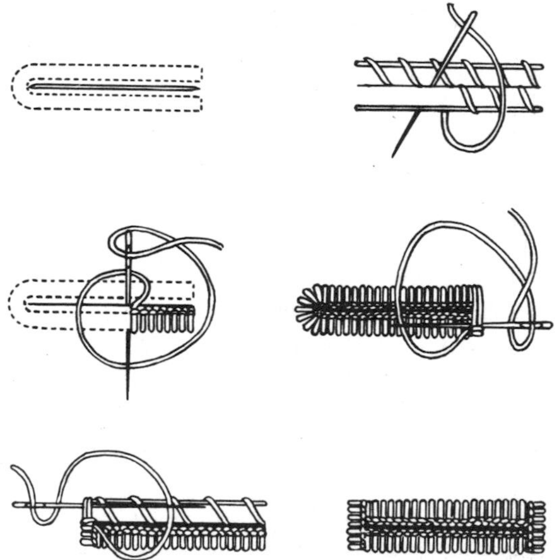

Worked Buttonholes. After garment is completed mark position of buttonhole. Baste marking following a thread of the fabric. Machine-stitch around. Cut on basting and overcast edges.

Work from right to left fanning stitches at end nearest edge of fabric. Finish with bar at other end. Buttonholes are worked vertically on shirt bands, fly fronts, and other narrow strips. In this case both ends have bar tacks.

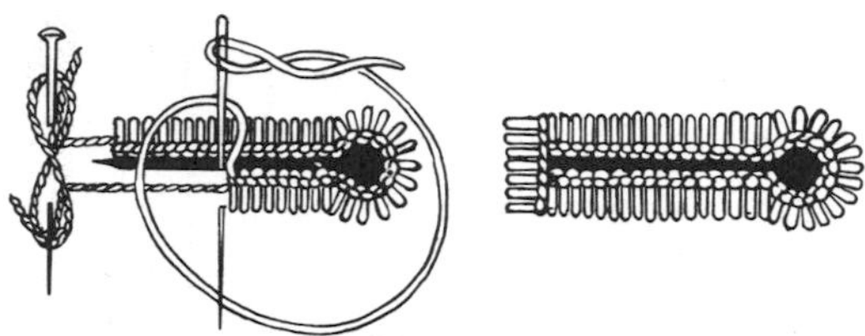

Tailored Buttonholes. Punch the end near edge of fabric with a stiletto. Baste and stitch as above. Cut on marked line and overcast edges. For a corded edge, work over a strand of buttonhole twist held taut with a pin. Work straight across end of buttonhole or work a bar tack.

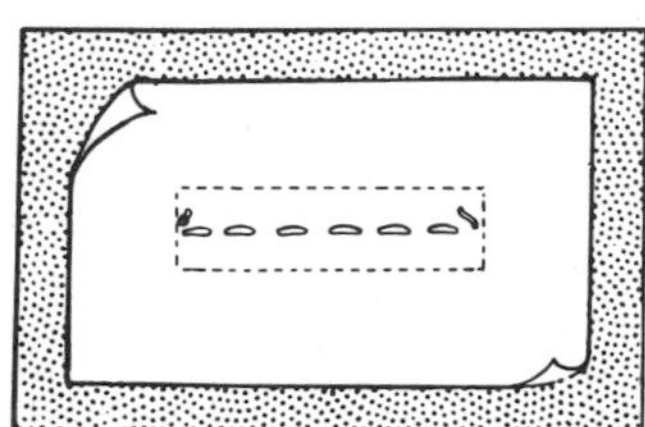

Patch-Bound Buttonholes. Cut a patch 2″ wide and 1″ longer than the buttonhole. The lengthwise grain of the fabric should run lengthwise of the buttonhole. The fabric can be cut on the true bias. This is often done on checks and plaids.

Note: The patch can be cut in one long strip and basted over all buttonholes at one time if the buttonholes are 2″ apart or more. After stitching around buttonholes, cut the strip half-way between each buttonhole.

If separate pieces are used, crease fabric patch through center lengthwise. Open out and, with right sides together, center and baste with the crease over the marked basting line. Stitch ⅛″ each side of basting and across ends, making square corners.

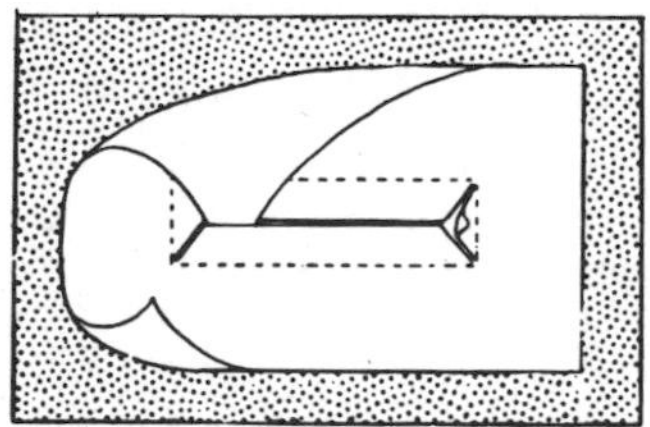

Slash on the center line to within ¼″ or ⅜″ of ends and clip diagonally to corners. Turn strip to inside. Form a piping with the patch by turning seams away from slash.

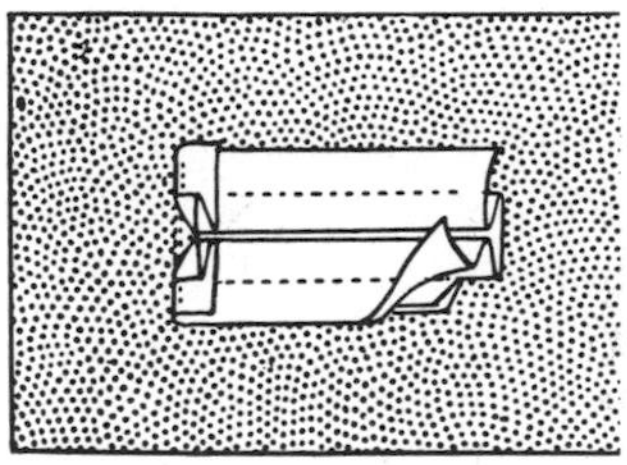

Make tiny box pleat at each end. Baste around. Stitch the small triangles to the patch by hand or by machine.

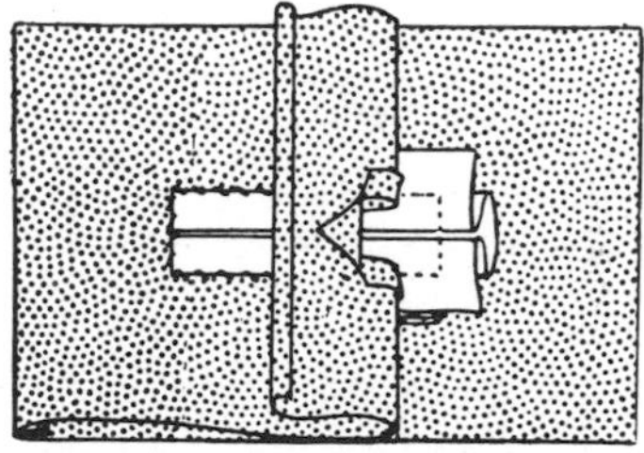

To face buttonhole, slash facing through buttonhole opening, clipping corners. Turn in edges and hem.

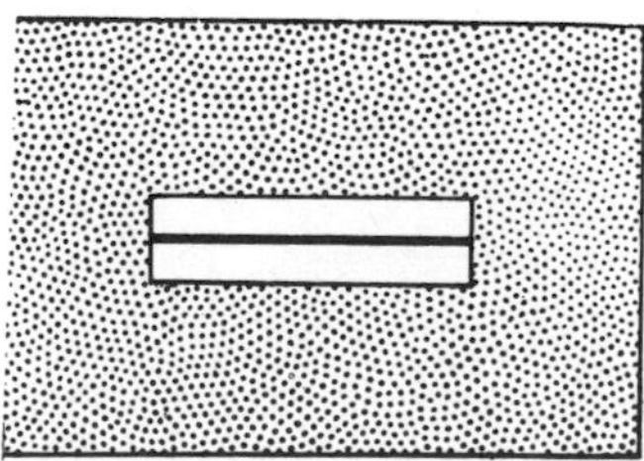

Corded or Two-Piece Buttonholes. For each buttonhole you will need a strip of cording twice its length plus two inches. Prepare enough for all buttonholes at one time. Cut a strip ¾″ to 1″ wide on the bias or straight of fabric. Fold lengthwise right side out and stitch close to encased cord. Size of cord depends upon size of buttonhole and fabric used.

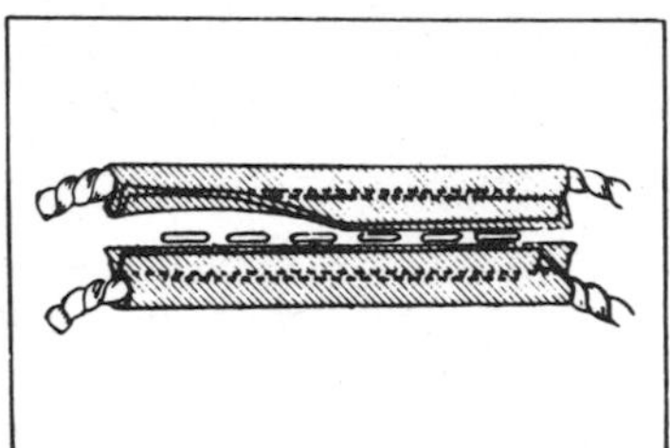

On right side baste the two strips with raw edges meeting on the line of marking for buttonhole. The line of stitching on the cording should be ⅛″ away from line of buttonhole (wider for heavy fabrics). Stitch both sides but not across ends. Slash and clip to corners. Turn strips to wrong side.

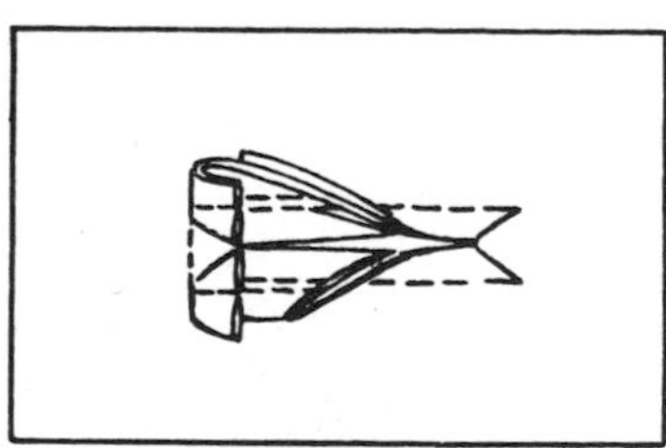

Stitch the triangular ends to the piping. This can be done by hand or machine. Press and face same as Patch-Bound Buttonholes.

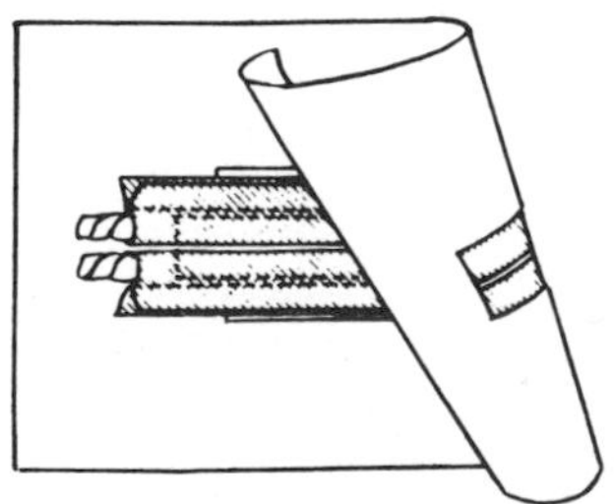

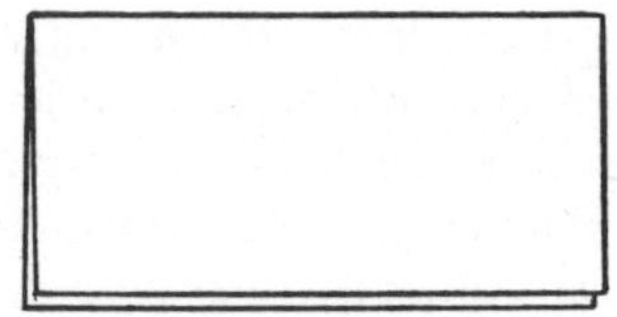

One-Piece Fold Buttonholes. Cut a strip 1″ wide and 1″ longer than finished buttonhole. Right side out, fold piece lengthwise down center and press lightly.

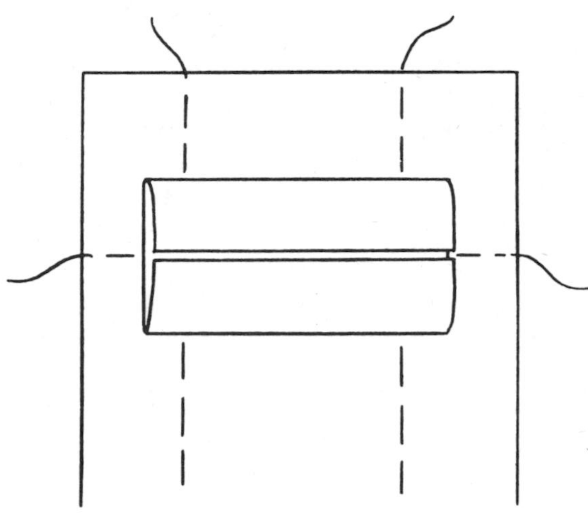

Fold with raw edges meeting at creased line. With raw edges up baste to right side of fabric, centering over marking.

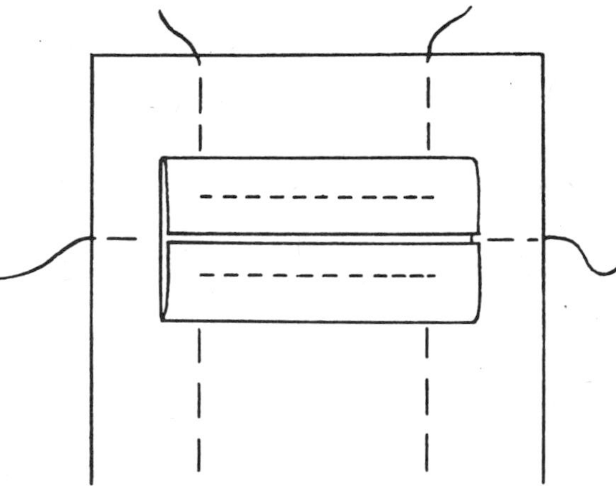

Baste and stitch ⅛″ each side of raw edges the length of buttonhole but not across ends.

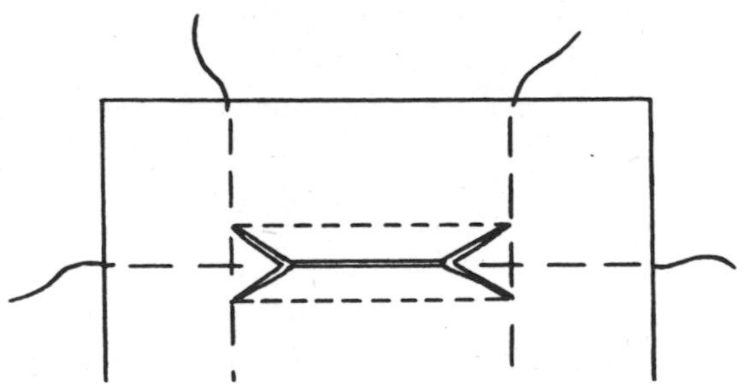

Slash center line and diagonally to corners.

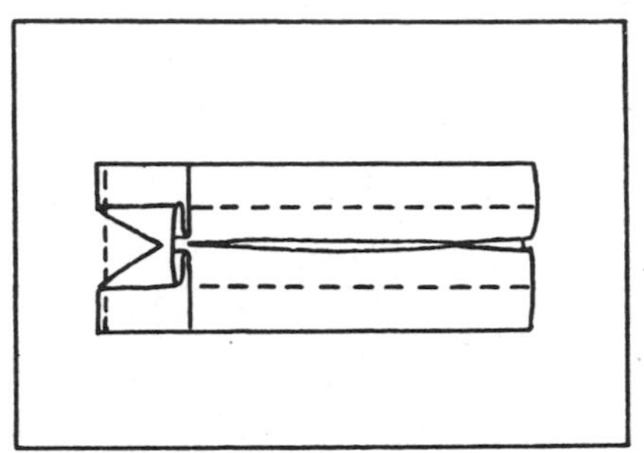

Turn patch to wrong side and stitch the small triangles to the patch by hand or by machine with very fine stitching. Keep cor-

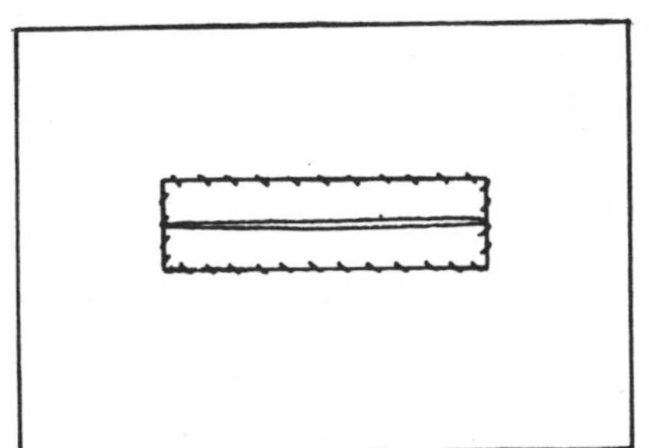

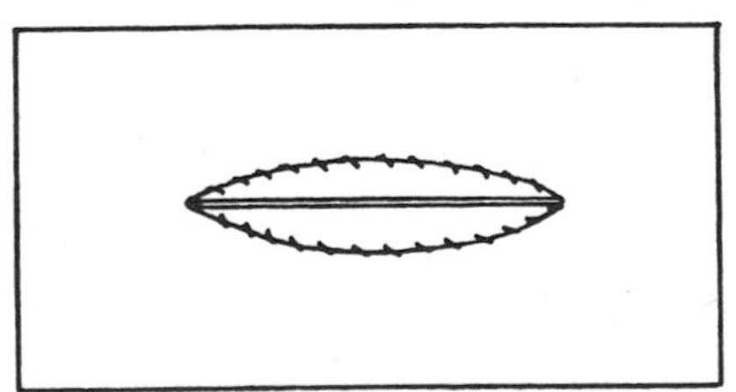

ners square. Press. If facing is called for, slash facing and hem by hand. Facing may be finished with square corners by slashing

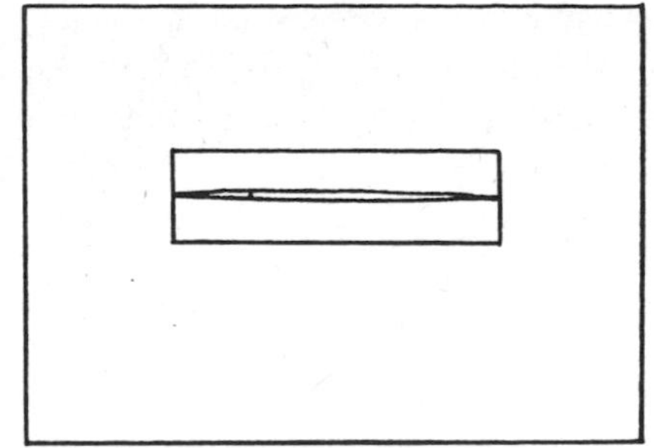

corners. Finished buttonhole should be true and square at corners and follow grain of fabric.

Sewing on Buttons

How to Mark. Lap garment properly and mark position of button, centering it at end of buttonhole nearest the edge of garment.

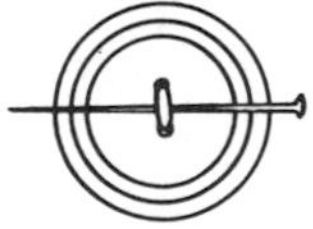

Set button in place with pin on top. Starting on right side, conceal knot under button.

Sew through button and over the pin, taking care that the stitches on wrong side are short and almost invisible. Remove pin and wind thread under button to form shank.

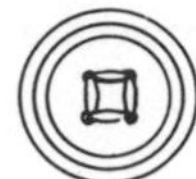

There are several ways of sewing on buttons.

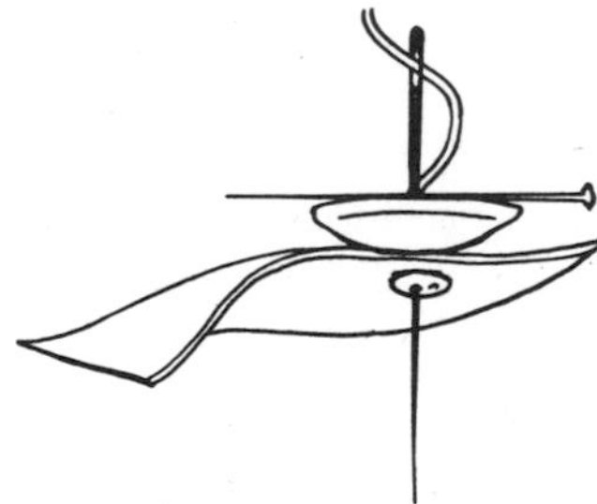

On coats and jackets where there is much strain, a small stay button may be used on the wrong side for reinforcement.

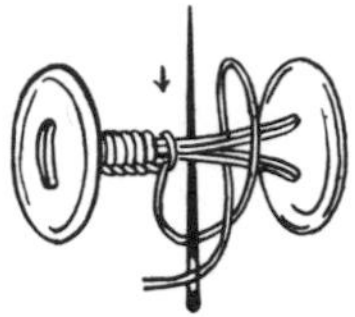

Link Buttons. These can be made by sewing buttons to the ends of a finished narrow fabric strip. The link can also be made like a French tack. Run thread several times between buttons, then work over the thread with close blanket stitch as shown.

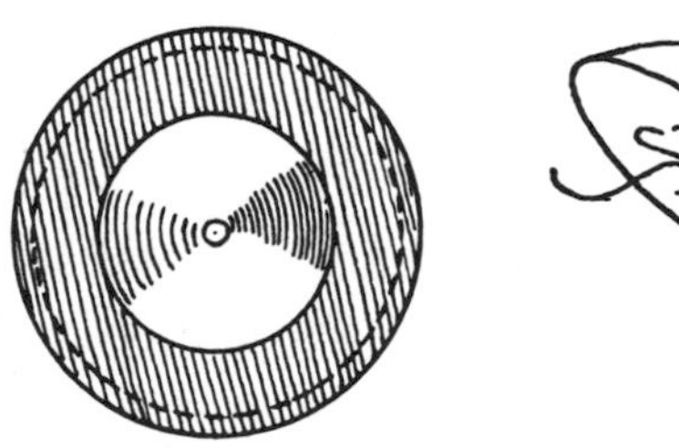

Covered Buttons. WOODEN MOLD: Cut a circle large enough to almost meet at back of mold. Run gathering stitches close to edge, insert mold and draw up. Sew over and over to fasten.

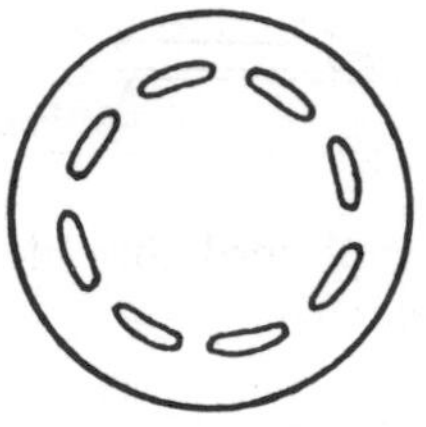

PERFORATED DISK: Disks or rings are covered in the same way as wooden mold. Using matching buttonhole twist, take stitches one at a time around edge through disk and fabric. Back-stitches or more decorative stitches may also be used.

On both mold and disk the back may be finished off neatly by cutting a small square or circle of the fabric and applying to the back of the button. Turn in edges and hem. This covers raw edges and serves as a shank for attaching button to fabric.

Shank Buttons. Place the shank so stitches will be parallel to edge of garment. This relieves strain. For removable buttons, make eyelets. (See Chapter 2, Embroidery.)

Loops and Tubing Fasteners

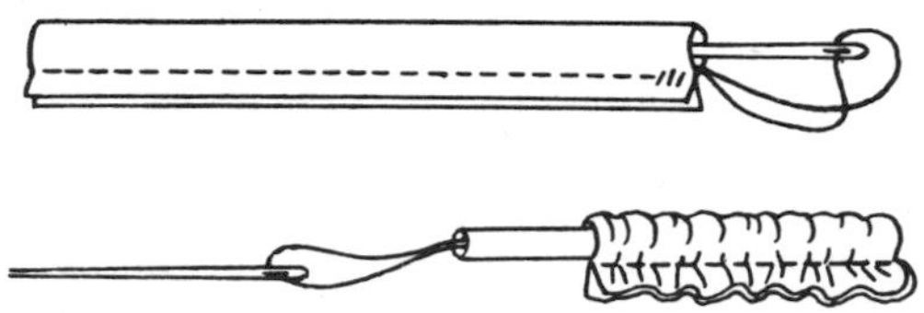

To Make Fabric Tubing. Fold lengthwise a bias strip of the desired width, then stitch and trim seam. Turn inside out with thread and bodkin or tubing turner. Or attach cord at one end of the bias strip, stitch with cord-

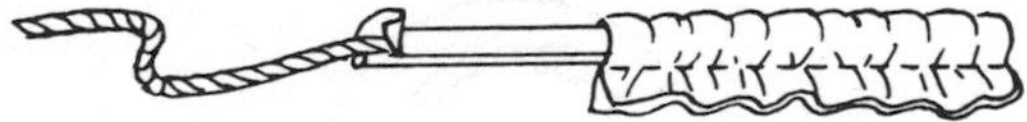

ing foot and pull cord through tube to turn bias inside out.

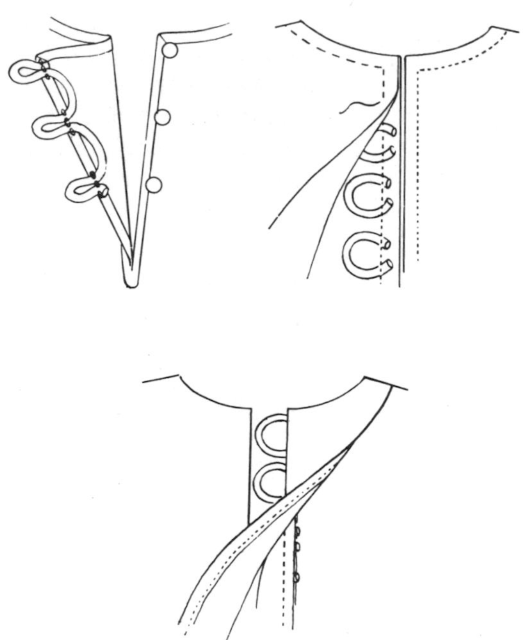

Applying Loops. Make cord as above or use purchased cord. Measure and mark spaces. Pin cord to inside of opening extending loops beyond the edge. Sew loops in place with overhand stitches. Loops may also be cut to fit buttons and sewed on separately. If facing is used place loops on right side with facing on top. Stitch and turn facing.

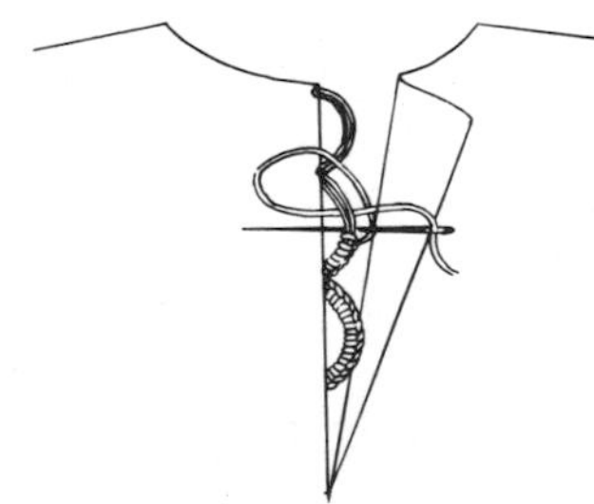

Buttonhole-Stitch Loops. Sew back and forth leaving thread the right length to fit over buttons. Cover with buttonhole stitch using needle with the eye as the point.

Frogs. Make fabric cord or use purchased cord. Twist cord into desired shape keeping seam underneath. Sew in place from wrong side. Attach to garment leaving one loop free to slip over button.

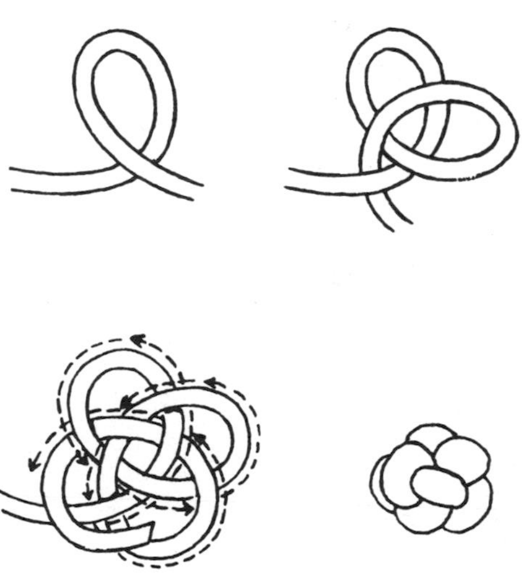

Chinese Buttons. Make a fabric cord 6 to 8 inches long, or longer if cord is thick. Follow carefully the steps given in the diagrams. Keep the loops open and rather loose while working; then ease them into a rather tight ball button. Tack the ends and clip.

Metal Fastenings

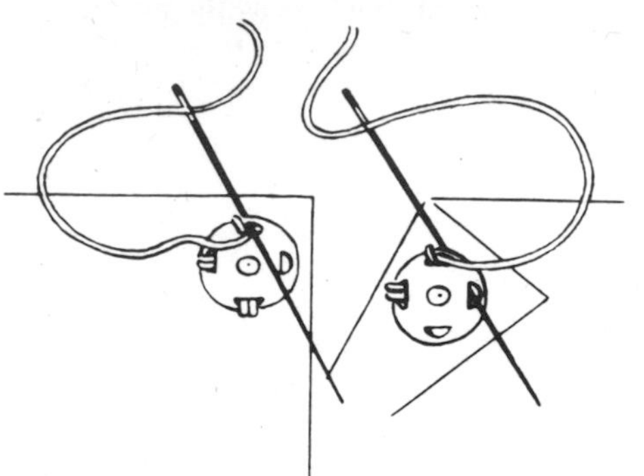

Snaps. The socket must be exactly opposite the ball. Sew in place with overhand stitches, taking several stitches in each hole.

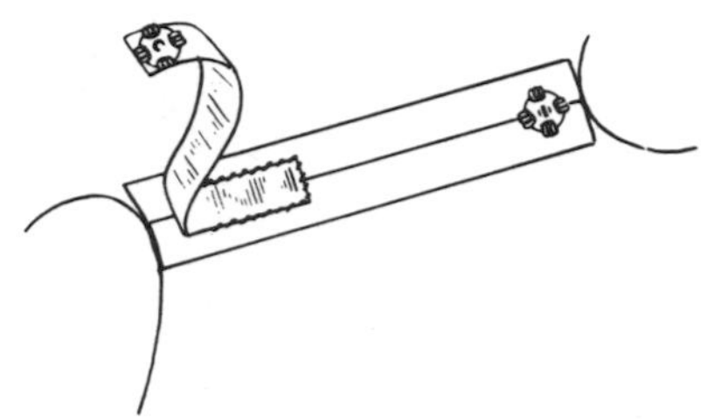

Lingerie Strap. Use tape or ribbon and attach on shoulder seam of garment as shown, using snap fastener.

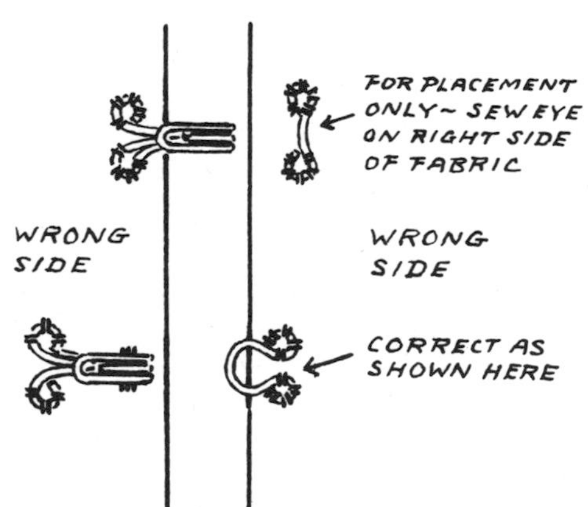

Hooks and Eyes. When using on edges, place eye slightly back from the edge and allow the hook to extend a little. Sew over and over in each ring and under the end of the hook. Thread eyelets may be made in place of the eyes. Make same as buttonhole-stitch loops, only smaller.

Belts

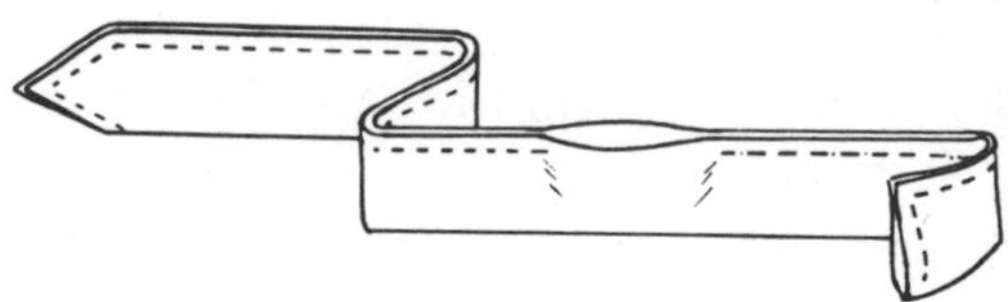

Plain Belt. Cut on lengthwise grain with one end pointed or diagonal. Fold with right sides together, stitch, leaving opening, trim

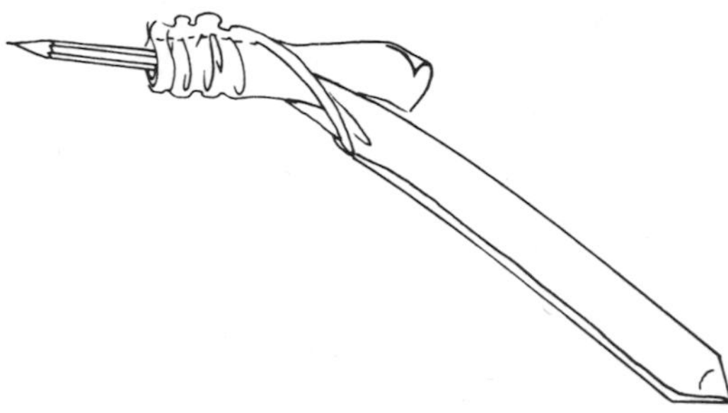

seam and turn. Slip-stitch opening. Sew buckle on straight end. Make eyelets if needed for heavy or stiff fabrics.

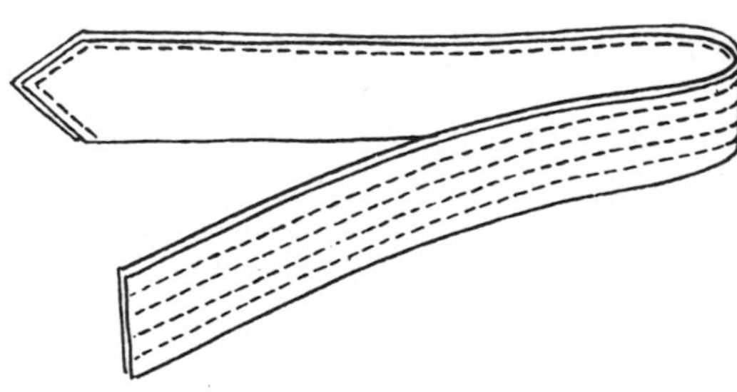

Interfaced Belt. For softer fabrics cut interfacing of pre-shrunk cotton and stitch to one half of belt on wrong side before folding and stitching. Make several rows of stitching to hold facing in place. Finish as for plain belt.

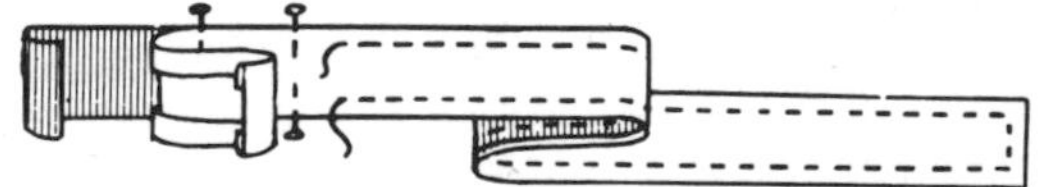

Belt with Stiffening. Use belting ribbon which serves as back and facing. Cut fabric ¾″ wider and longer than backing for turn-

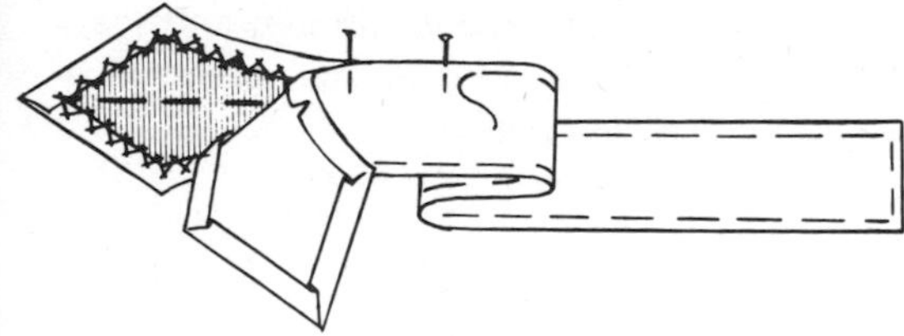

ing under. Pin and baste in place. Edge-stitch on right side. Sew on buckle.

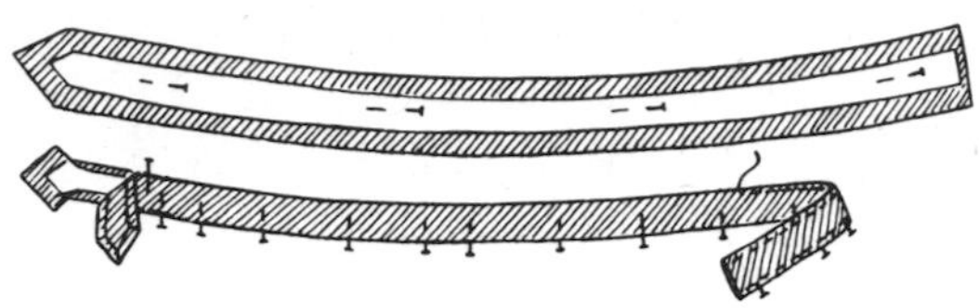

Shaped Belts. Cut belt size and shape desired. Cut lining the same size. Cut a stiff interlining the size and shape of belt without seam allowance. Turn belt edges over interlining, clipping curves if necessary. Pin and baste. Edge-stitch on right side if desired. Hem lining edges to belt.

Carriers

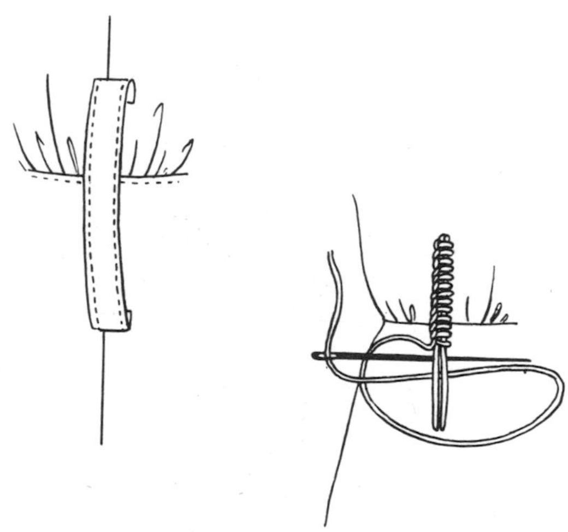

Fabric. Use a narrow strip of fabric, folded and stitched (about ¼″ wide when finished). Attach to dress, turning in ends.

Worked. Make like a French tack, the proper size to hold belt.

Pockets

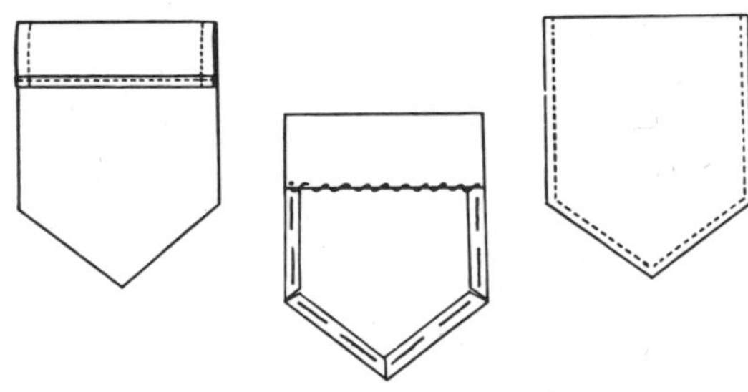

Patch Pockets Plain. May be pointed at bottom or not, as desired. Turn in seam allowance at top to wrong side, press, and stitch. Turn hem to right side and stitch seam at sides. Turn hem to wrong side. Turn and press side seams. If pocket is pointed at bottom, turn up point first, then turn remaining seams. Slip-stitch hem. Baste pocket in place on garment and top-stitch close to edge. On children's garments a small piece of tape may be used at corners on inside of garment for reinforcement.

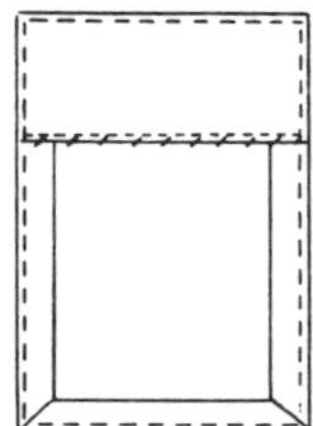

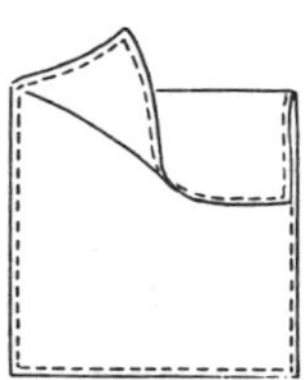

Flap Pocket. A loose flap may be made using same procedure as above, but the hem is cut wide enough to include flap. The extra width is later turned to the outside.

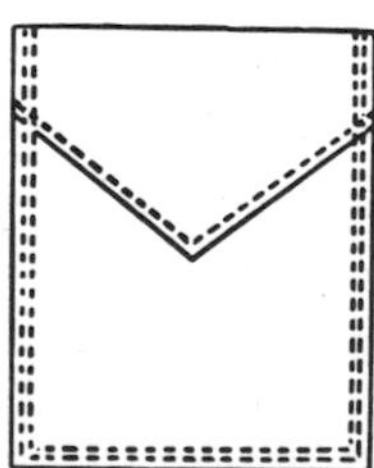

A stitched-down flap is turned to the outside and stitched.

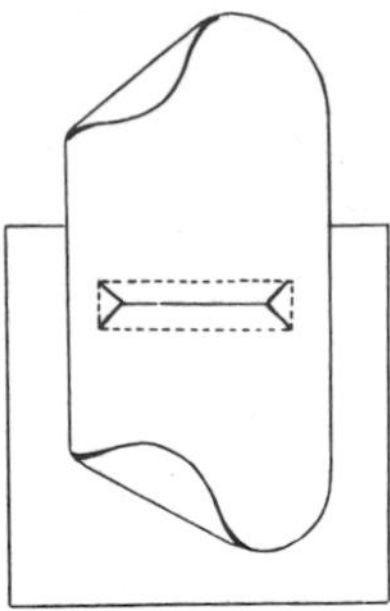

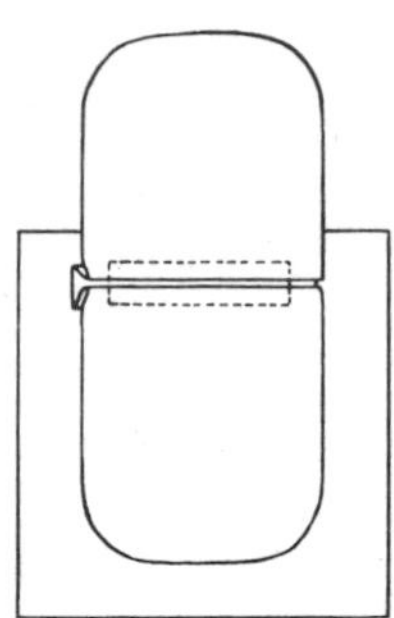

Bound Pocket. Made very much like a bound buttonhole. The pocket piece must be 1″ wider than the opening and twice the depth of pocket plus 1″.

On the pocket piece mark or press a line 1″ below center.

Right sides together, center this line over the pocket line. Baste on the line. Stitch ¼″ each side of basting and across ends. Slash on center line and diagonally to corners. Turn pocket to wrong side through slash.

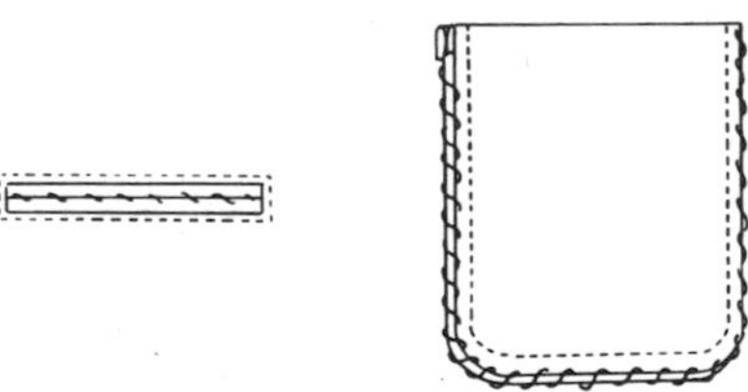

Turn seams back from opening and form a pleat at each end. Baste and press. If desired, pocket may be edge-stitched around on outside. On inside, fold together, baste and stitch around. Trim edges if necessary. Overcast raw edges.

Welt Pocket. Cut pieces for welt 1″ longer than pocket opening and twice as wide as finished width plus ½″. Cut pocket piece same as for bound pocket. With right sides together, fold welt lengthwise and stitch ends taking ½″ seams. Trim, turn, and press. (a) On right side of garment lay welt with raw edges just below pocket line.

Fold pocket piece 1″ below center. Right sides together, center the fold over opening. Open out, baste and stitch ¼″ each side of marking and across ends (see Bound Pocket) catching welt below marking but not across ends. Slash down center and diagonally to corners. (b) Push pocket through and seam together. (c) Turn welt up and press. Slip-stitch welt ends to position.

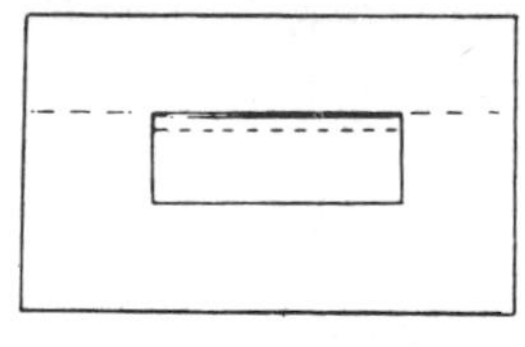

a

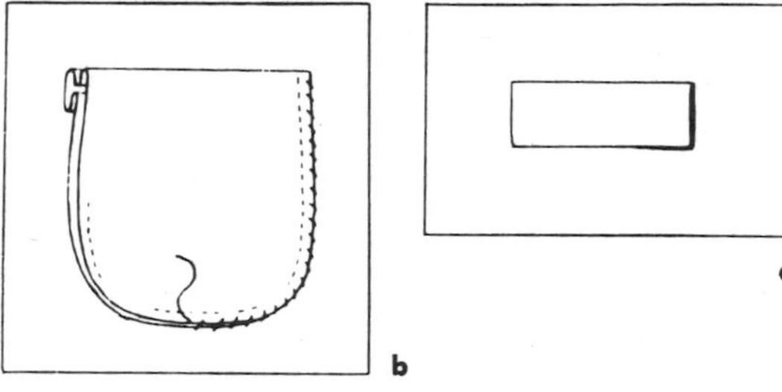

b c

Flap pocket is made the same way, except flap is made and placed *above* marking with raw edges on line.

Collars

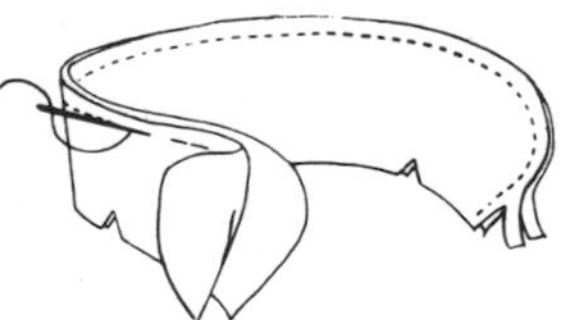

Applying with Bias Band. Interface, then face the collar, leaving neckline side open. Trim seam, turn, baste on folded edge and press. Pin and baste collar to neckline with back centers matched. Turn edge of front opening ¼″ to wrong side and stitch.

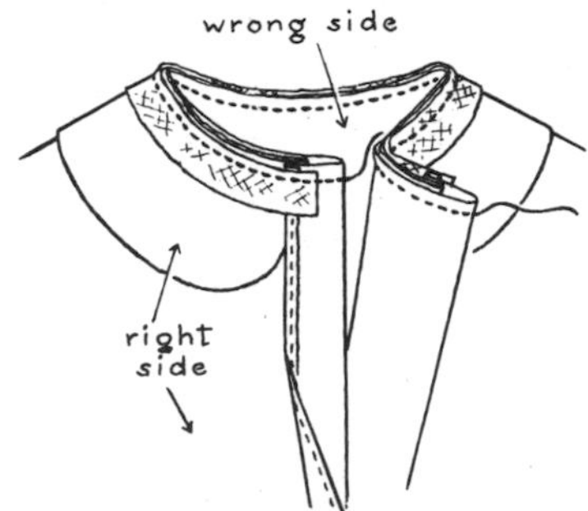

Turn hem of opening over the collar. Baste 1½″-wide bias at edge of collar and overlapping hem, easing bias so it will lie flat. Stitch around neck. Turn and clip curve.

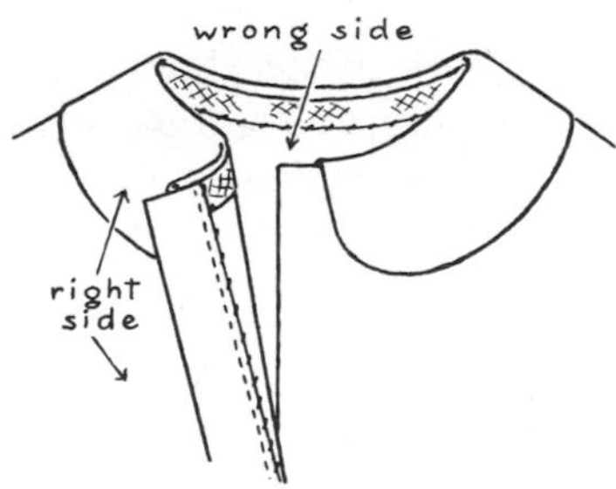

Trim seam, clip on curve, and press. Turn bias and front hem to wrong side and blind-hem.

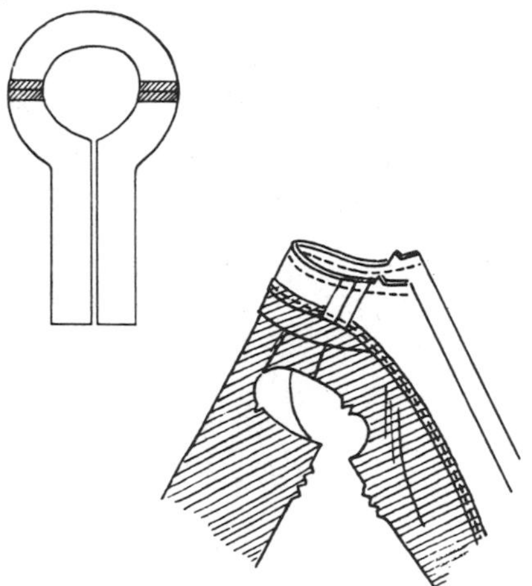

Applying with Facing. Face the collar leaving neckline edge open. Trim seam, turn, baste on folded edge, and press. Pin and baste collar to neckline with back centers matched and ends of collar an equal distance from front edges.

Seam back facing to front facings at shoulder line and press seams open. Pin and baste facings to neckline. Baste and stitch neck seam. Trim, clip curve. Turn facing edges ¼″ to wrong side and stitch.

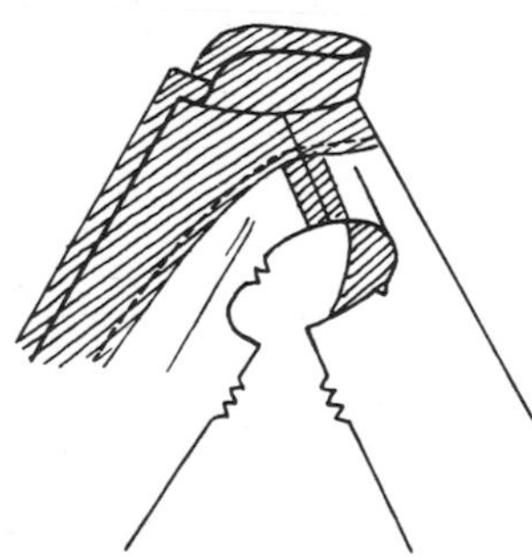

Turn facings to inside and press. Tack at shoulder seam.

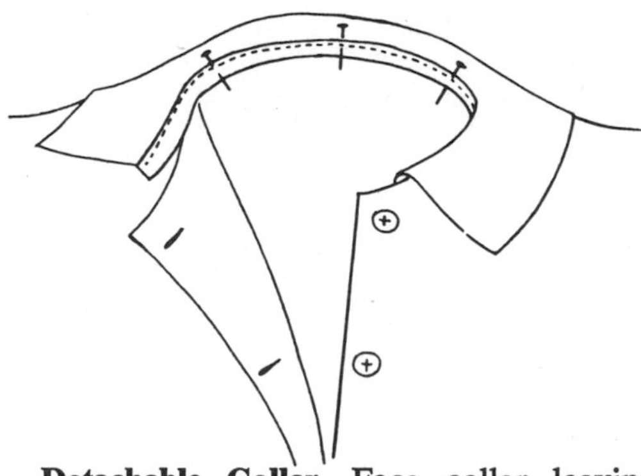

Detachable Collar. Face collar leaving neck edge open. Trim, turn, and baste on folded edge. Press. Bind edge of collar with 1″-wide bias strip, turning in ends.

Matching center backs, pin collar to neckline. Slip-stitch in place. Snaps may be used to hold collar in place.

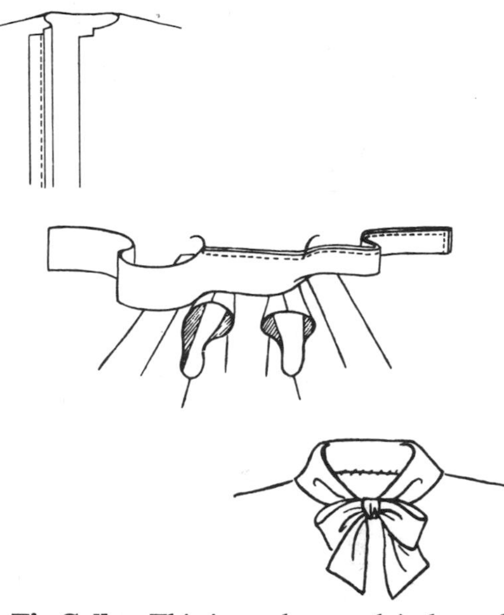

Tie Collar. This is used on a plain lapped closing. Cut tie the width and length desired. Turn front edges of blouse ¼″ to wrong side and edge-stitch. Turn front hems of blouse to right side and stitch at neckline. Clip where stitching ends. Turn hems to wrong side.

Right sides together and center backs matched, baste tie collar to neckline. Stitch as far as the clip.

Fold tie in half lengthwise, right sides together. Stitch ends and sides as far as the clip. Trim seams and clip corners. Turn right side out, turn under at neck edge, and slip-stitch. Press.

Necklines

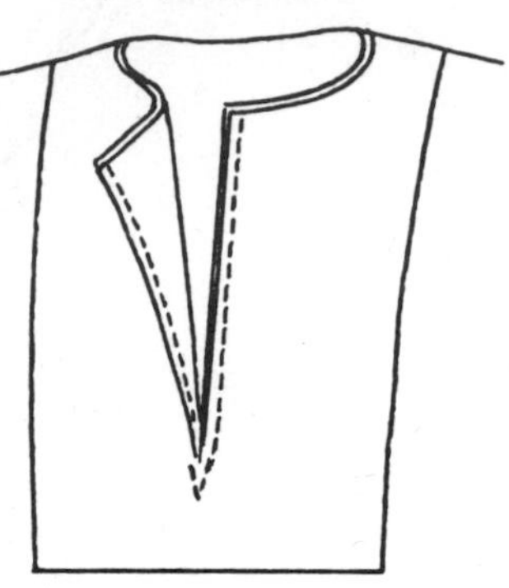

Slashed Neckline with Facing. Baste facing to garment, right sides together, down center of slash. Stitch ¼″ each side of basting, graduating to nothing at point. Stitch again around point. Slash to point and turn to wrong side, baste on fold, and press.

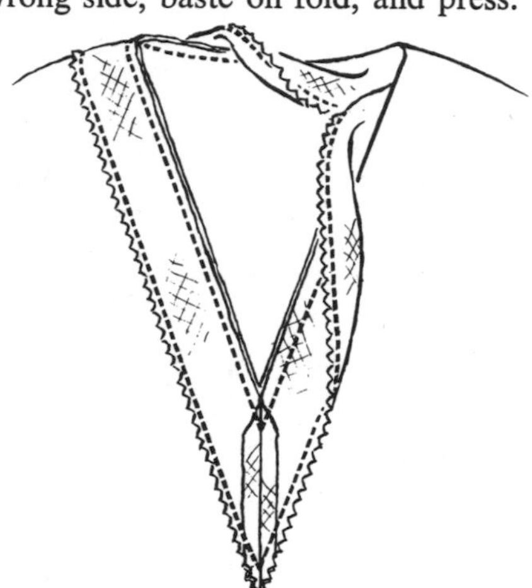

V-Neck with Bias. Use a true bias cut 1½″ wide. Right sides together, baste to neckline, mitering at point. Press mitered seam open. Stitch around, trim seam, clipping on curves and at point. Stitch ¼″ from outside edge and pink the edge. Turn and slip-stitch invisibly.

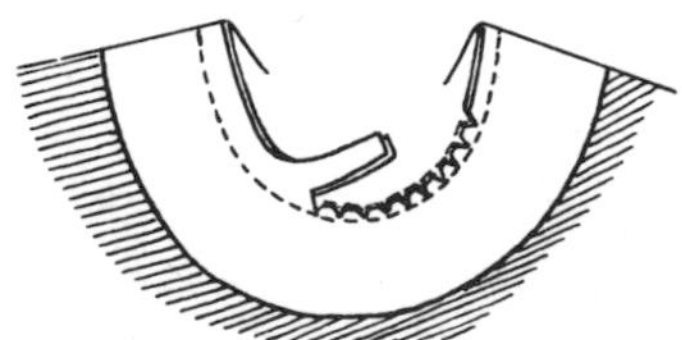

Shaped Facing. Cut and sew facing together at shoulder seam. Press seams open. With right sides together baste and stitch to neckline. Trim and clip seam and press seam

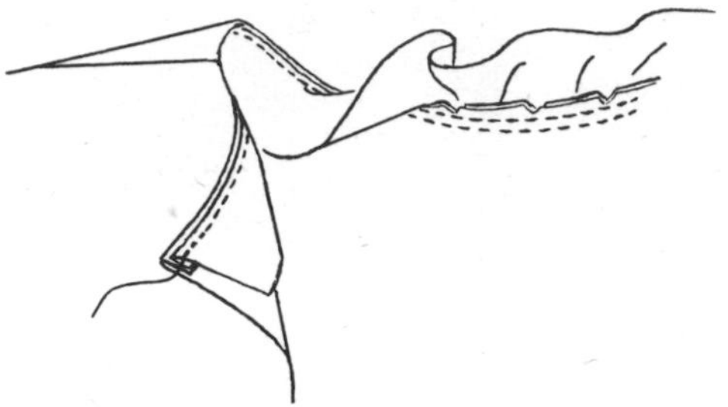

toward facing. On outer edges of facing, turn under seam allowance and stitch or apply bias seam binding. Hold facing away from bodice and do a row of understitching catching seam allowance near the seam line. Turn to wrong side and press. Tack at shoulders.

Sleeves and Sleeve-Finishes

Types of Full-Length Sleeves.

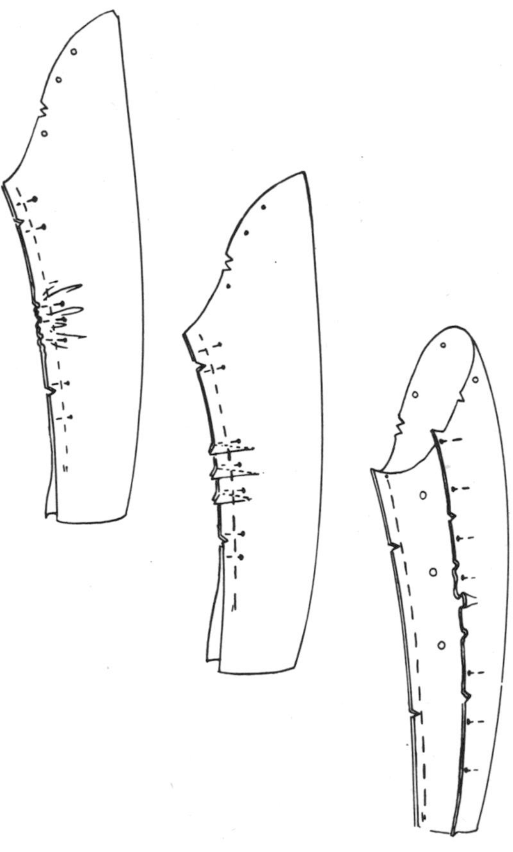

One-piece with gathers for ease at elbow.

One-piece with darts for ease at elbow. These may be left unstitched if desired.

Two-piece shaped for ease.

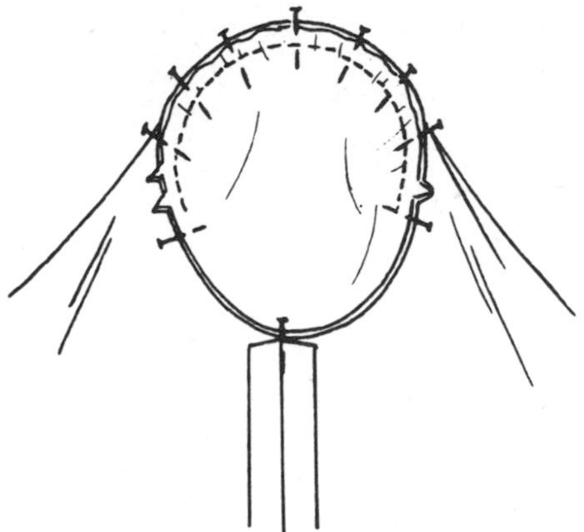

Setting in a Plain Sleeve. Machine-baste (use long stitch) between notches around sleeve top. Join underarm seam and press open.

Place right side of sleeve to right side of garment and hold so the inside of sleeve is toward you. Match and pin underarm seams or markings, match notches and the shoulder marking to the shoulder seam. Pull up machine-basting, easing fulness to fit armhole, avoiding pleats and gathers. Pin at close intervals and baste. Stitch around, starting at underarm and with sleeve side down.

Use a tailor's cushion or mitt and press seam allowance toward sleeve, shrinking out any remaining ease. (On very closely woven fabrics remove sleeve after fitting to armhole and press and shrink around top of sleeve after drawing up machine-basting and before basting sleeve into armhole.)

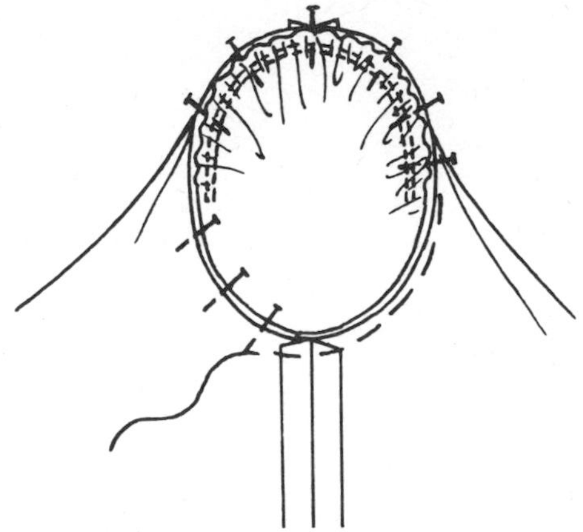

Gathered Sleeve. Use two rows of gathering between notches.

With sleeve toward you and right sides together, pin sleeve in armhole, matching all markings. Baste, stitch, and press.

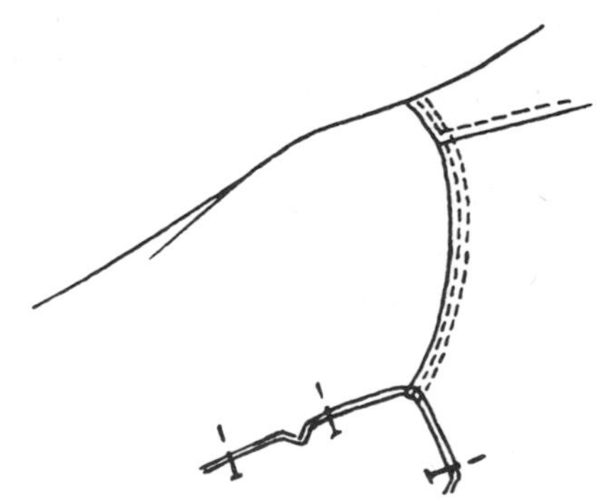

Shirt Sleeve. Use a flat felled seam to join sleeve to shirt armhole before making underarm seam. The shirt seam may be turned over the sleeve seam (which is trimmed) or the shirt seam may be trimmed and the sleeve seam be turned over it. *Note:* On wash-and-wear and durable press fabrics, plain seams with overcast edges are used. Avoid outside stitching which may cause puckering.

Gusset in Kimono Sleeve. A gusset may be added if sleeve is too tight at underarm. On front and back of blouse at underarm mark for a slash about 3″ long pointing toward the shoulder. Stitch ½″ each side of marking to nothing at the point.

Slash between stitching. Stitch underarm seams. Cut a piece of fabric on grain 4″ square. Working from wrong side, pin and baste gusset to slashed edge with ½″ seams

and tapering to nothing at points of slashes. Stitch.

Stay at Gusset. To reinforce underarm seam on kimono type sleeve, baste a 2-inch square piece of fabric over the point. Stitch on seam line to point, pivot and stitch back. Slash between stitching.

Hints: For added strength gusset may be edge-stitched close to seam line on outside. For a fine tailored finish, gusset is sometimes lined with a square of lining fabric. Cut same size as gusset, turn under edges and hem.

For a Fitted Sleeve. SLIDE FASTENER: Use the slot seam method shown under zipper insertions.

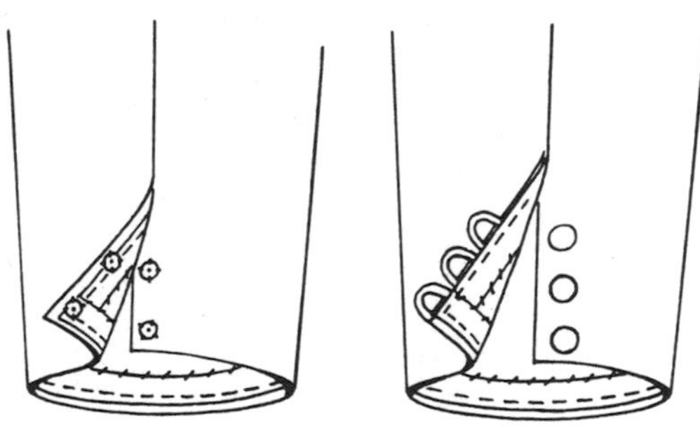

FACED WITH SEAM BINDING: Clip seam where opening ends; then baste and stitch seam binding to right side around edges, mitering corners. Turn to wrong side and hem edge of binding to sleeve invisibly. Lap and sew on snaps.

LOOP FASTENING: Sew fabric loops to front edge of seam. Apply seam binding as for faced sleeve. Lap and sew on buttons. Thread loops may be used and are applied after seam binding is put on.

A buttoned pleat may be used to fit sleeve to wrist. Try on, pin pleat. Sew on buttons and make thread loops.

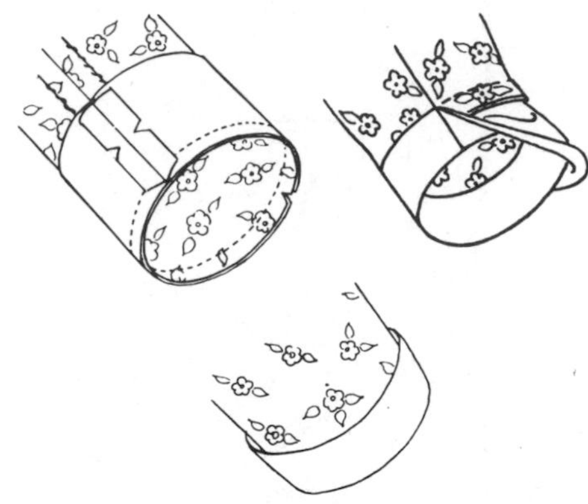

Turned-Back Cuffs. PLAIN: Pin right side of cuff to wrong side of sleeve, matching seams. Stitch and turn to right side. Turn under raw edge and hem over seam. Press. Turn cuff back and tack at seam.

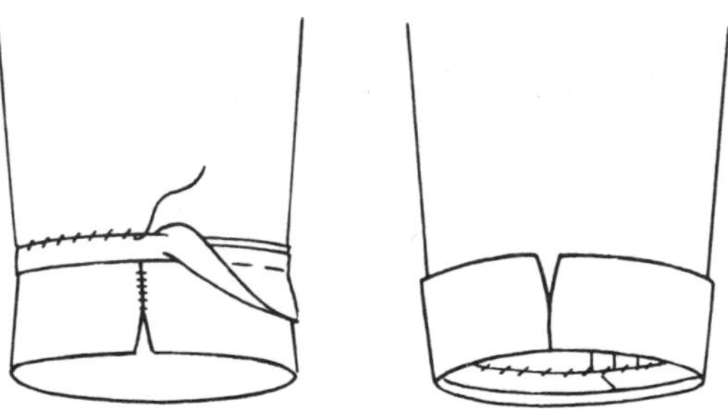

SHAPED: Make the cuff and pin to outside of sleeve, matching notches. Baste bias strip on top. Join ends and stitch on seam line through all thicknesses. Turn under raw edge of bias and hem. Press. Whip cuff edges together. Turn back cuff.

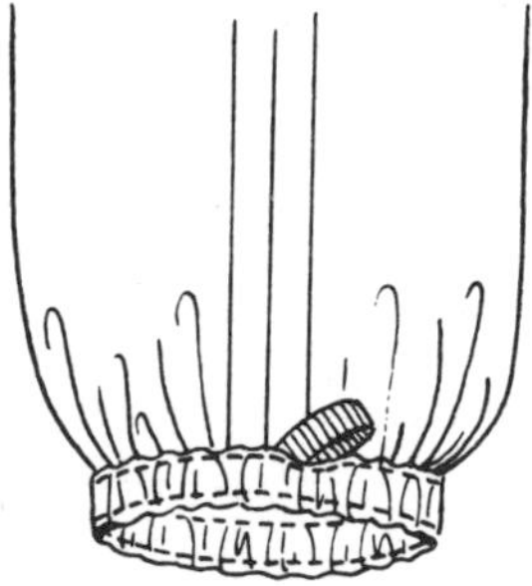

Casing Hem for Elastic. Face or hem lower edge of sleeve, leaving opening for elastic. Edge-stitch on fold. Insert elastic and close opening.

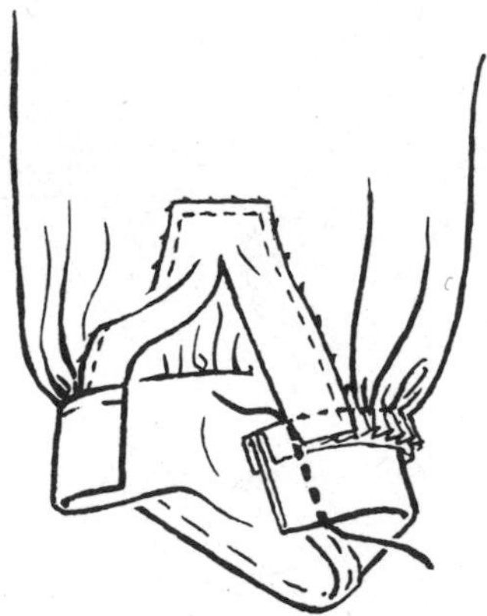

Cuff on Gathered Sleeve. Apply facing to slashed opening, turn to wrong side, and blind-hem. Gather sleeve edge and make cuff band. Baste right side of cuff to wrong side of sleeve, adjusting gathers evenly. Stitch, turn to wrong side, turn under edge, and edge-stitch over seam. Or baste right side of cuff to right side of sleeve, stitch, turn, and hand-hem to wrong side.

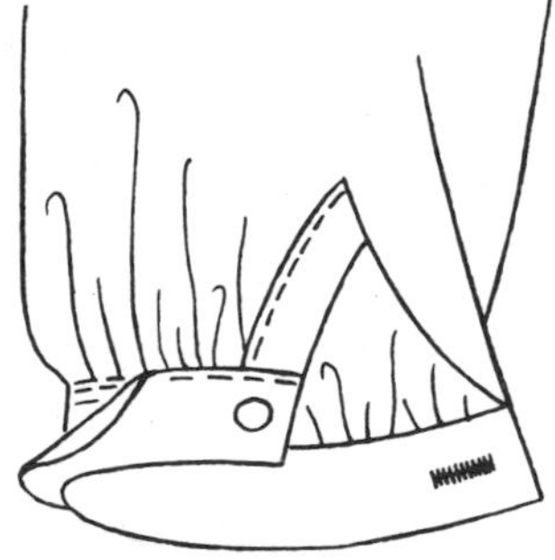

The slash may be bound instead of faced. Cut binding on straight grain and bind opening. Gather edge of sleeve and apply cuff. Let binding extend on underlap and fold it under on top lap.

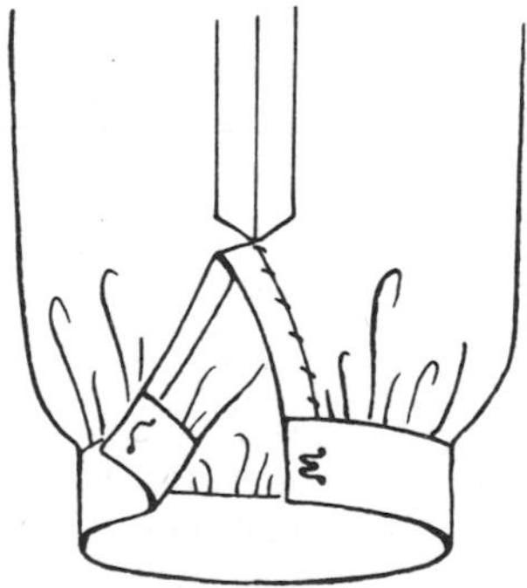

When sleeve opening is on a seam, clip seam at top end of opening and bind opening. Gather edge and apply cuff, turning under binding on top lap.

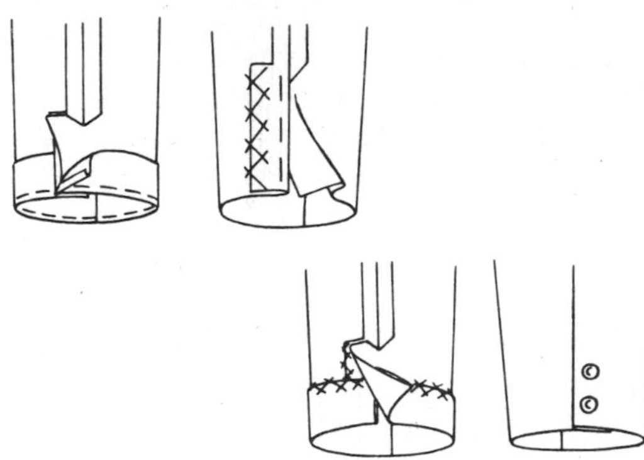

Vent with Buttons. A two-piece sleeve sometimes calls for this finish. Join front seam and back seam above opening. Make buttonholes in upper sleeve section if called for. Clip seam at top end of opening on under sleeve and press seam open above clip. Turn up hem and catch-stitch. Turn extension on upper sleeve, face buttonholes, miter corner, and catch-stitch in place. Turn back extension, miter corner, and catch-stitch. Sew on buttons.

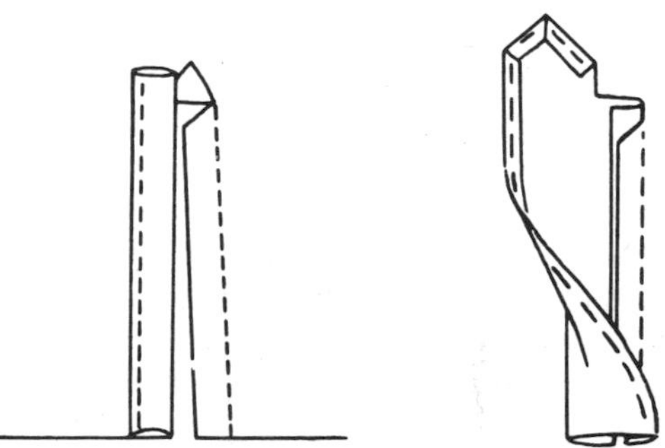

Classic Shirt-Sleeve Cuff. Stay-stitch each side of line for opening. Slash opening and diagonally to corners of seam allowance.

Two pieces are used to finish the opening: the underlap extension and the overlap band. Baste right side of underlap to wrong side of back edge. Stitch, taking ¼″ seam, and turn to right side. Turn edge over seam and stitch.

Baste right side of overlap to wrong side of front edge. Stitch, taking ¼″ seam. Turn to right side. Baste under ¼″ seam allowance on free edge and around point.

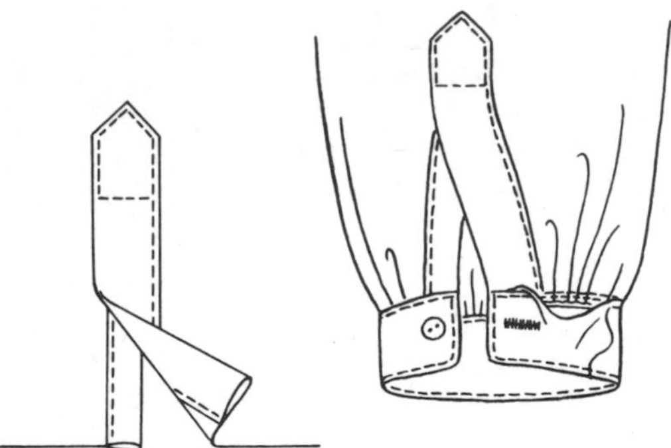

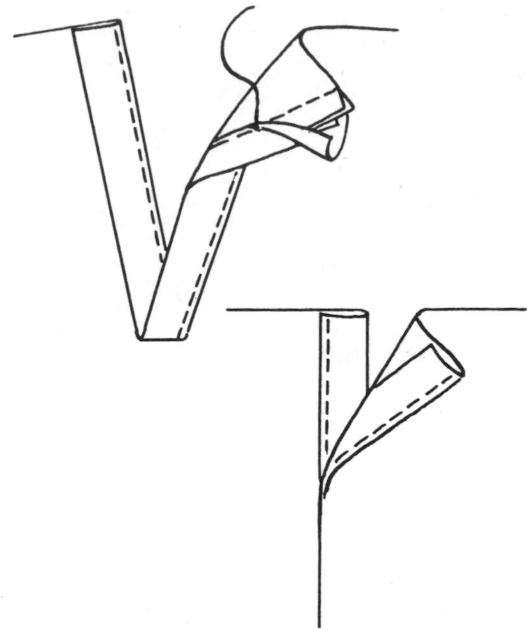

Fold and baste in position with the point in the center. Stitch across upper end, around point, and down side.

Cut interfacing for cuff facing, minus seam allowance on inner edge. Baste interfacing to cuff facing. Right sides together, pin and stitch cuff to facing, leaving open at inner edge. Trim seam, turn, and baste edges. Gather edge of sleeve.

With cuff facing to wrong side of sleeve, baste to gathered edge and stitch. Turn edge of outer cuff and baste over seam. Stitch all around cuff. Make worked buttonholes.

For French cuffs, which are wider, fold underlap to inside before putting on cuff.

Plackets

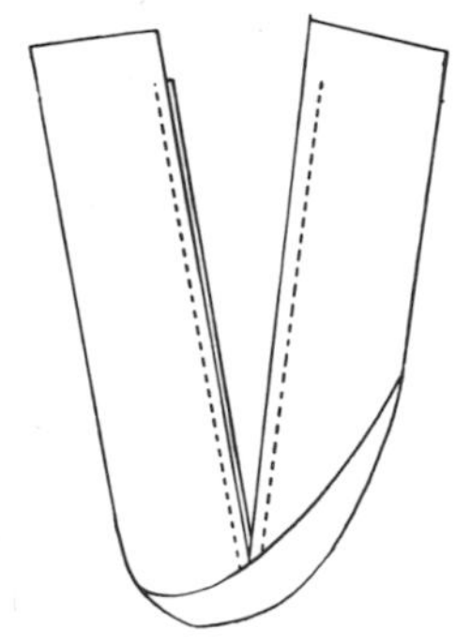

Slashed Placket with Binding. Use a strip twice as long as slash and at least 2″ wide. Baste right side of strip to wrong side of slash, tapering slash seam to nothing at point. Stitch and turn binding to right side. Turn under edge and stitch. On delicate fabrics start from right side, turn to wrong side and hem by hand.

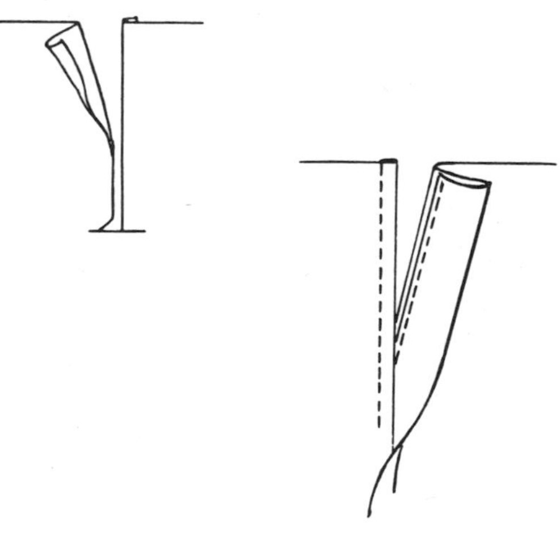

Placket with Pleat. Cut a slash, then cut at right angles each side at base of slash ¼″. Turn edges ¼″; then turn left edge again ¼″ and stitch. Turn right edge ½″ and stitch. Lap to form pleat at bottom of slash. Stitch across at lower end through all thicknesses. For a wider pleat make diagonal slash longer.

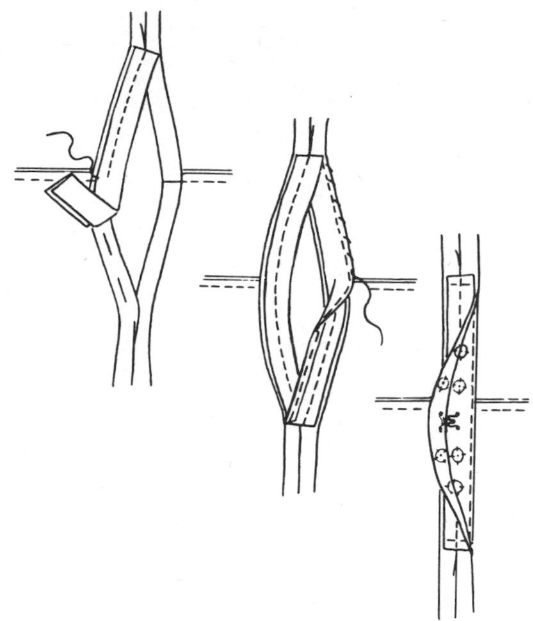

Dress Placket, Two-piece. Cut a bias strip for front of placket 1″ longer than opening and 1½″ wide. Cut back strip on straight grain the same length but 2″ wide. Turn under seam allowance on back opening, baste on fold, and press. Fold the wide strip down the center and press. Place under back opening, raw edges even, folded edge extending. Stitch on outside on basted edge. Face front with bias strip, turning edge ⅛″ past the seam line. Press. Lap and sew on snaps with hook and eye at waistline.

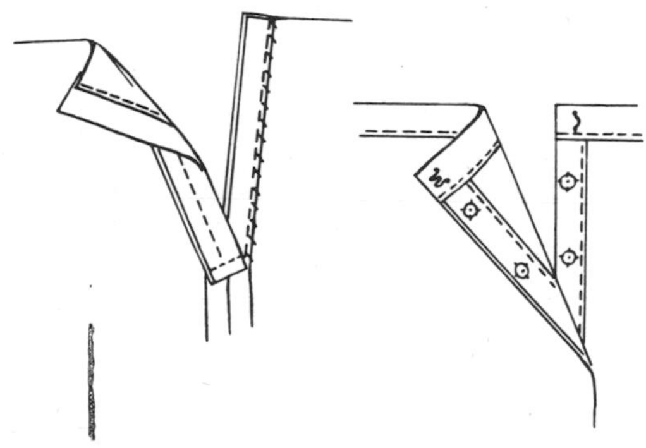

Skirt Placket. Use bias facing on front edge and straight piece on back as for dress placket. Stitch together at lower ends. Attach waistband. Sew snaps on placket and hooks and eyes on waistband.

Zippers

Skirt Zipper. Before you start, check to see if—

Opening has been stay-stitched.

The garment has been fitted.

Check the zipper opening; it should be as long as the metal part of the zipper plus one inch.

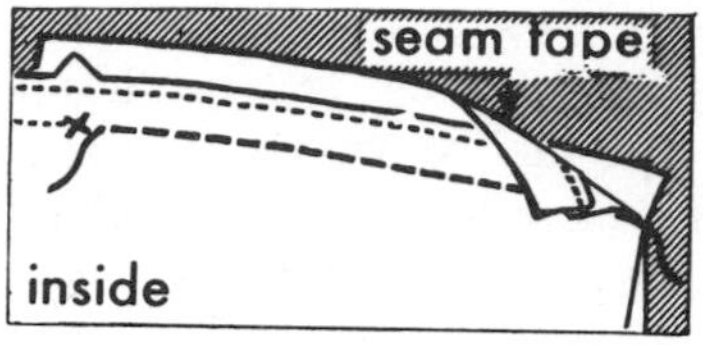

1. Machine-baste opening together (use longest stitch). Stitch seam tape to front seam allowance to widen it. Press seam open. Open the zipper.

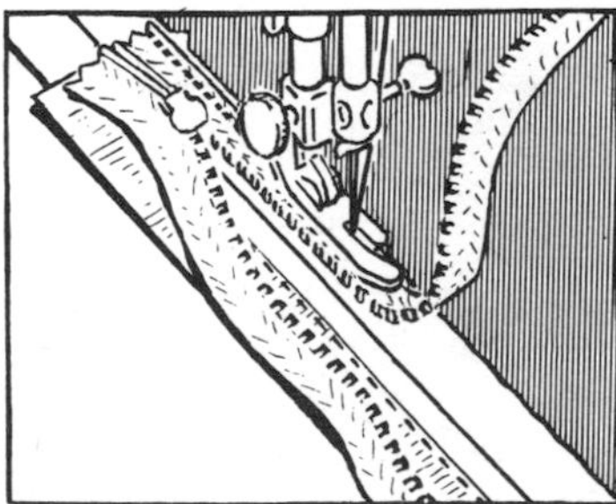

2. Working on the inside of the skirt throughout, put zipper in place face down on back seam allowance. Match bottom of zipper to bottom of opening. Have the full width of the chain on the back seam allowance and edge of chain along seam line. Stitch with the edge of the foot against chain. Keep checking position of chain. Use cording foot if desired.

3. Change cording foot to left of needle and close zipper. Turn the zipper right side up, folding seam allowance close to zipper chain. Stitch along the fold for the full length of tape as shown.

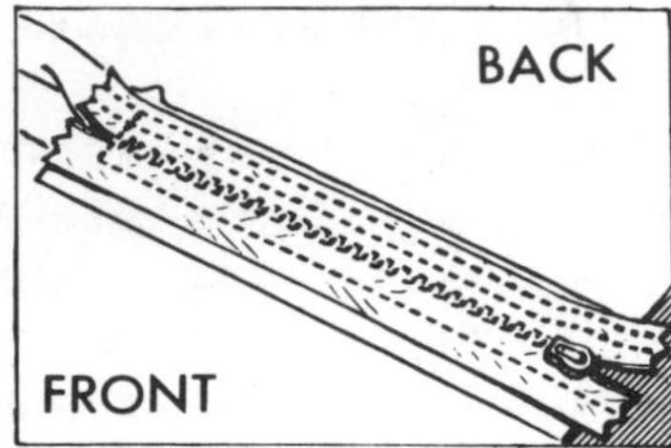

4. Open out garment, turn zipper face down over front seam allowance, making a small pleat at lower end as shown. Stitch across tape just below the stop and up the other side close to the chain, sewing through tape, seam allowance, and garment.

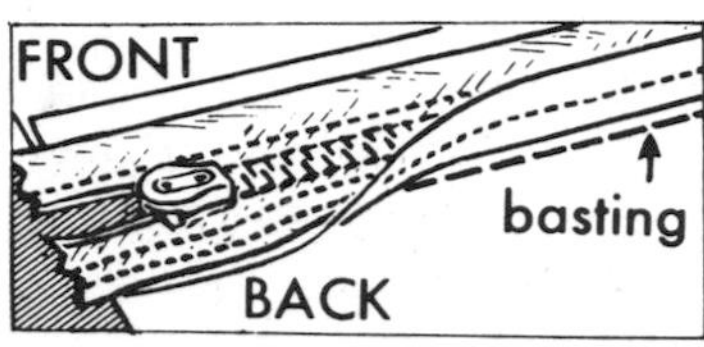

5. Press placket on wrong side. Remove machine basting (clip at intervals).

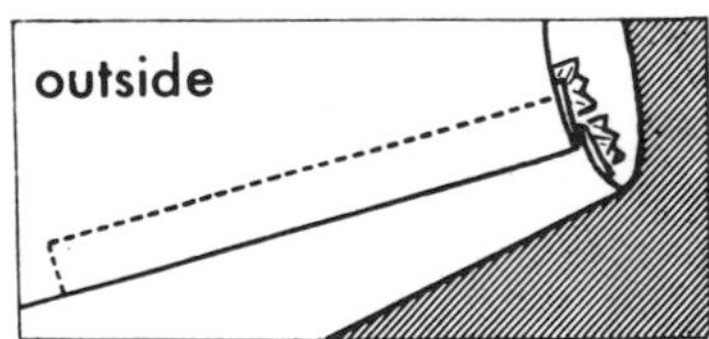

6. Press placket on right side using thick cloth to avoid shine. A tailor's ham is useful here.

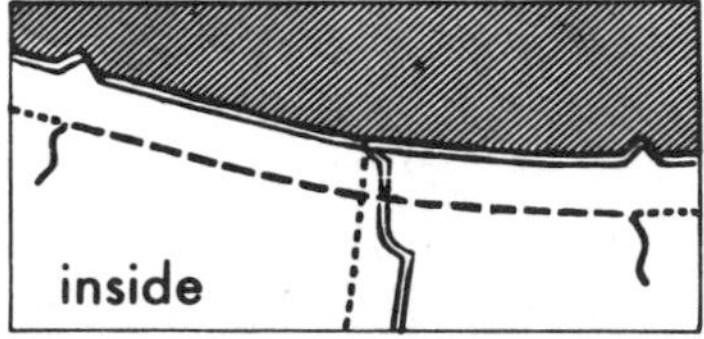

Dress Zipper. Check garment details in same manner as for skirt zipper. Machine-baste and press seam open.

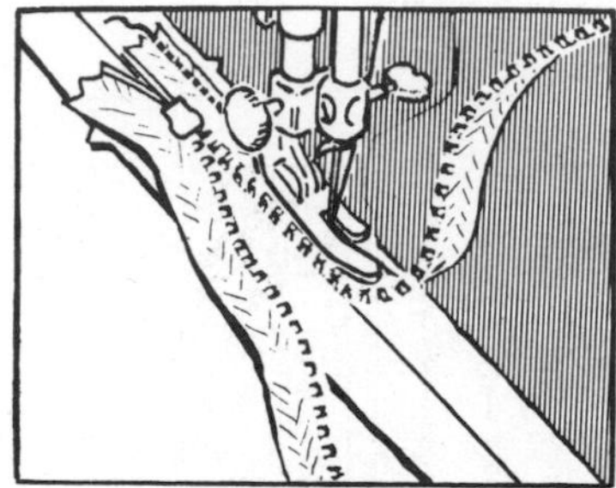

Steps 2 and 3 same as for skirt zipper.

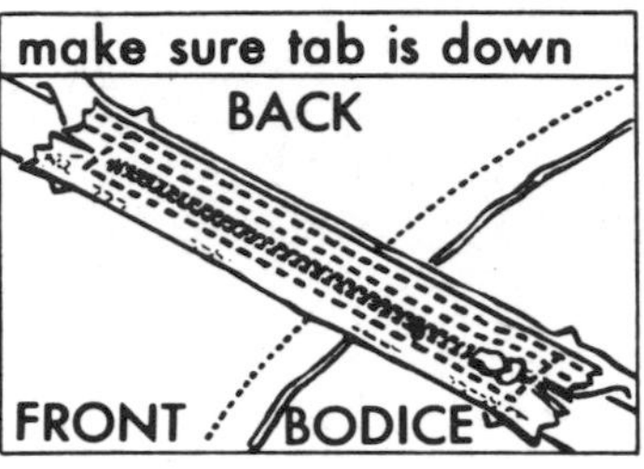

Open out garment, turn zipper face down over front seam allowance, making a small pleat at each end as shown. Stitch across tape just below stop and up the other side close to chain and across top.

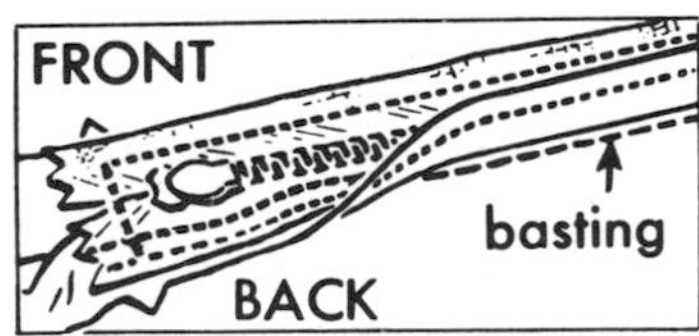

Press placket on wrong side and remove machine-basting.

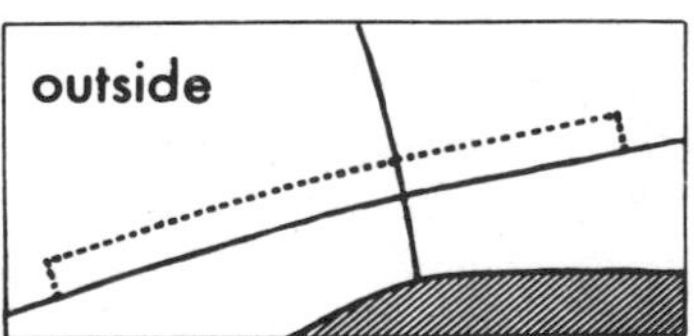

Press on right side using thick cloth to avoid shine.

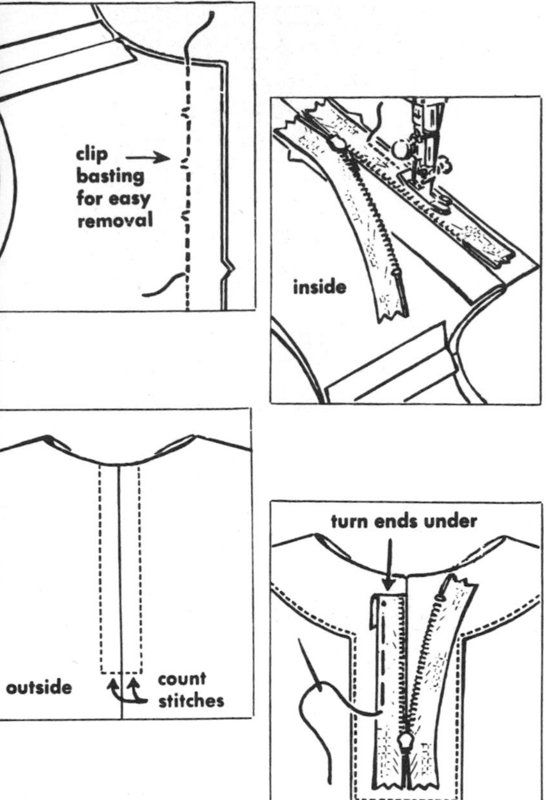

Neck Zipper. Check garment details as for skirt zipper, and machine-baste opening. Press seam open. Clip basting but do not remove.

Open zipper and place face down. Have one tape on single seam allowance with teeth against seam line. Stitch with edge of foot against teeth. Close the zipper.

Change to zipper foot. Turn garment to outside and, starting at neckline, stitch around zipper as shown making square corners at lower end. Press on wrong side and remove basting. Press on right side using thick cloth. Press nylon zippers with care.

For slashed opening, slip-baste edges together. Baste gripper face down as shown. Close gripper and stitch on right side.

For Faced Openings. Apply facing and hold opening together on right side with overcasting. Lay the open zipper face down with teeth against the seam line. Baste along tape turning under top ends. Close zipper and follow step 2 under Neck Zipper.

Interfacings, Linings, and Interlinings

The appearance, wear and warmth of a garment depend largely upon its construction. The inside construction involves the interfacing, interlining, and lining.

Interfacing is a layer of fabric used between a facing and the outer part of the garment such as jacket front, lapels, collars, cuffs, and pocket flaps. It can be used to hold shape in yokes (front and back) and to keep hems firm. (See section on Tailoring.)

Special fabrics have been created for interfacings, and you should choose the correct kind and weight for your fabric and pattern. Hair canvas is most often used in suits and coats. It comes in a variety of weights and quality. Interfacing helps keep fabrics from stretching, especially in areas of strain. It can help support an unusual shape or silhouette which stands away from the body. Patterns usually suggest where to use interfacing and include a pattern for cutting.

Lining is used in jackets and coats to provide a nice finish by covering seams and other raw edges; also to add warmth and help to hold the shape of the garment.

Interlining is used for additional warmth in coats. A layer of fabric, selected for its thermal quality, is added between lining and outer fabric. It can be assembled separately or sewn in with the lining (double construction). Lamb's wool is most often used.

Underlining is used to hold the shape of the garment, especially one made of a soft fabric. Here again, the proper weight fabric for the underlining must be selected. China silk, or its equivalent in weight, is most often used. This procedure is sometimes called "double construction." A piece of underlining is cut exactly like the outer fabric sections. It is then basted and sewed to the wrong side of the fabric and darts, if any, put in before the parts of the garment are sewn together. The section is then treated as one piece of fabric and the underlining is sewn in with the seams of the garment. Very firmly woven fabrics do not need to be underlined.

Underlining garments is sometimes called double construction or backing. The purpose of underlining is to keep the garment from stretching and to help bring out the shape and style of the design. The type and weight of the underlining to be used is determined by the type and weight of the outer fabric and also by the effect to be achieved. The underlining should be somewhat lighter in weight than the outer fabric but with enough body to serve its purpose.

Choose a material with a firm weave such as taffeta, china silk, sateen, muslin, silk organza, or one of the many fabrics made especially for the purpose.

Stretch fabrics should be lined with a material such as crepe or tricot which also will stretch. Be sure to choose a washable underlining for a washable garment.

SKIRTS. A skirt may be underlined partially or totally, front and/or back. It depends upon style and fabric.

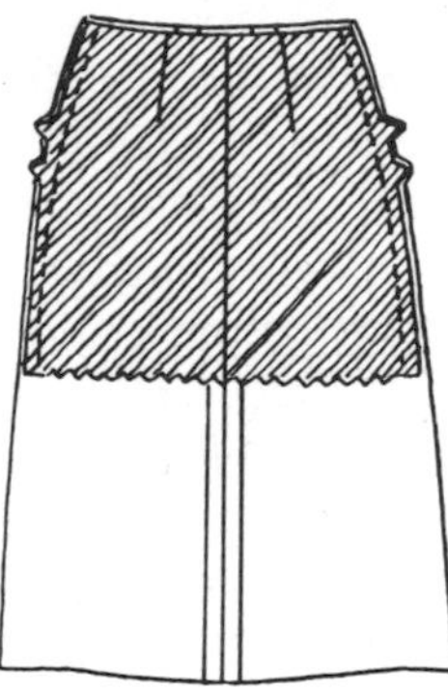

SKIRT BACK (HALF-LINING). To prevent a bulge in the back of a skirt a half-lining may be used. Choose a firm fabric which will not stretch, such as rayon taffeta. Do not use crepes. Cut fabric crosswise leaving selvage at lower edge.

To cut the lining use the back skirt pattern but cut it somewhat shorter. It should come well below the widest part of the hips. Staystitch skirt and lining and pink the lower edge of lining if it is not selvage. Make darts and seams same as in skirt and press. Wrong sides together, lay lining to skirt back and baste side seams. To take some of the strain from the skirt, the lining may be extended about ⅛″ each side on side seams when basting together. This makes it slightly narrower than the skirt back. Make up the skirt, treating the lined back as one piece. Jersey and other knitted fabrics should be lined both front and back.

STRAIGHT SKIRT. A fully lined skirt may have the lining attached only at waistline and around zipper or it may be sewn in as an integral part of the skirt. For the latter, use the skirt pattern and cut the underlining long enough to reach a little lower than the top of the hem. If the skirt has a pleat or vent, omit it when cutting the underlining, but keep a seam allowance.

Stitch the center front seam, if any, and center back seams of both skirt and lining and press open. If the skirt has a back pleat, stitch the seam of the underlining only to the point above the pleat. Turn edges below seam and double-stitch.

With wrong sides together, pin underlining back to skirt back. Machine-baste sides. Do the same on fronts and now treat as one piece of fabric.

Pin and stitch down center of darts through both lining and outer fabric (see Darts). Change to regular stitching and stitch darts. Pin side seams and stitch and proceed as usual for making a skirt. The hem (outer fabric) should cover the lower (raw) edge of underlining.

Note: When the underlining is left loose at the sides, the darts are made separate from outer fabric. The side seams are then sewn. The underlining (sometimes called a "drum"), is then sewn in with the belt and turned under and hemmed by hand around zipper. The lower edge is hemmed by hand or by machine.

ONE-PIECE DRESS. The procedure is much the same as described above for a fully lined straight skirt.

1. Cut underlining same as outer fabric.
2. Wrong sides together, pin and machine-baste around. Treat as one piece of fabric.
3. Stitch darts down center (long stitches), then make darts as usual.
4. Pin and sew front and back side seams, leaving opening for zipper.
5. Insert zipper, and neck and armhole facings (or set-in sleeve).

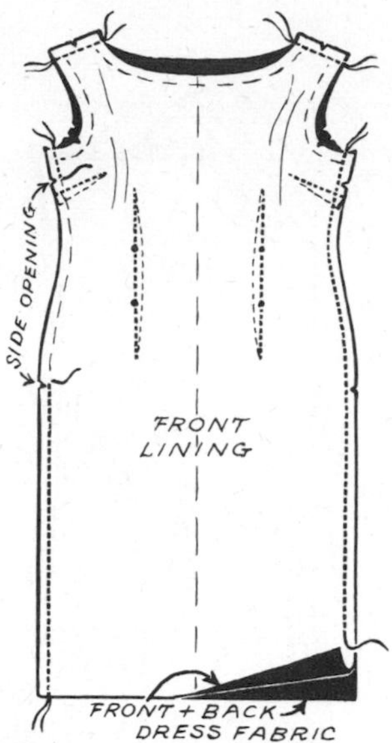

6. Try on, mark and finish hem.

DRESS WITH LINING LEFT LOOSE.

1. Cut underlining like dress and make darts and side seams in each separately. Press as you sew.
2. Wrong sides together, pin and baste-stitch underlining pieces to tops and armholes only.
3. Insert sleeves, facings, zipper, etc.
4. Turn under and hem lining around zipper opening.
5. Hem outer fabric and lining separately.

TAILORING

The classic jacket with notched collar presents some typical tailoring problems.

Preparation

In tailoring, great care in preparing the fabric is essential:

1. Be sure the fabric and interfacing are preshrunk. Do it yourself if necessary.
2. Straighten ends of fabric.
3. Make alterations on pattern before cutting.
4. When cutting, follow grain line with precision.
5. If fabric is medium weight, use a good quality hair canvas (or one that will withstand dry cleaning) of medium weight for interfacings.

After Cutting

Stay-stitch all curved seams. Trace the grain with basting lines across the bust and top of back and sleeves and down center back and front. These will be a great help in fitting.

The weight of the jacket is supported at the shoulder line and in fitting the grain line must be kept vertical and horizontal.

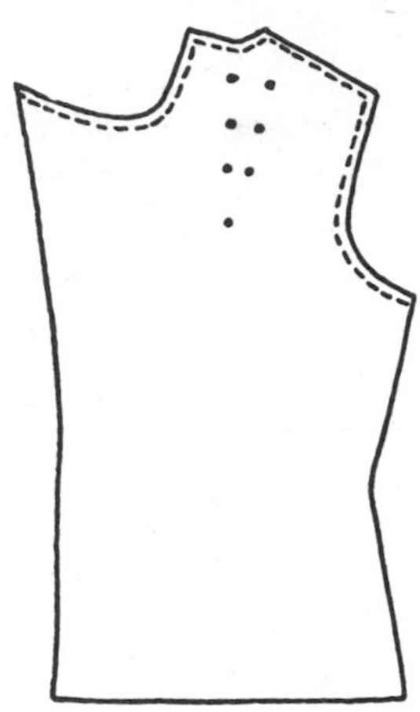

Fitting

Preparation for Basted Fitting. The first fitting should be a basted fitting. This permits adjustments to the figure in all areas, not just at the underarm. Fit over a blouse and skirt.

Baste all darts on front and back. Baste shoulder, underarm, and sleeve seams. Press seams open lightly. Baste-stitch sleeve seams

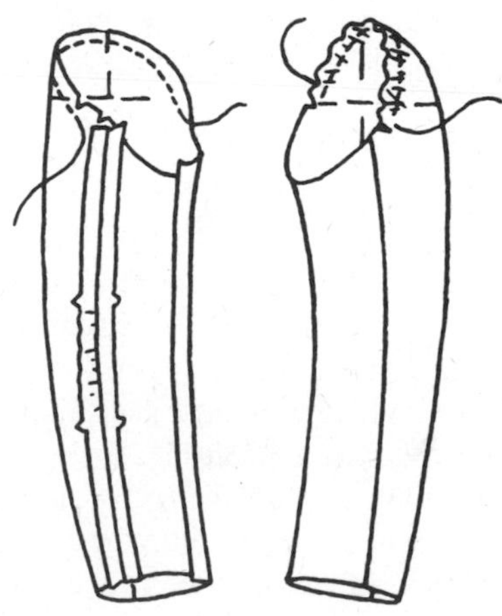

and tops of sleeves and draw up to fit armholes. Shrink-press and baste in place.

Baste interfacing to fronts of jacket. Baste undercollar pieces together and baste to neckline.

Fitting. Try on jacket right side out over blouse and skirt. Lap and pin at center front.

Add shoulder pads if called for. Fit with enough ease to allow for lining. Distribute any needed fulness or take in equally on

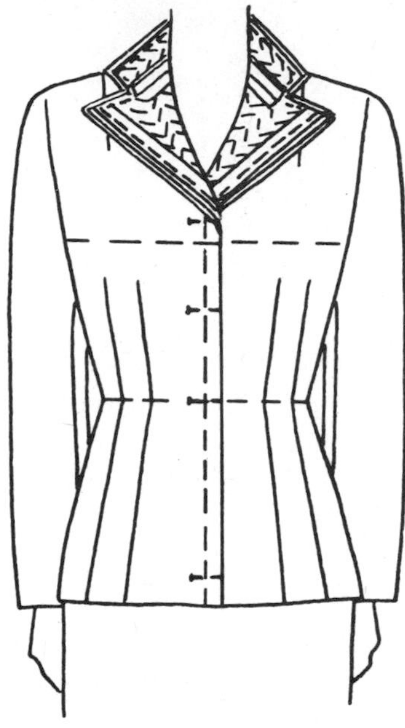

darts and seams. Check grain lines; do not pull these out of line when fitting.

If cross grain line sags, the shoulder may need raising. Adjust armhole and shoulder seams for wide or narrow shoulders. Bend elbow and check strain at armhole.

Pin together at top buttonhole to find where roll of lapel begins. Mark the roll line with pins.

Sewing

Balance up the adjustments, rebaste, if necessary, and stitch darts and seams. Slash darts, clip curved seams, press seams and darts open. When pressing, use tailor's ham and *mold* the garment on all curves. This is very important to a good fit. Certain places, such as points of darts, can be shrunk to smoothness with careful steam pressing.

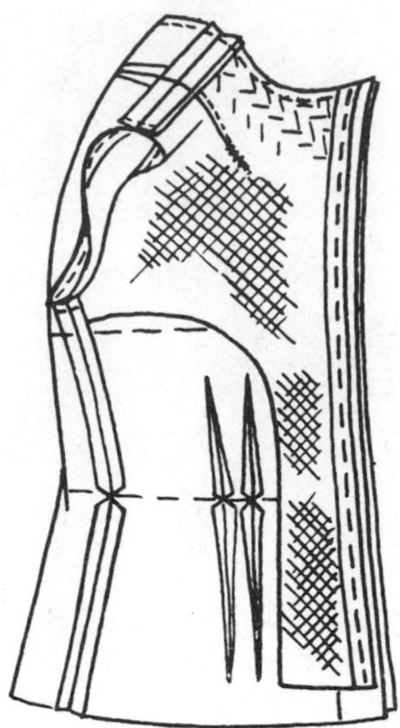

Interfacing. Prepare interfacing by cutting and lapping darts. (See section on Darts.)

The interfacing is tacked to the front of the jacket with padding stitches which are invisible on the right side. Starting at the shoulder and working toward the front on the roll line, work padding stitches on lapel section rather close together. Work several rows more loosely up and down fronts below lapels. For soft dressmaker-type suits omit the padding stitches on fronts.

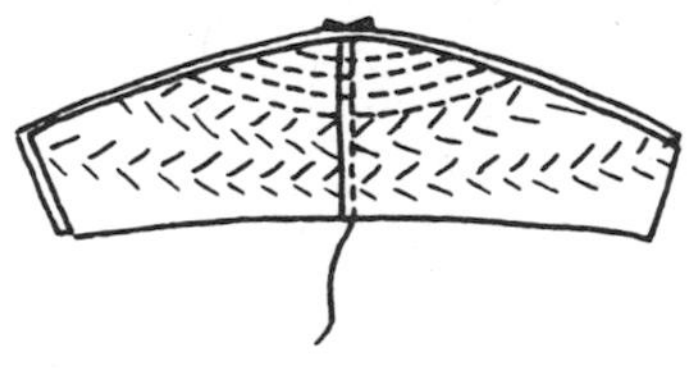

Lap, stitch, and trim collar interfacing and baste to undercollar around outer edges. Mark roll line and work rows of padding stitches outside of line, rolling and shaping in the hand. Inside of roll line stitch several rows by hand or by machine about ¼″ apart following curve. Preserve the roll. Rebaste collar to neckline and stitch only as far as seam line.

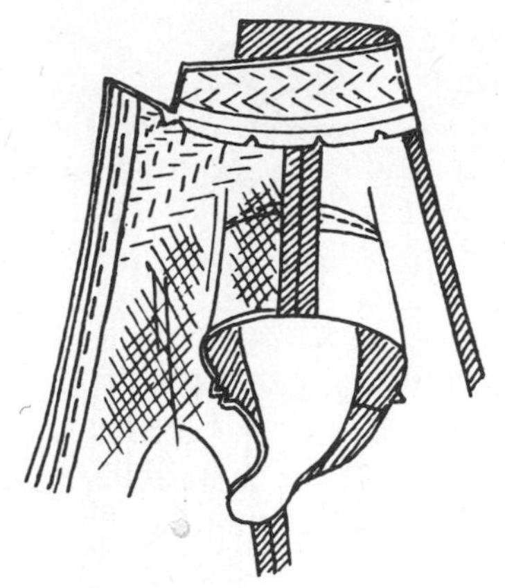

Buttonholes and Pockets. Set-in pockets and bound buttonholes are made at this point, before front facing is applied. Worked buttonholes are done after jacket is finished.

Facing. Seam together front jacket facings and back neck facing, if called for, at shoulder; then attach collar at neckline. If there is no back neck facing (patterns differ), attach collar to front facings at neckline. Clip on curves and press open. With right sides together, pin, baste, and stitch facing and collar to jacket. Match all seams carefully at notch. Take a few stitches at notch by hand.

On soft fabrics the edge seam of lapel may need taping. Use a preshrunk tape; baste, and whip edge to seam line. The width of tape lies inside (on jacket area).

The back neckline seam may also be taped to prevent stretching.

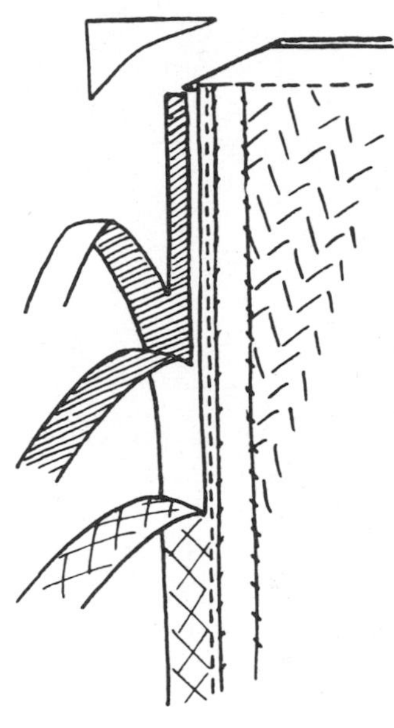

Beveling Seams and Turning. Thick seams must be trimmed to prevent ridges. Trim corners as shown. Bevel seams by trimming seam allowance of interfacing to seam line. Trim seams so that one is slightly wider than the other (¼″ and ⅜″). Trim neckline seam at notch. Cut away interfacing under neckline seam and press seam open.

For a sharper edge on seams, press them open before turning, using tip of iron. Turn facings, crease edges, and baste rolling edge of collar under slightly. Use point presser on corners. Below lapel, roll seam slightly to the inside. All neckline seams, pressed open, should match perfectly. Tack seams together invisibly. Steam-press edges using clapper (back of hair brush will do).

Sleeves. Rebaste sleeves in position. Fit again (with shoulder pads if called for) over skirt and blouse and make any further adjustments necessary. Mark sleeve and jacket length. Hem at bottom should not be less than 1″.

Shoulder Padding. For a lightly padded shoulder, cut a strip of cotton wadding 2½″ by 6″. Fold and sew together as shown. Place over shoulder seam and sew to edge of seam allowance as shown. Tack to top seam.

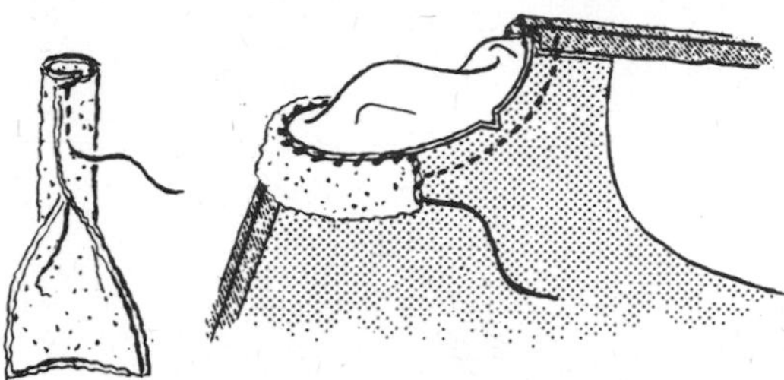

Finishing. Stitch in sleeves and steam-press to shrink any fulness at cap. (See Setting in Plain Sleeve.) Turn and baste hems on fold in jacket and sleeves. Trim hem and press flat. Trim hem under facing to regular seam allowance and catch-stitch. Turn front facing same length as hem.

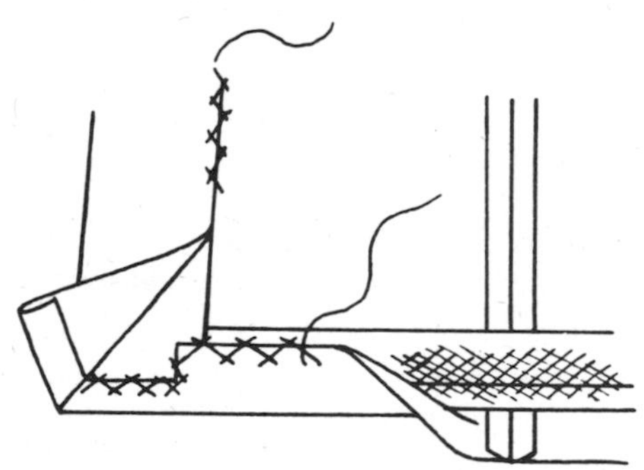

Reinforce hem line with interfacing, using bias strip of light weight interfacing (pre-shrunk muslin will do) cut ½″ wider than hem plus seam width. Turn and press seam allowance along one side. Lay muslin inside hem with fold on hem line, letting it overlap onto front facing. Slip-stitch along fold. Tack upper edge of interfacing to jacket with tailor's hem (see Hems and Hem Finishes). Catch-stitch edge of jacket hem to interfacing. Use same procedure in sleeve hems. Catch-stitch front facing to jacket, easing over bust.

Clip collar at shoulder seam and sew to seam at back of neck. If using back neck facing, tack at seam line.

Give jacket a final pressing from inside. If waistline is to be accented, sew seam binding by hand around waistline on inside. Hand picking, an almost invisible running stitch, is sometimes used near the edge of collars and lapels, or machine-stitch trimming is done before lining.

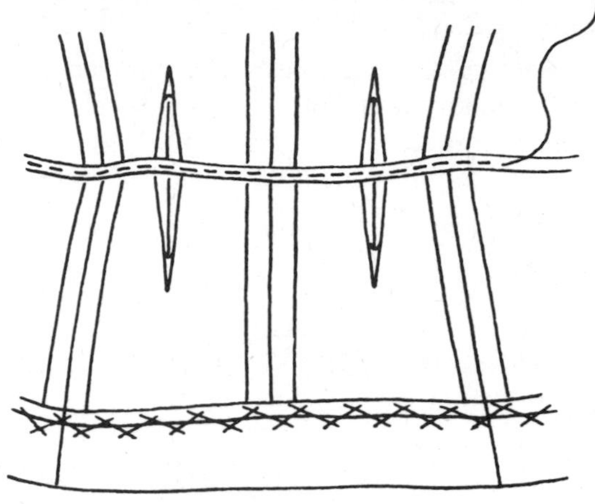

Lining Jacket. Make same alterations on lining as on jacket. Pin, stitch, and press darts and lengthwise seams of lining but leave shoulder seams open. Lay in and pin pleat at center back. Lining must have enough ease to prevent drawing.

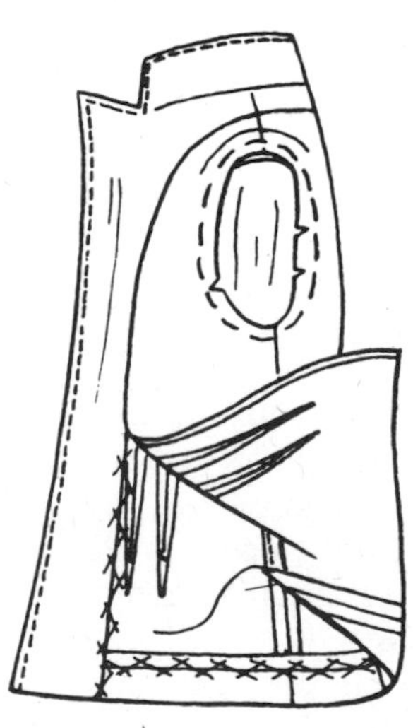

Turn jacket inside out; pin lining to jacket matching seams and center back. Tack underarm seams from inside. Baste around armholes, matching underarm seam and working up on each side, leaving 2 or 3 inches free at top on both front and back. Clip on curves. Turn under seam allowance on back shoulder and lap over front. Turn under seam at back of neck and down fronts, clipping on curves and easing slightly. Pin at frequent intervals and hem. Make a bar tack or catch-stitch the pleat just below neck edge and at waistline.

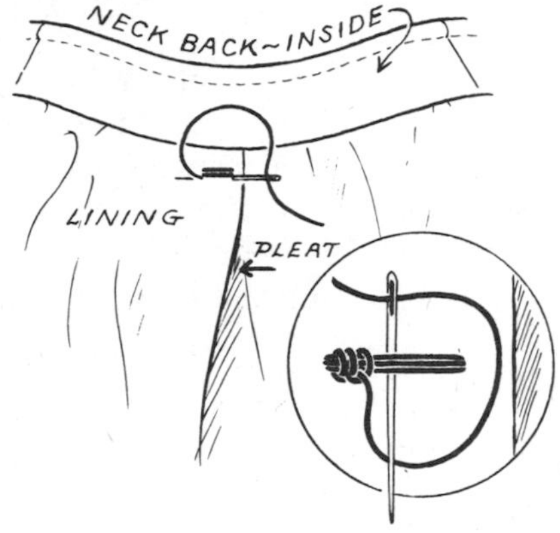

Finish lower edge of lining hem by catching to jacket hem with slip-stitching and allowing for ease to fold over. Edge of fold should come about ¾″ above lower edge of jacket. Baste-stitch top of sleeve between notches and draw up to fit.

Slip on sleeve lining, pin and hem, matching underarm seams. Turn under, pin and hem around armhole and at lower edge (allowing for ease as on hem of jacket).

Try on jacket, mark for buttons, and sew on. One button should be at the waistline.

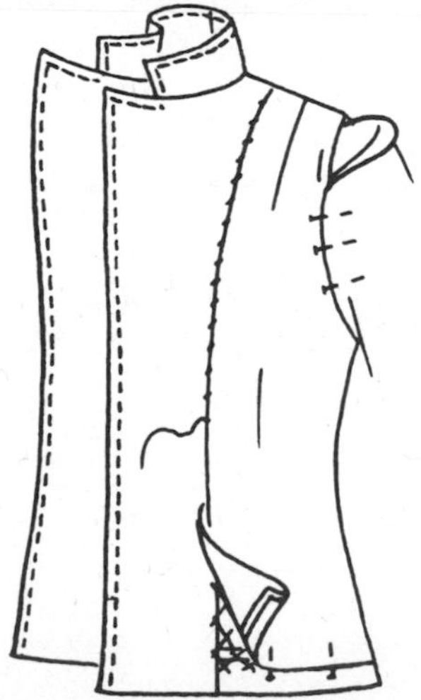

Tailoring Hints

Press lining and jacket thoroughly before setting lining into jacket.

When setting in lining, baste lining to jacket around armhole seam. Allow ample length in sleeve lining to prevent drawing.

Lay a soft pleat at center back of lining. Make bar tacks at neck, waistline, and near lower edge to hold.

For a professional appearance, press each section thoroughly as you work.

For a good fit at the waistline on a tailored dress make an inside belt of belting ribbon. Stitch along center of belt to the waistline seam, stopping 1″ from zipper and leaving ends loose. Finish with hooks and eyes to fit waistline.

On a kimono-type sleeve, before setting in gusset make a bar tack by hand at the point where slash ends at underarm. This will reinforce against strain.

After cutting a garment and before unpinning front and back pieces, run a basting down center front and back. Keep these lines vertical when fitting.

How to Stay a Dress at the Waistline. Use narrow belting on inside of dress.

1. With ends turned in and meeting, have belt fit waistline comfortably. Sew on hooks and eyes.

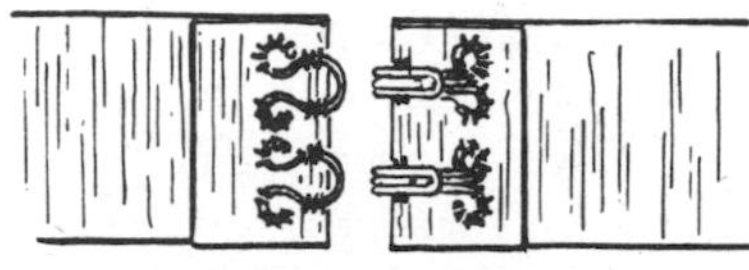

2. Cover raw edges with seam binding and hold with hemming stitches all around.

3. After bodice and skirt are sewn together, sew center of belting to waistline seam. Leave ends loose each side of zipper.

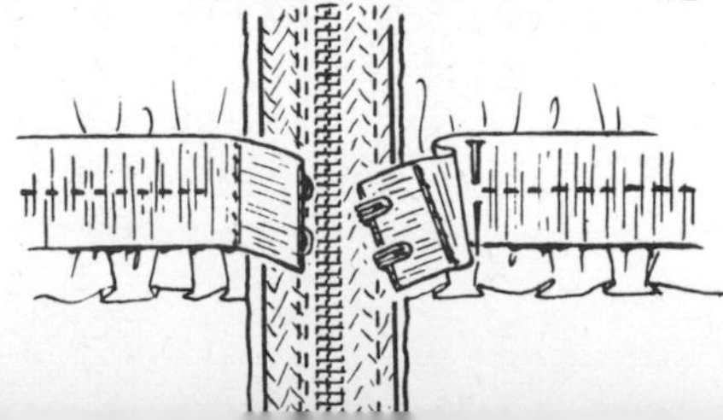

TRIMMINGS AND DECORATIVE DETAILS

Self-Fringe. There are various ways of making fringe. Self-fringe can be made on many fabrics. Cut fabric on grain. Draw a thread (or two on fine fabric) where you want the fringe to end. Machine-stitch on this line. Pull threads to the stitching.

Plain Fringe. Make a gauge of heavy paper the desired width and length of the fringe. Fasten end of yarn and wrap around the gauge, laying strands closely side by side. Stitch by machine about ½″ from the top. Cut loops at bottom and tear away paper. Turn under edge of fabric and stitch to fringe.

Knotted Fringe. Cut yarn twice the length of fringe plus allowance for knot. (This varies with size of yarn.) Take 2 or more strands, fold in middle. Insert crochet hook in edge of fabric or knitted piece. Pull loop through. Draw ends of yarn through the loop and pull up knot. Trim evenly when finished.

A more decorative knotting may be done. Pick up half the threads in each group and knot together. This may be repeated picking up alternate groups.

Cord. Cut yarn a little more than twice the length of finished cord. Use several strands for a heavy cord. Fold in half and catch the loop over something stationary, or work in the hand if cord is short. Keep taut and twist the strands until they are tight. Fold in half, slip off loop, and let the cord twist itself together. Tie ends.

Tassels. Cut a gauge of cardboard the length the tassel is to be. Wrap yarn or thread around it to thickness desired. Tie a self-thread around top strands, leaving long ends. Cut loops at bottom. Wind a thread around tassel near top and tie. Clip ends and slip the knot under the wrapping. Trim ends of tassel evenly.

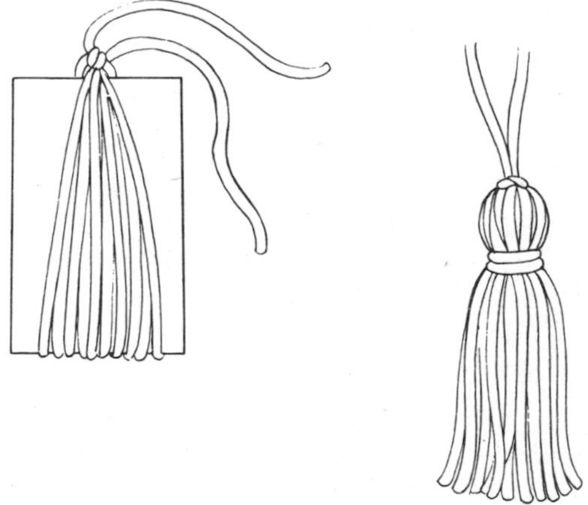

Pompons. Wind yarn back and forth between two heavy push pins (see diagram). Wrap and tie tightly at intervals, leaving ends of an inch or so. Cut between the wrappings. Trim pompons and fluff into balls.

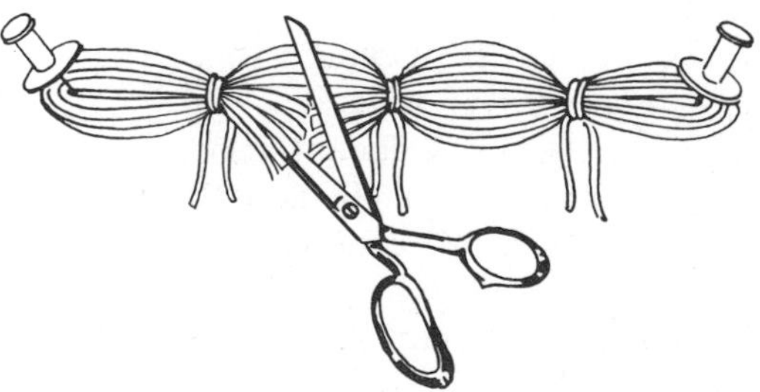

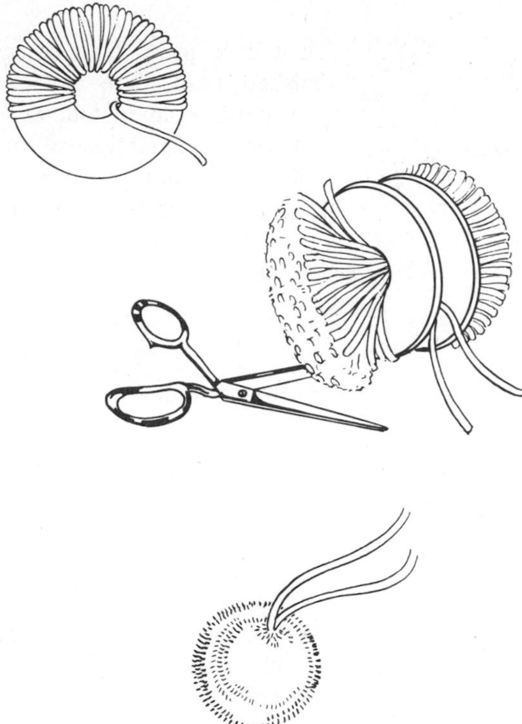

Or cut 2 cardboard disks the desired size with ¼″ hole in center. Cover the disks with yarn, using a blunt needle. Slip scissors between disks and cut around edge. Wind and tie thread around center, leaving ends for fastening.

Snow-Man Fringe. Suitable for trimming a child's scarf.

Cut two pieces of cardboard, one 4″ wide and the other 2½″ wide.

On the larger cardboard wind white knitting worsted around 40 times. Tie securely at top and slip off cardboard, leaving long end. To form a "head" wind a piece of yarn ¾″ from top. Tie and clip ends.

For arms, wind yarn around smaller cardboard 20 times. Cut through ends and wind and tie ends.

Cut through end loops of body. Divide in two and slip arms between. Tie beneath arms for waistline. Take a couple of short stitches with red yarn for mouth and with black thread for eyes.

Make as many dolls as needed. Place dolls' arms end to end and tack them together, catching into winding thread. Attach dolls to scarf with ends left at top, leaving about ½″ free.

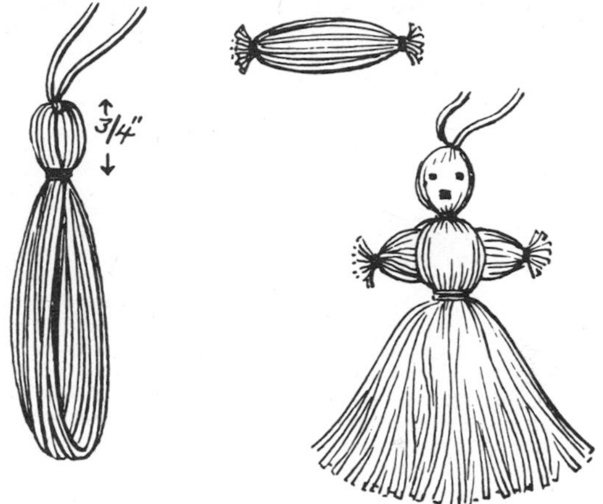

Monk's Cord. Calculate the length of cord desired and measure off 9 times this amount of heavy thread. (*a*) Fold in half and make a slip knot at the center. (*b*) Slip this loop over forefinger of left hand.

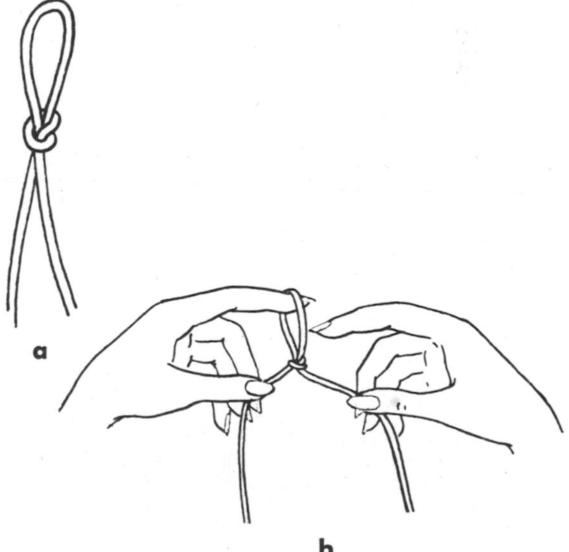

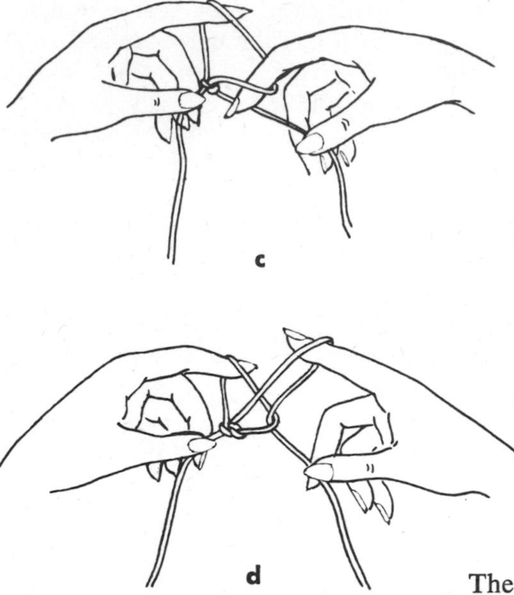

The string that pulls easily should be in the left hand and the string that does not, in the right (*c*) and (*d*).* Through the loop on the left hand, using right forefinger, draw right strand through to make a loop. Slip out left forefinger and insert right thumb in the loop and draw up pulling left strand tight. (*e*) and (*f*) The loop is on the right hand; insert left forefinger and draw left strand through, making a loop. Insert left thumb and pull up tight. Repeat from *, alternating from side to side. To end, pull last strand all the way through. Thread with needle and conceal in cord.

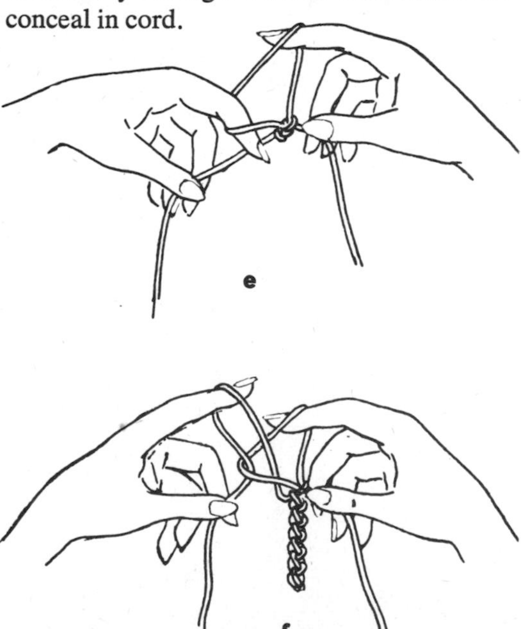

Sewing on Sequins in a Line. Follow the line of the design. Use a back-stitch and sew sequins on one at a time.

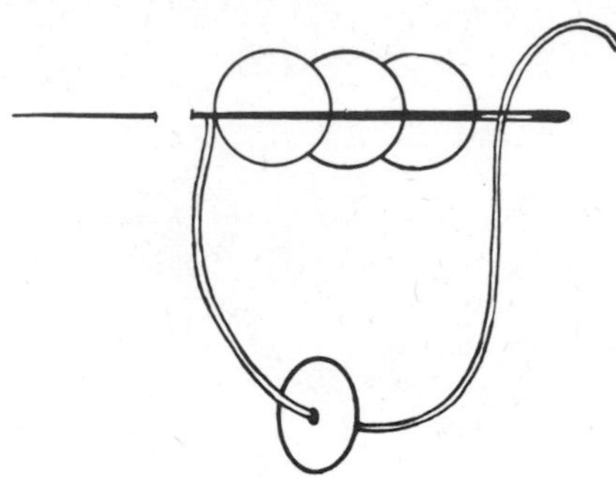

Sewing Sequins Singly. Use a very fine needle (a beading needle is best). Bring up from wrong side, thread through sequin, through small glass bead, back through sequin, and into cloth near where needle came out. Fasten thread securely or bring needle out at next place if not too far apart.

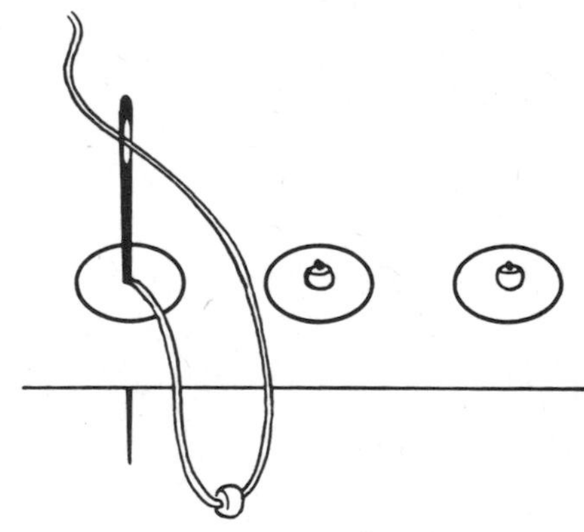

Beading. Beads are sewed on with backstitch, usually in rows. They can also be applied in loops.

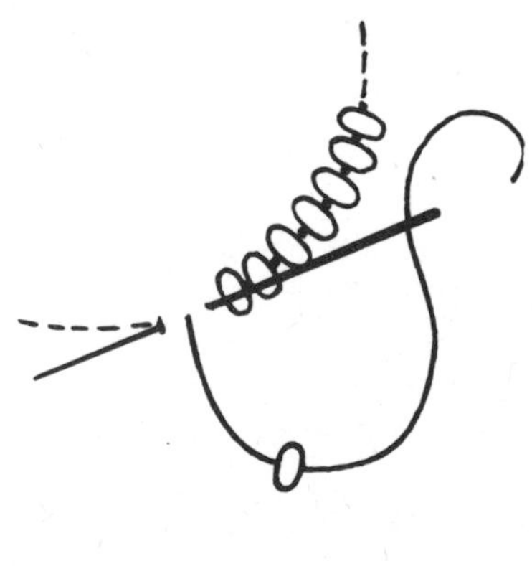

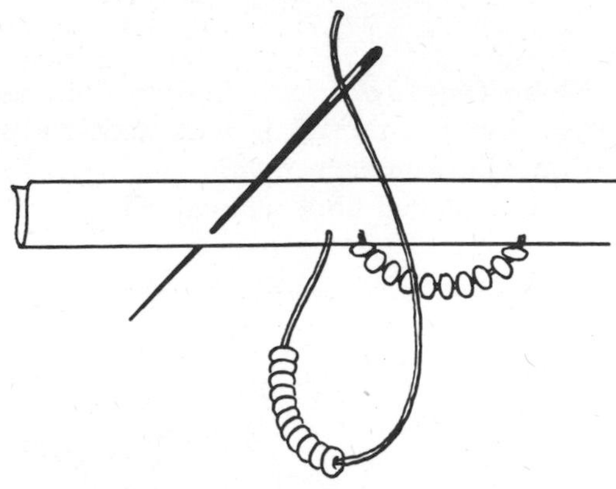

Rickrack. Rickrack can be sewed on by hand or by machine. Mark line for center of rickrack. Pin and baste. Sew with short stitches from point to point. If rickrack is very wide, take a stitch between points. Narrow rickrack can be stitched down the center by machine.

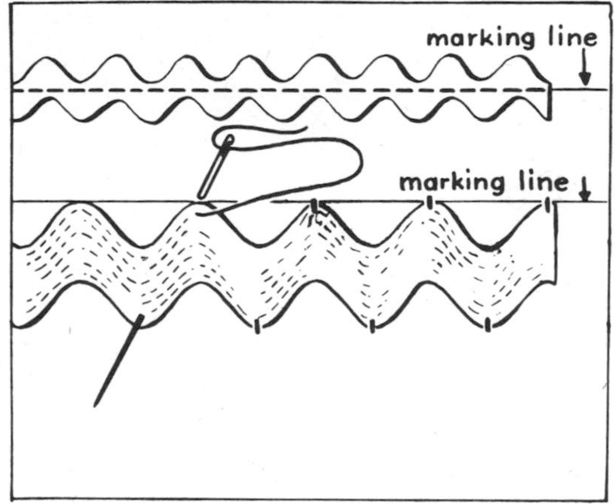

For an interesting effect, sew baby rickrack down center of wide rickrack.

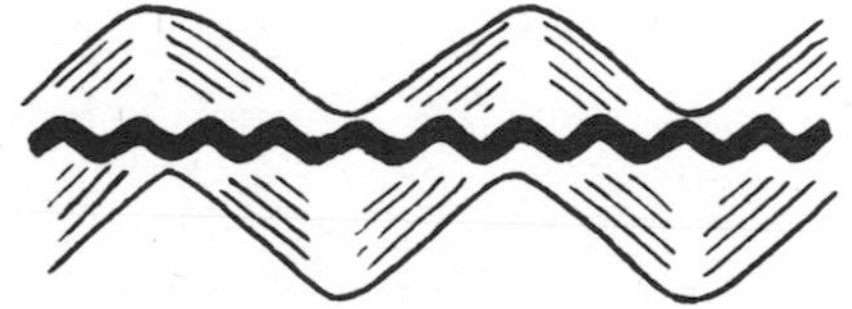

Place rickrack under folded edge of fabric with points showing and edge-stitch.

Or lay rickrack on top of fabric near edge and stitch down the center.

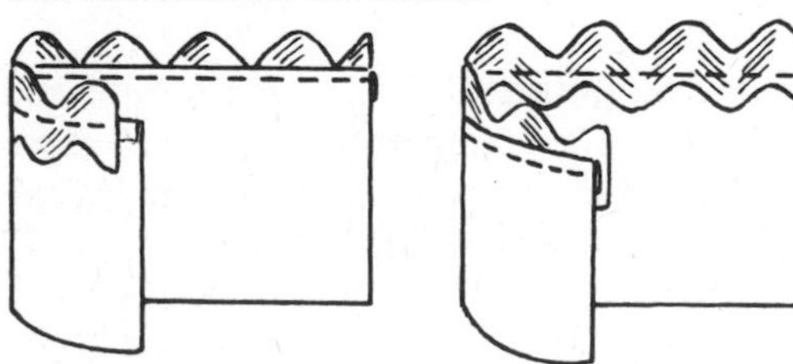

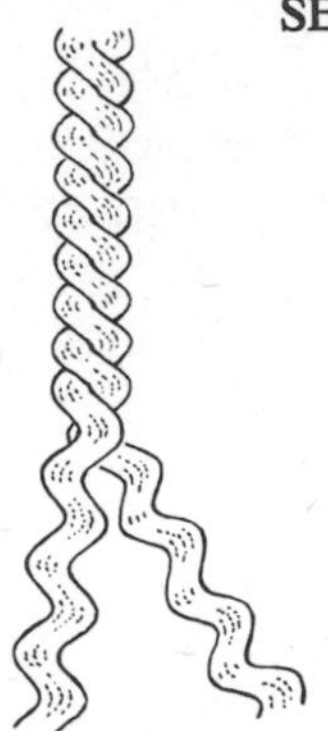

Rickrack may be "braided" or interlaced. Use two pieces of the same size rickrack and twist them together. Keep flat and press if necessary. Apply by sewing points down by hand, or stitching down the center.

Bar Tack. Take several vertical stitches. Work over and over with satin stitch, catching into the fabric. Work small bars at each end.

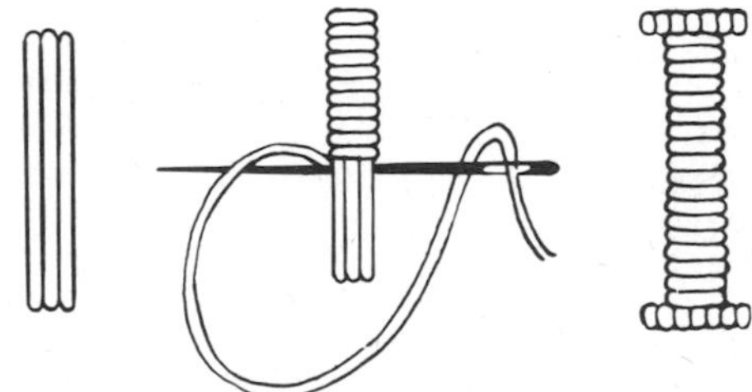

Arrowhead Tack. Mark a triangle. Bring needle out at left corner A. Take a short stitch from right to left at top of triangle B. Insert needle at right corner C and bring out slightly to the right of stitch at left corner A. Following line of triangle, take a stitch at top just below the first stitch. Insert needle at right corner just inside of first stitch. Repeat until triangle is filled.

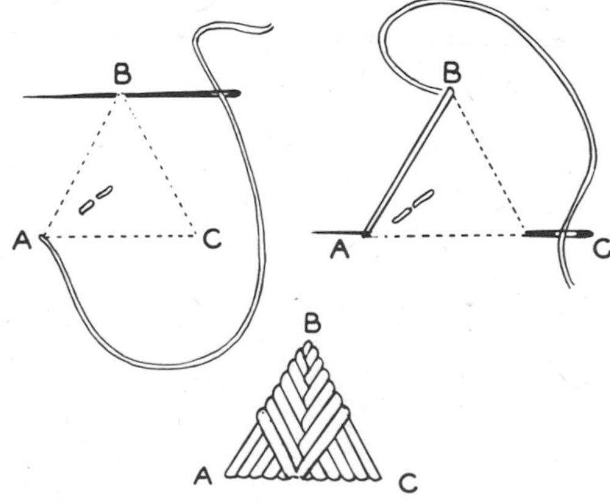

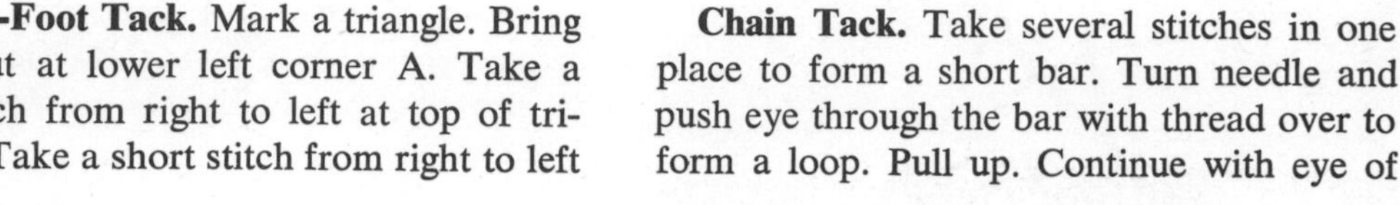

Crow's-Foot Tack. Mark a triangle. Bring needle out at lower left corner A. Take a short stitch from right to left at top of triangle B. Take a short stitch from right to left

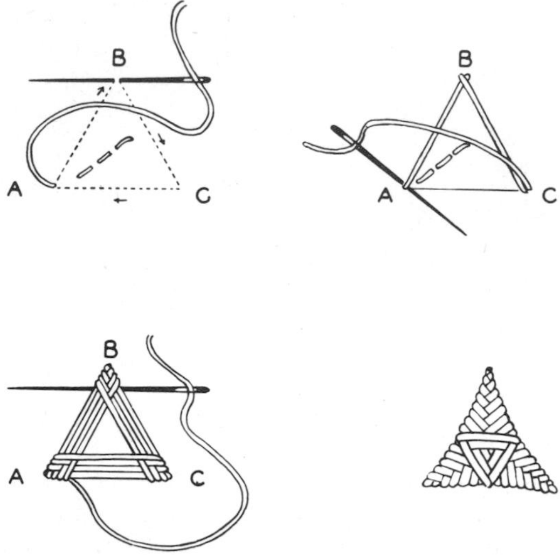

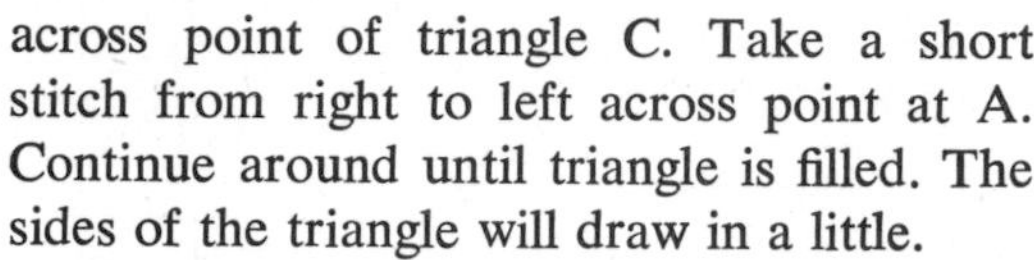

across point of triangle C. Take a short stitch from right to left across point at A. Continue around until triangle is filled. The sides of the triangle will draw in a little.

French Tack. (Sometimes called suspension tack.) This is used to hold two surfaces together loosely. For example, in tacking coat lining to coat at hem or belt to dress. Take several stitches back and forth between the two pieces. Work blanket stitch over them to cover. Use needle backward to avoid catching into stitches.

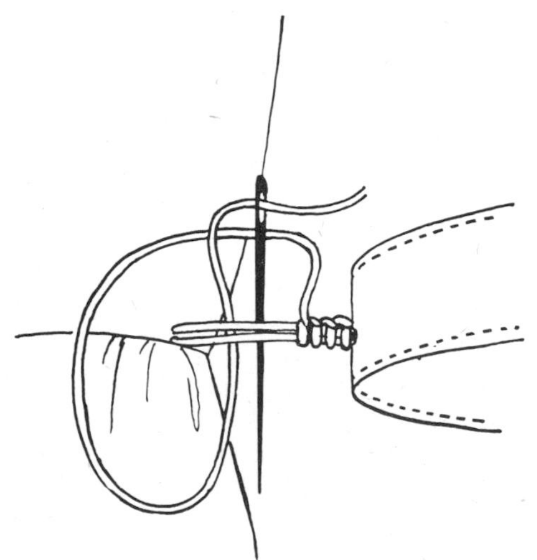

Chain Tack. Take several stitches in one place to form a short bar. Turn needle and push eye through the bar with thread over to form a loop. Pull up. Continue with eye of

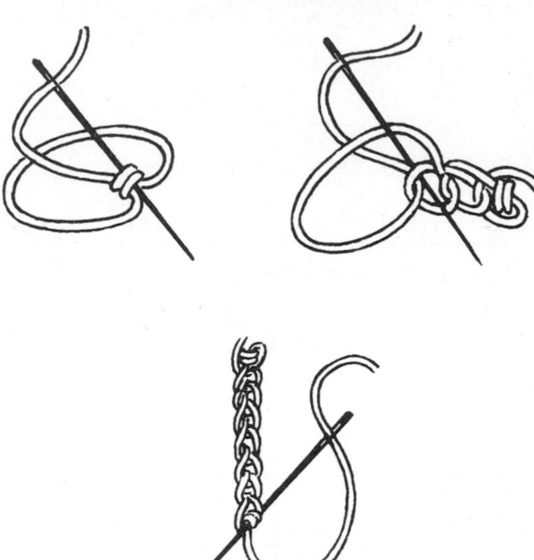

needle in each loop to form a chain. At the end, pull thread all the way through loop and sew to second piece of fabric. Used in the same way as a French tack.

Working with Lace

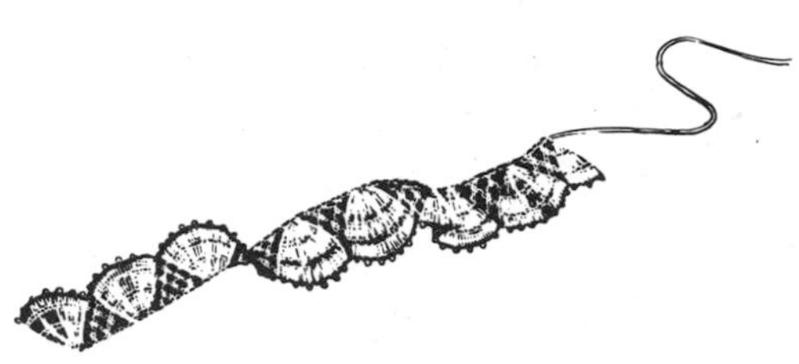

Lace Application. Use a fine needle and thread when working with lace. Some lace edgings (Val) can be gathered by pulling the edge thread. Otherwise they must be "fulled" while whipping on.

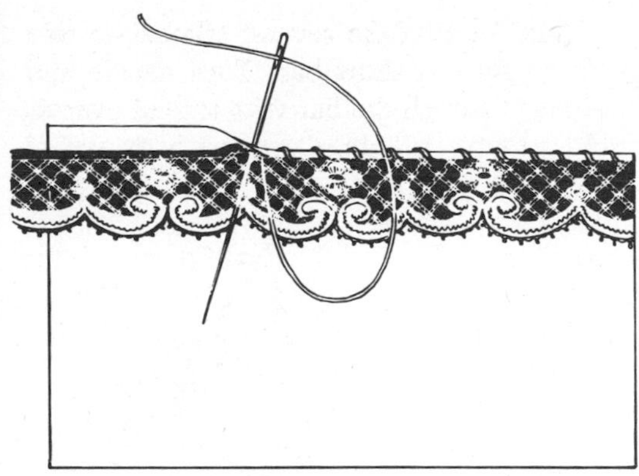

Lace on Rolled Edge. Make a rolled hem and sew on lace in one operation.

Lace on Hemmed Edge. After hemming, with right sides together, overhand lace to fabric.

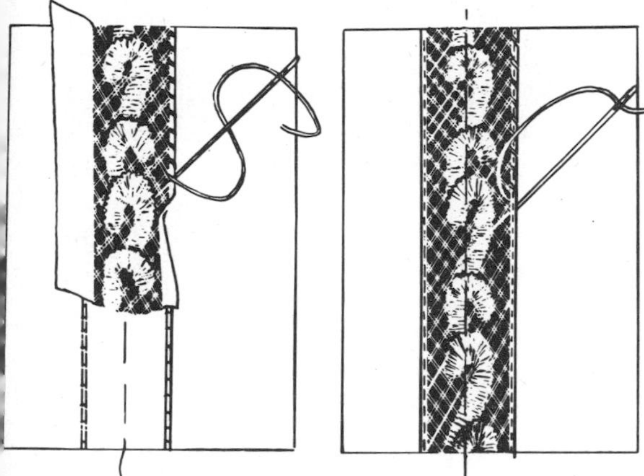

Setting in Lace Insertion. Baste insertion right side up to right side of fabric. Hem edges of lace to fabric. Cut away fabric underneath leaving narrow edges. Roll edges and whip with fine stitches.

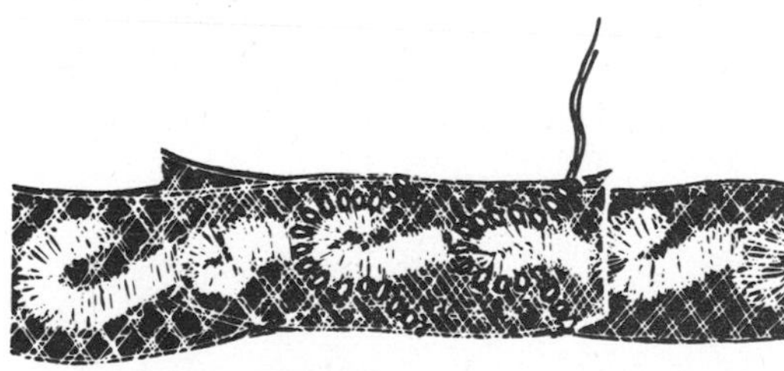

Joining Lace Invisibly. Overlap and match the pattern exactly and baste. Whip around the design and cut away excess close to stitches.

Joining Lace and Entre-deux. Roll and whip edges of entre-deux to fabric and lace. If entre-deux has finished edges, simply whip together.

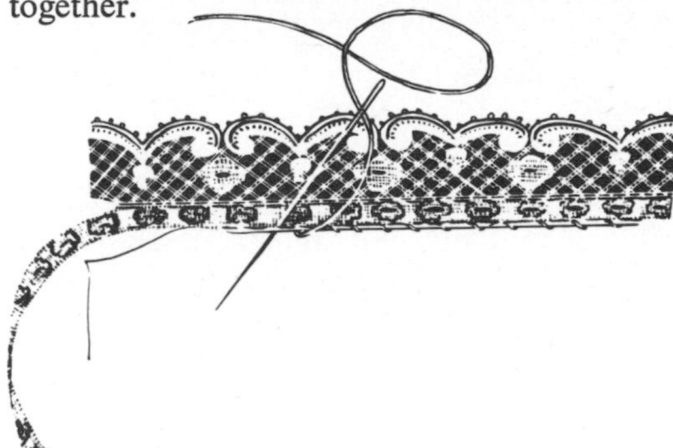

Setting in Lace Medallions. Baste motif on right side of fabric. Hold down edge with short over-and-over (satin) stitches and cut away fabric underneath close to stitches. Or sew edge with running stitches or back-stitches. Cut fabric away underneath, leaving enough to roll and whip, catching lace. Lace motifs may also be applied to fabric with machine zigzag stitch around edges.

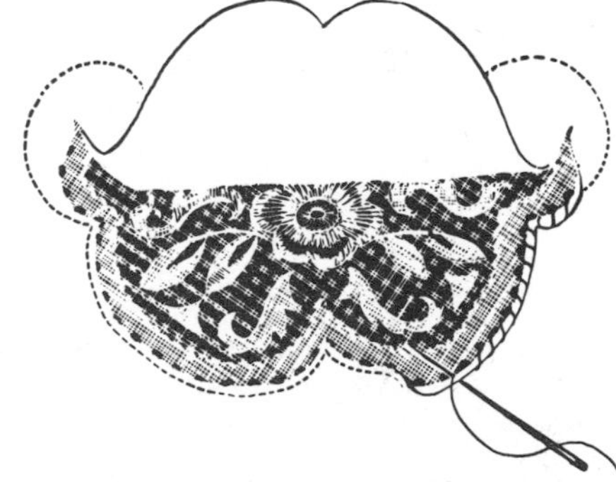

Flat Lace Corner. If possible have center of motif come at corner. Miter the corner, keeping the motif intact. Do not cut into edge. Lap corners and whip together. Trim close to stitch. Lace may also be gathered at corner by drawing up thread in edge of lace.

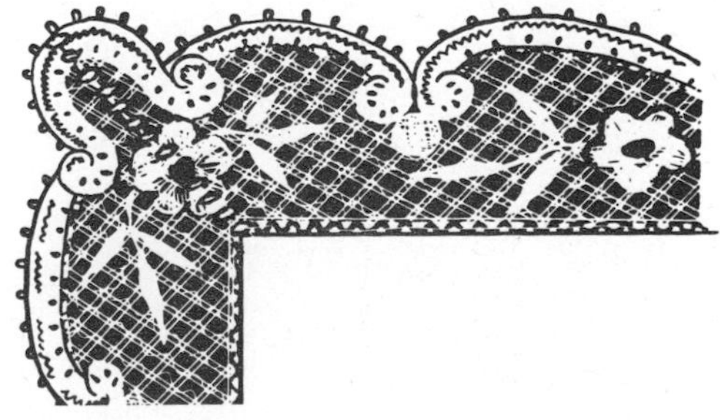

Working with Fur

Do not cut into good fur pieces unless you are reasonably sure of your own skill in following these instructions. Acquire experience by making a small piece first, using fur which is not too valuable.

Materials. Sufficient fur in good condition. Pattern. Muslin for fitting capes, stoles, etc. Lining and Interlining. Brush. Water Basin. Tape Measure. Thimble. Needle. Ruler. ½″-wide Tailor's Tape. (A good quality seam binding will do.) Chalk. (Ordinary white blackboard can be used. This must be kept sharpened. Rubbing over a piece of coarse screen will accomplish this.) Safety Pins. Thumbtacks. Scissors. Single-edge Razor Blade. Mercerized Cotton Thread. Flat Board—surface large enough for pattern.

General Procedure.

1. Test fur to be sure it is not too tender or brittle. This is done by pinching on the skin side. It will crack if it is too brittle.

2. For articles other than a straight scarf, make and fit on the wearer a muslin model-pattern of the article you intend to make of fur.

3. After the muslin model is fitted perfectly, take it apart and make a paper pattern from it. Be sure all corrections on the muslin are made on the paper pattern also. Cut off all seam allowances. *Note:* Fur is sewn edge to edge with no seam allowance; therefore it is necessary to eliminate all seam allowances from the pattern.

4. Disassemble your old fur piece and remove all attached linings and facings. Note the direction in which the fur lies (the grain), texture and color markings. These are important for matching while you work.

5. If you are using a large piece of fur, place the flattened fur on the working board with the skin-side up and mark the center back from neckline to bottom with a distinct chalk line. *Note:* This and Step No. 6 apply only if you are making (or remaking) a garment such as a shell (lining), jacket or stole.

6. Lay pattern on with the center back edge of pattern on the center line of the fur. Be sure all pattern pieces are placed with the grain (which is the direction of the flow of hair). Be sure to cut a right and left piece. Hold pattern in place with thumbtacks or tailor's pushpins. Outline the pattern with chalk. See Diagram 1. Reverse pattern and repeat. Continue marking all parts of the pattern.

For most small fur pieces such as collars, belts, etc., lay on pattern with fur grain or nap flowing toward the center back.

7. Following the chalk outlines, cut the fur with the single-edge razor blade. See Diagram 2. To avoid cutting the hair, the fur must be raised from the board. Do not cut darts (if any) at this time.

8. Examine the fur on the hair-side for worn spots. Mark these with safety pins in a triangle with one point toward the top of the piece. Turn fur to the skin-side and mark the triangle with connecting chalk lines from each pin. Cut on line of triangle and use the cutout section as a pattern for replacement piece of good fur. Be sure to match carefully the texture, color and grain. Sew in the replacement piece with close overcast stitch, sewing only the skin. Be sure all hair is free on fur side.

9. Mark all pattern pieces on working board. Using water basin and brush, wet fur on skin-side. Place fur, hair-side down, over pattern outline on board and tack carefully, matching the pattern. Allow to dry thoroughly (for at least 24 hours).

10. Remove thumbtacks. Replace pattern pieces on fur and carefully remark each pattern piece using a fine chalk line. Cut exactly on the chalk line. Cut out darts.

11. Lay tailor's tape flat around all edges, with edge of tape matching edge of skin. See Diagram 3. Hold in place with a flat zigzag stitch.

12. Join all seams and darts, using the same close overcast stitch with the skins edge to edge. See Diagram 4.

13. Sew tape to all outside edges using an overcast stitch. See Diagram 5.

14. Using a lukewarm iron, smooth out all the seams, making sure the iron touches only taped edges, not the skin.

15. Dampen the hair-side of fur, brushing

gently with the grain as you would brush your own hair. With ruler edge, fluff the fur slightly against the grain.

16. If the piece is to be interlined, cut the interlining (cotton flannel or sheet wadding) like the pattern. Lay it on the skin-side, fitting it carefully. Turn tape to wrong side over the interlining and hem down by hand. See Diagram 6.

17. The lining should be cut with seam allowance and sewn as you would line any garment.

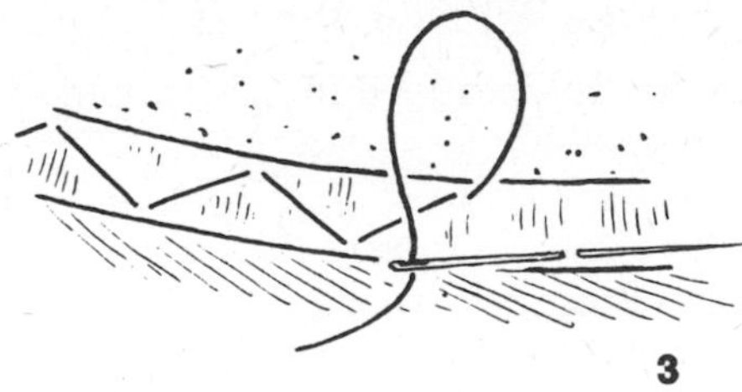
3

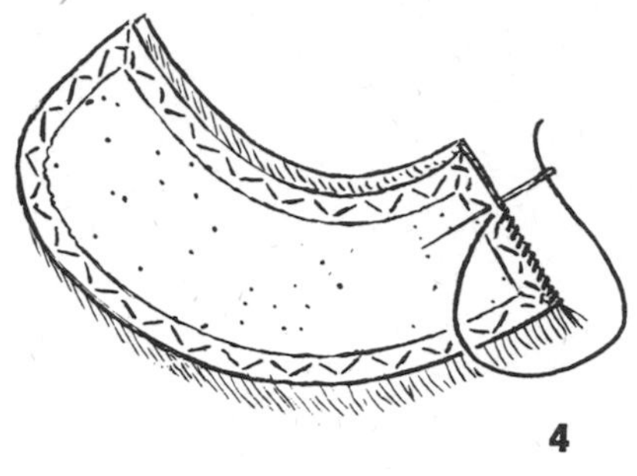
4

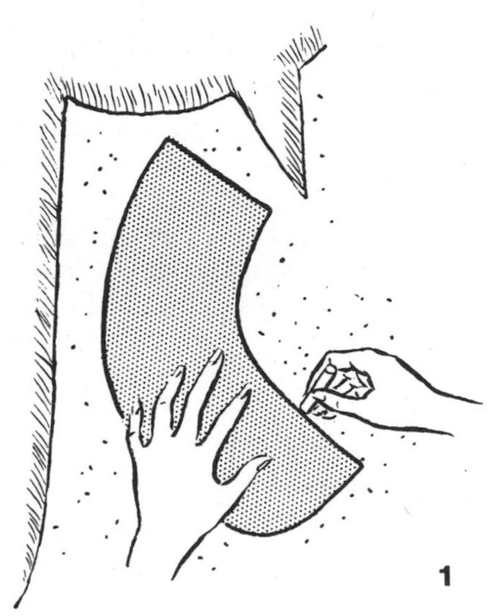
1

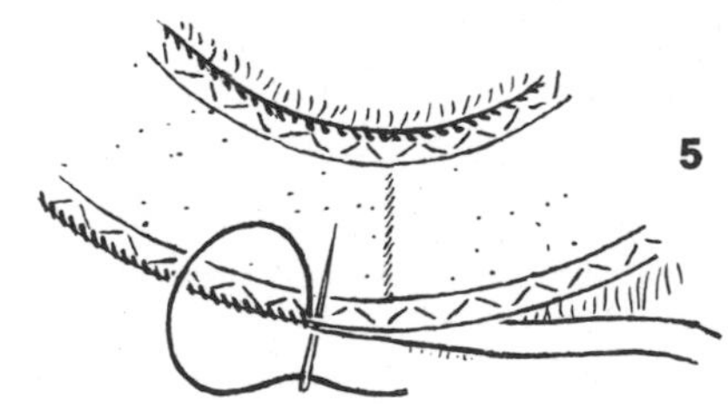
5

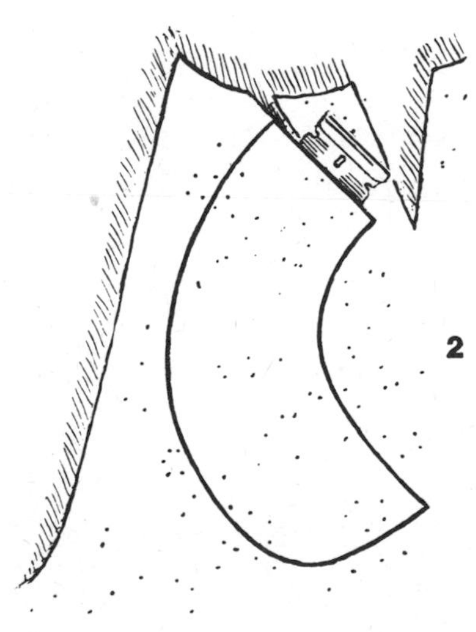
2

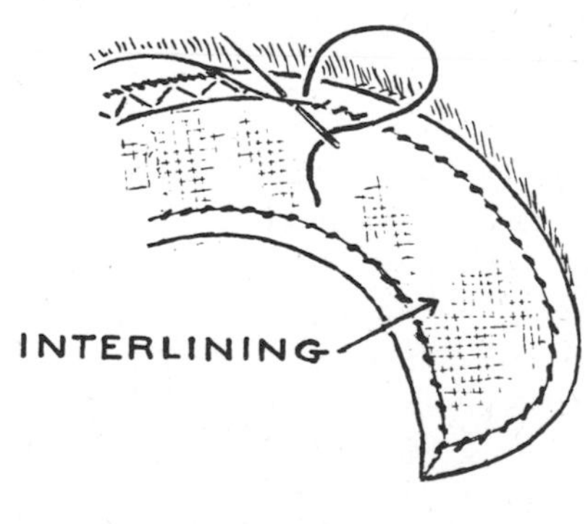

6

PATTERN ALTERATION

General Hints

Before buying your pattern take the following measurements over a simple dress of thin material and well-fitting foundation garments:

Bust. . . . . . . around the fullest part

Waist. . . fairly snug at natural waistline

Hip. . . around fullest part (about 7″ below waistline)

Waist length at center back.

Compare these measurements with those on the various charts in the front or back of the pattern catalog. Choose your type (Junior, Misses, Women's, Half-size, etc.) and then pick the size which is closest to your measurements.

If your measurements are between two sizes, choose the smaller if you like a snug fit, the larger if you like a looser fit. You will of course alter the pattern where necessary.

Buy dress and blouse patterns by bust measurement and skirt and slack patterns by hip measurement.

For a figure which is very much out of proportion (for example, very large hips and a small bust), it saves time and trouble to buy two patterns, one for the bust measurement and one for the hip measurement.

One thing which must be taken into consideration when altering a pattern is "ease." For a simple fitted bodice, for example, the pattern may allow for about 4″ ease (patterns differ in amount of ease). For a bust which actually measures 32″ (and the pattern says 32″) the pattern with seams and darts subtracted will measure 36″ (or more). About 2″ ease is allowed on hip measurements and ½″ around the waistline. If this were not done a dress or skirt would be too tight to be comfortable. Do not lose this ease when altering your pattern.

Also remember that the fashion and the style of the garment influence ease. A shirtwaist dress with full bodice will have much more ease than the tailored type. And the same is true of skirts.

If you are hard to fit, it is advisable, whenever possible, to make up a muslin of the garment (after making major adjustments in pattern) and fit it to the figure and use it for a pattern for cutting the fabric.

You can also buy a basic pattern or a simple dress pattern with long sleeves; make it up in muslin and fit it to your figure; and keep it on hand for reference when fitting any garment.

A dress form exactly like your figure is also a tremendous help when altering and fitting.

How to Alter Your Pattern

Most patterns indicate with printed lines where lengthening and shortening should be done.

To Lengthen. BODICE AND SKIRT: Cut across pattern and spread the necessary amount. Pin to a paper underlay.

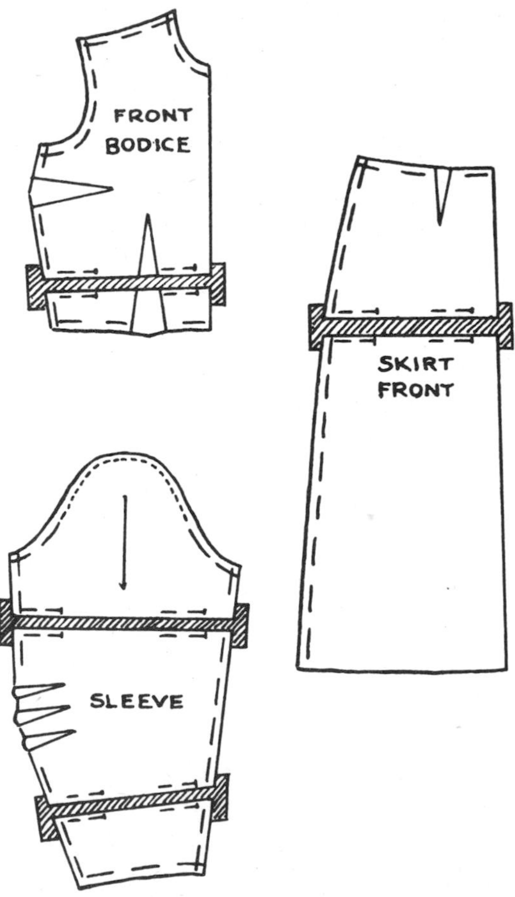

SLEEVE: Cut and spread above or below elbow, or both places if necessary.

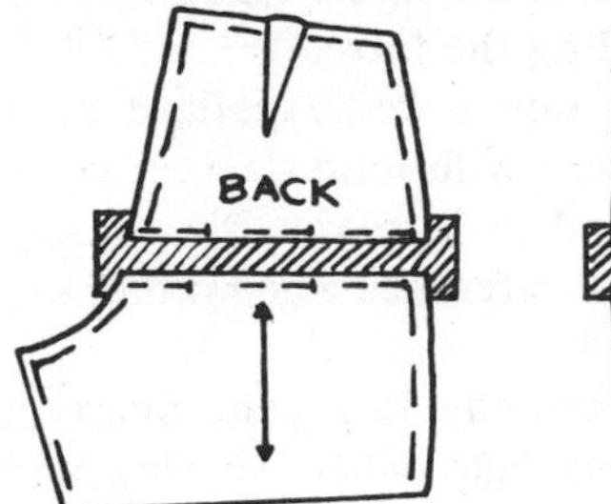

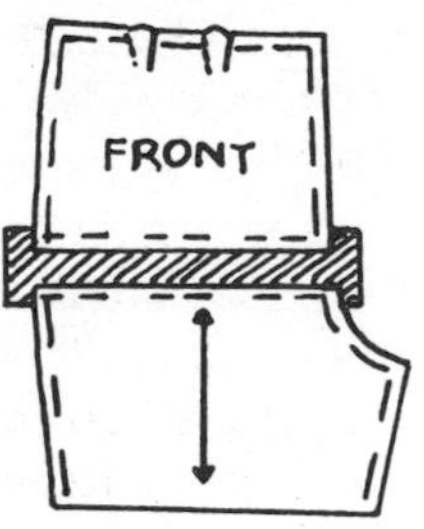

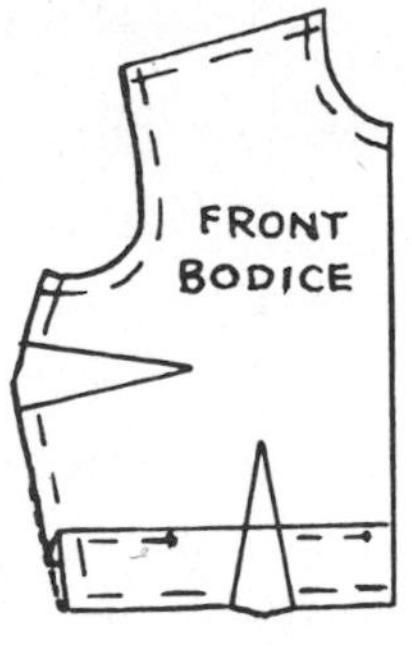

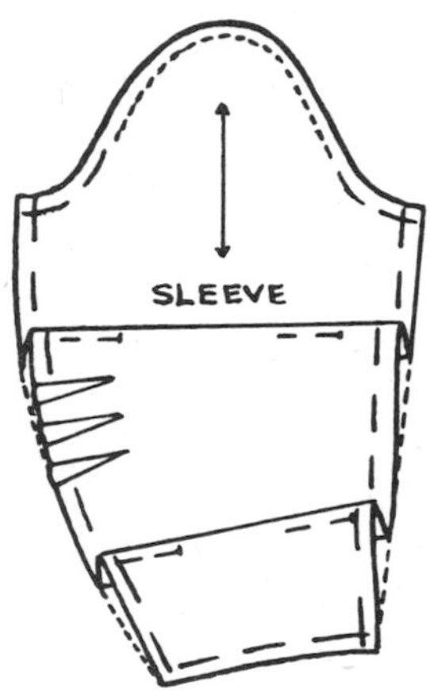

SLACKS AND SHORTS: While seated, measure the distance from the waistline to the chair and add ¾″. Measure *back* of pants pattern straight across from point of crotch (disallowing seams). If this is the same as your first measurement, the pants should fit. If it is less, cut pattern and spread as shown; if more, fold a tuck in the pattern.

If you have a large abdomen, take a full crotch measurement from front to back waistline between the legs. Add 3″ for ease. Now measure the front and back crotch seams of pattern (less seams). If less than your first measurement, add as shown on front, at crotch, tapering to nothing at sides.

Extra length may also be added at lower edge of slacks if needed.

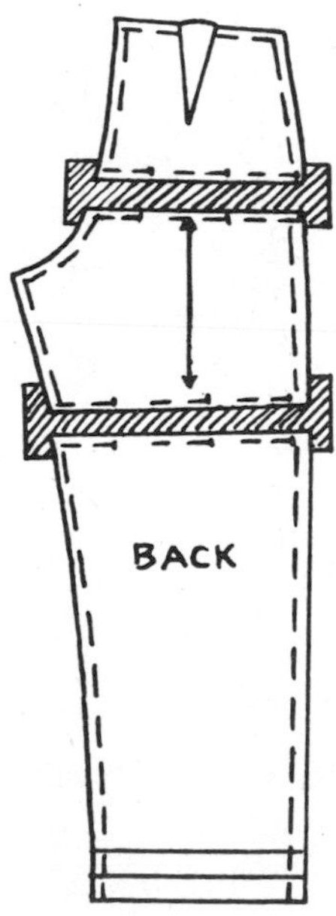

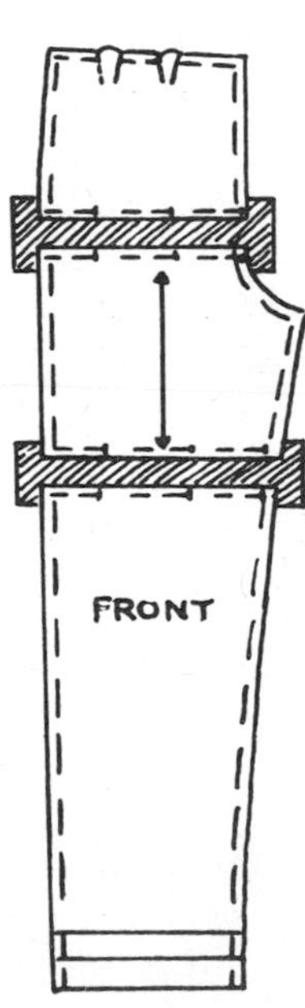

To Shorten. BODICE AND SKIRT: Fold a pleat or tuck across pattern the necessary amount.

SLEEVE: Fold a tuck above or below elbow or both if necessary.

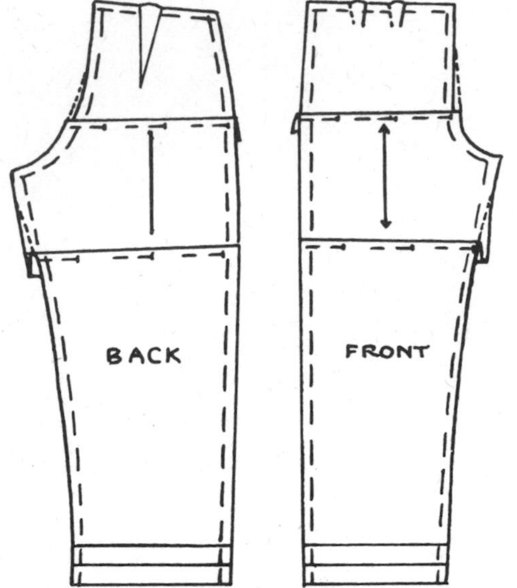

SLACKS AND SHORTS: Fold a tuck above and below crotch. Additional shortening may be done at lower edge of slacks.

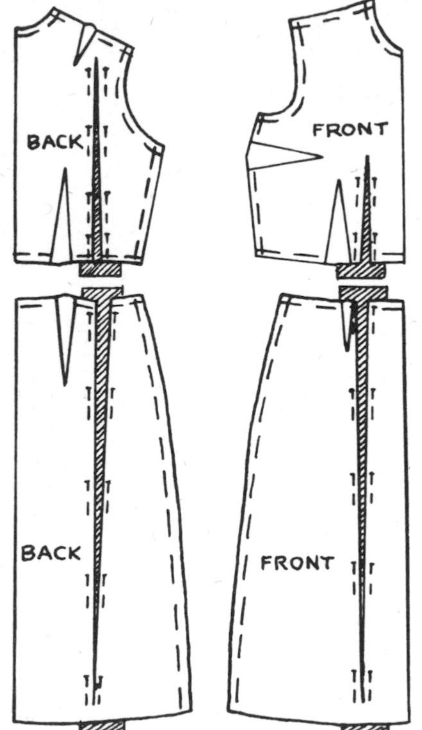

Large Waistline. Slash front bodice from waistline to crown of bust. Slash back bodice from waistline almost to shoulder. Spread correct amount and pin to paper underlay.

Slash skirt front and back directly below bodice slash, spread and pin to underlay.

Large Waistline and Abdomen. Adjust as for large waistline. Also slash across front 3″ or so above waistline, tapering to nothing at underarm, and spread desired amount. Slash skirt across front and spread desired amount.

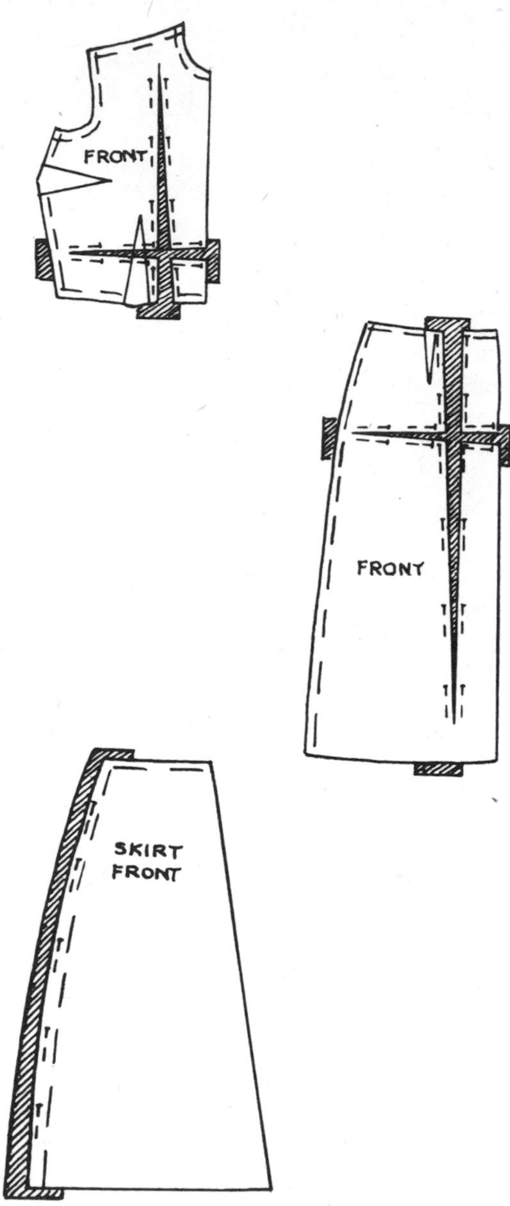

Large Hips. Determine how much needs to be added and add ¼ the amount to each side at front and back of skirt, tapering to nothing at the waistline if necessary.

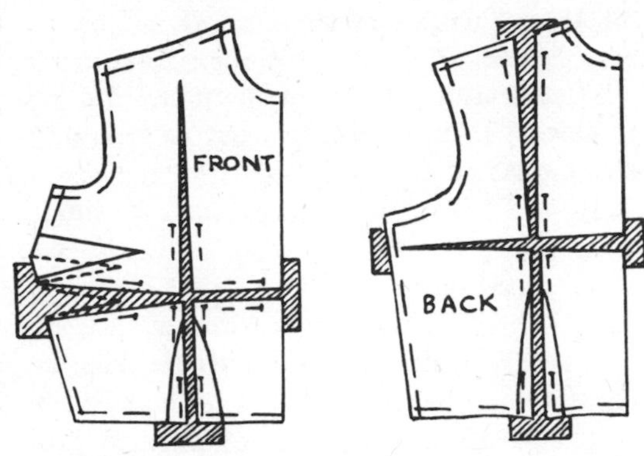

Large Bust Line. FRONT: Add to length as before. Slash from waistline and taper to shoulder. Spread desired amount. Adjust darts.

BACK: Add to length and spread desired amount adding dart at underarm if necessary. Slash from waistline and taper to shoulder.

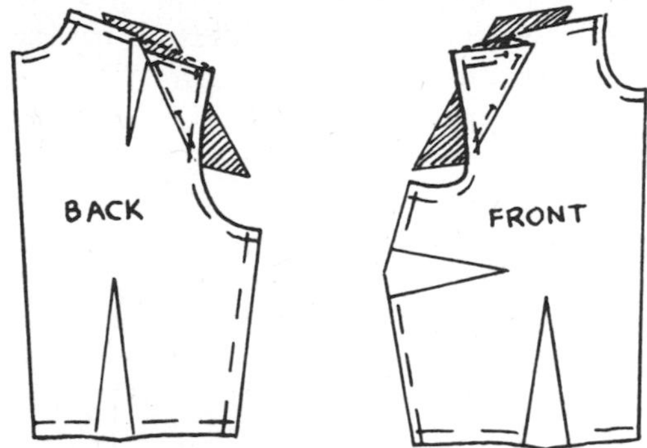

Narrow Shoulders. Make a slantwise slash from center of shoulder almost to armhole. Lap amount necessary and pin to underlay. Draw a new straight shoulder line.

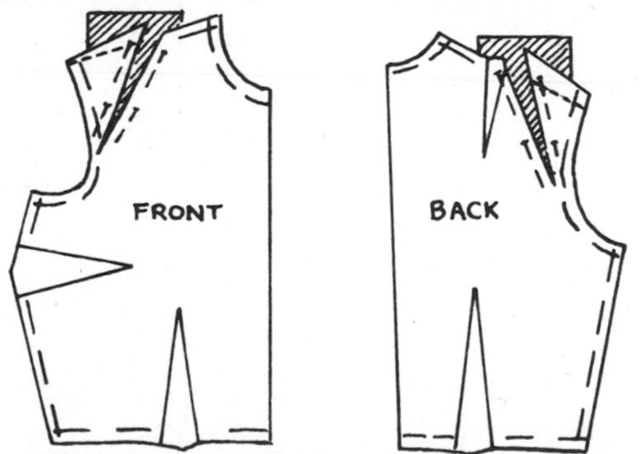

Wide Shoulders. Slash as for narrow shoulders and spread desired amount. Pin to underlay and draw new shoulder line.

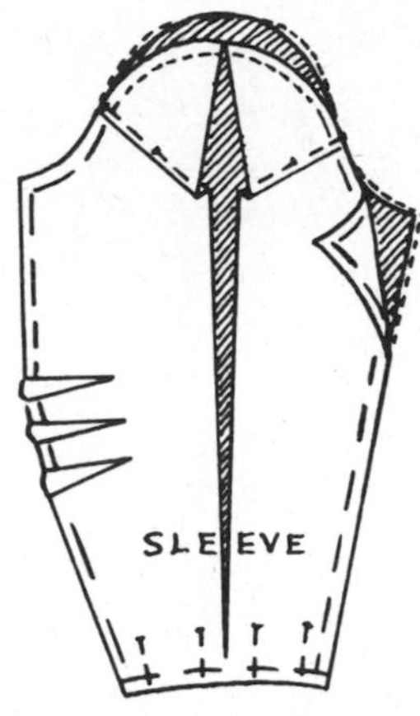

Large Upper Arm. Sleeve should allow "ease" of 1½″ to 2½″ around arm just below armhole. Slash lengthwise through center tapering to nothing at lower edge. Spread desired amount. To flatten pattern, bring together at top and fold in dart on each side. Retain curve at top of sleeve.

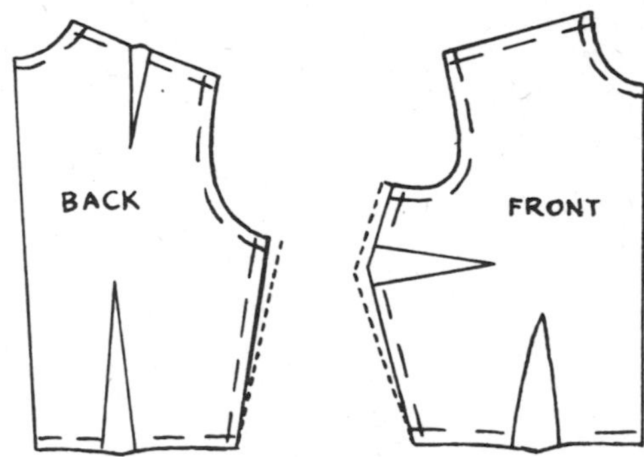

The same total amount must be added at underarm seam on front and back bodice.

For a thin arm make a fold lengthwise at center of sleeve. Take off an equal amount at underarm on front and back bodice.

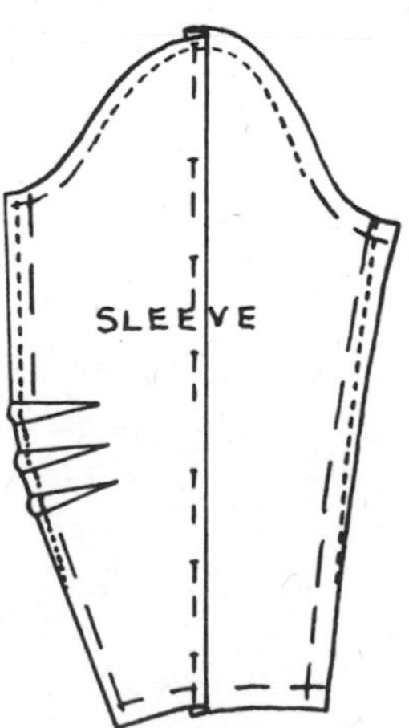

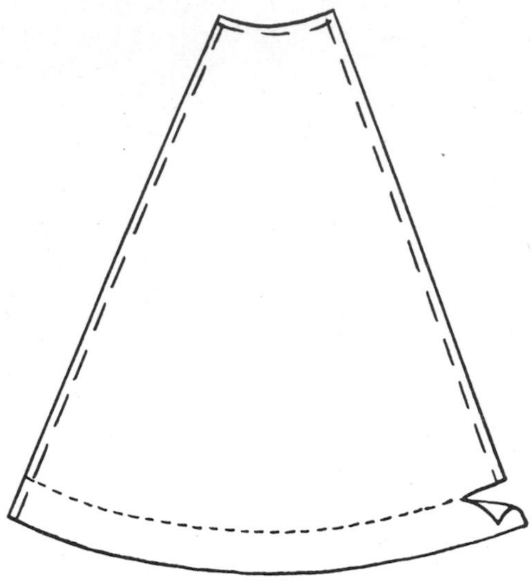

Shortening Circular Skirt. Take off the necessary amount at lower edge. Or cut across on a circular line 8″ or 9″ below waistline and lap. Correct the side seam lines.

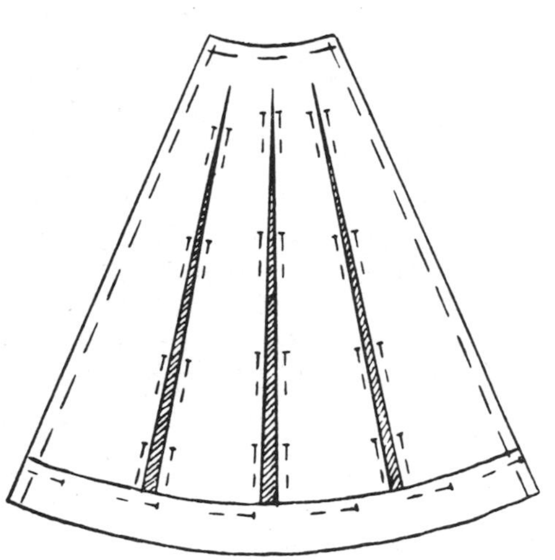

To preserve the width in shortening, slash from lower edge to waistline and spread apart enough to fit the original hem.

Lengthening Circular Skirt. Add to the hem line.

THINGS TO SEW

Here follow a number of articles for you to sew, with step-by-step, easy-to-follow instructions and diagrams.

If you are a beginner, choose a simple item to start with—the man's tie, the bed jacket, the apron, or a simple toy. The handbag accessories, although smaller, are not necessarily easier, as they must be done accurately and neatly or they lose their charm.

The bassinet is a more complicated project, but if directions are carefully followed it should come out well.

Man's Tie

Materials. ¼ yard 36″-wide lengthwise-striped heavy Silk or Cotton, for one tie, or ¾ yard 36″-wide crosswise-striped heavy Silk or Cotton for four ties. ¼ yard thin Muslin. Smooth Wrapping Paper for pattern.

Pattern. Make a paper pattern, following diagram. Use outside lines for tie and inside lines for lining.

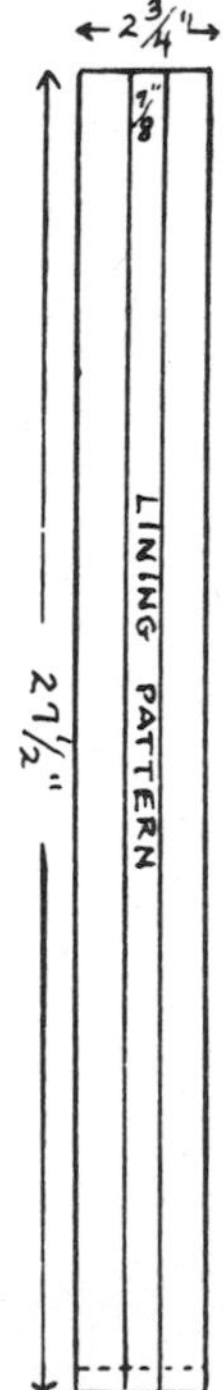

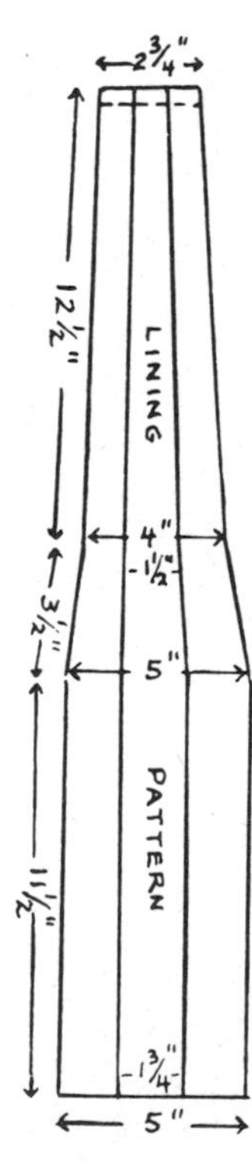

Cutting. 1/4" seams are allowed. No seam allowance is needed on lining, except at ends for piecing together. Pin tie pattern on fabric so stripes run crosswise on tie. Cut one narrow and one wide piece. Cut lining from muslin.

To Make. Right sides together, join the two pieces at narrow ends where seam allowance is shown on pattern (this is center of tie). Press seam open. Lap and sew center seam of tie lining. Place lining down center on wrong side of tie. Turn ends of tie 1/4" to wrong side. Slip-stitch across ends, and press. Fold sides of tie (as far as lining) to the center, pin, baste, press. Turn under one edge; pin, slip-stitch the full length of tie.

Bed Jacket

Materials. 1 yard 54″-wide White Wool Flannel. 1 yard 48″-wide Silk or Nylon Pink or White Sheer Print, for lining. 7 yards Baby Gold Rickrack. 3½ yards ½″-wide Gold, Pink, and White Woven Braid. 1 yard ½″-wide White Ribbon.

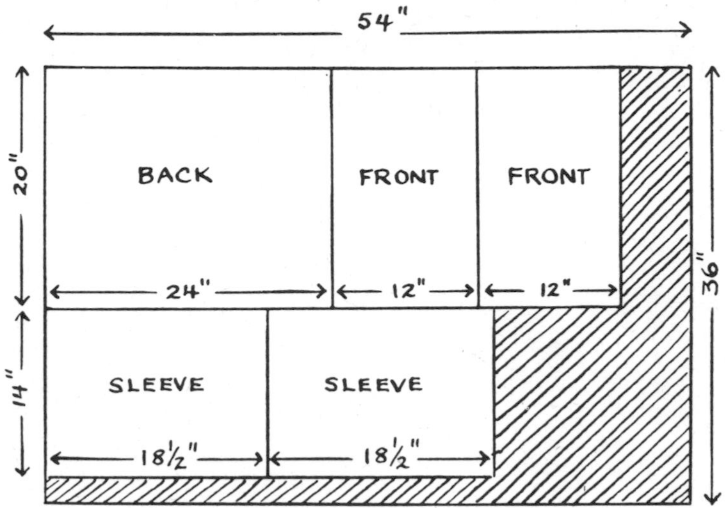

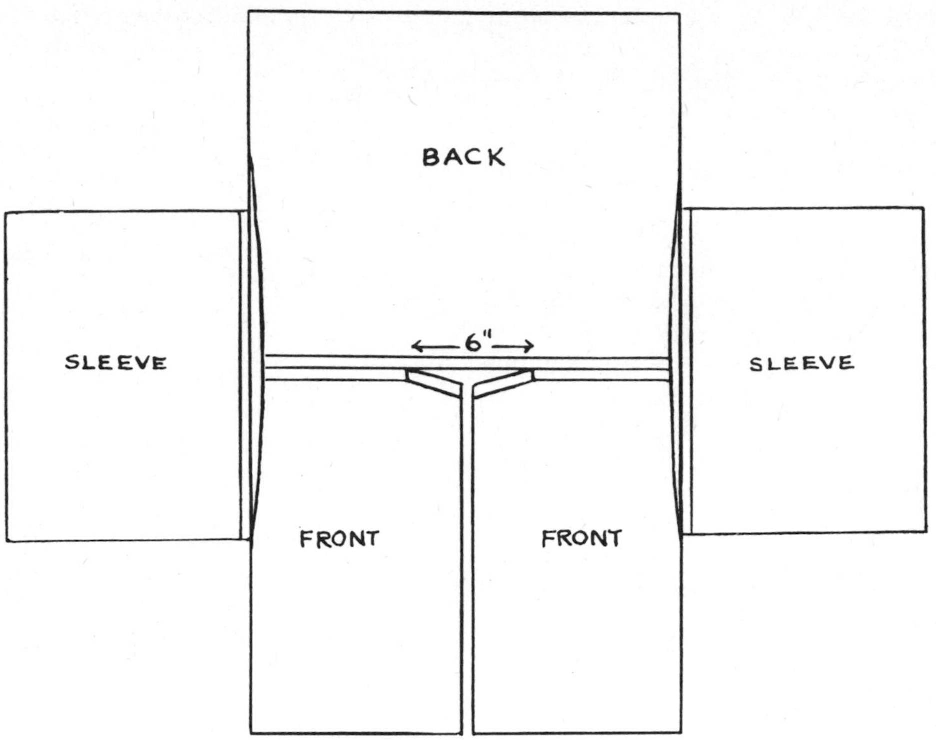
BACK
SLEEVE
6"
SLEEVE
FRONT
FRONT

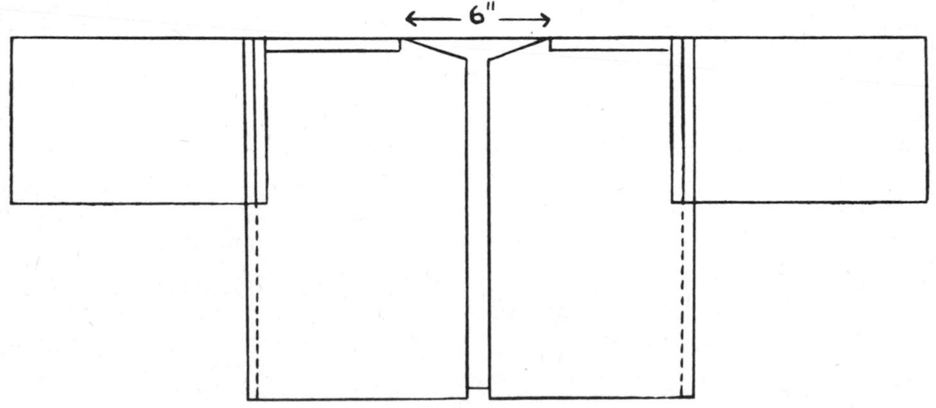
6"

Cutting (½″ seams allowed). To make pattern, follow cutting diagram, or mark directly on the flannel, and cut. Use flannel pieces as guides, and cut lining pieces for fronts, back, and sleeves.

To Make. Find top center back, and mark 3″ each side. Sew fronts to back at shoulder up to markings. (This leaves 6″ open at center back and a 3″ lapel on each side of front.) Press seams open. Mark center on one long side of each sleeve. With this center point matching shoulder seam of jacket, pin and stitch sleeves to jacket. Press seam. Clip jacket seam at underarm. With jacket wrong side out and folded at shoulder line, pin and sew sleeve and underarm seams. Turn and press ½″ seam allowance to wrong side on all jacket edges except lapels, which are turned to right side 9″ from top edge. Make lining in same way as jacket. Press seams open.

TRIMMING: On right side of fronts and lower edge of jacket, pin and stitch one row of gold rickrack ½″ from folded edge, starting and stopping 8″ from top. Pin and stitch braid 1/16″ in from rickrack, starting and stopping 7½″ from top and mitering corners on lower fronts. Stitch braid on both edges. Pin and stitch another row of gold rickrack on other side of the braid, starting and stopping 7″ from top. Trim lapels in same manner, mitering corners and ending lower ends of braids 1″ below turn of lapels. Trim sleeve edges in same manner. (The trimming of three rows of braid should be about 1″ wide when finished.)

LINING THE JACKET: Place lining and jacket wrong sides together. Pin along all seams. Turn under ½″ around sleeves, at back of neck, around lower edge, and up fronts to point where lapel begins. Cut away lining at lapel fold, leaving ¼″ for turning under. Turn under along fold, and pin. Blind-hem lining to jacket. Press carefully. Cut ribbon into two 16″ lengths, turn in ends, and sew to wrong side of fronts just below lapel.

Handbag Accessories

Materials (for entire set). ¾ yard 36″-wide Cotton Print (models are in small traditional pattern, blue and red on white background). 1 yard Plain Cotton (red in model). 10″×20″ piece heavy Cotton Batting for coin-purse interlining. 30″×36″ piece Single-Sheet Batting. ½ yard heavyweight nonwoven Interfacing. 1 package ½″-wide Bias Binding, to match plain fabric. 4 inches ¼″-wide Elastic. ½ yard fine Cord. 8″ neck-opening-type Zipper, to match plain fabric (for coin purse). Mercerized Sewing Thread, to match plain fabric. 1″ Graph Paper.

Notes. Quilting design for each accessory may be as simple or as elaborate as you wish. Machine-stitch lines diagonally across fabric, forming parallel lines, diamonds, zigzags, or any other pattern.

Where pattern is given on a graph, copy on 1″ graph paper, enlarging each square to 1″.

Single Spectacles Case

Cut 4″×8″ pieces, as follows: two sections from print fabric, on lengthwise grain; two sections from plain fabric; two sections from interfacing; two sections from sheet batting. Place together in this order: one plain section; one interfacing; one batting; one printed section, right side up. Baste together, matching edges. Quilt as desired. Make two such pieces.

Copy and cut pattern. Cut out quilted pieces from pattern; be sure to have them facing, one right side up, one wrong side up. Press open one fold of bias tape. Starting at one X point and folding end over as sketched, pin this edge of tape to edge of one quilted section, on right side, edges even. Stitch around, easing around curves. Let ends lap; cut. Turn to wrong side; hem down folded

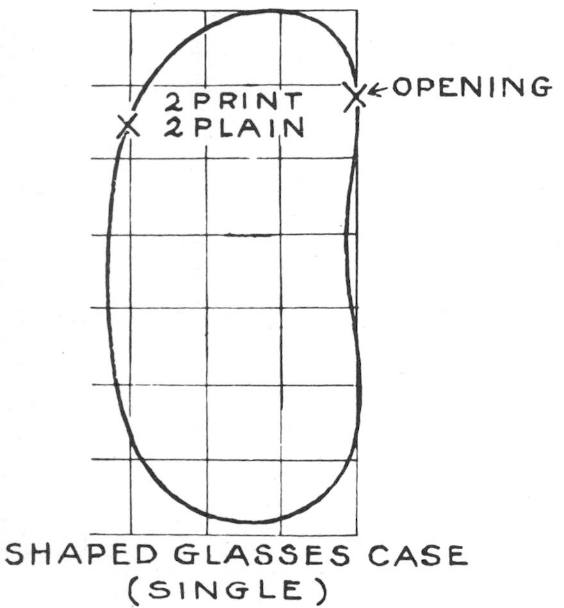

SHAPED GLASSES CASE (SINGLE)

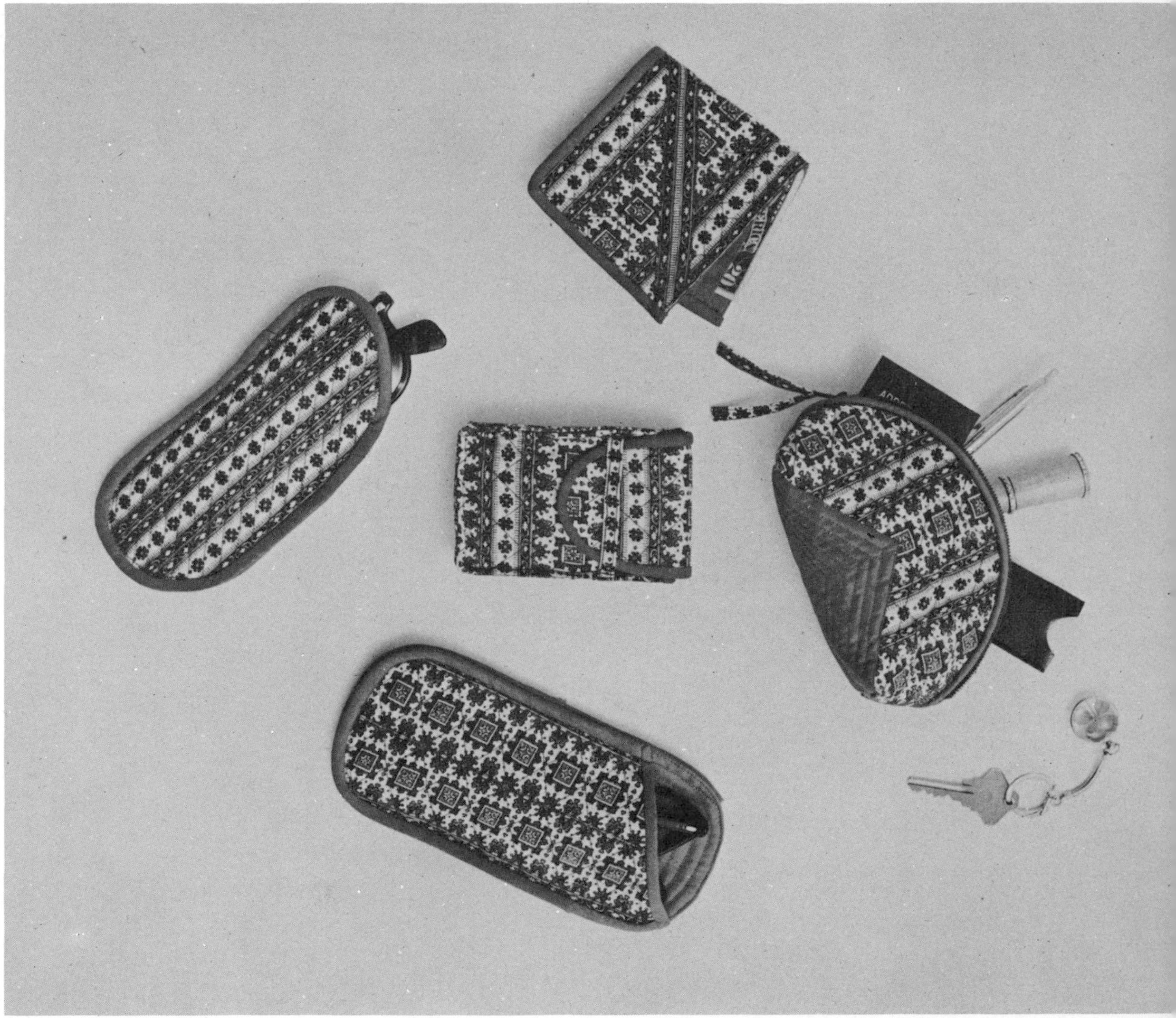

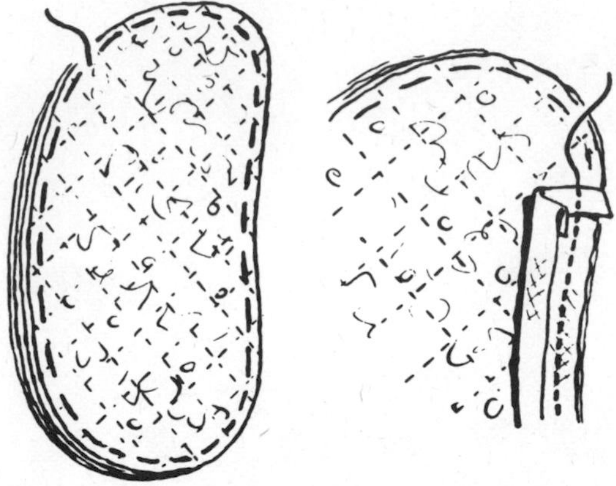

edge. Repeat on second section. Pin the two sections together, plain sides facing. Starting and ending at X points, stitch around through all thicknesses, just inside line of bias binding. Take a few backward stitches with machine at beginning and end of stitching line.

Double Spectacles Case

Prepare and cut pattern. Following it, cut two pieces of plain fabric and one piece of sheet batting, *adding ¼" seam allowance all around*. Place the three pieces together, with batting in center. Stitch all around, leaving one end open. Trim allowance to ⅛"; turn to right side through opening. Turn in raw edges; press and edge-stitch around. Quilt upper end as shown.

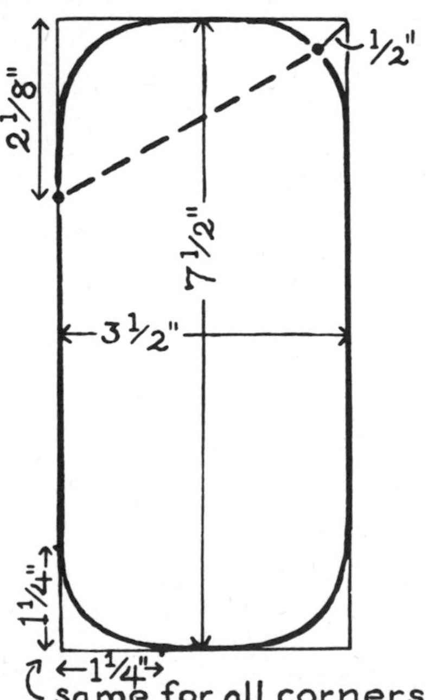

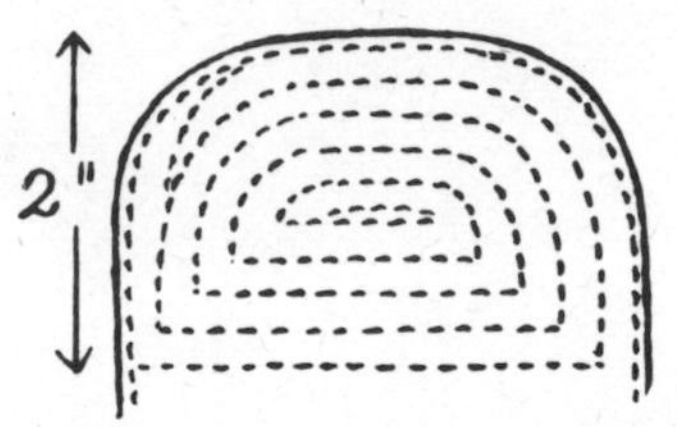

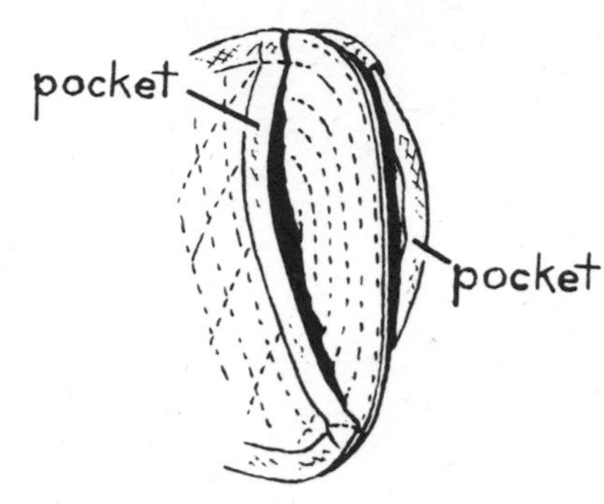

Follow directions for single spectacles case, but using pattern at left with top trimmed off at dotted line shown on sketch. Bind edges of the two outer pieces as instructed, finishing by hand at corners. Place the plain piece between the two printed ones before assembling.

Cigarette Case

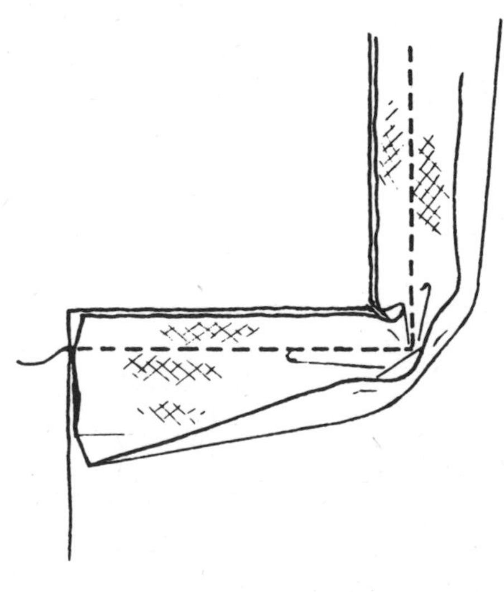

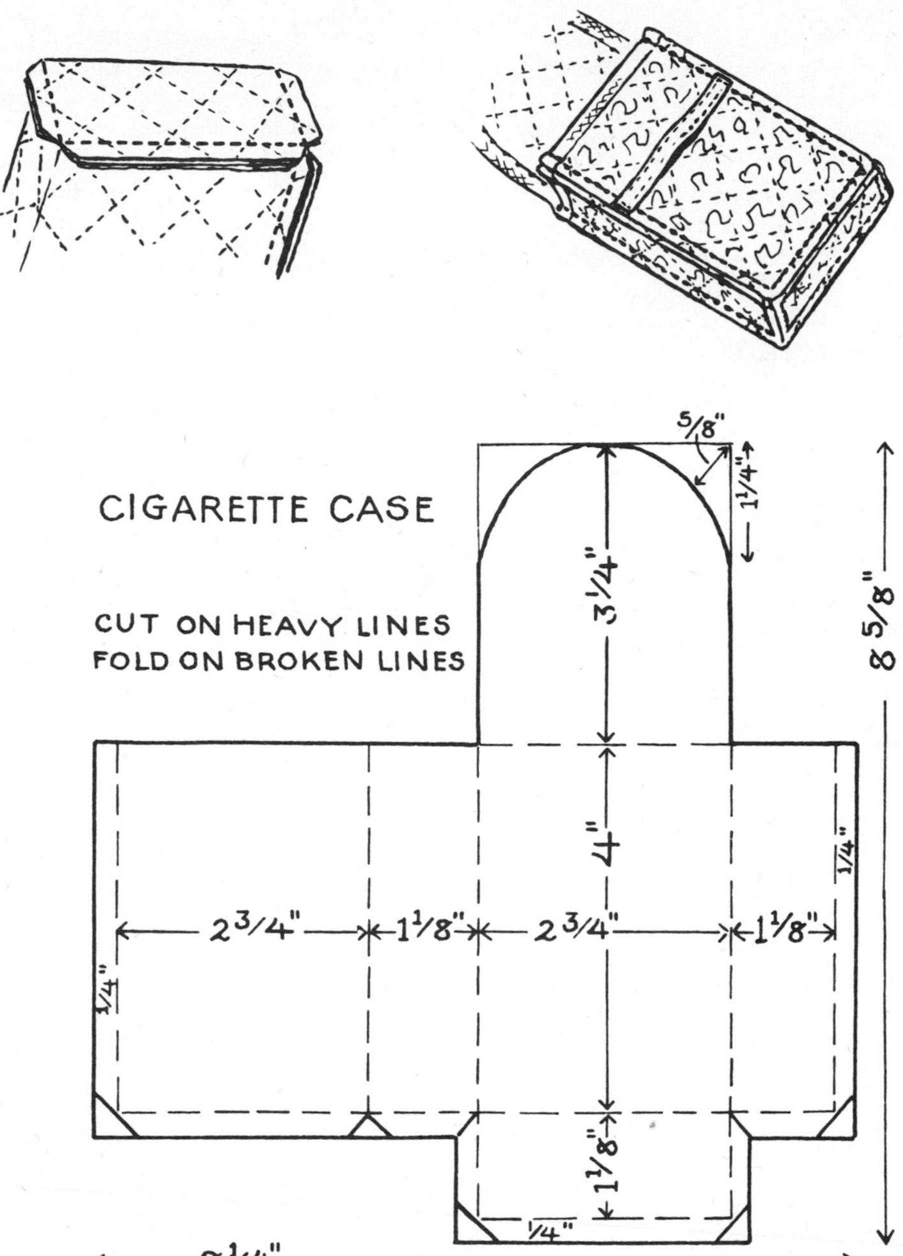

Cut one 10″×11″ square each of print fabric, plain fabric, and interfacing; two 10″ ×11″ squares of sheet batting. Place together as follows: plain fabric; batting; interfacing; batting; print fabric, right side up. Baste together, and quilt as desired.

Cut pattern as shown. Place pattern on right side of quilted piece; cut out carefully. Mark fold lines on right side with lines of basting.

Press open one fold of bias tape. Starting at one corner of top, baste and stitch open edge to right side of top edge and around flap, easing over curve. Turn to wrong side; hem down.

Stitch side hems together, wrong side out. Clip through seam allowance into the two corners. Notch other seam allowances as marked.

Fold bottom; match edges carefully to side

bottom edges; pin, and baste. Stitch around, and trim seam allowance to less than ⅛″. Turn case to right side.

Cut 1″×3¼″ strip of print fabric. Fold strip to about ¼″; stitch along two edges. Folding ends under, pin strip across front of case about 1″ below top edge, as shown.

Make a sharp crease at baste-marked corners; stitch along crease ⅛″ from edge. Do this along all four corners (treating seamed corners in the same manner) and around bottom.

Wallet

Cut 5″×9″ pieces as follows: one each from print fabric, plain fabric, and interfacing; two of cotton batting. Place together, edges even, as follows: one layer batting; interfacing; batting; print fabric, right side up; plain fabric. Stitch together along 9″ edge ½″ from edge. Trim away seam allowance on batting and interfacing as close as possible to stitching line. Press seam open. Turn plain fabric to other side, as shown, covering batting, etc. Press seam. Make a line of topstitching ⅛″ from seamline.

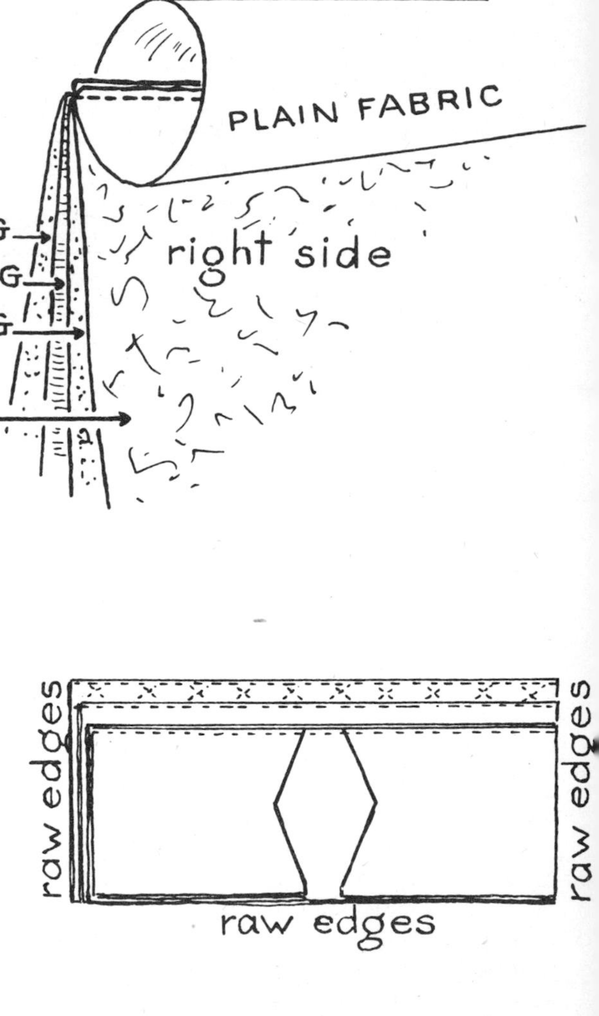

NOTCH
actual size
fold

Baste all layers together, and quilt as desired. Cut this quilted piece down to 4″×7½″. The diagonal band on the pictured wallet was made by cutting a 1″×7″ strip of print fabric, turning long edges ¼″ under and top-stitching to quilted piece. Trim ends even with wallet edges.

From plain fabric, cut one 6½″×7½″ piece; one 5½″×7½″ piece; two 5½″×3½″ pieces.

Fold each of the last two pieces crosswise (to measure 2¾″×3½″). Press. Trace notch, shown here in actual size, on tissue paper. Transfer markings to one end of a folded piece; stitch along marked line. Trim seam allowance to ⅛″; clip into corner of notch. Turn to right side, and press.

Fold the 5½″×7½″ piece in half lengthwise. Press. Place the two notched sections on it, matching folded edges, as shown. Make a line of top-stitching along folded edges. Fold remaining piece in half lengthwise. Top-stitch along fold.

Place these two prepared sections on plain side of quilted section, matching all raw edges. Stitched edges are graded, as shown. Baste and stitch around the three raw edges.

Press open one fold of bias tape. Starting at one top corner of wallet, on right side and letting end of tape extend, as shown, stitch tape around three sides of wallet, easing at corners. Turn ends in; turn tape to inside of wallet, and sew down by hand.

Zippered Coin Purse

Patterns. For purse, copy pattern on graph, enlarging each square to 1″. Cut out.

For quilted patch, measure and mark pattern as given at upper right. Cut out.

Quilting. Cut one 10″×10″ square each of print fabric, heavy batting, and interfacing. Baste together in that order, print right side up. Quilt as desired.

Cutting. From purse pattern, cut one section from quilted piece, one from plain fabric (lining); place pattern on folded fabric, as indicated.

From second pattern, cut one piece of plain fabric, on fold, as indicated.

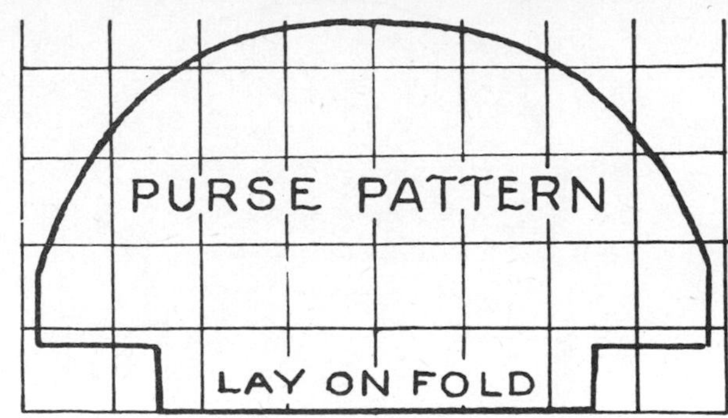

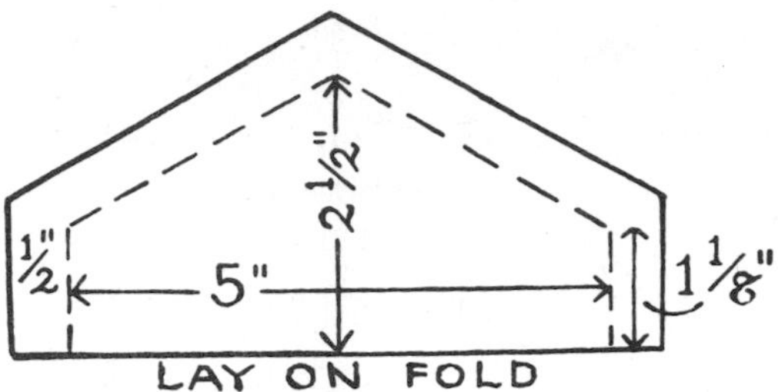

From plain fabric, cut two 1″×11″ bias strips (piece if necessary); one 2¾″×6″ piece; one 2¾″×3½″ piece.

To Make (½″ seams allowed). Turn under seam allowance on the two points of plain section cut from pattern. Press. Baste over quilted section as shown. Edge-stitch in place, and quilt as shown, using width of presser foot as a guide.

POCKETS: On both 2¾″-wide pieces, crease one long edge ¼″ to one side, and fold same edge ½″ to other side, as shown. Stitch side edges. Turn this hem to wrong side. Stitch hem on smaller piece. On longer

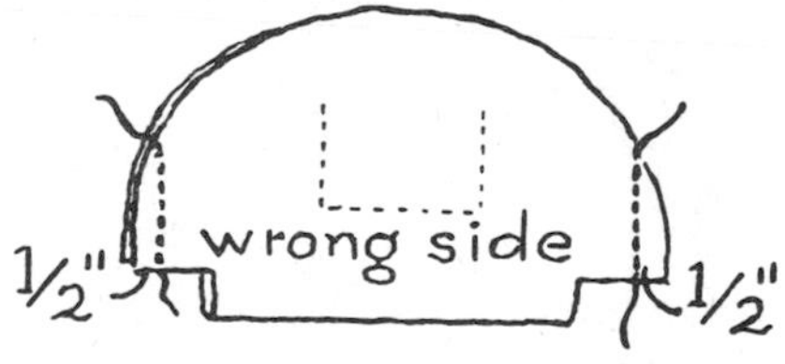

piece, attach each end of a 3¼″ piece of elastic inside each side seam of pocket hem. Stretch elastic as you stitch hem. Turn under seam allowance around other sides of pockets, trimming corners. On shirred pocket, gather bottom edge to match top. Center each pocket on pocket-lining section, top

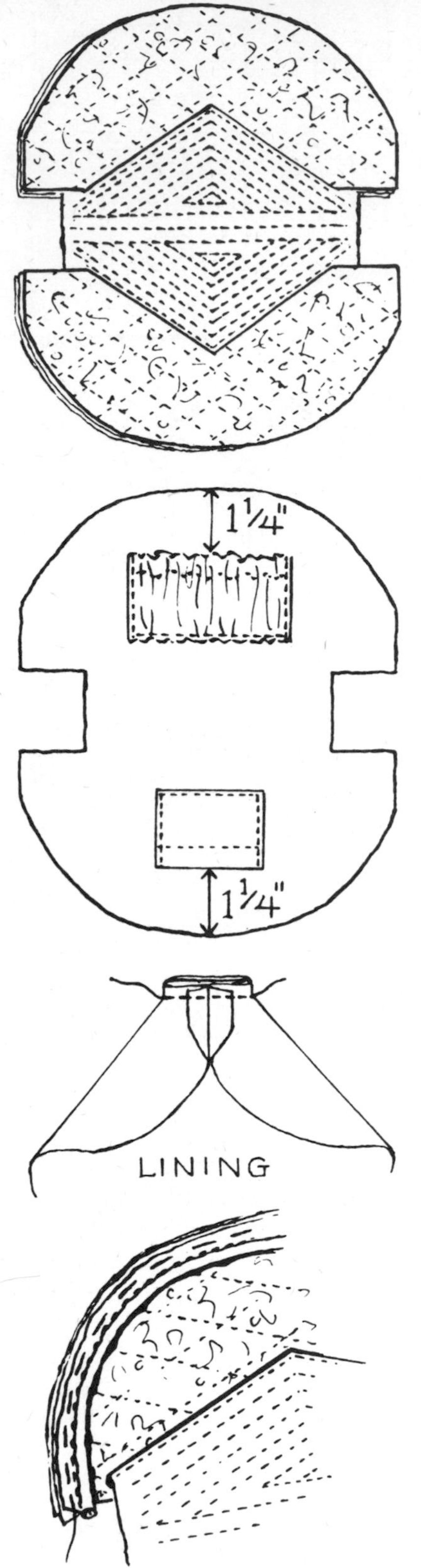

edge 1¼″ from each curved edge, as shown. Stitch around three sides.

Fold lining section across bottom, pockets together, and stitch up sides as shown.

Prepare two lengths of welting by placing cord inside bias strips and stitching close to cord.

Baste and stitch welting along curved edge of quilted piece, all raw edges even. Turn welting up; baste down all seam allowances against wrong side of quilted piece.

Fold piece across bottom, wrong side out. Stitch up sides the same way as for lining (left).

Open zipper. Place inside quilted section, pinning tapes to welting seam allowance, zipper teeth against welting. Sew securely by hand.

Turn both quilted section and lining wrong side out. Fold one open end of lining section as shown, seam in center. Fold one end of quilted section in same way. Place the two sections together, back to back and raw edges even. Seam across through all thicknesses. Do the same at other open end.

Turn so that lining is inside purse. On curved edge of lining, turn seam allowance under, and slip-stitch edge over zipper tapes.

Cut ½″×3″ strip of print fabric. Turn in raw edges, and top-stitch together. Stitch across ends. Fold in half crosswise, and attach fold securely to zipper tab as a pull.

Peasant Apron

Materials. ½ yard 36″-wide, solid-color Cotton Fabric. ¾ yard 36″-wide Cotton Print. 1 package double-fold Bias Tape in contrasting color. Mercerized Sewing Thread to match.

Cutting. Following cutting diagrams, cut print and plain fabric.

To Make. Bind print fabric with bias tape around inside edge (see diagram page 82).

Right sides together, join print fabric to plain fabric at sides and along lower edge.

Sew the bound edges at sides only to the plain fabric, and continue the stitching straight down to lower edge of apron. Also stitch down center to form two pockets.

Make ¼″ hem on long edges of ties and 1″ hem at one end of each tie. Fold band in half lengthwise. Pleat tie end; fit into end of waistband; stitch. Trim seam; turn, and press. Gather apron, and attach waistband.

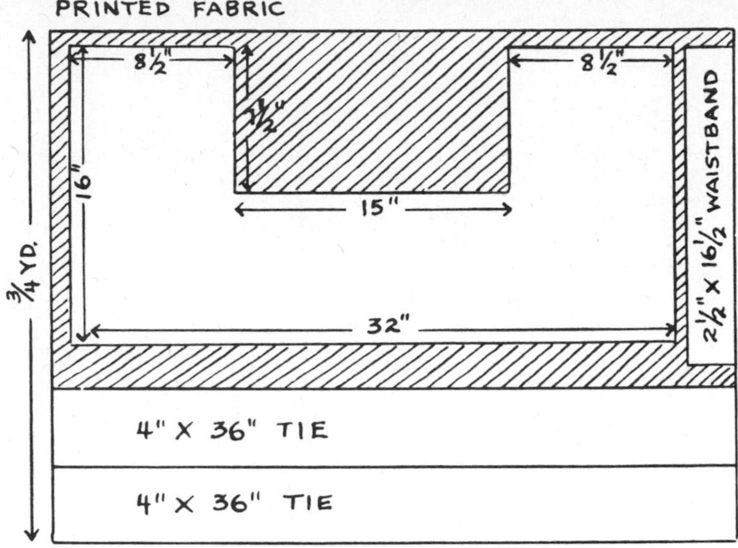
PRINTED FABRIC
8½"
8½"
2½"
16"
15"
3/4 YD.
32"
2½" X 16½" WAISTBAND
4" X 36" TIE
4" X 36" TIE

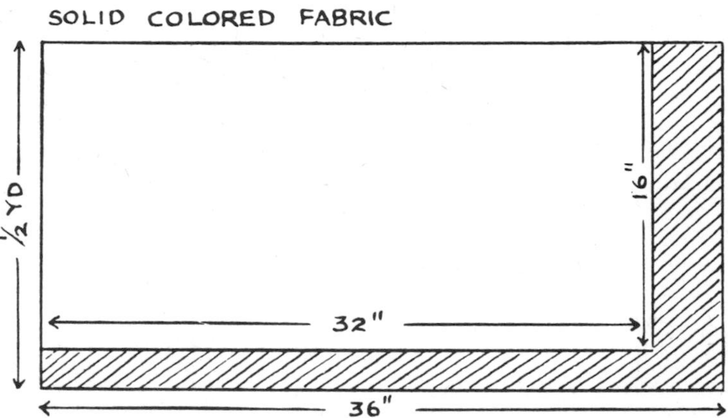
SOLID COLORED FABRIC
½ YD
16"
32"
36"

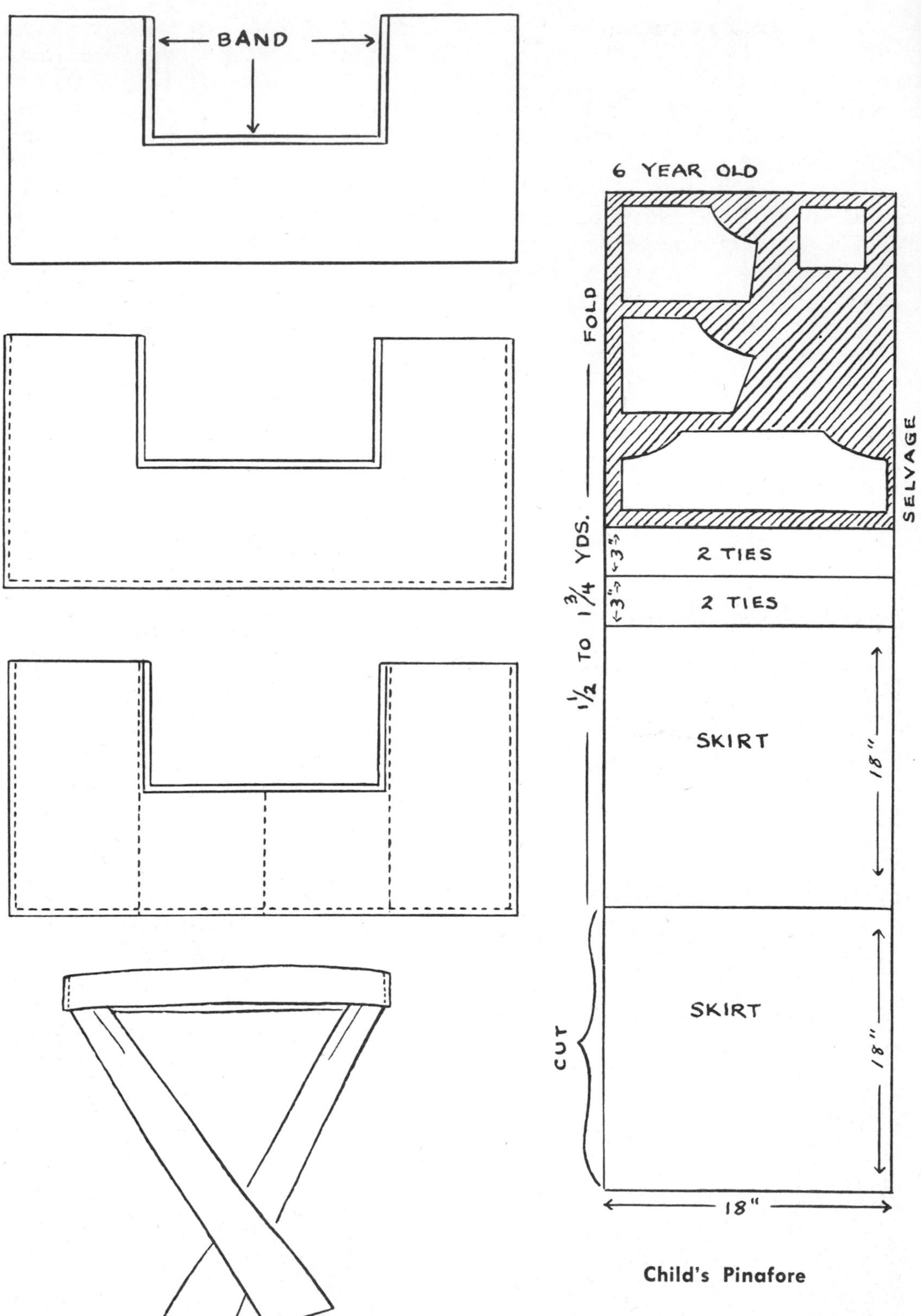

Peasant Apron

Child's Pinafore

Child's Pinafore

Materials. 1½ yards White Cotton Sateen, for size 2 and 4; 1¾ yards White Cotton Sateen, for size 6. Small pieces Red, Green, and Gold Cotton for appliqué. White Mercerized Sewing Thread. Six-Strand Embroidery Floss to match appliqué pieces. 1 yard White Twill Tape (½″ seams are allowed).

Pattern. Trace desired size of bodice pattern, pages 84 and 85.

Cutting. Cut pinafore, following cutting diagram, shown opposite.

To Make. 1. Right sides together, seam bodice front and back at underarm. Seam facing in same way. Press seams open. **2.** Right sides together, join facing to front bodice, stitching at sides and along top. Trim seams, and turn right side out. **3.** Join skirt sections. Pink seams, and press open. Make narrow hems at two ends, and gather across top. **4.** Right sides together, join skirt to bodice, adjusting gathers. Turn under seam allowance on facing, and slip-stitch to skirt. **5.** Make ¼″ hems on long edges of shoulder ties. Pleat; cut ends; turn under, and hand-stitch to bodice as shown. **6.** Attach twill tape in same manner to back of bodice. **7.** Hem pinafore (3″ hem allowed: adjust to child). **8.** Pockets, page 86. Make ¼″ hem at top of pockets. Trace design, and trace onto pockets, using dressmaker's carbon paper. Trace cherries, leaves, and flowerpot on various colors, as indicated. Cut out on line. Apply to pockets with blanket-stitch, using three strands of matching embroidery floss. Work stems in green outline stitch. **9.** Sew pockets in place, back-stitching at top to hold securely.

BODICE FRONT

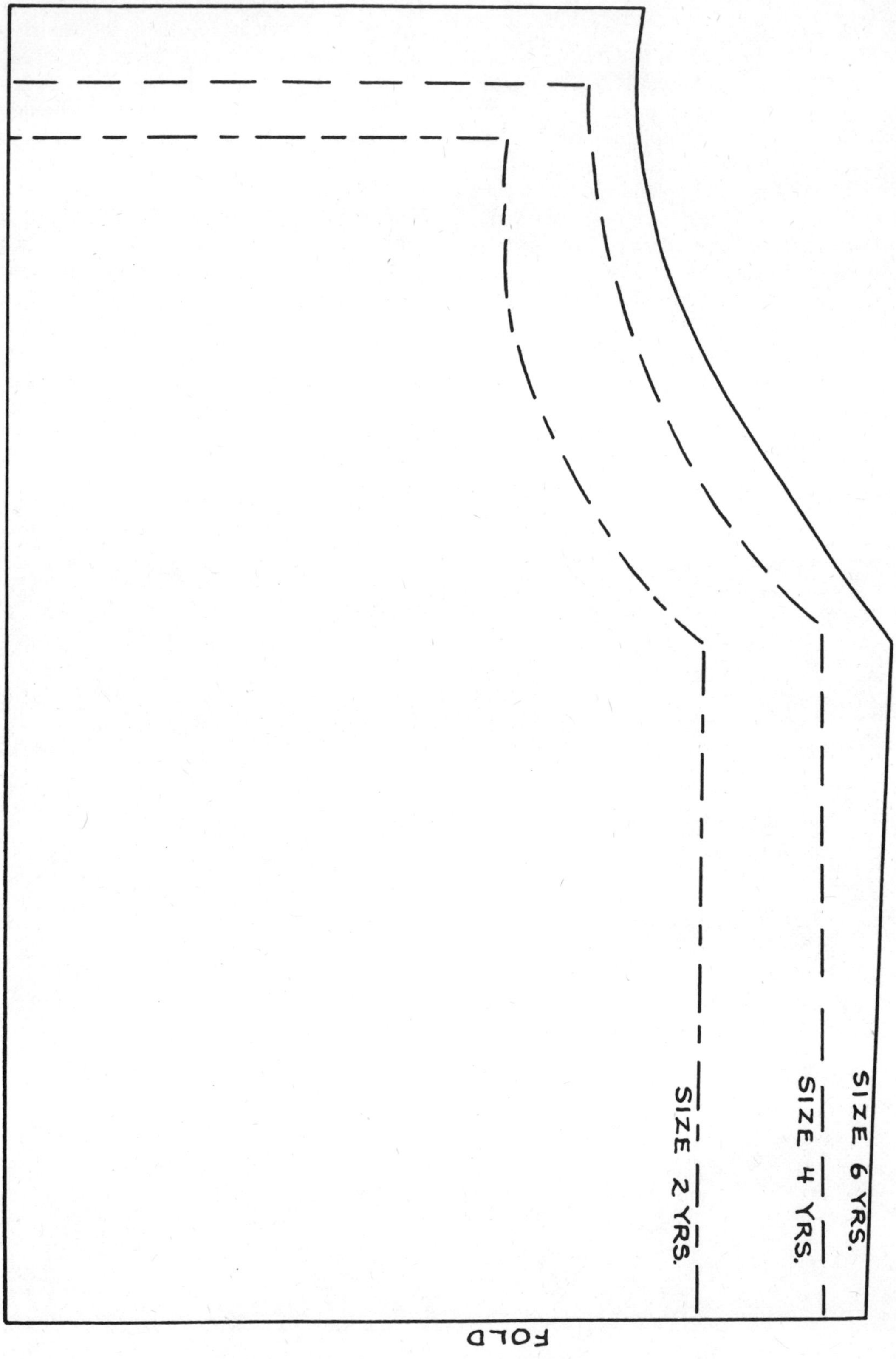

SIZE 6 YRS.

SIZE 4 YRS.

SIZE 2 YRS.

FOLD

ODICE BACK

SIZE 6 YRS.

SIZE 4 YRS.

SIZE 2 YRS.

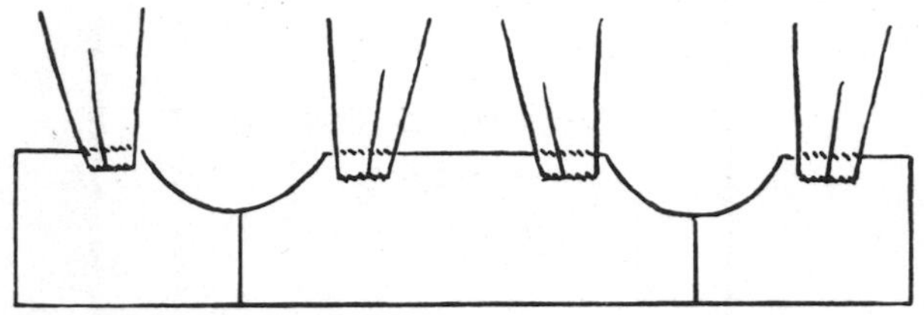

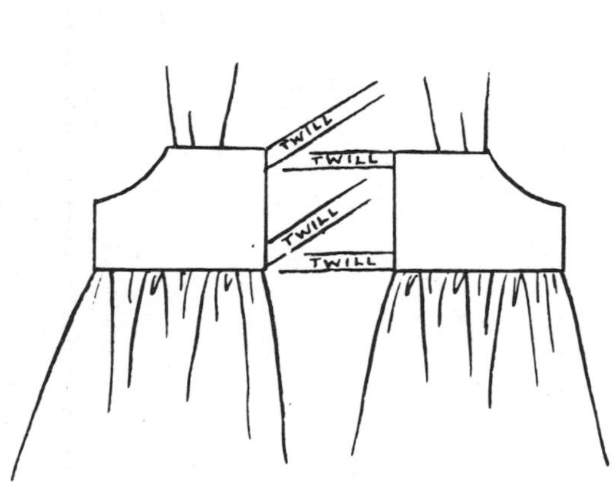
TWILL
TWILL
TWILL
TWILL

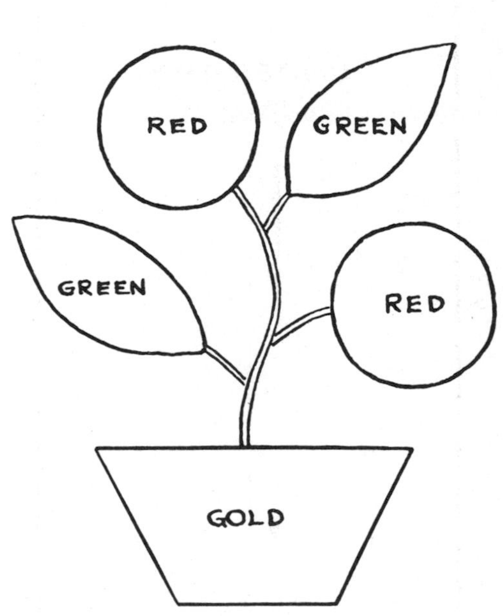
RED
GREEN
GREEN
RED
GOLD

Shepherdess Nightie

Materials. 4 yards 36″-wide Pale Pink Batiste. ⅜ yards Deep Pink Batiste. 1 yard milliner's Elastic. 1½ yards narrow Twill Tape.

Pattern. Make a pattern following diagram.

Cutting. Cut one back and one front, laying pattern on fold as indicated. Cut 2 underarm pieces. Cut 2 sleeves crosswise of fabric, laying pattern on fold as indicated. Cut 2 bands of deep pink fabric 6½″×36″, crosswise of fabric.

To Make. 1. Sew underarm pieces to back and front at sides. **2.** Sew sleeves at underarm (short seam). Sew in sleeves. **3.** Make a narrow (about ¼″) machine hem at lower edge of sleeves, leaving opening for inserting elastic. **4.** Make a 1″ hem at neck edge. Stitch again ⅜″ from edge. Open at one seam and insert tape. Insert elastic in sleeves. Try on, adjust neckline and sleeves, and sew up openings. **5.** Make narrow carriers 3¼″ long for sash by folding a ¾″-wide piece of fabric and stitching down the center. **6.** Join sash pieces end to end. Fold in half length-

3 3/4″
1 3/8″
6 3/4″
5″
1 1/2″
UNDERARM
cut 2
42″
17 1/2″

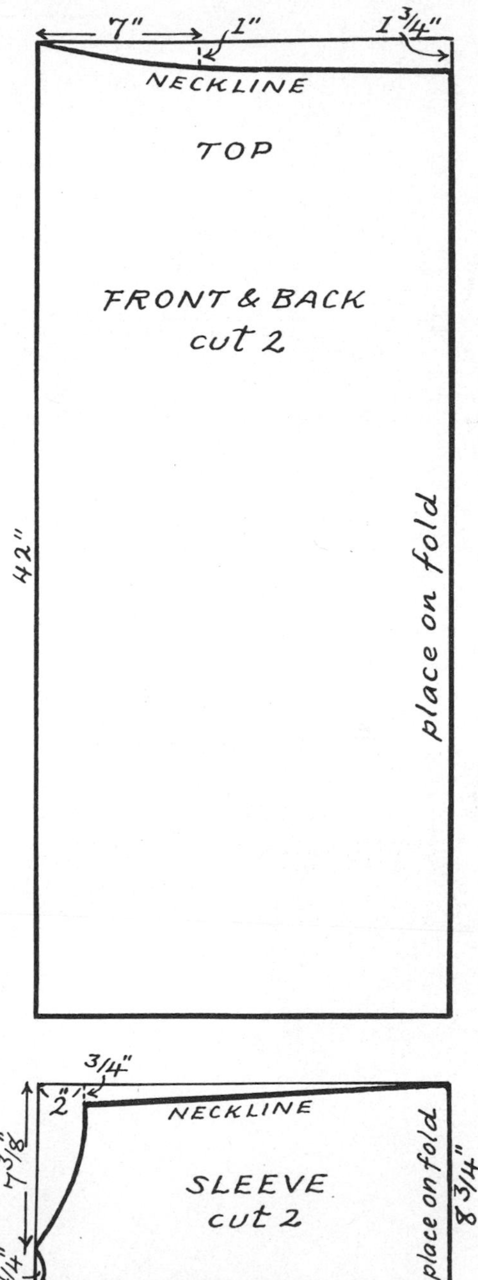

wise and stitch along the long side, but not across ends. Leave selvage ends open. Trim, turn and press. **7.** Try on nightie; mark length and hem by hand.

Baby Doll Dress

Materials. 2⅔ yards 36″-wide Navy and White Striped Cotton Fabric. 2⅔ yards 36″-wide Red and White Striped Cotton Fabric. 6 yards ½″-wide cotton woven Braid Trimming. 1¼ yards Cotton Tape for drawstring. ¼″-wide Elastic for sleeves.

Cutting. Make pattern from diagram. Follow cutting diagram and cut one left front, one left back and one sleeve of blue. Cut one right front, one right back and one sleeve in red. ½″-seams are allowed.

To Make. Right sides together, sew center

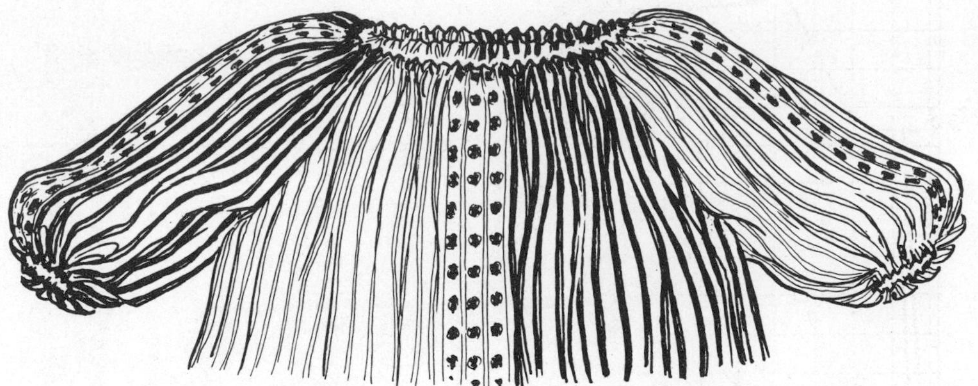

front, and center back seams. Pin and stitch three rows of braid down center front ¼″ apart. Now sew side seams. Pin and stitch 2 rows of braid down center top of sleeve ¼″ apart. Sew sleeve seams.

Pin and stitch red sleeve to blue side of dress, pin and stitch blue sleeve to red side of dress. Turn and stitch a ⅝″-hem at neckline, leaving 1″ open at center front for inserting drawstring. Turn and stitch ½″ hems at lower edge of sleeves. Insert ¼″-wide elastic for tightness desired and fasten. Insert drawstring at neck. (See diagram.) Try on dress, draw up neckline and adjust fullness. Mark and put up hem at desired length.

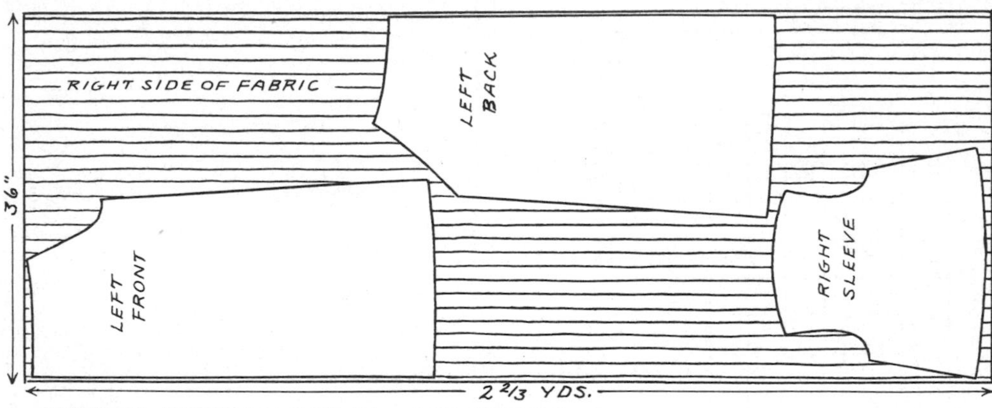

CUTTING DIAGRAM FOR BL. + WH. STRIPE

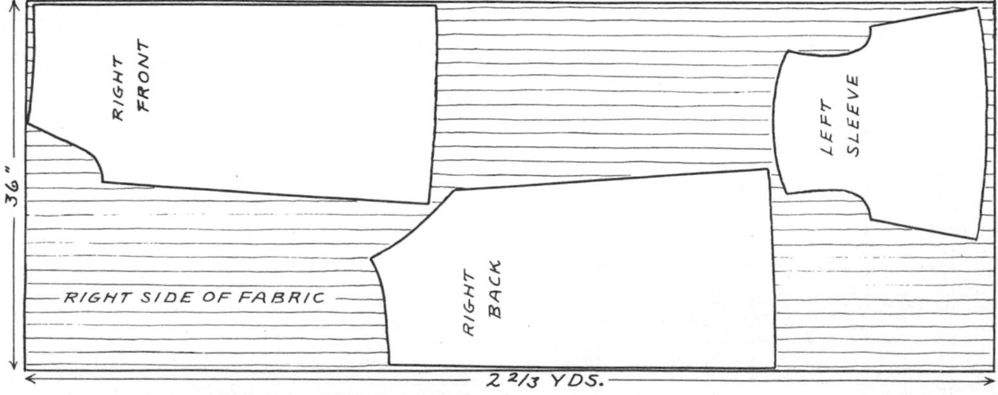

CUTTING DIAGRAM FOR RED + WH. STRIPE

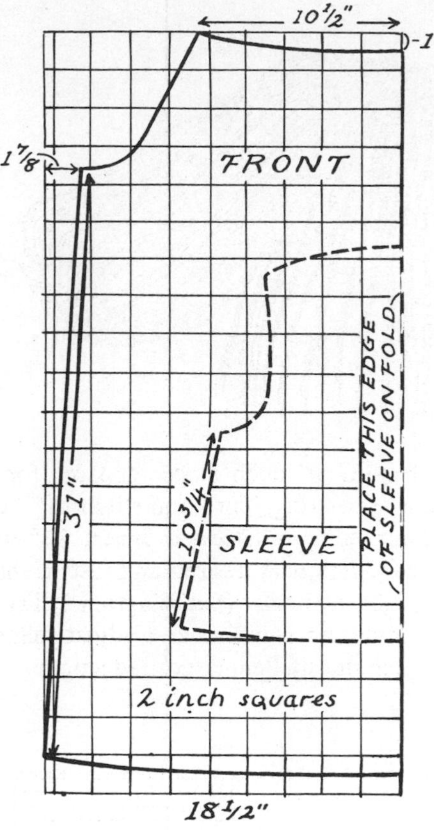

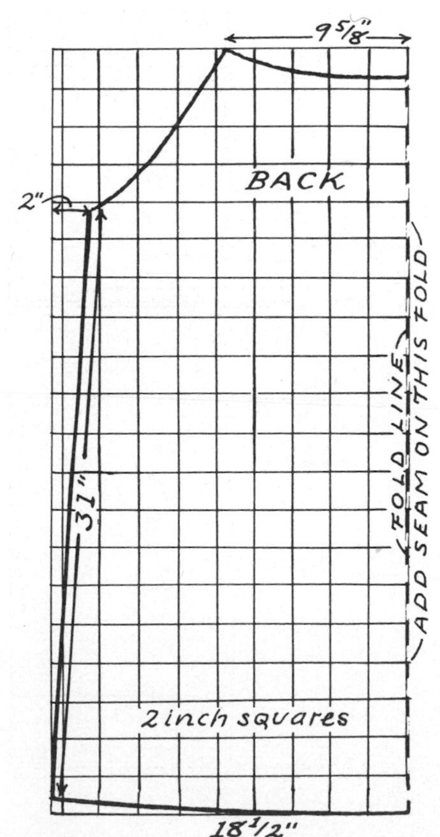

Polka Dot Appliqué Shift

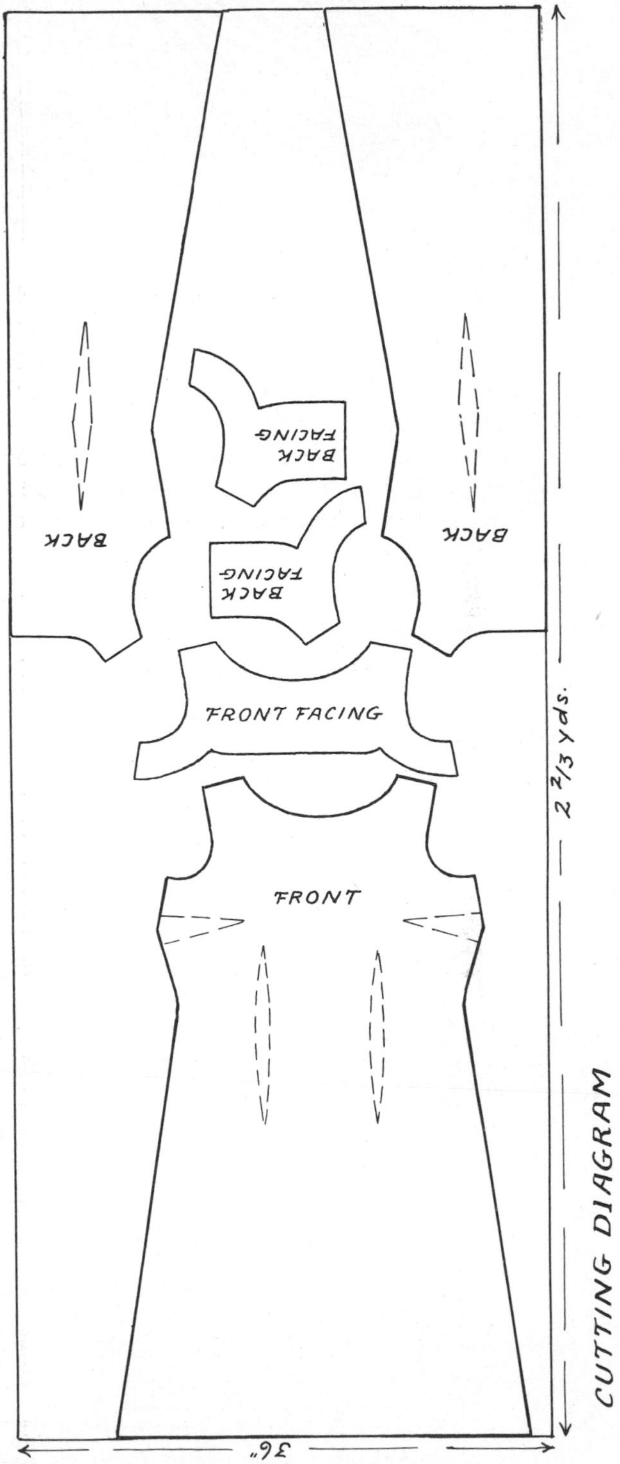

BACK
BACK FACING
BACK FACING
BACK
FRONT FACING
FRONT
2 ⅔ yds.
36"

CUTTING DIAGRAM

PANEL DESIGN

Materials. 2⅔ yards 36″-wide Cotton, large polka dot; ⅝ yard 36″-wide Cotton, small polka dot, for appliqué. 3¼ yards Black Bias Fold Tape. Interfacing for neckline. Black and White Thread. Long Zipper for back.

Cutting. Use a simple shift pattern and cut dress. Make pattern for floral panel design by enlarging diagram, and cut from the appliqué material.

To Make. First pin and sew all darts on the front and back of the dress. Hold dress front to figure and determine about what length it will be when hemmed, and mark edge of hem with pins. Fold and mark center front of dress. *Note:* Use the diagram of the panel design as a guide or enlarge it to actual size (each square equals 2″) and trace it lightly onto front of dress. Centering the design and with lower flowers about ½″ to 1″ from edge of hem, arrange the stems and motifs in tree-like pattern as shown on diagram. The design should be about 28″ to 29″ high.

Stem. Pin the bias tape directly on center line. Add side stems, cutting lower stems 4½″ long, upper stems 5″ long. Slip the side stems under the center stem. Narrow stems at top are done with zigzag satin stitch. Handling carefully so edges will not fray, pin the flowers and leaves in place lapping them over the ends of the stems. Now baste around

all parts of the entire design in order that the appliqué be held firmly in place while sewing the edges by machine with zigzag stitch.

(*Note:* If desired, the appliqué can be done by hand. Sew the bias tape on by hand hemming the edges. Sew the motifs on with blanket stitch using three strands of six strand embroidery floss in matching color.) Work narrow machine zigzag stitch around flowers and stems just inside the edge. Trim any frayed edges being careful not to cut the fabric. Pin side, back and shoulder seams and try on dress. Adjust if necessary. Stitch seams and press open. Stitch interfacing together, then pin and baste interfacing to underside of neckline. Make and apply neck and armhole facing. Stitch the facing near seam line through seam allowance. This is called understitching. Press.

Apply back zipper. Try on dress, adjust, turn up, and finish hem.

Calico Flower Garden Skirt

Materials. 1⅔ yards 45″-wide Black or Black-and-White Print (we used fine stripe) Cotton. Pieces of Calico-Type (small print) Cotton for flowers—10 pieces 7½″ by 7½″ for flowers—two of each color and print can be used. (We used 2 red, 2 blue, 2 yellow, 2 green, 2 navy. 10 3-inch pieces for centers are of plain colored fabric. Use various colors such as red on blue and green, green on red, blue on yellow, orange on navy.) ⅛ yard of Green Print for leaves. (We used green checked gingham.) 3 yards Red Bias Fold Tape for stems.

Cutting. Cut skirt following cutting diagram. Trace flower, center and leaf pattern and cut ten flowers, ten centers and 11 leaves.

To Make. Sew skirt together leaving one seam open. Following diagram, pin and baste on flowers, centers, stems, and leaves. Flowers should overlap stems. Stems should

overlap leaves.

With red thread, make narrow zigzag machine stitch just inside the edge of all flower and leaf appliqué. Do the same on the edge of stems. Sew remaining skirt seam leaving opening for zipper. Apply zipper. Gather top of skirt and apply waistband.

Try on skirt, mark and put in hem.

APPLIQUÉ PATTERNS

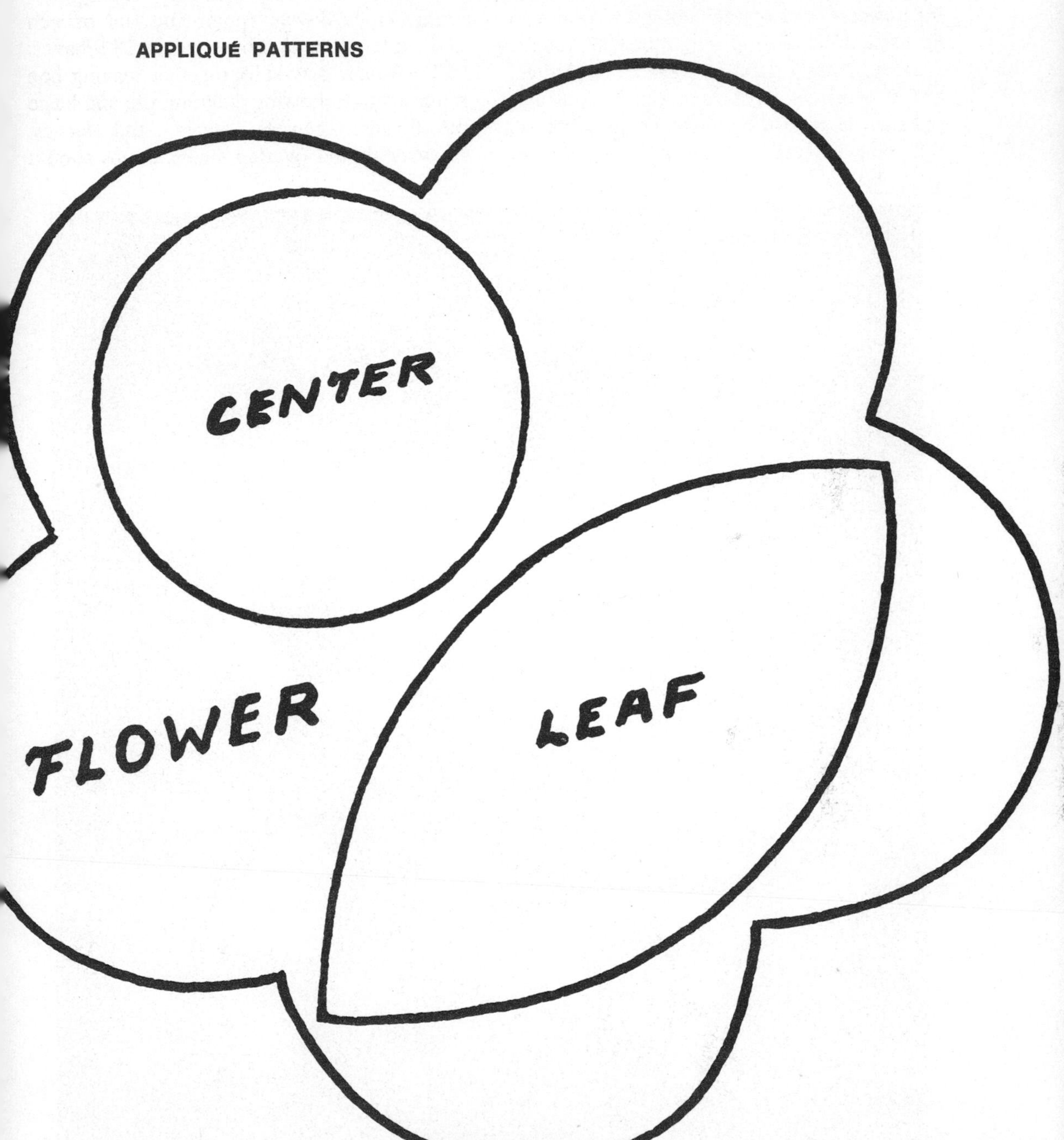

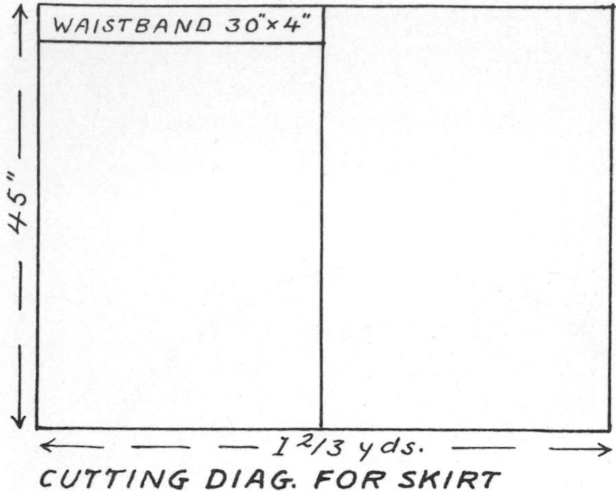

CUTTING DIAG. FOR SKIRT

COLOR KEY– CENTERS

a = GREEN
b = BLUE
c = TURQUOISE
e = YELLOW
f = RED
g = ORANGE

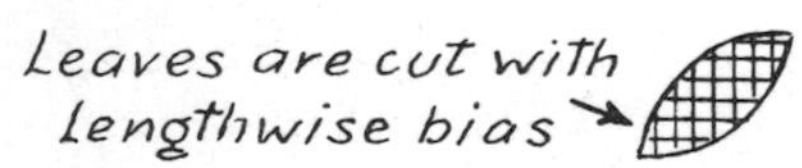

COLOR KEY~FLOWERS

1 = BLUE
2 = RED
3 = WHITE
4 = BLACK
5 = GREEN
6 = YELLOW

DIAGRAM– COLOR KEY + PLACEMENT

Bassinet with Flounce

For those who want to make an elaborate bassinet, this is a practical answer. The flounce, hood ruffle, and lining, all separate, can be removed for quick drip-dry laundering (nylon fabric used throughout). Although it looks intricate, almost anyone could attempt it—if the directions are followed step by step. We made ours in pale yellow and white, but any baby shade may be used.

Materials. Large bassinet on wheels. At rim, our bassinet measures 41″ long and 21″ wide. Mattress to fit bassinet. 38½″×42″ purchased pillowcase in light yellow or yellow-and-white stripe. 1¾ yds pale-yellow quilted nylon, 44″ wide, for lining. 6½ yds matching yellow nylon taffeta, 44″ wide. 6 yds white flock-dot nylon, 48″ wide. 5 yds lace-edged white nylon beading, 1¾″ wide. 11 yds embroidered white nylon edging, 2½″ wide. 7 yds pale-yellow nylon ribbon, ½″ wide. 4 yds pale-yellow nylon ribbon, 4″ wide. 3 yds snap-on tape. 1 ball pale-yellow yarn (Orlon or nylon). 1¼ yds elastic, ½″ wide.

Lining. In making this size bassinet, follow cutting diagram to cut lining and strips. (*Note:* If another size is used, measure both the inside of bassinet at the rim and the depth (from rim); add 4″ for top hem and 4″ at bottom.) Cut strips, 4″ wide, to attach lining to flounce.

With right sides together, sew the two lining pieces together at ends, tapering seam from ½″ at top to 2″ at bottom. Fig. 1. Press seam open.

Turn top edge ¼″ to wrong side, and stitch.

Place lining in bassinet, wrong side out, and fit by pinning a large dart at each side of end seams where bassinet curves. Remove lining and stitch darts. (Fig. 2.) Sew bias strips of nylon taffeta together (see cutting diagram for taffeta), and bind lower edge of lining. Place lining in bassinet.

Sew the two 4″-strips together, and trim to make a strip 64″ long, or length required to reach around top of bassinet (not including hood). Turn edges ¼″ to wrong side, and stitch.

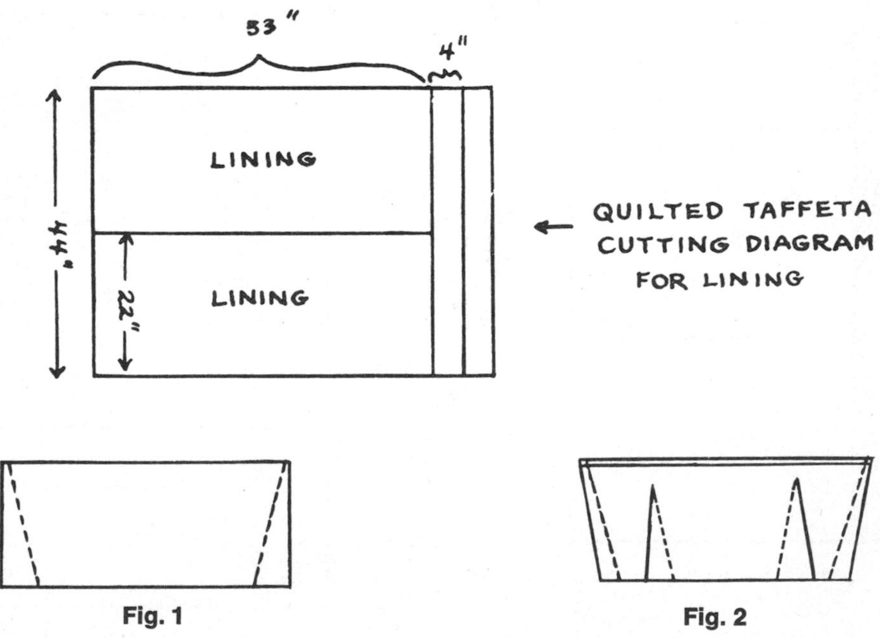

Fig. 1

Fig. 2

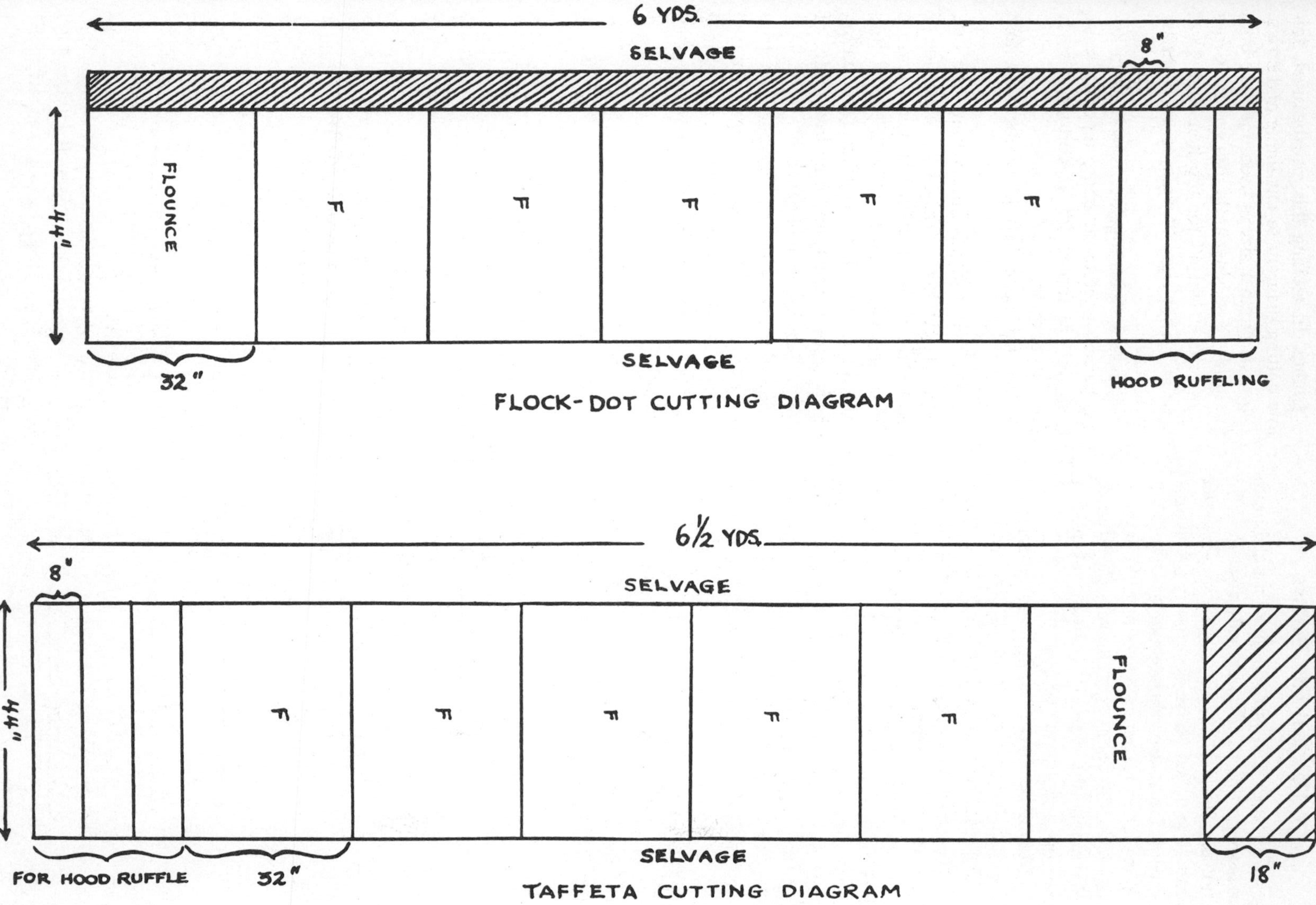
6 YDS.
SELVAGE
8"
FLOUNCE
F
F
F
F
F
44"
SELVAGE
32"
HOOD RUFFLING
FLOCK-DOT CUTTING DIAGRAM
6½ YDS.
8"
SELVAGE
F
F
F
F
F
FLOUNCE
44"
SELVAGE
FOR HOOD RUFFLE
32"
18"
TAFFETA CUTTING DIAGRAM

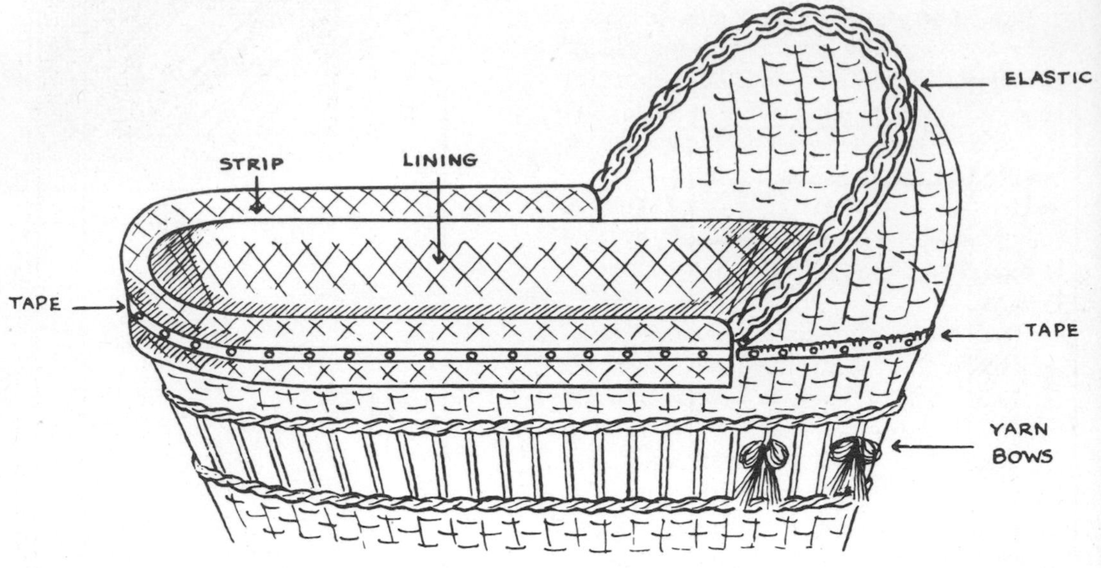

Fig. 3

Separate snap-on tape, and machine-stitch under part of tape along one edge of strip. Cut off remaining tape. Thread a thick needle with doubled heavy thread or crochet cotton. Whipstitch remainder of under part of snap-on tape to wicker around the base of the hood, in line with the rim of the bassinet. Start with first snap at the regular interval, and let end as it will at opposite side. Fig. 3. Turn 4″ at top of lining to wrong side. Slip strip under lining (with tape to outside), and pin around, adjusting so tape is in line with tape on hood of bassinet. Slipstitch strip to lining. Thread needle with doubled yarn. At three or four places at back of bassinet, just below hem of lining, insert needle through wicker from outside of bassinet, take a small stitch in lining, and bring needle out; cut off needle, and tie a bow on outside of bassinet —this holds lining in place. (Fig. 3.)

Flounce. Follow cutting diagrams for taffeta and flock dot. (*Note:* If another size bassinet is used, measure bassinet from just below rim to floor, and add 1″. Cut six pieces of nylon taffeta this same length. Cut six pieces of white flock-dot nylon this length minus 1″.)

Sew nylon-taffeta lengths together on selvage edges (½″ seams) to make a continuous piece. Do the same with the flock-dot pieces. Turn pieces with seams inside. Place yellow flounce inside white flounce. Turn top edges toward each other ½″, pin around, and edge-stitch. Set machine at longest stitch, and stitch ¼″ from top. Stitch again ¼″ below this. Now pull up bobbin threads of long stitching, gathering to fit around bassinet (about 3 yds) as follows: clip bobbin threads at seams, and pull threads evenly at each side of each panel until panel measures about 18″. Leave ends of threads free, or wind over pins.

Match upper strip of snap-on tape to fit the tape on quilted strip and tape around back of bassinet; cut length required. Divide into six portions (about 18″), and mark with pins. Starting at a seam on the flounce, pin this tape to inside of top, ⅛″ below edge. Fit the 18″ sections of flounce to 18″ sections of tape. Pin carefully. Using zipper or cording foot on machine, stitch top edge of tape to flounce.

Snap flounce to bassinet. Turn up lower edge of under layer of flounce (taffeta) 1″ from floor, and pin. Remove, and make 1″ hem around.

Lay embroidered nylon edging at edge of flock-dot flounce so lower edge is same length as underflounce. Pin around. Turn under raw edge of trimming, pin, and stitch. With pinking shears, trim away white flounce underneath edging to within ½″ of stitching.

Lay lace-edged beading over gathering on top of flounce. Pin and sew securely, by hand, at top edge of beading band. Snap flounce to bassinet.

Hood Ruffle. Sew taffeta pieces together, and make a 1″ hem along one edge. Sew flock-dot ruffling same as taffeta. Sew embroidered edging on one edge (as was done for flounce) so that white ruffling is same width as yellow. With seams down, lay white ruffle on top of yellow ruffle, and pin together. Turn in top edges toward each other ½″, pin, and edge-stitch. Stitch and gather as for flounce. Draw up threads to fit over hood, meeting top of flounce at sides. Sew on beading as on flounce.

With hammer and small tacks, fasten end of elastic on one side of hood (under rim). Stretch it over hood just under rim so it will fit snugly, and tack to other side. Fig. 3. Cut off excess elastic. Fasten small safety pins at intervals to under side of gathered edge of ruffle. Then open each pin, and enclose elastic so pin will slide along elastic. Run narrow ribbon through beading over hood, and fasten at each end. Run ribbon through beading at top of flounce, beginning at one side near hood, and leaving long ends. Tie in bow with long loops. With wide ribbon, make a large bow with four loops and streamers, and tack by hand at foot of flounce (see photograph, page 97).

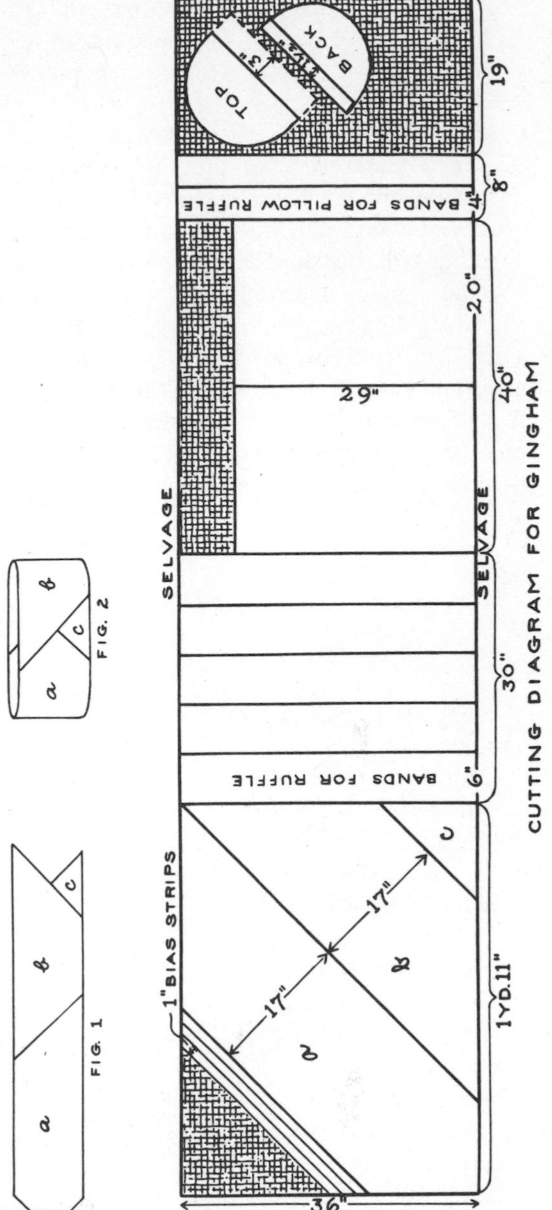

Clothesbasket Bassinet

Here's an inexpensive and quickly made bassinet for the new baby.

Materials. Large wicker clothesbasket, measuring 22″ across and 28″ in length at top. 1 firm bed pillow and plastic zip-on cover. 4 yds blue-and-white (or other baby color) checked gingham, 36″ wide with ⅛″ checks. 3 yds jumbo white rickrack. ½ yd muslin, 36″ wide. 6 oz. Dacron filling. 8 small snap fasteners. One 20″ zipper, white or to match gingham.

Cutting. Following sketch, cut paper pattern for pillow. Fold muslin in half with selvage edges together. Lay pattern with lower edge on fold, and cut.

Following cutting diagram, cut gingham.

Note: When cutting gingham pillow, add 3″ to lower edge of pattern for top. Fold lower edge of pattern up 1½″ for cutting pillow back.

Lining. Using a, b and c bias strips (Fig. 1), turn under edge of one strip about 3 squares of the gingham; lap to end of second strip, matching checks. Pin, and slipstitch together (piecing should not show). Pin ends together, points matching, lap, and slipstitch as before to make a continuous bias piece. (Fig. 2). Make narrow hem along one raw edge (this is bottom edge). Sew together the five 6″-wide ruffle strips to make a continuous band. Make narrow machine-stitched hem along one edge of band. Set machine for longest stitch, and stitch around ruffle ½″ from other edge. Pull up gathers with bobbin thread to fit top edge of lining. Distribute gathers evenly. With right side of ruffle facing right side of lining—and with edges even—pin, and stitch. Press seam toward bias. (Fig. 3). Lay rickrack on right side, covering seam; pin, and stitch down center of rickrack. Fit lining to basket, and cut a slot at each end for handles. Bind slots with bias, and sew on snaps to hold slot together inside handle. (Fig. 3.) Press.

Slip Cover for Pillow-Mattress. Using the two 20″×29″ pieces, apply zipper to one end. Then stitch together around remaining edges.

Decorative Pillow

Pillow Form. Stitch together around curved edge of muslin; leave opening for filling. Turn to right side. Stuff with Dacron, and sew opening by hand.

Gingham Cover. Stitch together the two 4″-wide strips to form one long strip (ruffle). Make narrow machine-stitched hem along one edge and ends. With longest stitch on machine, stitch ½″ from other edge, and gather. Make a ½″ hem at lower edge of both top and back of gingham pillow pieces. With right sides together and edges even, pin

GINGHAM PILLOW PATTERN

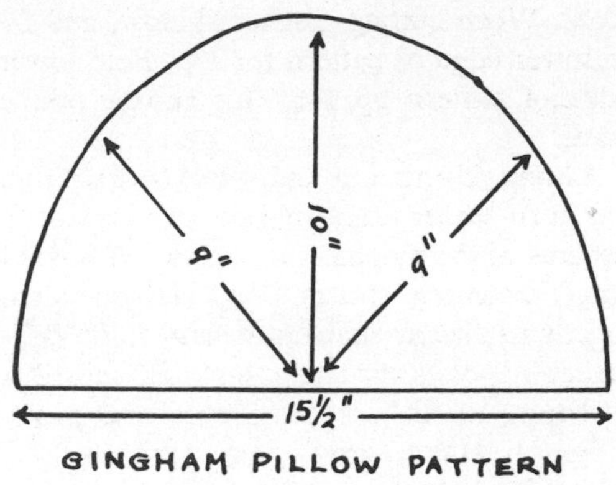

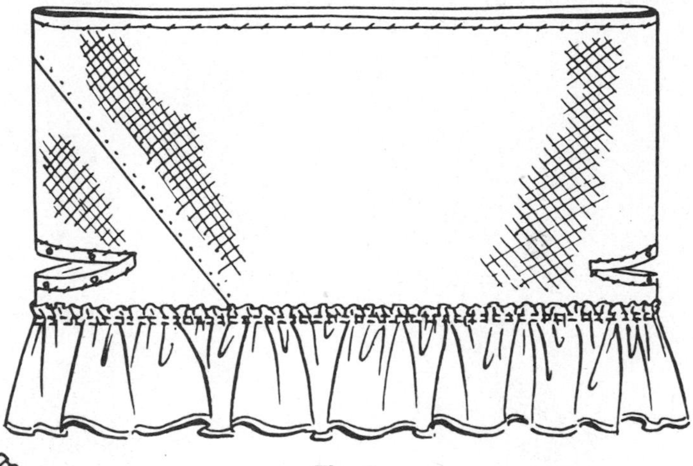

Fig. 3

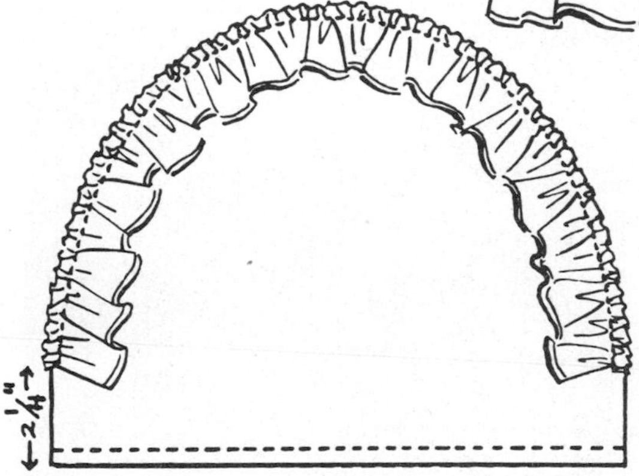

Fig. 4

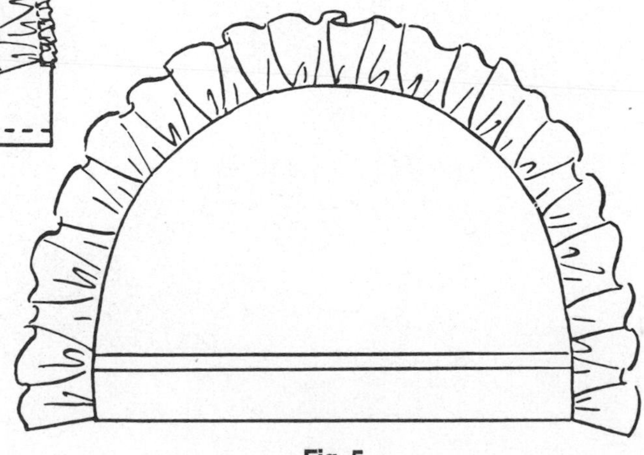

Fig. 5

ruffle to top to within 2¼″ of lower edge on each side. (Fig. 4.)

Lay back of pillow on top of front piece (ruffle between); fold front extension to the back, lapping hems. Pin, and stitch around. Turn, and press. Sew snaps on hems. (Fig. 5.) Sew on rickrack where ruffle meets the front.

Big Daisy Tent Dress

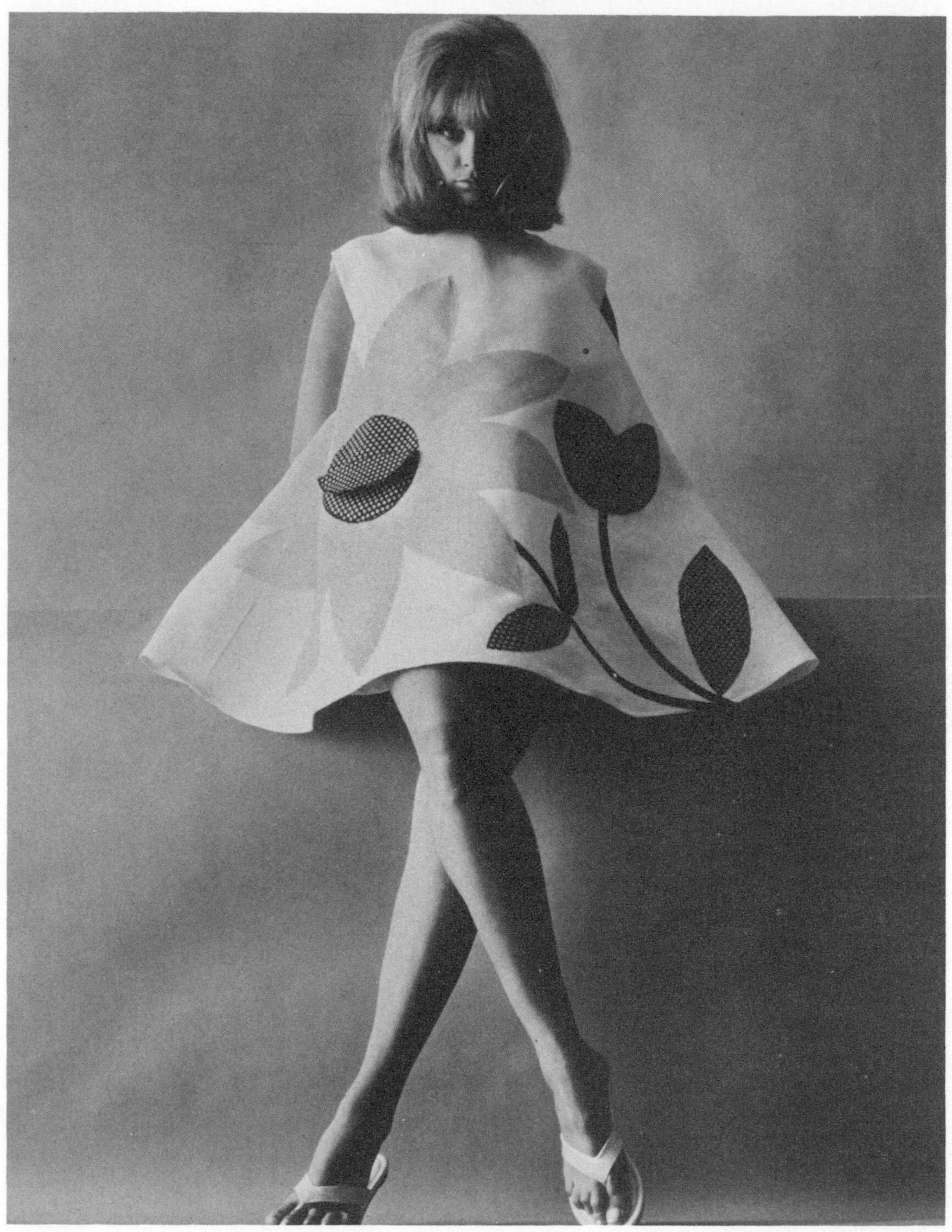

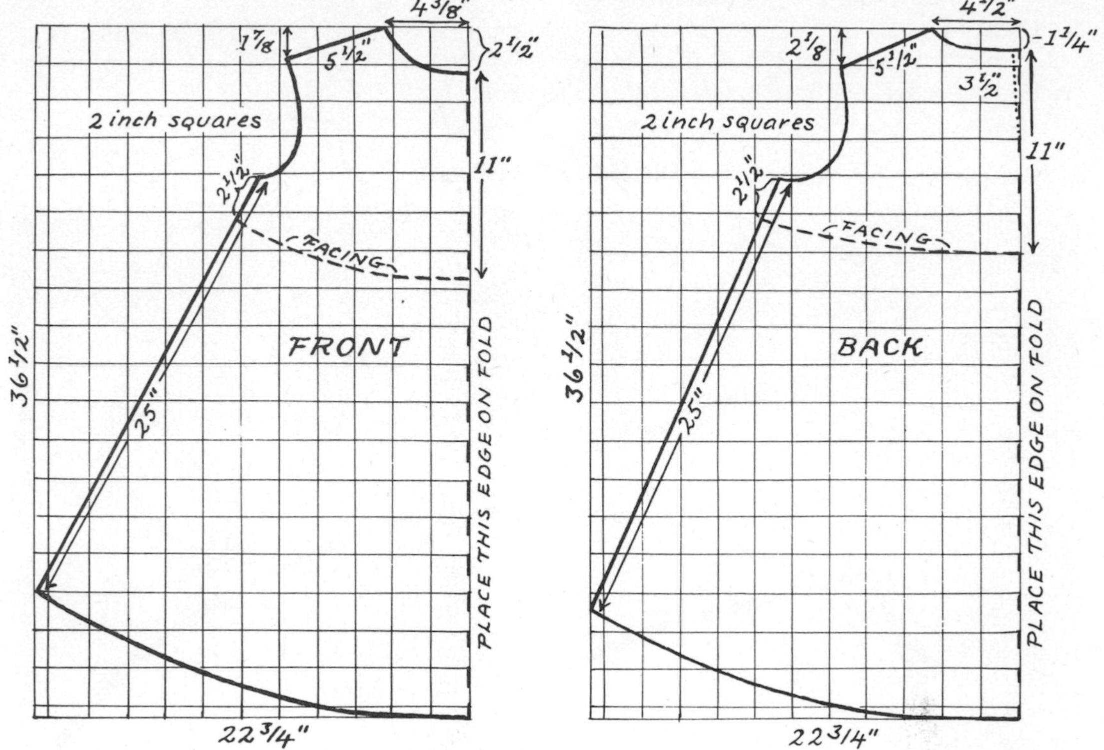

Materials. 2¾ yards 45″-wide ribbed (or other pattern) White Cotton Pique. ½ yard 36″-wide Bright Yellow Cotton Broadcloth. ¼ yard 36″-wide Black and Yellow Calico Print for leaves and centers. 1⅛ yards Black Bias Fold Tape for stems. Yellow, White, and Black Thread.

Cutting. From diagram, make pattern for dress. Following diagram, cut dress and facings. ½″ seams allowed. Trace and make pattern for motifs for daisy design. Cut flower petals (9) of yellow, cut centers (2), bud (2), and leaves (3) of print.

To Make. Sew front and back of dress together at right seam only. Fold and mark center front of dress with pins. Follow diagram for placing daisy design on front of dress. Pin the different parts, including stems of bias tape, to the dress. Reserve one bud and one daisy center. Daisy petals should overlap in the same direction all around. Three petals will overlap side seam a little. Daisy petal and bud should overlap end of stem and stem should overlap slightly the 2 small leaves. Baste the design to the dress fairly close to the edge of each piece. With matching thread, make a narrow machine zigzag stitch just inside the edge around each part of the design. Do the yellow petals first, stems next, and the leaves last. Trim edges.

Pockets. Using slightly wider and closer (satin) zigzag stitch, work around the remaining bud and daisy center. Trim. Pin this bud on top of the one already sewn on and stitch it around the lower curve just inside the satin stitch, using a straight stitch. Do the same with the extra center for the daisy. Sew it on around the lower half. This forms a pocket on the bud and on the daisy.

Sew front and back of dress together at side and shoulder seams.

Make and apply neck interfacing and facing as given in general instructions on page 44 with this exception. There is a 4″-slash at center back of neck. Stitch slash ¼″ wide at top tapering to nothing at bottom at same time facing is sewn to neckline. Cut the slash before turning. Try on dress, measure, mark for length desired. Trim if necessary. Turn a ⅜″-hem to wrong side, stitch twice ⅛″ apart.

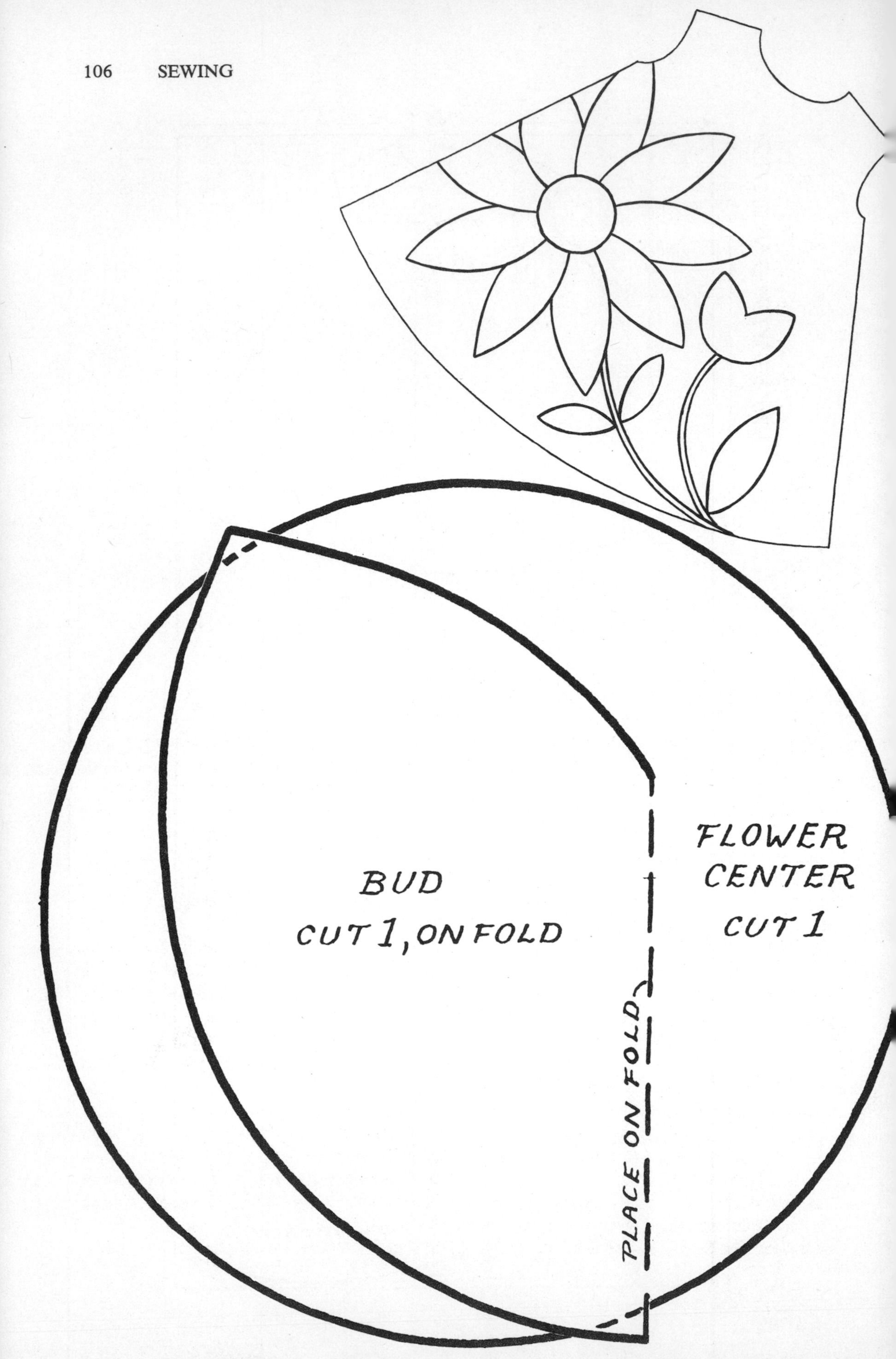
BUD
CUT 1, ON FOLD
PLACE ON FOLD
FLOWER
CENTER
CUT 1

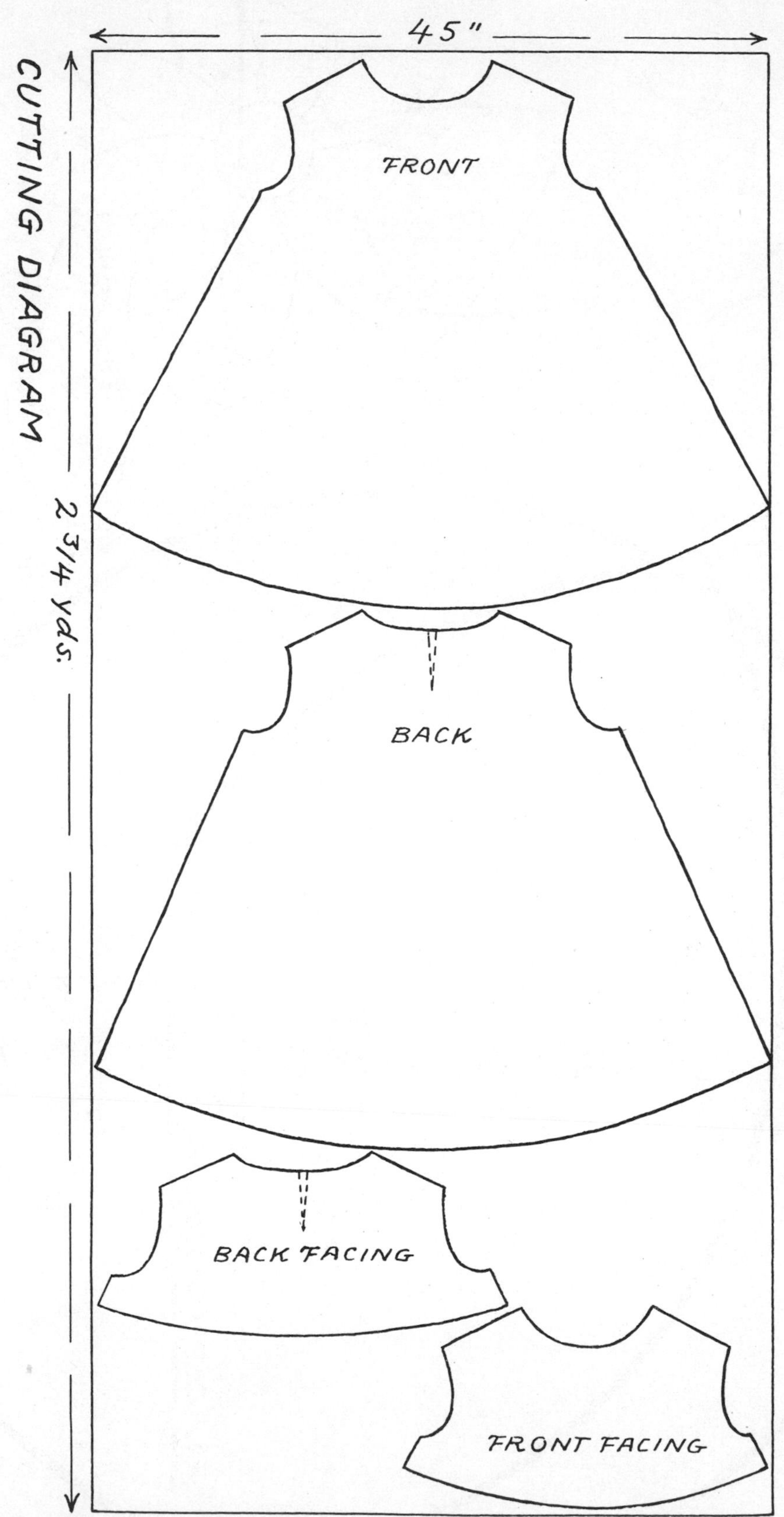
45"
CUTTING DIAGRAM
2 3/4 yds.
FRONT
BACK
BACK FACING
FRONT FACING

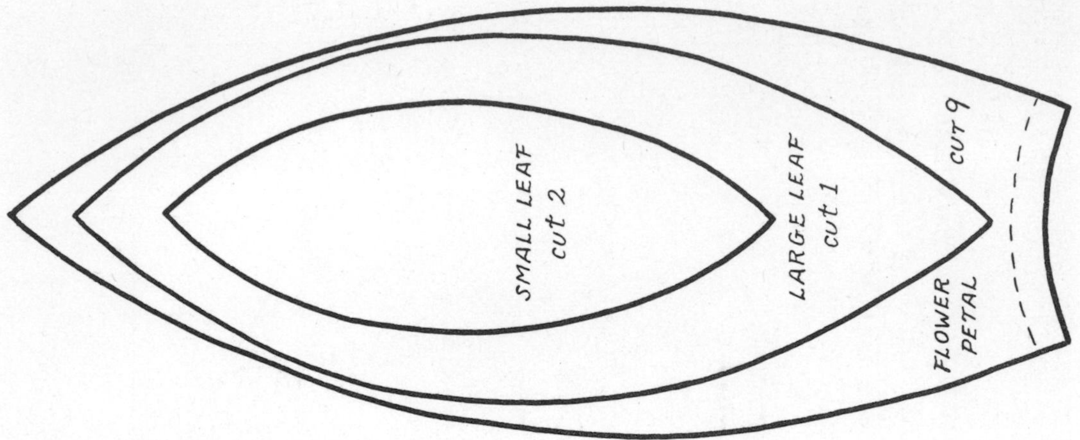

Cabana Coat

The popular cabana coat, long a seaside favorite of men, can be worn as robe or lounging jacket, at home or on business trips. And in summer it can go to the beach.

Materials. 2 yds striped Cotton, 38″ wide; 1⅛ yds Black Cotton, 38″ wide.

To Make. Following Fig. 1, cut robe of striped cotton, centering a stripe through center front and back.

Following Fig. 2, cut belt and neckband of black cotton.

Seam sleeve pieces together as in Fig. 3 (top of sleeve).

Fold robe; mark top of shoulder (Fig. 4). Pin and stitch sleeve to robe, matching seam to shoulder marking (Fig. 5). Press this seam toward sleeve.

Stitch underarm and sleeve seam in one operation. Clip underarm (Fig. 6). At bottom of robe, make 2″ hem.

Seam neckband pieces together; clip ¼″ at neck corners of robe; with right sides together and seam at center back, stitch band to neck and front (Fig. 7). Starting at center back, fold band to wrong side down center; turn under raw edge and slip-stitch over seam. Turn in ends even with hem; slip-stitch.

Make a 2″ hem at top of pocket; turn in ½″ on remaining 3 sides; pin in position (on right or left side and at height desired). Edge-stitch (Fig. 8). Make a 1¼″ hem at edge of sleeves.

Stitch belt pieces together to form one long strip; fold in half lengthwise and stitch leaving one end open; turn and slip-stitch open end. From leftover fabric, cut 2 pieces 3″× 1″; make belt carriers. Stitch at waistline.

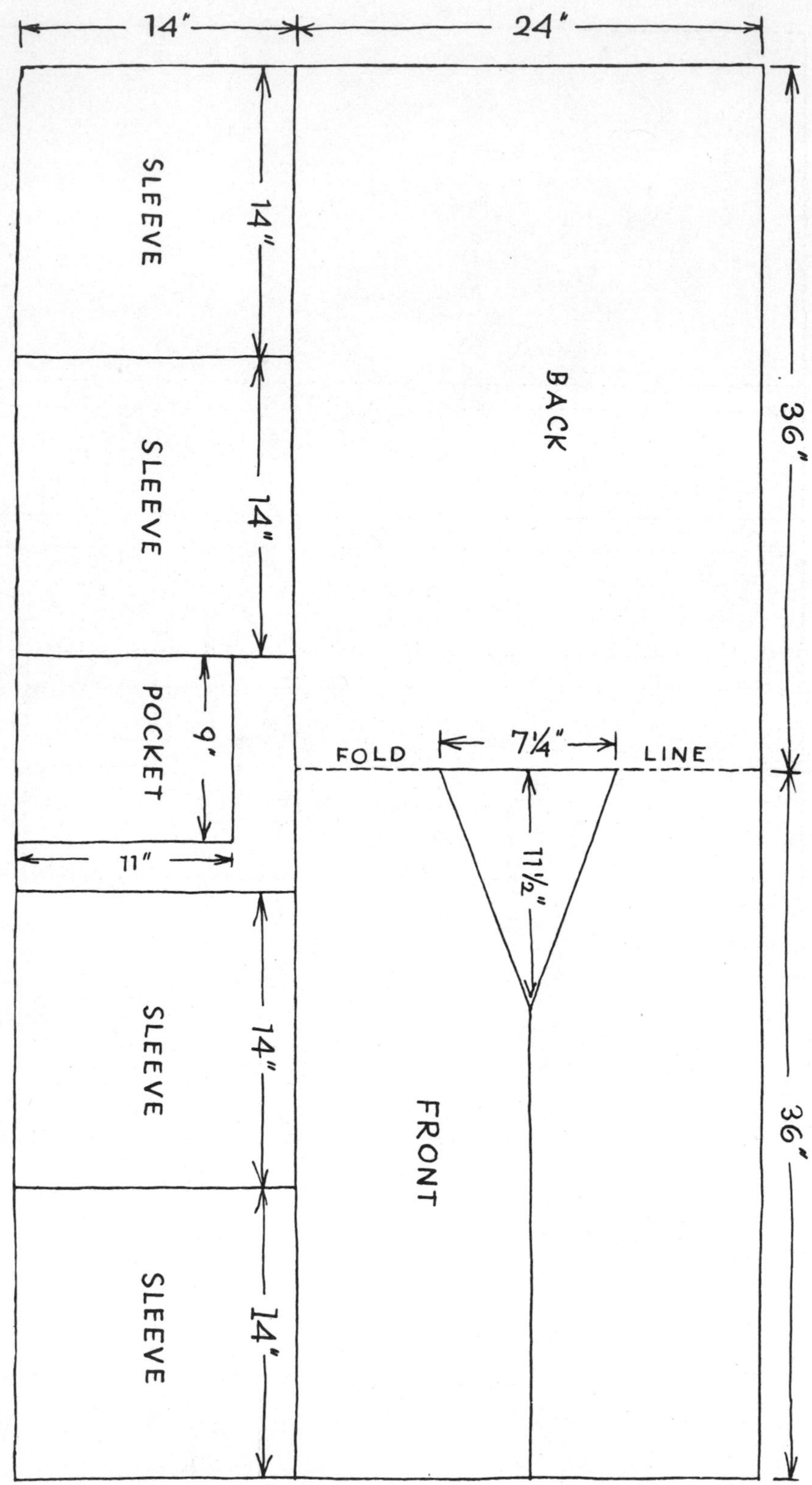

14"
24"
SLEEVE
14"
SLEEVE
14"
POCKET
9"
11"
SLEEVE
14"
SLEEVE
14"
BACK
FOLD
7¼"
LINE
11½"
FRONT
36"
36"

Fig. 1

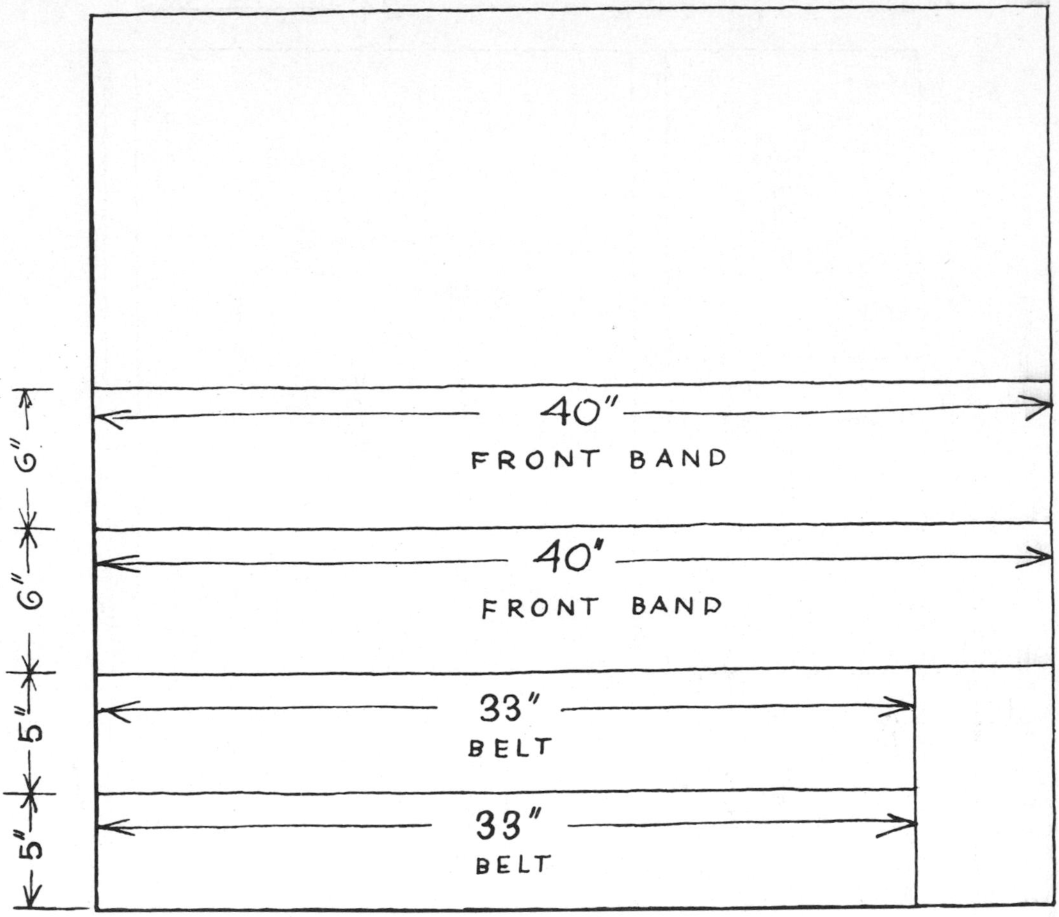

40"
FRONT BAND
40"
FRONT BAND
33"
BELT
33"
BELT
6"
6"
5"
5"

Fig. 2

SLEEVE

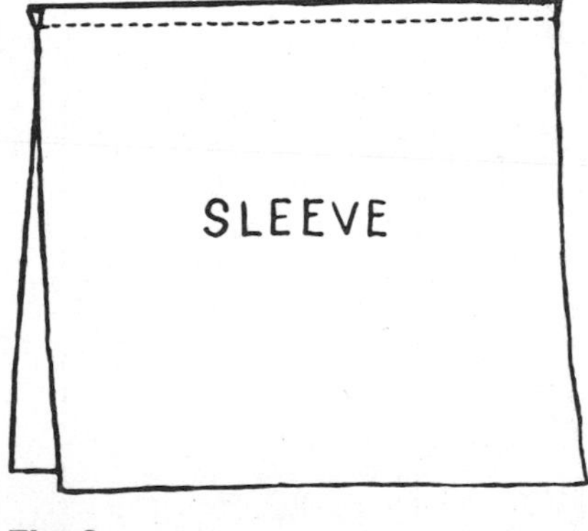

Fig. 3

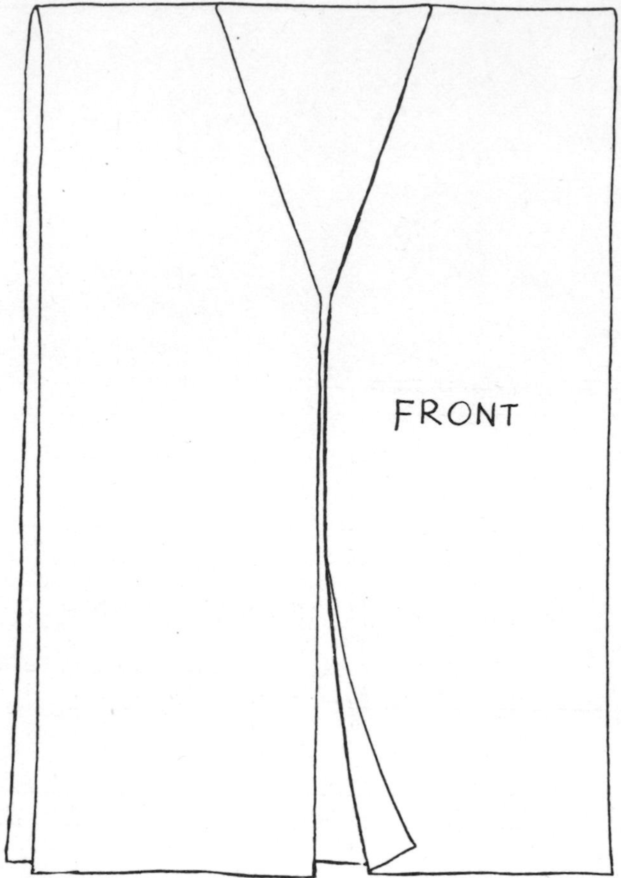

Fig. 4

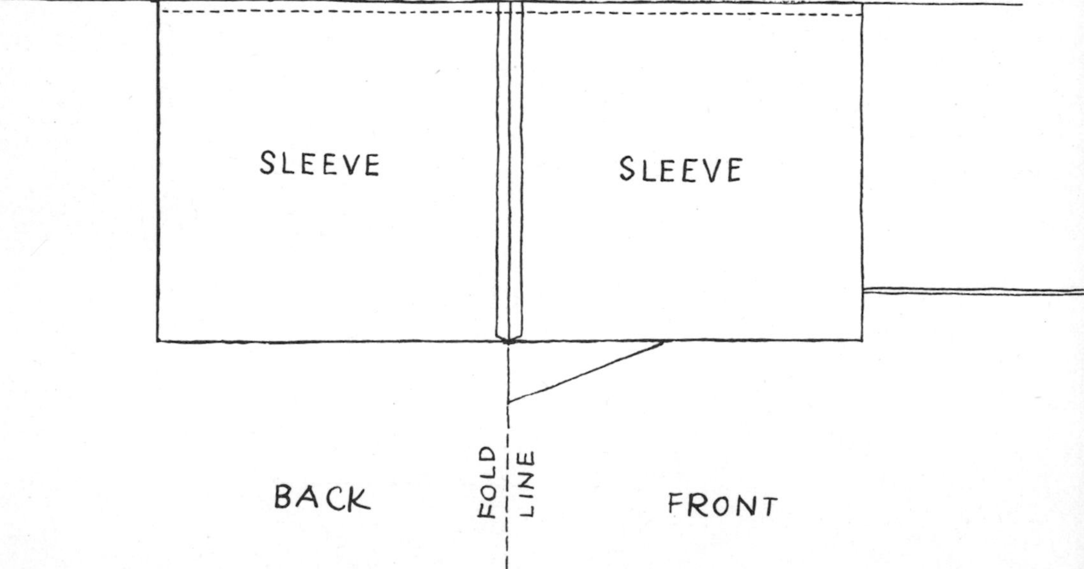

Fig. 5

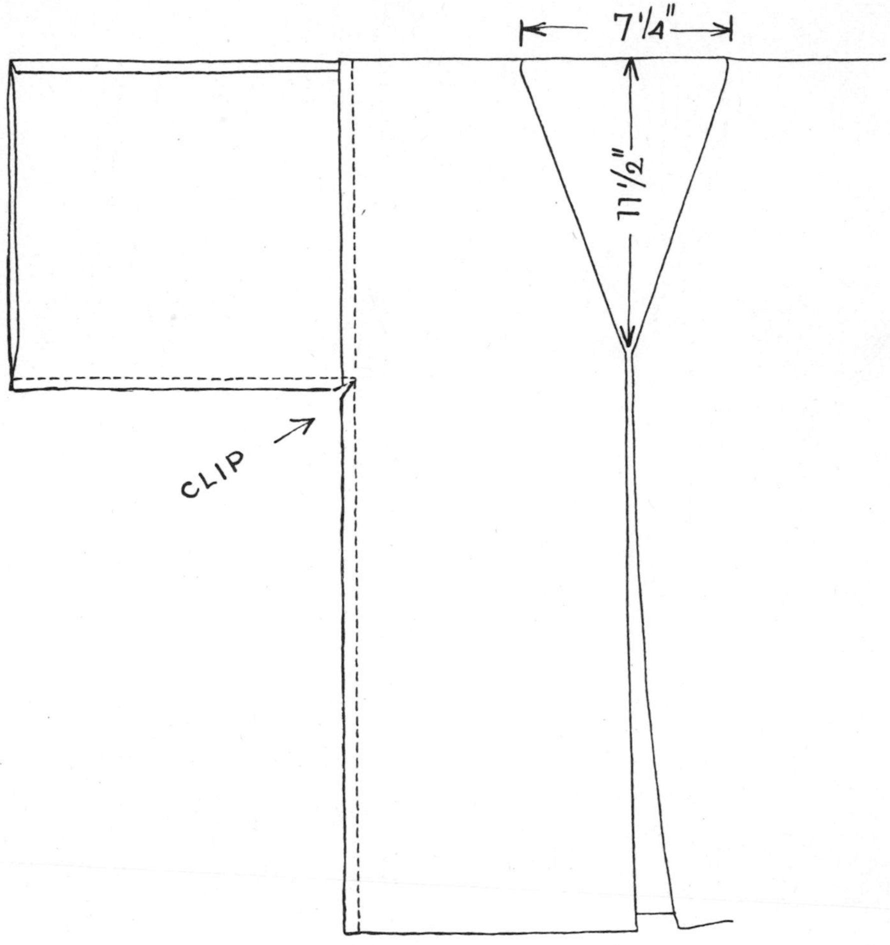

Fig. 6

Fig. 7

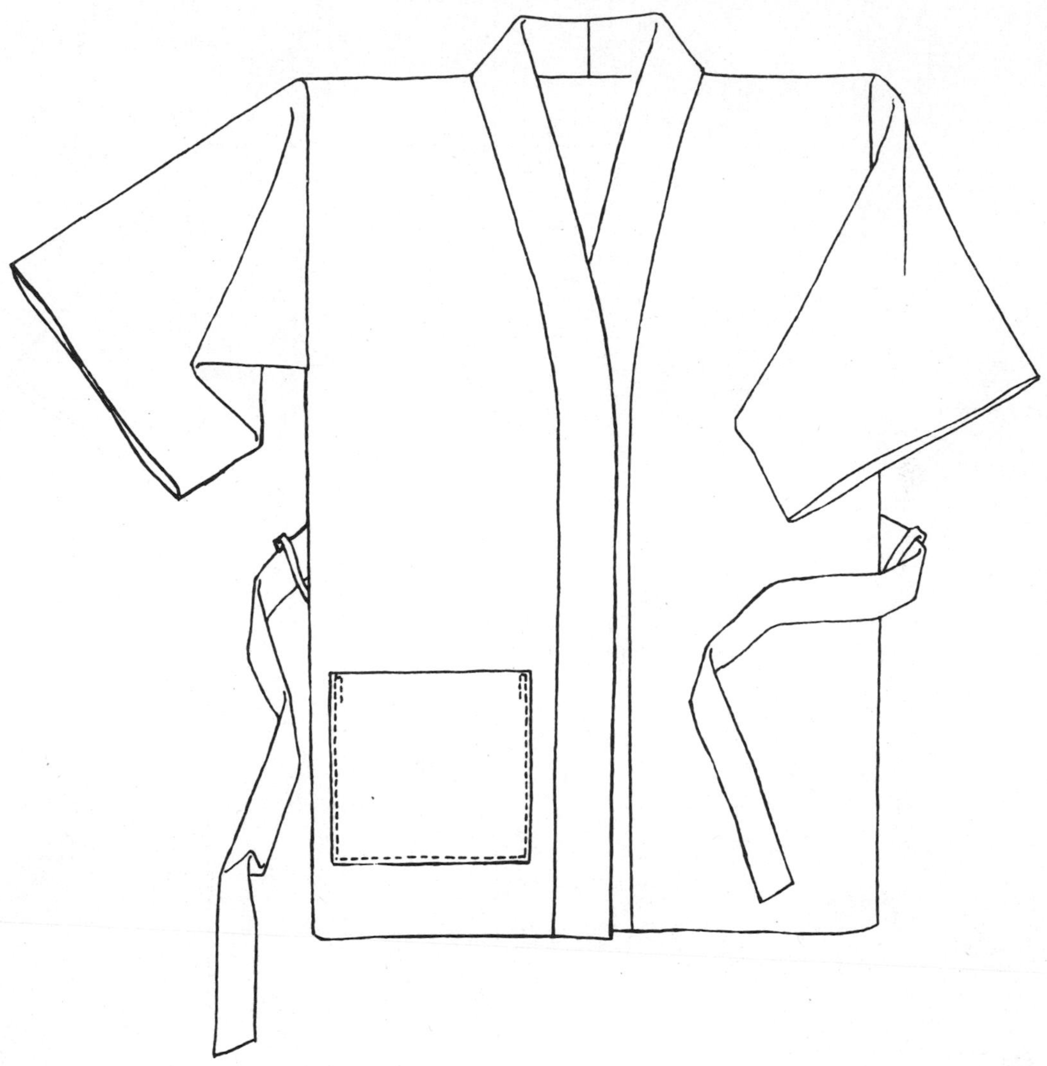

Fig. 8

Chapter 2

Embroidery

Needle and thread and a suitable fabric, plus a working knowledge of even a few embroidery stitches, will give you the means of producing many beautiful things for your home or wardrobe.

The art of embroidery is very old and has been part of the cultural development of every nation. If one were to study the collections of old embroideries in museums and other places, it would be possible to assemble over 300 embroidery stitches.

All of the well-known stitches and some of the more unusual ones are given here in the hope that they will act as a spur to the imagination of those who enjoy or wish to learn this lovely craft.

The old custom of making a sampler was not a bad one, since working each stitch until it is perfected gives one confidence. Also the sampler itself can be decorative.

Suitable round thread linen with an even count is difficult to find and counting threads is something which few women will attempt in these modern times. However, since it is well to have some means of keeping stitches evenly spaced while learning, we suggest woven checked gingham or a similar fabric as a background for learning the basic stitches and starting one on the path of becoming a fine embroideress. (See gingham sampler, page 137.)

FABRICS

Fabrics offer an infinite variety of textures to be decorated and therefore are a challenge to the imagination. Suiting the stitch, the thread, and the design to the fabric calls for much thought and some practice, as well as good taste.

Linen has long been used for embroidery, and rightly so because of its suitability to many articles such as table linens, mats, towels, etc., which are so often decorated with stitches. Cotton is also widely used, especially for wearing apparel. Woolen fabrics with suitable decoration make lovely bed throws or afghans. Silk and rayon fabrics are rather difficult to handle, and, with some exceptions, are not as well adapted to this work as other fabrics. In general, use fine stitches and threads on fine fabrics, bolder stitches and heavier threads on coarser ones.

Certain kinds of embroidery, such as Hardanger, can be done only on a suitable type of evenly woven fabric because of the necessity of counting threads. The most beautiful cross stitch work is also done by counting threads on round thread linen. These fabrics are not always available because the demand is not great enough to keep them on the market. These techniques are still practised by a relative few.

Many lovely designs can be purchased ready-stamped on linen. These are usually designed for cut work, cross stitch, or lazy daisy stitches and will answer the need of those who are not inclined to experiment on their own with stitches and fabric. Color Plate 3 shows a Swedish design called "Birds of Bright Plumage." Designs like this one are often sold in kits, complete with stamped linen, thread, and instructions.

THREADS

Many types of thread may be used for embroidery. The mercerized cotton threads such as six-strand floss and perle cotton in various sizes are the ones most commonly used and readily available.

It is interesting, however, to experiment with a variety of threads. Unusual effects can be obtained by using yarns or threads which were not originally intended for embroidery. For example, all types of wool yarns are very useful and the color ranges are magnificent. Cottons with a soft twist, linen, silk, rayon, and other synthetics have great possibilities. Metallics are now made strong and untarnishable and can be added for interesting glitter. Even jute will produce bold interesting effects suitable to contemporary interiors.

NEEDLES

To accommodate the larger threads, special needles with large eyes are used. Embroidery needles are fine to medium, chenille needles are much heavier. Blunt-pointed tapestry needles, also with large eyes, are used for canvas work or counted-thread embroidery on linen. Choose the correct needle for the thread you are using.

STITCHES

Running Stitch

Run the needle in and out of the fabric, making stitches of even length. This is a basic stitch in both sewing and embroidery. Stitches may be long or short as needed.

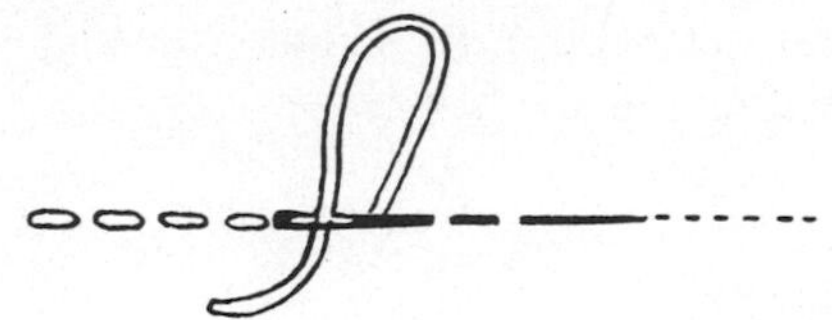

Whipped Running Stitch. Whip over each running stitch without picking up the fabric. A blunt needle or the eye of the needle instead of the point may be used to avoid splitting the thread of the running stitches.

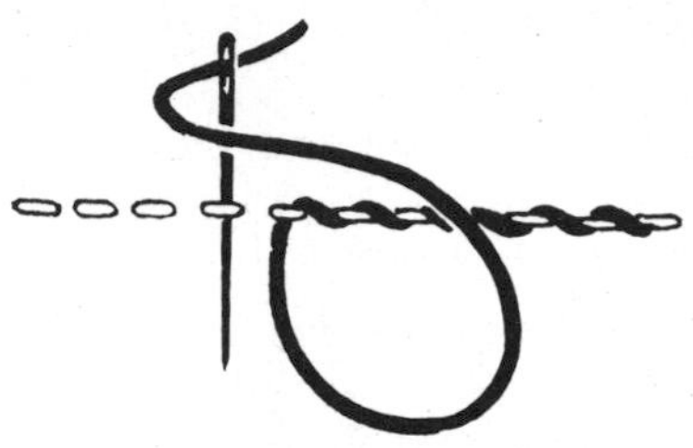

Holbein or Double Running Stitch. Work a simple running stitch with even spaces between. Turn and fill spaces left open. The stitch appears the same on both sides. Holbein designs are usually geometric, and often combined with cross stitches.

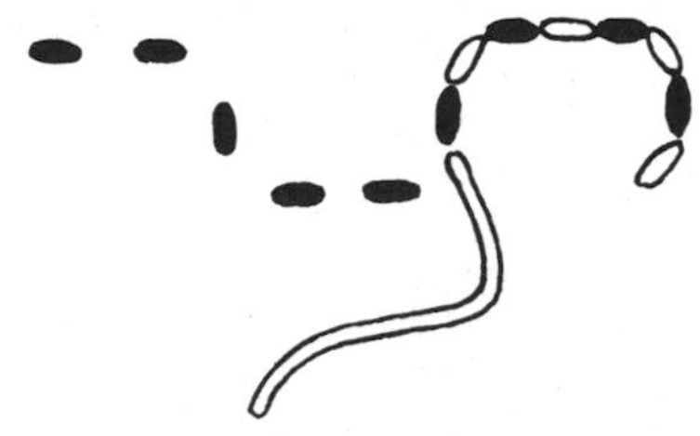

Back-Stitch

Work from right to left. Take a short stitch. Insert the needle at the beginning of this stitch and bring it out a stitch ahead.

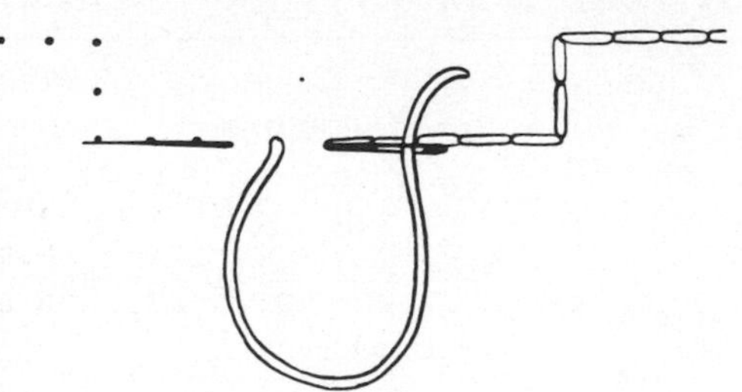

Repeat across. Result should resemble machine stitching and be neat and regular.

Wheat Stitch

Bring needle out at 1 (below) and insert it at center. Bring out at 2 and insert at center. Bring needle out a stitch below these two stitches. Run the needle through the two top stitches and insert again where needle came out last. Make two more straight stitches (3 and 4) and proceed as before.

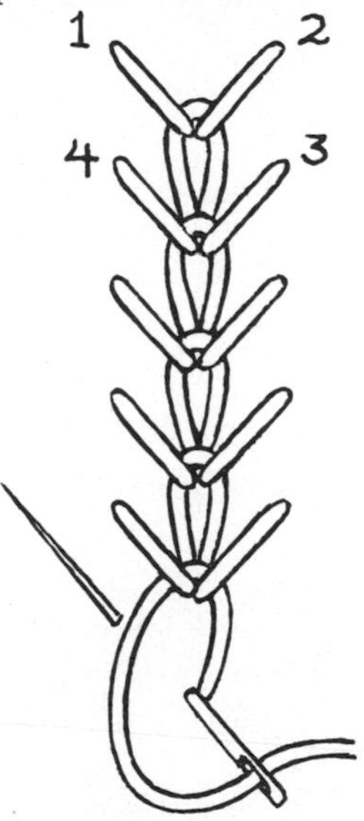

Pekinese Stitch. The foundation line is back-stitch. A second thread is interlaced as shown. This is frequently found in Chinese embroideries. If drawn tightly it gives a braided effect.

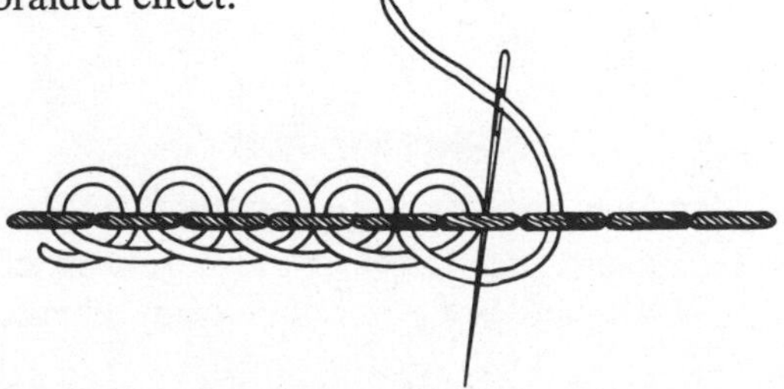

Seed or Dot Stitch

Each stitch consists of 2 back-stitches worked into the same place. It may be used in regular rows or hit or miss as a filling stitch, known as seeding.

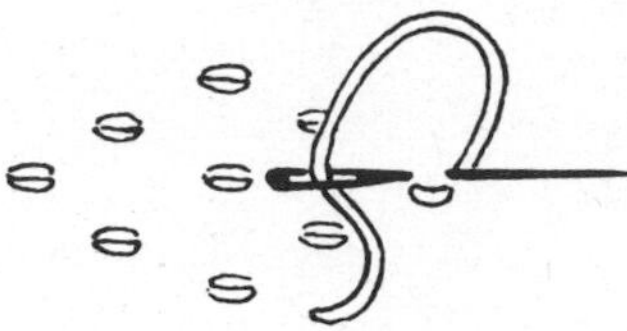

Fern Stitch

Work three straight stitches of equal length, all radiating from one point. If repeated along a curved line they give the effect of a fern-like leaf. It also may be used for veinings in large leaves.

Outline or Stem Stitch

Work from left to right, keeping thread always on same side of needle—either to left or right of it. Bring needle out where last stitch went in, following the line, which may be curved or straight.

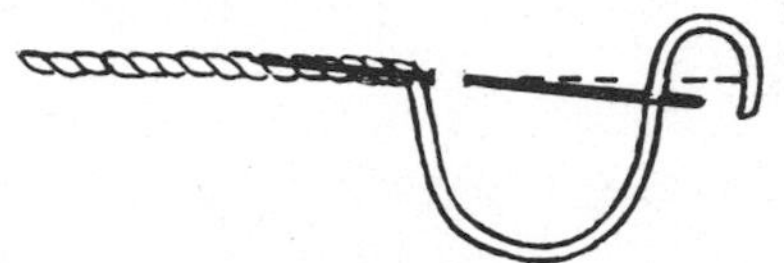

Whipped Stem Stitch. Work outline or stem stitch; then whip over it, spacing stitches evenly. Needle should not enter fabric. Used for bold lines.

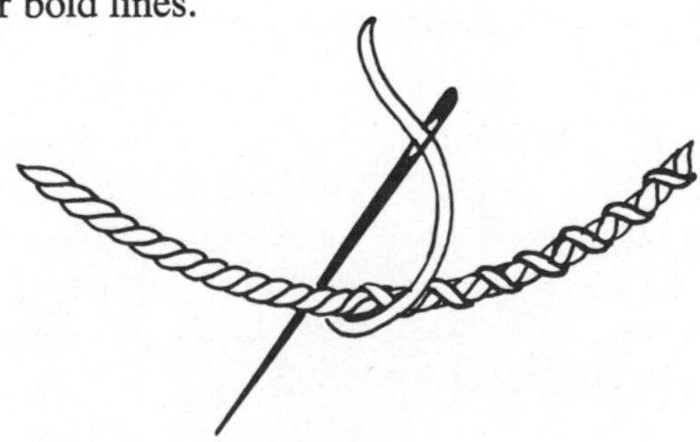

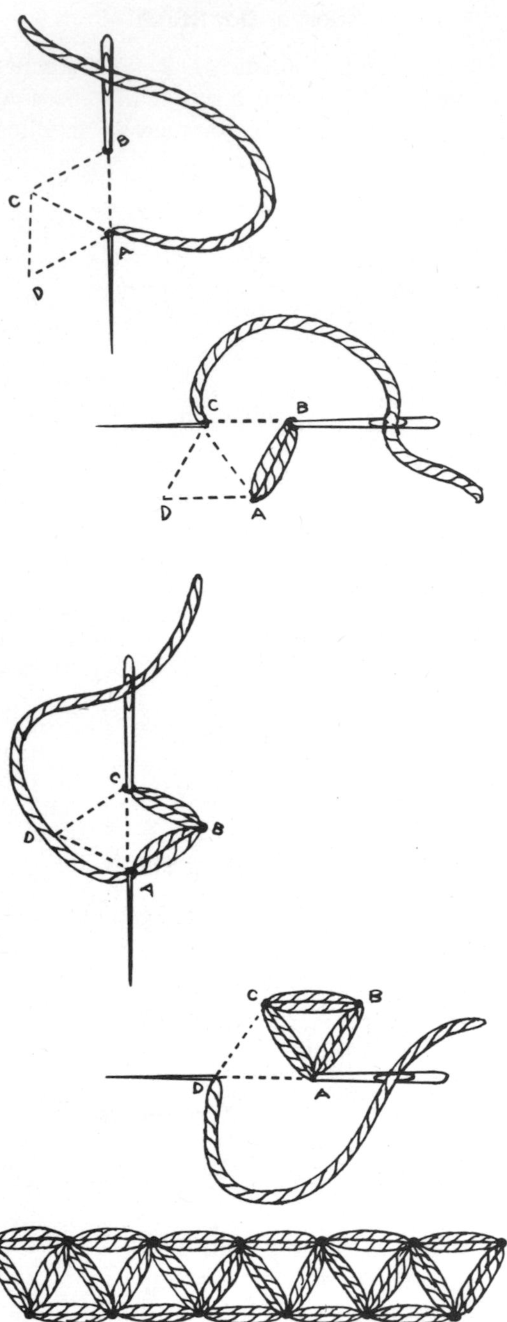

Bermuda Fagoting or Three-sided Stitch

Also known as Point Turc. When working on fine or sheer fabrics use a thick needle and fine thread to get a lacy or openwork effect. The stitch does not need to follow the thread of the fabric but can be used on curves, scallops, etc. It is often used to apply lace on fine lingerie, or for fine appliqué.

Punch Stitch

Similar to Bermuda Fagoting but with 4 sides. Follow the diagram, making upright stitches all the same length or over the same number of threads. Pull threads taut. Work a similar row back again. Continue until the space is filled. Turn work and repeat the process, completing the squares. Always work into holes made by previous stitch.

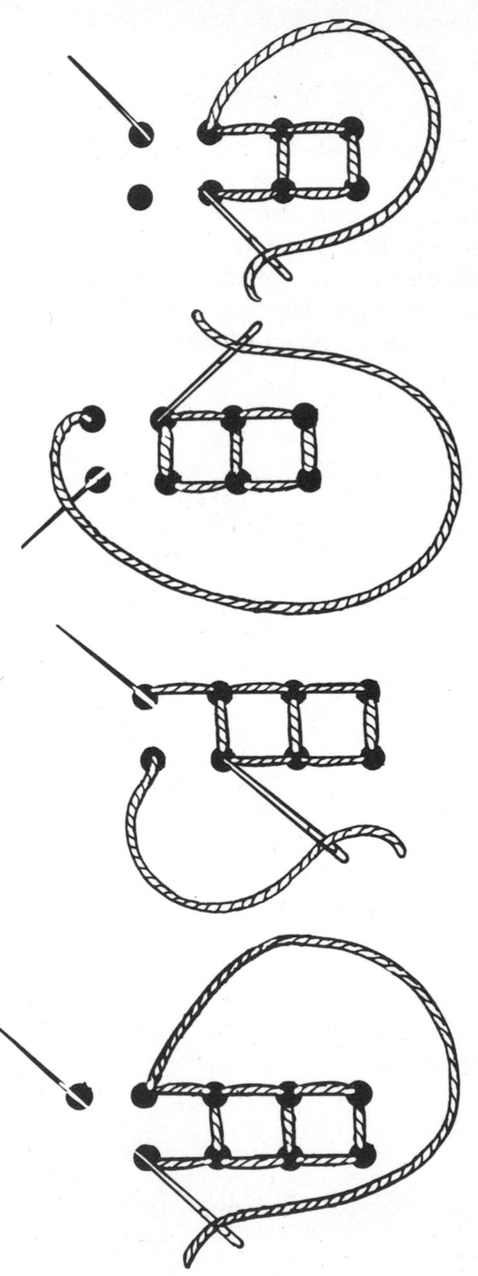

Split Stitch

This should resemble a fine chain stitch. Bring the thread out on the line. Take a short stitch and, at the same time, bring the needle through the thread which is making the stitch. Repeat.

Rambler Rose Stitch

Begin the center with a single outline stitch, or with several satin stitches for a raised center. Work closely around the center with outline stitch, keeping needle pointed to the left and the thread below the needle. Make rose the desired size.

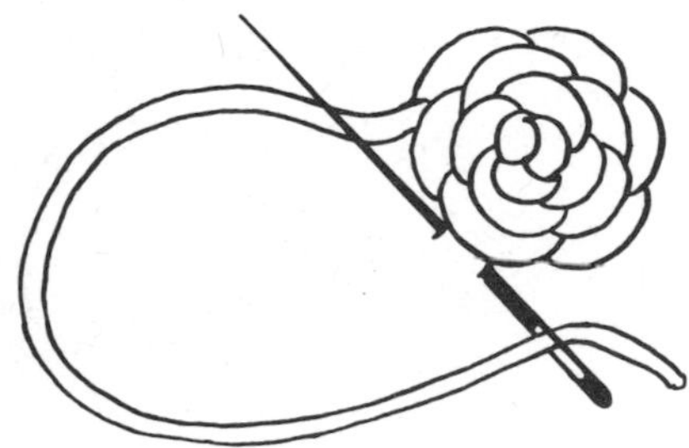

Straight or Spoke Stitch

Single straight stitches can be of any desired length and worked in any direction. It may be spaced as desired to form flowers, leaves, etc. Here, shown combined with French knots and running stitch.

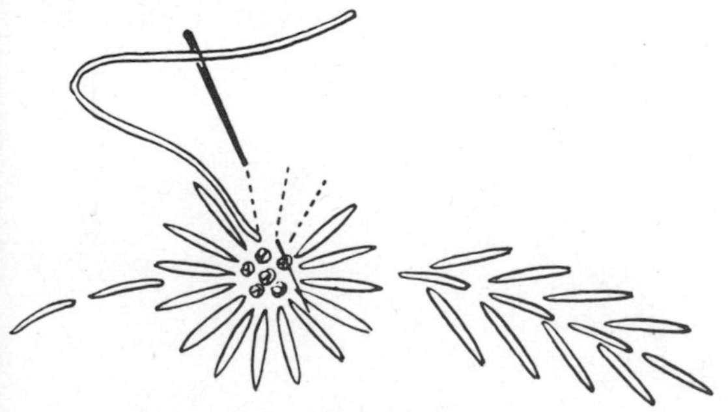

Algerian Eye Stitch

Each star or eye consists of eight stitches all taken into a central point. Arrange the stitches in a square. This can be done on canvas.

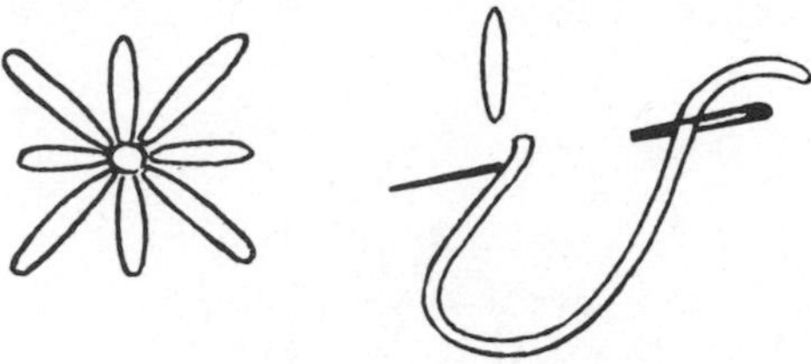

Satin Stitch, Plain

Stitches must be close enough together to cover the fabric; the edges should be very even and neat. This is not easily done and takes practice. The stitches may be slanted in any direction but they should not be too long. Large spaces may be broken up. Before working, the area may be padded with rows of running, back, or outline stitches.

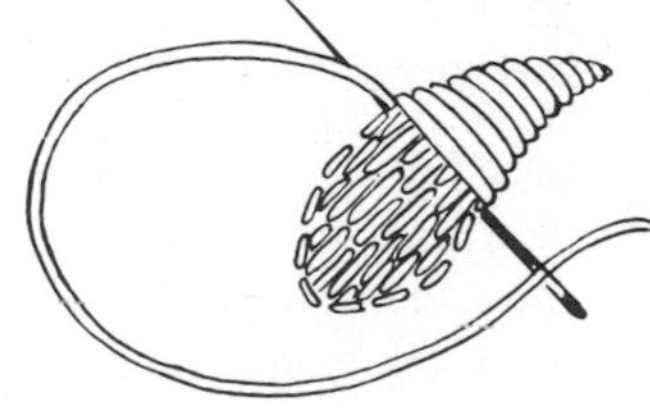

Satin stitch, slanted or straight, may be used in many ways for flowers and leaves. Variations for leaves are shown here.

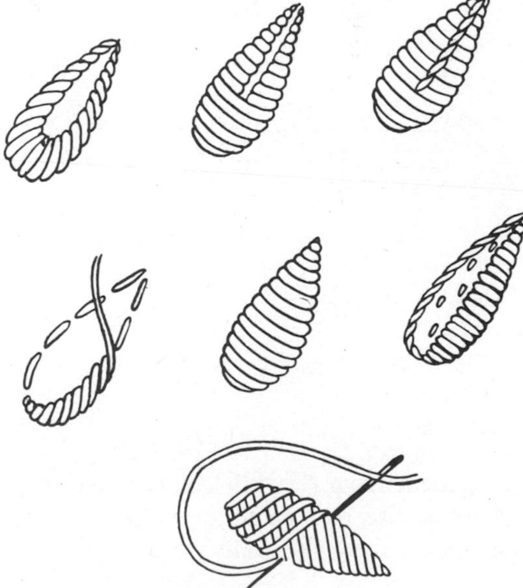

Long and Short or Kensington Stitch

Much like satin stitch except that stitches are long and short. A nice way to blend colors because one row encroaches upon another. It is used to shade and fill in designs of various shapes.

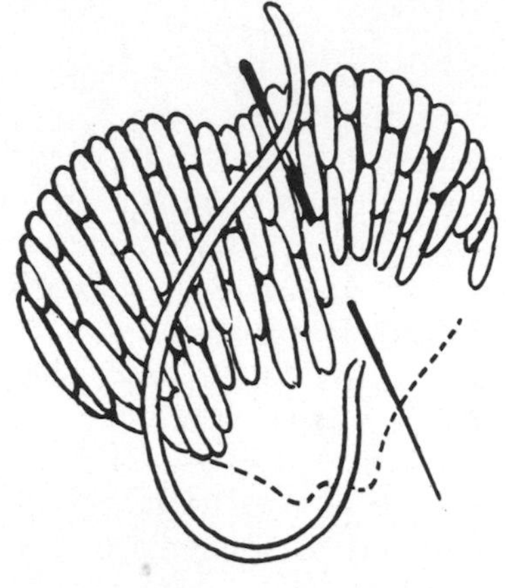

Horizontal Flat Stitch

Take a short horizontal stitch across the point of the leaf and bring needle out to the left of the center. *Insert needle at right top edge and bring out to right of center. Insert at left top edge and bring out at left of center. Repeat from * until leaf is filled. The stitch can also be slanted, in which case the first stitch is done vertically.

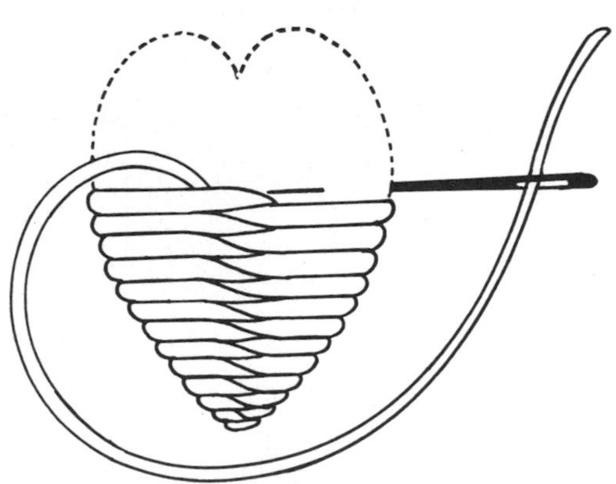

Fishbone Stitch

Bring the thread out at 1 and make a short straight center stitch. Bring the thread out at 2 and take a slanted stitch across the center inserting needle below first stitch and a little to the left of it. Bring needle out at 3 and take a similar stitch to the right. Continue until leaf is filled.

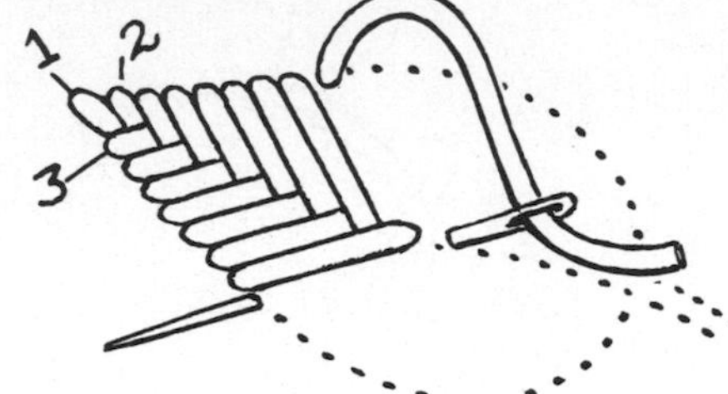

Open Fishbone Stitch. Work same as Fishbone stitch but omit center stitch. Bring needle out at 1, in at 2, out at 3, etc. These stitches present a more spread-apart appearance than in Fishbone stitch.

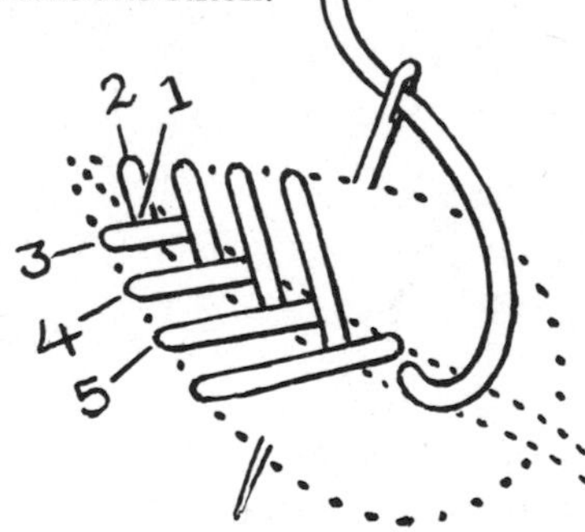

Dorondo or Raised Fishbone Stitch. Make a long vertical stitch (halfway down from point of leaf). Bring needle out at left side opposite the end of this long stitch. Take a short stitch at top of leaf from right to left and insert needle on opposite side of where first stitch came out. Bring needle out below stitch on opposite side. Take another stitch at top just below the first, and so on until space is filled.

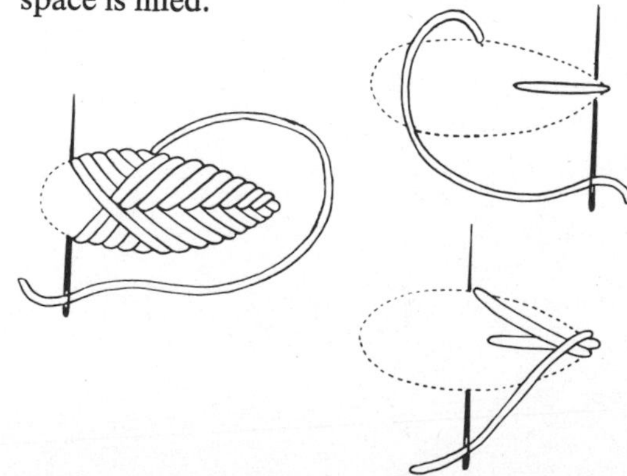

Leaf Stitch

Follow the diagram. Starting at bottom, bring needle out at 1 and insert at 2. Come out at 3, in at 4, and out at 5. Continue until leaf is filled.

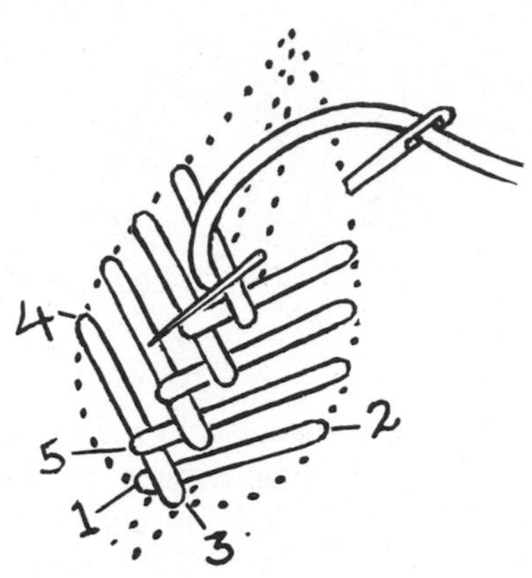

Open Herringbone Stitch

Sometimes called catch-stitch. There are many variations. Work from left to right along 2 imaginary parallel lines. These may be drawn lightly or one can follow the weave. Bring needle out on line at upper left. Take a short back stitch on lower line a little to the right, keeping thread under the needle. Take a back-stitch on upper line a little to the right with thread under the needle. Continue, keeping spaces even.

Closed Herringbone Stitch. Work herringbone with stitches touching so space is filled. Take very short stitches if you want to fill the space more closely. This stitch is used for "shadow embroidery" on sheer fabrics. The herringbone appears on the wrong side. (See next page.)

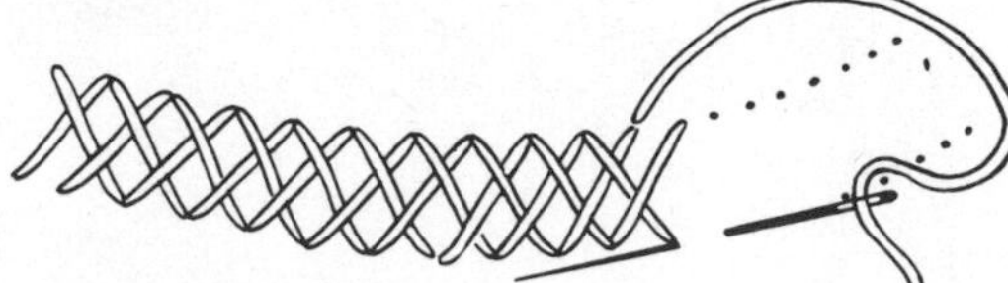

Double Herringbone Stitch. Work a row of open herringbone stitches with wide spaces. Work a second row using a contrasting color, placing stitches in spaces between and interlacing as you work.

Laced Herringbone Stitch. Work open herringbone stitch. Then lace a second thread around the crosses that have been formed. Make two complete circles around each upper cross and one and a half around each lower cross. Always interlace under and over the foundation stitches and under and over the thread being used.

Threaded Herringbone Stitch. Work open herringbone and lace in manner shown. When lacing do not let needle and thread enter the fabric.

Tacked Herringbone Stitch. Work a row of open herringbone. Work a small single vertical or horizontal stitch, entering the fabric, over each place where stitches cross. This holds the cross in place and allows a second color to be used.

Narrow and Wide Herringbone Stitch. Without changing thread, an ornamental border may be made by changing the width of the stitches at regular intervals.

Ornate Herringbone Stitch. Work a large single chain stitch over each point where herringbone stitches cross. Very effective in bold heavy thread or yarn in contrasting colors.

Shadow Embroidery. This is closed herringbone stitch worked "wrong side out." It is done on sheer fabric so the underneath stitches show through in shadow effect. It can be worked along parallel lines or to fill simple shapes such as leaves and petals. Take a back-stitch on upper line; then one on the lower line. Sometimes called double back-stitch.

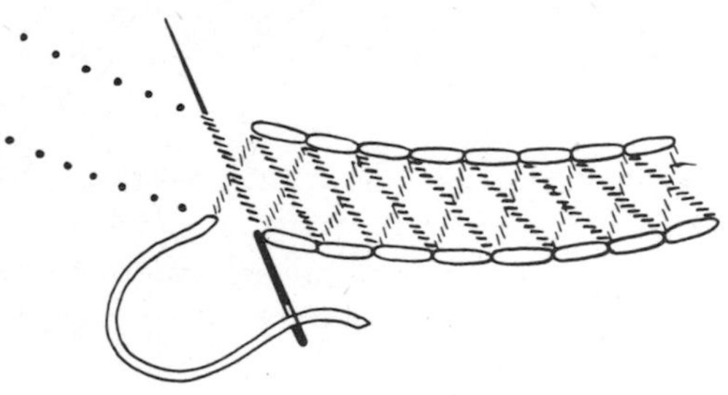

Chevron Stitch

This stitch is also worked on parallel lines and is somewhat similar to herringbone. Take a short stitch on the top line, and bring needle out in the center of this stitch. Take a stitch half the length of the top stitch on line below. Insert needle to the right and bring needle out where the last stitch went in. Arrange stitches so the cross threads come from the center of stitch taken on the line. See diagram.

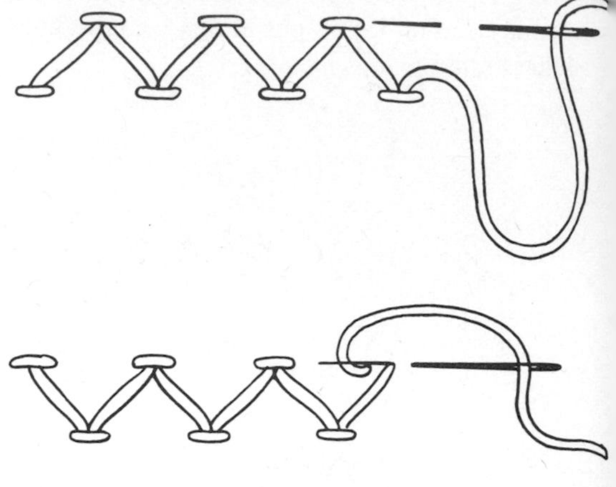

Cross Stitch

This can be started either at the right or the left. Make a row of slanted stitches of equal length and evenly spaced. Work back over them with the same stitch but slanting in the opposite direction. This makes a row of cross stitches. The reverse side will show a row of upright stitches.

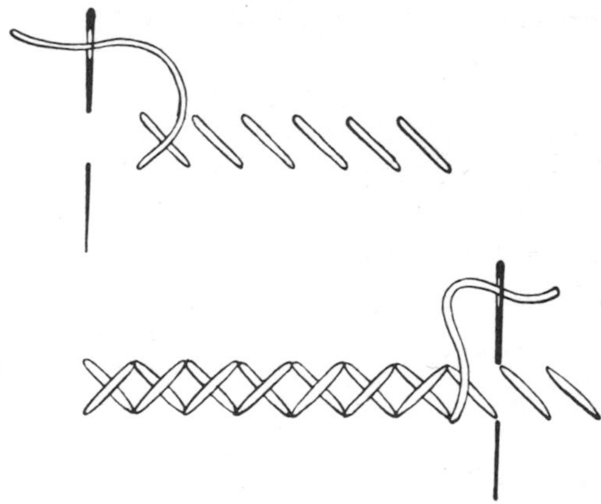

Double Cross Stitch. This consists of a cross stitch done on the diagonal (as above) with another cross centered over it. Arrange the length of the stitches to make a square.

Long-armed or Long-legged Cross Stitch. The first stitch of the cross is longer and more slanted than in regular cross stitch. The second stitch of the cross is done immediately after the first and is the usual length and slant. This gives a plaited effect. May be worked on linen or canvas.

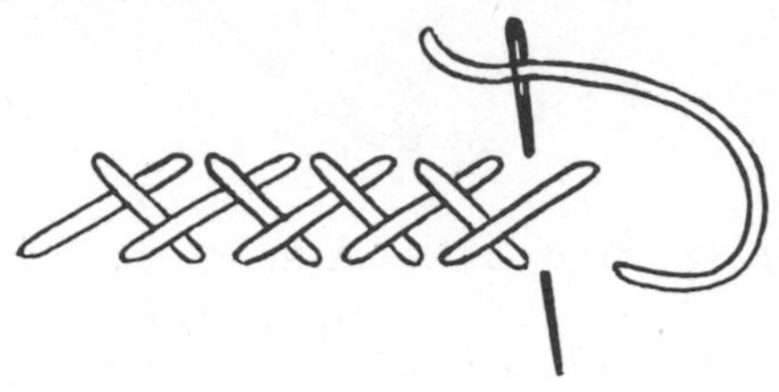

Plain Blanket Stitch

Work from left to right. Bring needle out on line (or very close to hem edge). Take an upright stitch to the right with needle pointed down, keeping thread under the needle, and come out on line or edge. Diagram also shows how to turn a corner with blanket stitch. Many variations of this stitch are possible.

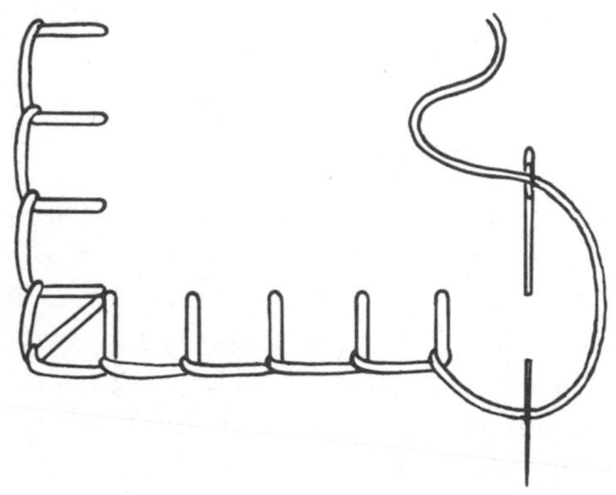

Tent Blanket Stitch. Slant stitches to form points (which resemble a row of tents).

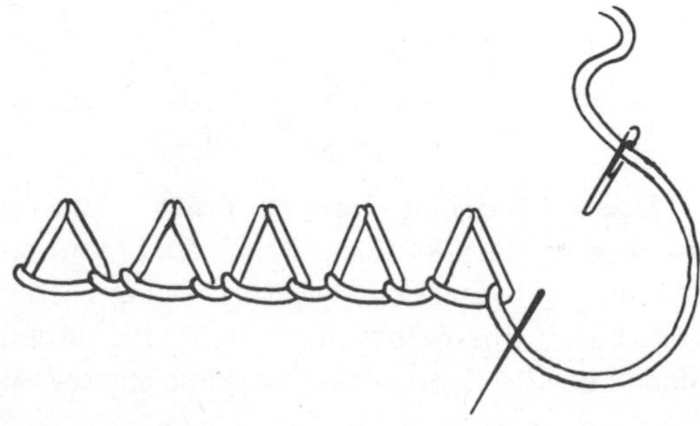

Crossed Blanket Stitch. Work a blanket stitch slanting needle from right to left. Work another over it slanting needle from left to right. Place it so stitches will cross.

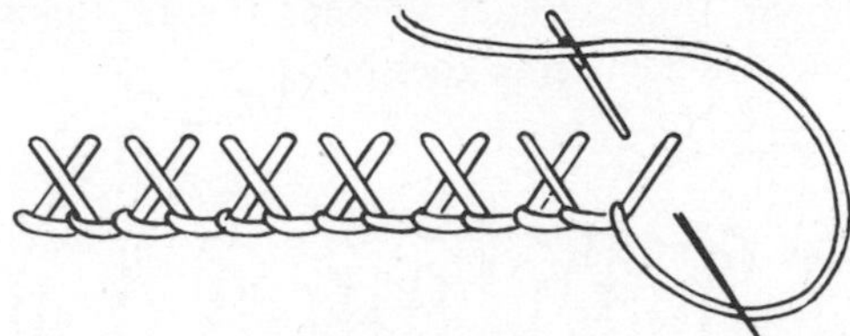

Graduated Blanket Stitch. Vary the length of stitches to make patterns. Great care must be taken to keep groups uniform.

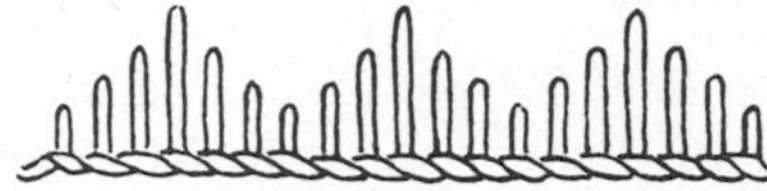

Long and Short Blanket Stitch. Worked same as plain blanket stitch, but with stitches of different lengths.

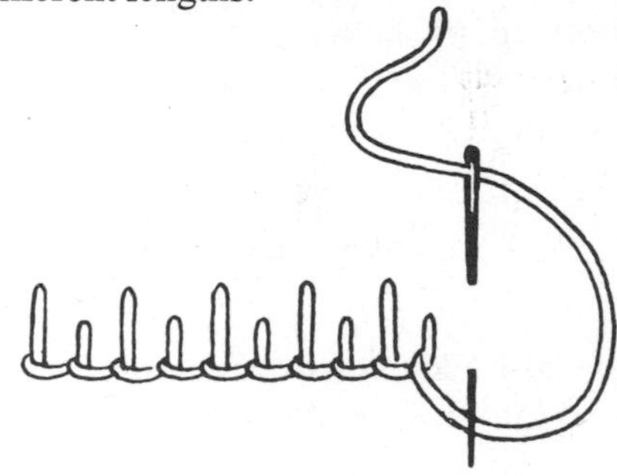

Grouped Blanket Stitch. Work stitches in groups of two or more with a wider space between each group. This makes a nice border on a narrow hem if not done too boldly.

Double Blanket Stitch. Work a row of plain blanket stitch. Turn work and make another row, taking stitches between those of the first row. Keep all stitches even and of equal length.

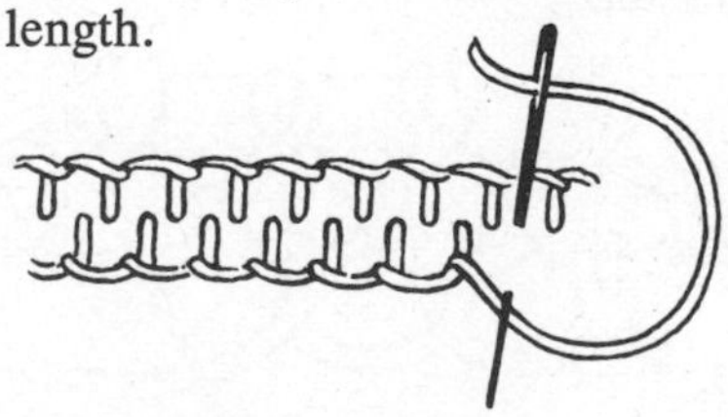

Knotted Blanket Stitch. Work from left to right. Start at lower edge like regular blanket stitch. Before inserting needle to make the stitch, twist the thread around the needle as shown. Pull through, keeping the knot close to where the needle goes in.

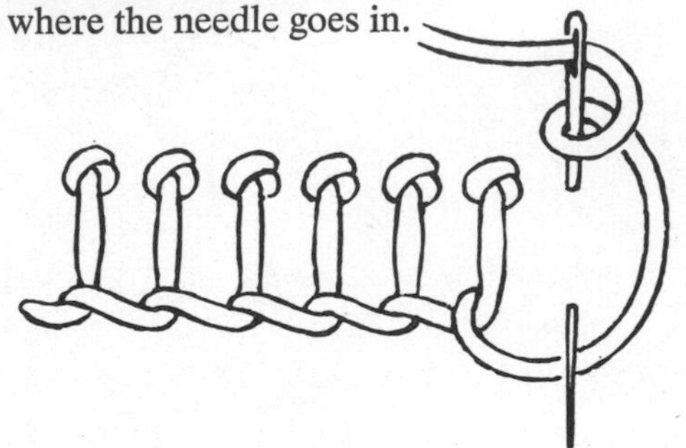

Knot Stitch Edging. Bring needle through at edge of fabric and do a simple blanket stitch. Run the needle behind the loop just made and over the thread coming from the needle as shown. Pull up, making a knot. If desired, a second row can be made, working over the loops between the knots of the previous row.

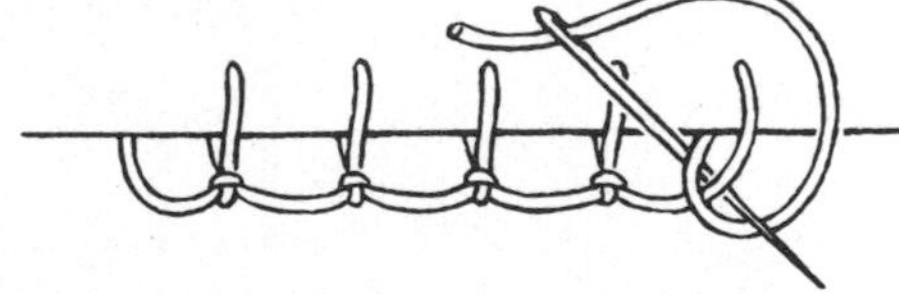

Looped Filling Stitch. Make rows of loops, catching into the row above as shown.

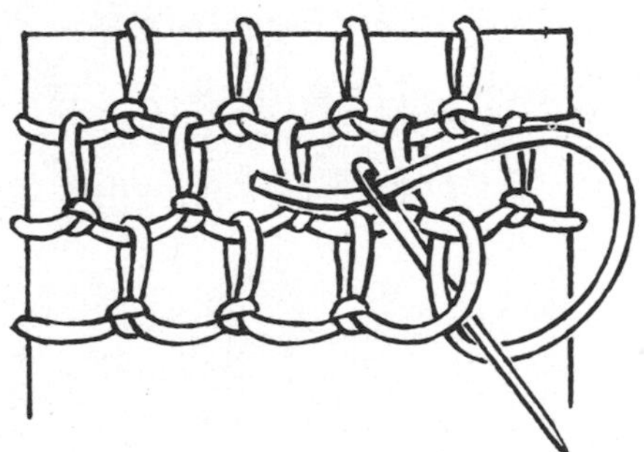

Knot Stitch Filling. Work Knot Stitch Edging in rows over fabric as shown but without catching into the fabric except at sides and top.

Mille Fleur. Draw a circle. Work blanket stitch around, inserting needle at or near center. Make all stitches the same length.

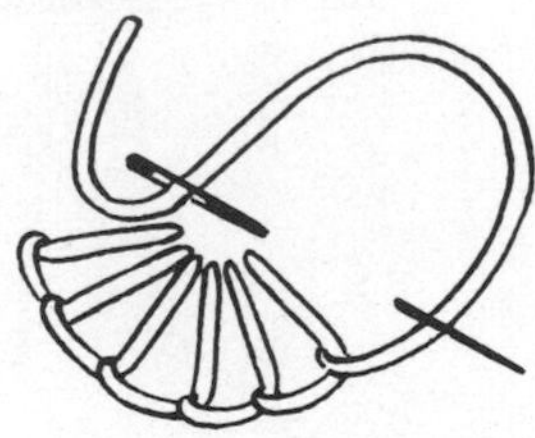

Spider Web Stitch. Usually done in a circle. Divide circle in five parts. Make a fly stitch over two of the sections with a long "tail" reaching to opposite side of circle. Make a straight stitch each side of the tail bringing needle out at center. Weave over and under the spokes until filled. In drawn work, the web is only partly filled to give a lacy effect.

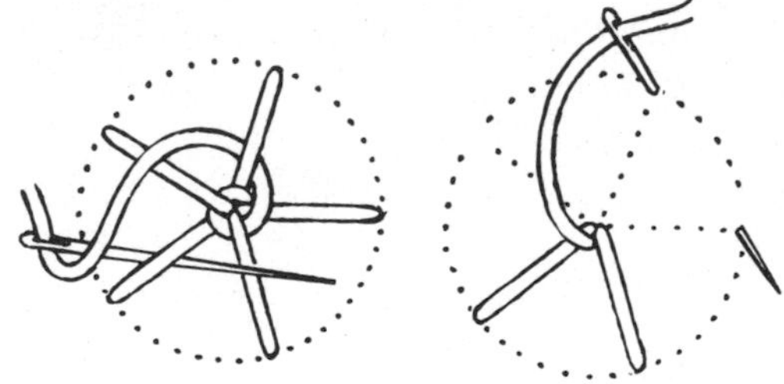

Simple Chain Stitch

Bring thread out on the line. Insert needle where thread came out and take a short stitch on the line, keeping thread under the needle. Draw up. This makes a loop which should lie flat. Insert needle where thread came out and take another stitch in same manner. Keep stitches the same length.

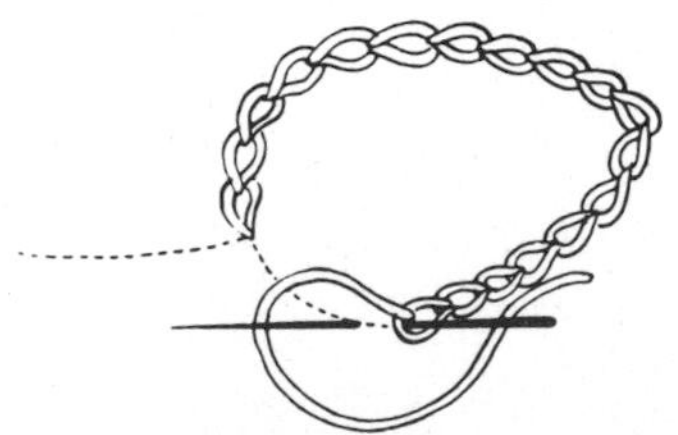

Open Chain or Ladder Stitch. This is worked on parallel lines. Bring needle out on left line and insert on right line. Bring needle out on left line below first stitch with thread under needle. Loop must be kept somewhat loose. Insert needle on right line with loop under it; bring needle out on left line and so on. Keep the spaces even. They may be any size desired.

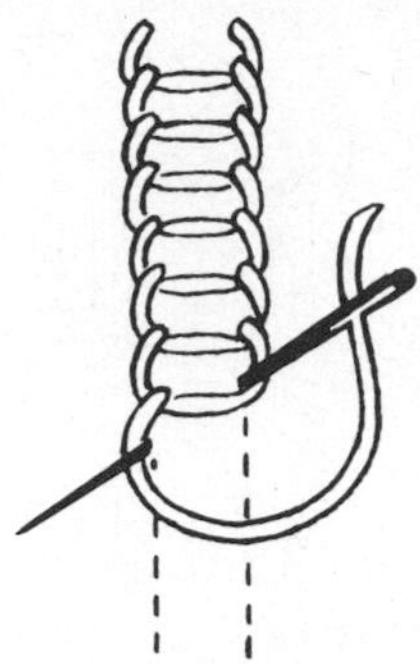

Heavy Chain Stitch. Work from top down. Bring needle out at 1 and make a short vertical stitch. Bring needle out at 2 directly below first stitch. Run the needle through the first stitch without catching fabric; insert needle just at the left side of where it came out. Bring needle out at 3 directly below second stitch. Run it again through the first stitch and insert at 3. Continue in this way, and running the needle under the two preceding loops.

Feathered Chain Stitch. Work on parallel lines. Starting on one of the lines, work a slanted chain. Following the slant, insert needle a little *inside* of the second line. Bring needle out *on* the second line a little above where it went in. Make another slanted chain. Continue back and forth.

Zigzag Chain Stitch. Worked the same as ordinary chain stitch, but with stitches slanted in such a way as to make a zigzag line.

Detached Chain or Lazy Daisy Stitch. Work as for chain stitch, but insert needle just outside (or below) loop. Bring needle out wherever next stitch is wanted. The stitches may be placed to form daisy petals or spaced evenly for filling stitches.

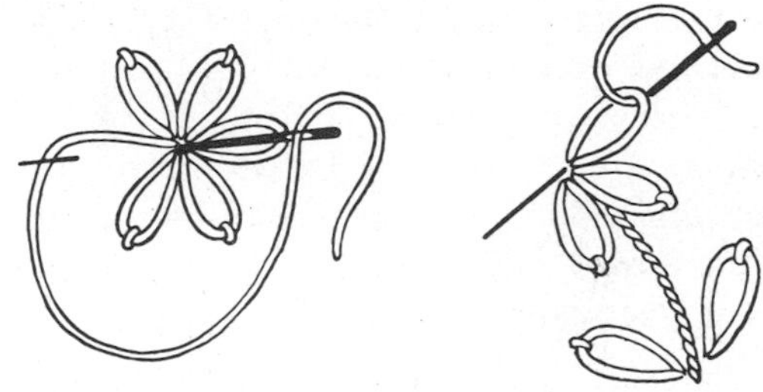

Fly-Stitch or Y-Stitch. This is a detached chain stitch worked open. Picture a V when inserting the needle. Hold the loop down at center below with a stitch as for detached chain or daisy stitch, but make it a little longer.

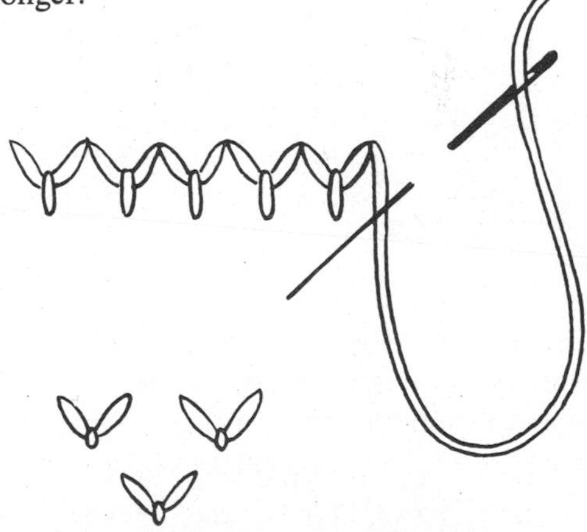

Feather Stitch

With thread under slanted needle, make a blanket stitch to the right of a straight perpendicular line. With thread under needle make a blanket stitch to the left. Repeat. Fancy feather stitch is made by working several stitches on each side. They may be evenly spaced or grouped. A further variation is made by pointing the needle straight down so the outside stitches are parallel and closed.

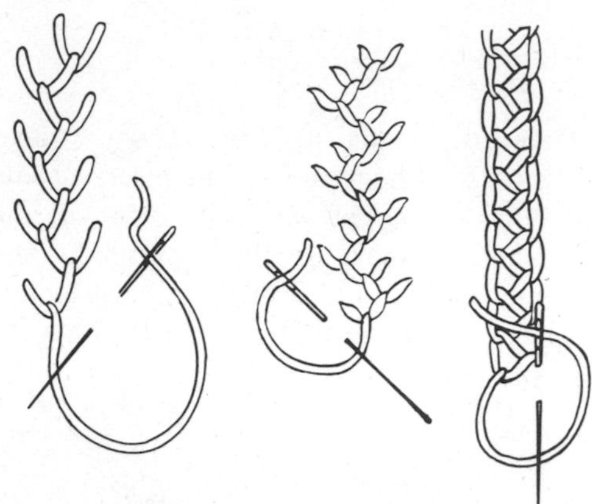

Cretan Stitch. A variation of feather stitch. With thread under needle, work back and forth, keeping needle pointing straight up or straight down.

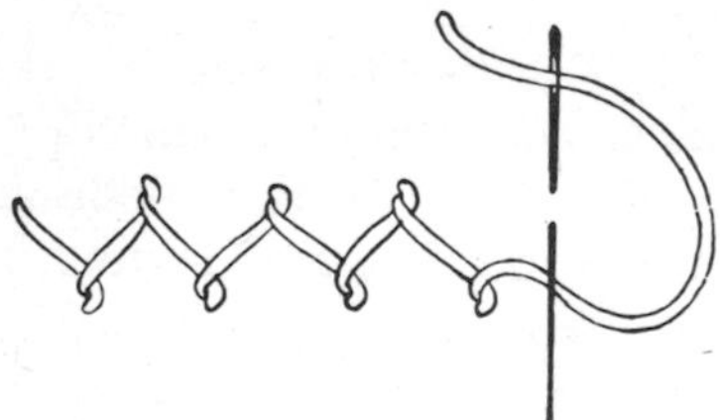

Closed Cretan Stitch. Can be used to fill a leaf or similar shape. Start at center top. Take a stitch to the right, bringing needle out at the left side of the leaf. Insert needle just above and in center of first stitch, bringing it out in center of and on top of second stitch. Insert needle at right side and bring it out on top of and at center of stitch being made. Bring needle out at left side, insert in center of same stitch. Continue in this manner following the diagram until space is filled.

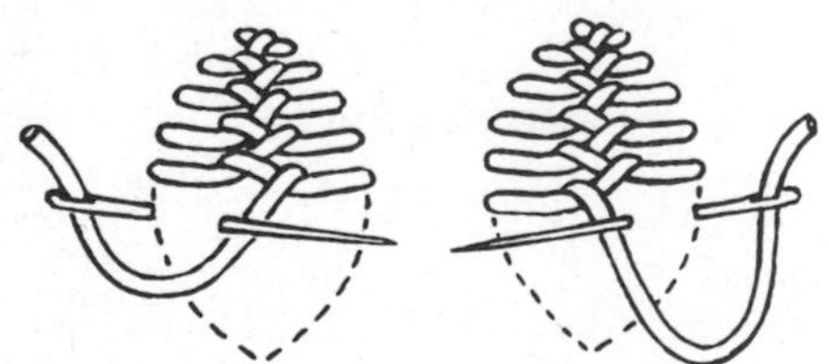

Fish-Bone Stitch. Another variation of feather stitch. Slant the needle more and take stitches longer than for regular feather stitch. Always bring needle out at center line.

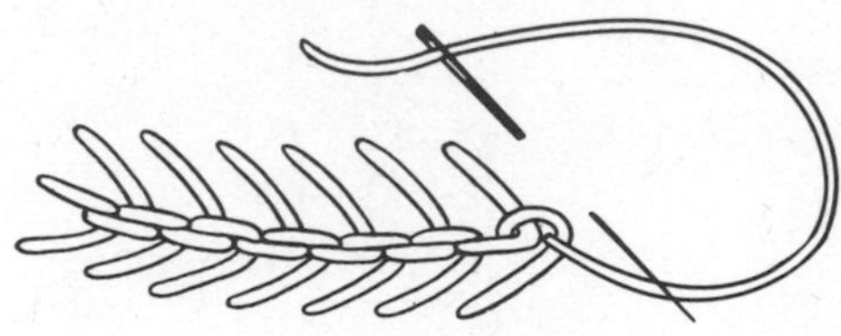

Spine or Loop Stitch. Work from right to left. Bring needle out at 1 and insert at 2. Bring out at 3 just below 2. Keeping thread to the left and under the needle, run needle under the first stitch without picking up fabric. Insert needle on top line again and continue as before.

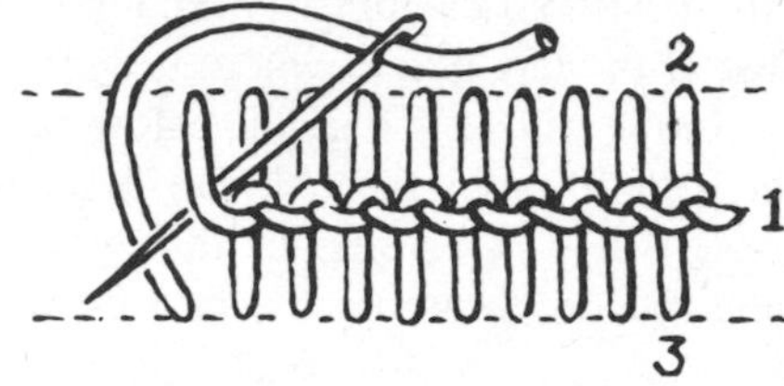

Van Dyke Stitch. Work from top down. Bring needle out at 1, then take a short horizontal stitch at center top, 2, from right to left. Insert needle at 3 and bring out at 4 (just below 1). Pass needle under crossed threads below 2, then insert again at 5. Continue in this manner.

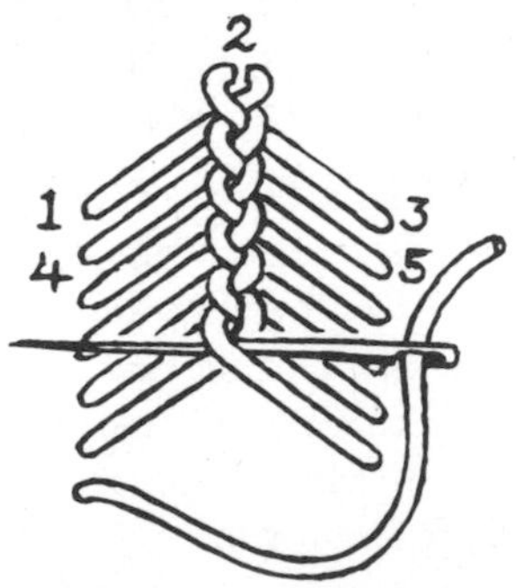

Plain Couching Stitch

A heavy thread or a group of threads are laid on the fabric. With another thread (usually of contrasting color), hold the heavy thread down with short stitches across it at regular intervals. Do not allow the heavy thread to pucker. This can be done on curved or straight lines.

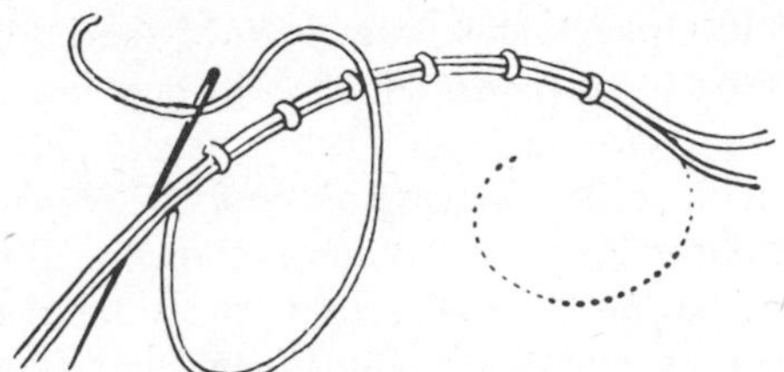

Fancy Couching Stitch. The couching stitch may be varied by slanting, grouping, or zigzagging. Stitches such as cross stitch, feather stitch, or blanket stitch may be used to hold down the heavy thread. Keep spaces even for the best effect.

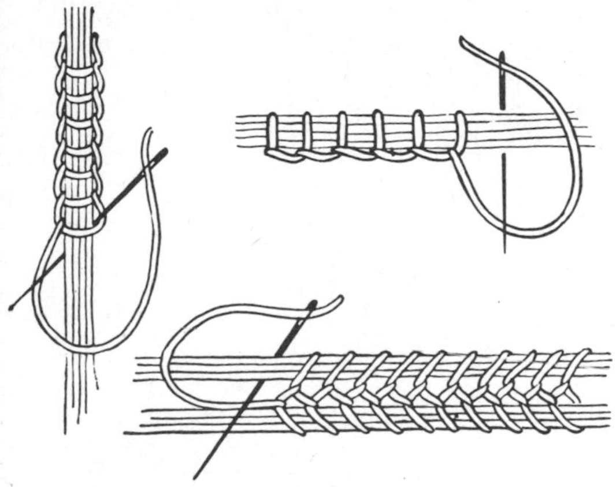

Bokhara Couching Stitch. Used for filling an enclosed space. The same thread is used for the laid thread as for holding it down. The thread to be couched is laid from left to right. This is held down on return by small slanting stitches evenly spaced. Roumanian couching is very similar, the difference being that the return stitches are taken at a very long slant. When finished, it is difficult to distinguish the laid from the couching stitch.

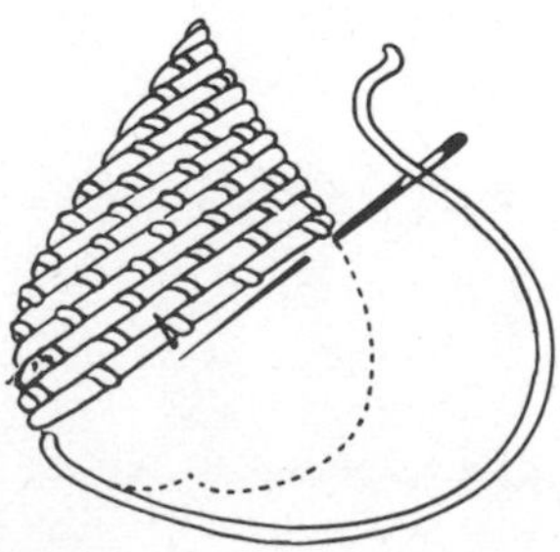

Couched Filling Stitch. This is a form of laid work and can be done in any shaped space. Take long stitches horizontally and again vertically, spacing evenly. Work either a half cross or full cross at intersections.

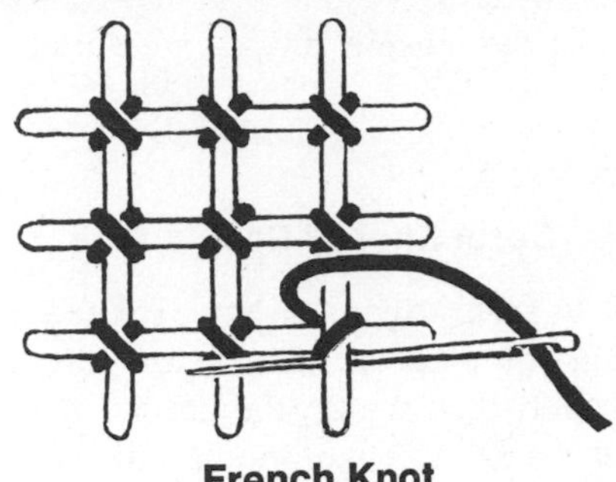

French Knot

Bring needle to right side. (*a*) With left hand wind thread over needle 2 or 3 times or more (depending upon size of knot desired).

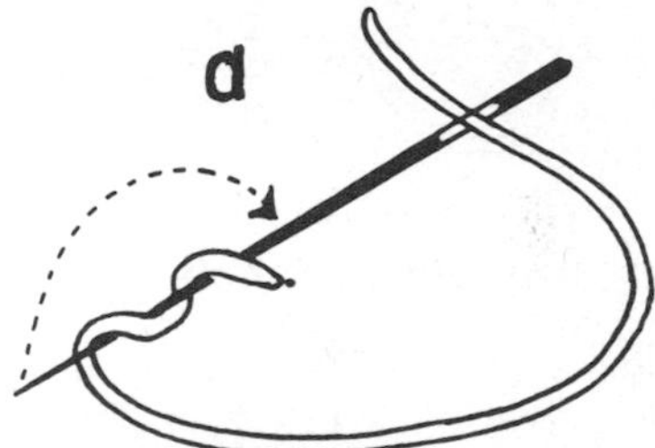

(*b*) Insert needle close to where it came out. (*c*) While adjusting tension with left hand, draw needle to wrong side, forming knot.

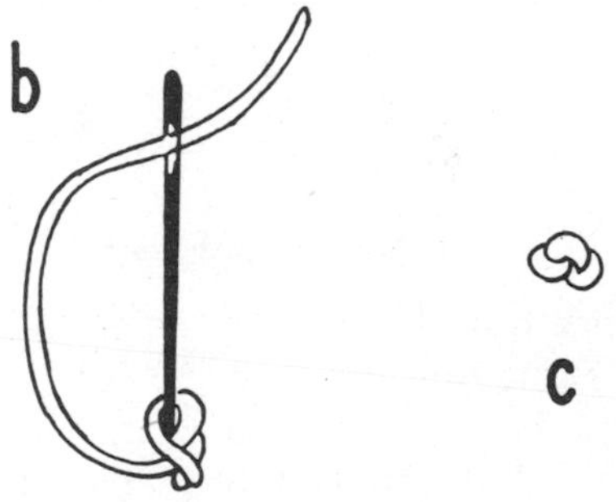

Bullion Stitch

Bring needle to right side. Take a short stitch (whatever length desired) and bring needle out at the same place as before. Wind thread over the needle several times—enough to fill space the length of the stitch taken. Hold the "wind" with left hand while pulling thread through so it will be smooth and even.

This may be used to make a rambler rose, daisy, or other design.

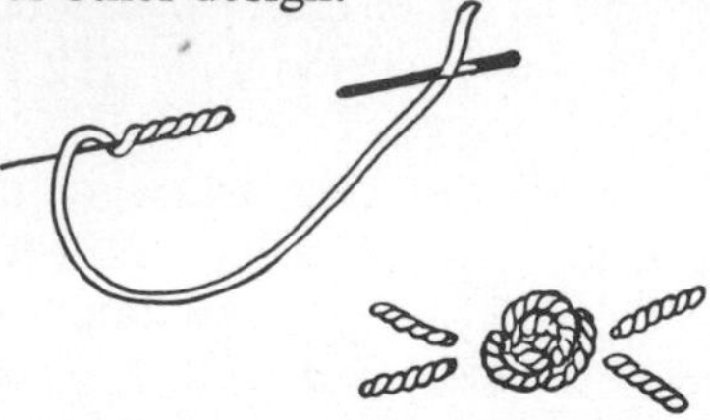

Coral Knot or Snail's Trail

Work from right to left. Take a short slanting stitch on the line. Allow the thread to lie over, then under, the needle. Draw up to make a knot. Take another stitch a little farther along and repeat.

Scroll Stitch

Similar to Coral Knot stitch and can be used as a border. Work from left to right. Bring needle out on the line, loop the thread and take a short slanted stitch inside the loop as shown. The needle is on top of the loop. Pull up. Space stitches evenly.

Armenian Edging

Work from left to right on the edge of a hem. Bring thread out on the very edge. Insert needle a little to the right, pointed up. Before pulling thread through, loop it around the needle as shown. Pull tight. This forms a knot on the edge. Effective in heavy thread. (See also Armenian needlepoint lace.)

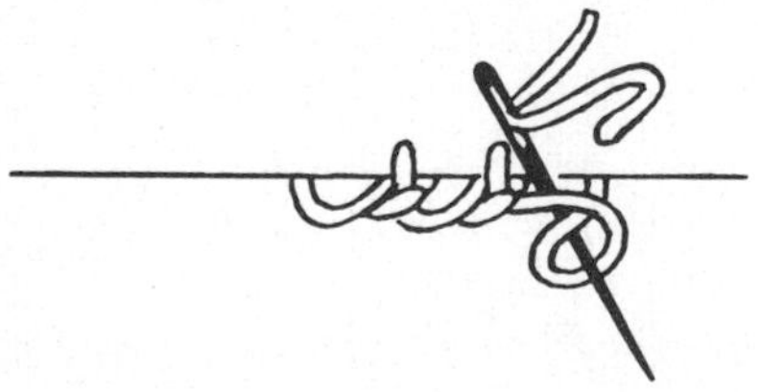

Swedish or Needle Weaving

Draw threads for a border of the desired width. Upper and lower edges of the border may be hand hemstitched to help group the stitches. Use no knot; bring needle out at edge of border, leaving an end. Weave over and under 2 sets of threads as shown. Fill the space closely by pushing darning stitches together as you work. Finish bar and fasten thread by running down center of bar. Do same with next starting thread. Bars may be grouped to form varied patterns. Whenever possible, pass needle under stitches to get from one group to another.

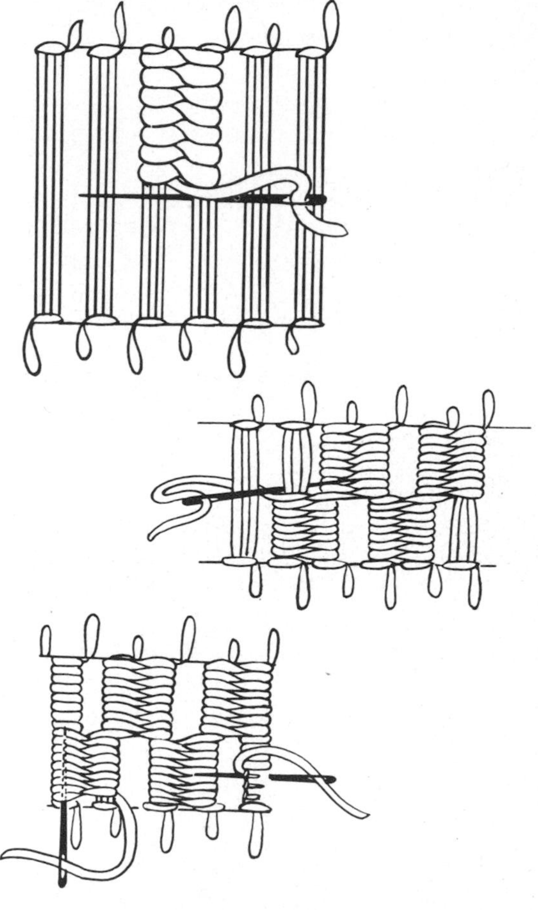

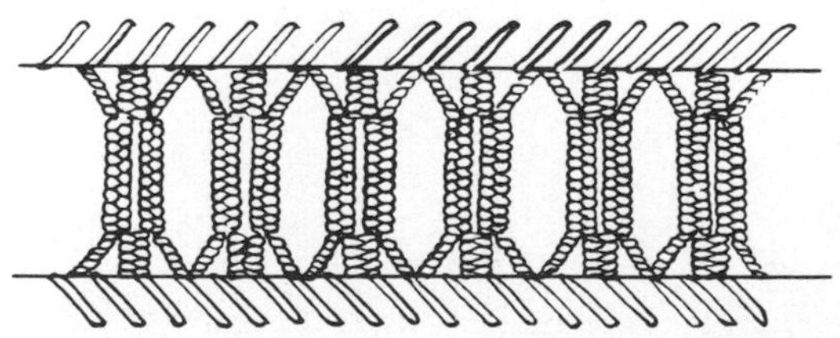

To finish a raw edge of material, first overcast edge, then work overhand stitches to give appearance of a woven bar.

Darning on Huck

This is a very old art and many lovely designs can be made with it. It is a simple but effective type of embroidery done on the surface of huckaback towelling. The raised thread of the fabric occurs at regular intervals and forms the basis of the work, which is simply a darning stitch. Choose the side of the fabric where the threads of the raised dots run up and down and parallel with the selvage. This is actually the wrong side of the fabric.

Use a blunt-pointed needle and either 6-strand floss or perle cotton size 5 or 8, depending upon the fineness of the weave of the huck. Start with a strand of thread long enough to reach across the border (of towels). Follow the chart below. Start at the center of the design and the center of the fabric and work from right to left. An enlarged detail of the center of the motif on the towel pattern is given on page 132 to show how the threads cross.

Pull the thread only half-way through, leaving an end long enough to work the other half of the design. You can later turn the towel up side down and work the other half of the border. Be careful not to go through the fabric to the wrong side. Fasten thread neatly by running back through a few stitches. Do not pull thread too tightly. Elaborate borders are traditional and varied, but simpler designs may also be made. Colored huck is now available and comes wider than formerly, giving greater scope to this fascinating technique.

The same principle may be applied on

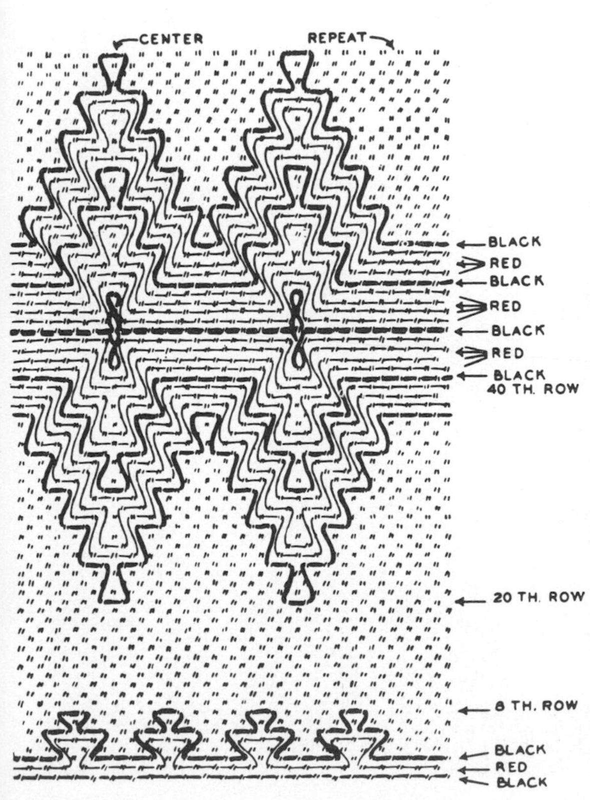

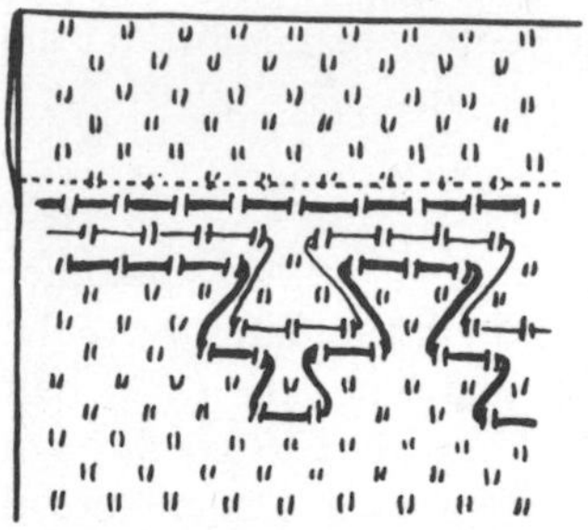

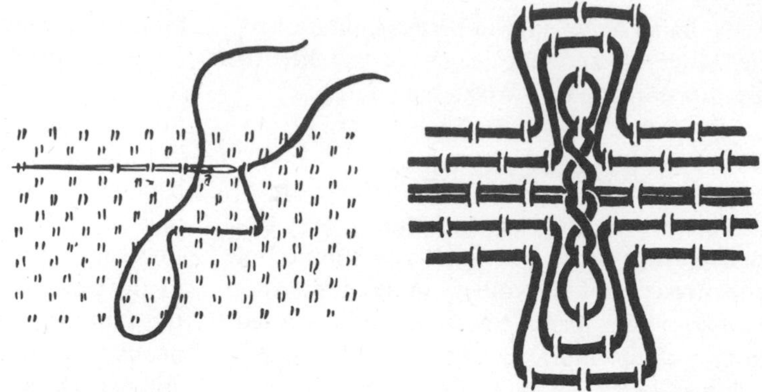

other fabrics, such as checked gingham or dotted Swiss, catching the squares or dots in place of catching the raised threads on the huck.

This work is sometimes done with wool on coarse huck for knitting bags, pillows, etc. It is also possible to work on the right side of the huck by inserting the needle from top and bottom of the raised threads instead of from the sides. A more squared-off pattern results.

Place Mat

Materials. ½ yard 36″-wide Red Huck. (*Note:* 1¼ yards, cut lengthwise, will yield four place mats.) 3 skeins White Six-Strand Floss. Red Mercerized Sewing Thread.

To Make. Work border along both ends, allowing for ½″ hems. Make narrow, rolled hems along long edges, ½″ hems at ends, all by hand.

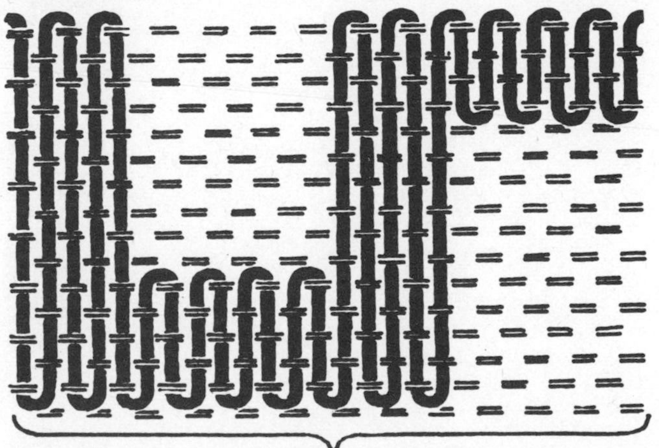

Border Patterns

Suitable for decorating aprons, towels, curtains, place mats, children's wear, etc. Follow general instructions when applying patterns in color combinations of your choice.

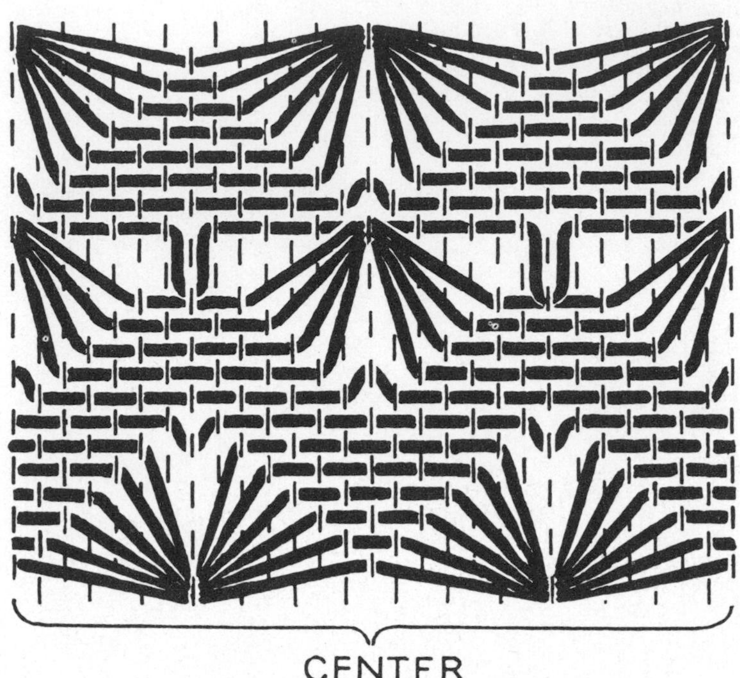

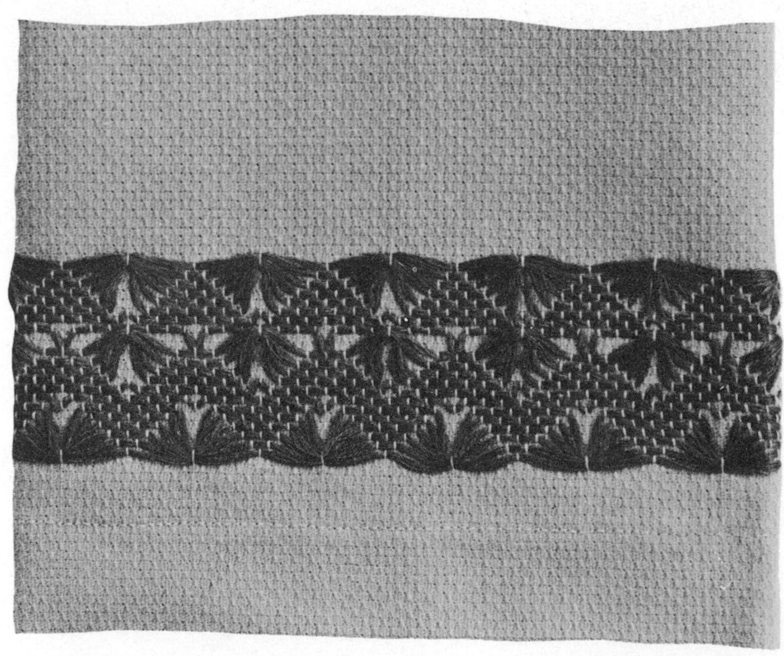

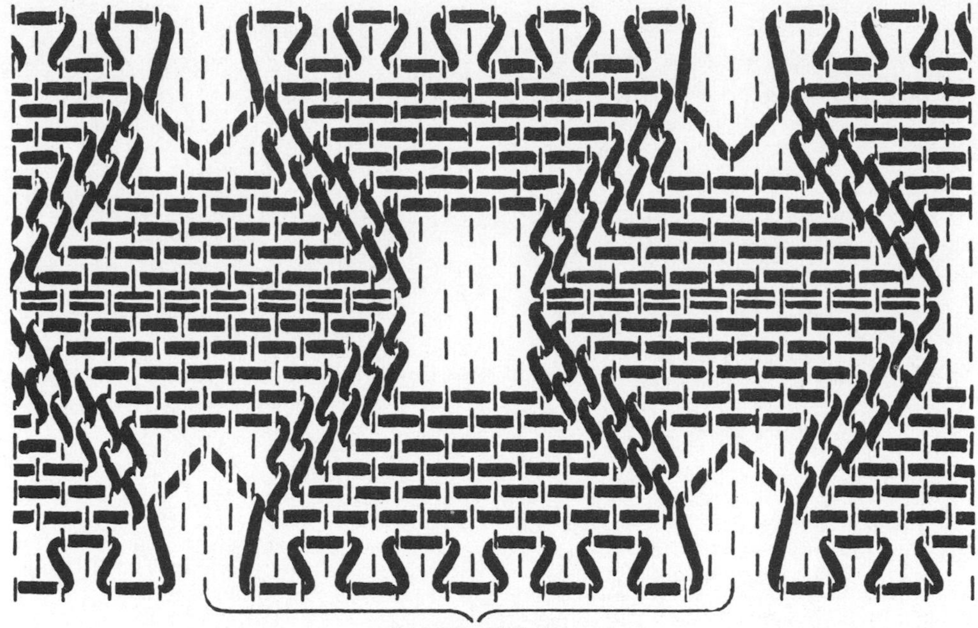
REPEAT

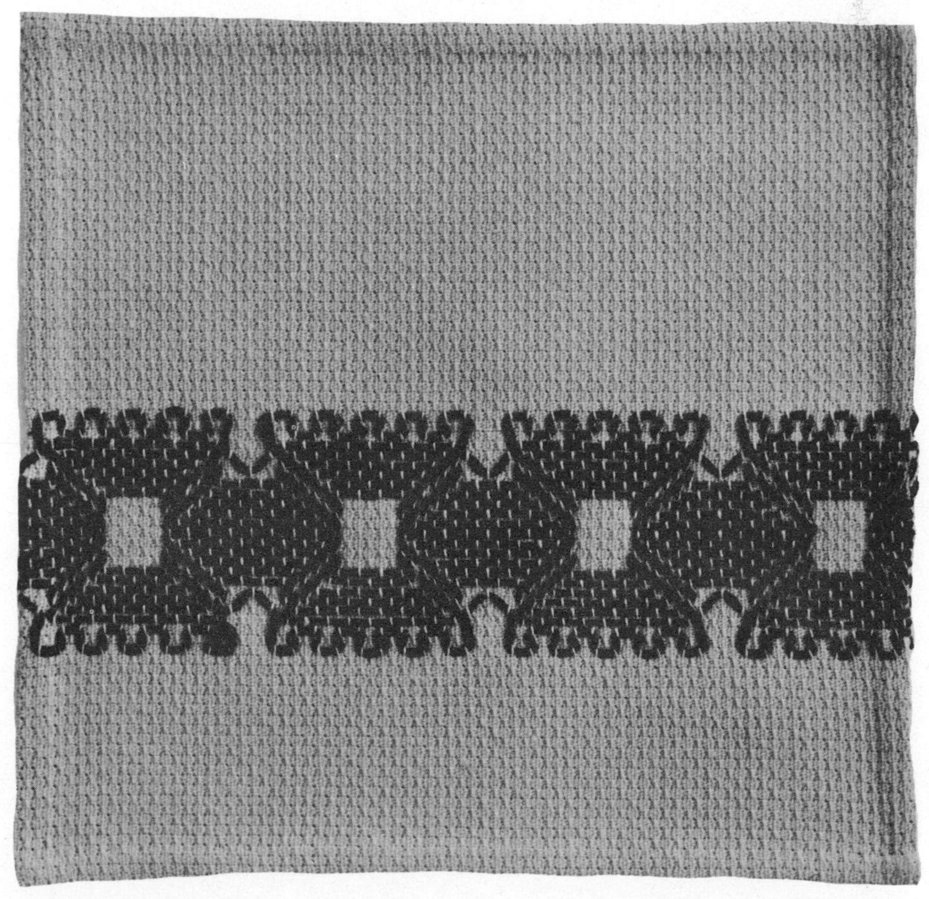

Buttonhole Stitch

(For true buttonhole stitch, see page 34.)

Work from left to right like blanket stitch but with the stitches placed close together. Buttonholing is used for scallops or edges of cut-work designs. The purling is always worked on the edge which is cut away. Scallops may be padded with running or outline stitch.

Buttonhole Bars. Work simple buttonhole stitch along one side of opening and along opposite side up to the place where bar is to be. Carry thread across to the finished row and bring needle up from below through one loop. Carry thread back and forth until there are 3 threads. Cover these threads with buttonhole stitches or simply wind them closely with thread to make a bar. Do not catch into fabric. A simple picot may be made in the center of the buttonholed bar by leaving the loop of the center stitch longer. Hold it with a pin. Then work next stitch around it. Finish working around opening.

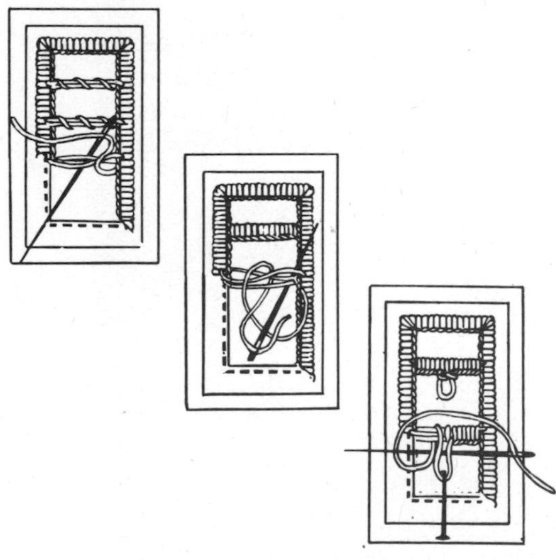

Eyelets

Mark a circle. Work running stitches on the line for padding. If circle is small, punch a hole with a stiletto. If large, cut a cross in the center. Overcast edges turning them under as work proceeds. Buttonhole stitch may

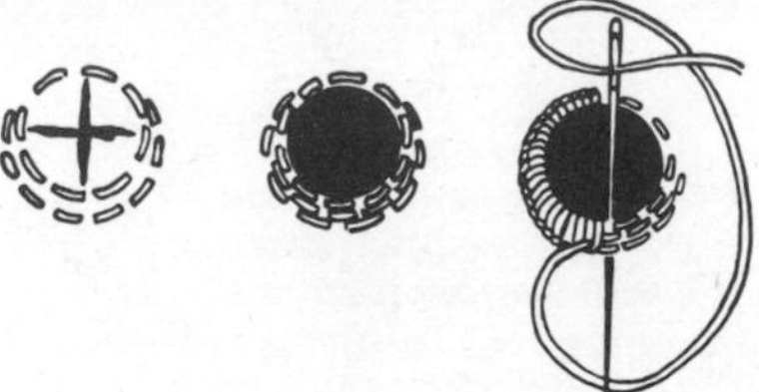

also be used. Leaves and petals may be worked in the same way. Slash fabric lengthwise. Round eyelets may be worked by gradually widening edge as shown.

Gingham Sampler

The sampler, "I Know My Stitches" (opposite) is worked on checked gingham and is not at all difficult to do. You can make it or a similar one by following the checks on the gingham and the diagrams given showing the stitches used in the various borders. Substitute other stitches as desired.

Follow the photograph for placement of designs and borders, or arrange them to suit yourself. The photograph has been reduced. Checked gingham with eight squares to the inch (measuring crosswise the fabric) was used. Have the selvage run lengthwise on the sampler.

You will need a piece of gingham about 14″ by 19″. This will leave a border of about 2″ around the embroidery. In order that the design be placed in the center, as well as to have it symmetrical, begin in the center and work outward.

Bright red, Kelly green, medium orange, and royal blue threads were used, but colors can be chosen which look well on the gingham you have selected.

Be sure to sign your sampler by working

ABCDEFGHIJKLM
NOPQRSTUVWXYZ
I KNOW MY STITCHES

ABCDE FGHIJ KLMNO
PQRSTUVWXYZ

your name or initials as well as the date in one of the lower corners. Back-stitch is good for this purpose.

Opposite is a typical modern sampler inspired by an old one in a museum. Many similar to this are stamped on linen, and are available with thread and instructions included. This one is not available.

Working Cross Stitch on Gingham

Almost anything that can be made of checked gingham can be decorated with a suitable cross-stitch design. Here is a partial list:

- Skirts
- Beach Cover-ups
- Maternity Smocks
- Blouses
- Children's smocks, aprons, dresses, bibs, overalls, coveralls, etc.
- Aprons
- Dresses
- Pot Holders
- Band trimming on towels
- Curtains
- Dressing-table skirts
- Bedspreads
- Luncheon cloths
- Place mats
- Doll clothes
- Pillows
- Picture frames
- Toys
- Pajama bags
- Cocktail napkins

Here are a number of cross-stitch and other designs suitable for working on gingham. Suggestions for where to use some of them are shown in the sketches.

Checked gingham furnishes a natural guide for working cross-stitch and many other stitches. Follow the design diagrams and work over the checks, skipping or filling in as necessary. The motif will become larger or smaller according to the size of the checks.

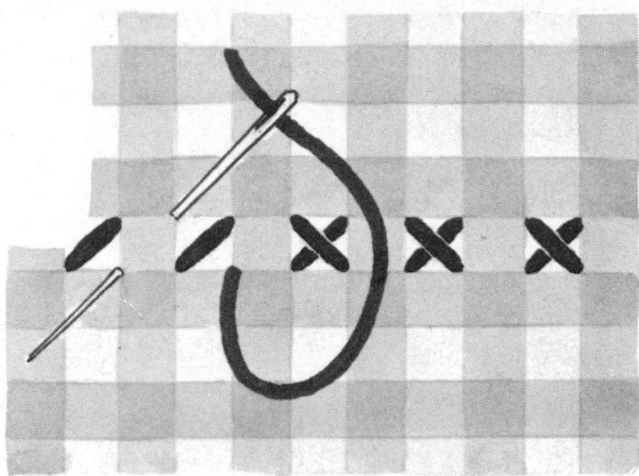

Cross-stitch may be worked from right to left, or left to right, but it looks best when all the top stitches slant in the same direction. Slant all the rows in a design in one direction, then work back over the rows in the opposite direction. Follow the diagram for slanting the needle.

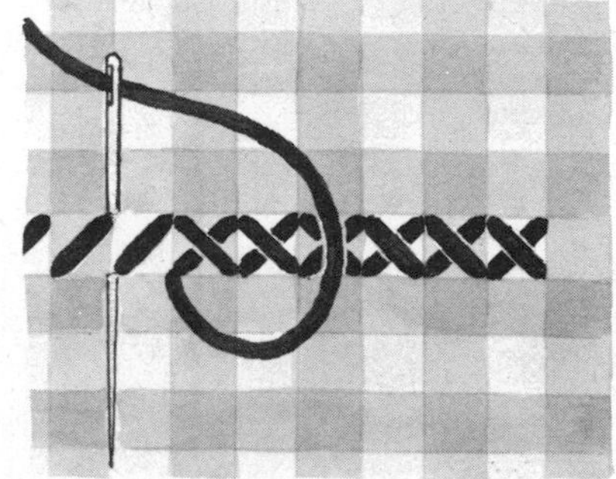

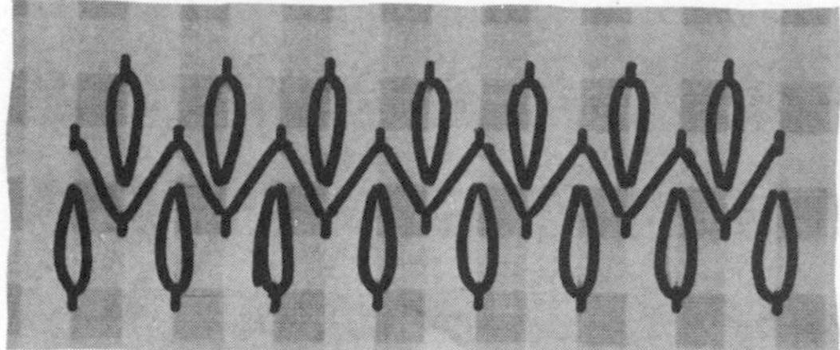

Try this on the front of a child's dress or around a skirt.

A simple design (at right) to work over pleated gingham. It consists of rows of blanket stitch, French Knots, and zigzag stitch.

Four quickly-made borders suitable for many decorative purposes such as curtains, skirts, aprons.

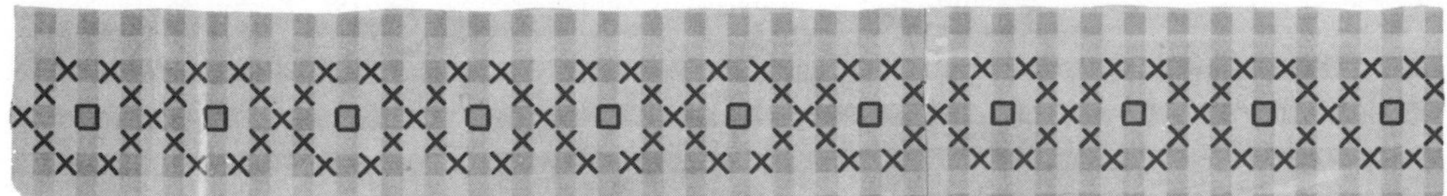

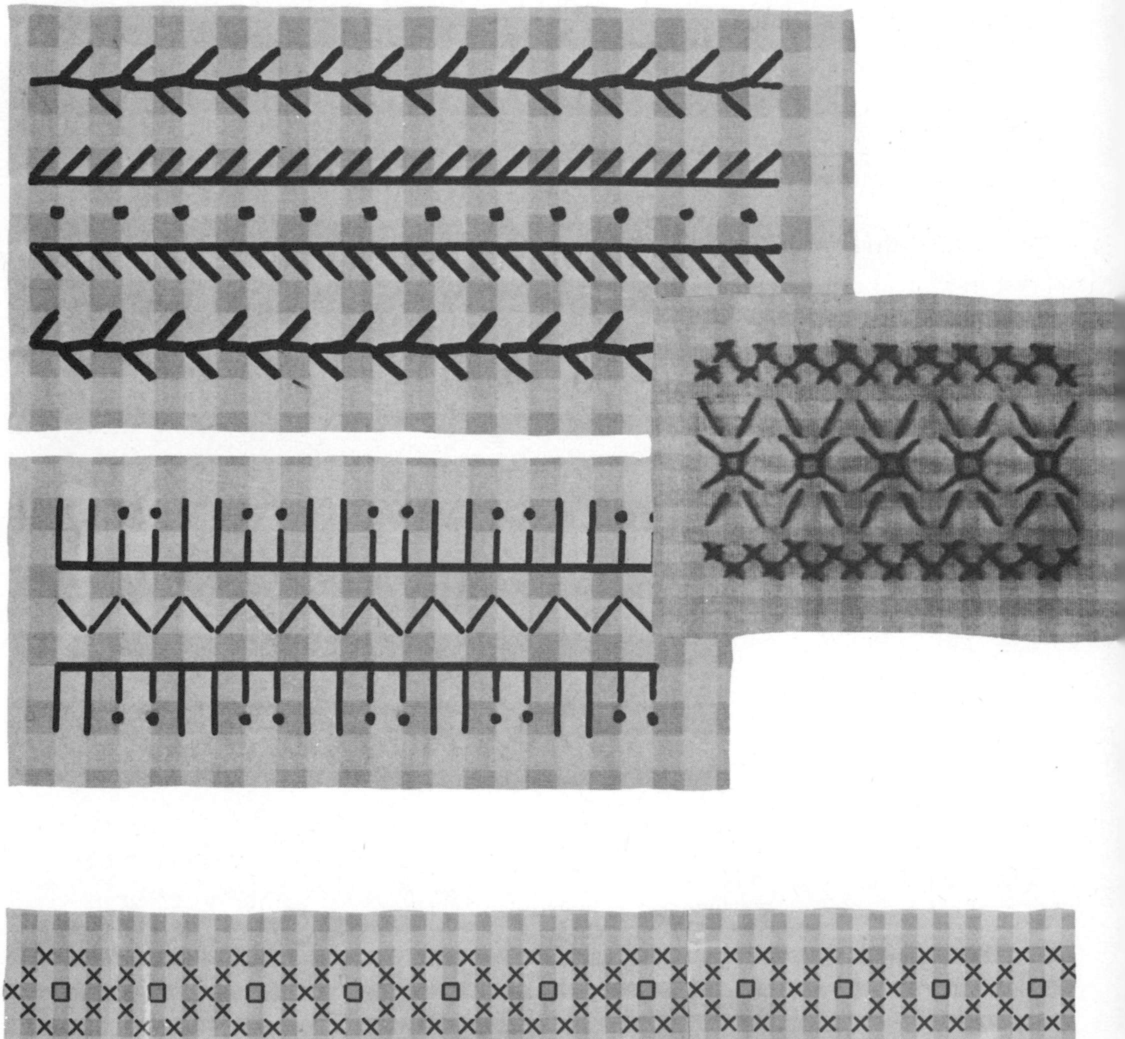

A simple and effective medallion (above) which can be worked on gingham cut on the bias or on the straight of the material.

Kerchiefs are always popular. For Mother: Cut a 27″ square of gingham in half diagonally. Hem the edges, then work a narrow border of cross-stitch on the two straight sides. For Daughter, start with a 20″ square.

A simple flower form cut from small-checked gingham and applied to larger checks and outlined with baby rickrack. Center is made of outline stitch and back stitch.

Big medallions make a lovely border on café curtains in kitchen or bedroom.

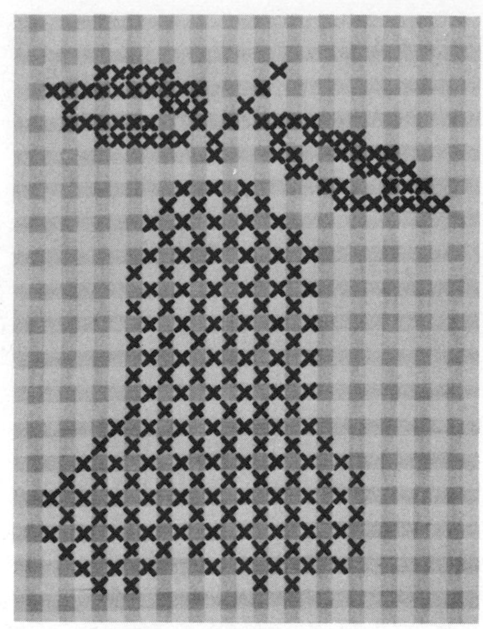

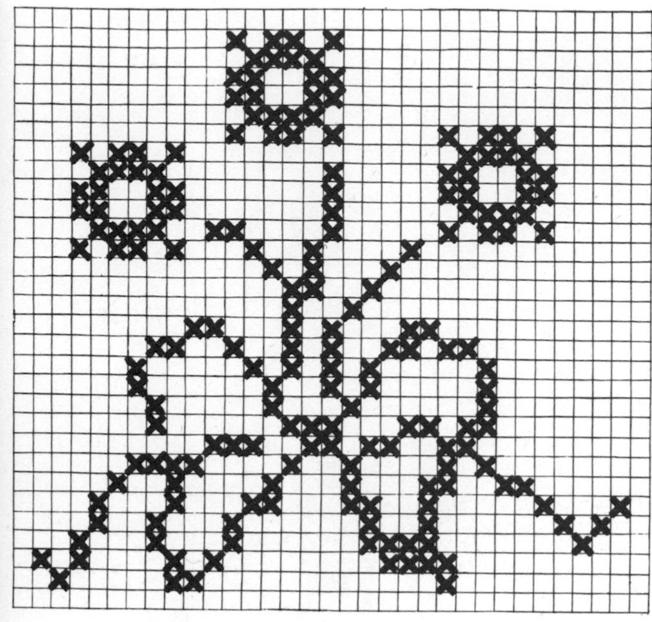

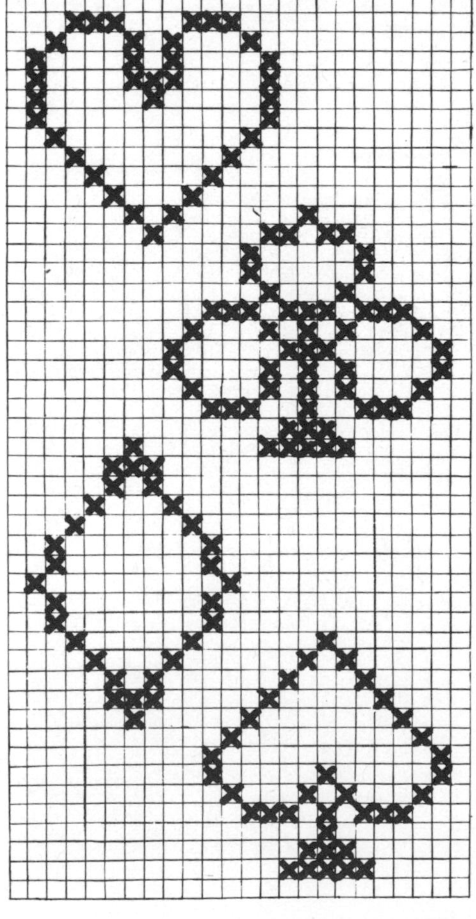

Animals, butterflies, fishes, or a charming border are fun to work and fun for the small fry to wear on dresses and play clothes.

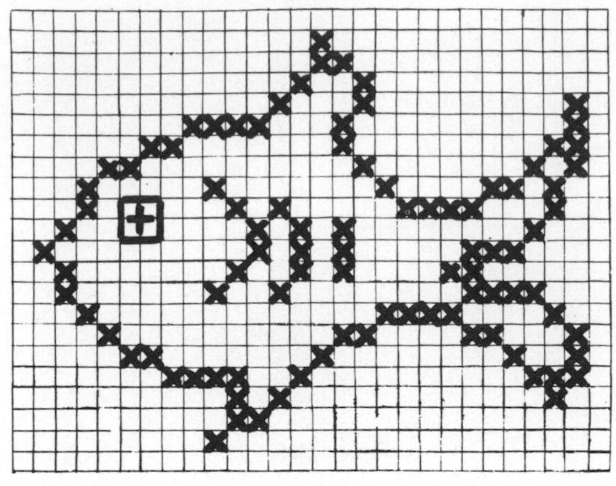

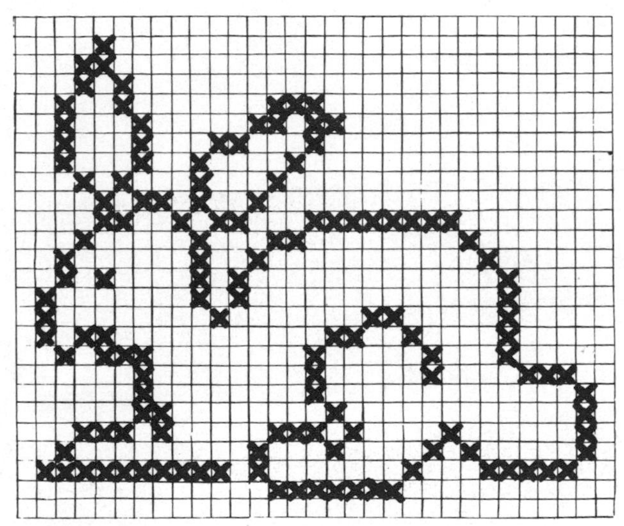

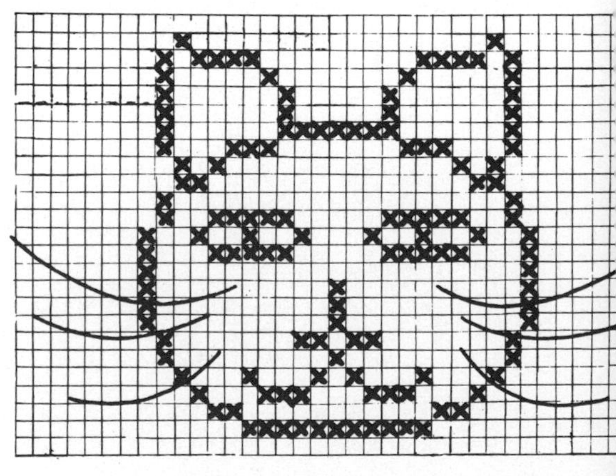

Mother's Skirt and Child's Pinafore or Sun Dress

Use any simple pattern for a child's pinafore with a yoke. Be sure there is enough fulness below the yoke to allow for pleating the gingham as shown. Embroider pinafore using 4 strands of floss. Work 2 rows of herringbone stitch and 2 rows of French knots holding pleats in place below yoke (see photograph on page 148). Work a row of double cross-stitch across center of yoke.

Applying Trimming Band on Mother's Skirt

See photograph on page 147

Fold a yard of small-checked gingham in half diagonally and cut enough 7½″-wide bands to make a little more than 3 yards (see diagram). Leave ends on the diagonal.

Sew pieces together with diagonal seams matching checks. Trim seams and press open.

Pin band on skirt an even distance from lower edge. Band should be about 7 inches above lower edge of skirt on a 26-inch long skirt. (This is optional and should be adjusted to look well on the length of skirt you are making.) Overlap bias ends, trim, allowing for seam. Turn in one end, match checks as well as possible and baste. Join with invisible hand hemming.

Turn under raw edges at top and bottom of band ½″ on each side and baste. Lay a row of rickrack on each edge, pin or baste in place and stitch.

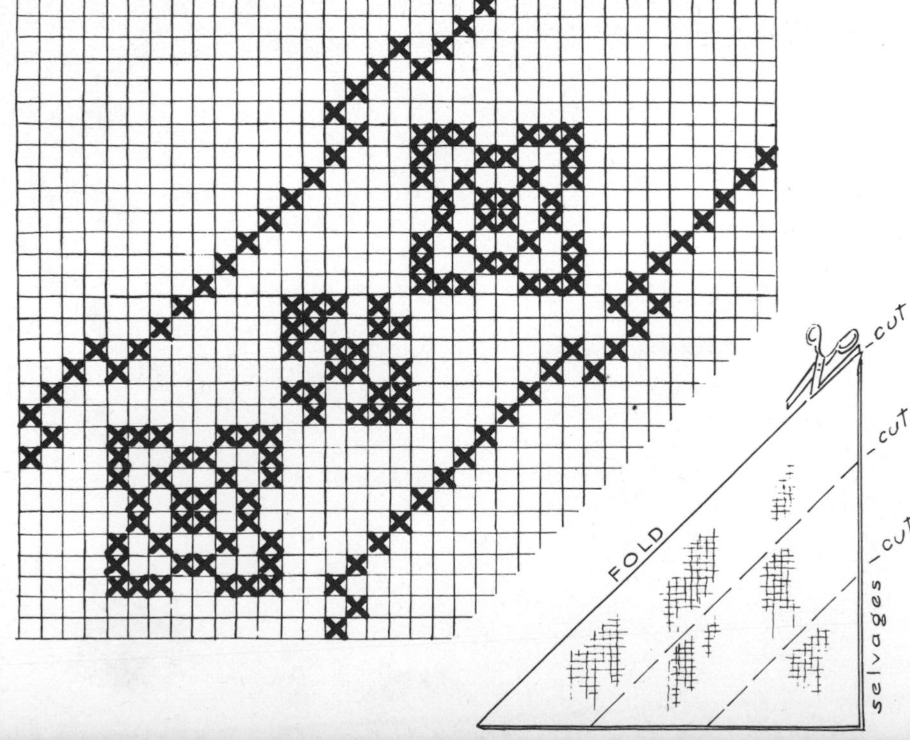

Color Plate 1 IN-A-WALL SEWING ROOM

A fully equipped sewing room can be tucked into a tiny space. Folding doors backed by full-length mirrors hide it from sight when not in use. *To order plans, see page 2.*

Color Plate 2 THE WORLD OF FABRICS

Here are some examples: Row 1. Fabrics of synthetic fibers: Fleece, printed tricot, plain jersey, printed linenlike fabric, nylon jersey, metallic sheer, quilted nylon, fur fabric, two-faced bonded flannel, rayon challis, shantung weave, rayon checked fabric, stretch, rayon velvet, stretch in woven checks, novelty crepe, diagonal knit, bonded lace, nylon organdy. Row 2. The top group is woolen fabric: Woven checks, novelty looped weave, sheer wool, coating, woven checked twill weave, wool crepe, wool fleece, chinchilla weave, novelty weave, slubbed crepe, tweed, diagonal-weave lightweight coating, wool jersey, hound's tooth check. The lower group is linen: Natural, fine dress, herringbone nubby-weave, coarser dress. Row 3. Silk fabrics: Silk organdy, chiffon, printed taffeta, plain taffeta, habuti, printed satin, shantung, printed silk, twill-weave shantung taffeta, plaid silk broadcloth, novelty weave, silk linen, china silk, raw silk, twill-weave Italian silk, printed surah, shantung taffeta, herringbone-weave silk tweed. Row 4. Cotton fabrics: printed sateen, corded weave, gingham, rep, printed lawn, broadcloth, woven plaid, woven stripe, watered print, plissé, seersucker, printed piqué, denim, printed poplin, striped dimity, printed voile, petit point piqué, outing flannel, ribbed weave, pinwale corduroy, corduroy, printed percale, duck, dimity, chambray.

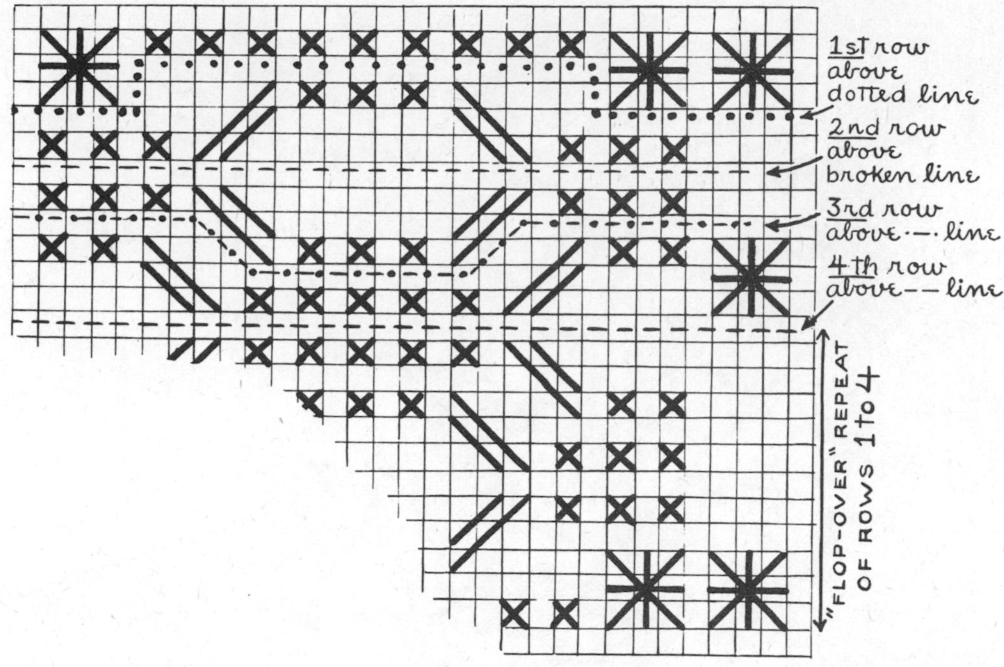

A rather elaborate band to decorate a favorite overblouse.

Follow diagram for cross-stitch and, using 5 strands of floss, work the pattern, *centering* it on the bias band.

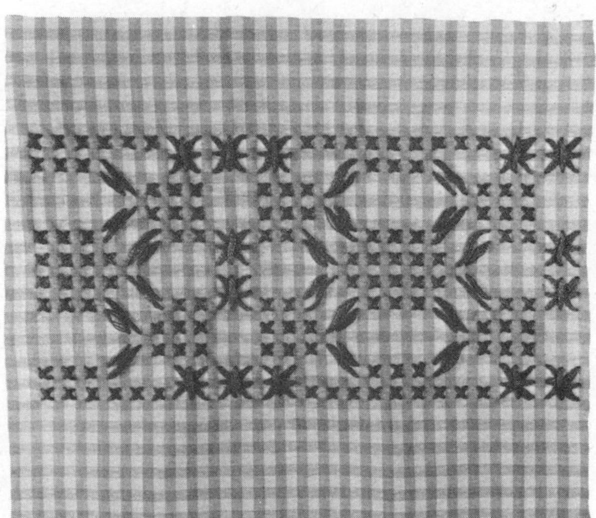

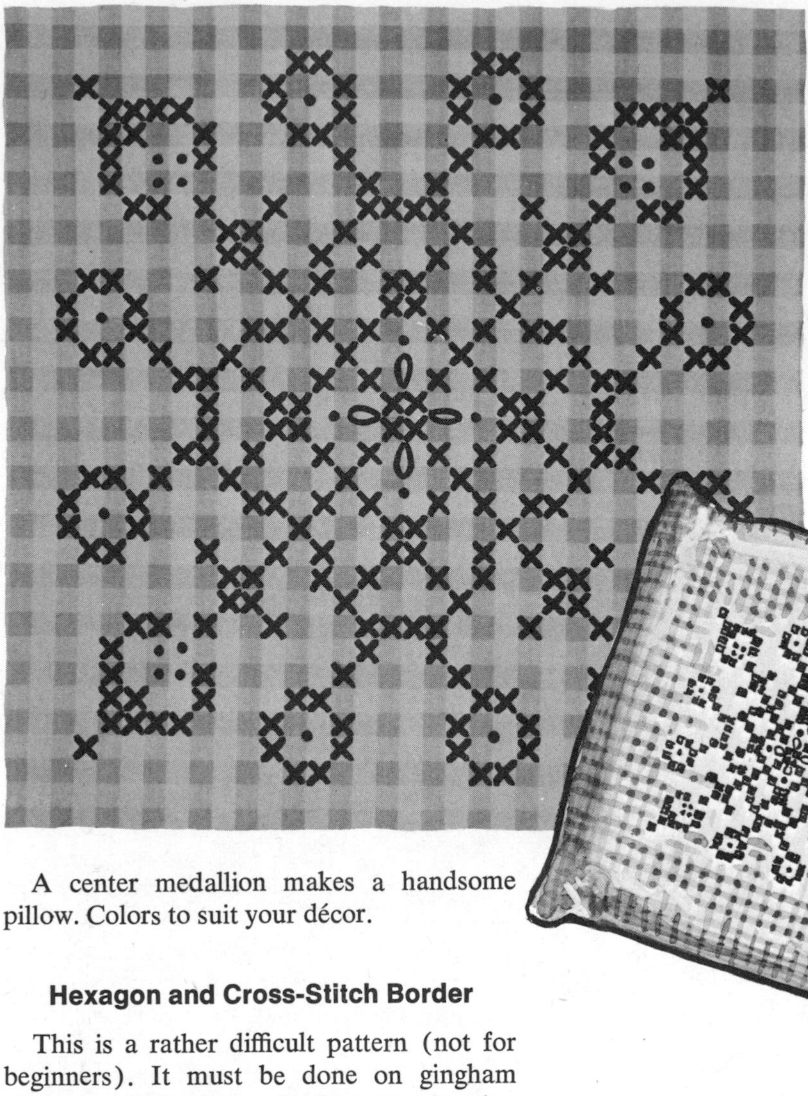

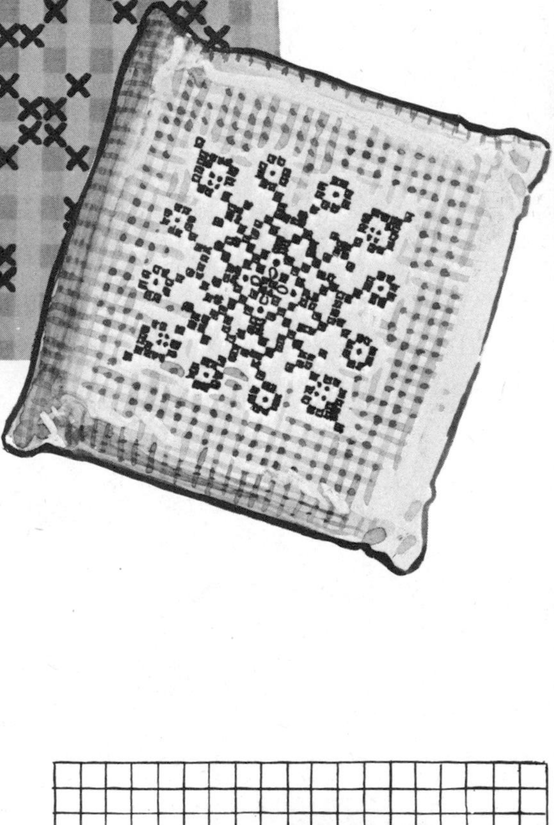

A center medallion makes a handsome pillow. Colors to suit your décor.

Hexagon and Cross-Stitch Border

This is a rather difficult pattern (not for beginners). It must be done on gingham which has been cut on the bias. A trimming band can be cut and applied, and this design worked on it.

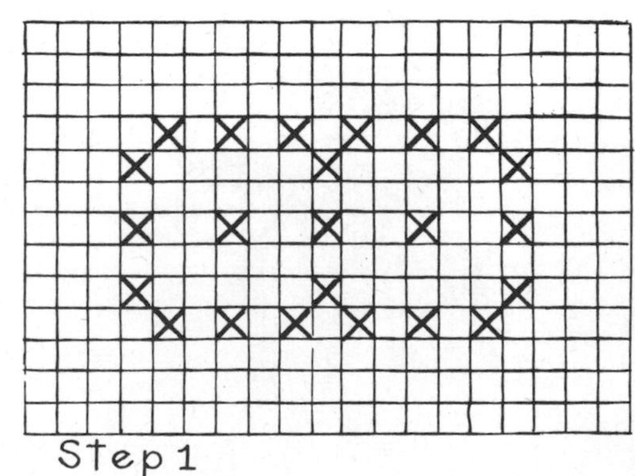

Follow the steps 1 through 7 shown in the diagrams. Also follow the numbering on the diagrams as you work. The design will be zigzag when finished and can be used on curtains, dressing-table skirts, bedspreads, or wearing apparel.

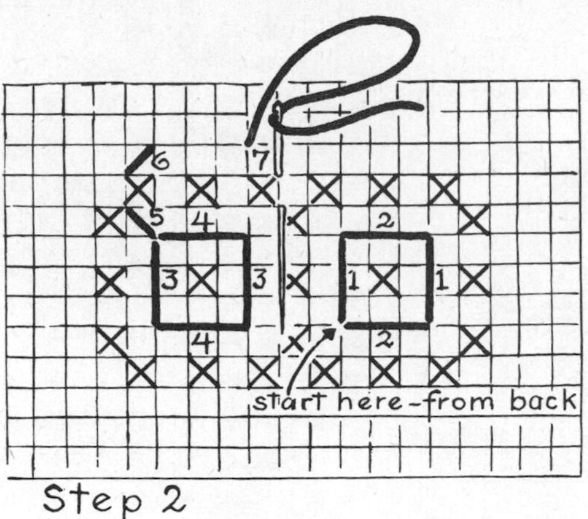

Step 2

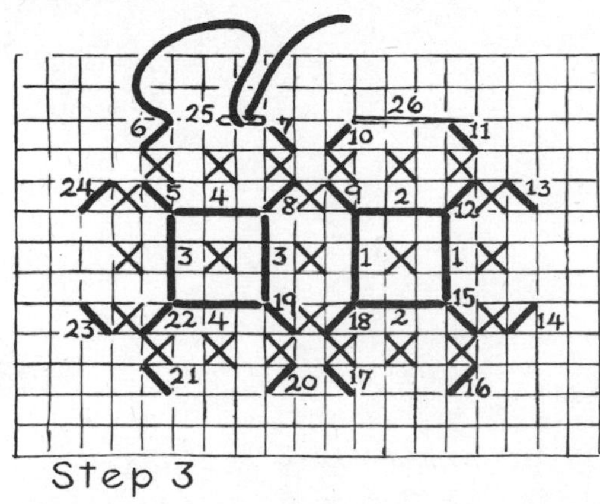

Step 3

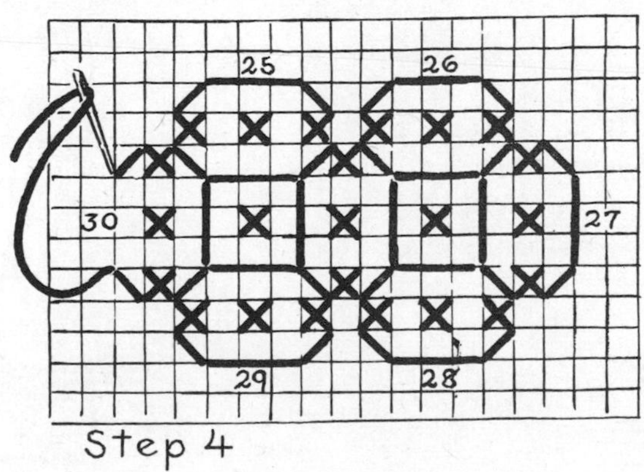

Step 4

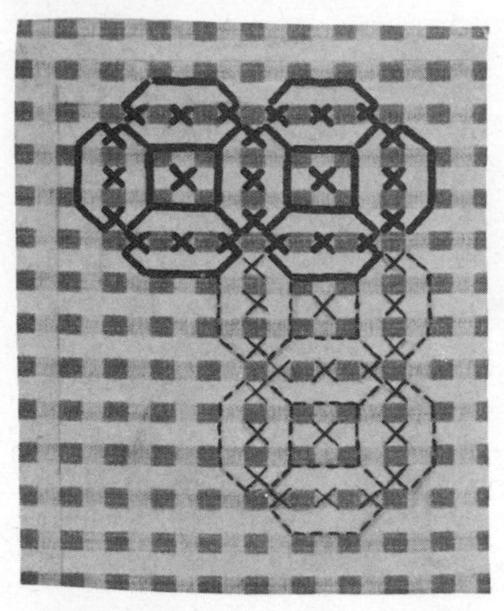

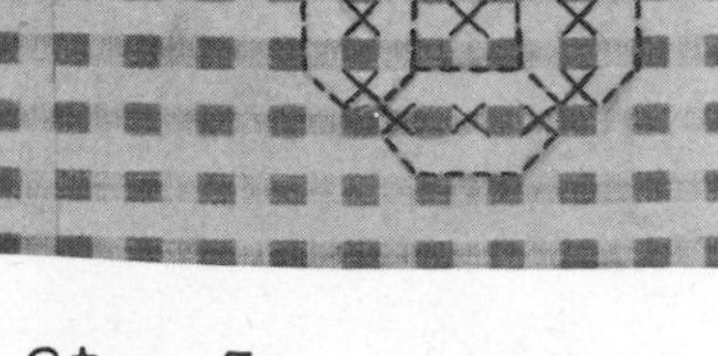

Step 5

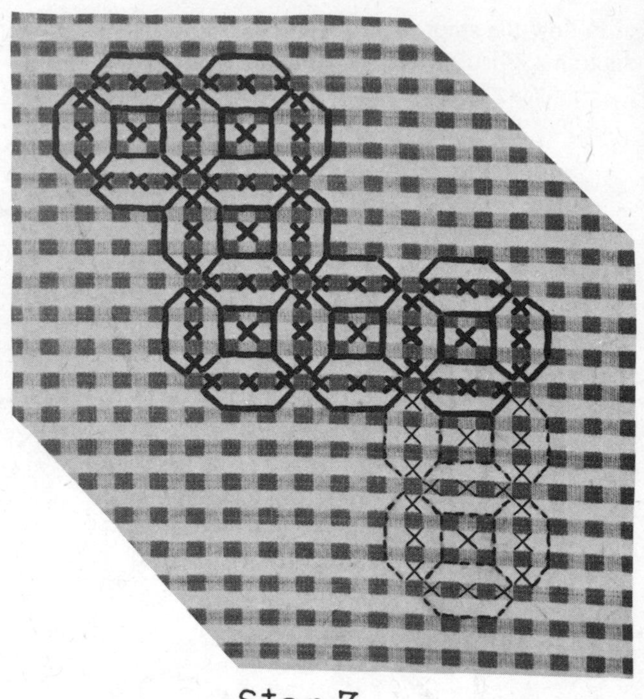

Step 7

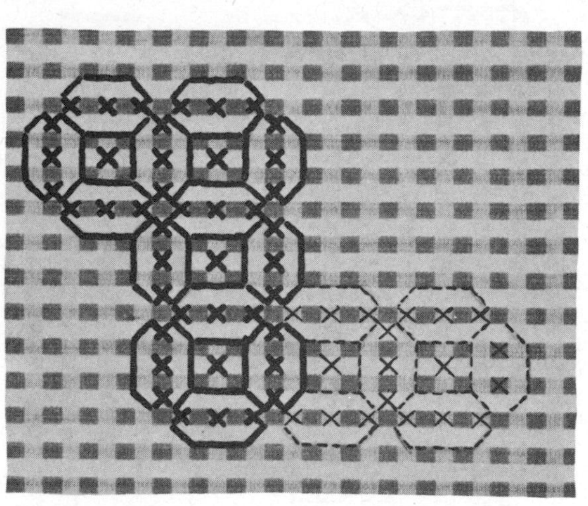

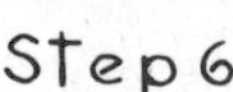

Step 6

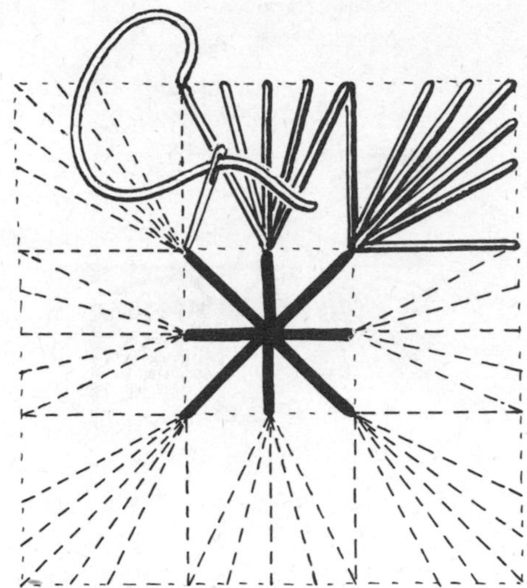
Fig. 1

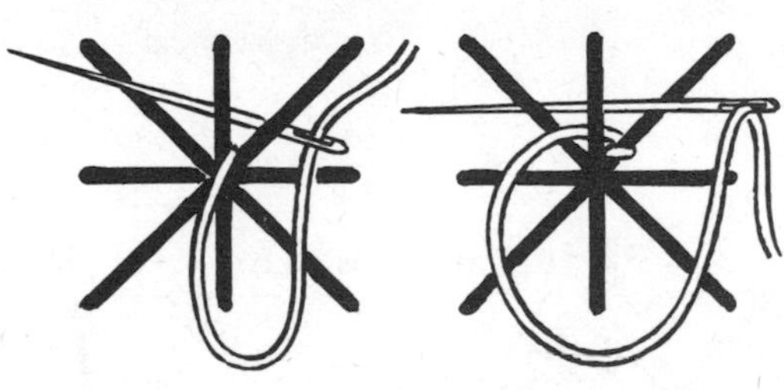
Fig. 2 Fig. 3

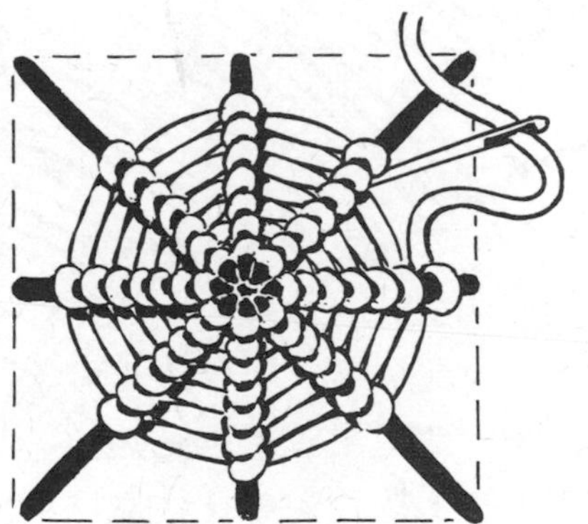
Fig. 4

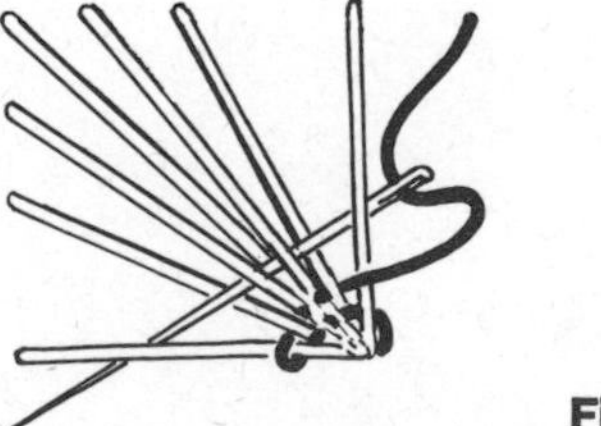
Fig. 5

TENERIFE

These motifs have the appearance of drawn work but are worked on top of the fabric. Since they are square in shape, they are easily done on checked gingham. Suitable for place mats, luncheon cloths, curtains, skirts, etc. Follow the diagrams.

1. In making webs, work from the outside to the point where lines converge. Make a large, double cross-stitch in the center.

2, 3, & 4. Weaving center: Bring needle out between any 2 stitches near the center. Slip the needle under 2 web threads (as shown) *each* time. This makes 1 back stitch. Work around, filling in almost to end of web stitches.

5. Weaving corners: Bring needle out where web stitches converge. Weave 7 loops (see diagram) over all web stitches. Then weave 5 loops over 5 web stitches. Then weave 6 loops over remaining 3 web stitches. Bring needle to back of work and fasten. Work remaining 3 corners the same.

The other Tenerife designs are worked in much the same way.

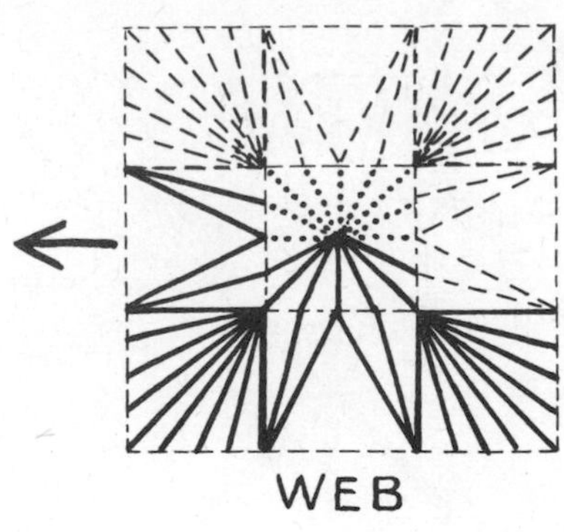

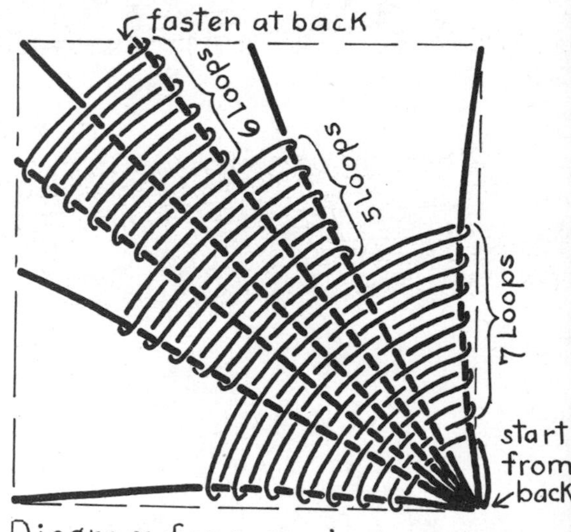

Diagram for weaving corners

Fig. 6

Our great-grandmothers combined stitches when they set their "crazy quilts" together. Some of the results of their imaginations are delightful. Here are a few taken from an old silk "crazy quilt." These would be particularly suitable for trimming baby things and little girls' dresses.

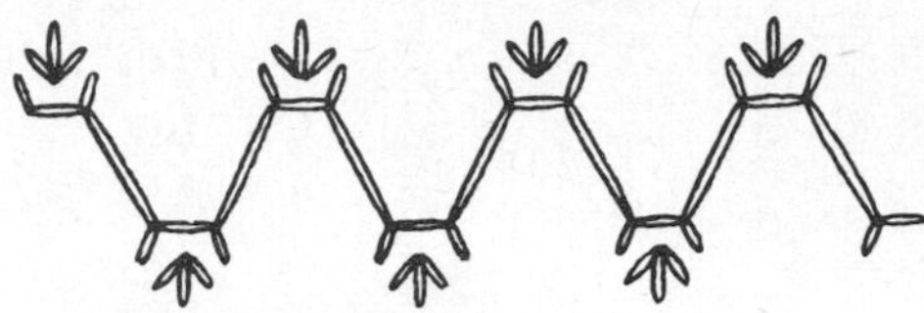

Briar and Hen Tracks

Ball and Briar

Fagot and Turkey Track

COMBINING STITCHES

After learning a few of the stitches shown here, try combining some of them to make interesting borders. Some unusual and lovely effects can result. They will be very useful for decorating any number of articles, such as children's wear, place mats, pillows, table cloths, and skirts, and on flat decorations.

Above are a few examples of combinations of stitches. They may be used on many articles, from place mats to aprons and little girls' dresses.

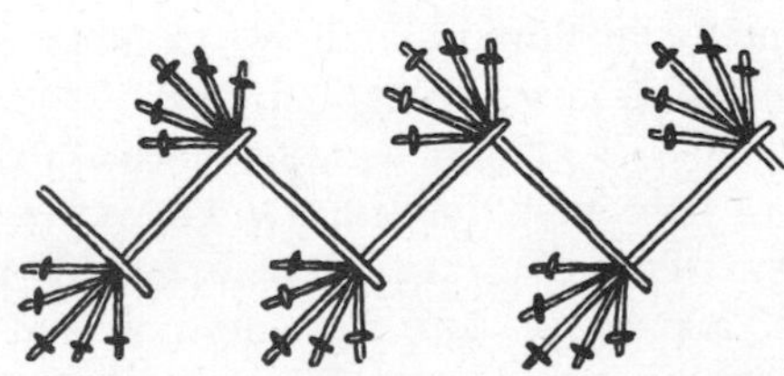

Witch Hazel

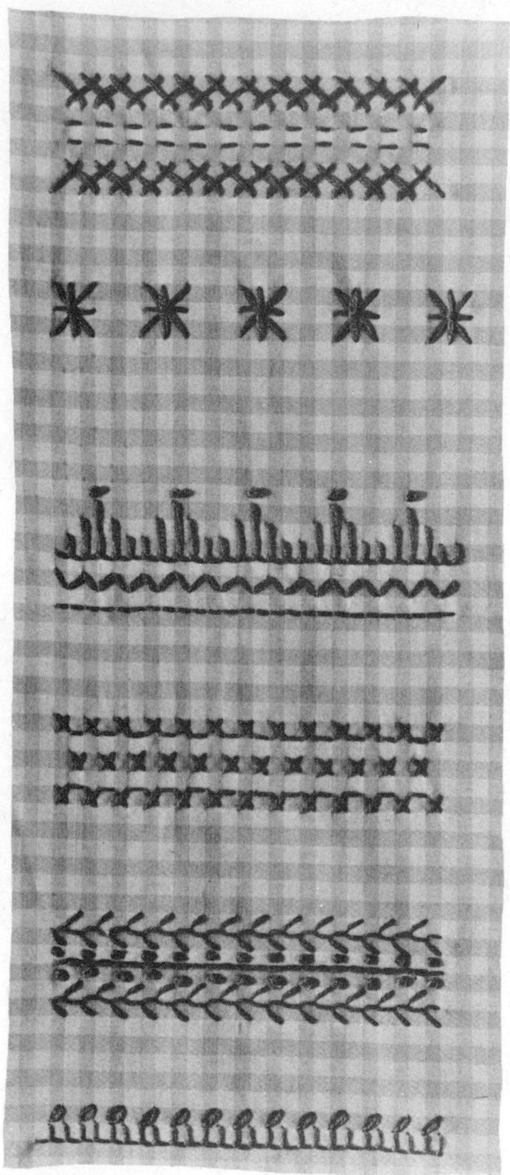

A border of rickrack in graduated sizes plus simple embroidery stitches gives an elaborate effect without much work. Running stitch and lazy daisy stitch were used. Bright red on white organdy is effective, but many other color arrangements would be equally good. Suitable for borders on place mats, aprons, or little girls' pinafores.

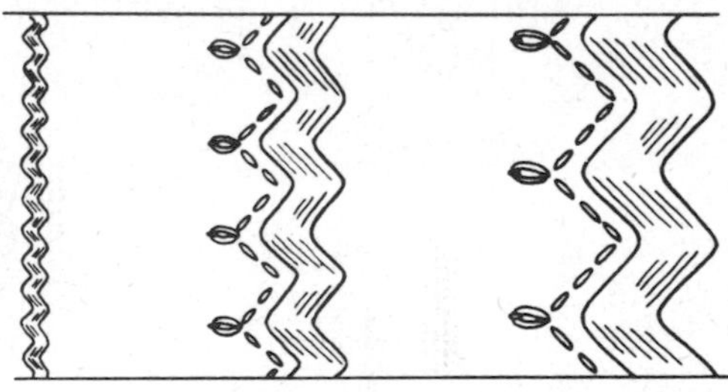

Rickrack Plus Embroidery

Arrange medium size rickrack into five-pointed star flowers, and sew to fabric with invisible stitches. Using 2 strands of embroidery floss, work blanket stitch around petals. Work stem in outline stitch and leaves in lazy daisy stitch. Finish edge with narrow hem and rickrack on top. This motif is suitable for trimming place mats, guest towels, aprons, children's garments, etc.

Appliqué

See quilt chapter for appliqué with edges turned under.

Appliqué patches may also be held in place with blanket stitches. Cut the patch on the line (no turn-under allowance) and hold in place with blanket stitches.

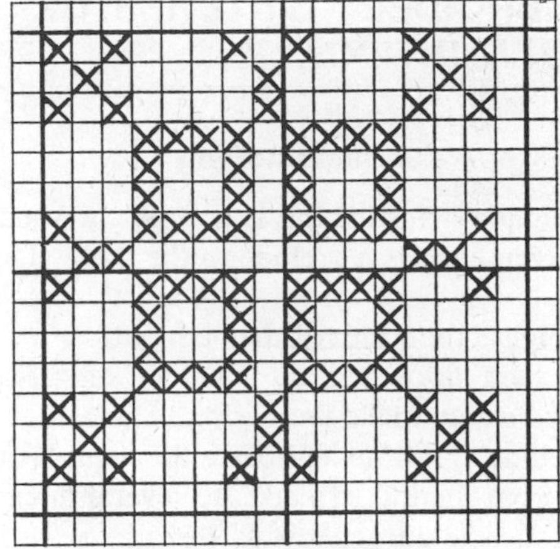

Cross Stitch Motif

This simple design in cross stitch can be done by counting threads on linen or other fabric with an even weave. It can be repeated any number of times to make runners, table cloths, pillows, etc.

The cross stitch is worked over 3 threads each way of the material. The dividing lines are worked in herringbone stitch over 6 threads in depth with 3 threads picked up on the needle.

Arrange the design as a border, corner pattern, or as an all-over design.

A suggestion for a color scheme: On cream linen, use deep beige or gray for the herringbone dividing lines and light red and black for the cross stitch motifs. Finish edge with a narrow hand hem. (Page 23.)

Follow the photograph when working the design.

EMBROIDERY STITCHES OF MORE INTRICACY

Hemstitching

Simple hemstitching is not difficult, and it is given here as a prelude to the more elaborate types.

Figure the width of the hem. At the top of the hem draw out the number of threads necessary to make the desired width of hemstitching. Turn up and baste the hem. Working from right to left, take up several threads; pull needle through with thread *under* the needle. Take next stitch through very edge of hem and draw up tightly. Continue these two stitches across row.

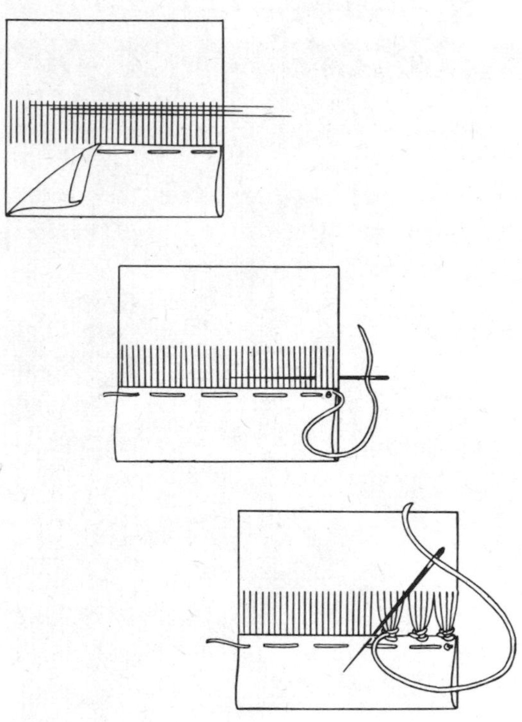

For double or ladder hemstitching with straight bars, work along other side of drawn threads picking up same group of threads.

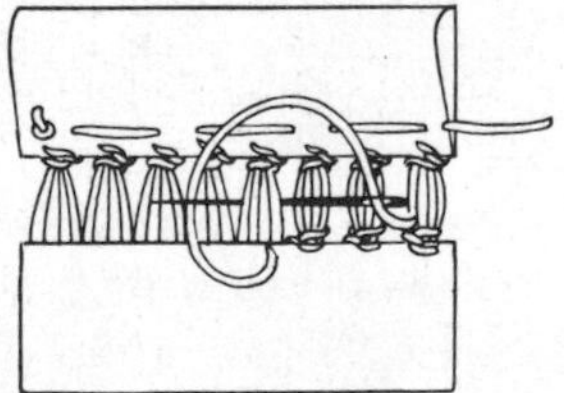

For diagonal hemstitching, be sure to pick up an even number of threads when working first row. When working second row, pick up half from each group, making a zigzag line.

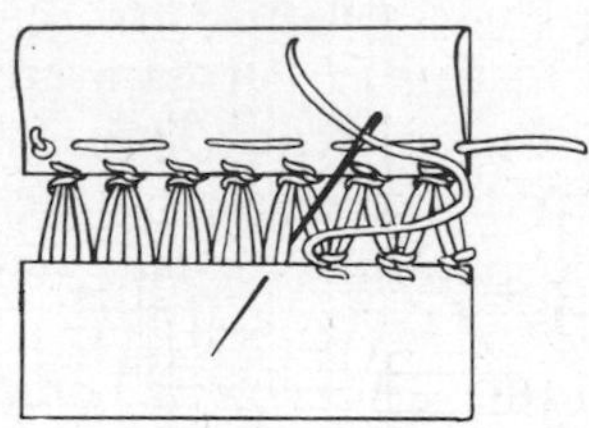

Italian Hemstitching. Draw out two rows of threads above hem, leaving a narrow space of linen between. Make a row of regular hemstitching just above the hem. Starting at right and using same clusters above and below, pass needle under first group of threads of lower row. *Insert needle at right of this group and bring out at left of group above.

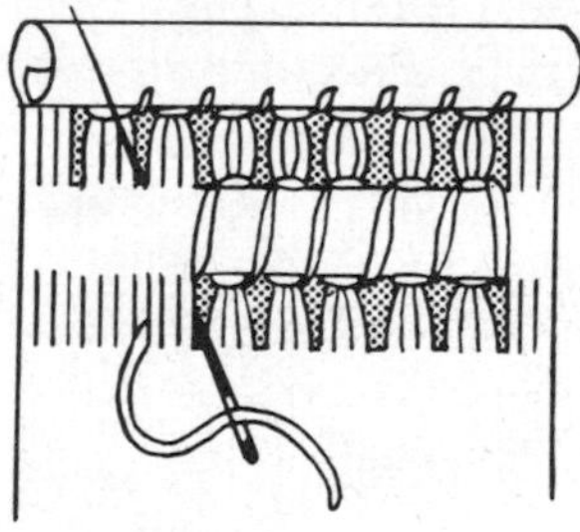

Pass needle under top group and draw up. Bring needle out at left of lower group. Repeat from * across.

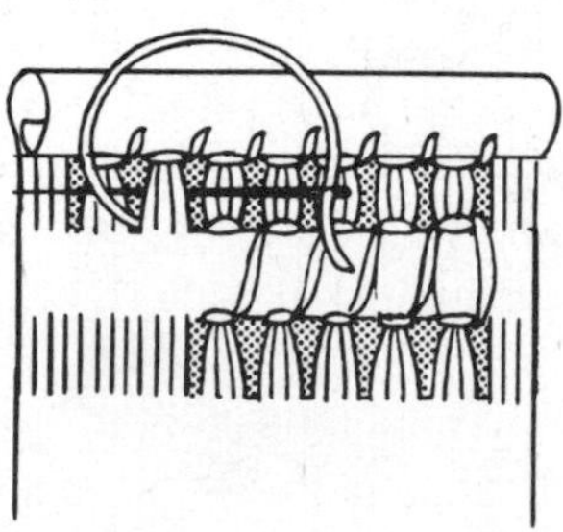

See top of next page for corner showing Italian hemstitching and drawn work.

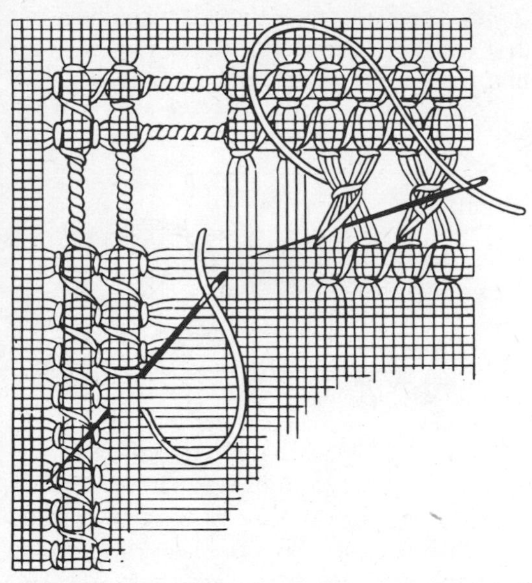

Drawn Work

Draw threads in a somewhat wider space than for regular hemstitching (½- to ¾-inch wide). Work plain hemstitching on both edges in spoke or ladder effect. Work down the center with a chain stitch which holds together groups of three clusters (see diagram). The thread is carried along between

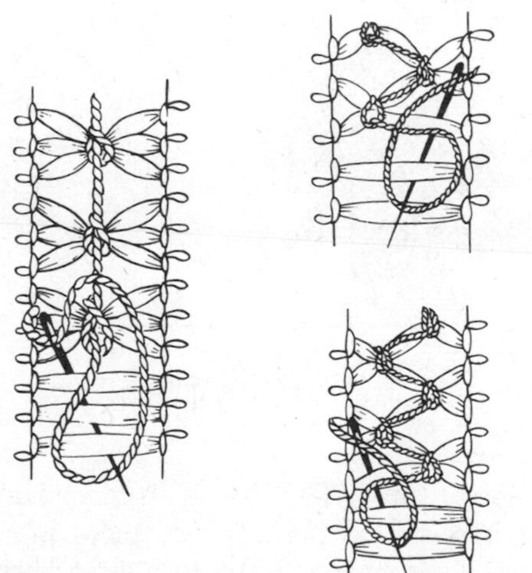

the stitches. In a wider space this same stitch may be used in zigzag fashion. Do not pull thread tightly between clusters.

Another simple drawn-work stitch: bring needle from right to left under the second cluster of threads. Turn needle from left to right on top of and picking up the first cluster. This causes the clusters to cross each other. Do not pull thread too tight.

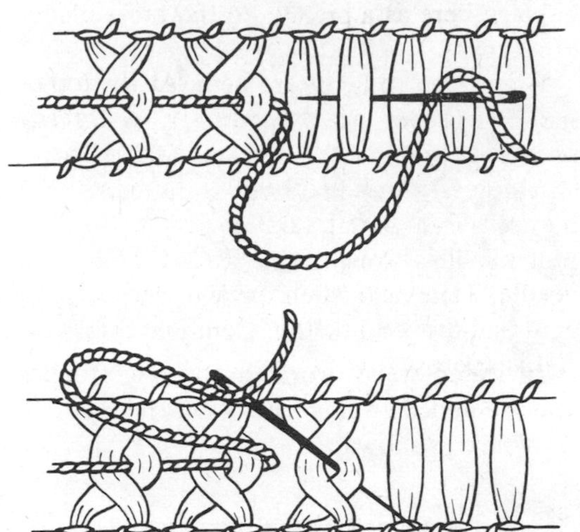

If working a corner, knot the second thread over the first.

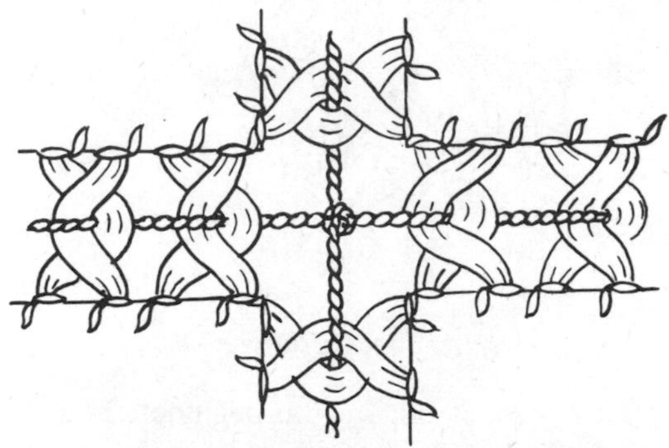

For a wider area, two rows or a double twist may be made.

Finishing corners in open drawn work:
Cut and loosen threads on both sides of corner and conceal ends in hem.

Work hemstitching on edges or overcast. Add long stitches from corner to corner and weave center in spider-web fashion.

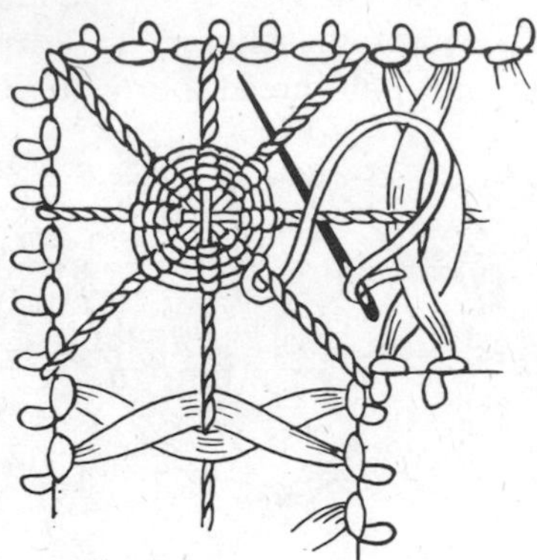

In wider drawn work, more long stitches may be added from corner to corner.

Weave as shown.

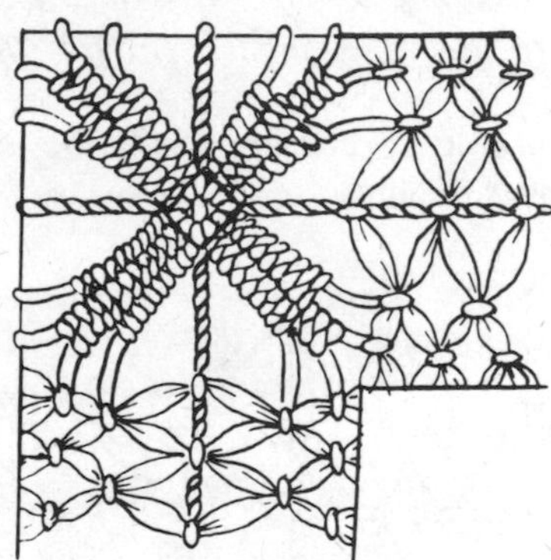

Italian Cutwork

This work is not for the beginner. It may be simple or elaborate, but must have the lines drawn or stamped on the linen as a guide for working.

To Work a Simple Design. Draw a simple diagram, as given here, on the linen. Make small running stitches from A to B, then from B carry the thread diagonally to C. Overcast this thread without catching fabric. Make running stitches from B to D; then carry thread diagonally from D to A catching diagonals together at center. Overcast this diagonal, which brings you back to D. Work running stitches from D to C, from C to A, and from A to E (center of side). Run

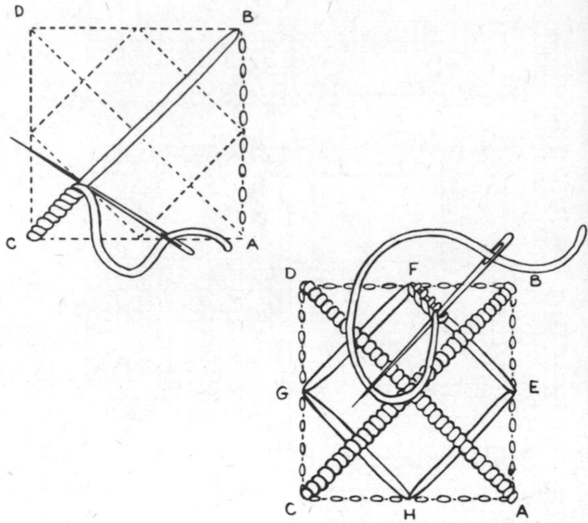

diagonal threads from E to F, from F to G, from G to H, and back to E, passing needle through diagonal bars and catching into fabric on the running stitches. Buttonhole over the diagonals, working picots in center if desired. Cut away linen close to running stitches and cover with overcasting or with buttonhole stitch.

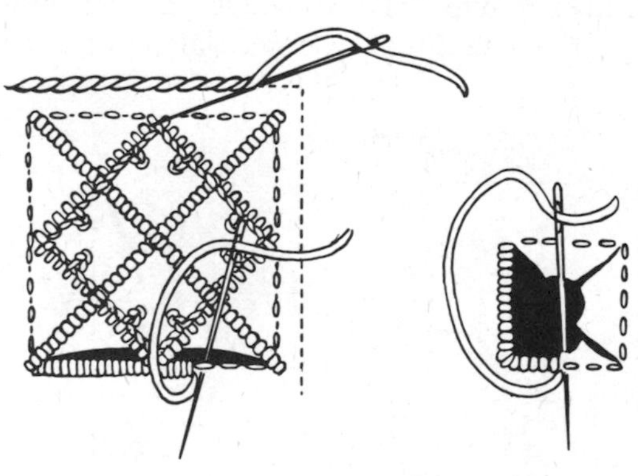

Picots

Single Picot. The thread is carried inside the hem to the point where picot is to be worked. Bring needle out; turn thread around needle 12 or 15 times. Draw thread through this spiral and insert needle in same place where it was drawn out. Slip needle through to next place.

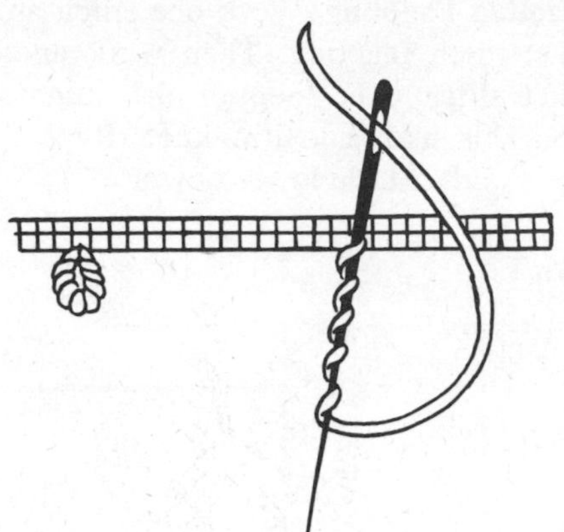

Buttonhole Stitch and Picots. Make a running stitch on the line where hem is to be turned. Turn the hem and, with edge of linen toward you, make several buttonhole stitches. Insert needle in last buttonhole stitch (not the fabric) and pull it through. Take another buttonhole stitch in the same thread. This makes a picot. Insert needle under last buttonhole stitch and bring needle out in correct position to continue buttonhole stitches.

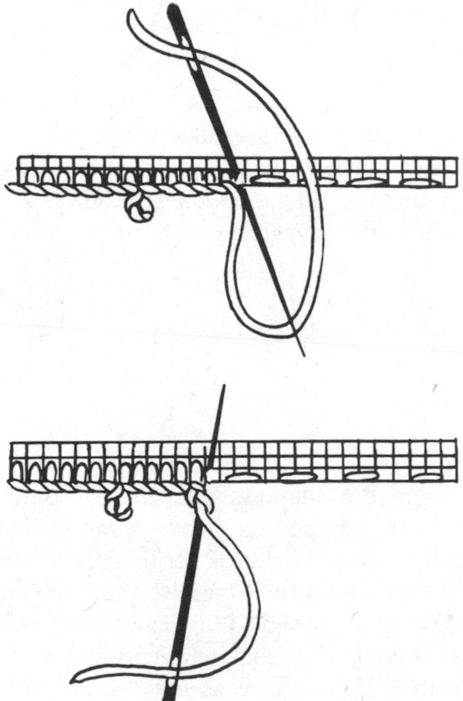

Overcast Edge with Picot. Hold edge away from you. Work overcast stitches and single picot as described at left.

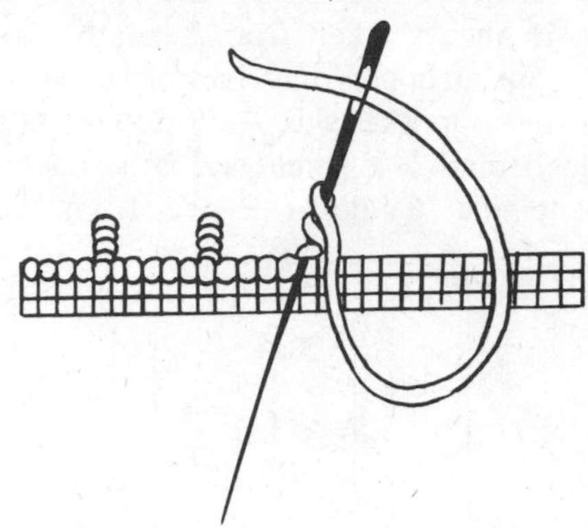

Cutwork

This type of work is sometimes called Richelieu embroidery and must be transferred to linen in some manner such as stamping or tracing so that there are clear-cut lines to follow. Very handsome designs can be purchased stamped on linen and ready to work.

The entire design is done in narrow buttonhole stitch and the background is then cut away to leave the design in relief. The purl of the buttonhole stitch must come on the edge which is to be cut away. A running stitch may be worked between the narrow lines before buttonholing to serve as padding. This gives a more raised effect. Some designs have bars added to connect the more open places. These are worked like the buttonhole bars described on page 136, without catching into the fabric.

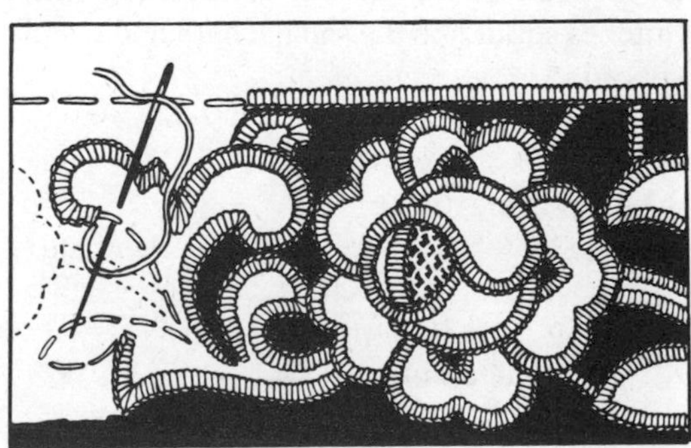

Fagoting

Criss-Cross Fagoting. Baste bias or straight folded edges on strips of paper an even distance apart. The stitch into the edge of the fabric is always taken from beneath. Bring needle out at upper right hand; then take a stitch on opposite side ¼″ down. *Pass needle behind last stitch and bring out on opposite side ¼″ down. Repeat from *.

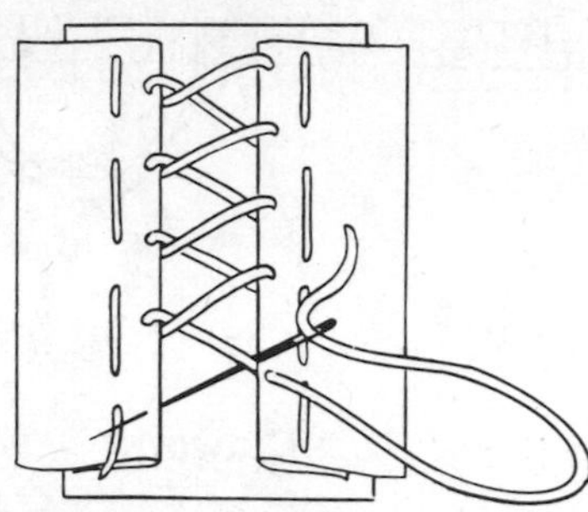

Bar Fagoting. Bring needle out at left side and insert directly opposite. Pull up stitch but leave enough to twist. Twist the stitch just made around the needle several times and bring needle out at left again. Slip needle down inside fabric to the place for the next stitch.

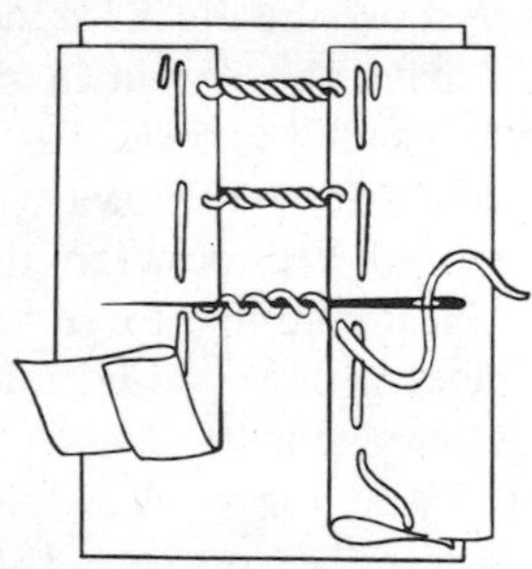

Blanket-Stitch Fagoting. A blanket stitch is worked first on one side then on the other. Stitches should be the same length and evenly spaced.

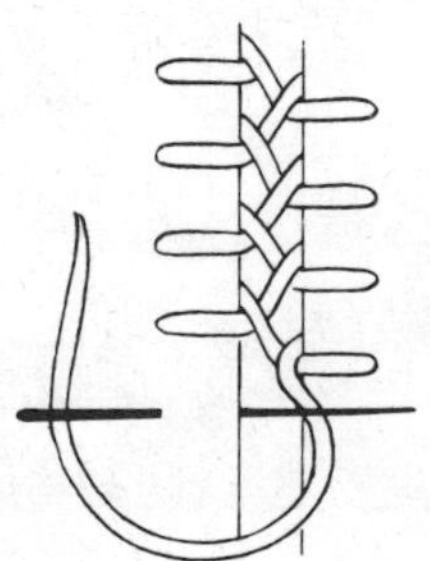

Knotted Fagoting. Work one stitch as for blanket-stitch fagoting. Then work another blanket stitch over loop of the stitch just made. This makes a firm knot. Repeat on opposite side a little lower down.

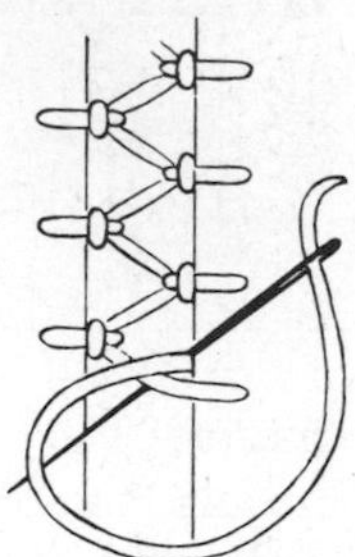

Whipped Blanket-Stitch Insertion. Work a row of blanket stitches along both edges of fabric. Hold together by catching into the loops of the blanket stitches.

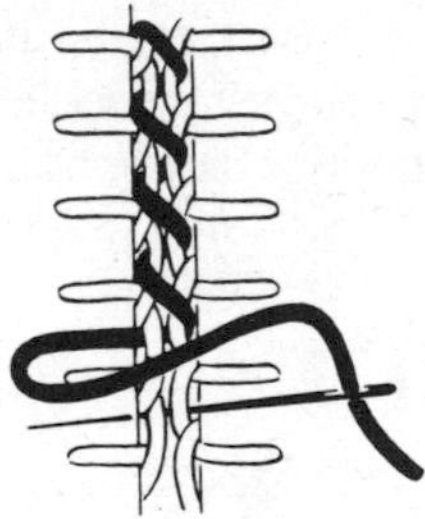

Blanket-Stitch Insertion. Work groups of blanket stitches (with center stitch longer) first on one side then on the other. Keep stitches evenly spaced and close together.

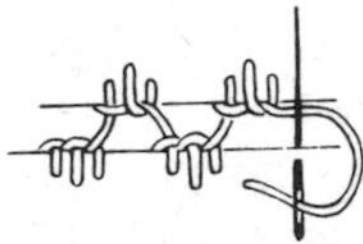

Fagoted Medallion. The design should be drawn or stamped on a foundation of heavy paper, stiff cambric, or scrim. Use double-fold bias binding and baste to the foundation following the design. Bias binding should be long enough to complete entire design if possible. If not, have as few "ends" as you can and always conceal them under another fold of the bias.

Use criss-cross fagoting to fill in the spaces, catching into the bias fold on each side.

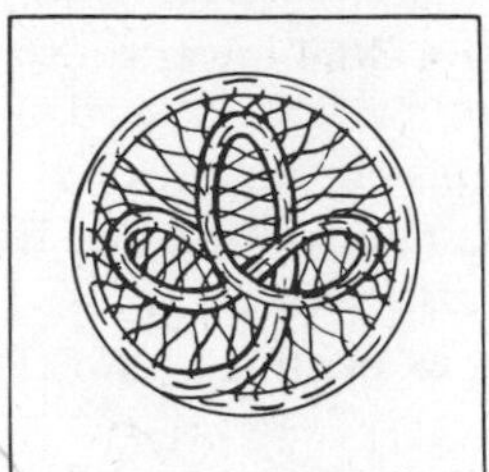

Remove the basting; this frees the medallion. Baste the medallion in place on the fabric. On the wrong side, attach with fine running stitch, catching outside row of bias fold. Cut away fabric from beneath, leaving a narrow edge. Roll and whip raw edge to medallion.

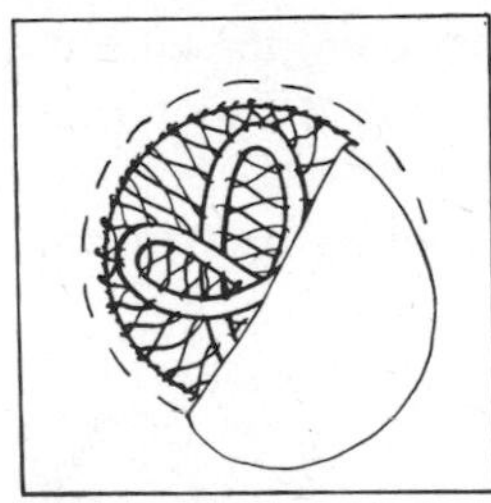

Candlewicking or Tufting

This stitch was used on early American coverlets. A special heavy soft thread is used. It is composed of many strands with little or no twist. Candlewicking thread, a large needle, and muslin which has not been laundered are needed.

The design is indicated by dots. The stitch is a simple running stitch. Pick up about ⅛″ on the needle and leave about ¾″ between stitches. Several stitches may be taken on the needle at one time. Do not draw thread tightly enough to pucker fabric.

Cut each top stitch in half. When all tufts have been completed, dip in water to shrink fabric. This will hold tufts in place. Dry without ironing. Shake and brush tufts to fluff them into little balls. Use single thread for small tufts, double thread for large ones.

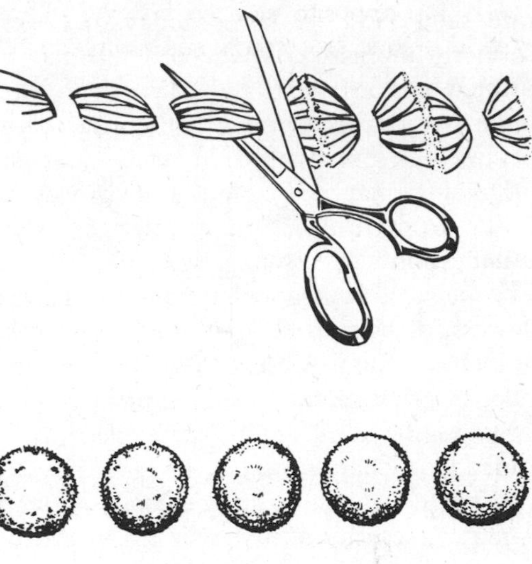

Maltese or Tassel Stitch

This stitch produces small tassels instead of tufts. It can also be used for tufting patterns. It was originally used for making rugs. Make a short stitch slanting slightly upward to the left and leaving an end (cluster of strands). Insert needle to right of center, in line with the point where it came out and bring it out at the center. Cut all strands the same length.

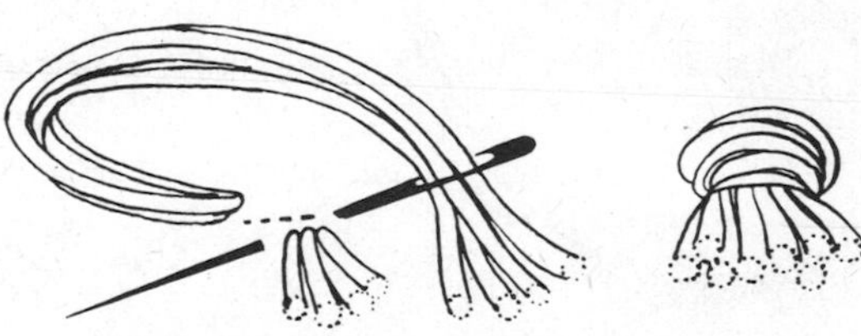

Crewel Embroidery

Crewel embroidery (occasionally called Jacobean embroidery) was very popular in England in the latter part of the seventeenth century.

The work is done with loosely twisted woolen yarn, known as crewel yarn, and is usually worked on linen, linen twill, and woolen fabrics. However, other background materials may also be used. Crewel embroidery is *always* worked with crewel yarns. Traditional English designs were more elaborate than those preferred today and were formerly thought to have been inspired by printed cottons from the Far East. After intensive research, many authorities now believe the opposite to be true—that the original design motifs found their way to India from England. The designs were usually floral or arboreal, with the Tree of Life being a popular motif; unusual leaves, flowers, or birds were often worked into the branches. Embroiderers seldom observed rules of proportion; birds or exotic leaves, as large as the deer in the same piece, only added to its charms.

When crewel embroidery came to colonial America, scarcity of materials led to greatly simplified designs and stitches. A variety of stitches were used to outline the motifs, and filling stitches were used for areas inside leaves and flowers. The colorings, soft rich blendings of blues, greens, muted reds, and tawny yellows and gold, look particularly well on natural linen.

Crewel embroidery is used, for the most part, on upholstery and drapery fabrics, pictures, wall hangings, chair and footstool coverings. It is also sometimes used on wearing apparel such as handbags, sweaters, blouses, and jackets.

The variety and combination of stitches are endless. Long-and-short (Kensington) stitch, blanket stitch, outline stitch, chain stitch, coral stitch, satin stitch, herringbone, French knot, feather stitch, couching and laid work, fishbone stitches, etc., are some of the stitches employed in this work. (See section on Stitches for diagrams and instructions.)

Some of the loveliest examples of crewel work can be seen in museums on early American bed draperies and spreads. It was probably the earliest form of embroidery done in this country by pioneer women.

Color Plate 3 EMBROIDERED WALL HANGING

This one is called "Birds of Bright Plumage." Worked on linen with linen thread, it is typical of the many beautiful designs available in kit form in stores and through the mail.

Color Plate 4 CREWEL-EMBROIDERED WALL HANGING

Inspired by an old-fashioned bell pull, this design is worked in finest crewel wool on linen. Crewel embroidery kits, including the yarn and instructions, are widely available.

This is a simple motif for crewel embroidery which may be traced, transferred onto your own fabric, and arranged for maximum advantage. It is suitable for a small pillow or footstool, or it can be used as a border. You may also arrange your own color scheme.

The solid lines can be worked in outline stitch or chain stitch, loops in lazy daisy, and so on. (Consult section on Stitches for other stitches and how to do them.)

Shown here, are several examples of the filling stitches sometimes used in leaves, flowers, etc. They are combinations of simple stitches such as cross stitch, French knot, satin stitch, running stitch, double cross stitch, etc., used in an all-over effect. Those shown here are worked inside of a simple floral shape, but they may be used in any space desired.

FILLING STITCHES

A variety of leaf and other motifs are illustrated here in detail to show how they are worked.

Color Plate 4 shows a wall hanging inspired by an old-fashioned bell pull. It is worked in soft glowing colors in the finest crewel wool on linen, and is typical of many designs to be found in kits sold in needlework shops.

This is an illustration of a crewel bed spread inspired by the Mary Breed quilt in the Metropolitan Museum. Similar designs are available in kit form.

Armenian Needlepoint Lace

All loops or meshes are made with knotted buttonhole stitch.

Hold fabric piece with edge away from

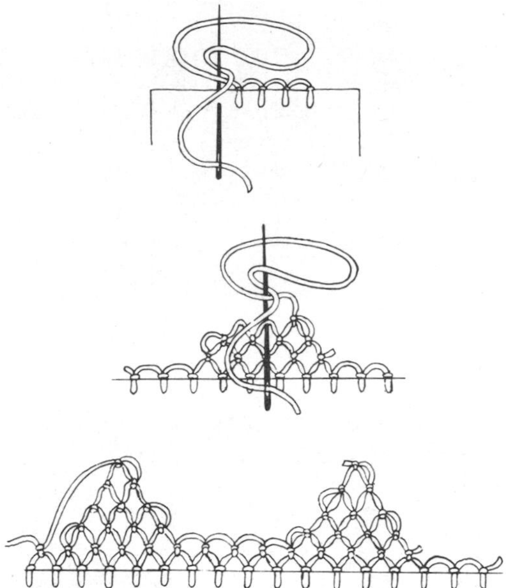

you and point the needle away from you. Fasten thread and insert needle. Thread coming from the cloth lies first over the needle, then under it. Thread coming from the eye lies under the needle, then over it (study diagram). Pull needle through and tighten the knot close to edge. Take the next stitch ⅛″ away. Succeeding rows are made in the same way, forming a knot in each loop.

Hardanger Embroidery

Hardanger work may be done on any fabric with an even weave. This means there are the same number of threads in a given space

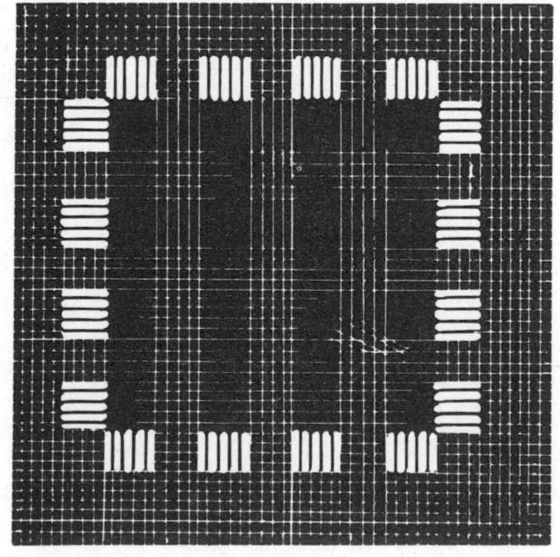

when counted either crosswise or lengthwise of the fabric. Fabric with 20 to 26 threads to the inch is best. This work can be done only by the accurate counting of threads as you work.

There are two principal stitches used in hardanger: satin or kloster stitch for the solid parts and a weaving stitch for the drawn work.

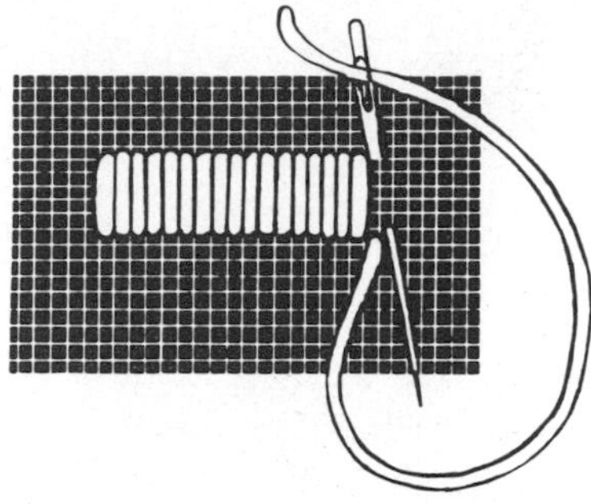

The satin stitch is usually worked in groups of five over four threads of canvas. This is called a kloster block.

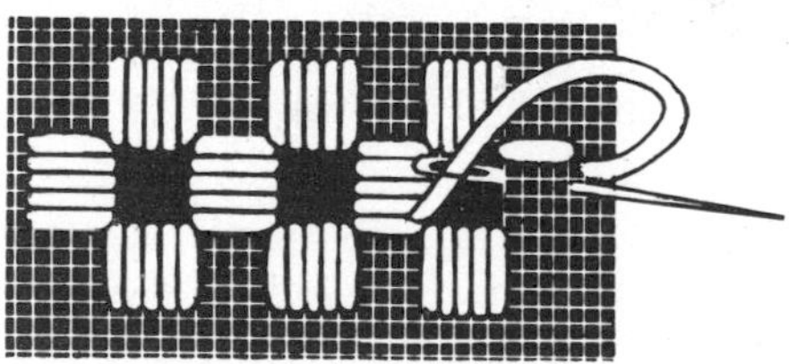

These groups are worked horizontally or vertically to form squares. The squares may be set together in rows on the straight or on the diagonal.

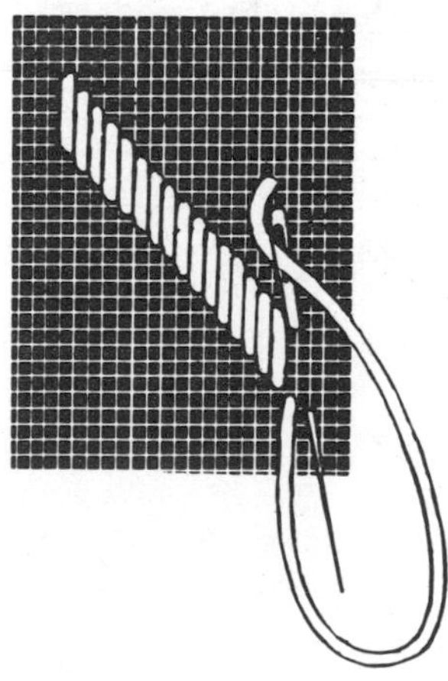

The satin stitch may be worked on the diagonal by raising (or lowering) each stitch

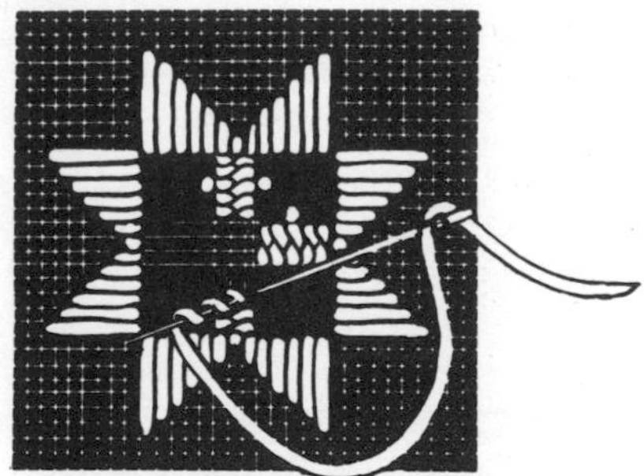

one mesh. Blocks with diagonal edges may also be made.

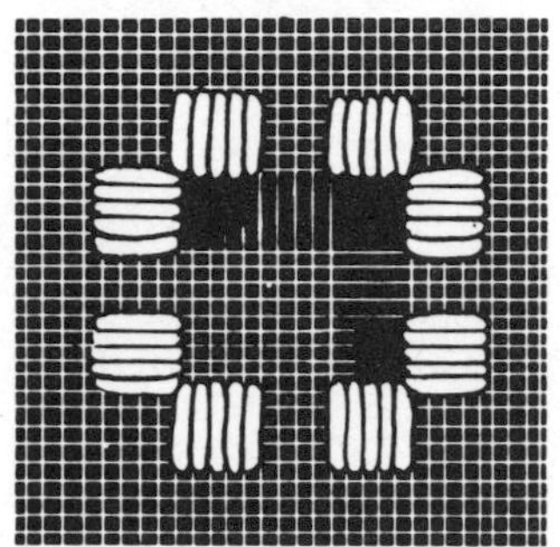

When blocks are completed the threads are cut. Care must be taken in cutting the threads for the openwork, being sure to leave attached those over which the weaving is to be done.

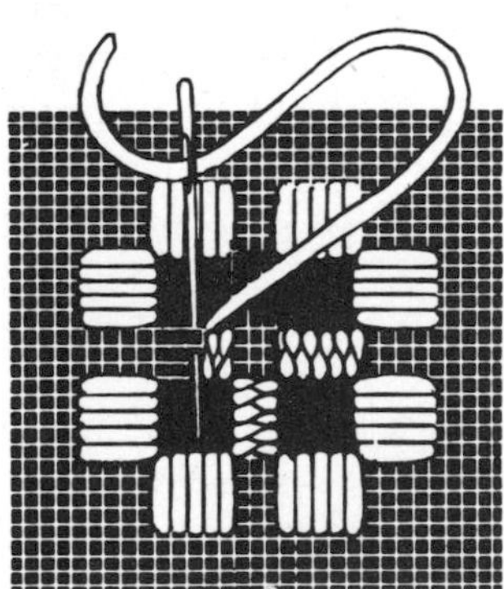

The remaining threads may be ornamented by weaving or by overcasting. Weave the bars closely and evenly. Picots may be worked on the woven bars (see previous illustration).

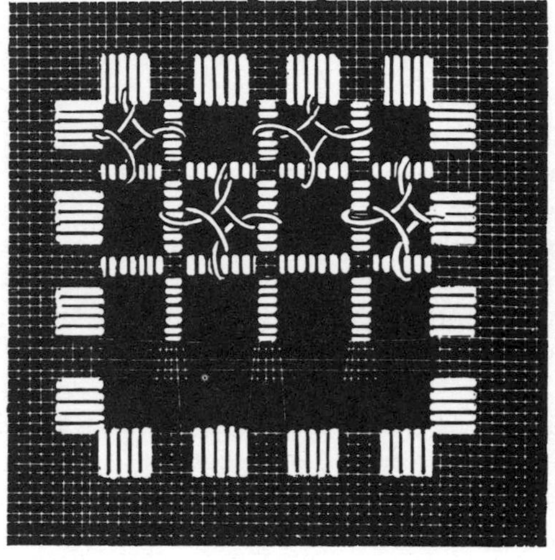

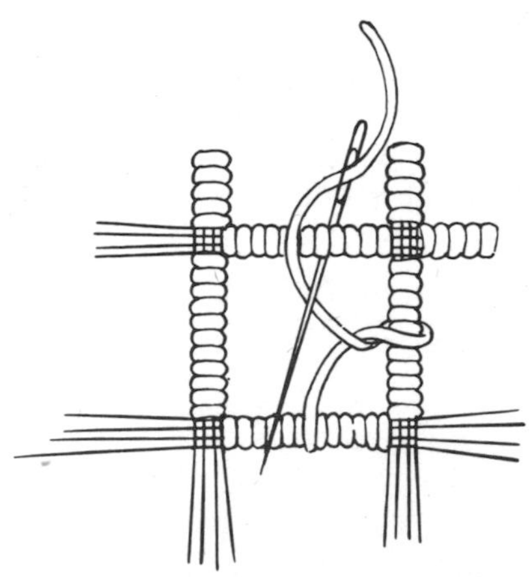

On more elaborate pieces the open spaces may be ornamented with loop stitch or twisted bars to make lace work.

Chapter 3

Quilting

The purpose of quilting is to hold together several layers of material and prevent the interlayer of cotton from slipping. In addition to this practical purpose, an infinite variety of decorative effects may be obtained. Quilting itself is an ancient art. It probably originated in a cold climate in an attempt to keep layers of cloth together for warmth. Examples of quilting have come down to us from many early sources. The knights of the Middle Ages wore quilted jackets under their armor for protection. And in ancient Egypt, quilting was used in place of armor. It is still worn in northern China for warmth, and it is revived periodically by today's fashion designers for robes, jackets, etc.

But a "quilt" in our minds is a bed covering, and pieced quilts are truly American. They were the result of the attempt of pioneer women to make the best of things. The pieced quilt came before the appliquéd one, and was born of necessity, since women in those early days had to use and re-use every inch of cloth which came into their hands.

The first quilts were of the "crazy quilt" variety, made with shapeless scraps without attention to design. Simple patterns developed next, and finally the more intricate designs with interesting names such as Turkey Track, Indian Hatchet, Washington's Plumes, Churn Dash, Log Cabin, Delectable Mountains, and so on. A thorough study of old American quilts is a study of American history revealing the sturdy character, ingenuity, and sense of humor of our pioneer mothers.

Every pioneer bride aimed to have at least a dozen quilts in her dower chest. When a girl became engaged, she started her "bride's quilt." These were especially beautiful and a great deal of work went into them.

Later the appliqué quilt appeared. Since two scraps pieced together go farther than one laid on top of the other, "laying on" a design was considered something of a luxury and was, therefore, indicative of better times. Appliqué, also, is very old as a technique, having been used by all people in all ages. But only in America was it associated with bed quilts.

The appliqué quilt offers more possibilities of variation in design than the pieced one. If at all possible, look at some examples of lovely old quilts in museums. They are a wonderful inspiration, and we can all take pride in this expression of the skill and imagination of our forebears.

For those whose enthusiasm for quilts is great enough for them to want to make one, we have tried to give here as many practical hints as possible. If you like to sew you will like to quilt; it takes only care and time.

CHOOSE YOUR DESIGN

Whether you make a pieced quilt or one

designed for appliqué is a matter of personal choice. Putting together small pieces by hand (certain patterns can be done on the machine), may seem monotonous and boring, or it may appeal to you as being as much fun as solving an interesting puzzle. Certainly the finished effect is lovely and the geometric designs highly suitable to modern interiors.

See Color Plate 5 for this type of quilt.

Appliqué work is also fascinating and since this technique allows for curves, it is possible to use florals and other natural shapes. These are usually simplified but can be very charming indeed.

FABRICS

The most important thing to keep in mind is to use the best materials you can afford. This is of course true of all handwork. Good quilt fabrics are not expensive, and it would be foolish indeed to put a great deal of work into a quilt made of cheap fabric which will not wear, and may run or fade in washing. Choose a fabric with a firm weave but with a soft texture, such as fine percale or broadcloth. A thin interlining or batting is best since it allows for closer rows of quilting. A cotton bat is better than flannelette as it gives that much wanted puffy effect. Sheet wadding is too stiff for easy quilting.

For the lining or backing choose a soft unstarched fabric which is similar in texture to the top.

Thread for piecing should be a good 6 cord No. 50 or 60. If the piecing is done by machine, No. 70 is best. Also use No. 70 for appliqué work.

PATCHWORK OR PIECED QUILTS

Making Patterns

Your design will be made up of basic units. Trace or draw the shape of these unit pieces onto tracing or bond paper. Cut out each piece. To make a more durable pattern place each piece on top of a blotter or fine sand paper (either of which has the advantage of not sliding around on the fabric while you are cutting) and cut out exactly on the edge. Make more than one pattern of each piece so that when one becomes worn another is at hand. Sheet brass or tin, thin enough to cut with shears, may be used in place of blotting or sand paper and is more durable still.

Cutting

Press fabric thoroughly. Use a damp cloth, if necessary, to remove wrinkles. Place the pattern on lengthwise grain. A square must be laid on true lengthwise and cross grain. Diamonds should be placed so that two opposite sides are on lengthwise grain, which gives two bias sides. Otherwise there will be four bias sides, which are difficult to piece without stretching.

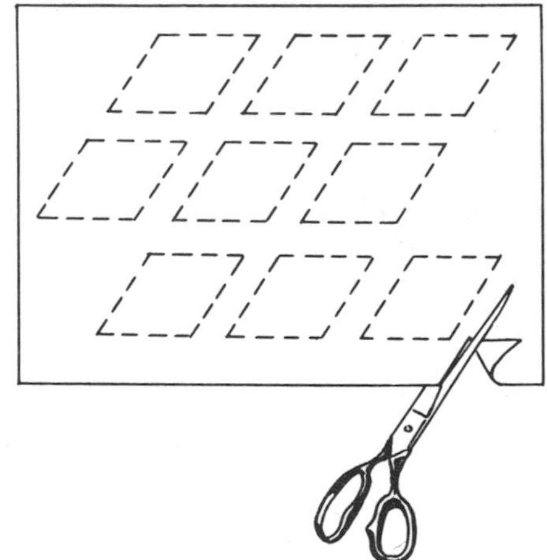

Trace around the pattern; then cut with a ¼″ seam allowance all around. All pieces must be cut exactly alike if the quilt is to fit together properly and be true to pattern.

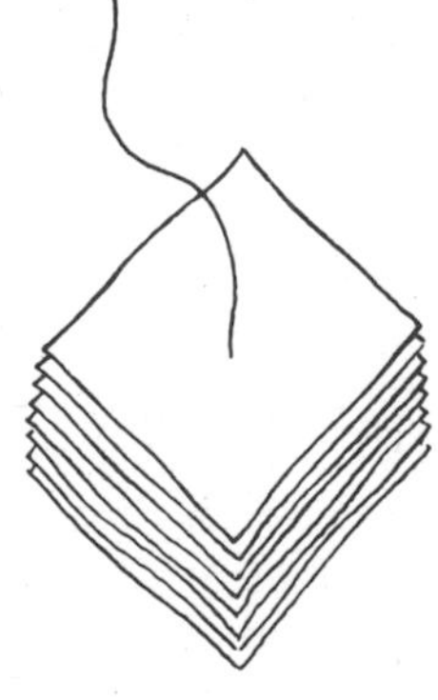

Each block must come out even at all corners and edges. If desired, after pieces are cut the pattern may be laid on the wrong side of each piece and the seam allowance pressed back over the edge. This slows down the work but insures uniform seams.

Group pieces of a kind together; our grandmothers ran a thread through each pile.

Piecing

A poorly pieced quilt can never be made to look right. Unless each small piece in a patchwork block is true and even, and unless all pieces are sewed to each other with the same width seam, the block will be crooked and will not lie flat. The next step of sewing blocks together or to strips will be difficult and the result disappointing.

A rule of patchwork is to join the patches or units from the center out. Lay 2 pieces with right sides together and join on the seam line with fine running stitches. An occasional back stitch will make a stronger seam. Use a short length of thread and be careful not to stretch any bias edges. Give special attention to corners where more than 2 pieces meet so that a perfect joining is made. Press seams open as you go; it makes for better-looking quilts. If this is not possible, press each block, taking care not to stretch bias seams.

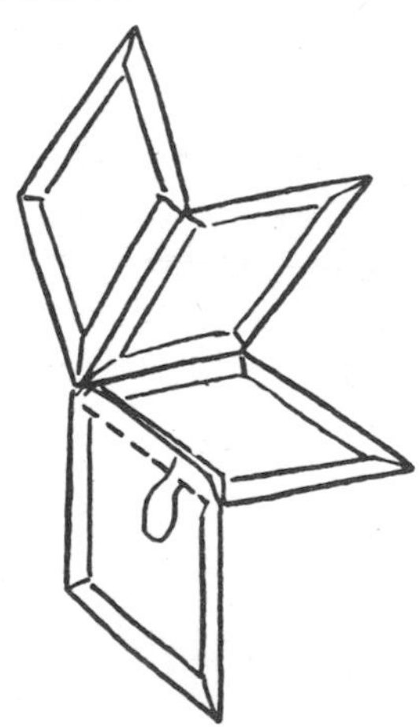

Setting the Blocks Together

There are many ways of varying the "set". First work out on paper the one you will use. After the blocks are finished, join blocks in strips, and sew the strips together. Put the border on last. Pieced blocks are often alternated with plain blocks, or plain strips are set between them in both directions. Make all seams match, and press the whole top carefully after it has been set together.

Marking the Quilting Pattern

Marking or transferring the quilting pattern onto the quilt is usually done before putting the quilt into the frame (see section on Quilting Frames, page 173). If you are using a hot iron transfer pattern it is best to do it at this point. Cut the pattern apart and lay it in the proper places. Be sure joinings match. If not using a hot iron transfer, run a colored basting up and down the center and crosswise for a guide, if needed.

If the marking is done after the quilt is in the frame, mark all reachable space on four sides. Quilt and roll.

In the early days, there were many methods of transferring quilting patterns onto the quilt top. Some of them are still practical. One was with models or templates. These could be wood, heavy paper, cardboard, even homely articles such as plates, cups, spools, or anything which could be used to make interesting scrolls, curves, etc. Some quilters scratched around the object, then worked quickly before the line disappeared. Others used pencil or chalk for marking.

A plain, all-over pattern such as diagonal lines or diamonds can be used and is very effective. One can change the direction of the lines for variation. If the quilt has plain and pieced blocks, it is more effective if the plain block is quilted more elaborately than the pieced one. Sometimes the design of the pieced or appliqué block is used for a quilting pattern on the plain. Also, transfer patterns for more elaborate designs can be purchased.

APPLIQUÉ QUILTS

This is an entirely different technique from piecing. To appliqué, one piece is laid upon another, edges turned under and secured with fine hemming stitches.

How to Appliqué

Trace each design part and make a cutting pattern of each piece using heavy paper or thin cardboard.

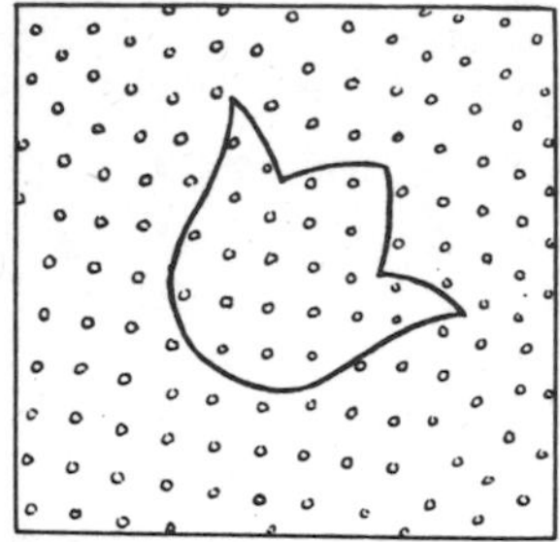

Lay the pattern on the fabric and trace around. Cut out, allowing 3/16″ for turning under. The traced line is the turning line.

Unless the design is very simple, it should be traced or stamped onto the quilt top to show where the cut-out patches are to be placed.

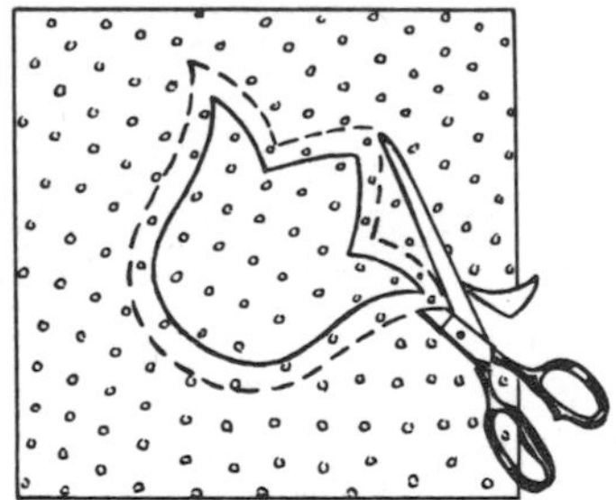

Place the patch where it belongs, pin carefully, turn under on the line, and baste in place. Clip corners where necessary. Let flowers, buds, leaves, etc., overlap stems. All raw edges are turned under unless they end at the edge of a block and will be sewed in with the seam. Sew patches on with invisible hemming stitches, barely catching the edge of the patch and keeping its true shape.

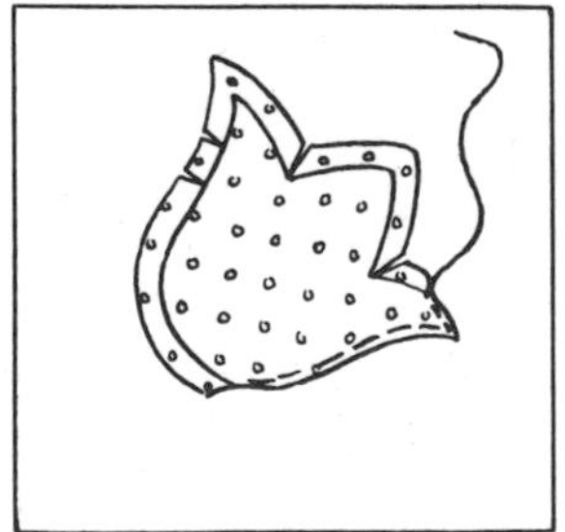

It is possible to purchase this type of quilt ready-stamped; that is, the top of the quilt is stamped with both the appliqué design and the quilting pattern and the patches are stamped with both cutting and turning lines.

PUTTING THE QUILT TOGETHER

Preparing the Backing

The backing is made of widths of fabric stitched together. Usually a 36″ width is used in the center and a narrower strip on each side. Remove selvages before sewing strips together. The back of the quilt is usually cut a little larger than a pieced top because the latter has more "give" to it. If you wish to bring the edges of the backing over the top for a binding, as is often done, cut the back about 3 inches larger all around.

Interlining

Cotton batting is most often used and is most practical. One bat is usually sufficient for a single-size quilt. Bats are sold in different sizes.

Placing Layers Together

Lay the quilt backing flat on the floor wrong side up, smoothing it out. Place cotton batting on top, one strip next to another (do not overlap), arrange it in an even thickness over the backing, with no wrinkles

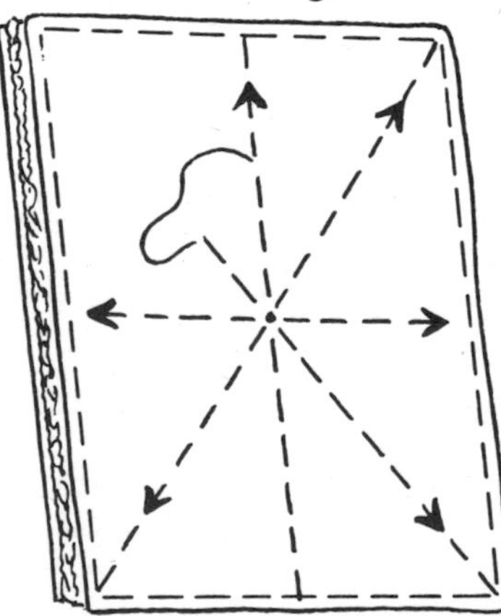

or lumps. Lay the quilt top in place right side up, and baste all three thicknesses together (see diagram).

Start at the center of the quilt and baste out to the mid-point of all four edges. Then, starting at the center, baste to the four corners. Baste all outer edges together.

QUILTING

Frames and Hoops

Perfect results require the use of a quilting frame of some kind. The purpose of the quilting frame is to hold the work taut while it is being quilted. Quilting frames may be made of four strips of wood; two short bars (2″ wide by 24″ to 36″ long) and two long bars (2″ wide by about 92″ long, or a little longer than the quilt is wide), and a contrivance (a clamp) at corners for control. The corners must be held at right angles. A tape or strip of muslin is tacked the length of the long bars and the top and bottom edges of the quilt are sewed to these tapes. Roll one side until the width of the narrow bars is reached. The part exposed should be as much as can be reached comfortably from either side. Clamp the corners. To hold sides taut, sew over and over through the edge of the quilt and around end bars using heavy thread. Some frames are made with two strips of wood a little longer than the quilt and two of a length corresponding to the width of the quilt, but these take more space when set up. A curtain stretcher may also be used as a quilting frame. The frame may be set on saw horses or four straight-back chairs.

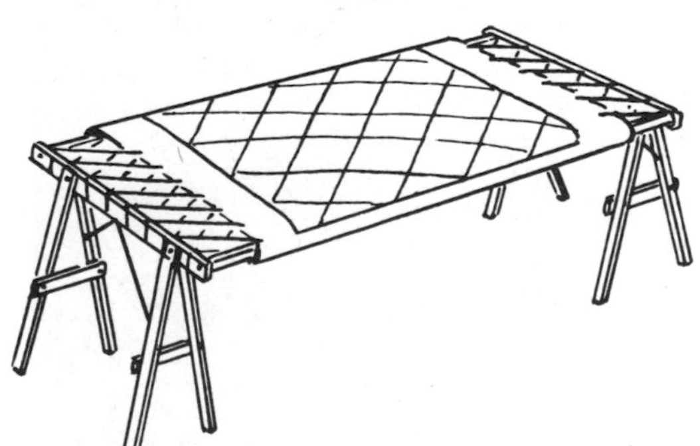

Large hoops, 22″ or more in diameter, are available and can be used on quilts. Begin in the center and work outward.

Quilting without a Frame. It is possible to quilt without a frame. Two things are necessary. (1) The quilt must be basted closely all over. Start by basting as explained under "Basting" and then add many rows between so that layers are held firmly together. (2) There must be space (such as a ping-pong table or even the floor) where the quilt may remain until finished. Always work on this surface and from the center out as much as possible. Unless you are agile, do not attempt quilting in this way.

How to Quilt

Use a short needle especially made for quilting to speed the work. Also use quilting thread; it is strong and smooth and less likely

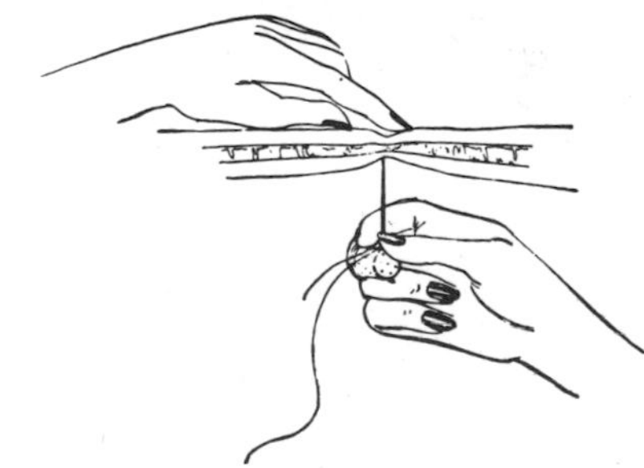

to knot. Use a short length of thread and pull the knot through to the batting so it will not show.

Place the forefinger of left hand over the spot where the needle should come through. From below, push needle through with right hand until it touches finger. Change hands and pull through with right hand. Forefinger

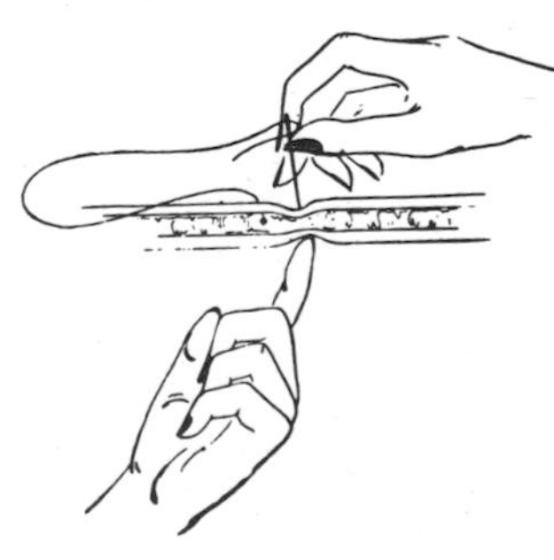

of left hand should now be underneath. With right hand push needle down through the 3 layers to touch forefinger. Pull through with right hand.

Continue working in this fashion. This upward and downward movement through the layers is one way to quilt. If the quilt is not too thick it may be possible to do a running stitch and pick up one or two stitches on the needle at the same time. Fasten end of each thread securely by running between layers.

If you are working in a frame and have quilted all space within reach, undo threads at sides, roll up until a new area is exposed, and continue.

After quilting is completed use art gum to erase pencil lines (if any), and bind the edges of the quilt.

Double Irish Chain Quilt

This is a variation of a favorite old pieced quilt. It may be made of plain or printed fabric combined with white. The blocks are 11″ square (finished) and are made up of the following units (all given without seam allowance).

Unit no. 1 is a rectangle 1″ by 7″.
Unit no. 2 is a rectangle 1″ by 5″.
Unit no. 3 is a rectangle 1″ by 3″.
Unit no. 4 is a 1″ square.
Unit no. 5 is a 3″ square.

Make a pattern for each unit.

Number of each unit to cut for one block:

Unit no. 1: cut 4 white.
Unit no. 2: cut 4 white.

Unit no. 3: cut 4 white.

Unit no. 4: cut 20 white and 32 print.

Unit no. 5: cut 1 print.

See general directions for Making Pattern Pieces and Cutting (allow ¼″ seams all around units). For a single quilt multiply the above numbers by 70. For a double quilt multiply the above numbers by 90. A single-size quilt takes 70 blocks set 7 by 10. A double-size quilt takes 90 blocks set 9 by 10.

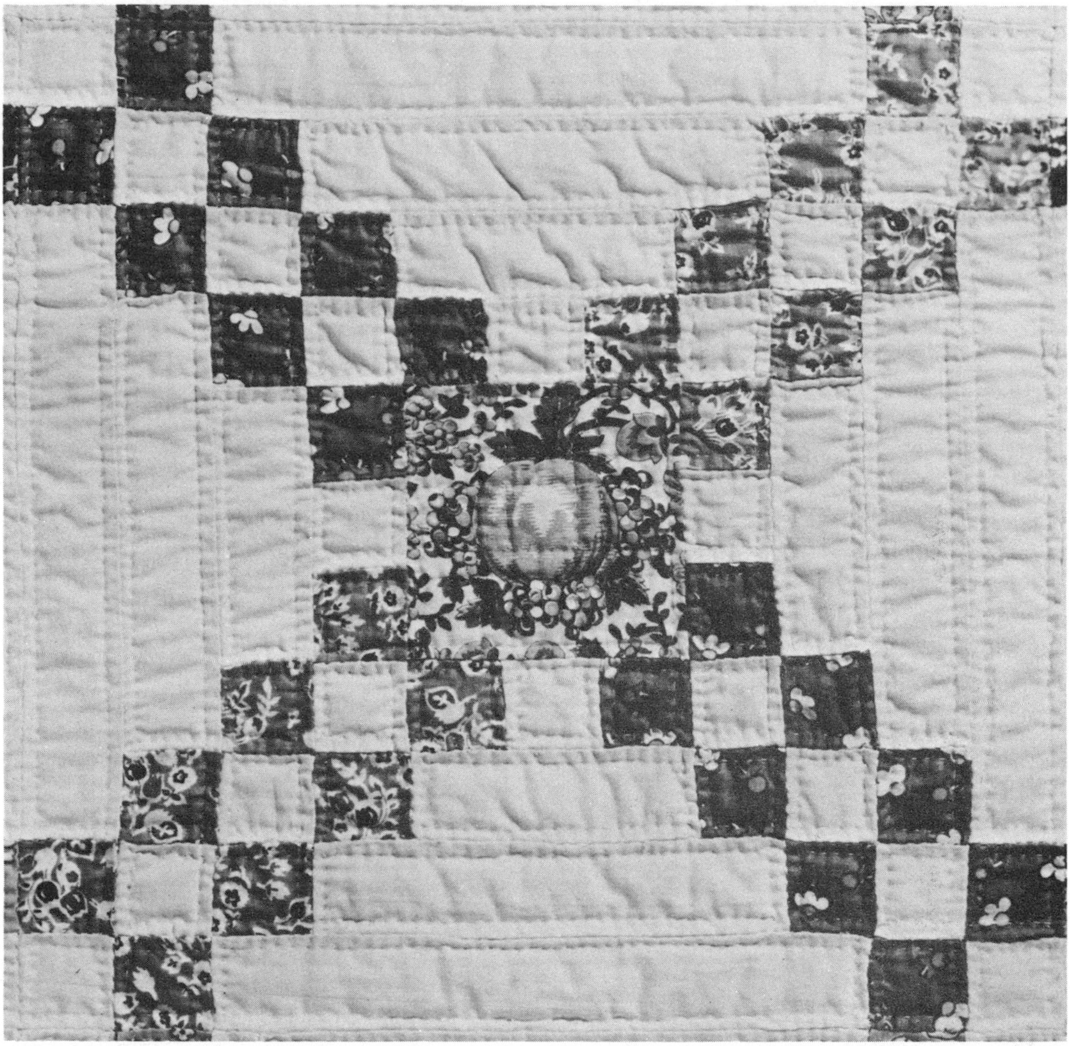

How to Join to Form a Block

Start with a no. 5 unit in the center. Follow diagrams for setting together. Piece together each narrow row before setting it to the block; this avoids having to sew a block into a corner. Match seams carefully.

After all blocks are made, set them together; see general directions for Backing, Interlining, and Quilting. As shown in the photograph, this quilt looks well quilted each side of all seams, ⅛″ away. Quilt the center block as though it were pieced of 9 (unit 4) 1″ squares. Bind edges with print or plain.

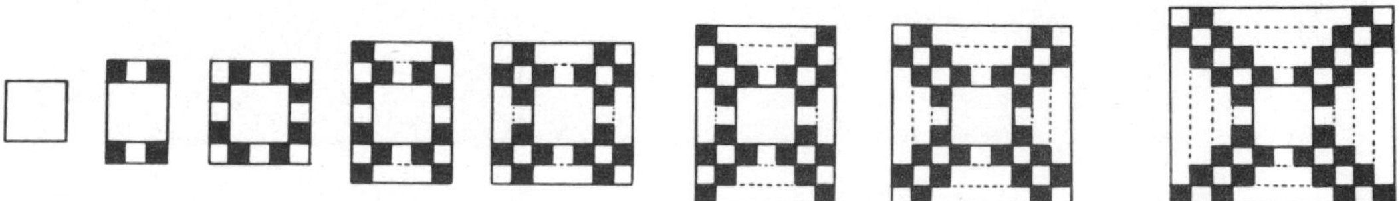

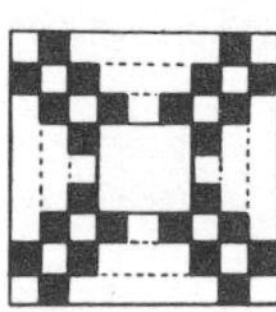

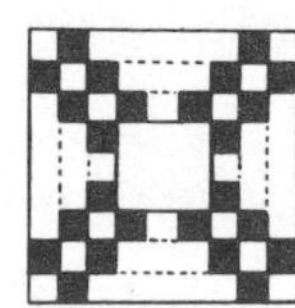

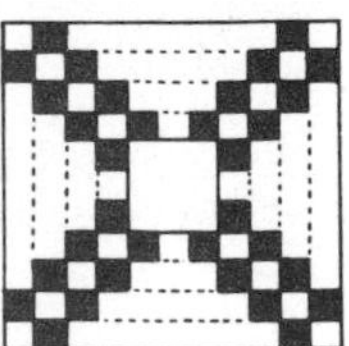

Log Cabin Quilt

Patterns and directions for the quilt pictured in Color Plate 5 are available. For information, write to Good Housekeeping Needlework and Sewing Center, 959 Eighth Avenue, New York, New York 10019.

Piece- and Quilt-as-You-Go Quilt

This is an unusual method of quilt making which holds much fascination because it has the advantage of being padded and "quilted" as you go. Each block is a square folded to make a triangle. Before folding, padding in the form of sheet wadding is laid on the square, edges of the square are turned and whipped together. These puffy triangular units are then whipped together. The quilt may be made of print or plain fabric combined with white, and block arrangements other than the one given here are possible. It is especially delightful done in a delicate color with white for a child's quilt. This is also a good way to use up silk or fine wool scraps for a bed throw or lap robe.

Child's Quilt or Carriage Cover

For a quilt 30 by 40 inches you will need:

1½ yards white batiste, broadcloth, or other fine cotton.

1½ yards colored cotton of fine quality.

3 yards sheet wadding.

Cotton batting.

Cut a piece of cardboard 3½″ square (this is guide for cutting wadding only).

Cutting. Cut 96 squares of each color (on grain of fabric) 4½″ square. This gives a seam allowance of ½″ all around. The easiest way to do this is to use a yardstick and pencil to mark off the squares on the fabric and then cut.

Cut 96 squares of sheet wadding the size of the cardboard guide.

To Make. Center the cardboard guide on each fabric square, fold seam allowance over edges, and press.

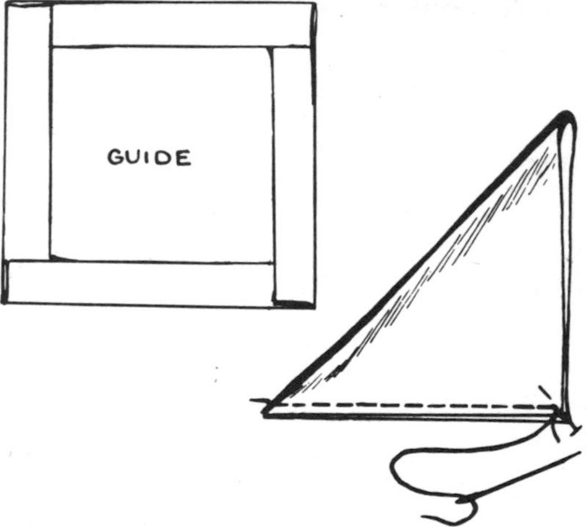

Place a square of sheet wadding inside the square of fabric; trim corners of fabric. Fold square diagonally, edges even, and pin at point. Insert a small amount of cotton batting into triangle to make it puff slightly. Baste edges of triangle together. Prepare all triangles in this manner.

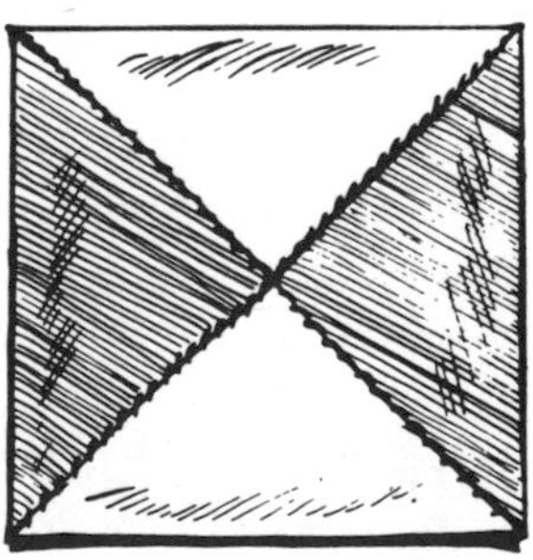

Pin the basted sides of two triangles together, matching white to a color. Whipstitch, taking in all thicknesses. Repeat; then assemble the two parts to form a block as shown.

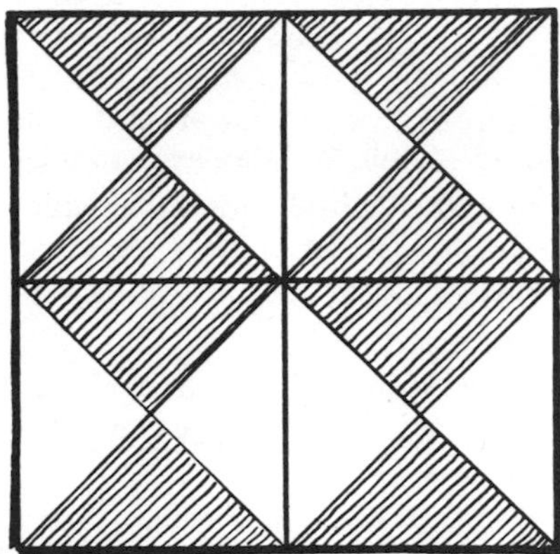

After making four blocks, whipstitch the folded edges together on the wrong side, white to white, color to color, as shown. Child's quilt is 6 blocks by 8 blocks. See photograph on opposite page. For larger quilts and throws, make desired size.

Biscuit Quilt

This is a puff quilt reminiscent of the "biscuit" pillows our grandmothers made from left-over pieces of silk. This is made of print and plain cotton, and stuffed with Dacron. It is practical for an extra coverlet, or can be used in place of a spread.

The quilt pictured (see page 179) is 64″ by 85″ in size. The squares are 2½″ finished and the quilt is 27 squares by 34 squares. Any size can be made.

Materials needed for this size:

- 6½ yards cotton print.
- 6½ yards plain color cotton.
- 4¾ yards white cotton for backing.
- 7 yards light weight unbleached muslin.
- 9 yards 1″ bias binding to match plain cotton.
- Cotton, Orlon, or Dacron for stuffing (large package).

Cutting. Cut one 3″- and one 4″-square from cardboard.

Use the cardboard patterns or mark off directly on the fabric with pencil and ruler. The plain and printed cotton is cut into 4″-squares. The unbleached muslin is cut into 3″-squares. The whole quilt may be cut at one time; or you may cut enough squares for one row across, which would be 14 squares print, 13 squares plain (alternate rows will be 14 squares plain and 13 squares print). Cut also 27 squares muslin.

To Make. ¼″ seams have been allowed. Pin the corners of a 4″ square to corners of a 3″ square (muslin).

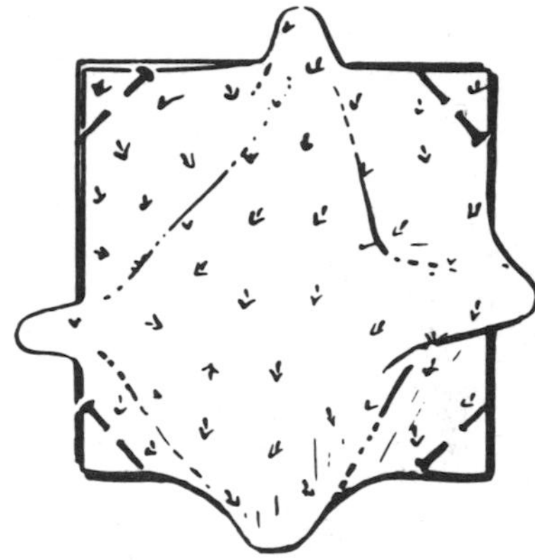

Fold and pin excess fabric into a pleat at center of each side. Always fold in the same

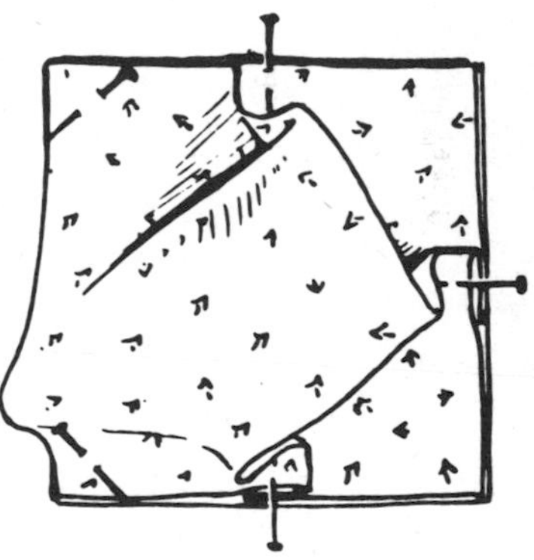

direction. Before pinning the fourth side, insert a wad of cotton about the size of a walnut. Baste square all around.

After preparing 27 squares in this manner, baste them together in a row, right sides together, taking ¼″ seams and alternating colors. Stitch and then press seams open. The row should begin and end with the same color.

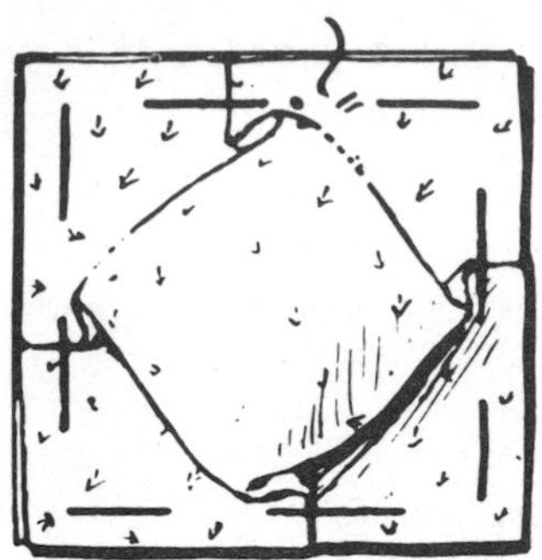

Make another row, beginning and ending with the second color. Rows are then sewed together in a crosswise seam.

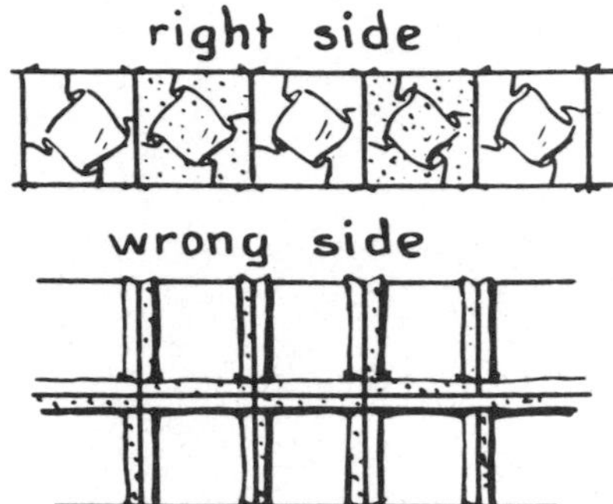

Lining. Cut white backing crosswise in two parts. Trim off selvages and sew the two pieces together lengthwise. Press seam open.

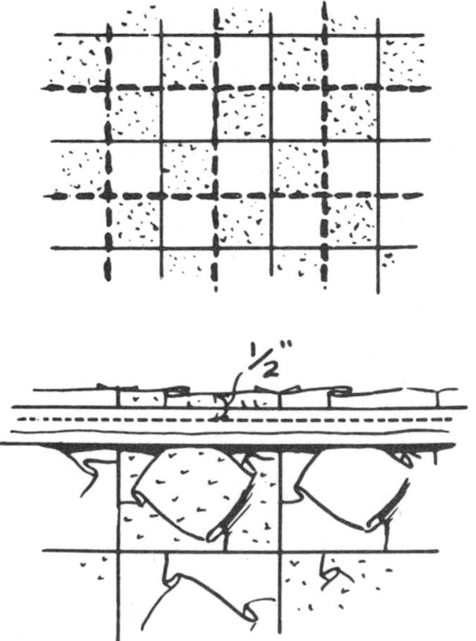

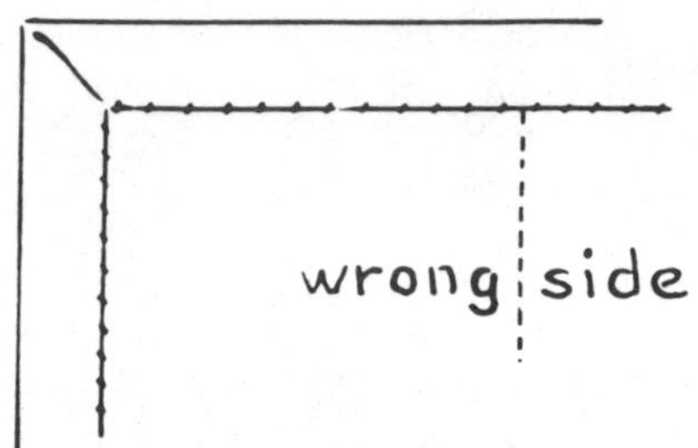

Quilting. Quilt on the seam lines. This may be done on every row or every other row as desired, and it may be done by hand or by machine. Bind edge.

MAKING A PIECED QUILT

Shown on pages 180 through 202 are 19 old-time pieced-quilt patterns and 1 appliqué pattern. The quaint names reflect the difficulties but also the sense of humor of our forebears. Often the same design was known by a different name in another section of the country. Designs for the old pieced blocks for the most part consist of squares, triangles, diamonds, bars, circles, or parts of circles. Use any color you wish or printed fabric for the darker part of the designs and white or cream for the white sections.

1. You should first determine the approximate size of the quilt you wish to make (single- or double-bed size). Then choose the block design. Plan the number of blocks the quilt will require for its width and length. At this time, also plan how the quilt will be set together. Some patterns look best if all the blocks are of the pieced design; others look more attractive with a plain block or strip between. This also affects the size, and must be taken into consideration. If the quilt is set together with plain blocks, use an odd number of blocks crosswise and lengthwise so that the corners will be alike. The quilt may be planned *with* or *without* a border; if a border is used, it may be wide or narrow. Sometimes quilts are made so the pieced blocks lie on top of the bed and the drop all around is a border which may be plain or pieced in rows. Make a rough drawing of how the quilt will look before starting to make it.

2. After choosing the design, and with tracing paper over the design, trace each unit exactly.

3. Cut out units exactly on the line—¼″ has been allowed for seams. With the paper pattern as a guide, cut a permanent pattern of each unit out of medium-weight cardboard. (Or use fine sandpaper, because it does not slip on the fabric.)

4. Determine, by counting, how many of each unit are required for a block and then for the entire quilt.

5. Lay pattern for each unit on the fabric (whenever possible, straight edges should follow fabric grain), and cut with accuracy. Separate colors and units, and run a thread through each pile. (See Cutting.)

6. Follow general instructions for piecing a quilt.

MAKING AN APPLIQUÉD QUILT

Follow the general directions for doing appliqué. Trace and make patterns of the design parts. Cut, then arrange on the block as shown in the illustration for the design you are making. Follow general instructions for planning a quilt, setting it together, and quilting. The broken lines around the design parts are seam allowances. The broken lines on the block itself represent quilting.

CRAZY-QUILT PATCHWORK

This kind of patchwork was done by our grandmothers and great-grandmothers, who used bits of silks and ribbons which they had saved from their dressmaking. No doubt they traded pieces with neighbors and friends in order to have a greater variety for their quilts and pillows. Almost any size and shape of piece was used. Sometimes a definite design was followed in a few of the blocks. For example, on some of the old quilts we find that they used old quilt-block patterns or made up a new design. Small embroidered motifs were often appliquéd on top of some of the patches. But almost invariably, in this kind of patchwork, rows of colored embroidery stitches were used to embellish the design. The embroidery was done over the line where the pieces joined, and it was often made quite elaborate by combining several stitches and colors.

Biscuit Quilt

Morning Star

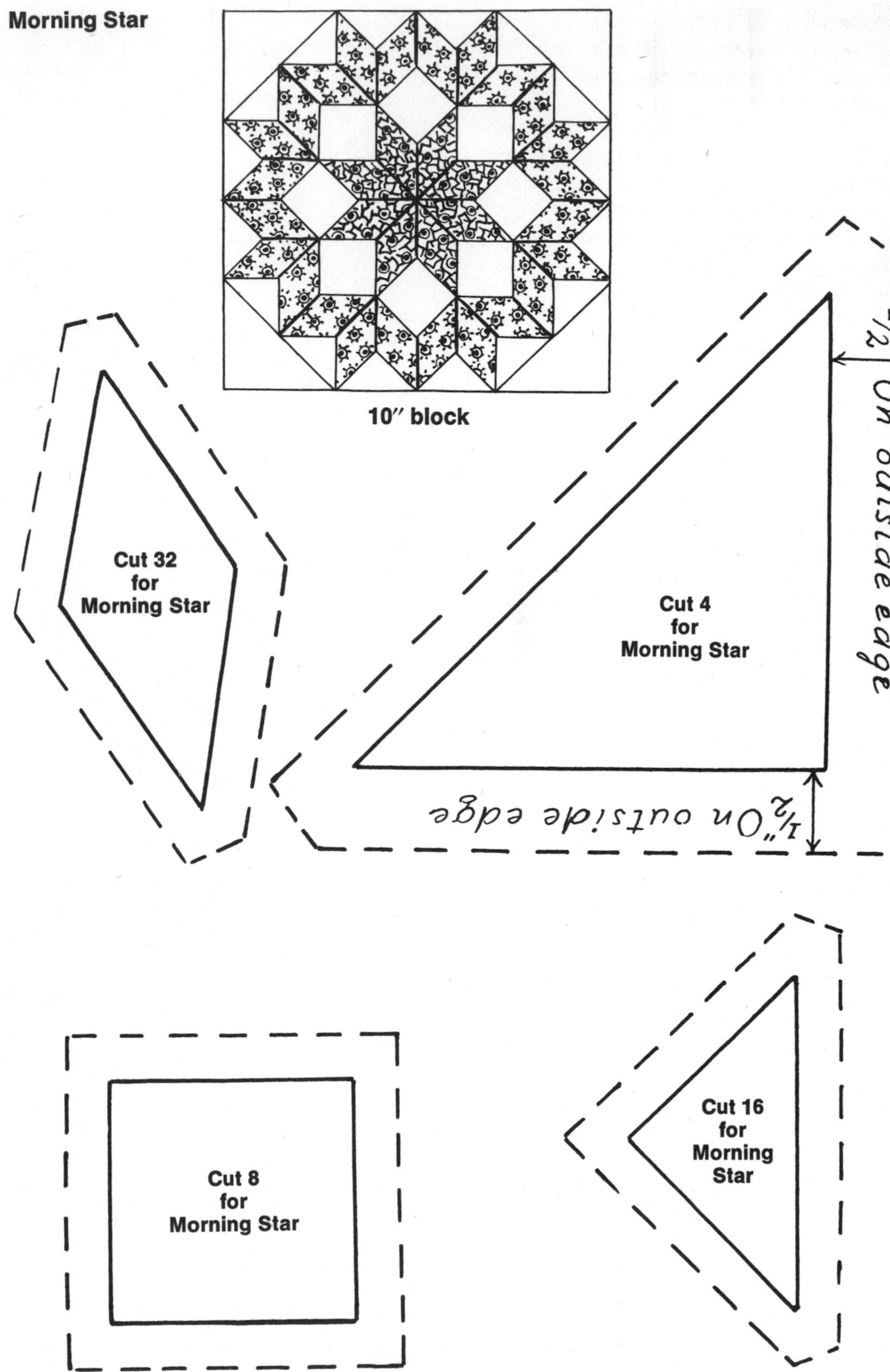

Color Plate 5 PATCHWORK QUILT

The time-honored, traditional design shown here is "Log Cabin." The piecing can be done either by hand or machine. To order the pattern and instructions, *turn to page 176.*

Color Plate 6 SMOCKING DESIGNS

Smocking is a beautiful old art which seems never to go out of style. The designs shown here are for real English smocking. Diagrams for copying them are on pages 209–212.

Windmill

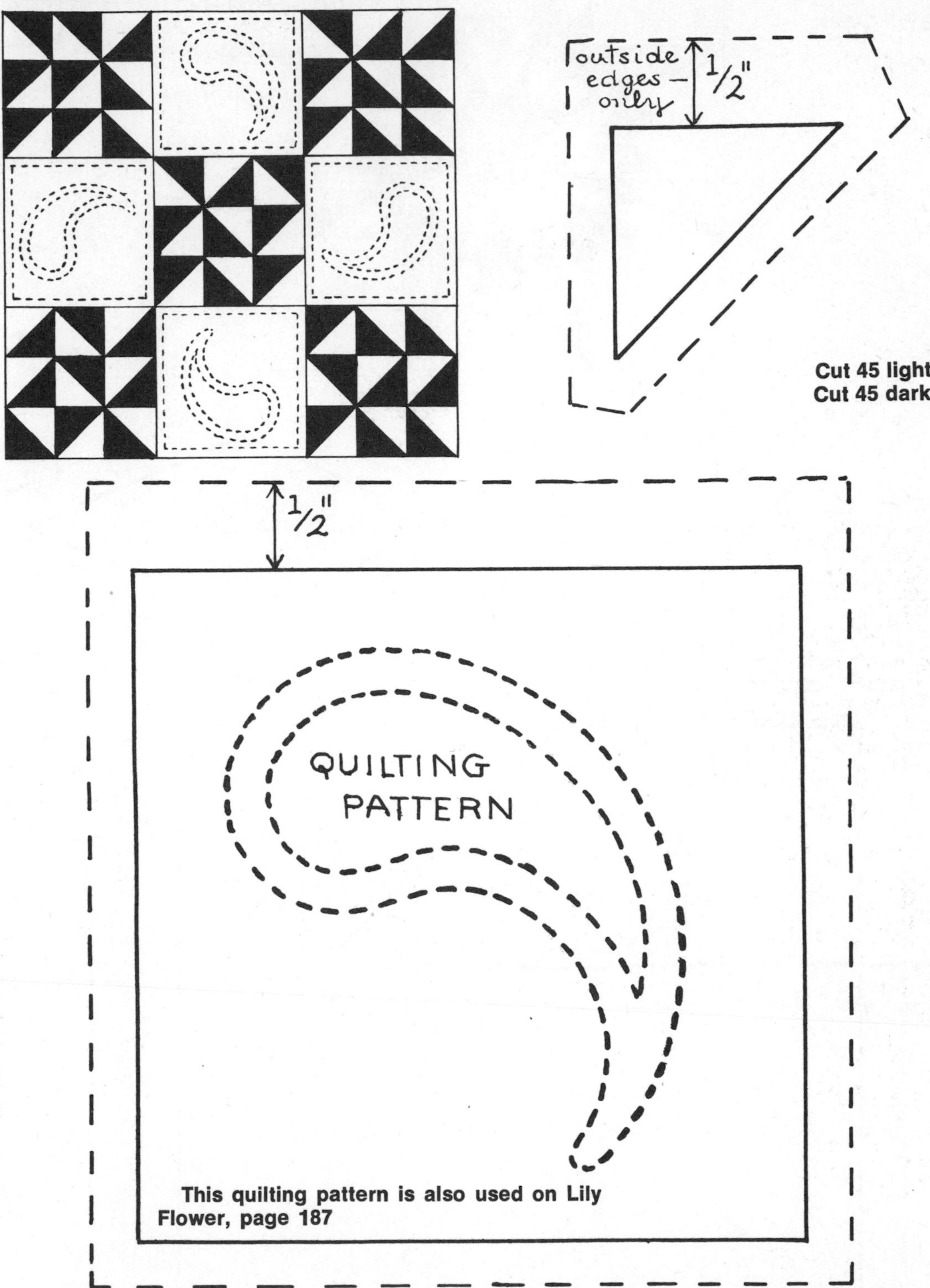

The number marked on each pattern piece is the number required to complete one block of the quilt. Cut as many of each piece as needed for making complete quilt.

Lone Star

13½″ block

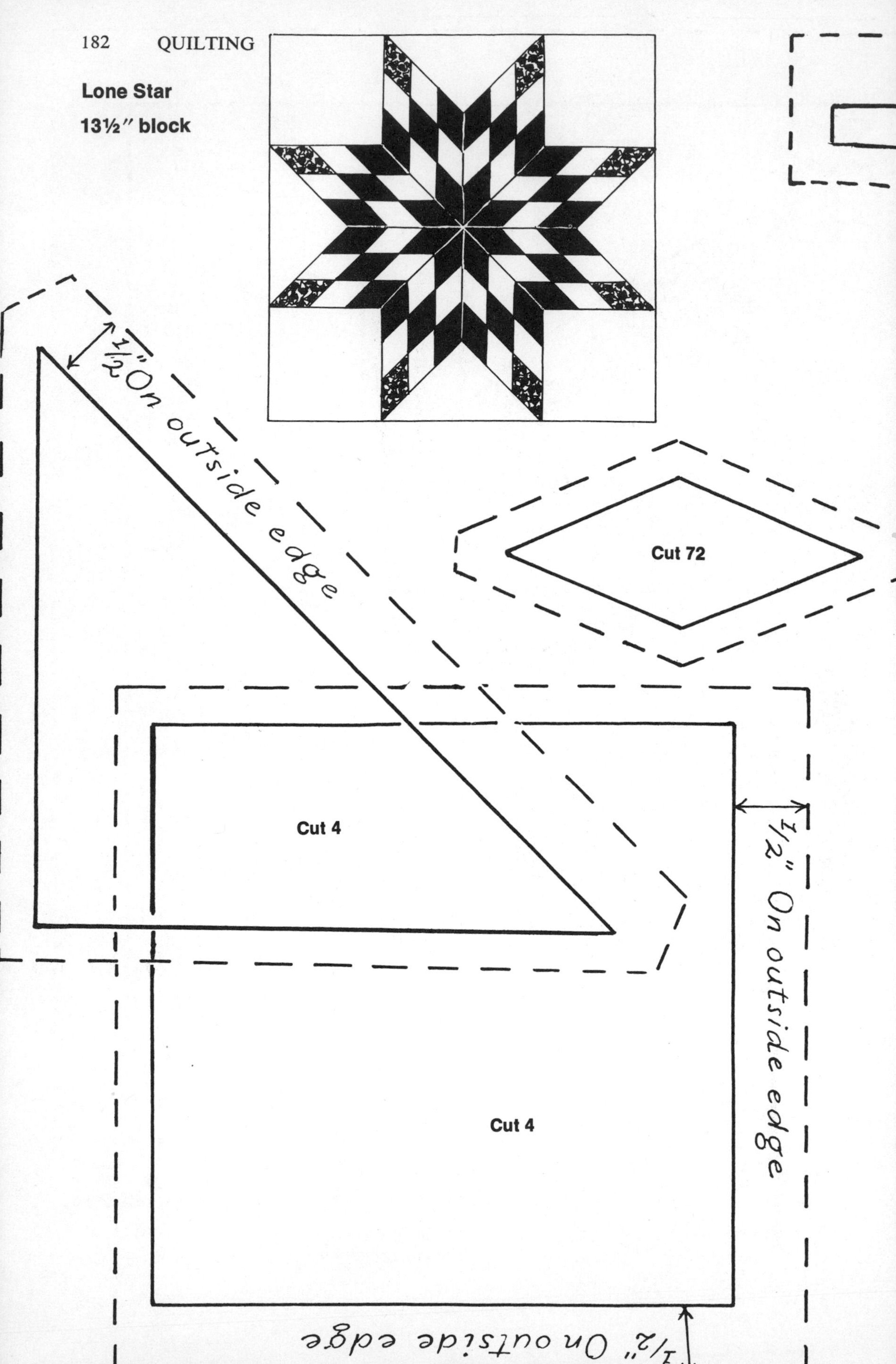

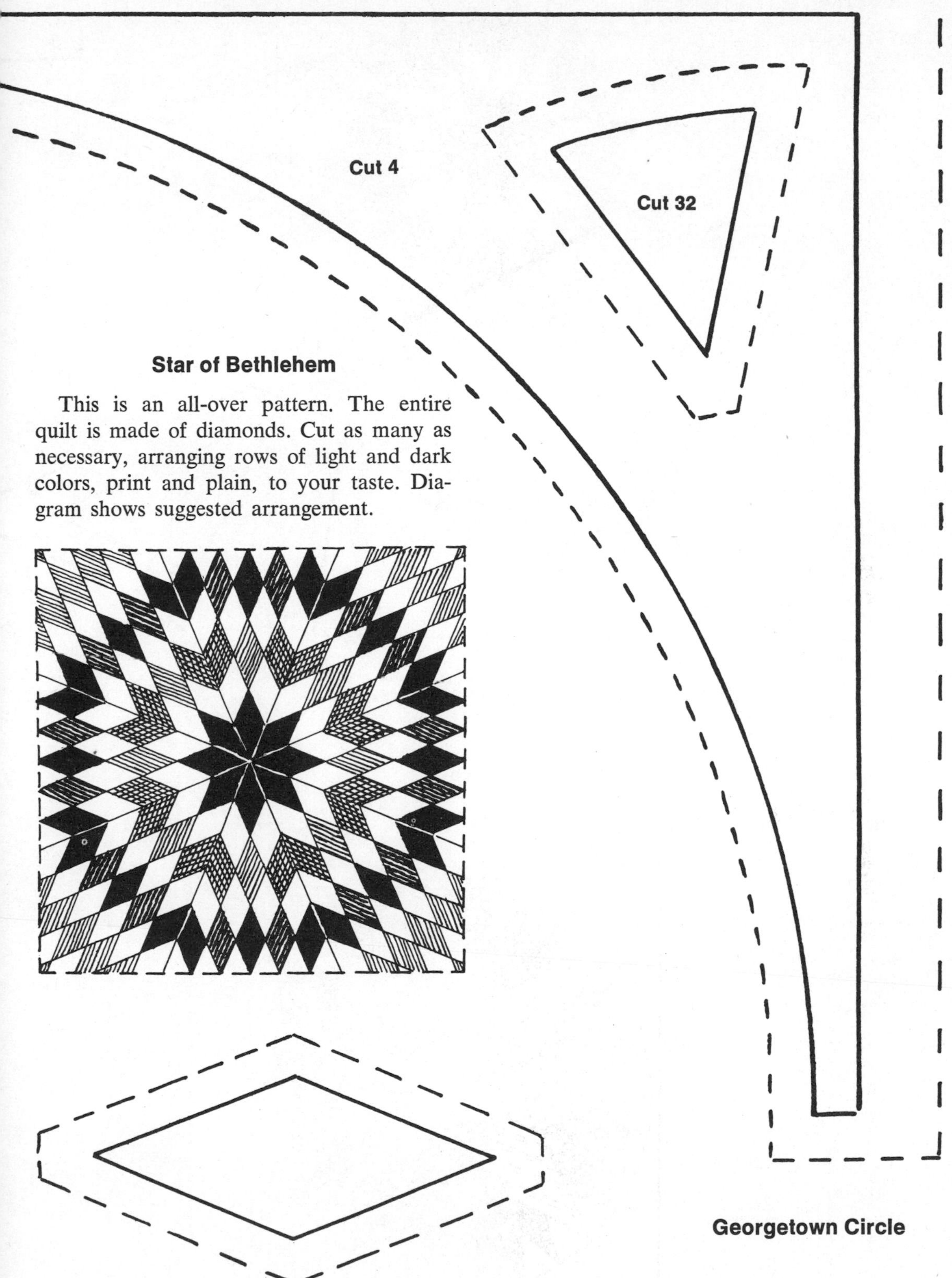

Star of Bethlehem

This is an all-over pattern. The entire quilt is made of diamonds. Cut as many as necessary, arranging rows of light and dark colors, print and plain, to your taste. Diagram shows suggested arrangement.

Georgetown Circle

Georgetown Circle (cont.)

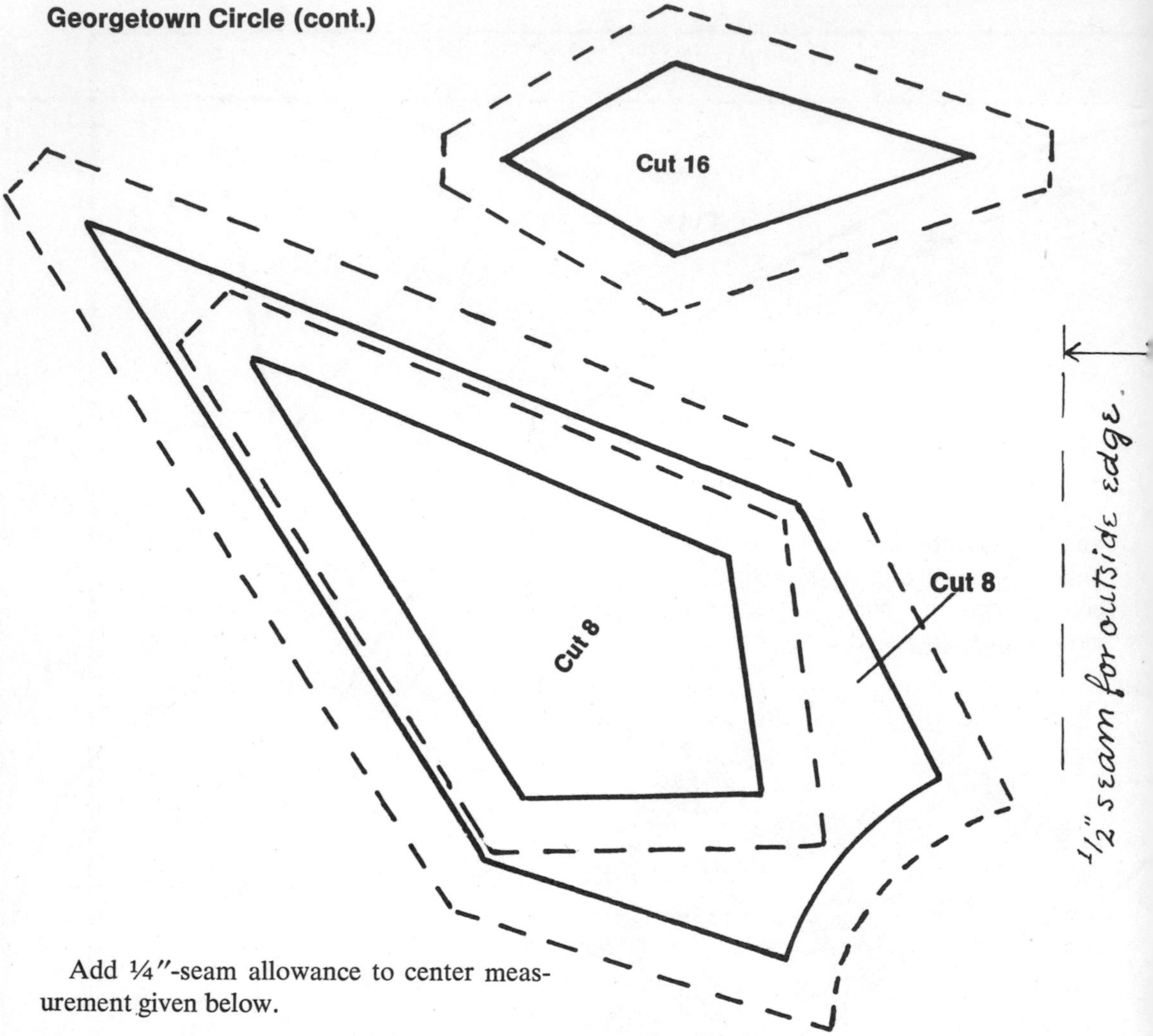
Cut 16
Cut 8
Cut 8
1/2" seam for outside edge.

Add ¼″-seam allowance to center measurement given below.

14″ block

3 1/4"

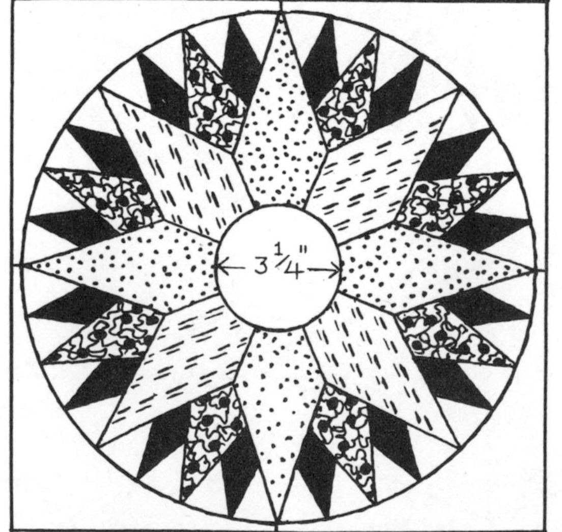

7″

allow 1/2″ seam for outside edge

Green

Dark rose

Dark rose

Pink

Rose

center

Pattern for ¼ block

14″ block

Tudor Rose

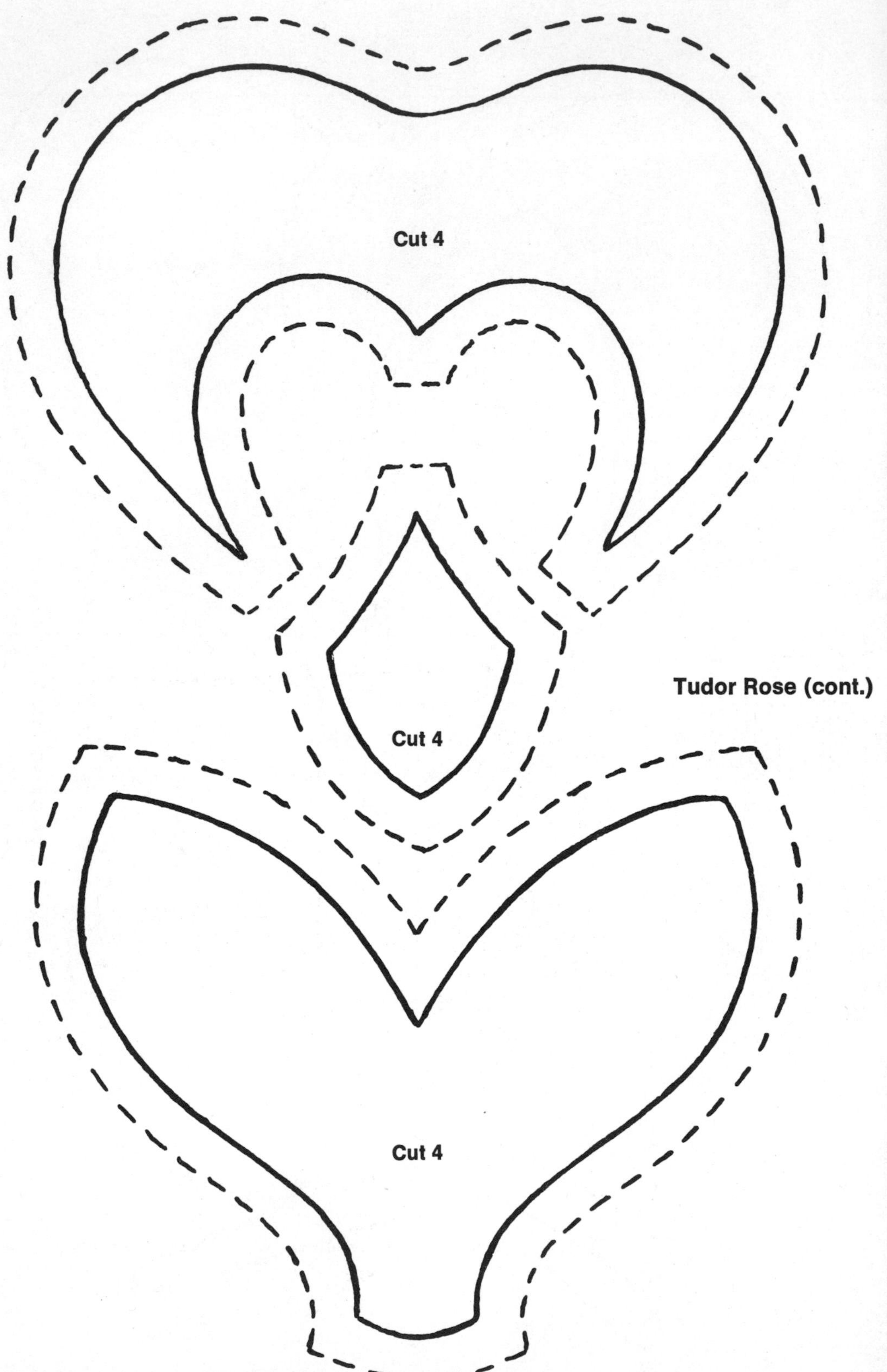

Tudor Rose (cont.)

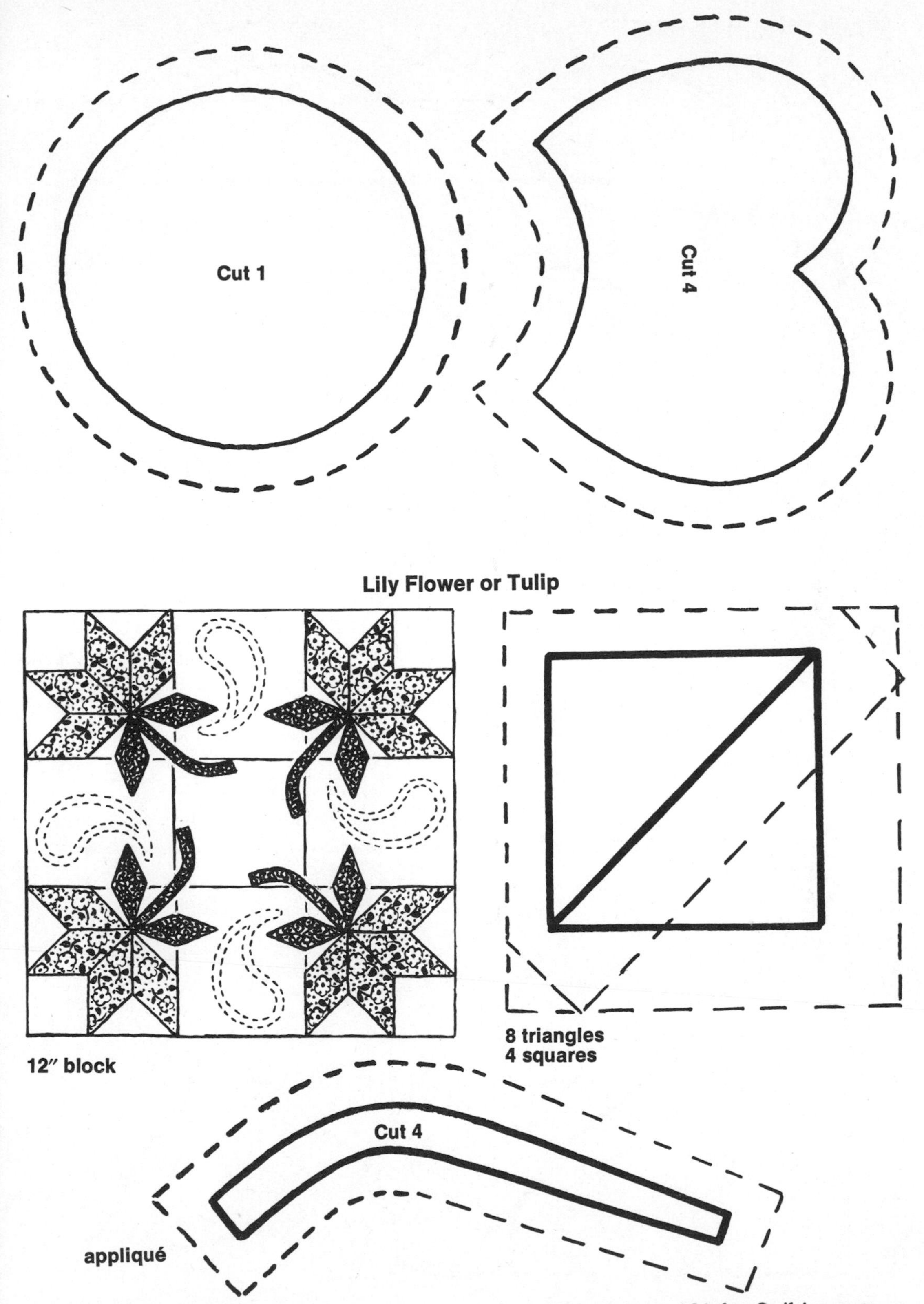

Also see page 181 for Quilting pattern.

Lily Flower or Tulip (cont.)

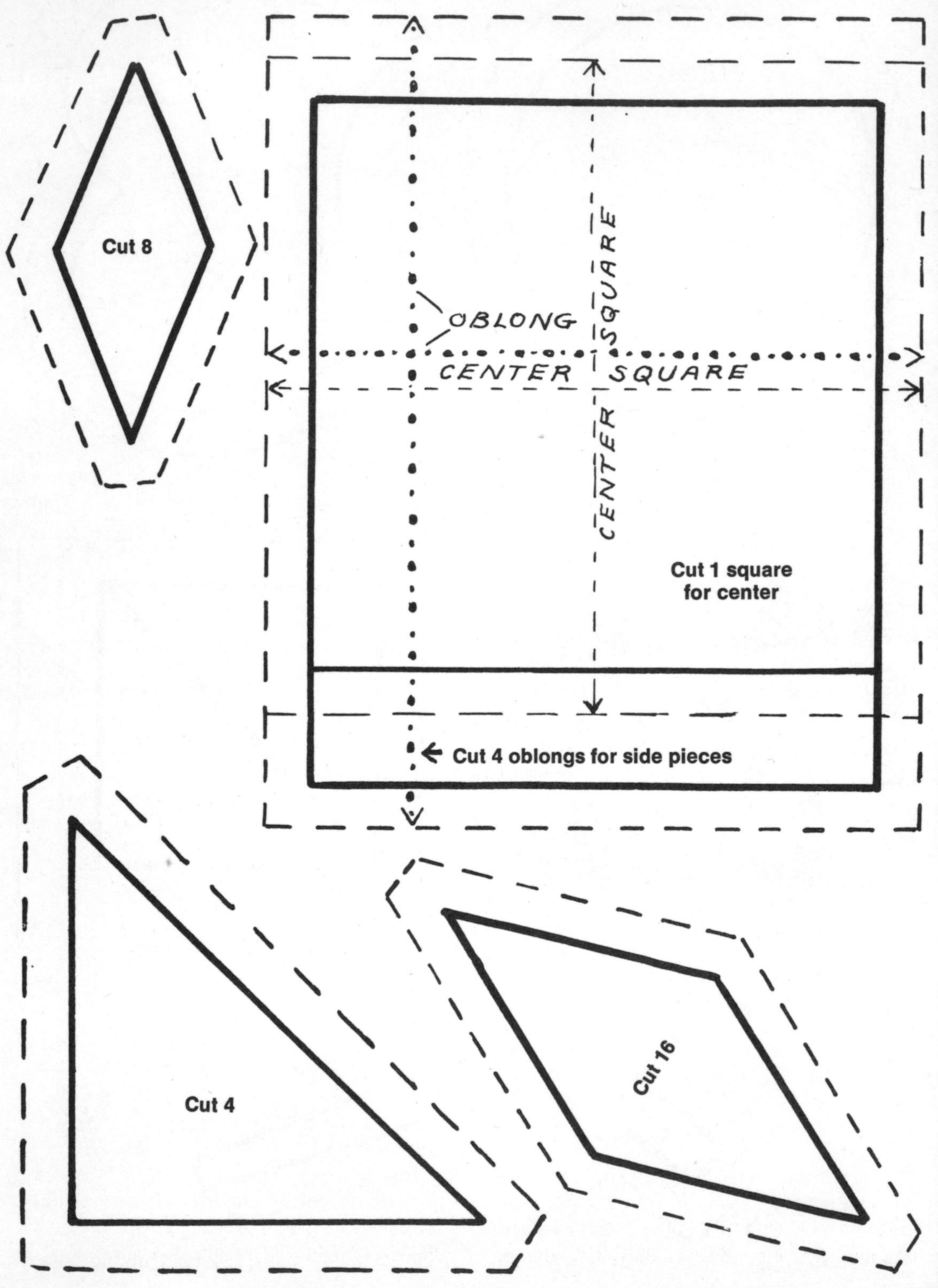

Grandmother's Flower Garden

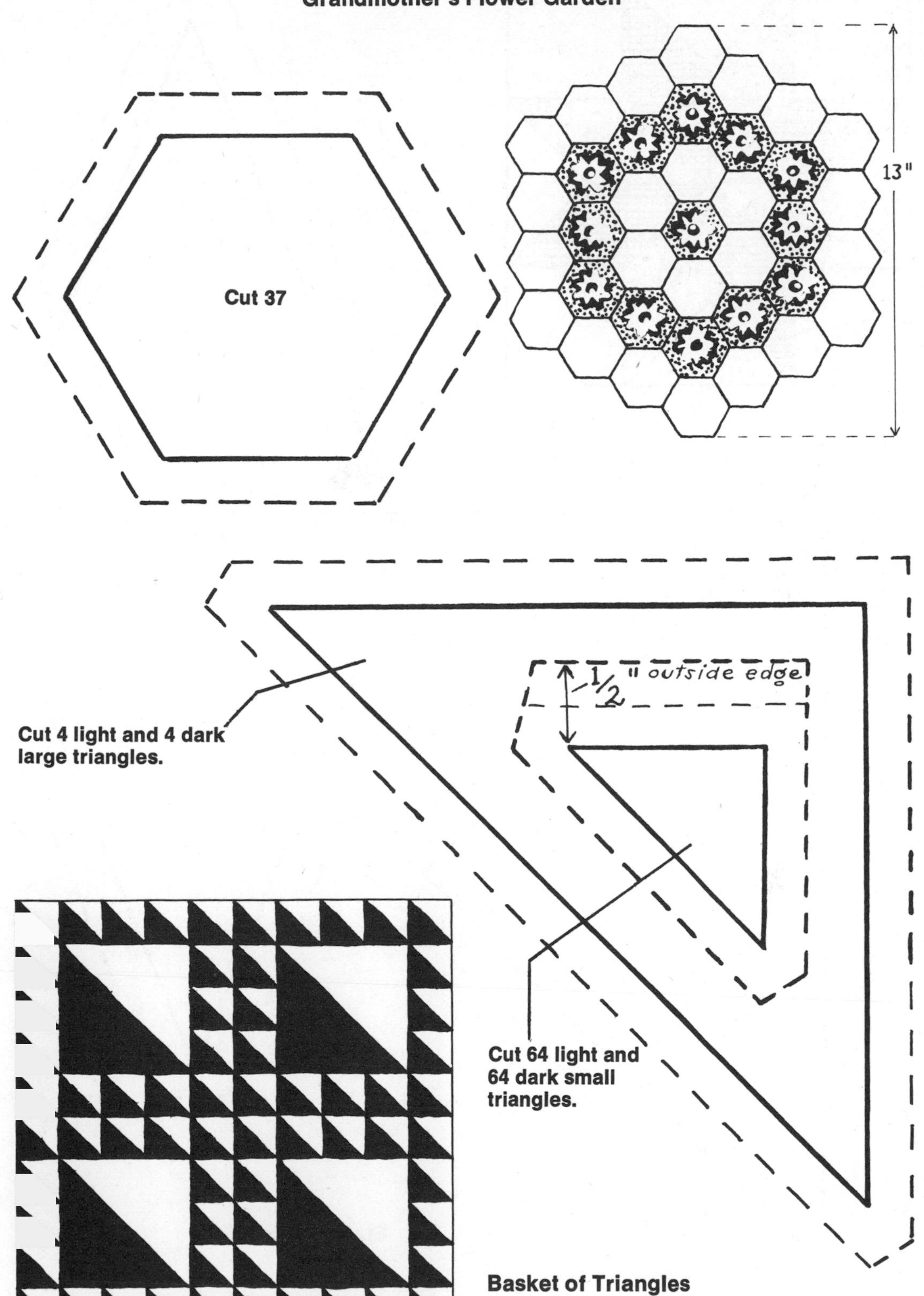

Basket of Triangles

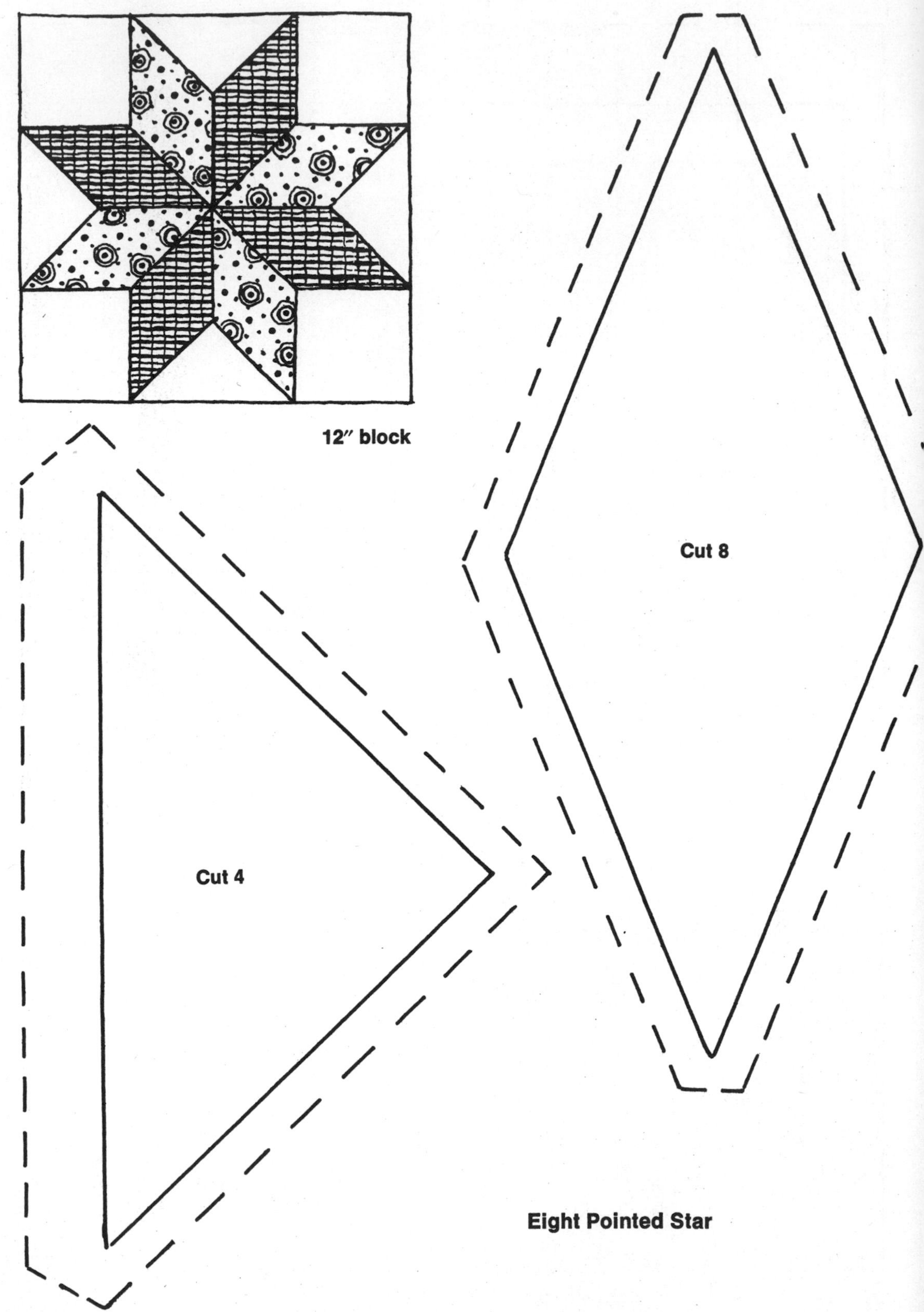

Eight Pointed Star

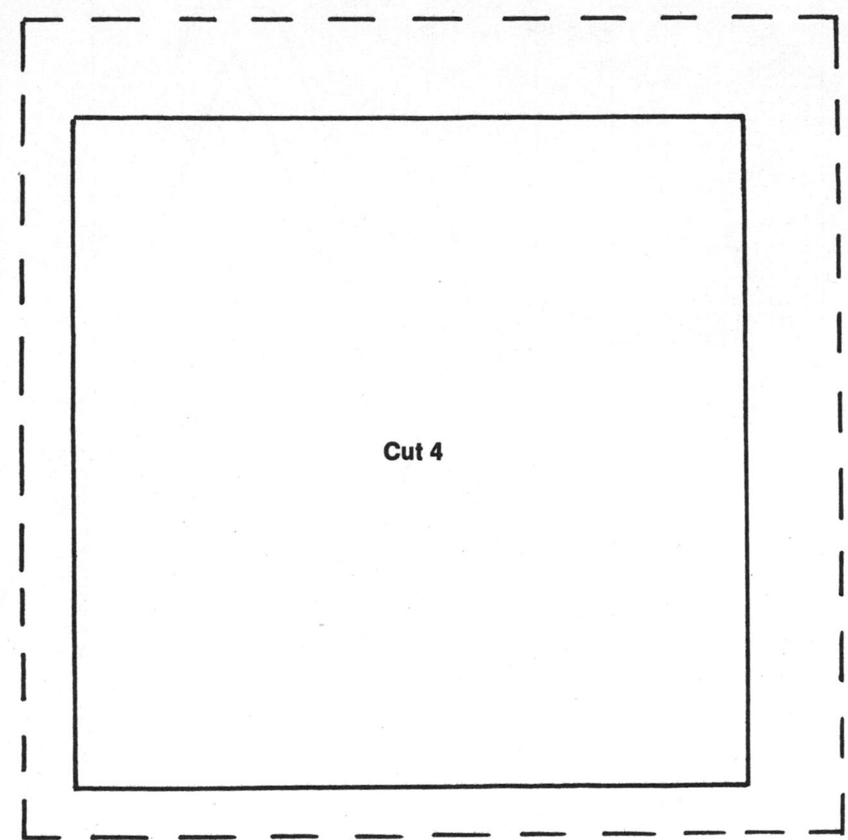

Noonday or Sunburst

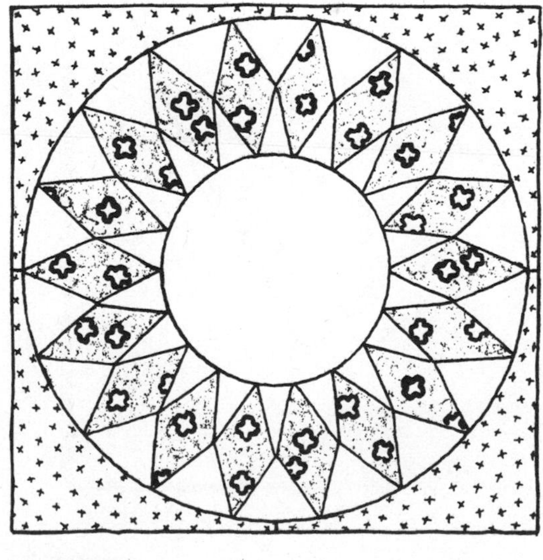

11″ block

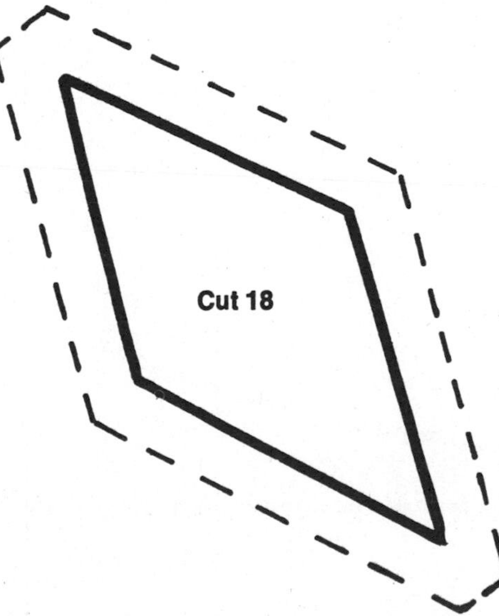

Noonday or Sunburst (cont.)

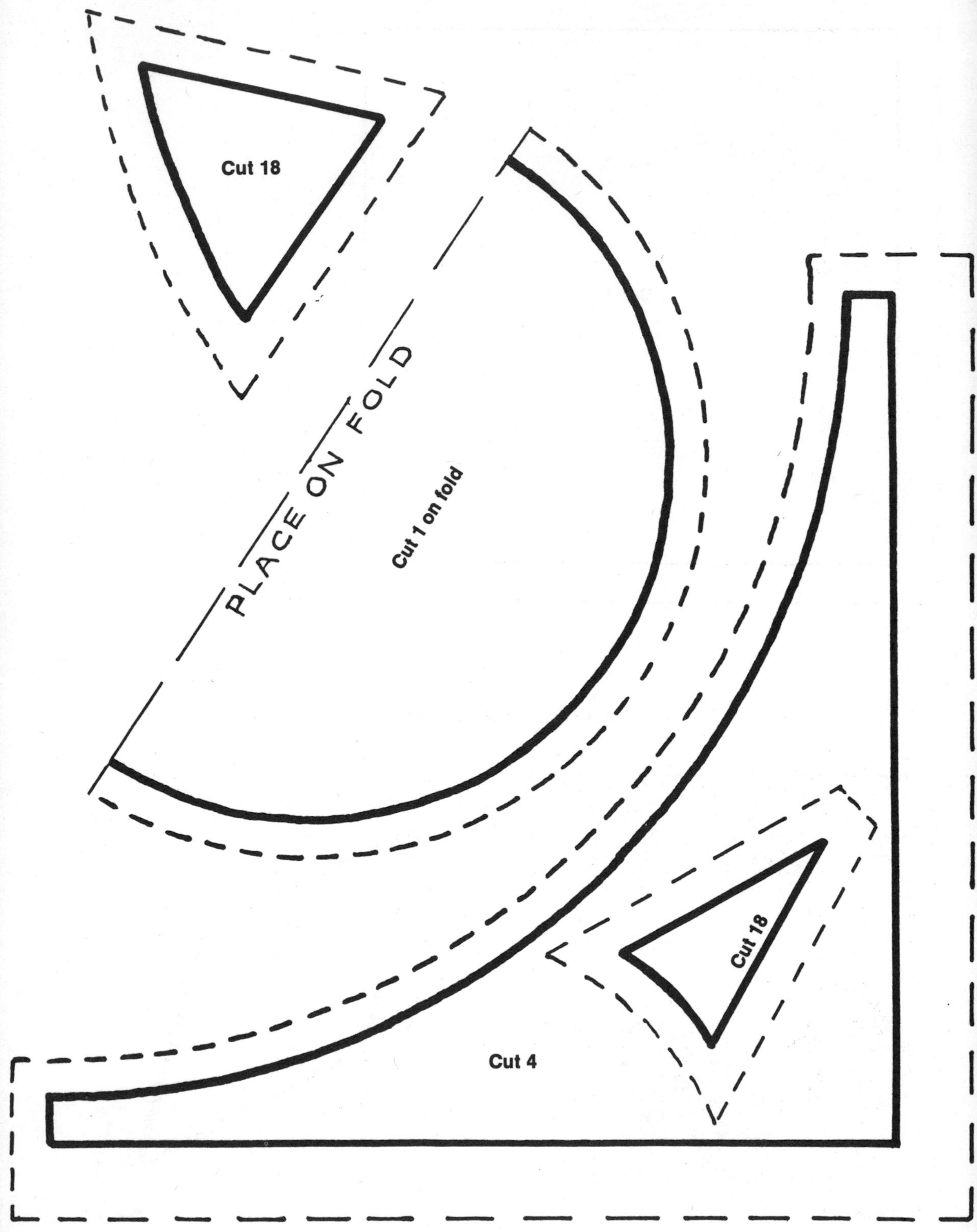

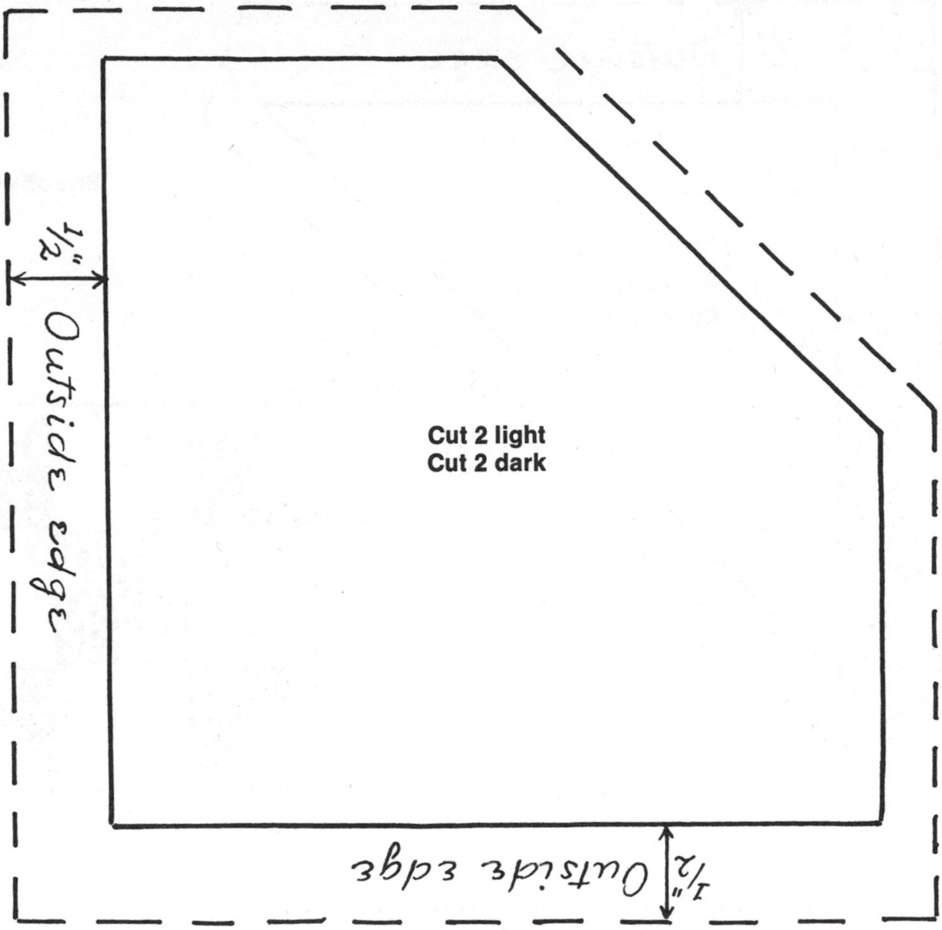

Cut 2 light
Cut 2 dark
1/2"
Outside edge
1/2"
Outside edge

Cut 1 dark

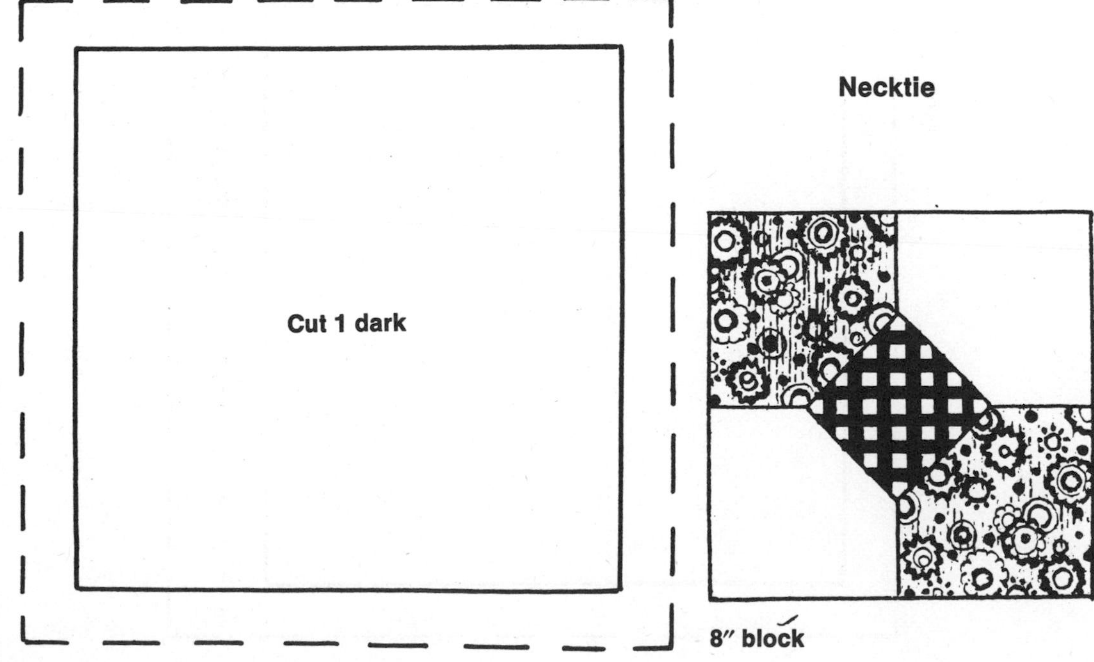

Necktie

8″ block

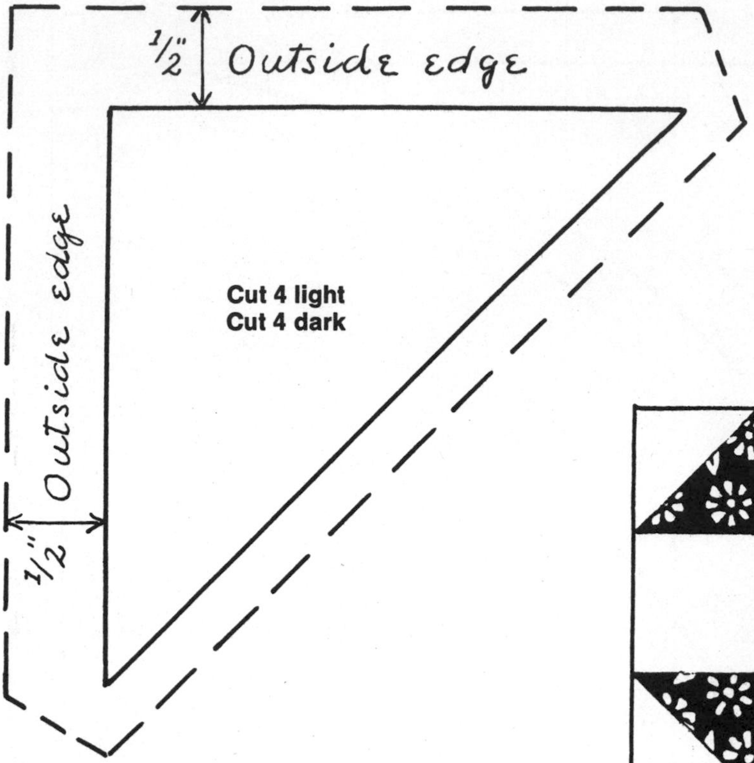

1/2"
Outside edge
Outside edge
1/2"
Cut 4 light
Cut 4 dark

Shoofly

9″ block

1/2"
Outside edge
Cut 4 light
Cut 1 dark

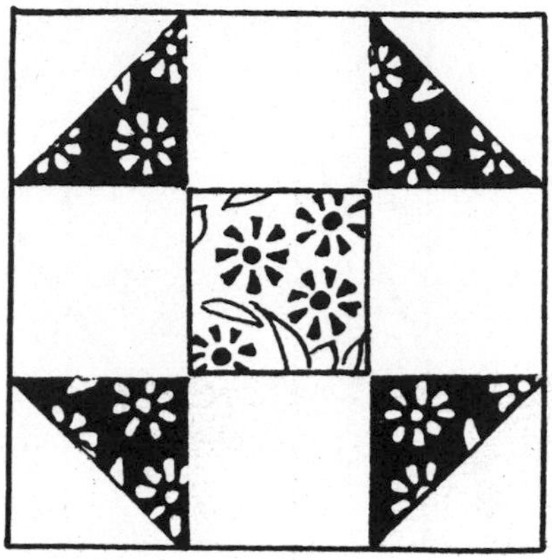

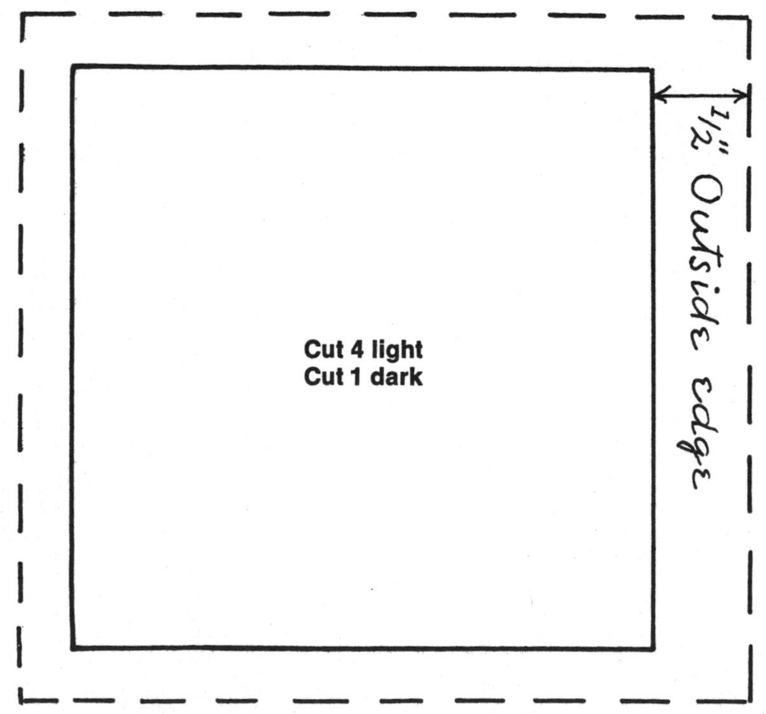

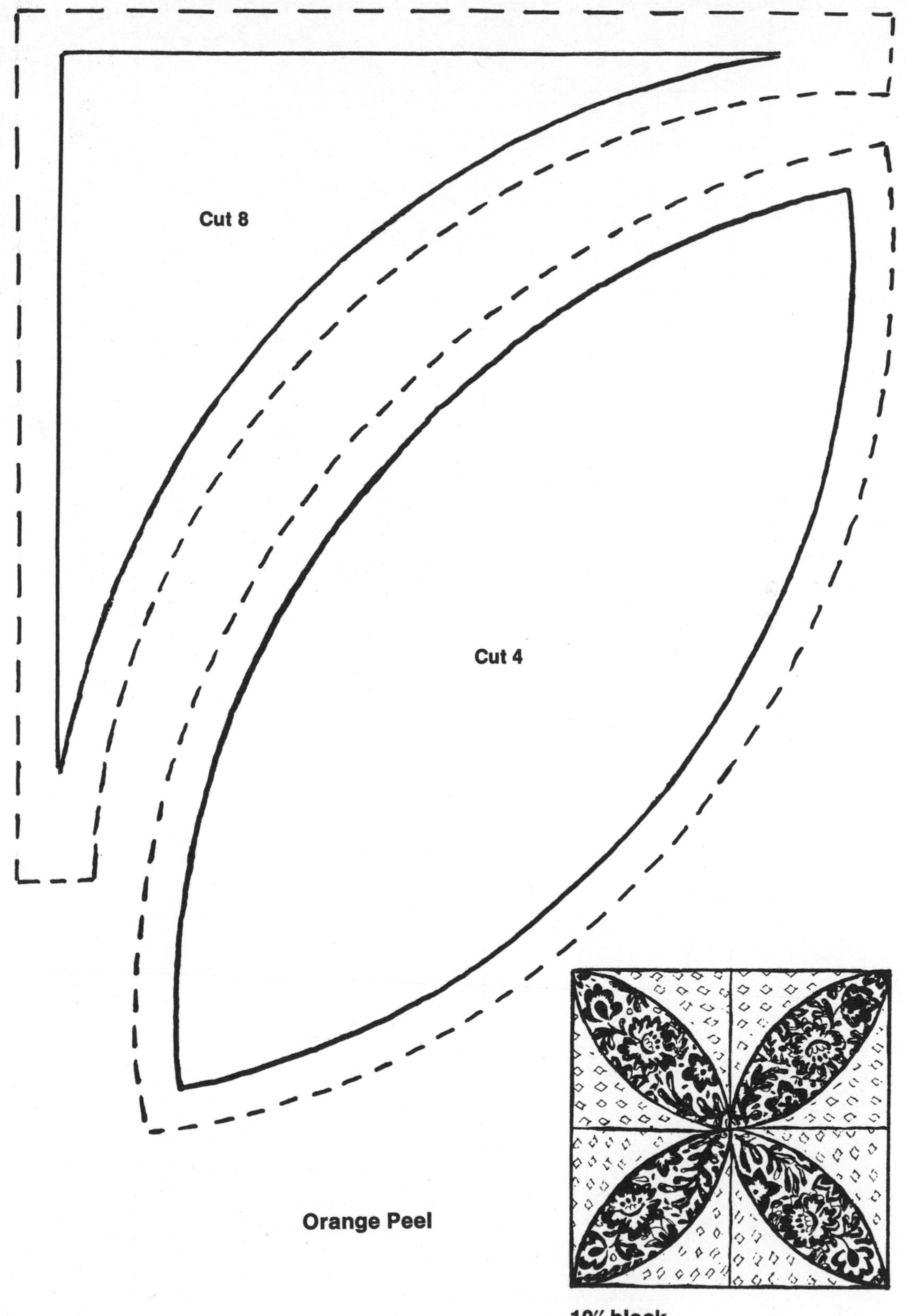

Orange Peel

10″ block

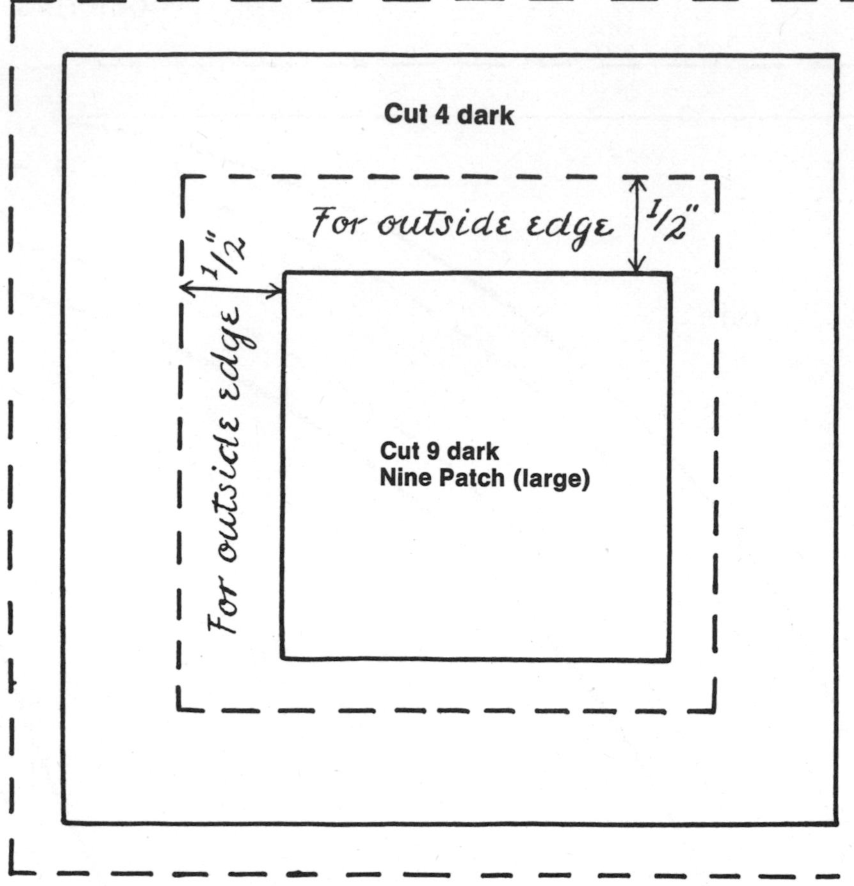
Cut 4 dark
For outside edge
1/2"
1/2"
For outside edge
Cut 9 dark
Nine Patch (large)

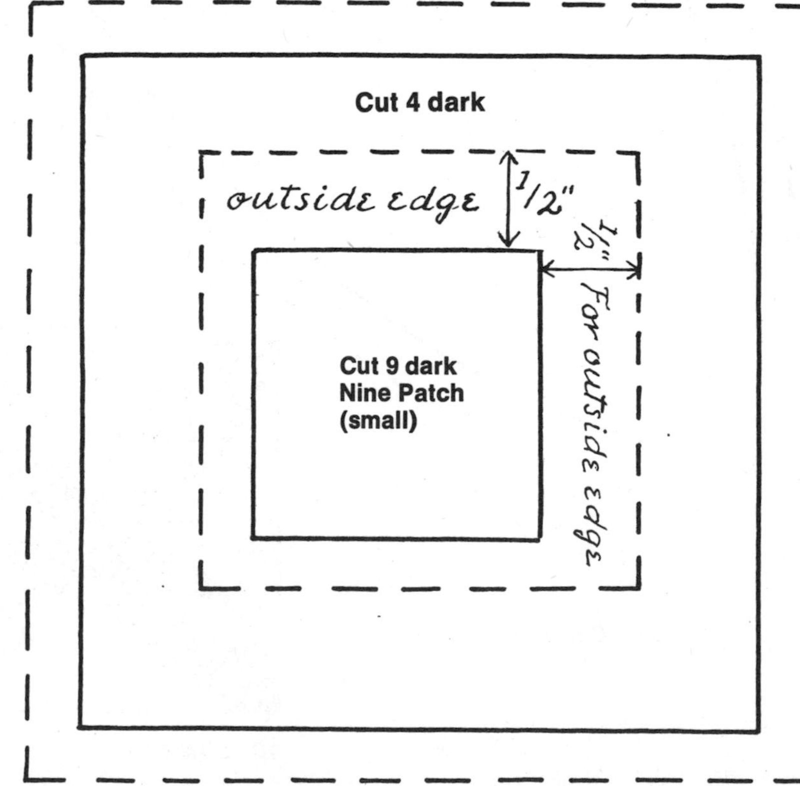
Cut 4 dark
outside edge
1/2"
1/2"
For outside edge
Cut 9 dark
Nine Patch
(small)

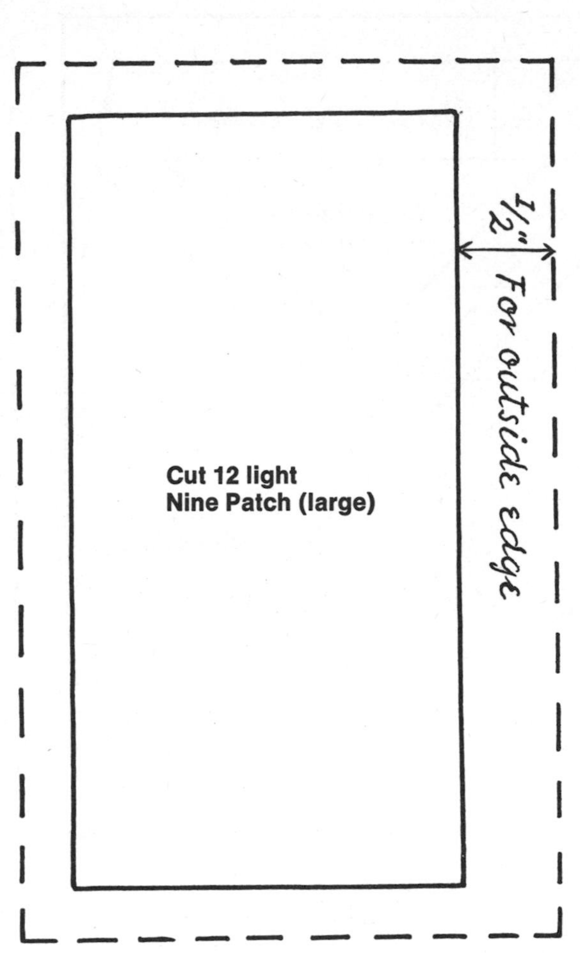

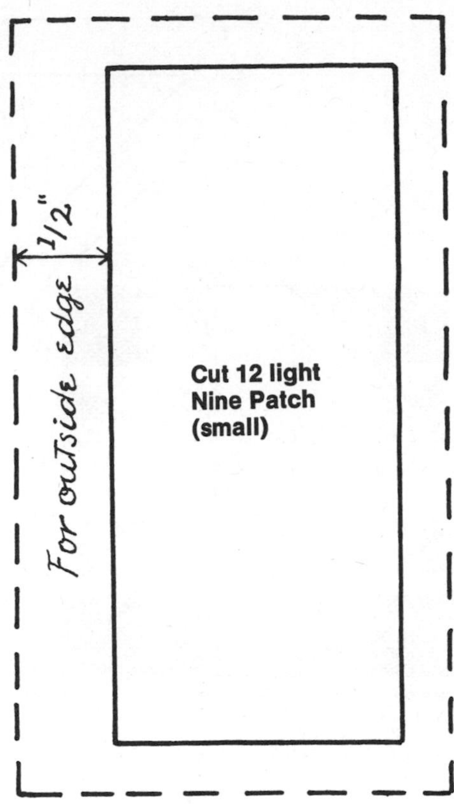

Nine Patch

large: 14″ block
small: 10″ block

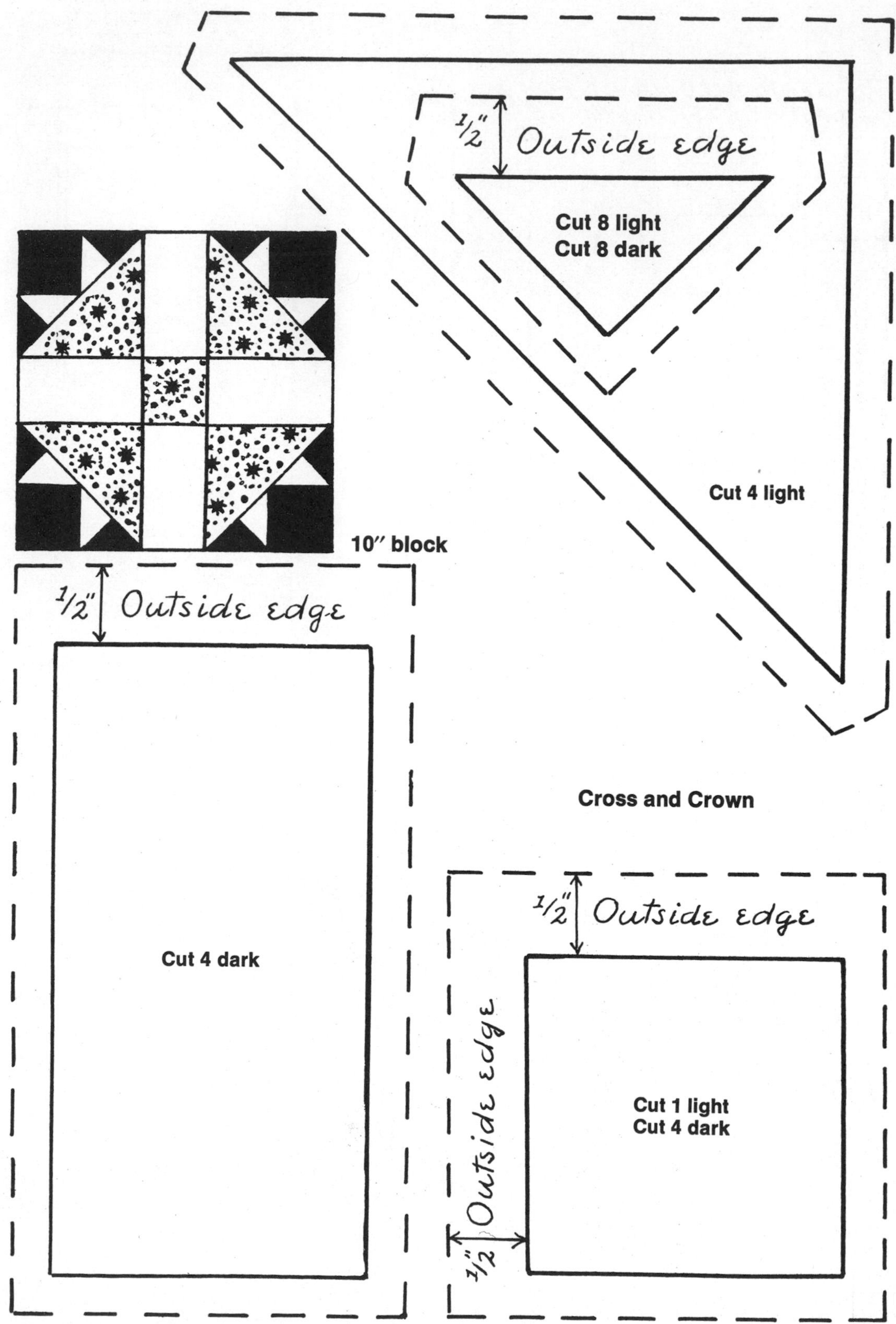

Cross and Crown

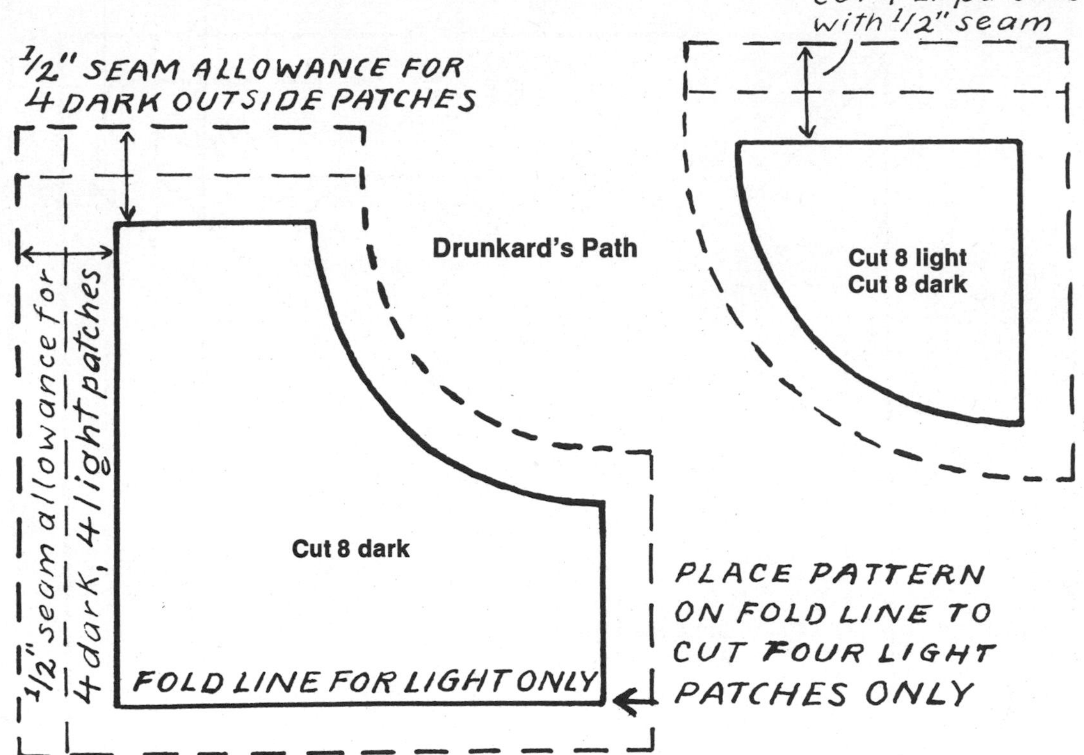

10″ block

Pinwheel

12″ block

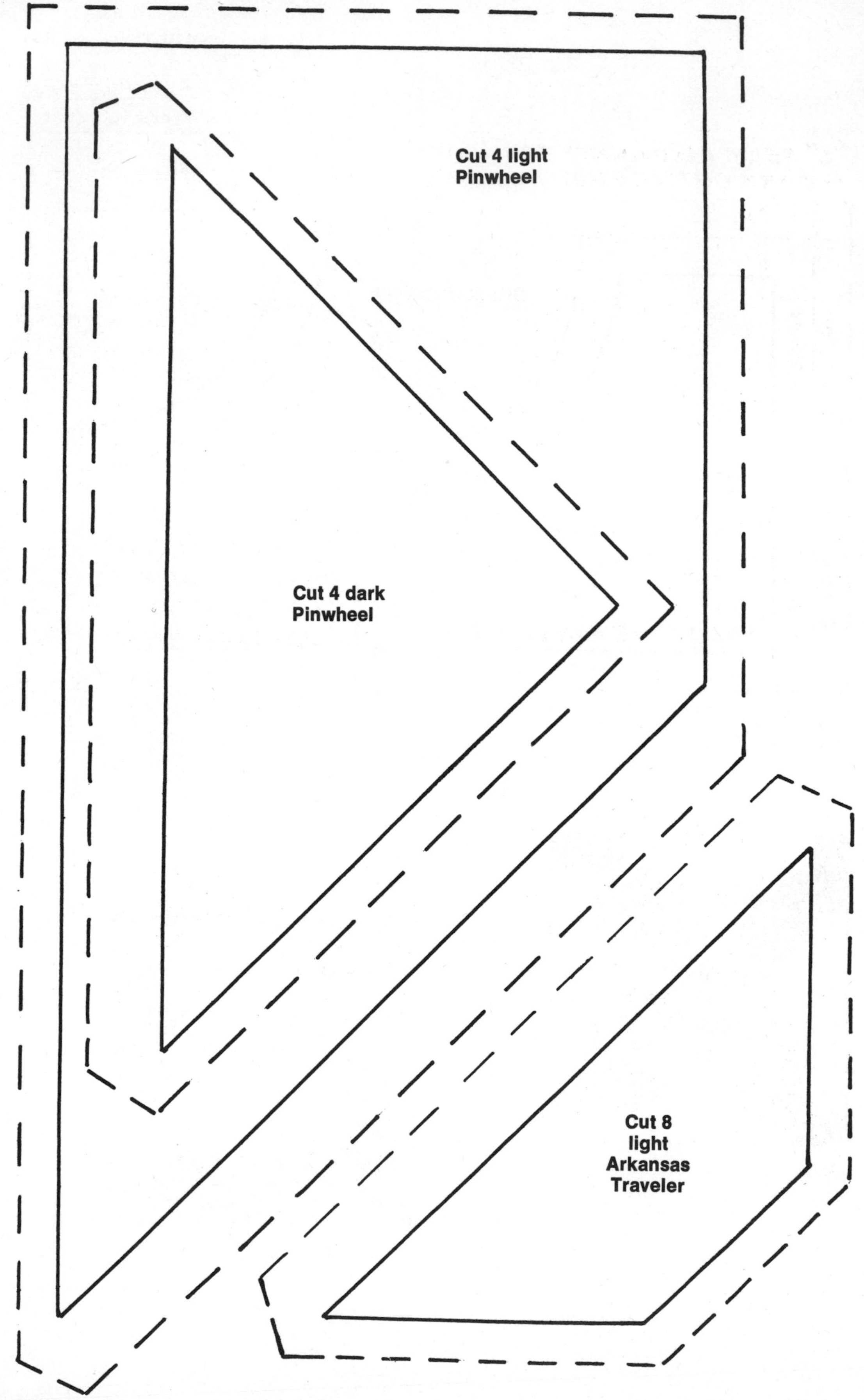
Cut 4 light
Pinwheel
Cut 4 dark
Pinwheel
Cut 8
light
Arkansas
Traveler

Arkansas Traveler

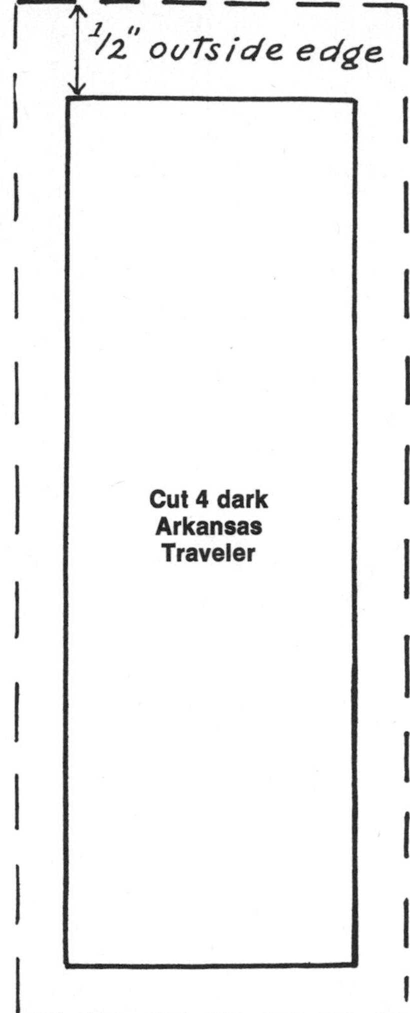

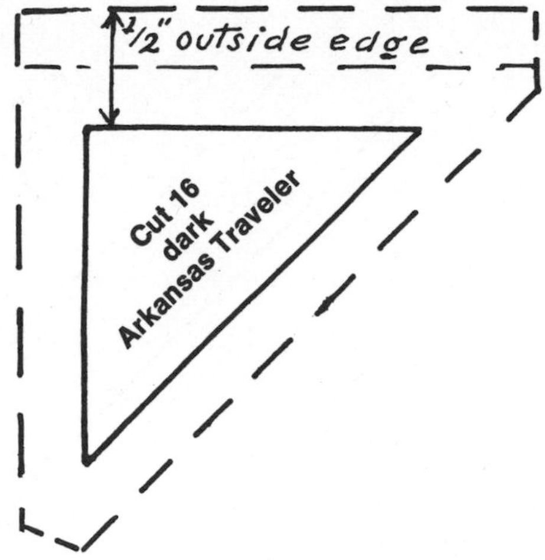

9″ block

Kansas Troubles

12″ block

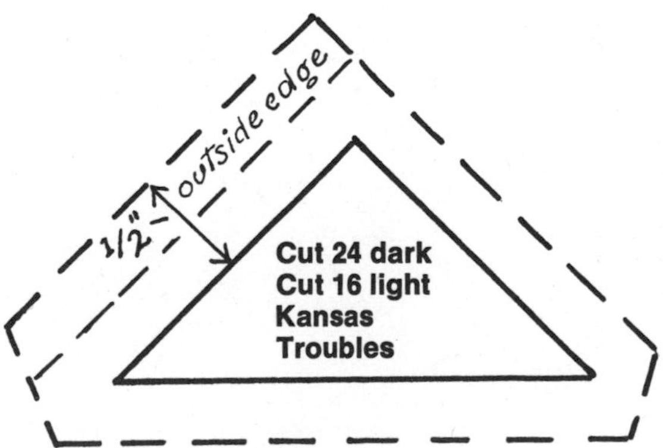

Kansas Troubles (cont.)

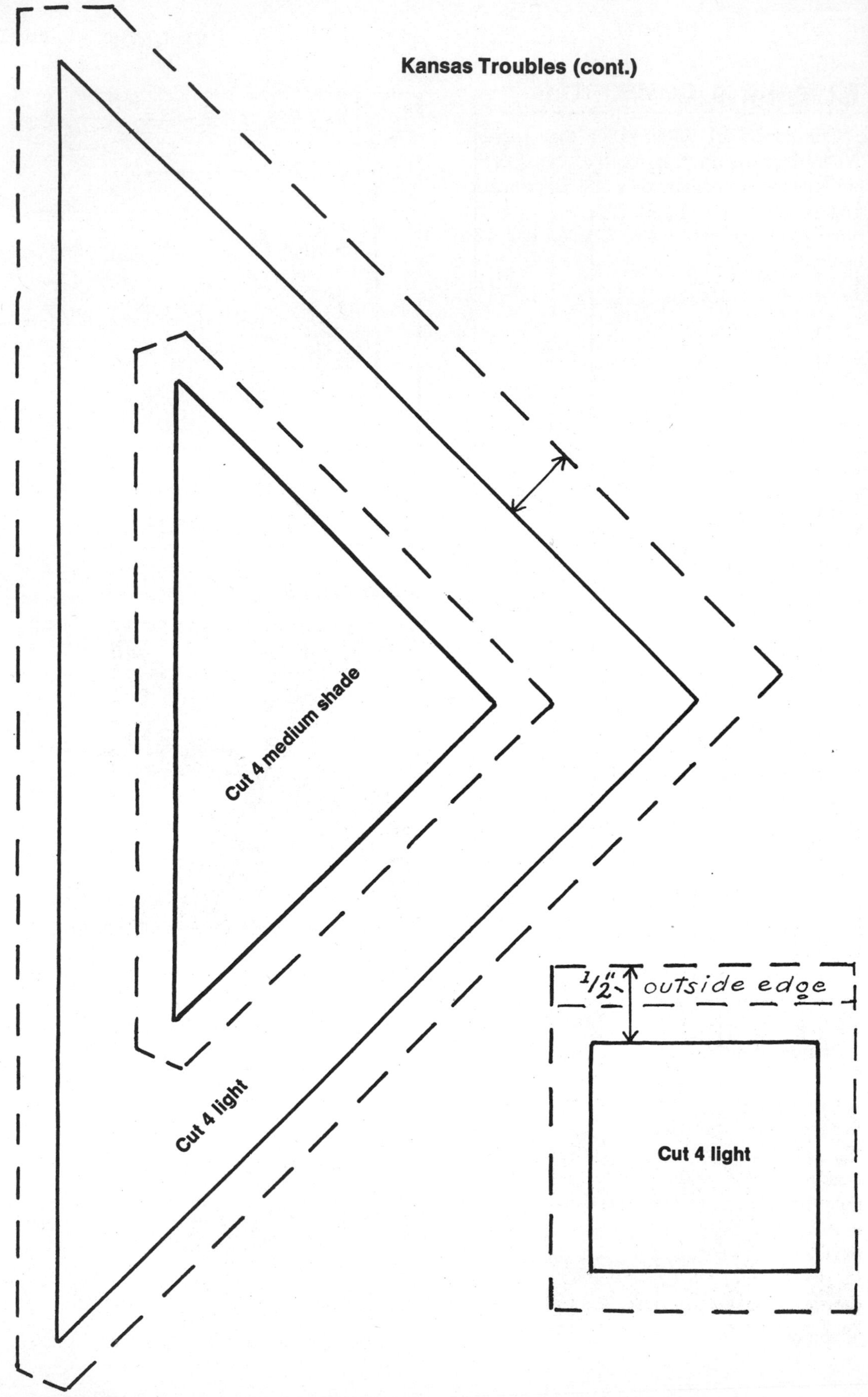

TO MAKE A COMFORTER

Comforters are tufted rather than quilted. Where more warmth is wanted, the interlining is made of feathers or wool. Dacron batting, or two layers of cotton batting are more often used. An old woolen blanket can also be used.

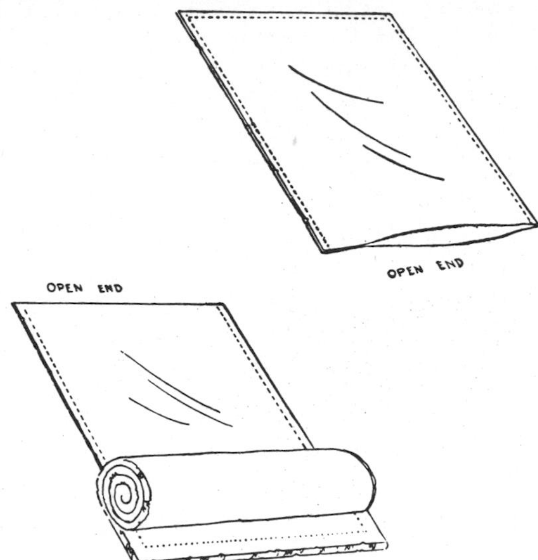

Sew the top and backing together to form a tube which is closed at one end. With tube wrong side out and on a flat surface, place the batting on smoothly and evenly. To give the comforter a nice rounded finish, allow the bat to extend beyond the edges about 1 inch all around. Baste the bat or interlining to all four sides of the top and turn right side out as you would a pillow slip. Sew up the open end and complete by tufting or by very wide quilting.

Tufting. Tufting is the process of tying the layers of a comforter together at intervals closely enough to hold them in place (4 to 6 inches). Use 4-ply Germantown or Knitting Worsted wool yarn or nylon yarn and a heavy needle (one large enough to make a hole for the yarn to go through). Use double thread. Force the needle straight down through the layers and then straight up about ¼″ away from where it went in. Pull yarn through leaving ends to tie. Tie a firm double knot and cut leaving ½″ ends for tufts.

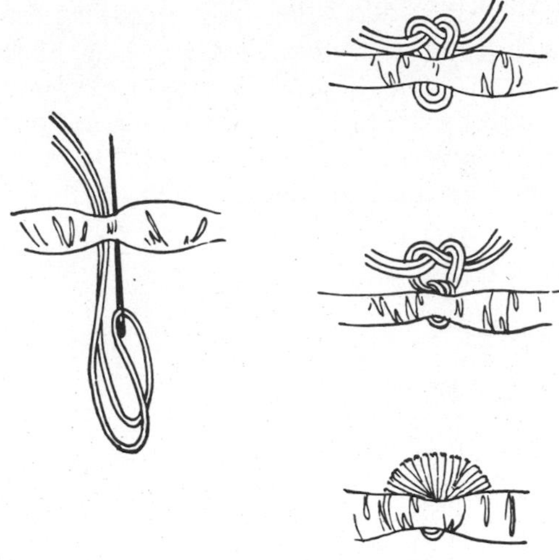

TRAPUNTO OR ITALIAN QUILTING

This type of quilting does not cover the whole area but is done only on certain parts. A design with double lines is used. Trace or stamp design onto a soft open-weave muslin or any thin loosely-woven cotton fabric. Baste muslin to under side of the top (which is often of satin or taffeta) with design showing. Work running stitch on all lines of the design, sewing through the muslin and taffeta.

To raise the design, a heavy yarn is inserted between the double lines. Use a blunt needle and soft yarn such as Germantown. Use double or as many strands as necessary to fill the space. Insert the needle through

muslin, and follow the design, pushing the needle between the double lines of stitching. To turn around curves bring needle out through muslin and insert again in same hole. On sharp corners yarn may be left to form a small loop outside. Insert needle and proceed.

STUFFED OR PADDED QUILTING

The all-white quilt (no piecing, no appliqué) originated in England. The only decoration is a very elaborate all-over quilting pattern, part of which is further enhanced with extra padding to make it stand out in relief. This is sometimes called "bas-relief" quilting. After the quilting is finished, the larger spaces (flower petals, leaves, etc.) are stuffed from the back of the quilt. A small hole is "punched" by pushing threads aside in the backing (do not cut), and tiny pieces of cotton are carefully inserted to raise these design parts and make them puffy. If the hole is small, the threads can be stroked back into place and the opening will not show. A very rich-looking quilt can be made in this way especially if the quilting pattern is elaborate and well-designed, and the quilting itself is precisely done.

CARING FOR QUILTS

A beautiful quilt deserves the best of care, and a well made one should keep its puffy shape after many launderings.

Quilts should not be allowed to become too soiled. It is then possible to wash them in the automatic washer using the short washing cycle intended for fine fabrics. Use a mild soap or detergent.

Never wring by hand or spin dry in the washer. Instead arrange the wet quilt on the line, matching corners, and let it drip dry. Never touch it with an iron.

After washing, look over carefully to see if any quilting stitches have broken and, if so, repair at once.

Chapter 4

Smocking

Smocking is a beautiful old art which seems never to go out of style. In Anglo-Saxon times, women wore a loose undergarment or "smock" with breeches and a woolen dress over it. It gradually became the fashion to decorate the upper part of the undergarment with fine stitching and to cut the neck of the overdress lower to display the hand work.

Later, as recently as 150 years ago, men wore loose smocks or dusters which were ornamented with a smocking design to denote their trade.

Today these lovely rows of stitches are used extensively on children's wear, such as dresses and coats, and to a lesser degree on women's blouses, lingerie, bed jackets, etc.

Real English smocking is done after very careful preparation of the foundation fabric. It is symmetrical and elastic, and a limitless number of designs, exquisite in coloring and stitch arrangement, can be achieved. It is not at all difficult if the rules are followed carefully.

ENGLISH SMOCKING

Fabrics and Thread

Many fabrics are suitable for smocking, but it probably is at its best on fine crisp cottons such as Pima cotton, fine gingham, chambray, dotted Swiss, fine lawn, muslin, and percale.

Use six-strand embroidery floss, varying the number of strands according to the fineness of the fabric and smocking pattern. Four strands is a good average. Use crewel needles for the smocking, and sharps or crewels for the gathering.

Preparation of the Fabric

There are several points to keep in mind when preparing the fabric for English smocking.

Amount or Width of Fabric. For every inch of finished smocking allow about 3 inches of fabric. Measure the yoke space or wherever the smocking is to be used, and multiply by three. This means adding width in cutting if the pattern was not designed to allow for smocking.

Marking. There are hot-iron transfers available for the rows of dots needed when gathering, or you can dot your own fabric (a tedious process). The *dots* should be ⅜″ to ⅝″ apart depending upon the fineness of the fabric. The *rows* are spaced ½″ apart. The dots must be spaced uniformly, and on the rows each dot must be exactly below the one above.

Instead of marking the dots it is entirely possible to follow the stripes on a striped fabric (rows will have to be marked), the checks on checked gingham, or the dots on dotted Swiss when doing the gathering or "gauging."

If using a transfer pattern, iron it onto the wrong side so that the larger pleat will come on the right side and the dots will not show on finished work. Also, when placing transfer in position, line up the dots with the thread or grain of the fabric, leaving a seam allowance at the top.

On a curved neckline clip the pattern at regular intervals to fit it to the curve.

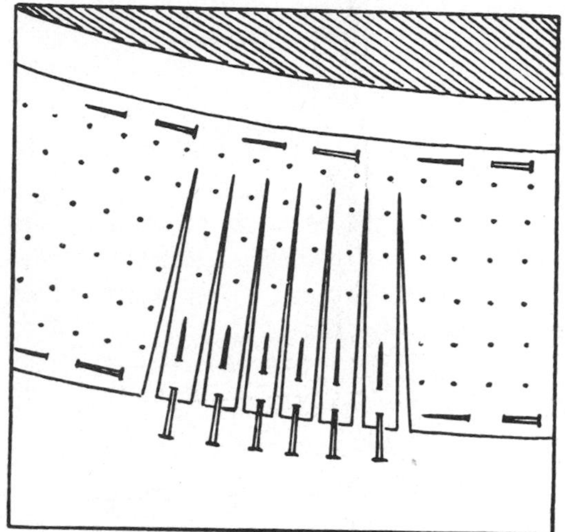

Gathering or Gauging

Each row of gathering must have a separate thread. Working on the wrong side, start with a knot and a double stitch at the right. Pick up a very short stitch (1/16″) on each dot, then slip the needle to the next dot. This makes a uniform running stitch.

By setting the stitches exactly below each other in rows, a foundation of small "organ" pleats is formed upon which the smocking stitches are worked. The rows of gathering serve as a guide for the rows of smocking as well as to hold the pleats in place. The gathering is removed after the smocking is completed.

Do not pull the gathers too tightly; pleats will form and they should be movable in order to insert the needle between them when smocking. Leave the threads in loose ends. Fasten them later by tying 2 together in a slip knot or winding each separately on a pin.

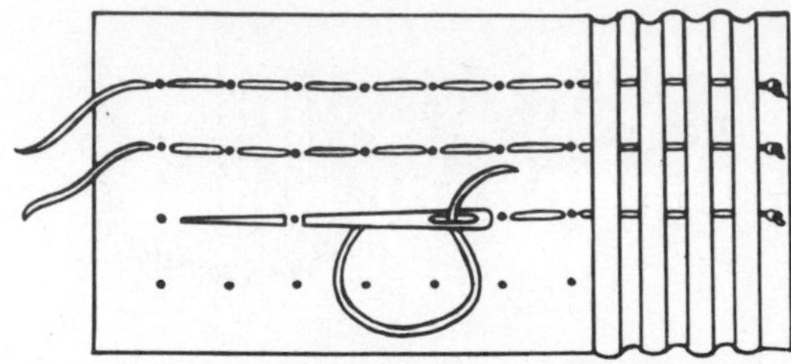

There is a small gathering machine available which does this part of the work for you in even and accurate rows. If you intend to do much smocking, it would be well to investigate it.

Smocking Stitches

There are several basic stitches in smocking. The lovely designs which can be made are the result of combining and arranging them in different ways.

Do not pull the smocking stitches too tight; the work should "give." Some calculation is necessary to make a design symmetrical if you wish the points or waves to come out even on each side.

Outline, Stem, or Rope Stitch. This is worked from left to right. Keep the thread under the needle and pick up one pleat at a time.

Cable Stitch. Work this the same as outline stitch but throw the thread first above the needle and then below, alternately.

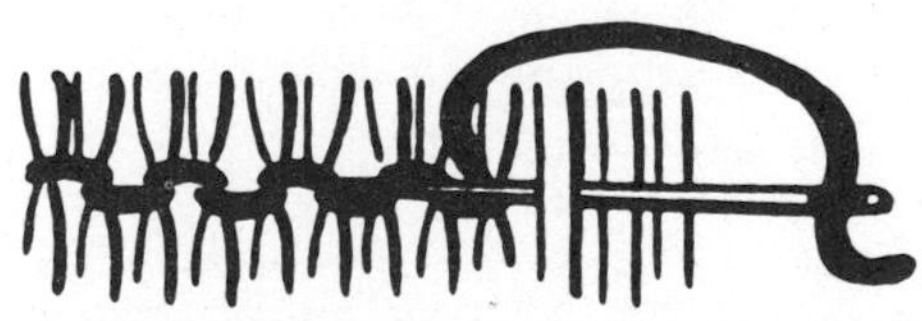

Double Cable. Two rows of single cable worked close together.

Single Wave Stitch. Work up and down from one row of gathers to another, picking up stitches as shown. A cable stitch is made at the top and at the bottom. This is sometimes called Van Dyke Stitch, and when several rows are used close together it may be called Surface Honeycomb or Diamond Stitch. It may be varied by working several cable stitches instead of one before moving up or down (see diagram for dress).

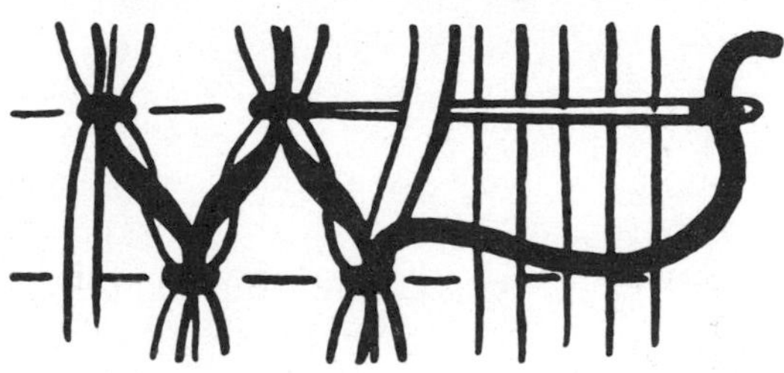

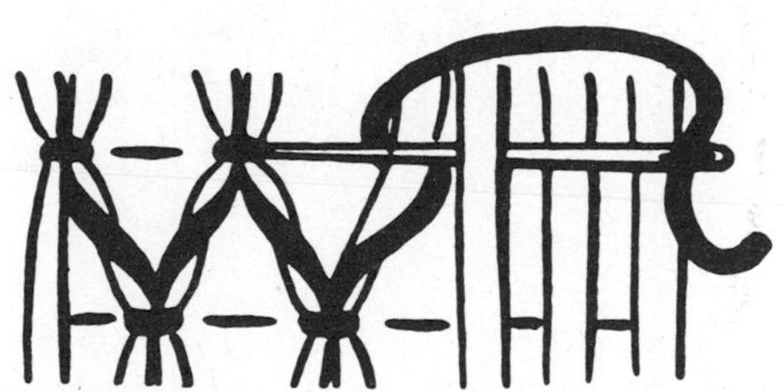

Trellis Stitch. Similar to Single Wave Stitch but with stitches closer together. It may be varied by taking 3, 4, or 5 stitches on each diagonal with the cable stitch at top and bottom. Keep stitches evenly spaced. This is sometimes called Chevron or Step Wave Stitch. Work from left to right.

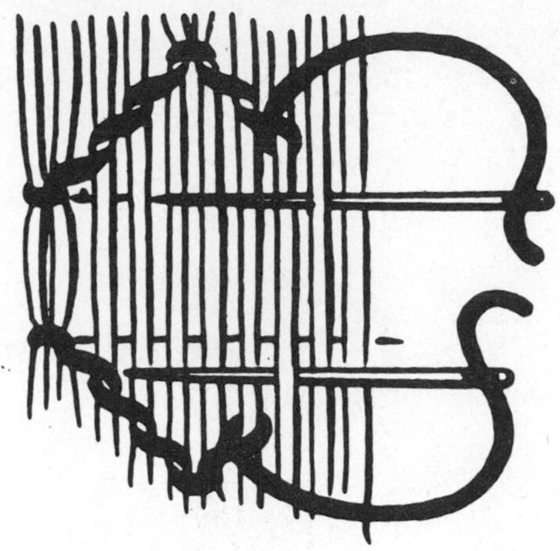

Honeycomb Smocking. This is more elastic than other types of smocking. It is usually worked from right to left and is done using 2 rows of dots. Two dots are picked up for each stitch, alternating from one row to the other. Follow the steps as shown in the diagrams and work as follows:

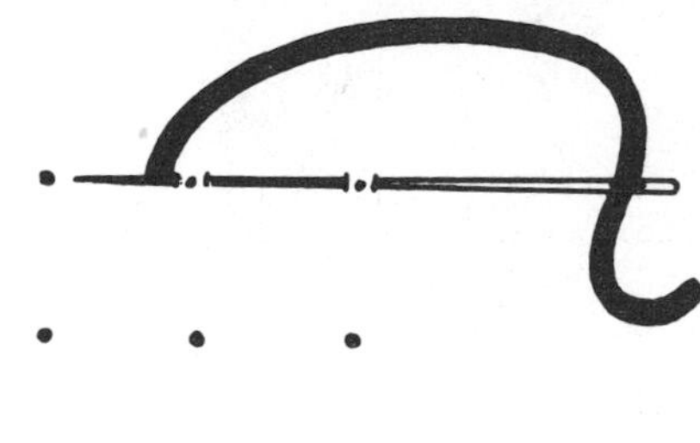

Bring the needle out at the second dot from the end at the right of the first row. Keep the thread above the needle and pick up the first dot of this row and also the second.

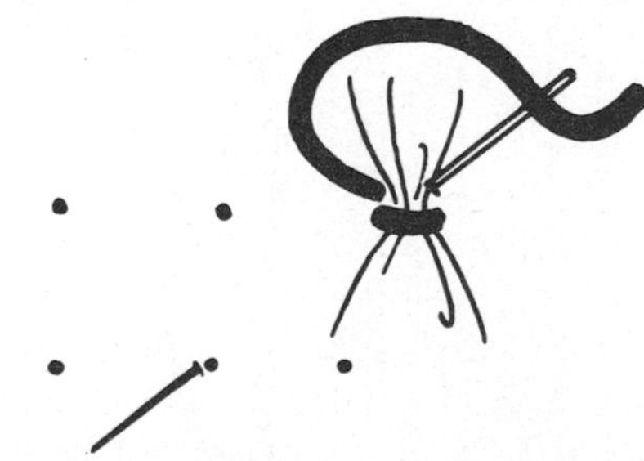

Draw up. Take a second stitch over the first, bringing needle out at third dot on the row below. Pick up the second and the third dot of that row and draw up. Take a second stitch over it, bringing needle out 2 dots to

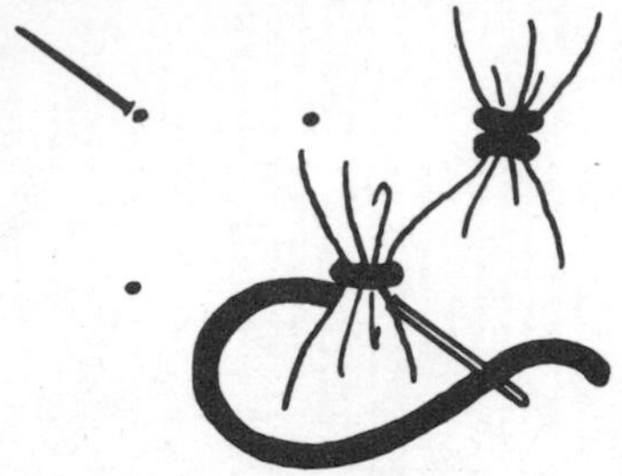

the left of stitch made on top row. Repeat the first stitch and continue back and forth in this manner. Repeat on the two rows below to cover as much space as desired. The long stitch between dots is on the wrong side of the fabric, leaving only dots on top forming a honeycomb effect.

Embellishments. Sometimes smocking is embellished in the open spaces of the design with embroidery stitches such as lazy daisy, rambler rose, bullion, French knots, etc. (See Chapter 2, Embroidery.)

Also, embroidered dots and bars can be added by sewing over and over in satin stitch.

Staying the Back. This is a "trick" which can be used on certain types of smocking patterns.

The pleating or gauging of English smocking is so attractive in itself that it is not necessary to cover it entirely with smocking stitches. Large areas can be left open with borders at top and bottom plus a scattered design (see strawberry design on Color Plate 6). To do this, it is necessary to hold the pleats in place by working rows of smocking outline stitch at about 1″ intervals on the *back* of the pleating. These stitches are elastic and will "give," holding the pleat in place since the gathering stitches are removed after the smocking is finished.

MOCK SMOCKING

This is done by working embroidery stitches over rows of machine gathering. Put in the rows of gathering ½″ to 1″ apart; then work the embroidery stitches on top of the stitching. There is no elasticity to this type of "smocking." The stitches used here are closed feather, creton, and back-stitch. Herringbone, chain, or other decorative stitches may also be used.

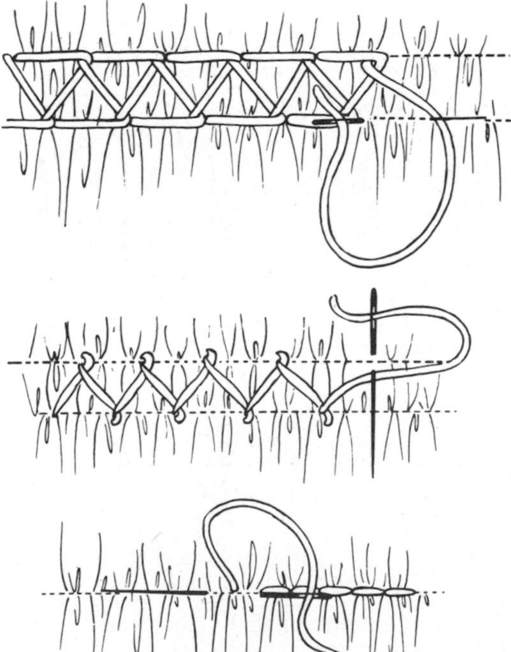

"BOX PLEAT" SMOCKING

A novel way of getting a smocked effect. Make 1″ tucks an inch apart and press them into small box pleats. Baste down the center of each pleat to hold it in place. Draw lines across the pleats lightly about 2″ apart and baste on the lines. Work fine feather or other decorative stitching on these lines. Using embroidery floss, pick up the two edges of the pleat half-way between the rows of embroidery and sew together with double back-stitches. The effect is somewhat like honeycomb smocking. There is no elasticity to this work.

DESIGNS FOR SMOCKING

Color Plate 6 shows four designs for English smocking; two are fairly simple and two are rather elaborate. Diagrams are given here for all four so they can be copied if desired.

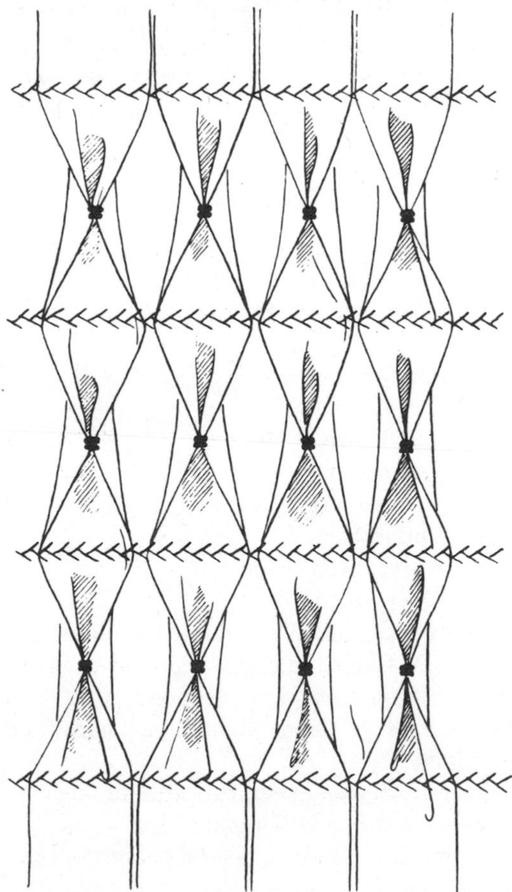

No. 1 Pattern (on white fabric)

Description of rows beginning at top:

2 rows Cable stitch, Kelly green

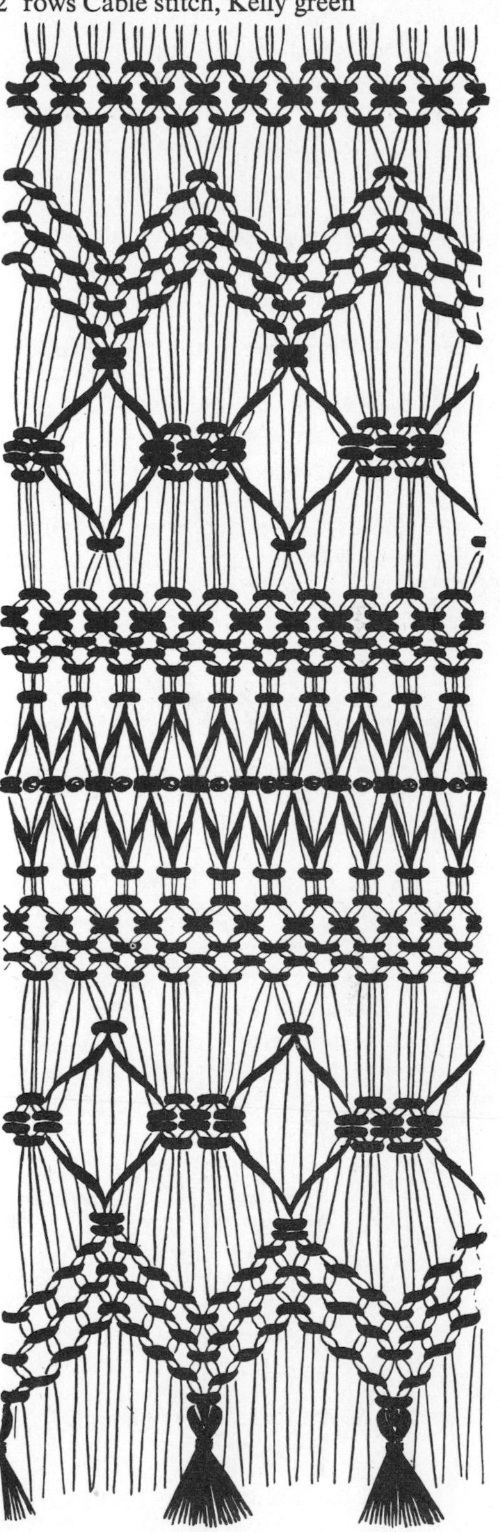

3 rows Trellis stitch, red
2 rows Single Wave stitch, royal blue (3 Cables where rows meet)
1 row Cable, gold
1 row Cable, green
* 1 row Cable, gold
2 rows Single Wave, red with gold French knots worked on top where they meet

Repeat in reverse from * ending with 3 rows Trellis stitch. Make small (½″ to ¾″ long) red tassels and sew one to every other point.

No. 2 Pattern (on light blue fabric)

Beginning at top:
2 rows Cable, red, about ⅜″ apart
1 row Trellis, white, with red dots between points
2 rows Trellis, royal blue, worked to form diamonds with red dot in center of each diamond
1 row Trellis, white, with red dots

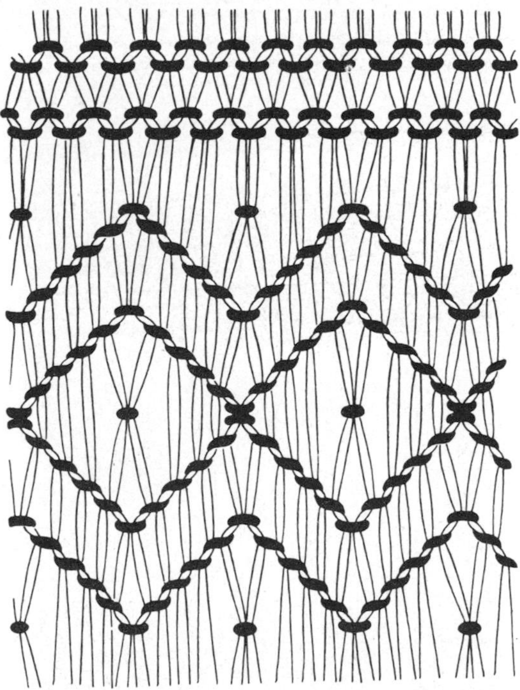

No. 3 Pattern (Strawberry Design)

Beginning at top:
1 row Cable, royal blue
1 row Cable, red
Space (about 1¾″) for scattered strawberry design. Work 3 rows Outline stitch on back in this space to keep pleats in place.
Strawberries are outlined and filled in with red Outline stitch, leaves in green Lazy Daisy stitch, seeds in yellow Seed stitch.

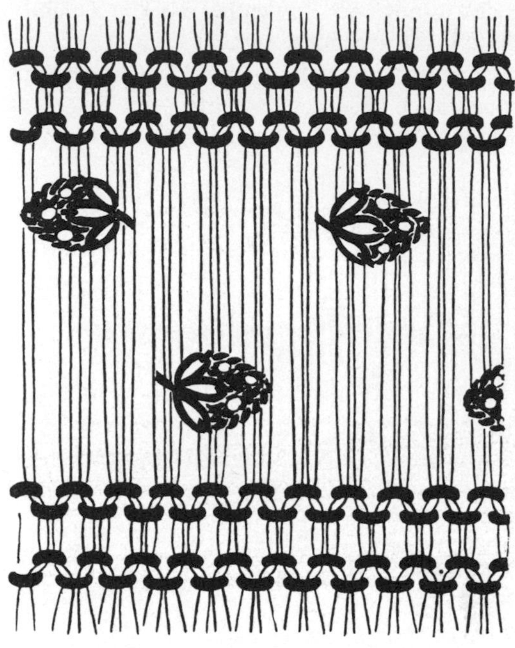

No. 4 Pattern (Dress)

Top half of pattern is given; repeat rows in reverse after center rows of cable stitch (the bottom row on the diagram) for lower half.

Beginning at top:
1 row Outline, navy
1 row Cable, bright blue } work close together
1 row Outline, navy
1 row Feather stitch, orange
1 row Outline, navy
1 row Cable, bright blue } work close together
1 row Outline, navy
* 2 rows Single Wave to form diamonds with 3 Cable stitches where they meet
Small x stitch inside of diamond, navy
Repeat from * using light blue instead of orange.
Repeat again using gold instead of orange.
Navy x stitch in all diamonds.

1 row Cable, bright blue. This forms cen-

ter of pattern. Do not repeat this row.

Repeat remainder of pattern in reverse ending with navy Outline stitch.

Any portion of the wide border patterns may be used.

Hot-iron transfers can be purchased for smocking designs. When using them it is not necessary to do the gathering or gauging. Follow the directions which come with the pattern for transferring and smocking. The appearance is somewhat different from English smocking but is attractive.

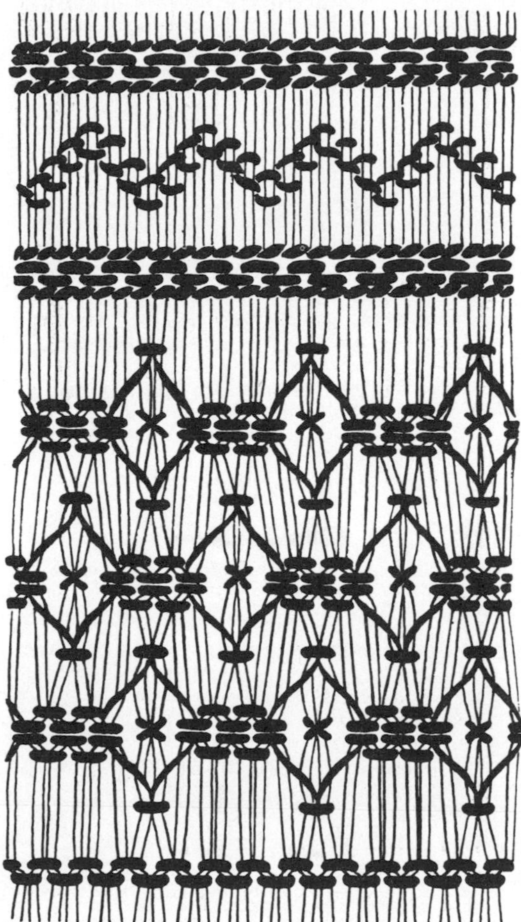

ADDITIONAL SMOCKING DESIGNS

A dainty all-over pattern is shown at right above.

Featured are rows of Trellis stitches, in a diamond pattern, and Lazy Daisy stitches.

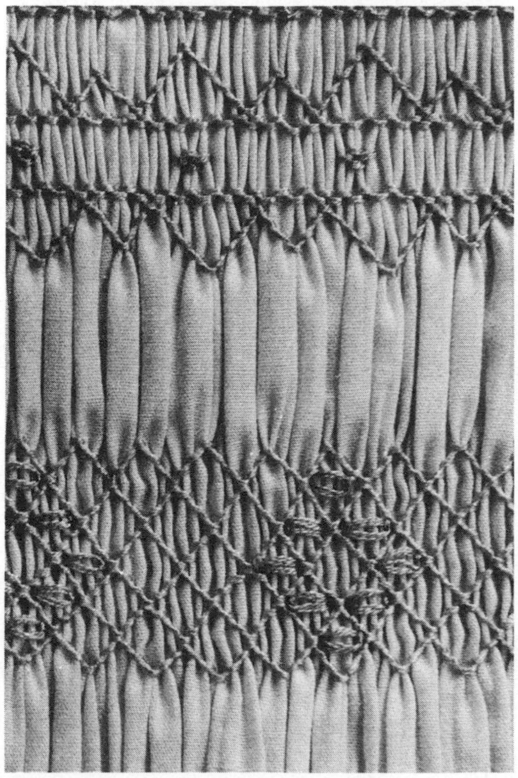

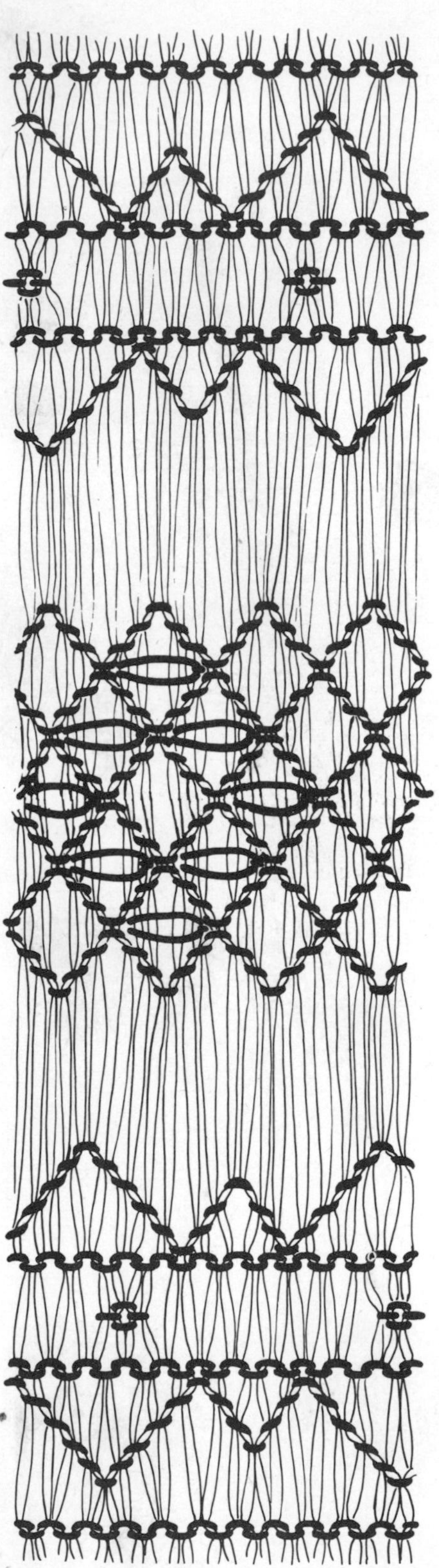

Pattern was worked in blue on white fabric.

Beginning at top, as shown in diagram at left and photograph on preceding page. Pattern was worked in all pink, with dots and Lazy Daisies in blue, on white fabric.

1 row Cable
1 row Trellis
1 row Cable
1 row "dots" made with Cable
1 row Cable
1 row Trellis

6 rows Trellis to make diamond pattern, embellished with horizontal Lazy-Daisy stitches

1 row Trellis
1 row Cable
1 row "dots" made with Cable
1 row Cable
1 row Trellis
1 row Cable

Beginning at top, as shown in photograph below. Pattern was worked in white on blue-and-white-striped fabric.

2 rows Cable
4 rows Trellis
2 rows Cable

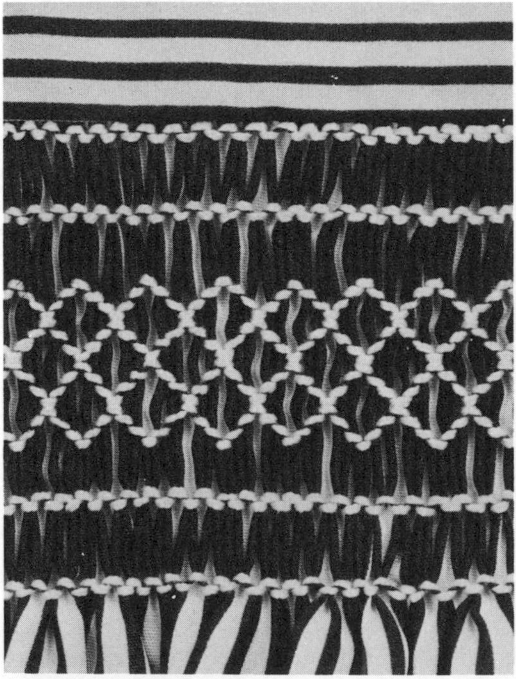

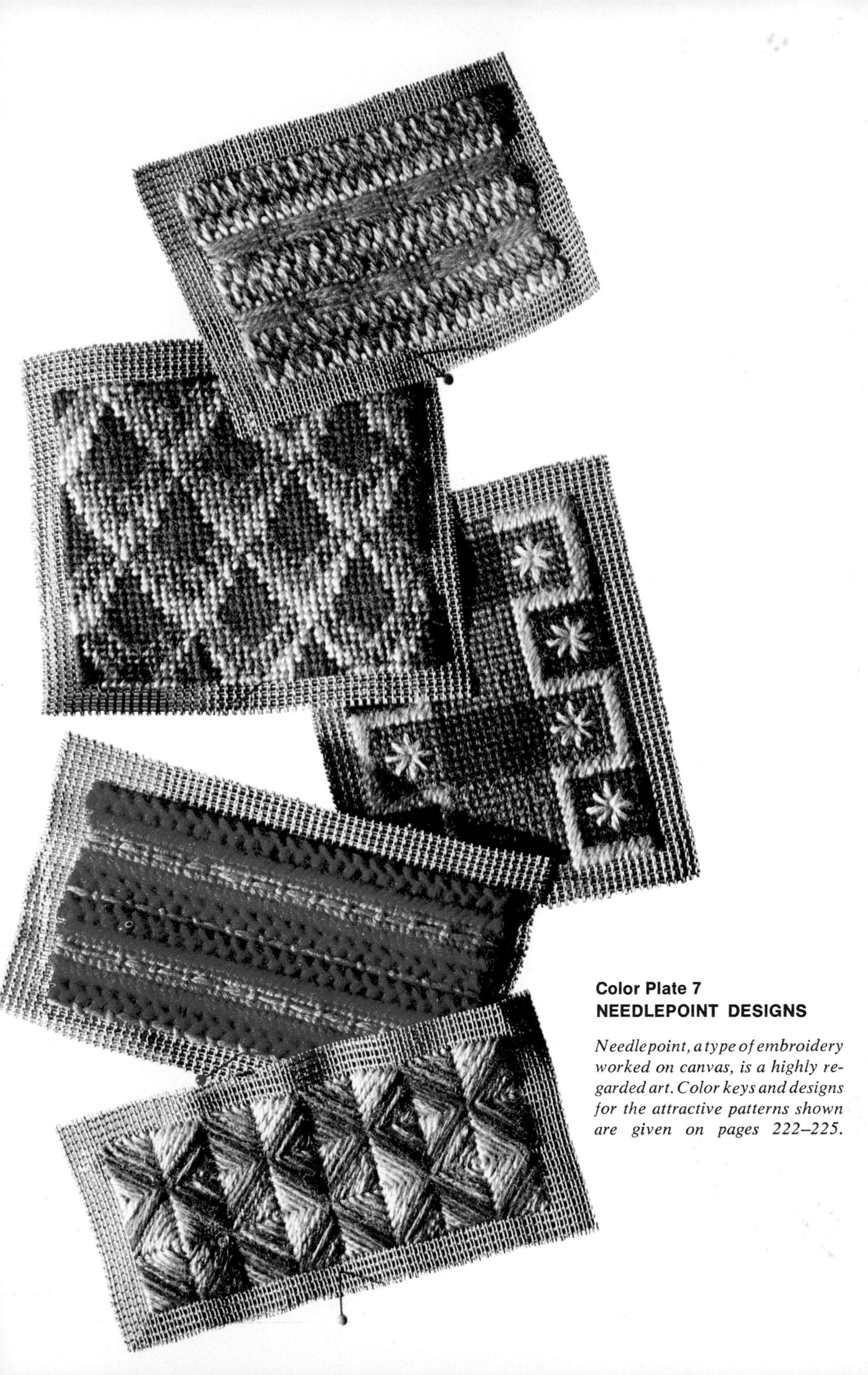

Color Plate 7
NEEDLEPOINT DESIGNS

Needlepoint, a type of embroidery worked on canvas, is a highly regarded art. Color keys and designs for the attractive patterns shown are given on pages 222–225.

Color Plate 8 NEEDLEPOINT SAMPLERS

Pieces like these with the design already worked and the background left to be filled in are often to be found in needlework and department stores or are sold through the mail.

Chapter 5

Needlepoint

Needlepoint is considered by some to be the highest art of the needle. Inspired by the old tapestries, it began in medieval times when queens and court ladies plied their needles, making lovely hangings for their castles while their lords were away. It was an aristocratic art, and the pieces usually told a story or recorded history or the fashions of the periods.

However, it has now been, for more than a hundred years, a popular needlework art at which any woman may try her hand. Tinted or started needlepoint patterns are widely available, or you may design your own or have one designed for you. There is a particular kind of fascination in watching these tiny stitches grow under your fingers into something decorative and useful.

Needlepoint is durable; it will outlast most other decorative materials. Used as upholstery it almost never needs to be replaced. It is adaptable; the stitch is extremely simple, but almost any type of design can be developed with it. Also, the uses to which this embroidery can be put are legion—from pictures to chair seats, from purses to pillows, and from screens to men's vests—all handsome and infinitely suitable.

Patterns may be geometric, naturalistic, or something in-between. Flowers, fruits, animals, houses, ecclesiastical designs, and many other motifs have been expressed in needlepoint. Original designs stemming from individual interests and hobbies or family activities have been the inspiration for rugs, pictures, hangings, and so on. After you have mastered the technique on a simple project you may wish to try your hand at an original creation.

If possible, visit museums and exhibits and look at fine tapestries and needlepoint pieces to appreciate this great hand art.

WHAT IS NEEDLEPOINT?

Needlepoint is a type of embroidery worked on canvas and is a general term used for petit point and gros point. These are really the same stitch, differing only in size. The size of the mesh of the canvas determines the size of the stitch.

Materials

As in other hand work, do not be satisfied with anything less than the best in materials. The labor involved merits the best in canvas and a fine quality of yarn.

There are two types of needlepoint canvas, single-mesh and double-mesh. The former has single, evenly-spaced threads running in both directions (crosswise and lengthwise). Double-mesh canvas, as the name implies, is woven with double threads instead of single, leaving evenly-spaced square meshes for the needle to work through.

Any stitch method (see Needlepoint Designs) may be used on double-thread canvas. Any stitch method *with the exception of Plain Half Cross Stitch* may be used on single-thread canvas.

Canvas is made in many qualities, sizes (number of meshes to the inch), and widths.

Choose a strong canvas with an even weave (square meshes). It should be somewhat stiff. Choose a yarn especially made for the purpose, with body enough to cover the meshes and in a good color selection.

Since needlepoint can be worked in the hand, it has the advantage that it can be carried about. Many people, however, prefer to use a frame which helps the piece to keep its shape better. An old picture frame, or strips of wood with clamps will do as a frame. If working in a rigid frame you do not have to hold the work. This is more time-consuming, but even arthritic people can work in this way. Never use a hoop as it pulls the work out of shape.

Use a tapestry needle, which is a blunt needle with elongated eye large enough to let the thread slide easily. These needles are especially made for working needlepoint. Size 18 or 19 is suitable for gros point, size 22 or 24 for petit point.

Purchase enough yarn of one dye lot to complete the piece. You will also need small scissors and a thimble.

General Rules

After measuring the space to be covered, add 1″ all around for turning under (add more for slip-seat furniture). Also make allowance for a slight shrinkage from working. On small items, such as handbags and glasses cases, work only a few meshes beyond the finished area.

The piece will look more uniform if you can develop a rhythm as you work. Pull the yarn evenly on each stitch. Work a little every day to avoid tension and to keep the rhythm. For a smoother finish, work in one direction only; do not turn work and go back.

Practice each stitch method to find which one is best suited to you and to the piece on which you are working. If you are left-handed turn the stitch diagrams upside down.

For blocking purposes, make a note of the size of the canvas before starting to embroider. Mark with crayon or basting stitch the outer edges of the background area to be covered.

The selvages of the canvas should be at the sides. If you are using a started piece the design will probably have a top and a bottom.

If you are not working in a frame, roll the canvas as you work—from bottom up and from top down. In this way the work can be grasped more easily.

If buying a started piece, be sure the canvas is large enough for the object for which you will use it. There should be at least 2″ of unworked canvas all around for attaching.

Also, choose a design that harmonizes in style and is in proportion to the chair or other piece on which you will use it.

NEEDLEPOINT DESIGNS

Needlepoint designs may be purchased with the motifs ready-worked and only the background to be filled in. One can also buy canvas with designs tinted or stamped on, in which case the whole piece must be worked.

Tramé patterns have the design and background indicated with threads "laid on." These are used as a guide and covered with needlepoint stitches.

One can also work from a chart. These can be purchased, or you may design your own. Use graph paper 10 squares to 1″ or a size corresponding to the mesh of the canvas you will use. Each square represents one mesh of canvas or one stitch. On your first design do not attempt much shading. Try simple motifs in all-over or border arrangements. All-over patterns can be very lovely;

they often resemble old brocades. Indicate the design in pencil, crayon, or water color on the graph paper. Find the center of the design and the center of the canvas and work outward, unless you are willing to do a great deal of mesh counting to locate the different parts of the design.

The tent or half cross stitch can be made in various ways. The appearance on the right side of the work is the same but the wrong side is different. The amounts of yarn used also differ.

Continental and diagonal stitches both work up with more thickness on the back than on the front. This is especially desirable for upholstery and rugs because it serves as a pad and saves wear on the needlepoint. Plain half cross stitch leaves little yarn on the back and is the most economical as to yarn.

Gros point means large point and petit point means small point. They both can be done in any of the various methods. The mesh size of the canvas determines the size of the stitch. *Plain half cross stitch cannot be done on a single-mesh canvas.*

Study the stitch diagrams and directions for making. One stitch method may be better than another for a certain article. For example, it would not be necessary to use continental stitch, which pads the back, on a picture.

To avoid fraying, use a strand of yarn in the needle not longer than 18″ to 20″. Use a shorter length for petit point.

To thread the needle, fold the yarn over the needle, then slip needle out. The resulting loop will easily thread through the eye. If you have to thread a short length, cover the end of the yarn with a small piece of folded paper or tape; then slip it through the eye.

For petit point, split the yarn or use stranded mercerized cotton, using as many strands as necessary to cover the mesh.

Gros Point

Continental Stitch. Start at upper right-hand corner and work from right to left. The needle is brought out a mesh ahead and slanting. Study the diagram and top photograph below. Tent or half cross stitch is produced on the top but a long slanting stitch

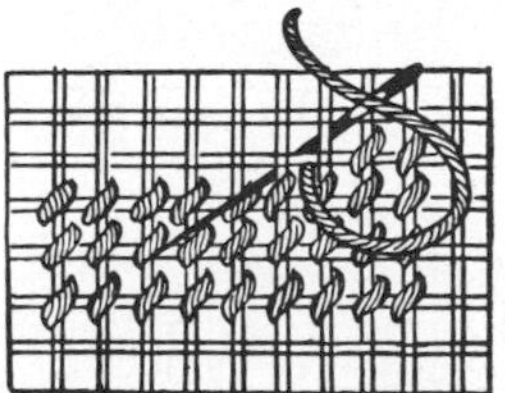

Right Side

Wrong Side

appears on the back (see photographs above). Very good for chair seats, foot stools, rugs, or any place where a padded back is desirable. This stitch uses about 1¼ yds of yarn to cover a square inch of canvas.

Plain Half Cross Stitch. This must be done on double-thread canvas. It may be done from right to left, from left to right, or from bottom to top working vertically. It forms a straight stitch on the back. Try all three methods and find the one which is easiest

Right Side

Wrong Side

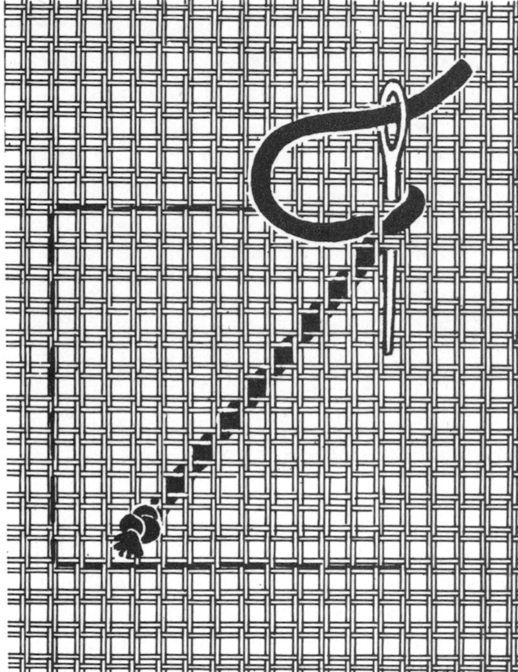

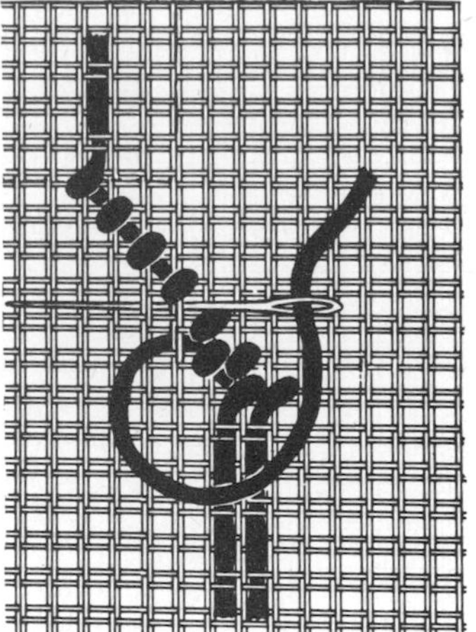
Right Side

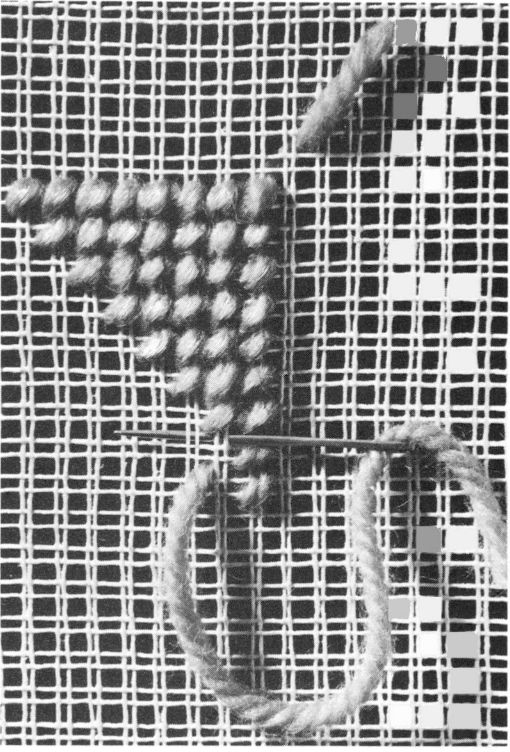
Right Side

for you. Follow the diagram. Plain Half Cross is adequate for small items which need no padding on the back. It uses about 1 yd of yarn for a square inch of canvas. This stitch has a tendency to pull the piece out of shape but this can be corrected in blocking.

Diagonal Stitch. Beginning at lower right hand corner, take a half cross stitch, bringing needle out horizontally under 2 groups of threads to the left. Follow diagram closely. For 2nd row, begin again at lower right corner, taking stitches between those of the previous row. This stitch also leaves a thick pad on the back, using about the same amount of yarn as continental stitch. This stitch does not pull the canvas out of shape.

Basket Weave or Bias Tent Stitch. This is started in the upper right hand corner (see next page). Fasten thread in usual way or insert needle a few meshes down and a few meshes to the left, leaving knot on the surface. The piece of yarn on the back will be covered with stitches as you work. Clip off the knot when you reach it. Bring needle out

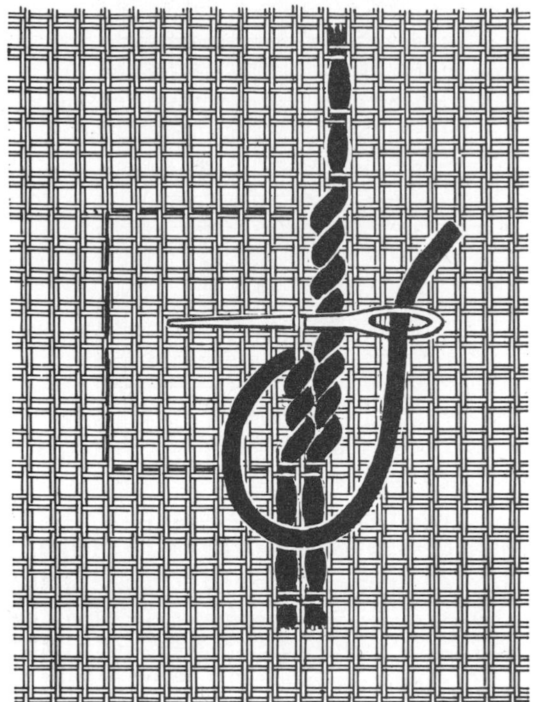

at upper right hand corner and take a stitch. Take another stitch to the left but bring

Right Side

needle out below first stitch. Follow diagrams. Rows are worked up and back diagonally, leaving a thick basket weave on the under side. This uses about 1¾ yards of yarn per square inch.

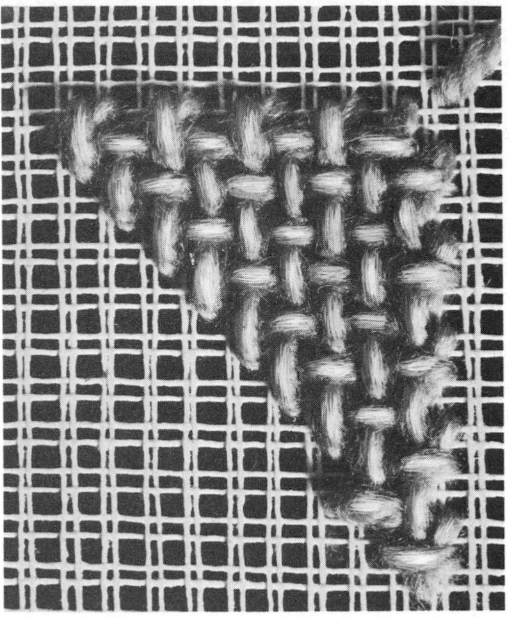

Wrong Side

Petit Point

Petit point is usually worked over a single-thread canvas but can be done on double-thread. Very fine double-thread (Penelope) is quite suitable if available.

All the stitch methods given except plain half cross can be done on single-thread canvas. Continental stitch is most often used for petit point.

When a portion of the design on a gros point pattern is to be done in petit point, the stitch is done over a single thread. To facilitate this, dampen this portion of canvas

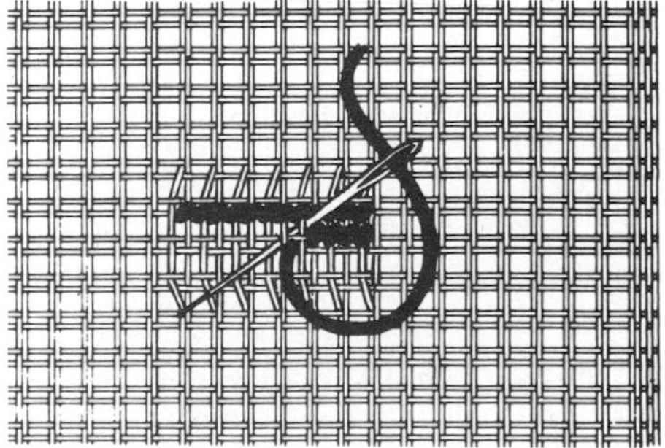

and push the threads until the spaces are even.

Work the areas of petit point first. Silk or mercerized thread is sometimes used for petit point. Use as many strands as necessary to cover the mesh. Wool is also used but the yarn must be split. Petit point is especially suitable for designs with fine detail, such as faces, flowers, figures, etc., because subtle shading is possible.

If you are working a piece with a petit point center and background of gros point, work gros point up as far as there are 2 canvas threads to work over. Work also any open spaces within the petit point area. Then split the background yarn and fill in the small spaces, working over 1 thread of canvas, in petit point.

Tramé

This type of needlepoint has long threads "laid on" indicating the design and change of colors.

Tramé pieces can be purchased and usually come complete with yarn in the correct amounts and colors for completing the piece. Half cross stitch is worked over these long stitches which also serve as padding.

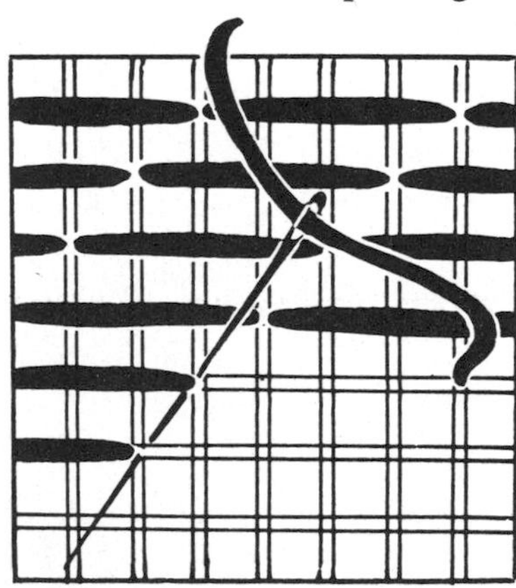

If you are working on tinted canvas, you may wish to prepare the piece in this manner yourself.

To lay on the stitches: Bring needle up through canvas from right-hand side between the double threads on one row. Carry it across the top of the double mesh and insert at point where color changes. Work half cross stitch back over the laid thread or you may do all of the tramé before covering with needlepoint stitches.

Other Canvas Stitches

Gobelin Stitch. Like gros point, this stitch is used for backgrounds. It is worked over 2 or more meshes in height but only one in width, which makes it slightly slanted; or it may be worked over meshes directly above, which gives a vertical stitch. This should be worked on double mesh canvas unless the stitches are long (over more than 1 mesh).

Long Oblique Stitch with Running Stitch. Work rows of oblique stitches and fill space between with 2 rows of running stitch, backstitch, or chain stitch.

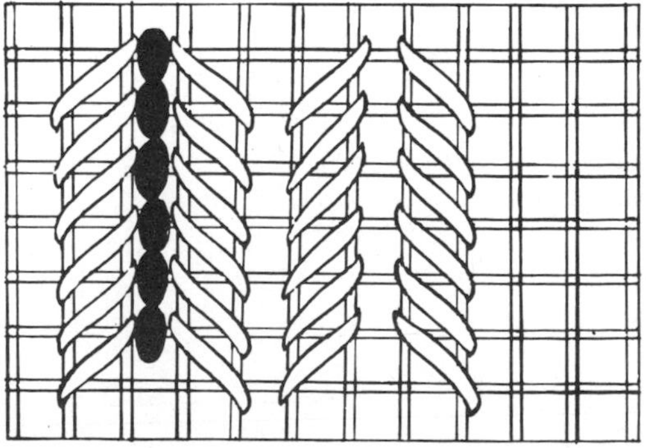

Greek Herringbone Stitch. This is a long-legged herringbone worked from left to right. Turn and work back.

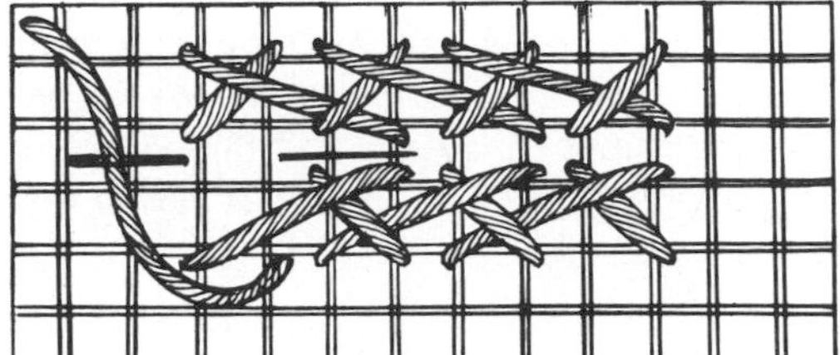

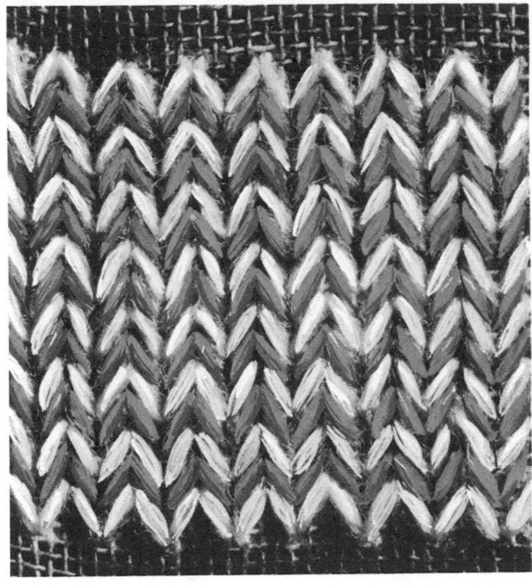

Kelim Stitch. Rows of oblique stitches slanted alternately. Two or more colors may be used. To save time use a needle for each color.

Bargello or Florentine Stitch. This is also called Flame embroidery and is a variation of long and short stitch. It is usually done on single-thread canvas following a chart, and is worked from left to right (or right to left) over 2 or more meshes. After working one or two rows the counting is simple because all repeats are alike. The shading can be soft and gradual or more striking contrasts can be used. Several charts are given here for designs from a simple diamond to the skyscraper effect.

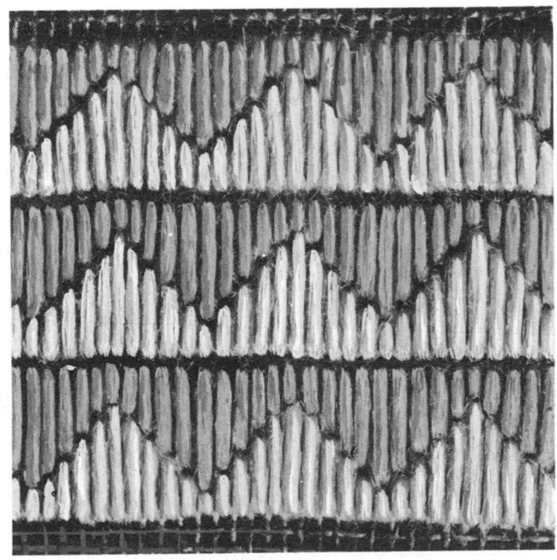

Simple Long and Short Stitch. In two shades of a color, this makes an attractive all-over pattern.

Shadow Design. Use three colors in soft shades for a subtle effect.

Forget-me-not. A floral-like pattern with lots of appeal.

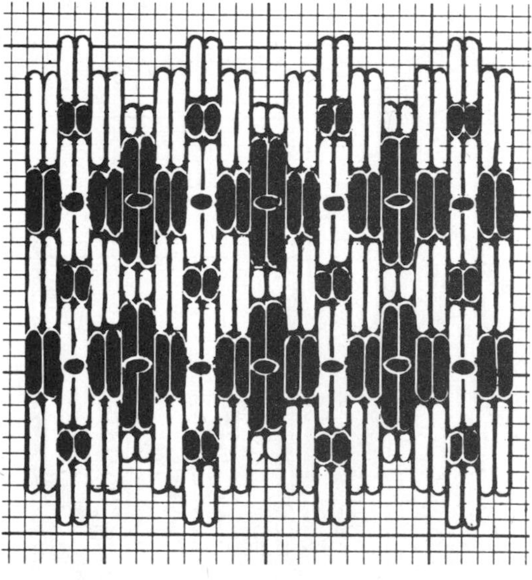

Shaded Diamond. Has many possibilities in color arrangements suitable for modern settings.

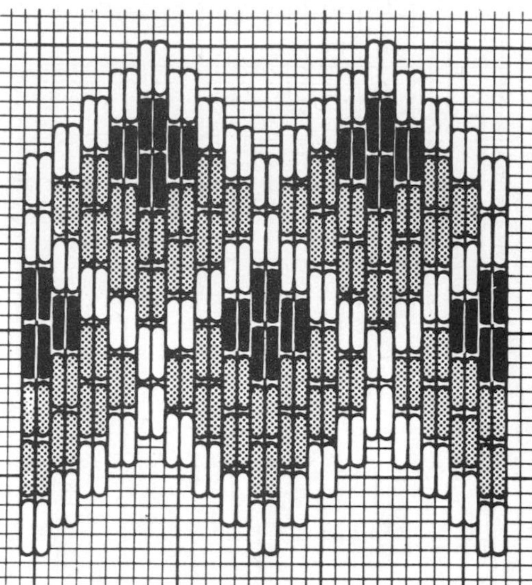

Simple Diamond. Useful for smaller articles.

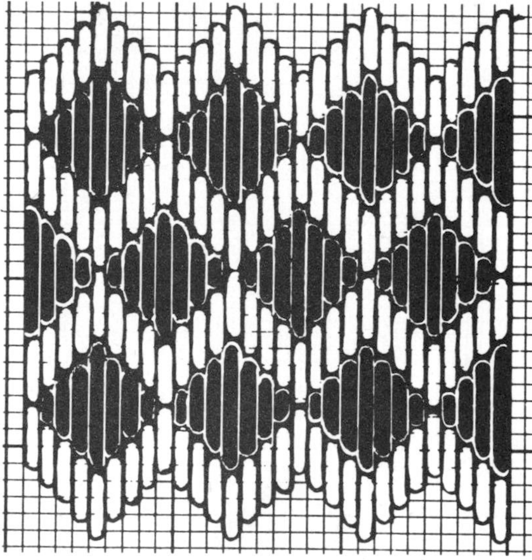

Sawtooth Design. A typical flame pattern with many possibilities for color shading.

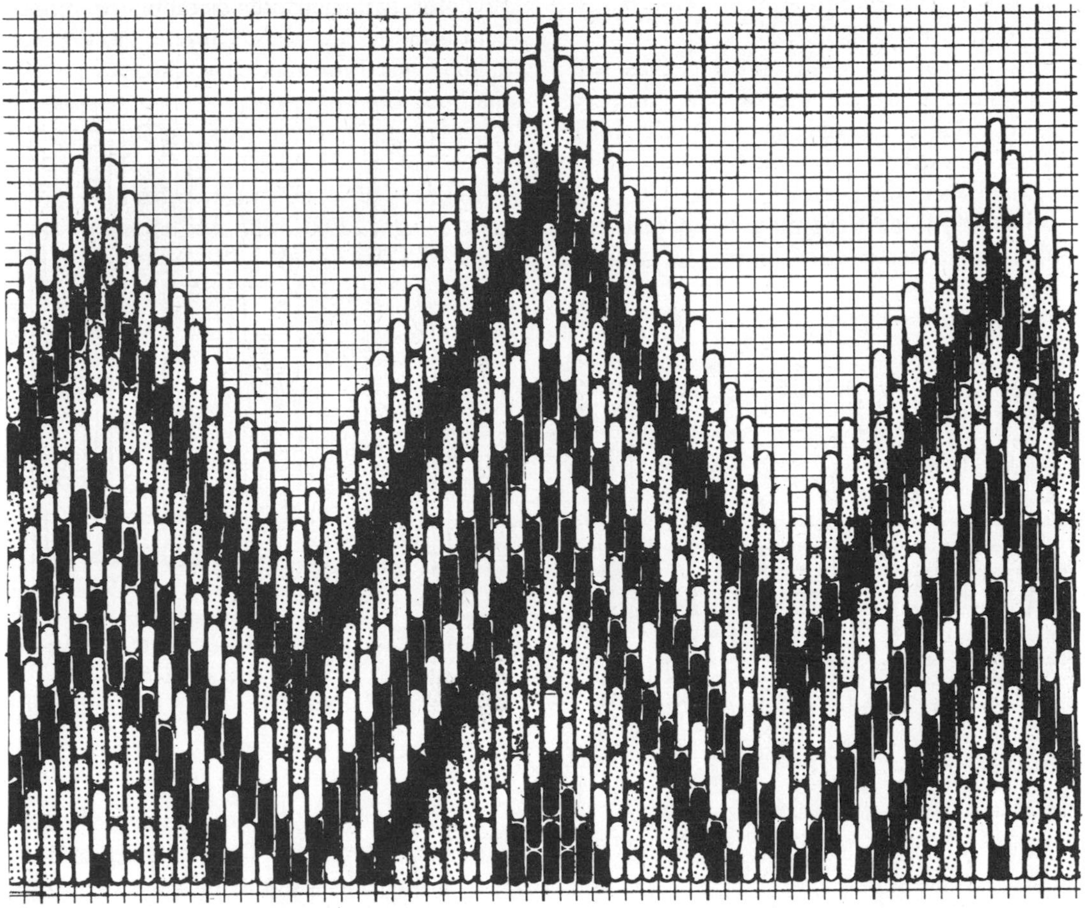

Skyscraper Design (see previous page). A typical Bargello or Florentine design which can be done in multicolor.

The size of the mesh of the canvas will determine the size of the design. An easy way to enlarge a design is to use a coarser canvas. A suitable yarn must be selected—one that covers the mesh well.

All of these patterns may be adapted for different articles. Worked on medium-coarse canvas (about 8 or 10 meshes to the inch) they are right for footstools, pillows, chair seats, and knitting bags. On finer canvas they might be used for handbags, glasses cases, or small bedroom pillows.

On coarse canvas, very handsome rugs can be fashioned in this type of work.

Color Plate 7 shows a number of needlepoint designs. Following are color keys and designs for these.

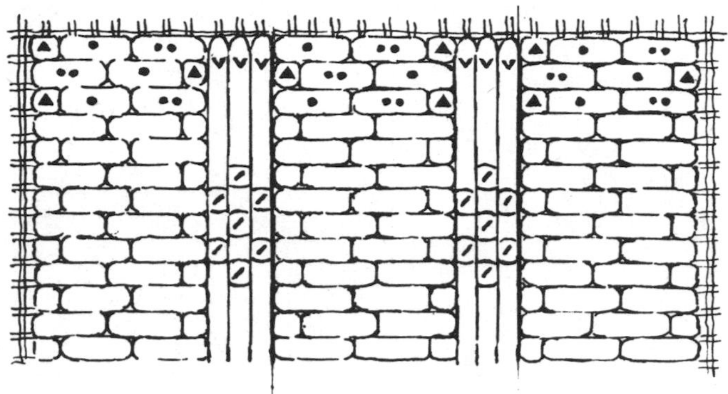

COLOR KEY

▲ = oyster white
•• = pale chartreuse
• = olive green
|v| = mustard yellow
/ = deep pink

Rows of long and short gobelin stitch in Eggshell, Pale Yellow, and Mustard-Green alternate with 3 rows of couching—Gold held down with Hot Pink. The couching is done by counting meshes and makes a pattern at intervals. See diagram.

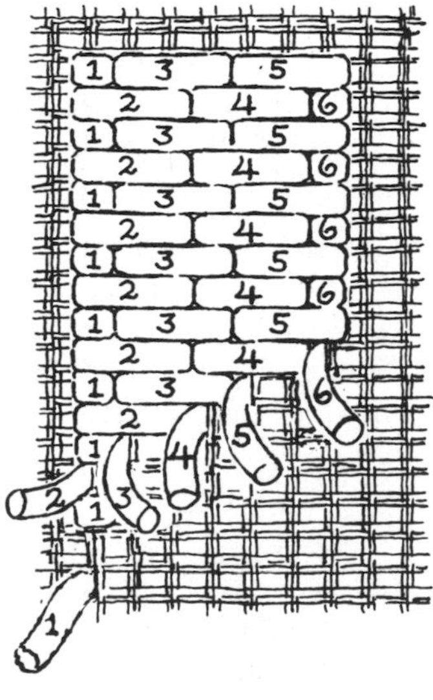

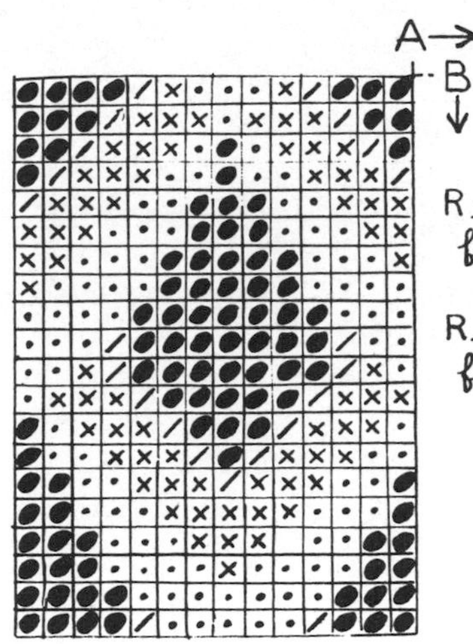

Repeat
from A
across

Repeat
from B
down

COLOR KEY

● = Royal blue
/ = Turquoise
× = Lt. moss green
• = Pale grey

All-over design in needlepoint (gros point). Follow the color chart or use your own selection of colors.

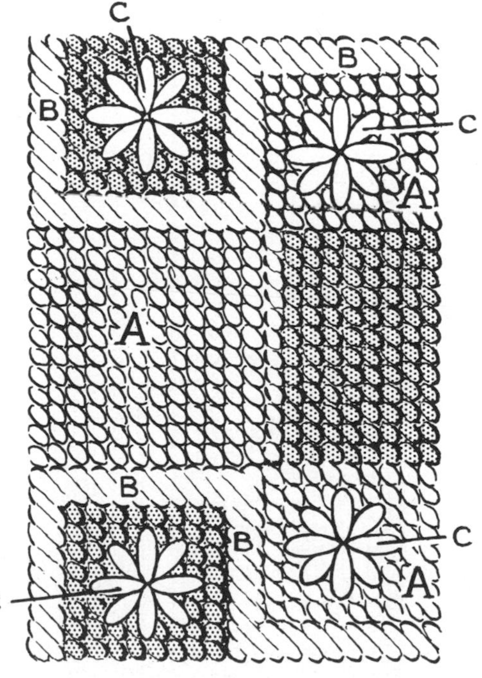

COLOR KEY

Shaded areas in very dk. brown
Areas A in medium brown
Border B, and flowers C
in old gold

Gros point in squares alternating black with brown. The Greek border is worked in oblique stitch in yellow beige as are the star flowers in straight stitch. The flowers are worked on top of the needlepoint.

COLOR KEY

A = Salmon
B = Maroon
C = Geranium
D = Bright pink

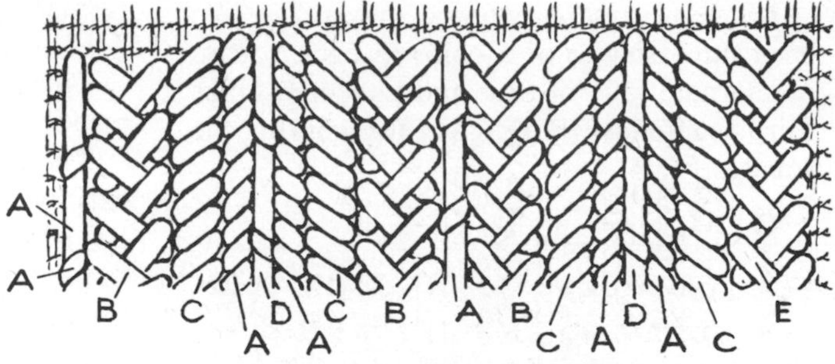

Stitch Details

Rows of herringbone stitch, couching, oblique stitch, and gros point make up this lovely striped pattern. It is worked in shades of bright Rose, Pinks, and Wine. Follow the working diagram.

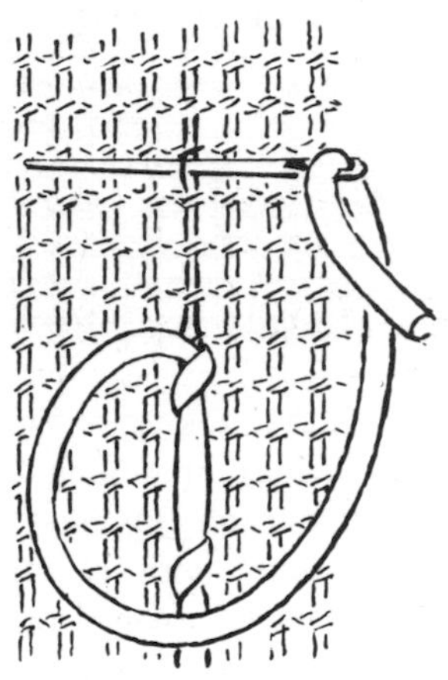

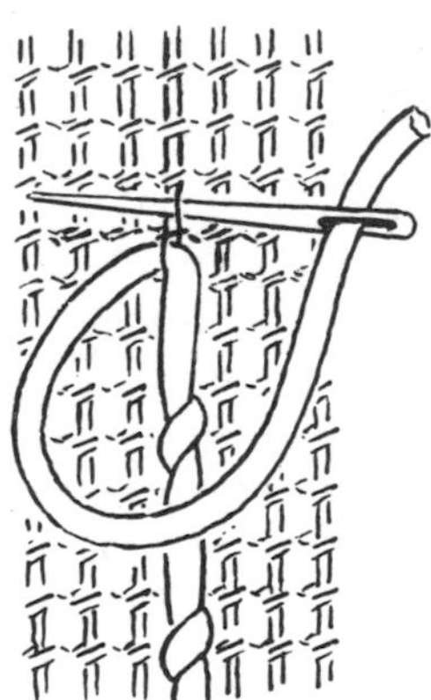

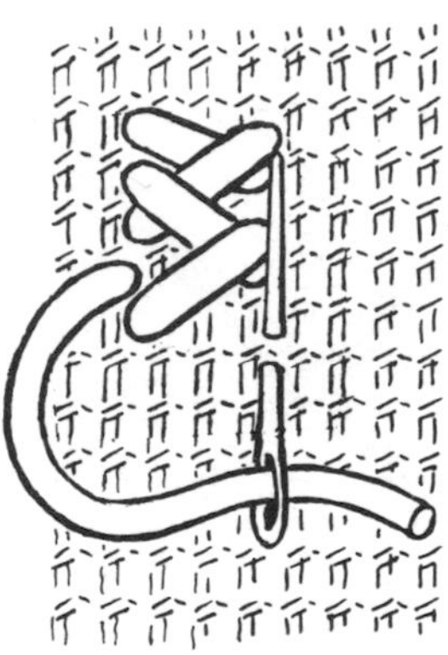

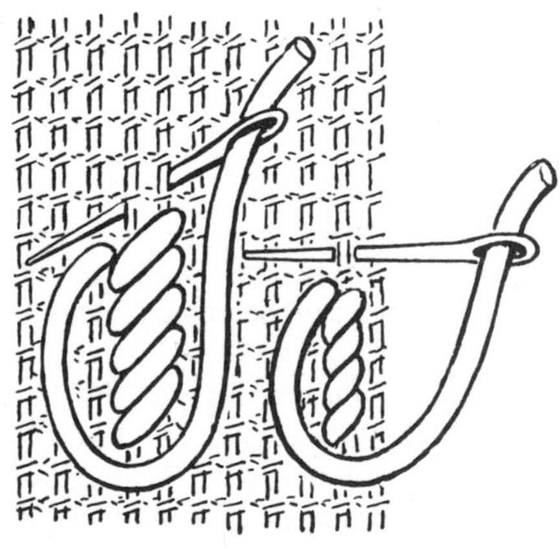

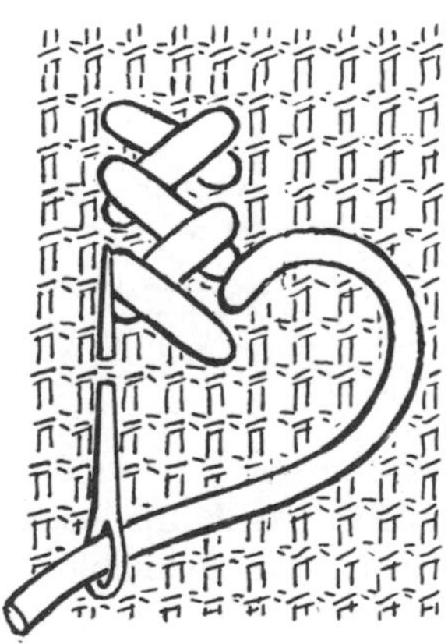

Diagonal squares worked on canvas. We used three shades of a color in each square in alternate rows of Blue and Lavender (plus Purple). Follow the diagram for working the squares.

COLOR KEY

R = Lavender O = Med. dk. blue
S = Violet X = Med. blue
T = Dk. violet Z = Light blue

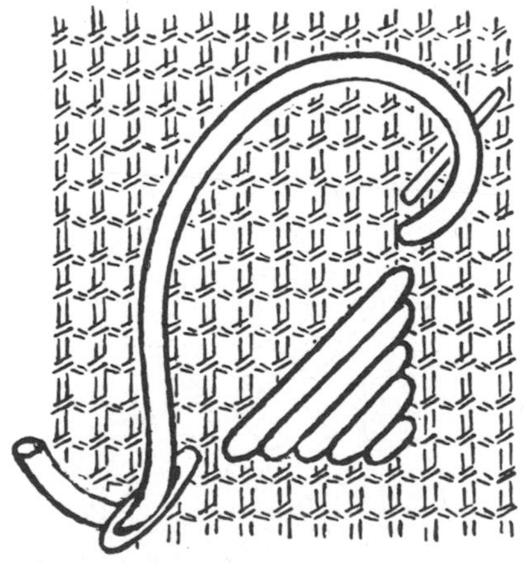

Needlework samplers in which the design is ready worked, with the background left to be filled in, are available. Some typical designs are shown in Color Plate 8.

HOW TO PIECE NEEDLEPOINT

There are times when it is necessary to piece needlepoint canvas.

The canvas to be added must always be of exactly the same size mesh as the original. Be sure that selvages are running in the same direction on both pieces so the double threads will match.

If these precautions are taken, canvas may be pieced either horizontally (crosswise) or vertically (lengthwise).

With right sides together and edges even,

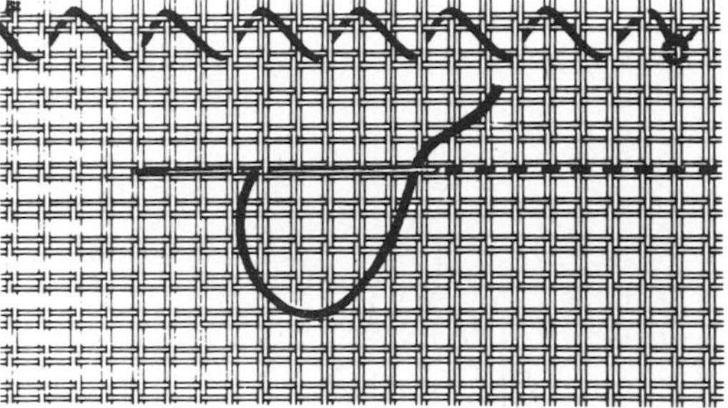

pin and baste canvas together taking a ⅝″ seam. Overcast the raw edges, matching 2 sets of double threads; back-stitch (by hand) through these double threads with strong linen thread or use a thread drawn from edge of canvas. Press seam open. The seam line on the right side is considered as a row of mesh when working over it.

Work up to and over this row *not catching* in the seam allowance. When working the seam line, instead of picking up the whole stitch from the right side, use an up and down movement, pushing needle to wrong side, catching with left hand, and pushing through to right side. Continue across row.

BLOCKING

If the piece has become pulled out of shape in working this can be remedied by correct blocking.

Do not cut into canvas before blocking. Roll the piece in a very damp Turkish towel and leave overnight or until thoroughly damp.

Using the dimensions you made note of

before starting work (see General Rules), lay the piece face down on marked board. Stretch into shape and tack with rust-proof thumb tacks ¾″ apart around edges. Allow piece to dry thoroughly even if it takes several days. It should not be necessary to press but if desired you may do so. Remove from board, cover with damp cloth, and steam with a hot iron to fluff the yarn. Do not touch iron to needlepoint.

Mounting, especially of upholstery, should be done by an expert.

Pictures are framed like any painting. Pillows are made up in the usual ways. Handbags should be mounted by specialists. Rugs must be hemmed or faced with heavy tape and are sometimes lined.

Fringing

If fringe is used on rugs and pillows, be sure to use the same yarn as was used in the background. See Trimmings and Decorative Details in Chapter 1.

Chapter 6

Rug Making

There are several ways of making hand-made rugs. None is very difficult nor does any of them, with the exception of a hand-woven one, require much equipment.

Hooking is a very old craft, highly popular in Colonial America. Many fine examples are to be found in museums and private collections. These early hooked rugs show much artistic feeling, as well as patience and industry. Some are primitive, quaint, and simple in design; others are more intricate and even elaborate. For the most part they were made of left-overs and partly worn fabrics.

Modern hooked rugs are still made of fabric strips, but many are made of yarn. There is a growing interest in hooking, using many types of materials such as fabric strips, yarn, jute, and even fur scraps in the same rug. Unusual texture effects are achieved in this way.

Braided rugs are also easy to make and lovely to look at when done with skill and taste. They are warm and cheerful and furnish a further use for scraps and pieces and partly worn clothing.

Needlepoint and cross stitch rugs are more elaborate in feeling and take longer to make. Designs with more detail can be executed in this technique and the effect is richer. It is fascinating and rewarding hand work.

The possibilities for achieving fine artistic effects for decorative use are very great in hand-woven rugs. They can be very handsome indeed. One must first master weaving in order to make them.

Crocheted rugs have a very definite place. Made in soft cotton or wool yarns, they are extremely useful in bedroom and bath or children's rooms. Some very interesting textured rugs are being made of jute, which is suitable for more general use.

The knotted rug is another technique growing in favor. It is a revival of an old method and is done on coarse canvas or base cloth by knotting in loops of yarn. This method of working has great possibilities.

These are the important basic techniques of making hand-made rugs and the methods are given in the following pages. Designs can be simple and still be in wonderfully good taste. You can even plan them yourself. Plan your rug for the place it is to be used, taking into consideration size, color, and texture in relation to the room and its furnishings. Ready-prepared designs in several of the techniques can be purchased.

HOOKED RUGS

Hooked rugs are easy to create, and since they can be made with leftover materials on inexpensive fabric, they are not costly. Until you have tried your hand at this simple craft, you cannot know how much real pleasure can be derived from it and from displaying a rug you yourself have made.

The rug shown on page 229 was hooked of strips of fabric much of which was specially dyed to produce a rich color arrangement. A

diagram of the pattern is given on the preceding page and it can be enlarged. The original rug was approximately 39″ × 69″ finished. To make your own pattern, draw this size on light weight wrapping paper and mark it off in 3½″ squares. Trace off the design given using tissue or tracing paper. Mark it off in ½″ squares. Both large and small patterns should be 10 squares wide and 19 squares long. To transfer the pattern onto the wrapping paper draw into the squares the lines of the design which appear in the corresponding small squares.

Cut burlap or other foundation material 39″×69″ plus 3 or 4 inches around for hemming. Place heavy carbon paper face down between pattern and burlap. Center the design and trace with blunt end of crochet hook.

The motifs are simple and lend themselves to other arrangements. If you wish a rug of different size and shape, the motifs can be arranged in various ways with good results.

If you do not wish to use fabric strips, we suggest jute, which comes in beautiful tones.

Another beautiful hooked rug is shown in Color Plate 9. Materials for making it are available. Write to Good Housekeeping Needlework and Sewing Center, 959 Eighth Avenue, New York, New York 10019 for information.

Foundation Fabric

For the foundation, heavy closely-woven burlap, warp cloth, monk's cloth, heavy linen, osnaburg, or any fairly coarse unbleached cotton may be used.

Fabric Strips and Yarns

Many types of materials can go into a rug: fabric of various kinds cut into strips or yarns in different weights. Yarn is almost always used in punch and automatic needles. Woolen fabric is better than cotton, although many of the lovely old rugs were cotton. As a general rule it is best to use the same fiber throughout in one rug. However, if you enjoy experimenting with textural effects you may use a variety of materials. There is no standardization as to materials and this lends to the charm of hooked rugs.

Preparing Fabric Strips

Be sure the fabric is clean before cutting. The strips should run lengthwise of the fabric. Strips may be cut in the hand using scissors (a rather slow process) or the fabric may be rolled (jelly-roll fashion) and cut with a sharp knife or razor blade. Also, a rug-cutting machine or stripper can be purchased. Never tear the strips, as this leaves threads which make the rug look fuzzy. Firmly woven fabrics can be cut ¼″ wide or even less for the more detailed parts of the design. If a quickly-made and coarse type of rug is desired cut the strips wider.

Designs

Designs can be simple. Several shades of a soft rich color can be arranged in blocks, rows, shells, diamonds, or scallops for a beautiful rug. Simple floral arrangements are not difficult to do if you have drawing ability. Many types of designs can be purchased ready-stamped or tinted on foundation fabric, but for many people half the fun of hooking a rug is creating the design. Remember that a border tends to make a rug look smaller. Draw the design on a light weight wrapping paper. If the paper is too heavy it is difficult to transfer. Trace the design onto the foundation fabric using heavy carbon paper, face down, under the pattern, and the blunt end of a crochet hook. If there are rows or straight lines in the design be sure they are in line with the weave of the foundation fabric when placing pattern. Leave a margin of 3 or 4″ for fastening to the frame and later hemming the rug. The piece is put into the frame by lacing, or tacking.

Ways to Hook

The method you use is a matter of personal taste and preference. It is wise to experiment with all of them before deciding which to use.

Hooking from the Right Side. Hold the fabric strip or yarn (use any length), underneath with the left hand; the hook is pushed through from the top with the right hand. Catch the end of the strip and pull it through. Push the needle in again a thread or two away (depending upon the foundation fabric) and pull up a loop (see photograph). Repeat, following the design. Keep loops about ¼″ in length and uniform throughout. Skill develops with practice. Any length of strip can be used. Always pull ends through to the right side. Loops should be left uncut on rugs made of fabric strips. If not working in a frame, always start in the center of the rug. Do the design and then the background. Hooking may be done in straight rows or following the contours of the design.

Hooking from the Wrong Side. Strictly speaking this is not hooking but "punching," but the final result is much the same. It is done with either a punch or shuttle type needle. The punch type needle is a tube-like affair through which the yarn runs. It is made in different sizes for different weights of yarn and it always has some sort of adjustable stop to prevent the needle from being pushed farther than is wanted. This makes it possible to produce loops of different lengths. The shuttle type of punch hook is worked up and down with both hands and "walks" along, punching through at regular intervals. It is the quickest way of hooking, and is usually done with yarn.

Hooking from the back requires that the rug be stretched in a frame. The frame may be very simple (an old picture frame will do) with thumb tacks for holding the rug in place. Excellent frames which are made especially for the purpose are also available.

Both types of needles, when raised, leave a loop on the under side (the right side of the rug). Do not lift the needle above the surface but push it in again a short distance away. Some rug makers recommend doing the whole rug in rows changing colors as needed (see photograph). Others prefer to work following the shape of the motifs (flowers, etc.), maintaining that a more natural result is achieved. Certainly it is much easier to shade flowers by this last method. When using the punch needle, hold the finished row back with the left hand so loops will not be caught with the needle. Leave an unhooked border 2″ to 3″ wide for hemming.

Clipping

Rugs made of yarn are often clipped and this is done while the rug is still in the frame. Use long, narrow, sharp scissors (some have bent handles for this purpose), and slide the points into the loops. Several loops can be cut at one time. Loops of fabric-strip rugs are left uncut.

Sculpturing or Beveling

Some designs lend themselves to sculpturing or beveling. This means shaping parts of

Hooking from the Right Side

Hooking from the Wrong Side

the design by clipping the pile. Exaggerated sculpturing is not practical because it is difficult to walk on, but there are times when a limited amount will bring out the design.

Sizing, Hemming, and Blocking

There is a special rug sizing which can be used on the back of burlap rugs. It is used only on unclipped rugs and its purpose is to prevent the loops from slipping out of the burlap. Many prefer not to size rugs, maintaining that it stiffens them and also causes them to slip easily. Remove the rug from the frame, trim, and make a 1½″ hem all around. The edge of the hem may be taped instead of being turned under, which makes a flatter finish. The rug may be steamed and pressed lightly over a soft surface, or it may be placed face down on the floor with paper underneath and walked on for a while to set the stitches.

Hooked Rug Design

Geometric squares. One square equals 1″. To enlarge: On a large piece of brown paper, draw a 27″ by 40″ rectangle, and mark off 1″ squares. Draw sections (squares, border, etc.), as shown in diagram. Lines within the pattern show direction of rows of hooking. Work rug in a mixture of light and dark colors (as shown in photograph), or in several shades of one color.

BRAIDED RUGS

Making braided rugs is a simple but fascinating old handcraft enjoying a popular revival. In olden times rug making was a necessity, but now it is a hobby which produces satisfaction as well as a useful article. Furthermore, it has the advantage of allowing you to fit colors to your decorating scheme.

Braided rugs are suitable in traditional homes but, as you see in the room photographed, are also perfectly suited to contemporary furnishings. Braiding is one of the easiest ways of making rugs, and in almost any size or shape.

Fig. 1

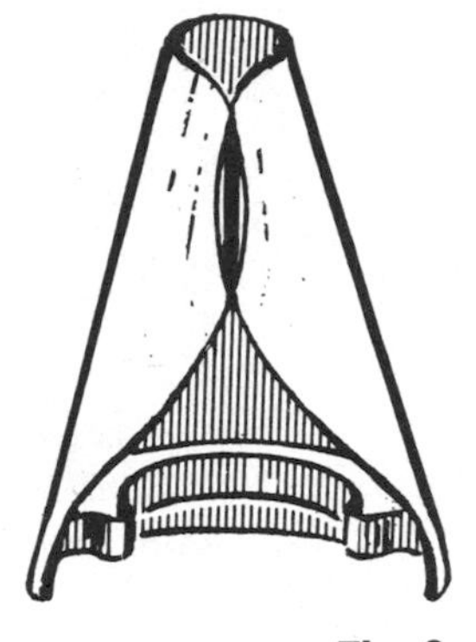
Fig. 2

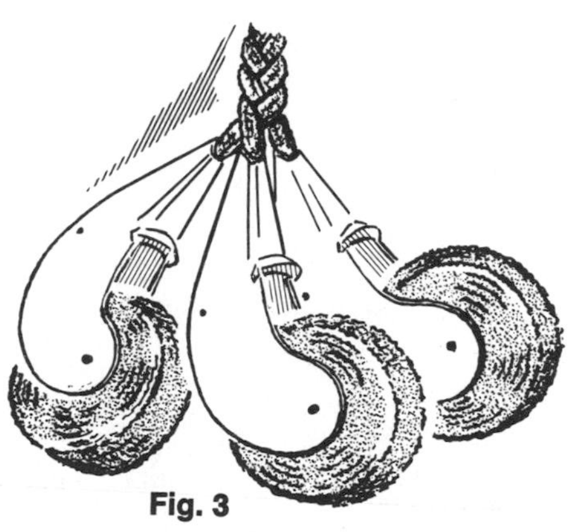
Fig. 3

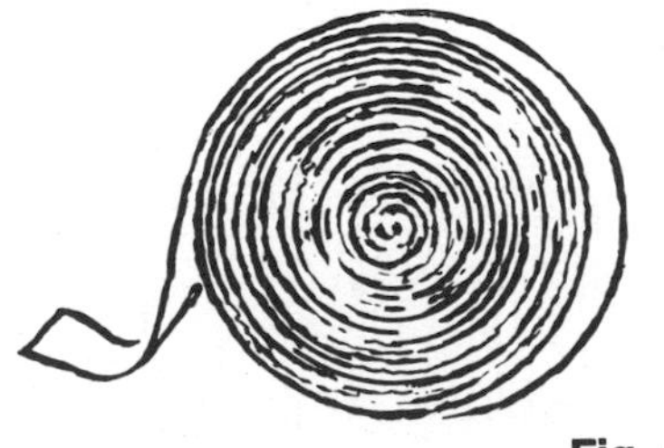
Fig. 4

Color

Most of these rugs have a plan of stripes, bands, etc.; therefore, you must decide on a color scheme and on how you wish in general to arrange the bands of color before starting the rug. Fabric may, of course, be dyed if you need certain colors (see Dyeing, page 243). Plan to have a darker color in or near the center, and repeat this at the edge. Make a color chart before you buy, collect, or dye your fabric.

A hit-and-miss rug, using short lengths, is the simplest to make since the color arrangement may be more or less ignored. Even in this type, however, a general color tone can be maintained.

Materials

Wool, cotton, and silk all can be used but should not be combined in the same rug. Cotton soils easily and, therefore, is more suitable for small rugs, which can be laundered. Silk can be braided into small mats and rugs for use where they will get little wear. Wool is best for sturdy rugs because of its body and wearing quality.

A heavy, closely woven, but soft and firm, woolen material is best. A harsh or wiry fabric is not as easy to use since it tends to crease into folds which change the appearance of the braids. If you wish to use these hard-finished worsteds (they wear very well), line them with a narrow strip of soft woolen to prevent wrinkles; or tear the strips very wide, and roll the edges in to the middle of the strip. Avoid using jersey except for small mats; it has too much stretch and does not wear well underfoot (nylon stockings may also be used for mats). You may use woolen pieces left over from sewing, or partly worn woolen articles (discard the much-worn parts)—such as skirts, trousers, coats, blankets, etc.—or use woolen fabric purchased from remnant stores or woolen mills by the pound, or use ready-cut strips from sources (write for list) which insure uniform braids.

In addition to the fabric which makes the rug, you will need heavy carpet thread

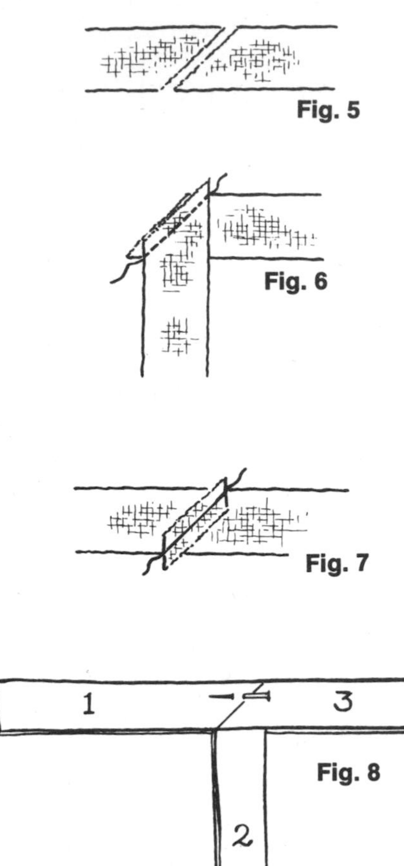

Fig. 5

Fig. 6

Fig. 7

Fig. 8

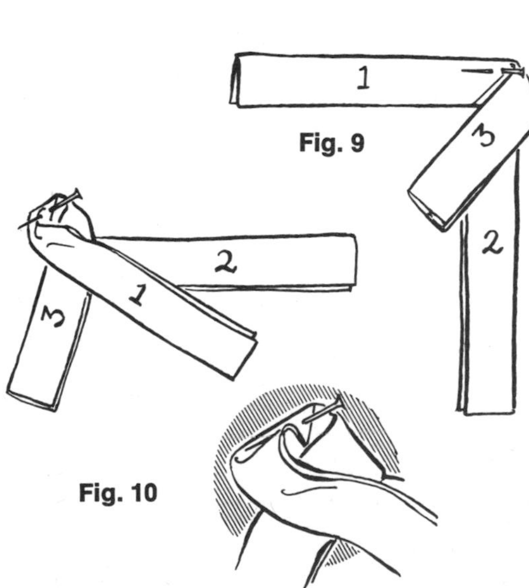

Fig. 9

Fig. 10

(threads made especially for this purpose are available); the newer lacing threads are multistranded and not too stiff. You will also need a blunt needle for lacing (see Fig. 1), a clamp for holding braid ends, and, if you wish, devices for folding the braids. Various kinds of folding devices, called cones or braid-aids, are on the market. One kind is constructed to hold the roll of ready-cut strips (see Figs. 2 and 3). A measuring guide for scissors is also a convenience.

Size and Shape

Braided rugs can be made in round, oval, square, or oblong shapes, and in many variations of these shapes. The oval rug is probably most popular. The place the rug is to be used usually determines the size and shape. Stair treads may be oval or rectangular.

The braiding technique can be used to fashion all sizes, from small mats to room-size rugs. The size of the rug influences the size of the braid. Narrow braids are used for mats and small rugs; larger, fatter braids for larger rugs. To learn how fabrics affect the size of braids, first make a small mat for a chair seat.

Amount of Material

Depending on the thickness of the braid, each square foot of rug requires about ¾ of a pound of wool. The large rug pictured on page 234 is made of very heavy braid and uses one pound of wool per square foot. In order to plan the best use of materials, you may wish to estimate the length of strands needed for each braid; therefore, you should know for figuring amounts that ⅓ to ½ the length of a strip is taken up in braiding, and that each braid is 7″ to 8″ longer than the one in the preceding row. If you are making complete rows (see Butting, page 240), allow about 7″ for interweaving ends of braids.

Preparation of Fabric

If you are using old materials, they should be carefully washed before being cut. If you want a colorfast rug, wash and rinse each

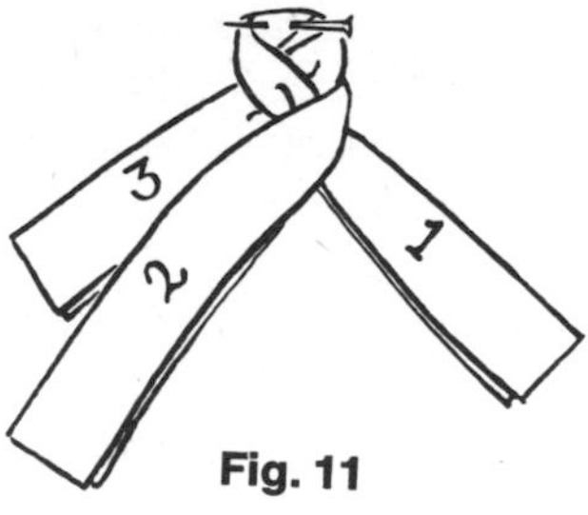
Fig. 11

color separately until the water is clear.

If you intend to dye fabrics, do it at this point (see Dyeing, page 243). Since dye lots differ, dye all pieces of one color that will be needed at the same time.

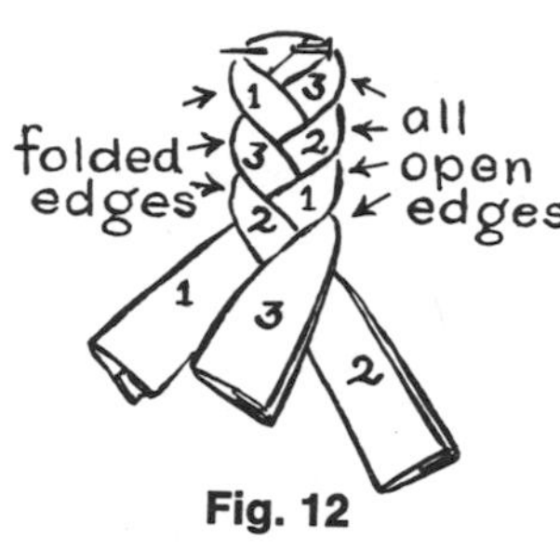

Fig. 12

Cutting and Piecing Strips

Before you cut strips for the entire rug, experiment to get the size of braid you want. The thickness of the fabric determines the size of the braid. The strips are usually cut from 1″ to 1½″ wide. Strips should be cut or torn crosswise, because crosswise fabric (selvage to selvage) has more give; if cut lengthwise, the strips tend to wrinkle more. Separate colors, and roll them into balls or rolls (see Fig. 4), which may be placed in separate paper bags.

Piece the strips by cutting the ends on the diagonal and by seaming them together (see Figs. 5, 6, and 7).

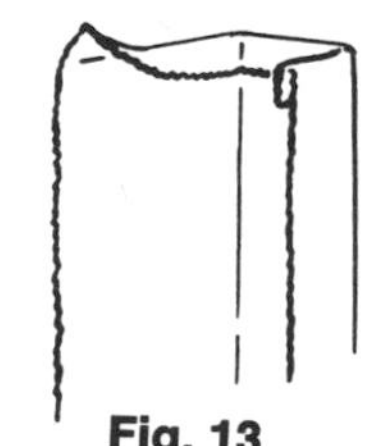
Fig. 13

How to Braid

The simplest type of braiding is that using 3 strips of fabric. It is possible to use 4 or more, but multiple braiding with folded fabric strips requires skill and long practice.

Avoid having seams on the 3 strips meet at one place in the braid, or a bulge will form. If necessary, cut the strip, and repiece it in a different place.

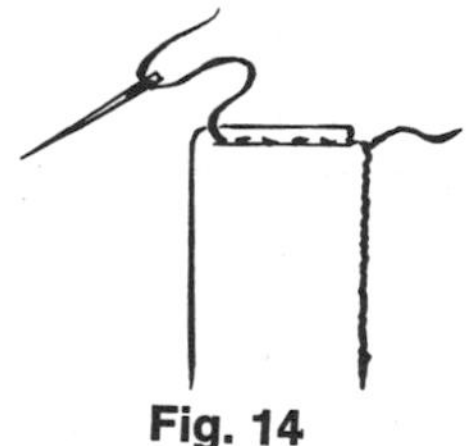
Fig. 14

If you are using cones or braid-aids, slip them on now before enclosing the ends. If you do not use braid-aids, turn the raw edges to the inside, and fold the strip down the center. Be sure the edges are turned all the way to the center so you will have four thicknesses of wool to make an even braid.

Note: While braiding, keep the open sides of all three folded strips to the right; this makes a more uniform braid and a reversible rug.

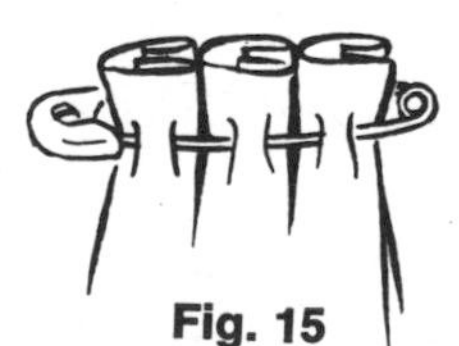
Fig. 15

There are two general methods of avoiding raw ends on the strips:

1. The T method (see Figs. 8 through 12): If you are making a 3-color braid, sew together the ends of 2 of the colors (piecing them as explained under Cutting and Piecing

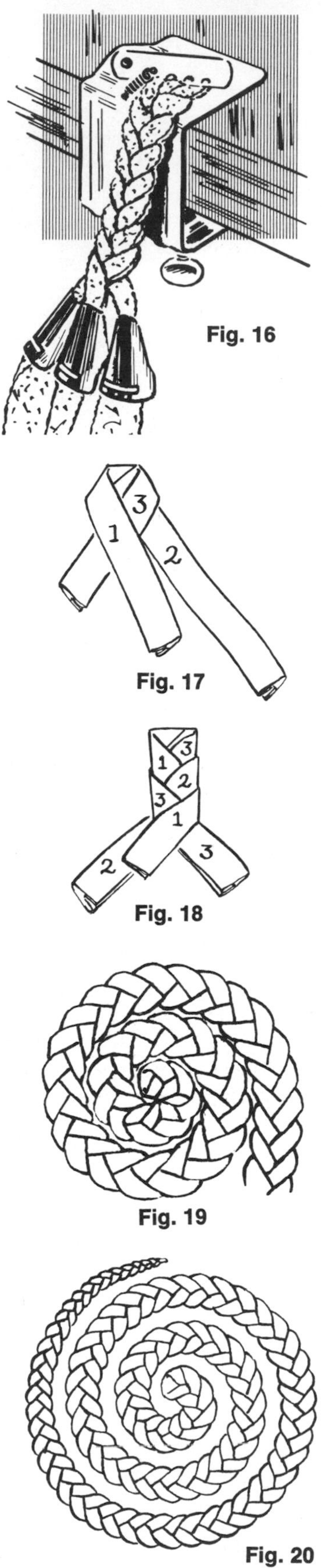
Fig. 16

Fig. 17

Fig. 18

Fig. 19

Fig. 20

Strips). Lay this strip with the open edges down and slip end of the third strip into the fold. If you are making a 2-color braid, make the top part of the T with the color used twice, and proceed as for a 3-color braid. Pin or sew in place where the T crosses. Start braiding with number 3. Following diagrams, pick up number 1, and twist it once before crossing it over, thus keeping open edges on all strips to the right.

2. The closed-ends method (see Figs. 13, 14, 15). Turn in the raw edges of the end of each strip, and slipstitch together. Slip all 3 ends, with open edges to the right, onto a safety pin or into a clamp and start braiding. Fold the braids, as explained above, or use braiders.

3. This method is plaiting (see Figs. 16, 17, and 18). As you braid, keep the strip flat and always with the same side of the strip up. Do not fold the strip over each time. Keeping open edges of strips to the right, make a firm, tight braid. When leaving the work or adding strips, hold the braid with a safety pin or clothespin.

Note: Before starting your rug, you should practice until you can make a neat, uniform braid.

Oval Rug. Decide on the size of the rug. Subtract the width from the length to get the length of the center starting braid. Braid a few yards or approximately the amount needed for the center color before starting to lace (see Lacing, below). Measure the length of the center braid; then turn it back on itself with open-edge sides of braid together (see Fig. 22).

Round Rug. Starting with end of braid, twist and turn it, in spiral fashion, to form a circle (see Fig. 19). Hold in place with safety pins after a few turns; then start to lace from the center. (Fig. 20 shows how to taper off the end of the spiral; narrow the ends by trimming to long points.)

Lacing

Years ago braided rugs were tediously made by sewing the braids together. Now they are joined by lacing, which makes stronger, better-looking rugs and the interwoven effect one sees in modern braided rugs.

Lacing is done on a flat surface with a coarse, blunt needle (see Fig. 21) and with heavy thread. Tie a knot in the end of the thread. Use a heavy darning needle to bring the knot through a place in the braid where it will be buried and hidden. Rethread with the lacing needle; or tie the end of the thread into a loop with a slip knot, and hide the end under a loop when finished.

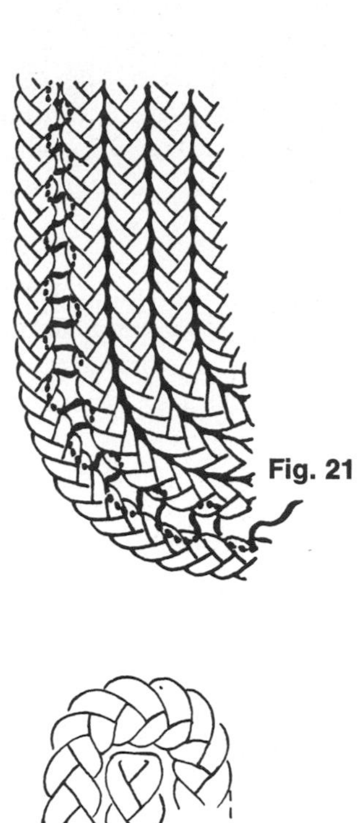

Fig. 21

Lacing Straight Braids

Slip needle through one loop of first braid, then through a loop of the adjoining braid. Work back and forth in this manner, pulling the thread tight so that the joining can scarcely be seen (see Fig. 22) because the braids fit so closely together. Proper lacing completely hides the thread.

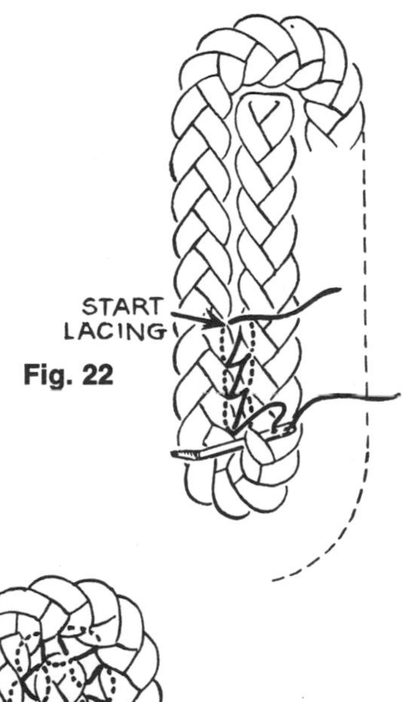

Fig. 22

Lacing on Curves

In making either an oval or a round rug, you must increase on the curves. The outside braid must be longer than the one before; you "full" it by skipping loops, while lacing as explained above. Do not skip loops on the straight sides of an oval or rectangular rug. Also, do not put the loops side by side while lacing; let them interlock (see Fig. 23) so the surface appears all one piece. On the curves, skip only *one* loop on the braid being added to produce fullness on a curve. Lace with a continuous thread by using a square knot to tie on a new piece (see Fig. 24). Hide the two ends in a loop, and proceed as usual. Usually three increases on each shoulder of a curve is sufficient. If the rug gets too full, add a row or two with no increases.

START
BACK

Fig. 23

If you are making a rug with indentations, *decrease* in the same way by skipping loops *on the body of the rug*. There are many novelty shapes which can be made with braiding.

Do not skip loops except on curves. Skipping speeds up the work but leaves loose spots, which catch dirt and spoil the shape of the rug.

Fig. 24

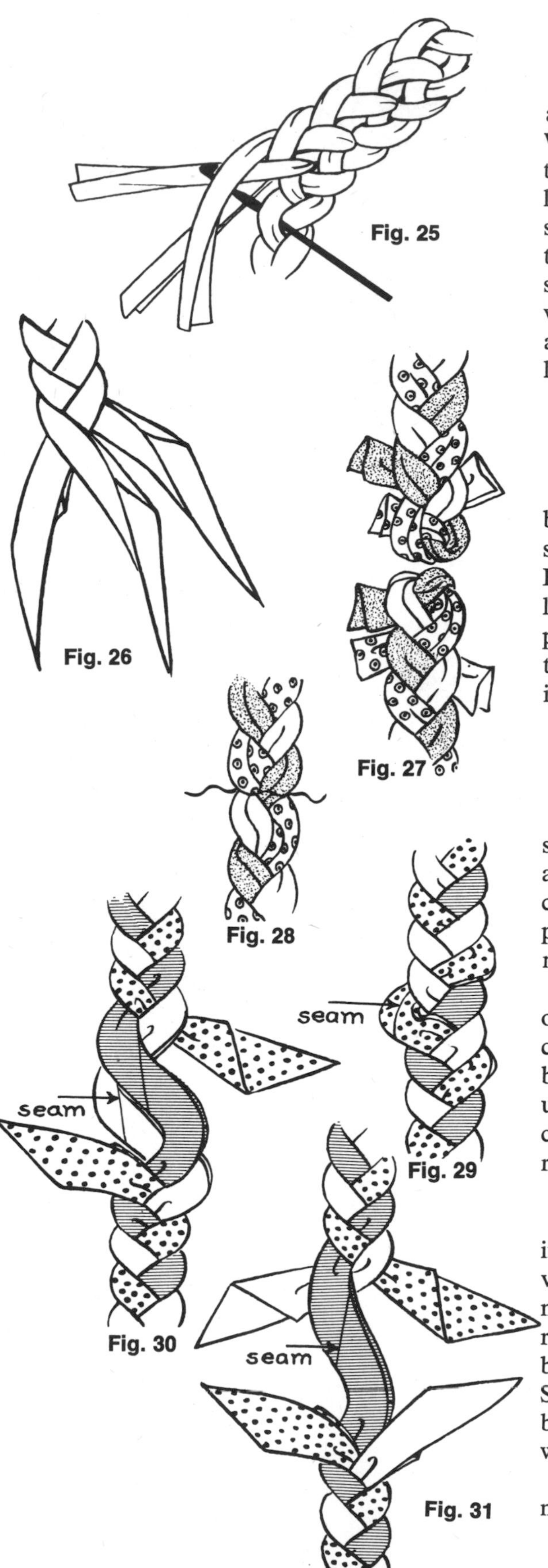

Fig. 25

Fig. 26

Fig. 27

Fig. 28

Fig. 29

Fig. 30

Fig. 31

Interbraiding. This method joins the braids as they are made, using a heavy crochet hook. When ready to join, as each strand comes to the inside it is pulled through the finished loop of the previous row with the hook, as shown in Fig. 25. On curves it is necessary to bring two successive strips through the same loop. This method of braiding makes a very neat and finished-looking rug. Work on a flat surface when joining the rug so it will lie flat.

Finishing Off

After completing the last row, remove braid-aids, if you have used them. With scissors, taper off each strip to a long point (see Fig. 26). Then braid to the end, and finish lacing, working the end slightly under the previous braid. Another method is to work the ends into the adjacent braid for a smooth, invisible finish on the border.

Butting

Rugs can, of course, be made entirely in spiral fashion, and many very handsome rugs are made this way. The changes from one color to another can be done gradually to produce a softly shaded rug. The second method is that of closed braids.

Butting is the process of joining each round of braid so that it forms a complete circle or closed braid. (The spiral rug is a continuous braid from beginning to end.) Butting can be used for the entire rug or, as is often done, can be used on the last few rows of a spiral rug in order to obtain a more tailored finish.

There are a couple of ways to do butting:

1. Probably the older method is just sewing the ends together. This must be done very carefully to avoid a bulge. (The rug will not be reversible.) On the wrong side of the rug, turn up the ends (see Figs. 27 and 28), bringing the braid together so it fits the rug. Sew the ends together by hand; then fold back the ends and press. Taper the ends and work them into the loops. Trim if necessary.

2. In this method, you join the braid by manipulating the ends so they come together in a perfect braid. Keep each strand flat; do not twist. If you have three colors and follow the diagrams (Figs. 29, 30 and 31), this is not difficult. If your strips are all the same color, mark each one in some way (colored thread, perhaps) so that they may be worked into a continuous braid. Sew the ends together by hand in diagonal seams.

Braid Holder or Clamp

In order to make a tight, firm braid, some means of anchoring the braid while it is being worked on is necessary. If it is heavy enough a weight can be used, but some kind of clamp is better. You can buy clamps for use on the edge of a table (see Fig. 16, page 238).

Another old-time and still practical method is anchoring the braid by tying or winding it around the top of a chair back. The feet are braced against a lower rung to hold the braid taut.

Making a Square or Oblong Rug

The length of the center strip of an oblong rug is arrived at in the same way as that of an oval rug (subtract the width from the length). After deciding on the size of your rug (2′ by 3′, 3′ by 4′, 3′ by 5′, 6′ by 9′, etc.) and finding length of center strip, make a paper pattern (see Fig. 32). Draw the center strip line, and connect to corners. Use the diagram as a guide while you work. The diagonal lines are the points where the corners are turned on each row of braid.

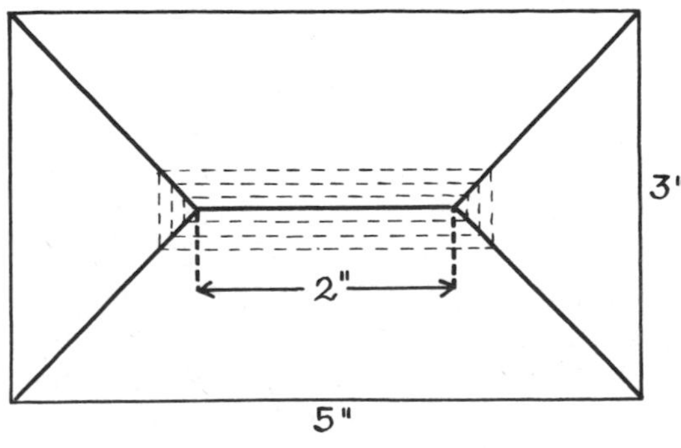

Fig. 32

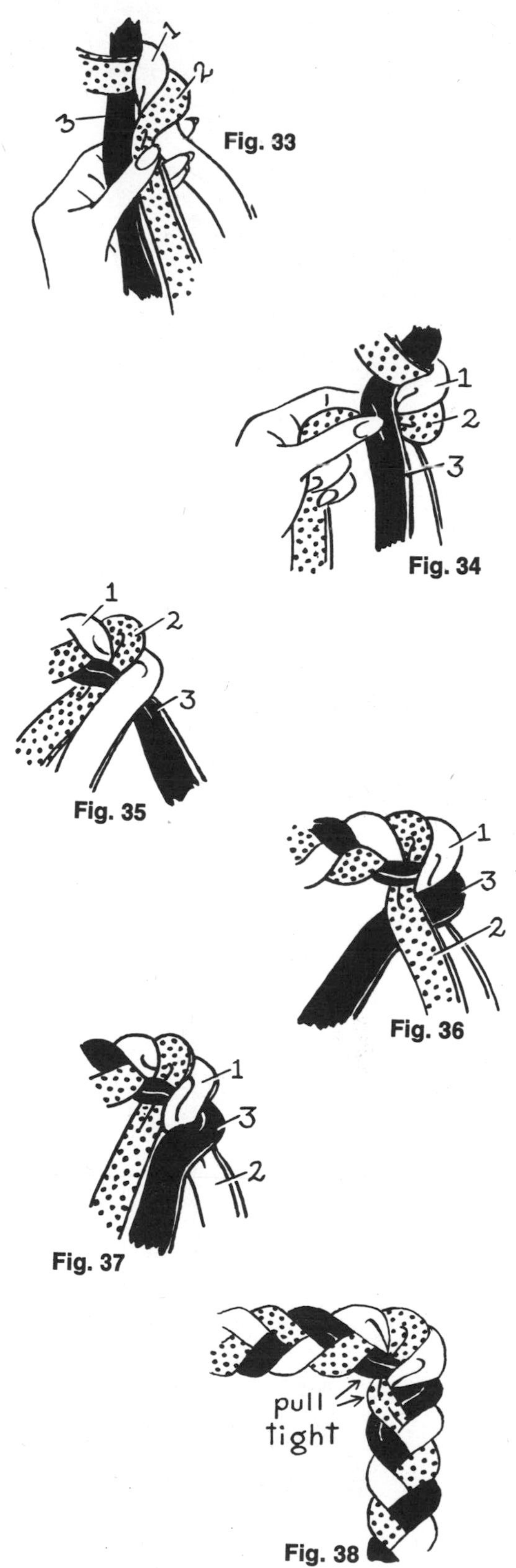

Fig. 33

Fig. 34

Fig. 35

Fig. 36

Fig. 37

Fig. 38

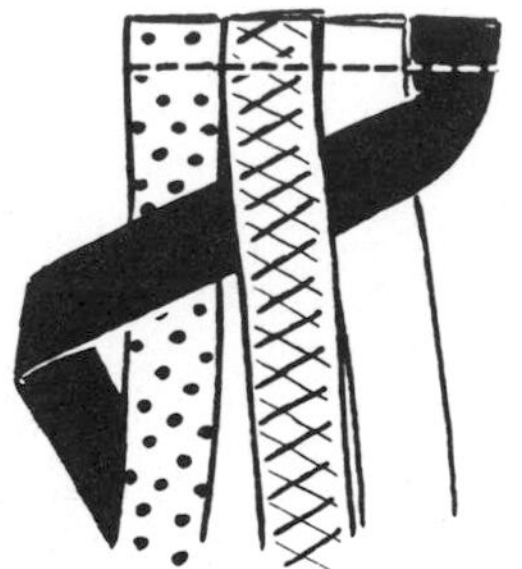
Fig. 39

There is a method of making double looping at the corners. This means that you cannot make several yards of braiding and then lace, but that you must braid to fit the pattern. This is the method of braiding in a corner. When you get to the corner (see Figs. 33 through 38), number your braids 1, 2, and 3, starting with the inside strip. Working tightly, place 1 over 2, then 2 over 1; now bring 3 over 2, and pull number 3 tight. Repeat as follows: place 1 over 3, 3 over 1, then 2 over 3. Then braid and lace as usual, and make the double-loop again at the next corner. Be sure to pull the inside loops tight. Lay the rug on the pattern each time to be sure you are making the double-loop at the proper place.

Rectangular rugs may also be made by lacing together the braids in lengthwise rows. These rugs are usually finished with a border of two or more rows all around (butted). The lengthwise braids in this case may be plaited of four or more strands (see Figs. 39, 40, and 41).

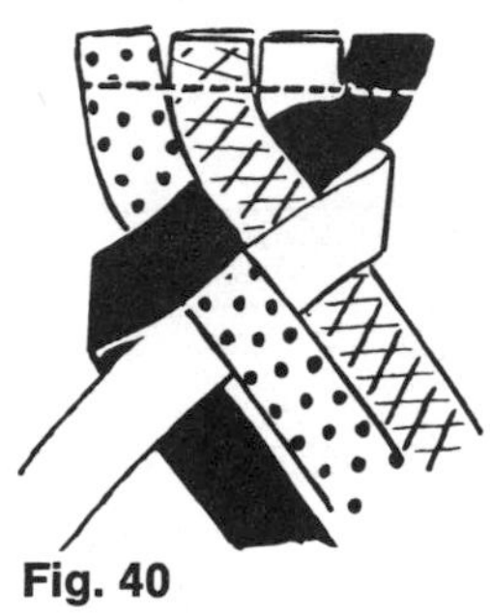
Fig. 40

Multiple Braiding

The principle is the same whether you braid with three strands or more. Begin with the last strip to the right and weave it over and under from right to left. Repeat, beginning again at the right (see Fig. 42).

Fancy Five-strand Braiding. Number the strips from left to right. Bring last strip (No. 5) over No. 4 and No. 3. Bring No. 1 over No. 2 and under No. 5. Re-number strips and repeat these two steps (see Fig. 43).

Heavy Five-strand Braiding. Number strips from left to right. Bring last strip, No. 5 over Nos. 4 and 3; bring No. 1 over Nos. 2 and 5. Re-number strips and repeat these two steps (see Fig. 44).

Fancy Eight-strand Braiding. Number strips from left to right. Bring No. 4 over No. 5, under Nos. 6, 7, and 8. Bring No. 5 over Nos. 3, 2, and 1. Grasp Nos. 6, 7, and 8 as one unit and bring under Nos. 1, 2, and 3 as one unit. Bring No. 4 over Nos. 1, 2,

Fig. 41

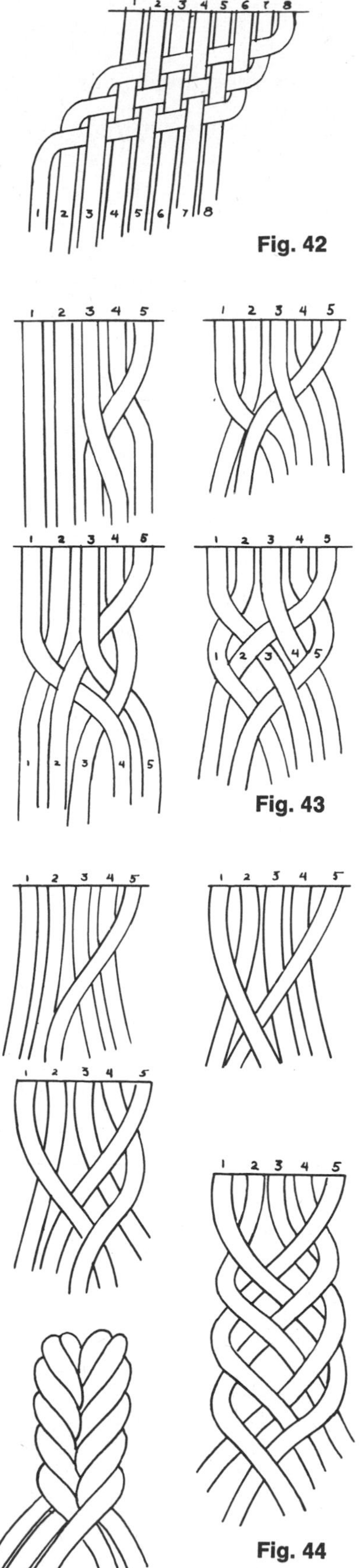

Fig. 42

Fig. 43

Fig. 44

and 3, and bring No. 5 under Nos. 6, 7, and 8. Bring No. 5 over No. 4 at center. Repeat these last two steps, continuing to braid first the three-strand units and then the single-strand units (see Fig. 45).

Since the wider the braid, the more difficult it is to turn curves and corners, it is better to use the wide braids in oblong rugs where strips run lengthwise only. Ends may be unravelled to form a fringe (see Fig. 46).

Dyeing

Since braided rugs are suitable for both traditional and modern furnishings, many people today are making room-size rugs. In this case, color is all important, and the color plan must suit the room. To achieve a planned color scheme, you may have to dye some of the needed colors.

There are many good dyes on the market. Follow the directions on the package. A bleach powder is available to remove the original color. Package directions are for dyeing over white to produce sharp, clear colors. You can get many lovely, muted shades by dyeing over light gray, beige, or any light color. Any light shade may be made darker, but if the color itself is to be changed, you must first use the color remover.

Because of new finishes (crease-resistant, etc.) some fabrics resist dyeing. Tightly woven fabrics absorb moisture slowly; to prevent uneven colors, they should be thoroughly soaked in warm water before being dyed. Loosely woven fabrics absorb dye quickly, and thick, closely woven ones take longer. A very loose fabric, which would be unsuitable for strips, sometimes shrinks in the boiling process and becomes thick enough to use.

It is possible to dye strips after they have been cut, but since they will probably shrink, cut them a little wider than desired. Colors may be mixed to get many varied, unusual shades. Here it is well to experiment. In case you wish to duplicate a color, it is a good idea to label the material after it has been dyed so you know exactly what combination of dye colors was used.

Fig. 45

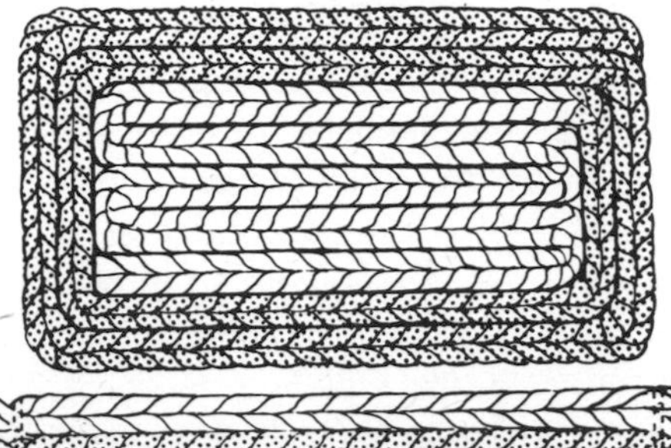

Fig. 46

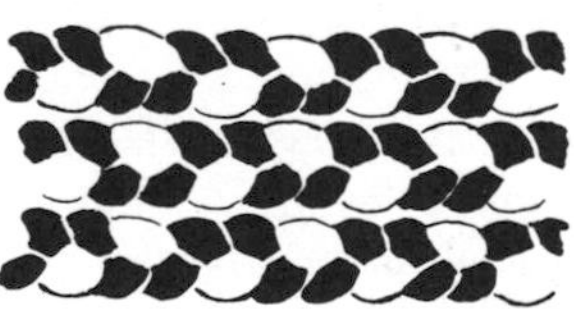

Fig. 47

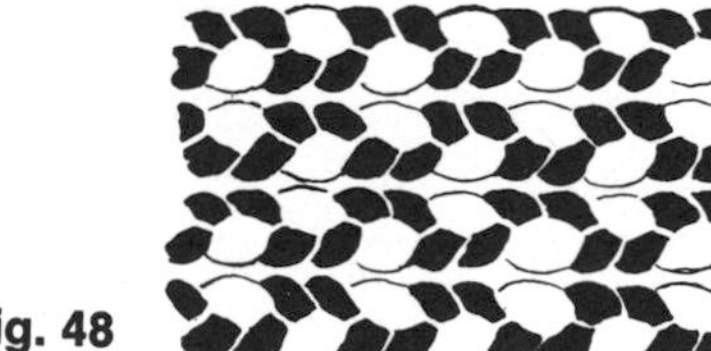

Fig. 48

Fig. 49

Braided Rug Patterns

To produce simple patterns, use contrasting colors in the braids and take care in the lacing to line up the colored strips so that a pattern is formed.

The pattern in Fig. 47 is braided with two strips of dark and one strip of light. When lacing, arrange to have a dark loop against a light (see diagram).

The pattern in Fig. 48 is also braided with two dark strips and one light. When lacing, lay a dark loop against a dark loop in the previous row. This will produce a different pattern (see diagram).

The pattern in Fig. 49 is plaited with one dark and three light strips. To produce the diamond pattern, follow the diagram when you lace the strips.

Shown here are three rugs in typical sizes and colorings you may wish to copy or use for inspiration. The colors in the parentheses indicate the colors of the strips in the braid. You may vary them to suit your materials and your color scheme.

Oblong Rug
29″ x 40″

Make center 12″ long, then:

4 rows Gray and Light Blue (2 Blue; 1 Gray)
3 rows Gray and Blue (1 Gray; 1 Light Blue; 1 Marine Blue)
2 rows Gray and Blue (1 Gray; 1 Light Blue; 1 Dark Gray)
3 rows Gray (1 Light Gray; 2 Dark Gray)
4 rows Gray and Red (1 Red; 1 Light Gray; 1 Dark Gray)
1 row Blue and Gray (1 Light Gray; 1 Light Blue; 1 Dark Gray)
1 row Blue and Gray (1 Light Gray; 2 Light Blue)
1 row Blue and Gray (1 Light Gray; 1 Light Blue; 1 Dark Gray).

Round Rug
Approximately 35″ to 36″ in diameter

Make a spiral until 8″ across, using braid made with 1 Light Green strip, 1 Gray mix-

Color Plate 9 HOOKED RUG

Called "Summertime," this is a beautiful example of a hooked rug made from narrow strips of fabric dyed especially for the purpose. For how to get these, see page 229.

Color Plate 10 CROCHETED MOTIF RUG

Made of small crocheted squares, this rug can be enlarged, or made smaller, simply by adding or subtracting squares. The diagram and gauge for the size shown are on page 251.

ture, 1 Tan, then:

3 rows (1 Tan; 1 Bright Green; 1 Gray mixture)
1 row (1 Tan; 1 Gray mixture; 1 Deep Bright Green)
1 row (1 Chamois; 1 Gray mixture; 1 Deep Bright Green)
2 rows (1 Chamois; 1 Gray mixture; 1 Brown)
1 row (1 Chamois; 2 Black)
1 row (1 Chamois; 1 Black; 1 Gray mixture)
2 rows (1 Gray mixture; 1 plain Gray; 1 Black)
3 rows (1 Gray mixture; 2 Deep Bright Green)
1 row (2 Brown; 1 Chamois)
1 row (1 Brown; 2 Chamois)
2 rows (1 Brown; 1 Chamois; 1 Brown mixture).

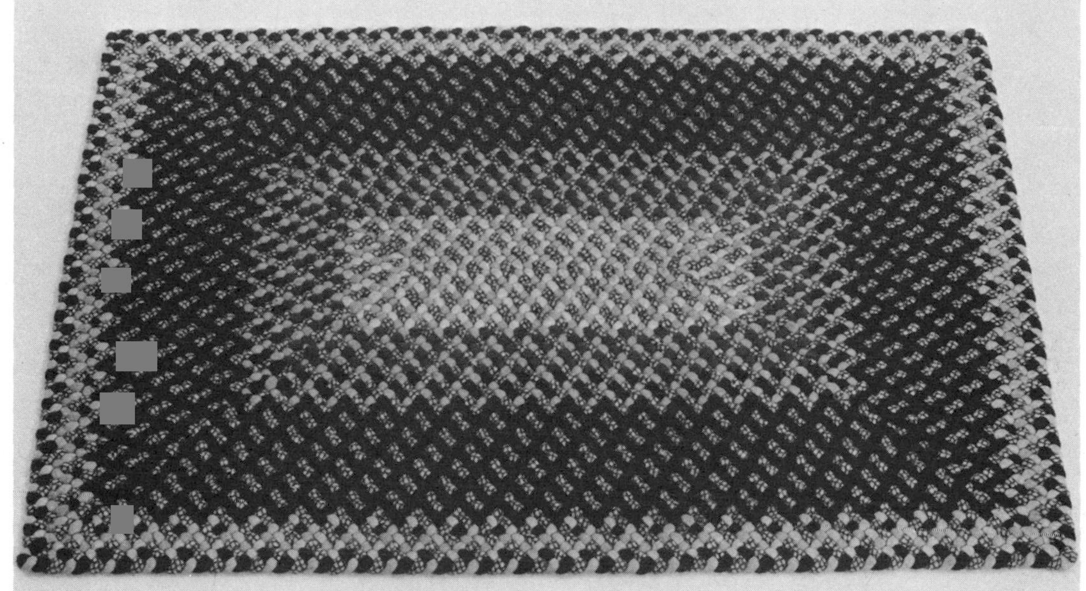

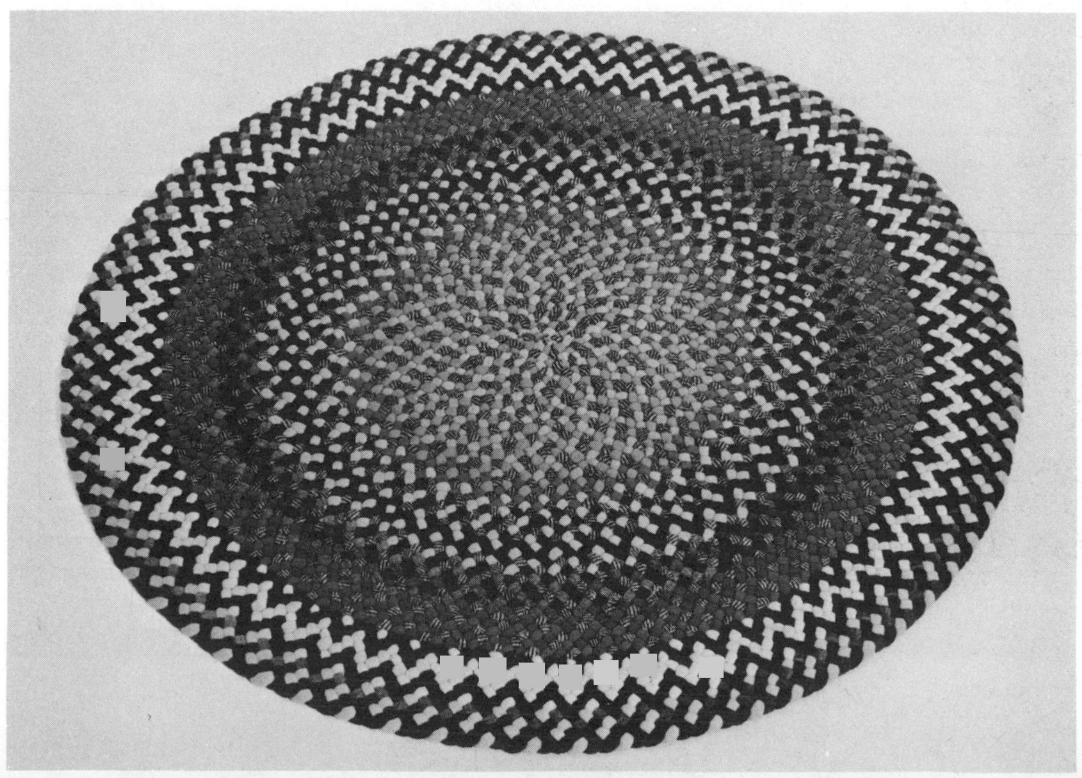

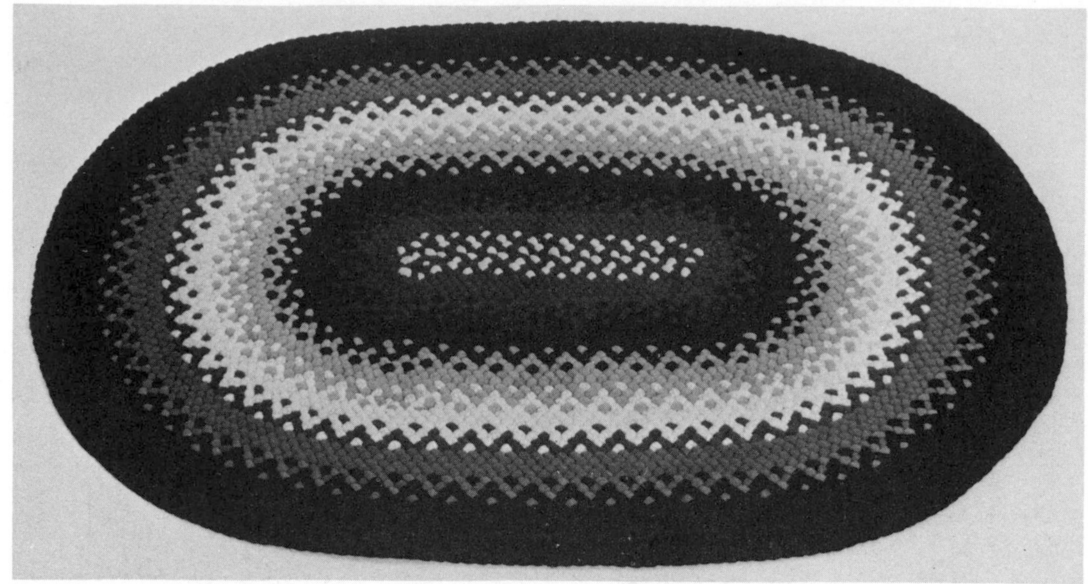

Oval Rug
Approximately 36″ x 48″

Make center 12″ long, then:
4 rows Pink and Red
2 rows solid Red
1 row Black and Red (2 Red; 1 Black)
1 row Black and Red (2 Black; 1 Red)
2 rows Black
1 row Black and Yellow (2 Black; 1 Yellow)
1 row Black and Yellow (1 Black; 2 Yellow)
1 row Yellow
1 row Yellow and Cream (2 Yellow; 1 Cream
1 row Yellow and Cream (2 Cream; 1 Yellow)
1 row Cream and Red (2 Cream; 1 Red)
1 row Cream and Red (1 Cream; 2 Red)
2 rows Red
1 row Red and Black (2 Red; 1 Black)
1 row Red and Black (2 Black; 1 Red)
4 rows Black.

Approximate Color Shading in Rug Shown Opposite (Bottom) and on Page 234

Center of rug
First braid 100″ long.
6 rows soft Green
3 rows brighter Greens
5 rows shading Green to Tan
3 rows Tan
1 row Tan and Brown
1 row Brown
2 rows Green and Brown
7 rows soft Greens
1 row brighter Green
4 rows Beige and soft Green
2 rows Green and Brown
2 rows Beige and Brown
1 row Beige and Orange
3 rows Beige
4 rows Beige and Orange
2 rows Orange and Brown
1 row Brown
1 row Brown and Rust
1 row Brown and Gray
2 rows Brown and Beige
1 row Chartreuse
2 rows Beige and Chartreuse
3 rows Orange and Brown
2 rows Brown and Rust.

RUGS WORKED ON CANVAS—KNOTTED RUGS

See photograph on page 247

Turkey Work, Smyrna Rug Stitch, or Pile Stitch

These are different names for the same stitch. It is done with needle and thread on canvas. A tapestry needle is used and it can be done on heavy single-thread linen canvas, rug, or base cloth, in which case it is called Turkey Work. Persian rug wool, which is a loosely twisted 3-ply yarn, is used; or regular rug yarn can be used if the canvas or base cloth is coarse enough. Have several needles at hand to avoid changing colors as much as possible.

When done on double-thread canvas using the same stitch it is sometimes called Smyrna Rug stitch or Pile stitch. Diagrams show working the stitch on canvas. It is not necessary to put the canvas in a frame as it can be worked in the hand or on a table top. It can be rolled up when not in use.

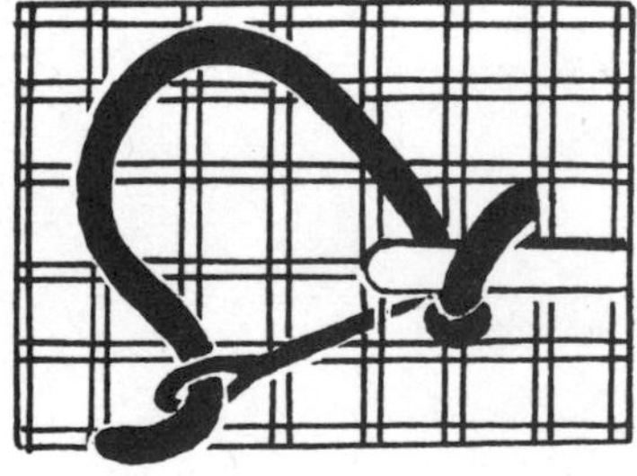

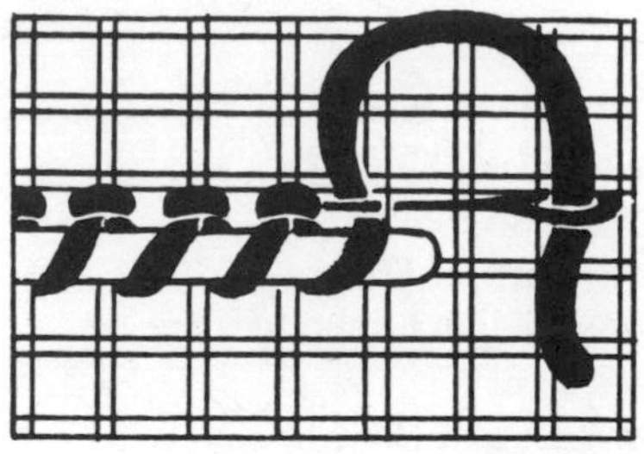

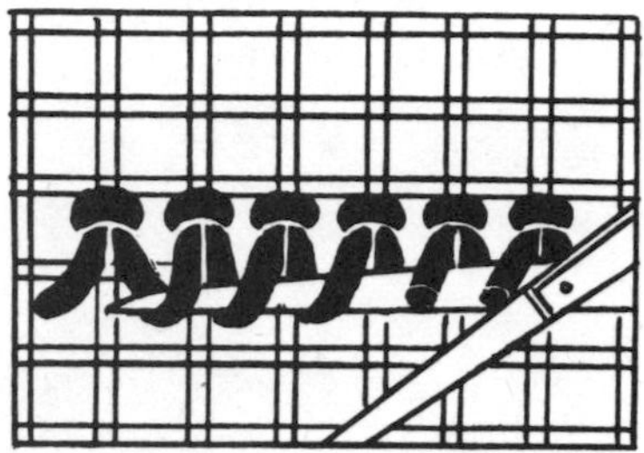

If working on a table, hold canvas down with a weight. Have the first row at edge of table. Start at the lower left hand corner leaving several squares for turning under. The stitch is very simple. First pass the needle horizontally to the left under a vertical thread. Draw up tight. Work the next stitch to the right of the first, holding the thread in a loop against the canvas, or use a ½″ wide gauge made of a tongue depressor. It is very important that all the loops be the same length. The design is done first and then the background, but each row is finished before going on to the next. After working a half dozen loops or so they are cut.

Finishing Edge. Fold edges under one square on coarse canvas or about ½″ on single thread canvas. Work over edge with close blanket stitch.

Needlepoint and Cross-Stitch Rugs

These rugs are made on regular needlepoint canvas for a fine textured rug or on coarser canvas which gives a bolder effect and works up more quickly.

Cross stitch on double-thread canvas is shown here. (See Needlepoint chapter for needlepoint and other canvas stitches, for which finer canvas may be used.)

Any cross stitch pattern can be followed. Simple borders can be repeated to make rows; or motifs can be arranged in block effect. On the whole, soft color combinations are more pleasing and easier to live with.

There are many stitches other than needlepoint and cross stitch which can be worked on canvas to make handsome rugs. (See chapters on Embroidery and Needlepoint for stitches.) Learn to experiment with various threads and yarns on different sizes of canvas for unusual and interesting texture. More than one stitch may be combined in the same rug. Also, cross stitch or other canvas stitches may be combined with knotting or pile stitch for very interesting effects.

Knotted with Latch Hook

This type of knotting is similar to but not exactly like knotting with needle and thread. It is done on coarse double-thread canvas with a special latch hook.

Rug yarn is used and it is cut in short lengths before knotting into the canvas. Cut yarn in lengths of about 3 inches and keep each color separate.

Place the canvas on the table and mark off a border of about 2″ all around. This is for turning under after rug is completed. Work with the rug on the table or in the lap; the selvage edges should be at the sides.

Start at the lower right-hand corner on the first row just inside of the margin. If you are working on tinted canvas, follow the colors of the tinting, selecting yarn to match.

Fold the piece of yarn in half over the shank of the hook just below the latch.

Match the two loose ends and hold with thumb and forefinger of left hand. Hold the hook in the right hand and keep the latch down with the forefinger.

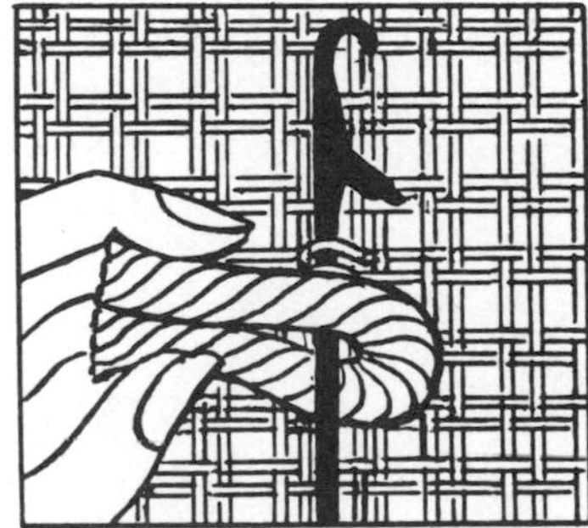

With yarn still folded over the hook, push the hook through the first hole under the first row of horizontal threads and up through the hole directly above. Push far enough so the latch is above the threads.

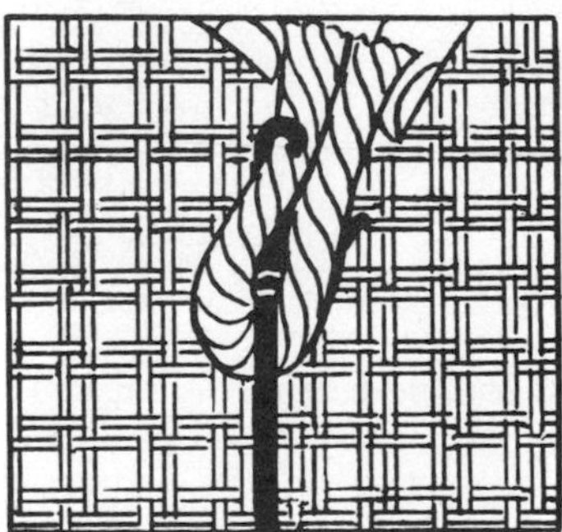

Now pull the hook toward you until the latch is almost vertical but not closed. Slip the ends (which are held in the left hand) between the latch and the hook.

Draw hook back until latch is closed; let

go of the ends and pull loose ends through the loop. The hook slips out.

Tighten the loop by pulling the loose ends. This is one stitch. Continue across, making a loop in each square. Work rows from right to left, keeping finished part toward you.

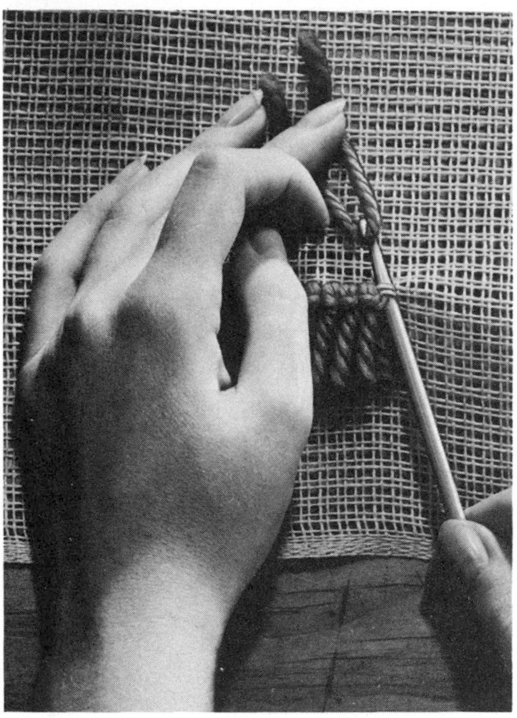

When complete, trim any uneven ends and shake rug well.

Turn under the margin and sew on rug binding. Apply binding flat, covering the raw edges. Hem down both edges, using a curved needle and strong thread. Apply binding loosely and miter the corners.

It is also possible to do the stitch with an ordinary crochet hook.

CROCHETED RUGS

Crocheted rugs can also be made of various kinds of yarn or thread or of fabric strips. Use all of one kind of fabric (wool or cotton preferably) in one rug. The strips are cut wider than for hooking but not as wide as for braiding (½″ to ¾″ depending on the thickness of fabric used). It is wise to make a swatch. Some prefer to cut the fabric on the bias for crocheting. Knitted fabrics work up well.

If you have many odds and ends of yarn, they can be worked up into a "hit or miss" round or oval rug in single crochet (picking up both top stitches) with a very pleasing result. All weights of yarn can be used by doubling the finer ones. Increase just enough to keep the rug flat and not enough to make it ripple. Increase equal amounts on each side.

There are many other stitches which make attractive crocheted rugs such as loop stitch, popcorn, etc. (See chapter on Crochet.)

Crocheted Motif Rug
Approximately 33½″ x 49½″

Shown on Color Plate 10

Materials. Heavy Rug Yarn—eight 70-yd. skeins each Chartreuse and Taupe. Nine

70-yd. skeins Ant. Gold. Fourteen 70-yd. skeins Moss. Aluminum Crochet Hook, Size J (or any size which will result in motif gauge specified).

Gauge. Each motif is a 6½″ square.

Note: Entire rug is worked with a double strand of yarn throughout. All motifs will be worked in same manner as motif no. 1, but in color scheme given. Make 7 of each motif.

Motifs. MOTIF NO. 1: With Moss, ch 2, work 8 s c in 1s st of ch, join in 1st s c. **2nd Round:** Ch 1, 3 s c in same space (corner), 1 s c in next s c, * 3 s c in next s c, 1 s c in next s c, repeat from * twice, join in 1st s c, cut yarn. **3rd Round:** Attach Chartreuse in center s c of any corner, 3 s c in same space, * 1 s c in each of the next 3 s c, 3 s c in next s c, repeat from * twice, 1 s c in each of the next 3 s c, join, cut yarn. **Next 4 Rounds:** Work in same manner as last round, always having 2 more sts between inc points in each round and working in following color scheme: 2 rounds Antique Gold, 1 round Taupe and 1 round Moss. MOTIF NO. 2: Work 2 rounds Antique Gold, 1 round Moss, 2 rounds Chartreuse, 1 round Taupe, and 1 round Moss. MOTIF NO. 3: Work 2 rounds Taupe, 1 round Moss, 2 rounds Antique Gold, 1 round Chartreuse, and 1 round Moss. MOTIF NO. 4: Work 2 rounds Chartreuse, 1 round Antique Gold, 1 round Moss, 2 rounds Taupe, and 1 round Moss. MOTIF NO. 5: Work 2 rounds Moss, 2 rounds Chartreuse, 1 round Taupe, 1 round Antique Gold, and 1 round Moss.

MOTIF 1	MOTIF 2	MOTIF 3	MOTIF 4	MOTIF 5
2	3	4	5	1
3	4	5	1	2
4	5	1	2	3
5	1	2	3	4
1	2	3	4	5
2	3	4	5	1

Finishing: Block all motifs. Sew motifs tog, sewing in back loop of sts only, arranging according to chart.

Edge: With a double strand of Moss work in s c and in back loop of sts working 1 s c in each s c, 1 s c in each joining and 3 s c in each corner, join, cut yarn.

Chapter 7

Knitting

Knitting was at one time considered to be a manly accomplishment. Although women now regard the craft as almost exclusively their own, they are relative newcomers to it. During the Middle Ages in England, in the years of the "Crafts and Guilds," a man worked six years to become a master-knitter. He served an apprenticeship under a qualified master, went abroad to learn foreign techniques, and returned to "sit" for an extremely difficult examination.

The machine age and the Industrial Revolution changed all that, and knitting was left to the women. In early America, women knit to provide warm clothing for the family. Every stocking had to be knit at home by hand and even children were obliged to help out. They often knew how to knit before they could read and carried their work to school to do during recess periods.

Knitting is a simple technique, done for the most part on two needles, but it can fashion things of delicate beauty or of sturdy warmth and practicality for children and adults. Every girl should learn to knit. At some time in her life she is almost sure to find this skill to be useful either from a practical point of view or as an outlet for her creative energy.

HOW TO BEGIN

Yarns

There are many types of yarns and threads suitable for knitting although they vary in size, twist, and texture. They also differ in fiber content and may be made of silk, wool, cotton, linen, or man-made fibers such as nylon, Orlon, Dacron, and others. A yarn may also be a combination of two or more fibers. The type and size of yarn determines its use, and this must be considered when choosing a suitable yarn for the article to be made.

The size or ply of yarn to be used is usually given with the knitting instructions (novelty yarns excepted) and should be followed as closely as possible for satisfactory results.

Only an expert knitter dares to make changes in size or type of yarn. Some yarns are interchangeable, but this must be carefully determined by knitting a swatch to check the gauge. Also, be sure to buy all of the yarn needed for a garment at one time because dye lots differ.

Knitting Needles

Knitting "pins" or needles vary in size and length and the proper ones are specified in the instructions. It is not advisable to change sizes unless necessary to obtain the proper gauge. (See Gauge.)

Straight Needles. These come in pairs. When using them, the work is done in rows back and forth. Sizes are numbered—the larger the number, the coarser the needle.

Circular Needles. These come in different sizes and in several lengths. The longest will hold enough stitches for a skirt width. They can also be used for smaller articles and in places where it is desirable to avoid a seam. They are usually used for knitting round and round instead of back and forth.

Double-Pointed Needles. These come in sets of 4 or 5 and, as the name implies, are pointed at each end. They also are used to knit in rounds, especially socks.

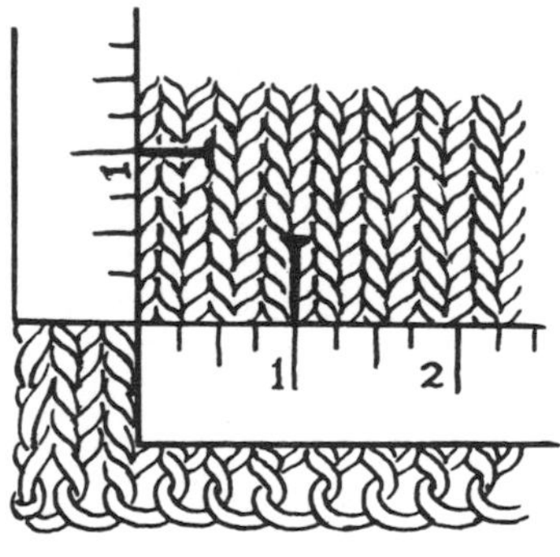

Gauge

Do not overlook the Stitch Gauge given at the beginning of each instruction. It is very important to the size and fit of your garment. Gauge is the number of stitches per inch knitted or crocheted with the specified size needle (or hook) and yarn. It is always well to make a swatch at least 2 inches square, block it, then measure. (See diagram.) The number of stitches and rows to the inch should be the same as those given in the instructions. If you get more stitches to the inch than called for, you are working too tightly, so change to larger needles (or hook). If you get fewer stitches to the inch than called for, you are working too loosely, so change to smaller needles (or hook). Remember, the size of the needles (or hook) used does not matter as long as your stitch gauge is correct.

Abbreviations

oz(s) .... ounce(s)
k .... knit
p .... purl
inc(s) .... increase(s)
dec(s) .... decrease(s)
rnd(s) .... round(s)
sl .... slip
st(s) .... stitch(es)
sl st .... slip stitch
yo .... yarn over
psso ... pass slip stitch over knit stitch
tog .... together
beg .... beginning
dp .... double pointed
pat .... pattern

* This symbol (asterisk) means that the instructions immediately following it are to be repeated the given number of times.

A row is once across the needle. "Work even" means to work without increasing, keeping the pattern as is.

Abbreviations for crochet may be found in chapter on crochet.

HOW TO KNIT

Basic Techniques

To Cast On means to put the first stitches onto the needle.

1. About 24 inches from the end of the yarn, make a slip knot as shown. (When starting an actual garment, allow about 1 inch per stitch for heavy yarn and ½ inch for lightweight yarn.) Slip needle into the loop. Pull up the knot to tighten.

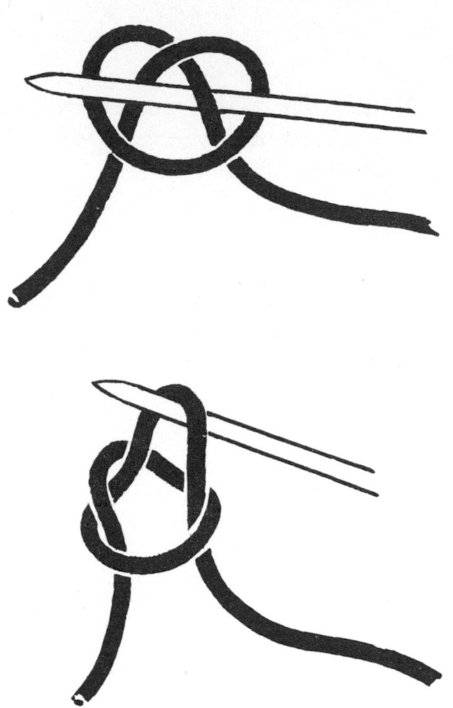

2. Holding the needle with the slip knot in the right hand, draw up the 2 strands of yarn between ring and little fingers of the left hand. Hold yarn securely.

3. Slip forefinger and thumb of left hand between the strands. The one coming from the ball should be at the back.

4. Bring thumb up and spread the fingers.

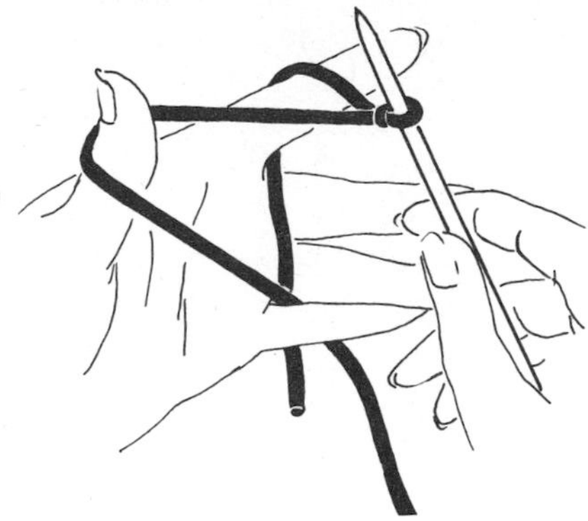

5. Put the needle under the front strand on the thumb.

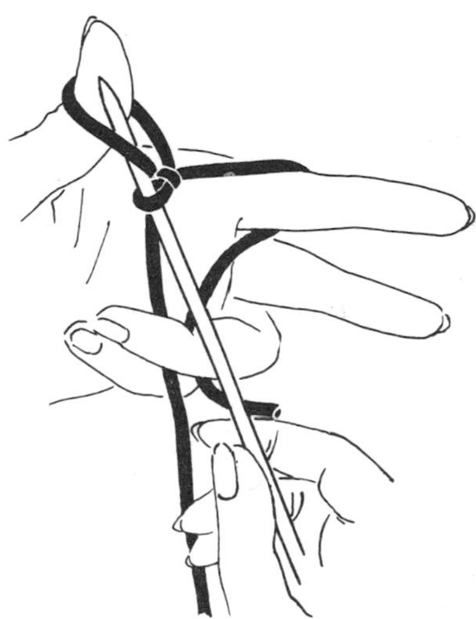

6. Then pick up the strand on the forefinger.

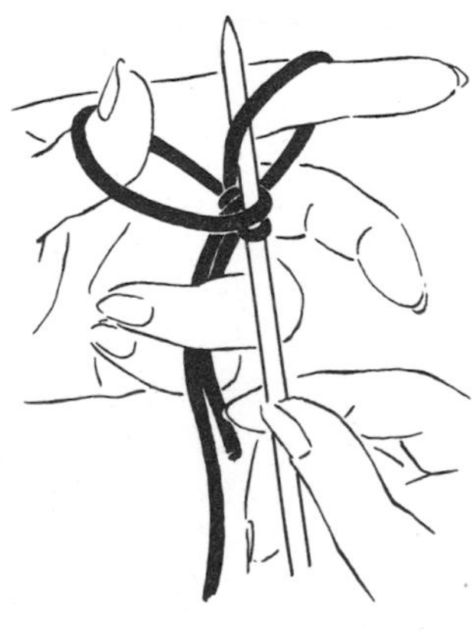

7. Pull it through the loop on the thumb.

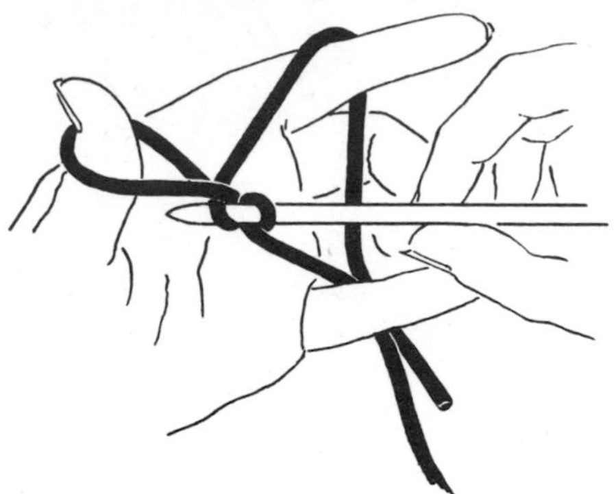

8. Let the loop slip from the thumb.

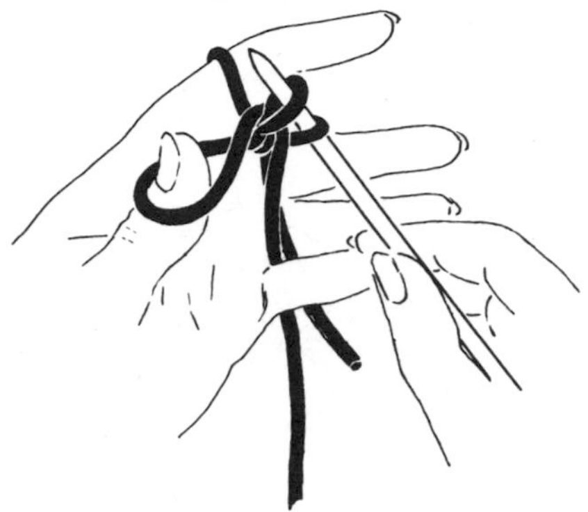

9. Tighten the stitch. Repeat from step 1 for as many stitches as you need.

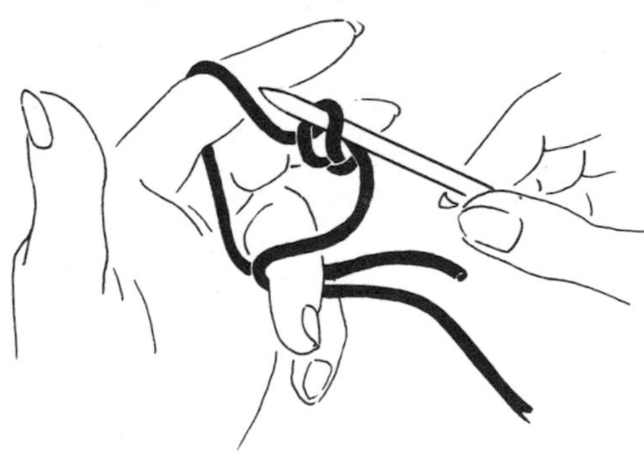

To Knit:

1. Hold the needle with the cast on stitches in the left hand as shown.

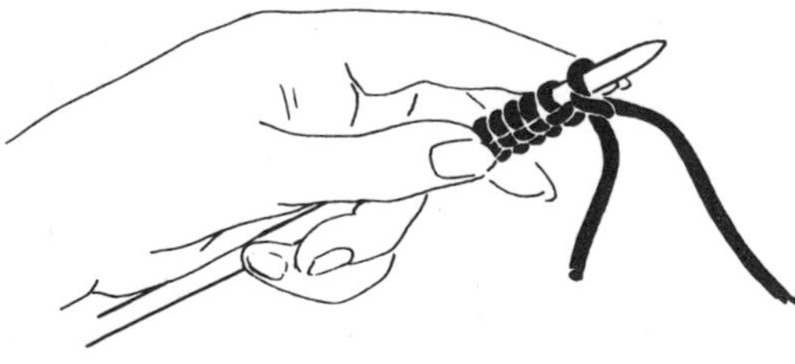

2. Right hand: Wrap yarn around the little finger, under the next two fingers and over the forefinger.

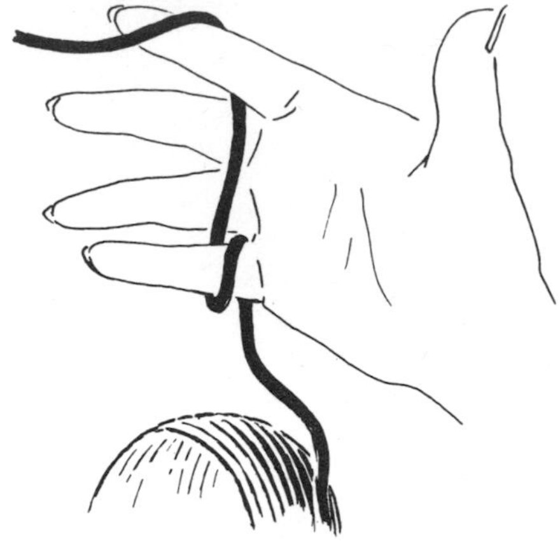

3. Holding second needle in the right hand, insert it into the front of the first stitch.

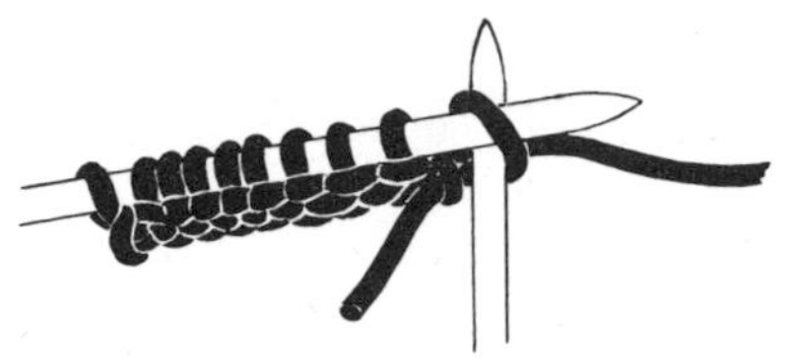

4. Throw the yarn under and over the point of needle in the right hand.

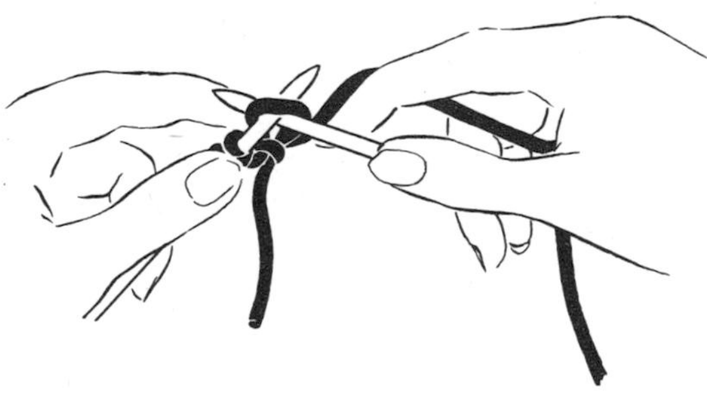

5. Draw yarn through the stitch.

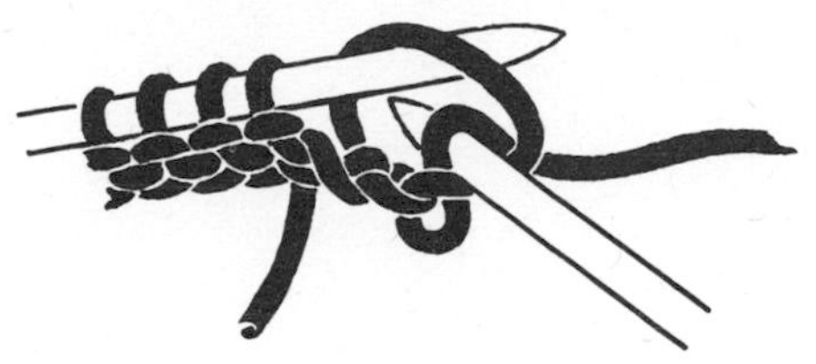

6. Slip stitch from left needle. Repeat steps 3 through 6 until all stitches are knit.

Repeat this row of knitting by twos and you have the garter stitch, pictured here.

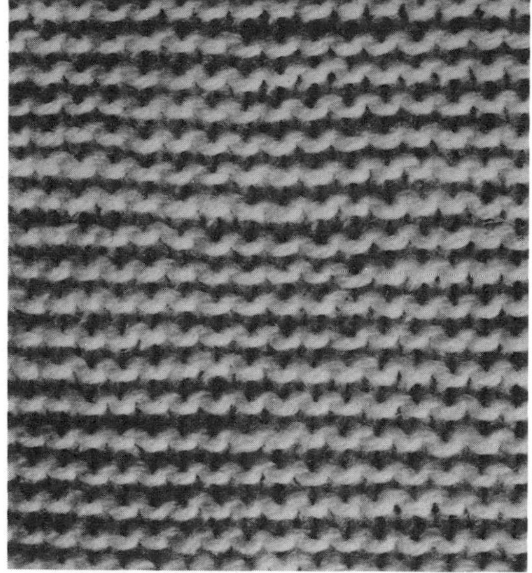

To Purl:

1. Hold the needle with the knit stitches in the left hand.

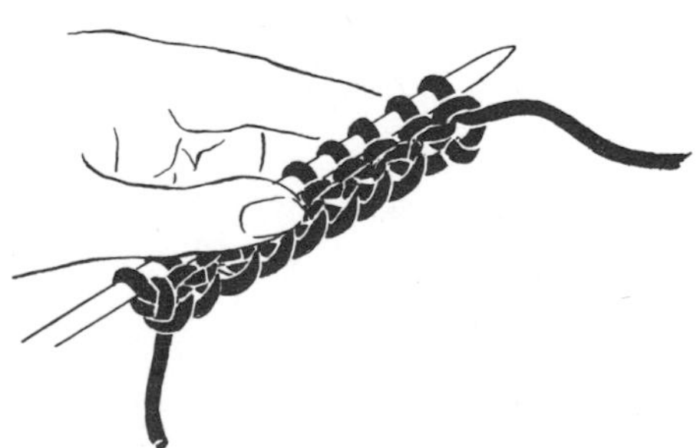

2. Hold the yarn in the right hand the same as before. With the second needle in the right hand, insert point of needle in *back* of first stitch. The right needle is now in front of the left.

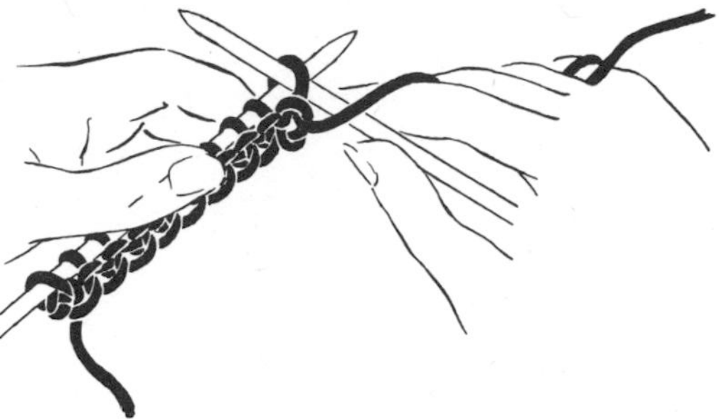

3. Bring yarn around needle the same as for knitting, under then over point of right needle.

4. Draw the yarn through to the back.

5. This forms a stitch on the right hand needle.

6. Slip the stitch off the left hand needle. Repeat steps 2 through 6 across row.

Knit across and purl back for the stockinette stitch shown here. Repeat these two rows. On circular or sock needles, knit continuously to produce stockinette.

To Bind Off:
1. Knit two stitches.

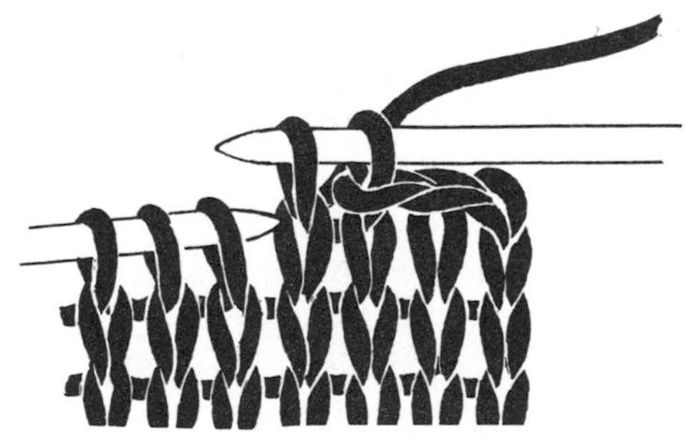

2. Insert left needle into the first of the two stitches which you have just knit.

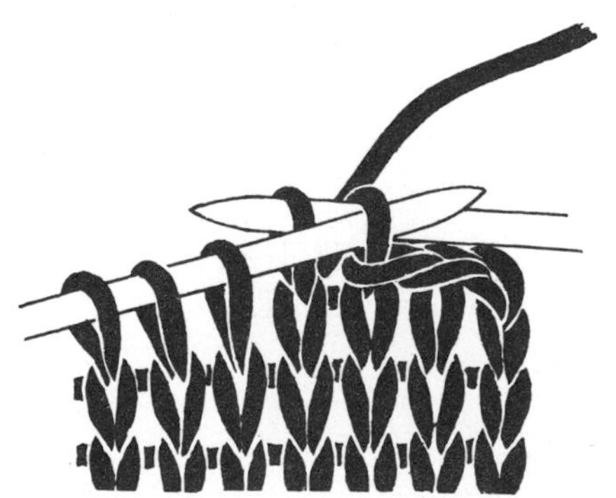

3. Now pull the first stitch over the second.

4. There will be one stitch remaining on right hand needle. Knit another stitch, then repeat from step 2.

To Increase (Method No. 1):
1. Insert needle into front of stitch.

2. Knit it but do not remove it from left needle.

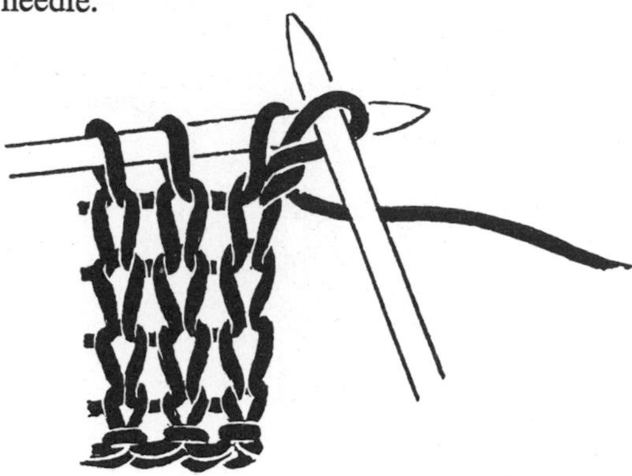

3. Insert right hand needle into back of the same stitch and knit again. Then remove the stitch from left needle.

To Increase (Method No. 2): This method is used to form a dart (as on thumb of mitten or glove).

1. Insert needle under the thread of yarn between the stitches and knit. This will leave a small opening. To prevent the opening, pick up the thread, twist it entirely over, slip it onto the left hand needle and then knit it off as shown.

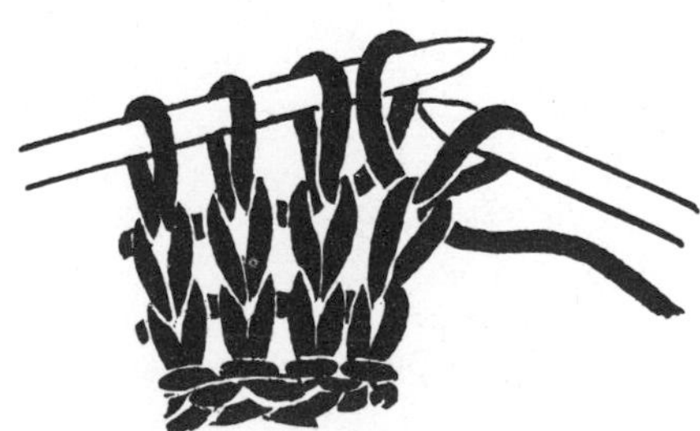

To Increase (Method No. 3): This forms an eyelet or opening and is generally used for lace stitches.

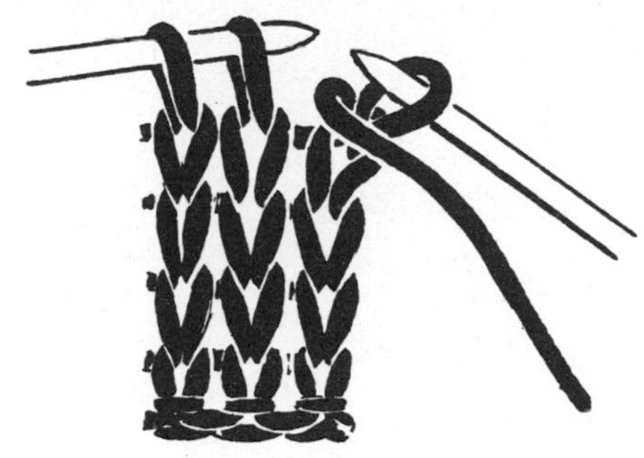

1. Bring yarn to the front between the needles and over the right hand needle—this is called "yarn over" (yo)—and then to the back.

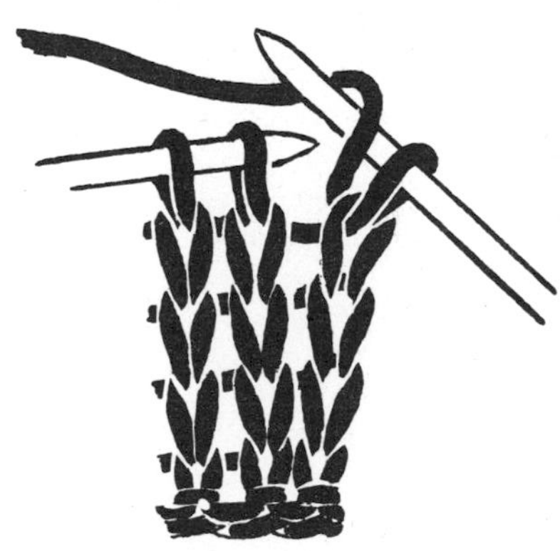

2. Knit the next stitch.

To Decrease (Method No. 1): This method is used when decreasing at the edge of a garment or when a slant to the right is desired.

1. Insert needle in front as for regular knitting. Knit 2 stitches together.

2. Slip the stitches off together.

To Decrease (Method No. 2): This method is used when a slant to the left is desired.

1. Insert needle in *back* of stitches and knit 2 stitches together.

2. Slip the stitches off together.

To Decrease (Method No. 3):

1. Slip one stitch from the left needle onto the right needle, then knit one stitch.

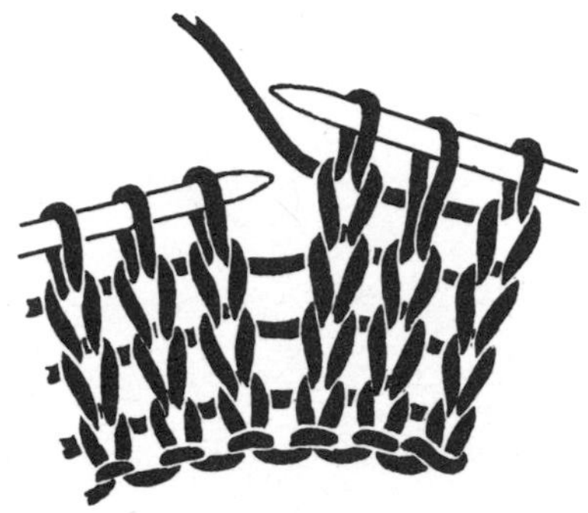

2. Pass the slipped stitch over the knit stitch.

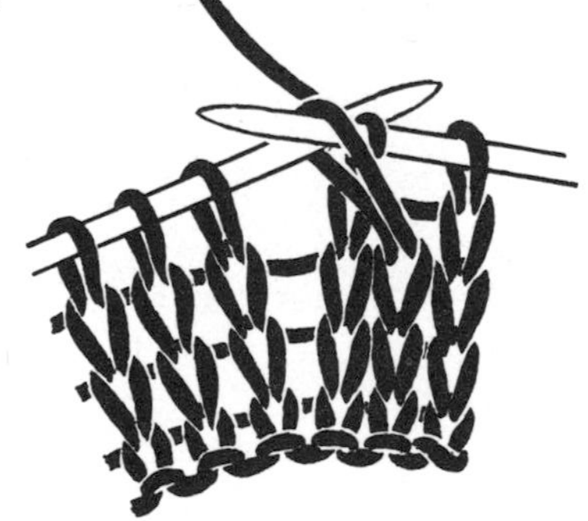

To Make a Smooth Edge. Insert right needle into front of first stitch on the left needle from the right side and slip the first stitch off and onto the right needle without knitting. Do this with the first stitch of each succeeding row and you will have a smooth edge known as chain edge.

Note: This chain edge is not used in all cases; it makes a smooth edge on straight knitting. However, the closed edge produced by knitting every stitch is used when shaping various parts of a garment.

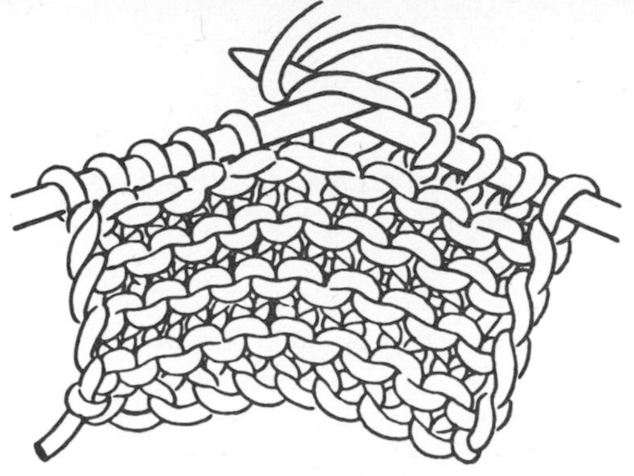

Bring yarn to the back of the work and proceed as before. Knit in this manner for a number of rows and you have garter stitch.

Ribbing. For a k 2 p 2 ribbing, cast on a multiple of 4 sts, then * k 2 sts, bring yarn forward and p 2 sts. Repeat from * across row and end with p 2. Turn work and repeat this row. In ribbing, when smooth side of stitch is toward you, the stitch is to be knitted; and when the rough side is toward you, the stitch is to be purled. There are other types of ribbing; the pattern depends upon changes in the number of k and p stitches.

To Slip a Stitch. Slip the stitch from the left to the right needle as for purling without knitting it.

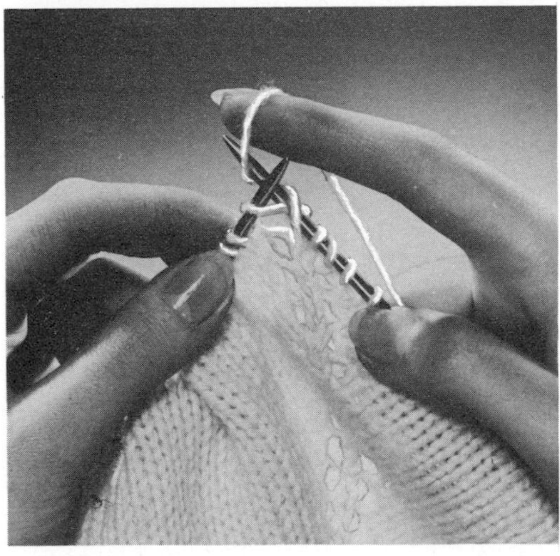

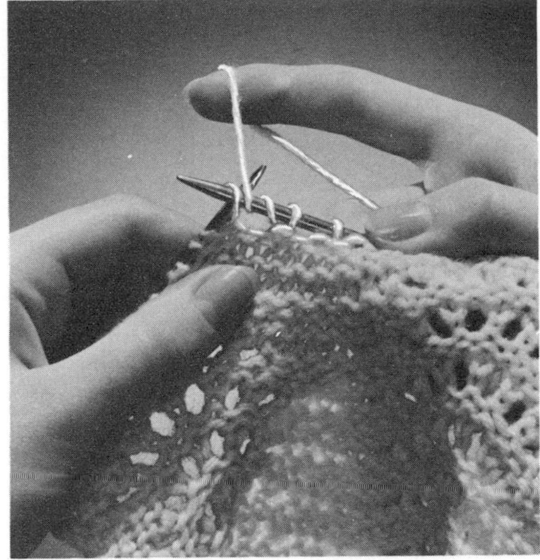

Yarn Over. Before a knit stitch, bring yarn in front of right needle and then knit the next stitch. This makes an extra stitch because a loop is formed on the right needle. Before a purl stitch, wrap yarn completely around right needle and purl the next stitch in the usual way. These "yarn overs" form holes and are used for open work patterns.

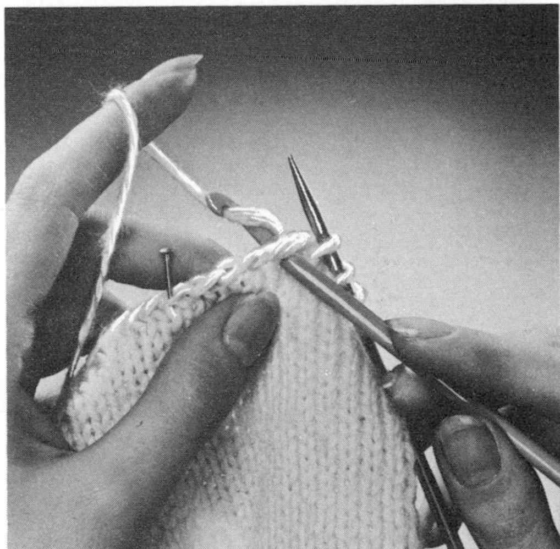

To Pick Up Stitches. Stitches are most frequently picked up around neck and armholes. Divide and mark the space into quarters. Be sure to pick up ¼ of the total number of stitches in each space so work will look smooth. On an irregular edge, insert needle into every row to avoid holes. With right side toward you, work from right to left. Hold free end of ball of yarn against back of garment with left hand until you get started. Insert crochet hook into first row in from edge and draw yarn through. Place stitch on knitting needle. Continue around. Stitches may also be picked up directly onto the knitting needle.

You should now be able to make any knitted article worked on 2 needles in stockinette stitch, garter stitch, and ribbing. Pattern stitches, unless very simple, take a little more practice.

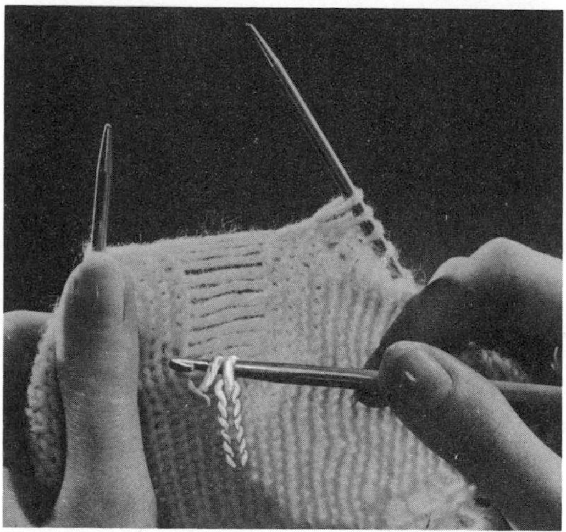

Dropped Stitches. In stockinette or ribbing, always pick up stitches with the knit side toward you. Insert a crochet hook in loop of dropped stitch; draw yarn of the row above through the loop. Continue until you reach the row on which you are working. Slip last loop onto needle. Do not twist stitches.

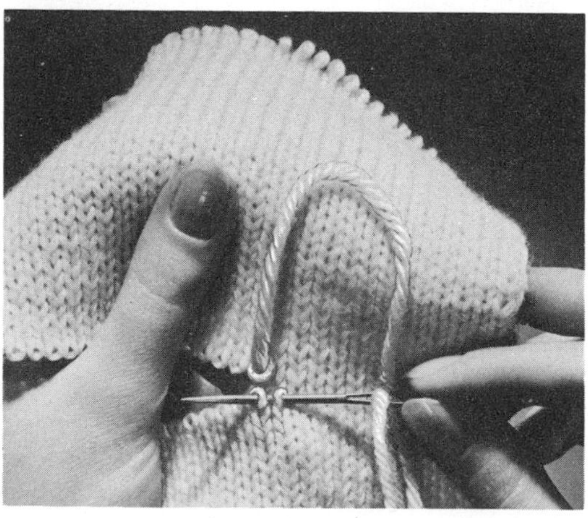

To Weave Stockinette. Use a wool needle (or any needle with blunt point) and the same yarn as the garment. Bring pieces to be joined close together. Fasten yarn on the under side at the right. Draw yarn from wrong side through first stitch on upper piece. Insert needle in first stitch on lower piece and bring through next stitch on lower piece from wrong side. Draw up yarn. * Insert needle in same stitch as before on upper piece and bring through next stitch on upper piece from wrong side. Draw up yarn. Insert needle from right side in same stitch as before on lower piece and draw through next stitch on lower piece from wrong side. Repeat from * until stitches are joined. Fasten yarn on wrong side.

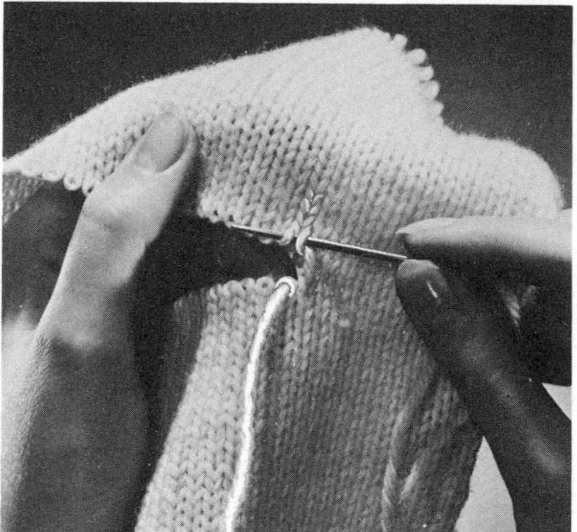

Weaving Toes of Socks. There must be an equal number of stitches on each of two needles. Break the yarn off from the ball, leaving a long length. Thread this into a wool needle. The knitting needles with the stitches are held even and parallel, having the end of yarn coming from right at back of needle.

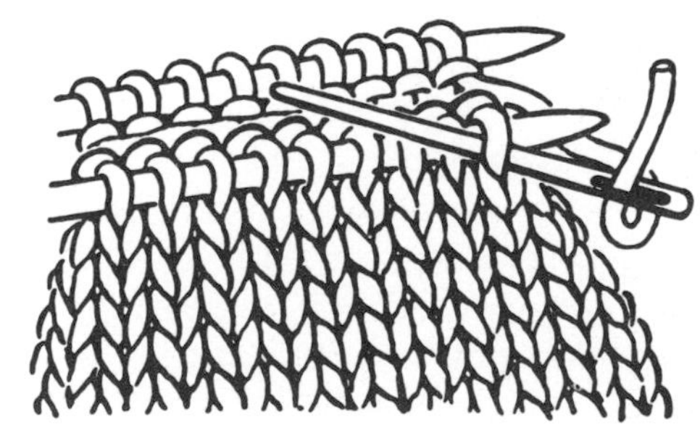

1. Insert the wool needle as if to purl in first stitch of front needle. Draw yarn through leaving stitch on needle.

2. Insert wool needle as if to knit into first stitch of back needle. Draw yarn through leaving stitch on needle.

3. Insert wool needle as if to knit in first stitch of front needle (same stitch as before) and slip the stitch off the needle. Insert needle in next stitch of front needle as if to purl; draw yarn through but leave stitch on needle.

4. Insert wool needle as if to purl in first stitch of back needle and slip this stitch off. Insert wool needle in next stitch of back needle as if to knit. Draw yarn through but leave stitch on needle.

5. Repeat steps 3 and 4 until all stitches are worked off.

How to Knit with Four Needles. This is round knitting and is usually used on socks. It is always worked in one direction. (See Casting On.) Using method number one, cast on one needle ⅓ the number of stitches required. Place another needle alongside of and a little forward of the first and cast on the second ⅓ of stitches. Repeat on third needle.

Arrange the three needles in a triangle with free end of yarn on right-hand needle. Make certain that the stitches haven't become twisted. With fourth needle start working on the first needle. This is called joining.

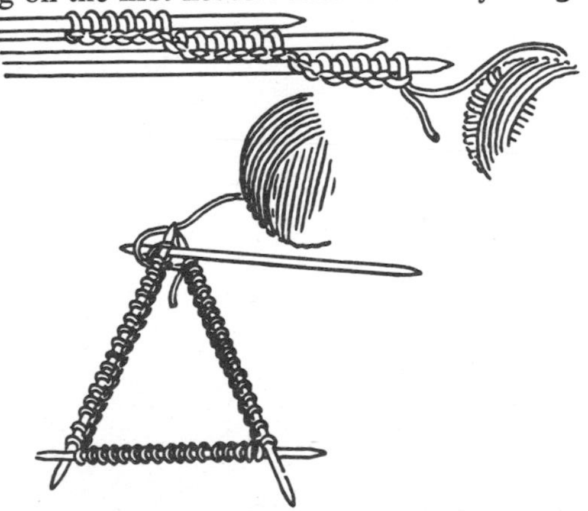

How to Knit with Circular Needle. Cast on the desired number of stitches using one or both points of the needle. Lay the needle on a flat surface and make sure the cast-on

edge is not twisted. Insert point of right needle (yarn from ball is attached at left needle) into first stitch of left side and begin to knit. In working on a circular needle, continue in one direction. This forms stockinette stitch.

Knots. Whenever possible, have knots come at the end of a row. If not possible, leave 3- or 4-inch ends on both pieces but do not make a knot. After several rows of knitting these ends can be tied firmly.

Raveling Stitches. Rip the last row stitch by stitch and place each stitch on a fine needle. Knit these onto the needle you are using.

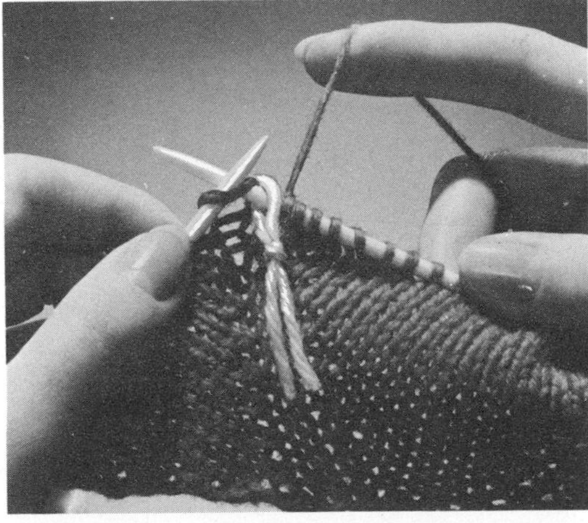

Markers. Instructions sometimes say to slip a marker on the needle. A small safety pin or a loop of yarn made with a slip knot and of contrasting color may be used. Slip onto right needle and on next row slip from one needle to the other.

There are many small knitting aids available such as stitch holders, counters, and bobbins for holding the various shades of yarn in multicolor knitting. These are usually made of plastic and are sold in needlework departments and yarn shops.

Buttonholes

Bind off the given number of stitches (to fit size of button desired). Cast on the same number of stitches on next row directly over the bound-off stitches. Work around holes with buttonhole stitch.

Girls' and women's cardigans can be faced with grosgrain ribbon down each side of front. Mark for buttonholes and machine-stitch around markings. Cut through for buttonholes and work buttonhole stitch around opening. Sew buttons on left side. Or make machine-made buttonholes through the grosgrain. These are usually done vertically.

Loop Buttonholes. Mark spaces at edge of opening for placing buttonholes. Thread needle with yarn and make a loop of 2

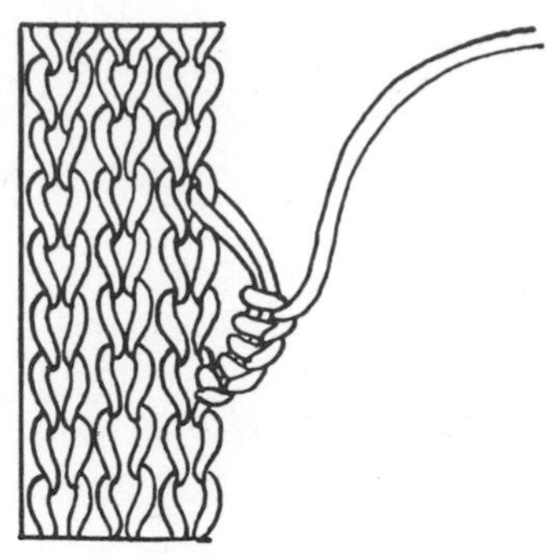

strands of yarn long enough to admit button. Work buttonhole st over the loop.

Crocheted Buttonholes. Sometimes used on edges which are finished with single crochet. Mark spaces. Work in sc to marking. Chain st for number of sts required for the button. Skip this space on the edge and work sc to the next mark. Buttonholes may also be made in the center of a wide crocheted band in the same way, by working rows of sc before and after making buttonholes.

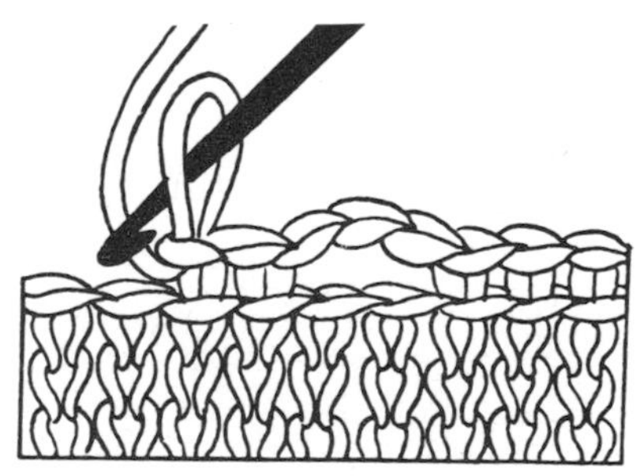

Knit-in Raglan Sleeve on Slipon Sweater

For this type of sweater, begin at the neck and work down. The following method tells how to arrive at the number of stitches to be cast on.

Measure the width at the back of the neck (we will assume it is 5 inches), and allow 1 inch for each sleeve top. This makes 7 inches; multiply this by the number of stitches per inch of your gauge (we will assume it is 6). This makes 42 sts. Now add 4 seam sts, 8 sts for raglan increasing, and 1 st for each side of front. This makes 56 sts in all. This total will vary with the width at the back of neck and the gauge.

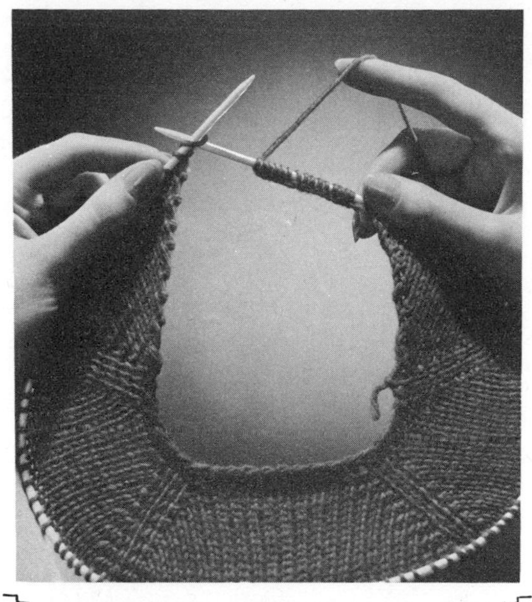

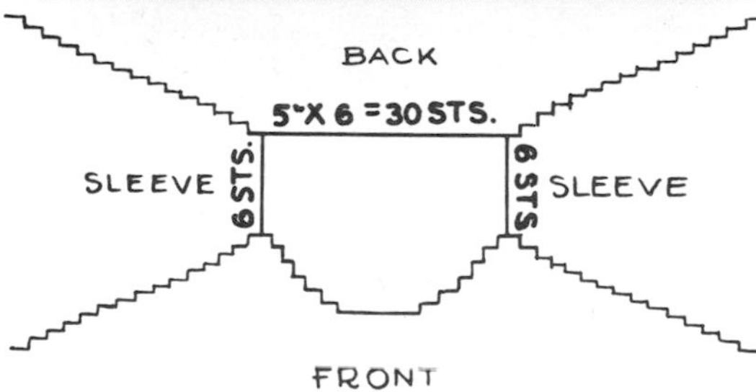

Cast stitches on circular needle. Mark the seam sts. Work back and forth, increasing on each side of the seam sts at the beginning and end of every alternate row (every knit row). At the same time, shape neck as follows: For a round neck increase 1 st at beg and end of every second k row 7 times (or as desired). Then cast on the number of sts required to complete neck (straight across front; see diagram). The number of sts for front must equal or exceed number of sts in back section. For example: if there are 58 sts in back and 20 sts in each front section, cast on 18 sts. Join and work round and round as in plain knitting. At the same time, continue to inc before and after each of four seam sts every other round until raglan seam is the required length (to reach to underarm plus "ease"), and the front and back are wide enough.

Now place front, back, and one sleeve on stitch holders and work on one sleeve only.

To sleeve sts, add ½ inch each side for underarm and work downward, decreasing as necessary for width and length of sleeve desired. Work second sleeve in same manner.

To body sts add ½ inch on each side of front and back for underarm. Join and work downward on total number of sts back and front for desired length. Rib at waistline as desired. Bind off.

If a shaped sweater is desired, select 2 sts at each underarm for seam line and dec 1 st each side of these 2 sts as desired.

For V neck, sts will have to be calculated when increasing on side fronts to get shape and depth desired.

For cardigan, divide measurements of front in half and add 1 inch to each side of center front for lap. Cardigans may have round or V neck.

Set-in Pocket

Knit the body of the sweater to proper placement of pocket. Bind off number of stitches desired for width of pocket. Knit to end of row. Drop this piece temporarily. On separate needles, cast on same number of stitches as were bound off for pocket and knit for desired depth of pocket. Be sure to end piece on the same row as stitches of body of sweater were bound off. Drop this piece of work. Pick up body of sweater. Knit across row as far as space made by stitches bound off; pick up needle with small pocket piece, slip these stitches onto left needle and knit across these stitches and to end of row. Continue knitting. When garment is completed, sew pocket lining to wrong side of garment.

How to Turn the Heel on a Sock

When it is time to make the heel, the stitches must be rearranged on the needles. The directions tell how many stitches to place on each needle.

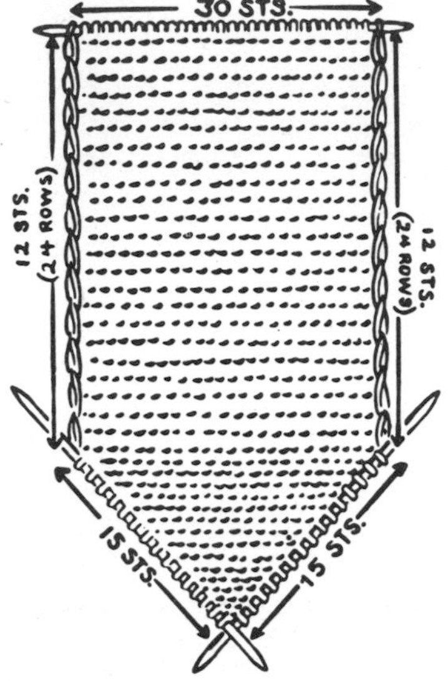

For example: if you are working with 60 sts, place 30 sts on the heel needle and 15 sts on the other two needles. These two needles are left idle while a heel flap is made on the 30 sts. Work straight for 24 rows. (For longer wear, nylon yarn may be substituted for the heel part or a thread of matching nylon sewing thread may be knitted in with the yarn.) For extra strength, the heel is knitted in alternate rows as follows:

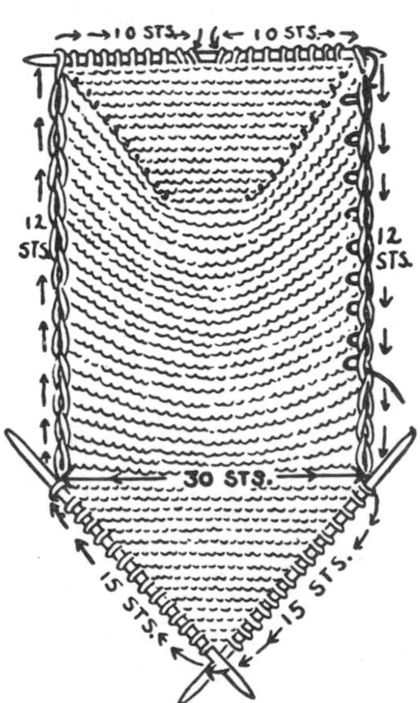

Row 1: P across. **Row 2:** * Sl 1, k 1, repeat from * across. Work for the number of rows (or inches) indicated in the directions —depending upon size of socks. Now this heel portion must be brought into position to make it possible to knit on three needles

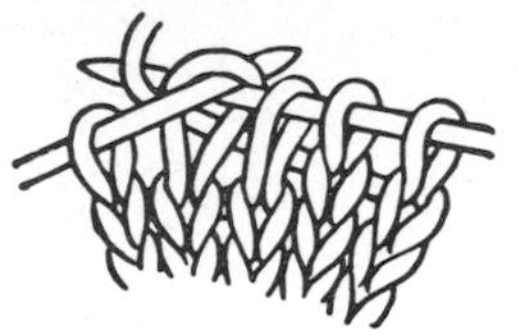

again. This shaping is achieved by a series of decreases on each side of work. This is called "turning the heel."

To make an even slant in opposite directions two kinds of decreases must be used. When working on the wrong side, dec by purling 2 tog. When working on the right side, decrease with sl 1, k 1, psso.

When shaping is completed, there are 20 sts on the needle (or as many as size indicates). Now pick up side sts according to directions and resume work on 3 needles. Pick up the inside loop of stitches at side of heel.

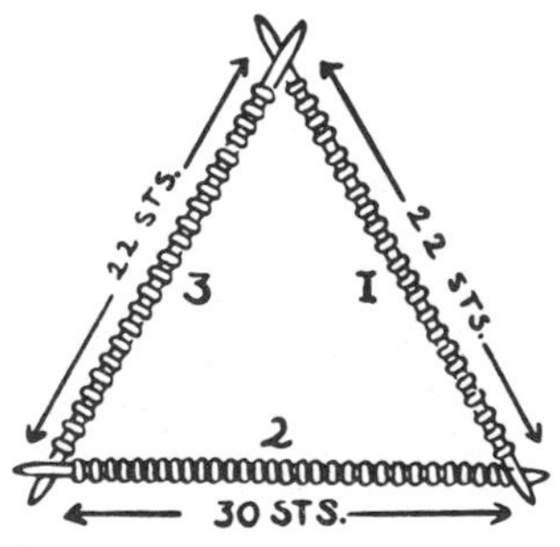

PATTERN STITCHES

Moss, Seed, or Rice Stitch. Cast on an uneven number of sts. **Row 1:** * K 1 st, p 1 st, repeat from * across row ending with k 1. Repeat this row. Always be sure to k above the p sts and p above the k sts of the preceding row.

Simple Rib Stitch. Cast on a multiple of 7 sts plus 2. **Row 1:** * P 2, k 5, repeat from * across row and end with p 2. **Row 2:** * K 2, p 5, repeat from * across row and end k 2. Repeat these 2 rows.

Smocked Ribbing. This is done on a simple rib pattern of k 5, p 1. The p 5, k 1 side is the right side of the garment. Thread a blunt-end needle with contrasting yarn. * Working from left to right and following the same row of knitting across, * bring needle from wrong side to the left of the first k st; insert needle from right to left under k st of next rib and under the first k st. Draw up. Work another stitch in the same place. Bring needle to wrong side at right of stitches just made. Bring needle out at left of k st on next rib. Do not draw up. Repeat from * across. Skip about 8 rows of knitting. On the next row, pick up alternate ribs and work across to form diamonds or "honeycomb" smocking. This may be worked on other types of ribbing and spacing can be varied.

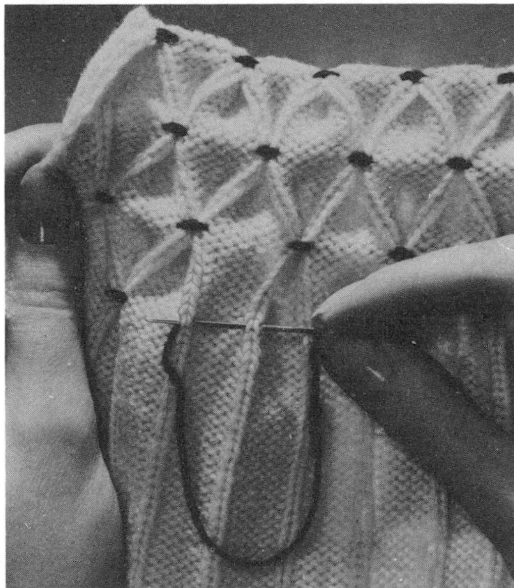

Block Stitch. Cast on a multiple of 10 sts. **Row 1:** * K 5, p 5, repeat from * across row and end with p 5. Repeat row 1 for 6 rows. **Row 7:** * P 5, k 5, repeat from * across row and end k 5. Repeat row 7 for 6 rows. Repeat these 12 rows to make pattern.

Diamond Stitch. Cast on a multiple of 8 sts plus one. **Row 1:** K 4, * p 1, k 7, repeat from * across row p 1, k 4. **Row 2:** P 3, * k 1, p 1, k 1, p 5, repeat from * across row and end p 3. **Row 3:** K 2, * p 1, k 3, repeat from * across row and end k 2. **Row 4:** * P 1, k 1, p 5, k 1, repeat from * across row and end p 1. **Row 5:** * P 1, k 7, repeat from * and end row p 1. **Row 6:** Same as row 4. **Row 7:** Same as row 3. **Row 8:** Same as row 2. Repeat these 8 rows for pattern.

Cable Stitch

Cable stitch is always done on a group of stitches of an even number. There are always a few purl stitches each side to set it off.

1. Work up to the cable section (stitches which are to be used for cable). Slip half the number of stitches of the cable section onto an extra needle (double-pointed cable needle). Hold these in back of the work.

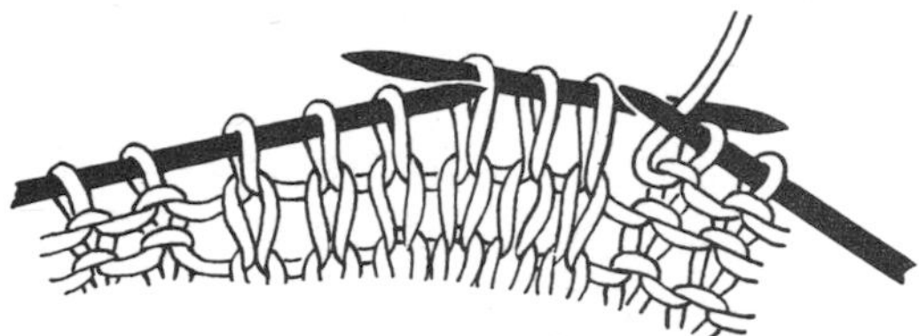

2. Knit remaining stitches of cable section.

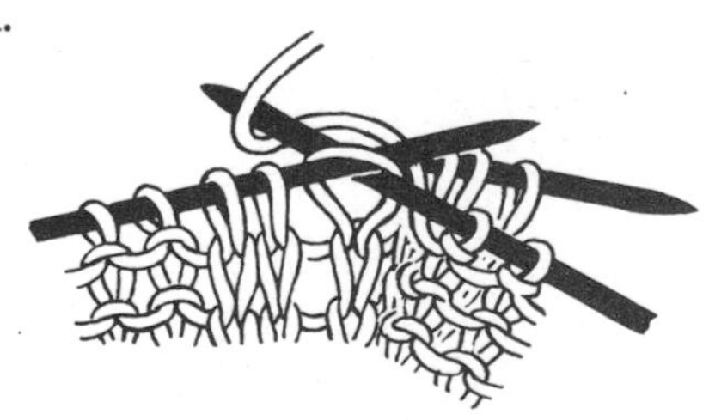

3. Knit the stitches from the cable needle and work the remainder of the row.

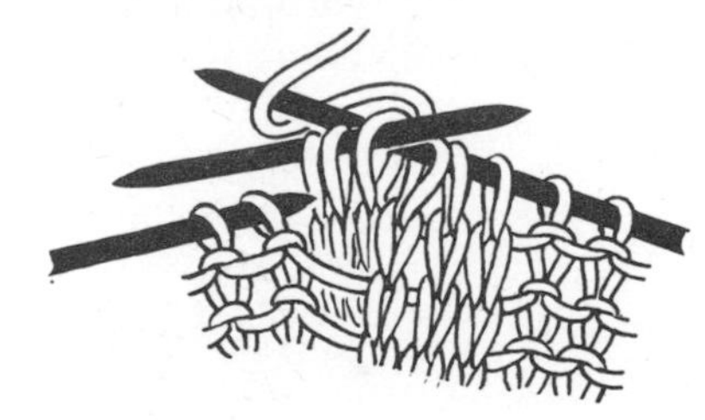

Mock Cable. Cast on a multiple of 6 sts plus 3. **Row 1:** * P 3 and k 3. Repeat from * across row and end p 3. **Row 2:** * K 3 and p 3. Repeat from * across row and end k 3. **Row 3:** * P 3, k into third st on needle and leave on needle, k into first st on needle then k into second st on needle, drop 3 sts off left needle. Repeat from * across row and end p 3. **Row 4:** Same as row 2. Repeat these 4 rows for pattern.

Simple Cable. Cast on a multiple of 14 sts. **Rows 1, 3, 5, 7, and 9:** K 2, * p 10, k 4, repeat from * across row and end with k 2. **Rows 2, 4, 6, and 8:** P 2, * k 10, p 4, repeat

from * across row and end p 2. **Row 10:** P 2, * slip next 5 sts onto double-pointed needle and place in back of work, k next 5 sts, then k 5 sts from double-pointed needle, p 4, repeat from * across row and end p 2. Repeat these 10 rows for pattern.

Plaited Cable. Cast on a multiple of 14 sts plus 1. **Rows 1 and 3:** * P 1, k 2, p 9, k 2, repeat from * across row and end k 2, p 1. **Row 2:** * K 1, p 2, k 9, p 2, repeat from * across row and end p 2, k 1. **Row 4:** K 1, p 2, slip next 3 sts onto double-pointed needle and place in front of work, k next 3 sts, then k 3 sts from double-pointed needle, k 3, p 2, repeat from * across row and end k 3, p 2, k 1. **Rows 5 and 7:** Same as row 1. **Row 6:** Same as row 2. **Row 8:** * K 1, p 2, k 3, slip next 3 sts onto double-pointed needle and place in back of work, k next 3 sts, then k 3 sts from double-pointed needle, p 2, repeat from * across row and end p 2, k 1. Repeat these 8 rows for pattern st.

Lattice Cable. Cast on a multiple of 4 sts plus 2. **Rows 1, 3, 5, and 7:** * K 2, p 2, repeat from * across row and end k 2. **Rows 2, 4, and 6:** * P 2, k 2, repeat from * across row and end p 2. **Row 8:** * P 2, slip next 4 sts onto double-pointed needle and place in back of work. K 2 from left needle, slip 2 p sts from double-pointed needle, repeat from * across row and end p 2. **Rows 9, 11, 13, and 15:** Same as row 1. **Rows 10, 12, and 14:** Same as row 2. **Row 16:** P 2, k 2, * p 2, slip 4 sts onto double-pointed needle and place in front of work, k 2 from left needle, slip 2 p sts from double-pointed needle to left needle and p these 2 sts, k 2 from double-pointed needle, repeat from * across row and end p 2. Repeat these 16 rows for pattern.

Chain Cable. Cast on a multiple of 15 sts plus 3 sts. **Row 1 (wrong side):** K 3, * p 12, k 3, repeat from * across. **Row 2:** P 3, * k 12, p 3, repeat from * across. **Rows 3 through 11:** Repeat Rows 1 and 2. **Row 12 (right side):** P 3, * sl next 3 sts on dp needle and hold in back of work, k next 3 sts, k sts from dp needle; sl next 3 sts on dp needle and hold in front of work, k next 3 sts, k sts from dp needle, p 3, repeat from * across. Repeat these 12 rows for pattern.

Lace Stitches

Lace Stitch with Pointed Border. Cast on a multiple of 13 sts, plus 1. **Row 1:** P across. **Row 2:** * K 1, yo, k 4, k 2 tog twice, k 4, yo. Repeat from * across row, end with k 1. Repeat these two rows for pattern.

Lace Stitch with Scalloped Border. Cast on a multiple of 18 sts. **Row 1:** K across. **Row 2:** P across. **Row 3:** K 2 tog 3 times, * (yo and k 1 for 6 times), k 2 tog 6 times, repeat from * across row and end k 2 tog 3 times. **Row 4:** K across. Repeat these 4 rows for pattern.

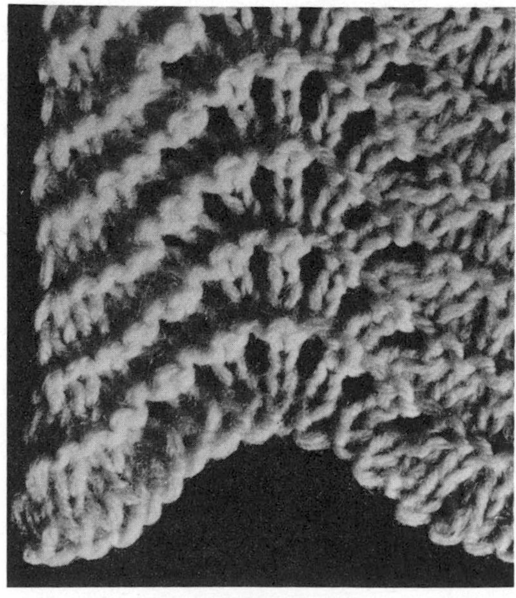

Medallion Lace Stitch. Cast on a multiple of 8 sts plus 2. **Row 1:** K 1, p 3, * k 2, p 6, repeat from * across row and end k 2, p 3, k 1. **Row 2:** K 4, p 2, * k 6, p 2, repeat from * across row and end k 4. **Row 3:** Same as row 1. **Row 4:** Same as row 2. **Row 5:** K 1, p 2, * k 2 tog, yo, slip 1, k 1, psso, p 4, repeat from * across row and end k 2 tog, yo, slip 1, k 1, psso, p 3. **Row 6:** K 3, * p 1, k into back of next st, then k into the front of the same st, p 1, k 4, repeat from * across row and end k 3. **Row 7:** K 1, p 1, * k 2 tog, yo, k 2, yo, slip 1, k 1, psso, p 2, repeat from * across row and end p 2. **Row 8:** K 2, * p 6, k 2, repeat from * across row and end k 2. **Row 9:** K 1, * k 2 tog, yo, k 2 tog, yo, slip 1, k 1, psso, yo, slip 1, k 1, psso, repeat from * across row and end k 1. **Row 10:** K 1, p 3, * k into the front and back on the next st, p 6, repeat from * to last 5 sts, then k into the front and back of the next st, p 4. **Row 11:** K 1, * yo, slip 1, k 1, psso, yo, slip 1, k 1, psso, k 2 tog, yo, k 2 tog, repeat from * and end yo, k 1. **Row 12:** K 1, k into back of next st, * p 6, k into the front and back of the next st, repeat from * and end k into back of next st, k 1. **Row 13:** K 1, p 1, * yo, slip 1, k 2 tog, psso, yo, k 3 tog, wrap yarn all the way around needle, p 2. **Row 14:** K 2, * k into back of next st, p 1, k into the front and back of the next st, p 1, k into back of next st, k 2, repeat from * across row and end k 2. **Row 15:** K 1, p 2, * yo, slip 1, k 1, psso, k 2 tog, wrap yarn around needle, p 4, repeat from * across row and end p 2, k 1. **Row 16:** K 3, * k into back of next st, p 2, k into back of next st, k 4, repeat from * and end k 3. Repeat the last 14 rows (rows 3 to 16 inclusive) for pattern.

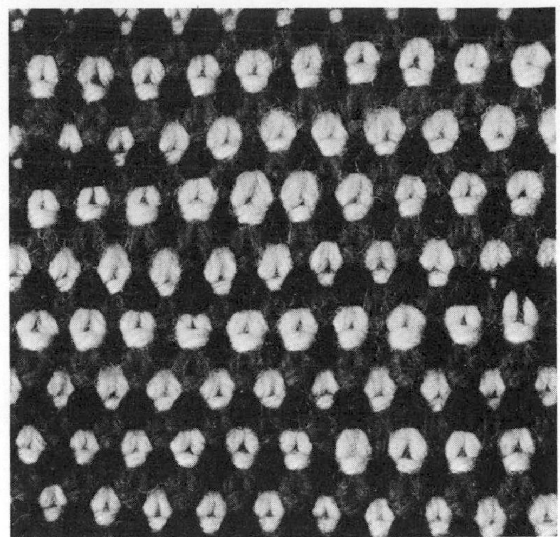

Tri-Color Stitch. Cast on an even number of sts. Use 3 colors—indicated by A, B, and C. **Row 1:** With B, * k 1, bring yarn to front of work and sl 1, repeat from * to end of row. **Row 2:** With C, * p 1, hold yarn in back of work and sl 1, repeat from * to end of row. Repeat these 2 rows for pat, working 1 row each of A, B, and C alternately.

Popcorn Stitch. Cast on a multiple of 4 sts. **Row 1 (right side):** Purl. **Row 2:** * K, p and k in next st (3 sts made in 1 st), sl 1, k 2 tog, psso, repeat from * to end of row. **Row 3:** Purl. **Row 4:** * Sl 1, k 2 tog, psso; k, p and k in next st (3 sts made in 1 st), repeat from * to end of row. Repeat these 4 rows for pattern.

Knitting Patterns in Colors

Known as Scandinavian or Fair Isle Knitting. Certain patterns are typical of certain countries.

There are two methods of carrying the yarn across the wrong side of the work.

Method 1: When the spaces between the color in the design are not more than 4 sts wide, the yarn not in use is carried loosely across the back. Try to keep it the same tension as the knitting, never taut.

Method 2: When the spaces are more than 4 sts, the colors should be caught in by twisting around the yarn being used. Hold the thread you are carrying in the left hand. K 1 st in the usual manner, but before catching thread to k, be sure yarn is over the yarn you are carrying. Break the yarn only when you are finished with that color. Leave an end 4 or 5 inches long on the back to be fastened in later with a sewing needle. In this type of knitting it is possible to work designs from cross stitch patterns. You can design your own on graph paper, using symbols to represent different colors. It is well to have the colors in quite strong contrast.

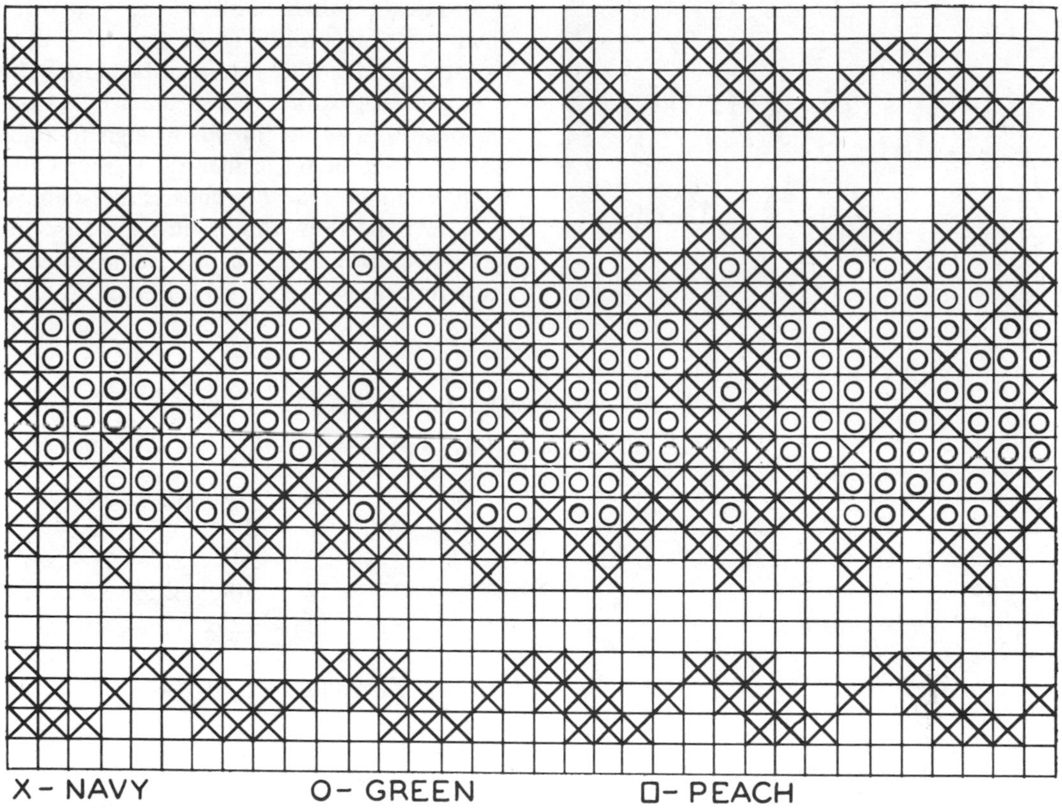

X - NAVY O - GREEN □ - PEACH

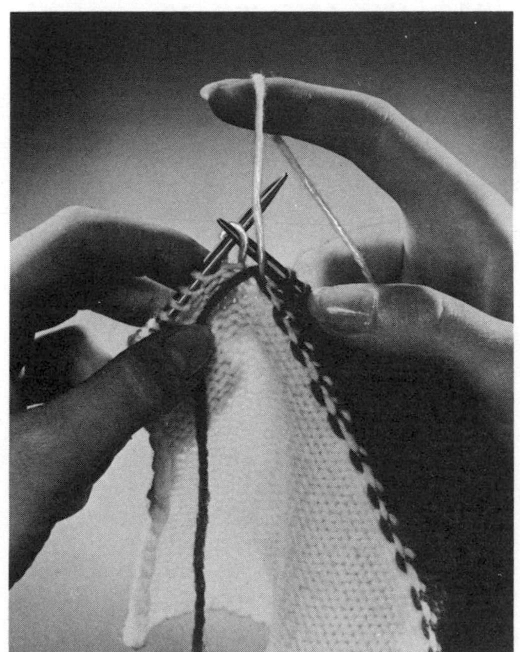

Changing Colors. When working with 2 or more colors for wide spaces, always be sure to twist the colors to prevent holes.

Duplicate Stitch. Follow the chart for placing sts according to design. Thread a tapestry needle with yarn and fasten on the wrong side of work. * Insert the needle from the back and bring thread through to right side of work in the center of a stitch. Slip the needle under the 2 strands of the st above as shown and draw thread through. Now insert needle in center where it came out and draw through to wrong side. Repeat from *.

BODY MEASUREMENT CHARTS

Infants and Children (boys and girls)

Size	6 mo	1	2	3	4	5	6	7	8	10	12	14
Chest	19	20	21	22	23	23½	24	25	26	28	30	32
Waist	19	19½	20	20½	21	21½	22	22½	23	24	25	26
Hip						25	26	27	28	30	32½	35
Back Waist Length								11	11½	12½	13	13¾
Sleeve Length	6	7	8	8¾	9½	10¾	11	11½	12	13½	14½	16

Misses and Women

Size	10	12	14	16	18	20	40	42
Bust	31	32	34	36	38	40	42	44
Waist	24	25	26	28	30	32	34	36
Hip	33	34	36	38	40	42	44	46
Back Waist Length	15¾	16	16¼	16½	16¾	17	17⅛	17¼
Sleeve Length	16¼	16½	17	17½	18	18	18	18

Men

Chest	32	34	36	38	40	42	44
Waist	28	30	32	34	36	38	40

Women's Half Sizes

Size	12½	14½	16½	18½	20½	22½
Bust	33	35	37	39	41	43
Waist	27	29	31	33	35	37
Hip	37	39	41	43	45	47
Back Waist Length	15¼	15½	15¾	16	16¼	16½

To Change Instructions for Individual Measurements

Take the measurements of the individual accurately. (See measurement chart to find which measurements to take, and to decide which size to follow in the directions.) Knitted garments, like other wearing apparel, are made with a certain amount of "ease";

that is, somewhat larger than actual body measurements. This varies with personal taste and also with the type of garment. For example, an evening top should fit more snugly than a ski sweater.

Instructions in this book are given with "ease" allowed for each size. When changing instructions for sizes not given here, compare the measurements you have taken with those given in the instructions and add or deduct the number of stitches equal to the difference in measurements. If the instructions are for a pattern stitch, be sure the number of stitches you are going to use is a multiple of this pattern stitch.

FINISHING HAND-KNITS

Blocking. This must be done properly and before the seams are sewed up in order to achieve a professional-looking job. Block each piece separately, using rust-proof pins. Place the pieces on a flat padded surface or pressing board wrong side up. Pin all edges, stretching to the blocking measurements given with the instructions. Use plenty of pins, placing them close together to avoid scalloped edges.

Place a damp cloth over the piece and press *lightly* with a moderately hot iron, allowing the steam to go through garment. Leave until thoroughly dry. A skirt knit on the round may be blocked double or on a skirt blocker. Do not stretch or press ribbing but steam lightly.

Sewing Seams. Place right sides of pieces together and pin, matching the pattern, if any. Beginning at bottom, sew ¼ inch from edge with back stitches. Do not draw stitches too tight. Press seams open.

If the garment has shoulder seams, reinforce them with seam binding to prevent stretching. Pin tape flat along seam on wrong side and sew to garment with invisible hemming stitches, using matching mercerized thread.

When sewing in sleeve, pin sleeve seam at underarm and center top of sleeve at shoulder seam. Ease in fulness.

Laundering. Use mild soap and lukewarm water. Squeeze suds through until garment is thoroughly clean. Handle carefully; do not stretch. Rinse thoroughly in several warm waters. Squeeze, do not wring. Place on a clean bath towel; roll tightly to absorb moisture. Do not hang garment, but leave flat on towel to dry. Block to measurements. Special soaps are available for washing woolens.

Casing for Top of Skirt. This is best done with crochet. With right side toward you, work several rows of sc around top of skirt. With wrong side toward you, work 1 sc in first st of first round of sc, * ch 5, skip 5 sts on last round and work 1 sc in the sixth st. Ch 5, skip 5 sts on first round and work 1 sc in sixth st. Repeat from * around. End with sl st in first sc. Skip more or less sts to produce an even beading.

HOME KNITTING MACHINES

Many different makes of home knitting machines are now available. They vary somewhat in the number of needles (width of knitting space), automatic devices for the different knitting processes, size, and ease in handling. Before purchasing, it is well to investigate several to find the one that suits your needs best.

Most of the machines will accommodate a number of kinds and weights of yarn and do a variety of stitches (but not all that can be done by hand). After developing skill in using a knitting machine, it is possible to make many types of garments and other articles such as afghans, stoles, scarves, etc.

KNITTING FOR THE HOME AND FAMILY

Baby's Surplice for Beginners

Materials. Jumbo Pompadour 3 ozs. Knitting Needles, No. 7. Plastic Crochet Hook, Size 3.

Gauge. 5 sts—1″.

Surplice. Cast on 45 sts for lower edge of back. Work even in garter st until 6″ from beg or desired length to underarm. Cast on 30 sts at beg of each of next 2 rows for sleeves—105 sts. Work even until sleeve edge measures 3″. Next row, k 44 sts, slip these sts on a holder; bind off 17 sts for back of neck; k 44 sts. Work even on 44 sts for 1″, ending at neck edge. Inc 1 st at neck edge on next row, repeat inc every 2nd row 6 times, then every row until sleeve measures 7″ from beg, ending at sleeve edge. Bind off 30 sts beg next row, inc 1 st at end. Continue increasing at neck edge every row until there are 45 sts on needle. Work even until front measures same as back. Bind off. Beg at neck edge, work other side to correspond, reversing shaping.

Finishing. Sew underarm and side seams. From right side, work 1 row sc around front and neck edge. Work 1 row sc around sleeve edges. Block. RIBBON TIES: Sew ribbon at top and bottom of even edge of each front and at corresponding places at underarm seams.

Garter-Stitch Baby Sacque

Directions are for Size 6 months.

Materials. Baby Wool—2 balls of Yellow, 1 ball of White. Knitting Needles, No. 7. Steel Crochet Hook, No. O. 3 small Buttons.

Gauge. 7 sts—1″; 14 rows—1″.

Blocking Measurements:

Chest	20″
Width of sleeve	5½″
Length from back of neck	8½″
Length of sleeve seam	4¼″

Note: Sacque is worked in vertical rows of garter stitch. The yoke is solid yellow and the rest is worked in stripes of yellow and white.

Sacque. Starting at left front edge with yellow, cast on 60 sts, K 2 rows. **Row 3:** Starting at lower edge with white, k 46, turn. **Row 4:** Knit. **Row 5:** Drop white, pick up yellow and k to neck edge. **Row 6:** K, drop yellow, pick up white. Repeat rows 3–6 for pattern. Work in pattern until lower edge measures 5½″ to underarm, ending with 2 rows white.

Sleeve. With yellow, k 26 and slip these sts to a holder, turn, cast on 30 sts, turn, k 2 rows yellow on 64 sts. Continue in pattern for 5½″, ending with 2 rows white. **Next row:** With yellow bind off 30 sts, k to neck edge. Turn, k to bound off sts, then k sts from holder.

Back. Work in pattern on 60 sts for 9½″, ending with 2 rows white. Repeat sleeve.

Right Front. Work in pattern for 5½″, having same number of ridges as on left front and ending with 2 rows yellow. Bind off.

Finishing. Sew sleeve seams. CROCHETED BORDER: With yellow and wrong side facing you, sc in left corner of neck, sc in end of every other ridge around neck. Ch 1, turn. Sc in each sc, 2 sc in last sc. RND 1: Ch 2 for buttonhole, sc in first cast-on st of left front edge and in next 4 sts, ch 2, skip 2 sts, sc in next 5 sts, ch 2, skip 2 sts, sc in each st to lower edge, 3 sc in corner, sc in each ridge around lower edge, 3 sc in corner, sc in each st to right front neck, 3 sc in corner. RND 2: Picot round. Sc in next sc, * ch

Color Plate 11 CHILDREN'S SWEATERS

A trio of classics—an embroidered cardigan and a shell with a ruffle for a little girl, a V-neck sweater for a boy. Knitting instructions for all three are on pages 288–289.

Color Plate 12 MAN'S OUTDOOR SWEATER

What man, whether he's the outdoor type or not, could resist this colorful ski sweater of banded diamonds with a boat neck? Complete knitting instructions are on page 305.

Color Plate 13 MAN'S ARAN KNIT SWEATER

A pullover in rugged wool, natural-colored. Strikingly handsome alone, its extra-wide collar also lets it pair with turtleneck sweaters. Knitting instructions are on page 306.

Color Plate 14 ONE DRESS TO KNIT, ONE TO CROCHET

The dress to knit (right) is a slim ribbed design with a scoop neckline. The one to crochet has a fringed sash trimmed with buttons. For instructions, see pages 330 and 385.

3, sl st in last sc made, skip 1 sc, sc in next sc. Repeat from * around, join with sl st in first sc, fasten off. With right side facing you, attach yellow to sleeve seam, sc in same st, * ch 3, sl st in last sc made, skip 1 ridge, sc in next ridge. Repeat from * around sleeve, join and fasten off. Work border on other sleeve to correspond. Sew on buttons.

Argyle Booties

Directions are for Infants' Size.

Materials. Fingering Yarn—One 1-oz. skein each Pale Blue, Yellow, Pink, and White. Knitting Needles, No. 3. Steel Crochet Hook, No. 4. 1 set of Bobbins.

Gauge. 7 sts—1″; 10 rows—1″.

Note 1: Wind 2 bobbins with yellow and 1 bobbin with pink. The cross-lines are worked in duplicate st after the bootie is completed.

Note 2: To prevent a hole when changing colors, always pass yarn to be used under yarn just used.

Booties. With blue, cast on 47 sts. P 1 row, k 1 row, p 1 row. Using bobbins, work in stockinette st (k 1 row, p 1 row) following chart for 23 rows. Break off all bobbins. With blue, p 1 row. **Beading Row:** * K 1, yo; repeat from * across row. **Next Row:** P, dropping all yo, thus making a large stitch). INSTEP: K 17 sts, and slip these sts to a holder, k across next 13 sts for instep, slip remaining 17 sts to a holder. P 1 row. Continue in stockinette st and follow chart until small diamond of instep is completed. P 1 row. Break yarn. **Next Row:** Slip sts from first holder to needle, join blue, pick up and k 11 sts along side edge of instep, k across

13 sts of instep, pick up and k 11 sts along other side edge of instep, k across remaining 17 sts. There are 69 sts on needle. P 1 row, k 1 row for 11 rows. **Next Row:** K 29, k 2 tog, k 7, k 2 tog, k 29. P 1 row. Bind off. Block. With white, work duplicate st over 1 st and 1 row following chart. Sew back seam. SOLE: With blue cast on 22 sts. Work in garter st (k every row). Inc 1 st each side every other row 3 times. There are 28 sts on needle. Work 4 rows even. Now dec 1 st each side every other row until there are 22 sts on needle. Bind off, DO NOT break yarn. With crochet hook work 1 row of sc around entire sole, taking care to keep edges flat.

Finishing. Holding right side of upper section and edge of sole, crochet the sole and upper section tog with a row of sc. Join, cut yarn. With 2 strands of yarn (1 blue, 1 pink), crochet a chain 18″ long. Fasten off. Make 2 small pompons and fasten to ends of chain as shown in photograph. POMPONS: Wind yarn around ½″ wide cardboard about 50 times. Tie at one edge and cut at opposite edge. Trim evenly.

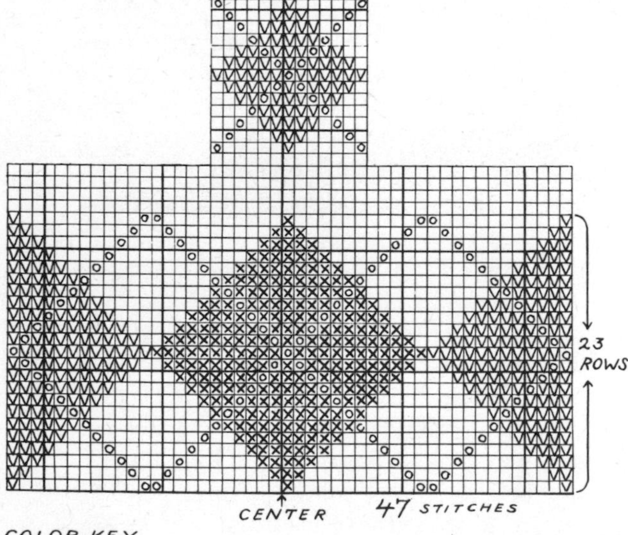

Four-Piece Knitted Baby Set

Directions are for Size 6 months to 1 year.

Materials. Orlon or Fingering Yarn 3 ply —5 ozs., Baby Pink. Knitting Needles, Nos. 1 and 2. 2 Stitch Holders. 1 Double-Pointed Needle, No. 2. Steel Crochet Hook, No. 3. 4 Buttons. 1½ yds. ¾″ Ribbon. 2 yds. narrow Ribbon.

Gauge. 8 sts—1″.

Sacque. RIGHT FRONT: With No. 2 needles cast on 55 sts and work in garter st for 7 rows. Next row p to within 4 sts from end. K 4 for border. Work these 4 sts in garter st for front border. Work in stockinette st until piece measures 5½″ ending with a p row. START PATTERN: **Row 1:** K 4 sts for border, then k 5, * with yarn in front of work slip next 5 sts to right-hand needle (slip as if to p), k 3, repeat from * across ending with k 1. **Row 2 and all even rows:** Purl, working 4 sts of border in garter st. **Rows 3 and 5:** Repeat Row 1. **Row 7:** K 4 sts for border, k 7, * insert right-hand needle under 3 loops of the 3 slipped rows, k into next st on left-hand needle, knitting the loops and st tog, k 7, repeat from * across ending k 3. **Row 9:** K 4 sts for border, k 1, * with yarn in front of work, slip 5 sts, yarn in back of work, k 3, repeat from * across ending k 5. **Rows 11 and 13:** Same as Row 9. **Row 15:** K 4 sts for border, k 3, * insert needle under 3 loops of the 3 slipped rows, k into next st knitting loops and st tog, k 7, repeat from * to end of row.

SHAPE ARMHOLE: At arm edge, bind off 5 sts. Dec 1 st at arm edge every row 2 times. Work even in pat until armhole measures 2½″ from last dec of underarm ending with last row of pat. SHAPE NECK: At front edge bind off 16 sts. Work 8 rows even. Dec 1 st at neck edge every other row 4 times. Work even on 28 sts for 7 rows. Sl sts on holder.

LEFT FRONT: Work to correspond to right front for 5½″, reversing the 4 border sts ending with a p row. **Next row:** Start pat: K 1, * sl 5, k 3, repeat from * across ending k 9. Last 4 sts are for border. Complete to correspond to right front. BACK: Cast on 25 sts for back of neck, cut yarn. Join to right front by picking up sts from holder to same needle, join yarn and p across row (81) sts. Keeping pat uniform, work in pat until 4 pat have been worked from the 25 cast-on sts of neck, ending with last row of pat. Inc 1 st each and every other row 4 times. Cast on 5 sts beg of next 2 rows. Work 13 more rows in pat, then work in stockinette st until same length as fronts, ending with border same as fronts. Bind off.

SLEEVES: Cast on 49 sts and work in garter st (K each row) for 7 rows. **Row 8:** K 1, * sl 5, k 3, repeat from * across row. Continue in pattern same as Sacque for 15 more rows. Work in stockinette st until sleeve measures 6″ from start. SHAPE CAP: Bind off 5 sts at beg of next 2 rows. Work 1 row even. Next row: Dec 1 st each end of row. Repeat last 2 rows until 19 sts remain. Bind off.

FINISHING: Block. Sew seams and set in sleeves. NECKBAND: With right side toward you and using No. 1 needles, pick up 70 sts around neck edge, k 6 rows. Bind off. CROCHETED EDGE TRIM: With right side of work toward you, join yarn at left side of neck edge, * ch 3 and working down left front, 1 sl st in each of the next 3 ridges, repeat from * down front, * ch 3, and working across lower edge, 1 sl st in each of the next 3 sts, repeat from * across lower edge, work up right front same as left front and work around neck edge same as lower edge, join, cut yarn. Work edge trim on sleeves in same manner. Sew buttons in place.

Cap. With No. 2 needles, cast on 17 sts. Work in stockinette st for 7 rows. On the next row inc 1 st each end and repeat this inc every 7th row until there are 29 sts. Work even until piece measures 4″. Cast on 30 sts at beg of next 2 rows—89 sts. PATTERN: **Row 1:** K 2, * sl 5, k 3, repeat from * ending k 2. Continue in pat until cap measures 9¾″ from start, ending with a p row. Work in garter st for 8 rows. Bind off.

FINISHING: Block. With wrong side facing you, work edge trim on bound off sts. Sew sides. Turn back garter st border. With No. 1 needles, pick up 40 sts along side of cap, 16 sts across back, and 40 sts along other side. K the next row, dec at even intervals to 83 sts. Work in garter st for 5 rows. Bind off. Crochet edge trim around neck edge. Sew ribbons in place as shown.

Bootees. With No. 2 needles, cast on 41 sts. Work in garter st for 7 rows. PATTERN: K 2, * sl 5, k 3, repeat from * ending k 2. Continue in pat for 15 rows. Work in stockinette st until piece measures 2½″ from start, ending with a p row. BEADING: K 1, * yo, k 2 tog, repeat from * across. Work in stockinette st for 3 rows. Divide for Foot:

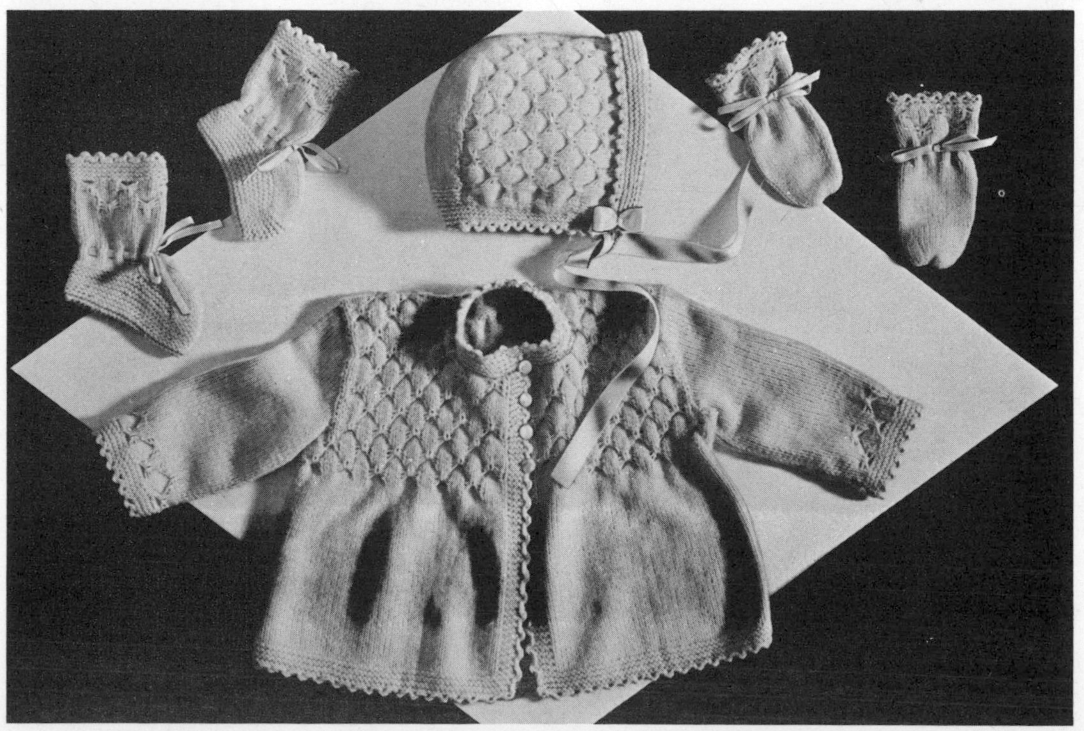

K 14 sts and slip them on a holder; k 13 sts for instep; slip remaining 14 sts on another holder. Work in stockinette st on instep sts for 2", ending with a p row. Slip these sts on a dp needle. Slip 14 sts from first holder onto needle, pick up 11 sts along side of instep, k 13 sts of instep, pick up 11 sts along other side of instep, k 14 sts from other holder. Work in garter st on 63 sts for 10 rows. K the next row, dec 4 sts at even intervals. K 3 rows. Dec 1 st in center of next row. Work 1 row even. Bind off.

FINISHING: Sew sole and back seams. Work edge trim around upper edge. Lace ribbon through beading.

Mittens. With No. 2 needles, cast on 41 sts. K 2 rows. PATTERN: K 2, * sl 5, k 3, repeat from * across ending k 2. Continue pat for 15 more rows ending with a p row. K 1 row. P 1 row. BEADING: K 1, * yo, k 2 tog, repeat from * across. Work in garter st for 3 rows. **Next row:** * K 8, k 2 tog, repeat from * 3 times, k 1 (37 sts). P 1 row. Work in stockinette st until piece measures 3½", ending with a p row. **Next row:** * K 5, k 2 tog, repeat from * 4 times, k 2 (32 sts). P 1 row. Work in stockinette st for 12 rows ending with a p row. **Next row:** K 2 tog across row. Cut yarn, leaving an end long enough to draw through remaining sts. Thread into blunt needle, draw through stitches and sew side of mitten. Join yarn at edge of mitten and crochet edge trim. Lace ribbon through beading.

Ruffled Baby Afghan
Approximately 32" x 38"

Materials. Super Fingering Yarn (1 oz. skeins)—12 skeins of White and 5 skeins of Light Pink. Knitting Needles, No. 7.

Gauge. 6 sts—1". 11 rows—1" (2 rows make 1 ridge).

Center Section. (Make 1 white and 1 pink.) Starting at narrow end, cast on 120 sts. Work in garter st (k every row) for 26 inches. Bind off. Make other piece exactly the same number of rows.

Border. With white and spare needle, pick up and k 1 st in each st across narrow end of pink section. With white, insert needle through first st on narrow end of white section and first st on needle and k 1; k tog 1 st from white section and 1 st from needle, across. Work these sts in garter st, inc 1 st at both ends of every other row 6 times. Bind off loosely. With spare needle, and white, pick up and k 1 st in each ridge along

side edge of pink section. Complete this border same as first border, then work border along other 2 sides in same way.

Ruffle. With white, cast on 30 sts. **Row 1:** K. **Row 2:** P. **Row 3:** K. Repeat these 3 rows until piece measures 132 inches unstretched. Bind off. Sew ends of ruffle together. Sew ruffle evenly around afghan, gathering at corners.

Baby Cardigan

Directions are for Infants' Size 2. Changes for Size 3 are in parentheses.

Materials. Baby Wool—3 (4) ozs. Knitting Needles, No. 3. Contrasting scraps of yarn for trim. 4 Buttons.

Gauge. 7 sts—1″. 9 rows—1″.

Border Pattern. Rows 1 and 2: * K 2, p 2, repeat from * across. **Row 3:** K 3, * p 2, k 2, repeat from * ending p 1. **Row 4:** K 1, * p 2, k 2, repeat from * ending p 2, k 1. Repeat these 4 rows for pattern.

Back. Cast on 72 (80) sts. Work in pat for 1½″. Now work in stockinette st until back measures 6½ (7)″ from start. SHAPE RAGLAN ARMHOLES: Dec 1 st each end every other row until 36 (40) sts remain. Bind off.

Left Front. Cast on 44 sts. Work in pat for 1½″. Keeping 10 sts in pat for front border, work remaining sts in stockinette st until piece measures same as back to underarm. SHAPE ARMHOLE AND NECK: Dec 1 st inside front border and 1 st at arm edge every other row until 14 sts remain. Keeping front edge even, continue to dec at armhole edge until 10 sts of front border remain. Continue in pat on these 10 sts for 1½″. Bind off.

Right Front. Work to correspond with left front, reversing shaping and working first buttonhole when piece measures ½ (1)″. BUTTONHOLE: Starting at front edge work 3 sts, bind off 2 sts, complete row. On the next row cast on 2 sts over 2 sts bound off previous row. Make 3 more buttonholes, evenly spaced, the last one to be made at start of neck shaping.

Sleeves. Cast on 44 (48) sts. Work in pat for 1″. K the next row inc 10 sts at even intervals. Continue in stockinette st until sleeve measures 7 (7½)″, or desired length to underarm. SHAPE CAP: Dec 1 st each end every other row until 28 sts remain, then dec 1 st each end every row until 8 sts remain. Bind off.

Finishing. Block pieces. Sew seams. Set in sleeves. Sew ends of front borders tog and sew in place to back of neck. Sew buttons in place. Embroider flowers as shown or as desired.

Child's Raglan Cardigan

Directions are for Size 2. Changes for Sizes 3 and 4 are in parentheses.

Materials. Sports Yarn—2 (2-3) 2-oz. balls. Circular Needles, Nos. 6 and 3. Knitting Needles, Nos. 3 and 6. 6 Buttons.

Gauge. 6 sts—1″; 8 rows—1″.

Seed Stitch. Multiple of 2 sts + 1. K 1, * p 1, k 1; repeat from * to end. Repeat this row for pat st.

Cardigan. Beg at neck edge with larger circular needle, cast on 67 sts. Do not join. Work back and forth as on straight needles. **Row 1:** P 12 (right front), p and mark next st (seam st), p 9 (right sleeve), p next st and mark (seam st), p 21 (back), p next st and mark (seam st), p 9 (left sleeve), p next st and mark (seam st), p 12 (left front). **Row 2:** K 3, seed st on next 7 sts, k 2, yo, k seam st, yo, k 9, yo, k seam st, yo, k 21, yo, k seam st, yo, k 9, yo, k seam st, yo, k 2, seed st on next 7 sts, k 3. **Row 3:** P 3, work seed st on next 7 sts, p to last 10 sts counting the 8 yo's as sts, work seed st on next 7 sts, p 3. **Row 4:** K 3, seed st on 7 sts, k 3, yo, k seam st, yo, k 11, yo, k seam st, yo, k 23, yo, k seam st, yo, k 11, yo, k seam st, yo, k 3, seed st on 7 sts, k 3. **Row 5:** Same as Row 3. Continue as established, shaping raglan same as before—always yo before and after each of the 4 seam sts until there are 20 (22-24) yos. P across all sts. There are 227 (243-259) sts on needle.

Divide sts as follows: Work 33 (35-37) sts including 1 seam st and slip to a holder for left front; with larger straight needles, k across 49 (53-57) sts of left sleeve, slip next 63 (67-71) sts including 2 seam sts to a holder for back, slip next 49 (53-57) sts to a holder for right sleeve, slip next 33 (35-37) sts including 1 seam st to a holder for right front.

Sleeves. P 1 row. Continue in stockinette st (k 1 row, p 1 row). Cast on one st at beg of next 2 rows (once each side). Work even on 51 (55-59) sts for 2″. Continue in stockinette, dec one st each side every 1″, 6 times. Work even on 39 (43-47) sts, until sleeve measures 8 (9-10)″ from underarm cast-on sts. Dec 1 st on last row. Change to smaller straight needles. Rib in k 1, p 1 on 38 (42-46) sts, for 1½″. Bind off in ribbing. Slip sts from right sleeve to larger straight needles and complete right sleeve same as for left sleeve.

Body. Slip sts of left front to larger circular needle. Tie in yarn. Cast on 2 sts for underarm, k across 63 (67-71) sts of back, cast on 2 sts for underarm, work remaining

33 (35-37) sts of right front. There are 133 (141-149) sts on circular needle. Keeping seed st as established, p 1 row. Continue in stockinette st, until body measures 6 (6½-7)" from underarm cast-on. Dec 1 st on last row. Change to smaller circular needle. Rib in k 1, p 1 on 132 (140-148) sts, for 1¼". Bind off in ribbing.

Left Front Band (made separately). With smaller straight needles cast on 10 sts. Rib in k 1, p 1, until band is long enough to reach from lower edge to neck edge. Slip sts to a holder. Mark places for 5 buttons in center of band (6th button will be in neck band). Have first marker ½" from lower edge and other 4 markers evenly spaced above.

Right Front Band. Work to correspond to left front band, forming buttonholes opposite markers as follows: Rib 3 sts, bind off next 3 sts. On the following row, cast on 3 sts over bound-off sts.

Finishing. Sew sleeve seams. Sew front bands to front edges.

Neckband. Working from right side and beg at right front edge, with smaller straight needles, pick up 96 sts around neck edge including sts of front bands. Rib in k 1, p 1 for 3 rows. Work a buttonhole in next 2 rows same as before. Continue in rib pat until band measures 1". Bind off in ribbing. Block. Sew on buttons.

Child's Embroidered Raglan Jacket

Directions are for Size 2. Changes for Sizes 4, 6, and 8 are in parentheses.

Materials. Super Fingering Yarn—5 (6-6-7) 1-oz. skeins, White. 1 skein Emerald Green for all sizes. Steel Crochet Hook, No. 1/0 (zero). Knitting Needles, No. 5.

Gauge. 6 sts—1". 10 rows—1".

Blocking Measurements

Body chest size . . . . 21 (23-24-26)".

Actual Knitting Measurements

Chest (buttoned) . . . . . . 23 (25-27-29)".
Width across back at underarm . . . . 11 (12-13-14)".
Width across each front at underarm (excluding border) . . . 6½ (7-7½-8)".
Length from back of neck to lower edge (excluding border) . . 12 (13-13¾-15)".
Length from underarm to lower edge (excluding border) . . . 6½ (7-7-7½)".
Length of sleeve seam (excluding border) . . . . 8 (9½-11-12½)".
Width across sleeve at upper arm . . . . 9 (10-11-11¾)".

Back. Starting at lower edge, cast on 67 (73-79-85) sts. **Row 1:** (wrong side) K across. **Row 2:** K 1, * p 1, k 1. Repeat from * across. Repeat these 2 rows for pattern. Work even in pat until length is 6½ (7-7-7½)", ending with a wrong-side row. RAGLAN SHAPING OF BACK: Keeping in pat, bind off 2 sts at beg of next 2 rows. Work 2 rows even. Dec one st at both ends of next and every other row thereafter until 21 (23-25-27) sts remain, ending with a wrong-side row. Bind off in pattern.

Left Front. Starting at lower edge, cast on 39 (43-45-49) sts. Work same as back to raglan shaping, ending with a wrong-side row. RAGLAN SHAPING OF LEFT FRONT: Bind

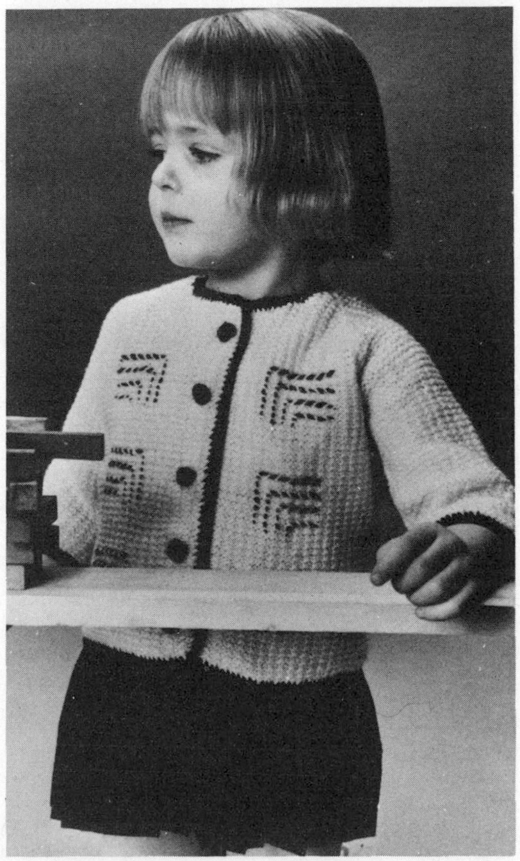

off 2 sts at beg of next row. Work 3 rows even. Dec one st at beg of next row and at same edge every other row thereafter until 22 (24-24-28) sts remain, ending at front edge. NECK SHAPING: **Next Row:** Bind off 10 (12-12-12) sts, complete row. Keeping in pat, dec one st at both ends of next and every other row thereafter until 2 sts remain, k 2 tog. Break off and fasten.

With pins mark the position of 5 buttons evenly spaced along front edge, having the first pin 1″ up from lower edge and the last pin ¾″ down from neck edge.

Right Front. Work as for left front, reversing all shapings and make buttonholes in line with pins on left front. **To make a buttonhole:** Starting at front edge, work in pattern over the first 3 sts, bind off 2 sts, complete row in pattern. On next row work across, casting on 2 sts over the bound-off sts.

Sleeves. Starting at lower edge, cast on 37 (41-45-49) sts. Work in pattern same as back for 1″. Keeping in pat, inc one st at both ends of next and every 6th (6th-7th-8th) row thereafter 8 times in all. Work even on 53 (57-61-65) sts until total length is 6 (6½-7-8)″, ending with a wrong-side row. RAGLAN SHAPING OF SLEEVES: Keeping in pattern, bind off 2 sts at beg of next 2 rows. Work 2 rows even. Dec one st at both ends of every row until 43 (49-57-59) sts remain, then dec one st at both ends of every other row until 7 sts remain, ending with a wrong-side row. Bind off in pat.

Buttons (Make 5). Starting at center with emerald green, ch 2. **Rnd 1:** 6 sc in 2nd ch from hook. **Rnd 2:** 2 sc in each sc around. **Rnd 3:** * Draw up a loop in each of the next 2 sc, yo and draw through all 3 loops on hook. Repeat from * around. **Rnd 4:** Sc in each sc around. Break off and fasten, leaving a 6″ length of yarn. Stuff with cotton batting or yarn. Thread the 6″ length into a tapestry needle, draw through remaining sts, pull up tightly and fasten securely.

Finishing. Block to measurements. Sew side and sleeve seams. Sew in sleeves. Work buttonhole st around buttonholes. Sew buttons in place. EDGING: **Rnd 1:** With right side facing, attach emerald green at left side seam at lower edge; making 3 sc in same place at each corner, and easing in neck to fit, sc evenly along lower edge, right front, neck, left front and remaining lower edge. Join with sl st to first sc. **Rnds 2 and 3:** Sc in each sc around, making 3 sc in center sc of each 3-sc group. Join. Turn at end of Rnd 3. With wrong side facing, sl st in each sc around. Break off and fasten. Omitting incs (for corners), work edging around sleeve edges the same way. EMBROIDERY: Using emerald green, follow diagram for embroidery, running yarn through loops of purled stitches. Place 3 patterns evenly spaced along center of left front as shown. Place 2 patterns evenly spaced across lower section of left back in line with lowest pattern of front. Work patterns on right front and right back sections in same way, reversing position of patterns.

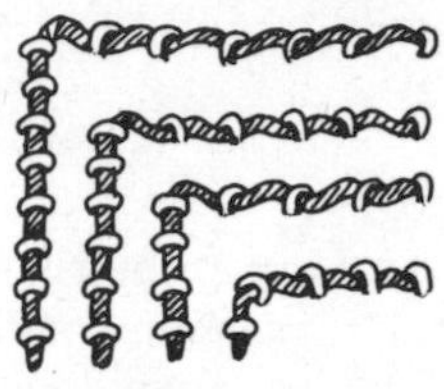

DIAGRAM FOR EMBROIDERY

Cabled Slipon

Directions are for Toddler Size 3.

Materials. Baby Wool—3 ozs. Knitting Needles, Nos. 1 and 4. Double-Pointed Needle. 2 small Pearl Buttons.

Gauge. 8 sts—1″. 10 rows—1″.

Pattern. Row 1 (wrong side): * P 4, k 1, repeat from * ending p 4. **Row 2:** * K 4, p 1, repeat from * ending k 4. **Row 3:** Same as Row 1. **Row 4:** K 4, p 1, k 4, * p 1, sl next 2 sts on dp needle and hold in back of work, k next 2 sts, k 2 sts from dp needle (cable twist), p 1, k 4, repeat from * until 7 cable twists have been made, p 1, k 4 twice. Repeat these 4 rows for pattern.

Back. With No. 1 needles, cast on 68 sts. K 1, p 1 in ribbing for 1¼″. Change to No. 4 needles. K the next row, inc at even intervals to 84 sts. Work in pat until back measures 8″. ARMHOLES: Work 6 sts and slip them onto a holder, work across to last 6 sts and slip these onto another holder. Continue in pat on remaining 72 sts for 3½″. SHAPE NECK: **Row 1:** Work in pat across 19 sts, * k 4 sts, k 2 tog, k 2, k 2 tog, repeat from * 2 more times, k 4, continue in pat to end of row. **Row 2:** Work in pat across 19 sts, k 28 sts, work in pat to end of row. Repeat Row 2 four more times. Bind off loosely in pat.

Front. Work in same manner as back until 2″ above armholes. Now work neck in same manner as back (do not bind off). SHAPE NECK: Work in pat across 19 sts, k 4, join another ball of yarn and bind off center 20 sts, complete row. Working on both sides at the same time, work 4 sts in garter st at each neck edge and remaining sts in pat until arm edge measures same as back. Bind off in pat.

Sleeves. Starting at arm edge, sew shoulder seam for 1½″. With right side toward you and No. 4 needles, sl 6 sts from one holder onto needle, pick up 52 sts around arm edge, then k across 6 sts of other holder. Work in pat as on front for 3 rows. **Row 4:** (K 4, p 1) 3 times; (cable twist, p 1, k 4, p 1) 4 times; k 4, p 1, k 4. Work in pat as set up for 2″. Continue in pat, dec 1 st each end every 1″ 7 times. Work on 50 sts until sleeve measures 9″, or 1½″ less than desired length. Change to No. 1 needles and k 1, p 1 in ribbing for 1½″. Bind off loosely in ribbing.

Finishing. Block. Crochet 1 row sc around each shoulder opening, making a ch-3 loop on each front edge. Sew seams. Sew buttons in place.

Child's Raglan Pullover

Directions are for Size 6. Changes for Sizes 8, 10, and 12 are in parentheses.

Materials. Knitting Worsted—2 (2-3-3) 100-gram skeins (Light Blue); 1 (2-2-2) 100-gram skeins (Navy); 1 (2-2-2) 100-gram skeins (White); Knitting Needles, Nos. 6 and 8. Double-Pointed needles, No. 6.

Gauge (on No. 8 needles). 9 sts—2″. 6 rows—1″.

Blocking Measurements:

Back or front at underarm . . . 13½ (14½-15½-16½)″.
Sleeve width at upperarm . . . . 10½ (11½-12-13)″.

Back. With navy and No. 6 needles, cast on 62 (66-70-74) sts. Work in ribbing of k 1, p 1 for 2 rows. Break off navy. With white, continue in ribbing for 8 rows, increasing 1 st at end of last row—63 (67-71-75) sts. Break off. Change to No. 8 needles and with light blue, work in stockinette st (k 1 row, p 1 row) until piece measures 10 (10½-11-11½)″ from beg, or desired length to underarm, ending on wrong side. SHAPE RAGLAN ARMHOLES: Bind off 2 sts at beg of next 2 rows. **Dec. Row** (right side): K 2, k 2 tog, k to last 4 sts, sl 1, k 1, psso, k 2 (2 sts dec). Repeat dec row on every k row 3 times. End on wrong side. Break off light blue. With white, repeat dec row on every k row 5 times. End on wrong side. Break off white (white stripe completed). With navy, repeat dec row every k row 8 (9-10-11) times. End on wrong side. Slip remaining 25 (27-29-31) sts on stitch holder for neckband.

Front. Work as for back until white stripe of armholes is completed—41 (45-49-53) sts. With navy, repeat dec row on every k row 7 times—27 (31-35-39) sts. End on wrong side. SHAPE NECK: K 2 sts, k 2 tog, k 6 (8-10-13) sts, join another ball of navy and bind off next 7 (7-7-5) sts for neck, k until you have 6 (8-10-13) sts on right hand needle after bound-off sts, sl 1, k 1, psso, k 2. Working on both sides at once, bind off 4 sts at beg of each neck edge 2 (2-2-3) times, then 1 (2-3-2) sts once; at same time, repeat raglan dec row at each arm side every k row 0 (1-2-2) times.

Sleeves. With navy and No. 6 needles, cast on 28 (30-32-34) sts. Work in ribbing of k 1, p 1 for 2 rows. Break off navy. With white, continue in ribbing for 8 rows, increasing 1 st at end of last row—29 (31-33-35) sts. Break off white. Change to No. 8 needles. With light blue, work in stockinette st, inc 1 st each side every ¾″ 4 (5-5-6) times, then every 1″ 5 times—47 (51-53-57) sts. Work even until sleeve measures 11 (11½-12-13)″ from beg, or desired length to underarm, end on wrong side. SHAPE RAGLAN CAP: Work as for back raglan armholes. Slip remaining 9 (11-11-13) sts on stitch holder.

Embroidery. Following chart, embroider design in duplicate stitch, working over 2 rows and 1 st wide, as follows: Start on Row 1 of chart and with center st on 6th row below white stripe, work toward sides. Embroider design across back, front and sleeves. (See chart below.)

Finishing. Matching stripes, sew sleeves to back and front armholes. Sew side and sleeve seams. NECKBAND: With dp needles (divide sts on 3 dp needles), working from right side, slip from holders 9 (11-11-13) sts at top of right sleeve, 25 (27-29-31) sts at back of neck, 9 (11-11-13) sts at top of left sleeve, pick up 33 (35-37-39) sts on front of neck—76 (84-88-96) sts. Work in ribbing of k 1, p 1 for 4″. Bind off loosely in ribbing. Turn neckband in half and sew loosely to inside of neck edge.

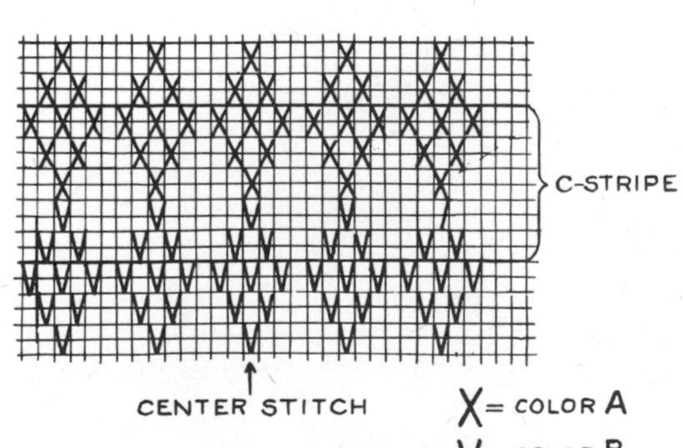

Chlld's Banded Jacket

Directions are for Size 2. Changes for Sizes 3 and 4 are in parentheses.

Materials. Knitting Worsted—7 (8-9) ozs., White. 1 oz. each Blue and Pink. Knitting Needles, Nos. 5 and 7; Steel Crochet Hook, No. 0; 5 (6-6) buttons.

Gauge. On No. 7 needles: 5 sts—1″. 7 rows—1″.

Back. With white and No. 5 needles, cast on 54 (59-64) sts. Work in ribbing of k 1, p 1 for 1½″. Change to No. 7 needles and work in stockinette st (k 1 row, p 1 row) until piece measures 7½ (8-8½)″ from beginning. SHAPING ARMHOLES: Bind off 4 sts at beginning of next 2 rows, then decrease 1 st at beginning of next 2 (4-4) rows. Work even in stockinette st until armholes measure 4 (4½-5)″ from first bind off. SHAPING SHOULDERS: Bind off 7 (7-8) sts at beginning of next 2 rows. Bind off 7 (8-8) sts at beginning of next 2 rows. Bind off remaining 16 (18-20) sts for back of neck.

Left Front. With No. 5 needles and white, cast on 32 (34-36) sts, work in ribbing for 1½″, inc 1 st in last row of ribbing. Change to No. 7 needles and work 2 (2-4) rows in stockinette st.

Pattern. Row 1: * With white k 1, with blue k 1, repeat from * across row, ending with k 1 in white. **Row 2:** * With white p 1, with blue p 1, repeat from * across row, ending with p 1 in white. **Row 3:** With blue k across row. **Row 4:** With blue p across row. **Row 5:** * With blue k 1, with white k 1, repeat from * across row, ending with k 1 in blue. **Row 6:** * With blue p 1, with white p 1, repeat from * across row, ending with p 1 in blue. Cut blue. **Next 6 rows:** With white, work in stockinette st. **Row 13:** * With white k 1, with pink k 1, repeat from * across row, ending with k 1 in pink. **Row 14:** * With white p 1, with pink p 1, repeat from * across, ending with p 1 in pink. **Row 15:** With pink k across row. **Row 16:** With pink p across row. **Row 17:** * With pink k 1, with white k 1, repeat from * across row, ending with k 1 in pink. **Row 18:** * With pink p 1, with white p 1, repeat from * across row, ending with p 1 in pink. Cut pink. **Next 6 rows:** With white, work in stockinette st. Repeat from first pattern row until front measures same as back to underarm ending at armhole side. **Next row:** Working in pattern, bind off 4 sts at beginning of row, then bind off 1 st at underarm every other row 1 (2-2) times. Continue working even in pattern until armhole measures 3 (3½-4)″, ending at neck edge. Discontinue pattern after 5 stripes are completed. **Next row:** Bind off 10 sts (all sizes) at neck edge, then dec 1 st at neck edge each row 4 (4-5) times. Work even until armhole measures same as back armhole. Bind off shoulder samc as back.

Right front. Work to correspond to left front, reversing the shaping and working a buttonhole in center row of ribbing and in each white stripe. BUTTONHOLE: Work 2 sts, yo, k 2 tog. Work to end of row. In next row, work the yo as a st.

Sleeves. With white and No. 5 needles cast on 32 (34-36) sts. Work in ribbing for 1½″. Change to No. 7 needles and work in stockinette st, inc 1 st at each end on next row, then inc 1 st at each end every 10th row until there are 42 (44-46) sts on needle. Work even until sleeve measures 8½ (9-9½)″ from beginning. SHAPING SLEEVE: Bind off 4 sts at beginning of next 2 rows, then dec 1 st each end every other row until 20 (20-22) sts remain. Bind off.

Finishing. Block each section. Sew underarms, shoulder and sleeve seams, sew in sleeves. Work a row of sc down each front section.

Collar. With white and No. 5 needles, and with wrong side facing you, pick up 66

(68-70) sts around neck, starting at 2nd st from front edge and ending at 2nd st from opposite front edge. Work in k 1, p 1 ribbing for 1″. Change to size 7 needles and work in ribbing for 1¼″, and bind off. Face fronts with grosgrain ribbon. Cut buttonholes in ribbon and overcast buttonholes. Sew buttons in position, sewing a snap fastener at neck front on small size only.

Girls' Striped Pullover

Shown in Color Plate 11

Directions are for Size 4. Changes for Sizes 6, 8, 10 and 12 are in parentheses.

Materials. Sport Yarn (2-oz. skein)—1 (1, 2, 2, 2, 2) skeins each Peach Glow (MC), and White (CC). Knitting Needles, Nos. 3 and 5. 3 Buttons. Crochet Hook No. 3.

Gauge. 6 sts—1″; 8 rows—1″.

Back. With No. 3 needles and MC, cast on 64 (70, 76, 82, 88, 92) sts. Work in St st (k 1 row, p 1 row) for 7 rows, k 1 row on p side for hemline. Change to No. 6 needles. Continuing in St st, work 8 rows of MC and 8 rows of CC for stripe pat. Work until piece measures 9 (10, 11, 12, 13, 14)″ from hemline, or desired length to underarm. ARMHOLES: Bind off 5 sts at beg of next 2 rows. Dec 1 st each end of needle every other row 5 times. DIVIDE FOR BACK OPENING: Work across 22 (25, 28, 31, 34, 36) sts, add another ball of yarn and work last 22 (25, 28, 31, 34, 36) sts. Working both sides at once, work until armholes measure 4¾ (5¼, 5¾, 6¼, 6¾, 7¼)″. At each arm edge, bind off 6 (7, 8, 9, 10, 11) sts twice. Bind off rem'ing sts.

Front. Work same as back until armholes measure 2¾ (3¼, 3¾, 4¼, 4¾, 5¼)″. Work across 14 (17, 19, 22, 24, 26) sts. Add another ball of yarn and bind off next 16 (16, 18, 18, 20, 20) sts. Working both sides at once, work last 14 (17, 19, 22, 24, 26) sts. Dec 1 st at each neck edge every other row 2 (3, 3, 4, 4, 4) times. When armhole is same as back, at each arm edge, bind off 6 (7, 8, 9, 10, 11) sts twice.

Finishing. Sew shoulder seams. Matching stripes, sew side seams. Turn up hem and sew in place. With crochet hook and MC, work 1 row sc around armholes. Work 1 row sc around neck and back opening, working in 3 button loops evenly spaced. FOR RUFFLE, (ch 6 and dc) twice in every sc around neck. Fasten off. Block lightly.

Girl's Mohair Cardigan

Shown in Color Plate 11

Directions are for Size 4. Changes for Sizes 6, 8, 10, 12 and 14 are in parentheses.

Materials. Mohair yarn (40-gram ball) 4 (4, 5, 5, 6, 7). Knitting Needles, Nos. 6 and 8. 4 (4, 4, 5, 5, 5) Buttons. Scraps of Red, Green and Pink Yarn.

Gauge. 4 sts—1″; 11 rows—2″.

Back. With No. 6 needles, cast on 48 (52, 56, 60, 64, 68) sts. Work in k 1, p 1 ribbing for 1½″. Change to No. 8 needles and work in St st (k 1 row, p 1 row) until piece measures 8 (9, 10, 11, 12, 13)″, or desired length to underarm. ARMHOLES: Bind off 2 sts at beg of next 2 rows. Dec 1 st each end every other row 3 (3, 4, 4, 5, 5) times—38 (42, 44, 48, 50, 54) sts. Work even until armholes measure 4½ (5, 5½, 6, 6½, 7)″. SHOULDERS: Work across 14 (16, 17, 19, 20, 22) sts. Add another ball of yarn and bind off center 10 sts, finish row. K 2 tog at each neck edge every other row twice. At arm edge, bind off 6 (7, 7, 8, 9, 10) sts once, 6 (7, 8, 9, 9, 10) sts once.

Left Front. With No. 6 needles, cast on 27 (29, 31, 33, 35, 37) sts. Work ribbing as on back. Change to No. 8 needles. **Next Row:** K to within last 5 sts, k 1 (p 1, k 1) twice. Keeping 5 sts at front in ribbing, work until piece measures 8 (9, 10, 11, 12, 13)″. ARMHOLE AND NECK: At arm edge, bind off 2 sts. Work to within last 6 sts of front edge, work 2 sts tog, rib to end. Continue to shape armhole as on back, and, *at the same time,* dec 1 st inside front ribbing every 6th row 4 times more. When armhole measures same as back, at arm edge bind off 6 (7, 7, 8, 9, 10) sts once, then 6 (7, 8, 9, 9, 10) sts once. Place rem'ing 5 sts on holder. Mark positions on front for 4 (4, 4, 5, 5, 5) buttons, the first ¾″ from beg and the last 1″ below first neck dec. Space remainder evenly between.

Right Front. Work to correspond to left front, reversing shaping. Make buttonholes opposite markers as follows: From front edge, work 2 sts, work 2 sts tog, yo, work to end.

Sleeves. With No. 6 needles, cast on 24 (25, 27, 28, 29, 31) sts. Work ribbing for 1½″. Change to No. 8 needles and work 4 rows St st. Inc 1 st each end of next row, then every 6 (6, 7, 8, 7, 8)th row until there are 36 (39, 41, 44, 47, 49) sts. Work even until sleeve measures 9½ (11, 12½, 14, 15½, 16½)″, or desired length to underarm. SLEEVE CAP: Bind off 2 sts at beg of next 2 rows. Dec 1 st each end of next 5 (5, 5, 7, 7, 7) rows, then every other row until 16 (17, 17, 18, 19, 19) sts rem. Bind off 3 (3, 3, 4, 4, 4) sts at beg of next 2 rows. Bind off.

Pocket. With No. 8 needles cast on 14 (16, 18, 20, 20, 22) sts. Work in St st for 2½ (2¾, 3, 3¼, 3½, 3¾)″. K 1, p 1 in ribbing for ½″. Bind off loosely.

Finishing. Join shoulder seams. Sl sts from holder onto needle. Work in k 1, p 1 ribbing until band, when slightly stretched, fits to center back of neck. Place on holder leaving end for weaving. Work other side in same way. Weave ends tog, sew in place. Sew in sleeves. Sew side and sleeve seams. Embroider pocket and sleeves as shown with lazy daisies. Sew pocket in place. Sew on buttons. Block seams very lightly.

Boy's Sleeveless Classic

Shown in Color Plate 11

Directions are for Size 4. Changes for Sizes 6, 8, 10, 12 and 14 are in parentheses.

Materials. Sport Yarn (2-oz. skein)—2 (2, 3, 3, 4, 4) ozs. Main Color (MC), 2 ozs. Contrasting Color (CC). Knitting Needles, Nos. 3 and 6. St Holders.

Gauge. 11 sts—2″; 15 rows—2″.

Back. With No. 3 needles and MC, cast on 68 (74, 80, 86, 92, 98) sts. K 1, p 1 in ribbing for 1½″. Change to No. 6 needles and work in St st until piece measures 8 (9, 10, 11, 12, 13)″, or desired length to underarm. ARMHOLES: Bind off 6 sts at beg of next 2 rows. Dec 1 st each end every other row 6 times—44 (50, 56, 62, 68, 74) sts. Work even until armhole measures 4¾ (5¼, 5¾, 6¼, 6¾, 7¼)″. Bind off 7 (8, 9, 10, 11, 12) sts at beg of next 4 rows. Sl rem'ing 16 (18, 20, 22, 24, 26) sts onto a holder for neck.

Front. Work same as back to armholes. At beg of next 2 rows, bind off 6 sts. Work across 28 (31, 34, 37, 40, 43) sts and sl them onto a holder. On rem'ing sts, dec 1 st at arm edge every other row 6 times, and, *at the same time,* k 2 tog at neck edge every 4th row 8 (9, 10, 11, 12, 13) times. When armhole is same as back, at arm edge bind off 7 (8, 9, 10, 11, 12) sts twice. Join yarn at neck edge and work sts from holder to correspond, reversing all shapings. Sew right shoulder of front to back.

Neckband. With No. 3 needles and MC, work across sts on holder, pick up 4 out of 5 sts on left neck front, put a marker on needle, pick up same number of sts on right neck front. Break off MC. With CC, k 1 row. Then work in k 1, p 1 ribbing, being sure to stay in pat, k 2 tog each side of marker at center V every other row for ¾″. Bind off loosely in ribbing.

Armbands. With No. 3 needles and MC, pick up 4 out of 5 sts around entire armhole. Break off MC, attach CC, k 1 row. Then work in k 1, p 1 ribbing for ½″. Bind off loosely in ribbing.

Finishing. Sew left shoulder and underarm seams, weaving ribbing tog. Block lightly.

Child's Turtle-Neck Pullover

Directions are for Size 6. Changes for Sizes 8, 10, and 12 are in parentheses.

Materials. Tweed or Knitting Worsted—4 (5-5-6) 100-gram skeins. Knitting Needles, Nos. 6 and 9. Double-Pointed needles, No. 6.

Gauge (Stockinette st on No. 9 needles). 4 sts—1″. 6 rows—1″.

Back. With No. 6 needles, cast on 54 (58-62-66) sts. Work in ribbing of k 1, p 1 for 1¾″. Change to No. 9 needles. Work even in stockinette st (k 1 row, p 1 row) until piece measures 10 (10½-11-11½)″ from beg, ending on wrong side. SHAPE RAGLAN ARMHOLES: Bind off 2 sts at beg of next 2 rows. **Dec Row:** (right side) K 3, k 2 tog, k to last 5 sts, sl 1, k 1, psso, k 3 (2 sts dec). Repeat dec row on every k row 16 (18-19-21) times. Place remaining 16 (16-18-18) sts on holder for neckband.

Front. Work as for back until 10 (12-13-15) raglan dec rows are completed, ending on k row—30 (30-32-32) sts. SHAPE NECK: Work 13 (13-14-14) sts, join another ball of yarn and bind off 4 sts, finish row. Working on both sides at once, repeat raglan dec row at each arm side 4 times; at same time, dec 1 st at each neck edge every k row 7 times. Bind off remaining 2 (2-3-3) sts of each side.

Sleeves. With No. 6 needles, cast on 24 (26-28-30) sts. Work in ribbing of k 1, p 1 for 1½″, inc 4 sts evenly across last row—28 (30-32-34) sts. Change to No. 9 needles. Work in stockinette st, inc 1 st each side every 1″ 7 (8-8-9) times—42 (46-48-52) sts. Work even until piece measures 11 (11½-12-12½)″ from beg on wrong side. SHAPE RAGLAN CAP: Work as for back raglan armhole until 13 (15-16-18) dec rows are completed—12 sts. Repeat dec row every 4th row twice. Bind off remaining 8 sts.

Finishing. Sew sleeves to back and front armholes. Sew side and sleeve seams.

Collar. With dp needles (divide sts evenly on 3 dp needles), slip from holders 16 (16-18-18) sts of back of neck, 8 sts at top of left sleeve, pick up 32 (32-34-34) sts on front of neck, slip from holder 8 sts of top of right sleeve—64 (64-68-68) sts. Work in ribbing of k 1, p 1 for 4 (4-4½-4½)″. Bind off loosely.

Earflap Hat

Directions are for Size 6 months to 1 year.

Materials. Sports Yarn—one 2-oz. skein or ball. Double-Pointed Needles, Set No. 3. 1 Button.

Gauge. 6 sts—1″. 8 rows—1″.

Right Earflap. Cast on 7 sts. Rib in k 1, p 1 for 2 rows. BUTTONHOLE: Work 3 sts, bind off next st, work to end of row. On the next row, cast on 1 st over bound-off st. Continue in ribbing until piece measures 3 inches. SHAPING: **Row 1:** Rib 2 sts, inc 2 sts in next st, rib 1 st, inc 2 sts in next st, rib 2 sts. Work even on 11 sts for 3 rows. **Row 5:** Rib 3 sts, inc 2 sts in next st, rib 3 sts, inc 2 sts in next st, rib 3 sts. Work even on 15 sts for 3 rows. **Row 9:** Rib 3 sts, inc 2 sts in next st, rib 7 sts, inc 2 sts in next st, rib 3 sts. Continue in this manner to inc 4 sts every 4th row until there are 31 sts. K 3 rows even. Sl sts to extra needle.

Left Earflap. Work same as for right earflap, omitting buttonhole.

Hat Cuff. Cast on 108 sts. Divide sts evenly on 3 needles. Join and work round and round in ribbing of k 1, p 1 for 10 rounds.

Join Earflaps as follows: Work 5 sts, put needle of left earflap in back of left-hand needle and work ribbing through sts of both needles until sts of earflap have been worked off, work ribbing over next 25 sts, join right earflap in same manner, work to end of round. Continue in ribbing until piece measures 3½″ above earflap joining.

Top. Rnd 1: * Rib 15 sts, k 3 tog, rib next 15 sts, p 3 tog; repeat from * all around (12 sts dec). **Rnd 2:** Work even. Repeat these 2 rounds, having 2 sts less between dec on each dec round, 5 times more. Break off yarn, leaving a 12″ end.

Finishing. Thread yarn needle with end of yarn and run through all sts on needles, tighten and fasten securely on wrong side. Block. Make a pompon and sew to top of hat as shown in photograph. Sew on button. POMPON: Wind yarn around 1″-wide cardboard 100 times. Tie tightly at one edge of cardboard, leaving yarn ends; cut at opposite edge. Use ends of yarn for sewing on pompon.

Child's Bavarian Sweater

Directions are for Size 4. Changes for Sizes 6, 8, 10 and 12 are in parentheses.

Materials. Knitting Worsted—13 (13–14–15–16) 1-oz. skeins, Oxford; 1 oz. Dark Green, and 5 yards Geranium for all sizes. Knitting Needles, No. 3. 8 buttons, ⅝″ in diameter.

Gauge. 5 sts—1″. 10 rows—1″.

Blocking Measurements:

Body Chest Size . . . 23 (24–26–28–30)″.

Actual Knitting Measurements:

Chest (buttoned) . . 25 (27–29–31–33)″.

Width across back at underarm . . . . 12 (13–14–15–16)″.

Width across back above armhole shaping . . . 9½ (10–10½–11–11½)″.

Width across each front at underarm (including borders . . . 7 (7½–8–8½–9)″.

Length from shoulder to lower edge . . . . 12½ (14–16–17–18½)″.

Length of side seam . . . . 7½ (8½–10–10½–11½)″.

Length of sleeve seam . . . . . . 10 (11½–13–14½–16)″.

Width across sleeve at upperarm . . . 10 (10½–11–11½–12)″.

Back. Starting at lower edge with dark green, cast on 60 (65–70–75–80) sts. Work 3 rows of garter st (k each row). Break off dark green, attach oxford. Mark first row of oxford as right side of work. Continue in garter st until total length is 7½ (8½–10–10½–11½)″. ARMHOLE SHAPING: Bind off 3 (3–4–5–5) sts at beg of next 2 rows. Dec one st at both ends of every 4th row 3 (4–5–5–6) times. Work even over remaining 48 (51–52–55–58) sts until length from first row of armhole shaping is 5 (5½–6–6½–7)″. SHOULDER SHAPING: Bind off 4 sts at beg of next 6 rows. Bind off 3 (4–4–5–6) sts at beg of next 2 rows. Slip onto a stitch holder for back of neck the remaining 18 (19–20–21–22) sts.

Left Front. Starting at lower edge with dark green, cast on 33 (35–38–40–43) sts. Work 3 rows of garter st. Break off dark green, attach oxford. Mark first row of oxford as right side of work. Continue in garter st until total length is 7½ (8½–10–10½–

11½)", ending with a wrong-side row. ARMHOLE SHAPING: With right side facing, bind off 3 (3–4–5–5) sts at beg of next row. Dec one st at same edge on every 4th row 3 (4–5–5–6) times. Work even over remaining 27 (28–29–30–32) sts until length from first row of armhole shaping is 3½ (4–4½–4½–5)", ending at front edge. NECK SHAPING: K 7, slip these 7 sts onto a safety pin to be used later, complete row. Keeping armhole edge straight, dec one st at neck edge on every other row 5 (5–6–6–7) times. Work even over remaining 15 (16–16–17–18) sts until armhole measures same as back, ending at armhole edge. SHOULDER SHAPING: Bind off 4 sts at armhole edge on every other row 3 times. At same edge, bind off remaining 3 (4–4–5–6) sts. With pins, mark the position of 8 buttons, evenly spaced on front edge, having the first pin just below the neck safety pin, and the last pin 2 (2¼–2¼–2½–2½)" up from lower edge.

Right Front. Work to correspond with left front, reversing shapings and making buttonholes in line with pins on edge of left front.

To Make Buttonholes. Starting at front edge, work 2 sts, bind off next 2 sts, complete row. On next row, cast on 2 sts over the bound-off sts.

Sleeves. Starting at lower edge with dark green, cast on 32 (35–37–40–42) sts. Work 3 rows of garter st. Break off dark green, attach oxford and continue in garter st until total length is 1½ (2–2½–3–3)". Inc one st at both ends of next row and every 8th (9th–10th–11th–13th) row until 9 inc rows in all have been made. Work even over these 50 (53–55–58–60) sts until total length is 10 (11½–13–14½–16)". TOP SHAPING: Bind off 3 (3–4–5–5) sts at beg of next 2 rows. Dec one st at both ends of every 4th row 3 (4–5–5–6) times. Dec one st at both ends of every other row 4 times. Dec one st at both ends of every row until there remain 18 (19–17–18–18) stitches. Bind off.

Finishing. Block pieces. Sew shoulder seams. NECKBAND: With right side facing, using dark green, k 7 sts from right front safety pin, pick up and k 15 (15–15–20–20) sts evenly along right neck edge, k 18 (19–20–21–22) sts across back of neck, pick up and k 15 (15–15–20–20) sts evenly along left neck edge, k 7 sts from left front safety pin. There are 62 (63–64–75–76) sts on needle. Work 3 rows garter st. Bind off loosely, purling the sts. FRONT BAND: With right side facing, using dark green, pick up and k 58 (66–76–78–86) sts along front edge (including bands). Work same as neck band. Work a front band along left front edge in same way. MOCK POCKET: With dark green, cast on 18 sts. Work 3 rows of garter st. Break off dark green, attach geranium and k 2 rows. Bind off, purling the sts. Sew this piece on upper left front. Sew side and sleeve seams. Sew in sleeves. Block. Sew on buttons.

Baby Jacket—Reversible and Double-Breasted

Directions are for Infants' Size 3 to 6 months. Changes for Size 1 year are in parentheses.

Materials (same for both sizes). JACKET: Baby Yarn—4 ounces Color A, and 4 ounces Color B. HOOD: 1 ounce Color A, and 1

ounce Color B. Knitting Needles, No. 3. Steel Crochet Hook, No. 6. 6 buttons.

Gauge. 7 sts—1"; 7 ridges (14 rows)—1".

Pattern Stitch. Garter stitch (knit every row).

Note: Because there is no right and wrong side, the directions are the same for boy or girl until lining is attached.

Raglan Yoke. Starting at neck edge with Color A, cast on 92 (96) sts. **Row 1:** K 22 (23) for front, place marker on needle, k 14 for sleeve, place marker on needle, k 20 (22) for back, place marker on needle, k 14 for sleeve, place marker on needle, k 22 (23) for other front. **Row 2:** K, increasing 1 st before and after each of the 4 markers. To keep track of the increase rows, mark this row with a colored thread. **Row 3:** K. **Row 4:** Repeat Row 2. **Row 5:** K 3, k 2 tog, yo for buttonhole, k 10, k 2 tog, yo for buttonhole, k to end of row. Repeat buttonholes every 2½ (3)″ twice more. Repeat Rows 2 and 3 until there are 260 (288) sts. Divide work for back, fronts and sleeves as follows: K 43 (47) sts and slip them to a holder for front, k 56 (62) sts and slip them to 2nd holder for sleeve, k 62 (70) sts and slip them to 3rd holder for back, k 56 (62) sts for sleeve, slip remaining 43 (47) sts to 4th holder for other front.

Sleeves. Cast on 1 st, turn and k across the 57 (63) sts, cast on 1 st, turn. K across the 58 (64) sts. Dec 1 st each side every 2½ (2)″ twice (3 times). Knit on the remaining 54 (58) sts until sleeve measures 6 (7)″ from underarm. Do not bind off, but leave long end for binding off later. Slip sts to a thread to be attached to lining of jacket later. Work other sleeve to correspond.

Body. Starting at underarm, k across the 43 (47) sts on 4th holder (front). Next row, k the 43 (47) sts, pick up and k 2 sts on cast-on sts of sleeve, k across the 62 (70) sts of back, pick up and k 2 sts on cast-on sts of other sleeve, k across the 43 (47) sts of other front. Knit the 152 (168) sts to 6¼ (7¼)″ from underarm, or desired length. Do not bind off but leave long end for binding off later. Sl sts on to a thread.

Lining. With Color B cast on 92 (96) sts. Work same as outside, working body and sleeves 3 rows less than on outside.

Hood (optional). With Color A cast on 96 (100) sts for back edge. Knit in garter st for 6½ (7)″. Break off Color A. With Color B work to 14 (15)″ from start. Bind off.

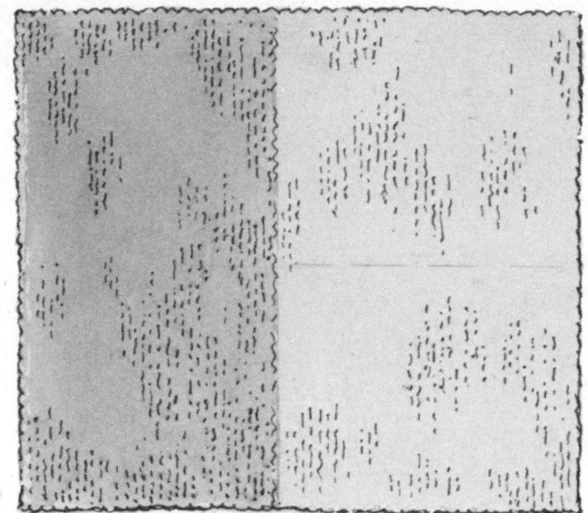

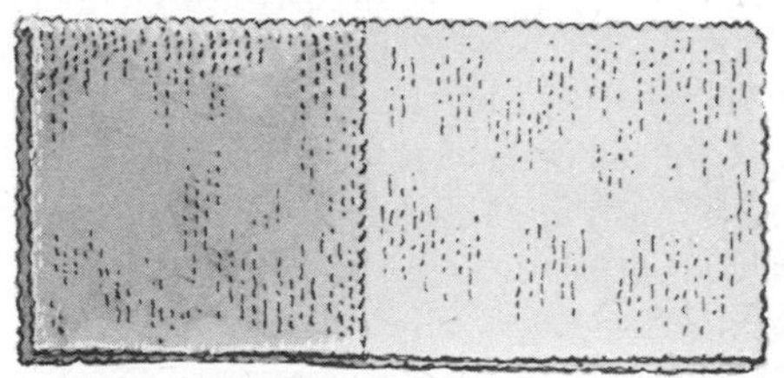

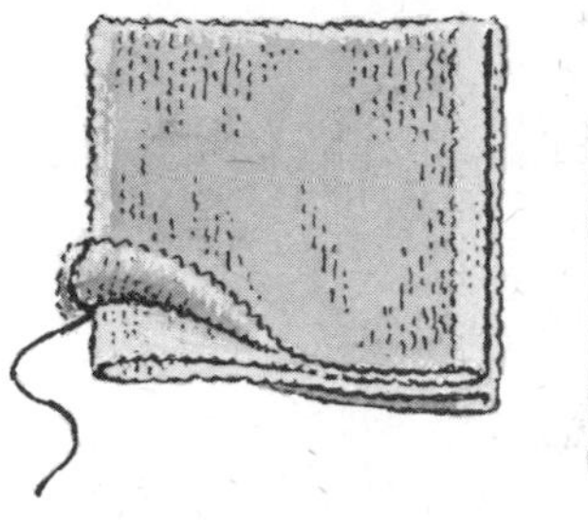

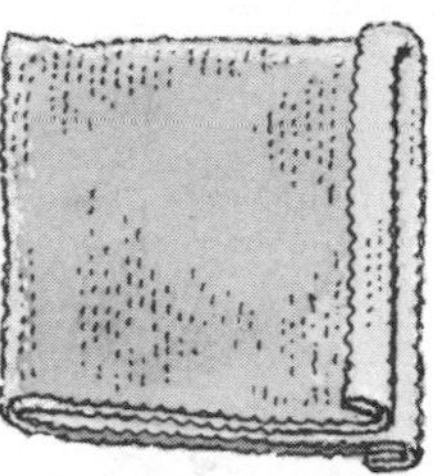

Assembling. For girl's jacket turn outside layer (Color A) so jacket laps from right to left with buttonholes on right front. For boy's jacket, turn so jacket laps from left to right with buttonholes on left front. Being careful to match buttonholes, insert lining; slip stitches of one sleeve edge onto a knitting needle; slip stitches of sleeve lining onto a spare knitting needle; hold both needles together and, with a third knitting needle, using main color, bind off both layers simultaneously, picking up both stitches at once. Repeat for other sleeve.

Sew sleeve seams of outside (Color A), and then of lining, together on the inside.

Join lower edges of jacket the same as

lower edges of sleeve (by binding off together). Whip edges of buttonholes together, joining the two layers. Join the two layers at neck and front edges with an overcast stitch.

Starting at lower right front edge on right side of work, using Color A, insert crochet hook between first 2 ridges, work 1 sc, ch 3 and 1 sc in same space, * skip next 2 ridges, work 1 sc, ch 3 and 1 sc in next space between ridges, repeat from * up right front, around neck and down left front edge. Fasten off.

Fold hood in half and sew cast-on edges (Color A) together for back seam; see diagram. Now sew bound-off edges together (Color B) for back seam of lining. Push lining to inside so back seams meet (lining will show on outside of hood at fold—front of hood). Turn back 1″ at front edge for cuff and tack in place, then join double edges of knitting at lower edge. Sew hood in place with edges 1″ in front of raglan seam (see photograph), sewing through the extra thickness of cuff of hood.

Boy's Peaked Cap

Materials. Sports Yarn—1 oz. Knitting Needles, No. 5. One ¾-inch button.

Gauge. 6 sts—1″. 8 rows—1″.

Note: The whole cap is worked in k 1, p 1 ribbing.

Center Section. Starting at back of neck, cast on 25 sts. **Row 1:** K 1, * p 1, k 1, repeat from * to end. **Row 2:** P 1, * k 1, p 1, repeat from * to end. Repeat these 2 rows until center section measures 7¾″, ending with Row 2.

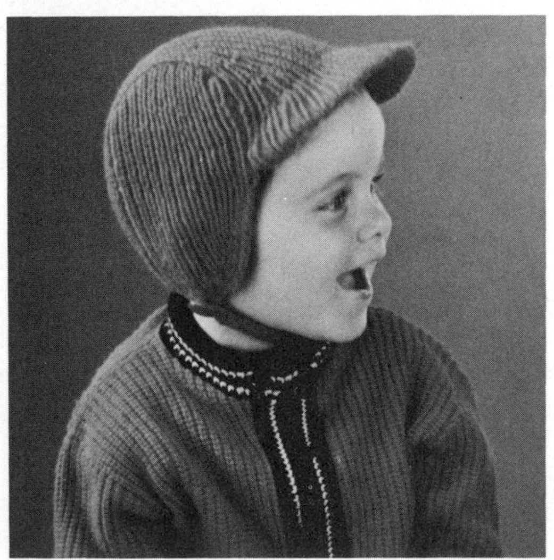

Peak. K 1, p 1, k 1, p 1; in the next st, k in the back of loop, p in the front of same loop, then k in the back of same loop (2 sts inc.) Work in rib pat to 5 sts of end. Inc 2 sts in next st as before, rib to end. Work even, keeping continuity of rib pat for 5 rows more. Repeat these last 6 rows 3 times more (4 inc rows in all) and 41 sts on needle. PEAK FACING: Bind off 2 sts at beg of each of next 12 rows. Bind off remaining 17 sts in ribbing.

Left Side. STRAP: Leave a long end for buttonloop and cast on 5 sts. **Row 1:** K 1, p 1, k 1, p 1, k 1. **Row 2:** P 1, k 1, p 1, k 1, p 1. Repeat rows 1 and 2 for 4½″, ending with row 1. SIDE PIECE: **Row 1:** With wrong side of strap facing you, p 1. In the next st k in the front of the loop, p in back of same loop, k in front of same loop (2 sts inc), p 1, inc 2 sts in next st same as before, p 1. (9 sts on needle.) **Row 2:** (and all even rows) K 1, * p 1, k 1. Repeat from * 3 times more. **Row 3:** Keeping continuity of established rib pat, work 3 sts, inc 2 sts in next st, k 1. Inc 2 sts in next st, work 3 sts. (You now have 13 sts on needle.) **Row 5:** Work 4 sts in pat. Inc 2 sts in next st. Work to end. **Row 6:** K 1, * p 1, k 1. Repeat from * to end. Repeat rows 5 and 6 five times more. Work even in rib pat on 25 sts for 7 rows; place marker on shaped edge. Continue in pat until right side measures 3 inches from last inc row.

Shape Top. Bind off 2 sts at beg of each of next 8 rows. Bind off remaining 9 sts. Using the long end of yarn at beginning of strap, work a ch buttonloop.

Right Side (no strap on this piece). Cast on 5 sts. **Rows 1, 2, 3 and 4:** Repeat Rows 1, 2, 3 and 4 of left side piece. **Row 5:** With wrong side of work facing you, rib 8 sts. Inc 2 sts in next st. Rib 4 sts. Complete right side piece to correspond with left side piece reversing all shaping. Break yarn.

Finishing. Fold center section in half along long edges by bringing cast-on end to first bound-off stitches of peak. Place a marker at center top on both sides. Find center top of each side piece and place a marker (center of the 9 bound-off stitches). Match center top of right-side piece to center top at right edge of center section, with seam at inside. Pin remainder of seam, easing where necessary, and sew together. Repeat with left-side piece. (See diagram.) Trace diagram for a pattern, cut heavy gauge clear plastic for peak stiffener. Fold peak under on row 1 of peak facing. Insert stiffener. Sew peak facing in place on wrong side. Sew button to right earlap.

Scandinavian Mittens

Direction are for children's medium size. Mittens measure about 6½″ around palm and back, and approximately 6″ from first thumb-gore increase to tip.

Materials. Sports Yarn—1 oz. Main Color (MC). 1 oz. Contrasting Color (CC). Double-pointed Needles, 1 set No. 4.

Gauge. 7 sts—1″. 8 rows—1″.

Note: When changing colors, always pass yarn to be used *under* yarn just used to prevent a hole. Be careful not to pull yarn on wrong side too tightly or work will pucker.

Right Mitten. With MC cast on 32 sts. Divide sts on 3 needles—12 on No. 1 needle, 10 on No. 2 and No. 3 needles. Join, being careful not to twist sts on needles. Rib in k 2, p 2 for 7 rnds. **Next Rnd:** With CC, rib in k 2, p 2. **Next Rnd:** With MC rib in k 2, p 2. Repeat last 2 rnds 3 times more, then rib 5 rounds more as follows: 1 rnd CC, 2 rnds MC, 2 rnds CC. This completes ribbing. Change to stockinette st (k every rnd). DIVIDE STITCHES: Slip first 8 sts to No. 1 needle for one half of palm. Slip next 8 sts to No. 2 needle for second half of palm. Slip remaining 16 sts to No. 3 needle for back of mitten. THUMB GORE: **Rnd 1:** Starting with No. 1 needle and MC yarn, k 2. Place marker on needle. Inc 1 st in each of next 2 sts for thumb gore. Place another marker on needle. K to end. (You now have 34 sts on 3 needles.) **Rnd 2:** With MC k 34 sts. **Rnd 3:** With MC, k 2, slip marker, inc 1 st in next st, k 2, inc 1 st in next st, slip marker, K 30 sts to end. **Rnd 4:** With MC k 36 sts. **Rnd 5:** K 1 MC, 1 CC, slip marker. K 1 MC. With CC yarn inc 1 st in bar between

sts. K 1 MC, 1 CC, 1 MC, 1 CC. With MC inc 1 st in bar between sts. K 1 CC. * K 1 MC, 1 CC. Repeat from * to end. **Rnd 6:** * K 1 CC, 1 MC. Repeat from * to end. (You now have 38 sts on 3 needles.) **Rnd 7:** Repeat Rnd 5 having 10 sts between markers. **Rnd 8:** (Palm) With MC k 12. * Inc 1 st in next st. K 2. Repeat from * 3 times more. (You now have 28 sts on No. 1 and No. 2 needles.) Back (No. 3 needle) * k 2. Inc 1 st in next st. Repeat from * 4 times more. K 2. (You now have 21 sts on No. 3 needle—49 sts in rnd.) **Rnd 9:** With MC, k 2. K the thumb gore sts increasing 1 st *after* first marker and 1 st *before* second marker as before. Place the 12 sts of thumb gore on a holder or strand of yarn to be worked later for thumb. K to end. (You now have 39 sts on needles.)

BEGIN PATTERN (see diagram): **Rnd 1** (palm): K 1 MC, 1 CC. With MC cast on 5 sts over thumb sts. K 1 MC. * K 1 MC, 1 CC, 2 MC. Repeat from * 2 times more. K 1 MC, 1 CC, 1 MC. Back (No. 3 needle): Following working chart, work Row 1 over 21 sts, placing colors as designated on chart. (You now have 44 sts on 3 needles.) **Rnd 2** (palm): Starting with No. 1 needle, * k 2 CC, 2 MC. Repeat from * 4 times more. K

3 CC. Back (No. 3 Needle): Following working chart, work Row 2 of chart over 21 sts. **Rnd 3** (palm): * K 1 MC, 1 CC, 2 MC. Repeat from * 4 times more. K 1 MC, 1 CC, 1 MC. Back (No. 3 needle): Following working chart, work Row 3 of chart over 21 sts. Continue in this manner, repeating Rnds 2 and 3 for Palm and following working chart for back until 25 rows of working chart are completed. SHAPE TOP (palm): Starting with No. 1 needle and Rnd 3 of palm pat, k 1 MC, 1 CC. With MC k 2 sts tog. Work in established pat to 4 sts of end of No. 2 needle. With MC k 2 sts tog. K 1 CC, 1 MC. Back —(No. 3 needle). With MC, k 2 sts tog. Following working chart, work next 17 sts. With MC k 2 sts tog. **Next Rnd** (palm): Starting with No. 1 needle and Rnd 2 of Palm pat, k 2 CC. With CC k 2 sts tog. Work in established pat to 4 sts of end of No. 2 needle. With CC k 2 sts tog. K 2 CC. Back —With MC k 2 sts tog. Following working chart work next 15 sts. With MC k 2 sts tog. Repeat last 2 rnds until only 1 Palm st and 1

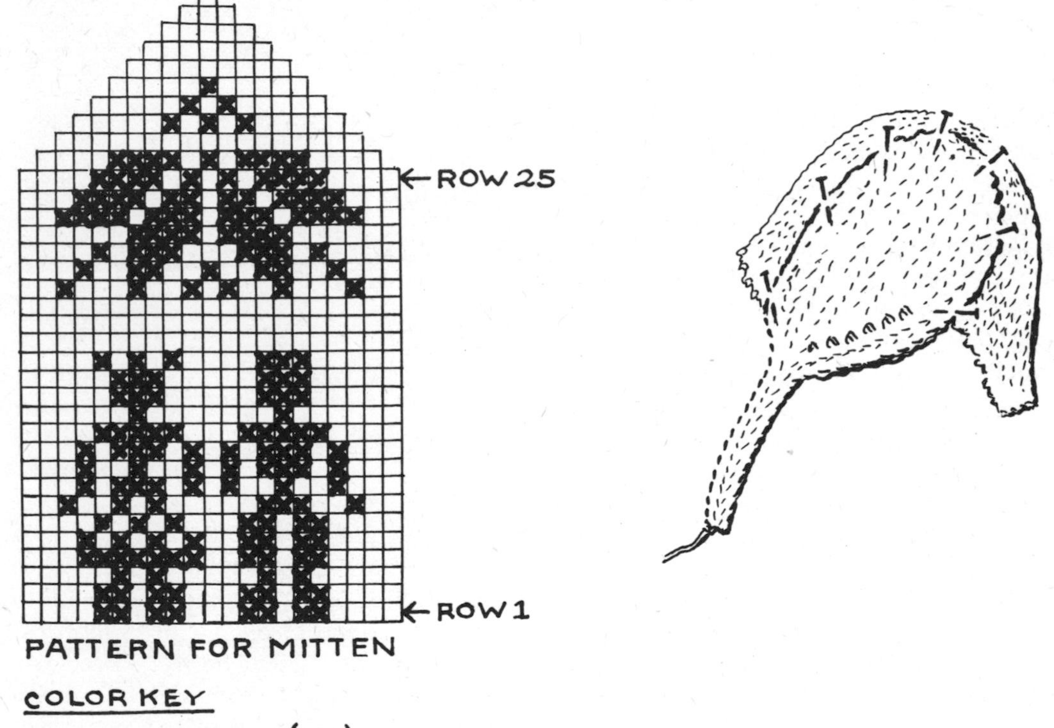

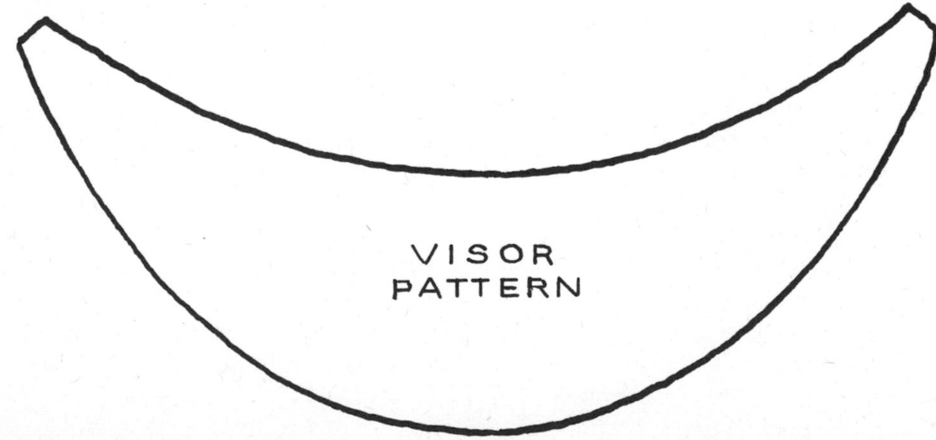

Back st remain. Draw yarn through last 2 sts. Break yarns. THUMB: Slip 6 sts of thumb gore to No. 1 dp needle. Slip next 5 sts of thumb gore to No. 2 dp needle. Slip last st of thumb gore to No. 3 dp needle, then pick up 1 st in each corner and 6 sts in the cast-on sts of Palm. (You now have 20 sts on 3 needles.) **Rnd 1:** Starting with No. 1 needle * k 1 MC, 1 CC, 2 MC. Repeat from * once. K 1 MC, 1 CC, 1 MC. Working over the 9 sts on No. 3 needle—k 2 MC, 1 CC, 3 MC, 1 CC, 2 MC. **Rnd 2:** Starting with No. 1 needle * k 3 CC, 1 MC. Repeat from * once. K 3 CC. No. 3 needle—k 1 MC, 3 CC, 1 MC, 3 CC, 1 MC. Repeat Rnds 1 and 2 five times more. (12 rows of thumb are completed.) SHAPE TOP: With MC k 2 sts tog. Work in pat to 2 sts of end of No. 2 needle. With MC k 2 sts tog. No. 3 needle—with MC k 2 tog. Work in pat to 2 sts of end. With MC k 2 sts tog. **Next Rnd:** With CC yarn k 2 sts tog. Work in pat to 2 sts before end of No. 2 needle. With CC k 2 sts tog. No. 3 needle—with CC k 2 sts tog. Work in pat to 2 sts before end. With CC k 2 sts tog. Repeat last 2 rnds until only 2 sts remain. Draw yarn through last 2 sts. Break yarns.

Left Mitten. Work to correspond to right mitten. When beginning thumb gore work as follows: Starting with No. 1 needle and with MC, K 12. Place marker on needle. Inc 1 st in each of next 2 sts for thumb gore. Place another marker on needle. K 2. No. 3 needle—with MC yarn k to end. Complete to correspond to right mitten having thumb at opposite side of palm.

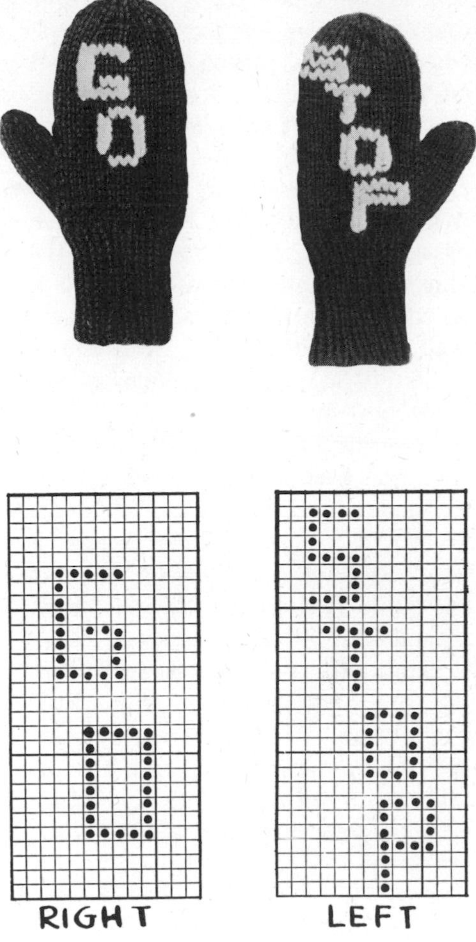

■ = WHITE DUPLICATE STITCH

Children's Stop-and-Go Mittens

Directions are given for Size 4½. Changes for Sizes 5, 5½ and 6 are in parentheses.

Materials. Knitting Worsted—1 (1–2–2) oz.(s) each of Geranium and Green, and a few yards of White for embroidery. Double-pointed Needles, 1 set each Nos. 3 and 5. Tapestry Needle, No. 18.

Gauge. 11 sts—2″. 8 rounds—1″.

Measurements Around Palm:

Inches 4½ 5 5½ 6

Left Mitten. Starting at cuff edge with geranium and No. 5 needles, cast on 26 (28–30–34) sts. Divide sts among 3 needles and join, being careful not to twist sts. Change to No. 3 needles and work in K 1, P 1 ribbing for 1¾ (1¾–2–2¼)″. Change to No. 5 needles and work in stockinette st (k each rnd) for 2 rnds. THUMB GORE: **Rnd 1:** K 1, place marker on needle, p and k in next st, k in front and back of next st, place a marker on needle, k to end of rnd. **Rnds 2 and 3:** K around, slipping markers. **Rnd 4:** K 1, slip marker, p and k in next st (one st increased);

k 2, k in front and back of next st (another st increased); slip marker, k to end of rnd. **Rnds 5 and 6:** K around, slipping markers. **Rnd 7:** Increasing one st following the first marker and one st preceding the 2nd marker as before, k around. Repeat last 3 rnds until there are 8 (8–8–10) sts between markers. Work 2 more rnds even. **Next rnd:** K 1, removing markers, place the 8 (8–8–10) sts of the thumb gore onto a safety pin to be worked later; cast on 2 sts for inner side of thumb, K to end of round. Knit over these 26 (28–30–34) sts until mitten, when tried on, reaches tip of little finger, or measures from last rnd of cuff 3½ (4–4½–5)″. TO SHAPE TIP: **Rnd 1:** K 2 (0–2–2), * k 2 tog (dec made); k 2. Repeat from * around, 6 (7–7–8) decs made. **Rnds 2 and 3:** K around. **Rnd 4:** Dec 6 (7–7–8) sts, k around. **Rnds 6 and 7:** K around. **Rnd 8:** * K 2 tog. Repeat from * around. Break off, leaving an 8″ length of yarn. Thread this yarn into needle and draw through remaining sts. Pull up tightly and fasten off securely. THUMB: Place sts from safety pin onto two No. 5 needles; with 3rd needle pick up and k 3 sts over the 2 cast-on sts. K around until thumb, when tried on, reaches ¼″ from tip, or measures 1½ (1¾–2–2)″. TO SHAPE TIP: **Rnd 1:** K 2 tog, * k 1, k 2 tog. Repeat from * around, ending *for size 6 only* with k 2 instead of k 1. **Rnd 2:** K around. Break off, leaving an 8″ length of yarn and finish same as tip of mitten.

Right Mitten. Using paddy green, work as for left mitten.

Embroidery. With a basting thread, mark an oblong section of 13 sts and 28 rows at center of back on each mitten to correspond with sts and rows shown on each chart. Each square on chart represents one knitted st; each dotted square a duplicate st (see photograph on page 274, for making duplicate st). Following charts, with white, embroider backs of mittens.

Child's Aran Pullover

Directions are for Size 2. Changes for Sizes 4, 6 and 8 are in parentheses.

Materials. Knitting Worsted—8 (9–11–12) oz., White. Knitting Needles, No. 8. Double-pointed Needle, 1 set (for popcorn).

Gauge. 9 sts—2″. 6 rows—1″.

Blocking Measurements:

Body Chest Size .... 21 (23–24–26)″.

Actual Knitting Measurements:

Chest .... 23 (25–27–29)″.

Width across back or front at underarm 11½ (12½–13½–14½)″.

Width across back above armhole shaping ...... 9½ (10–10½–11)″.

Length from shoulder to lower edge .... 12½ (13½–14½–15½)″.

Length of side seam .. 8 (8½–9–9½)″.

Length of sleeve seam .... 8 (9½–11–12½)″.

Width across sleeve at upper arm .... 9 (10–11–11½)″.

Back. Starting at lower edge, cast on 52 (56–60–64) sts. Work in k 1, p 1 ribbing for 2 (2–2½–3)″, increasing one st on last row in the 26th (28th–30th–32nd) st. Work Aran pattern over these 53 (57–61–65) sts as follows: **Row 1** (right side): P 9, k 2, p 5 (7–9–11), k 2, p 6, slip next 3 sts onto a dp needle and hold in back of work, k next 2 sts; p 1 and k 2 from dp needle—cross made; p 6, k 2, p 5 (7–9–11), k 2, p 9. **Row 2:** K 9, p 2, k 2 (3–4–5), in next st k 1, yo, and k 1—pc started; k 2 (3–4–5), p 2, k 6, p 2, k 1, p 2, k 6, p 2, k 2 (3–4–5), start pc in next st, k 2 (3–4–5), p 2, k 9. *Note:* Each yo counts as one st. **Row 3:** P 9, k 2, p 2 (3–4–5), (p in front and k in back of next st) twice—pc increased; p 3 (4–5–6), k 2, p 5, slip next st onto a dp needle and hold in back of work, k 2, p the st from dp needle—k 2 rib moved to right; p 1, slip next 2 sts onto a dp needle and hold in front of work, p 1, k the 2 sts from dp needle—k 2 rib move to left; p 5, k 2, p 2 (3–4–5), inc in next pc, p 3 (4–5–6), k 2, p 9. **Row 4:** K 9, p 2, k 2 (3–4–5), p 5 tog—pc closed; k 2 (3–4–5), p 2, k 5, p 2, k 1, start pc, k 1, p 2, k 5, p 2, k 2 (3–4–5), close next pc, k 2 (3–4–5), p 2, k 9. **Row 5:** P 9, k 2, p 5 (7–9–11), k 2, p 4, move rib to right, p 1, inc next pc; p 2, move rib to left, p 4, k 2, p 5 (7–9–11), k 2, p 9. **Row 6:** K 9, p 2, k 5 (7–9–11), p 2, k 4, p 2, k 2, close next pc, k 2, p 2, k 4, p 2, k 5 (7–9–11), p 2, k 9. **Row 7:** P 9, k 2, p 5 (7–9–11), k 2, p 3, rib to right, p 5, rib to left, p 3, k 2, p 5 (7–9–11), k 2, p 9. **Row 8:** K 9, p 2, k 2 (3–4–5), start pc, k 2 (3–4–5), p 2, k 3, p 2, k 1, start pc, k 3, start pc, k 1, p 2, k 3, p 2, k 2 (3–4–5) start pc, k 2 (3–4–5), p 2, k 9. **Row 9:** P 9, k 2, p 2 (3–4–5), inc next pc, p 3 (4–5–6), k 2, p 2, rib to right, p 1, inc next pc, p 4, inc next pc, p 2, rib to left, p 2, k 2, p 2 (3–4–5), inc next pc, p 3 (4–5–6), k 2, p 9. **Row 10:** K 9, p 2, k 2 (3–4–5), close next pc, k 2 (3–4–5), (p 2, k 2) twice; close next pc, k 3, close next pc, (k 2, p 2) twice; k 2 (3–4–5), close next pc, k 2 (3–4–5), p 2, k 9. **Row 11:** P 9, k 2, p 5 (7–9–11), k 2, p 2, rib to left, p 7, rib to right, p 2, k 2, p 5 (7–9–11), k 2, p 9. **Row 12:** K 9, p 2, k 5 (7–9–11), (p 2, k 3) twice; start pc (k 3, p 2) twice; k 5 (7–9–11), p 2, k 9. **Row 13:** P 9, k 2, p 5 (7–9–11), k 2, p 3, rib to left, p 2, inc next pc, p 3, rib to right, p 3, k 2, p 5 (7–9–11), k 2, p 9. **Row 14:** K 9, p 2, k 2 (3–4–5), start pc, k 2 (3–4–5), p 2, k 4, p 2, k 2, close next pc, k 2, p 2, k 4, p 2, k 2 (3–4–5), start pc, k 2 (3–4–5), p 2, k 9. **Row 15:** P 9, k 2, p 2 (3–4–5), inc next pc, p 3 (4–5–6), k 2, p 4, rib to left, p 3, rib to right, p 4, k 2, p 2 (3–4–5), inc next pc, p 3 (4–5–6), k 2, p 9. **Row 16:** K 9, p 2, k 2 (3–4–5), close next pc, k 2 (3–4–5), p 2, k 5, p 2, k 3, p 2, k 5, p 2, k 2 (3–4–5), close next pc, k 2 (3–4–5), p 2, k 9. **Row 17:** P 9, k 2, p 5 (7–9–11), k 2, p 5, rib to left, p 1, rib to right, p 5, k 2, p 5 (7–9–11), k 2, p 9. **Row 18:** K 9, p 2, k 5 (7–9–11), p 2, k 6, p 2, k 1, p 2, k 6, p 2, k 5 (7–9–11), p 2, k 9. Repeat last 18 rows for pattern. Work in pattern until total length is 8 (8½–9–9½)", ending with a wrong-side row. ARMHOLE SHAPING: Keeping continuity of pattern as established, bind off 3 (3–4–4) sts, at beg of next 2 rows. Dec one st at both ends of next row and every other row 2 (3–3–4) times in all. Work even on remaining 43 (45–47–49) sts until length from first row or armhole shaping is 4½ (5–5½–6)". SHOULDER SHAPING: Bind off 5 sts at beg of next 4 (4–2–2) rows. Bind off 6 sts at beg of next 0 (0–2–2) rows. Bind off loosely remaining 23 (25–25–27) sts.

Front. Work same as for back until length from first row of armhole shaping is 2 (2¼–2½–2¾)", ending with a wrong-side row. NECK SHAPING: **Next Row:** Work in pattern across first 13 (13–14–14) sts, place these sts on a stitch holder, bind off loosely next 17 (19–19–21) sts, work across remaining sts —13 (13–14–14) sts. Turn and work in pattern over this set of sts, decreasing one st at neck edge every other row 3 times. Work even on remaining 10 (10–11–11) sts until length from first row of armhole shaping is 4½ (5–5½–6)", ending with a right-side row. SHOULDER SHAPING: Bind off 5 sts at armhole edge every other row 2 (2–1–1) times. *On Sizes 6 and 8:* Work 1 row even. Bind off remaining 6 sts. *On all sizes:* Slip the sts from the stitch holder onto a needle. Attach yarn at neck edge and work to correspond with other side, reversing shapings.

Sleeves. Starting at lower edge, cast on 32 (34–36–38) sts. Work in k 1, p 1 ribbing for 1½ (2–2–2½)", increasing one st at beg of last row. Now work in pattern as follows: **Row 1:** P 5 (3–1–2), k 2, * p 5 (7–9–9), k 2. Repeat from * across, ending with p 5 (3–1–2). **Row 2:** K 5, (3–1–2), p 2, * k 2 (3–4–4), start pc in next st, k 2 (3–4–4), p 2. Repeat from * across, ending with k 5 (3–1–2). **Row 3:** P 5 (3–1–2), k 2, * p 2 (3–4–4), inc next pc, p 3 (4–5–5), k 2. Repeat from * across, ending with p 5 (3–1–2). **Row 4:** K 5 (3–1–2), p 2, * k 2 (3–4–4), close pc, k 2 (3–4–4), p 2. Repeat from * across, ending with k 5 (3–1–2).

Children's Spiral Socks

Materials. Fingering Yarn—two 1-oz. skeins. Double-pointed Needles, No. 3.

Gauge. 7 sts—1". 10 rows—1".

Pattern Stitch. Multiple of 6 sts. **Rnds 1, 2, 3 and 4:** * K 3, p 3; repeat from * all around. **Rnds 5, 6, 7 and 8:** P 1, * k 3, p 3; repeat from * ending p 2. **Rnds 9, 10, 11 and 12:** P 2, * k 3, p 3; repeat from * ending p 1. **Rnds 13, 14, 15 and 16:** * P 3, k 3; repeat from * all around. **Rnds 17, 18, 19 and 20:** K 1, * p 3, k 3; repeat from * ending k 2. **Rnds 21, 22, 23 and 24:** K 2, * p 3, k 3; repeat from * ending k 1. Repeat these 24 rows for pat st.

Socks. Cast on 52 sts. Divide sts evenly on 3 needles. Join, being careful not to twist sts. Rib in k 2, p 2 for 1½". Inc 1 st at beg of next round and again after knitting 26 sts. Work even on 54 sts until piece measures 9½" from beg, or desired length. Discontinue pat st, k in stockinette st for 3 rounds. TOE: **Rnd 1:** * K 7, k 2 tog; repeat from * all around (6 sts dec). **Rnd 2:** K. **Rnd 3:** * K 6, k 2 tog; repeat from * all around (6 sts dec). **Rnd 4:** K. Continue to dec 6 sts evenly around (having 1 st less between decs every other round) until there are 12 sts left. K 2 tog around. Break yarn leaving a 6" end. Run this end through remaining 6 sts, draw up tightly and fasten on wrong side. Steam slightly.

Red Stocking Hat

Materials. Knitting Worsted—one 4-oz. skein. Knitting Needles, No. 8.

Gauge. 5 sts—1". 7 rows—1".

Hat. Cast on 80 sts. Rib in k 1, p 1 for 10". **First Dec Row:** * Sl 1, k 2 tog, psso, (p 1, k 1) twice, p 1; repeat from * 9 times more (20 sts dec). Work 2 rows even. **2nd Dec Row:** * Sl 1, k 2 tog, psso, p 1, k 1, p 1; repeat from * 9 times more (20 sts dec). Work 2 rows even. **3rd Dec Row:** K 2 tog across row (20 sts dec). Work 1 row even. Break yarn, leaving a 12" end. FINISHING: Thread yarn needle with end of yarn and run through all sts on needle, tighten and fasten securely on wrong side. Sew back seam. Block. Make a large pompon and fasten to top of hat as shown in photograph. POMPON: Wind yarn around 2" cardboard about 150 times. Tie at one edge of cardboard and cut at opposite edge.

Pixie Hood

Materials. Sports Yarn—one 2-oz. skein. Knitting Needles, No. 5.

Gauge. 6 sts.—1″. 7 rows—1″ (measured on k 2, p 2 rib).

Hood. Cast on 86 sts. **Row 1:** * K 2, p 2; repeat from * ending k 2. **Row 2:** * P 2, k 2; repeat from * ending p 2. Repeat these 2 rows once more. **Row 5:** K 6, p 2, * k 2, p 2; repeat from * to last 6 sts, k 6. **Row 6:** P 6, k 2, * p 2, k 2; repeat from * to last 6 sts, p 6. **Row 7:** Same as Row 5. **Row 8:** K 8, work in rib pat as established to last 8 sts, k 8. **Row 9:** P 8, work in rib pat to last 8 sts, p 8. **Row 10:** Same as Row 8. **Row 11:** K 10, work in rib pat to last 10 sts, k 10. **Row 12:** P 10, work in rib pat to last 10 sts, p 10. **Row 13:** Same as Row 11. **Row 14:** K 12, work in rib pat to last 12 sts, k 12. **Row 15:** P 12, work in rib pat to last 12 sts, p 12. **Row 16:** Same as Row 14. Continue in this manner, working 2 sts more at each end in reverse stockinette st and 4 sts less in k 2, p 2, ribbing in center of every 3rd row, until 2 sts remain in ribbing in center. K next row. Break off yarn, leaving an 18″ end. Bind off and sew back seam, or sl 43 sts to a separate needle and, holding both needles tog, weave sts tog for center-back seam. NECKBAND AND TIES: Cast on 8 sts and work in garter st (k every row) for 38″. Bind off. Pin center-back seam of cap to center of neck band and sew together along neck, holding in to measure 4½″ either side of center seam. Steam lightly. Make 2 pompons; turn back center front of cap for 1″ and tack pompons in place as shown in photograph.

Boy's Knitted Cardigan

Directions are for 22″ size (to fit chest size 22″ and 24″). Changes for 24″ size are in parentheses.

Materials. Sirdar Baby Nylon—6 (7) balls. Knitting Needles Nos. 1 and 3. 1 dp or cable needle. 7 buttons.

Gauge. 7½ stitches—1″.

Back. With No. 1 needles cast on 107 (123) sts. **Row 1:** Sl 1, k 1, * p 1, k 1, repeat from * to last st, k 1. **Row 2:** Sl 1, * p 1, k 1, repeat from * to end of row. Repeat Rows 1 and 2 six times. Change to No. 3 needles. **Row 15:** Sl 1 (k 1, p 1) 7 (11) times, k 1, p 4, * sl next 3 sts onto dp needle and hold in back, k 3, then k the 3 sts from dp needle (for cable twist), p 6, sl next 2 sts onto dp needle and hold in back, k 2, then k 2 sts from dp needle (for "twist 4"), p 6, cable twist *, p 11, repeat from * to * once, p 4, (k 1, p 1) 7 (11) times, k 2. **Row 16:** Sl, (p 1, k 1) 7 (11) times, p 1, k 4, * p 6, k 6, p 4, k 6, p 6, * k 11, repeat from * to * once, k 4, (p 1, k 1) 8 (12) times. **Row 17:** Sl 1, (p 1, k 1) 7 (11) times, p 5, * k 6, p 4, sl next 2 sts onto dp needle and hold in back of work, k 2, then p 2 sts from dp needle (for "back twist"), sl next 2 sts onto dp needle and hold in front of work, p 2, then k 2 sts from dp needle (for front twist), p 4, k 6, * p 11, repeat from * to * once, p 5, (k 1, p 1) 7 (11) times, k 1. **Row 18:** Sl 1, (k 1, p 1) 7 (11) times, k 5, * p 6, (k 4, p 2) twice, k 4, p 6, * k 11, repeat from * to * once, k 5, (p 1, k 1) 7 (11) times, k 1. **Row 19:** Sl 1, (k 1, p 1) 7 (11) times, k 1, p 4, * k 6, p 2, back twist, p 4, front twist, p 2, k 6, * p 11, repeat from * to * once, p 4, (k 1, p 1) 7 (11) times, k 2. **Row 20:** Sl 1, (p 1, k 1) 7 (11) times, p 1, k 4, * p 6, k 2, p 2, k 8, p 2, k 2, p 6, * k 11, repeat from * to * once, k 4, (p 1, k 1) 8 (12) times. **Row 21:** Sl 1, (p 1, k 1) 7 (11) times, p 5, * cable twist, p 2, k 2, p 8, k 2, p 2, cable twist, * p 11, repeat from * to * once, p 5, (k 1, p 1) 7 (11) times, k 1. **Row 22:** Sl 1, (k 1, p 1) 7 (11) times, k 5, * p 6, k 2, p 2, k 8, p 2, k 2, p 6, * k 11, repeat from * to * once, k 5, (p 1, k 1) 7 (11) times, k 1. **Row 23:** Sl 1, (k 1, p 1) 7

(11) times, k 1, p 4, * k 6, p 2, front twist, p 4, back twist, p 2, k 6, * p 11, repeat from * to * once, p 4, (k 1, p 1) 7 (11) times, k 2. **Row 24:** Sl 1, (p 1, k 1) 7 (11) times, p 1, k 4, * p 6, (k 4, p 2) twice, k 4, p 6, * k 11, repeat from * to * once, k 4, (p 1, k 1) 8 (12) times. **Row 25:** Sl 1, (k 1, p 1) 7 (11) times, p 5, * k 6, p 4, front twist, back twist, p 4, k 6, * p 11, repeat from * to * once, p 5, (k 1, p 1) 7 (11) times, k 1. **Row 26:** Sl 1, (p 1, k 1) 7 (11) times, k 5, * p 6, k 6, p 4, k 6, p 6, * k 11, repeat from * to * once, k 5, (p 1, k 1) 7 (11) times, k 1. Repeat Rows 15 through 26 for pat. Continue in pat until piece measures 7 (8)″, end on wrong side. ARMHOLE SHAPING: Bind off 5 sts at beg of next 2 rows. Dec 1 st each end of next and every other row until 47 (59) sts remain. Now dec 1 st each end of every row until 27 (31) sts remain. Bind off in pat.

Sleeves. With No. 1 needles cast on 51 (55) sts. **Row 1:** Sl 1, k 1, * p 1, k 1, repeat from * to last st, k 1. **Row 2:** Sl 1, * p 1, k 1, repeat from * to end of row. Repeat Rows 1 and 2 six times more. Change to No. 3 needles. **Row 15:** Sl 1, k 1, * p 1, k 1, repeat from * to last st, k 1. **Row 16:** Sl 1, * p 1, k 1, repeat from * to end. **Row 17:** Same as Row 16. **Row 18:** Same as Row 15. Repeat Rows 15 through 18 for pat. Continuing in pat, inc 1 st each end of next and every 6th row until there are 65 (73) sts. Continue without shaping until pieces measure 8½ (10½)″ or desired length to underarm, end on wrong side. RAGLAN SHAPING: Bind off 5 sts at beg of next 2 rows. Dec 1 st each end of next and every 4th row until 47 (55) sts remain. Now dec 1 st each end of next and every other row until 3 (3) sts remain. **Next Row:** K 3 tog. Break off and fasten.

Left Front. With No. 1 needles cast on 59 (67) sts. **Row 1:** Sl 1, k 1, * p 1, k 1, repeat from * to last st, k 1. **Row 2:** Sl 1, * p 1, k 1, repeat from * to end. Repeat Rows 1 and 2 once. **Row 5:** Sl 1, k 1, * p 1, k 1, repeat from * to last 6 sts, bind off 2 sts, p 1, k 2. **Row 6:** Sl 1, p 1, k 1, p 1, cast on 2 sts, * k 1, p 1, repeat from * to last st, k 1. Repeat Rows 1 and 2 three times, then repeat Row 1 once. **Next Row:** Sl 1, (p 1, k 1) 4 times, slip these 9 sts onto a holder for front border, * p 1, k 1, repeat from * to end—50 (58) sts. Change to No. 3 needles. **Row 1:** Sl 1, (k 1, p 1) 7 (11) times, k 1, p 4, cable twist, p 6, twist 4, p 6, cable twist, p 1, k 1. **Row 2:** Sl 1, k 1, p 6, k 6, p 4, k 6, p 6, k 4, (p 1, k 1) 8 (12) times. **Row 3:** Sl 1, (p 1, k 1) 7 (11) times, p 5, k 6, p 4, back twist, front twist, p 4, k 6, p 1, k 1. **Row 4:** Sl 1, k 1, p 6, (k 4, p 2) twice, k 4, p 6, k 5, (p 1, k 1) 7 (11) times, k 1. **Row 5:** Sl 1, (k 1, p 1) 7 (11) times, k 1, p 4, k 6, p 2, back twist, p 4, front twist, p 2, k 6, p 1, k 1. **Row 6:** Sl 1, k 1, p 6, k 2, p 2, k 8, p 2, k 2, p 6, k 4, (p 1, k 1) 8 (12) times. **Row 7:** Sl 1, (p 1, k 1) 7 (11) times, p 5, cable twist, p 2, k 2, p 8, k 2, p 2, cable twist, p 1, k 1. **Row 8:** Sl 1, k 1, p 6, k 2, p 2, k 8, p 2, k 2, p 6, k 5, (p 1, k 1 7 (11) times, k 1. **Row 9:** Sl 1, (k 1, p 1) 7 (11) times, k 1, p 4, k 6, p 2, front twist, p 4, back twist, p 2, k 6, p 1, k 1. **Row 10:** Sl 1, k 1, p 6, k 4, (p 2, k 4) twice, p 6, k 4 (p 1, k 1) 8 (12) times. **Row 11:** Sl 1, (p 1, k 1) 7 (11) times, p 5, k 6, p 4, front twist, back twist, p 4, k 6, p 1, k 1. **Row 12:** Sl 1, k 1, p 6, k 6, p 4, k 6, p 6, k 5, (p 1, k 1) 7 (11) times, k 1. Repeat Rows 1 through 12 for pat. Continuing in pat, work until piece measures same as back to armhole, end on wrong side. ARMHOLE SHAPING: **Next Row:** Bind off 5 sts in pat, work in pat to last st, k 1. **Next Row:** Sl 1, work in pat to last st, k 1. Dec 1 st at armhole edge on next and every other row until 29 (37) sts remain. **Next Row:** Dec 1 st at armhole edge. Dec 1 st every other row until 26 (34) sts remain. NECK SHAPING: **Next Row:** Bind off 5 (7) sts in pat, work in pat to last st, k 1. Dec 1 st at armhole edge on next and every other row. At the same time dec 1 st at neck edge every row until 10 (15) sts remain. Now dec 1 st at armhole edge only every other row until 5 (7) sts remain, then dec 1 st at armhole edge only every row until 2 (2) sts remain. **Next Row:** K 2 together. Break off and fasten.

Left Front Border. With right side of work facing and No. 1 needles, attach yarn to first st on holder. **Row 1:** Sl 1, (k 1, p 1) 3 times, k 2. **Row 2:** Sl 1, (p 1, k 1) 4 times. Repeat Rows 1 and 2 three (4) times. ** **Next Row:** ** Sl 1, k 1, p 1, bind off 2 sts, p 1, k 2. **Next Row:** Sl 1, p 1, k 1, p 1, cast on 2 sts, k 1, p 1, k 1. Repeat Rows 1 and 2 eight (9) times **. Repeat from ** to ** 3 times. **Next Row:** Sl 1, k 1, p 1, bind off 2 sts, p 1, k 2. **Next Row:** Sl 1, p 1, k 1, p 1, cast on 2 sts, k 1, p 1, k 1. Repeat Rows 1 and 2 seven (8) times. Place these sts on a holder.

Right Front. Using No. 1 needles cast on 59 (67) sts. **Row 1:** Sl 1, k 1, * p 1, k 1, repeat from * to last st, k 1. **Row 2:** Sl 1, * p 1, k 1, repeat from * to end. Repeat Rows 1 and 2 five times, then Row 1 once. **Next Row:** Sl 1, * p 1, k 1, repeat from * to last 9 sts, slip remaining 9 sts onto a holder for front border—50 (58) sts. Change to No. 3 needles. **Row 1:** Sl 1, p 1, cable twist, p 6, twist 4, p 6, cable twist, p 4, (k 1, p 1) 7 (11) times, k 2. **Row 2:** Sl 1, (p 1, k 1) 7 (11) times, p 1, k 4, p 6, k 6, p 4, k 6, p 6, k 2. **Row 3:** Sl 1, p 1, k 6, p 4, back twist, front twist, p 4, k 6, p 5, (k 1, p 1) 7 (11) times, k 1. **Row 4:** Sl 1, (k 1, p 1) 7 (11) times, k 5, p 6, (k 4, p 2) twice, k 4, p 6, k 2. **Row 5:** Sl 1, p 1, k 6, p 2, back twist, p 4, front twist, p 2, k 6, p 4, (k 1, p 1) 7 (11) times, k 2. **Row 6:** Sl 1, (p 1, k 1) 7 (11) times, p 1, k 4, p 6, k 2, p 2, k 8, p 2, k 2, p 6, k 2. **Row 7:** Sl 1, p 1, cable twist, p 2, k 2, p 8, k 2, p 2, cable twist, p 5, (k 1, p 1) 7 (11) times, k 1. **Row 8:** Sl 1, (k 1, p 1) 7 (11) times, k 5, p 6, k 2, p 2, k 8, p 2, k 2, p 6, k 2. **Row 9:** Sl 1, p 1, k 6, p 2, front twist, p 4, back twist, p 2, k 6, p 4, (k 1, p 1) 7 (11) times, k 2. **Row 10:** Sl 1, (p 1, k 1) 7 (11) times, p 1, k 4, p 6, (k 4, p 2) twice, k 4, p 6, k 2. **Row 11:** Sl 1, p 1, k 6, p 4, front twist, back twist, p 4, k 6, p 5, (k 1, p 1) 7 (11) times, k 1. **Row 12:** Sl 1, (k 1, p 1) 7 (11) times, k 5, p 6, k 6, p 4, k 6, p 6, k 2. Repeat Rows 1 through 12 for pat. Continuing in pat, work until piece measures same as back to armhole, end on right side. ARMHOLE SHAPING: **Next Row:** Bind off 5 sts in pat, work in pat to last st, k 1. Dec 1 st at armhole edge on next and every other row until 29 (37) sts remain. **Next Row:** Dec 1 st at armhole edge, then dec 1 st every other row 27 (35) sts. NECK SHAPING: **Next Row:** Bind off 5 (7) sts in pat, work in pat to last 2 sts, k 2 tog. **Next Row:** Sl 1, work in pat to last st, k 1. Dec 1 st at neck edge every row. At the same time dec 1 st at armhole edge on next and every other row until 10 (15) sts remain. Dec 1 st at armhole edge only every other row until 5 (7) sts remain. Now dec at armhole edge only every row until 2 (2) sts remain. **Next Row:** K 2 tog. Break off and fasten.

Right Front Border. Work same as Left Border, omitting buttonholes. Do not break off yarn, slip these sts to a holder.

Finishing: Block pieces. Sew side, sleeve and raglan seams. NECKBAND: With right side of work facing and No. 1 needles sl 1, (k 1, p 1) 4 times from holder. Pick up and knit 23 (29) sts evenly along right side of neck, 2 sts from top of sleeve, 27 (31) sts from bound off sts at back of neck, 2 sts from other sleeve top and 23 (29) sts evenly along left side of neck, (p 1, k 1) 4 times, k 1, from second holder—95 (111) sts. **Row 1:** Sl 1, * p 1, k 1, repeat from * to end. **Row 2:** Sl 1, k 1, * p 1, k 1, repeat from * to last 6 sts. Bind off 2 sts, p 1, k 2. **Row 3:** Sl 1, p 1, k 1, p 1, cast on 2 sts, * k 1, p 1, repeat from * to last st, k 1. **Row 4:** Sl 1, k 1, * p 1, k 1, repeat from * to last st, k 1. **Row 5:** Sl 1, * p 1, k 1, repeat from * to end of row. Bind off loosely in ribbing. Sew front border seams. Sew on buttons.

FOR GIRLS: Work buttonholes in right front shoulder.

Cable Mittens

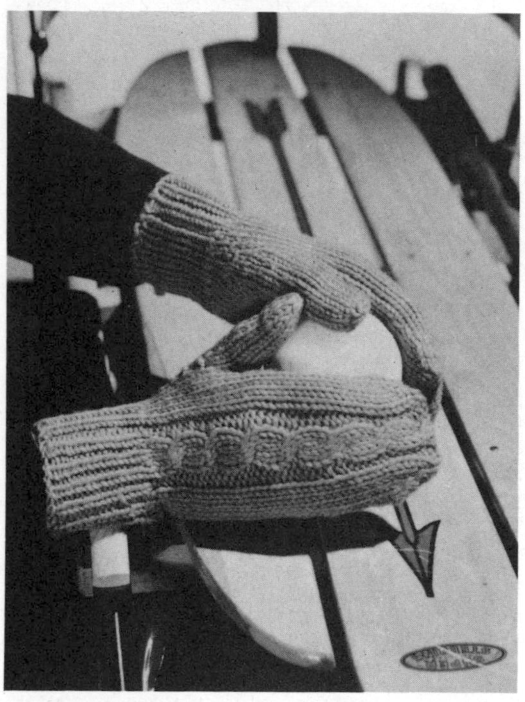

Directions are for Size 4. Changes for Sizes 5, 6, 7, 8, 9, 10, 11, 12, 13, and 14 are in parentheses.

Materials. Knitting Worsted, 4 ply—Sizes 4–12; 2 ozs. Sizes 13 and 14; 4 ozs. Double-Pointed Sock Needles, 1 set each No. 3 and No. 5.

Gauge. 5 sts—1″. 7 rnds—1″.

Right Mitten. Starting at cuff with No. 5 needles, cast on 26 (26–28–28–30–30–32–32–34–34–36) sts. Divide sts among 3 needles and join, being careful not to twist sts. Change to No. 3 needles and work in k 1, p 1 ribbing for 1¾ (2–2–2–2¼–2¼–2¼–2½–2½–2½–2½)″; inc 1 st on last rnd on Sizes 5, 7, 9, 11, and 13. Change to No. 5 needles and work as follows: **Rnd 1:** K 15 (16–16–17–17–18–18–19–19–20–20) sts, p 2, k 4 for cable rib, p 2, k 3 (3–4–4–5–5–6–6–7–7–8) sts. **Repeat rnd 1,** 1 (1–1–2–2–2–3–3–3–3–3) more time. THUMB GORE: **Rnd 1:** Place a marker on needle, p and k in first st, k in front and in back of next st, place a marker on needle, knit 13 (14–14–15–15–16–16–17–17–18–18) sts, p 2, k 4, p 2, k 3 (3–4–4–5–5–6–6–7–7–8) sts. Inc 1 st following the first marker and 1 st preceding the 2nd marker on every 3rd rnd, slipping the markers on every rnd until there are 8 (8–8–10–10–10–10–10–12–12–12) sts in thumb gore, *at the same time* making a cable over the cable rib on the 6th rnd and every 6th rnd thereafter (to make a cable, sl 2 sts onto a spare dp needle and hold in front of work, k next 2 sts on left-hand needle, k the 2 sts from the spare dp needle). When thumb gore is completed, work even for 2 (2–2–3–3–3–3–4–4–4–4) rnds. **Next rnd:** Slip the sts of the thumb gore onto a safety pin or stitch holder to be worked later, cast on 2 sts for inner side of thumb, join and work in pat over these 26 (27–28–29–30–31–32–33–34–35–36) sts until mitten, when tried on, reaches tip of little finger, or measures from last rnd of cuff 4½ (4½–4¾–5–5–5¼–5¼–5½–5¾–5¾–6)″. SHAPE TIP: **Rnd 1:** Sl 1, k 1, psso, k 9 (10–10–11–11–12–12–13–13–14–14) sts, k 2 tog, place a marker on needle, sl 1, k 1, psso, work in pat to within last 2 sts, k 2 tog. **Rnd 2:** Work in pat around without decreasing, sl the marker. **Rnd 3:** Sl 1, k 1, psso, k to within 2 sts preceding the marker, k 2 tog, sl marker, sl 1, k 1, psso, work in pat to within last 2 sts, k 2 tog. Repeat rnds 2 and 3 alternately until 14 (15–16–17–18–19–20–21–22–23–24) sts remain. **Next rnd:** On Sizes 5, 7, 9, 11, and 13, work in pat around, dec 1 st at center back of hand. **Next rnd:** Repeat rnd 3. On all sizes, place the sts of the palm on one needle and the sts of the back of hand on another needle and weave sts tog. THUMB: Slip the sts for the thumb onto 3 needles, pick up 2 sts over the 2 cast-on sts. K around until thumb reaches ¼" from tip, or measures 2 (2–2–2¼–2¼–2¼–2¼–2¼–2½–2½–2½)". SHAPE TIP: **Rnd 1:** * K 1, k 2 tog. Repeat from * around. **Next Rnd:** K around. **Next Rnd:** * K 2 tog. Repeat from * around. Break off, leaving an 8" length of yarn. Thread this length into a needle and draw through remaining sts. Pull up tightly and fasten securely on wrong side.

Left Mitten. Work as for Right Mitten until cuff has been completed. Change to No. 5 needles and work as follows: **Rnd 1:** K 3 (3–4–4–5–5–6–6–7–7–8) sts, p 2, k 4 (cable rib), p 2, k 15 (16–16–17–17–18–18–19–19–20–20) sts. Work as for Right Mitten to within first rnd of thumb gore. THUMB GORE: **Rnd 1:** Work in pat to within last 2 sts, place a marker on needle, p and k in next st, k in front and in back of next st, place a marker on needle—position of Thumb Gore has now been established. Complete as for Right Mitten.

Finishing. Press Mittens through a damp cloth.

Man's Outdoor Sweater

Shown in Color Plate 12

Directions are for small size (36–38). Changes for medium size (40–42) and large size (44–46) are in parentheses.

Materials. Knitting Worsted (2-oz. balls): Main Color (MC)—9 (10–11) balls. Color A—2 balls; Color B—1 ball; Color C—1 ball. Knitting Needles, 1 set each Nos. 6 and 10.

Gauge. 9 sts—2". 5 rows—1".

Back. With MC and No. 6 needles, cast on 80 (86–92) sts. Work k 1, p 1 ribbing for 1½". Change to No. 10 needles and work 2 rows of stockinette, increasing 5 sts across first row. Following the chart, work pattern on the 85 (91–97 sts until piece measures 13 (14–15)". ARMHOLES: Bind off 2 sts at beg of next 6 rows, then continue in pattern on remaining 73 (79–85) sts until armholes

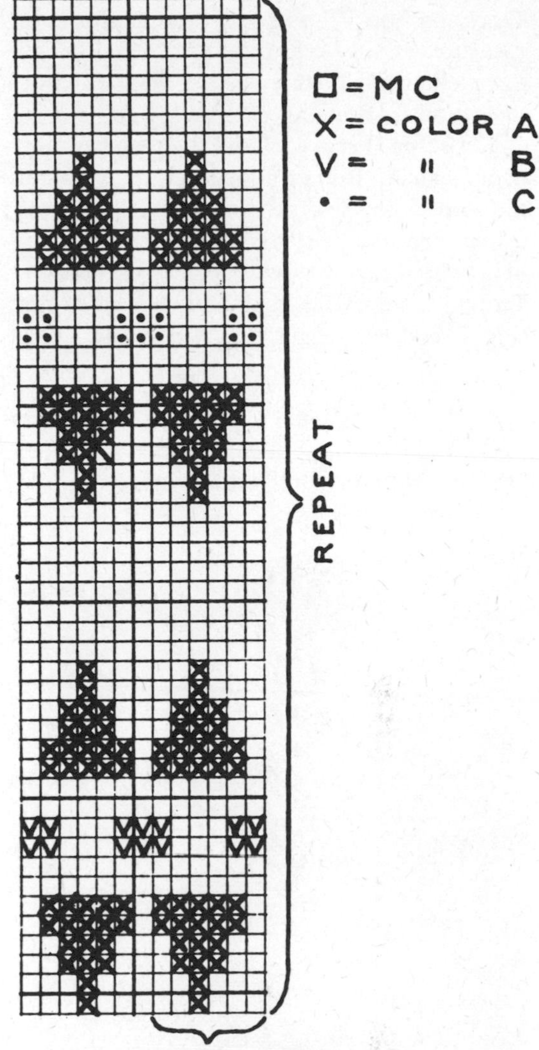

measure 8 (9–10)". *Note:* It is not necessary to end pattern at a certain point. SHOULDERS: Bind off 4 (6–6) sts loosely at beg of next 4 rows, then 6 (4–6) sts at beg of next 2 rows. With MC work in stockinette on remaining 45 (47–49) sts, decreasing 1 st at each side every other row 4 times. Bind off on 9th row.

Front. Work same as back.

Sleeves. With MC and No. 6 needles, cast on 40 (40–44) sts. Work k 1, p 1 ribbing for 2½". Change to No. 10 needles and work 2 rows of stockinette increasing 3 (3–5) sts in first row. Work pattern on the 43 (43–49) sts for 2 (1–1) inches following the chart; then keeping established pattern, inc 1 st at each side every 4th row 15 (18–18) times.

Work on the 73 (79–85) sts until sleeve measures 16 (17–18)″ above ribbing. SHAPE CAP: Bind off 2 sts at beg of next 6 rows, then bind off remaining 61 (67–73) sts.

Finishing. Press each piece on wrong side, using a steam iron or a medium-hot iron and a damp cloth. Sew seams and set in sleeves using a running back-stitch, except for ribbing which is sewn with an overcast stitch. Turn down hem at neck and sew to wrong side. Press seams lightly on wrong side.

Man's Aran Knit Sweater

Shown in Color Plate 13

Directions are for small size (36–38). Changes for medium size (40–42) and large size (44–46) are in parentheses.

Materials. Knitting Worsted (2-oz. ball) 14 (15–16). Circular Knitting Needles, Nos. 6 and 8. Cable-Stitch Needle.

Gauge. 5 sts—1″; 7 rows—1″.

Pattern Stitch for Back and Front. Row 1 (right side): P 2 (k 2, p 2) 5 (6–7) times, k 12 for cable, p 2 (k 2, p 2) 6 (6–7) times, k 12 for cable, p 2 (k 2, p 2) 5 (6–7) times. **Row 2 (wrong side):** K 2 (p 2, k 2) 5 (6–7) times, p 12 for cable, k 2 (p 2, k 2) 6 (6–7) times, p 12 for cable, k 2 (p 2, k 2) 5 (6–7) times. **Row 3:** (K 2, p 2) 5 (6–7) times, k 2, k 12 for cable, k 2 (p 2, k 2) 5 (5–6) times, p 2, k 2, k 12 for cable, k 2 (p 2, k 2) 5 (6–7) times. **Row 4:** (P 2, k 2) 5 (6–7) times, p 2, p 12 for cable, p 2 (k 2, p 2) 5 (5–6) times, k 2, p 2, p 12 for cable, p 2 (k 2, p 2) 5 (6–7) times. **Rows 5 through 8:** Repeat Rows 1 through 4. **Row 9:** P 2 (k 2, p 2) 5 (6–7) times, sl next 4 sts onto cable stitch needle and hold in FRONT of work, k next 4 sts, put 4 sts on cable stitch needle to BACK of work, k next 4 sts, k the 4 sts from cable stitch needle (cable twist), p 2 (k 2, p 2) 6 (6–7) times, work cable twist on next 12 sts, p 2 (k 2, p 2) 5 (6–7) times. **Row 10:** Repeat Row 2. **Row 11:** Repeat Row 3. **Row 12:** Repeat Row 4. **Rows 13 through 16:** Repeat Rows 1 through 4. Repeat these 16 rows for pattern stitch for back and front.

Back. Using size 6 needle, cast on 94 (102–114) sts. Work back and forth as follows: **Row 1:** K 2, * p 2, k 2, repeat from * across row. **Row 2:** P 2, * k 2, p 2, repeat from * across row. Repeat these 2 rows for 3 inches, ending with Row 2. Change to size 8 needle and work back and forth in pattern st until the entire piece measures 15 (15½–15½) inches, ending with a wrong-side row. SHAPE RAGLAN ARMHOLES: At the beg of each of the next 2 rows bind off 2 (3–3) sts. Dec 1 st each end of needle every other row 20 (21–23) times—you now have 50 (54–62) sts. On next row dec 6 sts at even intervals. Sl remaining 44 (48–56) sts onto a holder.

Front. Work same as back.

Pattern Stitch for Sleeves. Row 1: P 2 (k 2, p 2) 5 times, k 12 for cable, p 2 (k 2, p 2) 5 times. **Row 2:** K 2 (p 2, k 2) 5 times, p 12 for cable, k 2 (p 2, k 2) 5 times. **Row 3:** (K 2, p 2) 5 times, k 2, k 12 for cable, k 2 (p 2, k 2) 5 times. **Row 4:** (P 2, k 2) 5 times, p 2, p 12 for cable, p 2 (k 2, p 2) 5 times. **Rows 5 through 8:** Repeat Rows 1 through 4. **Row 9:** P 2 (k 2, p 2) 5 times, work cable twist on next 12 sts, p 2 (k 2, p 2) 5 times. **Row 10:** Repeat Row 2. **Row 11:** Repeat Row 3. **Row 12:** Repeat Row 4. **Rows 13 through 16:** Repeat Rows 1 through 4. Repeat these 16 rows for pattern stitch for sleeves.

Sleeves. With size 6 needle cast on 54 sts. Working back and forth, repeat Rows 1 and 2 of back ribbing for 3½ inches, inc 1 st each end of last row—56 sts. Change to size 8 needle and work back and forth in pattern st for sleeves, inc 1 st each end of needle every 1½ (1–1) inch 9 (13–15) times, forming new double seed st patterns as sts are increased. Work even in pattern as established on 74 (82–86) sts until entire piece measures 19 (19¼–19½) inches. SHAPE RAGLAN CAP: At the beg of each of the next 2 rows bind off 2 (3–3) sts. Dec 1 st each end of needle every other row 20 (21–23) times—you now have 30 (34–34) sts. On next row dec 4 sts at even intervals. Sl remaining 26 (30–30) sts onto a holder.

Finishing. Sew sleeves to back and front armholes. Sew underarm seams.

Yoke. With right side facing you, sl sts from holder onto size 6 needle. Join yarn and k 2, p 2 in ribbing for 6 inches. Bind off in ribbing. Roll last 3 inches of yoke to right side and tack loosely. Steam seams.

Man's Cable Pullover

Directions are for Size 36. Changes for sizes 38, 40, 42 are in parentheses.

Materials. Mohair Yarn (1-oz. balls) 13 (14–16–17). Knitting Needles, No. 3, 5, and 9, 1 set each.

Gauge. Pattern stitch on No. 9 needles; 9 sts—2″; 11 rows—2″.

Back. With No. 5 needles, cast on 86 (90–96–100) sts. K 1 and p 1 in ribbing for 2″, inc 1 st at end of last row. Change to No. 9 needles. Work in pat on 87 (91–97–101) sts: **Row 1 (right side):** P 2 (4–2–4), * k 3, p 2, repeat from * across, ending k 3, p 2 (4–2–4). **Row 2:** K 2 (4–2–4), * p 3, k 2, repeat from *, ending p 3, k 2 (4–2–4). **Row 3:** P 2 (4–2–4), * k 3 tog through back of sts but do not drop from left-hand needle, yo and k same 3 sts tog through back of sts once more, then drop them from left-hand needle for cable, p 2, repeat from * across, ending cable on next 3 sts, p 2 (4–2–4). **Row 4:** Repeat Row 2. **Rows 5 and 6:** Repeat Rows 1 and 2. Repeat these 6 rows for pattern, working to 15″ (or length desired), ending on right side. RAGLAN ARMHOLES: Bind off 4 sts at beg of next 2 rows. Decrease 1 st each side every other row until 21 (21–23–23) sts remain. Slip them to a holder for back of neck.

Front. With No. 5 needles cast on 86 (90–96–100) sts. K 1 and p 1 in ribbing for 2″, increasing 1 st at end of last row. Change to No. 9 needles and work in pattern on the 87 (91–97–101) sts to 15″ (or length desired) from start, ending with same pattern row as on back. RAGLAN ARMHOLES AND NECK: Bind off 6 sts at beg of next 2 rows. Next row work 37 (39–42–44) sts and slip them to a holder, p center st and slip to safety pin for neck, work to end of row. Next row dec 1 st at armhole edge, then every other row 22 (24–26–28) times more *and at the same time* dec 1 st at neck every 4th row 11 (11–12–12) times. Bind off remaining 3 sts. Starting at center front, work other side to correspond, reversing the shaping.

Sleeves. With No. 3 needles, cast on 46 (50–54–58) sts. K 1 and p 1 in ribbing for 3″, inc 6 (6–8–8) sts across last row. Change to No. 9 needles. Work in pattern same as on back on the 52 (56–62–66) sts. Inc 1 st each side every 6th row 10 (10–11–11) times, working added sts in pattern, careful to work new cables at each end 2 purl sts apart. Work on the 72 (76–84–88) sts to about 19″, or desired length from start, ending with same row as on back. RAGLAN SLEEVE CAP: On sizes 40 and 42, dec 1 st each side every row 4 times. On all sizes dec 1 st each side every other row 24 (26–26–28) times. For left sleeve, end on right side of work; for right sleeve, on wrong side.

Neck. Mark end of last row for front neck edge. Next row dec 1 st at neck edge. Dec 1 st at same edge every row 9 times more, then bind off 4 sts at the same edge twice *and at the same time* dec 1 st at back edge every 4th row 3 times. Bind off remaining 3 sts. With first dec on sleeve caps matching first dec on armholes, sew sleeve caps to front and to right back raglan only. End the seams with last dec on front matching start of neck on sleeve caps.

Neckband. With No. 3 needles, starting at open seam on right side of work, pick up and k 60 (62–66–68) sts on left neck edge, k st from safety pin and mark for center st, pick up and k 60 (62–66–68) sts on other side, k across sts on back of neck, decreasing 9 sts across. Work on the 133 (137–147–151) sts. **Row 1 (wrong side):** p 1, * k 1, p 1, repeat from * across. Continue in established ribbing, decreasing 1 st each side of center st every other row 6 times. Bind off in ribbing. Sew open seams, joining neckband. Sew underarm and sleeve seams with last 1¼″ at top of sleeve to bound-off sts at underarm.

Man's Muffler

Material. Fingering Yarn—four 1-oz. skeins. Knitting Needles, No. 4 (10-inch). Steel Crochet Hook, No. 3.

Gauge. 7 sts—1″.

Scarf. Cast on 67 sts. Work in pattern as follows: **Row 1:** * K 1; yarn forward, slip 1 as if to p; yarn in back, repeat from * across row, ending k 1. **Row 2:** P across row. **Row 3:** * Yarn forward, slip 1; yarn in back, k 1; repeat from * across row, ending slip 1. **Row 4:** P across row. Repeat these 4 rows for pattern until work measures 46″ from start. Bind off. Work 1 row of sc along sides.

Fringe. To make 4″ length strands, wind yarn over a 2″ cardboard. Cut loops at one edge. Fold 3 strands in half and with crochet hook, pull through and knot in every other st across each end of scarf.

Color Plate 15 CRAZY-QUILT AFGHAN

This splendid, colorful specimen is knit in lengthwise strips, embellished with bits of embroidery, then sewn together. The complete directions for making are on page 337.

Color Plate 16 AFGHAN SLIPON SWEATER

An outdoor sweater of colorful squares crocheted in afghan stitch and then embroidered in cross stitch. Instructions and diagrams for making are given on page 379.

Man's Argyles

Directions are given for Medium Length. Changes for Bermuda Length are in parentheses.

Materials. Nylon Sweater and Sock Yarn —Main Color (M)—2 (3) ozs.; 1 oz. each of the following colors: Diamond (X), Diamond (Z), Crossline (o), and Crossline (O); Knitting Needles No. 3; Double-Pointed Needles No. 2.

Gauge. 9 sts—1″ (No. 2 Needles). 8 sts —1″ (No. 3 Needles).

Cuffs. To prevent stitches from slipping off, place rubber band at one end of each of 2 No. 2 Needles and with M cast on 68 sts loosely. Work in k 2, p 2 ribbing for 3 (1½)″. Change to stockinette st (for Bermuda Length, change to No. 3 Needles and work 1″ with M), then work pat from Chart twisting strands when changing color (by picking up the next color from underneath the color being dropped). Repeat the 33 rows of Chart once more (4 times more) to heel, reversing colors, *at the same time,* when 3 Diamond Patterns have been completed, change to No. 2 Needles for remainder of Sock. Place 17 sts from each end onto st holders for heel. On center 34 sts, work 1 more Diamond, reversing colors. Sl these sts onto st holder.

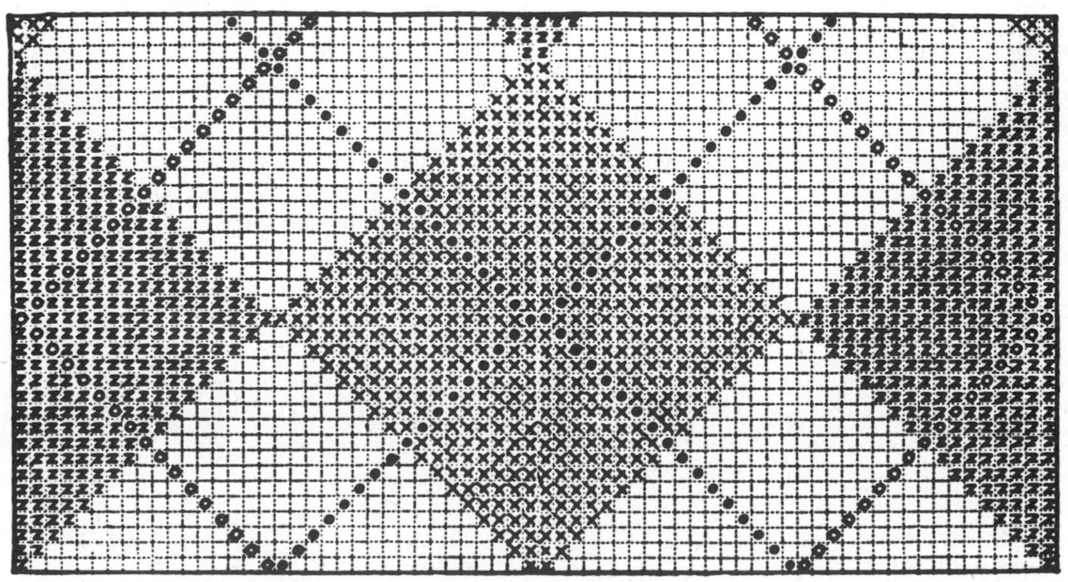

□—M—Main Color Z—Diamond X—Diamond o—Crossline ●—Crossline

Heel. Slip sts from holders onto one needle. Working on the 34 sts of heel only, work as follows: **Row 1:** (Right side of work) * sl 1, k 1, repeat from * across row. **Row 2:** Sl 1, then p across row. Repeat these 2 rows 17 times more (36 rows). TO TURN HEEL: **Row 1:** K 22, sl 1, k 1, psso, turn. **Row 2:** Sl 1, p 10, p 2 tog, turn. **Row 3:** Sl 1, k 10, sl 1, k 1, psso, turn. Repeat rows 2 and 3 until all sts are worked off each side (12 sts remaining on needle). Working on 2 needles, on wrong side of work, pick up and p 18 sts at side of heel, turn. **Row 1:** K across the 30 sts on needle, pick up and k 18 sts at other side of heel (48 sts). **Row 2:** P across row. **Row 3:** K 2 tog, work across row, ending k 2 tog. Repeat rows 2 and 3 until 34 sts remain.

Work even on the 34 heel sts until work measures same length as instep. K 17 to center of needle, then join sole to instep and work around as follows: 1st needle: k 17; 2nd needle: k across instep sts; 3rd needle: k 17. Work around (68 sts) until foot measures 9½″ from back of heel (or desired length)—allowing 2″ to finish toe.

To Shape Toe. Row 1: 1st needle: K to last 3 sts on needle, k 2 tog, k 1; 2nd needle: k 1, slip 1, k 1, psso, k to last 3 sts, k 2 tog, k 1; 3rd needle: k 1, slip 1, k 1, psso, k to end of needle. **Row 2:** K. Repeat last 2 rows until 24 sts remain. With 3rd needle k across 6 sts of 1st needle (12 sts on each of 2 needles). Weave sts tog. (See Weaving Toes of Socks.) Sew seams.

Travel Slipper

Directions are for Ladies' Sizes 5 to 8½.

Materials. Sports Yarn—one 1-oz. skein each of Color A and Color B (we used white with blue tops). Knitting Needles, 1 set No. 1.

Gauge. Garter stitch: 8 sts—1″. 18 rows (9 ridges) to 1″. Ribbing: 11 rows to 1″.

Slippers. With Color A, cast on 7 sts for strap. **Row 1:** With yarn at front, sl 1 as to p, with yarn at back, k to end of row. Repeat Row 1 twice more. **Next row:** Sl 1, k 2, yo, k 2 tog for buttonhole, k to end. Repeat Row

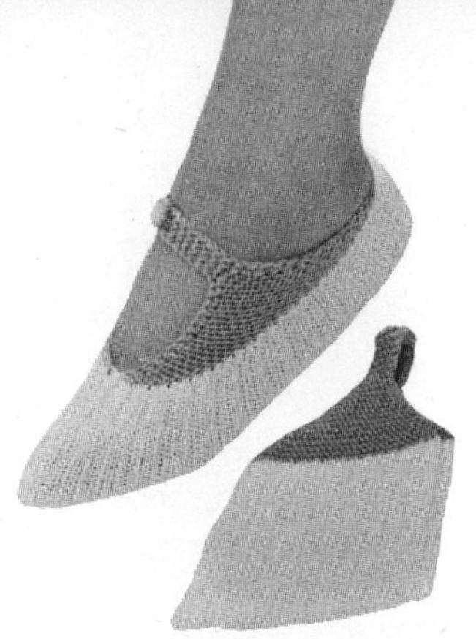

1 to 1½″ from start. **Inc Row:** Sl 1, inc 1 st in next st, k to end. Repeat inc row until there are 32 sts. Repeat Row 1 on the 32 sts. Break off A. With B, k 1 then inc 1 st in each of next 30 sts, k 1. Work on the 62 sts as follows: **Row 1 (wrong side):** P 2, * k 2, p 2, repeat from * across. **Row 2:** K 2, * p 2, repeat from * across. Repeat these 2 rows for 6½″, ending on wrong side. Break off B. With A, k 1 then k 2 tog 30 times, k 1. Repeat Row 1 on the 32 sts for strap. **Dec Row:** Sl 1, k 2 tog, k to end. Repeat dec row until 7 sts rem. Repeat row 1 on the 7 sts for strap. Work for 1½″. Bind off.

Fold in half and sew side eges of B sections tog with matching yarn. Sew on button opposite buttonhole.

Woman's Aran Cardigan

This is for experienced knitters only. Directions are for Size 12. Changes for Sizes 14, 16, and 18 are in parentheses.

Materials. Knitting Worsted—4 ply, 14 (14–15–15) 2-oz. skeins. Knitting Needles, Nos. 4 and 6. 1 Double-Pointed Needle. 7 Buttons.

Gauge. STOCKINETTE ST: 5 sts—1″; 7 rows—1″. PATTERN ST: 7½ sts—1″.

Blocking Measurements:

Bust (cardigan buttoned) . . . . 35½ (37½–41½)″
Width across back at underarm . . 17½ (18½–19½–20½)″
Width across each front at underarm . . . . . . 9½ (10–19½–11)″
Length from lower edge to underarm . . . . . 14 (14–14½–14½)″
Length of sleeve seam . . . . 13 (13–13½–13½)″
Width across sleeve at upper

arm . . . . 13 (13½–14–14½)"

Back. With No. 4 needles, cast on 88 (93–98–103) sts. Work in stockinette st for 9 rows. K 1 row on purl side of work to form hemline. Change to No. 6 needles and continue in stockinette st until back measures 14 (14–14½–14½)" above hemline. SHAPE ARMHOLES: Bind off 5 sts at beg of the next 2 rows. Dec 1 st each end every other row 5 (6–7–8) times. Work on 68 (71–74–77) sts until armholes measure 8 (8¼–8½–8¾)". SHAPE SHOULDERS: Bind off 6 sts at beg of next 6 rows; then bind off 4 (5–6–7) sts at beg of next 2 rows. Bind off remaining 24 (25–26–27) sts for back of neck.

Left Front. With No. 4 needles, cast on 63 (68–73–78) sts. Work in stockinette st for 9 rows. K 1 row on purl side to form hemline. Continue in stockinette st for 8 rows. Change to No. 6 needles and work in pat as follows: **Row 1:** K 1 (2–3–4) sts; skip next st, k in st below skipped st, k skipped st and pass first st over second st (raised k st); p 2, k 6, p 2 (for cable); work a raised k st; p 8 (k 4, p 8 for lozenge pat; work a raised k st; p 2, k 6, p 2; work a raised k st; p 12 (16–20–24) sts for popcorn pat; work a raised k st, k 5 (front border). **Row 2:** K 5; skip next st, p in st below skipped st, p skipped st and pass first st over second st (raised p st), * k, p and k in next st, sl 1, k 2 tog, psso, repeat from * 2 (3–4–5) times more for popcorn pat, raised p st, k 2, p 6, k 2, raised p st, k 8, p 4, k 8, raised p st, k 2, p 6, k 2, raised p st, p 1 (2–3–4) sts. **Row 3:** K 1 (2–3–4) sts; raised k st, p 2, k 6, p 2, raised k st; p 7; sl next st on dp needle and hold in back of work, k next 2 sts, p st from dp needle (k–2 rib moved to right); sl next 2 sts on dp needle and hold in front of work, p next st, k sts from dp needle (k–2 rib moved to left), p 7, complete same as Row 1. **Row 4:** K 5, raised p st, * sl 1, k 2 tog, psso; k, p and k in next st, repeat from * 2 (3–4–5) times more for popcorn pat (these 4 rows constitute popcorn pat), raised p st, k 2, p 6, k 2, raised p st, k 7, p 2, k 2, p 2, k 7, raised p st, k 2, p 6, k 2, raised p st, p 1 (2–3–4) sts. **Row 5:** K 1, (2–3–4) sts, raised k st, p 2; sl next 3 sts on dp needle and hold in back of work, k next 3 sts, k sts from dp needle (cable twist); p 2, raised k st, p 6, move k–2 rib to right, p 2, move k–2 rib to left, p 6; raised k st, p 2, twist cable, p 2, complete row. **Row 6:** Same as Row 2 through 3rd raised p st, k 6, p 2, k 4, p 2, k 6, complete same as Row 2. **Row 7:** Same as Row 1 to lozenge pat, p 5, move k–2 rib to right, p 4, move k–2 rib to left, p 5, complete same as Row 1. **Row 8:** Same as Row 4 through 3rd raised p st, k 5, p 2, k 6, p 2, k 5, complete row. **Row 9:** Work to lozenge pat, p 4, move k–2 rib to right, p 6, move k–2 rib to left, p 4, complete row. **Row 10:** Same as Row 2 through 3rd raised p st, k 4, p 2, k 8, p 2, k 4, complete row. **Row 11:** Work to lozenge pat, p 3, move k–2 rib to right, p 8, move k–2 rib to left, p 3, complete row. **Row 12:** Same as Row 4 to 3rd raised p st, k 3, p 2, k 10, p 2, k 3, complete row. **Row 13:** Working a cable twist as on Row 5, work to lozenge pat, p 2, move k–2 rib to right, p 10, move k–2 rib to left, p 2, complete row. **Row 14:** Same as Row 2 through 3rd raised p st, k 2, p 2, k 12, p 2, k 2, complete row. **Row 15:** Work to lozenge pat, p 1, move k–2 rib to right, p 12, move k–2 rib to left, p 1, complete row. **Row 16:** Same as Row 4 through 3rd raised p st, k 1, p 2, k 14, p 2, k 1, complete row. **Row 17:** Work to lozenge pat, p 1, move k–2 rib to *left,* p 12, move k–2 rib to *right,* p 1, complete row. **Row 18:** Repeat Row 14. **Row 19:** Work to lozenge pat, p 2, move k–2 rib to left, p 10, move k–2 rib to right, p 2, complete row. **Row 20:** Repeat Row 12. **Row 21:** Working cable twists as on Row 5, work to lozenge pat, p 3, move k–2 rib to left, p 8, move k–2 rib to right, p 3, complete row. **Row 22:** Repeat Row 10. **Row 23:** Work to lozenge pat, p 4, move k–2 rib to left, p 6, move k–2 rib to right, p 4, complete row. **Row 24:** Repeat Row 8. **Row 25:** Work to lozenge pat, p 5, move k–2 rib to left, p 4, move k–2 rib to right, p 5, complete row. **Row 26:** Repeat Row 6. **Row 27:** Work to lozenge pat, p 6, move k–2 rib to left, p 2, move k–2 rib to right, p 6, complete row. **Row 28:** Repeat Row 4. **Row 29:** Working

cable twists as on Row 5, work to lozenge pat, p 7, move k–2 rib to left, move next k–2 rib to right, p 7, complete row. **Row 30:** Repeat Row 2. **Row 31:** Work to lozenge pat, p 8, sl next 4 sts on dp needle and wrap yarn tightly around them twice, k these 4 sts, p 8, complete row. **Row 32:** Same as Row 4 to 3rd raised p st, k 8, p 4, k 8, complete row. Repeat these 32 rows for pattern. Work in pat until front measures same as back to underarm. SHAPE ARMHOLE: At arm edge bind off 5 sts. Dec 1 st at same edge every other row 5 (6–7–8) times. Work on 53 (57–61–65) sts until armhole measures 6 (6¼–6½–6¾)″. SHAPE NECK: At front edge work 14 (16–18–20) sts and slip these sts on a holder. (Work any broken popcorn pats in stockinette st.) Dec 1 st at neck edge every row 4 (5–6–7) times. Work on 35 (36–37–38) sts until armhole measures same as back. SHAPE SHOULDERS: At arm edge bind off 6 sts every other row 5 times, then bind off remaining 5 (6–7–8) sts.

Right Front. Work same as left front for 4 rows. BUTTONHOLE: Starting at front edge work 2 sts, bind off next 2 sts, complete row. On the next row cast on 2 sts over 2 sts bound off previous row. Complete hem as on left front, working a buttonhole on the 5th row above hemline. Change to No. 6 needles. Set up pat as follows: K 5 (front border), raised k st, p 12 (16–20–24) sts for popcorn pat; raised k st; p 2, k 6, p 2 for cable pat; raised k st; p 8, k 4, p 8 for lozenge pat; raised k st, p 2, k 6, p 2, for cable; raised k st, k 1 (2–3–4). Work to correspond to left front, reversing all shaping. Work 6 more buttonholes, evenly spaced, the last one to be made in neckband.

Sleeves. With No. 4 needles, cast on 42 (44–46–48) sts. Work in stockinette st for 7 rows, k next row on purl side to form hemline, continue in stockinette st for 7 rows. P the next row, inc at even intervals to 50 (52–54–56) sts. Change to No. 6 needles and set up pat as follows: **Row 1:** K 7 (8–9–10) sts, raised k st; p 2, k 6, p 2 for cable pat; raised k st; p 12 for popcorn pat; raised k st; p 2, k 6, p 2 for cable; raised k st, k 7 (8–9–10) sts. Working raised sts, cables, and popcorn pat as set up and remaining sts in stockinette st, inc 1 st each end every 6th row 11 (11–12–12) times. Work on 72 (74–78–80) sts until sleeve measures 13 (13–13½–13½)″ above hemline. SHAPE CAP: Bind off 5 sts at beg of next 2 rows. Dec 1 st each end every other row until 36 sts remain, then dec 1 st each end every row until 16 sts remain. Bind off.

Pockets. With No. 6 needles, cast on 25 sts. Work in stockinette st for 5″. Bind off. Make one more.

Finishing. Block pieces to measurements. Block without destroying raised effect of pattern sts. Fronts have more sts than backs. "Full" in front to back on shoulders. Sew shoulder seams. NECKBAND: With No. 4 needles and right side facing you, pick up 80 (84–88–92) sts around neck, including sts from holders. P 1 row, k 1 row, p 1 row. Work a buttonhole on right front of next 2 rows. K 1 row, p 1 row, k 2 rows (hemline). **Row 1:** K 5, p 2, * k 2, p 2, repeat from * to last 5 sts, k 5. **Row 2:** P 5, k 2, * p 2, k 2, repeat from * to last 5 sts, p 5. Repeating these 2 rows, work a buttonhole on the next 2 rows, work 3 more rows. Bind off. Leaving a 5″ opening on each side 2½″ above hemline for pockets, sew side seams. Sew shoulder and sleeve seams. Set in sleeves. Sew pockets to back edge of opening, tack to front on wrong side. Turn under hems and sew in place. Finish buttonholes. Press seams. Sew buttons in place.

Knitted Coat

Directions are for Size 10. Changes for Sizes 12, 14, 16 and 18 are in parentheses.
Bust Size 32½ (34–35½–37–39)″.

Materials. Mohair (40-gram ball); 17 (18–19–20–21) balls of Medium Blue, 15 (16–17–18–19) balls of Light Blue. 3 (3–3–3¼–3¼) yards of 45″ lining fabric. ¼ yard of bias Pellon. Knitting Needles, Nos. 10 and 11. Aluminum Crochet Hook, Size G.

Gauge. Stockinette stitch on size 11 needles 3 sts—1″; 4 rows—1″.

Note: Entire garment is worked with two strands (one strand of each color held tog).

Directions are for 38 (38½–39–39½–40)″ length measured (before blocking) from center back of neck. The knitted pieces will stretch about 3″ in length and 3″ in width in the blocking. For longer or shorter coat, make adjustment before first dec row.

Back. RIGHT SLEEVE SECTION: With No. 11 needles, cast on 3 sts. **Row 1:** Inc 1 st in first st, p 2. **Row 2:** Inc 1 st in first st, k 2, inc 1 st in last st. **Row 3:** Inc 1 st in first st, p to end of row. **Row 4:** Inc 1 st in first st, k to last st, inc 1 st in last st. **Row 5:** Repeat Row 3. **Rows 6 through 23:** Repeat Rows 4 and 5 nine times more. The beg of k rows is sleeve edge. Slip these 37 sts onto a holder. LEFT SLEEVE SECTION: With size 11 needles cast on 3 sts. **Row 1:** P 2, inc 1 st in last st. **Row 2:** Inc 1 st in first st, k 2, inc 1 st in last st. **Row 3:** P to last st, inc 1 st in last st. **Row 4:** Inc 1 st in first st, k to last st, inc 1 st in last st. **Row 5:** Repeat Row 3. **Rows 6 through 23:** Repeat Rows 4 and 5 nine times more. The end of k rows is sleeve edge. Slip these 37 sts onto a holder. Starting at lower edge of back with No. 11 needles, cast on 74 (76–78–80–83) sts. Work in stockinette st until back measures 14½″ (or length desired) from start. Dec 1 st each side of next row. Repeat, dec every 2″ 6 times more. Work on the remaining 60 (62–64–66–69) sts until back measures 28″ (or length desired) from start, ending with a p row. Break yarn. TO JOIN SLEEVE SECTIONS: K across sts of right sleeve, back and left sleeve. Mark each end of last row. *Sizes 14, 16 and 18 only,* continue in stockinette st, inc'ing 1 st each side every 2nd (4th–4th) row once. *On all sides,* continue in stockinette st on the 134 (136–140–142–145) sts for 4 (6–8–10–12) rows above markers ending on wrong side. SLEEVE AND SHOULDER: Dec 1 st each side every row 26 times. Bind off 4 sts at beg of next 6 rows. Place a marker on needle 13 sts in from each end on last row. Bind off 9 (9–10–10–11) sts at beg of next row, k across, dec 3 (3–4–4–4) sts evenly spaced between the 2 markers. Bind off 9 (9–10–10–11) sts at beg of next 3 (1–3–1–3) rows. *On sizes 12 and 16 only,* bind off 10 (11) sts at beg of next 2 rows. *All sizes:* Bind off remaining 19 (19–20–20–21) sts.

Left Front. Work sleeve section same as for right back. Starting at lower edge of front, with No. 11 needles cast on 49 (50–51–52–54) sts. Work in stockinette st for 14½″ (or same as back), ending with a p row. **Next row:** K 2 tog, k to end of row. Repeat dec at side edge every 2″ twice more. Work on the remaining 46 (47–48–49–51) sts until front has same number of rows as back to underarm, ending with a p row. Break yarn.

TO JOIN SLEEVE: K across 37 sts of sleeve and continue across sts of front. Place marker at sleeve edge. *On sizes 14, 16 and 18 only,* inc 1 st at sleeve edge every 2nd (4th–4th) row once. *On all sizes* work on the 83 (84–86–87–89) sts for 4 (6–8–10–12) rows above marker, ending on wrong side. SLEEVE, NECK AND SHOULDER: Dec 1 st at sleeve edge *every* row 26 times, placing a marker on needle 23 (23–24–24–25) sts in from front edge while working last row—there are now a total of 57 (58–60–61–63) sts on needle. **Next row:** Bind off 4 sts, k to within 2 sts *before* marker, k 2 tog, k to end of row. P 3 and sl them to a safety pin for neck facing, p next 6 sts and sl these to another pin to be woven to collar later, p next 8 sts and sl these to a holder for collar facing, p to end of row. *Note:* Neck and remainder of shoulder shaping are now worked at the same time from * to *. * Dec 1 st at neck edge *every* row 6 (6–7–7–8) times and repeat dec before marker every other row 3

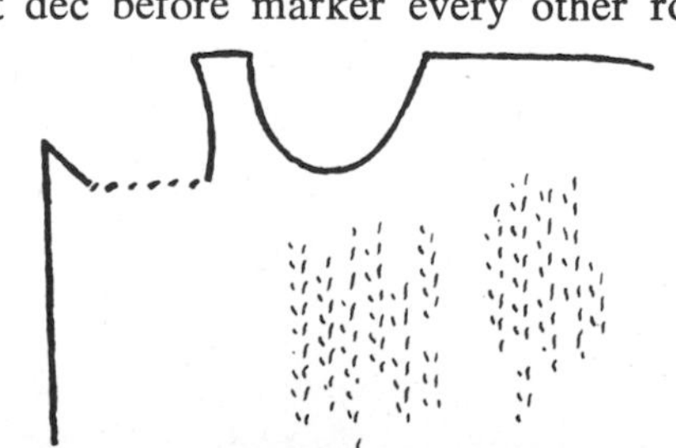

times more *while doing the following:* Bind off 4 sts at sleeve edge twice more, bind off 9 (9–10–10–11) sts at same edge 2 (1–2–1–2) times, then *on Sizes 12 and 16 only,* bind off 10 (11) sts at same edge once.* NECK FACING: Place the 3 sts of neck facing on needle. Dec 1 st at inner edge every 4th row twice. Fasten off. COLLAR FACING: Place the 8 sts of collar facing on needle. Dec 1 st at inner edge every 4th row 4 times. Work on the rem'ing 4 sts until straight edge measures 4½". Bind off.

Right Front. Work sleeve section same as for left back. Sl the 37 sts to a holder. Starting at lower edge, work to correspond to left front, reversing the shaping, ending with a p row. TO JOIN SLEEVE: K across sts of front, then k across sts of sleeve. *On sizes 14, 16 and 18 only,* inc 1 st at sleeve edge every 2nd (4th–4th) row once. Place a marker at sleeve edge. *On all sizes* work on the 83 (84–86–87–89) sts until 4 (6–8–10–12) rows above marker. SHOULDER AND NECK: Work to correspond to left front, reversing the shaping.

Collar. With No. 11 needles, cast on 66 (66–67–67–68) sts for outer edge. Work in stockinette st for 2½", ending with a p row. **Next row:** K, dec 9 sts evenly spaced across row. Work on the remaining 57 (57–58–58–59) sts until collar measures 4" from start, ending with a p row. **Next row:** K 6 and sl them to safety pin, k to last 6 sts, sl last 6 sts to another pin. Bind off 16 sts at beg of next 2 rows then bind off remaining 13 (13–14–14–15) sts.

Hem. With No. 10 needles and single strand of dark blue, cast on 180 (186–192–198–204) sts for lower edge. Work in stockinette st for 1½". Bind off.

Edging. Fold 9 sts in at right front edge for front facing and pin to wrong side. With double strand of dark blue, starting at lower edge on right side of work, crochet 1 sl st in each row up the front to the neck. Break yarn, leaving a 20" end to use later. Fold and pin in facing on left front to correspond. Starting at neck, crochet 1 sl st in each row to the lower edge.

Blocking Coat and Cutting Lining. We suggest that all knit coats be lined. Steam each knitted piece lightly, using a damp cloth and a moderately hot iron. Do not allow iron to rest on knitted pieces. Using knitted pieces for pattern, cut a lining piece like each knitted piece, allowing ⅝" around for each seam and about 2½" for a pleat at center back. In addition to taffeta collar, cut one of Pellon.

To Assemble Coat. Sew shoulder seams. Sew underarm and sleeve seams. Pin collar in place. Weave 6 sts of facing at neck to 6 sts of collar. With wrong sides tog, sew collar facing to front edge of collar. Sew collar in place to neck edge. Using long end of yarn, continue sl st all around collar. Baste inner edge of collar facing in place. Starting at lower edge of left front on wrong side of work, crochet 2nd row of sl sts in front loop of each st of previous row to within 2" below neck. Fasten off. On right front, starting 2" below neck, work 2nd row down right front to correspond. Fasten off. Starting 2" below neck edge on wrong side of work, crochet 2nd row of sl sts all around collar. Wrong sides together, pin hem piece in place along lower edge of coat with side edges meeting inner edge of front facings. Turn in ½" (or to length desired) at sleeve edge to wrong side and sew in place. LINING: Fold pleat at center back and make a tack. To set in lining: With wrong side out, place lining on a form or try it on. Slip knitted coat over lining, then pin lining and coat tog. Pin along seams, being sure coat hangs evenly. Sew lining in place by tacking along seams. Coat facings should overlap lining. Interface collar with Pellon, slipping it under facing; tack in place all around. Line collar and cut away excess lining at facings. Hem lining to meet top of coat hem.

Lacy Cardigan with Collar

Directions are for Size 12. Changes for Sizes 14, 16, and 18 are in parentheses.

Materials. Fingering Yarn—8 (9–9–10) skeins. Knitting Needles, Nos. 1 and 3. Steel Crochet Hook, No. 1. 7 small buttons. ⅛ yard nylon tulle.

Gauge. Pattern st. on No. 3 needles: 6 sts—1″. 7½ rows—1″.

Blocking Measurements:

Bust (cardigan buttoned) .... 35 (37–39–41)″
Width of back at underarm .... 17 (18–19–20)″
Width of each front at underarm ...... 9½ (10–10½–11)″
Width of sleeves at underarm ..... 13 (13½–14–14½)″

Pattern Stitch. Multiple of 10 sts plus 6 (2–8–4). **Row 1:** P 2 (5–3–1), * k 2, p 3, leaving yarn in front of work to form yo, sl 1, k 1, psso, p 3. Repeat from * ending with k 2, p 2 (5–3–1). **Row 2:** K 2 (5–3–1), * p 2, k 3. Repeat from * ending with p 2, k 2 (5–3–1). **Row 3:** P 2 (5–3–1), * k 2, p 3, yo, k 1, yo, k 1, p 3. Repeat from * ending with k 2, p 2 (5–3–1). **Row 4:** K 2 (5–3–1), * p 2, k 3, p 4, k 3. Repeat from * ending with p 2, k 2 (5–3–1). **Row 5:** P 2 (5–3–1), * k 2, p 3, yo, sl 1, k 1, psso, k 1, yo, k 1, p 3. Repeat from * ending with k 2, p 2 (5–3–1). **Row 6:** K 2 (5–3–1), * p 2, k 3, p 5, k 3. Repeat from * ending with p 2, k 2 (5–3–1). **Row 7:** P 2 (5–3–1), * k into 2nd st on left-hand needle, k first st and drop both sts from left-hand needle (cross st make), p 3, k 1, sl 1, k 1, psso, k 2, p 3. Repeat from * ending with cross st, p 2 (5–3–1). **Row 8:** Repeat Row 4. **Row 9:** P 2 (5–3–1), * k 2, p 3, sl 1, k 2 tog, psso, k 1, p 3. Repeat from * ending with k 2, p 2 (5–3–1). **Row 10:** Repeat Row 2. Making cross sts over the k 2 ribs on every 6th row, repeat these 10 rows for pattern. Next time, cross sts will fall on Row 3 of pattern, then on Row 9, then on Row 5, then on Row 1, then again on Row 7 of pattern.

Note: Rows 1, 3 and 5 increase each pattern by 1 st. Row 7 decreases each pattern by 1 st. Row 9 decreases each pattern by 2 sts. When counting sts, count each lace cable as 2 sts; if binding off or decreasing the sts of lace cable, take off any *extra* sts in the cable by making k 2 tog or k 3 tog as necessary to reduce cable to 2 sts.

Back. With No. 1 needles cast on 96 (102–108–114) sts. Work in k 1, p 1 ribbing for 1½″. Change to No. 3 needles and work in pattern for 2″. Work inc sts in reverse stockinette st (p on right side, k on wrong side), inc 1 st each edge on the next row and again every 2″ two more times; 102 (108–114–120) sts. Work even until total length is 11 (11½–11½–12)″. Mark last row. SHAPING ARMHOLES: Bind off 5 sts at beginning of next 2 rows. Dec 1 st each edge every other row 3 (4–5–6) times; 86 (90–94–98) sts, counting the lace cable as 2 sts. Work even until armholes measure 7½ (7¾–8–8¼)″ above marked row. SHAPING SHOULDERS: Bind off 7 (7–8–8) sts at beginning of next 6 rows, 8 (9–7–8) sts at beginning of next 2 rows. Bind off remaining 28 (30–32–34) sts for back of neck.

Left Front. With No. 1 needles, cast on 55 (58–61–64) sts. **Row 1:** K 0 (1–0–1), work in p 1, k 1 ribbing to last 11 sts, p 3; *on sizes 12, 14 and 18,* yarn back, yarn over, sl 1, k 1, psso, p 3, k 2, p 1. *On size 16 only,* k 2, p 3, yarn back, yo, sl 1, k 1, psso, p 1. **Row 2:** K 1, p 2 (2–3–2), k 3, p 3 (3–2–3), k 3, * p 1, k 1. Repeat from * across, ending with k 1 (p 1, k 1, p 1). These 2 rows start pattern on the 11 sts at front edge. Continue in pattern on the sts at front edge, and in ribbing as established on remaining sts, until piece measures 1¼″ ending at side edge. Change to No. 3 needles. **Row 1:** Work row 1 of pattern, ending with pattern as established at front edge. Keeping pattern as established, inc 1 st at side edge every 2″ 3 times; 58 (61–64–67) sts. Work even until piece measures same as back to underarm. Mark last row. SHAPING ARMHOLE: At side edge, bind off 5 sts once, dec 1 st every other row 3 (4–5–6) times; 50 (52–54–56) sts. Work even until armhole measures 5¼ (5½–5¾–6)" above marked row. NECK: At front edge bind off 10 (11–12–13) sts once, 4 sts once, dec 1 st every other row 7 times. SHAPING SHOULDER: At side edge, bind off 7 (7–8–8) sts 3 times, 8 (9–7–8) sts once.

Right Front. With No. 1 needles, cast on 55 (58–61–64) sts. **Row 1:** *On sizes 12, 14 and 18,* p 1, k 2, p 3, yarn back, yo, sl 1, k 1, psso, p 3; *on size 16,* p 1, yarn back, yo, sl 1, k 1, psso, p 3, k 2, p 3; *on all sizes* work in k 1, p 1 ribbing to end of row, ending with p 1 (k 1, p 1, k 1). **Row 2:** P 0 (1–0–1), work in k 1, p 1 ribbing to last 12 sts, k 3, p 3 (3–2–3), k 3, p 2 (2–3–2), k 1. These 2 rows start pattern at front edge. Complete to correspond with left front in reversed shaping.

Sleeves. With No. 1 needles, cast on 66 (66–72–72) sts. Work in k 1, p 1 ribbing for 1½". Change to No. 3 needles. Starting and ending right side rows with p 2 (2–5–5) and wrong side rows with k 2 (2–5–5), work in pattern for 10 rows. Inc 1 st at each edge on the next row and again every 1" 5 (7–5–7) times more; 78 (82–84–88) sts. Work even until total length is 11 (11½–11½–12)", ending with same row of pattern as back at underarm. SLEEVE SHAPING: Bind off 5 sts at beginning of next 2 rows. Dec 1 st each edge every other row until 34 (36–36–38) sts remain, then on every row until 22 sts remain. Bind off.

Collar. Starting at outer edge with No. 3 needles, cast on 118 (122–126–130) sts. **Row 1:** Right side. P 2, * k 2, p 2. Repeat from * across. **Row 2:** K 2, * p 2, k 2. Repeat from * across. **Row 3:** P 2, * cross st, p 2. Repeat from * across. **Row 4:** Repeat Row 2. **Rows 5–8:** Repeat Rows 1 and 2 twice. **Rows 9–14:** Repeat Rows 3–8 once. **Row 15:** P 2, * cross st, p 2 tog, cross st, p 2. Repeat from * to last 4 sts, cross st, p 2. **Rows 16–20:** Work in ribbing as now established. **Row 21:** P 2, * cross st, p 1, cross st, p 2 tog. Repeat from * to last 4 sts, cross st, p 2. Bind off in ribbing.

Finishing. Block pieces to measurements. Matching patterns, sew shoulder, side and sleeve seams. Sew in sleeves. Turn the 2 sts at each end of collar to wrong side and hem in place. With right side of collar against wrong side of cardigan, and matching center backs, sew on collar, leaving 1" free on each side of neck for overlap. Press. Mark position of 7 buttonloops evenly spaced on right front edge, with first one at center of waistband ribbing and top one ½" from neck edge. Attach yarn at lower right front corner, * sc to within ¼" of next marker, make a ⅝" chain for buttonloop, skip ½" of edge. Repeat from * until 7 buttonloops have been made, sc in remaining ¼", 3 sc in corner, sc across 1" of neck edge. Fasten off. Starting at opposite corner of neck and omitting buttonloops, work 1 row sc along left front edge to correspond. Face front edges with bands of nylon tulle 2" wide. Sew on buttons.

Shimmer of Crystal

Pattern stitch in long V yoke, at left in photograph on next page

Directions are for Size 12. Changes for Sizes 14, 16, and 18 are in parentheses.

Materials. Mohair with Tinsel (Blue)—7 (7–8–8) balls. Knitting Needles, Nos. 6 and 8. Crochet hook size F. 7 crystal Buttons. 10 dozen crystal Dewdrop Beads. 1 tube of tiny crystal Beads.

Gauge. Stockinette stitch. On No. 8 needles: 4½ sts—1". 6 rows—1". With No. 8 needles cast on 18 sts. Work in stockinette st for 24 rows. Piece should measure 4" square. If too small, try larger needles; if too large, try smaller needles, until correct gauge is obtained.

Blocking Measurements:

Bust . . . . 35 (37–39–41)"
Width of back at
underarm . . . . 17 (18–19–20)"
Width of each front at underarm, not
including borders . 9 (9½–10–10½)"
Width of sleeve at
underarm . . . . . 12½ (13–13½–14)"

Note: Fronts are worked first; pattern will determine exact length. Back will then be made to corresponding length.

Left Front. With No. 6 needles, cast on 40

(42–44–46) sts. Work in k 1, p 1 ribbing for 2″. Change to No. 8 needles. **Row 1:** K to last 7 sts, p 3, in next st make k 1, yo, k 1, yo and k 1 (5 sts made in 1 st for start of dewdrop), p 3. **Row 2:** k 3, p 5, k 3, purl to end of row. **Row 3:** K to last 11 sts, p 3, k 5, p 3. **Row 4:** Repeat Row 2. **Row 5:** K to last 12 sts, p 4, sl 1, k 1, psso, k 1, k 2 tog, p 3. **Row 6:** k 3, p 3, k 4, purl to end of row. **Row 7:** K to last 10 sts, p 4, sl 1, k 2 tog, psso (dewdrop completed), p 3. **Row 8:** K 8, purl to end of row. **Row 9:** K to last 9 sts, p 3, make 5 sts in next st, p 3, make 5 sts in next st, p 1 (2 dewdrops started). **Row 10:** K 1, p 5, k 3, p 5, k 3, purl to end of row. **Row 11:** K to last 17 sts, p 3, k 5, p 3, k 5, p 1. **Row 12:** Repeat Row 10. **Row 13:** K to last 18 sts, p 4, * sl 1, k 1, psso, k 1, k 2 tog, p 3. Repeat from * once more ending p 1. **Row 14:** K 1, p 3, k 3, p 3, k 4, purl to end of row. **Row 15:** K to last 14 sts, p 4, sl 1, k 2 tog, psso, p 3, sl 1, k 2 tog, psso, p 1 (dewdrops completed). **Row 16:** K 10, purl to end of row. **Row 17:** K to within 1 st of purl section, * p 3, make 5 sts in next st. Repeat from * ending with p 3 (2 dewdrops started). **Row 18:** K 3, * p 5, k 3. Repeat from * across pat section, purl to end of row. Continue in pat, working 1 st more in pat every 4th row, and having 1 more dewdrop in every other group of dewdrops, until there are 20 (21–21–22) sts in pat section, ending at side edge. (*On Sizes 12 and 16 only,* work 2 more rows.) SHAPING ARM-

HOLES: Working pat as before, bind off 4 sts at beg of next row, dec 1 st at same edge every other row 4 (5–6–7) times. You now have 32 (33–34–35) sts. Work armhole edge even until there are 28 (28–30–30) sts in pat, completing last set of dewdrops and ending at armhole edge. **Next Row:** Work in pat until 4 dewdrops have been started, purl to end of row. (*On Sizes 14 and 18 only,* work 4 more rows.) NECK: Working only 4 dewdrops, bind off 7 (7–8–8) sts at beg of next row, dec 1 st at neck edge every other row 6 times. You now have 19 (20–20–21) sts. If necessary, work even until armhole measures about 7½ (7¾–8–8¼)″. SHOULDER: Knitting together the sts of any uncompleted dewdrop as sts are bound off, at side edge bind off 7 sts twice, 5 (6–6–7) sts once.

Right Front. Work ribbing same as left front. Change to No. 8 needles. **Row 1:** P 3, make 5 sts in next st, p 3, k to end of row. **Row 2:** Purl to last 11 sts, k 3, p 5, k 3. **Row 3:** P 3, k 5, p 3, k to end of row. **Row 4:** Repeat Row 2. **Row 5:** P 3, sl 1, k 1, psso, k 1, k 2 tog, p 4, k to end of row. **Row 6:** Purl to last 10 sts, k 4, p 3, k 3. **Row 7:** P 3, sl 1, k 2 tog. psso, p 4, k to end of row. **Row 8:** Purl to last 8 sts, k 8. **Row 9:** P 1, make 5 sts in next st, p 3, make 5 sts in next st, p 3. Work to correspond with left front until armhole shaping has been completed and there are 28 (28–30–30) sts, in pat, completing last set of dewdrops and ending at front edge. **Next Row:** P 12 (12–14–14), * make 5 sts in next st, p 3. Repeat from * until 4 dewdrops have been started, finish row. Work 1 (5–1–5) more rows, ending at front edge. Shape neck and shoulder same as for left front.

Back. With No. 6 needles cast on 74 (78–82–86) sts. Work in k 1, p 1 ribbing for 2″, inc 3 (3–4–4) sts evenly across last row. You now have 77 (81–86–90) sts. Change to No. 8 needles and work even in stockinette st until total length is same as front to underarm. SHAPING ARMHOLES: Bind off 4 sts at beg in next 2 rows. Dec 1 st at each edge every other row 4 (5–6–7) times. You now have 61 (63–66–68) sts. Work even until armholes measure same as on front. SHAPING SHOULDERS: Bind off 7 sts at beg of next 4 rows, then 5 (6–6–7) sts at beg of next 2 rows. Bind off remaining 23 (23–26–26) sts for back of neck.

Sleeves. With No. 6 needles cast on 40 (42–42–44) sts. Work in k 1, p 1 ribbing for 2″. Change to No. 8 needles and work in stockinette st, increasing 1 st at each edge on the next row, then every 1″, 7 (7–8–8) times more. You now have 56 (58–60–62) sts. Work even until total length is 10½ (10½–11–11)″. TOP SHAPING: Bind off 4 sts at beg of next 2 rows. Dec 1 st at each edge every other row until 20 sts remain. Dec 1 st at each edge on every row until 12 sts remain. Bind off.

Finishing. Block pieces to measurements. Sew shoulder, side and sleeve seams. Sew in sleeves. Press. NECKBAND: With No. 6 needles and right side of work facing you, pick up 70 (72–74–76) sts evenly around neck edge. Work in k 1, p 1 ribbing for ¾″. Bind off loosely in ribbing. LEFT FRONT BORDER: **Row 1:** With right side of work facing you, work 1 row sc evenly along front edge. **Rows 2–5:** Ch 1, turn, sc in each sc. Fasten off. Mark position of 7 buttons evenly spaced on border with first one 1″ from lower edge and top one ½″ from neck edge. RIGHT FRONT BORDER: Work to correspond with left border, making buttonholes opposite markers on 2nd row. BUTTONHOLES: Ch 2, skip 2 sc. On the next row make 2 sc in each ch-2. TRIMMING: At base of each dewdrop on pat, attach thread securely, slip 2 small beads, 1 crystal dewdrop and 3 small beads, on thread, fasten securely at starting point, leaving beads loose enough to fall gracefully. Sew on buttons.

Monaco

At right in photograph opposite

Directions are for Size 10. Changes for Sizes 12, 14, and 16 are in parentheses.

Materials. Fingering Yarn—8 (8–9–9½) 30-gram balls. Knitting Needles, 1 pair each Nos. 2 and 4. 1½ yards grosgrain Ribbon 1¼″ wide. 6 iridescent Buttons ⅜″ size. 10

dozen iridescent glass Beads 5mm. size.

Gauge. 6½ sts—1″. 8 rows—1″. With 4 needles cast on 23 sts. Work in pat B for 28 rows. Piece should measure 3½″ square. If too small, try larger needles; if too large, try smaller needles, until correct gauge is obtained. You will work pat A or pat B depending on the number of stitches on the needle.

Blocking Measurements:

Bust (cardigan buttoned) .... 34 (36–38½–40½)″

Width of back at underarm ... 16¾ (17½–18¼–19)″

Width of each front at underarm ..... 9 (9¾–10¾–11¼)″

Width of sleeves at underarm ..... 12½ (13–13½–14)″

Pattern Stitch A. Multiple of 10 sts plus 9. **Row 1:** K 8, * yo, k 3 tog, yo, k 7. Repeat from * ending k 8. **Row 2 and all even rows:** Purl. **Row 3:** K 1, * yo, k 2, k 3 tog, k 2, yo, k 3. Repeat from * ending yo, k 1. **Row 5:** K 2, * yo, k 1, k 3 tog, k 1, yo, k 5. Repeat from * ending yo, k 2. **Row 7:** K 3, * yo, k 3 tog, yo, k 7. Repeat from * ending yo, k 3. **Row 9:** K 2 tog, k 1, yo, k 3, * yo, k 2, k 3 tog, k 2, yo, k 3. Repeat from * ending yo, k 1, k 2 tog. **Row 11:** K 2 tog, yo, k 5, * yo, k 1, k 3 tog, k 1, yo, k 5. Repeat from * ending yo, k 2 tog. **Row 12:** Purl. Repeat these 12 rows for pattern A. **Pattern Stitch B:** Multiple of 10 sts plus 3. **Row 1:** K 5, * yo, k 3 tog, yo, k 7. Repeat from * ending yo, k 5. **Row 2 and all even rows:** Purl. **Row 3:** K 2 tog, k 3, * yo, k 3, yo, k 2, k 3 tog, k 2. Repeat from * ending yo, k 3, yo, k 3, k 2 tog. **Row 5:** K 2 tog, k 2, * yo, k 5, yo, k 1, k 3 tog, k 1. Repeat from * ending yo, k 5, yo, k 2, k 2 tog. **Row 7:** K 2 tog, k 1, * yo, k 7, yo, k 3 tog. Repeat from * ending yo, k 7, yo, k 1, k 2 tog. **Row 9:** K 3, * yo, k 2, k 3 tog, k 2, yo, k 3. Repeat from * across. **Row 11:** K 4, * yo, k 1, k 3 tog, k 1, yo, k 5. Repeat from * ending yo, k 4. **Row 12:** Purl. Repeat these 12 rows for pattern B.

Note: When shaping, remember that every k 3 tog must be balanced by a yo on each side; each extra yo at ends of row must be balanced by a k 2 tog. Always make incs or decs on purl rows, then adjust pat at edges so that no sts are gained or lost on right-side rows. When binding off, the st remaining on right-hand needle becomes first st of pat.

Back. With No. 2 needles cast on 108 (112–118–122) sts. Work in k 1, p 1 ribbing for 1½ (1½–2–2)″, increasing 1 st at end of last row. Change to No. 4 needles and work even in pat A (B–A–B) until total length is about 13½ (13½–14–14)″, ending with Row 12 of pat. Mark last row. SHAPING ARMHOLES: Bind off 5 sts at beg of next 2 rows. Dec 1 st at each edge every other row 5 (5–6–6) times. You now have 89 (93–97–101) sts. Work even until armholes measure 7½ (7¾–8–8¼)″ above marked row. SHAPING SHOULDERS: Bind off 7 (7–8–8) sts at beg of next 6 rows, 6 (7–6–7) sts at beg of next 2 rows. Slip remaining 35 (37–37–39) sts on a holder for back of neck.

Left Front. With No. 2 needles cast on 58 (62–68–72) sts. Work in k 1, p 1 ribbing for 1½ (1½–2–2)″, increasing 1 st at end of last row. Change to No. 4 needles and work even in pattern A (B–A–B) until same length as back to underarm, ending with a purl row (side edge). Mark last row. SHAPING ARMHOLE: Bind off 5 sts at beg of next row. Dec 1 st at same edge every other row 5 (7–9–11) times. You now have 49 (51–55–57) sts. Work even until piece measures 5 (5¼–5½–5¾)″ above marked row, ending at armhole edge. NECK: Work to last 10 (11–13–14) sts and slip remaining sts on a holder. Dec 1 st at neck edge on every other row 12 times. You now have 27 (28–30–31) sts. Work even until armhole measures same as on back. SHAPING SHOULDER: From side edge, bind off 7 (7–8–8) sts 3 times, 6 (7–6–7) sts once.

Right Front. Work to correspond with left front, reversing shaping.

Sleeves. With No. 2 needles cast on 58 (62–62–68) sts. Work in k 1, p 1 ribbing for 3″, increasing 1 st at end of last row. You now have 59 (63–63–69) sts. Change to No. 4 needles and work in pat A (B–B–

A), increasing 1 st at each edge every 6th row 11 (11–12–13) times. You now have 81 (85–89–93) sts. Work even until total length is 13 (13½–14–14½)". TOP SHAPING: Bind off 5 sts at beg of next 2 rows. Dec 1 st at each edge every other row until 35 (37–39–41) sts remain, then on every row until 19 sts remain. Bind off.

Finishing. Block pieces to measurements. Sew shoulder, side and sleeve seams, matching pattern. NECKBAND: With No. 2 needles and right side of work facing you, slip the sts of right front holder on needle, attach yarn and pick up 19 sts evenly along side of neck, k sts from back holder, pick up 19 sts along other side of neck, k sts from left front holder. You now have 93 (97–101–105) sts. **Row 1:** P 1, * k 1, p 1. Repeat from * across. **Row 2:** K 1, * p 1, k 1. Repeat from * across. Repeat these 2 rows for 1". Bind off in ribbing. Face front edge with grosgrain ribbon, turning under 1 st at each edge. Make machine-stitched buttonholes on right front, placing one at center of neckband, another at center of waistband ribbing, the others spaced at center of every 3rd leaf pattern. Starting at outer edge of shoulder on each front, sew a bead to center of each leaf diagonally down toward center front. Sew a bead to each leaf above this diagonal line. Sew on buttons.

Inter-Laced-Leaf Shell

Far left in photograph on next page

Directions are for Sizes 32–34. Changes for Sizes 36–38 and Sizes 40–42 are in parentheses.

Materials. Fingering Yarn—4 (5–6) 1-oz. balls. Knitting Needles, No. 10. Steel Crochet Hook, No. 0.

Gauge. 4 sts—1". 9 rows—2".

Body Measurement:

At bustline . . . . 33 (37–41)"

Shell Measurement:

At bustline . . . . 35 (39–43)"

Length to underarms . . . . 10½"

Length to back of neck . . . . 18½ (19–19½)"

Pattern Stitch. A repeat of 16 sts plus 1. **Row 1:** K 1, * yo, k 5, k 2 tog, k 1, k 2 tog, k 5, yo, k 1; repeat from * to within 3 sts of end. Then yo, k 1, k 2 tog. **Row 2:** P 2, * yo, p 4, p 2 tog, p 1, p 2 tog, p 4, yo, p 3; repeat from *. End yo, p 3, yo, p 2 tog. Do not try to finish each pattern stitch before working the end instructions. **Row 3:** K 3, * yo, k 3, k 2 tog, k 1, k 2 tog, k 3, yo, k 5; repeat from *. End yo, k 3. **Row 4:** P 4, * yo, p 2, p 2 tog, p 1, p 2 tog, p 2, yo, p 7; repeat from *. End yo, p 4. **Row 5:** K 5, * yo, k 1, k 2 tog, k 1, k 2 tog, k 1, yo, k 9; repeat from *. End yo, k 5. **Row 6:** P 1, p 2 tog, p 3, * yo, p 2 tog, yo, p 1, yo, p 2 tog; yo, p 3, p 2 tog, p 1, p 2 tog, p 3; repeat from *. End p 2 tog, p 1. **Row 7:** K 1, k 2 tog, k 4, * yo, k 3, yo, k 4, k 2 tog, k 1, k 2 tog, k 4; repeat from *. End k 4, k 2 tog, k 1. **Row 8:** P 1, p 2 tog, p 3, * yo, p 5, yo, p 3, p 2 tog, p 1, p 2 tog, p 3; repeat from *. End yo, p 3, p 2 tog, p 1. **Row 9:** K 1, k 2 tog, k 2, * yo, k 7, yo, k 2, k 2 tog, k 1, k 2 tog, k 2; repeat from *. End k 2 tog, k 1. **Row 10:** P 1, p 2 tog, p 1, * yo, p 9, yo, p 1, p 2 tog, p 1, p 2 tog, p 1; repeat from *. End yo, p 1, p 2 tog, p 1. **Row 11:** K 1, k 2 tog, * yo, k 11, yo, k 2 tog, k 1, k 2 tog; repeat from *. End yo, k 2 tog, k 1. **Row 12:** Purl. Repeat these 12 rows for pat st.

Back. Cast on 71 (71–87) sts. Purl 1 row. Begin pat. **Row 1:** K 2 tog, k 1, yo, k 1; repeat from * of pat row 1, end yo, k 1, k 2 tog. **Row 2:** P 2 tog, yo, p 3; repeat from * of pat row 2, end yo, p 3, yo, p 2 tog. **Row 3:** K 6; repeat from * of pat row 3, end yo, k 6. **Row 4:** P 7; repeat from * of pat row 4, end yo, p 7. **Row 5:** K 8; repeat from * of pat row 5, end yo, k 8. **Row 6:** P 4, p 2 tog, p 3; repeat from * of pat row 6; end p 2 tog, p 4. **Row 7:** K 4, k 2 tog, k 4; repeat from * of pat row 7, end k 4, k 2 tog, k 4. **Row 8:** P 4, p 2 tog, p 3; repeat from * of pat row 8, end p 2 tog, p 4. **Row 9:** K 4, k 2 tog, k 2; repeat from * of pat row 9, end k 2 tog, k 4. **Row 10:** P 4, p 2 tog, p 1; repeat from * of pat row 10, end p 1, p 2 tog, p 4. **Row 11:** K 4, k 2 tog; repeat from * of pat row 11, end yo, k 2 tog, k 4. **Row 12:** Purl. Complete 3 patterns and work 11 rows of 4th pat. Piece should measure about 10½" from beginning. SHAPING ARMHOLES: **Row 1:** Bind off 3 sts, p to end. There are 68

(68–84) sts on needle. **Row 2:** Bind off 3 sts, leaving 1 st on right needle, repeat from * of pat row 1 to end. There are 65 (65–81) sts on needle. **Row 3:** P 2; repeat from * of pat row 2, end yo, p 2. There are 65 (65–81) sts on needle. **Row 4:** K 2 tog, k 1; repeat from * of pat row 3, end yo, k 1, k 2 tog. There are 63 (63–79) sts on needle. **Row 5:** P 3; repeat from * of pat row 4, end yo, p 3. There are 63 (63–79) sts on needle. **Row 6:** K 2 tog, k 2; repeat from * of pat row 5, end yo, k 2, k 2 tog. There are 61 (61–77) sts on needle. **Row 7:** P 2 tog, p 2; repeat from * of pat row 6, end yo, p 2, p 2 tog. There are 61 (61–77) sts on needle. **Row 8:** K 2 tog, k 2 tog, k 1; repeat from * of pat row 7, end yo, k 1, k 2 tog, k 2 tog. There are 59 (59–75) sts on needle. **Row 9:** P 2 tog, p 1; repeat from * of pat row 8, end yo, p 1, p 2 tog. There are 59 (59–75) sts on needle. **Row 10:** K 2 tog; repeat from * of row 9, end yo, k 7, yo, k 2 tog. There are 59 (59–75) sts on needle. **Row 11:** P 10, yo, p 1, p 2 tog, p 1, p 2 tog, p 1; repeat from * of pat row 10, end yo, p 10. There are 59 (59–75) sts on needle. **Row 12:** K 11, yo, k 2 tog, k 1, k 2 tog; repeat from * of pat row 11, end yo, k 11. There are 59 (59–75) sts on needle. **Row 13:** Purl. **Row 14:** K 2, yo, k 1, k 2 tog, k 1, k 2 tog, k 5, yo, k 1; repeat from * of pat row 1, end k 1, yo, k 2. **Row 15:** P 6, p 2 tog, p 4, yo, p 3; repeat from * of pat row 2, end p 2 tog, p 6. **Row 16:** K 1, yo, k 2, k 2 tog, k 1, k 2 tog, k 3, yo, k 5; repeat from * of pat row 3, end k 2, yo, k 1. **Row 17:** P 1, repeat from * of pat row 4, end yo, p 1. **Row 18:** K 2; repeat from * of pat row 5, end yo, k 2. **Row 19:** P 2 tog, p 1; repeat from * of pat row 6, end yo, p 1, p 2 tog. **Row 20:** K 2 tog, k 2; repeat from * of pat row 7; end yo, k 2, k 2 tog. **Row 21:** Same as row 9 of armholes. Repeat from row 10 of armholes until there are 35 (37–39) rows on armholes. SHAPING SHOULDERS: Work in stockinette st (p 1 row, k 1 row), bind off 8 (8–12) sts at beg of next 2 rows. **Next Row:** K on wrong side through back loops for hemline. K 1 row, inc 1 st each side. P 1 row, inc 1 st each side. Bind off loosely.

Front. Cast on 71 (87–87) sts. Work same as back to shoulders. SHAPING SHOULDERS: *For small size:* Bind off 8 sts at beg of next 2 rows. *For medium size:* Working 2 sts tog, bind off 16 sts at beg of next 2 rows. *For large size:* Bind off 12 sts at beg of next 2 rows. Complete same as back.

Finishing. Sew underarm and shoulder seams. Turn hem at neckline to wrong side and sew in place. Working from right side, work 1 row sc on lower edge, spacing sts to keep edge flat and dec at top of scallops. Working from right side, work 2 rows sc around armhole edges, holding in to desired length. Block to measurements.

Lace-Stitch Shell

At right in photograph opposite

These directions are written for Size 10. Changes for Sizes 12, 14, 16 and 18 are in parentheses.

Materials. Fingering Yarn—4 (4–5–5–6) 1-oz. balls. Knitting Needles, No. 10. Steel Crochet Hook, No. 0.

Gauge. 4 sts—1″. 5 rows—1″.

Body Measurement:

At bustline . . . . 32 (34–36–38–40)″

Shell Measurement:

At bustline . . . . 34 (36–38–40–42)″

Pattern Stitch. Multiple of 8 sts plus 1. **Row 1** (right side): K 1, * yo, k 2, k 3 tog, k 2, yo, k 1; repeat from * to end. **Row 2:** Purl. **Row 3:** K 2, * yo, k 1, sl 1 as if to p, k 2 tog, psso, k 1, yo, k 3; repeat from *. End last repeat k 2 instead of k 3. **Row 4:** Purl. **Row 5:** P 3, * yo, k 3 tog, yo, p 5; repeat from *. End last repeat p 3 instead of p 5. **Row 6:** Purl. Repeat these 6 rows for pat st.

Back. Cast on 65 (65–73–73–81) sts. Work in pat st until piece measures 11″ from beg. SHAPING ARMHOLES: Keeping continuity of pat, bind off 2 sts at beg of next 2 rows. Dec 1 st each side every other row twice. Work even on 57 (57–65–65–73) sts until armholes measure 7 (7½–8–8½–9)″. SHAPING SHOULDERS AND NECK: Bind off 6 (6–7–7–8) sts at beg of next 2 rows. You now have 45 (45–51–51–57) sts on needle. **Next Row:** Bind off 6 (6–7–7–8) sts, work 11 (11–12–12–13) sts, tie in another ball of yarn, bind off center 11 (11–13–13–15) sts, work to end. Continue working on each side with a separate ball of yarn, or work 1 side at a time if you wish. **Next Row:** Bind off 6 (6–7–7–8) sts, work to end. There are 11 (11–12–12–13) sts on each side. Bind off 6 (6–7–7–8) sts from each armhole edge every other row once more *and at the same time* bind off 5 sts from each side of neck edge once.

Front. Cast on 65 (73–73–81–81) sts. Work in pat st until same length as back to armholes. SHAPING ARMHOLES: Keeping continuity of pat, bind off 2 (3–2–3–2) sts at beg of next 2 rows. Dec 1 st at armhole edge every other row 2 (3–2–3–2) times. Work even on 57 (61–65–69–73) sts until armholes measure 6½ (7–7½–8–8½)″. **Next Row:** Work 23 (25–26–28–29) sts, tie in another ball of yarn, bind off center 11 (11–13–13–15) sts, work to end. Continue working on each side with a separate ball of yarn, or work 1 side at a time if you wish. Bind off 2 sts from each side of neck edge every other row 2 (3–2–3–2) times, then 1 st once, shaping shoulders as on back when armholes are same length.

Finishing. Sew shoulder and underarm seams. Working from right side, work 1 row sc around neck edge, spacing sts to keep edge flat. Turn sc row to wrong side and sew in place, being careful not to pull neck edge. Turn 1 st to wrong side around armholes and sew in place. Block to measurements.

Stockinette-Stitch Shell

Center in photograph on page 322

Directions are written for Size 10. Changes for Sizes 12, 14, 16 and 18 are in parentheses.

Materials. Fingering Yarn—4 (4–5–5–6) 1-oz. balls. Knitting Needles, No. 10. 1 yard 1″ wide grosgrain ribbon.

Gauge. 4 sts—1″. 5 rows—1″.

Body Measurement:

At bustline .... 30 (32–34–36–38)″

Shell Measurement:

At bustline ...... 32 (34–36–38–40)″

Back. Cast on 44 (48–52–56–60) sts. Work in stockinette st (k 1 row, p 1 row) for 1 inch. End with a purl row. **Eyelet Row:** K 1, * yo, k 2 tog; repeat from *. End k 1. This is hemline row. Continue in stockinette st (p 1 row, k 1 row) for 7 rows. End with a purl row. Repeat Eyelet Row. Continue in stockinette st, dec 1 st each side every 4th row twice. Work even on 40 (44–48–52–56) sts until piece measures 5″ from beg. Place a marker between the 16th and 17th sts from each end for dart markers. Continue in stockinette st, inc 1 st each side every 4th row 7 times *and* inc 1 st before first marker and after 2nd marker every 8th row 4 times. Work even on 62 (66–70–74–78) sts until piece measures 11½″ from beg. End with a purl row. NECK: **Next Row:** K 29 (31–33–35–37) sts, k 2 tog, join another ball of yarn, k 2 tog, k 29 (31–33–35–37) sts to end. Continue working on each side with a separate ball of yarn, or work 1 side at a time if you wish. Dec 1 st at neck edge every other row until piece measures 12½″ from beg. End with a purl row. SHAPING ARMHOLES: Continuing to work in stockinette st, dec 1 st at neck edge every 2nd row and *at the same time* bind off 4 sts from each underarm edge once, then dec 1 st at each armhole edge every other row 4 times. Keeping armhole edge even, continue to dec 1 st at each side of front edge every other row until there are 17 (18–19–20–21) decs in all at neck edge. Bind off remaining 5 (6–7–8–9) sts for shoulder.

Front. Cast on 48 (52–56–60–64) sts. Work same as back until piece measures 5″ from beg. There are 44 (48–52–56–60) sts on needle. Place a marker between the 12th and 13th sts from each end. Continue in stockinette st, inc 1 st each side every 4th row 7 times *and* inc 1 st before first marker and after 2nd marker every 8th row 4 times. Work even on 66 (70–74–78–82) sts until there is 1 row less on front than on back to beg of armholes. DIVIDE FOR NECK AS FOLLOWS: Work 31 (33–35–37–39) sts, k 2 tog, tie in another ball of yarn, work 2 tog, work 31 (33–35–37–39) sts. Continue working on each side with a separate ball of yarn, or work 1 side at a time if you wish. Dec 1 st at neck edge every other row *and at the same time* shape armholes as on back. Keeping armhole edges even, continue to dec 1 st at each side of neck edge every other row until there are 14 (15–16–17–18) decs in all at neck edge, then dec every row 5 times, binding off for shoulder when armholes are same length. BACK NECKBAND: Working from right side and beg at shoulder, pick up and k 38 (40–42–44–46) sts on right neck edge to beg of V, pick up and k 38 (40–42–44–46) sts on left neck edge to shoulder. **Row 1:** Purl. **Row 2:** Work Eyelet Row same as on back. **Row 3:** P 38 (40–42–44–46) sts, place a marker on needle, p 38 (40–42–44–46) sts. **Row 4:** K, dec 1 st at beg and end of row and 1 st before and after marker. **Row 5:** Purl. **Row 6:** Repeat Row 4. **Row 7:** Repeat Row 5. **Row 8:** Work Eyelet Row same as on back for hemline row. **Row 9:** Purl. **Row 10:** K, inc 1 st at beg and end of row and 1 st before and after markers. **Row 11:** Purl. Repeat last 2 rows once. Bind off loosely. FRONT NECKBAND: Working from right side and beg at shoulder, pick up and k 32 (34–36–38–40) sts on left neck edge to beg of V, pick up and k 32 (34–36–38–40) sts on right neck edge to shoulder. Work same as back neckband, placing marker at center between the 32nd (34th–36th–38th–

40th) st from each end. ARMHOLE BANDS: Sew shoulder seams, including neckbands. Working from right side and beg at underarm, pick up and k 48 (50–52–54–56) sts around armhole edge. P 1 row. **Next Row:** Work eyelet row same as on back for hemline row. Work in stockinette st (p 1 row, k 1 row) for 3 rows. Bind off loosely.

Finishing. Sew underarm seams, including armhole bands. Turn hemline row at lower edge, neckband and armhole bands to wrong side and sew in place. Block to measurements. Face neckband with grosgrain ribbon.

Lacy Knit Pullover

Directions are given for Size 12. Changes for Sizes 14 and 16 are in parentheses.

Materials. Super Fingering Yarn—3 Ply (1 oz. skeins): 5 (6, 7) skeins of light blue. Knitting Needles, Nos. 3 and 4. 1 Double-Pointed Needle for Cables.

Gauge. 23 sts (one pattern)—3⅛″. 9 rows—1″.

Blocking Measurements:

Sizes 12–14–16
Body Bust Size (In Inches) . . 32–34–36
Actual Knitting Measurements:
Bust 34–36–39
Width across back or front at underarm 17–18–19½
Length from shoulder to lower edge 18–19–20
Length of side seam (excluding armhole band) 11–11½–12

Back. Starting at lower edge with No. 3 needles, cast on 122 (128, 138) sts. Work in k 1, p 1 ribbing for 1½″, increasing one st on last row. Change to No. 4 needles and work in pattern over 123 (129, 139) sts as follows: **1st row (right side):** *For Size 14 Only,* k 3; *For Size 16 Only,* p 1, yo, k 2 tog, k 5; *For All Sizes,* p 1, k 6, * p 1, k 5, yo, sl 1, k 1, psso, p 1, yo, k 2 tog, k 5, p 1, k 6. Repeat from * across to within last 1 (4, 9) sts, complete row in pattern (to complete row in pattern, repeat from * as far as the number of remaining sts will allow you). **2nd and all even rows:** *For Size 14 Only,* p 3; *For Size 16 Only,* k 1, p 7; *For All Sizes,* k 1, p 6, * (k 1, p 7) twice; k 1, p 6. Repeat from * across to within last 1 (4, 9) sts; complete row in pattern. **3rd row:** *For Size 14 Only,* k 3; *For Size 16 Only,* p 1, k 1, yo, k 2 tog, k 4; *For All Sizes,* p 1, k 6, * p 1, k 4, yo, sl 1, k 1, psso, k 1, p 1, k 1, yo, k 2 tog, k 4, p 1, k 6. Repeat from * to last 1 (4, 9) sts; complete row in pattern. **5th row:** *For Size 14 Only,* k 3; *For Size 16 Only,* p 1, k 2, yo, k 2 tog, k 3; *For All Sizes,* p 1, k 6, * p 1, k 3, yo, sl 1, k 1, psso, k 2, p 1, k 2, yo, k 2 tog, k 3, p 1, k 6. Repeat from * to last 1 (4, 9) sts; complete row in pattern. **7th row:** *For Size 14 Only,* k 3; *For Size 16 Only,* p 1, k 3, yo, k 2 tog, k 2; *For All Sizes,* p 1, k 6, * p 1, k 2, yo, sl 1, k 1, psso, k 3, p 1, k 3, yo, k 2 tog, k 2, p 1, k 6. Repeat from * to last 1 (4, 9) sts, *For Size 14 Only,* p 1, k 3; *For Sizes 12 and 16 Only,* complete row in pattern. **9th row:** *For Size 14 Only,* k 3; *For Size 16 Only,* p 1, k 4, yo, k 2 tog, k 1, *For All Sizes,* p 1, k 6, * p 1, k 1, yo, sl 1, k 1, psso, k 4, p 1, k 4, yo, k 2 tog, k 1, p 1, k 6. Repeat from * to last 1 (4, 9) sts, *For Size 14 Only,* p 1, k 3; *For Sizes 12 and 16 Only,* complete row in pattern. **11th row:**

For Size 14 Only, k 3; *For Size 16 Only,* p 1, k 5, yo, k 2 tog, *For All Sizes,* p 1, slip next 3 sts on dp needle and hold in front of work, k next 3 sts, k 3 sts from dp needle—a cable made; * p 1, yo, sl 1, k 1, psso, k 5, p 1, k 5, yo, k 2 tog, p 1, make a cable. Repeat from * to last 1 (4, 9) sts, *For Size 14 Only,* p 1, k 3; *For Sizes 12 and 16 Only,* complete row in pattern. **12th row:** Repeat 2nd row. Last 12 rows form pattern. Work in pattern until total length is 11 (11½, 12) inches, ending with a wrong side row. ARMHOLE SHAPING: Keeping continuity of pattern, bind off 5 (5, 6) sts at beg of next 2 rows. Dec one st at both ends of every other row 6 (7, 8) times, ending with a wrong side row—101 (105), 111) sts. NECK SHAPING: **Next row:** Work in pattern over 50 (52, 55) sts. Place next st on a safety pin for center of neck; place remaining 50 (52, 55) sts on a stitch holder. NECK AND SHOULDER SHAPING: Work over set of sts on needle only, decreasing one st at neck edge every other row 26 (27, 29) times and at the same time when length from first row of armhole shaping is 7 (7½, 8)″, starting at armhole edge bind off 8 sts on every right side row twice. From armhole edge bind off remaining 8 (9, 10) sts. Place sts from holder on a No. 4 needle. Attach yarn to neck edge and work to correspond with other side, reversing shapings.

Neckband. With right side facing and No. 3 needles, starting at right shoulder pick up and k 50 (54, 58) sts along right side edge of neck, k st from safety pin, mark this st; pick up and k 50 (54, 58) sts along left side of neck to shoulder—101 (109, 117) sts on needle. **Row 1:** Work in k 1, p 1 ribbing to within 2 sts before the marked st, k 2 tog, p marked st, k 2 tog, work in p 1, k 1 ribbing to end of row. **Row 2:** Work in ribbing as established, to within 2 sts before marked st, p 2 tog, k marked st, p 2 tog, work in ribbing as established to end of row. **Rows 3, 4, and 5:** Repeat first, 2nd and first rows. Bind off in ribbing. ARMHOLE BAND: With right side facing and No. 3 needles, pick up and k 58 (62, 66) sts along armhole edge. Work in k 1, p 1 ribbing for 5 rows. Bind off in ribbing. Work band along other armhole edge in same way.

Front. Work as for Back until armhole shaping has been completed. Work even in pattern over 101 (105, 111) sts until length from first row of armhole shaping is 3″, ending with a wrong side row. NECK SHAPING: **1st row:** Work in pattern over 38 (40, 43) sts. Place remaining 63 (65, 68) sts on a stitch holder. Work over set of sts on needle only, decreasing one st at neck edge on every row 14 (15, 17) times. Work even over 24 (25, 26) sts until length from first row of armhole shaping is 7 (7½, 8)″, ending at armhole edge. SHOULDER SHAPING: **Row 1:** Bind off 8 sts, work in pattern across. **Row 2:** Work in pattern. **Rows 3 and 4:** Repeat 1st and 2nd rows. From armhole edge bind off remaining 8 (9, 10) sts. Leaving center 25 sts on holder for center of neck, slip remaining 38 (40, 43) sts on a No. 4 needle. Attach yarn to neck edge and work to correspond with other side, reversing shapings.

Neckband. With right side facing and No. 3 needles, starting at right shoulder, pick up and k 36 (40, 44) sts along side of neck, k sts on holder, pick up and k 37 (41, 45) sts along left side of neck—98 (106, 114) sts. Work in k 1, p 1 ribbing for 5 rows. Bind off in ribbing. Work armhole bands as for Back. Block to measurements. Sew side and shoulder seams.

Poorboy Sweater

Directions are for Size 12. Changes for Sizes 14, 16, and 18 are in parentheses.

Materials. Fingering Yarn—5 (5–6–7) balls. Knitting Needles, No. 4. Crochet Hook, No. 4.

Gauge. 7½ sts—1″. 9 rows—1″.

Back. Cast on 118 (126–134–142) sts. Work in ribbing as follows: **Row 1:** K 2, * p 2, k 2. Repeat from * across. **Row 2:** P 2, * k 2, p 2. Repeat from * across. Work in ribbing until piece measures 14 (14–14½–15)″. ARMHOLE SHAPING: Bind off 8 sts at the beg of next 2 rows. Dec 1 st at both ends of every other row 6 times in all. Work on remaining 90 (98–106–114) sts until armholes measure 2½ (2½–3–3½)″. NECK SHAPING: Work across the first 30 (32–34–

36) sts, attach another ball of yarn, bind off center 30 (34–38–42) sts, work across the last 30 (32–34–36) sts. Working on both sides, dec 1 st at neck edge every other row 10 times. Work on remaining 20 (22–24–26) sts until armholes measure 6 (6½–7–7½)″. SHOULDER SHAPING: At each armhole edge bind off 10 (11–12–13) sts every other row, twice.

Front. Work as for back.

Finishing. Sew side and shoulder seams. With right side facing work 2 rows of sc around neck and armhole edges.

Block Sweater

Directions are for Size 10. Changes for Sizes 12, 14, and 16 are in parentheses.

Materials. Sports Yarn—4 (5–5–6) 1-oz. skeins White (Color A); 4 (5–5–6) 1-oz. skeins Blue (Color B). *Or* Featherweight Knitting Worsted— 2 (3–3–3) 2-oz. skeins White (Color A); 2 (3–3–3) 2-oz. skeins Blue (Color B). Knitting Needles, Nos. 2 and 3.

Gauge. Stockinette stitch on No. 3 needles: 7 sts—1″. 10 rows—1″. *Note:* When changing colors, always pick up color to be used from *under* color being dropped to prevent a hole.

Back. With No. 2 needles and skein of A, cast on 61 (63–66–68) sts. On same needle, with skein of B, cast on 61 (63–66–68). With matching colors, starting with a K row work 7 rows in Stockinette stitch. K next row for turn. Change to No. 3 needles. With matching colors work in stockinette stitch on the 122 (126–132–136) sts to 12½″ from turn, ending with a P row. Break off colors. Reverse colors as follows: With A, K across 61 (63–66–68) sts, with B, K across 61 (63–66–68) sts. With matching colors work in stockinette st to 14″ from turn, ending with a P row. Width across back is 17½ (18–18¾–19½)″. ARMHOLE SHAPING: Bind off 7 (7–8–8) sts at beginning of next 2 rows. Dec 1 st each side every other row 7 times. Work on the 94 (98–102–106) sts to 6 (6¼–6½–6¾)″ above underarm, ending on wrong side. Width across shoulders is 13½ (14–14½–15)″. NECK SHAPING: Work across 30 (31–33–34) sts and slip them to a holder, work across center 34 (36–36–38) sts and slip them to a second holder. Work to end. Dec 1 st at neck edge every other row 4 (4–5–5) times. At the same time, when armhole measures 7 (7¼–7½–7¾)″ above underarm, bind off 7 sts at shoulder edge 2 (3–4–3) times; *Sizes 10,*

12 and 16 only, bind off 6 (6–8) sts at same edge 2 (1–1) times. Starting at neck edge work other side to correspond.

Front. Work same as back until armhole measures 6½ (6¾–7–7½)″. NECK SHAPING: Work across 30 (31–33–34) sts and sl them to a holder, work across center 34 (36–36–38) sts and slip them to a second holder. Work to end. Dec 1 st at neck edge every other row 4 (4–5–5) times. Work on the 26 (27–28–29) sts until armhole measures same as on back. SHOULDER SHAPING: Bind off 7 sts at side edge 1 (3–3–4) times; *Sizes 10, 14 and 16 only* bind off 6 (6–8) sts at same edge 3 (1–1) times. Starting at neck work other side to correspond.

Sleeves. With No. 2 needles and skein of A, cast on 37 (38–39–40) sts. On same needle with skein of B, cast on 37 (38–39–40) sts. With matching colors, starting with a K row work 7 rows in stockinette stitch. K next row for turn. Change to No. 3 needles. With matching colors, work in stockinette stitch on the 74 (76–78–80) sts increasing 1 st each side every 1½″ 6 times. Work on the 86 (88–90–92) sts to 12″ above turn, ending on wrong side. Width across sleeve is 12¼ (12½–12¾–13)″. Sleeve cap: Bind off 7 sts at beginning of next 2 rows. Dec 1 st each side every other row until 42 sts remain. Dec 1 st each side *every* row 6 times. Bind off 2 sts at beginning of next 8 rows. Bind off remaining 14 sts.

Finishing. Sew right shoulder seam. FACING: With No. 2 needles and right side facing you, with matching colors pick up and K 66 (68–70–72) sts around front neck including sts on holder, pick up and K 58 (60–62–64) sts around back neck including sts on holder. K next row for turn. Work 4 more rows in stockinette stitch. Bind off. Sew left shoulder seam. Sew sleeves in place. Sew sleeve and underarm seams. Turn in facing and sew in place. Turn up hems and sew in place.

Knitted Two-Piece Dress

Directions are for Size 10. Changes for Sizes 12, 14, 16, and 18 are in parentheses.

Materials. Tweed Yarn—15 (16–17–18–19) White (MC) 2-oz. balls. 1 ball Navy (A). 1 1-oz. skein Scarlet (B) Bouclé. Knitting Needles, No. 8. Crochet Hook, Size G. 1 yard ½″ Elastic. 5 Buttons.

Gauge. 9 sts—2″. 6 rows—1″.

Twisted Stockinette Stitch. Row 1: * K by inserting right-hand needle into back of next st, bring yarn from back to front over point of needle and draw through st, repeat from * across row. **Row 2:** Purl. Repeat these 2 rows for Twisted Stockinette Stitch.

Skirt. This skirt has been planned for 24 (24–24½–24½–24½)″ finished length, allowing 1″ for finishing. If you wish your skirt to be longer or shorter, work more or fewer inches before binding off.

Back. Starting at top of skirt, using MC, cast on 66 (68–72–77–81) sts. Work in twisted stockinette st for 4 rows. On next row inc 1 st each end of needle and repeat this inc every 4th row 6 (7–7–7–7) times more. Work even on 80 (84–88–93–97) sts until entire piece measures 23 (23–23½–23½–23½)". Bind off.

Front. Work same as back.

Finishing. Sew seams. EDGING: Using MC, with right side facing you, work 2 rounds sc around lower edge of skirt. Work 3 rounds sc around upper edge of skirt, holding in to desired waist measurement. Steam. CASING: Join yarn to inside waistband. With wrong side toward you, * ch 5, skip 2 sts, sl st in st ½" below next st, ch 5, skip 2 sts, sl st in next st ½" above next st; repeat from * around. Fasten off. Run elastic, cut to waist measurement, through casing and sew ends securely.

Pullover:

Back. Using MC, cast on 67 (71–77–81–85) sts. Work in twisted stockinette st, inc 1 st each end of needle every 2" 5 times. Work even on 77 (81–87–91–95) sts until entire piece measures 13 (13–13½–13½–13½)", ending with a p row. ARMHOLE SHAPING: At the beg of each of the next 2 rows, bind off 5 (5–5–6–6) sts. Dec 1 st each end of needle every other row 3 (3–4–4–4) times. Work even on 61 (65–69–71–75) sts until armholes measure 5¾ (6–6¼–6½–6¾)". NECK AND SHOULDER SHAPING: On next row work 25 (27–29–30–31) sts, join another ball of MC and bind off center 11 (11–11–11–13) sts, work to end of row. Working on both sides at once, at each neck edge dec 1 st *every row* 8 (9–9–9–9) times and, *at the same time,* when armholes measure 7¼ (7½–7¾–8–8¼)". At each arm edge bind off 8 (9–10–10–11) sts once and 9 (9–10–11–11) sts once.

Front. Work same as back until entire piece measures 9 (9–9½–9½–9½)", ending with a p row—75 (79–85–89–93) sts. FRONT OPENING: On next row work 35 (37–40–42–44) sts, join another ball of MC and bind off center 5 sts, work to end of row. Working on both sides at once, continue to inc 1 st at each arm edge every 2" once more. Work even in twisted stockinette st on 36 (38–41–43–45) sts of each side until entire piece measures 13 (13–13½–13½–13½)", ending with a p row. ARMHOLE SHAPING: At each arm edge, bind off 5 (5–5–6–6) sts. Dec 1 st at same edges every other row 3 (3–4–4–4) times. Work even in twisted stockinette st on 28 (30–32–33–35) sts of each side until armholes measure 4½ (4¾–5–5¼–5½)". NECK SHAPING: At each neck edge, bind off 5 (5–5–5–6) sts. Dec 1 st at same edges every other row 6 (7–7–7–7) times. Work even in twisted stockinette st until armholes measure 7¼ (7½–7¾–8–8¼)". SHOULDER SHAPING: At each arm edge, bind off 8 (9–10–10–11) sts once and 9 (9–10–11–11) sts once.

Sleeves. Using MC, cast on 44 (46–48–48–50) sts. Work in twisted stockinette st, inc 1 st each end of needle every 2 (2–2–2½–2½)" 5 (6–6–7–7) times. Work even on 54 (58–60–62–64) sts until entire piece measures 13½ (13½–14–14–14)", ending with a p row. SHAPING SLEEVE CAP: At the beg of each of the next 2 rows bind off 5 (5–5–6–6) sts. Dec 1 st each end of needle every other row for 4¼ (4½–4¾–5–5¼)". At the beg of each of the next 4 rows bind off 3 sts. Bind off remaining sts.

Finishing. Sew underarm, shoulder and sleeve seams. Set in sleeves. LOWER EDGE: **Rnd 1:** Using MC, with right side facing you work 1 row sc around lower edge, join with sl st. Fasten off. **Rnd 2:** Join Color A in first sc and work 1 sc in each sc, ch 1, turn. **Rnd 3:** Work 1 sc in each sc, join with sl st. Fasten off. **Rnds 4 and 5:** Using double strand Color B, repeat Rnd 2. Fasten off. SLEEVE EDGE: Work in same manner as for lower edge. FRONT EDGE: **Row 1:** Using MC, with right side facing you, starting at lower right front edge, work 1 row sc on right front, neck and left front edges, work 3 sc in each corner st. Fasten off. **Row 2:** BUTTONHOLES: Using Color A, with right side facing you, starting at lower right front edge, work 1 sc in each of next 4 sc, ch 2, skip 2 sc. Make 4 more buttonholes, evenly spaced, the last one to be made 1 st below corner st, work 3 sc in corner st, 1 sc in each sc around neck edge, 3 sc in corner st, 1 sc in each sc along left front edge, ch 1, turn. **Row 3:** Work 1 sc in each sc and in each ch st.

Fasten off. **Row 4:** Using Color B, repeat Row 1, ch 1, turn. **Row 5:** Work 1 sc in each sc, working 3 sc in each corner st. Fasten off. Steam lightly. Sew on buttons.

Cable Knit Dress

Shown in Color Plate 14

Directions are for Size 8. Changes for Sizes 10, 12, 14 and 16 are in parentheses.

Materials. Sport Yarn (2-oz. skein): 6 (7–8–8–8). Knitting Needles, Nos. 6 and 8. Double-Pointed Needle. 5/8″ wide Elastic for waistband.

Gauge. Ribbing slightly stretched: 6 sts—1″; 7 rows—1″.

Skirt Back. Starting at lower edge, with No. 8 needles, cast on 109 (113–119–125–131) sts. **Row 1 (right side):** K 1, * p 1, k 1. Repeat from * across. Mark this row as right side. **Row 2:** P 1, * k 1, p 1. Repeat from * across. Repeat these 2 rows for rib pat. Work in pat until piece measures 16½ (16½–17–17½–18)″ or 1″ less than desired length (1″ is allowed for stretching). Bind off in ribbing.

Skirt Front. Work same as back.

Pocket (Make 2): Starting at lower edge, with No. 8 needles, cast on 43 sts. **Row 1 (right side):** (P 1, k 1) 6 times; p 2, k 1, p 2, k 9, p 2, k 1, p 2; (k 1, p 1) 6 times. **Row 2:** (K 1, p 1) 6 times; k 2, p 1, k 2, p 9, k 2, p 1, k 2; (p 1, k 1) 6 times. **Rows 3 and 4:** Repeat Rows 1 and 2. **Row 5:** (P 1, k 1) 6 times; p 2, k 1, p 2, sl next 3 sts onto a dp needle, hold in back of work, k next 3 sts, bring dp needle to front, k next 3 sts on left-hand needle, then k the 3 sts on dp needle for a cable twist; p 2, k 1, p 2; (k 1, p 1) 6 times. **Rows 6 through 14:** Repeat Rows 2 and 1 four times more, then repeat Row 2 once more. Repeat Rows 5 through 14 once more, then repeat Row 5 and Row 2 once more. Change to No. 6 needles and work in rib pat on all sts for ½″. Bind off loosely in ribbing.

Bodice Back. Starting at lower edge, with No. 8 needles, cast on 99 (103–109–117–123) sts. Work in rib pat until piece measures 8 (8½–8½–8½–9)″; end on wrong side. ARMHOLE SHAPING: Continuing in pat, bind off 5 (6–6–7–8) sts at beg of next 2 rows. Dec 1 st each end every other row 5 (5–6–7–8) times. Work even in rib pat on remaining 79 (81–85–89–91) sts until length from first row of armhole shaping is 6½ (7–7½–8–8½)″; end on wrong side. SHOULDER SHAPING: Continuing in pat, bind off 6 (6–7–8–8) sts at beg of next 2 rows and 7 (7–8–8–9) sts at beg of following 2 rows. Change to No. 6 needles and continue in ribbing on remaining 53 (55–55–57–57) sts for 1″. Bind off loosely in ribbing.

Bodice Front. Starting at lower edge, with No. 8 needles, cast on 105 (109–113–125–129) sts. **Row 1 (right side):** Work in rib pat on 43 (45–47–53–55) sts, place a marker on needle, p 2, k 1, p 2, k 9, p 2, k 1, p 2, place a marker; starting with k 1, work in rib pat on remaining sts. **Row 2:** Work in ribbing as established to marker, sl marker, k 2, p 1, k 2, p 9, k 2, p 1, k 2, sl marker, finish row. **Rows 3 and 4:** Slipping markers, repeat Rows 1 and 2. **Row 5:** Work in pat to first marker, p 2, k 1, p 2, work a cable twist on next 9 sts as on Pocket, p 2, k 1, p 2, finish row. **Rows 6 through 14:** Repeat Rows 2 and 1 four times, then repeat Row 2 once more. Repeat Rows 5 through 14 for pat. Work in pat until piece measures 8 (8½–8½–8½–9)″; end on wrong side. ARMHOLE AND NECK SHAPING: Bind off 5 (6–6–7–8) sts at beg of next 2 rows. **Row 3:** Decreasing 1 st each end, work in pat. **Row 4:** Work even in pat. **Row 5:** Repeat Row 3. **Row 6:** Work in pat across first 41 (42–44–49–50) sts, place remaining sts on stitch holder to be worked later. Continuing in pat, dec 1 st at armhole edge 3 (3–4–5–6) times more. *At the same time,* remove marker and dec 1 st at neck edge every row until 13 (13–15–16–17) sts remain. Work even until armhole measures 6½ (7–7½–8–8½)″, end at armhole edge. SHOULDER SHAPING: **Row 1:** At armhole edge, bind off 6 (6–7–8–8) sts, finish row. **Row 2:** Work across. Bind off remaining sts. Leaving the last 9 sts on stitch holder for center of neck, slip remaining 41 (42–44–49–50) sts onto No. 8 needle; attach yarn at neck edge and work to correspond with opposite side, reversing shapings. With right side facing and No. 6 needles, starting at left shoulder, pick up and k 40 (44–48–52–56) sts along left neck edge to front holder, k the 9 sts on st holder, pick up and k 40 (44–48–52–56) sts along right neck edge. Work in rib pat on the 89 (97–105–113–121) sts for 1″. Bind off in ribbing.

Sleeves. Starting at lower edge, with No. 8 needles, cast on 63 (67–71–75–79) sts. Work in rib pat for 4 rows. Continuing in pat, inc 1 st each end of next row; then every 4th row, 4 times in all. Work in ribbing on 71 (75–79–83–87) sts until sleeve measures 3 (3–3½–3½–3½)″; end on wrong side. SLEEVE CAP: Bind off 5 (6–6–7–8) sts at beg of next 2 rows. Dec 1 st each end every other row until 31 sts remain. Bind off 4 sts at beg of next 4 rows. Bind off remaining sts.

Belt. With No. 6 needles, cast on 18 sts. Work in k 1, p 1 ribbing for desired length (waist measurement plus 5″). Bind off. Attach buckle.

Finishing. Block pieces lightly. Sew side seams of skirt. Sew pockets along side seams 3″ below top of skirt. Sew side, shoulder and sleeve seams. Sew in sleeves. Sew top edge of skirt to lower edge of bodice, gathering skirt to fit. *Casing:* Thread a tapestry needle with a long strand of yarn. On wrong side of dress, working from left to right, insert needle ½″ above waistline seam, then insert needle ½″ below seam. Continue to alternate above and below seam until casing is complete. Cut elastic to waist measurement, draw through casing and sew ends together.

Chin-Chin Cap and Mittens

Materials. *Mohairspun* (1-oz. pull skeins) —2 for headband, 3 for mittens. Knitting Needles, Nos. 6 and 11. 1 Double-Pointed Needle or Cable Holder.

Gauge. 7 sts—2″. 4 rows—1″.

Note: Yarn is used double throughout.

Headband. Using larger needles and a double strand of yarn, cast on 28 sts. Work even in stockinette st until piece measures 7″, ending with a k row. **Dec row:** Change to smaller needles and p 2 tog across row—14 sts. Put a marker in work. Then k 1, p 1 in ribbing until piece measures 6″ above marker, ending with a right-side row. **Inc. row:** On the next row p, inc 1 st in each st—28 sts in all. Change to larger needles and work even in stockinette st until entire piece measures 20″. Bind off. FINISHING: Sew back seam. Steam lightly. Brush vigorously with nylon brush, if desired.

Mittens. Medium size (9½″ long, not including ribbing). To lengthen, add more rows of ribbing; to shorten, omit some ribbing rows. Hand may be lengthened or shortened just before shaping top. CABLE TWIST: To be worked on 6 sts as designated. Sl first 2 sts onto dp needle and hold in front of work, K next 2 sts, place dp needle in back of work, k the next 2 sts on left-hand needle, then k the 2 sts from dp needle.

Right Mitten. Using smaller needles and a double strand of yarn, cast on 26 sts. K 1, p 1 in ribbing for 3″. Change to larger needles. Row 1: K 2, p 2, k 6, p 2, k 14. Rows 2 and 4: P·14, k 2, p 6, k 2, p 2. Row 3: K 2, p 2, work cable twist on next 6 sts, p 2, k 14. SHAPE THUMB GUSSET: **Row 1:** K 2, p 2, k 6, p 2, k 2, put a marker on needle, k in front, in back and in front of next st (2 sts increased), put a marker on needle, k 11. **Row 2 and all even rows:** P up to last 12 sts, k 2, p 6, k 2, p 2. **Row 3:** K 2, p 2, k 6, p 2, k to end of row. **Row 5:** K 2, p 2, k 6, p 2, k 2, inc 1 st in next st, k 1, inc 1 st in next st, k to end of row. Being sure to work a cable twist on the 6 sts of back in same manner as before every 8th row, continue to inc 1 st after first marker and before 2nd marker every 4th row until there are 9 sts between markers. With right side facing you, work to first marker and sl these 14 sts onto a holder, k 9 sts of thumb, sl remaining 11 sts onto another holder. THUMB: Cast on 1 st at end of thumb sts and work even in stockinette st on these 10 sts for 2¼″ or desired length. K 2 tog across row. Break off yarn, leaving a 12″ end. Run end through all sts and draw up tightly. Fasten off. Seam thumb. HAND: With right side facing, sl 14 sts from holder onto larger needles, join a double strand of yarn and pick up 3 sts over thumb, k 11 sts from other holder onto same needle. Continue in pattern as established on 28 sts until piece measures 4″, ending with a wrong-side row. SHAPE TOP: **Row 1:** K 2, p 2 tog, k 6, p 2 tog, k 4, k 2 tog, k 6, k 2 tog, k 2—24 sts. **Row 2:** Work in pattern as established. **Row 3:** K 2, k 2 tog, k 4, k 2 tog, k 4, k 2 tog, k 4, k 2 tog, k 2—20 sts. **Row 4:** Work in pattern as established. **Row 5:** K 2 tog across row—10 sts. Break off yarn, leaving a 12″ end. Run end through all sts and draw up tightly. Fasten off. Seam mitten. Steam lightly. Brush back of mitten vigorously with nylon brush if desired.

Left Mitten. Using smaller needles and a double strand of yarn, cast on 26 sts. K 1, p 1 in ribbing for 3″. Change to larger needles. **Row 1:** K 14, p 2, k 6, p 2, k 2. **Rows 2 and 4:** P 2, k 2, p 6, k 2, p 14. **Row 3:** K 14, p 2, work a cable twist on next 6 sts, p 2, k 2. SHAPE THUMB GUSSET: **Row 1:** K 11, put a marker on needle, k in front, in back and in front of next st (2 sts inc), put a marker on needle, k 2, p 2, k 6, p 2, k 2. Finish to correspond to right mitten.

Plain Skirt

Not shown

Directions are for Size 12. Changes for Sizes 14, 16, 18 and 20 are in parentheses.

Materials. Bouclé or other Dress Yarn—12 (12–14–14–16) ozs. Circular Needle No. 2. Steel Crochet Hook Size 2.

Gauge. 8 st—1″.

Note: To make skirt longer or shorter, work more or less inches before first dec rnd.

Body of Skirt. Cast on 410 (420–430–440–450) sts. Join, being careful not to twist sts. K around for 8 (9½–11–11–12½)″. Next rnd dec 10 sts at evenly spaced intervals. Continue to dec 10 sts (having 1 st less between dec on each dec rnd) every 1½″ 10 (9–8–8–7) times more—300 (320–340–350–370) sts on needle: (Hipline—23″ from start). Work even 1″, dec 10 sts as before, then every 1″ 2 (1–1–1–1) times, then every ½″ 6 (8–8–8–8) times—210 (220–240–250–270) sts on needle. When skirt measures 30″ (or desired length) from start, bind off.

Finishing. Work 1 rnd sc around lower edge of skirt. CASING: Join yarn to inside waistband. With wrong side toward you, * ch 5, skip 2 sts, sl st in st ½″ below next st, ch 5, skip 2 sts, sl st in next st ½″ above next st, repeat from * around. Fasten off. Run elastic, which has been cut to waist measurement, through beading and sew ends tog.

Narrow Rib Skirt

Directions are for Size 12. Changes for Sizes 14, 16, 18, and 20 are in parentheses.

Materials. Bouclé or other Dress Yarn—12 (13–14–15–16) ozs. Circular Knitting Needle No. 2. Steel Crochet Hook Size 2.

Gauge. 8 sts—1″.

Note: To make skirt longer or shorter, work more or less inches before first dec rnd.

Body of Skirt. Cast on 363 (374–385–396–407) sts. Join, being careful not to twist sts. **Rnd 1:** * K 5, p 6, repeat from * to end of rnd. Repeat this rnd until piece measures 17″. **First Dec Rnd:** * K 5, p 2, p 2 tog, p 2, repeat from * to end of rnd—33 (34–35–36–37) sts dec. Now k 5, p 5 in ribbing for 6″. On the next rnd, dec 1 st in center of each p rib. You now have 297 (306–315–324–333) sts. Work in k 5, p 4, ribbing for 2½″. On the next rnd, dec 1 st

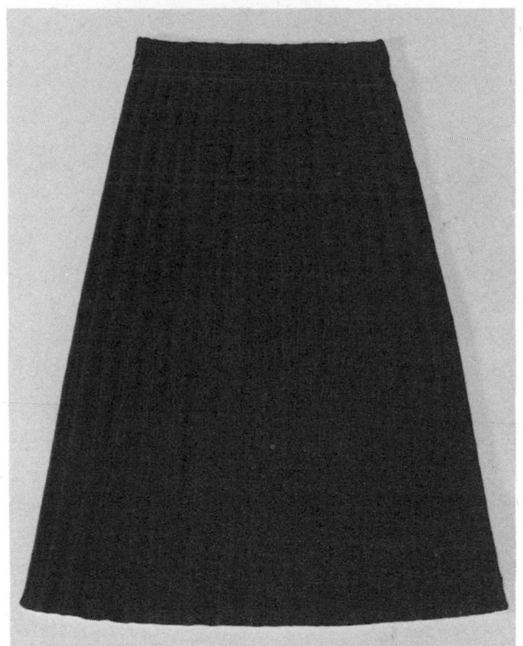

in center of each p rib and repeat this dec every 2½″ once more—231 (238–245–252–259) sts. Work in k 5, p 2 ribbing until skirt measures 30″, or desired length.

Waistband. K the next rnd, dec 31 (26–21–12–3) sts at even intervals. K 1, p 1 in ribbing for 1¼″. Bind off in ribbing.

Finishing. Crochet 1 rnd sc around lower edge of skirt. CASING: Join yarn to inside waistband. With wrong side toward you, * ch 5, skip 2 sts, sl st in st ½″ below next st, ch 5, skip 2 sts, sl st in next st ½″ above next st, repeat from * around. Fasten off. Run elastic, cut to waist measurement, through beading and sew ends tog.

Wide Graduated Rib Panel Skirt

Directions are given for Size 12. Changes for Sizes 14, 16, 18, and 20 are in parentheses.

Materials. Bouclé or other Dress Yarn—1-oz. balls—13 (14–16–17–19). 29″ Circular Knitting Needle No. 2. Steel Crochet Hook Size 2.

Gauge. 8 sts—1″.

Body of Skirt. Cast on 360 (360–396–396–432) sts, join, being careful not to twist sts. **Rnd 1:** * K 18, p 18, repeat from * around. Repeat Rnd 1 for 17″ (for 30″ Skirt—for shorter or longer skirt adjust accordingly). **Next row:** dec 1 st at center of each panel and work even for 2 (3–2–3–2)″. Dec as before, then every 2″ 2 times (3″ 1 time, 2″ 2 times, 3″ 1 time, 2″ 2 times) more. There are now 280 (300–308–330–336) sts on needle and skirt is at hipline, 23″ from start. When skirt measures 24½ (24½–25–25–25)″, dec 1 st in each panel as before, then every 1½″ 3 times (1½″ 3 times, 2″ 2 times, 1½″ 3 times, 2″ 2 times) more. There are now 200 (220–242–242–264) sts on needle. Work even until skirt measures 30″ or desired length from start.

Waistband. Work in ribbing of k 1, p 1, dec 8 sts for Size 14, 18 sts for Size 16, and 8 sts for Size 20, across row. Work even for 1½″, bind off loosely in ribbing. Crochet casing for elastic inside of Waistband. Crochet 1 row of sc around lower edge.

Bow-Bedecked Scarf

An easy-to-knit scarf which lies softly about your face and shoulders and is decked with a bright, contrasting bow.

Materials. Mohair—ten 1-oz. balls. Featherweight Knitting Worsted—one 2-oz. skein. Knitting Needles, No. 13; Steel Crochet Hook, Size 1.

Gauge. 5 sts—2″.

Scarf. With double strand of Mohair, cast on 50 sts. Work in stockinette st (k 1 row and p 1 row) for about 50″, or until all but about 1½ yards of yarn are used. Bind off. Fold in 2″ hem on one long edge and sew to wrong side. Steam very lightly, stretching slightly lengthwise; then brush very gently to bring up a soft "fuzzy" nap.

Crocheted Bow. With single strand of Featherweight, ch 9. **Row 1:** 1 single crochet in ch 2 from hook and in each of next 7 chs. Ch. 1, turn. **Row 2:** 1 single crochet in each st. Ch. 1, turn. Repeat Row 2 for 20″ and tie.

Shoulderette

Materials. Fingering Yarn 3 ply—6 ozs. Knitting Needles, Nos. 3 and 10. Steel Crochet Hook Size 2.

Gauge. 5 sts—1″.

Jiffy Garter Pattern. Row 1: With No. 10 needles, knit across. **Row 2:** With No. 3 needles, knit across. Repeat these 2 rows for pattern, continuing to change needles. Starting at cuff, with No. 3 needles, cast on 50 sts. K 1, p 1 for 5″. On the next row knit, inc 1 st in each st. Now work in pat until piece measures 45″ from start, or 5″ less than desired length. K 2 sts tog across the next row. With No. 3 needles, k 1, p 1 in ribbing for 5″. Bind off in ribbing.

Finishing. Sew cuffs and sleeves for 12″ from each end. EDGING: Join yarn at one end of opening. Crochet 1 row sc around opening. **Row 2:** * Ch 3, sc into first ch, skip 1 st, sc in next st, repeat from * around. Fasten off.

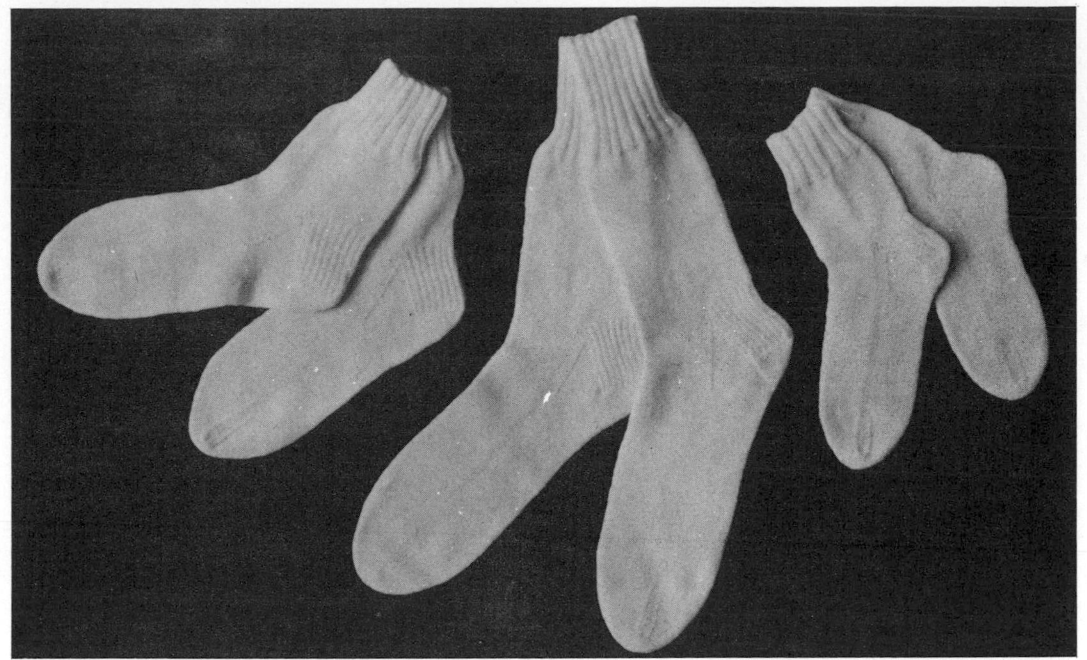

Socks for the Family

Directions are for Children's Size 7½. Changes for Women's Size 9½ and Men's Size 11½ are in parentheses.

Materials. Nylon and Wool, 3 ply—1 oz. for children and women, 2 ozs. for men. Double-Pointed Sock Needles, No. 2.

Gauge. 9 sts—1″. 12 rows—1″.

Cuffs. Cast on 52 (64–68) sts, 18 (22–24) sts on each of 2 needles and 16 (20–20) sts on third needle. Join, being careful not to twist sts. K 2, p 2 in ribbing for 1¾ (2¼–3½)″. *Children's socks only:* Dec 2 sts on last rnd. Now k round and round until work measures 4½ (5–11)″ from start, working to within last 12 (17–17) sts of 3rd needle. Slip last 12 (17–17) sts of 3rd needle and first 12 (17–17) sts of 1st needle onto one needle for heel and remaining 26 (30–34) sts onto 2 needles for instep.

Heel. Row 1 (right side): * Sl 1, k 1, repeat from * across row. **Row 2:** Sl 1, p to end of row. Repeat these 2 rows 11 (15–15) times more—24 (32–32) rows. TURN HEEL: K 14 (19–19), k 2 tog, k 1 turn. **Row 2:** Sl 1, p 5, p 2 tog, p 1, turn. **Row 3:** Sl 1, k 6, k 2 tog, k 1, turn. **Row 4:** Sl 1, p 7, p 2 tog, p 1, turn. Continue in this manner (k or p 1 st more every row) until 16 (20–20) sts remain on Row—8 (14–14). *Children's socks only:* **Row 9:** Sl 1, k 12, k 2 tog, turn. **Row 10:** Sl 1, p 12, p 2 tog—14 sts on needle. *On all sizes:* K 7 (10–10) sts to center of heel. Divide sts on 3 needles as follows: 1st needle: K remaining 7 (10–10) sts of heel, pick up and k 12 (16–16) sts at side of heel—19 (26–26) sts; 2nd needle: Work across instep sts; 3rd needle: Pick up and k 12 (16–16) sts at other side of heel, k 7 (10–10) sts to center of heel. Work around as follows: **Row 1:** K to last 3 sts on 1st needle, k 2 tog, k 1; work across sts on 2nd needle; 3rd Needle; K 1, sl 1, k 1, psso, k to end of row. **Row 2:** Knit. Repeat these last 2 rows 6 (8–8) times more. *Children's socks only:* dec 2 sts on instep needle. *Women's and men's sizes only:* sl 1 st from 1st and 3rd needles onto 2nd needle (32 sts on 2nd needle and 16 sts on 1st and 3rd needles). *All sizes:* K round and round until foot measures 6¼ (7½–9½)″, or desired length, allowing 1¼ (2–2)″ to finish toe. SHAPE TOE: **Row 1:** 1st Needle: K to last 3 sts on needle, k 2 tog, k 1; 2nd Needle: K 1, sl 1, k 1, psso, k to last 3 sts, k 2 tog, k 1; 3rd Needle: K 1, sl 1, k 1, psso, k to end of needle. **Row 2:** Knit. Repeat these last 2 rows until 20 (24–24) sts remain. With 3rd needle, k 5 (6–6) sts from 1st needle—10 (12–12) sts on each of 2 needles. Weave or sew sts tog.

Gloves for the Family

Directions are for Size 4. Changes for Sizes 5, 6, 7, 8, and 9 are in parentheses.

Materials. Nylon and Wool, 3 ply—1 oz. for Sizes 4 through 6; 2 ozs. for Sizes 7 through 9. Double-Pointed Needles, No. 2.

Gauge. 9 sts—1″. 12 rows—1″.

Right Glove. Cast on 46 (50–54–60–64–68) sts. Divide sts onto 3 needles and join, being careful not to twist sts. K 1, p 1 in ribbing for 2 (2–2½–2½–3–3)″. K around for 6 rnds, then start thumb increases as follows: **Rnd 1:** Inc 1 st in each of first 2 sts (4 sts in thumb), k to end of rnd. **Rnds 2 and 3:** Knit. **Rnd 4:** Inc 1 st in first st, k 2, inc 1 st in next st, k to end of rnd. **Rnds 5 and 6:** Knit. **Rnd 7:** Inc 1 st in first st, k 4, inc 1 st in next st, k to end of rnd. Continue to inc 2 sts in this manner (having 2 sts more between increases) every 3rd rnd until there are 16 (18–18–20–20–22) sts in thumb. Slip these sts onto a holder and cast on 2 sts over these sts. K around on 46 (50–54–60–64–68) sts until piece measures 5 (5½–6½–6¾–7½–7¾)″ from start, or desired length to base of fingers. FIRST FINGER: K first 7 (7–8–8–9–9) sts of 1st needle (palm), cast on 2 sts, then k last 7 (8–8–9–9–10) sts of 3rd needle (back of hand) and place remaining sts on a holder. Divide sts on 3 needles. Join and k around on these 16 (17–18–19–20–21) sts for 2 (2¼–2¾–2¾–3–3)″. **Next Rnd:** * K 2 tog, k 1, repeat from * ending k 2 tog (k 2–0–k 2 tog–k 2–0). K 1 rnd even. **Next Rnd:** * K 2 tog, repeat from * to end of rnd. Cut yarn, draw through remaining sts and fasten. SECOND FINGER: Join yarn and k 6 (6–7–7–8–8) sts from palm of hand, cast on 2 sts, k next 6 (7–7–8–8–9) sts from back of hand, pick up 2 sts over the 2 sts cast on first finger. Join and k around for 2¼ (2½–3–3–3¼–3¼)″. Dec and finish as for first finger. THIRD FINGER: Join yarn and k next 5 (5–6–7–7–8) sts from palm of hand, cast on 2 sts, k next 5 (6–6–7–8–8) sts from back of hand, pick up 2 sts overcast on sts for second finger. Join and k around. Finish as for first finger. FOURTH FINGER: Pick up remaining sts and pick up 2 sts over the cast-on sts of third finger. Join and k around for 1¾ (1¾–2–2–2½–2½)″. Finish as for other fingers. THUMB: Pick up sts from st holder and 2 sts over cast-on sts of hand. Join and k around on 18 (20–20–22–22–24) sts for 1¾ (2–2¼–2¼–2½–2½)″. Dec and finish as for other fingers.

Left Glove. Work to correspond to right glove, reversing all shaping.

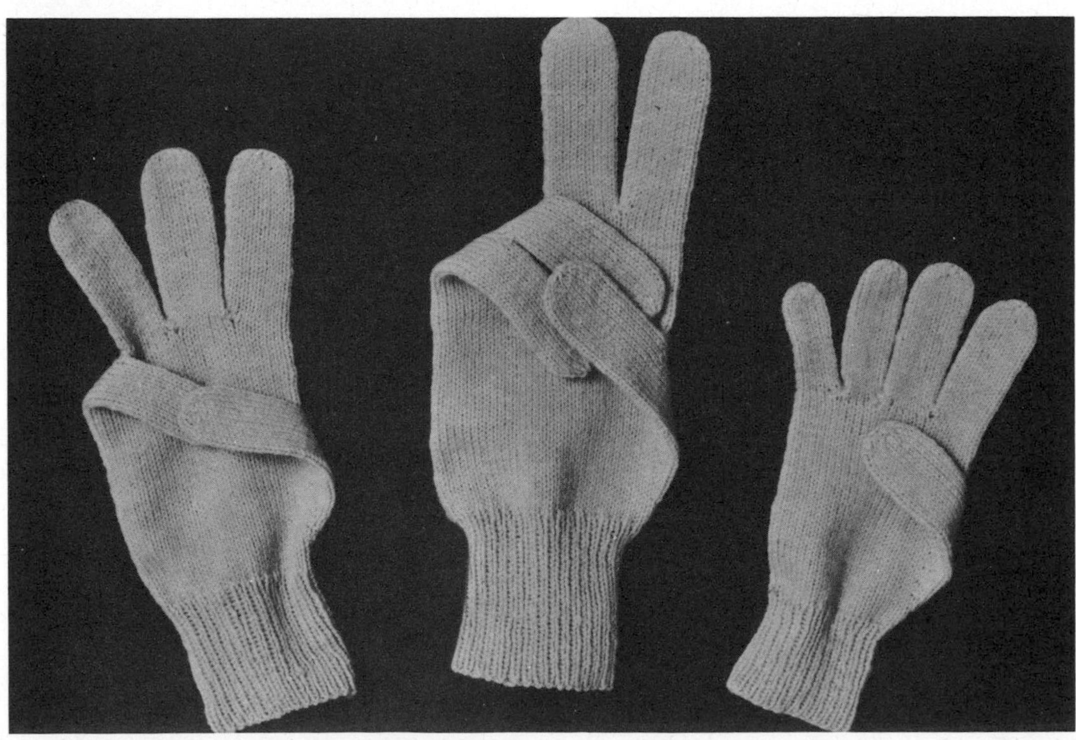

Cable Socks

Sizes 7½–12½

Materials. Nylon and Wool—3 ply. Sizes 7½–9½, 3 ozs. Sizes 10–12½, 4 ozs. Double-Pointed Sock Needles, No. 1.

Gauge. 9 sts—1″. 12 rnds—1″.

Cuffs. Starting at cuff, cast on 68 sts loosely. Divide sts among 3 needles. Join, being careful not to twist sts. Work in k 1, p 1 ribbing for 2″, inc evenly to 72 sts on last rnd. Work in pat as follows: **Rnd 1:** * P 2, k 2, p 2, k 6. Repeat from * around. **Rnd 2:** * P 2, k 2, p 2, make a cable over next 6 sts (to make a cable, slip the first 3 sts onto a spare needle and place in back of work, k the next 3 sts, then k the 3 sts from spare needle). Repeat from * around. **Rnds 3 to 7:** Repeat rnd 1. Rnds 2 to 7 constitute the pattern. Work in pat until piece measures 11″ in all, or desired length. Divide sts for heel as follows: With 4th needle, k across first 16 sts; sl 22 sts from 3rd needle onto other end of 4th needle (38 sts on heel needle). Divide remaining 34 sts on 2 needles for instep. Work back and forth over the heel sts only as follows:

Heel. Row 1: Sl 1, p across, dec 4 sts evenly. **Row 2:** * Sl 1, k 1, repeat from * across. **Row 3:** Sl 1, p across. Repeat last 2 rows alternately until piece measures 2¼″, ending with a p row. TURN HEEL: **Row 1:** K 21, k 2 tog, k 1, turn. **Row 2:** Sl 1, p 9, p 2 tog, p 1, turn. **Row 3:** Sl 1, k 10, k 2 tog, k 1, turn. **Row 4:** Sl 1, p 11, p 2 tog, p 1, turn. **Row 5:** Sl 1, k 12, k 2 tog, k 1, turn. **Row 6:** Sl 1, p 13, p 2 tog, p 1, turn. **Row 7:** Sl 1, k 14, k 2 tog, k 1, turn. **Row 8:** Sl 1, p 15, p 2 tog, p 1, turn. **Row 9:** Sl 1, k 16, k 2 tog, k 1, turn. **Row 10:** Sl 1, p 17, p 2 tog, p 1, turn. **Row 11:** Sl 1, k 18, k 2 tog, k 1, turn. **Row 12:** Sl 1, p 19, p 2 tog, p 1, turn. **Row 13:** K across (22 sts on heel needle).

Instep. With heel needle, 1st needle, pick up and k 16 sts along side of heel; with 2nd needle, work in pat across instep sts; with 3rd needle, pick up and k 16 sts along other side of heel; k 11 sts from heel needle. There are 27 sts on 1st and 3rd needles; 34 sts on

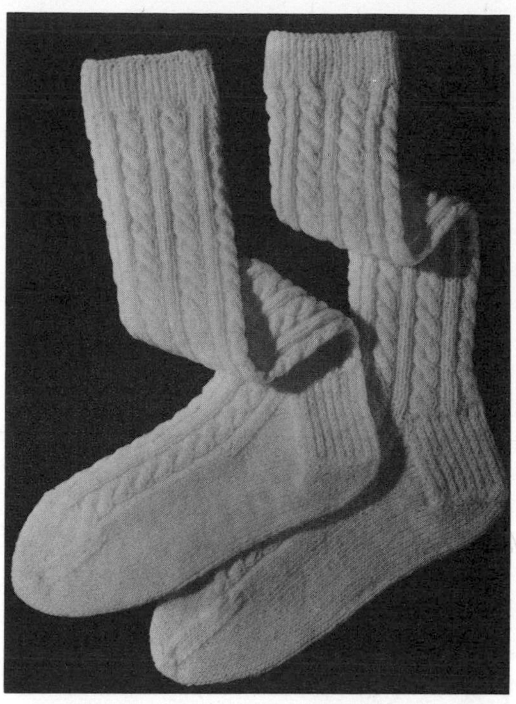

2nd needle. SHAPE INSTEP: **Rnd 1:** K to last 3 sts on 1st needle, k 2 tog, k 1; work in pat across 2nd needle; on 3rd needle k 1, sl 1, k 1, psso, k to end of rnd. **Rnd 2:** K across 1st needle, work in pat across 2nd needle; k across 3rd needle. Repeat the last 2 rnds until 34 sts remain on 1st and 3rd needles. Work even until piece measures 2½″ less than required foot size.

Shape Toe. Rnd 1: On 1st needle, k to last 3 sts, k 2 tog, k 1; on 2nd needle, k 1, sl 1, k 1, psso, k across to last 3 sts, k 2 tog, k 1; on 3rd needle k 1, sl 1, k 1, psso, k to end of rnd. **Rnd 2:** K around. Repeat the last 2 rnds until 20 sts remain. With 3rd needle, k across sts of 1st needle (10 sts on each of 2 needles). Weave sts tog.

Crazy-Quilt Afghan

Shown in Color Plate 15

About 46″ by 60″ plus fringe.

Materials. 4-ply Knitting Worsted (2-oz. skein)—2 skeins each Purple Glow, White, Turquoise, Luscious Pink, Tangerine; 1 each Winter White, Beige, Cranberry, Sapphire, Kelly Green, Orange, Charcoal Brown Heather, Moccasin, Dark Turquoise;

3 each Celery Leaf. Knitting Needles, No. 10. Crochet Hook, Size H.

Gauge. Stockinette st: 4 sts—1″; 6 rows —1″.

Note: Afghan is knit in 8 strips, then sewn together.

Pattern Stitches. PAT. 1: Stockinette st (k 1 row, p 1 row). PAT. 2: **Row 1 (right side):** * P 1, k 3, repeat from *, end p 3, k 2. **Rows 2, 3 & 4:** K the k sts and p the p sts. **Row 5:** * K 3, p 3, repeat from *, end p 2 instead of 3. **Rows 6, 7 & 8:** K the k sts and p the p sts. Repeat these 8 rows for pat. PAT. 3: **Row 1 (right side):** K 1, * p 1, k 1, repeat from * across. **Row 2:** P. **Row 3:** P 1, * k 1, p 1, repeat from * across. **Row 4:** P. Repeat these 4 rows for pat. PAT. 4: **Row 1 (right side):** * P 4, k 2, repeat from *, end p 4, k 1. **Rows 2, 3 & 4:** K the k sts and p the p sts. **Row 5:** K. **Row 6:** P. **Row 7:** P 1, k 2, * p 4, k 2, repeat from *, end p 2. **Rows 8, 9 & 10:** K the k sts and p the p sts. **Row 11:** K. **Row 12:** P. Repeat these 12 rows for pat. PAT. 5: Stockinette st as follows: 4 rows Tangerine, 2 rows Kelly Green (7 times), then 4 more rows Tangerine. PAT. 6: **Rows 1 and 2:** With Purple k 1 row, p 1 row. **Row 3:** With Celery k 3, * with yarn at back sl 1 as if to p, k 3, repeat from * across. **Row 4:** With Celery p 3, * with yarn at front sl 1, p 3, repeat from * across. **Rows 5 and 6:** With Purple k 1 row, p 1 row. **Row 7:** With Celery k 1, sl 1, * k 3, sl 1, repeat from *, end k 1. **Row 8:** With Celery p 1, sl 1, * p 3, sl 1, repeat from *, end p 1. Repeat these 8 rows for pat. PAT. 7: (*Note:* When changing colors, pick up new color from under dropped color to avoid hole.) **Row 1 (right side):** K 2 White, * k 2 Moccasin, 2 White, repeat from *, end k 1 Moccasin. **Row 2:** P 2 Moccasin, * 2 White, 2 Moccasin, repeat from *, end p 1 White. **Row 3:** K 2 Moccasin, * 2 White, 2 Moccasin, repeat from *, end 1 White. **Row 4:** P 2 White, * 2 Moccasin, 2 White, repeat from *, end 1 Moccasin. Repeat these 4 rows for pat. PAT. 8: **Row 1 (right side):** K 2 White, * 2 Purple, 2 White, repeat from *, end 1 Purple. **Row 2:** P 2 White, * 2 Purple, 2 White, repeat from *, end 1 Purple. **Row 3:** K 2 Purple, * 2 White, 2 Purple, repeat from *, end 1 White. **Row 4:** P 2 Purple, * 2 White, 2 Purple, repeat from *, end 1 White. Repeat these 4 rows for pat. PAT. 9: **Row 1 (right side):** P 1, k 4, * p 2, k 4, repeat from * across. **Rows 2, 3 and 4:** K the k sts and p the p sts. **Row 5:** K 1, p 4, * k 2, p 4, repeat from * across. **Row 6:** K 2, p 2, * k 4, p 2, repeat from *, end k 1. Repeat these 6 rows for pat. PAT. 10: K 1, * p 1, k 1, repeat from * across. Repeat for moss st. PAT. 11: Stockinette st as follows: 4 rows White, 4 rows Kelly Green (3 times). PAT. 12: **Row 1 (right side):** With Sapphire k 3, * p 1, k 3, repeat from * across. **Row 2:** P. Repeat these 2 rows for pat. PAT. 13: **Row 1 (right side):** K. **Row 2:** P. **Row 3:** K 1, * p 1, k 1, repeat from * across. **Row 4:** P. Repeat these 4 rows for pat.

Afghan. STRIP 1: With Purple cast on 23 sts. Work Pat. 1 for 9½″, end with a k row. Break off. With Tangerine p 1 row, then work Pat. 2 for 9½″, end with Row 7. Break off. With Turquoise p 1 row. Work Pat. 3 for 9½″, end on right side. Break off. With Celery p 1 row. Work Pat. 4 for 9½″, end on wrong side. Break off. Work Pat. 5 for 9½″, end on wrong side. Break off. Work Pat. 6 for 9½″, end on wrong side. Break off. Join Beige, work Pat. 1 for 4¾″. Bind off. With 1 strand Tangerine embroider 8 stars (below) on Purple block. With 2 strands Purple embroider 4 diagonal stripes in running st from right to left evenly spaced on Turquoise block. STRIP 2: With White cast on 23 sts. Join Moccasin, work Pat. 7 for 4¾″, end on wrong side. Break off Moccasin. With Purple and White work Pat. 8 for 9½″, end on wrong side. Break off. With Pink and Kelly Green work Pat. 5 for 9½″, end on right side. Break off.

Star Stitch. Begin star by making a ½-inch vertical stitch. Then work a cross stitch over the vertical stitch evenly to form a star.

With Orange p 1 row. Work Pat. 9 for 9½″, end on wrong side. Break off. With White and Sapphire work Pat. 6 for 9½″, end on right side. Break off. With Pink p 1 row, then work Pat. 2 for 9½″, end with Row 7. Break off. With Celery p 1 row. Work Pat. 3 for 9½″. Bind off. STRIP 3: With White cast on 23 sts. Work Pat. 1 for 9½″, end with a p row. Break off. With Turquoise work Pat. 10 for 9½″, end on right side. Break off. With Charcoal Brown p 1 row. Work Pat. 2 for 9½″, end on wrong side. Break off. With Beige work Pat. 1 for 9½″, end on wrong side. Break off. With White and Celery work Pat. 7 for 9½″, end on wrong side. Break off. With Pink and Winter White work Pat. 8 for 9½″, end on wrong side. Break off. With Orange work Pat. 10 for 4¾″. Bind off. With lazy daisy st (below) embroider 3 Pink and 3 Dark

Lazy Daisy Stitch. Bring thread up at base of loop; insert needle in same place. Take a short stitch with thread under needle, forming loop; hold down loop with a short stitch.

Turquoise daisies on White block. On Brown block embroider 8 Tangerine stars. On Beige block embroider Purple diamonds in duplicate st (below) over 2 rows. STRIP 4: With White cast on 23 sts. Work Pat. 11 for 4¾″, end on right side. Break off. With Celery p 1 row. Work Pat. 4 for 9½″, end on right side. Break off. With Sapphire p 1 row. Work Pat. 12 for 9½″, end on wrong side. Break off. With Cranberry and Winter White work Pat. 5 for 9½″, end on right side. Break off. With Purple p 1 row. Work Pat. 2 for 9½″, end on wrong side. Break off. With Winter White work Pat. 10 for 9½″, end on wrong side. Break off. With Dark Turquoise work Pat. 13 for 9½″. Bind off. With Orange crochet a ch in each p rib of Sapphire block. Embroider 8 Tangerine stars on Winter White block. Repeat Strips 1, 2, 3 & 4 once more, working 7 Dark Turquoise stars on Orange block of Strip 2 and omitting embroidery on White block of Strip 3 and on Winter White block of Strip 4. Sew strips together. With Beige on right side along side edges work 2 sc in first row, * skip 2 rows, 2 sc in next row, repeat from * to end. Fasten off. FRINGE: Cut strands 13 inches long. Knot 8 strands of 1 color in first st. Repeat across having 8 fringes in each strip, varying colors as desired. Repeat at other end.

Duplicate Stitch. *Draw yarn to right side at base of stitch. Insert needle under 2 strands at top of 2nd stitch above; draw through. Insert needle back into base of first stitch. Repeat from*.

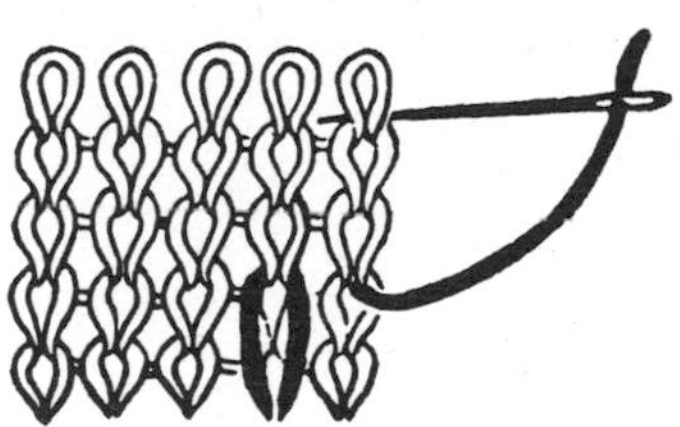

Bedspread

Materials. Mercerized Bedspread Cotton: Single Size Spread, 72×106″ (including fringe)—24 balls of White, Ecru, or Cream; Double Size Spread, 92×106″ (including fringe)—30 balls of White, Ecru, or Cream. Steel Double-Pointed Knitting Needles, No. 0.

Gauge. Block measures 10″ square.

Block. Starting at the center, cast on 8 sts on 4 needles. **Rnd 1:** * Yo, k 1, repeat from * around (16 sts). **Rnd 2:** K around. **Rnd 3:** * Yo, k 1, repeat from * around (32 sts). **Rnd 4:** K around. **Rnd 5:** * Yo, p 2, (k 1, yo) twice; k 1, p 2, yo, k 1, repeat from * around. **Rnd 6:** * P 3, k 5, p 3, k 1, repeat from * around (48 sts). **Rnd 7:** * Yo, p 3, k 2, yo, k 1, yo, k 2, p 3, yo, k 1, repeat from * around. **Rnd 8:** * P 4, k 7, p 4, k 1, repeat from * around (64 sts). **Rnd 9:** * Yo, p 4, k 3, yo, k 1, yo, k 3, p 4, yo, k 1, repeat from * around. **Rnd 10:** * P 5, k 9, p 5, k 1, repeat from * around (80 sts). **Rnd 11:** * Yo, p 5, k 4, yo, k 1, yo, k 4, p

5, yo, k 1, repeat from * around. **Rnd 12:** * P 6, k 11, p 6, k 1, repeat from * around (96 sts). **Rnd 13:** * Yo, p 6, place thread at back of work, sl 1, k 1, psso, k 7, k 2 tog, p 6, yo, k 1, repeat from * around. **Rnd 14:** * P 7, k 9, p 7, k 1, repeat from * around. **Rnd 15:** * Yo, p 3, yo, k 1, yo, p 3; sl 1, k 1, psso, k 5, k 2 tog, p 3, yo, k 1, yo, p 3, yo, k 1, repeat from * around. **Rnd 16:** * P 4, k 3, p 3, k 7, p 3, k 3, p 4, k 1, repeat from * around (112 sts). **Rnd 17:** * Yo, p 4, (k 1, yo) twice; k 1, p 3; sl 1, k 1, psso, k 3, k 2 tog, p 3, (k 1, yo) twice; k 1, p 4, yo, k 1, repeat from * around. **Rnd 18:** * P 5, k 5, (p 3, k 5) twice; p 5, k 1, repeat from * around (128 sts). **Rnd 19:** * Yo, p 5; k 2, yo, k 1, yo, k 2; p 3, sl 1, k 1, psso, k 1, k 2 tog, p 3; k 2, yo, k 1, yo, k 2; p 5, yo, k 1, repeat from * around. **Rnd 20:** * P 6, k 7, p 3, k 3, p 3, k 7, p 6, k 1, repeat from * around (144 sts). **Rnd 21:** * Yo, p 6, k 3, yo, k 1, yo, k 3, p 3, sl 1, k 2 tog, psso, p 3, k 3, yo, k 1, yo, k 3, p 6, yo, k 1, repeat from * around. **Rnd 22:** * (P 7, k 9) twice; p 7, k 1, repeat from * around (160 sts). **Rnd 23:** * Yo, (p 7, k 4, yo, k 1, yo, k 4) twice; p 7, yo, k 1, repeat from * around. **Rnd 24:** * P 8, k 11, p 7, k 11, p 8, k 1, repeat from * around (184 sts). **Rnd 25:** * Yo, p 8, sl 1, k 1, psso, k 7, k 2 tog, p 7, sl 1, k 1, psso, k 7, k 2 tog, p 8, yo, k 1, repeat from * around. **Rnd 26:** * P 9, k 9, p 7, k 9, p 9, k 1, repeat from * around (176 sts). **Rnd 27:** * Yo, p 9, sl 1, k 1, psso, k 5, k 2 tog, p 7, sl 1, k 1, psso, k 5, k 2 tog, p 9, yo, k 1, repeat from * around. **Rnd 28:** * P 10, k 7, p 7, k 7, p 10, k 1, repeat from * around (168 sts). **Rnd 29:** * Yo, p 10, sl 1, k 1, psso, k 3, k 2 tog, p 7, sl 1, k 1, psso, k 3, k 2 tog, p 10, yo, k 1, repeat from * around. **Rnd 30:** * P 11, k 5, p 7, k 5, p 11, k 1, repeat from * around (160 sts). **Rnd 31:** * Yo, p 11, sl 1, k 1, psso, k 1, k 2 tog, p 7, sl 1, k 1, psso, k 1, k 2 tog, p 11, yo, k 1, repeat from * around. **Rnd 32:** P 12, k 3, p 7, k 3, p 12, k 1, repeat from * around (152 sts). **Rnd 33:** * Yo, p 12, sl 1, k 2 tog, psso, p 7, sl 1, k 2 tog, psso, p 12, yo, k 1, repeat from * around. **Rnd 34:** * P 35, k 1, repeat from * around (144 sts). **Rnd 35:** * Yo, k 35, yo, k 1, repeat from * around. **Rnd 36:** * K 2, (yo, k 2 tog) 17 times; k 2, repeat from * around. Turn. **Rnd 37:** * Yo, p 37, yo, k 1, repeat from * around (160 sts). Now work back and forth across 1 needle only as follows: **Row 1:** Bind off 1 st, k across (39 sts), turn. **Row 2:** (right side): K 1, k 2 tog, * yo, k 2 tog, repeat from * across. **Row 3:** K 2 tog, * yo, k 2 tog, repeat from * across. **Row 4:** K 2 tog, * yo, k 2 tog, repeat from * across, ending k 1. **Row 5:** K 1, k 2 tog, * yo, k 2 tog, repeat from * across, ending k 1. Repeat the last 4 rows (2nd to 5th rows incl) until 4 sts remain. **Next row:** K 1, k 2 tog, k 1. Bind off. With wrong side facing, join thread at next needle and, starting with Row 1, work across the next group of sts. Complete remaining two sides to correspond. *For single-size spread* make 6 rows of 10 Blocks. *For double-size spread* make 8 rows of 10 Blocks. Sew Blocks neatly together on wrong side. Finish edges with Plain or Knotted Fringe or Tassels.

Plain Fringe. Cut 10 strands of thread, each 12″ long. Double these strands to form a loop. Insert hook in space on edge of bedspread and draw loop through. Draw loose ends through loop and pull up tightly to form a knot. Make a fringe in every other space (or every ½″) around spread. When fringe is completed, trim ends evenly.

Knotted Fringe. Cut 8 strands of thread, each 16″ long, and make a Plain Fringe around edges of spread. Pick up 8 strands of the first fringe and 8 strands of the second fringe and make a knot 1″ down and in the center between 2 previous knots. Pick up remaining strands of second fringe and first 8 strands of next fringe and knot as before. Continue in this manner around. Trim ends evenly.

Tassel. Cut a cardboard 4″×5″. Lay two 8″ strands across width of cardboard. Wind thread around length of cardboard 60 times. Pick up the two 8″ lengths and tie securely. Remove from cardboard and cut loops at opposite end. Wind a strand of thread several times around top, 1″ down from where tassel was tied. Trim ends evenly.

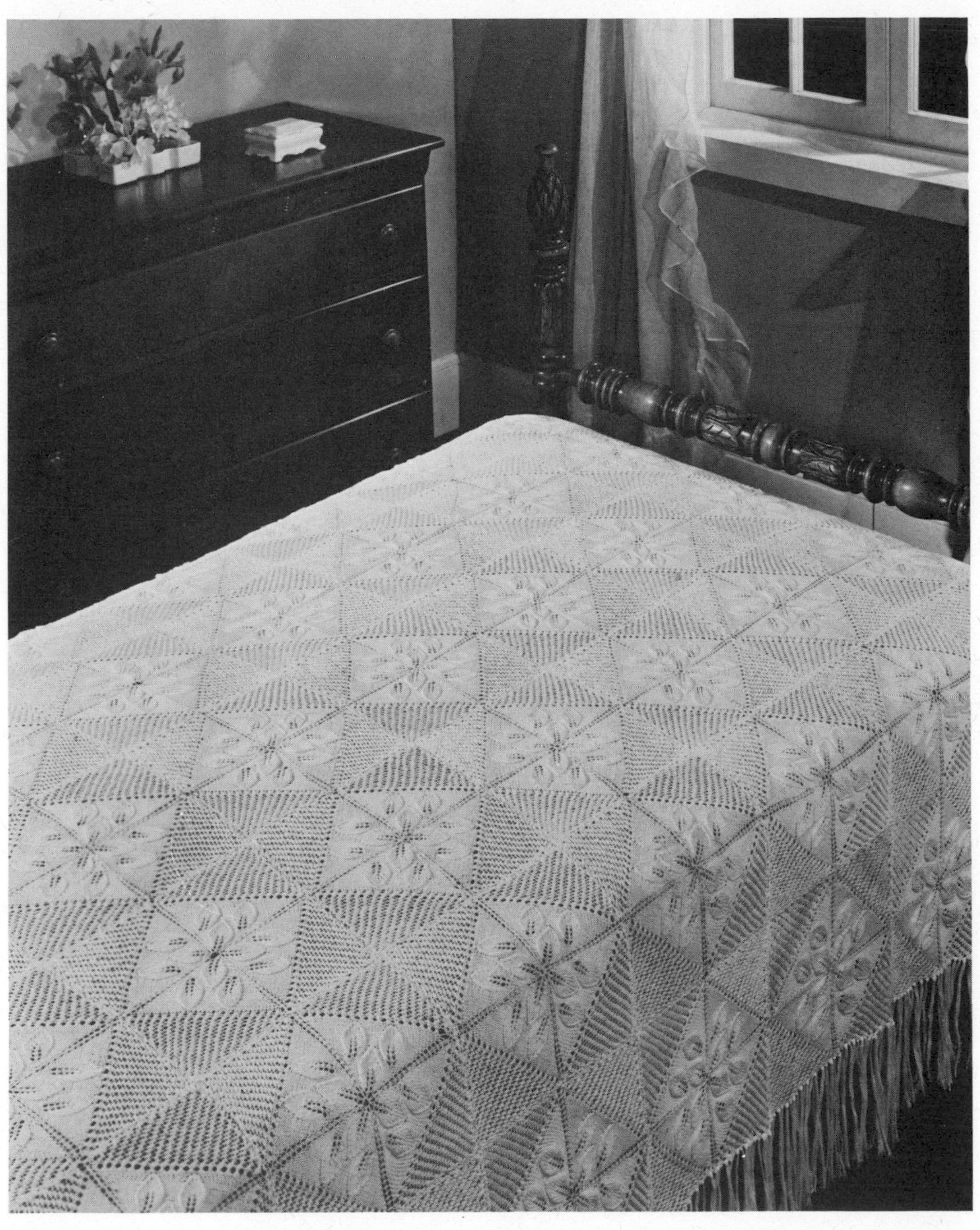

Chapter 8

Crochet

The word crochet is derived from the French word "croche" meaning hook. Originally one of a number of lace-making tools, the hook came to be used alone to fashion a multitude of designs.

For many years crochet was carried on almost entirely in convents. The terrible Irish famine of 1846 gave it a great impetus, for pupils of the nuns made and sold crocheted articles, with the proceeds used to alleviate suffering. Rare patterns of old lace were skillfully copied by the Irish girls. One of the loveliest types of crochet work—"Irish Crochet"—was famous as far back as 1743, when the Royal Dublin Society awarded prizes for outstanding examples of the art. Crochet gradually became one of the graceful accomplishments of the well-born ladies of the time.

Because it is so fascinating and versatile, crochet has become a well-loved hand art. Hook and thread plus agile fingers can produce an endless variety of tasteful designs, both modern in feeling and traditional, each with its special charm.

New threads, new stitches, or rather, variations of old ones, constantly appear and open up further possibilities to challenge the imagination of the crochet enthusiast.

ABBREVIATIONS

ch . . . . chain
sc . . . . single crochet
hdc or half dc . . . . . . half double crochet
dc . . . . double crochet
tr . . . . treble
d tr . . . . double treble
sl st . . . . slip stitch
st(s) . . . . stitch(es)
tog . . . . together
dec . . . . decrease
inc(s) . increasing, increased, increase(s)
incl . . . . inclusive
rnd . . . . round
sp . . . . space
bl(s) . . . . block, blocks
pat . . . . pattern
beg . . . . beginning
pc . . . . picot
yo . . . . yarn over
rem . . . . remaining

* This symbol (asterisk) means that the instructions immediately following it are to be repeated the given number of times.

Repeat instructions in parentheses as many times as specified. For example: "(ch 5, sc in next sc) 5 times," means to do everything in parentheses 5 times in all.

GAUGE

Gauge in crochet, as in knitting, is extremely important. It means the number of stitches and the number of rows equivalent to one inch and is given with each instruction when necessary. Make a swatch or practice piece at least 2 inches square, using the hook and thread specified in the instructions. Block it; then measure. If it does not correspond with the gauge given, it will be necessary to use a smaller or larger hook. If you have more stitches to the inch, you need a larger hook; if you have fewer, you need a smaller hook. Practice until it is correct.

THREADS

Many types of threads and yarns may be used for crochet and will produce a variety of effects. With very fine thread and a fine hook, laces can be fashioned which rival those made in almost any other way. Heavy threads and yarn give the bold effects often wanted in modern furnishings. Choose a tightly twisted thread for hard surface effects and long-wearing quality. Select a soft thread or yarn for softer textures. Crochet may be done with cotton, linen, silk, wool, man-made fibers, or combinations of any of these. The texture desired and the purpose of the article being made should determine the choice of thread.

Because sizes and dye lots vary and often cannot be matched, it is advisable to purchase enough thread or yarn to complete an item before beginning to work.

HOW TO CROCHET

1. Begin by making a loop. Make a slip knot near the end of the yarn or thread. Hold the loop between thumb and forefinger of left hand. Hold hook in right hand. Insert hook in loop and pull up close around end of hook but not too tight.

2. Pick up yarn (coming from ball) with little finger of left hand and throw it over once. Slip forefinger of left hand under the yarn.

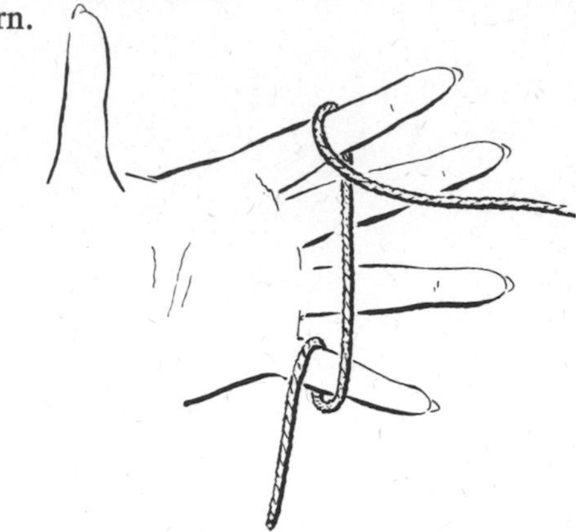

3. With hook still in the loop, hold hook in right hand as you would a pencil.

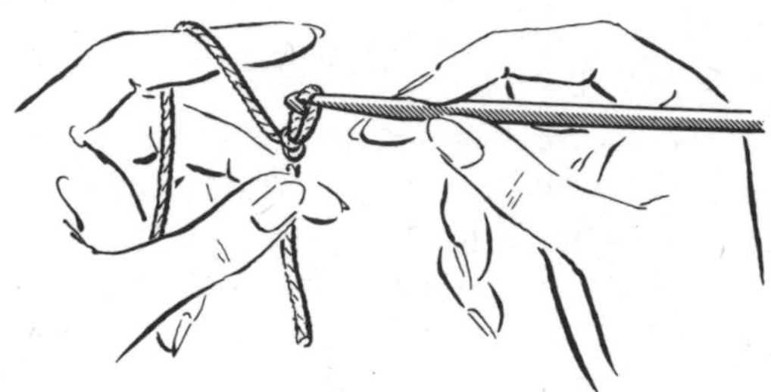

4. Slip hook under the yarn coming over the finger of left hand and pull yarn through the loop on the hook.

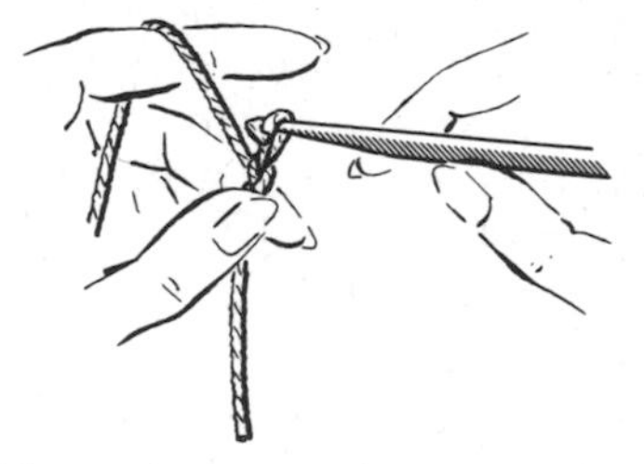

5. This makes one chain. Do not pull tight. Repeat until you have as many chains as needed. One loop always remains on the hook. Keep thumb and finger of left hand near stitch you are working.

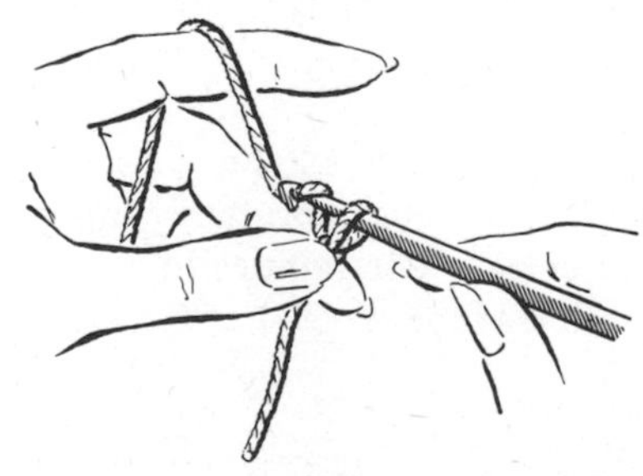

Single Crochet

1. Make a foundation chain of about 20 stitches for a practice piece. Insert the hook from the front under the two top threads of the second chain from hook.

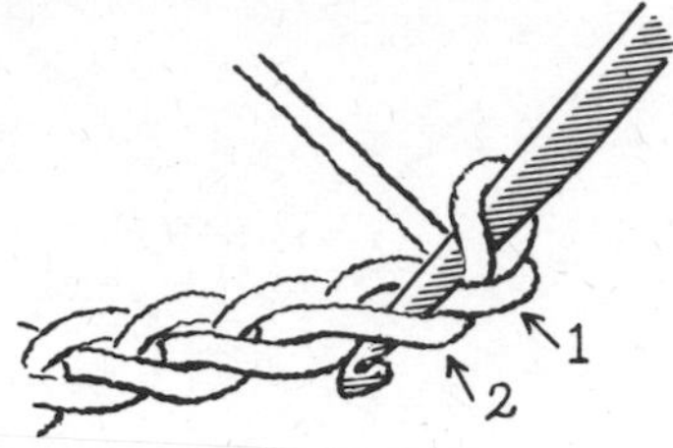

2. Catch the thread with the hook ("yarn over" or "thread over") and draw it through the stitch.

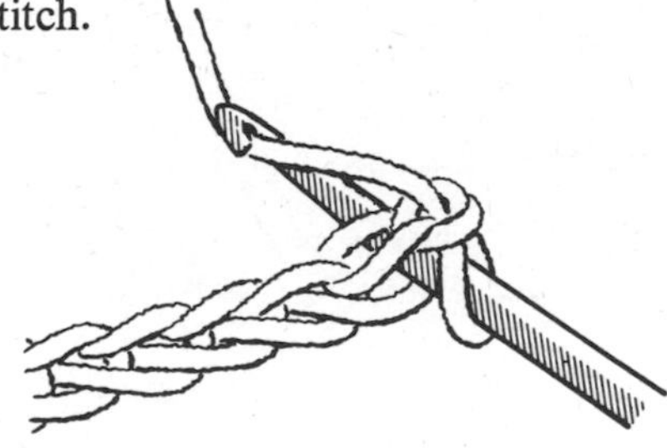

3. There are now 2 loops on the hook.

4. Yarn over again and draw it through the 2 loops.

5. One loop remains on the hook. This completes one single crochet.

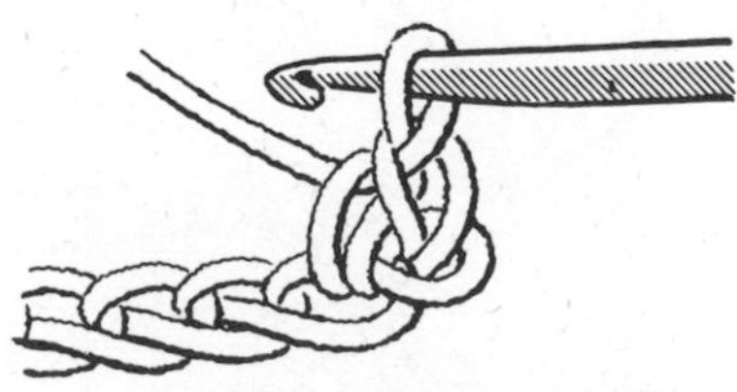

6. Now insert hook under 2 top threads of next stitch and proceed as before.

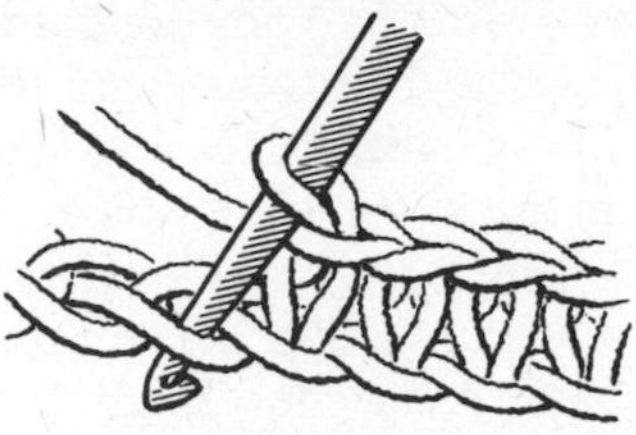

7. Repeat until you have made a single crochet in every chain; then chain 1 for turning.

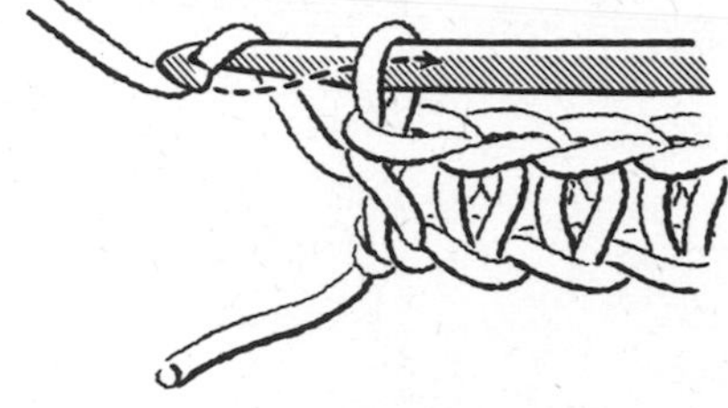

8. Turn work, insert hook from front under 2 top threads of 2nd stitch from hook and work as on 1st row.

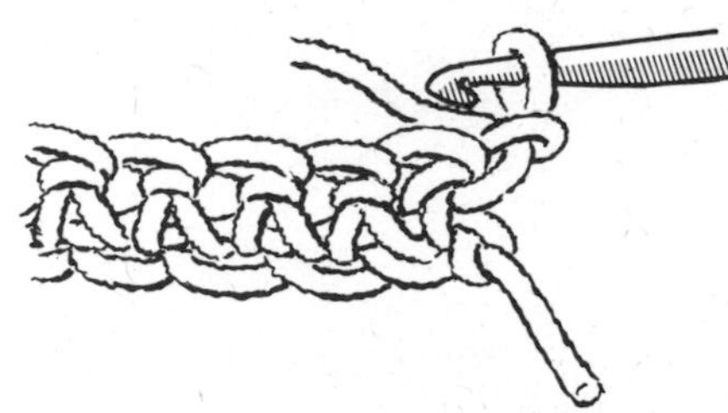

Note: In all crocheting it is customary to pick up the 2 top threads of every stitch unless otherwise specified. Picking up the back stitch only, makes what is known as a rib stitch. This gives a different effect.

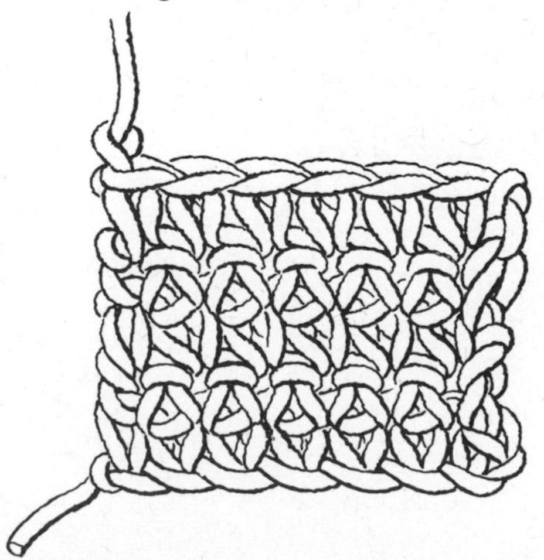

Turning Work. At the end of a row, a certain number of chain stitches is usually added to bring work into position for the next row. The piece is then turned and the work proceeds. The number of turning chains depends upon the stitch with which the next row begins. This is given in the directions for the article you are making. The turning chain always counts as the 1st stitch except in single crochet when ch 1 only raises the work to position. JOINING TO FORM A RING: Many instructions start with a row of chain stitches which must be joined to form a ring. This is done by making a slip stitch into the 1st chain stitch.

Slip Stitch

This stitch is used only in joining or where an invisible stitch is required. Insert hook from front through 2 top threads of stitch. Thread over and with one motion draw thread through stitch and loop on hook.

Double Crochet

1. Make a chain foundation. Thread over and insert hook from front under the 2 top threads of 4th chain from hook.

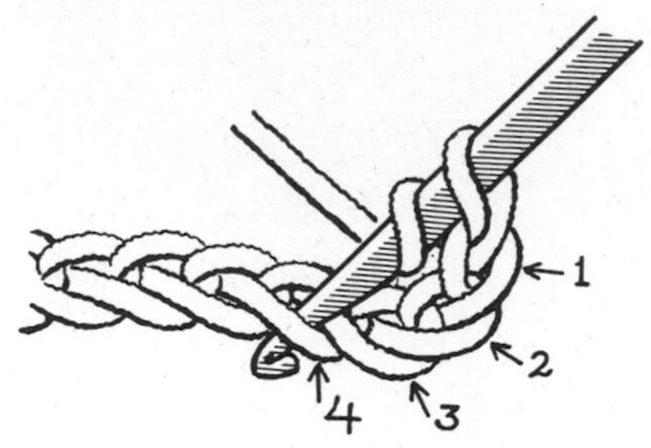

2. Thread over and draw through the stitch. There are now 3 loops on the hook. Thread over.

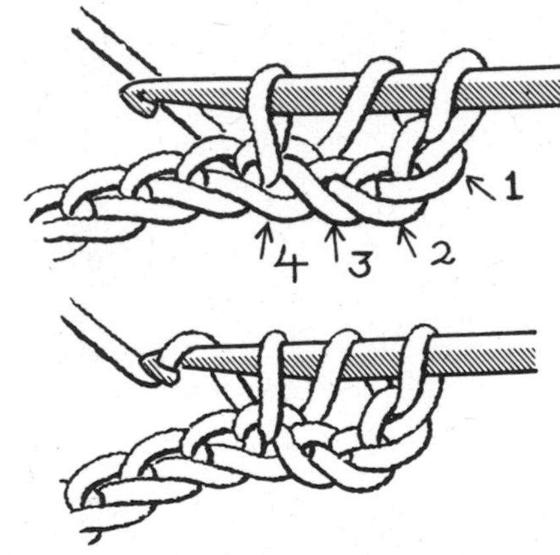

3. Draw through 2 loops. Two loops remain on the hook. Thread over.

4. Draw through 2 loops. One loop remains. This completes 1 double crochet. Thread over, insert hook from front under 2 top threads of next stitch and proceed as before.

5. Repeat across row. At end of row, chain 3 and turn. The chain 3 counts as 1st double crochet in next row.

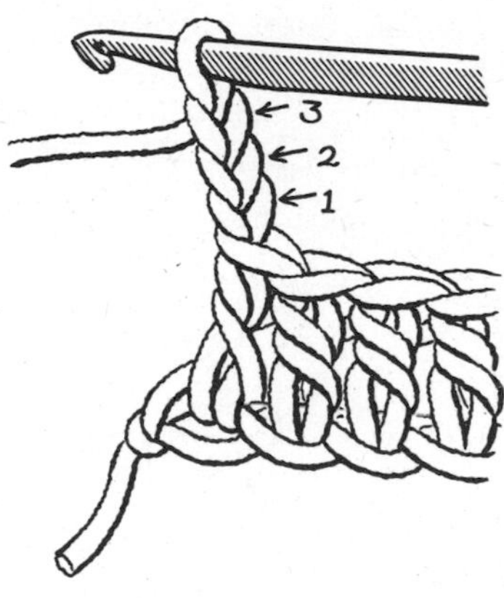

6. Second and following rows: Thread over, insert hook from front under 2 top threads of 2nd stitch on previous row.

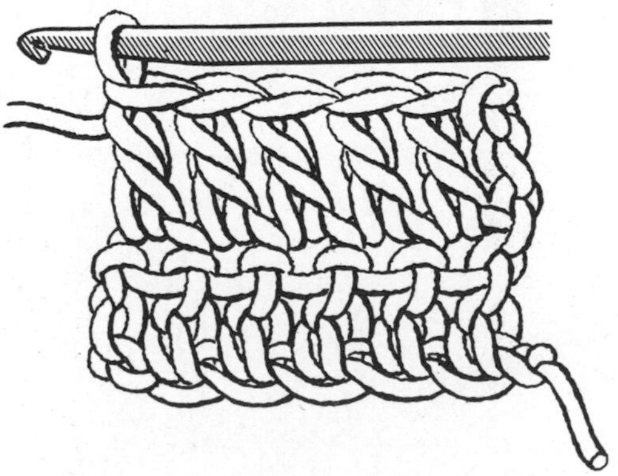

Half Double Crochet

This stitch is made by repeating the first 2 steps of double crochet (to the point where there are 3 loops on the hook). Then thread over and draw through all 3 loops at once. Chain 2 to turn.

Increasing and Decreasing

Instructions always indicate where to increase and decrease.

To Increase on any Stitch. Make 2 stitches in 1 stitch. Each time you do this you make an extra stitch on the row.

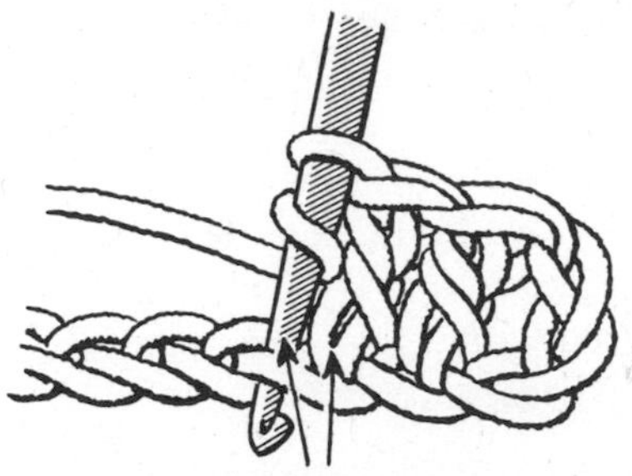

How to Decrease Single Crochet:

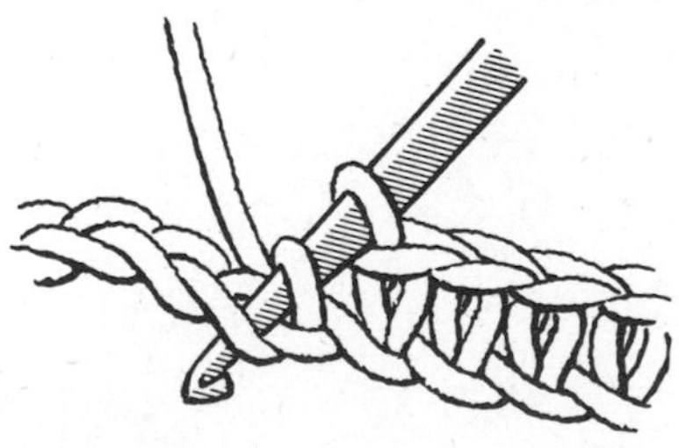

1. Work a single crochet to the point where 2 loops remain on the hook.

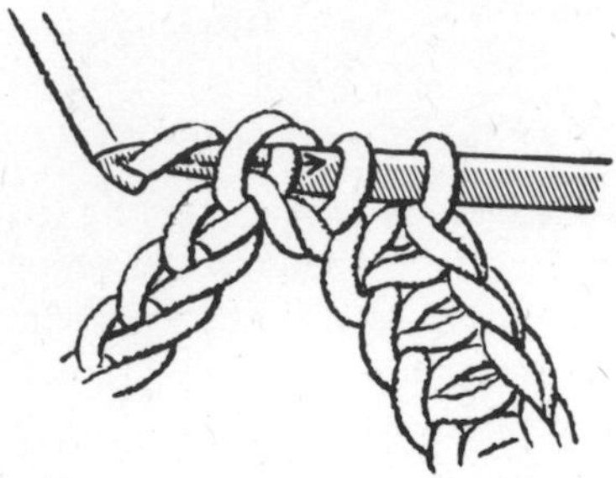

2. Insert hook from front under 2 top threads of next stitch.

3. Thread over and draw through 1 loop. There are now 3 loops on the hook.

4. Thread over and draw through the 3 loops at once. One loop left on hook. You have now worked 2 sc together.

How to Decrease Double Crochet:

1. Work a double crochet to the point where there are two loops on the hook.

2. Thread over and insert hook from front under the two top threads of next stitch.

3. Thread over and draw through one loop. There are now 4 loops on hook.

4. Thread over and draw through two loops. There are now 3 loops on hook.

5. Thread over and draw through 3 loops. One loop on hook. You have now worked 2 dc together.

You are now ready to make almost any simple crocheted article.

Treble Crochet

Make a foundation chain.

1. Thread over twice and insert from front under 2 top threads of 5th chain from hook.

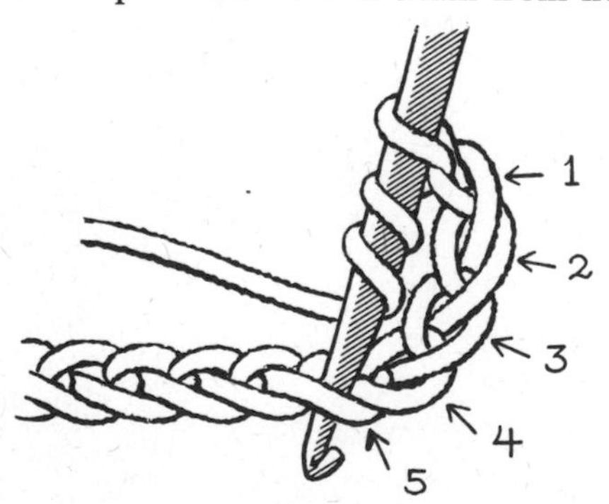

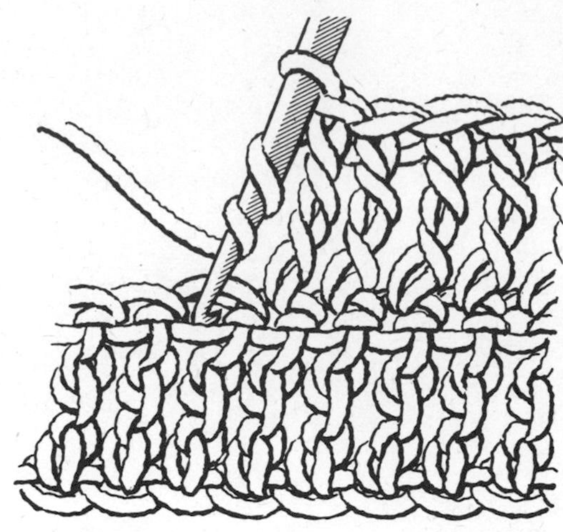

2. Thread over and draw through chain. There are now 4 loops on hook.

3. Thread over and draw through 2 loops. Three loops remain.

4. Thread over and draw through 2 loops. Two loops remain.

5. Thread over and draw through 2 loops. One loop remains.

6. For next treble, thread over twice and proceed again with step No. 1, inserting hook under 2 top threads of next stitch.

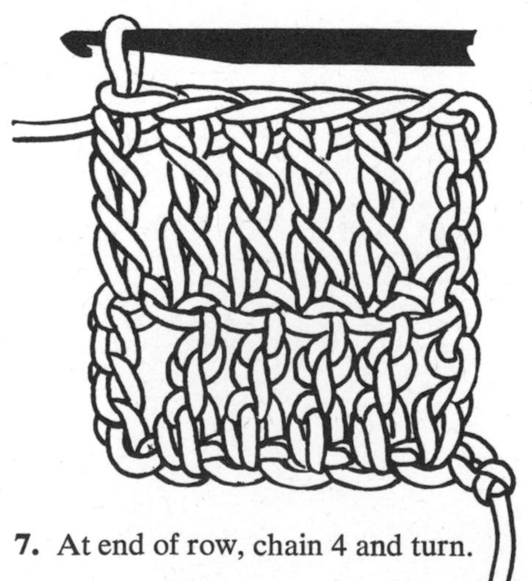

7. At end of row, chain 4 and turn.

Double Treble. Thread over 3 times, insert hook in stitch and draw loop through. Now 5 loops are on the hook. Thread over and draw thread through 2 loops at a time, 4 times. This completes a double treble.

Triple Treble. Thread over hook 4 times, insert hook in stitch and draw loop through. Now 6 loops are on hook. Thread over and draw thread through 2 loops at a time 5 times. This completes a triple treble.

Finishing and Care

Blocking. For woolen articles, blocking should be done before the seams are sewed up in order to achieve a professional-looking job. Block each piece separately, using rust-proof pins. Place the pieces wrong-side up on a flat padded surface. Pin all edges, stretching to the blocking measurements. Use plenty of pins, placing them close together to avoid scalloped edges.

Placc a damp cloth over the piece and press lightly with a moderately hot iron, allowing the steam to go through garment. Leave until thoroughly dry. Do not stretch or press ribbing, but steam lightly.

Cotton articles usually have to be stretched and pinned carefully to a flat padded surface and let dry to retain their design and shape.

Sewing seams. Place right sides of pieces together and pin, matching the pattern, if any. Beginning at bottom, sew together with whipping stitches. Do not pull too tight.

Laundering. Measure garment before washing. For woolen articles, use special cold-water soap, following instructions on package. Handle carefully; do not stretch. Rinse thoroughly. Squeeze, do not wring. Place on a clean bath towel, roll tightly to absorb moisture. Do not hang garment; leave flat on towel to dry. Block to measurements.

All crochet is based upon these fundamental stitches. By combining them in various ways, many interesting effects may be produced. Some of the more popular fancy stitches are given here.

Picot

There are two ways of making picots.

Method 1: Work a sc in edge of foundation, ch 3 or 4 or length desired, sl st in top of sc.

Method 2: Work a sc, ch 3 or 4 for picot and sc again in same space. Work as many sc's between picots as desired.

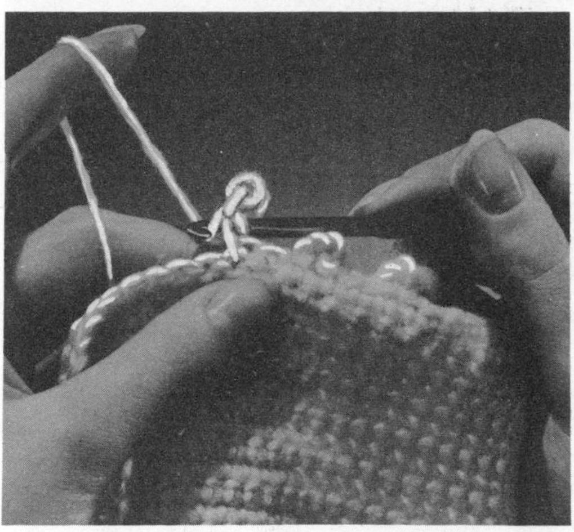

Changing Colors in Crochet

Begin the sc or dc as usual and at the second step of the last sc or dc (inserting hook from front under two top threads of stitch), pick up the second color and pull it through loop or loops on hook. Drop first color, leaving thread to hang until it is picked up in the next row. Work across. If the first color is to be discontinued, lay it along top of row and work over it for 3 or 4 stitches, then cut thread. The thread at the back must be loose enough to allow work to lie flat.

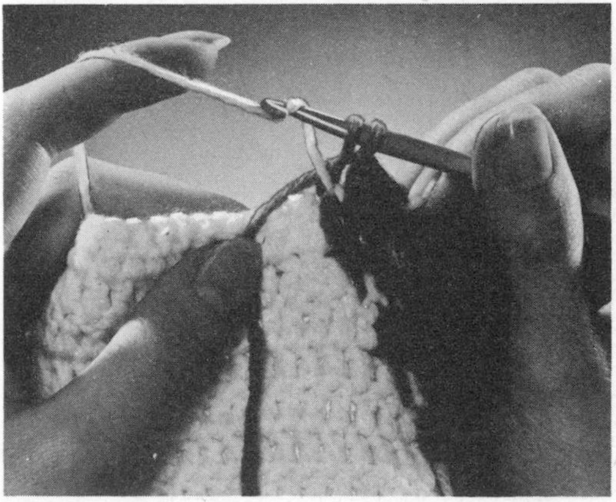

PATTERN STITCHES

Open Mesh

Make a foundation chain and 5 extra ch sts to turn. **Row 1:** 1 dc in 6th ch from hook, * ch 2, skip 2 ch, 1 dc in next ch. Repeat from * across row and end with 1 dc in last ch. Ch 5 to turn. **Row 2:** * 1 dc in dc of previous row, ch 2, skip 2 ch of previous row. Repeat from * across row and end with 1 dc in 3rd ch of 5 ch of previous row. Repeat Row 2.

Block or Solid Mesh

A block is formed of 4 dc; or 3 dc are required for each additional block when pattern calls for several blocks adjoining. For example: 2 adjoining blocks are formed of 7 dc and 3 adjoining blocks are formed of 10 dc. Spaces and blocks or "open and solid mesh" are used to make filet crochet, arranged to produce an interesting design. Filet designs are worked from a chart of squares. The dark squares represent solid mesh or blocks and the light squares represent open mesh.

Lace Stitch

Make a foundation chain plus 8 extra ch sts. 1 sc in 9th st from hook, * ch 3, skip 2 ch, 1 dc in next st, ch 3, skip 2 ch, 1 sc in next ch. Repeat from * across row and end with 1 dc in last ch. **Row 2:** Ch 8, 1 dc in 2nd dc * ch 5, 1 dc in next dc, repeat from * across row and end 1 dc in 6th ch of original group. **Row 3:** Ch 5, * 1 sc in 3rd ch, ch 3, skip 2 ch, 1 dc in next dc, ch 3, repeat from * across row and end with 1 dc in 6th ch of original group of 8 ch. Repeat Rows 2 and 3 throughout.

Star Stitch

Make a foundation chain. **Row 1:** Skip 1 ch and draw up a loop in each of next 5 sts, thread over and draw through 6 loops on hook. Ch 1, * draw a loop through the eye formed by ch just made, draw a loop through back of last loop of star just made, draw a

loop through same ch where last loop of previous star was made, draw a loop through each of next 2 ch sts, thread over and draw through the 6 loops on hook, ch 1. Repeat from * across row and end ch 1. **Row 2:** Ch 4 and turn. Skip first ch, draw up a loop in each of the next 3 chs, draw a loop through side of first star, draw a loop through eye of next star, thread over and draw through 6 loops on hook. * Ch 1, draw a loop through eye formed by ch just made, draw a loop through back of last loop of star just made, draw a loop through same ch where last loop of previous star was made, draw a loop through side of star of previous row, draw a loop through eye of next star, thread over and draw through 6 loops on hook, ch 1. Repeat from * across row and end ch 1. Repeat Row 2 throughout.

Shell Stitch

Make a foundation chain and 3 extra ch sts to turn. **Row 1:** 4 dc in 4th ch from hook, * skip 2 ch, 1 sc in next ch, skip 2 ch, 5 dc in next ch. Repeat from * and end with 1 sc. **Row 2:** Ch 3, turn, 4 dc in first sc, * 1 sc in 3rd dc of previous row, 5 dc in next sc of previous row. Repeat from * across row and end with 1 sc in 3rd dc of last group. Repeat Row 2 throughout, working 5 dc in each sc of the previous row and 1 sc in the center dc of the group of 5 dc of the previous row. Shells may be made with as many dc in a group as desired.

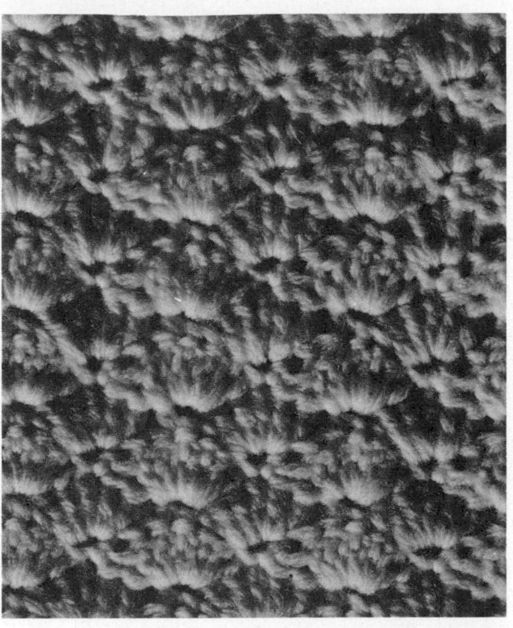

Brick or Crazy Shell

Make a foundation chain and 3 extra ch sts to turn. **Row 1:** 3 dc in 4th ch from hook,

* skip 3 ch, 1 sc in next ch, ch 3, 3 dc in same ch. Repeat from * across row, and end with 1 sc. **Row 2:** Ch 3 and turn, 3 dc in sc of previous row, * 1 sc in the space made by ch 3 of previous row, ch 3 and 3 dc in same place. Repeat from * across row and end with 1 sc in last ch 3 of previous row. Repeat Row 2 throughout.

Shawl Stitch

Make a foundation chain and 3 extra ch sts to turn. **Row 1:** 1 dc in the 4th ch, ch 2, 2 dc in same ch. * Skip 3 ch, 2 dc in next ch, ch 2 and 2 dc in same ch. Repeat from * across row. **Row 2:** Ch 3 and turn, 1 dc into space made by ch 2 of previous row, ch 2, 2 dc in same space, * 2 dc in next space made by ch 2 of previous row, ch 2 and 2 dc in same space. Repeat from * across row. Repeat Row 2 throughout.

Fancy Puff Stitch

Make a foundation chain plus 3 extra ch sts to turn. **Row 1:** Work 8 dc in 4th ch from hook. * Skip 4 ch and work 1 sc into next ch. Skip 4 ch and work 8 dc in next ch. Repeat from * across row and end with 4

dc. **Row 2:** Turn without making a ch, 4 dc in first sc, then work 4 dc in the last dc of the group of 4 dc of row below (this almost conceals the 4 dc just completed), * 1 sc between the 4th and 5th dc of next group of 8 dc, 4 dc in the next sc, then work 4 dc in the last dc of the previous group of 8 dc of row below (this almost conceals the 4 dc just completed). Repeat from * across row and end with 1 sc between the 4th and 5th dc of last group of 8 dc and 4 dc in the last dc of this group. Repeat Row 2 for pattern.

Knot Stitch

Make a foundation chain the desired length. **Row 1:** * Draw up a loop ½″ long, thread over and draw through ch, 1 sc in back strand of loop (this is a single knot); repeat from * to make a double knot. Skip 2 chs, 1 sc in each of next 2 chs. Repeat from first * across. End with one sc in last ch. Ch 3 to turn. **Row 2:** Make a single knot, * 1 sc in center of double knot of previous row, make a double knot; repeat from * across row. Ch 3 to turn. Repeat Row 2 for pattern.

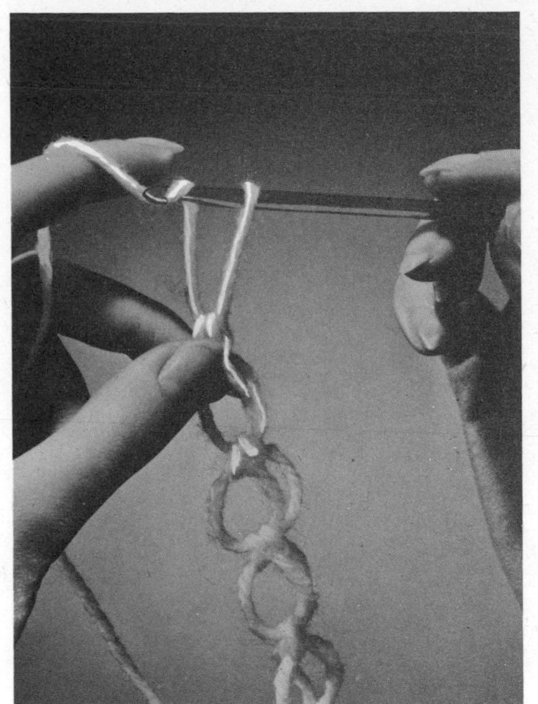

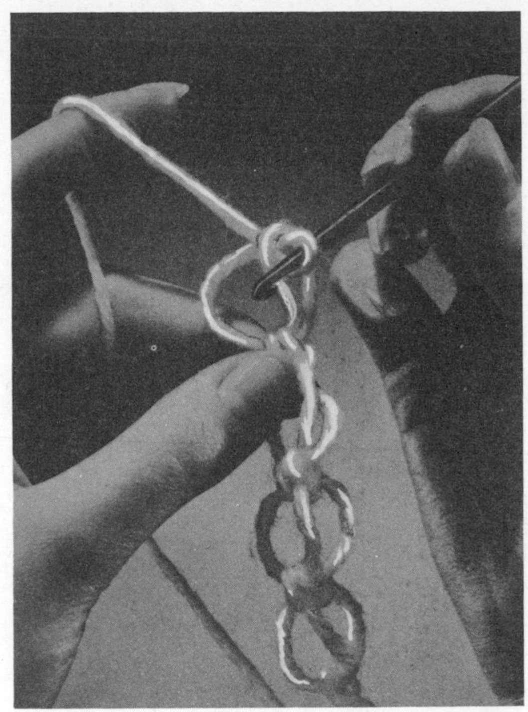

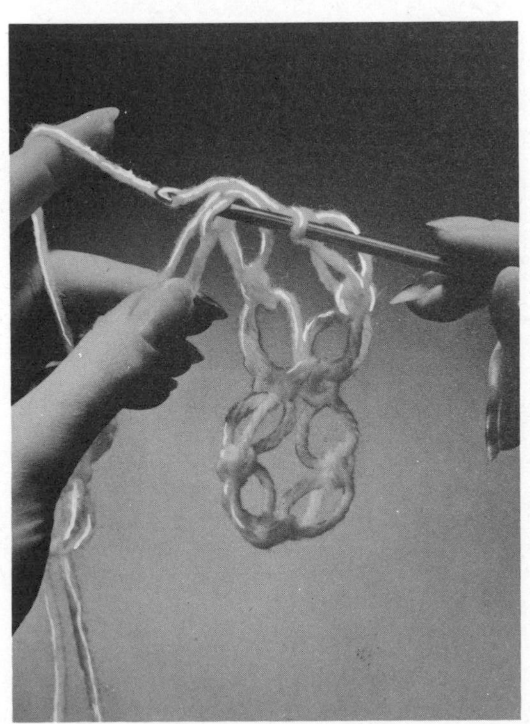

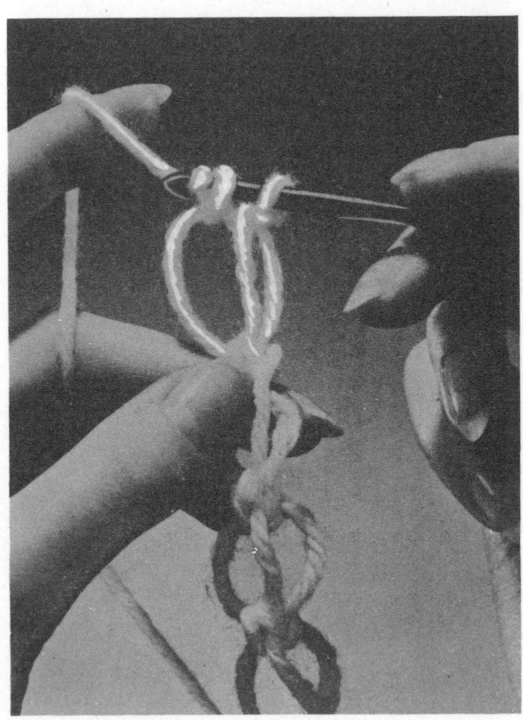

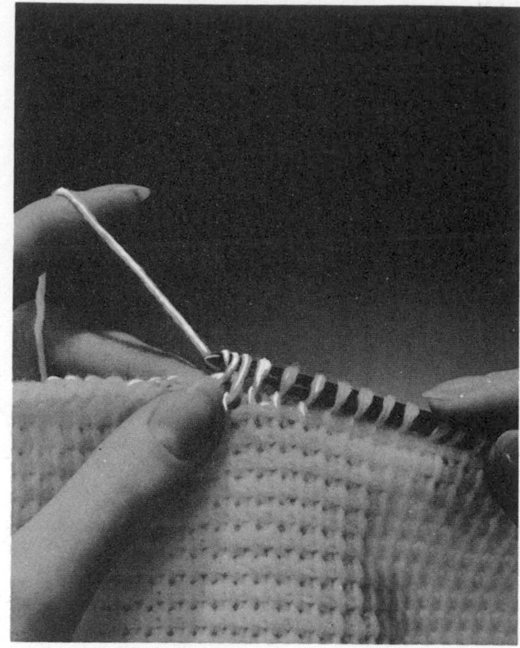

Afghan Stitch

Make a foundation chain plus 1 to turn. **Row 1:** Beginning in 2nd ch from hook, draw up a loop through each ch and keep all loops on hook. **Row 2:** Yo and draw through 1 loop, * yo and draw through 2 loops. Repeat from * until there is 1 loop left on hook. **Row 3:** Draw a loop through 2nd upright st

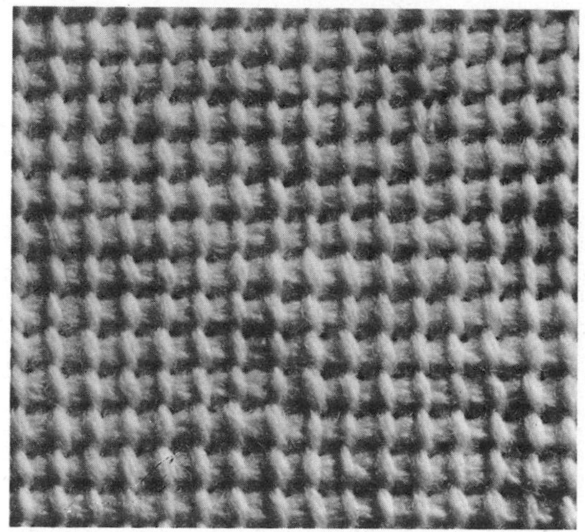

and through each one across row, keeping all loops on hook. Repeat Rows 2 and 3 for pattern.

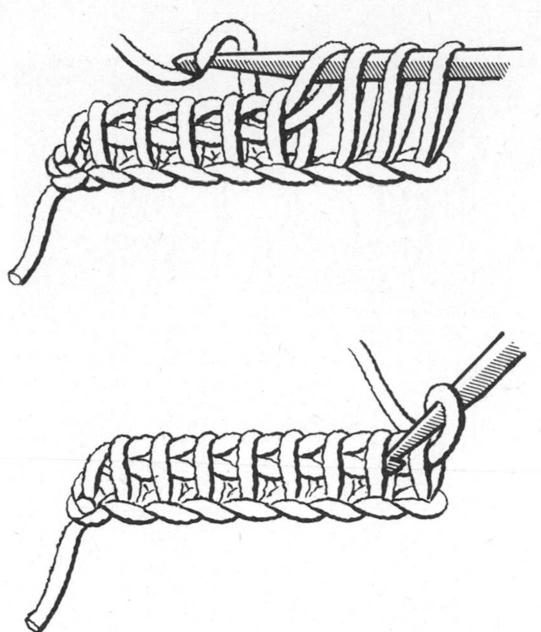

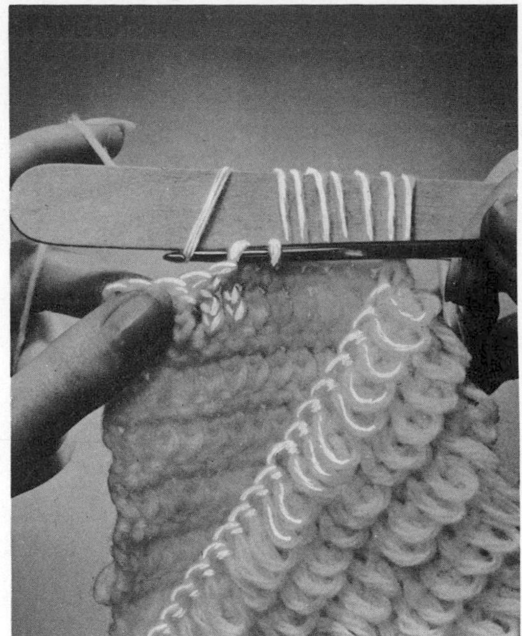

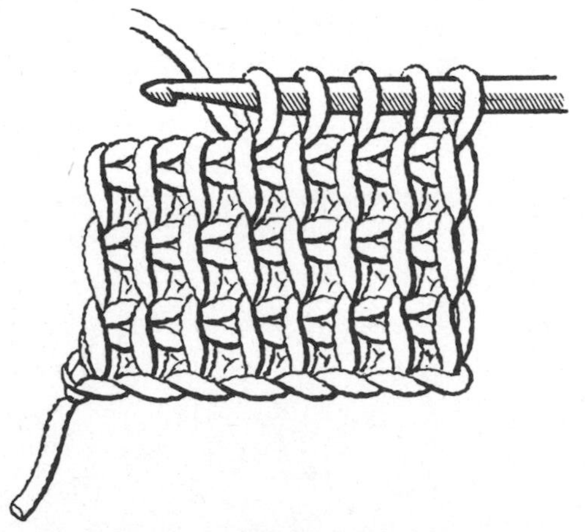

Loop Stitch

Use a piece of cardboard ¼″, ½″, or ¾″ wide or a tongue-depressor for a gauge. Make a ch desired length. **Row 1:** Work sc in each st across row. **Row 2:** * Hold cardboard in back of work, insert hook in next sc, wind yarn around cardboard from back to front, yarn over hook and draw loop through st, yo and draw through 1st loop, yo and draw through 2 loops on hook. Repeat from * to form each loop. Work 1 loop in each st. Repeat Rows 1 and 2 for pattern. This st can also be done by looping the thread over forefinger of left hand instead of using a gauge.

Hairpin Lace

This is made on a hairpin fork or staple which comes in several sizes ½", 2", and 3" wide. This work probably originated by using fine thread and crocheting over an ordinary straight hairpin.

Hairpin lace is very simple to make and goes quickly. After learning the basic steps, you can make many attractive variations.

Uses of Hairpin Lace. With wool yarn and a large fork, a soft fluffy lace results which can be used for afghans, baby wear, carriage covers, stoles, etc.

With fine cotton thread, lace edgings and insertions of great delicacy can be made for various uses.

With coarse cotton, linen, or jute threads, bold lace for curtains, mats, pillows, or trimmings can be made.

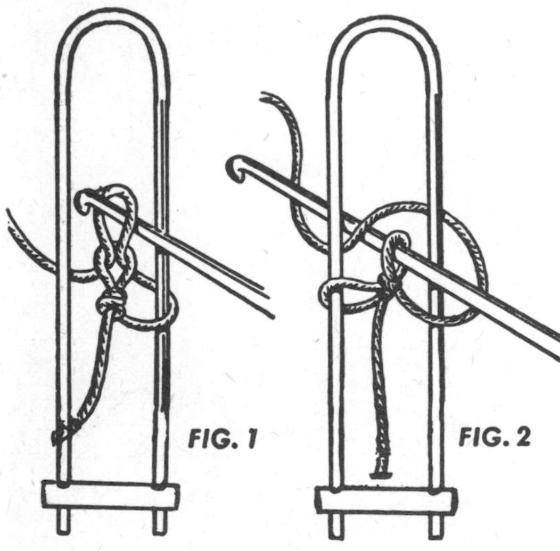

How to Make Hairpin Lace. BASIC STEPS: Hold staple with curve at the top. Bar at lower end is to keep stitches from slipping off.

1. Make a loop near the end of the ball of thread. Insert hook in loop and wind ball thread around right prong of staple. Thread over hook and draw through loop, keeping loop at center (Fig. 1).

2. Raise hook to a vertical position and turn staple to the left (Fig. 2).

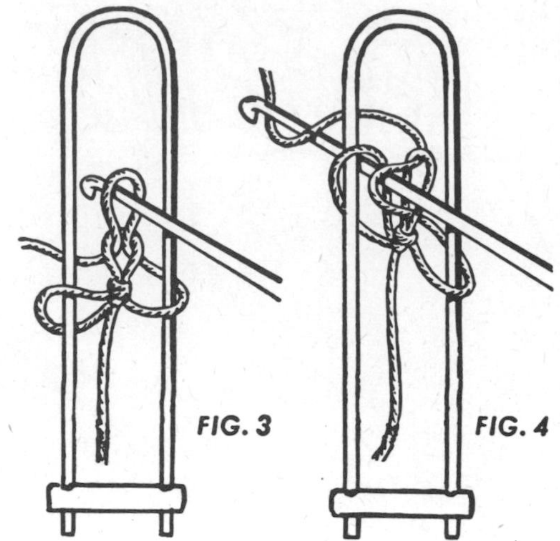

3. Thread over hook and draw through on hook (Fig. 3).

4. Insert hook in loop of left prong (Fig. 4). Thread over hook and draw loop through (2 loops on hook), thread over and draw through 2 loops.

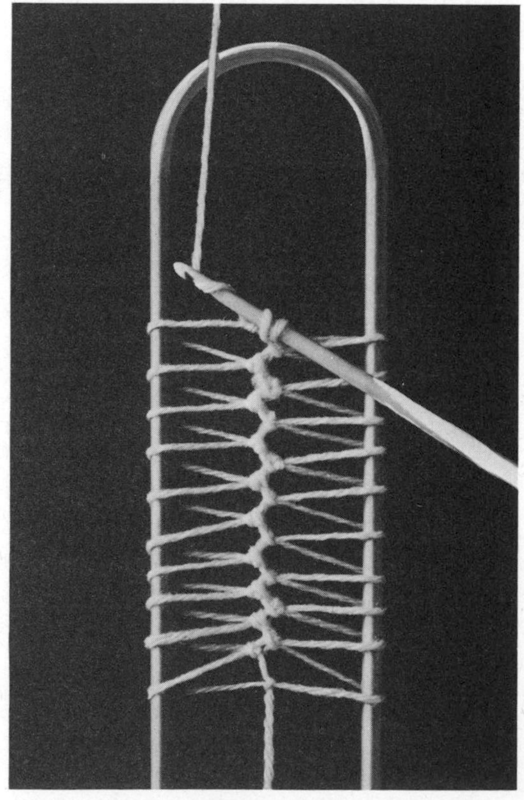

Repeat steps 2, 3, and 4 until staple is filled. Remove bar, slip off all but last few loops, replace bar, and proceed as before for length desired.

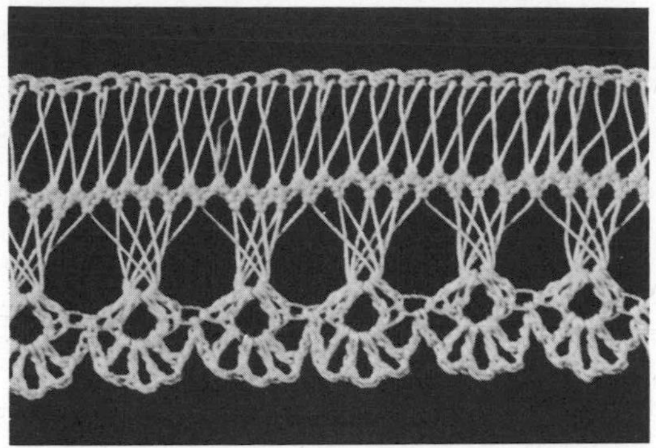

Pattern No. 1. Work hairpin lace for length desired, keeping the twist in the loops. Across one side work a sc in each loop.

Scallop, **Row 1:** Working on opposite side, attach thread through first 4 loops, ch 3, 1 dc in same space, ch 3, 2 dc in same space, * 2 dc through next 4 loops, ch 3, 2 dc in same space (shell), repeat from * across row, turn. **Row 2:** * Ch 2, 4 dc with ch 2 between each dc in next shell, ch 2, sc between shells, repeat from * across row.

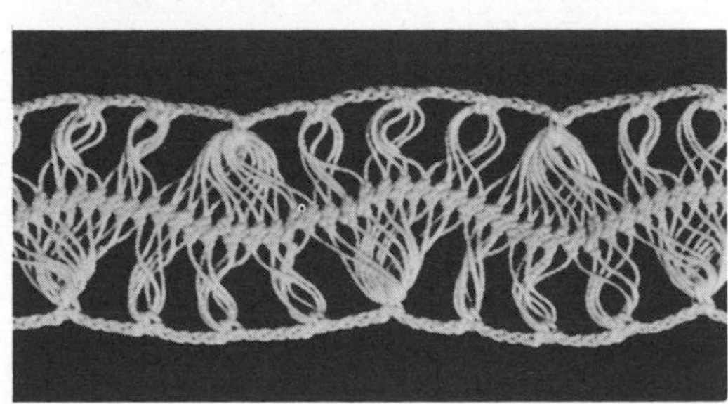

Pattern No. 2. Work hairpin lace for length desired. Join thread in 3 end loops and work 1 sc in same space, * ch 5, 1 sc over next 3 loops, repeat from * once, ** ch 5, 1 sc through next 9 loops, * ch 5, 1 sc over next 3 loops, repeat from * twice, repeat from ** across length. Join thread in first 9 loops of opposite side and work in same manner as first side, reversing the clusters.

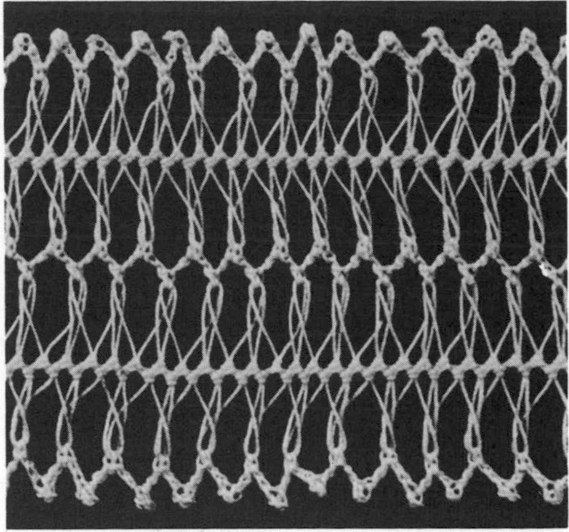

Pattern No. 3. Work 2 lengths of hairpin lace the desired length. Join thread in 2 end loops of 1st length and work 1 sc in same space, * ch 2, 1 sc over 2 corresponding loops of 2nd length, ch 2, 1 sc over next 2 loops of first length, repeat from * across length.

Edge: Join thread in 2 end loops of lace, 1 sc in same space, * ch 5, sl st in 3rd st from hook for picot, ch 2, 1 sc over next 2 loops, repeat from * across length. Work other side to correspond.

IRISH CROCHET

This distinctive type of crocheted lace never goes out of style. It has a kind of timeless beauty of which one does not tire. It is suitable for many things from linens to wearing apparel and baby articles.

Irish crochet is worked not in rows like ordinary crochet but with a mesh background. The motifs are worked separately. The mesh can be worked in around the motifs or the motifs can be applied to the finished background. The latter is a more simplified method.

The most beautiful examples of Irish crochet are done with very fine thread. The motifs are varied: flowers, tendrils, leaves, buds, stems, etc. The picot is used generously on both background and motif.

Given here is a typical background pattern

and the rose motif which is also typical. Here also is a round medallion which can be repeated and used in many ways. On page 373 you will find instructions for an exquisite round mat using an elaborate border of Irish crochet on linen. It could be an extra special mat for dining or be used in the bedroom.

Background Pattern

Ch ½″ to 1″ longer than actual measurement calls for. **Row 1:** Sc in 3rd st from hook (this forms the picot), ch 2, sc in 9th ch from picot. * ch 5, sl st in 3rd st from hook for picot, ch 2, skip 4 chs, sc in next ch (a single picot loop). Repeat from *. Ch 9, turn. **Row 2:** Sl st in 3rd st from hook for picot, ch 2, sc in next loop, * work a single picot loop, sc in next loop, repeat from * and repeat 2nd row.

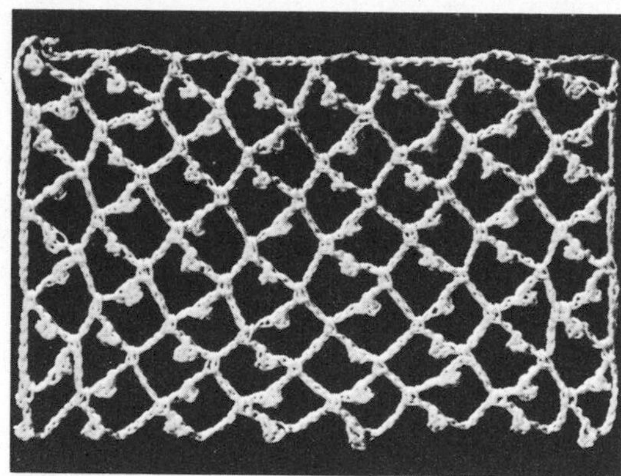

Irish Crochet Motif

Ch 5, join to form a ring, ch 6, dc in ring, * ch 3, dc in ring, repeat from * twice, ch 3, join in 3rd st of ch.

Rnd 2: Ch 1, * 1 dc, 7 tr c, 1 dc in next ch 3 loop, sc in next dc, repeat from * all around.

Rnd 3: * Ch 6, sc in next sc in back of petal, repeat from * all around.

Rnd 4: * 1 dc, 8 tr c, 1 dc in next loop, sc in next sc, repeat from * all around.

Rnd 5: Sl st to 2nd tr c, * ch 7, sl st in 5th st from hook for picot, ch 7, sl st in 5th st from hook for picot, ch 2 (double picot loop), skip 4 tr c, sc in next tr c, make an-

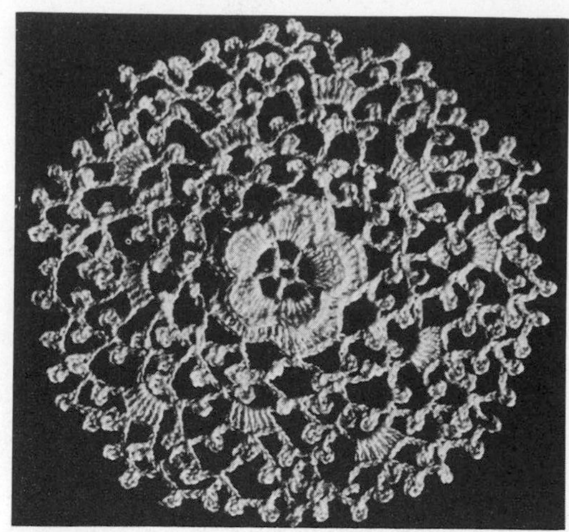

other double picot loop, sc in 2nd tr c of next petal, repeat from * all around.

Rnd 6: Sl st to center of loop between picots, * double picot loop, sc between picots of next loop, repeat from * all around.

Rnd 7: Ch 10, * sl st in 5th st from hook for picot, ch 7, sl st in 5th st from hook for picot, ch 2, sc between picots of next loop, ch 9, sc between picots of next loop, double picot loop, dc in next sc, ch 7, repeat from * 3 times, sl st in 5th st from hook for picot, ch 7, sl st in 5th st from hook for picot, ch 2, sc between picots of next loop, ch 9, sc between picots of next loop, double picot loop, join in 3rd st of ch 10.

Rnd 8: Sl st between next 2 picots, * double picot loop, 7 dc in next ch 9 loop, double picot loop, sc between picots of next loop, ch 9, sc between picots of next loop, repeat from * 4 times ending with sl st in same space as beginning.

Rnd 9: Sl st between next 2 picots, * double picot loop, sc in 4th dc, ch 5, sc in same space, double picot loop, sc between picots of next loop, double picot loop, 7 dc in next ch 9 loop, double picot loop, sc between picots of next loop, repeat from * 4 times ending with sl st in same space as beginning.

Rnd 10: Sl st between next 2 picots, * double picot loop, sc between picots of next loop, double picot loop, sc between picots of next loop, double picot loop, sc in 4th dc, ch 5, sc in same space, double picot loop, sc between picots of next loop, double picot loop, sc between picots of next loop, repeat from * around, join, cut thread.

Irish Crochet Rose

Ch 7, join to form a ring, ch 5, dc in ring, * ch 2, dc in ring, repeat from * 5 times, ch 2, join in 3rd st of ch.

Rnd 2: Ch 1 and over each mesh work 1 sc, 4 dc, 1 sc, join.

Rnd 3: * Ch 5, sl st in back of work between next 2 petals, repeat from * 7 times.

Rnd 4: Ch 1 and over each loop work 1 sc, 6 dc, 1 sc, join.

Rnd 5: * Ch 6, sl st in back of work between next 2 petals, repeat from * 7 times.

Rnd 6: Ch 1, and over each loop work 1 sc, 1 hdc, 7 dc, 1 hdc, 1 sc, join, cut thread.

CROCHETING FOR CHILDREN

Infant's Surplice for Beginners

Materials. Baby Yarn—3 ozs.; Plastic Crochet Hook, Size 6.

Gauge. 9 sts—2″.

Back. Ch 47 for lower edge; 1 dc in 4th ch from hook and in each st to end (45 dc). Ch 3, turn (ch 3 counts as first dc), 1 dc in 2nd dc and in each st across. Repeat last row

until 5½″ from beginning or desired length to underarm. Ch 29 at end of last row for sleeve, turn. Work 1 dc in 4th ch from hook and in each ch across, work 1 dc in each dc to end of row; with another strand of yarn, ch 27 sts for 2nd sleeve, join this ch to end of row below; continue last row, working 1 dc in each st to end of ch (99 dc). Work dc on all sts until sleeve edge measures 3¼″. Work across 42 sts for front. Work on these 42 sts only for 1″ (end at sleeve edge). Shape opposite edge for neck as follows: **Row 1:** Ch 3, turn, work across row, working 3 dc in last st (44 dc). **Row 2:** Ch 3, turn, 1 dc in 3rd ch from hook, 2 dc in next dc, work to end of row (47 dc). Repeat these two rows until sleeve edge measures 6½″ (end at neck edge). **Next Row:** Continue incs. at neck edge, work to within 27 sts of sleeve edge. Leave these 27 sts free for sleeve. Continue shaping neck edge as before until there are 45 dc. Work even until same length as back. Fasten off. Skip center 15 sts for back of neck. Join yarn in next st and work other side to correspond, reversing shaping.

Finishing. Sew side and sleeve seams. Work 1 row sc around sleeve edges and around entire surplice, keeping an even edge. Steam lightly. Sew ribbon at top and bottom of even edge of each front and at corresponding places at underarm seam.

Add-a-Block Baby Sacque

Infants' size 6 to 9 months.

Materials. Baby Yarn—2 ozs. White; Baby Blue (or your choice), 3 ozs. Plastic Crochet Hook, Size F. 1 yard ⅜″ ribbon. 6 small buttons.

Gauge. Motif is a 1½″ square.

Sacque. FIRST HALF: Work 67 motifs as follows: MOTIF: With White, ch 4, 2 dc in 4th st from hook, * ch 1, 3 dc in same space, repeat from * twice, ch 1, join in 3rd st of ch, cut yarn. **Rnd 2:** Attach Baby-Blue in any ch-1 space, ch 3, 2 dc, ch 1, 3 dc in same space, * 3 dc, ch 1, 3 dc in next ch-1 space, repeat from * twice, join in 3rd st of ch, cut yarn. Work 4 half motifs as follows: HALF MOTIF: With White, ch 5, 3 dc in first st of ch, ch 1, 3 dc, ch 1, 1 dc in same space, cut yarn, do not turn. **Row 2:** Attach Baby-

Blue in first loop, ch 3, 2 dc in same space, 3 dc, ch 1, 3 dc in next ch-1 space, 3 dc in next ch-1 space, cut yarn.

Finishing. Sew motifs tog according to chart. Then sew A to B and C to D along dotted lines. Sew one motif in position to free edges of motifs for underarm gusset. Work another section in same manner, reversing the shaping. Sew edge of 6 motifs of each section tog for center back. EDGE: With right side of work toward you, work a row of sc around entire sweater, working button loops as follows: one at center of lowest motif, 1 loop at joining above and 1 button loop at corner of next motif. See photograph. BUTTON LOOP: Ch 2, skip the length of a dc, sc in next st, continue in sc to next button loop.

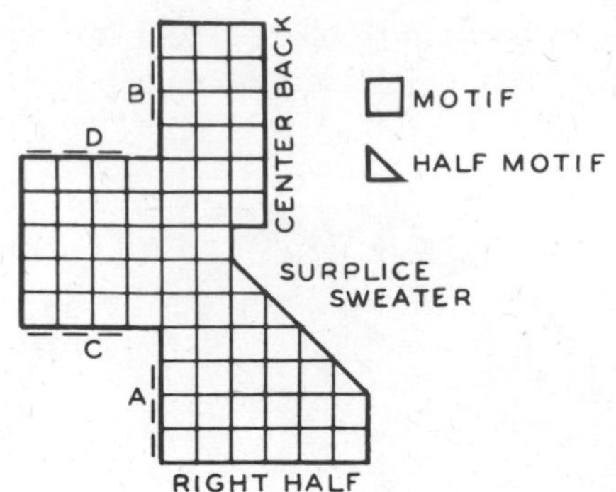

Work a row of shells around entire sweater: * Ch 3, 1 dc in same space, skip 1 st, sl st in next st (shell) repeat from * all around, join, cut yarn. Sew buttons in position, sewing 3 to side seam on right side and 3 to wrong side of other side seam. SLEEVE BEADING AND EDGE: Attach baby blue in joining at underarm seam, work 1 sc in each dc and in each joining, join. **Row 2:** (Beading) Ch 4, skip next st, dc in next st, * ch 1, skip 1 st, dc in next st, repeat from * all around, join in 3rd st of ch. **Row 3:** Ch 3, 1 dc in same space, skip 1 st, sl st in next st, (shell), repeat from * all around, join, cut yarn. Lace ribbon through beading and tie in a bow.

Crocheted Baby Set

Materials. Fingering Yarn—5 ozs. Baby Pink; 1 oz., White for trim. Plastic Crochet Hook, Size E. 3½ yards narrow Ribbon; 1½ yards ⅝″ Ribbon.

Gauge. 4 rows of pat—1″. 5 single knot sts—2″.

Sacque. With Pink, starting at neck, ch 61 to measure about 12½″, sc in 2nd st from hook, 1 sc in each remaining st of ch, ch 1, turn. **Row 2:** 1 sc in each of the next 12 sc (front), 3 sc in next sc, 1 sc in each of the next 4 sc (shoulder), 3 sc in next sc, 1 sc in each of the next 24 sc (back), 3 sc in next sc, 1 sc in each of the next 4 sc (shoulder), 3 sc in next sc, 1 sc in each of the next 12 sc (front), ch 1, turn. **Row 3:** 1 sc in each sc, ch 1, turn. **Row 4:** 1 sc in each of the next 13 sc, 3 sc in next sc, 1 sc in each of the next 6 sc, 3 sc in next sc, 1 sc in each of the next 26 sc, 3 sc in next sc, 1 sc in each of the next 6 sc, 3 sc in next sc, 1 sc in each of the next 13 sc, ch 1, turn. **Row 5:** 1 sc in each sc, ch 1, turn. **Row 6:** 1 sc in each sc and 3 sc in center st at each of the 4 inc points, ch 1, turn. **Row 7:** 1 sc in each sc; ch 1, turn. **Rows 8, 9, 10, 11:** Repeat Rows 6 and 7 twice. **Row 12:** Draw up a ⅜″ loop on hook, yo and pull through loop forming a ch st, sc over single loop of st (single knot st), sc in next sc, repeat from beg across row, turn. **Row 13:** * Work a single knot st, sc over the 2 loops of next single knot st (pat), repeat from * across row, turn. Repeat the last row 3 times (16th row is right side of work). **Row 17:** * Single knot st, sc over the 2 loops of next single knot st, repeat from * 16 times, ch 3, skip 15 single knot sts for sleeve, sc in next single knot st, work 34 pat across back, ch 3, skip 15 single knot sts for other sleeve, sc in next single knot st, work 17 pat across other front, turn. **Row 18:** * Single knot st, sc in next single knot st, repeat from * 16 times, single knot st, skip 1 st of ch, sc in next st of ch, * single knot st, sc in next single knot st, repeat from * 33 times, single knot st, skip 1 st of ch, sc in next st of ch, * single knot st, sc in next single knot st, repeat from * 16 times, turn. Work even in pat until Sacque measures 8″ from neck edge, fasten off.

Sleeve. Working on wrong side of armhole, attach yarn at underarm and work 18 pat around armhole, join in 1st single knot st, turn. **Next Row:** * Single knot st, sc in next single knot st, repeat from * all around dec 1 pat at underarm (17 pat), join, turn. **Next Row:** * Single knot st, sc in next single knot st, repeat from * all around, join, turn. Repeat last row until sleeve measures 4″ from underarm. **Next Row:** Working on right side of sleeve, * work 1 sc in each of the next 2 single knot sts, sc in next sc, repeat from * all around ending with sc in last single knot st, join. **Next Row:** Ch 1, 1 sc in each sc, join. Repeat the last row once, fasten off. **Next Row:** Edge: Attach White and * work a single knot st, skip 1 sc, sl st in next sc, repeat from * all around, join, fasten off. Work other sleeve in same manner. Beading: With right side toward you, attach Pink in 1st st at neck edge, ch 3, skip 1 sc, hdc in next sc, * ch 1, skip 1 sc, hdc in next sc, repeat from * across neck edge, fasten off. Attach White at opposite side of neck edge, * work a single knot st, sc in next hdc, repeat from * across neck edge, then work in pat down front skipping about ⅜″ space between knot sts, work a single knot st in each single knot st across lower edge and work up opposite front to correspond to 1st front, join, fasten off. Lace ribbon through beading.

Cap. With Pink, ch 4, join to form a ring, ch 1 and work 8 sc in ring; do not join this or following rnds. Place a marker at beg of each rnd. **Rnd 2:** 2 sc in each sc. **Rnd 3:** * Sc in next sc, 2 sc in next sc, repeat from * all around. **Rnd 4:** Work 1 rnd sc. **Rnd 5:** Same as rnd 3. **Rnd 6:** Inc in every 3rd sc. **Rnds 7 and 8:** Work 2 rnds even in sc. **Rnd 9:** Inc in every 4th sc, sl st in next sc to even rnd. **Rnd 10:** Draw up a ⅜″ loop on hook, yo and pull through loop forming a ch st, sc over single loop of st (single knot st), skip 1 sc, sc in next sc, * single knot st, skip 1 sc, sc in next sc, repeat from * around then sl st in 1st single knot st (30 single knot sts), turn. **Rnd 11:** * Work a single knot st, sc over the 2 loops of next single knot st, repeat from * 28 times, single knot st, sc in same sp as beg, then sl st in 1st single knot st, turn. **Rnd 12:** * Single knot st, sc over the 2 loops of next single knot st (pat), repeat from * 26 times (3 pat left free for back of cap), turn. **Rnd 13:** * Single knot st, sc over the 2 loops of next single knot st, repeat from * 26 times, turn. Repeat Rnd 13 until pat section measures 6″ from Rnd 9, fasten off. Leaving last 6 rows or 1½″ free for Turn Back and working on right side, attach Pink in next st, working across lower edge of cap, work 38 sc across to same sp at opposite side. **Next Row:** Ch 1, turn and work 1 sc in each sc. Repeat last row once, fasten off. With wrong side of work toward you, attach White at side edge of Turn Back and work a row of single knot st pat around Turn Back only. Fasten off. Trim with ribbon ties as illustrated.

Bootees. With Pink, ch 14, 3 sc in 2nd st from hook, 1 sc in each of the next 11 sts of ch, 3 sc in end st, working on other side of ch, 1 sc in each of the next 11 sts, do not join this or following rnds, place a marker at beg of each rnd. **Rnd 2:** 2 sc in each of the next 3 sc, 1 sc in each of the next 11 sc, 2 sc in each of the next 3 sc, 1 sc in each of the next

11 sc. **Rnd 3:** * 1 sc in next sc, 2 sc in next sc, repeat from * twice, 1 sc in each of the next 12 sc, 2 sc in next sc, * sc in next sc, 2 sc in next sc, repeat from * once, 1 sc in each of the next 11 sc. **Rnds 4 and 5:** 1 sc in each sc on sides, inc 3 sc, evenly spaced around each end in each rnd (52 sc in last rnd), sl st in next st to even rnd, turn. **Rnd 6:** 1 sc in each st, picking up entire st by inserting hook around entire st, join, ch 1, turn. **Rnd 7:** 1 sc in each sc, do not join. **Rnds 8 and 9:** Repeat Rnd 7. Fold in half lengthwise and mark center for toe. **Rnd 10:** 1 sc in each sc dec 3 sts evenly spaced around toe. **Next Row:** 1 sc in each sc to within 3 sts from center st at toe, then working in back loop of sts only, work 1 sc in each of the next 7 sc. Working through both loops of sts, 1 sl st in each of the next 2 sts, ch 1, turn. **Next Row:** Skip the 2 sl sts and working in back loop of sts, 1 sc in each of the next 7 sc, working through both loops of sts, sl st in each of the next 2 sc on side of bootee, ch 1, turn. Repeat the last row 6 times. **Next Row:** Skip the 2 sl sts and working in back loop of sts, 1 sc in each of the next 7 sc, sl st in same st on side of bootee, do not turn. **Next Rnd:** Beading: Ch 3, skip 1 sc, hdc in next sc, * ch 1, skip 1 sc, hdc in next sc, repeat from * around, ch 1, join in 2nd st of ch. **Next Rnd:** 2 sc in each ch 1 mesh, join in 1st sc. **Next Rnd:** Single knot st, skip 1 sc, sc in next sc, * single knot st, skip 2 sc, sc in next sc, repeat from * around, sl st into next single knot st, turn. **Next Rnd:** * Single knot st, sc over the 2 loops of next single knot st, repeat from * around, sl st in next single knot st, turn. Repeat the last rnd 3 times, fasten off. Attach White and work a row of single knot st pat around top of bootee, fasten off. Lace ribbon through beading. Work other bootee in same manner.

Mittens. With Pink, ch 25 (to measure about 4¾″), join, being careful not to twist ch, ch 1 and work 1 sc in each st of ch. Without joining rnds and working in sc, work even until piece measures 2″ from beg. **Next Rnd:** 1 sc in each of the next 3 sc, dec in next 2 sts, repeat from beg 4 times. Work 1 rnd even. **Next Rnd:** * 1 sc in each of the next 2 sc, dec in next 2 sts, repeat from * 4 times. Work 1 rnd even. Work 2 sts tog until 7 sts remain, cut yarn leaving a 4″ length. Thread into needle and draw tog, fasten off. BEADING: Attach Pink on opposite side of starting ch, ch 3, skip 1 st, hdc in next st, * ch 1, skip 1 st, hdc in next st, repeat from * around, ch 1, join. **Next Rnd:** Ch 1 and work 2 sc in each ch 1 mesh, join in 1st sc. **Next Rnd:** * Single knot st, skip 1 sc, sc in next sc, repeat from * around. **Next Rnd:** Sl st in 1st single knot st, turn, * single knot st, sc in next single knot st, repeat from * around. Repeat the last rnd once, sl st in 1st single knot st, fasten off. Attach White and work a row of single knot st pat same as bootees. Lace ribbon through beading. Work other mitten in same manner.

Soaker in Afghan Stitch

Size 1 year.

Materials. Nylon and Wool, 3 ply—3 skeins, White. Afghan Hook, Size F. 10 small Buttons. 1¼ yards white Ribbon, ¼″ wide.

Gauge. 13 sts—2″. 6 rows—1″.

Blocking Measurements:

Width around hips . . . . 21″
Length from waist to crotch . . . . 10″
Length of side seam . . . . 6½″

Back. Starting at waist, ch 66 to measure 10½″, having 13 ch to 2″. **Row 1** (First Half of Row): Retaining all loops on hook, draw up a loop in 2nd ch from hook and in each ch across (Fig. 1). There are the same number of loops on hook as there were ch sts. (Second Half of Row): Yo and draw through 1 loop, * yo and draw through 2 loops. Repeat from * across (Fig. 2). The loop which remains always counts as the first st of next row (Fig. 3). **Row 2** (First Half of Row): Retaining all loops on hook, draw up a loop in 2nd vertical bar (formed by loop of previous row) and in each vertical bar across to within last vertical bar (Fig. 4); insert hook through last vertical bar and the st directly behind it (arrow on Fig. 4) and draw up a loop (this gives a firm edge to this side). There are the same number of loops as on first row. (Second Half of Row): Yo and draw through 1 loop, * yo and draw through 2 loops. Repeat from * across. Repeat 2nd row for pattern. Work in pat until total length is 6″. SHAPE LEG OPENING: **Dec row** (First Half of Row): Insert hook under 2nd and 3rd vertical bars and draw up one loop—1 vertical bar dec, work in pat across to within last 3 vertical bars, dec 1 vertical bar over next 2 vertical bars, draw up a loop in last vertical bar. (Second Half of Row): Repeat second half of 2nd row. Repeat dec row until 32 vertical bars remain. Work 1 row even. Break off and fasten.

Front. Work same as Back. Block pieces lightly.

Waistband. With right side of work facing, attach yarn to first vertical bar at waist of Front. **Row 1:** Ch 1, sc in first 3 vertical bars, * insert hook under next 2 vertical bars, thread over and complete a sc, sc in next 3 vertical bars. Repeat from * across, ending with sc over next 2 vertical bars, sc in last vertical bar. Ch 3, turn. **Row 2:** Skip first sc, dc in each sc across. Ch 1, turn. **Row 3:** Sc in each dc and in top of turning chain. Ch 1, turn. **Row 4:** Sl st in each sc across. Break off and fasten. Work waistband of Back in same way. Sew back and front pieces neatly together at crotch. Now work across one complete side edge as follows: With right side of work facing, attach yarn at top edge. **Row 1:** Ch 1, sc closely across side and leg opening. Ch 1, turn. With pins, mark the position of 5 buttonholes evenly spaced on side edge of Front, having first buttonhole ¼″ down from top edge and last buttonhole ¼″ up from first row of leg opening. **Row 2:** * Sc in each sc across to next marker, ch 3, skip next 2 sc. Repeat from * across until 5 buttonholes have been made, sc in each remaining sc. Ch 1, turn. **Row 3:** Sl st in each sc and in each ch of buttonholes across. Break off and fasten. Work across other side edge to correspond. Sew on buttons to correspond with buttonholes. Cut ribbon in half and lace through 2nd sc row of each waistband. Tie in bows at sides.

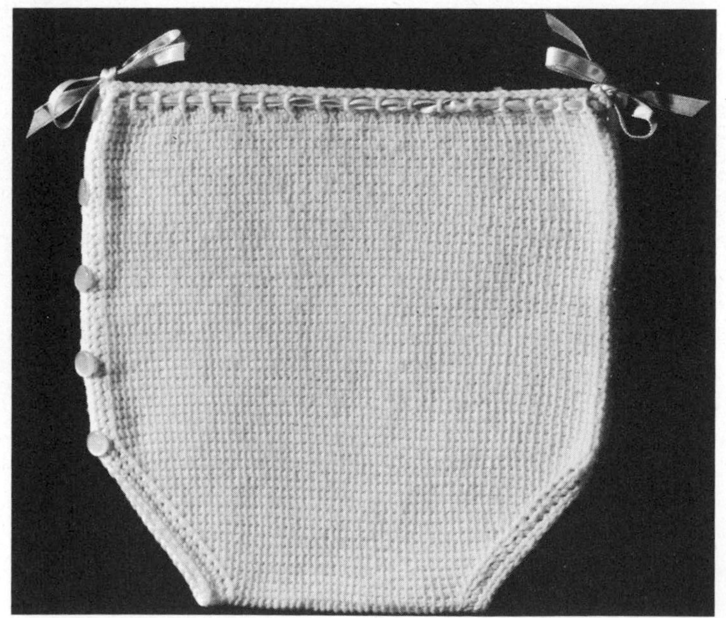

Fig. 1

Fig. 2

Fig. 3

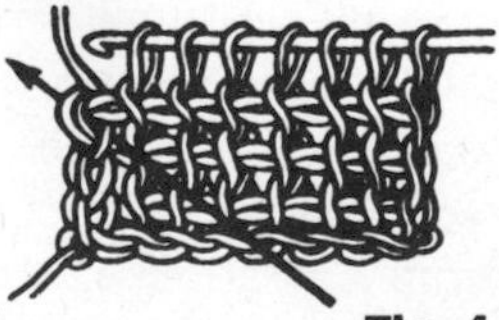

Fig. 4

Boy's Blazer Set

Directions are for Size 6 months. Changes for Sizes 1 and 2 are in parentheses.

Materials. Baby Wool, 3 ply—(2-oz. skeins), 3 skeins White, Plastic Crochet Hook, Size 3. 8 Buttons, 2½ yards Red Bias Binding. ½ yard Elastic, ¼″ wide.

Blocking Measurements:

Chest . . . . 18 (20–22)″
Length from shoulder to lower edge . . . . 9 (10–10½)″
Length of sleeve seam . . . 6 (6½–6½)″
Pants—Waist . . . . . . 18 (19½–20½)″
Pants—Length from top edge to crotch . . . . 9½ (9¾–10)″

Gauge. 6 sts—1″; 6 rows—1″.

Jacket. BACK: Starting at lower edge, ch 55 (61–67) to measure 10 (11–12)″. **Row 1:** Sc in 2nd ch from hook, * hdc in next ch, sc in next ch, repeat from * across—54 (60–66) sts, ch 1, turn. **Row 2:** * Sc in next hdc, hdc in next sc, repeat from * across, ch 1, turn. Repeat Row 2 until piece measures 6 (6½–7)″, ch 37 (41–41) for sleeve. Drop yarn. Join another ball at opposite end of last row and ch 36 (40–40) for other sleeve. Fasten off. Pick up dropped yarn and make sc in 2nd ch from hook, * hdc in next ch, sc in next ch, repeat from * across ch, then continue in pat across back and other ch. Ch 1, turn. Work in pat until piece measures 3 (3½–3½)″ from first row of sleeve shaping. Fasten off.

RIGHT FRONT: Starting at lower edge, ch 33 (37–41) to measure 6 (7–7½)″. Work in pat until there are 32 (36–40) sts on row. Work in pat as for back until piece measures 5 (5½–6)″, ending at neck edge. Keeping pat, dec 1 st at neck edge on next row and every other row until 12 (13–13) sts in all have been dec; *at the same time,* when piece measures 1″ from first row of neck shaping, ending at side edge, shape sleeve as follows:

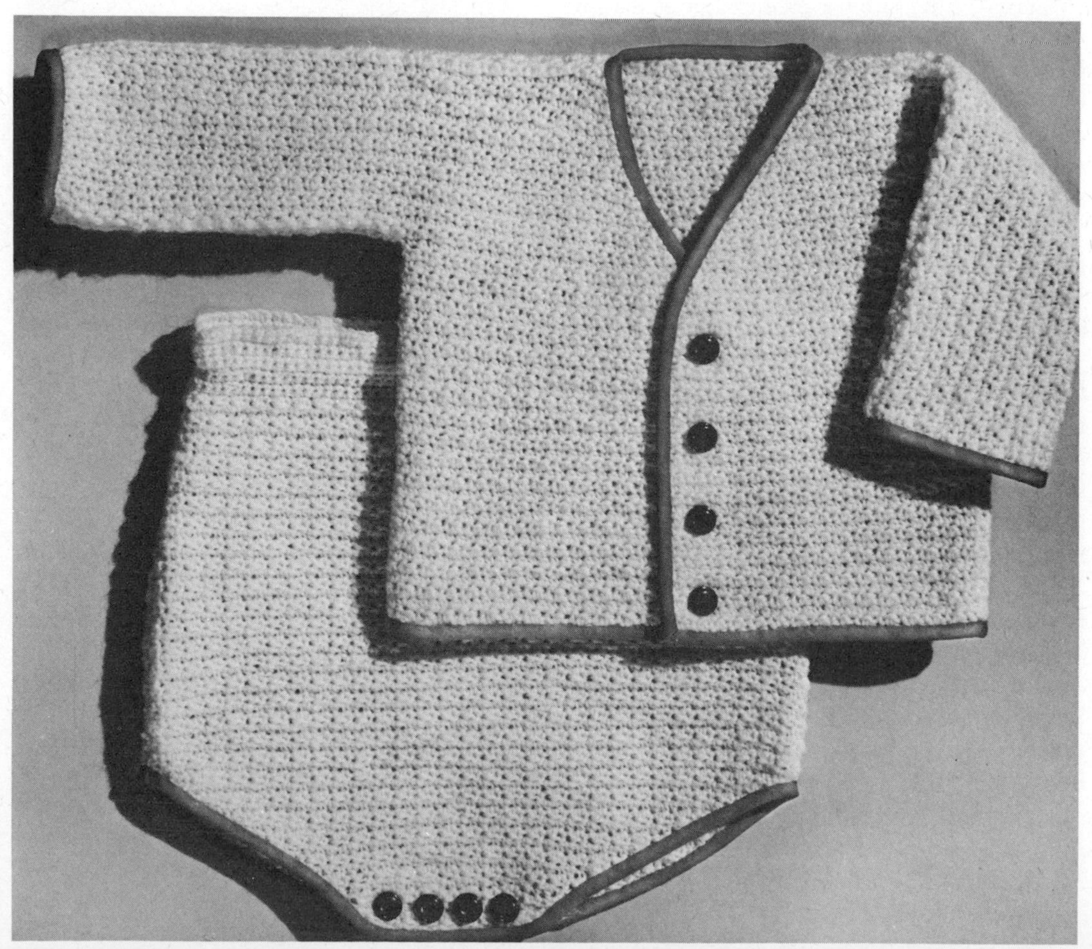

Ch 37 (41–41), turn. **Next row:** Sc in 2nd ch from hook, hdc in next ch. Continue to work in pat across ch and sts to end of row. Ch 1, turn. Continue in pat without dec at sleeve edge and continue to dec at neck edge as before, until piece measures 3 (3½–3½)″ from first row of sleeve shaping. Fasten off. With pins, mark the position of 4 buttons on Right Front, having the first pin mark ½″ up from lower edge and last pin mark 1″ down from first row of neck shaping.

LEFT FRONT: Work exactly as for Right Front, making a buttonhole ½″ in from front edge opposite each pin mark. Make a buttonhole as follows: **Row 1:** Ch 2, skip 2 sts, work in pat across. **Row 2:** Work in pat across, including ch sts.

FINISHING: Block to measurements. Sew side, shoulder, and sleeve seams. Sew bias tape all around jacket and cuff edges. Sew buttons in place.

Pants. BACK: **Row 1:** Starting at top edge, make a ch to measure 9½ (10–10½)″. **Row 2:** Sc in 2nd ch from hook, sc in each ch across, having an even number of sc on row, ch 1, turn. Repeat Row 2 until piece measures 1¼″. Now work in pat, inc 1 st at both ends of row every inch 3 times, being careful to keep pat. Work even until piece measures 6¾″. TO SHAPE CROTCH: **Row 1:** Work in pat across, dec 2 sts at both ends, ch 1, turn. **Row 2:** Work in pat across, dec 1 st at both ends, ch 1, turn. Repeat Rows 1 and 2 9 (9–11) times more. Work even for ½″. Fasten off.

FRONT: Work as for Back until last dec row of crotch has been completed. Next row: Work in pat across, making 4 buttonholes evenly spaced. Now continue in pat for 2 rows more. Fasten off.

FINISHING: Block to measurements. Sew side seams. Beading: Join yarn to inside of Pants, 3 rows down from top edge, sc in same place, * ch 3, skip 2 sc, sc in next sc, 2 rows below, ch 3, skip 2 sc, sc in next sc 2 rows above. Repeat from * around. Join. Lace elastic through Beading and fasten securely. Sew bias binding all around lower edges of pants. Sew buttons in place.

Mother and Baby Elephant Toys

Materials. Knitting Worsted—6 ozs. Melon, 2 oz. White. 1 yard No. 4 Blue double-fold Bias Tape. Scraps of White, Black and Blue Felt. 12″ each ¾″ Blue Ribbon. One striped or printed White and Blue Wash Cloth. Cotton Batting for stuffing.

Gauge. 4 sc—1″. 4 rnds—1″.

Mother Elephant. HEAD: Starting at tip of trunk with Melon, ch 4. Join with sl st to form ring. **Rnd 1:** 7 sc in ring. Work rnds continuously but mark beginning of each rnd. **Rnd 2.** 2 sc in each sc around (14 sc). **Rnds 3 through 9:** Sc in 14 sc. **Rnd 10:** * 2 sc in next sc, sc in next 6 sc. Repeat from * once (16 sc). **Rnds 11 through 16:** Sc in each sc. **Rnd 17:** Increasing 2 sc evenly spaced, sc in each sc. **Rnd 18:** Sc in each sc. **Rnds 19 through 24:** Repeat last 2 rnds alternately 3 times (24 sc). **Rnd 25:** * Sc in 5 sc, 2 sc in next sc. Repeat from * around (28 sc). **Rnd 26:** * Sc in 2 sc, 2 sc in next sc. Repeat from * 3 times (4 sc inc across face); sc in each of remaining sc. **Rnd 27:** * Sc in 3 sc, 2 sc in next sc. Repeat from * 3 times; sc in each of remaining sc. Continue to sc in each sc, inc 4 sc evenly spaced across face on each rnd until there are 56 sc around. Work even until length from tip of trunk is 10½″. **Next rnd:** * Draw up a loop in each of next 2 sc, yo and draw through all 3 loops on hook (a dec made); sc in next 6 sc. Repeat from * around (7 decs made). Stuff trunk and head firmly before opening becomes too small, dec 7 sc evenly on each rnd until 7 sc remain. Continue to dec until all sts have been worked off. Break off and fasten.

BODY: Starting at neck with Melon, ch 4, join with sl st to form ring. **Rnd 1:** 6 sc in ring. **Rnd 2:** 2 sc in each sc around (12 sc). **Rnd 3:** * 2 sc in next sc, sc in next sc. Repeat from * around. Increasing 6 sc evenly spaced on each rnd, sc in each sc until there are 54 sc on last rnd. Work even until total length is 8½″. FIRST LEG: **Rnd 1:** Ch 9 (for crotch), skip next 27 sc, sc in next 27 sc. **Rnd 2:** Sc in next 9 ch and in next 27 sc (36 sc). Continue to sc in each sc around until leg measures 3½″ from crotch. Sl st in next sc. Break off and fasten. Attach Melon to the sc preceding crotch ch; working along opposite side of ch, sc in 9 ch and in next 27 sc on body (36 sc). Complete 2nd leg to correspond with 1st leg.

DISC (make 2): Starting at center with White, work as for body until the 3rd rnd has been completed. Continuing to inc 6 sc evenly spaced on each rnd, sc in each sc until there are 36 sc on last rnd. Sl st in next sc. Break off and fasten. Stuff body and legs firmly; sew a disc to bottom edge of each leg. Sew head securely to body.

ARM (make 2): Starting at top with Melon, work as for body until 3rd rnd has been completed. Inc 6 sc evenly on each rnd, sc in each sc until there are 30 sc. Work even until arm measures 4″. Sl st in next sc. Break off and fasten. Work as for bottom disc of leg until there are 30 sc on rnd. Sl st in next sc. Break off and fasten. Stuff arms firmly. Sew a disc to edge of each arm. Sew arms to sides of body about 2½″ from neck.

EAR (make 2): Starting at center with White, ch 12. **Row 1:** Sc in 2nd ch from hook, sc in next 9 ch, 3 sc in last ch; working along opposite side of chain, sc in 10 ch (23 sc). Ch 1, turn. **Row 2:** Sc in 10 sc (sc in next sc, 2 sc in next sc) 3 times; sc in 10 sc. Ch 1, turn. **Row 3:** Sc in 10 sc (sc in 2 sc, 2 sc in next sc) 3 times; sc in 10 sc. Ch 1, turn (29 sc). **Rows 4 and 5:** Inc 3 sc evenly spaced along curved edge, sc in each sc (35 sc). Break off and fasten. Gather straight end to measure 1″. Sew ears to sides of head, 3½″ from top of head.

TAIL: With White ch 13. **Row 1:** Sc in 2nd ch from hook and in next 11 ch. Ch 1, turn. **Rows 2 and 3:** Sc in 12 sc. Ch 1, turn. At end of 3rd row, break off. Sew top edge to starting ch. Wind White 5 times around a finger. Tie at one edge, cut at opposite edge. Sew to one end of tail. Sew tail in place.

APRON: Cut a bibbed apron from the washcloth, making side edges 5″ and center front about 7¼″ long. Cut a 6″ piece of bias tape for neckband. Allowing ends of remaining 30″ piece to extend free for ties, sew tape over top (shaped) raw edges of apron. Place apron on toy and sew neckband in place. Cut two White felt circles, 1″ in diameter and two Blue felt circles, ¾″ in diameter for eyes. Sew a Blue circle and a White circle in place for each eye, 1½″ apart. Cut a narrow curved strip of black felt, 3½″ long for mouth. Sew mouth in place, under trunk. With the wide piece of ribbon, make a bow and tack to top of head.

Baby Elephant: HEAD: Starting at tip of trunk with Melon, ch 4. Join with sl st to form ring. **Rnd 1:** 5 sc in ring. Work continuously in rnds but mark beginning of each rnd. **Rnd 2:** Sc in 5 sc. **Rnd 3:** 2 sc in next sc (1 sc increased); sc in each of remaining sc around. **Rnd 4:** Sc in each sc around. **Rnd 5:** Inc one sc, sc in each sc around (7 sc). **Rnds 6 and 7:** Repeat rnds 4 and 5. **Rnds 8 through 11:** Inc one sc on each rnd, sc in each sc being careful not to have inc directly above previous inc (12 sc on last rnd). **Rnd 12:** * Sc in next sc, 2 sc in next sc. Repeat from * around (18 sc). **Rnd 13:** * Sc in 2 sc, 2 sc in next sc. Repeat from * around (24 sc). **Rnd 14:** Sc in each sc. **Rnd 15:** (Sc in 2 sc, 2 sc in next sc) 4 times—4 sc increased across face; sc in each of remaining sc. **Rnds 16, 17, and 18:** Repeat Rnd 14. **Rnd 19:** * Draw up a loop in each of next 2 sc, yo and draw through all 3 loops on hoop —1 sc dec; sc in next 2 sc. Repeat from * around—7 sc dec. Stuff trunk and head firmly before opening becomes too small, and dec 7 sc evenly on each rnd until 7 sc remain. Continue to dec until all sts have been worked off. Break off and fasten.

BODY: Starting at neck with Melon, ch 4. Join with sl st to form ring. **Rnd 1:** 5 sc in ring. **Rnd 2:** 2 sc in each sc (10 sc). **Rnd 3:** * 2 sc in next sc, sc in next sc. Repeat from * around (15 sc). **Rnd 4:** * 2 sc in next sc, sc in 2 sc. Repeat from * around (20 sc). Work even until total length is 3″. **Next Rnd:** * Sc in next 2 sc, dec one sc over next 2 sc. Repeat from * around (5 sc dec). Stuff body firmly, and dec 5 sc evenly spaced on each rnd until 5 sc remain. (Dec one sc over next 2 sc) twice; sl st in next sc. Break off and fasten. Sew head securely to body.

LEG (make 2): Starting at top, work as for body until Rnd 2 has been completed. **Rnd 3:** Sc in each sc, inc one sc. **Rnds 4, 5, and 6:** Sc in each sc. At end of last rnd, sl st in next sc. Break off and fasten.

BOTTOM DISC (make 2): Starting at center with white, ch 4. Join with sl st to form ring. **Rnd 1:** 6 sc in ring. **Rnd 2:** 2 sc in each sc around. Sl st in next sc. Break off and fasten. Stuff leg firmly. Sew disc to bottom edge of leg.

ARM (make 2): Making 5 rnds (instead of 6), work as for leg. Sew legs and arms in place as shown.

EAR (make 2): Starting at center with White, ch 7. **Row 1:** Sc in 2nd ch from hook, sc in next 4 ch, 3 sc in last ch; working along opposite side of chain, sc in 5 ch (13 sc). Ch 1, turn. **Row 2:** Sc in 5 sc, 2 sc in 3 sc, sc in 5 sc. Ch 1, turn. **Row 3:** Sc in 5 sc, (sc in next sc, 2 sc in next sc) 3 times; sc in 5 sc. Break off and fasten. Gather straight end to measure 5/8″. Sew ears to sides of head.

Cut two 3/4″ White felt circles, and two 1/2″ Blue felt circles, for eyes. Sew a Blue and a White circle in place for each eye. Cut a curved strip of black felt, 1 1/4″ long for mouth. Sew in place, under trunk. With narrow piece of ribbon make a bow and tack above one ear. Using remainder of wash cloth, cut a triangle for diaper. Fold in raw edges, and pin diaper in place.

Crocheted Baby Cap and Mittens

Directions are for Child's Medium Size (about 13″ head measurement).

Materials. Sports Yarn—2 ozs., Main Color (MC); 2 10-gram balls Baby Yarn—(CC). 1 Crochet Hook, Size O or E. 1 Crochet Hook, Size OO or G.

Gauge. 6 sts—1″. 8 rows—1″.

Cap. Starting at neck edge, with MC and Size O crochet hook, make a chain 13″ long, plus 2 extra ch sts. Turn. **Row 1** (Right Side of Cap): Skip last 2 ch, * 1 sc in next ch, ch 1, skip next ch. Repeat from * to end, ending with 1 sc in last ch. Ch 2, turn. **Row 2:** Skip first sc, * 1 sc over ch-1 space, ch 1, skip next sc. Repeat from * across row, ending 1 sc in turning ch, ch 2, turn. Repeat Row 2 until piece measures 6 1/2″ to 7″ from beg. (Longer measurement will make hat to fit larger child.) Break yarn. With wrong side of cap facing you, fold sides to exact center. Work 1 row sc across top, inserting hook through both front and back pieces each time. Break yarn. This finishes top and forms bunny ears.

Trim. FRONT: With right side of cap facing you, size 0 crochet hook, and baby yarn, work 1 sc at lower point of cap. * Ch 1, 1 sc over next ch 2 turning ch. Repeat from * up one front edge and down second front edge. (You will have 50 to 54 sc in all with ch 1 between each sc.) Ch 2. Turn. **Row 2:** Skip first sc, * 1 sc over ch 1, ch 1. Repeat from * across row, ch 2, turn. Repeat Row 2 five times more. Break yarn. NECKBAND: With baby yarn, work 1 sc over each ch along neck and both ends of front trim, ending ch 2, turn. Work 1 sc, ch 1 between each sc of previous row, ch 2, turn. BEADING ROW: Skip first sc, * 1 sc over ch 1, ch 3, skip the following: (1 sc, ch 1 and next sc), 1 sc over next ch 1. Repeat from * across row ending with 1 sc over turning ch. Ch 2, turn. **Next Row:** Sc, ch 1 across row having 1 sc between the 2 sc of beading row and (sc, ch 1, sc, ch 1) in each ch 3 space of beading row. End ch 2, turn. **Next Row:** Repeat Row 2 of Trim above. Make a twisted cord about 40″ long as follows: Cut 7 lengths of yarn 85″ long. Twist them tightly in opposite directions at each end and let double back on itself. Knot ends for tassels. Thread cord through beading.

Mittens. CUFF: With baby yarn and size 00 crochet hook, ch 38. Insert hook in first ch and sl st to form ring. Ch 1. **Rnd 1:** 1 sc in first ch, ch 1, * skip 1 ch, 1 sc in next ch, ch 1. Repeat from * to end. **Rnd 2:** Continuing around, skip first sc of previous rnd, * 1 sc over next ch-1 space, ch 1. Repeat from * to end. Continue in rnds, repeating rnd 2 seven times more. BEADING RND: * 1 sc, ch 1 and 1 sc over next ch-1 space, skip next sc, ch 1 and next sc. Repeat from * around. HAND SECTION: Change to MC and size 0 crochet hook. Repeat Rnd 2 of Cuff 15 times. SHAPE TOP: **Rnd 1:** 1 hdc over ch-1 space. **Rnd 2:** 1 hdc between each hdc of previous rnd. **Next Rnd:** * 1 hdc between next 2 hdc, skip next space, 1 hdc in next space. Repeat from * until 2 hdc remain. Break yarn, draw up tightly and fasten off. Make second mitten. Make 2 twisted cords each 17″ long using 3 strands each 40″ long and proceeding as for hat.

Crocheted Lion Cub

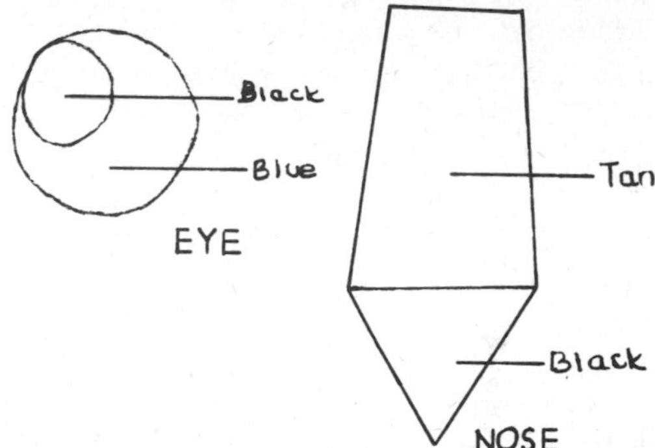

Materials. Knitting Worsted—two 2-oz. skeins Yellow; one 2-oz. skein Blush Pink. Six-Strand Embroidery Floss—1 skein each Black and Devil Red. Metal Crochet Hook, Size G. Stuffing (cotton batting, cut-up nylon hose, etc.). Scraps of Black, Blue and Tan Felt.

Gauge. 9 sc—2″. 4 rnds—1″.

Body. Starting at neck with Yellow, ch 4. Join with sl st to form ring. **Rnd 1:** 6 sc in ring. Work rnds continuously but mark last sc of every rnd to insure proper shaping. **Next 6 rnds:** Sc in each sc, inc 6 sc evenly on each rnd (to inc 1 sc, work 2 sc in 1 sc). **Next 7 rnds:** Sc in 42 sc (work even). Break off Yellow, attach Pink and work even for 26 more rnds (pants). **Next rnd:** * Sc in 4 sc; insert hook in next sc and pull loop through, twice; yo and draw through all 3 loops on hook (a dec made). Repeat from * 6 more times (7 decreases on rnd). **Next 4 rnds:** Dec 7 sc on each rnd. Break off and draw remaining 7 sts together; fasten.

Head. Starting at nose with Yellow, work 6 rnds same as body (36 sc). Count off the next 25 sts, mark the 25th st—this is forehead area; remainder is chin area. Inc 7 sc evenly across forehead area on every other rnd until there are 64 sc on rnd. Work 7 rnds even. Dec 8 sc evenly on next 5 rnds. Stuff, then adding stuffing as needed, continue dec as before, until opening is closed. Pin 10th rnd of chin area to 4th rnd of body; then sew head to body.

Front Leg (make 2): Starting at foot with Yellow, work 4 rnds same as body (24 sc). Work 2 rnds even. On next rnd, dec 6 sc next to each other for toe area. Work 9 rnds even on 18 sc. Break off and fasten. Stuff. Flatten out first 4 rnds and pinch across toe area. With Red embroidery floss, indent toes with four long overcast sts. Sew in place just above top edge of pants.

Back Leg (make 2). Work same as front leg until 10 rnds are completed. Change to Pink and work 12 rnds even. Break off and fasten. Finish same as front leg and sew in place.

Tail. With Yellow, ch 8. **Row 1:** Sc in 2nd ch from hook, sc in next 6 ch. Ch 15, turn. **Row 2:** Sc in 2nd ch from hook, sc in 13 ch, sc in 7 sc. Ch 1, turn. **Row 3:** Sc in 14 sc. Break off and fasten. Fold in half and sew starting chains to stitches. Sew in place. Wind Yellow 10 times around 4 fingers. Slip strands from fingers and tie around middle—(this is top of tassel). Cut loops at each end. Fold in half and wind Yellow around strands ¼″ from top. Sew to end of tail.

Ear (make 2). With Yellow, ch 4. **Row 1:** Sc in 2nd ch from hook, sc in next ch, 3 sc in last ch, sc in base of next 2 ch. Ch 1, turn. **Row 2:** Sc in 2 sc, 2 sc in next 3 sc, sc in next 2 sc. Ch 1, turn. **Next 2 rows:** Sc in each sc, inc 3 sc evenly across curved end on each row. Ch 1, turn. At end of 4th row break off and fasten. Line with blue felt.

Suspenders. Ch 2, sc in 2nd ch from hook, ch 1, turn. * Sc in sc, ch 1, turn. Repeat from * for 10″. Fold in half. Sew fold at center front; pass over shoulders, cross at back, then sew ends in place.

Mane—Tuft (makes 28). Wind Yellow 5 times around a 5″ cardboard. Slip strands from cardboard and tie around middle. Cut loops at each end (20 ends). Tie 8 tufts evenly around neck. Tie 17 tufts evenly along 15th rnd across top and sides of head. Sew on ears; then tie 3 more tufts across forehead between ears. Following diagrams, cut felt features and sew in place. Using embroidery floss, embroider mouth with Red, eyes with Black. Cut three 6-inch strands of Black; knot them together in middle. Sew knot on lip for whisker. Make another whisker and sew in place.

CROCHETING FOR THE HOME

Potholders

Materials. Mercerized Crochet Cotton—one 250-yard ball White, one 175-yard ball Red. Steel Crochet Hook, Size 7. 3 Bone Rings. 1 pkg. each White and Red Rickrack.

Round Potholder. With White, ch 2, 8 sc in 1st st of ch, join in 1st sc. **Rnd 2:** 2 sc in each sc, join. **Rnd 3:** Ch 3 (ch 3 counts as 1st dc), 1 dc, ch 1, 1 dc in next sc, * 1 dc in next sc, 1 dc, ch 1, 1 dc in next sc, repeat from * all around, join in 3rd st of ch. **Rnd 4:** Ch 3, 1 dc in next dc, 1 dc, ch 1, 1 dc in next ch 1 space, * 1 dc in each of the next 3 dc, 1 dc, ch 1, dc in next ch 1 space, repeat from * all around ending with 1 dc in last dc, join. Continue in same manner for 6 more rounds, having 2 more dc between each inc point in each round. **Rnd 11:** Work 1 sc in each dc and 1 sc, ch 1, 1 sc in each ch 1 space, join. **Rnd 12:** Ch 3, 1 dc in each dc, and 1 dc, ch 1, 1 dc in each ch 1 space, join. **Rnd 13:** * Ch 3, 2 dc in same space, skip 3 dc, sc in next dc (shell), repeat from * all around, join, cut thread. Work another section in same manner. Place the 2 sections tog and crochet them tog working through both thicknesses as follows: Ch 3, sc over ch 3 of shell, * ch 3, sc over ch 3 of next shell, repeat from * all around, join, cut thread. Cover bone ring with sc and sew to top of pot holder. With Red, work 2nd pot holder in same manner. TRIM: Form a circle of Rickrack White on Red and Red on White and sew to both sides of pot holders below the shell row. Cut and form a small circle of Rickrack having 12 points. Sew ends tog. Arrange and sew to center of pot holders and sew down at points on both sides of Rickrack. Work straight stitches from inner points to center.

Square Pot Holder. BACK SECTION: With White, ch 2, 8 sc in 1st st of ch, join in 1st sc. **Rnd 2:** 2 sc in each sc, join. **Rnd 3:** Ch 3, * 2 dc, ch 2, 2 dc in next sc, 1 dc in each of the next 3 sc, repeat from * all around ending last repeat with 1 dc in each of the last 2 sc, join in 3rd st of ch. **Rnd 4:** Ch 3, 1 dc in each of the next 2 sts, * 2 dc, ch 2, 2 dc in next ch 2 space, 1 dc in each of the next 7 sts, repeat from * all around, ending to correspond, join. Continue working 6 more rnds in same manner, having 4 more dc between inc points in each rnd. **Rnd 11:** Work 1 sc in each dc and 2 sc, ch 2, 2 sc in each ch 2 space, join. **Rnd 12:** 1 dc in each dc and 2 dc, ch 2, 2 dc in each ch 2 space. **Rnd 13:** * Ch 3, 2 dc in same space, skip 3 sts (counting ch 2 at each corner as 2 sts), sc in next st, repeat from * all around, join, cut thread. Work another section in same manner as follows: 1st 3 rows Red, 3 rows White, 3 rows Red, 1 row White, 1 row Red, 1 row White, 1 row Red. Place the 2 sections tog and working through both thicknesses, crochet them tog as follows: With Red, ch 3, sc over ch 3 of shells, * ch 3, sc over ch 3 of next shell, repeat from * all around, join, cut thread. With Red, cover bone ring with sc and sew to corner of pot holder.

Place Mat

Size 12″ x 19″, including fringe.

Materials (for 4 place mats): Mercerized Crochet Cotton—7 skeins Size 30, White. Steel Crochet Hook, Size 13.

Note: Work tightly for best results.

Mat. Starting at bottom edge, make 20″ chain. **Row 1:** Dc in 9th ch from hook (ch 2, sk 2 ch, dc in next ch) 8 times, * ch 24, sk 2 ch, sc in remaining 22 ch, sl st in side-top of last dc ** (ch 2, sk 2 ch, dc in next ch) 18 times. Repeat from * 3 times, and from * to ** again. (Ch 2, sk 2 ch, dc in next ch) 9 times (to measure about 16″ long). Cut and rip excess chain. **Row 2:** Ch 3, turn (2 dc in next sp, dc in next dc) 7 times, * 2 dc in next sp, holding back the last lp of each dc on hook make dc in next dc, dc in next sp, dc in first sc on added bar, sk next sc, dc in next 2 sc, yo and draw through all loops on hook for a 5-dc cluster-decrease in angle, dc in next 18 sc on bar, 7 dc in 1 lp at end of bar. Dc in next 18 sts on opposite side of bar, holding back the last lp of each dc on hook, dc in next 2 sts, sk 1 st, dc in final st, dc in next ch-2 sp, dc in next dc, yo and draw through all loops on hook for a 5-dc cluster-decrease in angle **, (2 dc in next sp, dc in dc) 15 times (15 blks). Repeat from * 3 times, and from * to ** again, (2 dc in next sp, dc in dc) 7 times; 3 dc in end sp. **Row 3:** Ch 5, turn, sk 3 dc, dc in next dc (ch 2, sk 2 dc, dc in next dc) 6 times (6 sps), * sk 5 dc in angle, dc in next dc (ch 2, sk 2 dc, dc in next dc) 5 times (ch 2, sk 1 dc, dc in next dc, ch 5, dc in same dc for corner, ch 2, sk 1 dc, dc in next dc) twice, (ch 2, sk 2 dc, dc in next dc) 5 times, sk 5 dc in angle, dc in next dc **; (ch 2, sk 2 dc, dc in next dc) 14 times. Repeat from * 3 times, and from * to ** again. Make 7 sps to end of row. **Row 4:** Ch 3, turn, * make blks across to third dc from cluster-decrease in next angle, 2 dc in next sp, holding back the last lp of each dc on hook, dc in next dc, dc in next sp, dc between 2 dc in angle, dc in next sp, dc in next dc, yo and draw through all loops on hook for a cluster-decrease, make 5 blks (2 dc in corner sp, 7 dc in third st of same sp, 2 dc in balance of sp, dc in next dc) 3-blk corner made, make blks across end of bar, 2 dc in corner sp, 7 dc in center st of sp, 2 dc in balance of sp, dc in next dc, make 4 blks, 2 dc in next sp, make a 5-dc cluster-decrease in angle as in opposite angle. Repeat from * 4 times. Make blks to end of row, putting final dc in third st of end ch 5. **Row 5:** Ch 5, turn, sk 3 dc. Dc in next dc, * make sps across to third dc from angle, sk 5 dc in angle, dc in next dc, 6 sps to center dc at next corner, ch 5, dc in same corner dc, make sps across to center dc at next corner, ch 5, dc in same corner dc, make 6 sps, sk 5 dc in angle, dc in next dc. Repeat from * 4 times. Make sps to end of row. (The dc in this row and in all other sp rows should be exactly above dc in previous sp rows.) Repeat rows 4, 5 and 4. **Row 9:** Ch 5, turn, sk 3 dc, dc in next dc; * sk 5 dc in angle, dc in next dc, 6 sps to corner, make corner sp, 14 sps to next corner, make corner sp, 6 sps, sk 5 dc in angle, dc in next dc **, 2 sps. Repeat from * 3 times, and from * to ** again, make 1 sp. **Row 10:** Turn, sk last 3 dc (2 dc in next sp, dc in dc) 6 times to corner sp, * make a 3-blk corner in corner sp, 14 blks across to corner sp, make 3-blk corner **; 4 blks, 2 dc in next sp, make 5-dc cluster-decrease in angle (dc in next sp, dc between 2 dc in angle, dc in next sp, dc in next dc) made into a 4-dc cluster-decrease in angle, 5 blks to corner sp. Repeat from * 3 times, and from * to ** again. Make 5 blks, 2 dc in next sp, sl st in third st of ch-5 sp. Fasten off. To sew tog the 4 slits across last row, start at center dc at each upper corner of one slit and sew 2 sides tog, going through both lps of each dc and exactly matching sts to bottom of slit. Repeat across. **Row 11:** Turn and attach thread to center dc at corner, ch 5, sk 2 dc, dc in next dc, make 8 sps, * ch 24, sk 2 ch, sc in remaining 22 ch, sl st in side-top of last dc **, make 9 sps to next sewn slit, make 9 more sps to center of next pattern. Repeat from * 3 times and from * to ** again. Make 9 sps across to center dc at end corner. Repeat Rows 2 through 11 twice, and 2 through 10 once more (40 rows).

Edge. Rnd 1: Turn wrong side up and attach thread to bottom corner (Row 1) and working across narrow end of mat, ch 5, dc between rows (ch 2, dc between next 2 rows) 8 times, * make 8 more sps (ch 2, dc between next 2 rows) 9 times. * Repeat from * to * up to center dc at corner, ch 5, dc in same corner st (18 sps across to next sewn slit) 4 times, 18 sps across to center dc at next corner, ch 5, dc in same st, repeat from * to * across next end to corner. **Rnd 2:** Ch 3, turn, 6 dc in first dc (make blks across side to next corner, make 3-blk corner in corner sp) repeated around 4 sides, join to first ch-3, sl st in next 3 dc (to corner). * Ch 5 (sk 2 dc, dc in next 4 dc, ch 2) repeated across end to next corner, dc in corner st. Fasten off. * Attach to next corner and work across opposite end, repeating from * to *.

FRINGE: Wind thread 12 times around a 2″ card, cut at one edge, fold strands in center, and knot into first sp at one end. Tie a fringe in each sp across each end. Trim fringe to an even length.

BLOCKING: Stretch and pin mat right side down in true shape. Steam through a doubled wet cloth, then press dry through a doubled dry cloth.

Irish Crochet Table Mat
14½″ diameter

Materials. Six-Cord Mercerized Crochet, Size 50—5 balls White. Few yards White Pearl Cotton. One-half yard Linen, 36″ wide. Steel Crochet Hook, Size 12.

Cut a circular piece of linen, 4¾″ in diameter. Make a narrow hem around linen and make 240 sc closely all around outer edge. Join with sl st.

Shamrock Edge. Rnd 1: Sc in same place as sl st, * (ch 2, picot) twice, ch 8, sl st in 6th ch from hook (this ch-6 loop is center of shamrock), turn, (ch 5, sc in center loop) 3 times, turn, in each of last 3 ch-5 loops make sc, 9 dc and sc, sc in ch-6 loop at center of shamrock, ch 2, picot, ch 1, sc between the first and second picots, ch 2, picot, ch 2, skip 4 sc, sc in next sc, (ch 2, picot) twice, ch 2, skip 4 sc, sc in next sc, repeat from * around (24 shamrocks). Fasten off. **Rnd 2:** Join thread to 7th dc of first petal (counting from stem), (ch 2, picot), 3 times, ch 2, sc in center of 2nd petal, * (ch 2, picot) 3 times, ch 2, sc in 3rd dc on 3rd petal, ch 2, tr in next loop on center, ch 2, sc in 7th dc on first petal of next shamrock, ch 2, picot, ch 1, turn and work sc between 1st and 2nd picots of last picot-chain, turn, (ch 2, picot) twice, ch 2, sc in center of 2nd petal. Repeat from * around. Do not fasten off.

Edging—Rose. With another ball of thread, work as follows: Starting at center, ch 7, join with sl st to form ring. **Rnd 1:** Ch 6, (dc in ring, ch 3) 6 times, join with sl st to 3rd ch of ch-6 (7 sps). **Rnd 2:** In each sp around make sc, 8 dc and sc. **Rnd 3:** * Ch 5, sc (from back of work) in next dc on first rnd, repeat from * around, ending with ch 5, sc in same place as sl st on rnd 1. **Rnd 4:** In each loop around, make sc, 10 dc, and sc. **Rnd 5:** * Ch 6, sc in the sc between next 2 petals on Rnd 3, repeat from * around, ending with sc between last and first petals. **Rnd 6:** In each loop around make sc, 12 dc and sc. **Rnd 7:** * Ch 7, sc in the sc between next 2 petals on Rnd 5, repeat from * around. **Rnd 8:** In each loop around make sc, 14 dc, and sc. **Rnd 9:** Sl st to 3rd dc of first petal, sc in same place, * (ch 6, sl st in 4th ch from hook—picot made—ch 2, picot, ch 2, skip 3 dc, sc in next dc) twice; (ch 2, picot) twice; ch 2, sc in 3rd dc of next petal, repeat from * around, ending with sl st in first sc. **Rnds 10 and 11:** Sl st to center of next loop, sc in same loop, * (ch 2, picot) twice; ch 2, sc in next loop, repeat from * around, ending with sl st in first sc. Fasten off at end of Rnd 11.

Edging—Thistle. Rnd 1: Wind thread 20 times around a match, slip off and make 21 sc in ring, join with sl st to first sc. **Rnd 2:** Ch 6, * tr in next sc, ch 2, repeat from * around, join last ch-2 with sl st to 4th ch of ch-6 (21 sps). **Rnd 3:** Working over 2 strands of Pearl Cotton, make 4 sc in each sp around, join, fasten off the 2 strands. **Rnd 4:** Sc in same place as sl st, * ch 4, sc in front loop of next sc, repeat from * around, ending with sl st in first sc. **Rnd 5:** Sc in same place as sl st, * (ch 2, picot) twice; ch 2, skip 3 sc, sc in back of next sc, repeat from * around, join with sl st to first sc. **Rnd 6:** Repeat Rnd 10 of Rose. **Rnd 7:** Sl st to center of next loop, sc in same loop, ch 2, picot, ch 1, sl st in any loop on last rnd of Rose, ch 1, picot, ch 2, sc in any loop on Thistle and complete as for last rnd of Rose, joining 2nd and 3rd loops to corresponding loops of Rose as first loop was joined. Make 5 more Roses and 5 more Thistles, joining them in alternate order as shown in illustration (as first Thistle was joined to Rose), and having 9 free loops on outer edge and 6 free loops on inner edge. Now work around inner edge as follows: **Rnd 1:** Attach thread to 2nd free loop on any flower, sc in same place, * (ch 2, picot) twice; ch 2, sc in next loop, repeat from * 3 more times, ch 2, picot, ch 2, sc in next free loop on next flower, turn, (ch 2, picot) twice; ch 2, sc in last loop on previous flower, turn, (ch 2, picot) twice; ch 2, sc in last loop made, ch 2, picot, ch 2, sc in next free loop on flower, (ch 2, picot) twice; ch 2 and continue thus around, join and fasten off. Lay this piece aside.

Join Edging to center as follows: With thread from Shamrock Edge, sl st to center

of first loop, ch 2, picot, ch 1, sc in a loop on Edging, * ch 2, picot, ch 2, sc in next loop on center, ch 2, picot, ch 1, sc in next loop on Edging, repeat from * around. Fasten off. Now work along outer edge of Centerpiece as follows: Attach thread to joining of flowers, * ch 2, picot, ch 2, tr in next loop, ch 2, picot, ch 6, insert hook in 2nd ch from hook and draw up loop (yo, insert hook under same ch and draw loop through) 10 times; yo and draw through all loops on hook, ch 1, sl st in next ch to hold strands tightly in place (*clones* knot made), ch 2, picot, ch 2, tr in same loop as last tr was made, ch 2, picot, ch 2, sc in next loop, repeat from * around, join and fasten off.

Star Wheel Tablecloth
68 × 85″—16 × 20 Motifs (320)

Materials. Six-Cord Mercerized Crochet, Size 20—37 balls White or Ecru. Steel Crochet Hook, Size 9.

Motif. Ch 10, join with sl st to form ring. **Rnd 1:** Ch 3, 23 dc in ring, join with sl st to 3rd ch of ch-3 first made. **Rnd 2:** Ch 10, and complete a cross st as follows: yo twice, insert hook in 8th ch from hook, draw thread through (4 loops on hook), yo once, skip 1 dc and insert hook in next dc, draw thread through (6 loops on hook), yo and take off 2 loops at a time, 5 times; * ch 3, yo 4 times, insert hook in next dc and draw thread through (6 loops on hook), yo and take off 2 loops at a time, twice; then yo, skip 1 dc, insert hook in next dc, draw thread through (6 loops on hook), yo and take off 2 loops at a time, 5 times; ch 3, dc in center point of the cross, thus completing the cross. Repeat from * until there are 8 cross sts around the circle. Join last ch-3 with sl st to 7th ch of ch-10 made first. **Rnd 3:** 5 sc in each sp. **Rnds 4 through 7:** Sc in each sc of previous rnd. **Rnd 8:** Ch 4, dc in first sc, * ch 1, dc in next sc, repeat from * around. Then ch 1 and join with sl st to 3rd ch of ch-4 made first. **Rnd 9:** Ch 10 and complete cross st as before, skipping 2 dc between

each leg of cross st and inserting hook under ch-1 sp, ch 3, skip 2 dc, make a cross st as before, inserting hook in ch-1 sps and skipping 2 dc between each leg of cross st. Repeat thus around (20 cross sts), join last ch-3 with sl st to 7th ch of ch-10 made first. **Rnd 10:** Sl st in first 2 sts of first sp, ch 5, * dc in same sp, ch 3, sc in next sp, ch 3, dc in next sp, ch 2, repeat from * around, join last ch-3 with sl st to 3rd ch of ch-5 first made. **Rnd 11:** Ch 6, dc in same sp, * ch 4, sc in next sc of previous rnd, ch 4, dc in next ch-2 sp, ch 3, dc in same sp, repeat from * around, joining with sl st to 3rd ch of ch-6 first made. Fasten off. Make necessary number of motifs and place in position. With neat over-and-over sts, sew 3 points of one motif to corresponding 3 points of the adjacent motif (thus leaving 2 points free on each motif).

Filet Monogram Sheet

Materials. Six-Cord Mercerized Crochet, Size 50—5 balls White. Steel Crochet Hook, Size 12; 1 Sheet.

Gauge. 7 sps—1″. 7 rows—1″.

Center. Cut a piece of graph paper 27 × 61 sps (not including border). With a pencil draw your middle initial at center, then space the others evenly on each side (see illustration). Starting with center, ch 96. **Row 1:** Dc in 4th ch from hook and in next 59 ch (20 bls made), (ch 2, skip 2 ch, dc in next ch-sp made) 3 times, dc in next 9 ch, make 3 sps, dc in next 6 ch, ch 3, turn. **Row 2:** Skip first dc, dc in next 3 dc (bl made over bl), ch 2, skip 2 dc, dc in next dc (sp made over bl), ch 2, dc in next dc (sp made over sp), make 9 more sps, (1 bl, 1 sp) 9 times; 1 bl, ch 3, turn. **Row 3:** Make 1 bl, 2 dc in next sp, dc in next dc (bl made over sp), make 27 sps, 2 bl, ch 3, turn. **Row 4:** Make 1 bl, 29 sps and 1 bl, ch 3, turn. Repeat Rows 3 and 4, following chart for initials, ending with Row 3. **Row 64:** Repeat Row 2. **Row 65:** Make 20 bls, 3 sps, 3 bls, 3 sps, 2 bls, ch 3, turn. Now follow insertion chart from A to B until piece is long enough to reach edge of sheet. Fasten off. Attach thread to opposite side of starting ch and complete to correspond. Pin insertion in place on sheet and cut away material in back, leaving ⅛″ for hem. Sew neatly in place.

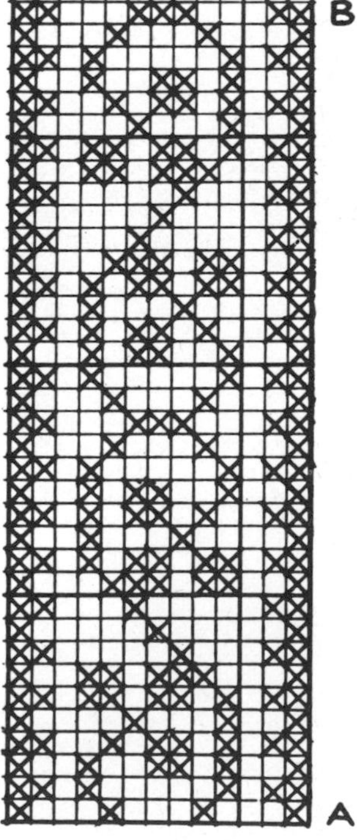

Curtain-Towel Edgings

Crochet is used to decorate the modern bathroom.

Materials. Six-Cord Mercerized Crochet, Size 30—6 balls White. Knit-cro-sheen—1 ball White. Steel Crochet Hooks, Sizes 10 and 9. Hairpin Lace Loom, ½″ Wide. 2 Bath Towels.

Materials are sufficient for a pair of organdy ruffled curtains 36″×54″ long (not including ruffles).

Make a strip of hairpin lace slightly longer than side and bottom ruffle. Fasten off. Make another strip the same way, having the same number of loops on each strip. TO JOIN STRIPS: Keeping the twist in all loops, insert hook in first loop of First Strip, draw first loop on Second Strip through loop on hook, * draw next loop on First Strip through loop on hook, draw next loop on Second Strip through loop on hook, repeat from * across, fasten last loop securely.

Heading. Keeping all loops straight, attach thread to first loop on opposite side of First Strip, sc in same place, * ch 1, sc in next loop, repeat from * across, fasten off. SCALLOPED EDGE: Still keeping all loops straight, attach thread to first loop on opposite side of Second Strip, sc in same place, * ch 5, sc in 3rd ch from hook, (picot made), ch 2, sc in next loop, repeat from * across, fasten off. Sew edging to curtain. Make another piece to fit across top ruffle and a piece for tie-back. Sew in place. Complete other curtain the same way. Starch edging lightly and press. Make edgings for towels the same way.

Pineapple Popcorn Spread

Materials. Single Size: Knit-cro-sheen—67 balls White or Ecru. Mercerized Bedspread Cotton—120 balls any color. Double Size: Knit-cro-sheen—79 balls White or Ecru. Mercerized Bedspread Cotton—140 balls any color. Steel Crochet Hook, Size 7.

Note: Each motif measures about 7″ from side to side, 8″ from point to point diagonally. For single-size spread (about 75″ × 108″ incl fringe) make 148 motifs. For double-size (about 90″ × 108″ incl fringe) make 175 motifs.

Motif. Starting at center, ch 8, join with sl st to form ring. **Rnd 1:** Ch 3, 17 dc in ring, sl st to top of ch 3. **Rnd 2:** Ch 3, 4 dc in same place as sl st, drop loop from hook, insert hook in top of ch-3 and draw dropped loop through (a starting pc st made), * ch 4, skip 2 dc, pc st in next dc (ch 1, 5 dc in same place, drop loop from hook, insert hook in ch preceding the 5 dc and draw dropped loop through), repeat from * around, ending with ch 4, sl st in tip of first pc st made. **Rnd 3:** Ch 3 and complete a starting pc st in same place as sl st, * ch 3, dc in next sp, ch 3, pc st in tip of next pc st, repeat from * around,

ending with ch 3, sl st in tip of first pc st. **Rnd 4:** Ch 3 and complete a starting pc st in same place as sl st, * (ch 2, dc in next sp) twice, ch 2, pc st in tip of next pc st, repeat from * around, ending with ch 2, sl st in tip of first pc st. **Rnd 5:** Ch 3, 7 dc in same place as sl st (this is base of pineapple), * (ch 2, dc in next dc) twice, ch 2, 8 dc in tip of next pc st, repeat from * around, ending with ch 2, sl st in top of ch 3. **Rnd 6:** Ch 4, (dc in next dc, ch 1) 6 times, dc in next 2 dc, * ch 2, dc in next 2 dc, (ch 1, dc in next dc) 7 times, dc in next dc, repeat from * around, ending with sl st in 3rd st of ch-4. **Rnd 7:** Sl st in sp, ch 3 and complete a starting pc st in same place, (ch 1, pc st in next sp) 6 times, * ch 2, skip next dc, dc in next dc, ch 2, dc in next dc, ch 2, skip next dc, (pc st in next sp, ch 1) 6 times, pc st in next sp, repeat from * around, ending with ch 2, sl st in tip of first pc st made. **Rnd 8:** Sl st in sp, ch 3 and complete a starting pc st, (ch 2, pc st in next sp) 5 times (6 pc sts in pineapple), * (ch 2, dc in next sp) 3 times, (ch 2, pc st in the next sp) 6 times, repeat from * around (4 ch-2 sps between pineapples), ending with ch 2, sl st in tip of first pc st. **Rnd 9:** Work as for Rnd 8, having 5 pc sts in each pineapple, and 5 ch-2 sps between pineapples. **Rnd 10:** * Make 4 pc sts, (ch 2, dc in next sp) 3 times, ch 2 dc in same sp (inc sp made), ch 2, dc in next sp twice, ch 2, repeat from * around, join. **Rnds 11, 12, and 13:** Work as for Rnd 10, making 1 pc st less on each pineapple on each rnd, and working dc, ch 2 and dc in each inc sp, join. **Rnd 14:** Sl st in next ch, sc in sp, ch 5, * dc in next sp, ch 2, repeat from * to the inc sp, in inc sp make 3 dc, ch 2 and 3 dc, ch 2, dc in next sp. Continue in this manner around, join with sl st to 3rd st of ch-5. Fasten off. Make necessary number of motifs and sew together on wrong side with neat over-and-over sts.

Fringe. Make fringe in each sp around as follows: Cut 8 strands, each 12″ long. Double these strands, forming a loop. Pull loop through sp and draw loose ends through loop. Pull tight. Trim evenly.

CROCHETED APPAREL

Afghan Slipon Sweater

Shown in Color Plate 16

Materials. Germantown or Knitting Worsted (4-oz. skeins)—1 each of:

Black	Fern
Orange	Watermelon
Lavender	Aqua
Daffodil	Temple Blue

For Embroidery a few yards of:

Orange	Lavender	Aqua
Daffodil	Fern	Watermelon
Temple Blue	Lettuce	White

Note: There may be enough of some colors left from the sweater to do the embroidery. The Lettuce and White are additional colors.

Afghan Hook, Size 7 or G.

Gauge: 5 sts—1″. 4 rows—1″.

Important: The directions for this Slipon are written in medium size only for a specific gauge. Please check measurements below before commencing your Slipon. If you wish a smaller size, change to a smaller gauge by using a smaller hook. If you wish a larger size, change to a larger gauge by using a larger hook. Remember that a change in stitch-gauge, in most cases means a change in row-gauge. Check your gauge as you progress.

Slipon Measurements:

Width across back at underarms . . . 18″
Width across front at underarms . . . 18″
Length from lower edge to underarms . . . 13″
Length from lower edge to back of neck . . . 22″
Width of sleeve at underarm . . . 18″
Length of sleeve to underarm . . . 20″

Note 1: Each square should measure approximately 4½″.

Note 2: Black is used only for edging, neckband and embroidery.

Note 3: When plain Afghan stitch is worked as a foundation for Cross Stitch Embroidery, avoid drawing loops too high. Work loops off loosely, forming perfect squares on which to embroider.

A—Aqua
G—Fern Green
W—Watermelon
O—Orange
L—Lavender
Y—Daffodil
B—Temple Blue

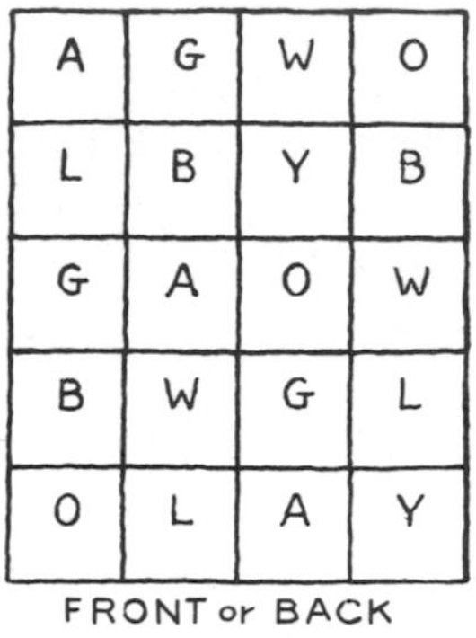

A	G	W	O
L	B	Y	B
G	A	O	W
B	W	G	L
O	L	A	Y

FRONT or BACK

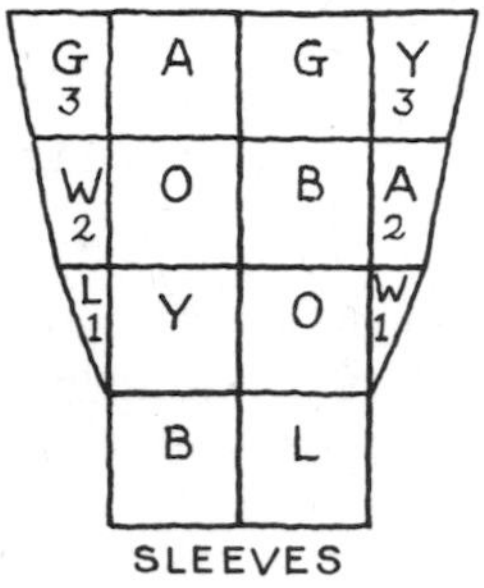

G 3	A	G	Y 3
W 2	O	B	A 2
L 1	Y	O	W 1
	B	L	

SLEEVES

CHART
FOR SETTING TOGETHER AFGHAN SWEATER

Pattern Stitch. PLAIN AFGHAN STITCH: Make a ch of desired number of sts. **First Half of Row 1:** Retaining all loops on hook, draw up a loop in 2nd and in each remaining st of chain. **Second Half of Row 1:** Yo hook and draw through 1 loop, * yo hook and draw through 2 loops; repeat from * across row. There will be same number of sts as chains. **First Half of Row 2:** Retaining all loops on hook, draw up a loop through front loop of 2nd and each succeeding upright st. Work 2nd half of row same as Second Half of Row 1. Repeat Row 2 for pattern st.

Bind Off. Work sl st through front loop of each upright st. Fasten off.

Large Squares (Make 56). With afghan hook, ch 20—should measure 4½″. Work plain afghan st for 16 rows. Your piece should be a perfect square.

Finishing. Bind off—do not break off yarn; work sl st around remaining 3 sides of square. Fasten off.

Embroidery. Colors given on the 9 charts are the suggested colors. Use the colors for 9 squares, then vary colors to suit your own color scheme. Embroider all squares following the 9 charts. Vary colors of designs to harmonize or contrast with color of each square. Stems are worked in outline stitch using full strand of yarn. Use one strand for small lazy daisies and double strand for large daisy.

Back. Following Chart, sew together 20 squares so that no two adjoining squares are the same background color.

Front. Same as Back.

Dec Squares (For Sleeves): RIGHT DEC SQUARE NO. 1 (Make 2): Ch 20. Work Row 1 of pat st. **Row 2:** Work sl st same as for bind off in next 2 sts (a dec), work pat to end. Continue to dec 2 sts at same edge 4 times more; then 5 sts, twice. Finish same as large square. RIGHT DEC SQUARE NO. 2 (Make 2): Ch 20. Work in pat st for 8 rows. **Next row:** Work sl st same as for bind off in next 5 sts, work pat to end (a dec). Continue to dec 5 sts at same edge 3 times more. Finish same as large square. RIGHT DEC SQUARE NO. 3 (Make 2): Ch 20. Work in pat st for 12 rows. **Next row:** Dec same as on Right Dec Square No. 2. Finish same as large square. LEFT DEC SQUARE NO. 1 (Make 2): Ch 20. Work Row 1 of pat st. **Next row:** Work pat to within 2 sts of end (a dec). Continue to dec 2 sts at same edge 4 times more; then 5 sts twice. Do not break off yarn; work sl st around all 4 sides of square. Fasten off. LEFT DEC SQUARE NO. 2 (Make 2): Ch 20. Work in pat st for 8 rows. **Next row:** Work pat to within 5 sts of end (a dec). Continue to dec 5 sts at same edge 3 times more. Finish same as Left Dec Square No. 1. LEFT DEC SQUARE NO. 3 (Make 2): Ch 20. Work in pat st for 12 rows. **Next row:** Dec same as on Left Square No. 2. Finish same as Left Dec Square No. 1.

Embroidery. Embroider all Dec Squares, using part of any of the 9 charts depending on size of square.

Sleeves. Following Chart, sew together 14 squares including 3 Right and 3 Left Dec

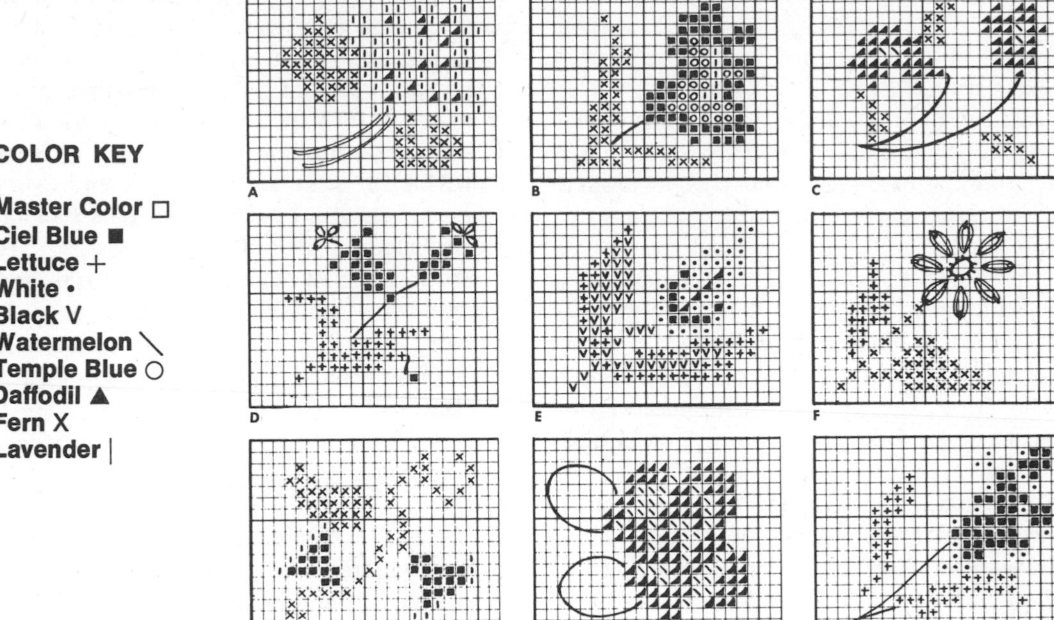

Squares. No two adjoining squares should have same background color.

Finishing. FRONT NECKBAND: From right side, work Row 1 of pat st across center 2 squares picking up 42 loops. Work in pat st, dec 1 st at each end for 5 rows. Bind off. Work Back Neckband the same way. Sew together 2 squares at each shoulder for seam. Weave ends of Neckband together. Sew together 3 squares at each side of Front and Back for underarm seam. Sew sleeve seams. Sew in sleeves. From right side, work 2 rows of sc around lower edge of Slipon and wrists, spacing sts to keep edges flat. Block.

Crocheted Slipon Sweater

Directions are for Size 30–32. Changes for Size 34–36 and for 38–40 are in parentheses.

Materials. Sports Yarn—6 (7–8) 2-oz. balls. Plastic Crochet Hook, Size F.

Gauge. 5 cross patterns—2″. 2 rows—1″.

Body Measurements 30 (34–38)

Slipon Measurements 32 (36–40)

Back. Ch 81 (91–101) sts loosely to measure 16 (18–20)″. **Row 1:** Sc in 2nd ch from hook, sc in each sc across. There are 80 (90–100) sc. Ch 1, turn. **Row 2:** Sc in each sc across. Ch 1, turn. **Row 3:** Sc in each sc across. Ch 3, turn. **Row 4:** 1 dc in first sc, * skip 1 sc, 1 dc in next sc, 1 dc in skipped sc (this is called a cross pat); repeat from *.

End 2 dc in last sc. Ch 3, turn. **Row 5:** Skip first dc, 1 dc in next dc, * skip 1 dc, 1 dc in next dc, 1 dc in skipped dc (1 cross pat); repeat from *. End 2 dc in last dc. Ch 3, turn. There are 40 (45–50) cross pats across row. Repeat Row 5 for pat, work even until piece measures 14½″ from beg, or desired length to underarm. Ch 1, turn. ARMHOLES: **Row 1:** Work 1 sl st in each of the next 6 dc, ch 3, work 1 dc in same st as last sl st, continue even in pat to within 6 dc of end, work 2 dc in next dc, turn. **Row 2:** * Work 1 sl st in each of the next 4 dc, ch 3, work 1 dc in same st as last sl st, continue even in pat to within 4 dc of end, work 2 dc in next dc, turn; repeat from * 1 (2–3) times more. Work even on 32 (35–38) cross pats, until armholes measure 7½ (8–8½)″. Ch 1, turn. SHOULDERS: **Row 1:** * Work 1 sl st in each of the next 10 dc, ch 3, work 1 dc in same st as last sl st, continue even in pat to within 10 dc of end, work 2 dc in next dc. Ch 1, turn; repeat from * once. Fasten off.

Front. Work same as back until armholes measure 5½ (6–6½)″. Ch 3, turn.

Neck and Shoulder Shaping. FIRST SHOULDER: **Row 1:** 1 dc, 11 cross pats across row, ch 3, turn. **Row 2:** Work 10 cross pats across row, 1 dc in last st, ch 3, turn. **Row 3:** Work 10 cross pats, 1 dc in last st, ch 3, turn. **Row 4:** Work 10 cross pats, ch 3, turn. **Row 5:** Work 10 cross pats, ch 3, turn. **Row 6:** Work 7 cross pats, turn. **Row 7:** Sl st in next 5 sts, work 4 cross pats, 1 dc in last st, break yarn and fasten off. SECOND SHOULDER: Skip 12 (15–18) cross pats at center of last complete row; join yarn in next dc, ch 3, do not turn. **Row 1:** 1 dc in next dc, 11 cross pats, 2 dc in last sp, ch 3, turn. **Row 2:** 1 dc in same space, 10 cross pats, 1 dc in last dc, ch 3, turn. **Row 3:** 10 cross pats, 2 dc in last sp, ch 3, turn. **Row 4:** 1 dc in first st, 10 cross pats, ch 3, turn. **Row 5:** 1 dc in first st, 9 cross pats, dc in last sp, turn. **Row 6:** Sl st in first 5 sts, ch 3, dc in next st, 6 cross pats, dc in last sp, ch 3, turn. **Row 7:** 4 cross pats, break yarn.

Sleeves. Ch 51 (55–59) sts loosely to measure 10 (11–12)″. Work first 5 rows, same as on back. There are 25 (27–29) cross pats. Continue in pat and inc 1 pat at each end on next row by working 2 extra dc in first and last st. Work even on 27 (29–31) cross pats until sleeve measures 5½″ from beg, or desired length. CAP: Work Row 1 and 2 of armhole shaping back. **Next Row:** Dec 1 cross pat st at each end every other row until 7 (9–11) cross pats remain. Fasten off.

Finishing. Sew shoulder, underarm and sleeve seams matching patterns. Sew in sleeves. Working from right side, work 3 rows of sc around entire neck edge. Fasten off. Block.

Crocheted Dress of Blocks

Shown in Color Plate 17

Block motif is made the same way for both sizes of the dress. Make 240 motifs for Small Size (10 to 12); 272 for Medium Size (14 to 16).

Materials. Fingering Yarn (1-oz. skein) —6 (7) skeins of Color A, 6 (7) skeins of Color B, and 4 (5) skeins of Color C. Steel Crochet Hook, Size 3.

Gauge. Each motif measures 2½″ square.

Note: Repeat instructions in parentheses as many times as specified. For example: "(ch 5, sc in next sc) 5 times," means to do everything specified in parentheses 5 times in all.

Motif. Starting at center with Color A, ch 6. Join with a sl st to form a ring. **Row 1:** Ch 4 to count as 1 dc, 3 dc in ring, remove hook, insert into top of ch 4 and draw loop through. This forms a cluster. (Ch 2, make a 4 dc cluster in ring, inserting hook into first dc of group) 7 times, ch 2, join to 4th dc at start, break off Color A and fasten. **Row 2:** With Color B, make a loop on hook, 1 sc in top of any cluster, (ch 1, 1 sc in next space, ch 1, 1 sc in next cluster) 7 times, ch 1, 1 sc in space, ch 1, sl st to first sc. **Row 3:** Ch 4, in same space make (dc, ch 1) twice, * (1 dc in next space, ch 1) 3 times, in next space make (dc, ch 1) 3 times for corner, repeat from * around, ending sl st to 3rd ch at start, break yarn and fasten. **Row 4:** With Color C, make loop on hook. Work

1 sc in any ch-1 space at side, * ch 1, 1 sc in next space, repeat from * to center dc of next corner, (ch 1, 1 sc) twice in this dc, repeat from * around, join to first sc with a sl st. **Row 5:** Sl st in next space, ch 4, * 1 dc in next space, ch 1, repeat from * to center space of corner, work (dc, ch 1) 3 times in this space, repeat from * around, ending sl st to 3rd ch of ch 4 at start. Break yarn and fasten. **Row 6:** With Color A, make loop on hook. Work 1 sc in any ch-1 space at side, * 1 sc in next space, ch 1, repeat from * around to center dc of corner, work ch 2 over this dc, repeat from * around, ending sl st to first sc. Break yarn and fasten.

Dress. Sew motifs together on right side of work, joining as in diagram A. Shaded section is for *Medium Size*. On *Small Size* make opening of 4 motifs for center front of neck,

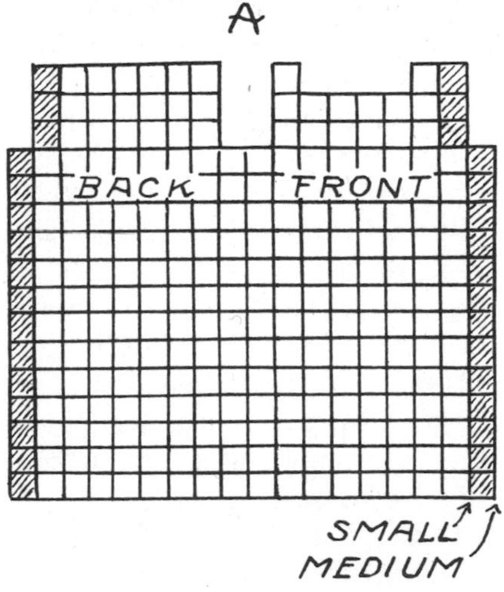

5 for *Medium Size*. BELT: With Color B, make a twisted cord, using 12 strands of yarn about 12 feet long. Fasten one end to a stationary object. Twist cord tightly. Fold strands in half and allow cord to twist upon itself. Tie knot at each end. EDGINGS: (Lower edge): Fasten Color B in any ch-1 space at lower edge. **Rows 1, 2 and 3:** Work 1 sc in space, * ch 1, 1 sc in next space, repeat from * around, join to first sc with a sl st. **Row 4:** Work "Italian" edging as follows: Working from left to right, ch 1, 1 sc in last space, * ch 1, 1 sc in next space, repeat from * across to beg. Break yarn and fasten. NECK: Work same edging around neck, working Row 1 to within 1 space of corner, work 1 hdc in next space, 1 dc in corner, 1 hdc in next space. On next 3 rows omit ch 1 at each side of corner st. ARMHOLES: **Row 1:** Fasten yarn in any ch-1 space, work 1 sc in each space around, omitting ch 1, working corner as on neck. **Row 2:** 1 sc in space, * ch 1, skip 1 st, 1 sc in next st, repeat from * around, sl st to first sc. **Rows 3 and 4:** Same as on neck.

Crocheted Suit

Directions are for Size 10. Changes for Sizes 12, 14, 16, 18, and 20 are in parentheses.

Materials. Sports Yarn (1-oz. skein)—29 (31–33–35–37–39) skeins. *Or* Featherweight Knitting Worsted (2-oz. skein—15 (16–17–18–19–20). Seven ⅜-inch Button Molds. Steel Crochet Hook, Size 0 or 1.

Gauge. 2 groups—1″. 2 group rows—1″.

Skirt. BACK: Ch 126 (132–138–144–150–156) loosely. **Row 1** (wrong side): Work 3 dc for "group" in 6th ch from hook, * skip 2 ch, 1 group in next ch, repeat from * across, ending skip 2 ch, 1 dc in last ch-40 (42–44–46–48–50) groups, ch 1, turn. **Row 1:** 1 sc in space before first group, * ch 2, 1 sc in space between next 2 groups, repeat from * across, ending ch 2, 1 sc in last space, ch 3, turn. **Row 3:** 1 group in each ch-2 space, ending with 1 dc in last sc, ch 1, turn. Repeat Rows 2 and 3 for pat, working to 5″ from start, ending with Row 2. Directions are for a 26″ skirt, allowing 1″ for blocking. For longer or shorter skirt, make adjustment here. Dec as follows: **Row 1:** 2 dc in first space, work to last space, 2 dc in last space, 1 dc in last sc, ch 1, turn. **Row 2:** 1 sc in first space, ch 1, 1 sc in next space, work across, ending ch 1, 1 sc in last space, ch 3, turn. **Rows 3 and 4:** Repeat Rows 1 and 2. **Row 5:** 1 dc in first space, work across, ending 1 dc in last space, 1 dc in sc, ch 1, turn. **Row 6:** Repeat Row 2. **Rows 7 and 8:** Repeat Rows 5 and 6. **Row 9:** Skip first space, * 3 dc in next space, repeat from * to last space, skip last space, 1 dc in last sc, ch 1, turn. **Rows 10, 11 and 12:** Work in pat. Repeat these 12 rows until 30 (32–34–36–38–40) pats rem. Work to 25″ or 1″ less than desired length from start. Fasten off. FRONT: Same as back.

Jacket. BACK: Ch 105 (108–114–117–126–132). Work in pat on the 33 (34–36–37–40–42) groups, working to 13″ from start, ending with a group row. ARMHOLES: **Row 1:** Sl st over first 4 dc, ch 1, sc in 2nd space, * ch 2, 1 sc in next space, repeat from * to 2nd space from end, ch 3, turn. Continue in pat, dec'ing 1 st each side every group row until 27 (28–30–31–32–34) pats rem. Work on rem'ing pats until armholes measure 8 (8–8½–8½–9–9)″, ending with a group row. SHOULDERS: **Row 1:** Sl st over first 3 groups, work to last 3 groups, ch 3, turn. **Row 2:** Work on the rem'ing 21 (22–24–25–26–28) groups. **Row 3:** Repeat Row 1. **Row 4:** Work on the 15 (16–18–19–20–22) groups. **Row 5:** Sl st over the first 2 (2–3–3–3–4) groups, work to last 2 (2–3–3–3–4) groups. Fasten off 11 (12–12–13–14–14) groups for back of neck.

RIGHT FRONT: Ch 60 (63–66–69–75–78) loosely. Work on the 18 (19–20–21–23–24) groups to same length as back to underarm, ending with a group row. ARMHOLE: Work to 2nd space from end, ch 3, turn. Continue in pat, dec'ing 1 st at armhole edge every group row until 15 (16–17–18–19–20) groups rem. Work until armhole measures 5 (5–5½–5½–6–6)″, ending at front edge with a group row. NECK AND SHOULDER: Sl st over first 3 (4–4–5–6–6) groups, work to end of row. Dec 2 sts at neck edge on every group row until 8 (8–9–9–9–10) groups rem and when armhole measures same as on back, * work to last 3 groups, ch 3, turn. Work 1 row. Repeat from * once more. Work 1 more row on the 2 (2–3–3–3–4) groups. Fasten off.

LEFT FRONT: Work to correspond to right front, reversing the shaping.

SLEEVES: Ch 66 (66–72–72–78–78). Work on the 20 (20–22–22–24–24) groups for 2″, ending with row of ch-2 spaces. Inc as follows: **Row 1:** 1 dc in first sc, * 3 dc in next space, repeat from * across, ending 2 dc in last sc, ch 2, turn. **Row 2:** 1 sc in base of turning ch, work across, ending ch 1, 1 sc in last space, ch 3, turn. **Row 3:** 2 dc in first space, work across, ending 2 dc in last space, ch 2, turn. **Row 4:** 1 sc in base of ch, * work across, ending ch 1, 1 sc in turning ch, ch 3, turn. **Row 5:** 3 dc in first space, work across, ending 3 dc in last space, 1 dc in top of turning ch, ch 1, turn. **Row 6:** 1 sc in space before first group, * ch 2, 1 sc in space between next 2 groups, repeat from * across, ending ch 2, 1 sc in last space, ch 3, turn. Repeat these 6 rows until there are 26 (26–28–28–30–30) groups, ending with row of ch-2 spaces. Continue to work in pat to 13″ from start, ending with a group row. SLEEVE CAP: **Row 1:** Sl st over first 4 dc, ch 1, 1 sc in 2nd space, work in pat to 2nd space from end, ch 3, turn. **Row 2:** 1 sc in first space, work in pat to last space, 1 dc in last space, 1 dc in last sc. **Row 3:** Sl st in first 2 dc, 1 sc in next space, work to 2nd space from end, ch 3, turn. Repeat Rows 2 and 3 until 6 groups rem. Fasten off.

Finishing. Steam all pieces. Cut lining for skirt, allowing 1″ for seams and for hems at top and bottom. Sew side seams of skirt, matching pats. Starting at top of right side seam, crochet 1 row of sc around waistline. Starting at lower edge at one side seam, on wrong side of work, crochet 1 row of sc around hemline. Join with a sl st, ch 1, turn. ITALIAN EDGING: On right side of work, * skip 1 sc to right, work 1 sc in next st to the right, ch 1, repeat from * working backwards from left to right around hemline. Join with a sl st, fasten off. Cut 1¼″ elastic for inside waistline, adjusting to size. Make lining and sew over elastic then attach inside waistline. Jacket: Cut lining, allowing 1″ for seams, allow for pleat at center back, dart at center shoulder on each front and for gathering at outer edge of elbow on sleeves. Sew shoulder seams. Sew sleeves in place then sew underarm and sleeve seams. Starting at left front edge on right side of work, crochet 1 row of sc on lower edge, ch 1, turn. **Row 2:** Crochet 1 sc in each sc. Fasten off.

Front Border. Starting at lower right front edge, crochet 1 row of sc on front edges and around neck, adjusting sts on neck for proper fit, ch 1, turn. **Row 2:** 1 sc in each sc, inc at corners to keep work flat. Place markers for 7 buttons on left front edge, having first marker 1½″ above lower edge and 7th marker 4 sc below neck. **Row 3:** Crochet 1 sc in each st to first marker, ch 3, skip 3 sc, 1 sc in next sc for buttonhole, repeat buttonhole opposite markers then finish row, inc at corners. **Row 4:** Work same as Row 2, working 3 sc over each ch-3. **Row 5:** Same as Row 2, ch 1. Continue around on right side, working Italian Edging around all edges as on skirt. Fasten off. Starting at sleeve seam, work edging around sleeves same as on hem of skirt.

Buttons. Cover button ring with sc. Break yarn, leaving 10″ end. Turn outer edge to center and sew tog.

Crocheted Wool Boots

Directions are for Size 6½. For larger or smaller sizes, inc or dec the number of rows over instep.

Materials. Knitting Worsted—3 ozs. Navy, 1 oz. Red. I pair Slipper Soles. Two 5″ Zippers. Plastic Crochet Hook, Size 5.

Note: Each boot is made in two parts.

Row 1: With Navy, starting at tip, ch 11, hdc in 3rd ch from hook and in each ch

across, ch 2, turn. **Row 2:** Hdc in each st across, inc 1 st in last st, ch 2, turn. **Row 3:** 2 hdc in first st, 1 hdc in each st across. **Rows 4 through 13:** Repeat Rows 2 and 3. **Row 14:** 1 hdc in each st across, ch 14, turn. **Row 15:** Hdc in 3rd ch from hook and in each st to end of row. Work even for 9 rows. Fasten off. Make two parts alike. With Red, make 1 sc in each of the 9 hdc of the tip, ch 1, turn. Work 5 more rows. With Navy, sew back of boot together; make a row of sc all around the top and down the front opening. With Red, make 2 rows of sc around top and 1″ of front opening. Cross red part of tip (see photograph). With Red, work 1 row sc around bottom part. For heel, work 2 rows sc for 15 sts on either side of back seam. Work another row sc all around bottom. Sew boot to sole, sew in zipper, join tassel to zipper tab.

Crocheted Dress

Shown in Color Plate 14

Directions are for small size (6–8). Changes for medium size (10–12) and large size (14–16) are in parentheses.

Materials. Sport Yarn (2-oz. ball) 10 (11–12) balls. Crochet Hook, Size H. 35 small Buttons.

Gauge. 7 sc—2″; 2 rows—1″.

Note: Instructions are for 32 (32½–33)″ finished length, hem to shoulder. If you wish your dress to be longer or shorter, work more or fewer inches before first dec row.

Pattern Stitch: Row 1 (right side): Skip 1 st, 3 dc (1 shell) in next st, * skip 2 sts, 1 shell in next st, repeat from * across, ending skip next st, dc in last st, ch 1, turn. **Row 2:** Sc in each dc across, working last sc in top of turning ch, ch 3, turn. Repeat these 2 rows for pat.

Back. Ch 72 (78–84) loosely to measure 20 (22–24)″ for lower edge. 1 sc in 2nd ch from hook, 1 sc in each of remaining sts, ch 3, turn—71 (77–83) sts. Work even in pat until piece measures 3″, ending with row 1 of pat. **Decrease Row:** Dec 1 st (by working 2 tog) at each end of next row—2 sts decreased. Being careful to keep pat as established, repeat dec row every 3″ 5 times more. Work even in pat on 59 (65–71) sts until entire piece measures 25″, ending with Row 1 of pat. SHAPE ARMHOLES: Sl st across 4 (5–6) sts, work in pat to last 4 (5–6) sts, ch 1, turn. Dec 1 st each end of next 2 rows. Work even in pat on 47 (51–55) sts until armholes measure 7 (7½–8)″, end with Row 1 of pat. SHAPE SHOULDERS: Sl st across 7 (8–9) sts, work in pat to last 7 (8–9) sts, turn. Work 1 row even. Repeat last 2 rows once more. Fasten off.

Front. Work same as back until entire piece measures 18½″—59 (65–71) sts, ending with Row 1 of pat. FRONT OPENING, RIGHT FRONT: **Row 1:** Work across first 29 (32–35) sts, ch 3, turn. Work even in pat on these sts only until piece measures 25″, end at arm edge. SHAPE NECK AND ARMHOLE: Sl st across 4 (5–6) sts, work in pat to end of row. Dec 1 st each end of next row. Dec 1 stitch at beg of following row (arm edge); work in pat to end of row. Now, working even at arm edge, dec 1 st at front edge every other row until 14 (16–18) sts remain. *At same time,* when armhole measures 7 (7½–8)″, shape shoulder as for back. LEFT FRONT: **Row 1:** Attach yarn at start of front opening, ch 3, 1 sc in 2nd ch from hook and in next ch st, work across 30 (33–36) sts. The added sts are for underlap. Work even in pat on the 32 (35–38) sts until piece measures 25″ ending at front edge. SHAPE NECK AND ARMHOLE: Sl st across first 3 sts, work to last 4 (5–6) sts, turn. Finish to correspond to right front, reversing shaping.

Sleeves. Ch 42 (45–48) sts. 1 sc in 2nd ch from hook, 1 sc in each of remaining sts, ch 3, turn—41 (44–47) sts. Work even in pat for 6 (6–8) rows. SHAPE CAP: Sl st across 4 (5–6) sts, work in pat to last 4 (5–6) sts, ch 1, turn. Dec 1 st at each end of work every row until 23 (22–21) sts remain. Fasten off.

Sash. Ch 15. 1 sc in 2nd ch from hook, 1 sc in each of remaining sts, ch 3, turn—14 sts. Work even in pat for 54″. Fasten off.

Finishing. Sew underarm, shoulder and sleeve seams. Set in sleeves. EDGING: With right side facing you, work 1 row sc along front opening. Fasten off. **Row 2:** Join yarn in first sc, sc in next st. FOR BUTTONHOLE: Ch 1, skip 1 sc, sc for about ½″. Work 6 more buttonholes evenly spaced—the last one to be made at start of neck shaping; then sc along neck edge to end of row. Fasten off. Lap right front over left front at opening and sew lower end of lap in place. Sew 7 buttons to left front. FOR SASH: Work 1 rnd sc around entire sash. For each end, thread 14 buttons onto yarn. Working across narrow end, join yarn at edge of work. Insert hook in first st, pass yarn over hook and hold in place, slide a button 7″ from hook, and, forming a 7″ loop, pass yarn over hook for a second time; draw hook through st with both loops on hook (3 loops on hook now), yo and draw through all loops (a button loop st made). Work 13 more loops in same manner across. Repeat at other end.

Chapter 9

Tatting and Netting

Tatting is a knotting technique with which many lovely things can be made. The size of the shuttle and the thread determine the fineness or coarseness of the finished piece. Tatting has been used principally for trimmings on table linens, handkerchiefs, blouses, children's dresses, etc. By making small motifs and joining them as you work, it is also possible to make very beautiful all-over lace pieces suitable for place mats, table covers, etc.

ABBREVIATIONS

r	ring
lr	large ring
sr or sm r	small ring
ds	double stitch
p	picot
lp	long picot
sm p	small picot
sep	separated
cl	close
rw	reverse work
sp	space
ch	chain
beg	beginning

* Repeat instructions following asterisks as many times as specified.

SHUTTLES AND THREADS

Shuttles can be made of various materials such as bone, tortoise shell, steel, or plastic. The points should come together closely enough to prevent the thread from feeding too rapidly. Some shuttles are made with a hook at the end but this tends to hinder the work. A crochet hook or pin can be used instead. Use larger shuttles for heavy thread and for wool yarn.

Fasten thread to shuttle by tying around the bar or through the hole in the bar if there is one. Wind thread evenly and not beyond the edge of the shuttle.

Cotton thread with a hard twist is customarily employed for this craft but other types of thread and yarns can also be used.

There are threads especially made for tatting, fine and with a hard twist. Coarser threads may be used and even woolen yarn, but all must have a twist to work well.

How to Tat

Holding Thread. With left hand grasp the free end of thread between thumb and forefinger. Spread the other fingers and bring the thread around them to make a circle. Hold securely with thumb and forefinger. Bend the little finger toward the palm to catch the thread and extend the middle finger to make the circle taut. This middle finger does most of the work of drawing up stitches or knots.

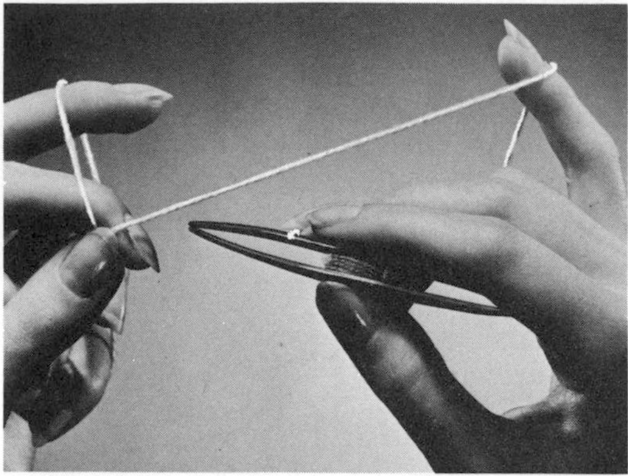

Double Knot, First Half. With right hand, hold shuttle by flat sides, pointing to left hand and with thread coming from back of bobbin. Extend little finger of right hand to support the thread.

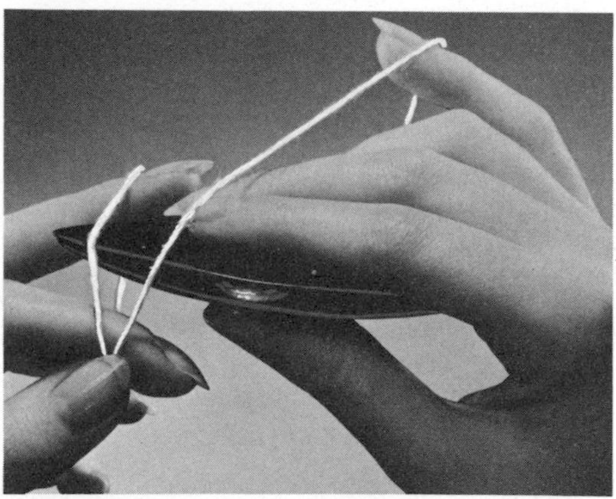

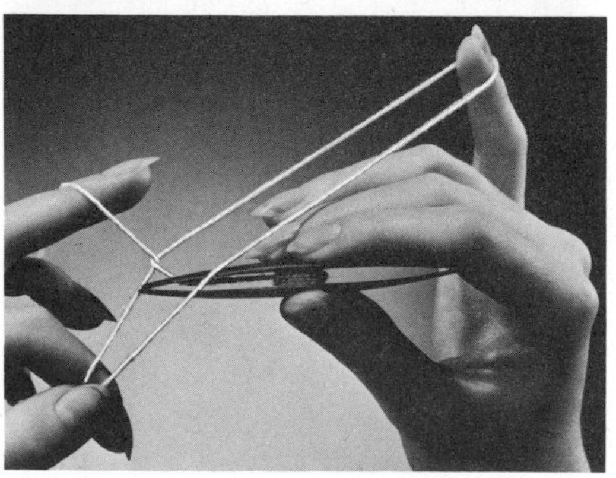

Without turning the shuttle, slide it first under, then over the thread held between middle and forefinger of left hand.

Drop middle finger of left hand. Draw shuttle thread taut; a loop will form with the thread around left hand.

Extend dropped finger of left hand, sliding the stitch down the shuttle thread which is held taut. This makes a tight stitch between thumb and forefinger. This completes first half of a double stitch.

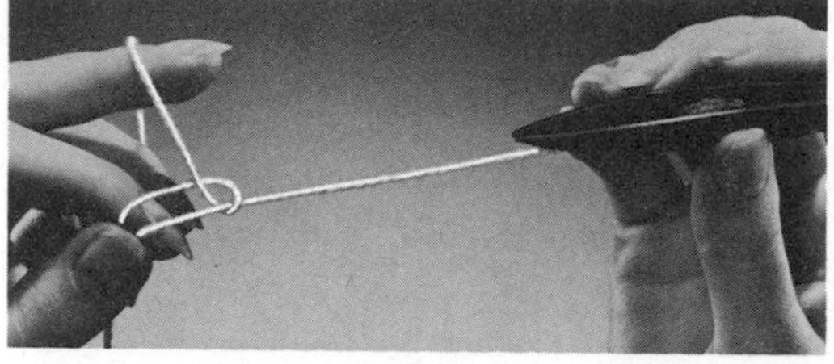

Practice this step until you do it with ease. The shuttle thread should slide easily through the stitches.

Second Half of Double Knot Stitch. Hold shuttle in horizontal position. Slide shuttle first over, then under thread between middle and forefinger of left hand. Draw up as for first half of stitch. This completes double stitch.

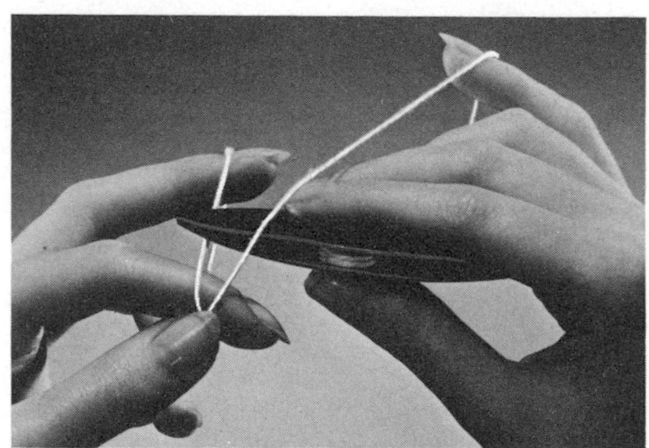

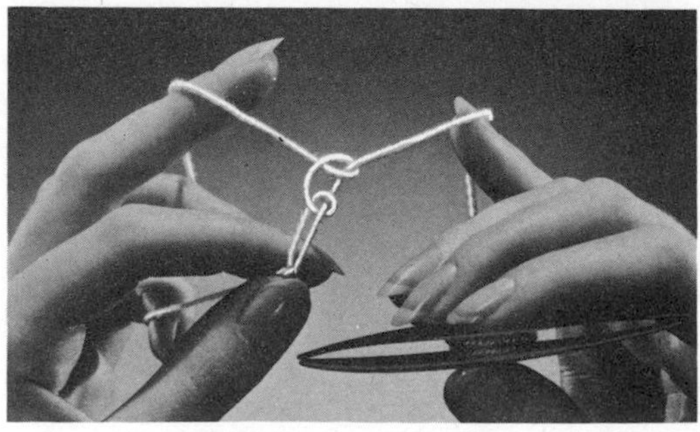

To Make a Ring. All tatting is made of rings, chains, and picots. The rings and chains are the basis of the design and picots are used for decoration and for joining.

After making several double stitches, draw up the thread on the shuttle so the first and last stiches touch, giving you a ring.

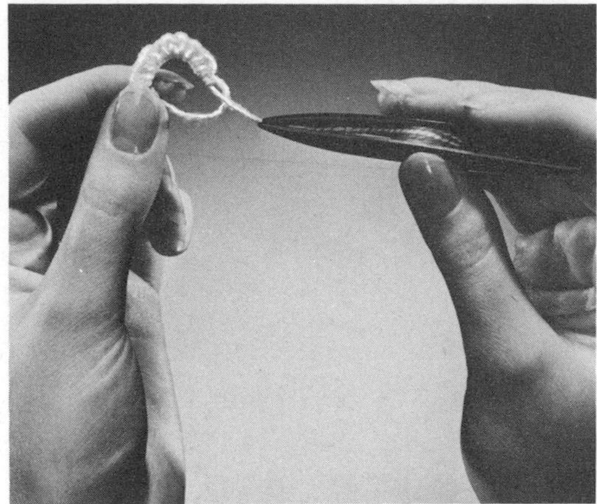

To Make a Picot. Make first half of a ds, but as you slide it into position, stop about ¼″ (or less) from preceding ds. Make the second half of ds; then slide entire ds close to preceding ds. The resulting loop is the picot. A picot means only the loop and does not include the ds which fastens it.

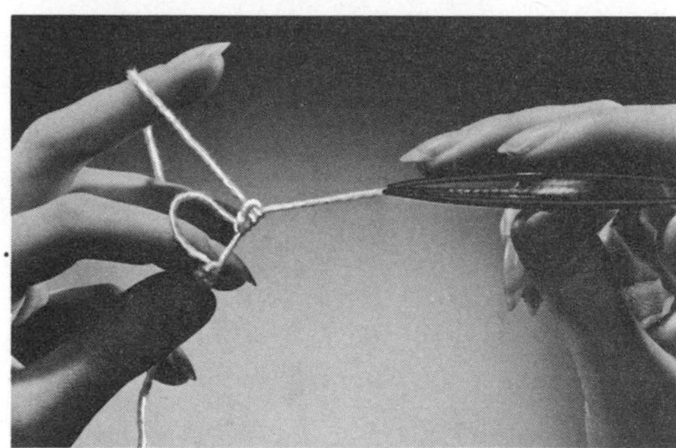

To Join Rings. When starting a second ring, leave a free space of about ¼ of the circumference of the first ring (this varies with the design).

For example (see abbreviations, page 387): Make first ring of 3 ds, p, 3 ds, p, 3 ds, p, 3 ds, draw up. Make 3 ds of 2nd r about ¼″ away from first r. Insert pin through last p of first r, catch thread encircling left hand and draw a loop through. Slip shuttle through this loop and draw shuttle thread taut. This joins 2nd r to first r and counts as first half of next ds. Complete ring as for first r.

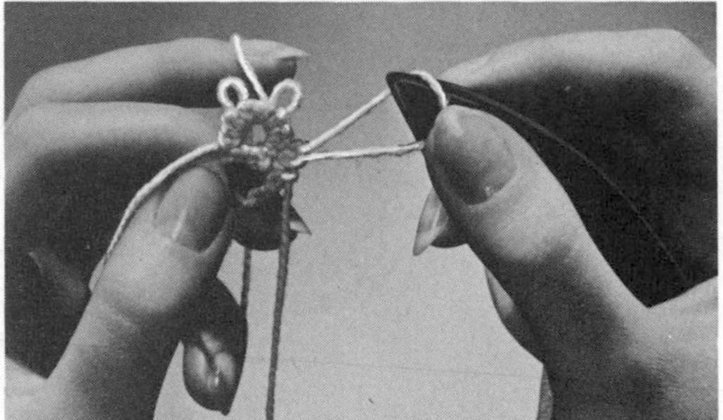

Using Two Shuttles, or a Ball and Shuttle to Make Chains. This is a way of covering the thread which passes from one ring to another. It also makes it possible to use two colors.

Rings can be made only with the shuttle thread wound completely around the left hand. Chains are made with the shuttle working on the ball (or second shuttle) thread.

Tie end of ball thread to end of shuttle thread. When making a ring use the shuttle thread in the regular manner.

When completed, turn it upside down so the base of the ring is held between the thumb and forefinger. Stretch the ball thread over the back of the fingers but instead of making a complete circle, wind it twice around the little finger to control the tension. Work over the ball thread with the shuttle as in making rings. (Picots and joinings are made in same way as on rings.) When chain

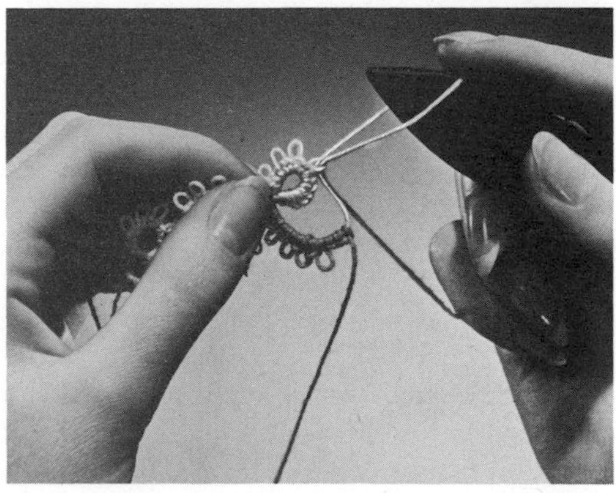

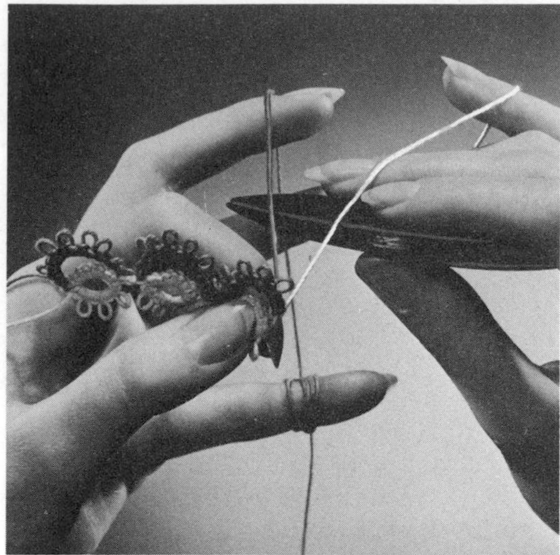

is finished, pull stitches close together and pull down ball thread. Pick up shuttle thread, turn work and make another ring.

Reversing Work. The round part of the ring is at the top as you work. By reversing the work, a loop can be made on the opposite side. This allows for wider edgings and insertions. To do this, the ring you have just worked is turned so the base of the ring is at the top and the new ring is worked as usual with the loop side up. Then reverse and make another ring beside the first and so on.

Joining Thread. When a new thread is required, make a square knot close to the base of the last ring or chain. Do not cut off ends as the strain of the work may loosen the knot. This is the only place to make knots, as they will not pass through the double stitches and therefore will prevent the ring from being drawn up if they occur on the thread encircling the hand. Cut off loose ends later.

Josephine Knot. This is an ornamental ring consisting of the first half of a double stitch made a specific number of times.

Long Picots. Make like regular picot but leave a longer space between double stitches.

Using Two Shuttles. When working rings in two colors use two shuttles, one color in each. Alternate shuttles. Drop the shuttle which has made the first ring and pick up the second. When separated by a chain, hold thread of second shuttle like the ball thread.

TATTING DESIGNS

Tatted Baby Cap

Materials. Six-Cord White Mercerized Crochet Cotton, Size 30. Tatting Shuttle. 3½ yards of narrow Ribbon, ¼″ wide.

Directions. 1st rnd: With shuttle thread only, r of 2 ds, 12 p's sep by 2 ds, 2 ds and cl, sp of ⅛″, tie threads to form a picot (13 p's). Tie and cut. **2nd rnd:** Sr of 6 ds, join to 1st p of r, 6 ds and cl, rw, sp of 3/16″, r of 5 ds, 3 p's sep by 5 ds, 5 ds and cl, * rw, sp as before, sr of 6 ds, join to next p of r, 6 ds and cl, rw, sp, r of 5 ds, join to last p of previous r, 5 ds, 2 p's sep by 5 ds, 5 ds and cl. Repeat from * around, sp, join at base of 1st sr (13 r's). Tie and cut. **3rd rnd:** Sr of 6 ds, join to center p of any r on previous rnd, 6 ds and cl, rw, sp of 3/16″, r of 5 ds, 3 p's sep by 5 ds, 5 ds and cl, * rw, sp as before, sr of 6 ds, join to same p, 6 ds and cl—increase made; rw, sp, r of 5 ds, join to last p of previous r, 5 ds, 2 p's sep by 5 ds, 5 ds and cl, rw, sp, sr of 6 ds, join to center p of next r, 6 ds and cl, rw, sp, r as before, joining to previous r. Repeat from * around, ending with r, sp, join at base of 1st sr (26 r's). Tie and cut. **4th rnd:** Sr of 6 ds, join to center p of any r on previous rnd, 6 ds and cl, rw, sp of 3/16″, r of 5 ds, 3 p's sep by 5 ds, 5 ds and cl, * rw, sp as before, sr as before, joining to same, p, rw, sp, r as before, joining to previous r, (rw, sp, sr joining to center p of next r, rw, sp, r, joining to previous r) twice; rw, sp, sr, joining to center p of next r, rw, sp, r, joining to previous r. Repeat from * around, making inc in last 2 r's (10 incs), join as before. Tie and cut. **5th rnd:** Tie ball and shuttle threads together, r of 7 ds, p, 7 ds and cl, rw, ch of 8 ds, join to center p of first r on previous rnd, 8 ds, join to center p of next r, 8 ds, rw, r as before, rw, ch as before, joining to next 2 r's as before, joining last ch to base of first r (18 chs). Tie and cut. **6th rnd:** With shuttle thread only, r of 5 ds, p, 8 ds, join to p of any r on previous rnd, * 8 ds, p, 5 ds and cl, r of 5 ds, join to last p of previous r, 8 ds, 2 p's sep by 8 ds, 5 ds and cl, r of 5 ds, join to last p of previous r, 8 ds, join to p of next r, 8 ds, p, 5 ds and cl, (r of 5 ds, join to last p of previous r, 8 ds, 2 p's sep by 8 ds, 5 ds and cl) twice, joining last r to 1st r—flower made. Tie and cut. R of 5 ds, p, 8 ds, join to p of same r and repeat from * around joining last flower to 1st flower (18 flowers). Tie and cut.

Now work in rows as follows: **1st row:** R of 5 ds, join to center p of 4th r on 1st flower of previous rnd, 8 ds, p, 8 ds, join to center p of 5th r on next flower, 5 ds and cl, r of 5 ds, join to previous joint p, 8 ds, 2 p's sep by 8 ds, 5 ds and cl, (r of 5 ds, join to previous r, 8 ds, 2 p's sep by 8 ds, 5 ds and cl) 3 times; joining last r to 1st r on same flower. Tie and cut. R of 5 ds, p, 8 ds, join to center p of 2nd r on previous flower, 8 ds, join to center p of 4th r of adjacent flower on previous rnd, 5 ds and cl, r of 5 ds, join to previous joint p, 8 ds, p, 8 ds, join to center p of 5th r of next flower on previous rnd, 5 ds and cl. Complete flower as before. Continue to work until 15 flowers are completed. **2nd row:** Tie threads as before, r of 7 ds, join to center p of 5th r on 1st flower of previous row, 7 ds and cl, * rw, ch of 8 ds, 2 p's sep by 8 ds, 8 ds, rw, r of 7 ds, join to joint p between same and next flower of previous row, 7 ds and cl. Repeat from * across. Tie and cut. **3rd row:** Sr of 6 ds, join to 1st p of first ch on previous row, 6 ds and cl, rw, sp, r of 5 ds, 3 p's sep by 5 ds, 5 ds and cl, * rw, sp, sr as before joining to next p of same ch, rw, sp, r of 5 ds, join to last p of previous r, 5 ds, 2 p's sep by 5 ds, 5 ds and cl, rw, sp, sr joining to next p of next ch, rw, sp, r joining to previous r. Repeat from * across making an inc in next p of same ch (6 incs, 36 r's). Tie and cut. **4th row:** Sr of 6 ds, join to center p of 1st r on previous row, 6 ds and cl, rw, sp, r of 5 ds, 3 p's sep by 5 ds, 5 ds and cl, * rw, sp, sr as before joining to center p of next r, rw, sp, r joining to previous r. Repeat from * across making 4 increases evenly spaced (40 r's). Tie and cut. **5th row:** R of 5 ds, p, 5 ds, join to center p of first r on previous row, 5 ds, p, 5 ds and cl, rw, sp, r of 5 ds, 3 p's sep by 5 ds, 5 ds and cl, rw, sp, r of 5 ds join to last p of 1st r, 5 ds, join to center p of next r, 5 ds, p, 5 ds and cl, * rw, sp, r as before, joining to next-to-last r, rw, sp, r joining to next-to-last r and to next r on previous row. Repeat from * across. Tie and cut. **6th row:** R of 5 ds, p, 8 ds, join to center p of 2nd r on previous row, 8 ds, join to next r, 5 ds and cl, r of 5 ds, join to previous joint p, 8 ds, join to next r and complete flower. Tie and cut. Make flower as before, skipping 3 r's and join to next 3 r's as before. Continue until 7 flowers are completed. **7th row:** R of 5 ds, 2 p's sep by 8 ds, 5 ds and cl, r of 5 ds, join to last p of previous r, 8 ds, join to joint p between 4th and 5th r's of first flower on previous row, 8 ds, p, 5 ds and cl, complete flower as before. Tie and cut. R of 5 ds, p, 8 ds, join to center p of 3rd r on previous flower, 8 ds, p, 5 ds and cl, r of 5 ds, join to last p of previous r, 8 ds, join to joint p between 3rd and 4th r's of first flower on previous row, 8 ds, p, 5 ds and cl, complete flower. Tie and cut. Continue working across the same way until 14 flowers are completed.

EDGING: Work across front of Cap exactly as for 2nd row. *Work across neck edge as follows:* Attach thread to base of 1st r on front edge, ch of 3 ds, 3 p's sep by 3 ds, 3 ds, rw, r of 7 ds, join to center p of 1st r on 1st flower of last row, 7 ds and cl, rw, ch as before, rw, r as before, joining to 1st p of 2nd r on 5th row, * rw, ch, rw, r, joining to next free p holding in slightly at back of neck. Tie and cut. Trim Cap with 3 rows of ribbon and make 2 rosettes as shown; cut two 15″ lengths of ribbon for ties. Sew both ties and rosettes firmly in place, as pictured.

Wide Edging with Medallions

At top in photograph above

Materials. Six-Cord White Mercerized Crochet Cotton, Size 30. Tatting Shuttle. Edging Measures 1¼″ wide.

Directions. With ball and shuttle thread, r of 3 ds, 6 p's sep by 3 ds, 3 ds and cl, rw, ch of 1 ds, sm p, * 7 ds, sm p, 2 ds. R of 2 ds, join to last sm p of previous ch, 6 ds, p, 6 ds, sm p, 2 ds and cl; r of 2 ds, join to last sm p of previous r, 6 ds, p, 8 ds and cl. Rw, r of 6 ds, join to last p of previous 6 p's, r, 2 ds, p, 8 ds and cl. Reversing curve of chain, ch of 11 ds, r of 10 ds, p, 2 ds, p, 8 ds and cl, ch of 9 ds, p, 3 ds. Rw, r of 6 ds, 3 p's sep by 3 ds, 6 ds and cl. Rw, ch of 3 ds, 2 p's sep by 3 ds, 3 ds, join to p of 4th r, 3 ds, p, 3 ds. (Rw, r of 6 ds, join to last p of previous r, 3 ds, join to center p of same r, 3 ds, p, 6 ds and cl. Rw, ch of 3 ds, 4 p's sep by 3 ds, 3 ds) 4 times; joining last ch at base of 6th r—medallion made. Ch of 3 ds, join to p of adjacent ch, 9 ds. R of 8 ds, join to last p of adjacent r, 2 ds, p, 10 ds and cl. Ch of 11 ds. Rw, r of 8 ds, join to 2nd p of last ch of previous medallion, 6 ds, p, 2 ds and cl. R of 2 ds, join to last p of previous r, 6 ds, 2 p's sep by 6 ds, 2 ds and cl. Rw, r of 8 ds, p, 2 ds, p, 6 ds and cl. Reversing curve of chain, ch of 2 ds, join to last p of next-to-last r, 7 ds, p, 1 ds. Rw, r of 3 ds, join to last p of previous r, 5 p's sep by 3 ds, 3 ds and cl. Rw, ch of 1 ds, join to p of previous ch. Repeat from * for desired length. Tie and cut.

Scalloped Edging

At center in photograph above

Materials. Six-Cord White Mercerized Crochet Cotton, Size 30. Tatting Shuttle. Edging measure ¾″ wide.

Directions. 1st row: With ball and shuttle thread, r of 4 ds, 3 p's sep by 4 ds, 4 ds and cl, * rw, ch of 5 ds, p, 5 ds, rw, lr of 4 ds, join to last p of previous r, (6 ds, p, 6 ds) twice; 4 ds and cl, rw, ch as before. Rw, r of 4 ds, join to last p of previous lr, 4 ds, 2 p's sep by 4 ds, 4 ds and cl. Repeat from * for desired length. Tie and cut. **2nd row:** Tie ball and shuttle threads together and attach to center p of 1st r, ch of 2 ds, sm p, 9 ds, sm p, 2 ds, * skip next lr and join to center p of next r, ch of 2 ds, join to last sm p of previous ch, 9 ds, p, 9 ds, sm p, 2 ds. Repeat from * for desired length. Tie and cut.

Narrow Edging

At bottom in photograph opposite

Materials. Six-Cord White Mercerized Crochet Cotton, Size 30. Tatting Shuttle. Edging measures ¾″ wide.

Directions. With shuttle thread only, r of 9 ds, p, 2 ds, p, 7 ds and cl, rw, r of 9 ds, p, 7 ds, p, 2 ds and cl, * sp of ¼″, lr of 2 ds, join to last p of previous r, 2 ds, 9 p's sep by 2 ds, 2 ds and cl, sp as before, r of 2 ds, join to last p of previous lr, 7 ds, p, 9 ds and cl, rw, r of 6 ds, join to last p of 1st r, 3 ds, p, 9 ds and cl, sp as before, sr of 6 ds and cl, sp, r of 9 ds, p, 3 ds, p, 6 ds and cl, rw, r of 9 ds, join to last p of 4th r, 7 ds, p, 2 ds and cl. Repeat from * for desired length. Tie and cut.

Wide Insertion with Rickrack

Materials. White Mercerized Crochet Cotton, Size 30. Tatting Shuttle. Rickrack.

Directions. R, 2 ds, p, 3 ds, join to point of rickrack, 3 ds, p, 2 ds, cl r. * R, 2 ds, join to last p of last r made, 3 ds, join in base between points of rickrack, 3 ds, p, 2 ds, cl r.

R, 2 ds, join to last r made, 3 ds, join to next point of rickrack, 3 ds, p, 2 ds, cl r, turn. Ch, 3 ds, 5 p sep by 3 ds, 3 ds, turn. R, 2 ds, p, 3 ds, join to same point of rickrack as last r made, 3 ds, p, 2 ds, cl r. Repeat from * for desired length.

Work other side in same manner.

Tatted Edging

Materials. White Tatting-Crochet Thread, Size 70. One Linen Handkerchief, 11 inches square. Tatting Shuttle.

Edging. 1st row: With ball and shuttle threads, r of 2 ds, lp, 2 ds, cl. Rw, ch of 4 ds, lp, 4 ds. Rw, r as before. Rw, ch as before. Continue to work this way for necessary length. Tie and cut. 2nd row: Tie ball and shuttle threads together. R of 2 ds, join to lp of *1st* ch of previous row, 2 ds, cl. Rw, ch of 4 ds, lp, 4 ds. * Rw, r of 2 ds, join to lp of next ch, 2 ds, cl. Rw, ch as before. Repeat from * across. Tie and cut. Sew edging to handkerchief.

Tatted Edging

Materials. White Tatting-Crochet Thread, Size 70. One Linen Handkerchief, 11 inches square. Tatting Shuttle.

Edging. R of 5 ds, lp, 5 ds, cl. Sp of ⅛″. Rw, r of 5 ds, lp, 5 ds, cl. Sp, as before. Rw, r as before. Continue to work this way for necessary length. Tie and cut. Sew edging to handkerchief.

Tatted Edging

Materials. White Tatting-Crochet Thread, Size 70. One Linen Handkerchief, 11 inches square. Tatting Shuttle.

Edging. * R of 1 ds, 8 lp's sep by 1 ds, 1 ds, half cl. Sp of ½″, r as before. Sp as before. Repeat from * for necessary length. Tie and cut. Sew edging to handkerchief.

Tatted Edging

Materials. White Tatting-Crochet Thread, Size 70. One Linen Handkerchief, 11 inches square. Tatting Shuttle.

Edging. With ball and shuttle threads, r of 2 ds, 3 lp's sep by 2 ds, 2 ds, cl. Rw, ch of 2 ds, 3 lp's sep by 2 ds, 2 ds. * Rw, r of 2 ds, join to last lp of previous r, 2 ds, 2 lp's sep by 2 ds, 2 ds, cl. Rw, ch as before. Repeat from * for necessary length. Tie and cut. Sew edging to handkerchief.

Tatted Luncheon Cloth 36″ Square

Materials. Six-Cord White Mercerized Crochet Thread, Size 30. Tatting Shuttle.

1 large and 1 small motif measure 2″.

Motifs. FIRST MOTIF: **1st row, 1st rnd:** Center r of 1 ds, 8 lp's sep by 3 ds, 2 ds, cl. Tie and cut. **2nd rnd:** Tie ball and shuttle threads together. * R of 7 ds, p, 7 ds, cl. Rw, ch of 7 ds, join to first lp of center r, 7 ds, rw, r of 7 ds, join to p of previous r (joint p), 7ds, cl. Repeat from * around, joining next ch to next lp and last ch at base of first r. Tie and cut. (Large motif made.)

SECOND MOTIF: (R of 7 ds, p, 7 ds, cl) 3 times. R of 7 ds, join to first joint p of previous motif, 7 ds, cl. Tie and cut. (Small motif made.) THIRD MOTIF: **1st rnd:** Work exactly as for First Motif. **2nd rnd:** R of 7 ds, join to p of 2nd r of previous motif, 7 ds, cl. Rw, ch of 7 ds, join to first lp of center r, 7 ds. Complete as for First Motif, no more joinings. FOURTH MOTIF: Work exactly as for Second Motif, joining to a joint p of previous motif directly opposite previous joining of motifs. Continue to work in this way until 18 large motifs have been completed. **2nd row:** Make a small motif as before, skip 1 joint p of First Motif and join to next joint p of same motif. MAKE A LARGE MOTIF AS FOLLOWS: **1st rnd:** Work exactly as for First Motif. **2nd rnd:** R of 7 ds, join to p of 3rd r of previous motif, 7 ds, cl. Rw, ch of 7 ds, join to first lp of center r, 7 ds. Rw, r of 7 ds, join to same p of previous motif, 7 ds cl. R of 7 ds, join to joint p of First Motif (between small motifs), 7 ds, cl. Rw, ch as before, joining to next lp of center r. Rw, r as before, joining to same p of First Motif. R as before, joining to free p of adjacent r of Second Motif. Rw, ch as before, joining to next lp. Rw, r as before, joining to same p of Second Motif. R as before, joining to adjacent joint p of Third Motif. Rw, ch, joining to next lp. Rw, r, joining to same joint p. Complete as First Motif, no more joinings. MAKE ANOTHER SMALL MOTIF AS FOLLOWS: (R of 7 ds, p 7 ds, cl) twice. R of 7 ds, join to next joint p of previous motif, 7 ds, cl. R as before, joining to next joint p of Third Motif. Tie and cut. Continue in this way, making small and large motifs alternately and joining to adjacent motifs until 17 large motifs have been completed. **3rd row:** Make a large motif as follows: **1st rnd:** Work exactly as for First

Motif. **2nd rnd:** R of 7 ds, join to p of 2nd r of first small motif of previous row, 7 ds, cl. Rw, ch as before, joining to first lp of center r. Rw, r as before, joining to same p of small motif. R as before, joining to adjacent joint p of next motif of previous row. Rw, ch as before, joining to next lp. Rw, r as before, joining to same joint p of large motif. Complete as before, no more joinings. Now make a small motif, joining to adjacent large motifs as before. Continue as before until 18 large motifs have been completed. Repeat last 2 rows until piece is a square.

Edging. Tie ball and shuttle threads together. ** R of 7 ds, join to joint p (joining First Motif of 1st row and First Motif of 2nd row), 7 ds, cl. R as before, joining to free p of small motif. Rw, ch of 15 ds. Rw, r, joining to same p of small motif. R, joining to joint p (joining First Motif of 2nd row and First Motif of 3rd row). * Rw, ch as before. Rw, r as before, joining to same p. (R as before, joining to next joint p. Rw, ch. Rw, r, joining to same p. Rw, ch. Rw, r, joining to same p) 3 times. R, joining to next joint p between motifs. Rw, ch. Rw, r, joining to same p. Join to free p of small motif. R, joining to next joint p between motifs. Repeat from * across to within joining of last small motif. R, joining to point p between motifs. Rw, ch. Rw, r, join to same p. R, joining to free p of small motif. Rw, ch. Rw, r, join to same p. R, joining to next joint p between motifs. Rw, ch. Rw, r, joining to same p. (R, joining to next joint p. Rw, ch. Rw, r, joining to same p. Rw, ch. Rw, r, joining to same p) 5 times. Repeat from ** around, joining at base of 1st r. Tie and cut.

Tatted Bootees

Materials. Tatting-Crochet Cotton, Size 70—2 balls Pink, White or Blue. Tatting Shuttle. 1 yard of Ribbon, ¼″ wide.

To start. 1st rnd: With shuttle thread only, starting at sole, r of 3 ds, 5 p's sep by 3 ds, 3 ds and cl, sp of ⅛″, r of 3 ds, join to last p of previous r, 3 ds, 4 p's sep by 3 ds, 3 ds and cl, rw, sp as before, r of 3 ds, join to 1st p at opposite side of 1st r, 3 ds, 4 p's sep by 3 ds, 3 ds and cl. * Rw, sp, r of 3 ds, join to last p of r at opposite side. Repeat from * until there are 10 r's on both sides, then make another r as before, joining at both sides at 1st and last p's. Tie and cut. **2nd rnd:** R of (3 ds, p) twice, 3 ds, join to center p of 1st r on previous rnd, (3 ds, p) twice, 3 ds and cl, rw, sp, r of 3 ds, 5 p's sep by 3 ds, 3 ds and cl, rw, sp, r of 3 ds, join to 1st p of 1st r made, 3 ds, p, 3 ds, join to same p where last r was joined, (3 ds, p) twice, 3 ds and cl—1 r increased. Rw and continue as for 1st rnd, joining center p of each r on one side to center p of each r of previous rnd and making another increase as before at opposite end. Join last r at both sides at 1st and last p's.

Toe. Count off the center 8 r's at one end of sole and mark with a pin; then work over these 8 r's as for 1st rnd, joining center p of one side to center p of adjacent r (toe).

Medallion. Starting at center, r of 1 ds, lp, (2 ds, lp) 11 times, 1 ds and cl (12 lp's). Tie and cut. Sr of 3 ds, join to lp of previous r, 3 ds and cl, rw, sp of 1/4″, lr of (3 ds, p) twice, 3 ds, skip end r of toe, join to center p of next r (next to toe end), (3 ds, p) twice, 3 ds and cl. Rw, sp as before, sr of 3 ds, join to next p of center r, 3 ds and cl, rw, sp, lr of 3 ds, join to p of previous lr, 3 ds, p, 3 ds, join to center p of next toe r, (3 ds, p) twice, 3 ds and cl, rw, sp, sr as before, join to next p of center r, rw, sp, lr of 3 ds, join to last p of previous lr, (3 ds, join to next r of toe) 3 times, 3 ds, p, 3 ds and cl, rw, continue around, joining center p's of next 2 lr's to center p's of next 2 r's of toe and complete rnd, alternating lr's and sr's as before. Make 5 more medallions, joining center p's of 3 r's to adjacent p's of previous medallion and joining center p's of 3 r's to adjacent p's on sole, leaving a lr free between medallions on sole.

Beading: 1st rnd: R of 2 ds, 3 p's sep by 2 ds, 2 ds and cl. * Rw, sp, r of 2 ds, join to last p of 1st r (2 ds, p) twice, 2 ds and cl. Rw, sp, r of 4 ds, join to last p of adjacent r, 4 ds and cl, rw, sp, r of 2 ds, join to last p of previous r (2 ds, p) twice, 2 ds and cl. Repeat from * around, joining to center p's of r's in each medallion. Tie and cut. **2nd rnd:** * R of 4 ds, p, 4 ds and cl, rw, r of 4 ds, join to center p of each 2 r's of previous rnd, 4 ds and cl, rw, r of 4 ds, p, 4 ds and cl, rw, r of 4 ds, join to same p's as last r was joined, 4 ds and cl, rw and repeat from * around. Tie and cut. Cut ribbon in half, insert and pull ribbon through beading, and tie.

Tatted Doily

Doily measures 11½″ in diameter.

Materials. Six-Cord White or Ecru Mercerized Crochet Cotton, Size 30. Tatting Shuttle.

Directions. CENTER MEDALLION: **1st rnd:** With ball and shuttle thread, make a r of 4 ds, 7 ps' sep by 4 ds, 4 ds and cl, sp of 1/8″, tie thread to form p. Do not cut thread, pull thread through last p. **2nd rnd:** * Ch of 6 ds, join to next p, make sm p. Repeat from * around. Join. **3rd rnd:** * Ch of 8 ds, join to next sm p, make sm p. Repeat from * around. Join. **4th rnd:** * Ch of 10 ds, join to next sm p, make sm p. Repeat from * around. Join. **5th rnd:** * Ch of 6 ds, sm p, 6 ds, join to next sm p, make sm p. Repeat from * around. Join. Tie and cut. **6th rnd:** With shuttle thread only, * sr of 4 ds, join to next sm p, 4 ds and cl, sp of 3/8″. Repeat from * around, joining to 1st sr (16 sr's). Tie and cut. **7th rnd:** Work as for previous rnd, sp of 1/2″ instead of 3/8″ and joining to sp between sr's. Tie and cut. **8th rnd:** Tie ball and shuttle threads together, sr of 3 ds, join to any sp of previous rnd, 3 ds and cl. * Rw, ch of 6 ds, 3 p's sep by 3 ds, 6 ds. Rw, sr as before, joining to next sp. Repeat from * around, joining to base of first sr. Tie and cut. **9th rnd:** Tie threads as before and attach to center p of any ch on previous rnd, lr of 9 ds, p, 9 ds and cl, * rw, ch of 9 ds, p, 9 ds, rw, lr as before, joining to center p of next ch. Repeat from * around, ending with ch, join to base of 1st lr. Tie and cut. **10th rnd:** With shuttle thread only, sr of 3 ds, join to p of 1st lr, * 3 ds and cl, sp of ⅜″, sr as before, joining to same p, sp as before; r of 6 ds, join to p of next ch, 6 ds and cl, sp, sr of 3 ds, join to p of next lr and repeat from * around, join at base of 1st sr. Tie and cut. **11th rnd:** With shuttle thread only, r of 3 ds, join to 1st sp of previous rnd, 3 ds and cl, sp of ⅜″, * sr as before, joining to same sp (sp as before, sr, joining to next sp) twice, sp, sr as before, joining to next sp and repeat from * around, sp, join as before. Tie and cut. **12th rnd:** With shuttle thread only, sr of 3 ds, join to 1st sp of previous rnd, 3 ds and cl, * sp of ⅜″, sr as before, joining to same sp, sp, (sr joining to next sp) 3 times; sp, sr joining to next sp, sp, sr joining to same sp and repeat from * around, sp, join at base of 1st sr. Tie and cut. **13th rnd:** Tie ball and shuttle threads together, sr of 3 ds, join to 1st sp of previous rnd, 3 ds and cl * (rw, ch of 6 ds, p, 6 ds, rw, sr as before, joining to same sp) twice, rw, ch of 6 ds, 3 p's sep by 3 ds, 6 ds, rw, r of 6 ds, join to next sp, 6 ds and cl, rw, r as before, skip next 3 sr's and join to next sp, rw, ch as before, rw, sr, joining to next sp and repeat from * around, ending with 3 p-ch, join at base of first sr. Tie and cut. **14th rnd:** Tie threads as before, r of 6 ds, join to p of 1st ch on previous rnd, 6 ds and cl, * rw, ch of 9 ds, p, 9 ds, rw, r as before, joining to p of next ch, rw, ch as before. Rw, r of 9 ds, join to center p of next ch, 9 ds and cl, r as before, joining to center p of next ch, rw, ch as before, rw, r of 6 ds, join to p of next ch, 6 ds and cl. Repeat from * around, ending with ch, join at base of 1st r. Tie and cut. **15th rnd:** Tie threads and attach to p of 1st ch on previous rnd, * ch of 6 ds, 3 p's sep by 3 ds, 6 ds, join to p of next ch. Repeat from * around, join last ch to beg of 1st ch (48 loops). Tie and cut. **16th and 17th rnds:** Tie threads and attach to center p of 1st ch on previous rnd, * ch of 6 ds, 3 p's sep by 3 ds, 6 ds, join to center p of next ch. Repeat from * around, joining last ch as before. Tie and cut. **18th rnd:** Work round of half medallions as follows:

FIRST HALF-MEDALLION: R of 4 ds, 6 p's sep by 4 ds, 4 ds, join to 1st p of 3rd ch on previous rnd of doily, 4 ds, skip center p of same ch and join to last p of same ch. Tie and cut. Tie threads and attach to next p of 2nd ch on doily and working around ring, ch of 8 ds, join to adjacent p of r, sm p (8 ds, join to next p of r, sm p) 5 times, 8 ds, join to next p of 4th ch on doily, join to center p of same ch, turn. (Ch of 10 ds, join to sm p of previous ch around r, sm p) 6 times, ch as before, joining to center p of adjacent ch on doily, turn. (Ch of 6 ds, sm p, 6 ds, join to sm p of previous ch, sm p) 6 times, ch as before, joining to next p of same ch on doily, tie and cut.

SECOND HALF-MEDALLION: Work exactly as for First Half-Medallion, joining to 6th ch on doily. Continue in this manner until 16 Half-Medallions are completed. **19th rnd:** With shuttle thread only and working around Half-Medallions, sr of 3 ds, join to sm p of last ch on any Half-Medallion, 3 ds and cl * (sp of ⅜″, sr as before, joining to next sm p between chains, sp as before, sr joining to sm p of next ch) 6 times, sr, joining to p of adjacent ch on next Half-Medallion. Repeat from * around. Tie and cut. **20th rnd:** Sr of 3 ds, join to 1st sp of previous rnd, 3 ds and cl * (sp of ⅜″, sr as before, joining to next sp) 11 times, sr, joining to 1st sp of next Half-Medallion. Repeat from * around. Tie and cut. **21st rnd:** Sr of 3 ds, join to 1st sp of previous rnd * (sp of ⅜″, sr as before, joining to next sp) 10 times—scallop made, sr, joining to 1st sp of next Half-Medallion. Repeat from * around (16 scallops). Tie and cut. **22nd rnd:** Tie threads, sr of 3 ds, join to last sp of any scallop and to first sp of next scallop, 3 ds and cl * (rw, ch of 3 ds, 3 p's sep by 3 ds, 3 ds, rw, sr of 3 ds, join to next sp, 3 ds and cl) 8 times, rw, ch as before, rw, sr of 3 ds, join to last sp of same scallop and to 1st sp of next scallop, 3 ds and cl. Repeat from * around, ending with ch, tie at base of 1st sr. **23rd rnd:** Tie threads and attach to center p of 2nd ch of any scallop, * (ch of 3 ds, 3 p's sep by 3 ds, 3 ds, join to center p of next ch) 6 times; ch as before, joining to center p of next ch on same scallop and to center p of 1st ch on next scallop, ch, join to center p of next ch and repeat from * around, joining last ch to beg of 1st ch. Tie and cut. Press lightly.

NETTING

Netting is an ancient handicraft of unknown origin. It is a simple technique once you have mastered the fundamentals. Tying the knots and drawing up uniform loops is the only skill required. Netting can be exceedingly fine and delicate, or bold and coarse; the size of needle, gauge and thread determine the result. It can be done with or without a gauge, depending upon the skill acquired. Experienced fishermen never use a gauge. A netting needle and a gauge can be purchased or whittled from any thin wood.

Netting consists of loops secured to one another by knots. It is begun on a foundation loop of strong twine or thread. This must be firmly attached to something so one can pull against it while working. The loop can be tied to a chair or otherwise secured.

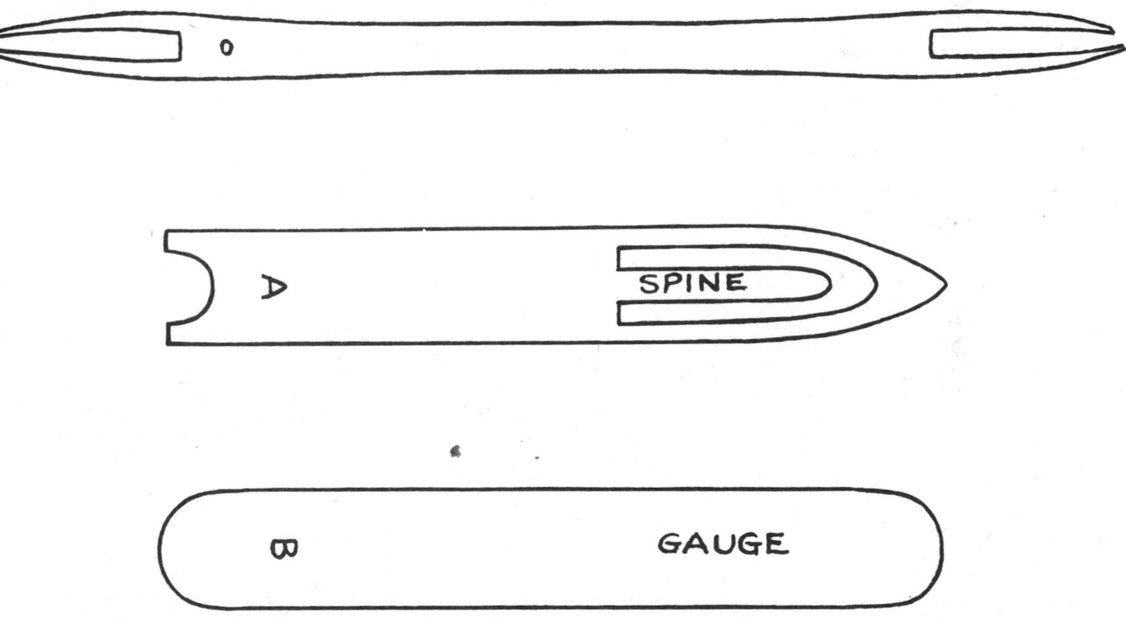

Materials Needed

Netting needle, mesh sticks (gauge), and thread or yarn. Foundation cord. The gauge and two types of netting needles are shown.

The foundation cord should be from 4″ to 12″ long. Tie ends of this cord together to make a loop and anchor the loop to some object.

To Thread Needle. Fasten thread to the spine. Wind down over end A (see diagram) and up over spine on opposite side. Then down over end A and up over spine on first side. Alternate from side to side, turning the needle. Fill the needle leaving ¼″ at tip of spine free.

How to Net

On end of thread coming from needle make a loop twice the width of the gauge, tying it around anchor loop. Place this knot in middle of left side and hold gauge in left hand in position shown. With needle in right hand, pass it through loop from right to left. Use gauge to measure space of mesh.

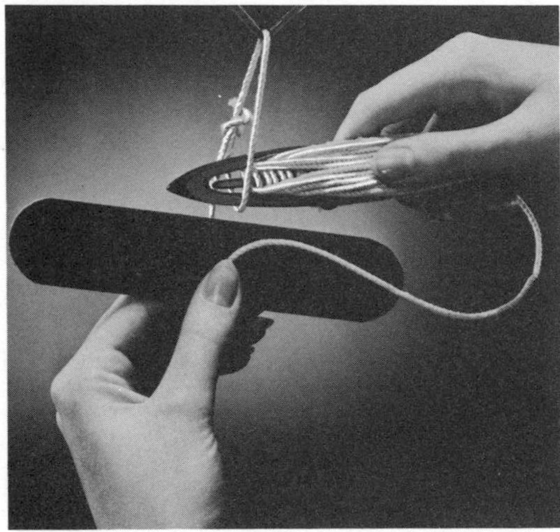

Pull thread to position and hold it firmly to the gauge with thumb.

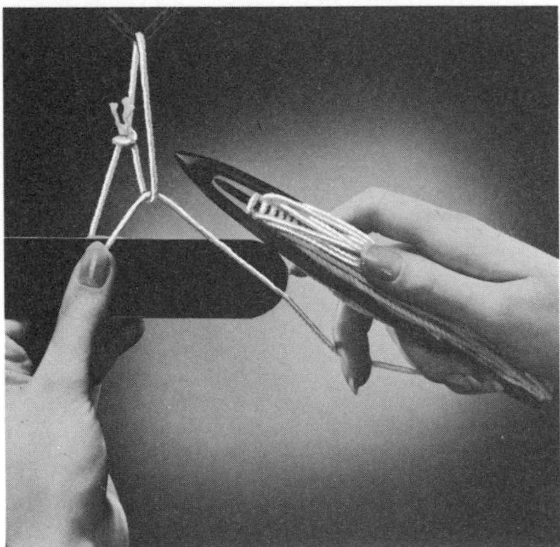

Loop twine down at right of first loop and hold with thumb. Pass needle under first two strands and over third and fourth strands above gauge.

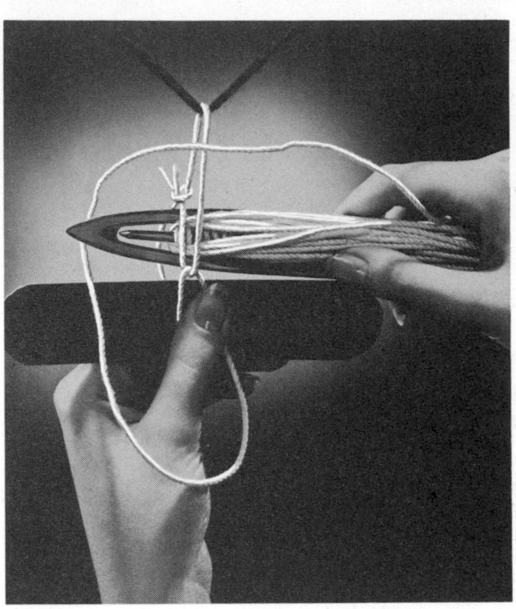

Pull knot hard and tight.

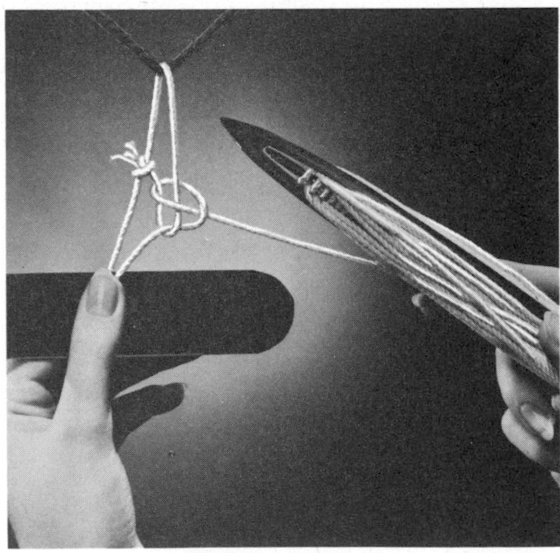

Do not remove thumb from below knot until the knot has been made tight by pulling toward right.

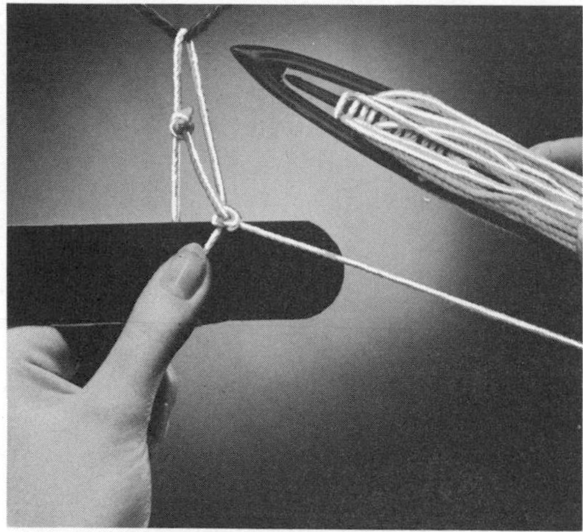

Remove gauge and place the new knot on the left and repeat until desired number of meshes have been made. This first row is a string of knotted loops the length of which depends upon the width of the article being made.

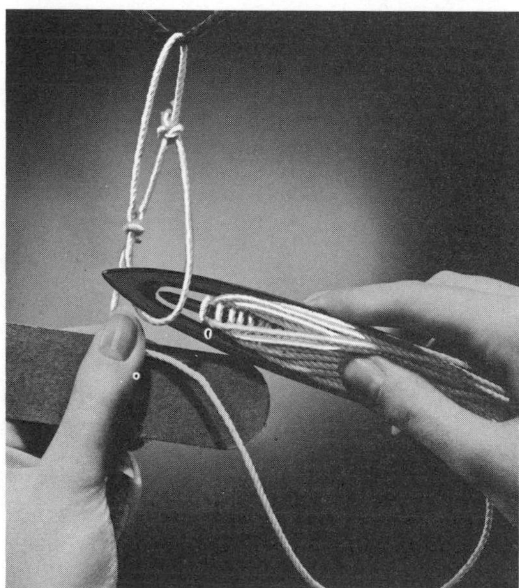

Now thread a heavy cord through the first row of meshes. This is the new anchor loop. Shorten the first anchor loop and leave tied on to locate starting mesh.

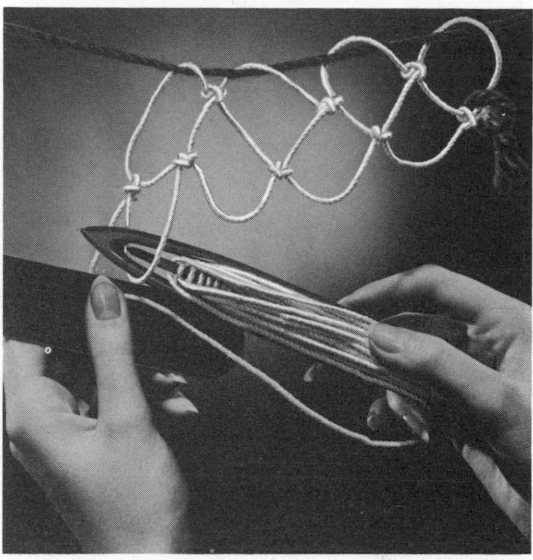

Now work across instead of down. Starting a knot at the first mesh to the left, continue working across to right until row is completed.

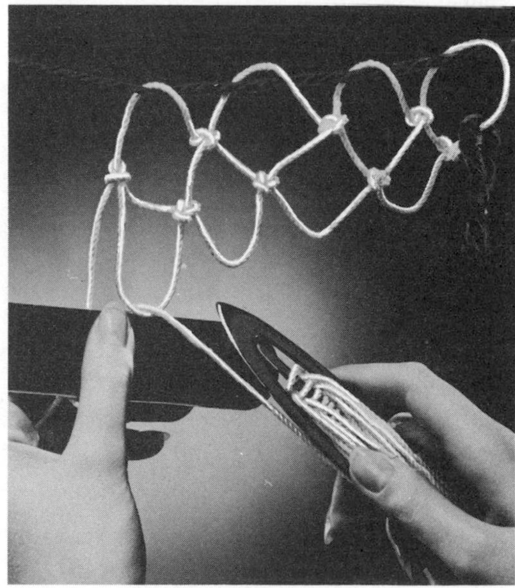

When row is completed change needle to left hand and gauge to the right hand. Work this row from right to left starting as shown.

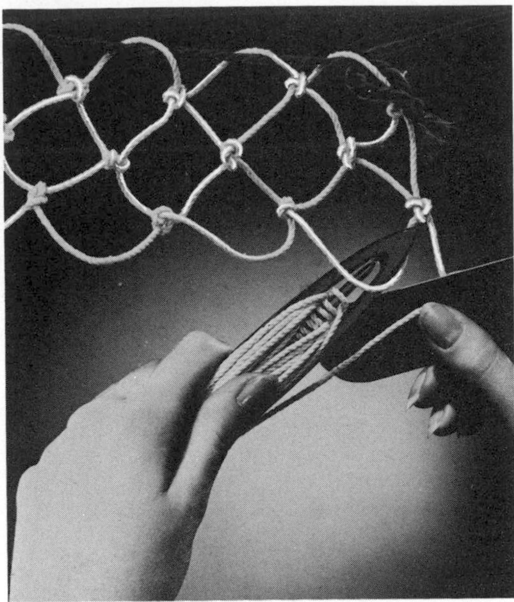

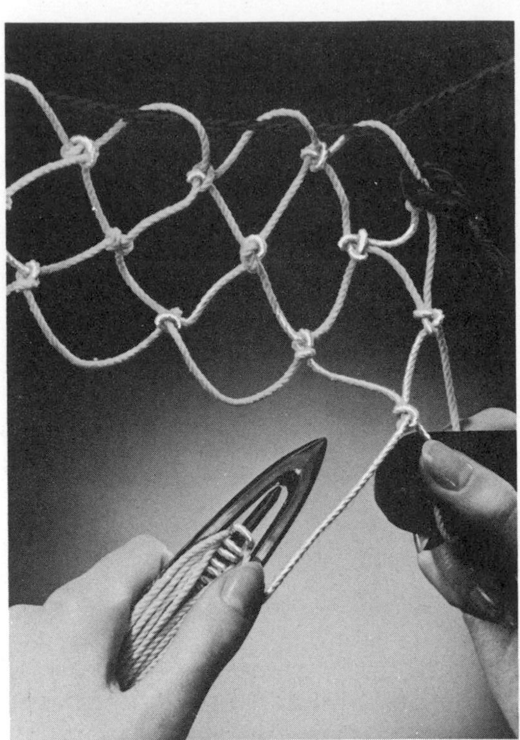

Hold thread firmly with thumb at bottom of loop and reverse steps as shown. Continue working to left across row. Repeat alternate right and left rows for desired length.

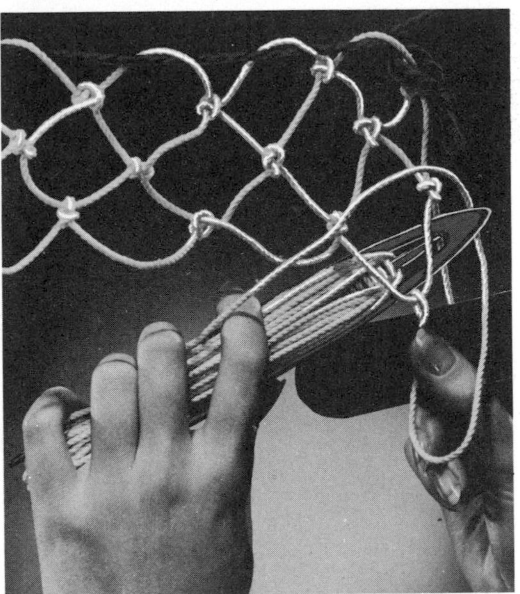

To Reduce a Mesh at End of Row. Do not net last mesh.

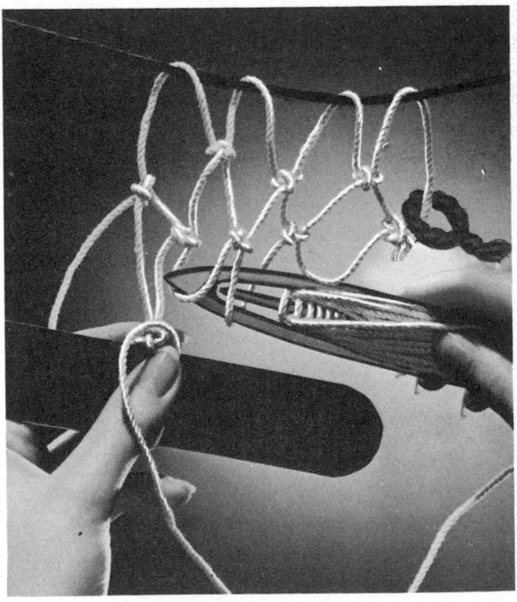

To Reduce a Mesh in the Middle of a Row. Net 2 meshes at one time by sliding needle through two loops instead of one and complete the knot.

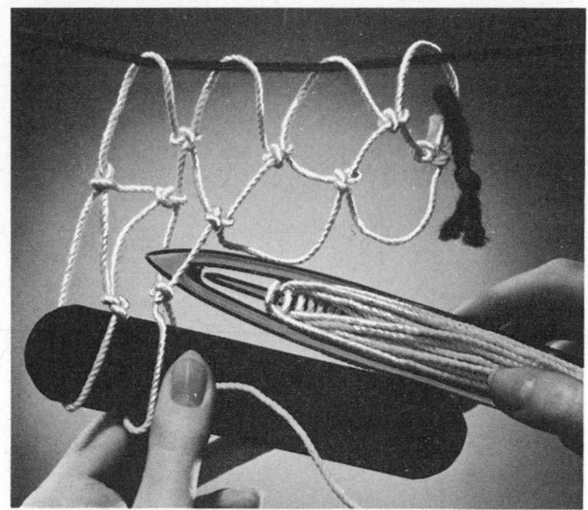

To Increase a Mesh. Make 2 knots in the same loop.

To Make a Triangle. Cast on required number of stitches. Decrease down to one stitch by joining the last two loops of every row with one knot.

Net Embroidery

Motifs and borders can be embroidered or woven on hand-made or machine-made net. Since net is the foundation upon which you work, its construction influences the planning of the design and choice of thread to be used.

Darning Stitch. This is the simplest stitch. Weave back and forth through the net, filling the space but not crowding enough to bulge. Various sizes of thread may be used.

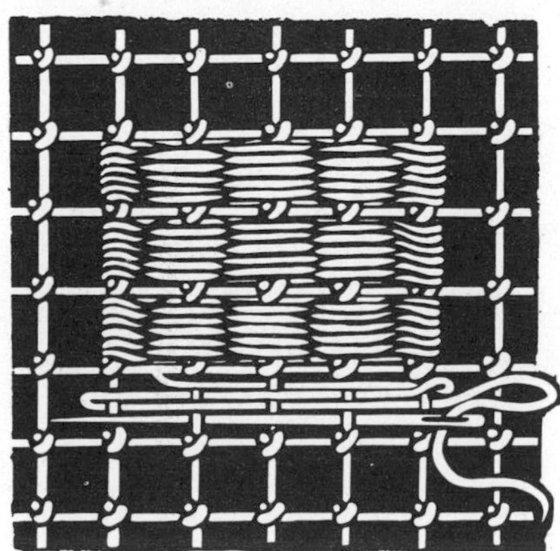

Linen Stitch. This is the one most often used. Weave over and under the net but fill the space loosely (back and forth, 2 times, will usually be enough). Turn and weave or darn over and under the threads just laid as well as those of the net. The result should be "plain weave." A knitting needle placed at the first and last row will prevent the stitches from slipping when second darning is done.

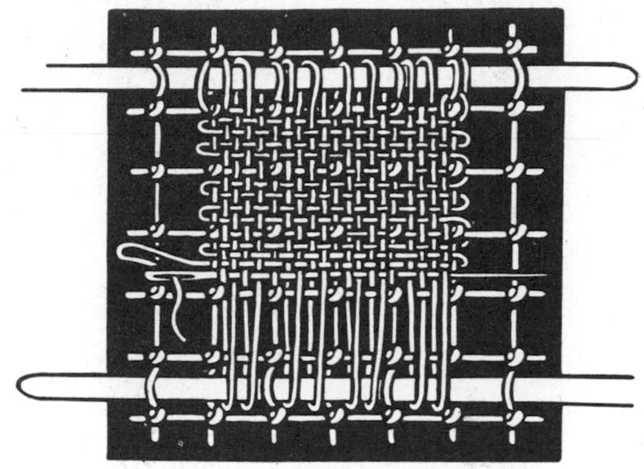

Simple Loop Stitch. Basically it is a blanket stitch. Keep the loop at least half the height of the bars of the net. On return row, make a stitch over the vertical bar of the net as shown in the diagram.

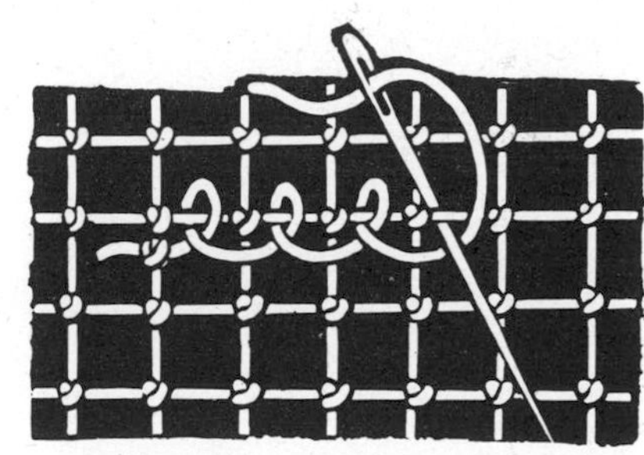

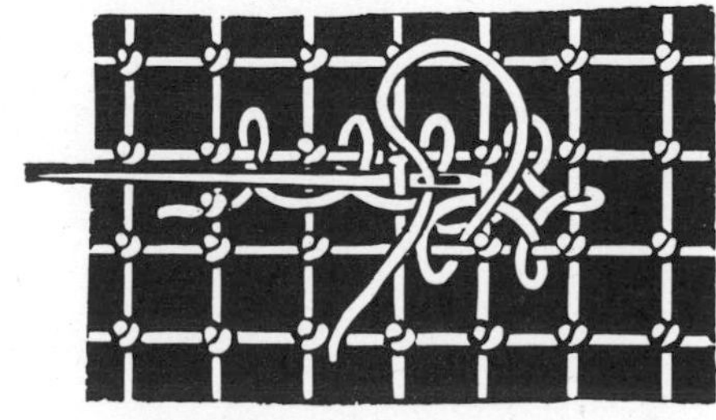

Color Plate 17 CROCHETED DRESS OF BLOCKS

Another dress to crochet, this one a simple classic composed of crocheted blocks sewed together. Make it to the length you like. *Instructions and diagrams are on page 382.*

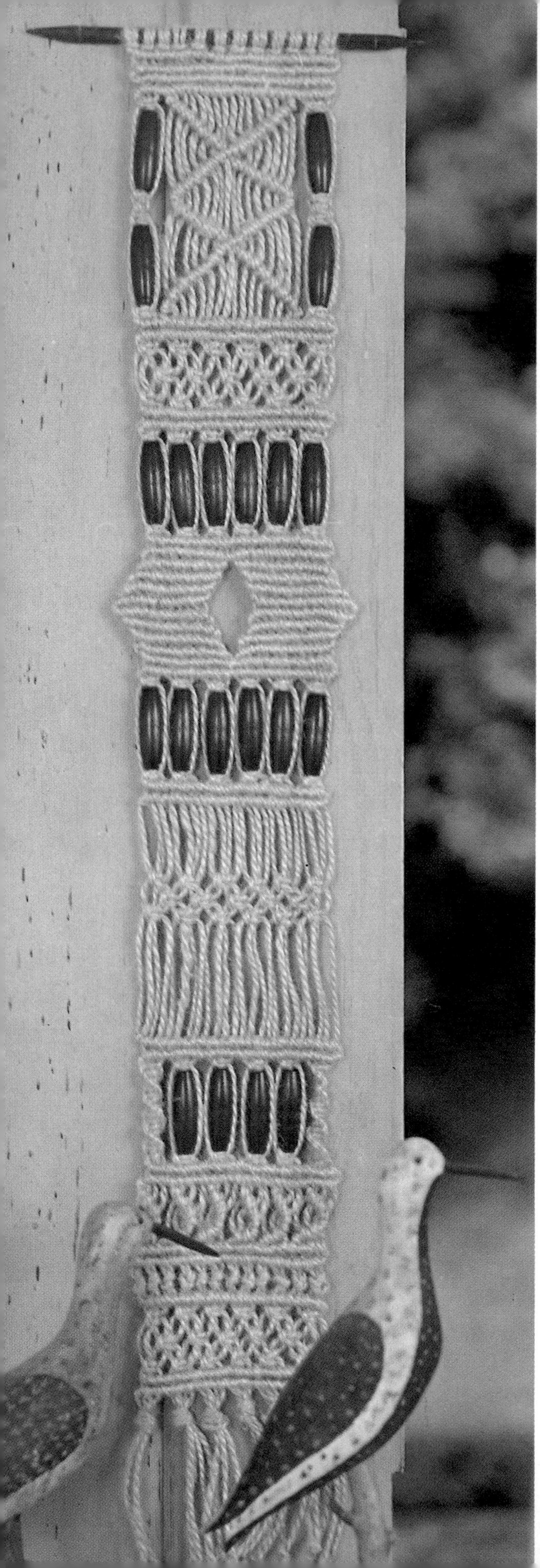

Color Plate 18 MACRAMÉ

The wonderful old technique of decorative knotting was used to make this wall hanging, two belts, and a pillow. Instructions for all are given on pages 408–416.

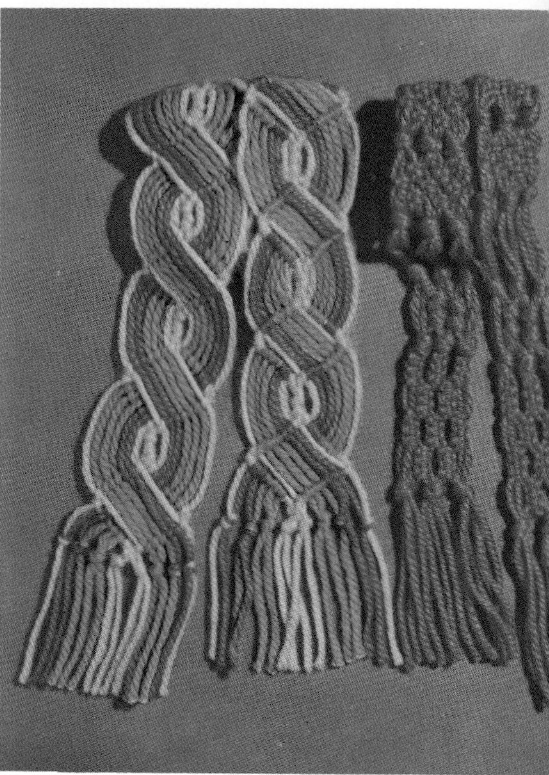

Chapter 10

Macramé

Have you ever carefully examined a knot? If you do, you will find it has dimension, texture, and very interesting design. As Girl Scouts, Boy Scouts, sailors, fishermen or as we go about life every day, we have all tied knots. Most of us think of knots in a purely functional way—mainly to fasten two ends of string together. There is also a very creative, decorative approach to knotting which is called macramé. The term is of Arabic origin, said to have meant fringe on a shawl or kerchief, but now used to encompass the art of decorative knotting in general.

There have been numerous uses for macramé through the ages. It was worked on the unwoven ends of material instead of hems. It was used in a fine form on religious garments and items for the church, as a fashion touch on clothing, table linens and towels. In a heavier form, it was worked by the sailors (the sailors called it square knotting). They would spend idle hours making both decorative and useful items, examples of which appear in maritime museums throughout the country. This wonderful old art has been updated to complement and blend with the fashions and decor of today (both traditional or contemporary) depending on the material used. It is an art for the whole family—and can prove to be a creative challenge once the basic technique of knotting is mastered. As the knots begin to form different textures and patterns, you find yourself completely engrossed in a captivating pastime.

The following is an introduction to a few of the basic knots. With practice, these knots will become automatic and you will find your fingers flying through the steps with ease. There are literally thousands of knots. However, if you learn these few basic ones, you can produce countless patterns, designs and textures by changing the weight of material used, or by varying the distance between knots and the length or number in groupings. This is only the beginning. You can constantly increase your vocabulary of knots.

GENERAL DIRECTIONS

Macramé is made up entirely of knots. It has no specific tool but certain accessories are necessary while the knotting takes place. You must have a firm working base such as a foam rubber pillow, T-head pins, or glass-headed pins such as the kind used for map marking. These are available at most notion counters. Hat pins can also be used. You will also need elastic bands, yardstick, scissors, plus whatever cord or thread you will use for the actual knotting (jute, twine, wool yarn, etc.).

A feel for the tension or tightness of the knots will come with a little practice. The amount of stress or pull necessary to produce a trim knot will become automatic in time. This varies slightly with the type of cord used. There is a correct pull which will insure the beauty of each type of thread. Each person will find a way of his own which is most convenient and relaxed while performing the actual knotting.

Mounting. Each cord is mounted on a holding cord with an overhand knot. For the holding cord (practice piece), cut a length of cord long enough to stretch across pillow plus a knot at each end. Tie a knot at each end and secure it to the sides of the pillow with pins. The space in the middle is where you work. Cut 5 lengths of knotting cord 4′ long and cut one length 6′ long. (In order to show ends, shorter lengths are used for photograph.) Fold the 6′ cord so you have a 2′ and a 4′ length. Start at the left side.

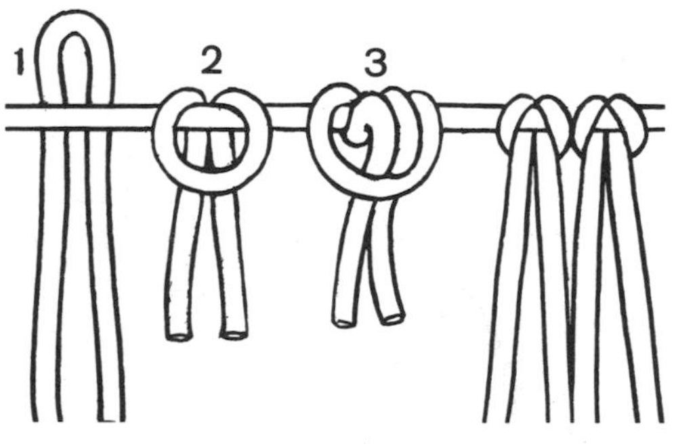

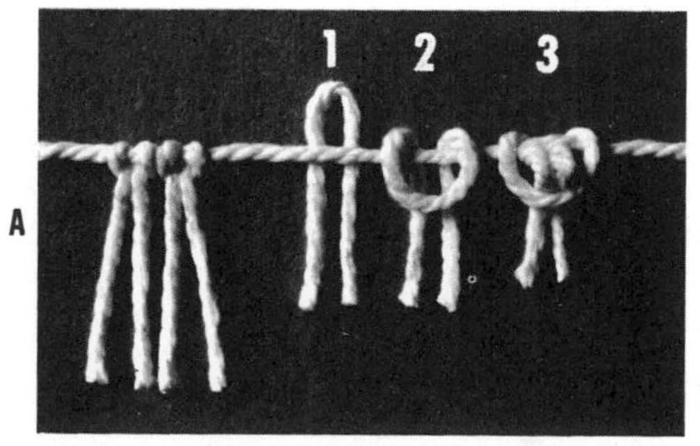

With 4′ length to the outside, place loop under holding cord (see photograph A1 and diagram 1). Fold loop over and pull cords through it (see steps 2 and 3). Fold the remaining 5 cords exactly in half and mount them one after the other to the right of the first one. You should have one cord 4′ and 11 cords 2′ making a total of 12 cords on which to practice the basic knots.

Horizontal Double Half Hitch. Place a number of extra pins along the holding cord to secure it. Tighten the holding cord itself by moving one of the original two pins. Make certain that the left side is secure as it will have to stand the pull of the knot-bearing cord. Hold the first and longest cord in your right hand. This will be known as the knot-bearing cord. Hold it parallel to the holding cord across the vertical cords. (See photograph B1 and left side of diagram B.) Using the 2nd cord as the knotting cord, make 2 half hitches as indicated. This will be called the double half hitch. Place a pin so that it holds these knots securely. Continue from left to right, using each cord in succession until you have reached the last cord. These knots should lie neatly next to each other and if the knot-bearing cord is kept taut they will wind around easily. The knot-bearing cord should always be pulled taut and straight so the knotting cord will be even. Use plenty of pins to hold in place. Now the long cord is on the right. Secure the last knot with a pin and take the long knot-bearing cord in your left hand. Holding it parallel to the previous row of knots, reverse the order of the knotting process. Starting on the right side, do a row of horizontal double half hitches using each cord in succession from right to left until you have completed the row and the long cord is again on the left. This motif is used to separate designs. The directions will read: "Work 2 rows of horizontal half hitches."

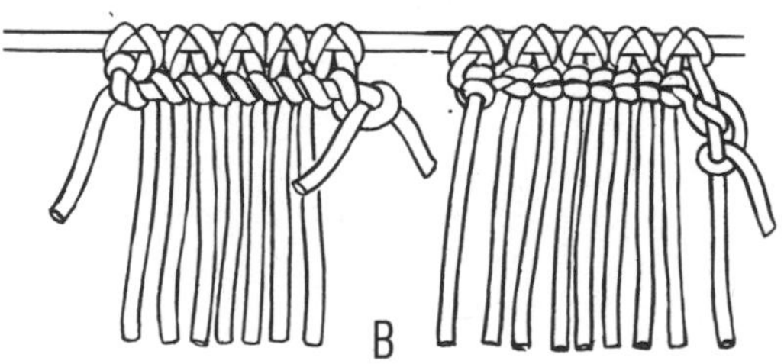

Vertical Double Half Hitch. In the vertical double half hitch, the vertical cords become the knot-bearing cords around which the first and longest cord is knotted. Holding the second cord in a vertical position in your left hand (taut), make 2 half hitches with knotting cord as indicated in photograph B2 and right side of diagram B. Place knotting cord under each knot-bearing cord before starting knots. Holding each cord in your left hand in succession, continue across from left to right until the long cord is on the right. Secure the last knot on the right with a pin. Reverse the order of knotting process. Using the same long cord as the knotting cord, hold the next in line taut in your right hand and make 2 half hitches. Continue from right to left holding each cord in succession, using the long cord as the knotting cord until it is back on the left.

B

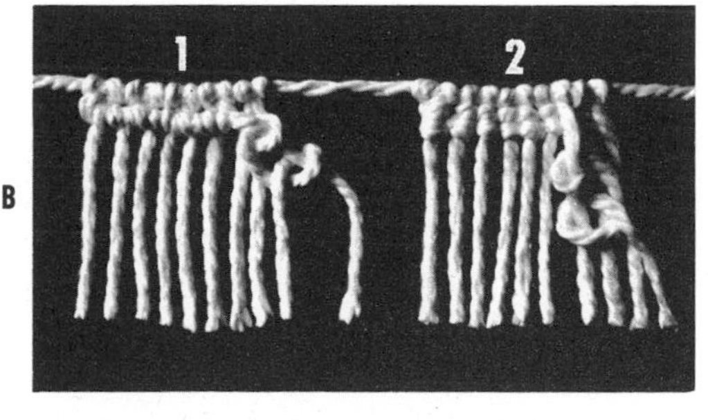

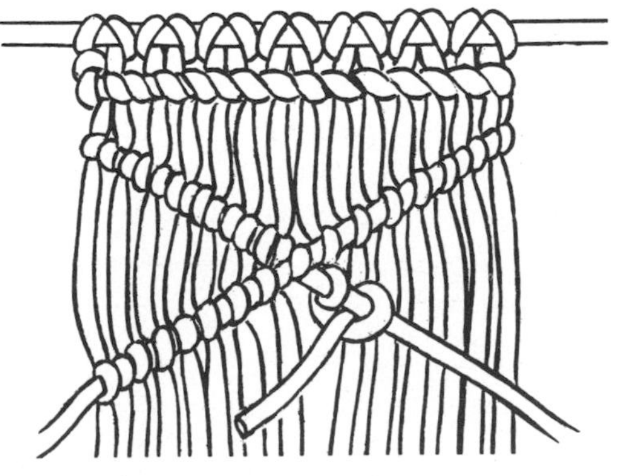

C

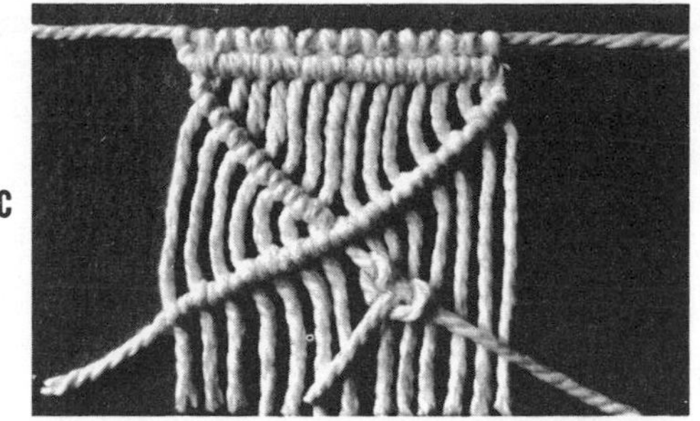

Diagonal Double Half Hitch. This is made exactly like the horizontal double half hitch except that the knot-bearing cord is held diagonally (see photograph C). Starting at the left side, knot each cord around the diagonal cord in succession as far as the center. Then start at upper right side (keeping cord on slant) and knot all the way across at a slant, crossing the 1st cord. Then finish the left hand cord for the remainder of its slanted line.

Half Knot and Square Knot. The square knot is considered to be the basis of macramé. It is actually a square knot tied around 2 other cords. All designs which include square knots must have a number of cords divisible by 4. The cords are divided into groups of 4. The first half of the square knot is known as the half knot. See diagram and photograph D, steps 1 and 2. The 2 middle cords are held between the first 2 fingers and the outer 2 cords go over and under the middle 2 cords as indicated. After you complete steps 1 and 2, work the 2nd half by reversing the process as indicated in steps 3 and 4. When the knot is carefully tightened, the pattern begins to form. Take the next 4 cords and repeat the steps. Continue until the knots are completed to the right side. To form the pattern shown in photograph E, leave the first 2 cords free on the 2nd row and starting with cord 3, divide into groups of 4. Dropping the knots down a bit to form the pattern, continue across to the right side. This will leave 2 free cords on the right side. On the third row, returning to the left side, divide cords into groups of 4 as on 1st row—drop down same distance as

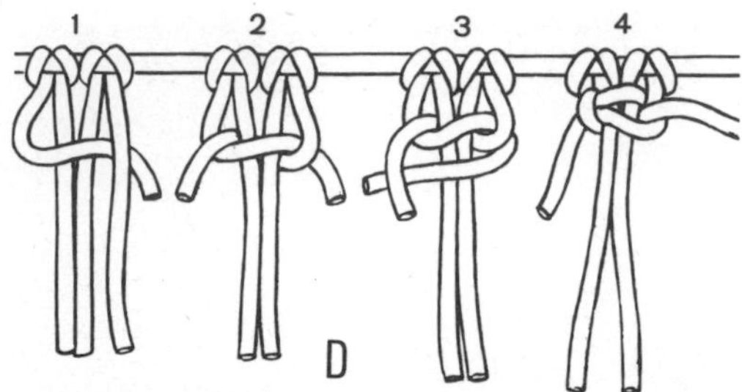

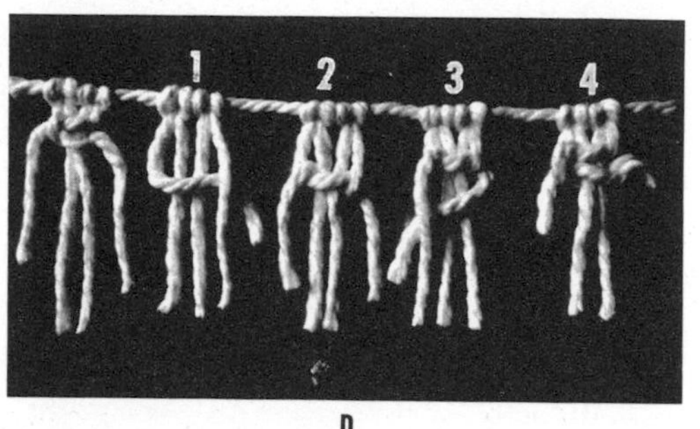

D

in previous row and continue across to the right. Experiment with this, for many patterns can be easily formed by changing the length of the space between rows. If the rows are knotted closely together, an entirely different pattern is formed.

Sinnets of Half Knots and Square Knots. After you master the square knot you can easily make these. The half-knot sinnet is merely the first step of the square-knot repeated. See photograph F. This knot becomes quite fascinating for it twists by itself. Continue until you feel it pull, turn it and continue as before. If you wish to turn it in the reverse direction, work the second half of the square knot as in photograph F2. The square knot sinnet (photograph F3) is a series of square knots. The two steps are repeated until the desired length is completed. This sinnet lies in a flat position.

E

F

MACRAMÉ DESIGNS

Three-Color Belt

Left-hand figure in photograph at far right on opposite page. Also shown in Color Plate 18

Materials. Rug Yarn (see below)—72 yards (total overall weight, 3 oz.).

Gauge. Cut yarn 3 times desired length of finished belt. To make a 56″ long belt, cut yarn into 4½ yd. lengths as follows:

6 Yellow cords	27 yds. yarn
4 Orange cords	18 yds. yarn
6 Turquoise cords	27 yds. yarn
Total	72 yds. yarn

See photograph H1. Tie overhand knots 5″ from ends, using two strands (shown in photographs G2 and 3). Pin knots so they are close together on foam rubber working pillow in the following order:

1. one Yellow and one Orange
2. one Orange and one Turquoise
3. two Turquoise
4. two Yellow
5. two Yellow
6. two Turquoise
7. one Turquoise and one Orange
8. one Orange and one Yellow

After knots have been tied and pinned in place, check order to make certain each strand falls in proper color sequence.

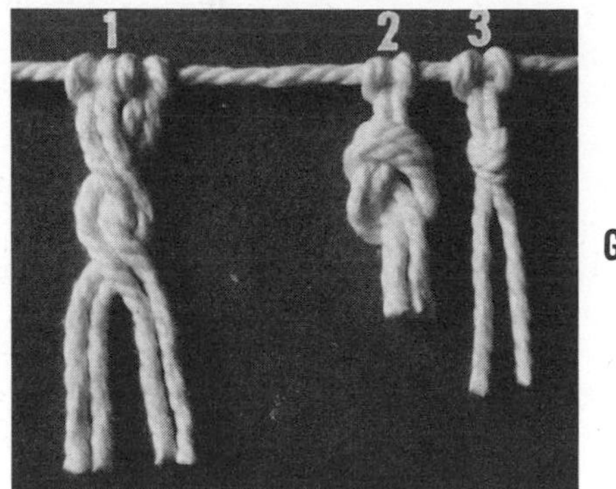

G

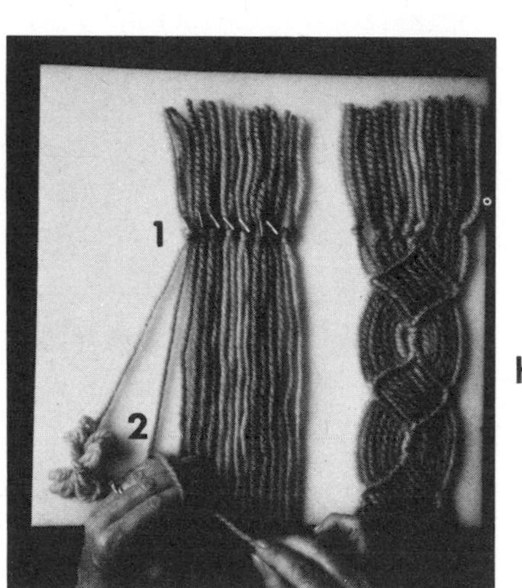

H

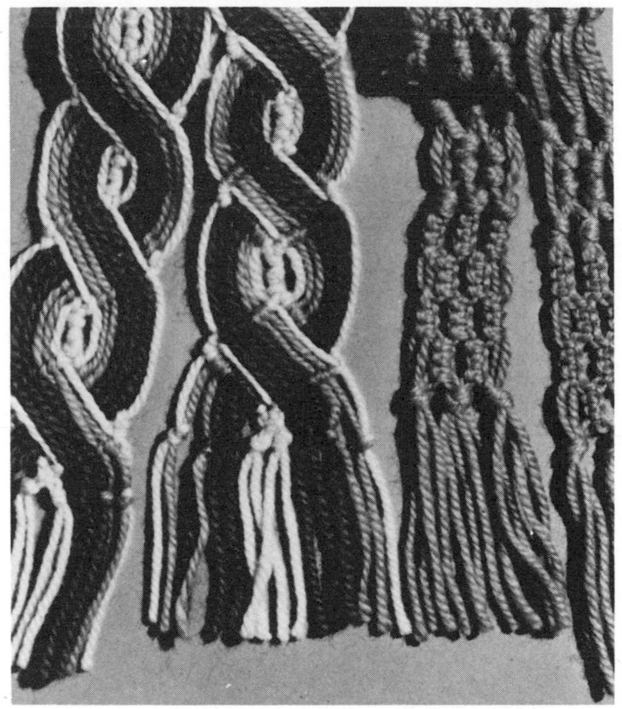

Tying Long Cords into Skeins. (See photograph H2.) To assist in working, wind each cord into a small skein. Hold first cord 12″ from knot (or holding cord). Wind cord around your four fingers until you reach end. Remove from fingers, wind it around several times to form a little skein and secure with rubber band. Continue until all the cords are wound. This process is used whenever the length of the cord is unwieldy, and enables you to pull more cord easily from the skein as it is needed

Using middle 4 Yellow cords, tie one square knot (see photograph D). Place pin in square knot to hold securely. * Middle 2 Yellow cords will be knot-bearing cords. Place left middle Yellow cord on top of cords to left of center and hold with left hand in a downward, diagonal direction. Tie diagonal double half hitches (per General Directions) with each cord in succession. Place pin at end and put knot-bearing cord to left side (photograph I).

Take right, middle Yellow cord in right hand and hold in a downward diagonal direction on top of cords to right of center. Tie diagonal double half hitches with each cord in succession. Place pin in end and put knot-bearing cord to right side (photograph I).

Grasp cords to right of center in right hand—cords to left of center in left hand (omitting knot-bearing cords placed to each side). Crisscross left-hand cords over right-hand cords so each group runs in a diagonal direction parallel to row of diagonal double half hitches (see photograph I).

Take left knot-bearing cord in right hand and hold in a diagonal downward right direction over bottom group of cords and parallel to top right row of double half hitches. Tie diagonal double half hitches to middle, using bottom group of cords in succession (see photograph I).

Take right knot-bearing cord in left hand, holding it in a diagonal left downward direction over top group of cords. Tie diagonal double half hitches to middle using top group of cords in succession. Using two knot-bearing Yellow cords (now in middle), tie 3 overhand knots (see photographs G2 and 3). Pin to hold securely. **Repeat from** *—leaving cords loose enough to make an arc to each side to form design. **Repeat until desired length** (Belt shown has 14 repeats). End with square knot at bottom of last diamond. Tie overhand knots in groups of 2 to correspond to beginning motif, leaving 5″ ends.

Note: Move up on pillow as work progresses, using as many pins as necessary. Keep design as uniform as possible. Other color combinations can be substituted or a solid color can be used.

I

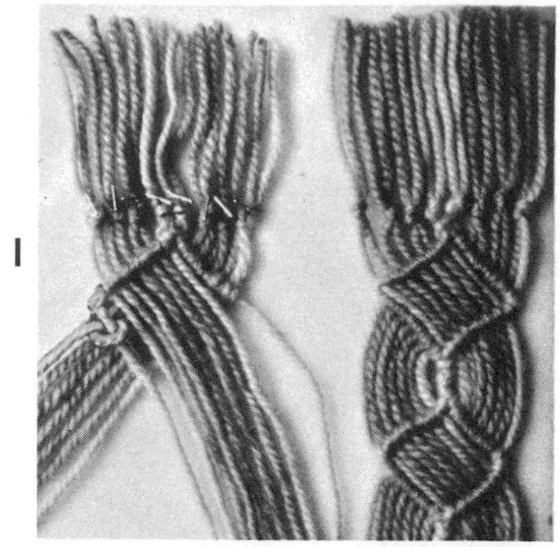

J

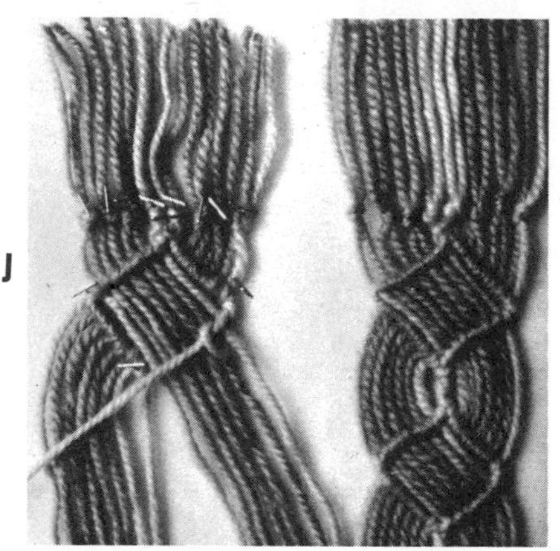

Belt or Neck Sash

Right-hand figure in photograph, page 409. Also shown in Color Plate 18

Materials. Rug Yarn—¼ lb. skein.

Gauge. Cut yarn 2⅔ times desired length of finished belt. For a belt approximately 54″ long, cut 12 cords of yarn each 4 yards long. Tie groups of 4 together with overhand knot, leaving tassels 5″ long when trimmed. Pin securely to foam rubber working pillow approximately 1″ apart. Starting at a point at least 12″ from knots, roll each cord into a skein and fasten with an elastic band (see photograph H2 and instructions for same under Three-Color Belt).

Note: It is necessary, especially in the beginning when skeins are large, to make a large loop for the overhand knot so the four skeins can be slipped through. After a little practice, you will develop the ability to tighten these knots so they will fall in the proper place. As the work progresses the skeins become smaller and easier to manage.

Motifs. BEGINNING MOTIF: * Place cords 1 and 2 of first group to left side. Using remaining 2 cords of first group and 2 cords from second group, tie 3 square knots close together. Using remaining 2 cords of 2nd

K

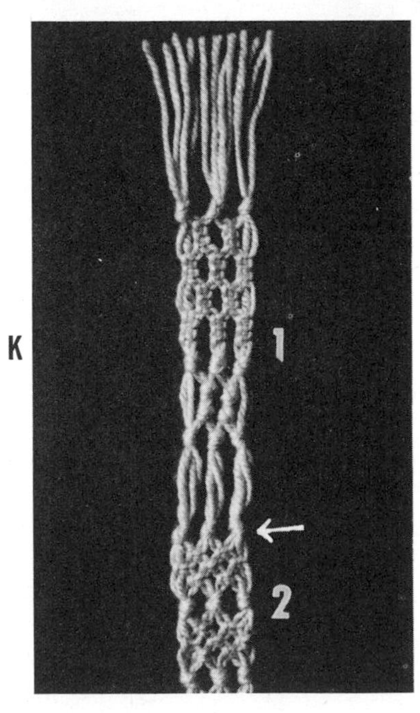

group and 2 cords from 3rd group, tie 3 square knots close together. ** Using all cords, divide into 3 groups of 4 cords each. Tie 3 square knots in each group. Repeat *; repeat **. Using 4 cords in each group, tie overhand knot close to 3 square knots. Place 2 cords of 1st group to left side. Using remaining 2 cords from 1st group and 2 cords from 2nd group, tie 2 overhand knots close together. Using remaining 2 cords from 2nd group and 2 cords from 3rd group, tie 2 overhand knots close together. Using all cords, divide into 3 groups of 4 cords each and tie an overhand knot in each. Leave a drop of 2″ and tie another overhand knot in each group. (See arrow on photograph K.) NEXT MOTIF: **Row 1.** Place 2 cords from 1st group to left side. Using remaining 2 cords from 1st group and 2 cords from 2nd group, tie square knot. Using 2 remaining cords from 2nd group and 2 cords from 3rd group, tie square knot. **Row 2.** Using 1st 2 cords and 2 cords from square knot of previous row, tie square knot. Using remaining 2 cords from square knot of previous row and 1st 2 cords of next group, tie square knot. Using remaining 4 cords, tie square knot. **Row 3.** Repeat Row 1. **Row 4.** Divide into 3 groups of 4 cords each and tie overhand knot in each. *Note:* Repeat from * until desired length. When length is reached where you wish to start Beginning Motif, reverse directions as follows: BEGINNING MOTIF REVERSED: Pin end already worked down side of working pillow so pattern can be duplicated for second end. Repeat motif, end up with three overhand knots. Drop 2″ and tie another overhand knot in each group. Place 2 cords of 1st group to left side. Using remaining 2 cords from 1st group and 2 cords from 2nd group, tie 2 overhand knots close together. Using remaining 2 cords from 2nd group and 2 cords from 3rd group, tie 2 overhand knots close together. Using all cords, divide into 3 groups of 4 cords each and tie an overhand knot in each. * Tie 3 square knots in each group of 4 cords. ** Place 1st 2 cords to left side. Using remaining 2 cords of 1st group and 2 cords from 2nd group, tie 3 square knots close together. Using remaining 2 cords of 2nd group and 2 cords from 3rd group, tie 3 square knots close together. Using all cords repeat *. Repeat **. Divide into 3 groups of 4 cords each and tie an overhand knot in each. Cut so that 5″ ends corresponds with beginning motif.

Wool Jersey Stole

Materials. Wool Jersey (either bonded or tubular)—1¾ yards. Rug Yarn for fringe —approximately 1 lb. 32 large Bugle Beads about ⅞″ long (optional).

Sewing Directions. If bonded jersey is used, fold lengthwise with right sides together. Stitch a ½″ seam along side and turn right side out. Turn back a ½″ hem on raw edges and run a row of machine stitches ¼″ from edge (see photograph M, next page).

Cutting and Mounting Cords. Cut yarn into lengths 4½ times desired finished length. For 14″ finished length as on our stole, cut yarn into 63″ lengths. (After mounting, the cords will be 2¼ times the finished length.) Place stole on flat surface. With edges even, start work at left. **Step 1.** (See photograph M.) Thread large yarn needle with cut strand.

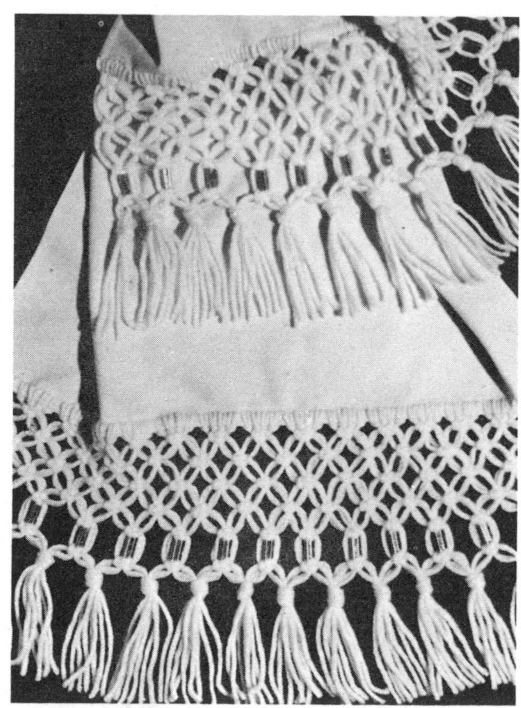

Starting from underneath, bring needle up through fabric close to left side about ½″ up from end (see photograph M1). Pull through approximately half of length of cut strand. Place point of needle about ¼″ to right of place where yarn came through fabric. Push through to underside, holding loop on surface with finger of left hand. Still holding finger through loop, hold ends with right hand and pull to even up lengths of cords. **Step 2.** (See photograph M2.) Pull the 2 even lengths of yarn through loop and tighten. You must end up with a number of individual hanging cords divisible by 8 (double the usual multiple of 4 shown in General Directions). In order to achieve this, it may be necessary to count off the spacing and mark with pins. The stole shown has 16 groupings of 8 cords each at each end. A foam rubber pillow or any flat surface can be used for working space. Very few pins will be necessary as the square knot used for this design does not require great tension while tying. Move across pillow as work progresses. *Note:* Work double strand in order to create the heavy textured appearance (see photograph M). Try to keep knots and design as uniform as possible so both ends will look alike.

Directions. Row 1. Using first 4 sets of double cords, tie a square knot. (General Directions, diagrams D and E.) Continue across until row is completed. **Row 2.** Place 1st 2 sets of double cords to left side (see photograph M3). Taking 2nd 2 sets of 1st group and 1st 2 sets of 2nd group, tie square knot, dropping down 1″ to form pattern. Continue across row, using 2 double sets of cords from each adjacent group. (You will end up with 2 extra sets of double cords on right side.) **Row 3.** Using all cords, repeat Row 1, dropping down 1″ for pattern. **Row 4.** Repeat Row 2. **Row 5.** Using all cords, tie 1 square knot in 1st group. To attach beads to middle 4 cords (use 2 brass bugle beads for each group), thread large yarn needle with individual strands and run 2 strands through each bead. Place beads close together and tie square knot at bottom of beads using all 8 cords, leaving outside cords slightly loose to form an arc (see photograph L1). If you do not wish to use beads, work alternating half hitches down center as in motif used for pillow on page 414. **Row 6.** (See photograph L.) Using 2 double cords from adjacent groups, tie overhand knots (see photograph G, page 409 and photograph L2). There will be a total of 8 single cords in each overhand knot with the exception of the first and last knots. Since these will have only 4 cords, tie 2 overhand knots one directly over the other to simulate size of other knots. Trim, leaving 5″ ends. Repeat fringe on other end, following spacing on first end as closely as possible.

L
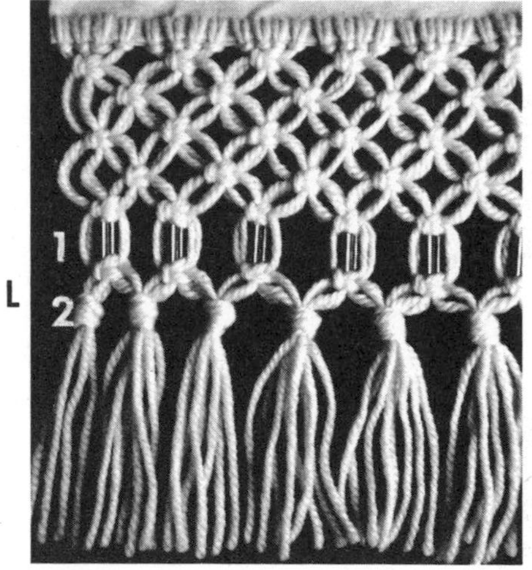

M
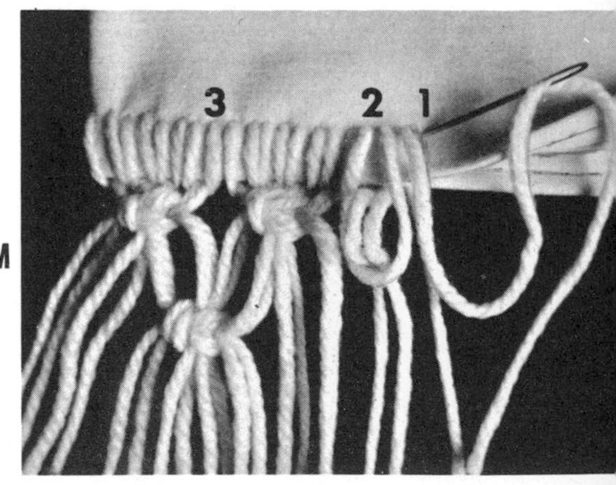

Square Pillow with Tassels

Shown in Color Plate 18

Materials. Rug Yarn—½ lb., for pillow top and tassels, Turquoise. Two pieces Felt, one 14″ x 14″ and one 14″ x 16″, Shocking Pink. Matching heavy-duty Sewing Thread. 10″ Zipper.

Directions. Draw 13″ square outline with dressmaker's chalk on foam rubber working pillow (this allows ½″ margin all around for seams). Cut holding cord 30″ long and pin in place along top line of area to be covered. Cut lengths of yarn 8′ long. Fold in half and attach to holding cord (see General Directions, diagram A) so there are 40 cords measuring 4′ each. Spread these evenly along the holding cord so the top line of the square area is covered. Starting at a point approximately 12″ from top, roll into skeins and fasten with elastic bands (see photograph H2 and directions page 409). **Row 1.** (See General Directions, photograph D.) Using multiples of 4 cords, tie 2 square knots in each group across entire top. **Row 2.** (See photograph N for pattern.) Place first 2 cords to left side. Using remaining 2 cords of first group, and first 2 cords of second group, tie 2 square knots, dropping down 1″ to form open pattern. Continue across row. Match distance between rows of knots so pattern is uniform. You will have 2 extra cords at end of row. *Note:* Place as many pins as you feel necessary to hold knots in place. As the work progresses, it is helpful to place pins down the sides, too, so knotting can be worked as evenly as possible. **Row 3.** Repeat Row 1, dropping down 1″ to form open pattern. **Row 4.** Repeat Row 2. Approximately 10 or 11 rows of double square knots with 1″ drop between will be needed for 12″ square. This figure may vary due to the slight variation of distance between rows of knots and the individual tension of the knots. When last row of double square knots is completed, tie adjacent groups together, using side cord of each group, so design is held in place along edge. Cut, leaving 1½″ ends. Make 4 tassels following directions, page 416. Wind yarn around cardboard 14 times for tassel center. Follow directions, page 416, for making pillow.

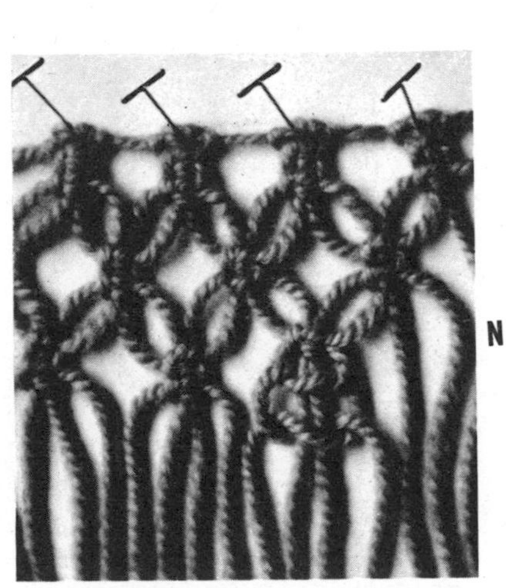

N

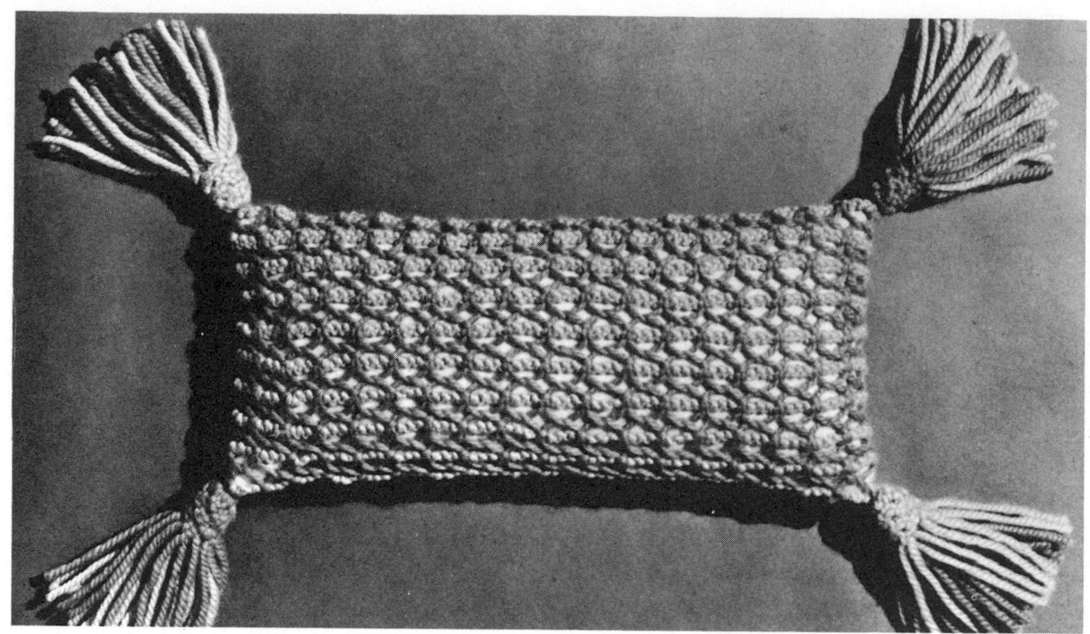

Oblong Pillow with Tassels

Materials. Rug Yarn—¼ lb. Shocking Pink, ¼ lb. Chartreuse. Two pieces Felt, one 10″ x 20″ and one 10″ x 22″. Matching heavy-duty Sewing Thread. 16″ Zipper.

Pillow. Draw 9″ line with dressmaker's chalk across working pillow approximately 2″ down from top edge. Cut holding cord of Pink 16″ long. Place along guide line of chalk, holding in place by tying knots around pins (see photograph O). Cut 10 lengths of Shocking Pink yarn each 4 yds. long. Cut 10 lengths of Chartreuse each 4 yds. long. Fold in half a length of Chartreuse yarn and attach to holding cord following steps 1, 2 and 3 in diagram A, General Directions. Double a length of Shocking Pink yarn, place loop under holding cord so Pink yarn falls on either side of Chartreuse cords already on holding cord (see photograph O1). Fold top loop of Pink yarn down over holding cord and pull 2 Pink cords through loop (see photograph O2). Tighten loop so 2 Chartreuse cords are in the middle with 1 Pink cord on either side (see photograph O3). Continue attaching cords in this manner until there are 10 groups of 4 cords (each cord will be 2 yds. long). Spread out evenly so chalk line is covered. Starting at a point 12″ from top, roll into skeins and fasten with elastic bands (see photograph H2 and directions page 409). **Step 1.** With Pink cord, tie 1 row of square knots (see General Directions, diagram D). Pink outside cords will be tied around 2 middle Chartreuse cords. **Step 2.** Pin knots in place. Using 2 middle Chartreuse cords, tie alternating half hitches as follows: Hold right cord in right hand and tie half hitch with left cord (see photograph P2). Hold left cord in left hand and tie half hitch with right cord (see photograph Q). Repeat 2 more times. *Note:* Before tying square knot at bottom of half hitches, place Pink cord from 2nd group over Pink cord from 1st group so they are interlaced (see photograph P1). Do this on both sides of alternating half hitches before tying square knot at bottom of each motif. This locks design together. **Step 3.** (See photograph R.) Tie square knot at bottom of alternating half hitches with Pink cords, leaving arc to form

O

Q

P

R

design. Keep as even as possible. Continue across to right side. Repeat until 18 rows of motifs have been worked, or measurement is 19″. As you progress, move up on working pillow and use plenty of pins to hold it in place. When work is completed, spread last row to measure 8½″. Pin in place. Using Pink cord from each adjacent group, tie knots to hold groups together along edge. Leave a slight drop so this knot can be caught under when pillow is constructed. Trim off leaving at least 2″ ends. Remove from pillow.

4 Tassels. See directions, page 416. Wind yarn around 6″ card 16 times. Make the following exceptions. There is approximately an equal amount of yarn of each color left from the pillow top which will be used for the tassels. Make 2 tops of each color and 2 middle tassels of each color. Use the 2 Pink middles with the 2 Chartreuse tops, and 2 Chartreuse middles with the 2 Pink tops. If you prefer solid-colored tassels, simply make two of each color. Attach so matching tassels are in opposite corners. Follow Construction Directions, page 416.

Construction Directions for Macramé Pillows

Materials. Two pieces matching Felt. Heavy-duty Sewing Thread. Zipper 2″ shorter than side of pillow (example: for 12″ pillow use 10″ zipper).

To Attach Macramé to Felt Top Facing. Starting with measurement of macramé pillow top, add 1″ all around. Example—12″ square pillow would require a piece of felt for top facing 14″ x 14″. Draw lines with dressmaker's chalk 1″ from each edge as guides for placement of macramé top. Place piece of felt on flat surface. Place macramé piece on top of felt. Stretch and shape macramé so ½″ of it extends on all sides of chalk lines. Carefully pin and baste to felt along chalk lines, catching the macramé knots at regular intervals. Keeping as straight a line as possible, stitch on basting line. This line of stitching will be used as a guide for seam line of the pillow so extra care at this point will assure a professional trim look to the finished article.

Felt Backing. Starting with measurement of macramé pillow top, add 1″ at each side and 2″ at top and bottom (this allows for flap for zipper). Example—12″ square pillow would require a piece of felt for backing 14″ x 16″. Cut felt piece apart approximately ⅓ distance from bottom of pillow. Insert zipper so it is not visible. Close zipper.

To Attach Back to Top. Zipper can remain closed while stitching 3 sides, but must be opened before stitching 4th side so item can be turned right side out. With right sides pinned together, using heavy duty thread, start at lower right bottom corner and run a line of stitching along bottom edge following the machine stitching around edge. Continue for 3 sides. Open zipper and complete 4th side. Check evenness of edges. Run a 2nd row of stitches over the 1st to reinforce and correct irregularities. Trim edges and corners of felt. Carefully turn right side out. Ease edges with fingers and push corners in shape with blunt end of pencil. Attach tassels.

Macramé Tassels

Materials. Rug Yarn—approximately ¼ lb. for 4 tassels.

Tassel Top. (See photograph S.) Cut holding cord 30″ long. Pin on working pillow. Cut 8 lengths of yarn 24″ long. Tie on holding cord so there are 16 cords 12″ long. (See General Directions, diagram A.) **Row 1.** (See photograph S1.) Work 1 row of square knots. (See General Directions, diagram D.) Remove from pillow and untie knots in holding cord. Tie around empty standard size spool of thread. Tie loose knot so it can be opened to tighten later. (See photograph S2.) **Row 2.** Using 2 cords from each first and last knot in Row 1, work 1 square knot (see photograph S2). Continue around row using 2 cords from adjacent knots of preceding row to form pattern shown in General Directions, photograph E. Do not drop rows. Work close to preceding row. **Row 3.** Repeat Row 2, using 2 cords from adjacent knots of preceding row. Push work up on spool as necessary. **Rows 4 and 5.** Repeat Row 3. Remove spool.

Tassel Center. Cut cardboard 6″ deep. Wind yarn around cardboard specified number of times. (See photograph T3.) Cut length of yarn 20″ long. Tie tassel at top. Cut through yarn at bottom (see photograph T4). Poke ends of tassel center tied with yarn up through center of macramé top so tops are even. Untie and tighten knot on macramé top so it closes snugly around center tassel. Using the two cords from center and the two cords from top, tie knot. Trim ends evenly. To attach to pillow, thread large needle with each strand at top of tassel and separately run them through to wrong side of pillow at each corner. Tie a firm knot on inside to hold securely in place.

Wall Hanging with Wooden Beads

Shown opposite, far right, and in Color Plate 18

Materials. Jute (or other heavy cord)—2 tubes. 20 Wooden Beads (1⅝″ deep with

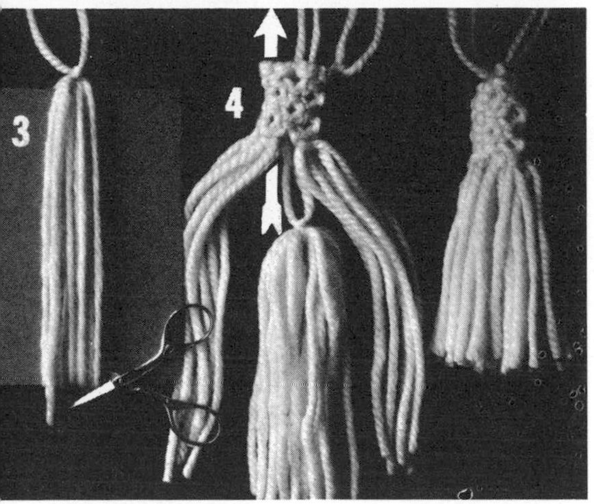

S

T

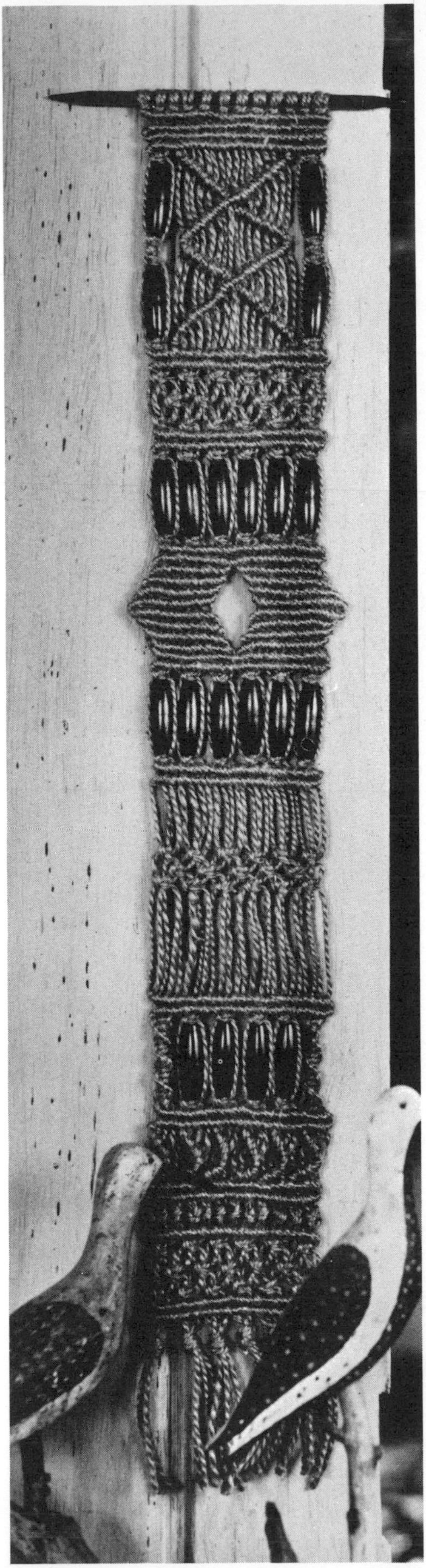

large hole). 9″ long piece of ¼″ dowel. (Make points on ends in pencil sharpener. Stain to match wooden beads and varnish. Let dry thoroughly.)

Cutting and Mounting Cords. Cut jute or cord in lengths as follows: One cord 12 yds. long. Eleven cords each 8 yds. long. Mount cords (see General Directions, diagram A) using dowel as holding cord. Use 12-yd. length as first cord, dividing it so the 1st single cord is 8 yds. long and the second 4 yds. long after mounting. Mount remaining 11 cords so the single cords are 4 yds. long. After mounting is completed, you will have 1 cord 8 yds. long and 23 single cords each 4 yds. long. Pin through jute to top of working pillow. When 1 or 2 rows of knots are completed, work is easily held in place by pins. Wind into skeins (see photograph H2,

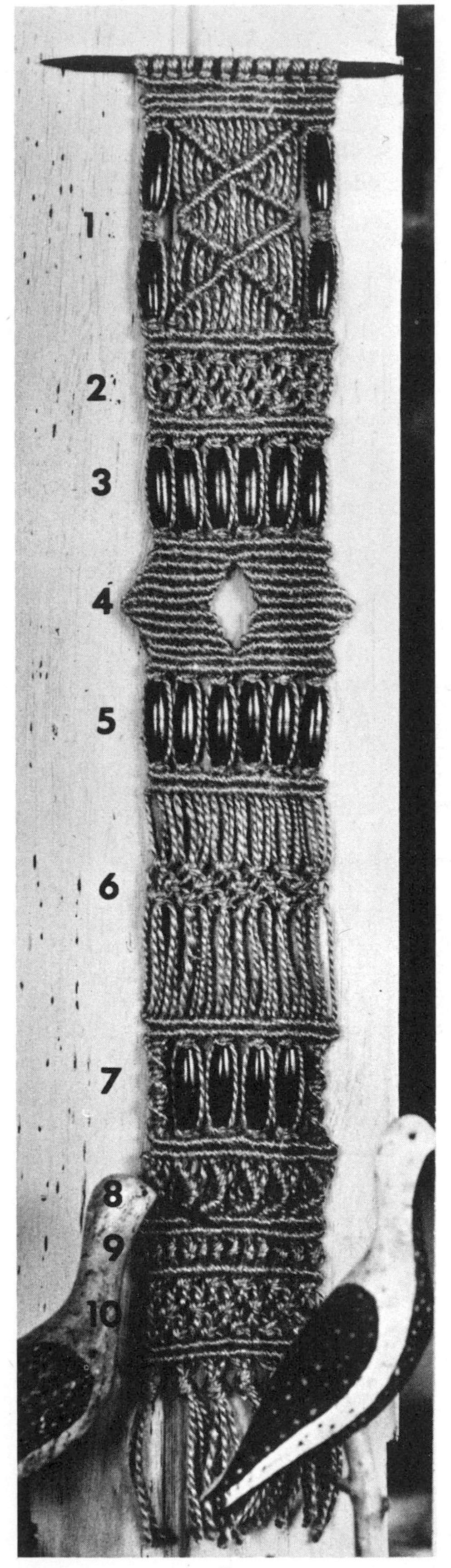

U

V

W

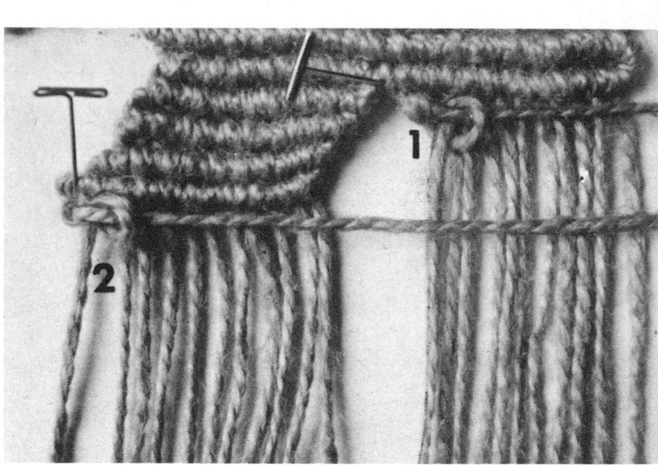

X

Y

page 409). Move up on pillow as work progresses.

To Attach Beads. (Follow photographs V1, 2 and 3 for attaching beads.): Tie square knot at top (see General Directions, diagram D). Insert 2 middle cords through hole in bead with large yarn needle if necessary. If needle is used, thread cords separately. Skeins must be untied during this process and retied when completed. Slip bead up in place (see photograph V2). *Note:* If you do not wish to use wooden beads, design shown in photograph W can be used. In place of bead, work alternating half hitches with middle two cords. Work one-half hitch to right and one-half hitch to left. Repeat 8 times to equal the length of beads. PHOTOGRAPH U—MOTIF 1. Work 4 rows of horizontal double half hitches, using long cord as the knot-bearing cord. Now, using 1st 4 cords, tie 1 square knot (see General Directions, diagram D) close to previous row. Undo skeins on 2 middle cords and attach wooden bead following steps in photograph V as outlined above. Tie 3 square knots at bottom before inserting 2nd bead and repeat process, tying 1 square knot at bottom. Place to side after rewinding skeins. Using last 4 cords, repeat process on right side. MIDDLE MOTIF. Divide remaining middle cords in half so there are 8 cords in each group. Work diagonal double half hitches (see General Directions, diagram C) crossing the center when the 8th cord is used and continuing on to make the cross. Make 2nd cross to complete the design. Gauge slant of diagonal so design falls in line with outside motifs as in photograph. *Work 2 rows of horizontal double half hitches using long cord as the knot-bearing cord.* After working the 2 rows the long cord will be on the left side again. MOTIF 2. Tie 3 rows of square knots (see General Directions, photograph E, for pattern, dropping down ¼″ between rows). *Work 2 rows of horizontal double half hitches.* MOTIF 3. Attach 1 row wooden beads with 1 square knot at top and 1 square knot at bottom. *Work 2 rows of horizontal double half hitches.* MOTIF 4. To make diamond-shaped opening work as follows: Divide cords into 2 groups of 12 cords each. Place #12 cord of 1st group to left (on top of all cords to left of center) parallel to preceding row of double half hitches. Repeat on right side, using 1st cord of 2nd group (#13) and place to right (on top of all cords to right of center) parallel to preceding row of double half hitches. (See photograph X1.) Work left side first—already worked in photograph. Hold cord #12 in left hand along preceding row on double half hitches. Work 1 row of double half hitches, using each cord to left of center in succession. Pick up cord nearest center of left side in left hand and repeat previous row. Repeat this 2 more times, using cord nearest center as knot-bearing cord. Use plenty of pins so cords can be taut and knots firm. When the 4 rows are completed, place pin at left side and hold 1st cord in right hand along preceding row. Tie double half hitches to center. Repeat for 4 rows using 1st cord in each row as knot-bearing cord. (See photograph X2.) Repeat on right side, using center cords as knot-bearing cords for 4 rows and last cords on right side as knot-bearing cords for next 4 rows. Place so bottom centers are adjacent and pin in place. *Using long cord at left side as knot-bearing cord, work 2 rows of horizontal double half hitches.* MOTIF 5. Attach 1 row wooden beads with 1 square knot at top and 1 square knot at bottom. *Work 2 rows of horizontal double half hitches.* MOTIF 6. Leaving a drop of 1½″, work 3 rows of square knots with ¼″ between rows, following pattern in General Directions, photograph E. Leave drop of 2¼″. *Work 2 rows of horizontal double half hitches.* MOTIF 7. Using first 4 cords, tie 17 half knots (see General Directions, photographs F1 and D1 and 2 only). Repeat with last 4 cords on right side. Using remaining cords in groups of 4, tie in 4 beads. Spread or squeeze end sinnets to length to correspond to center bead motif. *Work 2 rows of horizontal double half hitches.* MOTIF 8. (See photographs Y1, 2 and 3.) Design is worked in groups of 4 cords. Place pin at left side to secure. Using 1st cord as knot-bearing cord, hold in right hand in a downward right diagonal direction (see photograph Y1). Using next 3 cords in succession, tie diagonal double half hitches. Secure with pin at right of group (see photograph Y2) and hold same knot-bearing cord in left hand in a downward left diagonal direction. Tie diagonal double half hitches with remaining 3 cords in group in succession. (See completed design, photograph Y3.) Continue across until all groups have been worked. Pin securely in place at bottom of each group. *Work 2 rows of horizontal double half hitches.* MOTIF 9. Using groups of 2 cords, tie row of overhand knots leaving slight drop of ¼″ between knot and preceding row. (See photograph G, page 409.) Leave drop of ¼″ below knot. *Work 2 rows of horizontal double half hitches.* MOTIF 10. Repeat Motif 2. *Work 2 rows of horizontal double half hitches.*

Tassels. Using groups of 4 cords, tie overhand knots so there is ½″ drop between knot and preceding row of double half hitches. Continue across row. Trim, leaving 3″ ends.

Color Plate 19 HAND-WOVEN FABRICS

A variety of interesting textures and designs can be achieved in hand weaving. For reproducing the samples shown here, drafts and instructions are given on pages 432–433.

Color Plate 20 AUBUSSON TAPESTRY

A lovely example of an ancient type of weaving named for a famous French weaving factory. The name applies to the way the tapestry is made, not to its design. *See page 433.*

Color Plate 21 GOBELIN TAPESTRY

Another French weaving establishment gave its name to the type of weaving that is represented by this sample. Tapestries make marvelous wall hangings and upholstery fabrics.

Color Plate 22 SEWING FOR THE HOME—SLIPCOVERS

Slipcovers are easy to make if you know how. Detailed instructions for covers similar to these (as well as cafe curtains like the ones shown) are on pages 437–459.

Chapter 11

Hand Weaving

Like many of the other handcrafts, weaving was at one time a very practical and necessary occupation in the home. In the early days, weaving by the housewife or by the itinerant or village weaver was a matter of regular occurrence. In spite of the limitations as to threads, colors, etc., many early examples of this craft are still cherished for their beauty, ingenuity, and fine workmanship. Because of the introduction of power looms, weaving as a hand art was for a time almost lost in this country. However, it did survive, and in late years has enjoyed a thorough and enthusiastic revival among craftsmen throughout the country.

Weaving by hand is no longer a necessity, but it has become a very practical and delightful hobby. After a glimpse at some of the exquisite designs, colors, and textures in fabrics it is possible to produce in hand weaving, it is easy to understand the urge to buy a loom and try one's hand at this lovely craft. Weaving is fun. It is a sensible and practical hobby, and although it is not a cheap hobby, it is not necessarily an expensive one. Many women and men as well have made it a money-making hobby. There is, furthermore, much that could be said for its therapeutic value in this modern fast-moving life of ours. It is the most widely used of all the crafts by occupational therapists in restoring the physical and mental balance of their patients. The rhythmic movements of weaving have a definite curative effect.

This chapter cannot possibly be a full course in weaving. It is, rather, a bird's-eye view of the craft to give you some idea of the equipment needed, what must be learned, and some of the possibilities it offers.

For the procedure of setting up a loom, it is strongly urged that you have personal help from someone who knows the craft thoroughly. After you have learned this, you can proceed on your own.

BUYING A LOOM

This takes much careful consideration. Do not buy the first loom you see. Before buying, consider your needs: what kind of things do you want to weave? Will you be doing large things such as drapery and upholstery fabrics, possibly tweeds, or will you be making small things such as table mats, runners, babywear, etc.?

Also, fit the loom to your physical build.

Are you short or tall? Try the loom to find out if you are comfortable working at it. Even if the first one seems to be right, try several other models. How much will the budget allow? This is a big investment, so choose wisely. A cheap, unsuitable loom is not an economy, but it is possible to find an adequate one for a price you can pay. Also, many successful looms are made at home and it is possible to get good working drawings for them. How much space do you have for a loom? If you are fortunate enough to have the space for a wide loom, keep in mind that it is possible to weave narrow fabrics on a wide loom but not the other way around. Probably the most practical width for a loom is the greatest width that a shuttle can be thrown by hand with ease. This is 42″ for some and 50″ for others. Try before you buy.

Choose a loom made of well-seasoned wood that will not warp, and with hard wood in the parts that get the wear. Ratchets should be made of metal and easy to release. Heddles may be of metal (with fairly large eyes) or string and the reed should be metal.

Whether to use a sectional or plain warp is a matter of personal preference.

Another question that will arise is the number of harnesses in the loom. On a two-harness loom, only tabby (or plain weave) can be woven. However, many lovely fabrics can be made by variations in thread and coloring, and this may be all that you care to do. For pattern weaving you will need four harnesses, and here the possibilities are endless. Naturally, the more harnesses you have, the more variation.

WEAVING EQUIPMENT

In addition to the loom you will need:

Some sort of warping device.

A bobbin winder.

Skein holder.

Spool rack.

Extra shuttles and perhaps a flat pick-up shuttle.

Reed hook.

As you proceed you will find you may need other small tools such as paddle, scissors, pliers, etc.

KNOW YOUR LOOM

1. Warp beam.
2. Rachet and paul.
3. Back beam.
4. Top castle.
5. Horses.
6. Heddle frames.
7. Heddles.
8. Heddle eyes.
9. Lamms.
10. Treadles.
11. Part of beater.
12. Reed.
13. Beater bar.
14. Dents.
15. Breast beam.
16. Cape.
17. Cloth beam.
18. Shuttle race.

Note: There are many kinds of looms; not every one will look exactly like this one. This is generally representative of looms which are all basically the same. They vary in the way of working the harnesses.

HOW TO SET UP A LOOM

The whole process from making the warp to putting it on the loom ready for weaving is called "setting up a loom" or "dressing a loom."

How to Make a Warp

The first process in all weaving is the process of warping. This is done in the same manner regardless of the material chosen.

The warp is made by winding on a frame the threads which will run lengthwise on the loom. After winding, these threads are taken from the frame and finger crocheted (use the fingers as a crochet hook pulling one loop through another) into a long chain called the warp chain.

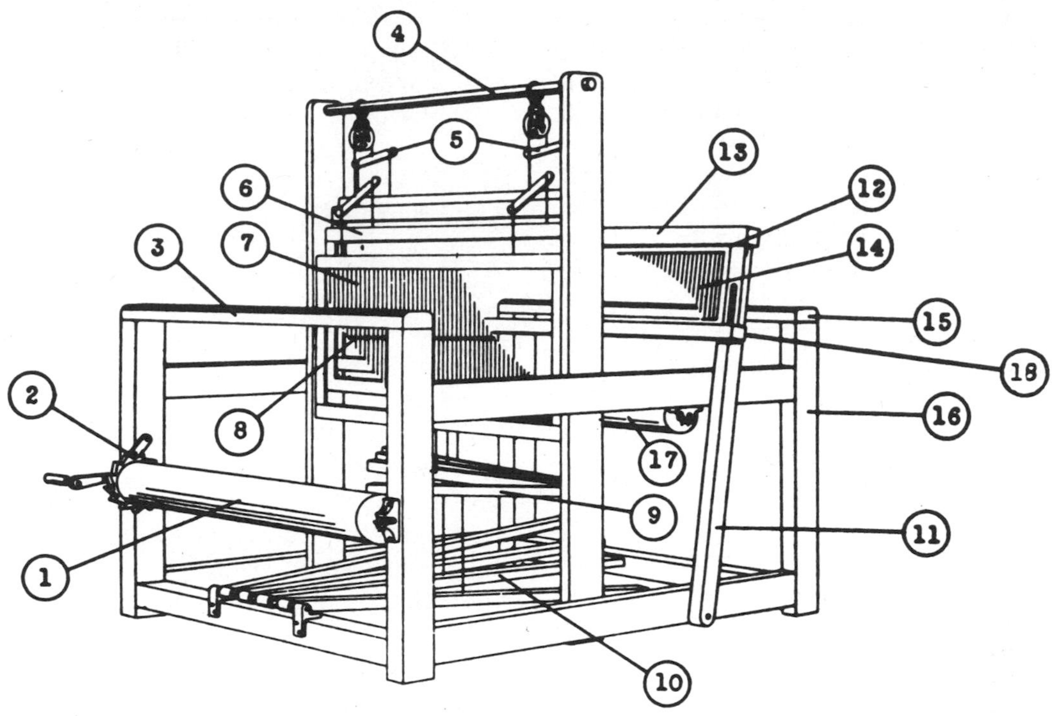

Warping may be done on a frame which limits the length of the warp but takes up little space. Or it may be done on a reel which allows for longer warp but takes up more space.

The most important single step in weaving is making the warp—it is the foundation for the whole thing. Therefore, learn to make a good warp.

Although a warping board limits the length of warp, it is still used in many cases, and a brief explanation on how to use one may be helpful.

A warp may be wound using a single thread but this is an unnecessarily long procedure. Two strands (not more) can be wound at one time and not get tangled, if the yarn is not the kind that will twist back on itself. It is, therefore, customary to use a number of threads at a time with a paddle. Any number of threads up to 20 can be used in this way.

The following procedure is for using 2 threads that have little or no tendency to twist. In order for the spools to unwind freely, use a spool rack or place each spool in a separate receptacle.

Tie the ends together and loop them over peg A. Guide threads under B and over C, then follow the dotted line as shown, passing threads around the outside pegs, back and forth and then under peg D, over and around E and back over D, then back in the same course to the top of the board where they go under C, over B, under and around A. Repeat from the beginning as many times as necessary for the number of threads needed in the warp. This forms a cross between B and C and another between D and E, which are the important ones. Whether they cross between A and B is unimportant.

Securing the crosses is very important, and if not done the warp will be spoiled when removed from the board.

The warp is wound with a cross in order to prevent the threads from twisting around each other. Whether made on a frame or on a reel, the warp threads are placed one after the other. This position is held by a cross near the end. It is important that when the

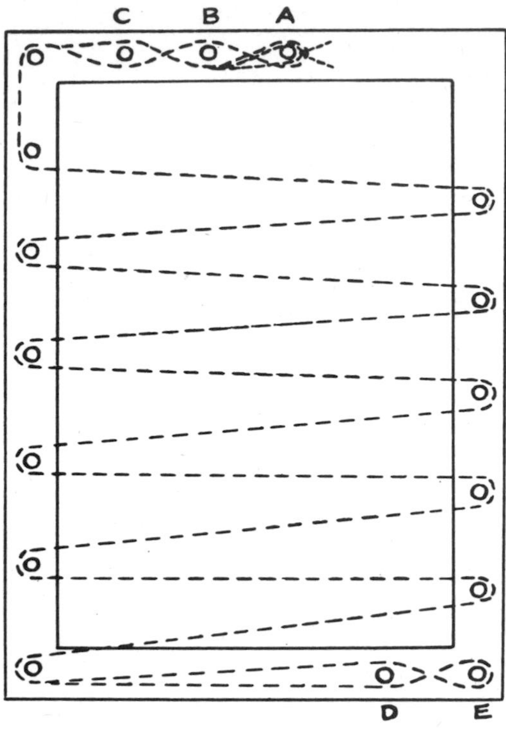

warp goes onto the loom the threads do not have a chance to twist and tangle. This is the function of the cross.

Tie the crosses as shown in the diagrams between C and B and between D and E. The threads may all be tied together at loop A.

The cross at the top of the board is the threading cross and the lower one is the counting cross.

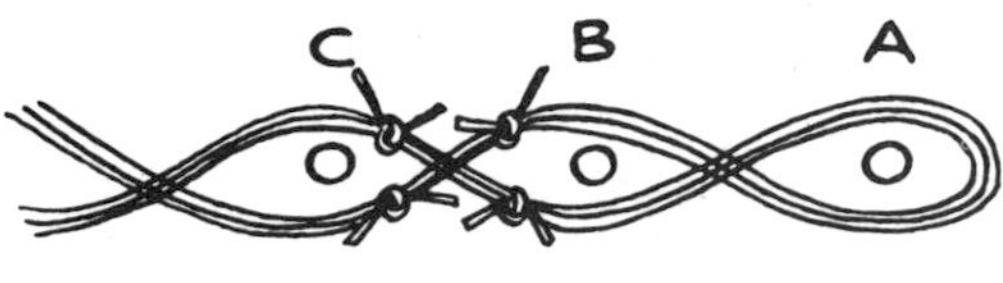

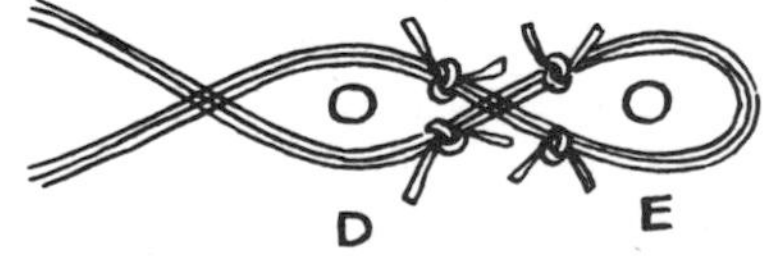

Taking Off the Warp

If you are beaming first (fastening warp ends to warp beam), cut all threads at A and chain from that end. If threading first, chain from D, E end which may or may not be cut. At end of the chain, cut all warp threads at dead center at A.

To chain. Hold with the left hand and make a big loose chain with the right hand (like chain stitch in crocheting, using the hands instead of a hook).

Putting the Warp on the Loom

After making a good warp, the next most important step is putting the warp on the loom. Even the best weavers cannot get good results with a poorly warped loom.

There are various methods of doing this, depending upon the kind of yarn being used and the type of fabric to be woven.

1. The warp may be wound onto the warp beam and then threaded through the heddles and reed.

2. Or the warp may be threaded through the reed and heddles and then wound onto the beam.

3. Or the warp may be tied onto a "dummy" or short warp already on the loom and then pulled through the heddles.

Beaming

If the beaming is done first, the loops are put through a raddle or spreader (a reed may be used for a spreader); the loops are then slipped over a stick which is fastened securely to the warp apron. (The apron is a length of cloth or tapes fastened to the warp beam or the cloth beam and to which the warp ends are fastened in order to save length of warp.)

The warp must be wound very tightly onto the beam; every end must be under equal tension. Laying sticks on the beam as you wind the warp is the old tried-and-true way of keeping the warp threads at an even tension. In recent years, however, many weavers have found that heavy brown paper wound with the warp is more efficient.

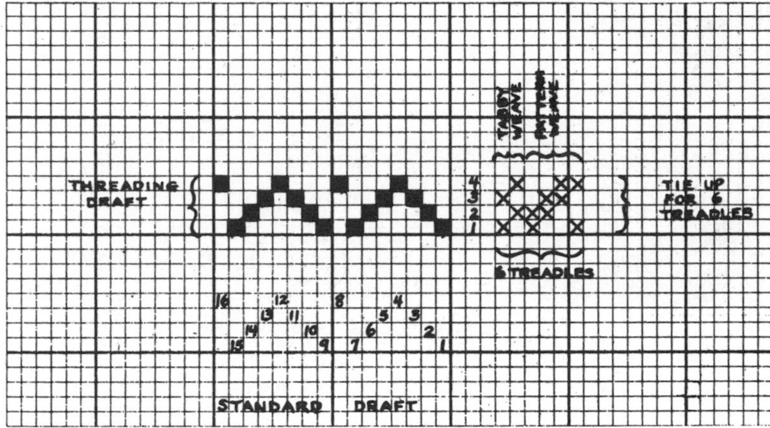

Standard Threading Draft

Threading Warp Through the Heddles and Sleying

The directions for threading are called a "draft."

The most usual way of writing a draft is given here.

The rows of squares from front to back represent the harnesses. The rows of squares from right to left represent the heddles.

For convenience in threading we start at the right. One black square represents 1 thread through 1 heddle eye on a single harness.

Following the draft given here, this means that the first warp thread is pulled through the eye of a heddle on number 1 harness, the second through the heddle eye of number 2, etc., as shown on the numbered squares. Finish threading across row, repeating the black squares.

Tie-Up

The group of x's at the side of the draft is called the "tie-up," which is a short way of saying "combination of harnesses used." The one given here is standard or most often used.

1 and 3 harnesses are used together alternating with 2 and 4 to produce tabby or plain weave.

If a loom has 6 treadles, harnesses 1 and 3 may be tied to one treadle and 2 and 4 to another for tabby. For pattern weaving, harnesses 1 and 2 are tied to treadle #3, 2 and 3 to #4, 3 and 4 to #5, and 1 and 4 to #6.

On larger looms with more harnesses and more treadles and using other patterns, the tie-up will be different.

Sleying

After the threads are through the heddles in the proper order, they must be brought through the reed. This is known as "sleying." The purpose of the reed is to spread and to determine how close the warp threads will be in the finished cloth. A reed may be threaded 1 or more threads to a dent (opening). Reeds come in various sizes (different number of dents to the inch). Fifteen dents to the inch is most often used.

Now the ends of the warp are tied (keeping the tension uniform) to the apron of the cloth beam.

The loom is now dressed and you are ready to weave.

WEAVING

Developing a good rhythm in weaving is the secret of good finished fabric.

First weave in a few strands of coarse wool for a "buffer," then proceed as follows:

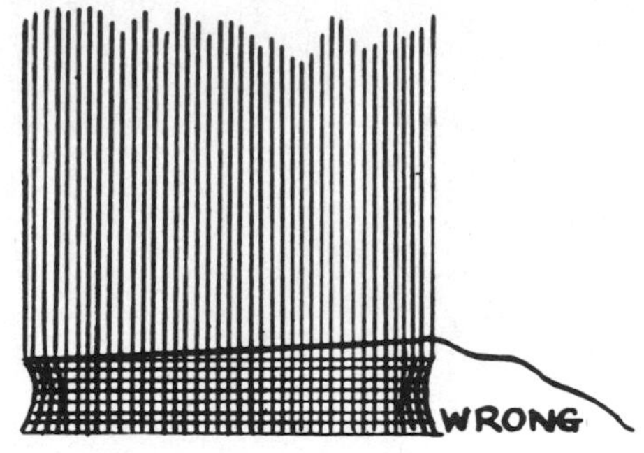

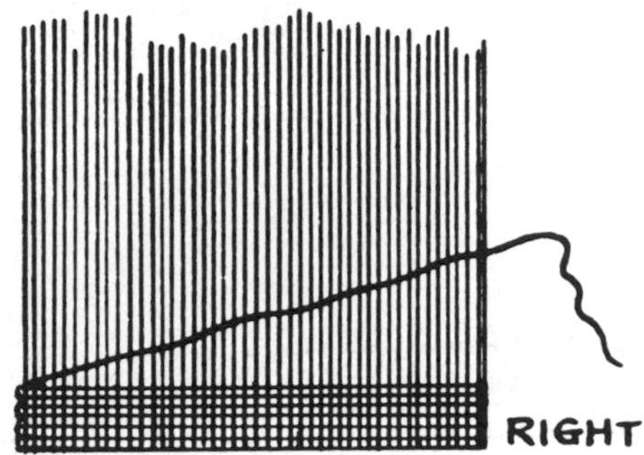

Open the shed (treadling), throw shuttle through with shed open, pull beater toward you. With beater in this position change to the next shed and push the beater back (away from you); throw shuttle. Repeat until you develop a rhythm.

To simplify:—tramp (open shed), back (beater back), throw, and beat. When the rhythm becomes even, the weaving will be even and the selvages good.

The beat must be regular or the fabric will show bands of close and loose weaving.

The thread left behind by the shuttle should lie close to the edge warp thread but not tight enough to draw it in. It should lie at a slant across the warp, not close to the fabric. In fact the weft should be allowed to lie as loosely as it will without making loops. If pulled too tightly the edges will be drawn in, resulting in broken warp threads.

Before proceeding very far examine the fabric for possible mistakes in sleying or threading. Correct any mistakes.

A streak where the fabric appears to be thin probably means a mistake in sleying. Re-sley. Sleying is a simple process but like every other step in weaving must be done with great accuracy. Avoid or correct crossed threads, missed dents, or dents with too few or too many threads. If 2 or 3 threads fail to tabby there is a mistake in the threading.

No two weavers have the same touch; therefore, as in knitting, it is not advisable for two people to work on the same piece.

After practicing several inches of tabby, try other treadlings (pattern combinations of harnesses) in various sequences. All variations in weaving are obtained by changing the order in which the combinations of harnesses are used.

The pattern given is a point twill known as "Rosepath."

There are more than 200 variations possible with this pattern when using only one shuttle.

When two shuttles are used, one shuttle using the pattern combination and each shot or "pick" followed by a tabby shot (second shuttle), the possibilities are endless.

Remember that the most fun and satisfaction to be had from weaving a pattern are in following one's own ideas and imagination rather than the directions written by someone who has woven it before. Color Plate 19 shows hand-woven fabrics in a variety of textures and designs.

TYPES OF WEAVING

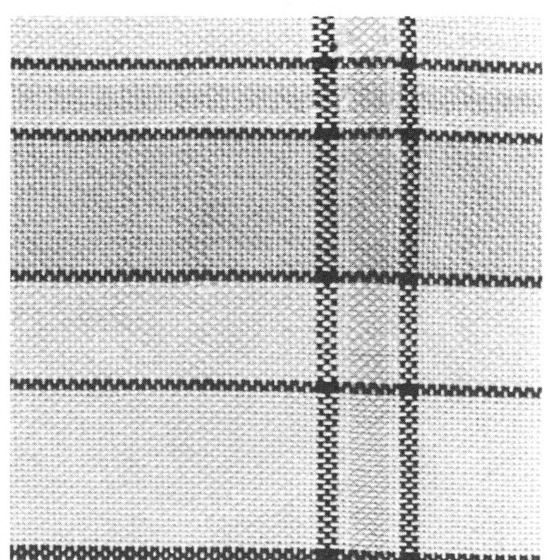

Tabby is the simplest type of weaving. However, it may be varied in use of color—stripes, checks, and plaids—or it may be varied in texture by the use of different kinds of yarn. The possibilities are very great with this one simple weave.

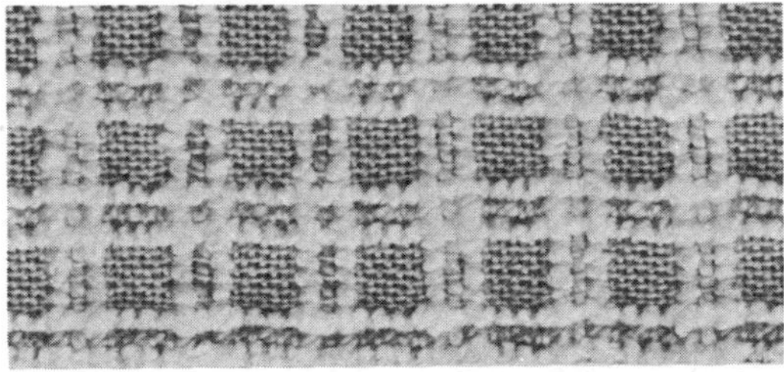

Twills open a large field of pattern variation. A direct twill is one in which the slant is in one direction only (serge). A point twill has the slant going in both directions to make chevrons (herringbone and irregular twill). A broken twill is a point twill with the draft arranged so there is never a skip of more than 2 warps. Plain tabby cannot be woven on a broken twill threading. The twills may be varied in color and texture indefinitely. We need not know any more

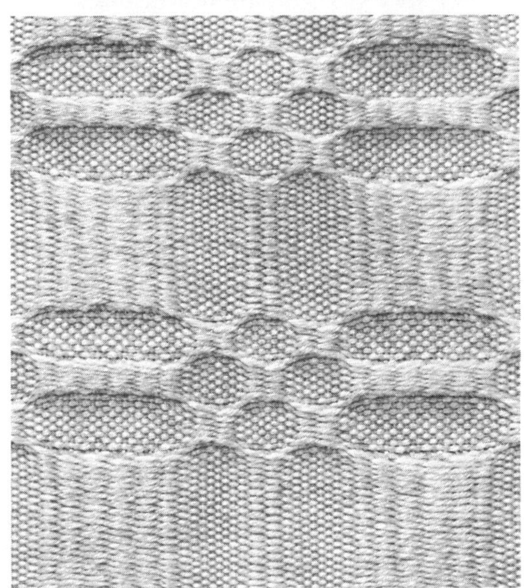

about weaving than twills in order to keep ourselves busy for a very long time.

If you wish to go to other types of weaving, they are divided according to structures. To name a few:

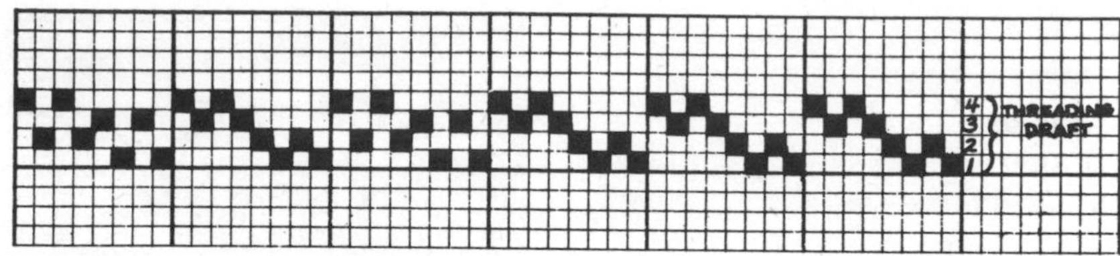

M's and O's Threading Draft

M's and O's is a development of twill often used for linens in Colonial times.

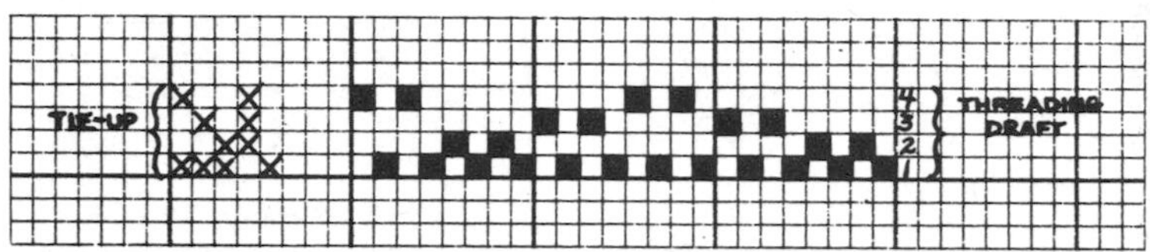

Spot Bronson Threading Draft

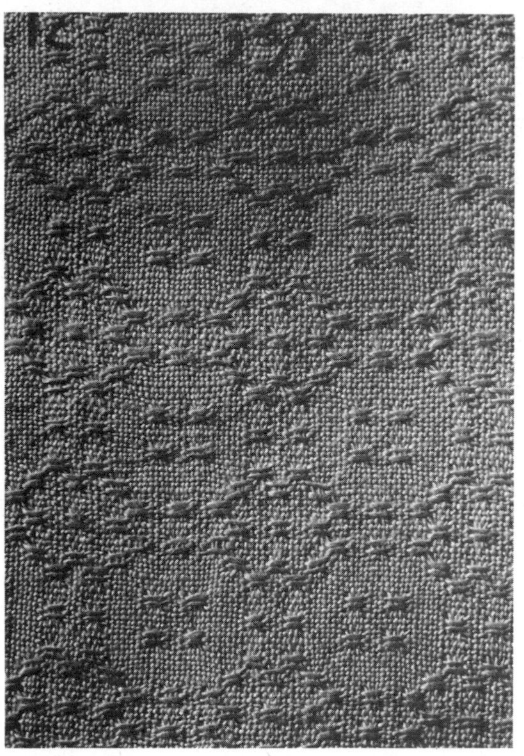

Huck can be elaborated to become Spot Bronson, or rearranged to become a lace weave.

Summer and Winter is the only truly American type of weave. It was popular from about 1775 to 1825.

Summer and Winter Threading Draft

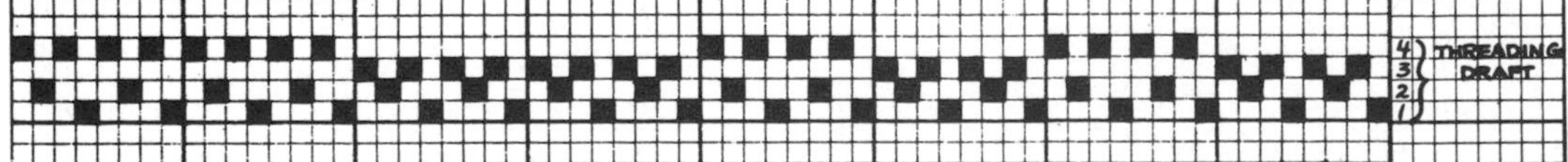

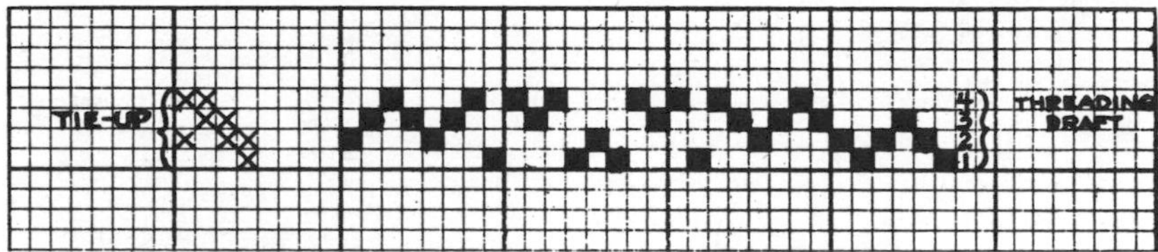

Crackle Threading Draft

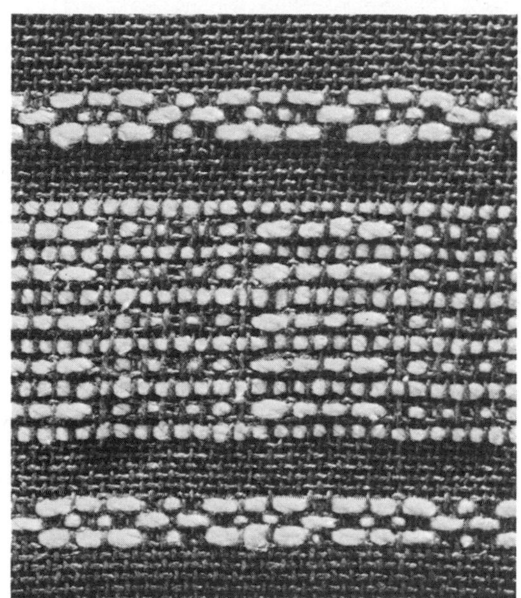

Crackle is an American name for a Swedish weave.

This example is linen with a silk border

Narrow band

Treadle 3–4
1–2 (white)
3–4

With 1 rose tabby between
6 rose tabby shots

Wide band

1 white tabby
1 rose tabby
2–3 white (repeat 5 times)
1 rose tabby
6 rose tabby shots

Repeat narrow band.

Colonial Overshot is probably the most familiar of the pattern weaves and was used on the old coverlets.

There are also many finger-controlled weaves which may be done on any tabby draft. These allow for more freedom of design than the so-called pattern weaves.

Some examples of these are Spanish Lace Borders, Leno Weave, Brooks Bouquet, Danish Medallion.

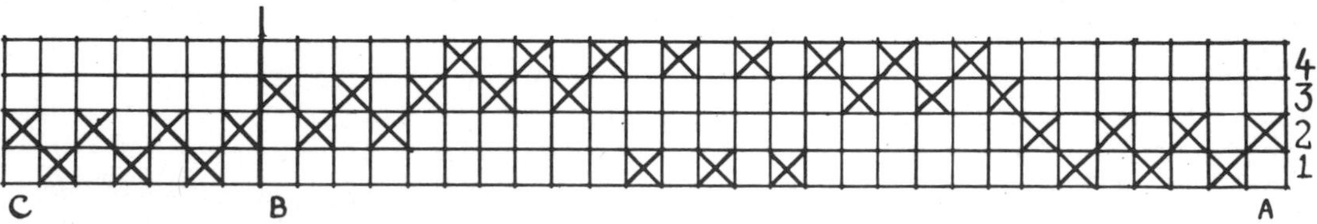

Colonial Overshot Threading Draft

Spanish Lace

Spanish is one of the easiest kinds of lace weaves and has many variations. It is merely a tabby that weaves back and forth over a few warps at a time instead of completely across the web.

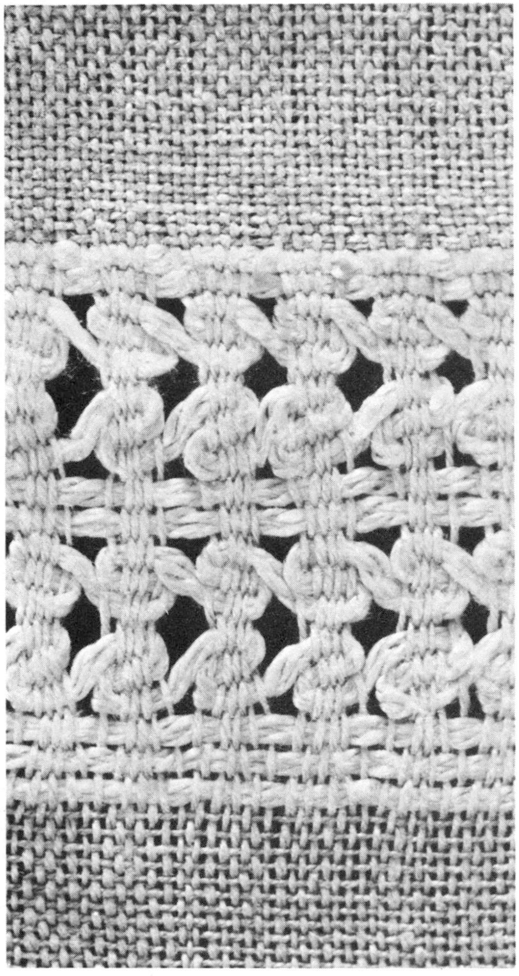

In all types of Spanish, the most important single factor is the tension; the weft must be pulled just the right amount and always the same amount. This is a matter of practice. Borders are effective and not really slow, for usually they are woven with a very heavy weft and so grow rapidly. The effectiveness of all types of Spanish depends on tension and on balance of warp and weft.

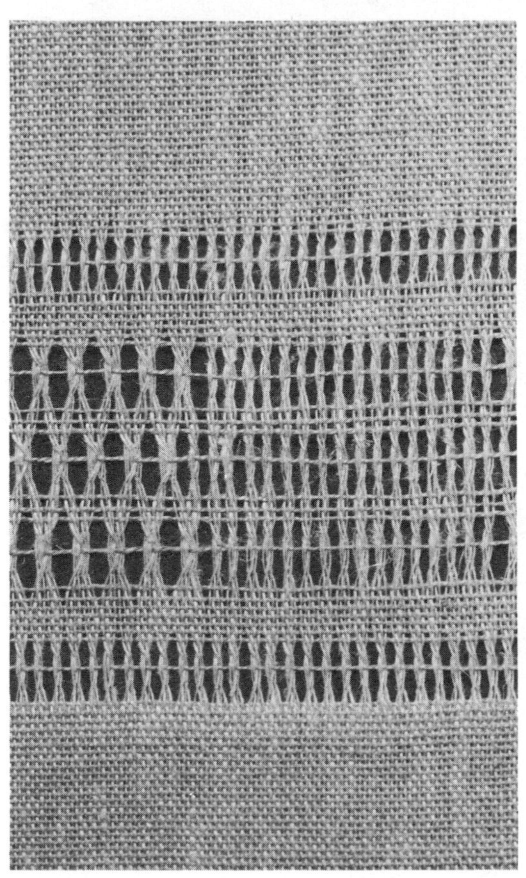

Leno

Leno is a general term for any type of weaving where the warp threads cross each other. There are hundreds of variations.

When making the twists, it is usually easier to work from right to left. A knitting needle can be used to cross the threads and a shed stick inserted as the work progresses; or, if the cloth is narrow, a smooth pointed stick can serve as both pick-up and shed stick. When the shed is opened for the first row of twists and the passage of the shuttle from right to left, the first warp thread *must* be a *top shed* thread. This is important. If the first thread is on the bottom shed, no twist will result. Also, it is much easier to work if the tension is not too tight.

Proceed as follows:

Open the shed. Insert the forefinger of the left hand into the shed a couple of inches from the edge; with the thumb and forefinger of the left hand, pull the top shed threads a little to the left to make the work easier. With the pick-up stick, pick up the first thread from the bottom shed and pass the stick *over* the first thread of the top shed, dropping it from the fingers of the left hand. This is the fundamental principle of all Leno handweaving. Continue across the web in the same way to pick up 1 and drop 1, moving the left hand as needed. When the pick-up stick has been taken across the width of the loom, look carefully to see that there are no mistakes in the crossing of the warps. It is easier to make corrections before the weft is put through. Turn the stick on edge to make a shed and pass the shuttle from right to left. Leno has a tendency to pull in and be narrow, so do not pull the weft thread too tightly. Beat the weft well back, but *do not* tighten the weft at the left edge. Because of the twist, the weft will not go completely back to the plain weave; if it did there would be no lace effect. But it does need a good beat or it will be too loose and too much open lace is not attractive. Change the shed and pass the shuttle back to the right edge of the web. This will untwist the warps and return them to their proper sequence.

Simple Rules for Weaving Leno.

1. The first warp thread *must* be a top shed thread.
2. Begin at the right edge, pick up a lower warp and drop a top warp.
3. Pass the shuttle through the shed made by (2) from right to left.
4. Change the shed and pass the shuttle from left to right.
5. Beat well after each weft.

Brooks Bouquet

Square. Enter the shuttle at the right edge and bring it out of the shed to the top about one inch from the edge. Count 3 warp threads to the right and enter the shuttle into the shed at this point. Bring the shuttle to the top 3 top warps to the left of where it came out before. This is essentially "back-stitching" over 3 warp threads and progressing 3

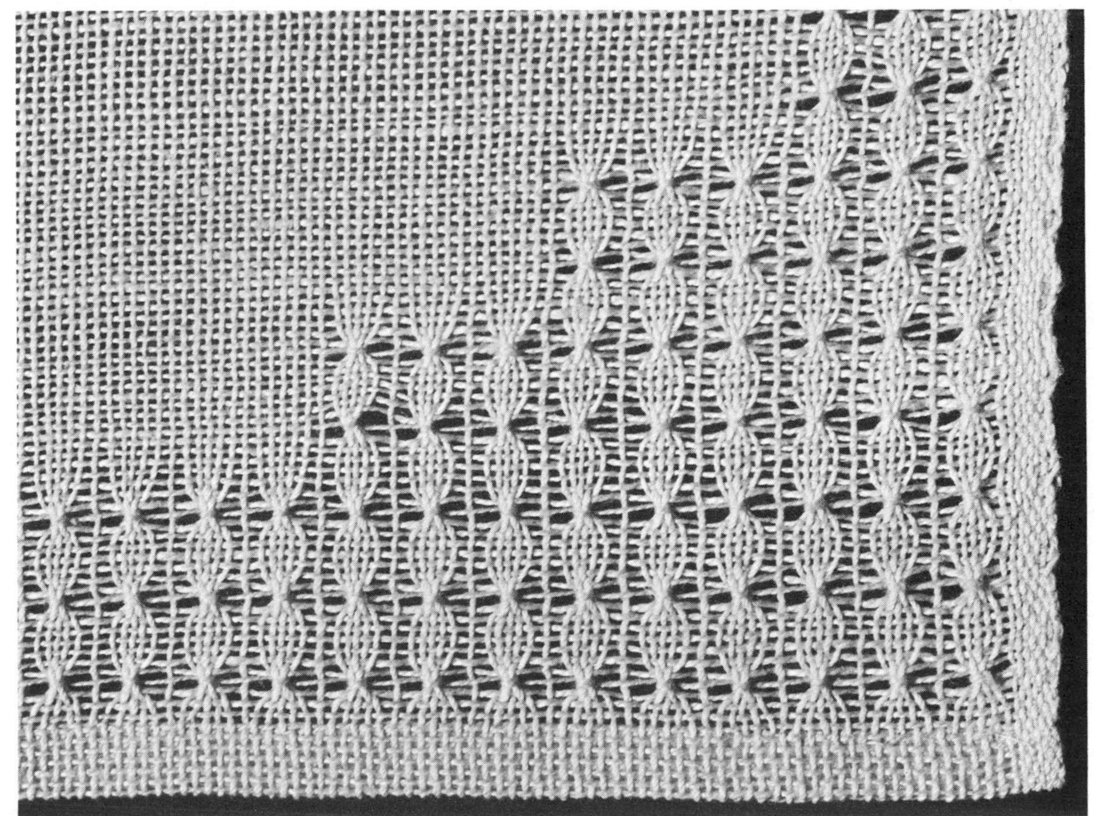

warps—all on the top shed. The weft should be drawn tightly enough to pull the 3 warps together but not so tightly that the weft cannot be beaten back. Weave *three* tabbies. On the next row, back-stitch over the same warp threads as before. In square Brooks you may back-stitch over an even or an odd number of warps; but there must be an *odd* number of tabbies between the rows of "bouquets" and the back-stitching is always done from right to left. The lace can follow a pattern or it can be a straight band.

HAND-WOVEN FABRICS

Shown in Color Plate 19

1. Tabby weave using plain and nubby threads.
2. Tabby weave in plaid arrangement.
3. Light weight woolen shawl. Draft as follows:

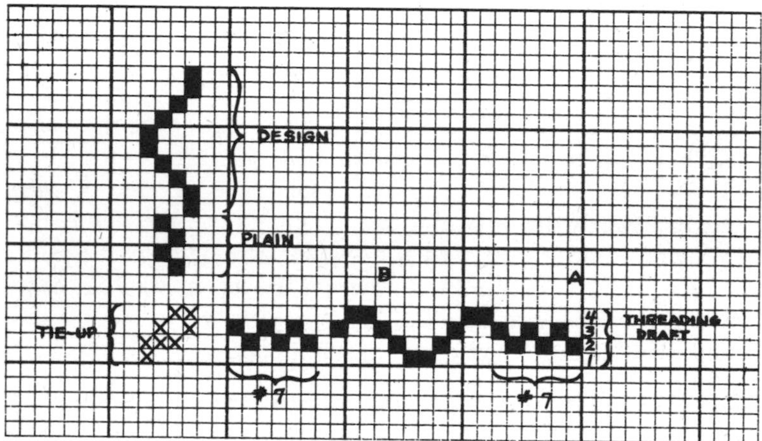

4. Rich texture with a variety of threads. Draft as follows:

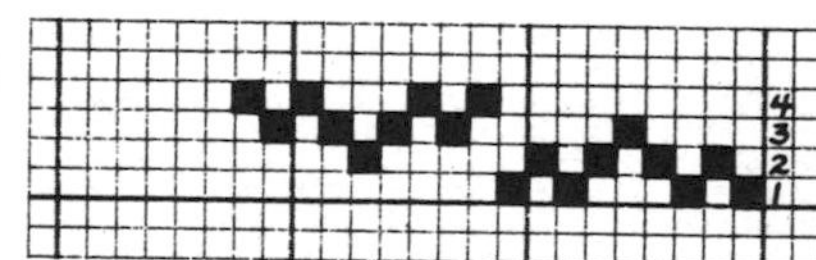

5. Stripes in tweed wool yarn suitable for upholstery fabric. Draft as follows:

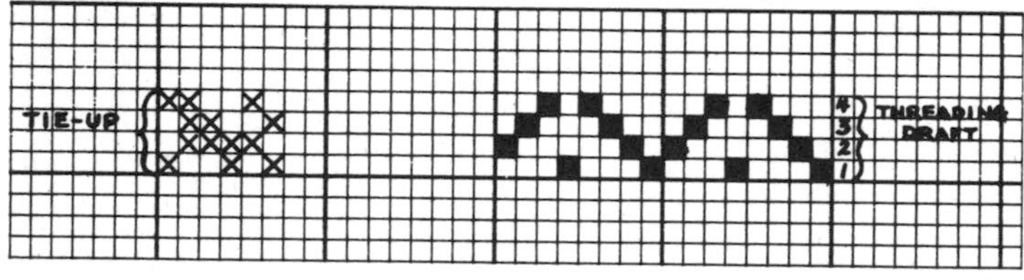

6. Striped drapery fabric using light weight and heavy yarns in an interesting effect. Draft as follows:

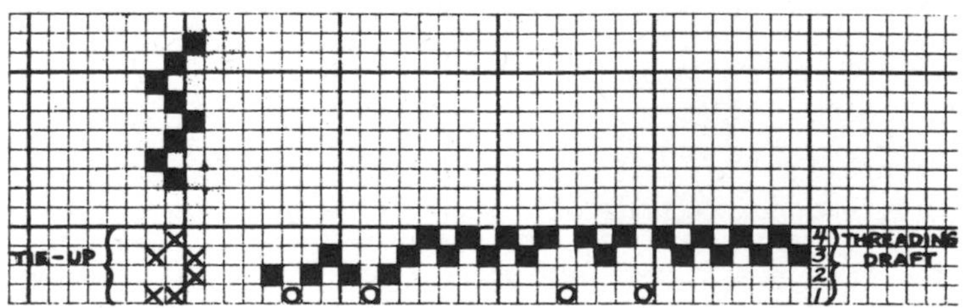

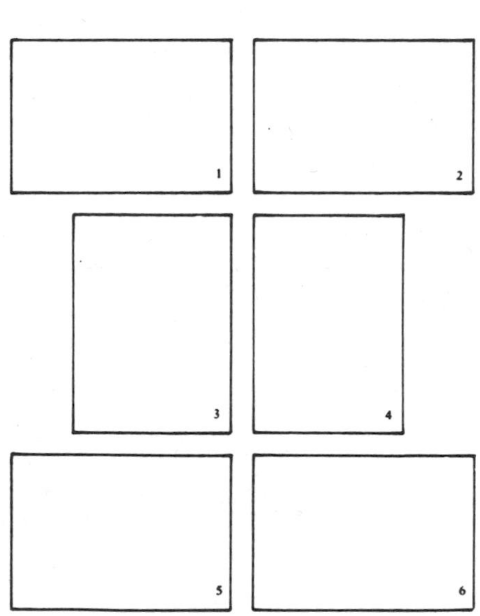

Danish Medallion

This may be varied indefinitely, but only the basic principles will be given here. The regular weft thread may be used to make the "medallions" or an extra weft may be added. If the extra weft is added, it should be a heavier weight, or a color—there is no point in adding the extra weft if it does not contrast with the one being used. Medallions may be used as a border or groups can be used as surface decoration.

Without cutting the original weft, splice in a heavier colored weft at the right selvage and weave to the left. With the regular weft, weave 4 or 6 tabbies. After the fourth or sixth tabby, change the shed as usual. Enter the heavy pattern weft into the shed, weave far enough into the shed to bring the shuttle out of the shed and on top between the sixth and seventh warp thread of the top shed. At this point and with a crochet hook, go *under* the heavy weft previously woven; pick up a loop of the pattern weft and bring it to the top of the web. Pass the shuttle through the loop to form a slip knot; then pull the weft to tighten it.

TAPESTRY WEAVING

Shown in Color Plates 20 and 21

Tapestry weaving is an old technique which is enjoying a revival. The term is often misused because it actually means a certain type of weaving and not "picture making."

One characteristic of tapestry weaving is that the warp is completely hidden by the weft and plays no part in the design.

In regular weaving the weft extends across the entire width of the warp; in tapestry weaving the color may change at any point and a color is carried across only as far as it is wanted. It is then turned back and therefore a whole section of color may be woven separately.

When colors meet they may interlock over the same warp thread. This makes a fairly smooth surface. Or they may turn back over adjacent warp threads, which leaves a "slit." Both are old techniques. The first is the Aubusson method and the second is the Gobelin way of working. In the ancient "slit" tapestries the slits were left open but later they were more often sewed together.

HAND-WOVEN MATS

1. Tabby weave using linen with bouclé type yarn.
2. Tabby weave of linen with Leno border.
3. Tabby weave with Danish medallion border, linen and rayon yarns.
4. Tabby weave using linen, Crackle border in novelty yarn. See Types of Weaving for draft and instructions for border.
5. Tabby weave of linen with stripes of heavier yarn.
6. A colonial overshot pattern. Jute plus pearl cotton. Draft is available.

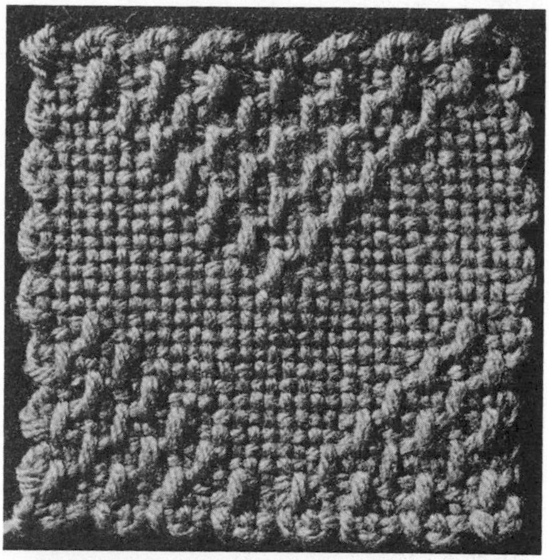

SIMPLE LOOMS

Small "looms" are available for teaching the fundamentals of weaving to children. They are also useful for those who like to work on something small which can be carried about. These come in various sizes. The 2″ and 4″ square weave is the most widely used. Several patterns can be made and the small squares set together in various ways to make many lovely things such as babywear, afghans, etc. Full instructions and needle come with the looms.

Some patterns which can be made on a weave-it loom are shown above.

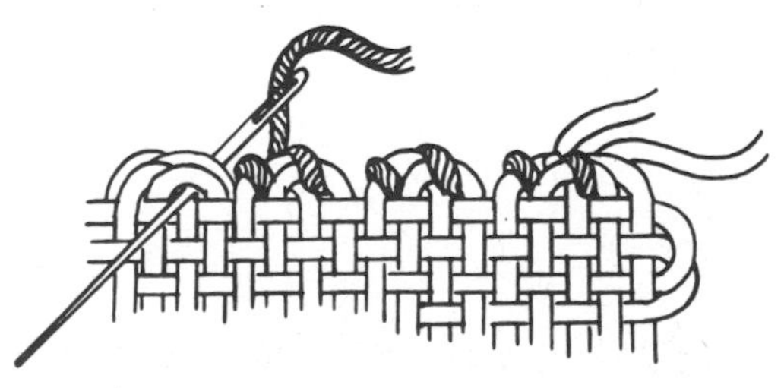

Sewing squares together

Color Plate 23 SEWING FOR THE HOME—DRAPERIES

Lined draperies that look as though they were custom made can be created at home at a much lower cost. Step-by-step instructions for the type shown are on pages 451–455.

Color Plate 24 APPLIQUÉ PLACE MATS

Machine embroidery can be used for many decorative accessories. These delightful place mats are appliquéd in zigzag satin stitch. For full instructions for making, see page 476.

Chapter 12

Sewing for the Home

One of the most satisfying occupations for a woman is furnishing and decorating or "redoing" her home. New draperies, slipcovers, curtains, and bedspreads can lift the spirits of family and house alike and become an exciting project.

This type of sewing is not at all difficult although it does take care and accuracy, and many women prefer it to making wearing apparel. There is a wealth of beautiful and practical decorator fabrics now available. The many new fibers and blends, and the special finishes which make fabrics easy to care for, are a great incentive to all of us to plunge in and turn decorator.

There are many good methods of making draperies and slipcovers. We have chosen to give you those methods which are quickly done and which give a custom look. In general, the more hand work, the more "custom-made." However, in the interest of durability and keeping the shape it is advisable to do certain things by machine.

MAKING SLIPCOVERS

Each chair, settee, or sofa is a problem in itself, but certain general rules and procedures for making slipcovers apply to all.

Slipcovers vary with the style and construction of the furniture; they may be casual, such as the temporary tie-on or snap-on variety, or they may be so carefully fitted that they may scarcely be distinguished from upholstery.

GENERAL RULES AND SUGGESTIONS ABOUT SLIPCOVERS

Slipcover your furniture while it is new. Although you may not keep the covers on at all times, they keep the upholstery fabric looking new much longer and give you (if you wish) two completely different color schemes for summer and winter.

Club or lounge chairs, wing chairs, and sofas are made with plain or with T cushions. The same general rules for making covers apply to both. It is difficult to slipcover a chair with a wooden frame. Occasionally, on a style with a small amount of wood showing, it can be done by using quilted fabric.

Unless the fabric is bulky, the flounce is cut twice the length for proper fullness. For heavy fabric, use a straight flounce with box pleats at the corners; it should be lined.

Do not use slippery-backed fabrics; they will never stay in place.

Tufted and channeled chairs cannot be slip-covered successfully. A *lightly* tufted back can be covered fairly satisfactorily if quilted fabric is used over the tufted area. Combining quilted and unquilted fabric is often a good idea on other styles of chairs also.

The tuck-in or lap at the inside back and sides should be deep enough to push in the hand up to the wrist. We have specified 5″, but your chair may need more. If the slipcover fabric is expensive or if you are running short, another fabric may be pieced on for the tuck-in. Rolls or tubes from paper towels may be pushed in at the back and sides to hold in the tuck-in (see *Note,* page 450). This is especially advisable on a curved-back sofa with no separate cushions, because the lap must stay pushed in to keep the back very smooth.

The upholstered look is newer (see lower finish on the Federal sofa). This makes it possible to use lighter colors, because they are removable.

General Procedure

Although slipcovers are not difficult to make, it might be advisable, if you are a beginner, to choose a chair with simple lines for your first project. Also, as a novice you should perhaps try your first cover with an inexpensive fabric. For the same reason, choose for your first try a plain fabric or one with a small pattern which does not require much matching. Keep in mind also that stripes are difficult and need careful handling when they are being cut.

Straighten one end of the fabric before you start cutting. Pull a thread (if it is a plain color or a woven design) and straighten the fabric by pulling and stretching, or draw a straight line at right angles to the selvage with yardstick or T square (if it is a printed fabric).

Unless the chair is old and badly out of shape or the piece of furniture is not symmetrical (such as certain styles of settees and chaise longues), the fabric may be placed and fitted wrong side out, to save turning the seams later. This is especially helpful when welting or fringe is used in the seam. If for any of the reasons given the fabric must be placed right side out, pin seams as usual then open out and mark with pencil near the seam and also across the seam on curve so seams can be matched and sewed accurately from the wrong side. See diagram.

The pieces must be cut and pinned so that the lengthwise grain of the fabric runs up and down on the chair and the crosswise grain is parallel with the floor as nearly as possible (even when the panel on the chair slants).

Do not try to work with one long piece of fabric. Measure and cut a section for each part of the chair *in the order given in the measuring instructions.* Allow for tuck-in and seams, plus a little more (2″ or 3″). Choose preshrunk fabric if possible. You can shrink it yourself if necessary and if the material is washable. Do not try to get around this step by allowing for shrinkage as you make the slipcover; it will not fit properly and will always look sad and droopy. Choose washable trimmings also if you plan to launder your slipcovers.

After cutting each section, lay it on the chair wrong side out, and stay-pin it to the part where it will be used (see Figs. 3, 4, 5, and 6). In this way, you will know which pieces have been cut.

If Your Fabric Has a Center Motif

Center the motif on the inside back of the chair with the cushion in place. Center the motif on the outside back of chair, and match the inside arms, placing the heavy part of the motif at top (depending on the design). Center the pattern on the cushion top and bottom (make both sides alike so it will be reversible). Center the pattern on the border (boxing) of the cushion and on the front border of the chair (apron).

If the fabric is printed with a large amount of white (or other background color) at the sides, trim off part of it before cutting sections or you will have wide areas of plain color and no pattern (this happens especially when the fabric is pieced).

Measuring Fabric for Chair

Grain should run up and down on all vertical parts, and from front to back on seat.

1. Decide how deep the flounce is to be

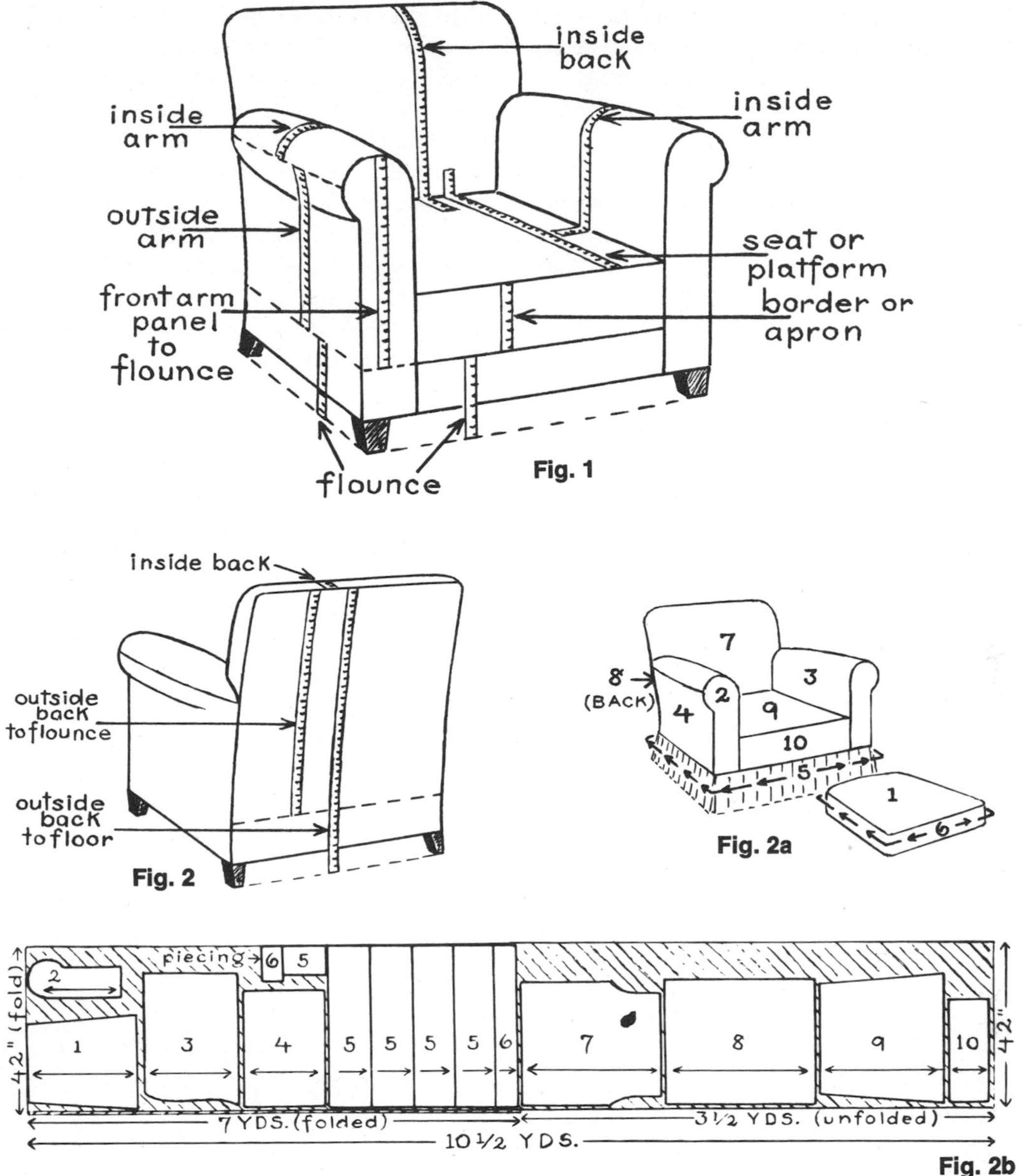

Fig. 1

Fig. 2

Fig. 2a

Fig. 2b

(Fig. 1), measuring from the floor up. This depends somewhat on the style of the chair, on whether it has a cushion, and on whether legs are straight or curved. Flounces vary in depth from 8″ to 12″ on average-size chairs and usually start at the lower edge of the front border. If a chair has a loose cushion, remove it before measuring. The "platform" is the part beneath the cushion. If the chair has no loose cushion, this area is called the "seat."

2. Measure. FRONT BORDER—from the top of the flounce to the platform or seat. It reaches all the way across the front of the chair on some styles (T cushion), and as far as the arms on others. SEAT OR PLATFORM—from the front edge to the back, with a 5″ tuck-in allowed at the back and sides. INSIDE BACK—from the top of the chair to the platform or seat, with a 5″ tuck-in allowed at the lower edge. OUTSIDE BACK—from the top of the chair to the top of the flounce (Fig. 2). OUTSIDE ARMS—from the farthest point of the curve at the outside, to the top of the flounce. INSIDE ARMS—from the outside of the curve over the arm, down to the seat or platform, plus 5″ for tuck-in. FRONT ARM PANEL—from the top of the arm to the top of the border or to the flounce, as the case may be. These pieces can usually be cut alongside other pieces, but make sure they are accounted for. CUSHION. Measure front to back (allow for 2 sides); boxing strip is cut crosswise on fabric (Fig. 2a). FLOUNCE. It should be made on up-and-down (lengthwise grain) of the fabric; it will have to be pieced at intervals. Allow for ½″ seam at the top and a 2″ hem. In length, allow for kick pleats or shirring as desired. Allow double the amount for shirring and 3 times as much for all-around pleating. Kick pleats (at corners) vary in size: allow 12″ to 16″ for each pleat (24″ to 32″ for each corner).

As mentioned above, allow about 3″ on each piece for leeway in fitting, and add sufficient allowance if the pattern must be matched or centered (this depends on the pattern), a yard or two perhaps. Now figure the total amount needed for the chair. See a typical layout (Fig. 2b which is related to Fig. 2a); it will help you figure yardage. Also, the table on page 450 gives approximate yardage requirements.

Keep these various measurements handy to be used when cutting.

Cutting

Following the same order used to measure the fabric, measure and cut each rectangular piece which will cover the portion of the chair for which it is intended (no shaping at this point). Be sure to make an allowance to cover the area more than adequately. The only exceptions are the front border and the flounce (also the top border and the side panel, if any; see Fig. 11 under Pinning Outside Back). The front border is a straight piece and can be cut exactly (with seam allowances), to avoid trimming later when it is difficult to get at; the flounce is left to the last and can also be cut exactly.

As you cut each piece, lay it, wrong side up, on the place it is to be used. Hold with pins. This is a check on what you have cut and keeps pieces from being mixed up.

If the Fabric Is Printed

As you go, plan the placement of motifs, centering one on the cushion (from right to left and front to back), the inside back above the cushion, the outside back, the front border, and the arms. Arrangement of the motifs should be as symmetrical as the pattern allows. If the fabric has a small, all-over design, centering and matching is not difficult but must be considered.

Piecing

On a settee or love seat, piecing will have to be done on the seat, the cushion, and the inside and outside back if you are using 36″ fabric.

Match or arrange the motifs when doing this. The piecing seams should be pinned, stitched, and pressed open as soon as the sections are cut.

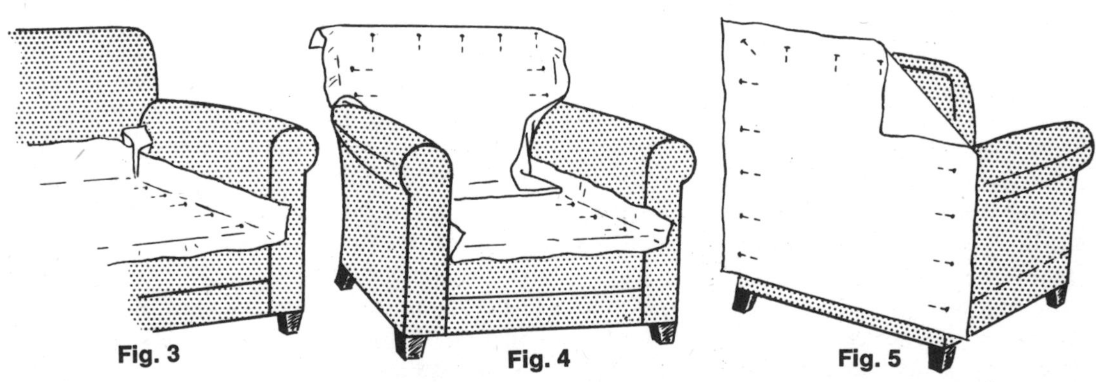

Fig. 3 Fig. 4 Fig. 5

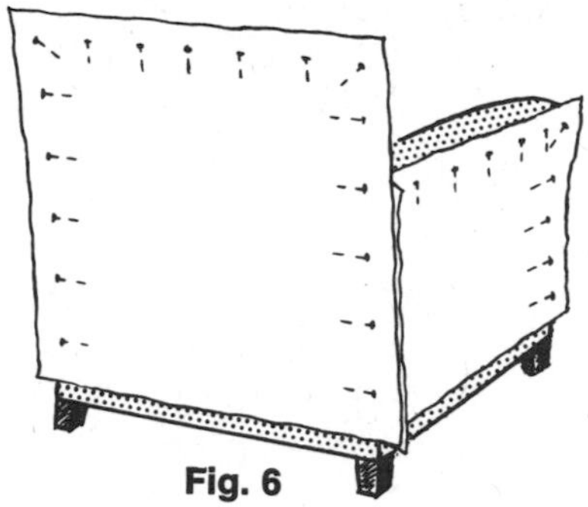
Fig. 6

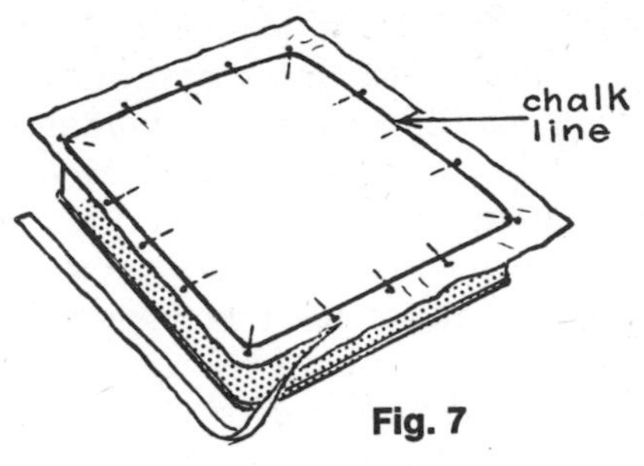

Fig. 7

PINNING AND FITTING

General Directions

Start with the seat or platform. Smooth out the piece, centering and adjusting (Fig. 3). Pointing pins inward, stay-pin the piece to the chair near its edge all around. Be sure tuck-in allowance is placed at back and sides.

Do the inside back next, smoothing, centering, and fitting as before, and stay-pin this piece to the chair around outside edge (Fig. 4). Cut away any large corners to within 2″ or 3″ of seam.

The outside back is next (Figs. 5 and 6), then the outside and the inside arms, the front arm panel, and the front border. In each case, pin the respective piece 2″ or 3″ away from the seamline, not on it. Cut away any unneeded large corners, so the remainder can be easily grasped.

Final Pinning

Cushion. Lay the cushion on a table. Place the fabric piece on it, wrong side up, centering the pattern (Fig. 7). Smooth the fabric over the cushion, and pin near the edge. With white chalk (do not use wax crayon), mark exactly over the welting or seam beneath. Trim ½ of the piece just outside the chalkline, allowing for the seam and rounding the corners a little. Fig. 7 shows top only partly cut.

Fold the cut half over the remaining half, matching to the chalklines on the underneath piece as nearly as possible; cut the remaining half (this makes the 2 sides symmetrical). Cut another piece like this one for the other side of the cushion. Measure the width of the

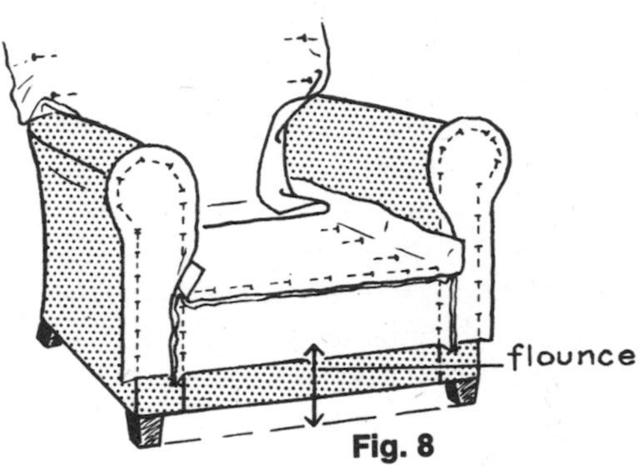

Fig. 8

Fig. 9

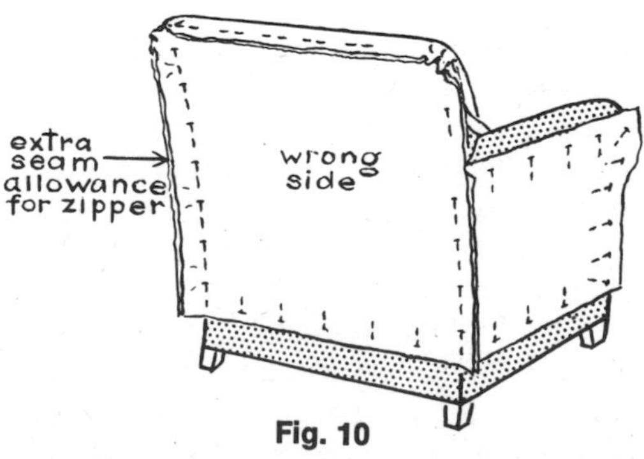

Fig. 10

side border (boxing) from seam to seam (or welting), add seam allowances, and cut a strip long enough to go *halfway* around the cushion plus seam allowance at each end. Before cutting, arrange so that pattern is centered in the front. Cut two more strips like this (needed for inserting zipper) These strips should be cut crosswise on the fabric and may have to be pieced.

Chair. As on the cushion, the final pinning is done exactly on the seamline. If the covering underneath has welting, it can be used as a guide. Start at the center-front border where it meets the platform or seat (Fig. 8). Pick up the fabric on each side of seamline, and pin on the seamline, fitting snugly as you go. Measure from the floor up to the lower edge of border from time to time, as this distance must be kept even for the flounce. You can trim the seams to the desired width as you go, or do it at one time later (see Trimming Seams). Pin across the top of the border along the edge of the seat. Pin the ends of the border to the front arm panel or outside the arm piece if the arm panel stops at the platform.

Keep measuring from the floor up, so lower edge is straight and is the correct distance from the floor.

Pin the seat cover or platform to the inside back (Fig. 9). Line up the tuck-in on the seat with the one on the inside back, and pin along the seamline. Leave the sides until you come to the inside of the arms.

Outside Back. Work from the floor up. Since you know the width of the flounce, you know where the back must end—same as on front border (Fig. 10). Allow for the seam. Find the lower center, and pin to the chair; pull the lower sides taut, and pin to the chair. Smooth up and pin the top edge along the seamline to the inside back. This is a hard edge and anchors the line of the back. Fit and pin the top corners.

Note: If there is a top border and side panel on your chair (see Fig. 11), you are pinning to this, instead of to the inside back. The top border, a straight piece, has been measured and cut accurately with seams allowed; so trim the back and front but not this border.

Fit and pin at the sides to the outside arm

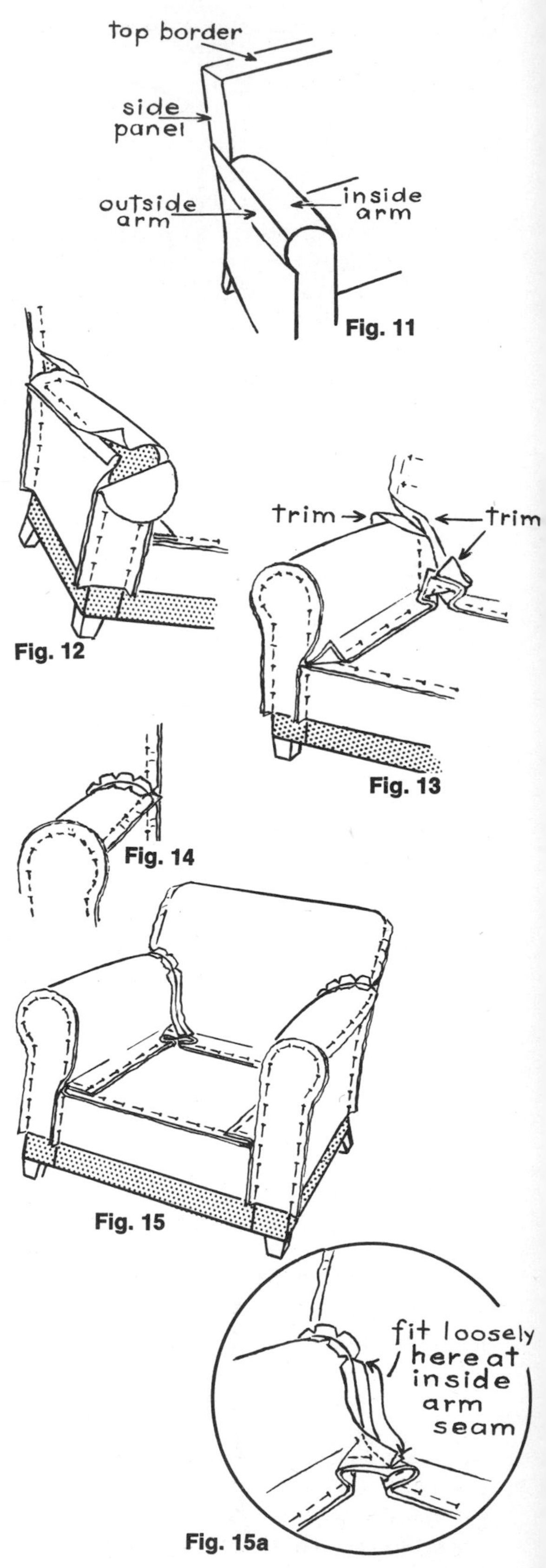

Fig. 11

Fig. 12

Fig. 13

Fig. 14

Fig. 15

Fig. 15a

pieces. Leave a wide seam at the right side for a zipper.

Outside Arm Panel. If the arm of the chair is curved, determine the outermost point of the curve; this is where the outside arm piece starts. Pin along this line to the inside arm panel (Fig. 12). Adjust and pin to the outside back, leaving a wide seam for a zipper on the right side of the chair.

Inside Arm Panel. Smooth the fabric over the arm and down the inside (Fig. 13). Match the tuck-in piece to that of the platform piece. Trim evenly, and pin along the seamline.

Note: On some chairs, because the tuck-in allowance is not needed toward the front, it can be tapered off. On the curve at the back where the arm meets the back of the chair, trim to fit, allowing for the tuck-in. Pin to the inside back. If no tuck-in is needed here (see Fig. 14), pin a curved seam, and clip on curve.

The back corner of the seat is probably the most difficult spot on the chair; this is where side and back tuck-ins meet (Figs. 15 and 15a). Leave plenty of allowance, which is eventually pushed into the corner of the chair, the sides, and the back. This gives "bounce" room and relieves strain on the cover during use.

Front Arm Panel. See Figs. 12, 13, 14, and 15. Keeping the grain of the fabric vertical, pin this section to the outside and the inside arm pieces. If chintz is used, the top of the inside arm piece may be pulled and stretched for a closer fit over the front curve of the arm. Do this while pinning the front arm panel. Not all fabrics will stretch.

The lower inside part of the front arm panel is pinned to the front border unless the border reaches all the way across the front.

Go over the chair carefully to see that everything fits and that you have enough pins in the seams (Fig. 15). They should be quite close together (1″ apart) and run parallel to the seams. Correct any errors.

Trimming Seams

During the final pinning and trimming, there is a great advantage in leaving a seam allowance exactly the width of that on your welting. This means that you can match the

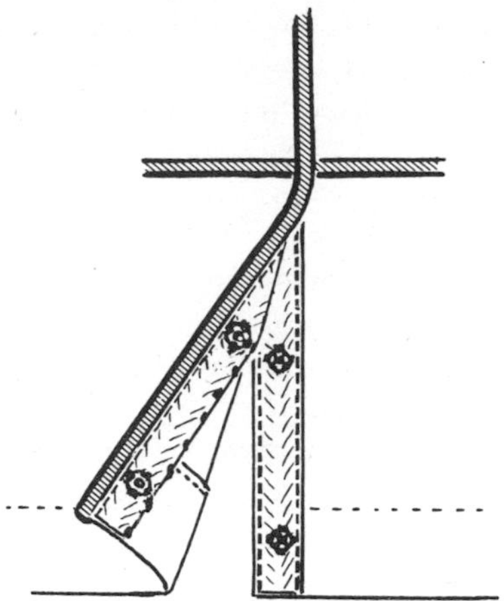

Fig. 16

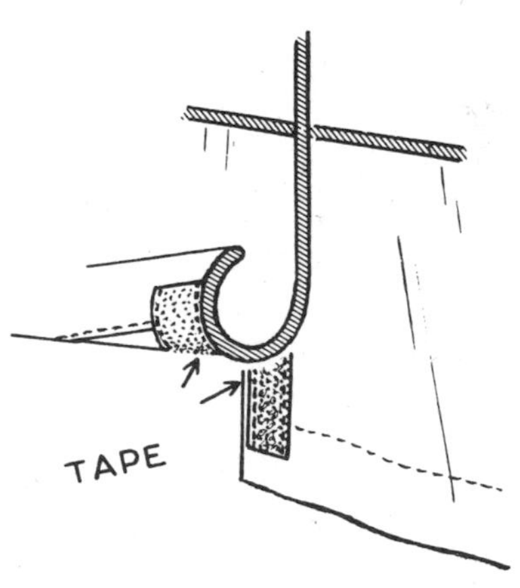

Fig. 16a

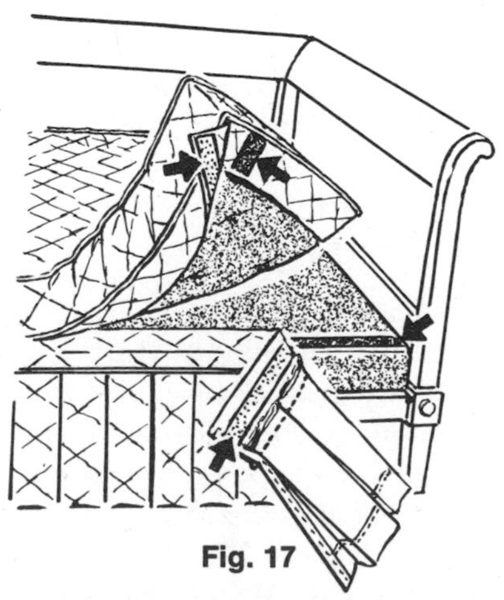

Fig. 17

raw edges of both the welting and the seams as you baste and sew in the welting. If you make your own welting, you yourself can decide the width of the seam (½″ is a good width; many professionals leave only ⅜″ on closely woven fabrics).

If you are using purchased welting, trim the seams of the slipcover to match the welting unless it is very narrow and the slipcover fabric is loosely woven.

The seam at the right side of the back should be trimmed wider than the others. The opening for zipper or snap tape is left here (Fig. 16). Trim this seam 1″ wide or wider, if desired, but mark it on the seamline. The opening should extend several inches above the arm. Zippers for slipcovers come in lengths of 24″, 27″, 30″, and 36.″ Insert the length suitable to your chair (see Inserting Zipper in a Welted Seam, opposite.)

There is a new burred nylon-tape closure which can be used for openings on slipcovers. Separate the strip, and sew the burr side to the top and the cushion side to the bottom (Fig. 16a). This new metal-less closure can also be used to advantage on the chair cushion and in various other ways. (See Fig. 17, which shows a slipcover on a daybed mattress, held at the corners by the tape. The pleated skirt is also held by the tape. It is hand-sewn to the cover of the box spring and to the skirt. A quick rip, and the tape comes apart for removal of the cover.)

Removing and Sewing

Unpin the seams to be used for the zipper opening. Slip off the cover, and stitch all inside seams where there is to be no welting. Baste the welting in the remaining seams, and stitch, using a cording or zipper foot (Fig. 18).

The Flounce

If you have worked carefully per directions, the slipcover will end at the top of the flounce and be even all around. Recheck the distance from the floor all around, and mark with pins or chalk. Cut the flounce 2½″ wider than the distance from floor; this allows ½″ for seam at top and 2″ for hem at bottom. For a gathered flounce, allow twice

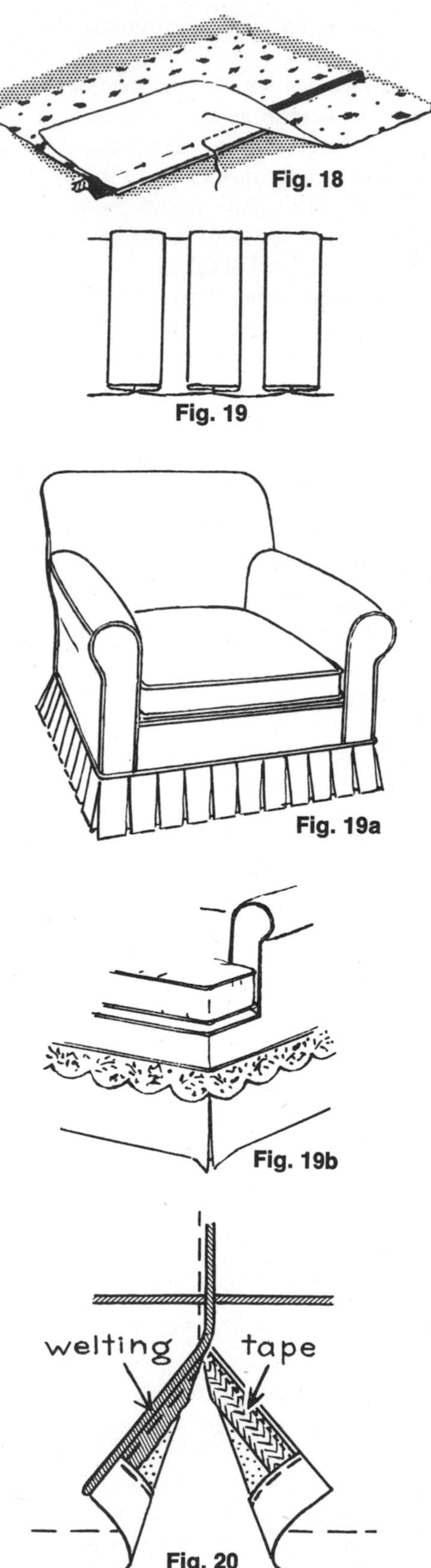

Fig. 18
Fig. 19
Fig. 19a
Fig. 19b
Fig. 20

the length of the distance around the chair, plus seams.

Piece and hem the flounce. If the flounce is to be gathered, measure into eighths, and mark with pins. Mark the lower edge of the slip cover at the center sides, center back and front. Adjust the gathers; start at the back opening, and pin the flounce to the cover, fitting each section (⅛ of the length) into ½ of each side of the cover.

For box pleats, allow 3 times the distance (plus seams). Pleats may be close together or spaced (Fig. 19). If the flounce is box-pleated all around (Fig. 19a), arrange the pleats so the center of a pleat comes in the center front and the others are evenly spaced.

If kick pleats are used (Fig. 22), pin around, making a deep, inverted box pleat at each corner (6″ or 8″ pleat at each side of a corner). Pin and baste in the welting, and stitch.

A decorative overskirt (Fig. 19b) must be lined; cut 2 pieces the wanted depth and the length of the distance around chair. Lay on lining, with right sides together; trace on scallops; stitch; trim; turn; and press. Baste the overskirt to the top of the flounce before attaching it with welting to the slip cover.

To attach the flounce to the cover. On the outside of the slipcover, baste the trimming or welting to the lower edge at the pinned or chalked line, with all raw edges together. Pin the right side of the skirt to the right side of the slip cover, with edges even, and stitch.

Inserting Zipper in a Welted Seam

1. Prepare the opening as follows: Baste and stitch the welting in place on one side, and face the opposite side with twill tape (unless you have left a wide enough seam). Fold the hem of the flounce over the welting and tape (Fig. 20).

2. Pin the welted edge over the zipper tape, with the stitching line close to the zipper teeth and with the tab a little above the hem edge. Fold under the ends of the zipper tape. Baste and stitch on the right side, using cording or zipper foot (Fig. 20a).

3. Pin opposite side to zipper tape so edges of opening meet. Baste, open zipper, and stitch (Fig. 20a).

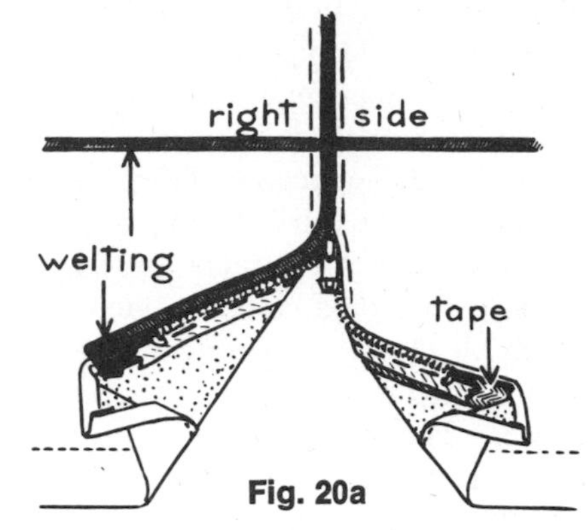

Fig. 20a

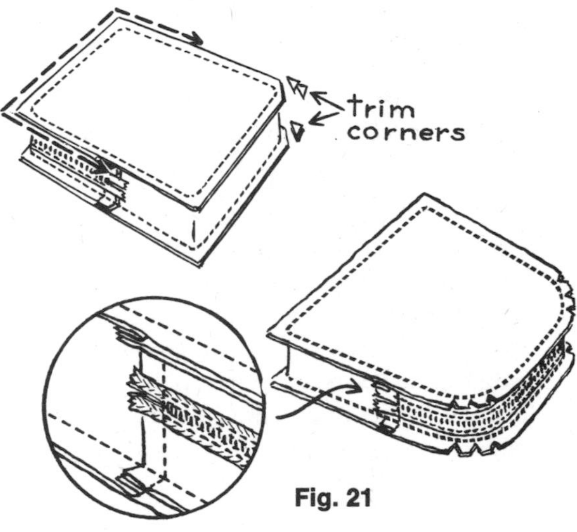

Fig. 21

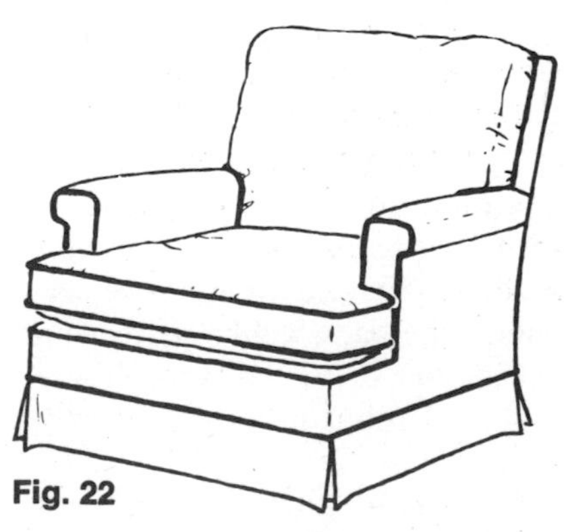
Fig. 22

Cushion

Fold two boxing strips in half lengthwise, and press on the fold. Place so that the folded edges meet with the zipper centered beneath. Pin, baste, and stitch down each side as for slot-seam zipper application (Fig. 21). Attach one end of the third strip to one end of the zipper strip, with the seam on the wrong side; this seam should come at side of cushion. With all the pieces wrong side out, pin the boxing strip to the top and bottom cushion pieces. The ends of the strips should meet on the opposite side of the cushion. Trim to fit, and seam the strip ends together. Remove pins, insert the welting at the top and bottom edges of the cushion, pin, baste, and stitch.

Note: This method can also be used on a round, square, or other cushion shape.

Lounge Chair with Semi-Attached Back Cushion

Many lounge chairs are now made with the back cushion attached to the back of the chair at the top and sides (Fig. 22). Although there is no hard edge at the cushion front, it is treated like a top border and side panel at the top and sides (Fig. 11), with the welting set in on both sides of the boxing panel.

Slipcovering a Sofa

When covering a sofa, a studio couch, or a sectional piece, follow the general procedure given for the lounge chair.

Follow the contour and structure of the sofa (or other piece of furniture) or the lines of the upholstery, cutting and fitting each piece as directed for a lounge chair. On a sofa with 3 cushions, the back will be pieced in 3 sections (Fig. 23). On a love seat with 2 cushions, the back will be pieced in 2 sections (Fig. 24) or, if the fabric has a large motif, place 1 motif in the center and piece it on each side.

For the skirt on a large sofa or chair, the plain box finish with kick pleats at corners is probably most often used. A gathered or all-around pleated skirt is also appropriate, depending on the style of your decor.

There are a number of other suitable and simple skirt or valance finishes and combinations of solid colors and prints.

Federal Sofa

Follow the general instructions for covering a lounge chair.

Stripes are very appropriate for this type of sofa, and care should be taken, when cutting the fabric, to match them (Fig. 24a).

The outside and inside arms meet at the farthest point (on the outside) of the curve as mentioned in connection with covering a lounge chair. Welting is used at this joining.

Since the arms on a Federal sofa have an exaggerated undercurve, fitting the outside of the arm (under the curve) is a problem.

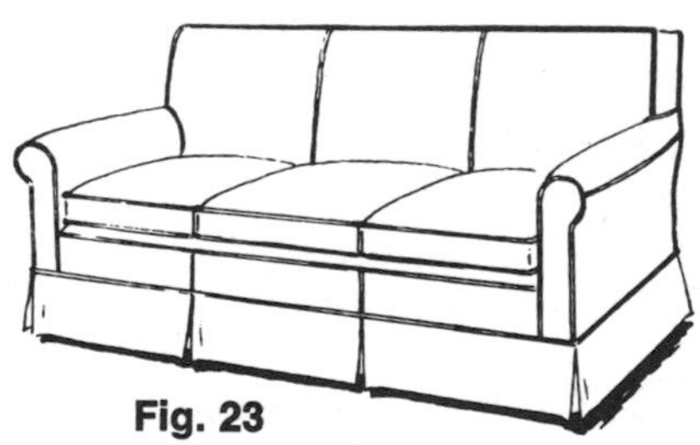

Fig. 23

Fig. 24

Fig. 24a

It should be fitted as closely as possible so it will not fall away from the chair; however, it is not possible to make the slipcover fit as snugly here as upholstery. Don't pin or anchor the arm covering in any way for it may pull and tear when someone is seated on the sofa.

At the lower edge of the border, only welting (no skirt or valance) is the usual finish on this type of sofa. (Finish it all around so that the sofa may be used with the back showing.) A tacking strip is added to keep the welting in place.

This is how it is done, and it may be used on chairs, as well as on sofas. Cut the front border, back, and sides to end at the lowest point of the frame (plus seam allowance). Pin welting along the lower edge. Cut a strip of sateen or of the cover fabric (if it is not too heavy) 3½″ wide and long enough to reach across the front. Also, cut strips for the ends and back. Fold the strips in half lengthwise, right side out. With all raw edges even, pin and stitch on the strip, covering the welting (Fig. 25).

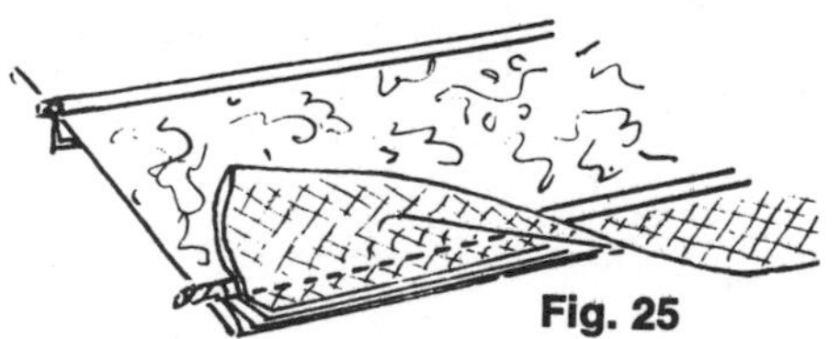

Fig. 25

When the cover is put on the sofa or chair, this strip is pulled to the underside and tacked to the frame (Fig. 25a). If you have cut and fit accurately, the row of welting will be exactly on the lower edge of the frame.

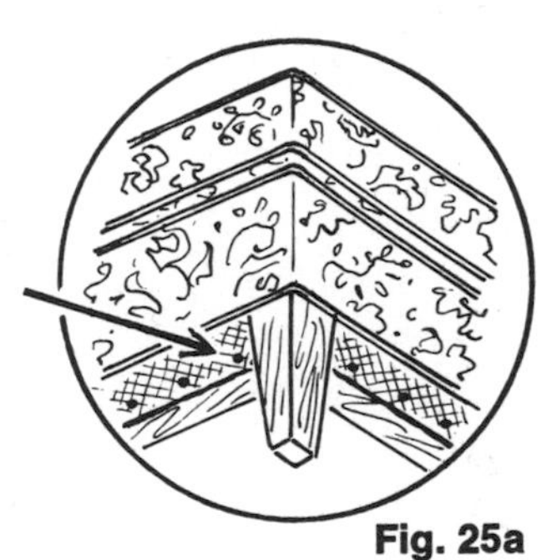

Fig. 25a

Wing Chair

Follow the general instructions for covering a lounge chair with the following changes:

After cutting the inside back of the chair, measure and cut the inside of the wings. Depending on the construction of the chair pieces, these usually stop at the inside arm. Then cut the outside pieces for the wings. This piece is attached to the outside arm and the outside back (Fig. 26).

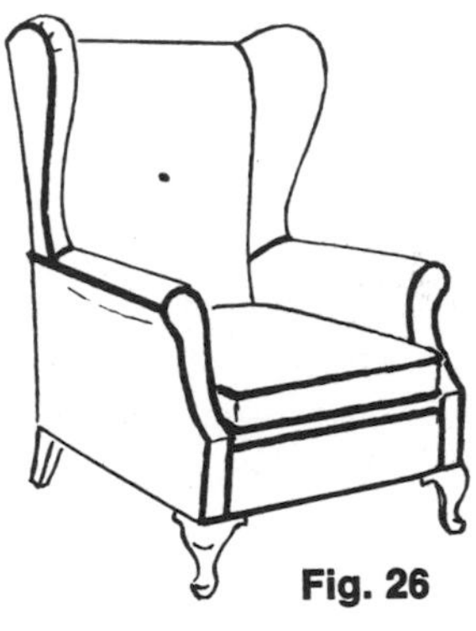

Fig. 26

Small Armchair

To slipcover an occasional chair or a small armchair, follow the general instructions for a lounge chair. Cut the inside and outside back and the seat; cut the side and top panel (boxing) for the back (if needed). Cut the arm pieces; these may be one continuous piece which fits over the arm and snaps un-

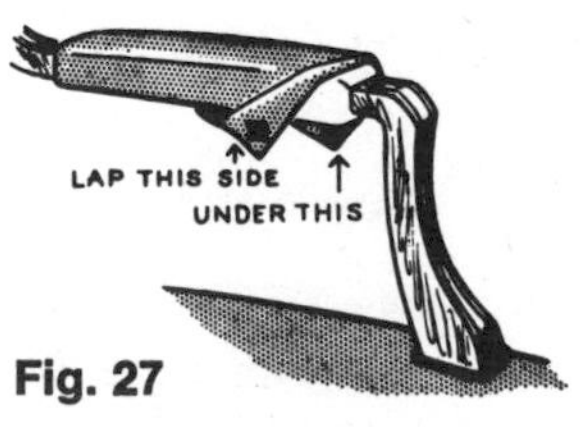

Fig. 27

derneath (Fig. 27). The top may be cut separately and set in with welting as shown on Fig. 27a, where all necessary parts of slip-cover for this style of chair are shown.

Fit and pin the inside and outside back as for a lounge chair. Fit and pin the seat carefully.

For a heavy arm or leg, fold back at each side and slash a V shape, ending about ½″ from the post as shown in Fig. 28. Turn under, and face with or without welting (Figs. 31 and 31a).

To fit around a narrow post, make a straight cut to within about a half inch of the frame (Fig. 29).

To fit a round post, clip a space for the post after making the slit, turn under, and face with bias strip with or without welting (Figs. 30, 30a, 30b).

CUT BORDERS FOR THE SEAT AS FOLLOWS: Cut 1 piece long enough to go across the front and part of the sides and to overlap at the posts. Cut 2 pieces for the sides to overlap the back at the posts. Cut 1 back piece.

Attach to the seat cover with welting between (Fig. 32). Finish the lower edge with welting or deep ruffle as desired, depending on style of chair (Fig. 32a). A short ruffle may be used in place of a border if desired (Fig. 32b). Finish the lapped ends with snap tape fasteners (Fig. 32c).

After fitting and cutting the proper shape for the front and back, the covering for the back is made like a pillowcase with one end left open. A panel or boxing strip may be needed at the sides or at the sides and top if the chair is so constructed as to need it (Fig. 32d). On a straight chair with no arms, this can be 1 continuous piece. If the chair narrows toward the bottom, an opening (about 9″) must be left at one side of the back and a zipper or snap tape fastener inserted. On an armchair, shorter pieces will be needed below the arm opening. These are finished with snap tape (Fig. 32c).

Slipper Chair

Follow the general instructions for making a lounge chair. Since there are no arms, cutting and fitting are simplified. There is no tuck-in, the seat cover is pinned to the inside

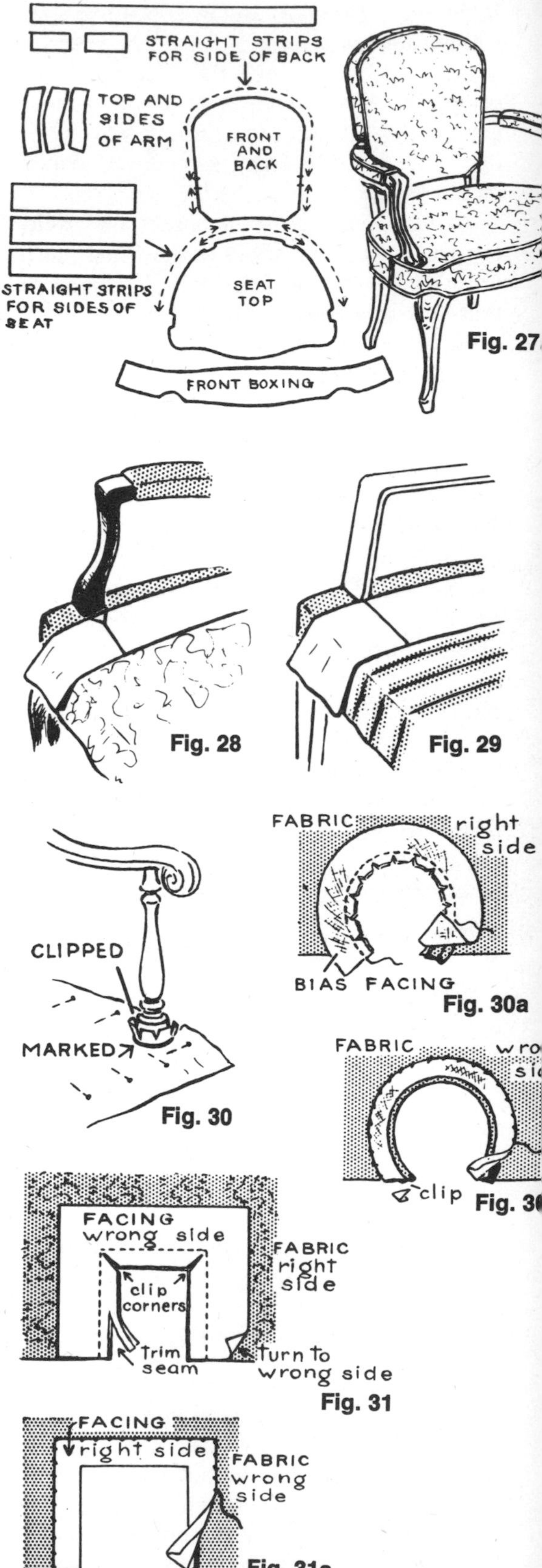

Fig. 27

Fig. 28

Fig. 29

Fig. 30

Fig. 30a

Fig. 30b

Fig. 31

Fig. 31a

back, and the borders and panels are pinned to the seat and the back.

The sewing procedure is same as that used for a lounge chair.

Fig. 32

Fig. 32a

Fig. 32b

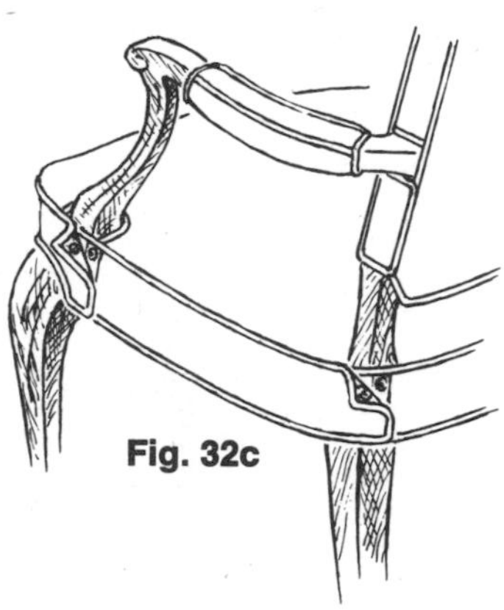

Fig. 32c

Fig. 32d

Slipper Chair with Arm

Small chairs of this type sometimes have arms. These are covered in the usual way. If the style is similar to the pictured chair, it might be advisable, for easy removal, to leave openings and to insert a zipper or snap tape at the curve at the back of the arms on both sides of the chair (Fig. 33).

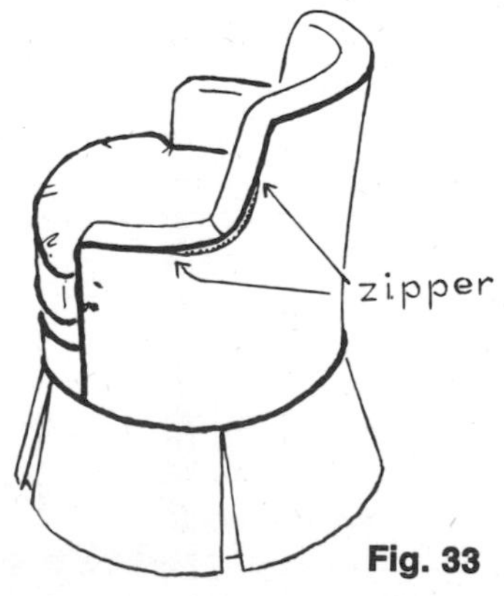

Fig. 33

Slipcovering Sectionals

Slipcovers for sectionals are made in the same way as those for lounge chairs and sofas, the only difference being that no part of the section has two arms (Fig. 34). The open side would be handled as is the front.

Note: If you are plagued by slipping slipcovers, try this: Save the fiber tubes around which waxed paper, paper towels, aluminum foil, etc., are rolled, and push them into the space made by the extra material tucked between the sides and backs and seats of chairs or sofas (Fig. 35). The slipcover will stay in place.

Color Plate 22 shows examples of the kinds of slipcovers and cafe curtains that can easily be made at home.

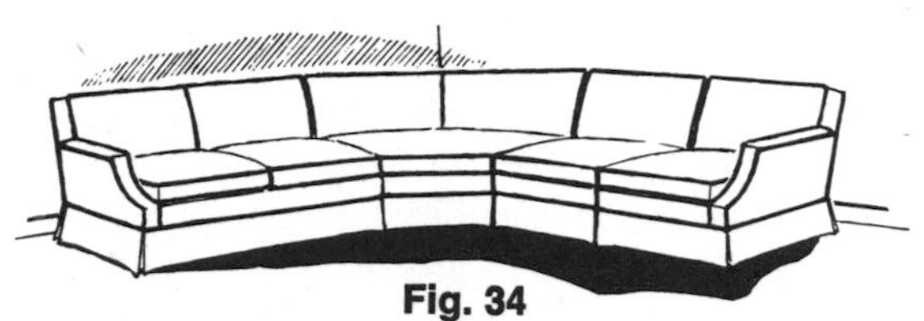

Fig. 34

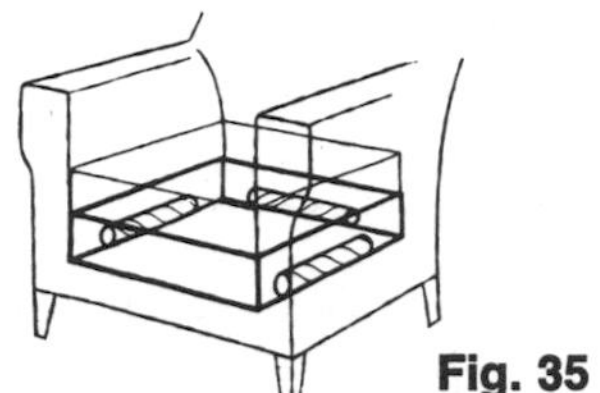

Fig. 35

Yardage Chart

Approximate—consult salesperson for large repeat pattern yardage. Does not allow for gathered or pleated flounces.

Type	CUSHIONS	48" WIDE		36" WIDE		WELTING or TRIMMING
		PLAIN	FIGURED or STRIPED	PLAIN	FIGURED or STRIPED	
Sofa	3	14 yds.	15½ yds.	21 yds.	23 yds.	36 yds.
	I L C	13½	15	20½	22½	33
	0	10	11	15	17	21
Love Seat	2	10	11	15	16½	24
	1	10	11	15	16½	23
	0	8½	9¼	12¾	14¼	14
Arm Chair	1	7½	8¼	11¼	12¼	18
	0	6	6¾	8⅓	9½	13
Boudoir Chair	1	5	5¾	7¾	8¾	15
	0	4½	5¼	6½	7½	12
Wing Chair	1	8	9	12	13½	18
	0	6½	7¼	9¾	10¾	13
Cogswell Chair	1	7	8	10½	12	16
	0	5½	6	8¼	9	11
Daybed and Mattress	3	14½	16	21¾	23¾	42
	0	11	12	17½	19½	27
Daybed	3	11	12	16½	18	29
	0	7½	8¼	11	12¼	14
Ottoman	0	2	2½	3	3½	6
Chaise Lounge	1	10	11	15	16½	23
	0	8	9	12	13¼	16
Dining Room Chair	0	1½	1¾	1⅚	2⅙	5½
Extra Cushion	1	1¼	1¾	1⅚	2⅙	5

LINED DRAPERIES— A SEMI-CUSTOM METHOD

How to Measure

Decide on the length of your draperies. Depending upon your furnishings and decorative scheme, they may begin at the ceiling, top of window, or beneath a cornice and come to the sill, lower edge of apron, or to the floor. The width will be the length of the curtain rod plus the "return" (the part that curves to the wall) plus the overlap, if any. Add to this the wanted fulness and allowance for seams and hems on each panel.

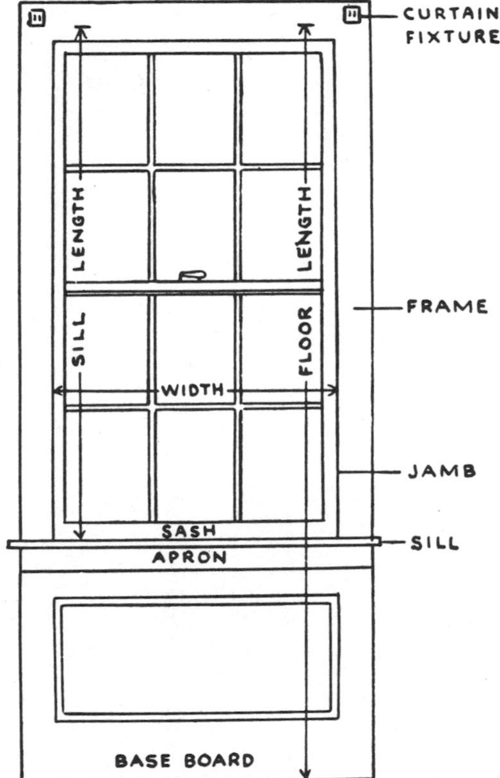

Have the fixtures in place or know where they are to go before measuring. Usually the fixture is placed so the heading of the drapery covers the frame of the window at the top. Also the top of drapery or heading should cover the metal part of the fixture. It is well to measure each window separately as they may vary slightly.

Hem allowances vary with the type of fabric and length of drapery. Allow 4″ for top hem and 8″ for a 4″ double hem at bottom on each panel (3″ at top and a 3″ double hem at bottom will do if draperies are not long and heavy). On very long panels, 5″ to 10″ double hems at the bottom are more suitable. The top hem is not usually wider than 4″.

Draperies as a rule are made with 100% fulness; that is, twice the width of the space they are to cover. If fabric is sheer, 150% is better (3 times the width).

Linings

Linings are used to give more body to draperies and cause them to hang better. They also protect from dust and sunlight which cause wear and fading. Cream or beige is a good choice although stronger colors are sometimes suitable. On draperies with a white background, to be used where light will come through, a white lining is desirable so the colors will be clearer.

You will not need as much lining as drapery fabric since each lining piece is cut approximately 9″ shorter than the outside panel (depending upon width of hem).

Cutting

Since no housewife is likely to have a table large enough to accommodate a length of drapery, the best place to cut is on the floor. If the fabric is a plain color or has a woven pattern, straighten ends by pulling a thread and stretch into shape (see Fabric Preparation in Sewing section, page 8). If the fabric is printed, cut without pulling threads; cut by pattern, not by weave.

On short draperies, if you are using a repeat pattern arrange it so that a motif will come above the hem. It does not matter what happens to the pattern at the top because of the fulness. On long draperies, arrange for a full motif at the top since a part motif near the floor will not be so noticeable. When cutting the panels, be sure that the motif placement is the same on every panel. Cut off selvage edges. After cutting one panel, use it for measuring the others. Lay it on the fabric and match the design carefully before cutting. If there is an up and down to the design, be sure it runs in the same direction on all panels.

Hemming

Make a 2″ machine hem at bottom of lining, press, and lay aside.

Hem lower edge of panels with a 4″ double hem as follows: Turn 8″ to wrong side at lower edge of drapery panel and press on fold. Bring the raw edge back to the pressed fold and press again on the new fold. Pick up double hem and turn again on the first fold and pin. This makes a 4″ double hem. Pin, press, and blind-hem by hand or machine (some machines do blind-hemming).

Note: On side panel draperies the front edge and outside edge are made differently because the outside edge on a side panel usually ends against the wall (due to the "return" on the rod) and does not show. Very often a ring is sewed to the top and lower corner of the outside panel and this slips over a hook on the baseboard or wall to hold the drapery in place.

Front Edge Hem. To make front edge on panel, place right sides together and edges even on one long side, lay the lining to the panel so that hem of lining comes 2″ above lower edge of hemmed panel. Top edges will not meet. Pin a 1¼″ seam down the side and stitch by machine.

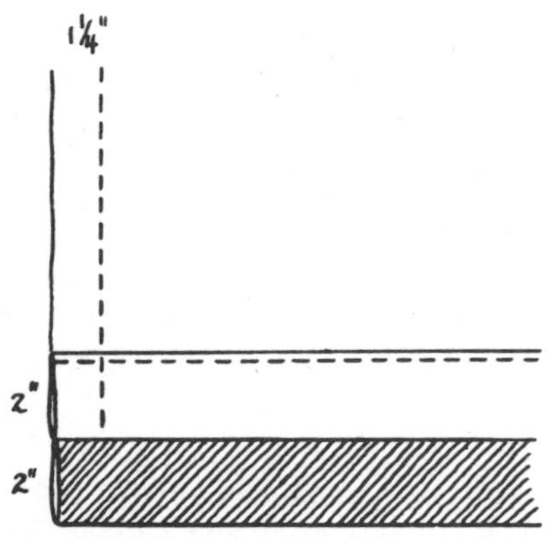

Open out lining and press this wide seam toward the center of the panel.

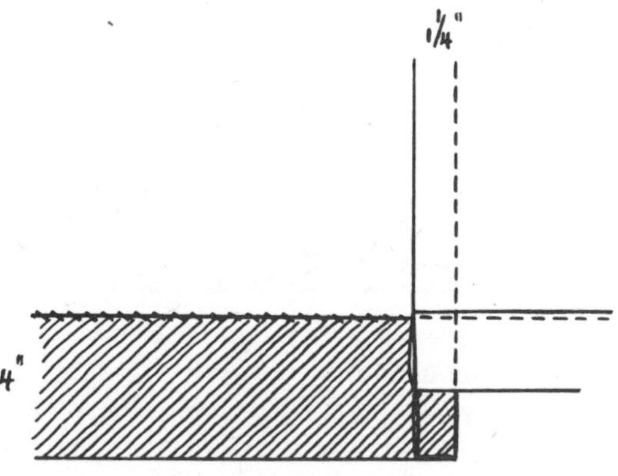

Fold lining into position, turning far enough so outside fabric shows 1¼″. Seam should lie inside this edge. Press and pin along seam.

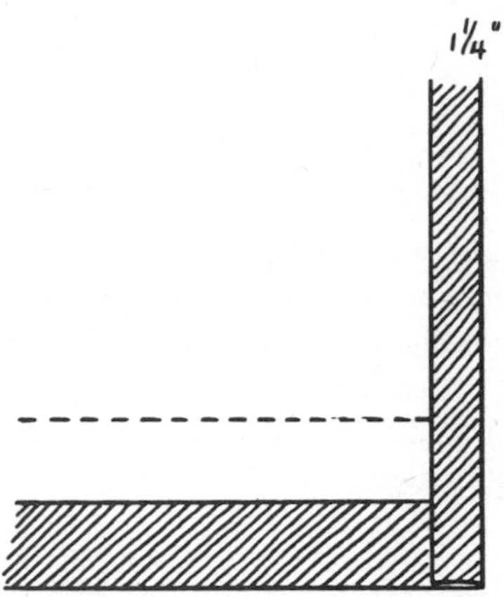

Top Hem. Turn top of panel 4″ to wrong side and press. Cut a piece of 4″ wide crinoline (permanent finish) long enough to reach across top of panel plus 1″. Turn under 1″ at one end and press. With this end at the seamed side, slip crinoline under the 4″ top hem and press. The crinoline is "tacky" and will cling to most fabrics.

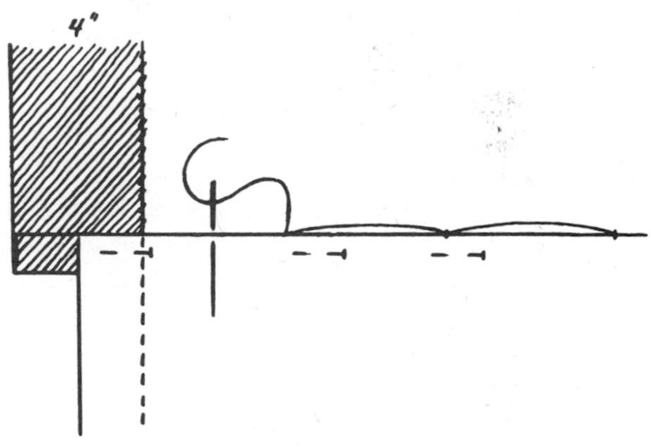

Working Again on Side Edge of Panel. Fold lining back (wrong side out) to the seam. Tack the lining the full length of the outside seam edge with long stitches and needle pointed toward you as shown. Pick up a few threads only of outside fabric on needle. Stitches should not show on outside.

Weighting Lower Hem. Slip a covered weight inside lower hem of the panel at the corner and tack with a few stitches through the center.

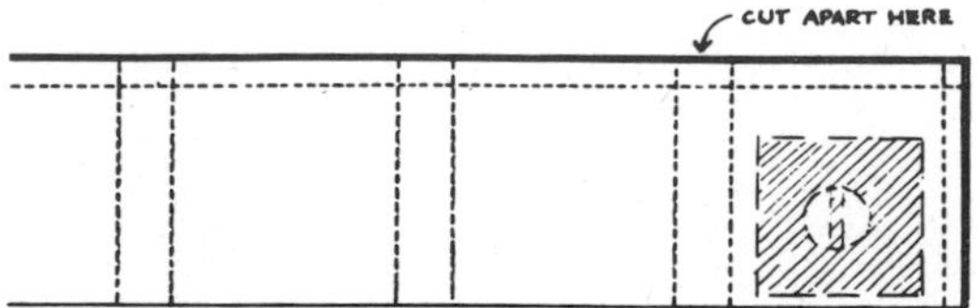

To cover weights. Cut a piece of muslin wide enough to fold double and seam, and enclose weights in it. Stitch a pocket for each weight, stitching 2 rows between pockets with space for cutting apart. Slip in weights and stitch along top of pockets. Cut apart.

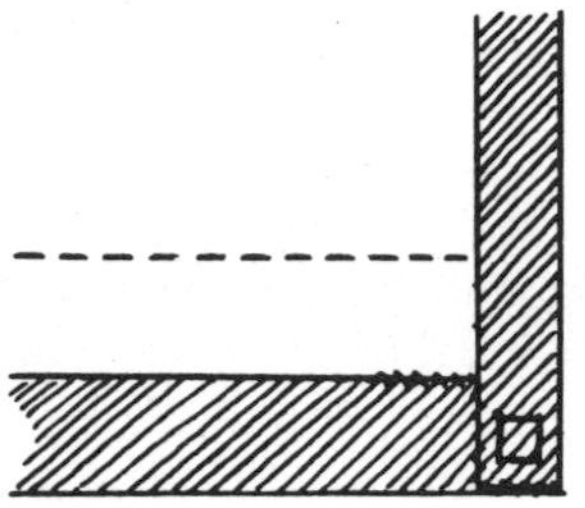

Fold lining back to wrong side. Hand-hem open edges of corner and also hem edge of lining for about 1½″.

At top of lining press seam allowance to wrong side. If measuring has been accurate, top of lining and panel will match. Turn and press 1¼″ seam allowance to wrong side on remaining long side of panel.

Note: On wide panels where more than one width of fabric has been used, fold lining back at piecing seams and tack the full length of the seam with long stitches as done on front edge. Also, insert a weight in the lower hem at each seam.

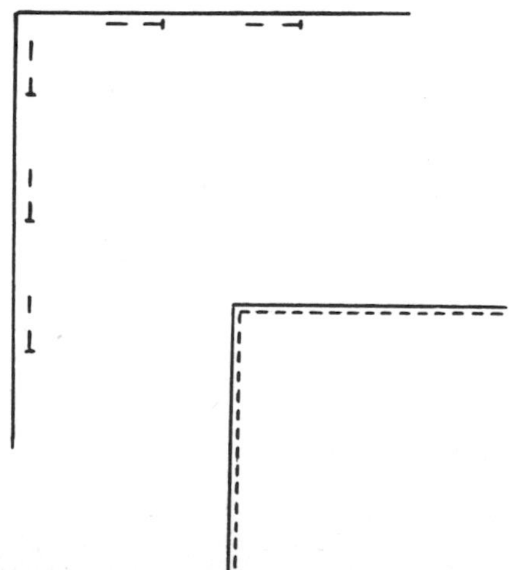

Fold lining to wrong side and smooth out. Pin across top, keeping folded edge of lining even with top of panel hem. Pin down side, turning in edge of lining even with turned edge of panel.

Edge-stitch across top and down side. This is the outside edge of the panel and goes against the wall. Make another panel with sides reversed so there will be a right and a left hand panel. If desired, instead of machine stitching, the top edges may be secured with blind-hemming done by hand for a finish which looks more custom-made.

Note: If the panel is to be used in the center instead of at the side, both sides are finished to look like the front edge with a 1¼″ of the outside fabric turned to the wrong side.

Proceed in this fashion:

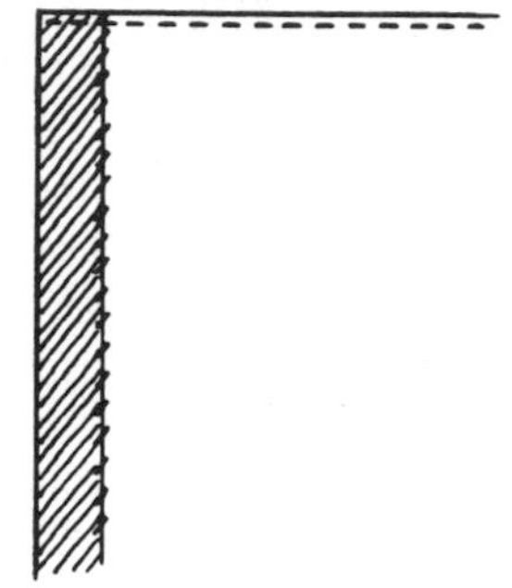

When ready to finish the last side, turn raw edges of both lining and outside fabric to wrong side 1¼″ and press. Pin folded edges together. Turn this whole edge to the wrong side 1¼″. Pin and slip-stitch by hand, catching both edges.

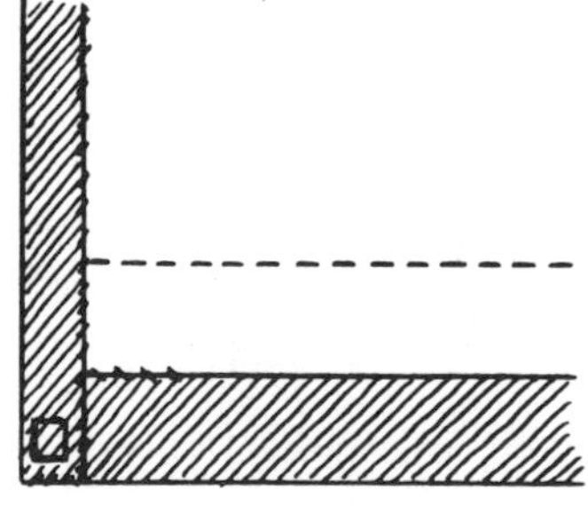

Finish lower corner like the first with weight and hemming of corner. Panels are now ready for pinch pleats or other finish at top.

Pleats

Pinch Pleats. Measure the panel and arrange to have pleats approximately 4″ apart and 4″ in from each side. Allow four inches for each pleat.

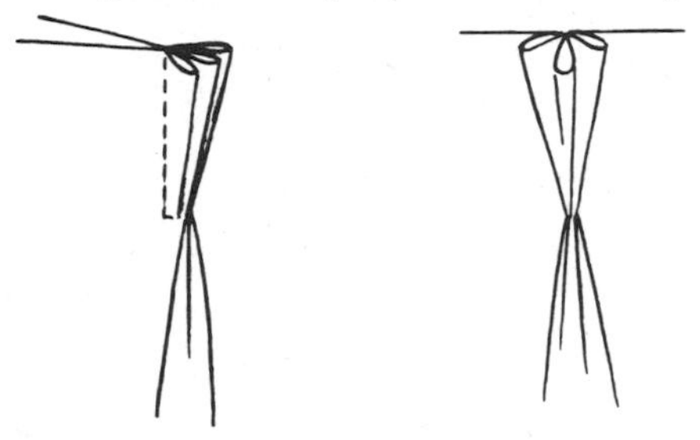

Fold the pleat and stitch 2″ from the fold to the depth desired (width of crinoline).

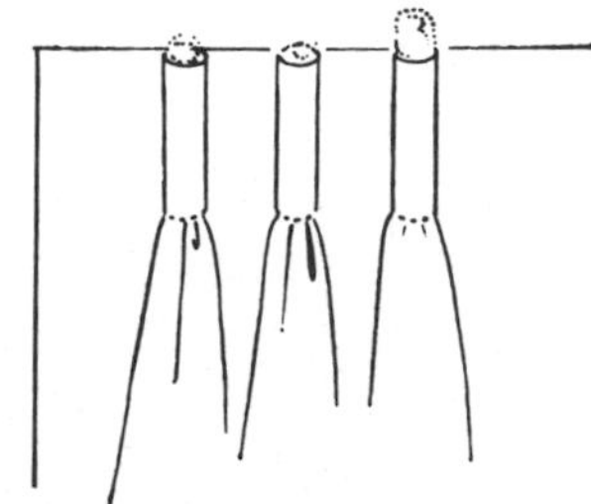

Divide each pleat evenly into 3 small pleats at the lower end of the stitching and stitch across by machine or sew by hand to hold securely.

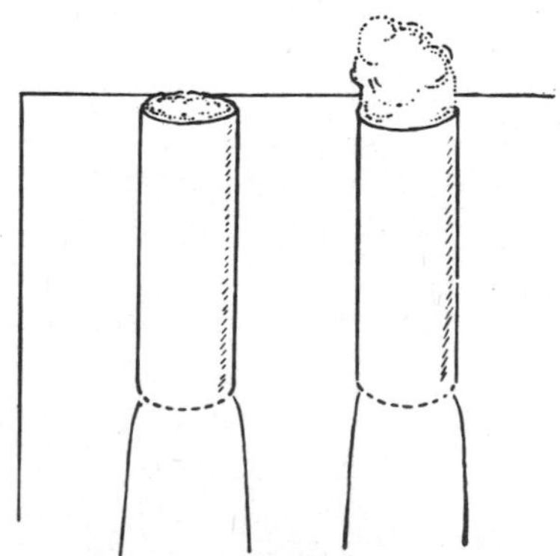

Cartridge Pleats. Make smaller pleats (stitch about 1″ from fold) and stuff with cotton or cord. They can be made extra large for long heavy draperies.

Insert drapery pins on back of panels on pleat seams and at each end. Place pins so that panel covers rod.

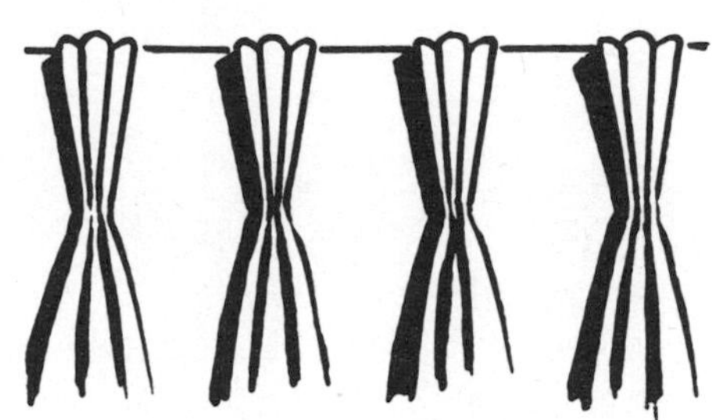

Pinch pleats may be made in a great variety of sizes and spacings. They may be made extra deep and closely spaced.

Or widely spaced and shallow.

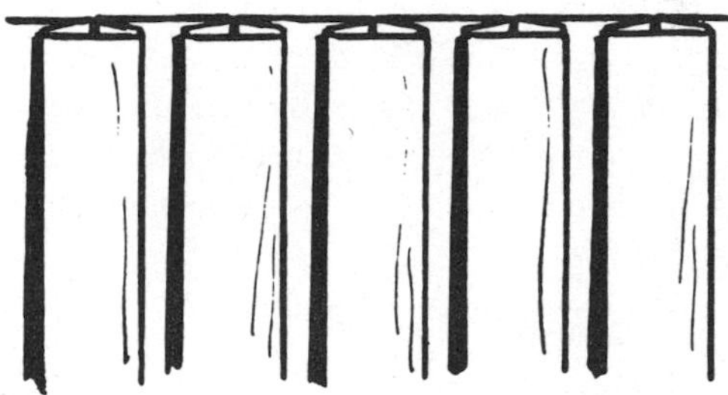

In place of pinch pleats, box pleats are sometimes used. Fold and stitch the pleat (see first step of pinch pleat), then press flat with seam down the center. These may also be made in any size desired.

An example of the handsome draperies that may be made at home is shown in Color Plate 23.

CAFE CURTAINS

Cafe curtains are now used on practically every type of window. They may be long or short, formal or informal, depending upon the fabric used, and almost any type of fabric *can* be used. It must be remembered that on cafe curtains the rod is exposed, and this must be taken into consideration in the final effect. Brass rods and black rods are available, or the rod can be painted to match the woodwork if there is not too much wear on it. Buy good quality rods that will not sag.

Cafe curtains may have scallops or V-points at the top with rings or clips for hanging, or they may be made straight across with straps, pinch pleats, or shirring.

Sometimes they appear on one-half the window only, and sometimes 2 or 3 tiers will cover the window. There are many variations and arrangements.

Cafe curtains are easily made and have many possibilities for decorative effects.

Several ways of finishing the tops are given here.

General Directions

Width. The width of the curtain should be at least twice the width of the window and may be fuller.

Length. Where straps or rings are used the curtain starts just below the rod. Some finishes require a facing and others do not. Allow 3″ for over-lap and 2½″ to 3″ for lower hem.

Scalloped Top No. 1

This makes its own loop.

1. Measure and cut panels the required length, allowing 6″ for top facing, plus 2″ to 3½″ for lower hem.

2. Make narrow hems on the side edges (see step No. 6 for panels wider than 35″).

3. Turn top edge ¼″ to wrong side and stitch.

4. Fold top edge 4″ to the right side. Pin and press.

5. For a finished 35″ panel use a 6″

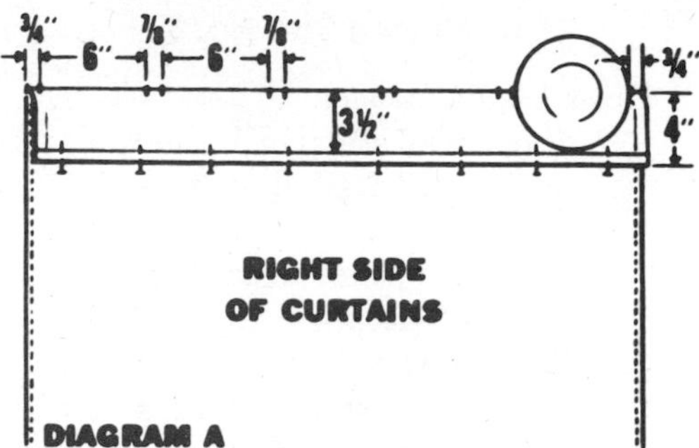

saucer or plate and mark as shown.

6. On wider panels continue across in same way, leaving 1¼″ beyond last scallop and trim off excess. Hem side edge.

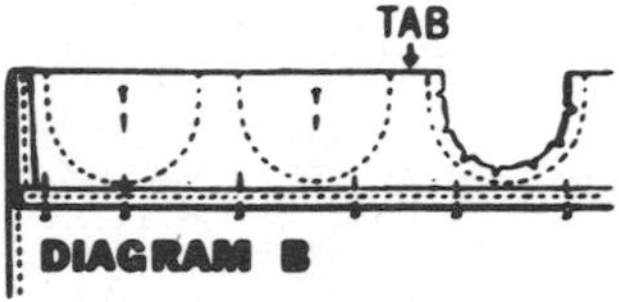

7. After marking scallops, pin near fold. Stitch scallops on marked line. Cut ¼″ away from stitching and clip on curves.

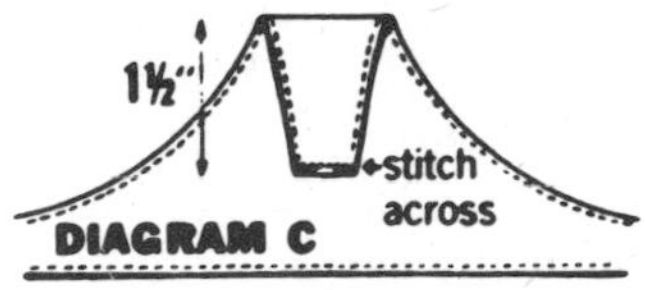

8. Turn to right side, pulling out corners sharply. Top-stitch along edge.

9. Fold tabs 1½″ to wrong side to form a loop and stitch end of tab.

10. Hem panel.

Scalloped Top No. 2

Follow directions for Scalloped Top No. 1 through step no. 8. Then, instead of folding the tab over and stitching to make a loop, attach metal clips at top of each one. This makes a deeper scallop suitable for a longer panel.

Scalloped Top No. 3

This is without facing.

1. Measure and cut panels, allowing ½″ at top and hem of desired width at bottom. Hem the sides.

2. Using a 6″ plate or cardboard circle, mark scallops 2″ deep leaving 1¼″ between scallops and at ends.

3. Turn a ¼″ hem to wrong side along scalloped edge and baste, being careful not to stretch fabric on curves. Clip curves before turning if necessary.

4. Pin medium-sized rickrack on top of hem and stitch down center of rickrack.

5. Sew plastic or metal rings at points.

Note: This may be made *with* facing by cutting panels 4″ longer, then turn ¼″ to wrong side and stitch. Turn 3¾″ to right side before measuring with plate. Stitch on curved lines, cut ¼″ away. Clip on curves and turn.

V-Point Tops

1. Measure and cut curtains, allowing for ¼″ seam at top and for hem at bottom (desired width). Hem the sides.

2. Turn top edge ¼″ to right side and baste without stretching.

3. Pin narrow fancy braid over turned edge and stitch on both edges of the braid. Pin metallic rickrack (gold or silver) just below the braid and stitch down center. Use metal clip-on rings at points.

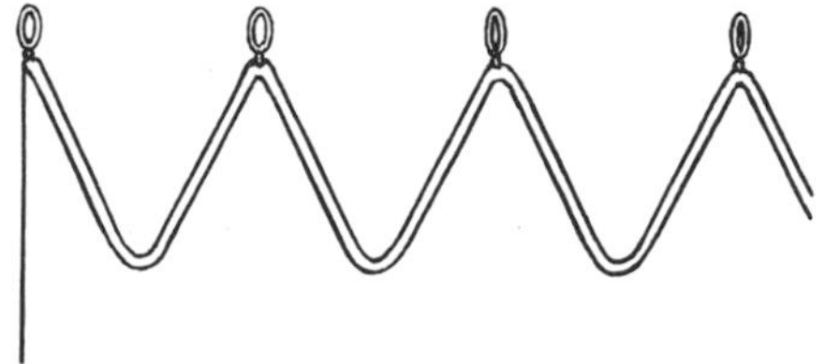

Straight Top with Straps

1. Measure and cut curtains, allowing ¼″ seam at top and desired hem at bottom.

2. Strips for making straps can all be cut and sewed at the same time. Allow about 3½″ for each strap (depending upon length

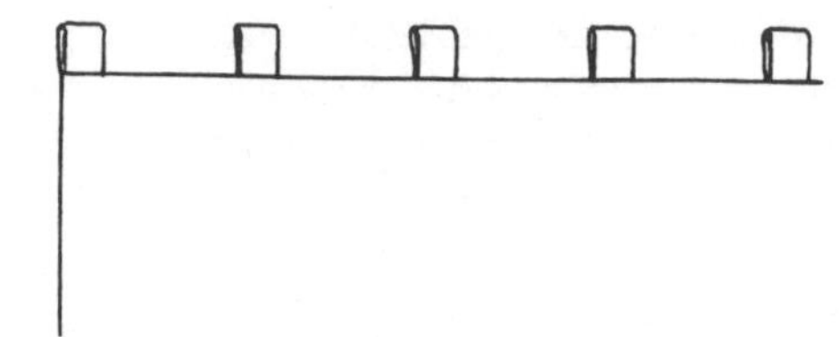

desired and size of rod). Cut strips 2½″ wide unless curtains are long and heavy, in which case they should be wider.

3. Fold strip down the center right side out. Turn raw edges ¼″ to inside and baste together, edges even. Match grain when basting or strip will buckle. Edge-stitch on both sides of the strip. Pin sample length to the curtain and try over the rod before cutting into lengths. Adjust as necessary before marking off and cutting remaining straps.

4. Turn top edge of curtain ¼″ to wrong side and press. Fold strips in half and pin to wrong side of curtain (3″ to 4″ apart), matching raw edges to those of curtain top. Have a strap at each end of panel. Cover raw edges with bias-fold tape, with edge of tape even with top of curtain. Turn in ends of tape. Stitch on both edges of bias.

Or pin straps on right side of curtain with raw edges even with raw edge of top. Face with 3″ wide piece of the fabric (cut on same grain as the curtain). Turn edge of facing and stitch; then blind-hem to curtain.

Ready-Scalloped Pleater Tape

There is available a ready-scalloped tape with "pockets" for hooks which makes scalloped cafe curtains with pinch pleats. This is done easily and quickly with no measuring and marking for scallops necessary.

Cut the tape to fit the top of the curtain being sure it is centered between the sides. Mark at ends and make side hems.

The right side of the tape is the one where the little pockets have an opening at the lower end (the end opposite the scallops).

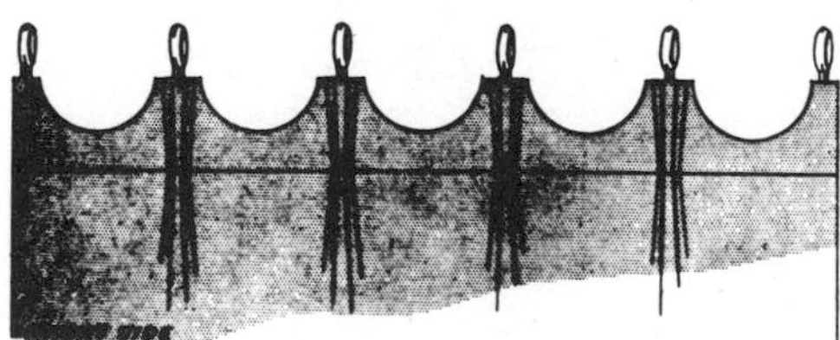

Lay wrong side of tape to right side of fabric, edges even with scallops at the top. Stitch across top and around scallops. Trim, clip curves, and turn to wrong side. Turn edges neatly and press. Turn under ends of tape ¼″. Sew across bottom of tape on woven line.

Insert ring pleaters and ring end hooks.

AUSTRIAN SHADES

The elegant and graceful Austrian shade has come back into favor. This lovely window treatment is not too difficult to make if shirring tape, available at trimming counters, is used and directions are followed carefully.

The shades are made by sewing long strips together; the shirring is done at the seam line and on the outside edges. In order for the shades to hang properly the strips must be tapered in width, being slightly narrower at the top than at the bottom.

There is no rule about the width of the strips but they average from 8″ to 12″. They may, of course, be narrower than this and would quite probably be wider on a shade used on a large picture window. The desired effect is the guide. On a 36″ wide shade, 3 strips would be sufficient to look well.

To measure and cut:

1. Measure the desired width of the finished shade.

2. Measure the desired length of the finished shade.

3. Decide how many strips (shirred spaces) you wish and divide the spaces to determine how wide each finished panel will be.

4. Each panel is cut 3 times the length of the finished shade.

5. Each outside panel is cut 4½″ wider than its finished width.

6. Each inside panel is cut 2½″ wider than its finished width.

Cut the panels, centering on grain, and then trim each panel so that it tapers and is 1½″ narrower at the top than at the bottom (take ¾″ off each side so panel will remain centered on grain).

Sewing Austrian Shades

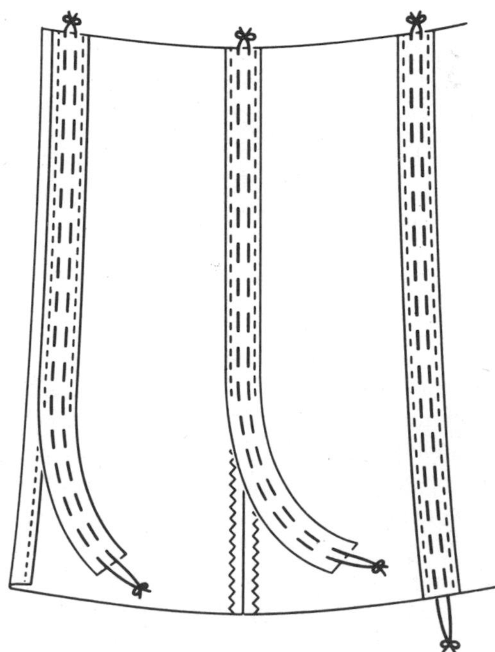

1. Stitch strips together lengthwise with ½″ seams, keeping narrow ends at top. Press seams open.

2. Cut shirring tape 4″ longer than seams. Baste and edge-stitch shirring tape centered over seam on wrong side leaving 2″ extending at top and bottom. Pull out cords a little inside edges of shade and knot at top and bottom. Trim ends of tape.

3. On outside strips turn 1″ to wrong side and stitch. Baste and stitch shirring tape ¾″ from edge, covering raw edge of hem.

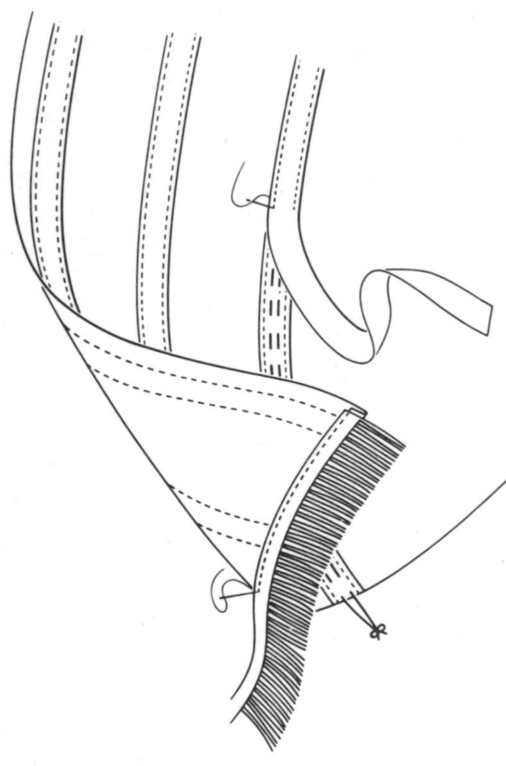

4. Sew a narrow facing over each length of shirring tape on the wrong side. Turn bottom edge of shade ⅜″ to right side (leaving knotted cords free) and finish with 2″ matching or contrasting fringe. A chainette fringe is the most authentic but other types are used. Small tassels may be attached at ends of shirring tapes.

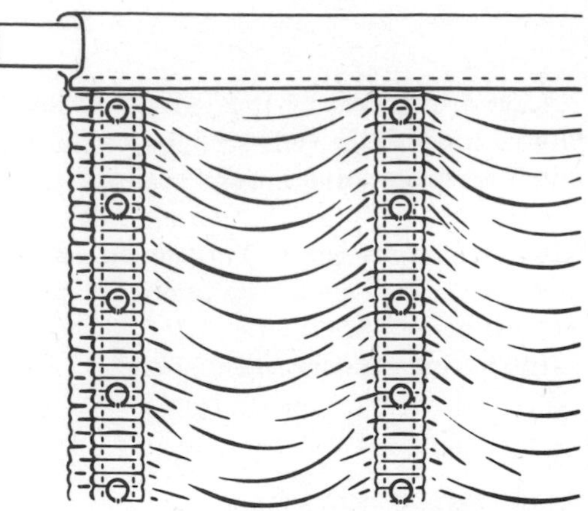

5. Make a fabric extension at top of shade as follows:

Cut a strip 3″ wide and as long as the width of the shade plus 2″ for end hems.

Turn 1″ at each end and hem. Right sides together, stitch extension along top edge of shade. Turn to wrong side, turn under raw edge and stitch over seam and knotted cord ends. Insert ½″ wide flat strip of wood in the finished hem. On windows wider than 36″, this strip must be heavier (and fabric extension wider) or shade will sag.

(If shade fabric is very sheer this piece should be of stronger material such as sateen.)

6. Pull up cords of shirring tape from the bottom, until shade is the desired length. Knot cords firmly and cut off ends.

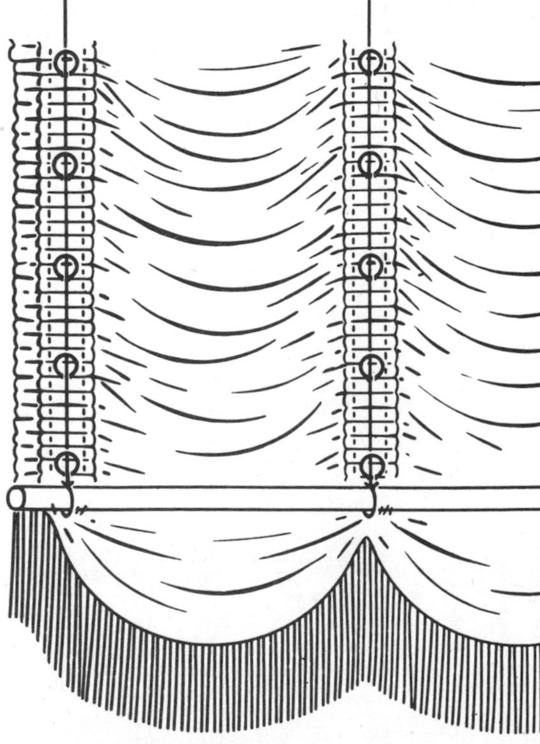

7. Sew small plastic rings about 3″ apart on wrong side of each shirring row from top to bottom. Space them so one will come close to each end.

8. Cut a ¼″ brass rod the finished width of the shade and cover as follows:

Cut a strip of firm material 2″ longer than rod and 2″ wide. Seam lengthwise with ½″ seam. Turn right side out and insert rod. Turn in ends and finish by hand.

Pin covered rod at bottom of shade at shirring strips on the wrong side.

Tie one end of long lengths of No. 3 traverse cord firmly to rod at center of each shirring strip. Sew casing of rod firmly to each shirring strip where pinned.

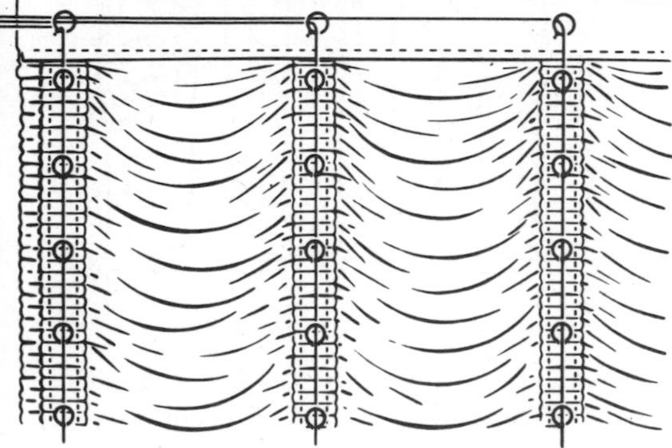

Fasten small screw-eyes to back of wooden strip at top of shade at center of each shirring strip. Carry traverse cords from rod at bottom up through screw-eyes at top. Carry all cords to right of window.

Attach shade to inside top of window frame with angle irons. Thread cords through eye-screw attached at upper right hand corner of window.

Pull and adjust cords until curtain rises and lowers evenly. Knot cords together and finish with heavy tassel.

SHEER CURTAINS

Sheer fabrics are no longer reserved for glass curtains, sash and casement curtains, or cottage and ruffled curtains.

Many decorative treatments now call for long sheer curtains with no other drapery, in which case decorative headings are permissible. On curtains used with draperies, the top is finished with a simple hem or casing with heading. They are usually made to draw, although this depends upon where they are used. They are, of course, made quite full —at least double and sometimes triple the width of the space they cover.

They are treated at the top somewhat like lined draperies although, since they are not lined, the method of finishing is different.

This is the general procedure for long sheer curtains of the draw type:

1. Plan for 3″, 4″, or 5″ double hem at the top; 4″ double hem at the bottom. The inside edges should have 1¼″ double hems, the outside edges should have ½″ double hems.

2. Trim off selvage and make side hems.

3. Make bottom hem. See Draperies, Hemmings, page 452, for directions on how to make a double hem.

4. Make top hem by inserting thin crinoline the full width of the hem on the first fold. Press, fold again, and stitch.

5. Make pinch pleats and use drapery hooks as on draperies.

Sheer curtains on large windows may also be made with shirred heading.

For glass, sash, and casement curtains several things must be kept in mind.

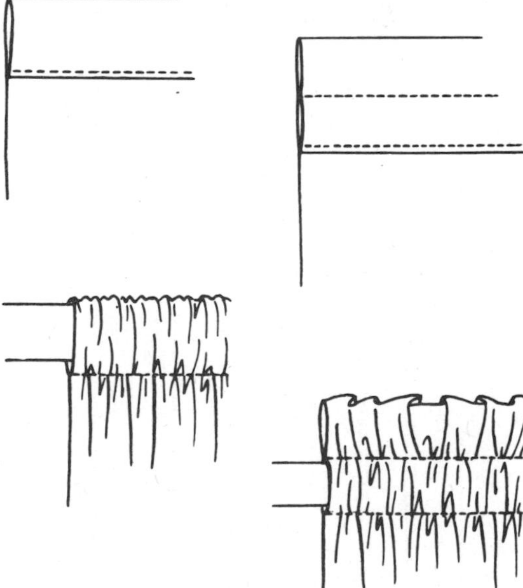

1. The size of the rod determines the width of the top hem. It must allow the rod to slide in and out easily.

2. Either a simple casing or a casing plus heading may be used.

3. A 1″ to 1¼″ (finished) heading is usually sufficient.

Note: A heading which is too wide on a sheer fabric will not stand up unless interfacing is used.

4. A ½″ wide rod will need a 1″ wide casing (finished). A 1″ wide rod will need a 1½″ wide casing. Round rods take a somewhat wider casing than flat ones.

5. Side hems are made first. One inch is a good width. This is stitched by machine.

6. The bottom hem is made next. 2½″, 3″, or 4″ double hems are used according to length of the curtains. Use a 4″ double hem on long curtains. They may be stitched by machine or by hand.

7. The top hems are made last. Turn under ½″ and press; then turn the hem, baste, stitch, and press. Stitch the casing line (if you have planned for a heading) above the hem line. Leave ends open for inserting rods.

8. Work on one pair of curtains at a time measuring them against each other for length, width of hems, etc.

Other Kinds of Curtains

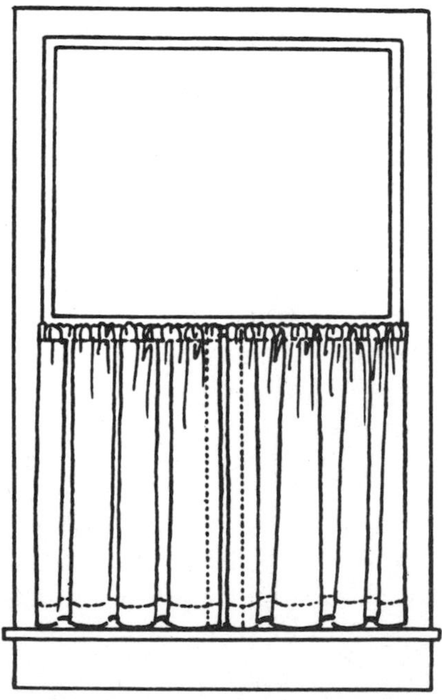

Sash, casement, cottage, and ruffled curtains are made in a manner similar to that of making glass curtains.

Sash curtains cover the lower half of the window only and end at the sill.

Cottage or Dutch curtains are a combination of sash curtains and short curtains which may or not be trimmed with ruffles. The lower section may be drawn and the upper be left open to admit light.

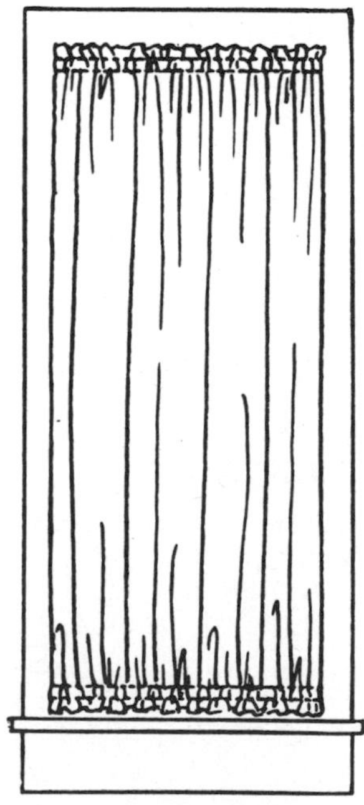

Casement curtains are for windows which swing in and out instead of up and down. They may be attached to the windows with a rod at top and bottom or be hung in some other manner. It is well to investigate new types of curtain hardware.

Ruffled curtains usually end at apron or floor. There is no hem at the bottom as the ruffle extends down the inside edge and across the bottom. Ruffles are usually 3″ or 4″ wide and 1½ times the combined length of the area of application to allow for fulness.

A ruffled valance may be used on a separate rod, or a ruffle may be sewed to the curtain at the lower edge of the casing. It should be the same width as the ruffles on the curtain.

Ruffled curtains may cross at the top, in which case two rods are used and the curtains are made extra wide and quite full. These are known as Priscilla curtains.

Printed fabrics may also be used for curtains made with casing or casing plus heading.

COLLECTION OF PILLOWS

Quilted Pillow

Materials. ⅝ yd. 48″ Shantung or other decorator fabric. Heavy-duty Thread to match. 12 ounces Kapok for stuffing.

Cutting. Cut two 20″ squares from fabric.

To Make. Place front to back, right sides together, pin and stitch ½″ seam around four sides, leaving 5″ opening for stuffing at center of last side. Turn right side out.

Measure in 5½″ from each side, and mark (lightly) to form center square. Machine-stitch square on three sides and part of fourth, leaving opening to correspond to opening on outside edge.

Stuff center square, firmly but not hard. Stitch opening by machine. Stuff outer square all around pillow. Slip-stitch opening by hand.

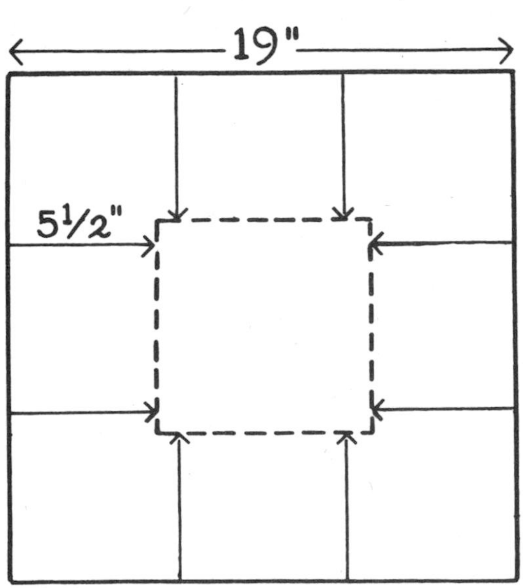

Tufted Pillow

Materials. ⅞ yd. 48″ wide Silk Shantung or other decorator fabric. Heavy-duty Thread to match. 2¼ yds. ¼″ wide Cording. 24 ⅝″ diameter Button Molds. 16 ozs. Kapok for stuffing. Carpet thread. Darning Needle.

Cutting. Cut two 21″ squares from fabric. Cut 1½″ wide bias strips from remaining fabric; piece to make strip 85″ long. Use remaining fabric to cover buttons.

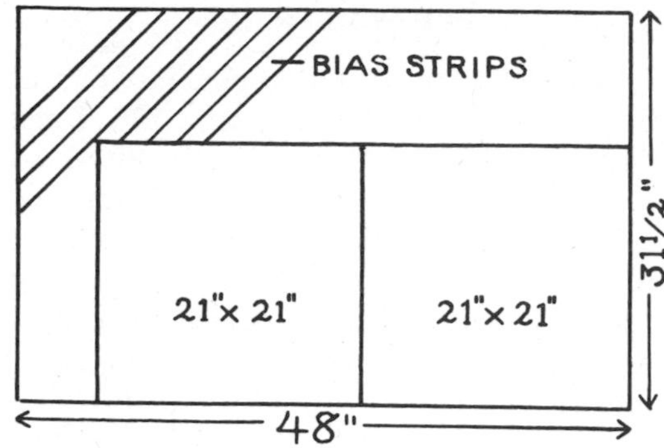

To Make. CORDING: Fold bias strip in half lengthwise, wrong sides together. Insert cord close to fold, and stitch (use cording foot) close to cord.

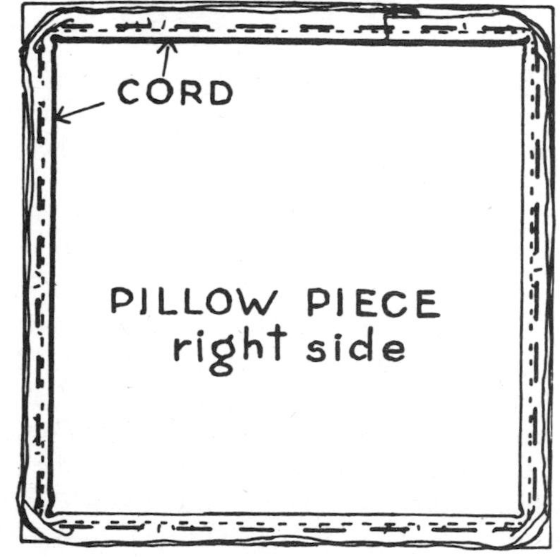

PILLOW: Beginning at the side and starting basting 1″ from end of cording, baste cording with raw edges even to right side of one square of fabric all around, finishing ends as follows: Rip back and cut ¾″ of cord out of first end, and fold in the bias strip ¼″. Insert other end of cording. If so long that cording does not lie flat, trim off raw end before inserting. Stitch all around (use cording foot) close to cord. Place the second square of fabric on top, right sides together, and stitch around same as first square, leaving 5″ on center of one side open for stuffing. Turn right side out.

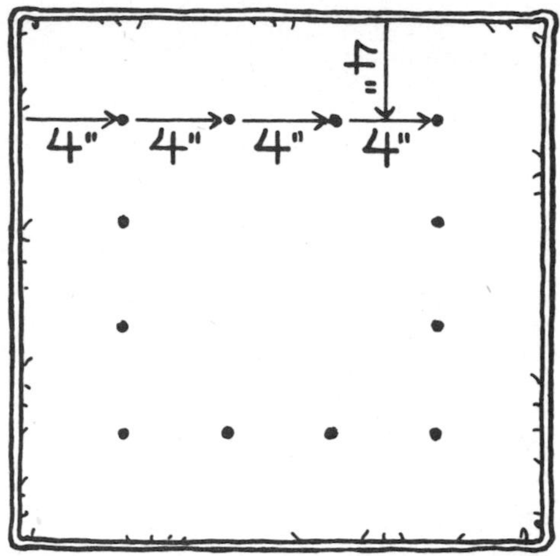

MARKING FOR BUTTONS: Before stuffing, measure in and mark 4″ from all sides of pillow, both front and back. On this mark, mark corners and points 4″ apart at sides (12 markings; see diagram). Do same on opposite side of pillow. Cover buttons, following directions on package.

Stuff pillow rather loosely. Turn in open edge, and slip-stitch along seam line of cording.

Using carpet thread and darning needle, sew button on one side, draw thread through to opposite point and sew on second button. Bring thread back through under first button; draw up tightly to make a puffed effect; tie securely. Repeat for remaining buttons.

Oriental Floor Cushion

Material. ¾ yd. 48″ wide heavy Silk Shantung, or other decorator fabric; or 1½ yds. 36″ wide fabric. Heavy-duty Thread to match. ⅛ yd. 4″ wide Black Rayon Fringe. Two 1½″ diameter Wooden Buttons. Black Perlesheen. Small amount of Carpet Thread. 1½ yds. Muslin for pillow form. 2 lbs. Kapok for stuffing. Darning Needle.

To Make. PILLOW FORM: Cut two 24″ squares from muslin. Pin together, matching edges, and stitch ½″ from edge around 4 sides, leaving an opening in center of 1 side for stuffing. Stuff firmly and evenly, but not hard. Sew opening by hand. PILLOW: Cut two 24″ squares from shantung. With right sides together and edges matching, pin and stitch around 4 sides ½″ from edge, leaving 16″ opening at center of 4th side.

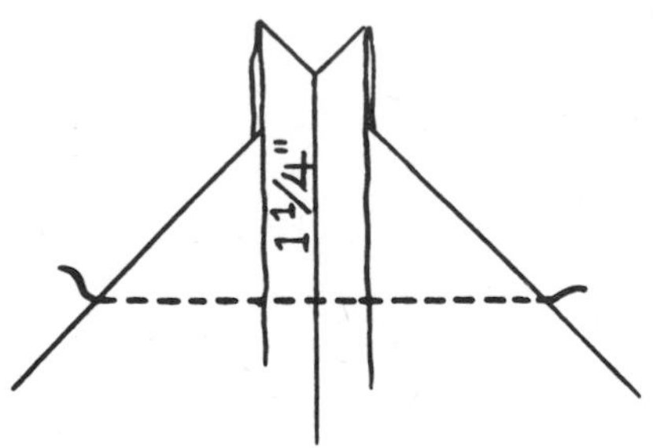

Open seams at corners; fold, matching seams; and stitch across 1¼″ from point. Turn right side out. Insert pillow form, and slip-stitch opening.

Cut four 1″ lengths of fringe. Roll, sew, and tie to form tassels. With double-strand Perlesheen, take 1″ long stitches each side of corner on seam line. Do not pull tight. Bring needle out at corner, and sew on tassel. Repeat on other 3 corners.

BUTTONS: Cut 2 circles of fabric twice diameter of button. Gather edge, insert button, pull up thread, and sew at back of button. Measure and mark center of pillow on both sides. With carpet thread (use double) and darning needle, sew a button at center of one side of pillow, bringing needle out at center of opposite side. Pull tightly to puff the pillow. Sew on 2nd button; bring needle through to opposite side under 1st button. Draw tightly and tie securely.

Fur-Fabric Pillow

Materials. ⅜ yd. Orlon-pile Fur Fabric. Heavy-duty Thread to match. 12″ Dress Zipper to match. Package single Bias-Fold Tape to match. 13″ square Pillow Form.

To Make. Cut two 13″ squares of the fur fabric (measure on wrong side). Place right sides together, and stitch around three sides ½″ from edge. Leave fourth side open for zipper.

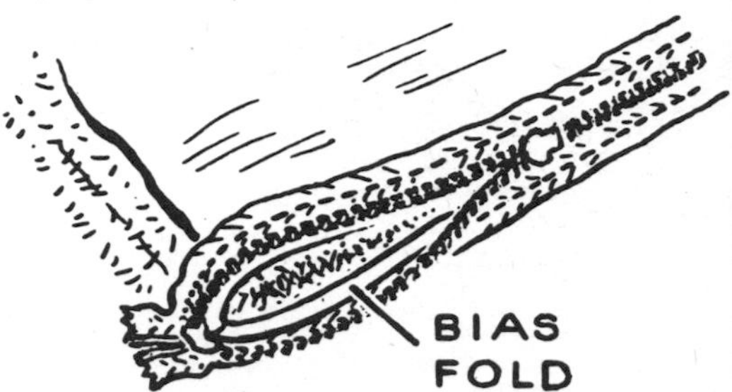

Right sides together, sew bias tape ½″ in from edge on both sides of opening. Center the zipper in the opening, pin, and sew in place by hand, using back-stitch.

Boxed Round Pillow

Materials. ¾ yd. 36″ wide fine ribbed Corduroy. Heavy-duty Thread to match. 10″ Dress-Placket Zipper. 2 yds. ¼″ diameter Cord. 11″ round foam-rubber Pillow Form.

Cutting. Cut pillow, boxing strips, and bias strips, following diagram. Cut enough bias strips, 2¼″ wide, to make 2 strips, each 36″ long after piecing.

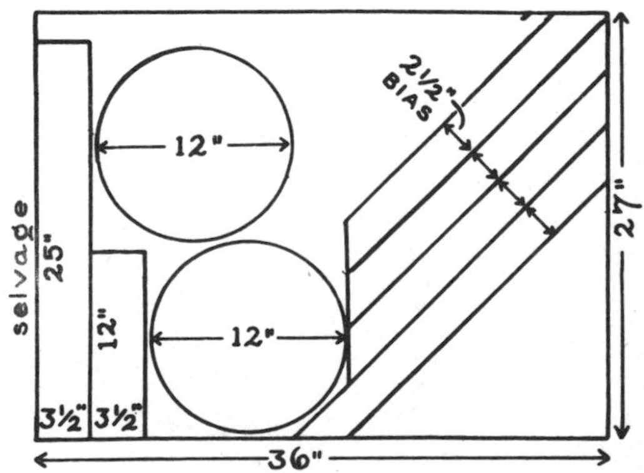

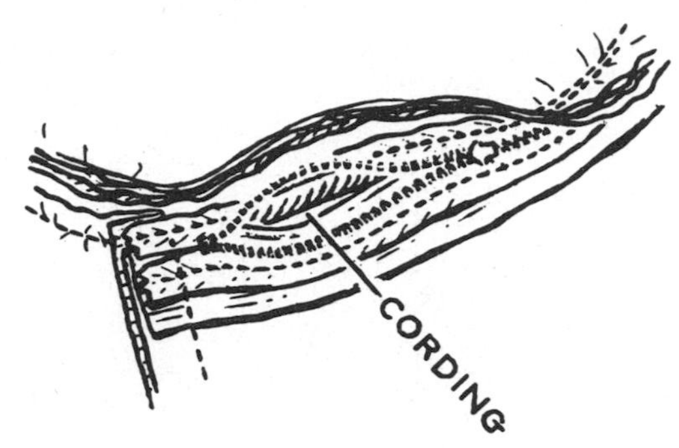

Cording. Fold bias strips in half lengthwise, right side out; insert cord, and stitch (use zipper or cording foot) close to cord.

To Make. Right sides together and raw edges even, baste cording around each circle. See "Tufted Pillow" for how to end cording neatly. Stitch close to cording. Turn back ¾″ on long side of shorter boxing strip, and press. Lay folded edge over metal part of zipper, centering ends. Baste and stitch to zipper tape ½″ from folded edge.

Right sides together, pin and baste boxing strips together, end to end. Stitch 1 end only.

Right sides together and zipper closed, pin and baste boxing to one side of pillow around edge. If too long, adjust at basted end of boxing; then stitch this end, and stitch around. Baste and stitch other side of boxing to second pillow top. Turn right side out, and insert filler.

BEDSPREADS

Bedspread with Two Flounces

How to Measure. Diagram shows basic measurements needed for making flounced bedspreads. A bed should be made up with sheets, blankets and pillows when taking measurements. Since all beds are not the same height, it is not possible to give exact yardage.

1. For top piece of spread, measure length A plus 1″ for seam, plus 12″ for tuck-in, and width B plus 1″ for seam. Cut one piece of organdy and one of lining (broadcloth) of these measurements.

Note: Fabric may have to be pieced lengthwise to fit the width of the bed. Allow for this when calculating amount of fabric needed.

2. For side lining pieces, measure F plus 1″, plus 12″ for tuck-in, and E plus 1″ for hems. Cut 2 pieces of broadcloth using these measurements.

3. For end lining piece, measure B plus 1″ and D plus 1″. Cut 1 piece using these measurements.

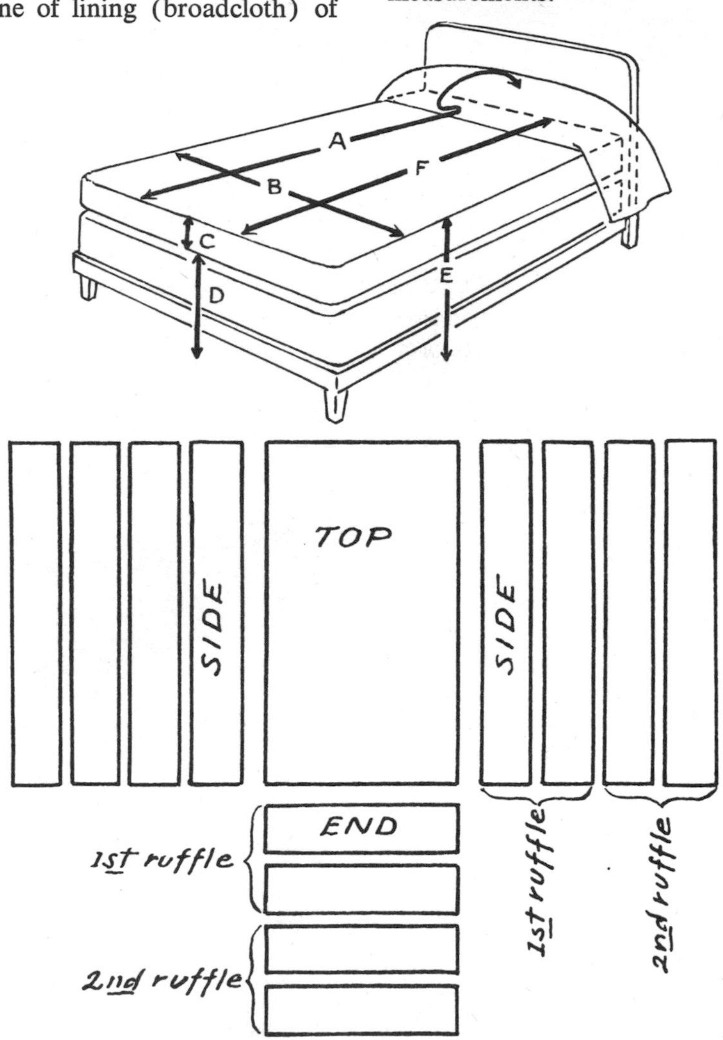

4. Cut top side flounce twice the length of top piece of spread, and ½ the measurement of E plus 3″ for lap and hems.

Note: If fuller ruffles are wanted, cut 2½ times the length of top piece of spread.

5. Cut lower side flounce twice the length of side lining piece and ½ measurement of E, plus 3″ for lap and hems. See note above.

6. Cut top end flounce twice width of top of spread and same width as side top flounce. See note above.

7. Cut lower end flounce twice width of

lining end and same width as lower side flounce. See note above.

To Make.

1. Lay large organdy piece on top of lining piece, pin and stitch all around, leaving 12″ opening at one end. Trim seam and turn. Slip-stitch opening.

2. Make narrow hems on 1 long side and on ends of each side lining piece, and also on end lining piece. Make 1″ hem along remaining long side on each piece.

3. Pin and stitch side and end lining pieces to top piece, lapping top over sides and end about ½″.

4. Sew side and top ruffles together to make 1 long strip for top ruffle and 1 long strip for bottom ruffle. Make a very narrow hem at top edge and each end of ruffles. Make a 1″ hem at lower edge of each ruffle. Do same with end ruffles.

5. Stitch with longest machine stitch ½″ from top edge of top side ruffle and draw up to fit side of spread. Adjust gathers and pin and stitch in place over the seam.

6. Repeat for lower ruffle and place on side lining with lower edge even with lining. Then pin and stitch in place over gathering line.

7. Repeat for opposite side and for end of spread.

Bedspread with One Flounce

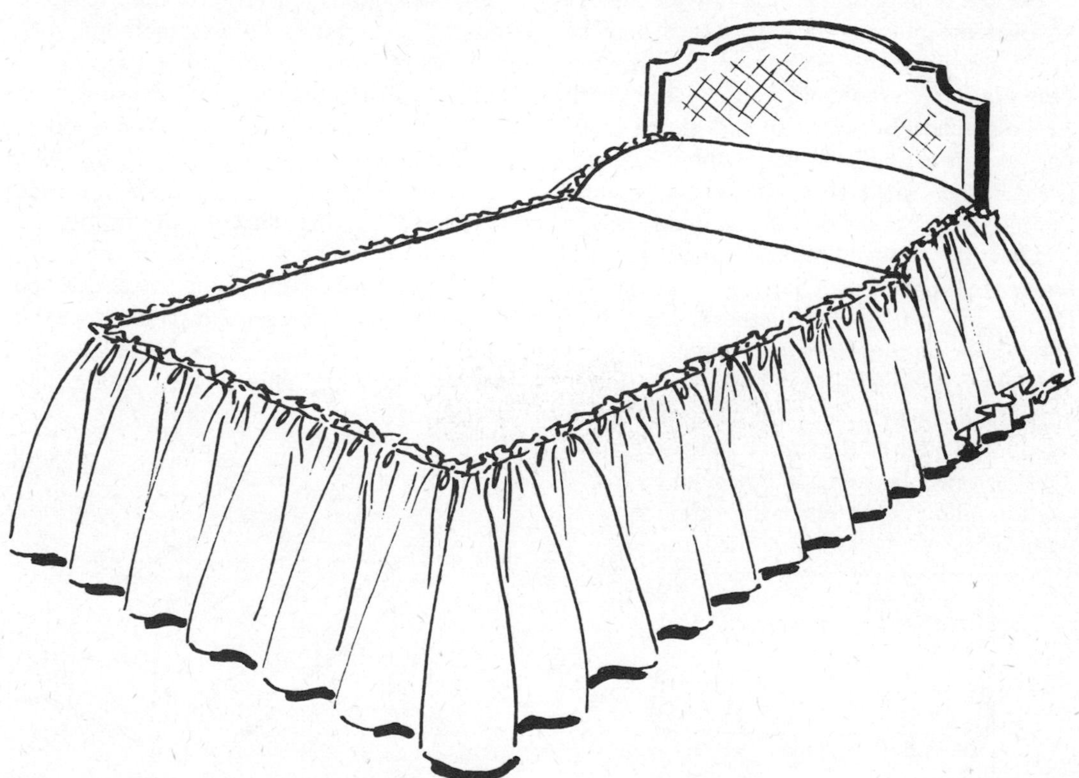

1. Make top and side linings as for bedspread with two flounces.

2. For flounce, measure from top of bed to floor (E in diagram) and add 3″ for hems. Cut a piece this wide and 2 times (or 2½ times if very full flounce is wanted) the length of side of top of spread, plus 1″ for hems. Proceed as for top ruffle on bedspread. Repeat for opposite side.

3. Cut end flounce 2 (or 2½) times the width of the end of the spread plus 1″ for hems. Apply same as side flounces.

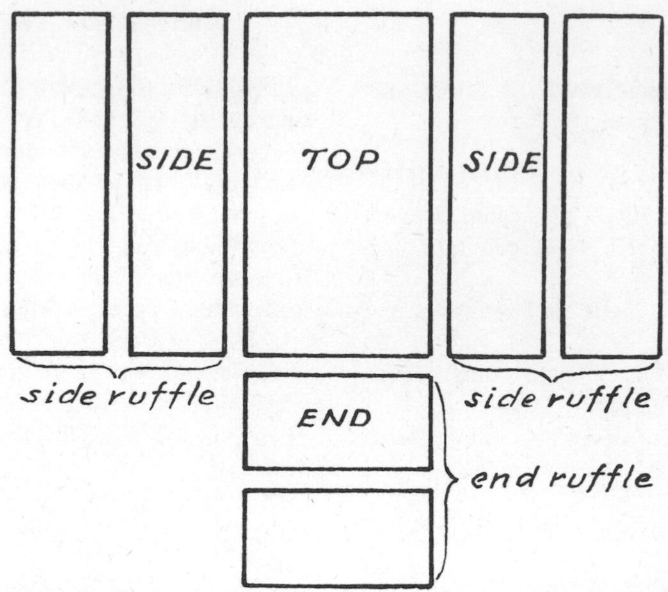

Pillow Throw Attached to Spread

Instead of making a spread long enough to go over the pillows, an extra piece may be made and sewed to the spread near the top (see diagram). It should be the same width as the spread, the seams should match those on the spread, and the edges should be finished in the same way. If the spread is lined, the pillow throw should also be lined.

The throw must be long enough to tuck under the front of the pillow, go over the pillow, and then tuck in at the headboard. Add enough for seams and for a 2″ hem.

Right sides together, pin and sew the lower edge of throw to the spread about 12″ from headboard edge of the spread (see diagram). Turn in raw edge and stitch or hem by hand. Center pillow over seam line and cover it with the throw, tucking in at headboard.

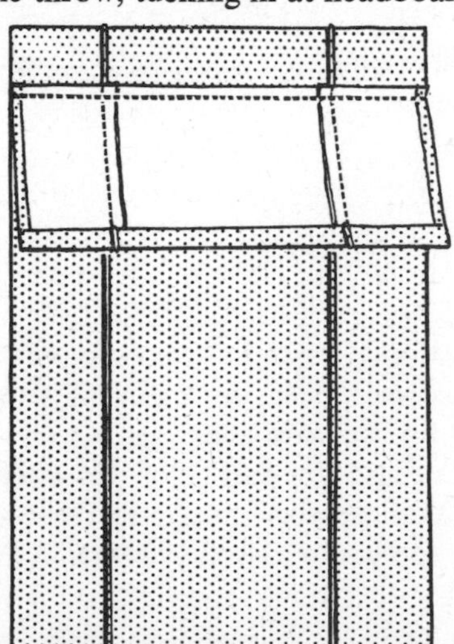

Throw Spread

To Measure. LENGTH: Measure length of bed and up and over pillows, including tuck-ins, plus overhang at foot of bed (to floor if desired) plus hems. WIDTH: Measure width of bed plus desired overhang (both sides), plus hems. For a 3-section spread, the width of the center panel depends upon the width of the bed and the width of the fabric. The seams should come fairly close to the edge of the bed. Measure the same as above, but allow for seams for sewing panels together.

A throw spread can be made with a shorter overhang and a dust ruffle used with it.

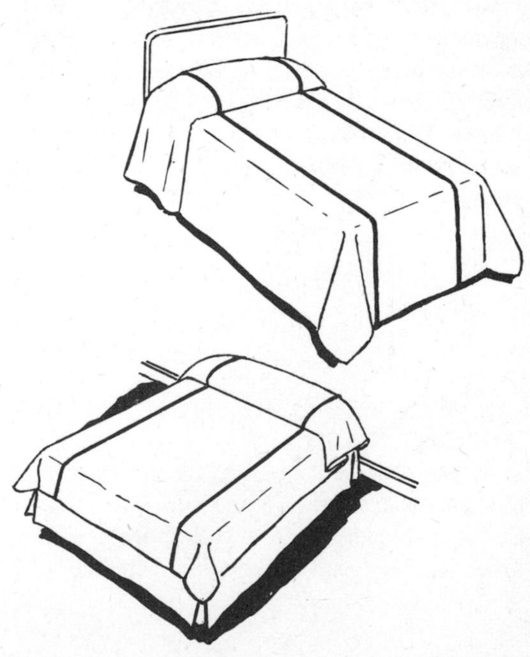

Fitted Spread

To Measure. TOP SECTION: Length and width of bed plus tuck-ins and seams. Sew cording around 3 sides if desired (not across top). SIDES: Cut 2. Length same as top section plus 3″ for pleat, plus seams. The width will be the length of the overhang (top of bed to floor) plus 2½″ for hem. END PIECE: Cut 1. Length is the width of the bed plus 9″ for pleat, plus seams, and is same width as sides.

Join side sections to end section. Make a 3″ pleat each side of corner of bed. Pin, fold and press. Right sides together, stitch top to side piece with pleats at corners. Stitch. Hem lower edge and across top of spread.

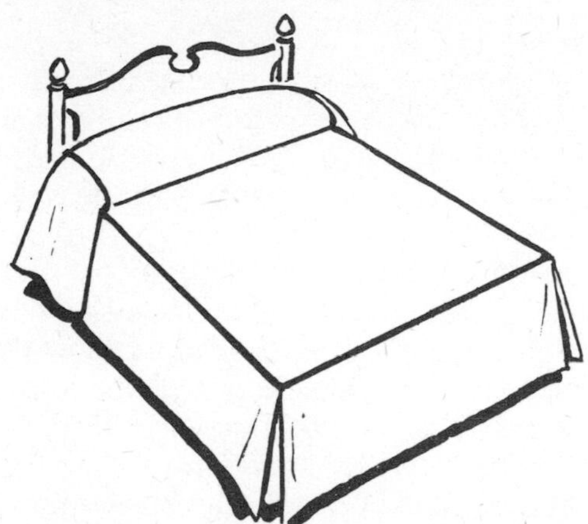

Note: A "fake" pleated corner can be made by not adding allowance for pleat. End side and end pieces at corner, hem the edges. Add a piece about 7″ to 8″ wide and same length (from top of bed to floor) as side pieces. Center it at corner and sew to the seam each side of corner. Hem it same as sides.

The side section may end where mattress and springs meet. A flounce may be added to reach to the floor.

Dust Ruffle for Box Springs

This fits top of box springs and lies between it and the mattress.

Make a muslin cover to fit top of mattress, extending ½″ beyond edge. Cover sides and end of this cover with 5″ wide strips of the same fabric as the ruffle. Miter the corners, turn under, and stitch inside edge to the muslin cover. Hem edge near headboard. Keep other 3 raw edges pinned together.

Dust Ruffle. For width, measure from top of box spring to the floor. Add ½″ for seam allowance and 2½″ for hem. Length is determined by fulness desired. It may be pleated or gathered. For a gathered ruffle, allow 2½ to 3 times the measurement around box spring (2 long sides and across foot of bed). Cut the pieces crosswise the material and piece them together. Make a 2″ hem along one long edge and a narrow hem at each end. Gather the other long edge and, right sides together, pin it to the top. Distribute the gathers evenly, baste, and stitch.

Chapter 13

Machine Embroidery

Machines for home sewing have developed so rapidly in recent years that a new skill has been added for the woman who sews at home.

These modern machines not only do straight sewing but perform miracles in machine embroidery. This is accomplished by the swing of the needle from side to side; for straight sewing it moves only up and down.

While straight sewing stitches look like this:

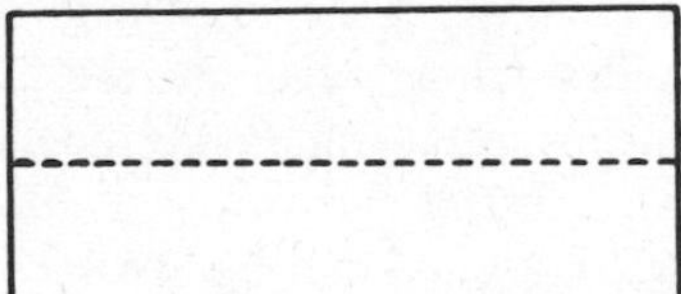

machine embroidery will look something like this:

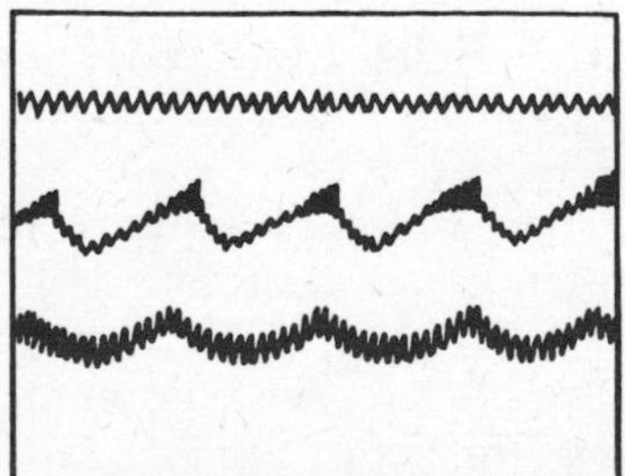

These are zigzag stitches which may lie close together:

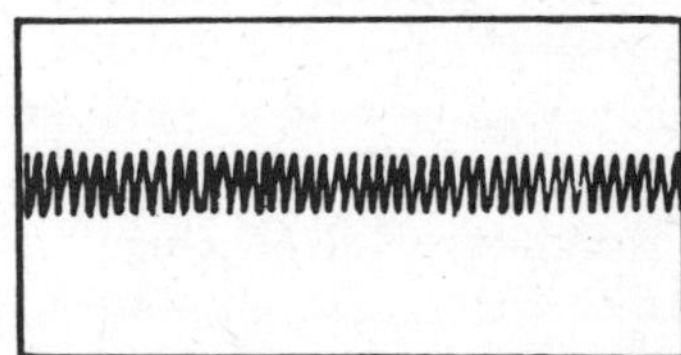

or be spread apart:

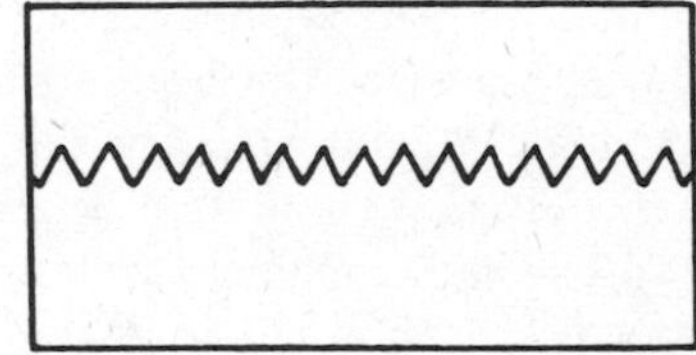

They may be of different widths of straight rows

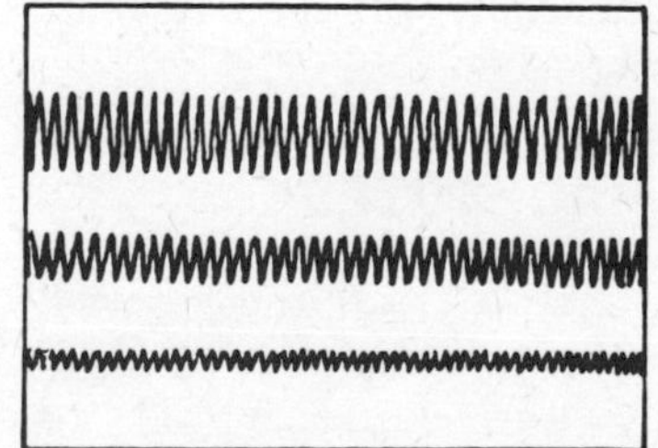

or varied in such a way as to make fancy patterns:

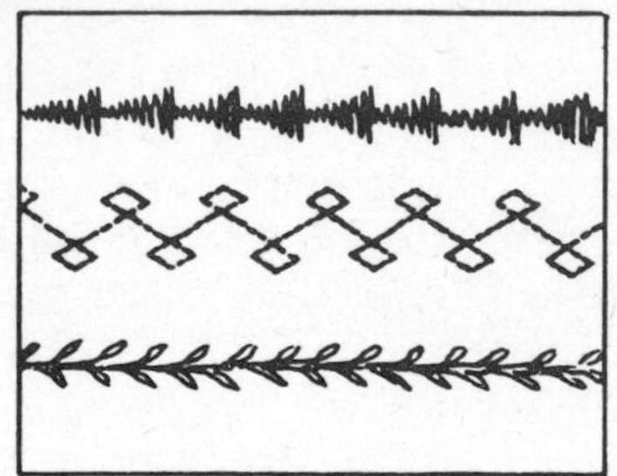

On the newest models it is possible to make many patterns automatically:

There are also zigzag attachments which can be used on regular sewing machines to make a number of stitch designs.

The possibilities of arrangement and variation of the stitches are endless. Also, the uses to which these new decorative stitches may be put are only limited by the imagination.

Sewing machines differ, and each woman should choose the one which suits her own needs best. She should also try out more than one model before making a decision.

Learn to use the machine you have purchased by having it thoroughly demonstrated and then practice on it yourself until you are skillful in using it.

The following pages are suggestions for using the decorative possibilities of your modern machine, with some reminders of its more practical points.

GENERAL NOTES

Use a mercerized thread especially made for machine embroidery. It should be extra-fine and lustrous, which will make the stitches more attractive.

Use a fine needle.

Study carefully the book of instructions which comes with the particular machine or attachment you are using.

Learn to run the machine at an even speed and run it slowly if you are a beginner.

Do the embroidery before the article is sewed up and finished.

Embroidery with a zigzag machine is done on the right side of the fabric.

The design area should, in most cases, be backed with paper, organdy, or a non-woven interfacing. The organdy or interfacing may remain, if needed, or be cut away after embroidery is completed. The paper of course is torn away.

Always make a practice swatch first. Work a part of the design on the fabric you are to use (with backing), and experiment with the stitches until they look right and you can execute them well.

Study the design. Where a line ends at another line, the latter should cover the former.

Keep bobbin case clean with a soft brush.

Adjust pressure on presser foot according to the weight of the fabric (see manual).

The three most important adjustments to be made are:

1. Needle position (center; left of center; right of center).
2. Width of stitch (known as bight).
3. Closeness of stitches. The lever that regulates the number of stitches to the inch for straight stitching regulates the closeness of the stitches in machine embroidery.

To fasten thread ends when making close satin stitch, start and end the work by taking a few stitches with bight lever at neutral; pull ends of thread to wrong side.

DESIGNS FOR MACHINE EMBROIDERY

Some stamped goods patterns and hot-iron transfers are suitable for machine embroidery; these are available in needlework and pattern departments. Here are some suggestions for some simple uses of the decorative stitches which are not too difficult to accomplish.

Double Needle on Zigzag Machines

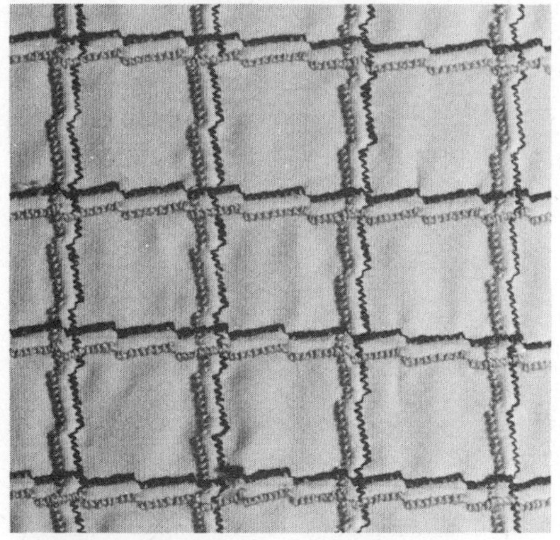

Two-color effects are possible when using the double needle, although the width of the stitches is somewhat limited. Trapunto effects and simulated tucks may be achieved.

GENERAL TYPES OF MACHINE EMBROIDERY

Borders and Bands

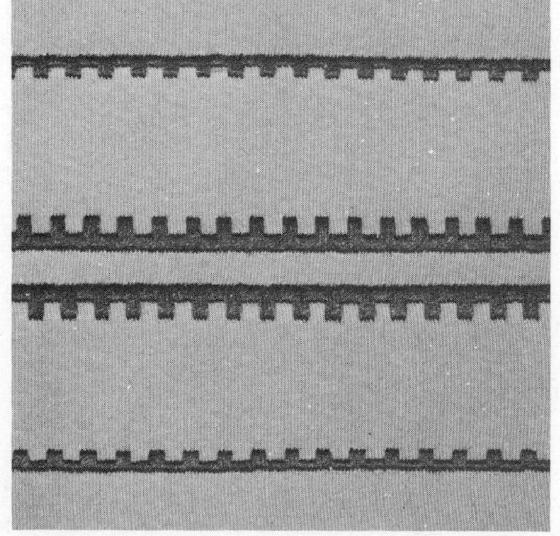

The decorative stitches, with many variations of design, can be worked in straight or curved lines.

These can be used in many ways and need not become monotonous. Done in bright colors on a dark fabric, they produce a peasant effect on skirts and blouses. Aprons, place mats, pillows, valances, and other suitable articles can also be decorated in this way.

A child's skating skirt can be trimmed with rows of bright stitching. Use a circular skirt pattern and work the embroidery before lining the skirt.

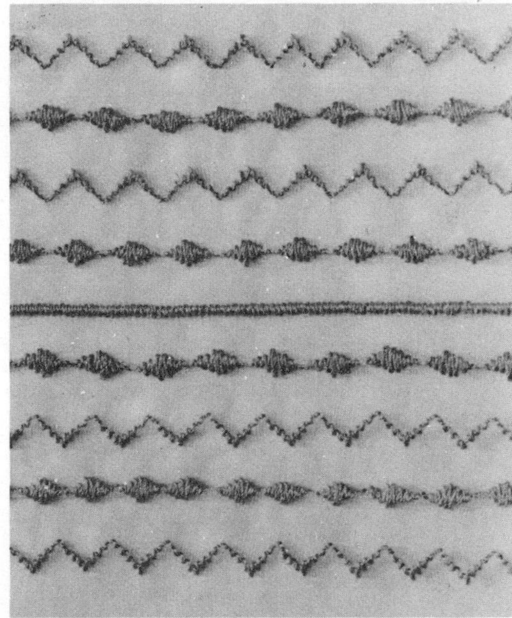

When worked in self-tone or monotone on organdy the effect is delicate and attractive and suitable for bridesmaids' and graduation dresses. With the addition of rows of lace (applied with zigzag stitch), the result is even daintier.

Appliqué

The possibilities with appliqué are limitless. Almost any shape, even quite intricate ones, can be applied with either satin stitch or open zigzag.

Transfer the design to the appliqué fabric (patch). When cutting out the design, leave

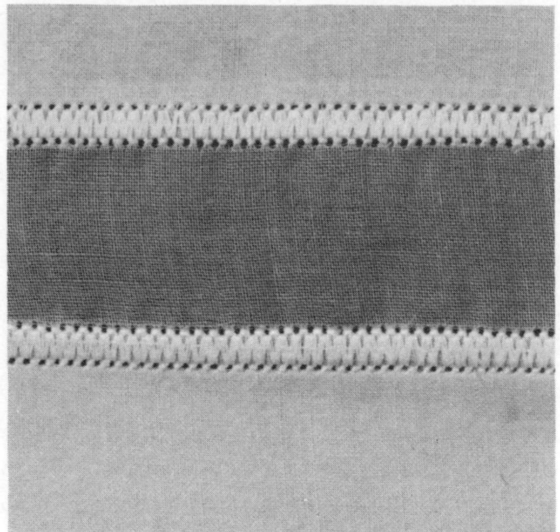

a margin of about ½″ all around the outline. Baste the appliqué to the background fabric. Stitch over the outline with either a close satin or open zigzag stitch. Trim away excess fabric.

A delicate transparent look may be had by using organdy for the appliqué over a heavier fabric, then cutting away the fabric beneath.

It is possible also to find many attractive designs in printed fabrics which can be cut out and used for decoration in this manner. These are more often found on decorator fabrics.

An old-fashioned "crazy quilt" can easily be made by machine, using the decorative stitches for joining the pieces. Arrange, pin, and baste pieces on a foundation square. Use the same color thread throughout but vary the stitch design.

Apple Tree Place Mats (finished size 14″ by 20″)

Shown in Color Plate 24

Materials. 1 yd. 45″-wide Black Heavy Cotton. 1 yd. Emerald-Green Cotton for tree. ¼ yd. each Red and Yellow-Green Cotton for apples and leaves. Matching Thread.

To Make. Cut four place mats 15″ by 21″ from black. Using patterns given, cut one green tree, eight red apples and 12 yellow-green leaves for each mat. Following diagram for placement, pin and baste tree in place. With matching thread and zigzag satin stitch, stitch all around tree. Again following diagram, pin and baste apples and leaves in place and zigzag edges with matching thread.

Adjust zigzag for a slightly more open stitch and with black thread, stitch all around edge of place mat. Turn and press

½″ hem all around and sew by hand.

Hand Appliqué. Patches may also be held in place with small blanket stitches.

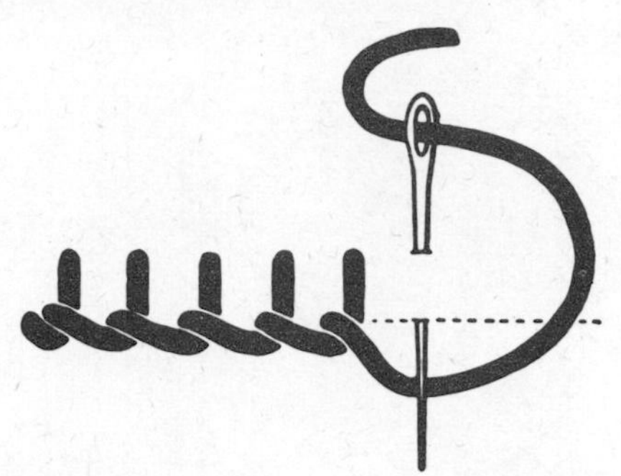

Monograms and Lettering

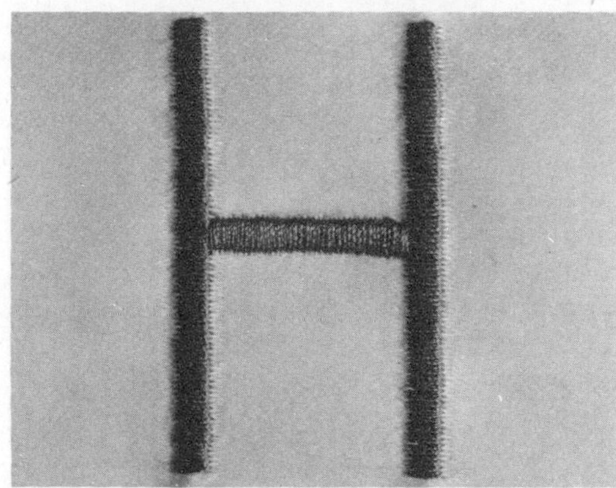

Block letters or monograms are quite easily made by tracing the design onto the fabric and then using close satin stitch over it. The satin stitch may be any width which is suitable to the size of the letter being made.

Script monograms should be done with the fabric stretched in an embroidery hoop to get the best results. The fabric is moved freely as if the operator were writing or drawing on the fabric with the needle. Perfection depends upon moving with a steady hand. Almost any size or shape of design can be done in this way.

Some types of machines now have automatic devices for monogramming and doing small motifs. However, these limit the design in size and style.

Fill-in and Large Designs

Fill-in designs can be done by using small motifs spaced at regular intervals. Also, the stitches may be used in rows or crossed over each other (see Double Needle on Zigzag Machines).

When doing large line or scroll designs, it is well to work in a hoop as described above.

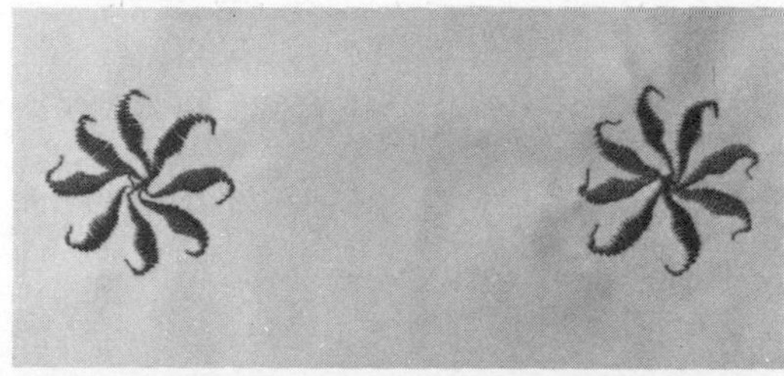

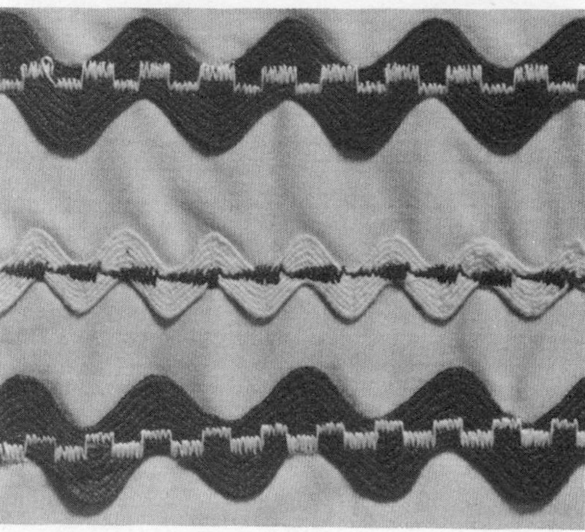

A novel use for these machine embroidery stitches is sewing on rickrack and other trimmings. Vary the stitches, the size of the rickrack, and the spacing as desired. A single row for edging may be all that is needed.

Rickrack may be set in as an insertion as follows:

1. Sew rickrack on top of fabric where wanted, catching points at each side.

2. Cut fabric underneath rickrack down the center. Press raw edges apart allowing openwork to show.

3. From right side, stitch each folded edge of fabric, using zigzag stitch. Clip away raw edges underneath.

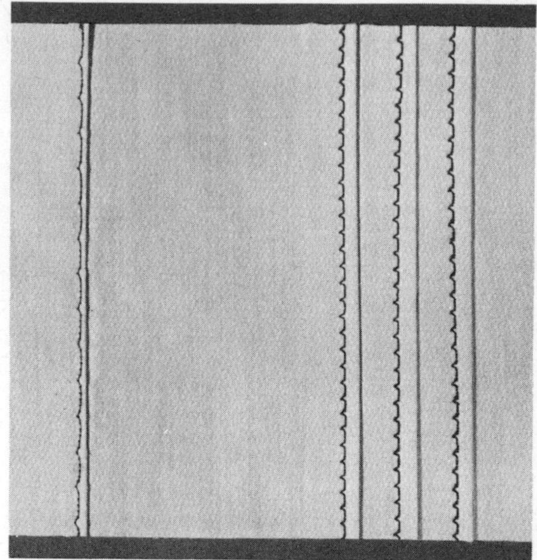

Buttons and Buttonholes

Because of this same zigzag movement of the needle, it is now also possible to sew on buttons and make buttonholes with these new machines. The needle can be set for various sizes of buttons and almost any length buttonhole can be made.

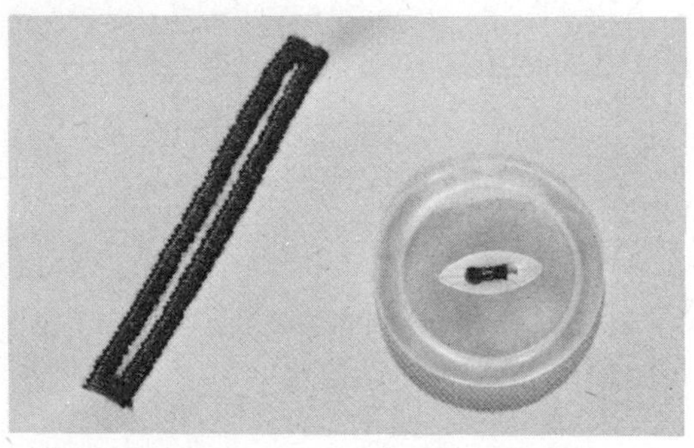

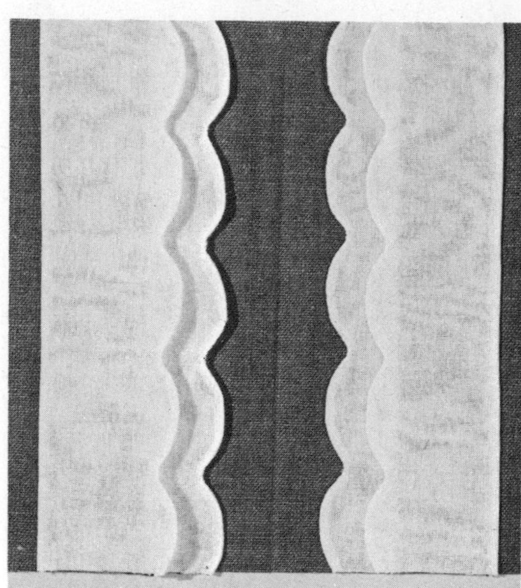

Tucks

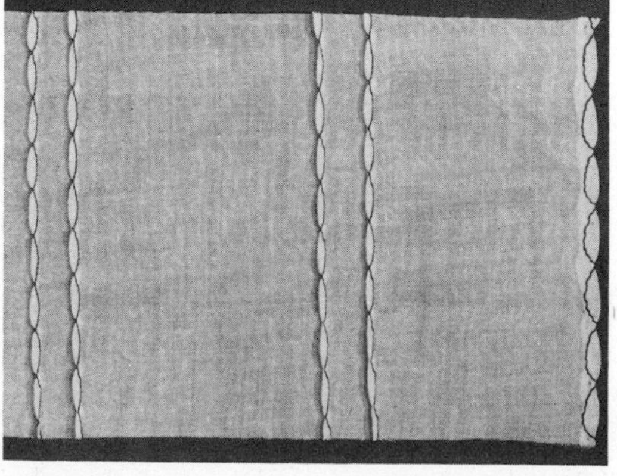

Decorative tucks of various kinds and widths are easily and quickly made. Any of the daintier decorative stitches can be used to sew in the tuck. For the narrow scalloped tucks, the blind-stitch is used.

This is set so the sideways stitch will catch over the folded edge forming the scallop.

The wider scallops can be used on tucks or on hems. They are especially attractive on little girls' dresses.

PLACE MATS

A neat and attractive arrangement of stitches is shown here for place mats and napkins, using narrow satin stitch and one of the decorative stitches.

Measure carefully and mark lightly with pencil where the lines should come on the mats, being sure they are all marked alike. Many arrangements are possible. Try your own ideas.

PRACTICAL USES FOR ZIGZAG

Seam Finishes

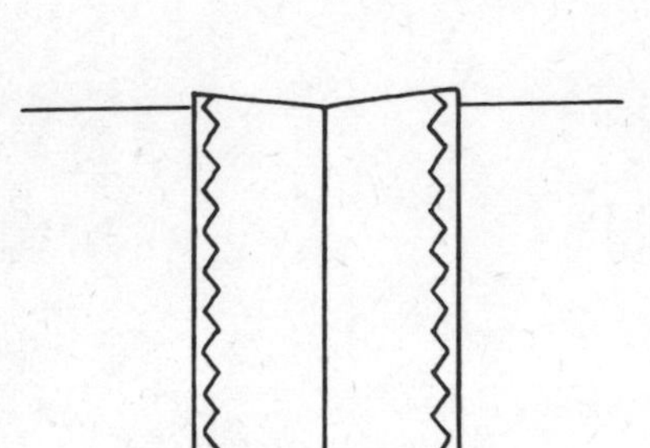

Plain seams. Zigzag stitch is excellent for seam edges on fabrics that ravel easily. Stitch near the edges and trim close to the stitching. Press seam open.

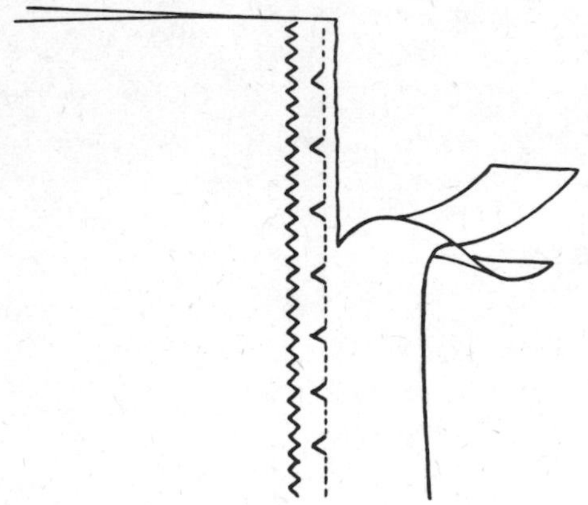

For seams in tricot lingerie, zigzag stitching is practical because it is flexible and will not break on stretching. Use light tensions and fine needle and thread. Do not press open. Finish if desired by stitching seam edges together with automatic blind stitch. Trim away the excess close to stitching.

Lapped seams. Zigzag stitching is fine for closing a dart on interfacings. Cut the dart down the center all the way to the point. Lap dart so the seam markings match. Stitch on the seamline and a little beyond. Trim close to the stitching on both sides.

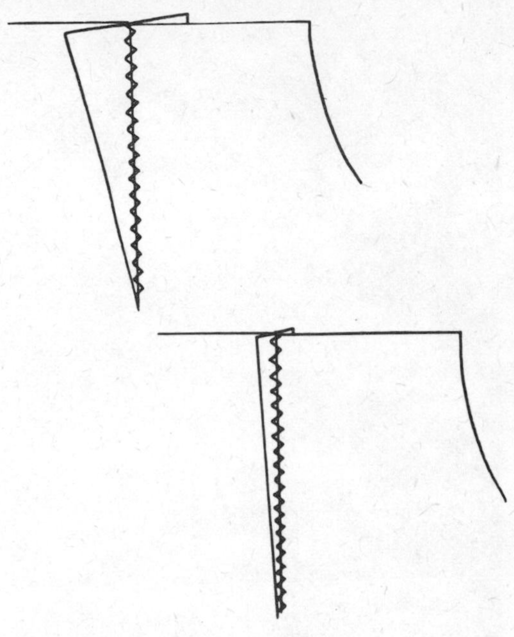

Hems. The machine blind-stitch is a form of zigzag stitching. It saves time on simple hems and is especially good on soft spongy fabrics. Turn the hem and baste on the fold.

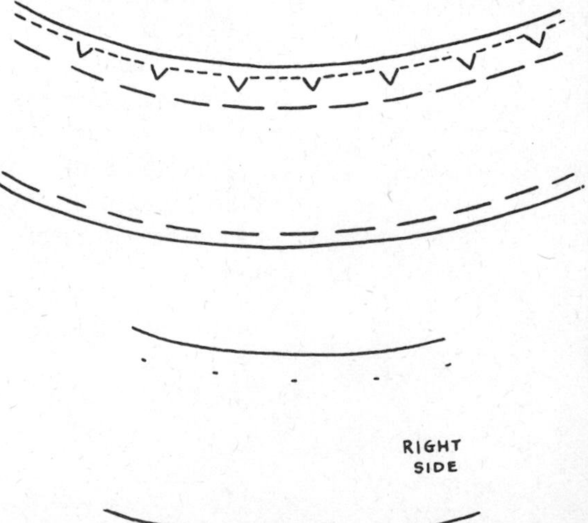

Measure and turn in the top edge and baste ½″ from the edge. Fold the *garment* back leaving a fold at the basting line. Blind-stitch so the straight stitches come at the top of the hem and the sideward stitches come into the garment fold. This makes a blind-stitch on the right side. Turn back and press.

Trim the narrow hem of a petticoat and finish it at the same time with a decorative stitch pattern in this manner:

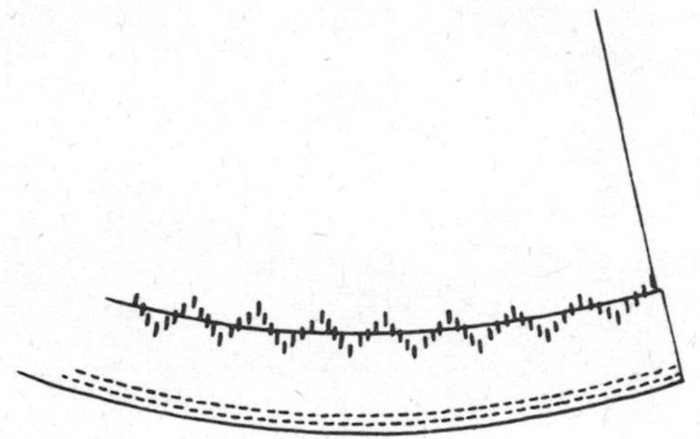

Turn hem edge ¼″ to the right side and press. Lay bias-fold tape on top with edges even. Top-stitch at lower edge and finish top edge with decorative stitching.

Other Uses for Zigzag Stitching

1. Sew elastic to waistlines of lingerie and pajamas with zigzag stitching. This is especially good for knitted fabrics.

2. To prevent breaking under normal strain, use zigzag stitching for seams and darts on knitted fabrics. It is also good for finishing the edge of facings on bulky fabrics instead of turning under and edge-stitching.

3. Use zigzag stitching to reinforce gussets at the underarm on kimono-type sleeves. Also at underarm on kimono sleeves where there is no gusset.

Chapter 14

Mending and Care

DARNING

Since the appearance of nylon, not as much sock and stocking darning is done as formerly. Even on children's socks the heels and toes are often reinforced with nylon, which prevents wear at these points.

However, there are other things which do wear out in spots so it is well to know how to darn. It may be done on almost any fabric.

Use thread as nearly the same color and weight of the fabric as possible. Sometimes threads can be pulled from the seam edges or from left-over fabric for darning.

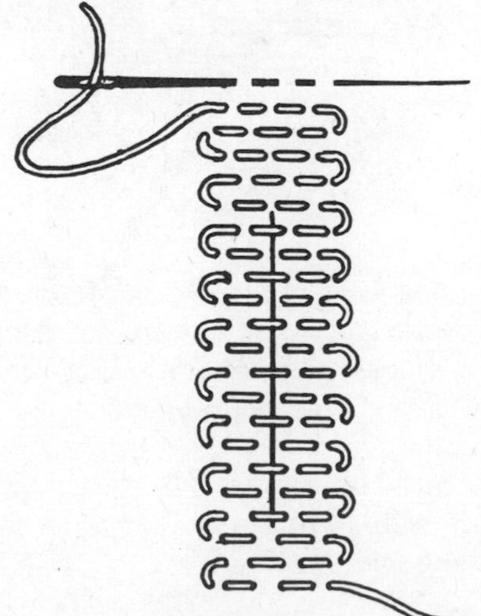

Darning is a combination of running stitch over edges and thin parts and weaving over the hole itself. Do not use a knot. Work on the right side of the fabric. Start and end with running stitch beyond the hole. Do not pull threads tight.

Straight Tear. Fit edges together and reinforce with fabric underneath if desired. Work back and forth with small running stitches, covering a space wide enough so it will not pull out. For a quicker job, use zigzag stitch with sewing machine.

Three-cornered Tear. Darn as for straight tear in both directions, lapping at the corner. This may also be done with zigzag stitch.

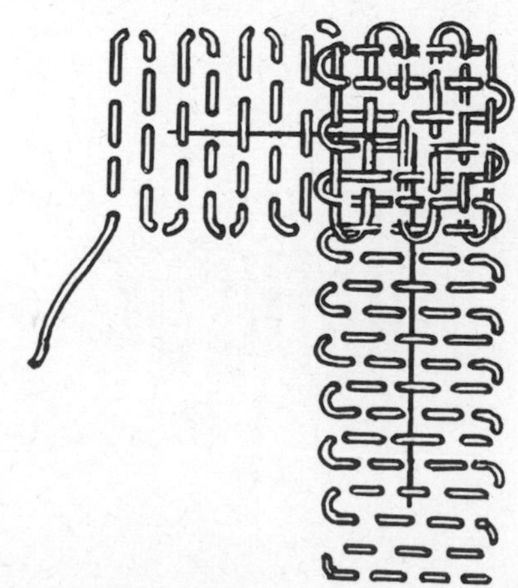

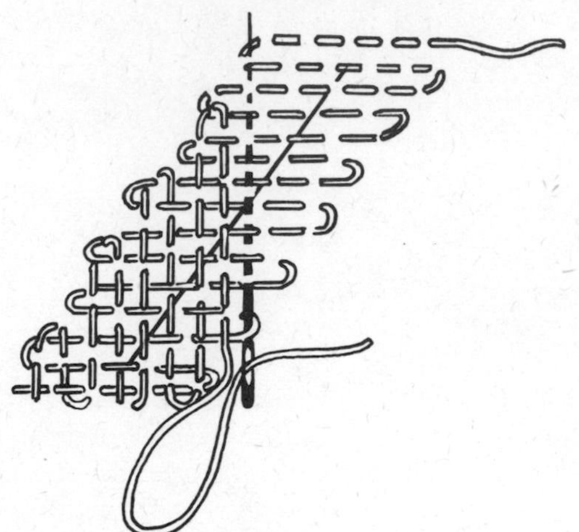

Diagonal Tear. Darn as shown, covering a diagonal-shaped space. Turn and darn in the opposite direction to reinforce.

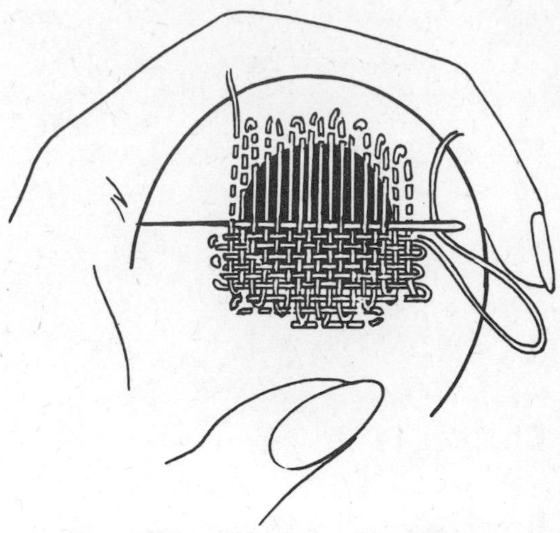

Darning a Hole. Trim the edges of the hole. Weave very closely over the hole. Follow the design of the fabric if possible.

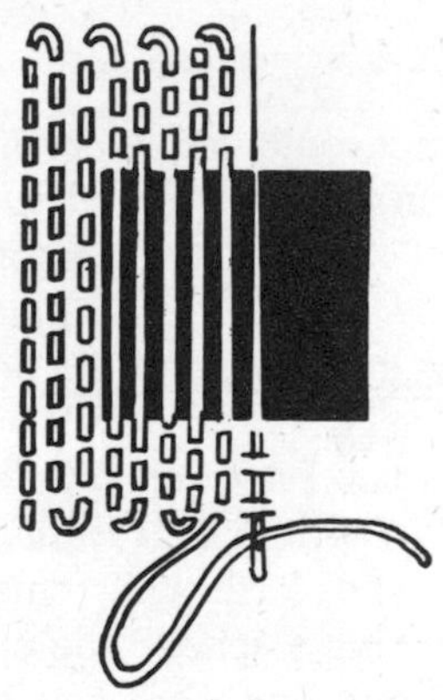

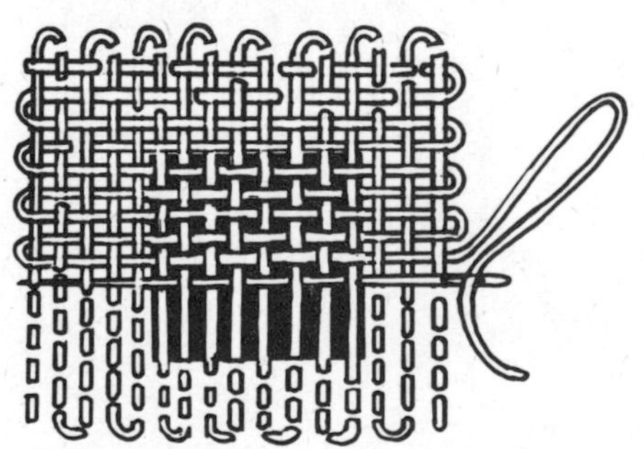

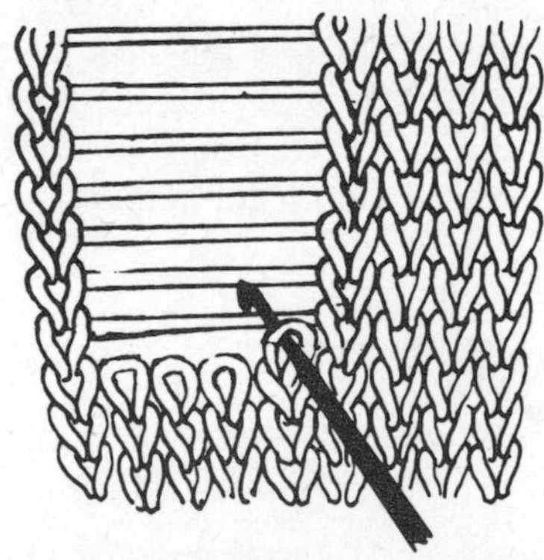

Darning Knit Wear. To reinforce a thin spot, work rows of duplicate stitch over it (see previous page and Knitting section). For weaving stockinette together, see Knitting section.

To mend a run in knit wear, pick up stitches with a crochet hook. Fasten threads on wrong side.

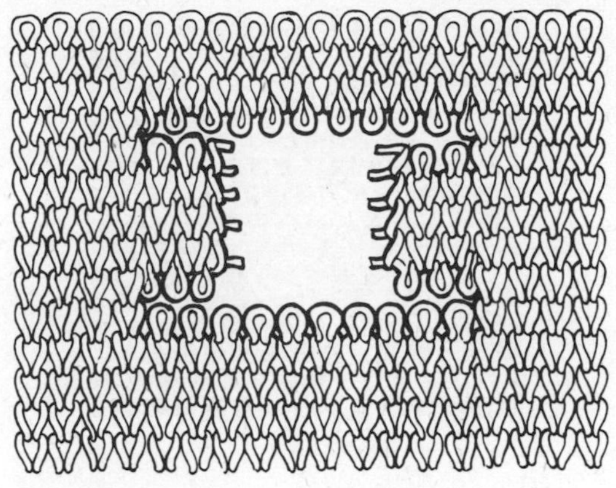

To Weave a Hole in Knit Wear. Unravel broken stitches to make a square or rectangle. Turn stitches along the sides to wrong side and hem. With needle and thread pick up the stitches (plus one beyond the hole on each side) working back and forth.

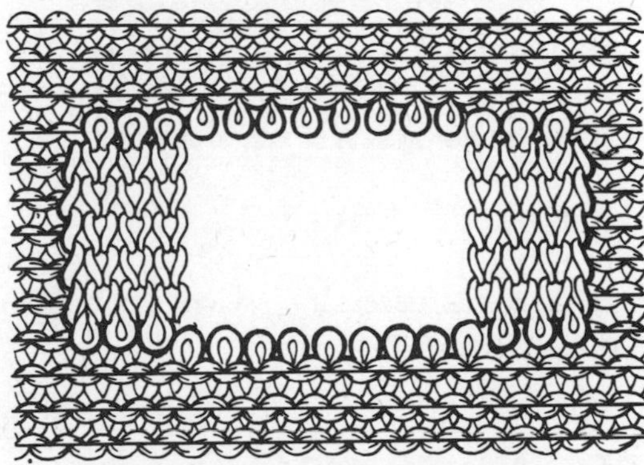

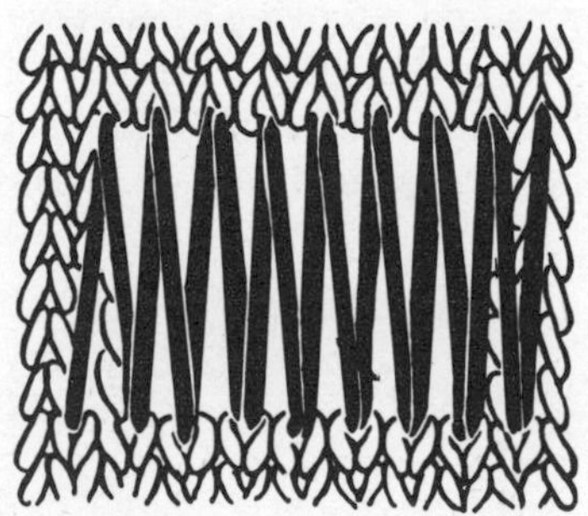

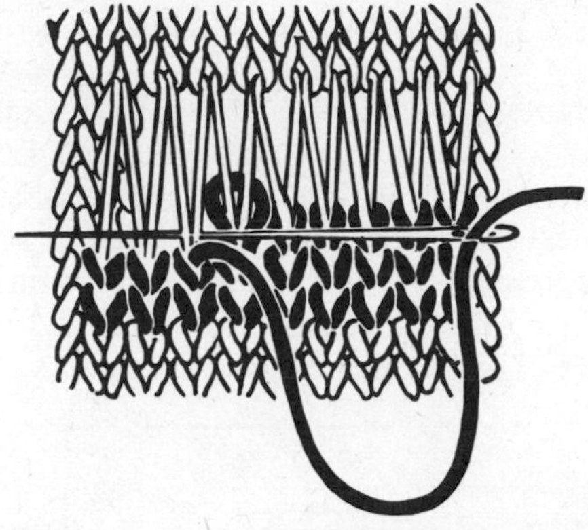

Fasten yarn on right side at lower right hand corner. Make stitches on the diagonal threads somewhat in the manner of duplicate stitch. Continue across row and work back in reverse. Keep stitches same size as those of the knitting.

PATCHING

When a hole is large it is better to patch than to darn. Follow the grain of the fabric and trim the hole into a square or rectangle. Cut the patch ½″ to 1″ larger than the hole on all sides. Be sure to use pre-shrunk fabric for patches on garments which have been washed. Match stripes, prints, etc., as nearly as possible.

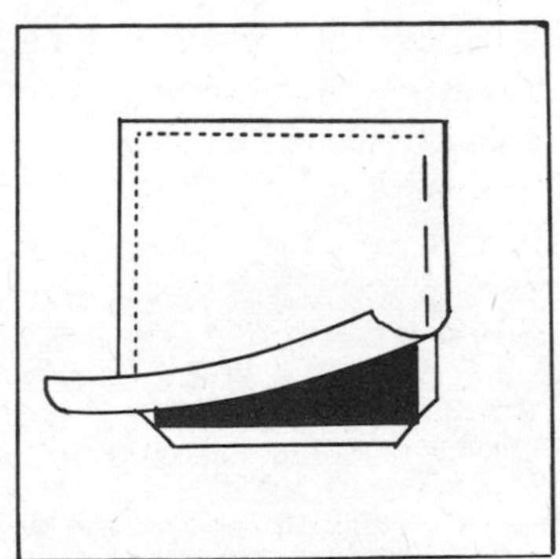

Hemmed Patch. This is suitable for many types of fabrics. Cut the patch 1″ larger than the hole all around. Clip the hole at corners ¼″ and turn edges under. Baste hole, centering it over patch. Hem the turned edges on the right side. Turn under and hem edges of patch on wrong side.

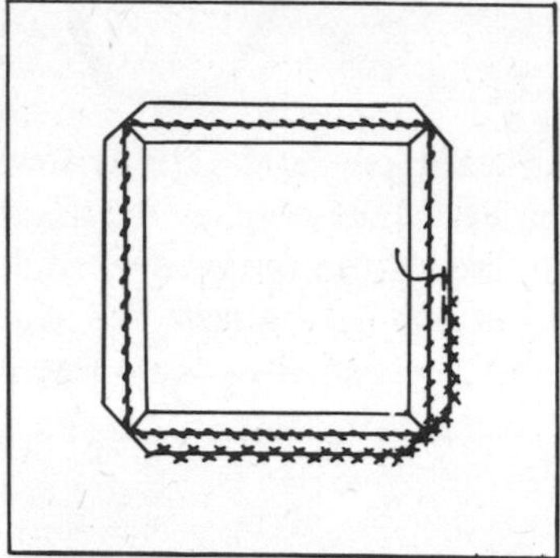

Or after hemming on the right side, press seams open and catch down on wrong side with herringbone stitch.

MENDING NET OR LACE

Weave horizontal threads as for ordinary darning, starting and ending 3 or more meshes on each side of hole.

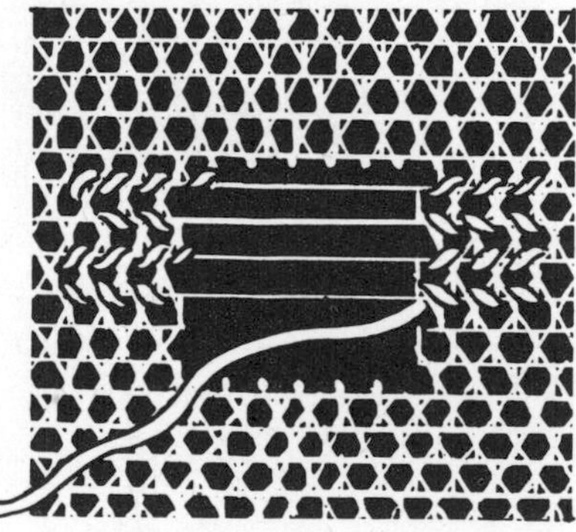

Now weave diagonally from upper right hand corner to lower left, catching around the horizontal threads.

If it seems necessary, weave again from the opposite diagonal.

RECLAIMING WOOL

Do not attempt to unravel knitting or crochet yarn which is matted. If yarn is worth reclaiming, then rip the seams carefully by clipping and removing threads with which seams are sewed. Find the last bound-off stitch and unravel each piece separately. Wind the yarn around a piece of heavy card-

board, keeping ends free. Tie together in about 4 places. Remove from cardboard and dip in warm water. Let drip dry. The weight of the water will remove the kinks.

CARE OF LACES

Fine lace should last indefinitely if properly cared for. The really fine laces were made in the seventeenth and eighteenth centuries and are mostly to be found in museums, but if you own some good lace of more modern vintage it is well to give it good care.

The enemies of lace are dampness, folding, and yellowing. Since dampness encourages mold, keep laces in a dry place but avoid dry heat.

Never pack laces tightly; lay tissue paper in the folds to avoid creasing.

To delay yellowing, store in a cool dry dark place. Avoid chemically treated papers. Yellowed lace can be restored but it should be done by an expert. Handle lace as little as possible.

CARE OF LINENS

Your good linens deserve careful treatment.

Wash linens in hot water with a mild soap or detergent; a water softener may be used if necessary. Linen yields dirt easily so one sudsing may be sufficient. Rinse thoroughly.

Where there are stains on white linen, a bleach may be used with care but it should be mixed with water in the washer or tub instead of being used on each spot. Rinse out thoroughly.

To give a light gloss to linen follow the directions on the package for "light starching," being sure it is well dissolved.

Straighten linen when hanging to dry. Dampen several hours before ironing. Use a hot iron, but be careful not to scorch. Do not press creases in with a hot iron as it may break the fibers. Fold by hand.

Fold large cloths down the center and roll on a mailing tube. Store unstarched to avoid attracting silverfish.

CARE OF SYNTHETICS

None of the new so-called miracle fibers will take too much heat. They rate in heat sensitivity as follows: Dynel is most sensitive, acetates are next; Orlon and Dacron are medium and nylon is the least sensitive. Use a low temperature until you are sure how much they will stand.

Blends can be a problem if you do not know the fibers in the fabric. When you buy, find out the fiber content and what the recommendations are for care. Keep labels for reference when laundering.

Always separate white from colors when laundering. This is especially important for synthetics because some fibers have a strong attraction for dye and soil.

Wash frequently and before garments become too soiled. Most of the new fibers give up soil readily if it has not become imbedded.

With the exception of some of the filmy, delicate fabrics, well-made garments of synthetics can be machine-washed. Use warm, not hot, water and add a water softener if necessary. Use a short washing cycle (4 to 6 minutes) and do not spin overlong. Avoid creasing with wringer or hand twisting. Hand wash delicate fabrics.

Grayed nylons can be whitened with a chlorine bleach, following directions on the bottle. Rinse thoroughly. If this is not sufficient use a color remover.

In washing permanent pleats, do not use too-hot water. They were put in by heat and heat can take them out. Rinse at the same temperature and drip dry on a hanger. "Finger-press" if necessary.

When pressing synthetics, use low heat and press on the wrong side.

MENDING LEATHER

Tears in leather articles (gloves, jackets, etc.) can be mended satisfactorily to extend their wearing period. Seams in gloves should be mended by using the same stitch as used in the construction of the glove—whipping, buttonholing, or saddle stitching.

To mend tears in leather, reinforce both edges with blanket stitches, drawing the tear together as you work. Use fine thread for thin leather and coarser thread for heavy leather.

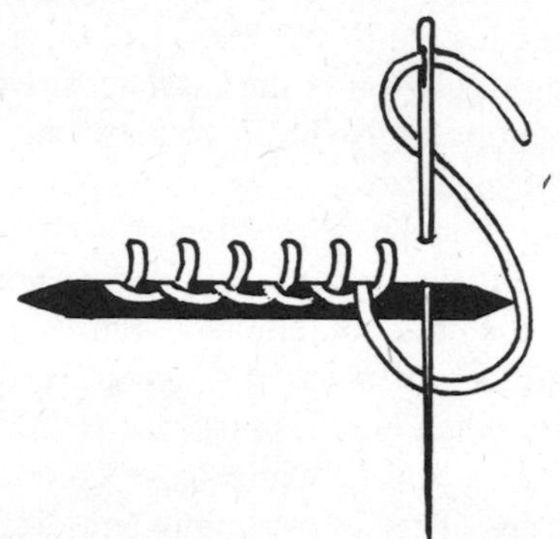

For small holes, start in the same way with a row of blanket stitches around the edge of the hole. Fill in with rows of blanket stitch worked into the preceding row. Decrease the number of stitches (by skipping a stitch) toward the center.

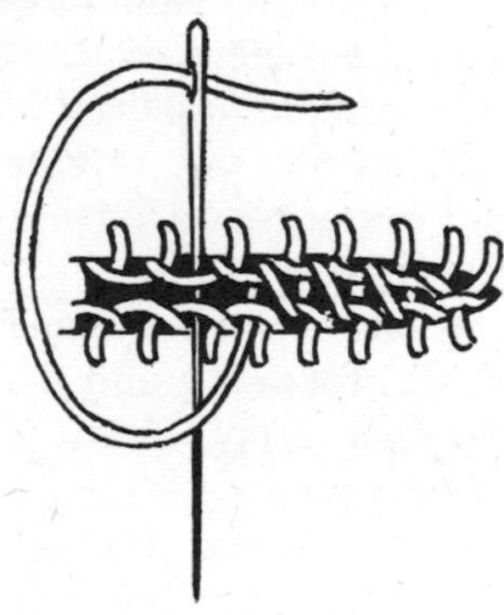

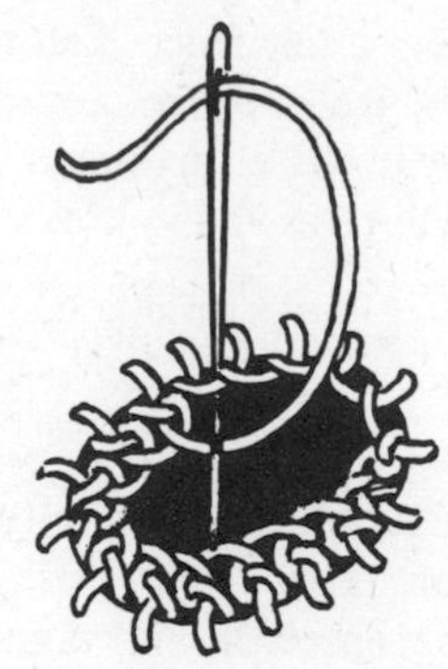

Large holes in leather will probably need to be patched. Cut a piece of leather, lay underneath the hole, and attach with fine overhand stitches around edge of hole. Turn to wrong side, trim edges of patch, and overhand edges of patch to the garment.

There are a number of products, such as press-on tape, mending tissue, and cement, available for doing quick jobs of mending and patching. For the most part they are satisfactory for certain jobs and withstand several washings and dry cleanings. Look for these at notion counters and follow directions which come with the package.

REINFORCEMENTS

It is well to look over a garment (even a new one) before wearing. Check for the following:

• If a hem is broken, repair at once, as heels can catch in a loose hem. The chain stitch often used in ready-made garments is best removed and replaced with hand hemming.

• Reinforce pocket corners by hand or machine.

• Examine binding to see if it is caught properly by the stitching. Rip and restitch if necessary to prevent binding from coming loose.

• Trim all dangling threads or fasten off securely.

• Puckered or crooked stitching should be ripped and restitched.

• If a garment has a kimono sleeve, to prevent from tearing under the arm, stitch narrow tape on top of the seam stitching.

• Weak buttonholes should be reworked with buttonhole stitch. If too far gone, stitch around close to the edge by machine then work buttonhole stitch over it.

• Resew loose snaps, and hooks and eyes. Check buttons and resew if necessary.

For special reinforcements in any area that needs strengthening, set the machine to about 20 stitches per inch and sew the seam or area in question.

Chapter 15

Gifts to Make

Throughout this book instructions are given for making many articles which can be used as gifts and bazaar items. The following pages give a further selection of gifts suitable for many occasions and for the various members of the family.

Cowboy or Cowgirl Kerchief Bibs

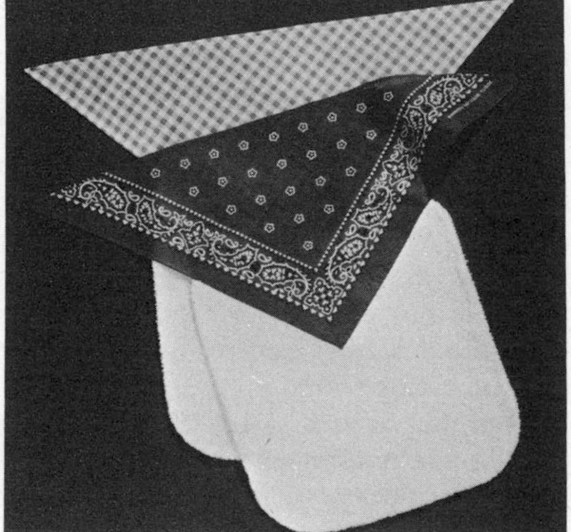

Materials. ½ yd. 36″ wide White Terry Cloth (makes 2 bibs). 1 Bandanna 17″ square (makes 2 bibs). Or ½ yard bright-colored Gingham (makes 2 bibs).

Pattern and Cutting. Enlarge pattern (one square = 1″) which is for half of the bib. Make a full pattern of brown paper. Place the pattern on fold of terry cloth, pin and cut. Cut bandanna in half to make 2 triangles. If you are making the bib with gingham, cut an 18″ square and cut it in half to make 2 triangles.

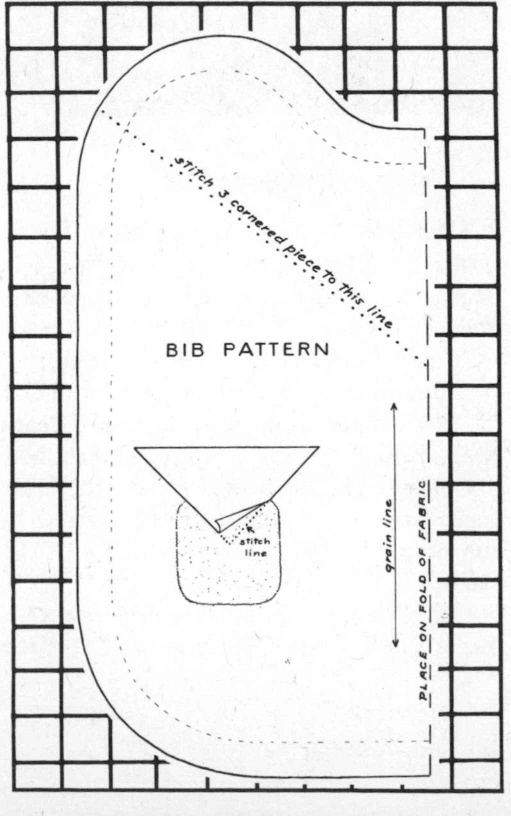

To Make. Turn a narrow hem and stitch all around terry-cloth bib, press. Turn a narrow hem and stitch the raw edge of one triangle or hem edges of one gingham triangle, press. Place point of triangle on bib as indicated on pattern and stitch.

Set of Bean Bags

Girl Bean Bag

Materials. 1/8 yd. Printed Cotton Fabric. Scraps of Light Pink (old lingerie) Silk, Rayon or Synthetic Jersey. Scraps of Red Felt. 1 package White medium Rickrack. Scraps of Red and Black Iron-on Fabric. 3 yds. Brown Rug Yarn. Small amount of Cotton Batting for stuffing. 1/4 lb. small Beans. Narrow Red Ribbon or Yarn for hair bow.

Cutting. Out of cotton print, cut body, head, and shoes as directed in pattern. Also cut piece 4″ x 17″ for skirt and 2″ x 10″ for ruffle.

Out of jersey fabric, cut 2 head pieces, 2 pieces 2¼″ x 3¼″ for arms and 2 pieces 2¼″ x 4¼″ for legs.

Cut about twenty 5″ lengths and six 6″ lengths of rug yarn.

Cut felt and iron-on fabric as indicated on pattern.

Note: Use ¼″ seam allowances throughout.

Body. With right sides together, sew around curved edge of body pieces, leaving straight edge open. Turn. Match 2 head pieces and stitch around, leaving bottom of neck open. Turn and stuff head (neck only slightly) with cotton. Fill body ¾ full with beans, then slip-stitch entire neck into body opening. Turn in raw edges of body and stitch across neck. Fold each piece for arms and legs lengthwise in half. Stitch 3/16″ from long raw edge and around one short end, leaving other end open (a). Trim and turn to right side. Stuff with cotton and slip-stitch opening. With seam in back, fold end of legs up ½″ for feet in front and sew in position (b).

Shoes. Fold felt for shoes as marked on pattern and whip-stitch around front and back, leaving top open. Slip over feet and tack to back of leg.

Arms and legs. Sew arms and legs to shoulder of body at side seams.

Skirt. Make ½″ hem on one long edge. Stitch rickrack to skirt ¼″ from edge of hem. Sew 2nd row of rickrack to skirt ¼″ above 1st row. With right sides together, join ends of skirt. Turn. Fold under ¼″ edge on top of skirt and gather, using double thread, about 1/8″ from folded edge. Sew skirt to body about ¾″ below neck.

Ruffle. Make 3/8″ hem on one long edge. Sew rickrack to ruffle ¼″ from edge. Turn in ¼″ of raw edge and gather same as skirt to fit around doll's neck. Draw up gathers and sew ruffle to neck.

Eyes and mouth. Place eyes, nose and mouth on face, using pattern and photograph as a guide. Set iron control at "wool," press down firmly on iron-on fabric, then rotate iron for about 12 seconds. Let cool.

Make a tiny stitch with Red thread at each corner of mouth and a short stitch with Black thread over each eye in this way: bring thread through head from back, take stitch and bring needle through head again. Draw both ends of thread out and tie off. This procedure gives a little shape to the face.

Hair. Place 5″ lengths of yarn across head of doll from eyebrows down to back of neck and tack to head across top and in back of head. Place 6″ lengths across top of head from side to side and tack to top and sides of head. Place Red ribbon or yarn around head (underneath hair in back) and tie in a bow on top of head.

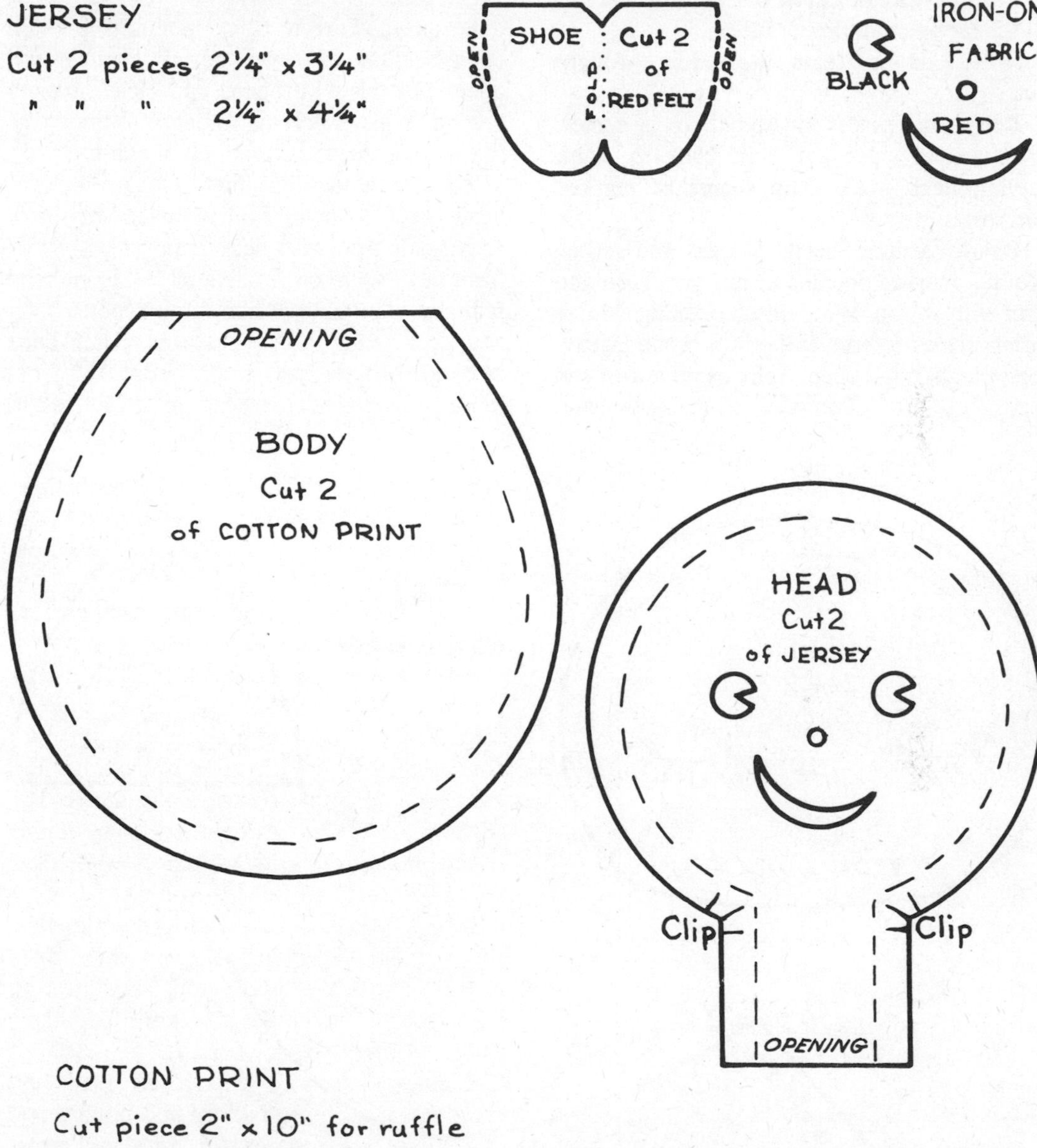

GIRL
BEAN BAG

Cat Bean Bag

Materials. ¼ yd. Checked Gingham Fabric (¼″ checks). Scraps of contrasting Cotton Fabric for lining ears. Mercerized Sewing Thread to match fabric. Six-Strand Floss, 1 skein, Black. Small amount Cotton Batting for stuffing. About 6 ozs. small Beans.

Cutting. Cut fabric as marked on pattern. Cut 2 ear pieces of lining fabric.

Note: Use ¼″ seam allowances throughout.

Body. Join pieces for body back at center. With wrong sides out, join back to front, leaving neck open. Clip seams as marked and turn.

Head. Match head pieces and stitch around, leaving opening at bottom. Turn and stuff with cotton. Whip-stitch opening. Match lining pieces to ears and stitch around, leaving straight edge open. Trim seam at top and turn. Fold ¼″ of raw edges to inside, and slip-stitch opening. Make tiny fold in center and whip-stitch ears to head, just in back of seam at corners. With 3 strands of floss, make half circle of outline stitches for eyes. Make 7 small single stitches below curved line for lashes and one small stitch between eyes for nose (see pattern). Stitch pieces for tail together along inner curve and ⅓ of outer curve. Turn to right side and slip-stitch open section of outer curve, leaving end open. Fill tail with beans and close opening on end. Whip-stitch tail to body. Fill body ¾ full with beans and slip-stitch opening.

To attach head to body. Place back of head upside-down against back of body (right side up) with neck seam of body ¼″ from head seam on 1 side and ½″ from head seam on other side. Whip-stitch head to body and neck seam in this position. Catch back of head to body back seam about ¼″ from joining. This gives the head an attractive tilt.

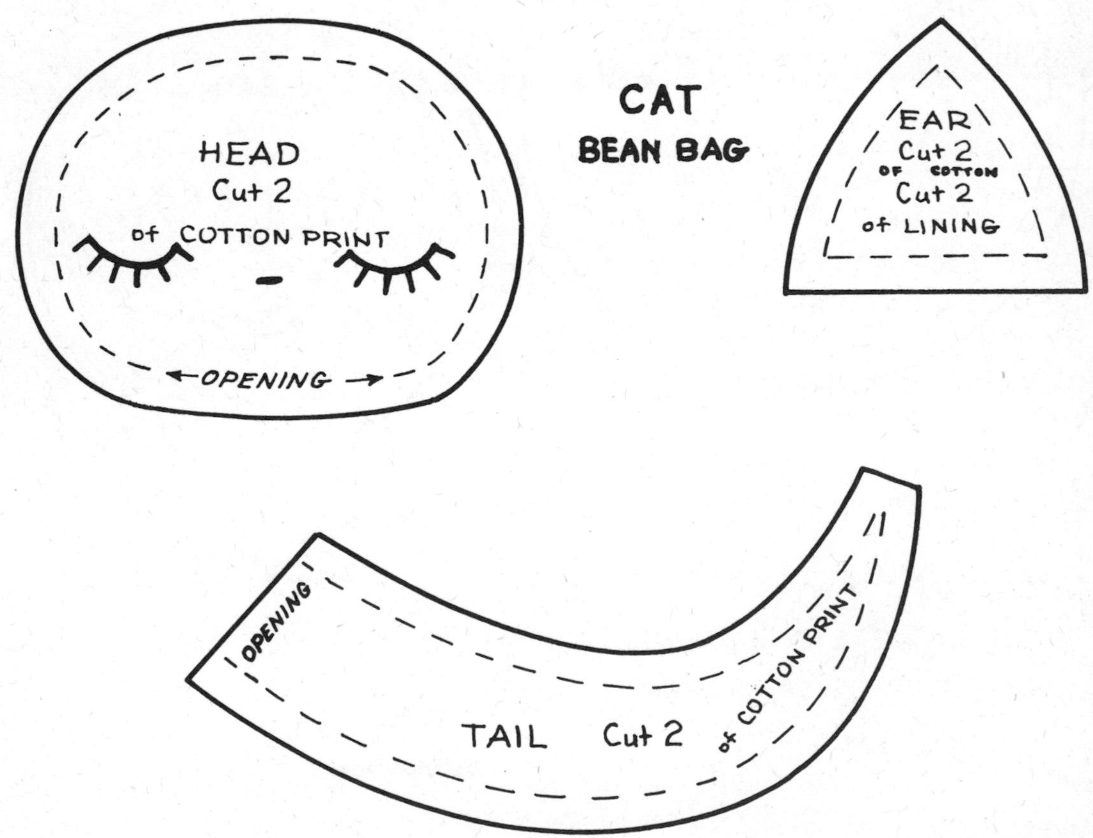

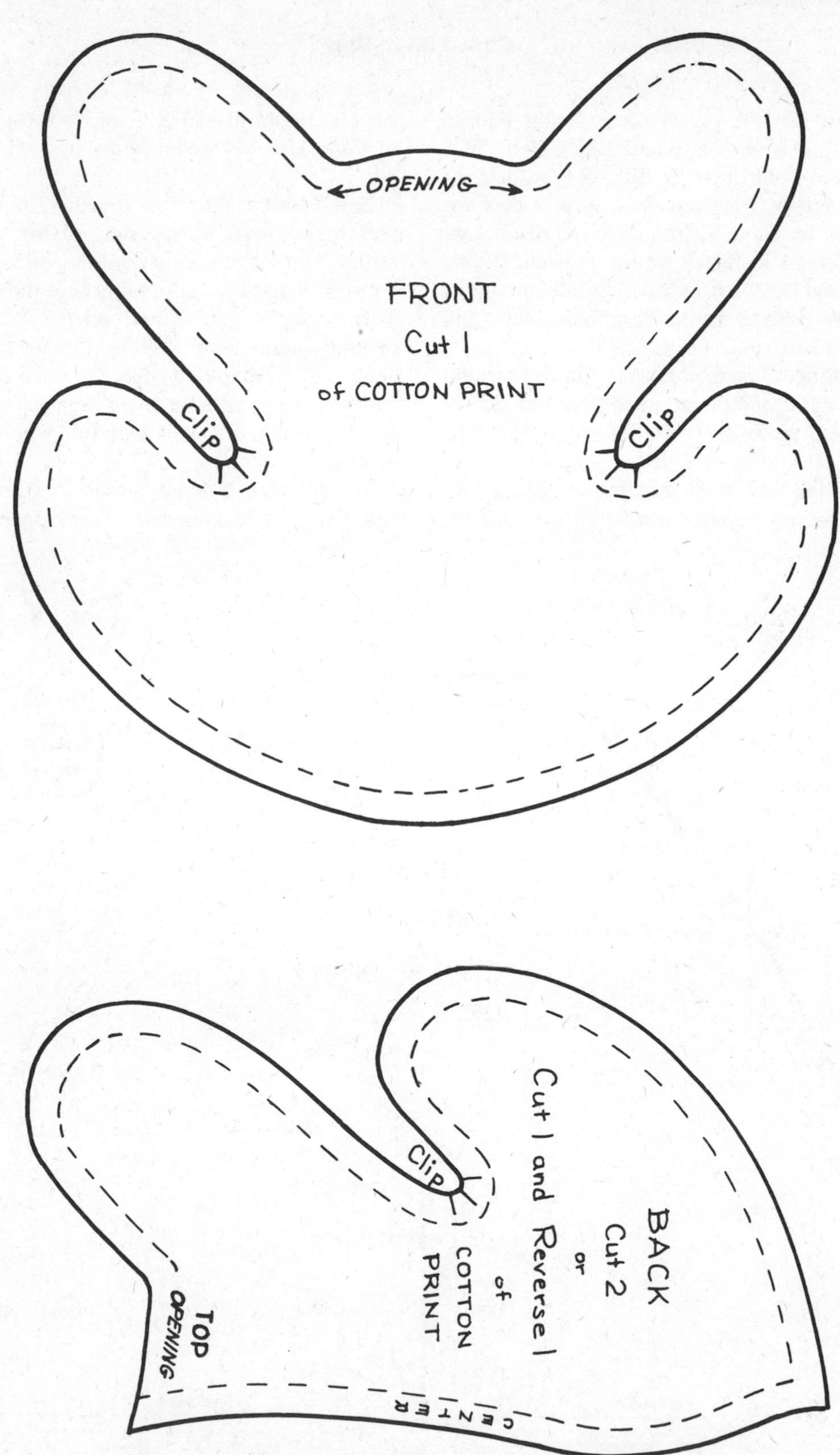
OPENING
FRONT
Cut 1
of COTTON PRINT
Clip
Clip
Clip
BACK
Cut 2
or
Cut 1 and Reverse 1
of
COTTON
PRINT
TOP
OPENING
CENTER

Clown Bean Bag

Materials. ¼ yd. Printed Cotton Fabric. Scraps of Red, White and Black Felt. 5″ x 7″ piece (old lingerie) Silk, Rayon or Synthetic Jersey. Red Iron-On Fabric. 1 package of Red medium Rickrack. Mercerized Sewing Thread to match fabric and felt. 2 yds. any bright color Rug Yarn. Small amount of Cotton Batting for stuffing head, feet and arms. ½ lb. small Beans.

Cutting. Trace patterns. Out of cotton print, cut 2 of suit and head and 4 of sleeve. Also cut piece 2″ x 10″ for ruffle. Cut 2 of hat piece out of Red felt, 2 of hand out of White felt and 4 of shoe out of Black felt. Cut nose and mouth out of Red iron-on fabric. Cut about fifteen 2″ lengths of rug yarn.

Note: Use ¼″ seam allowances throughout.

Suit. With right sides together, match 2 pieces for suit. Stitch side seams. Stitch around slot for leg as marked on pattern. Cut between leg seams, clipping where indicated. Turn to right side. Turn under ¼″ at leg opening and, with double thread, gather about ⅛″ from folded edge. Draw up gathers and sew back and forth through gathers to close opening. Fill suit half full with beans through top opening.

Head. Place 2 head pieces together and stitch around, leaving end of neck open. Clip

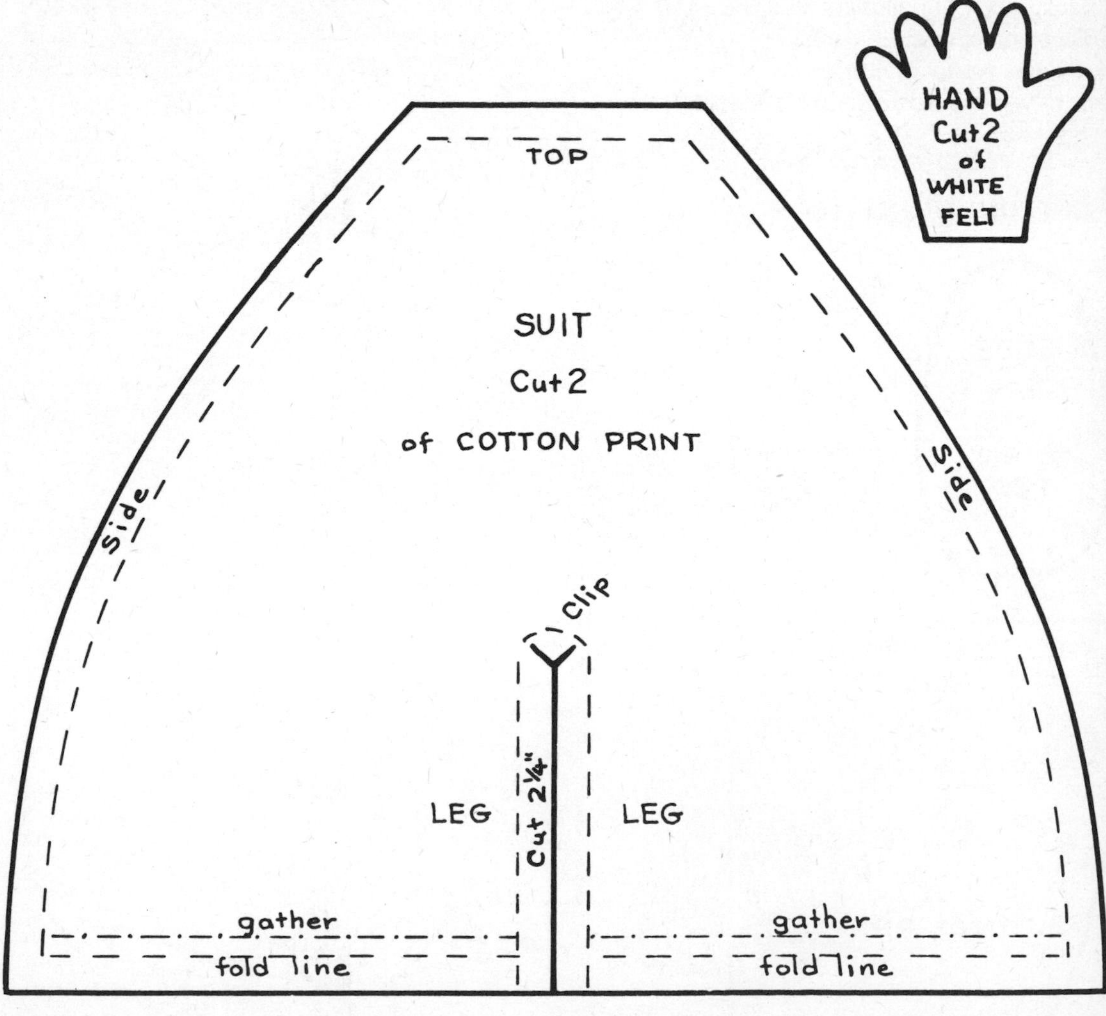

where marked and turn to right side. Stuff head well (neck only slightly) with cotton. Slip neck into opening of suit. Turn in raw edge of suit and machine-stitch across neck.

Sleeves. With right sides together, stitch 2 sleeve pieces together, leaving straight edge open. Turn. Fold raw edge under ¼″ and gather edge, ⅛″ from fold. Stuff sleeve with cotton. Slip wrist of felt hand into sleeve opening and draw up thread. Sew back and forth through felt and sleeve. Turn in ends at top of sleeve and whip-stitch. Attach top of sleeve to side seam and shoulder. Repeat for other sleeve.

Ruffle. Machine stitch a ¼″ hem on one long side of ruffle and sew on rickrack by hand, using machine-stitched line as a guide. Join ends of ruffle. Turn in raw edge ¼″ and gather. Slip ruffle over head, place seam in back, draw up gathers and tie off thread. Tack end of seam to back of clown.

Face. Apply mouth and nose to face, using iron at wool setting, and using pattern and photograph as a guide for placement. Press down firmly, then rotate iron slowly for 12 seconds. Allow to cool for a few minutes. With Black thread, make a ¼″ cross for each eye, as shown in photograph, bring thread through head and fasten on back of head.

Hat. Whip-stitch sides of hat together. Tack center of each 2″ length of rug yarn to inside of hat, spacing all around edge. Place hat on head at an angle and tack to head. POMPON: To make small pompon, wind yarn around finger 10 times. Slip yarn off finger carefully and tie doubled sewing thread around center of loops. Knot tightly and cut thread 3″ below knot. Hold pompon by ends of thread, cut loops open and trim pompon. Sew to center front of suit, about halfway between neck edge and top of leg.

Shoes. Whip-stitch together 2 shoe pieces, stuffing slightly before closing. Sew top of shoe to gathers at bottom of leg. Repeat for other shoe.

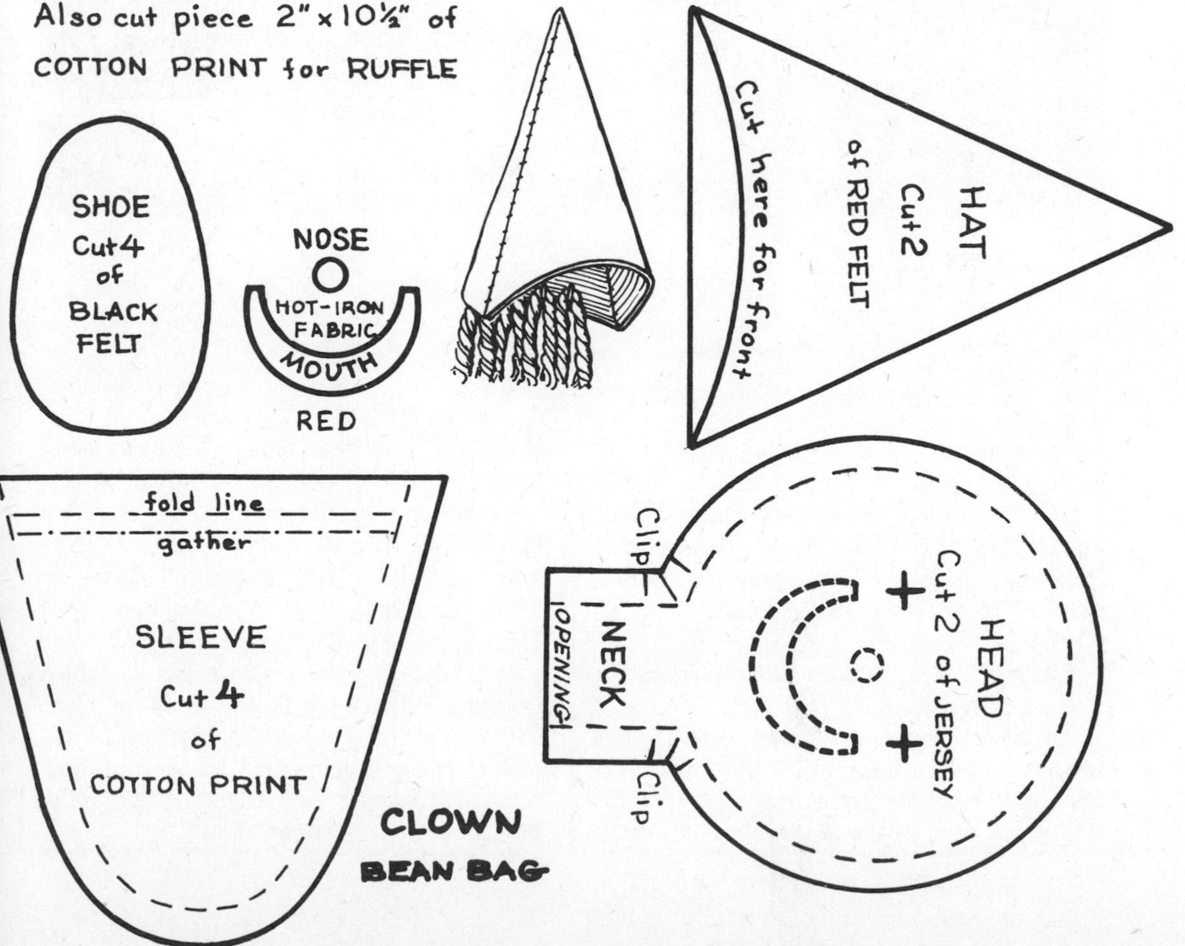

Child's Half Circle Pinafore

Materials. ½ yd. Red Cotton Fabric. 2½ yds. White giant Rickrack. 5 yds. White double-fold Bias Tape. 1½ yds. small-flowered Venice Lace. ¼ yd. White baby Rickrack. ⅓ yd. White regular-size Rickrack. 4″ x 7″ piece Red Percale. 6″ x 8″ piece Pink Percale.

Cutting. Trace pinafore pattern and cut on Red percale.

To Make. Bind with bias tape in this order: armholes, back and lower edge, then neck edge, leaving remaining tape free for ties. Stitch giant rickrack, leaving a ½″ space from tape. Clip apart flowers and tack separately in every 3rd rickrack V, alternating sides. Trace pattern and cut Red heart and Pink heart. Center and top-stitch Red to Pink. Stitch to apron. Top-stitch Red heart with lace flower strip to cover raw edges. Top-stitch Pink with rickrack to cover raw edges. Stitch baby rickrack stems as shown. Cut and stitch Pink flower motif in place. Cut Red center, fold under edges and hand-tack over motif. Top stitch petals with baby rickrack to cover raw edges. Add a small bow at joining of stems to heart.

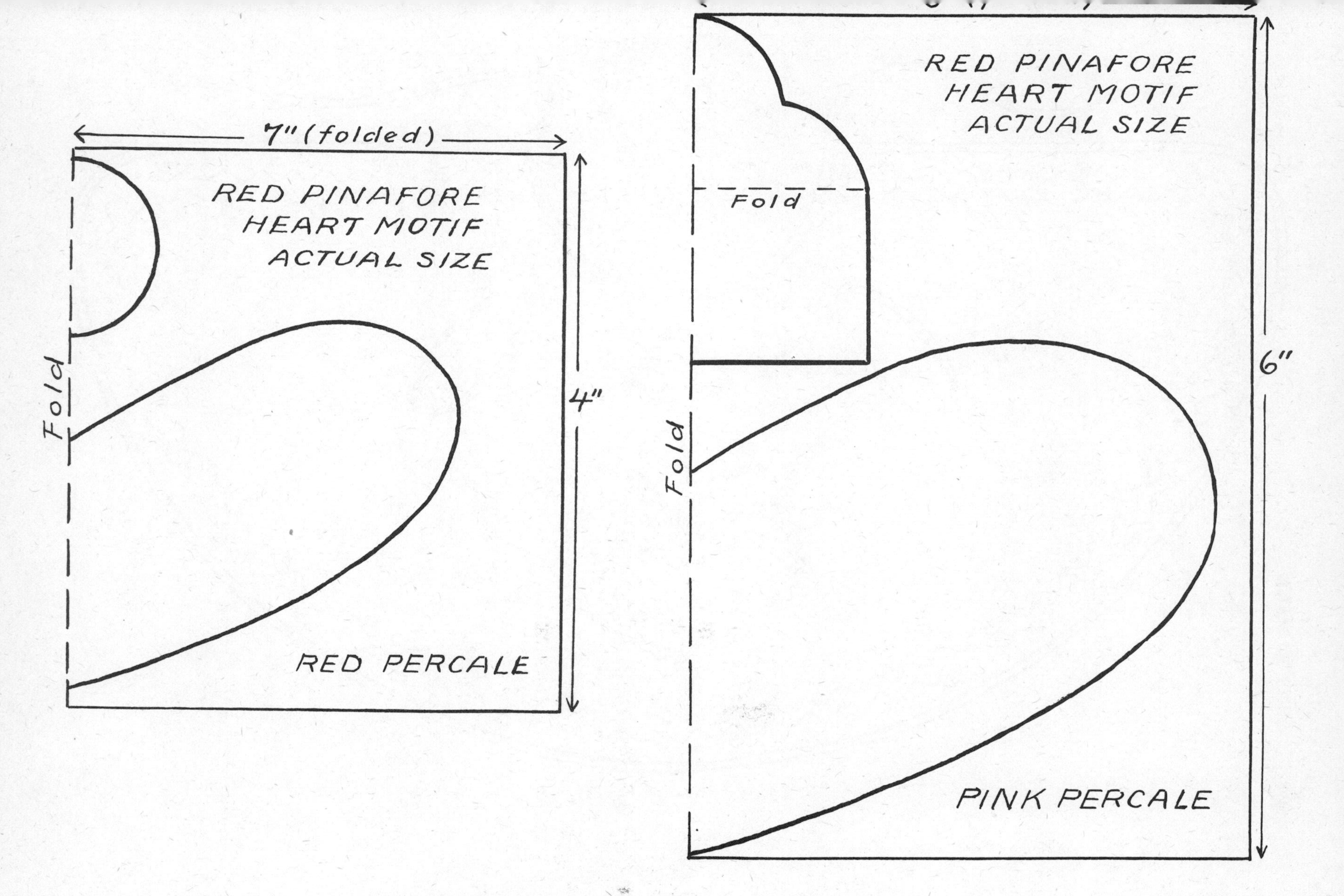
7" (folded)
RED PINAFORE
HEART MOTIF
ACTUAL SIZE
Fold
4"
RED PERCALE
RED PINAFORE
HEART MOTIF
ACTUAL SIZE
Fold
Fold
6"
PINK PERCALE

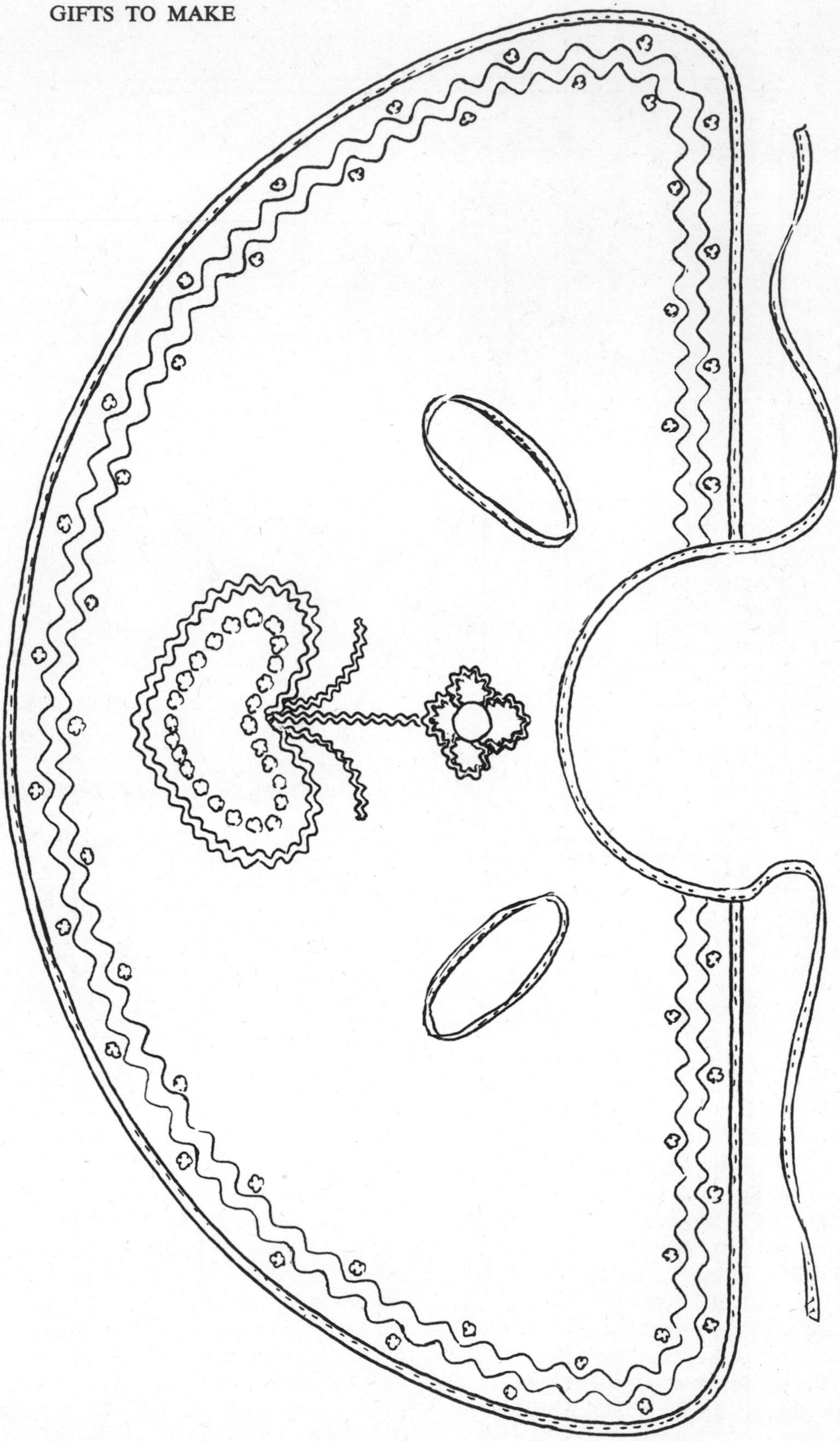

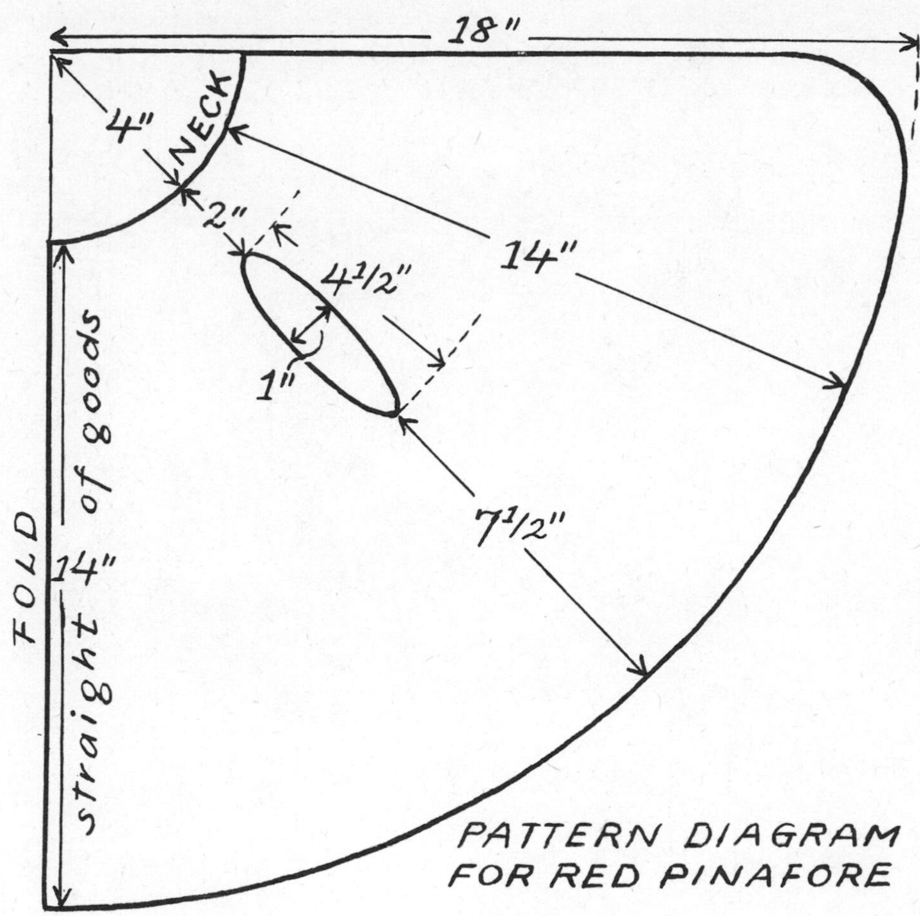

Doll

Materials. Knitting Worsted, 4 ply—4 ozs. of White and 1 oz. of Yellow. One 10″ Styrene Ball. Red and Brown Felt Scraps for face. 12″ by 24″ Petticoat Fabric.

Body. Cut 90 strands of White yarn, 25″ long, for each arm. Divide in 3 equal parts; braid tightly. Wrap 1½″ from each end with yarn; tie. Cut 102 strands of White, 56″ long; tie at center. Insert ball and tie strands around it for neck. Divide strands in 2 equal parts. Insert center of arms between halves and tie below arms for waist. Divide strands in 2 equal parts for legs, then divide each half in 3 equal parts and braid. Tie each braid 1½″ from end.

Hair. Cut a 4″ by 6″ piece of cardboard. Wind Yellow evenly 72 times around the 6″ width, covering the entire cardboard. Being sure to catch all strands, back-stitch over strands along one end for center part. Cut strands at opposite edge. Sew hair in place. Clip a few strands at center front for bangs. Cut 2 Black felt triangles, with 1″ sides, for eyes; a ⅝″ by 1″ red felt oval for mouth.

Sew these 3 pieces in place.

Petticoat. Sew narrow edges of fabric together for back seam. Fold in half lengthwise. Turn ½″ of raw edges to inside; gather this edge to fit waist.

Aprons

Materials (child's is for about age 3). ½ yd. of 36″ wide Striped Fabric. Scraps of contrasting Plain Fabric for pockets (dimensions below). 5 yds. Bias Tape. Sewing Thread to match.

To Make: With stripes running lengthwise, cut one 8″ by 14″ piece for doll's apron; 18″ by 22″ piece for child's. From plain fabric, cut two 3″ by 7″ pieces for doll's apron pockets; two 6″ by 14″ pieces for child's. Fold pocket pieces in half and stitch sides (¼″ seams). Turn, fold in raw edges and press. With fold-edge up, pin to aprons (doll's 1″ from side and bottom, child's 2″ from side and 3″ from bottom). Stitch around 3 sides. Gather apron tops, doll's to 4″ and child's to 6″. Bind remaining raw edges. Then bind tops, leaving 12″ tape ends on the doll's apron and 18″ ends on child's to be used for tying.

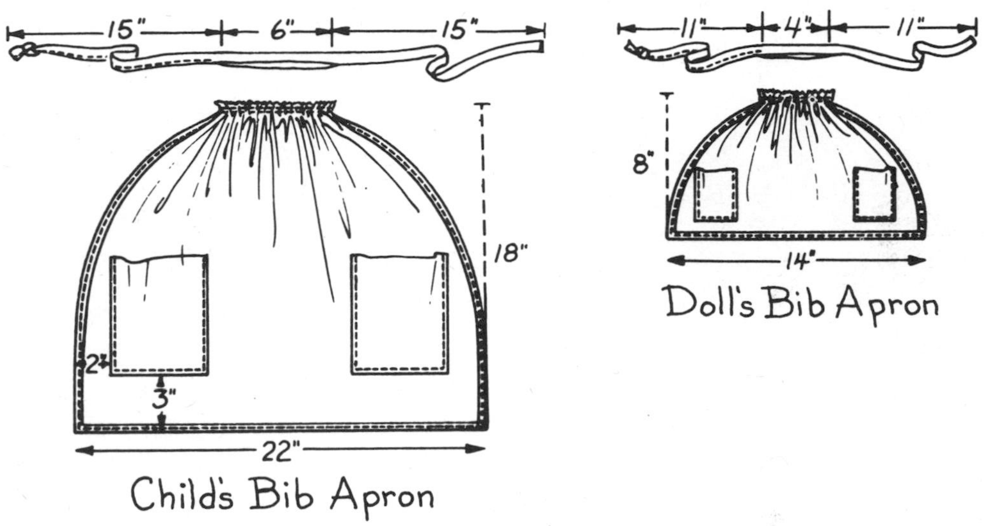

Child's Bib Apron

Doll's Bib Apron

Folding Tote Bag

Materials. 1 yd. 36″ wide sturdy Print Fabric. 1 yd. 36″ wide heavy non-woven Interfacing. Heavy-Duty Mercerized Sewing Thread, to match main color of print. 1 pkg. White baby Rickrack. 7½″ square of heavy Cardboard.

Cutting. From print fabric and interfacing cut:

1 piece 33″ x 18″—for bag

1 piece 9″ square—for bottom

From print fabric, also cut 2 pieces, 14″ by 3½″—for handles.

Note: ½″ seams allowed.

To Make. Pin interfacing to wrong sides of outer fabric pieces. Bring 18″ edges of bag pieces together, wrong side out, and stitch along 18″ edges. Press seam open. To make hem at top edge, turn down ½″ and press, then turn down 2″, press. Stitch around both edges of hem (a). Turn right side out. To form sides, press folds at seam and opposite seam, then bring those folds together to make 2 remaining folds (b). Select a motif on one side and outline with baby rickrack. Stitch rickrack in place. Turn bag wrong side out. Place right sides of bottom and lower edge of bag together, matching corners of bottom to folds in bag. Stitch all 4 sides. Fold under ½″ on all 14″ edges of handles. For each handle, bring folds together, right sides out, and press. Stitch along both long edges on each handle. Pin or baste handles in place with sides of handles 1″ from folds of bag (c). Stitch handles to bag over both stitching lines on bag hem. Topstitch along folds of bag and around bottom seam. Turn bag inside out. Slit bottom interfacing along one side. Slip cardboard into slit. Turn bag to right side.

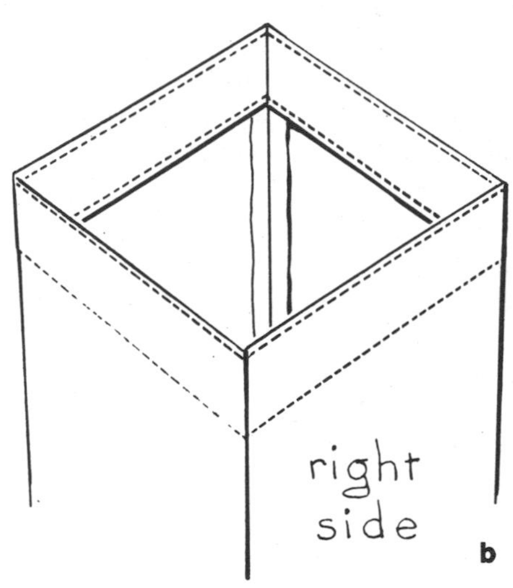

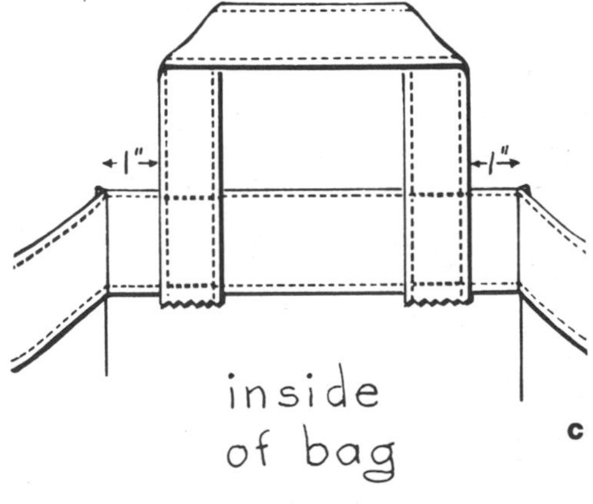

Drawstring Shift

Materials. 2⅜ yds. Pale Aqua 36″ wide fine Cotton Fabric. ⅜ yds. Deep Aqua 36″ wide fine Cotton Fabric.

Cutting. Cut shift and draw string of pale Aqua fabric, following cutting diagram. Cut 2 facing pieces (width of top of shift) 5″ wide of the deep Aqua fabric. Taking ⅝″ seams, stitch sides of shift together, leaving arm opening near the top as indicated on the diagram.

To Make. Press seams open. Finish edges of the seams and hem around armholes. Stitch ends of deep Aqua facing together to make a continuous piece. Right sides together to make a continuous piece. Right sides together, pin and stitch facing to top of shift. Turn to inside and press on the stitching line at the top. Turn under and press seam allowance at lower edge of facing. Pin the lower edge of facing to shift. Measure center front of shift 4″ down from top and mark. Measure and mark, ¾″ each side of the center front, a ½″ vertical buttonhole. This should be just between the eventual stitchings for the casing. See diagram. Unpin facing at this point and make the 2 buttonholes either by machine or by hand. Repin facing and stitch it to shift on the very edge and again ¾″ above. Sew the drawstring pieces together end to end. Fold lengthwise wrong side out and stitch a ¼″ seam. Stitch across ends but leave a 3″ opening at center side. Turn with tubing turner. Press and slipstitch opening. Run the drawstring through the casing. Make a simple knot about 1″ from each end. Try on, mark length and hem the shift.

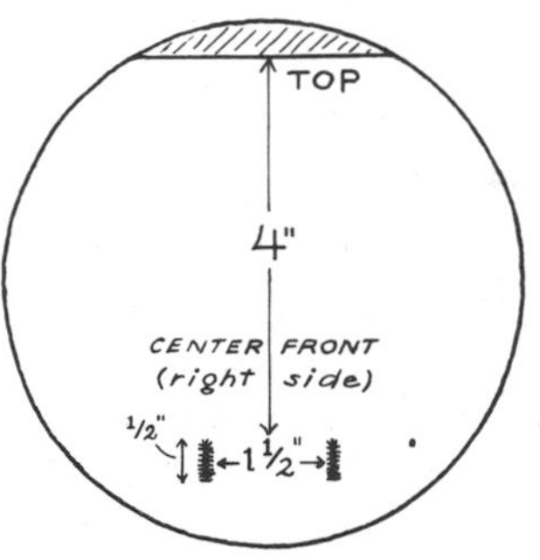

BUTTONHOLES FOR DRAWSTRING

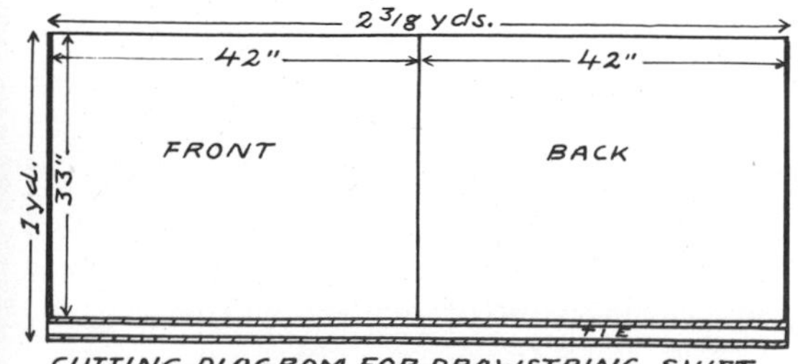

CUTTING DIAGRAM FOR DRAWSTRING SHIFT.

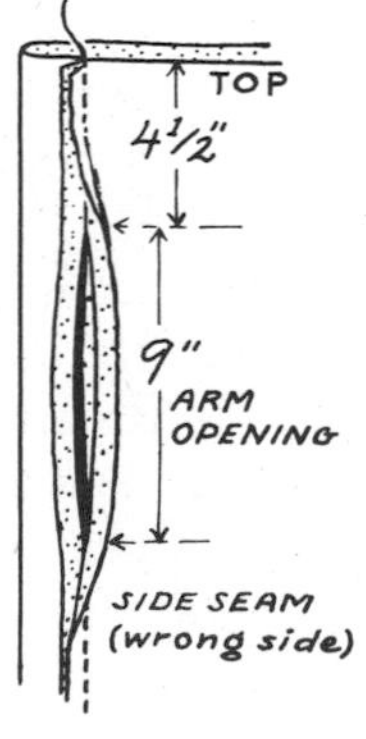

Tote Bags

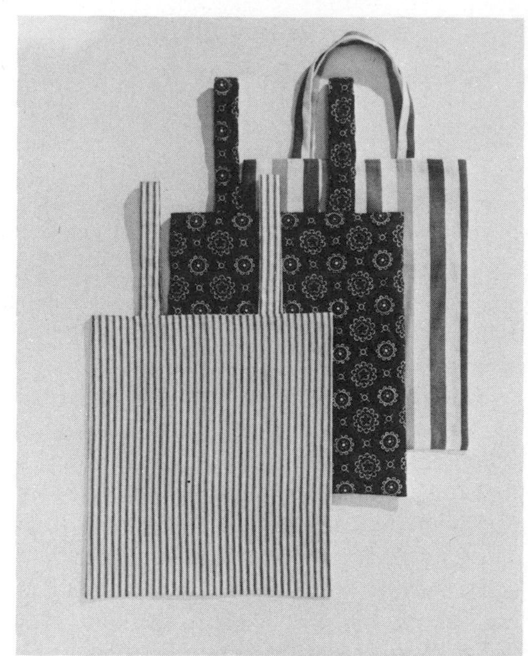

Materials. ⅝ yd. 36″ wide Striped Denim or other fabric. Two pieces 5″ x 14½″ of contrasting color for facing top of bag.

Cutting. Cut bag and handles as shown on cutting diagram.

To Make. Fold bag piece wrong side out lengthwise (the way the stripes run). Pin and stitch side seams and across the bottom, turn and press. Sew facing pieces end to end to make a continuous piece. Press seams. It should exactly fit top edge of bag. Turn under one raw edge and stitch. Fold handle pieces lengthwise right side out, turn in long raw edges, pin and stitch close to edge. Stitch on folded edge. Pin handles in place (see diagram) one on each side. Place facing on top with wrong side out and raw edge matching top of bag. Pin and stitch around top of bag. Push facing to inside and tack at sides. Press.

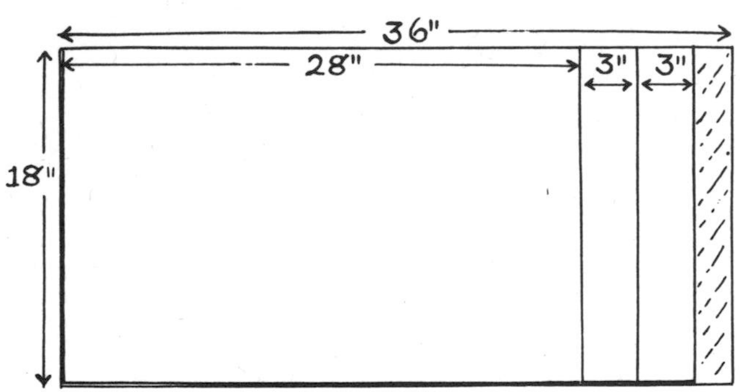

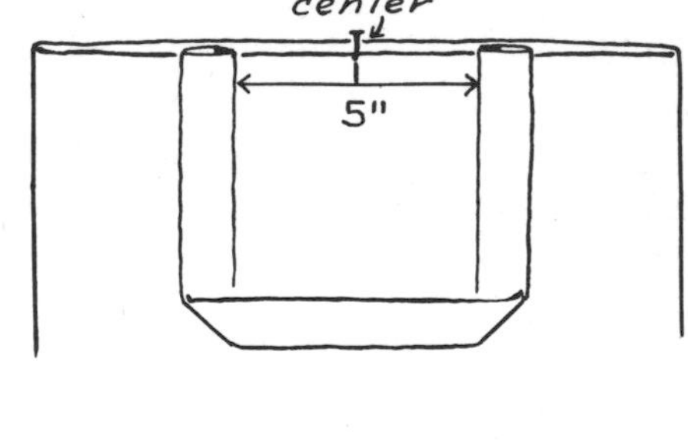

Patch-Pocket Aprons

Woman's Apron

Materials. 1 yd. 36″ wide Black Denim. A variety of Printed Fabrics for pockets.

Cutting. Trace and make apron pattern from diagram for man's apron, page 507, making 18″ long at side or length desired. Cut apron and ties from denim, following cutting diagram.

To Make. Stitch a 1″ hem at the top of bib. Stitch a very narrow hem all around the remainder of the apron. NECK STRAP: Turn in long edges, pin and stitch close to the edge and also along fold edge. Turn in one end, lap under top of bib at right side and stitch. Adjust to neck and attach other end to the opposite side of bib. TIES: Turn in one end, then edges toward each other and stitch. Attach ties at back of apron. POCKETS: Make various-sized pockets of the printed fabrics as shown on diagram or change sizes and placing to suit your own taste. Pockets may be made with a hem at the top or they can be made of double fabric as follows: Cut 2 pocket pieces the desired size plus seams all around. Place pieces right sides together, pin

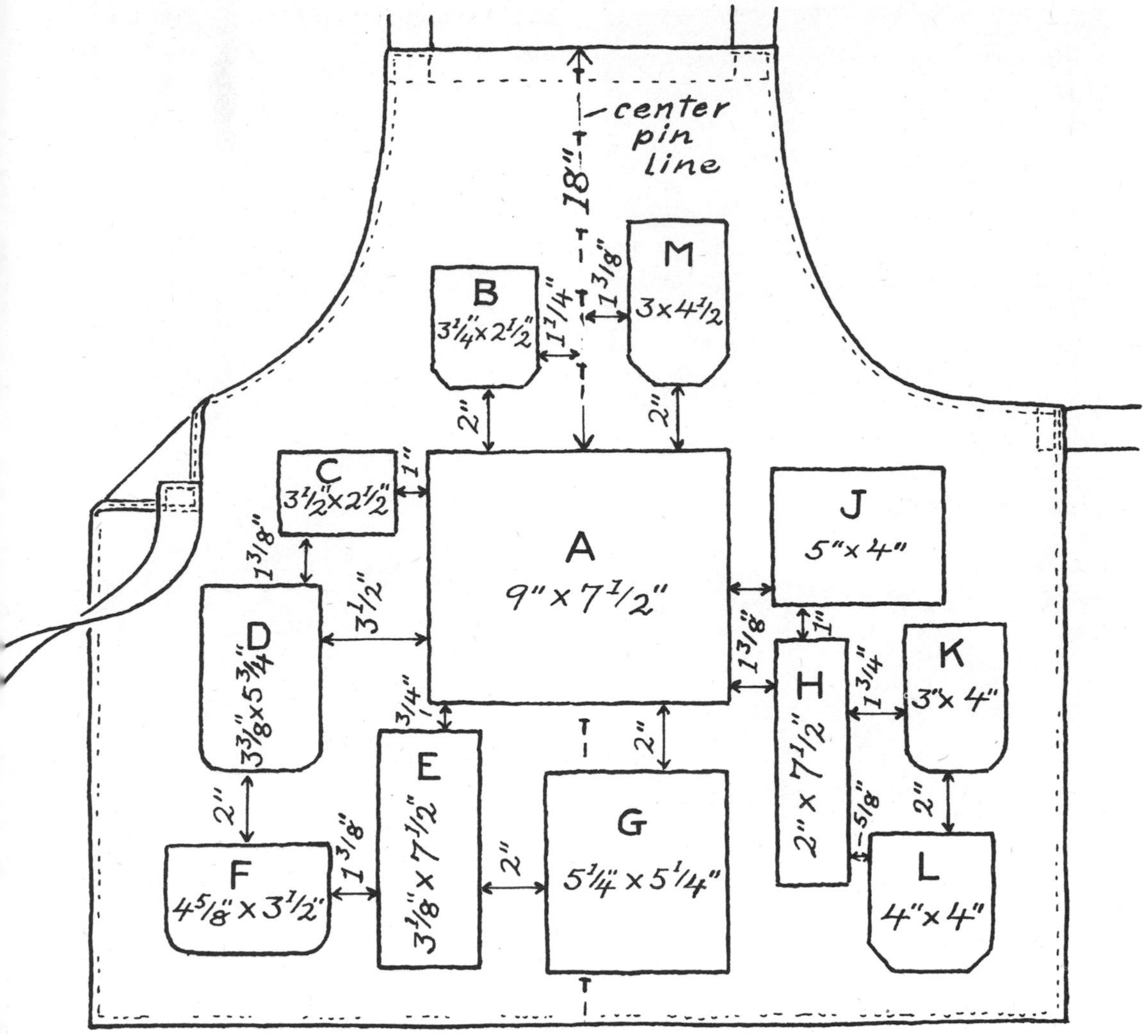

center pin line
18"
B
3¼"x2½"
1¼"
M
3x4½
1⅜"
2"
2"
C
3½"x2½"
1"
A
9"x7½"
J
5"x4"
1⅜"
D
3⅜"x5¾"
3½"
1⅜"
1"
H
2"x7½"
K
3"x 4"
1¾"
¾"
2"
E
3⅛"x7½"
G
5¼"x5¼"
2"
⅝"
2"
F
4⅝"x3½"
1⅜"
2"
L
4"x4"

PATCH POCKET PLACEMENT

36
(cut 2)
HALTER (cut 1) 2"x24"
TIES 1½"x12"
APRON
18"
FOLD

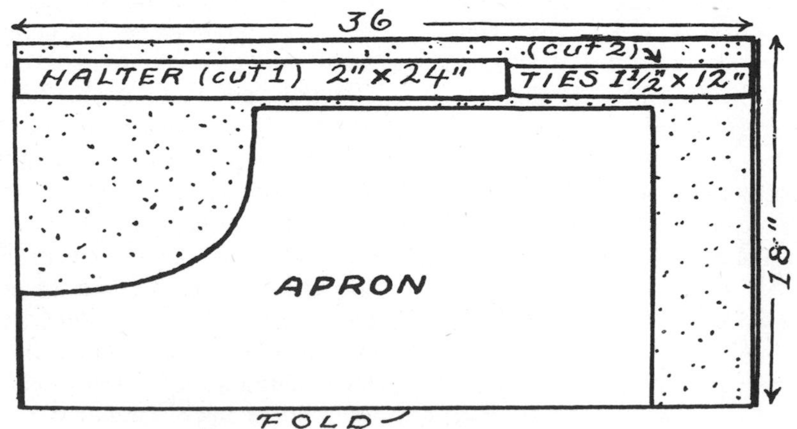

CUTTING DIAGRAM

and stitch all around leaving space for turning. Trim seam, turn and press. Slip-stitch opening. Place pockets as shown or as desired and attach to apron, stitching close to the edge at sides and bottom.

Man's Apron

Materials. 1 yd. Black and White Striped Cotton. Trimming pieces of Cotton for "pockets" as follows—like those in photograph or similar. 7½″ x 20″ wide Red and White stripe, pocket A. 6½″ x 23″ narrow Red and White stripe, pocket B. 6¼″ x 7¼″ Black and White checked gingham (1″ checks), pocket C. 2½″ x 5″ Black and White polka dot for neck tie. 1½″ x 2¾″ Black and White polka dot for neck tie.

To Cut. ½ of pattern for apron is given. Trace off and make a full pattern. Cut apron; cut 2 apron ties (1½″ x 25½″) and one neck band (2¾″ x 29½″); all should run lengthwise of fabric.

To Make. Stitch a ¾″ hem at top of bib and narrow hems on curved and one straight side (raw edge). Turn ½″ hem at top of pocket A and pocket C. Stitch a narrow hem on one long edge of pocket B. This will be top of pocket. Place pocket pieces on apron, following diagram and photograph, turn under edges; pin in place. Turn under and stitch the bottom edge of crosswise pocket B (narrow red and white stripe) to the up-and-down pocket A (wide red and white stripe) not catching to apron (unpin to do this). Repin and stitch pockets in place. Stitch other lines as shown to make more pockets on horizontal pocket piece. Hem top of checked pocket C. Turn in edges, pin in place and stitch. NECK BAND AND TIES: Turn in long edges toward each other and stitch. Stitch opposite side near edge. Turn under one end of neck band. Pin to side of bib. Stitch. Adjust length and sew other end to

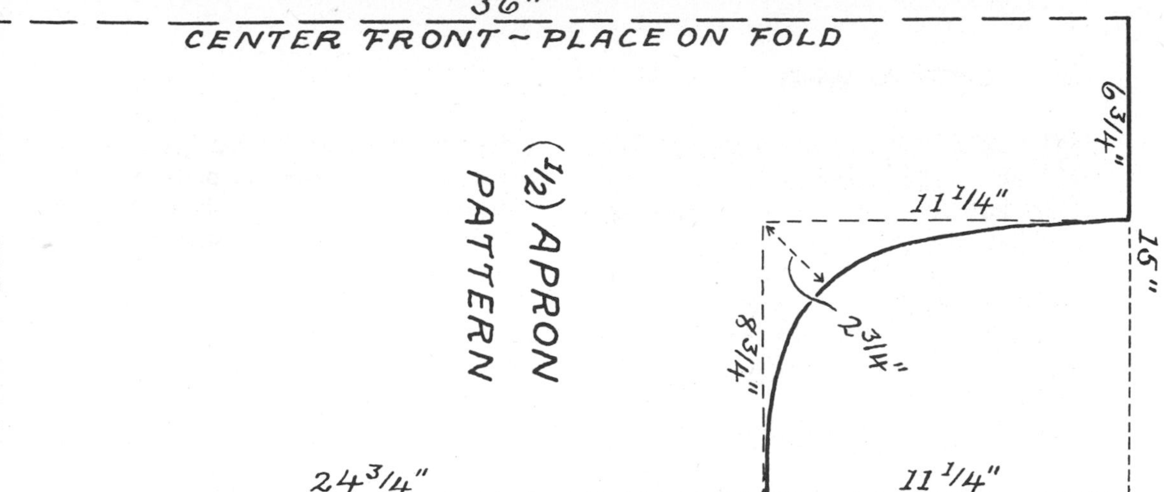

opposite side of bib. Attach ties in same way at sides of apron. Turn in ends of ties and slip stitch. Make 1″ hem at lower edge of apron.

Man's Shirt Holder

Materials. 2¼ yds. heavy Plaid Denim, 36″ wide. ¾ yd. heavy-gauge clear Plastic, 54″ wide or 1¼ yds., 36″ wide, 2 packages matching dominant color of plaid, double-fold Bias Tape. 1 spool Heavy-Duty Mercerized Sewing Thread to match bias tape. Decorative Cord, Black or Colored 1½ yds. Small nails (brads). Wooden Dowel, ¾″ diameter, 26″ long.

Cutting. DENIM FABRIC: Straighten fabric and cut a piece 78″ x 26″. Make a crosswise fold in center and press. Pin and machine-baste around piece so it can be handled as one thickness. PLASTIC: Cut 3 pieces of heavy plastic, 15″ x 26″.

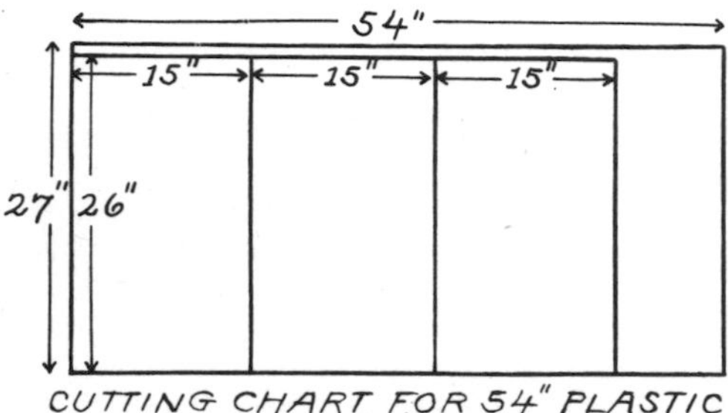

CUTTING CHART FOR 54" PLASTIC

To Make. HOW TO APPLY DOUBLE-FOLD BIAS TAPE: Insert edge of fabric between edges of folded tape, with narrower side of tape on right side of fabric. Stitch on right side along edge of tape. Bind fold of fabric with double-fold bias tape. This will be top edge. Bind one 26″ edge of each plastic piece. TOP POCKET: Keeping bound edges of fabric and plastic toward top, place one plastic piece 10″ down from top of fabric as shown (a) and secure with paper clips or bobby pins. Stitch lower (unfinished) edge of plastic to fabric, ⅛″ from edge. SECOND POCKET: Apply second plastic piece in same way, with top (bound edge) of plastic 17″ from upper bound edge of fabric. BOTTOM POCKET: Third piece of plastic is applied with lower (unfinished) edge of plastic, even with lower edge of fabric.

Finishing. Stitch a strip of bias tape, with wider fold on top, down center of entire shirt bag. Start 6″ from top and end at lower edge, stitching through all thicknesses of fabric and plastic. Stitch down center of tape. Use a line of the plaid to guide placement of bias strip. Apply binding down both side edges and across bottom, being careful to catch in all layers of plastic and fabric. Turn 3″ of entire bound top edge to front of bag. Pin, making sure bound edge follows a line of the plaid. Stitch across on stitching line of bias tape. Leave ends open so dowel can be inserted. Insert dowel and tack in place (b).

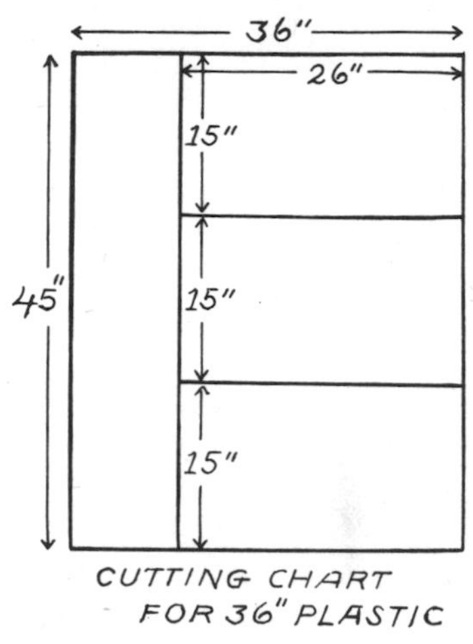

CUTTING CHART FOR 36" PLASTIC

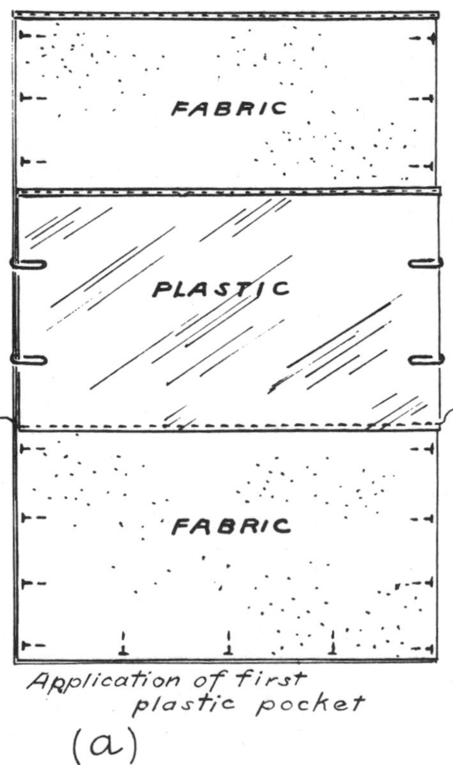

Application of first plastic pocket
(a)

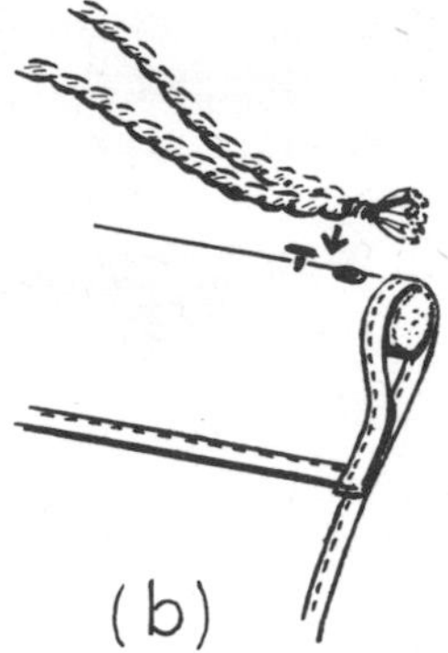

Hanger. Cut cord in half. With two lengths together, ends even, whip both pair of ends together to prevent fraying. Sew ends of cord securely to fabric at ends of dowel.

Round Place Mats

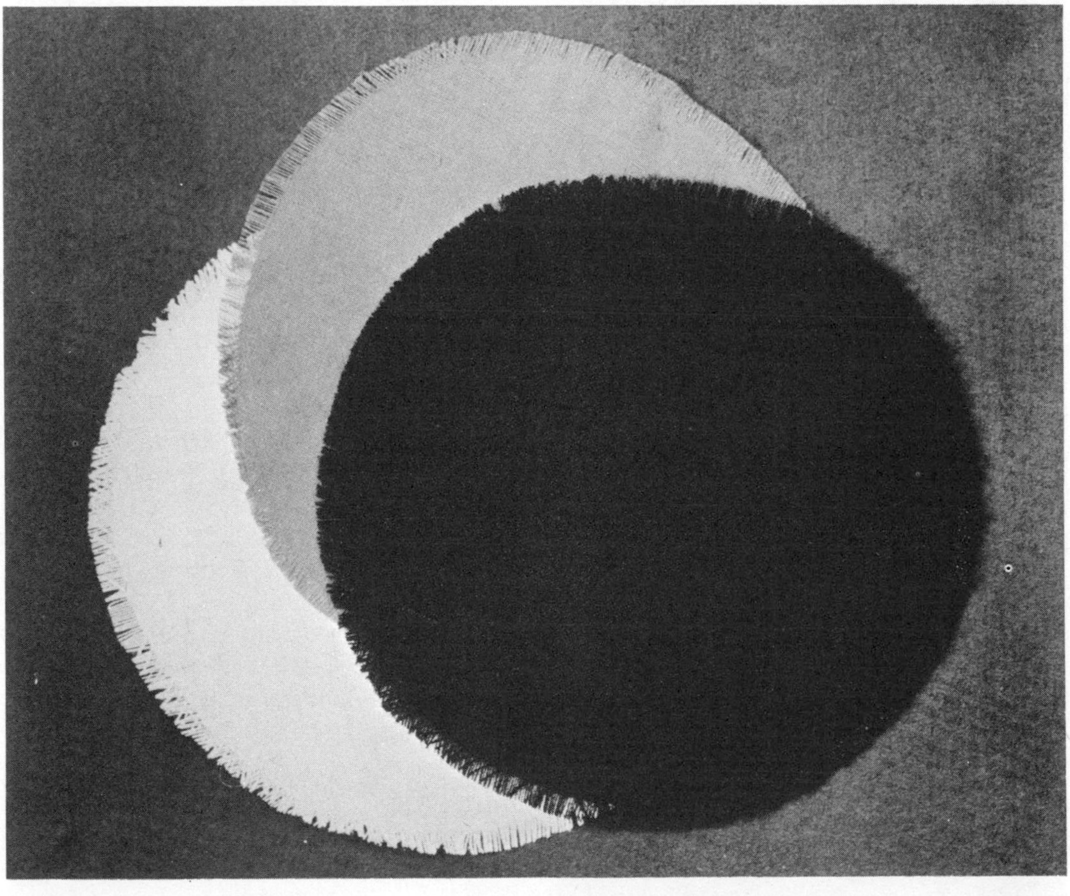

Materials. Mats are 17″ across, finished. ½ yd. 52″ wide Burlap will make 3. Use a variety of colors or make them all of one color.

Directions. With compass or string and pencil, draw a circle 17″ in diameter on brown paper (string should be half this length). Cut out and use as pattern. Pin pattern on burlap and cut around. Measure in ½″ from edge all around; mark and stitch on line twice. Fringe all around, clipping ends at stitching where necessary. On the four bias "sides" the threads can be separated to look fringed and not be clipped.

Dog Basket

Measurements given are for round basket 13″ in diameter and 4½″ high. Measurements must be adjusted for other sizes.

Materials. ⅝ yd. Red-and-White-Checked Gingham (¼″ checks), 36″ wide. ½ yd. Red Cotton Broadcloth, 36″ wide, for pillow. Dacron Batting. Heavy-Duty Mercerized Sewing Thread to match. Six-Strand Embroidery Floss, Black. Embroidery Needle, Size 7.

Pillow Pattern and Cutting. Using heavy paper, cut a circle the diameter of the basket plus 1″ for seam allowance (14″). Using paper pattern, cut two circles from Red fabric.

To Make Pillow. With wrong sides out, pin Red circles together. Stitch around, taking ½″ seam and leaving 3″ opening for turning. Trim, clip and press seam open. Turn right side out and stuff with batting. Slip-stitch opening securely.

To Make Skirt. Cut crosswise strips of gingham for skirt (width of strip should be the height of basket plus about 2½″ for hem). Our strips were 7″ wide. Circumference of skirt (length of strips sewn together) should be 2½ to 3 times circumference of basket. Seam ends of strips together to make one continuous piece.

Embroidery. Design is worked in cross stitch, using all six strands of embroidery floss. Work underneath rows of stitches slant-

ing in one direction, then work back over them slanting stitches in opposite direction. Follow Chart, starting from A, 3″ up from lower edge of gingham. First cross (A) should be on light Red square, next cross on Red. Follow Chart from A to B for motif. Repeat motif for entire length of strip, B of first motif will connect with A of next motif and so on.

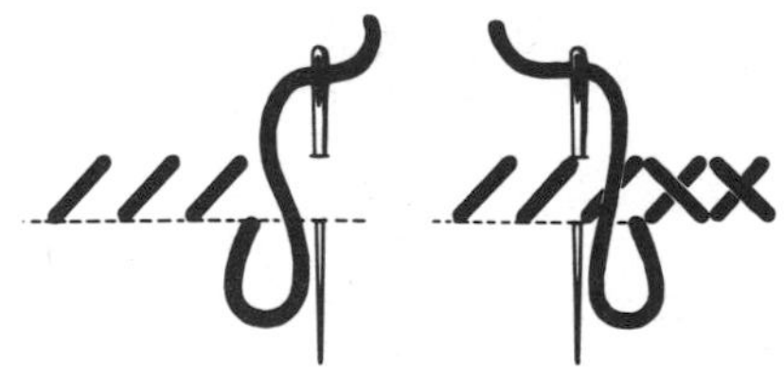

To Finish Skirt. Pleat or gather upper edge of skirt to fit basket (we used ½″ pleats). Stitch along edge, ½″ from edge to anchor pleats. Folding up ⅜″ below embroidery, make about a 2″ hem. Press and hem by hand. Skirt should end about ¼″ above floor. To attach skirt to basket, place it upside down against basket, right side of skirt against outside of basket, stitched line on skirt just under rim of basket (see diagram). Sew by hand through wicker.

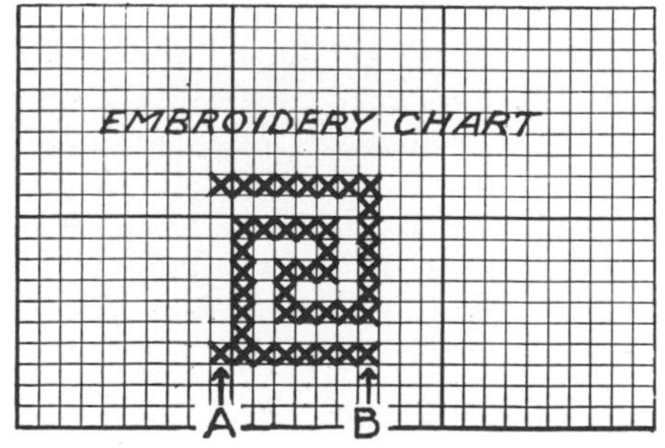

String Holder

Materials. ¼ yd. Burlap, 36″ wide. ¼ yd. Iron-On, nonwoven Interfacing. Iron-On Fabric, in Orange, Green, Brown, Yellow, Red and White. Knitting Worsted to match burlap. Heavy-Duty Mercerized Sewing Thread. 1 large metal Eyelet (¼″ hole). Tracing Paper and Dressmaker's Carbon.

Cutting. Cut a 9″ x 18″ piece from burlap and a matching piece from interfacing.

To Make. Match interfacing to burlap and apply with iron. Using dressmaker's carbon, trace appliqué pieces on fabric side of Iron-On fabric and cut out. Red body, Orange breast and wing, Yellow beak and feet, White eye with Black pupil, Green grass. Apply Iron-On pieces to burlap, following directions on package. Use photograph and cutting diagram as a guide for placement. Bird's back is about 5″ down from top edge, keep long edges of burlap at sides. Apply eyelet to burlap about 1½″ from side, and 8″ from top. Turn under ¼″ on all raw edges including top and stitch. Press. Fold bag wrong-side out and stitch up the sides ½″ from finished edges. Press seams open. Turn bag to right side. Turn down ¾″ around top to inside and hem. Crochet with yarn, using chain stitch to make a 9″ length. Sew ends of chain to back of holder at top about 1″ from the sides. Place ball of string in bag and bring loose end of string out through eyelet.

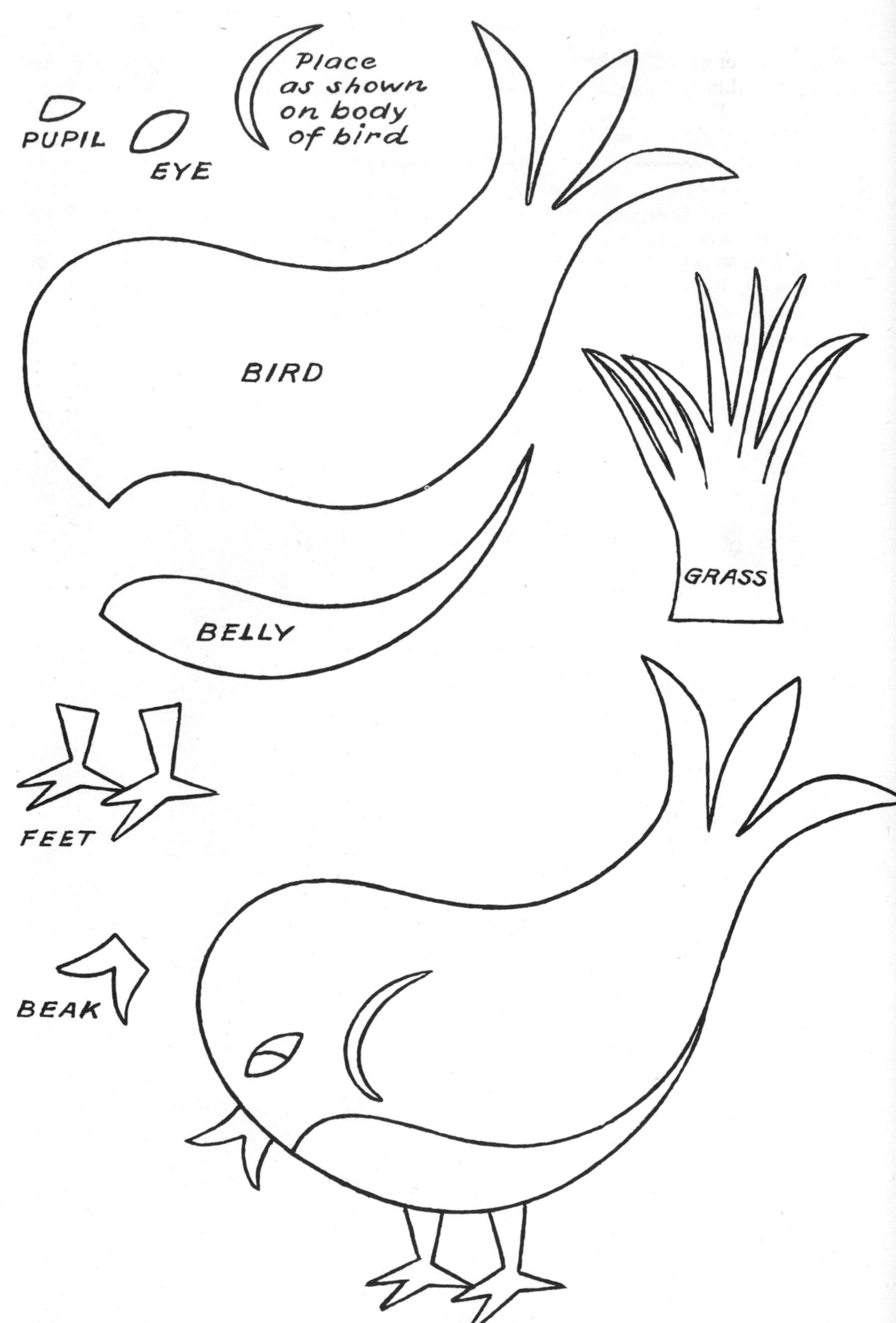
Place
as shown
on body
of bird
PUPIL
EYE
BIRD
GRASS
BELLY
FEET
BEAK

Little Linen Napkins

Materials. For napkins: use scraps of various colors of Linen or buy 1/4 yd. each of several colors. For appliqué, use scraps of bright-colored Cotton or Linen fabric. Embroidery Floss: Black, Brown and colors to match appliqués.

Cutting. Measure, pull threads and cut napkins 5 1/4" x 7". Pull threads to make fringe all around about 3/8" deep.

Appliqués. Trace designs and transfer them to the appliqué fabric using light-colored dressmaker's carbon lightly. Cut out motifs. Also, trace the design onto the napkin, placing it about 1/2" in from edge at left and centering it top and bottom. Pin and baste appliqué motifs in place on napkins and hold by embroidering around edge with matching blanket stitch. Stems, feelers, and other lines are worked in outline stitch; small dots in French knots; spots in satin stitch; birds' feet in lazy-daisy stitch. (Specific stitches are explained in Chapter 2, Embroidery.)

Knitted Ball

At right below

Materials. Super Fingering Yarn—¼ skein Paddy Green, ¼ skein Periwinkle, ¼ skein Emerald, a few yards Blue Jewel. Knitting Needles, No. 1. Acrilan Wadding.

Gauge. Each side of motif—1¼″.

Motifs. 1ST AND 2ND MOTIFS: Starting at outer edge with Emerald, cast on 51 sts. **Row 1:** Knit. **Row 2:** K 4, sl 1, k 2, tog, psso, * k 7, sl 1, k 2 tog, psso. Repeat from * ending with k 4 (41 sts). **Row 3:** With Periwinkle, k across. **Row 4:** With Periwinkle, k 3, sl 1, k 2 tog, psso, * k 5, sl 1, k 2 tog, psso. Repeat from * ending with k 3 (31 sts). **Row 5:** With Emerald, k across. **Row 6:** With Emerald, k 2, sl 1, k 2 tog, psso, * k 3, sl 1, k 2 tog, psso. Repeat from * ending with k 2 (21 sts). **Row 7:** With Periwinkle, k across. **Row 8:** With Periwinkle, k 1, * sl 1, k 2 tog, psso, k 1. Repeat from * across (11 sts). **Row 9:** Knit. Break yarn, leaving 9″ end. Thread end of yarn through remaining sts, draw tight and fasten. Sew ends of rows tog, matching ends of stripes. With Blue Jewel, make 5 lazy daisy sts, covering the 2 center stripes on each decreased point. Make another motif the same, then make 10 more motifs—3RD AND 4TH MOTIFS: Start with Periwinkle; make Periwinkle and Emerald stripes. 5TH AND 6TH MOTIFS: Start with Emerald; make Emerald and Paddy Green stripes. 7TH AND 8TH MOTIFS: Start with Paddy Green; make Paddy Green and Emerald stripes. 9TH AND 10TH MOTIFS: Start with Periwinkle; make Periwinkle and Paddy Green stripes. 11TH AND 12TH MOTIFS: Start with Paddy Green; make Paddy Green and Periwinkle stripes.

Finishing. Embroider all motifs with Blue Jewel lazy daisy sts (see diagram). Using 1 motif of each color combination, sew 5 motifs around 1 motif. Sew sides of the 5 motifs tog where they meet. This completes ½ of ball. Make other half to correspond. Leaving an opening, join the two halves, fitting motifs tog. Insert wadding, sew opening.

Embroidered Feltball

At center in photograph on page 515

Materials. Six-Strand Embroidery Floss—1 skein each of the following colors: Aquatone, Crimson, Signal-red, Orange, Russet, Mermaid-Green, and Nile-Green. Crewel Needle, No. 8. A piece of Beige Felt 8″ x 16″ for small ball or 12″ x 24″ for larger ball. Acrilan Wadding, Tracing Paper and Carbon Paper.

Pattern. Trace designs and outline of the 6 sections (this is for half of the ball; repeat for second half). With carbon paper trace onto the felt.

Embroidery. (See Chapter 2, Embroidery, for stitch diagrams.) Using 3 strands throughout, embroider sections as follows: **1.** Work in daisy stitch. Work center with Signal-red, the 5 large loops with Crimson and stitches inside large loops with Signal-red. Make 2 Orange and 1 Russet stitch between each large loop. Outline center stitches with Crimson. **2.** Work center in Orange French knots and surround with Signal-red daisy stitches. Make Nile-green fly stitch spokes, with Russet French knots at tips. **3.** Work center in Aquatone daisy stitches. Make rows of fly stitch to form star using Yellow, Orange, Red, and Nile-green in that order beginning at center. **4.** Work center in Aquatone French knots and surround with 5 Nile-green daisy stitches. Make 1 Signal-red and 2 Mermaid daisy stitches at tip of each center daisy stitch. Make Aquatone French knots as shown. **5.** Work center in Russet buttonhole stitch. Make Orange and Aquatone daisy stitches alternately around center. Make Orange fly stitches over each Orange daisy stitch and a Mermaid daisy stitch in each fly stitch. **6.** Work center daisy stitches and outline in Russet. Work spokes in Mermaid daisy stitch. Make dotted line in Crimson back stitch, and solid circle with Signal-red stem stitch.

Finishing. Cut sections apart along outlines. To preserve the arrangement, pin the sections together as you cut. Holding wrong sides together and using 3 strands of Russet, overcast edges of the 5 outer sections to the 6th center section as shown. Join side edges of the 5 outer pieces where they meet. Embroider 6 more sections in the same way and sew together as before. Now sew the two halves together, shifting, so that two matching designs do not meet. Leave 3 edges open for stuffing. Insert wadding and sew opening.

Note: This makes a ball approximately 3½″ in diameter. If a larger ball is wanted (5½″ diameter), use the larger pattern.

Crocheted Ball

At left in photograph on page 515

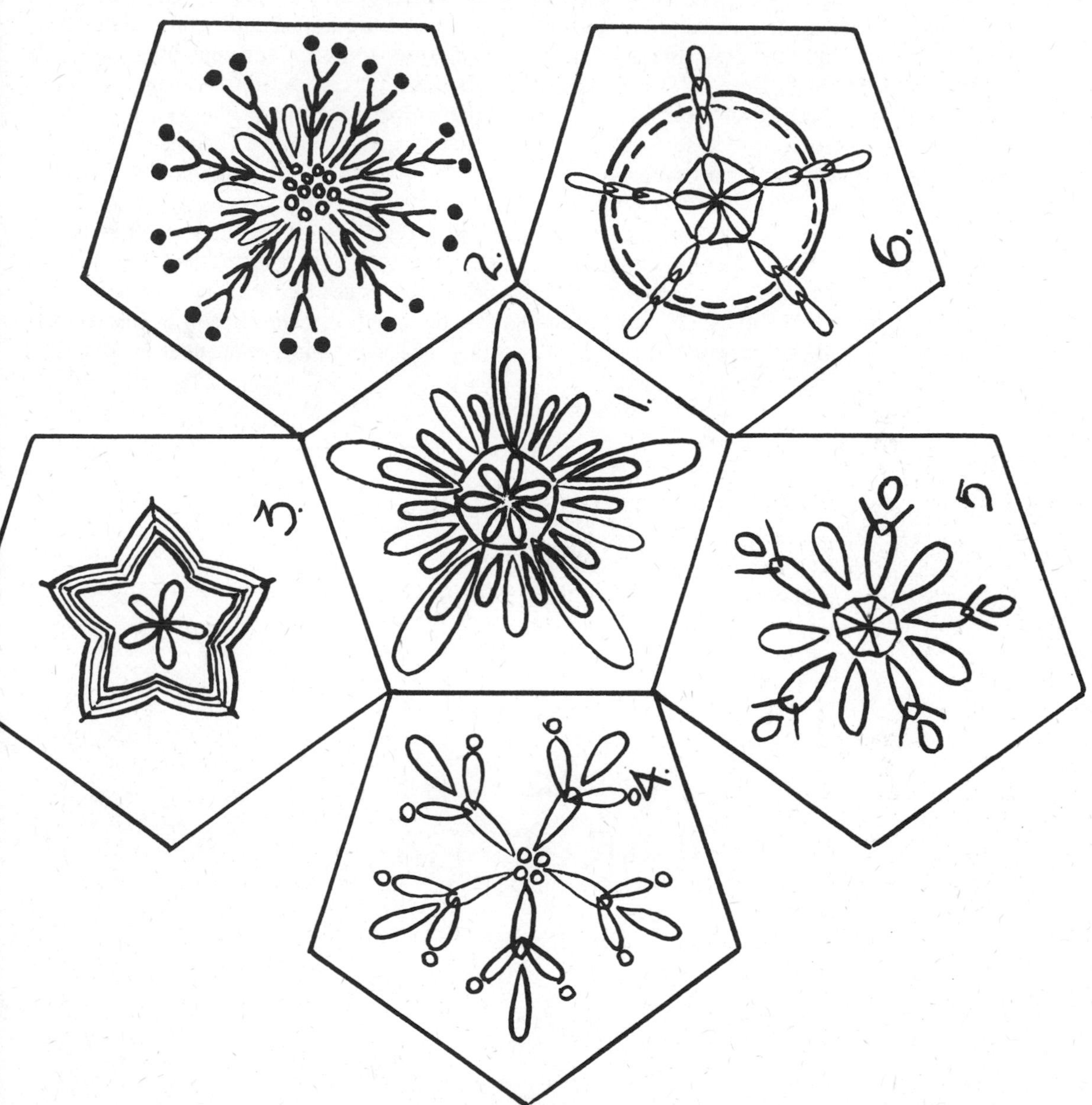

Materials. Super Fingering Yarn—1 skein each Flamingo, Blue Jewel, Yellow. Steel Crochet Hook, No. 1. Acrilan Wadding.

Gauge. Each side of motif—1¼″.

Motifs. 1ST MOTIF: Starting at center with Flamingo, make a loop over 1 finger, insert hook in loop and draw yarn through, ch. 1. **Rnd 1:** Make 10 sc in loop, draw up end of yarn to tighten loop, join with sl st in first sc. Break off and fasten. **Rnd 2:** With Blue, make a loop on hook. Starting in any st except joining, * sc in next sc, 3 sc in next sc.

Repeat from * around (20 sc). Join, break off and fasten. **Rnd 3:** With Yellow, make loop on hook. Starting in any st except joining sc in each sc around (20 sc). Join, break off and fasten. **Rnd 4:** With Flamingo, make loop on hook. Starting in center st over any 3-sc group, * make 3 sc in center st over previous 3-sc group, sc in next 3 sc. Repeat from * around (30 sc). Join, break off and fasten. **Rnd 5:** With Blue, make loop on hook. Starting at center of any 3-sc group, * make 3 sc in center st of 3-sc group, sc in next 5 sc. Repeat from * around (40 sc). Join, break off and fasten. **Rnd 6:** With Yellow, make loop on hook. Starting at center of any 3-sc group, * make 3 sc in center st of 3-sc group, sc in next 7 sc. Repeat from * around (50 sc). Join, break off and fasten. **Rnd 7:** With Flamingo, repeat 3rd rnd. Now make 5 more motifs, using colors as directed.

2ND MOTIF: Start with Flamingo, work Blue and Flamingo alternately for each rnd. 3RD MOTIF: Start with Yellow, use Flamingo and Yellow alternately. 4TH MOTIF: Start with Blue, use Yellow and Blue alternately. 5TH MOTIF: Start with Blue, use Flamingo and Blue alternately. 6TH MOTIF: Start with Yellow, use Blue and Yellow alternately. With right sides together and matching yarn, sew one edge of last 5 motifs to first motif in order given, then sew the sides of last 5 motifs together where they meet. This completes ½ of ball. Make other half exactly the same. Press each half.

Finishing. With right sides together, taking care not to have same motifs meet one another, sew edges of both halves together, until one motif remains unsewn. Insert wadding. sew remaining seam neatly from right side.

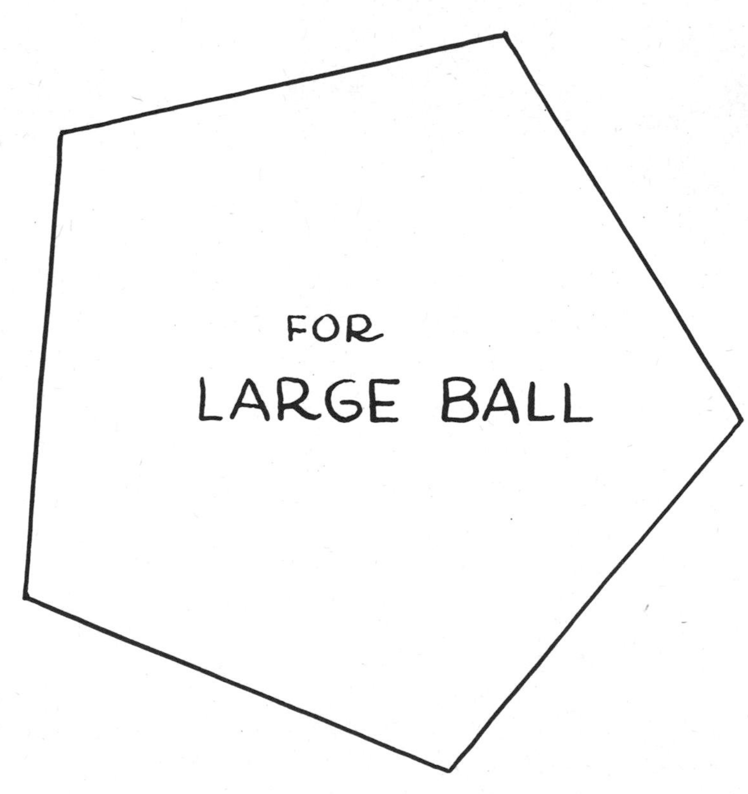

Wound Yarn Ball

Materials. Man's old Cotton Sock. Stuffing and some ordinary String. Odds and ends of Yarn in several colors. (We used 3 colors—Yellow, Orange and Brown.) Large-eyed Needle.

To Make. Cut off toe of sock about 4½″ from end. Turn in edges and run a gathering thread around. Before pulling up, stuff tightly to make as round a ball as possible. Pull up and fasten gathering thread. Mark sides of ball into 6 even sections. Thread needle with ordinary string and after knotting thread, pick up a short stitch at the point opposite gathering. Bring string over one of the markings to gathering point and pick up a stitch. Carry string to starting point over another mark. Continue until all marks are covered with a line of string "spokes." Thread needle with yarn. Make a knot and hide it under gathered edge. Slip needle under first "spoke," then over and under it, then under and over and under the next spoke. Continue around, pulling yarn taut but not tight. Repeat until ball is covered with yarn; each row should lie alongside the last one and completely cover the sock beneath. The color of the yarn may be changed periodically to form stripes or it may be used "hit and miss." Fasten yarn at opposite end after all the surface is covered.

Slippers

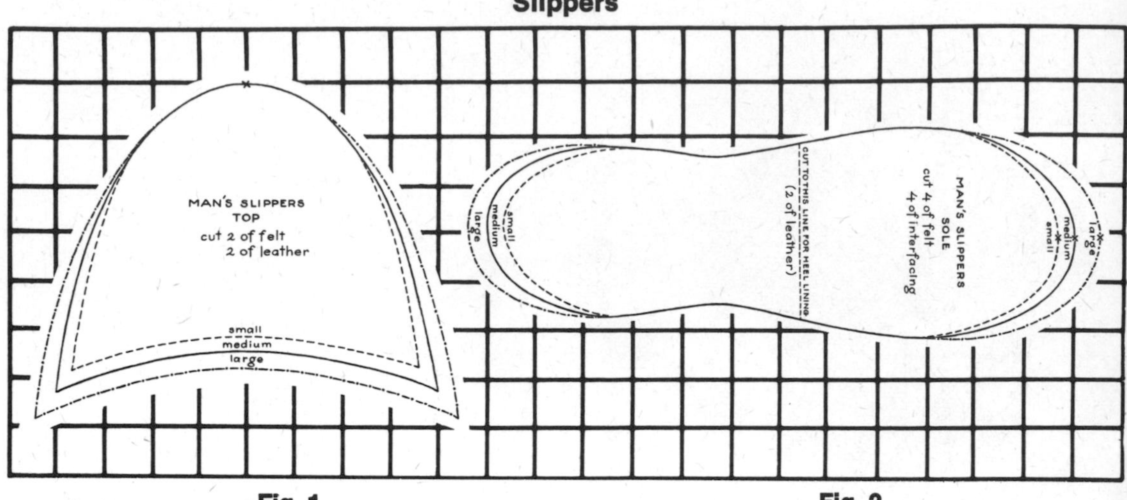

Fig. 1 Fig. 2

Men's Slippers

Materials. ¼ yd. 72″ wide Tan Felt. 2 4″ x 7″, and 2 6″ x 7½″ pieces soft Tan Leather or Suede Cloth. 2 1¾″ x 5½″ strips soft Beige Leather or Suede Cloth. ¼ yd. heaviest-weight nonwoven Interfacing. 1 package medium Brown Bias Tape. Mercerized Sewing Thread to match bias tape. Tracing or Tissue Paper.

Pattern and Cutting. Enlarge pattern in desired size from Figs. 1 and 2 (one square = 1″). Cut out. Cut fabric and leather as marked.

To Make. 1. Stitch tog two interfacing pieces. Place between two felt pieces. Baste together. **2.** Place leather heel lining over sole. Stitch around close to edge (Fig. 3). **3.** Topstitch together one leather top and one felt top close to edge. Center strip of Beige leather over this section; stitch in place along the two straight edges. Cover these edges with a strip of bias tape, stitching along both edges, as in Fig. 4. **4.** Open one edge of bias tape. Right sides tog, stitch to instep edge of top (Fig. 5). Turn bias to wrong side, and hem free edge by hand. **5.** Pin top to sole, as in Fig. 6, matching edges carefully and being sure the two ends of bound edge extend equally over leather part of sole. Stitch around, very close to edge. **6.** Starting at center back, apply bias binding all around slipper, stitching opened edge to right side and taking in all thicknesses of slipper (Fig. 7), lap ends of tape at center back. Hem free edge to bottom of sole (Fig. 8).

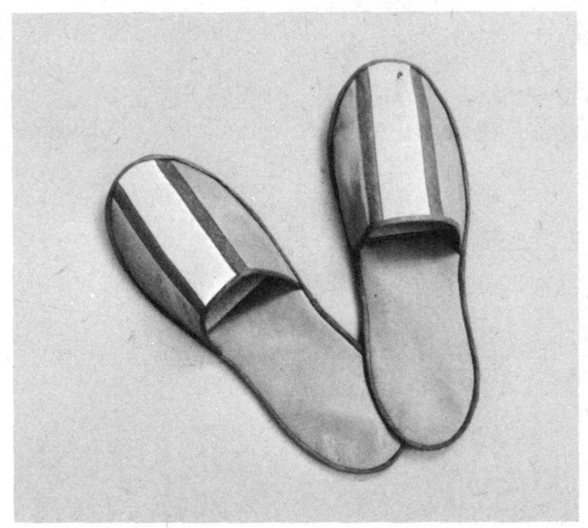

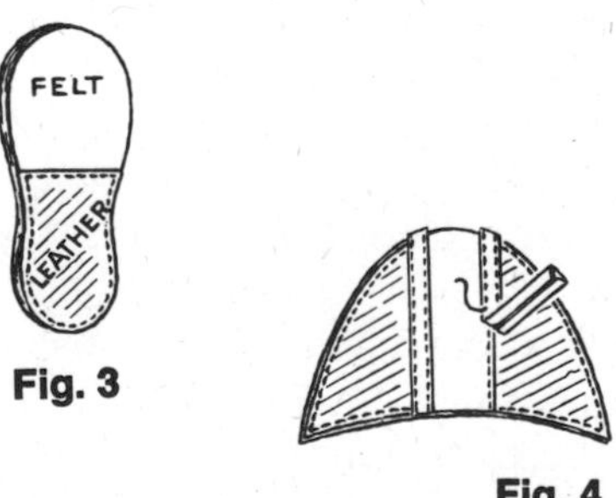

Fig. 3

Fig. 4

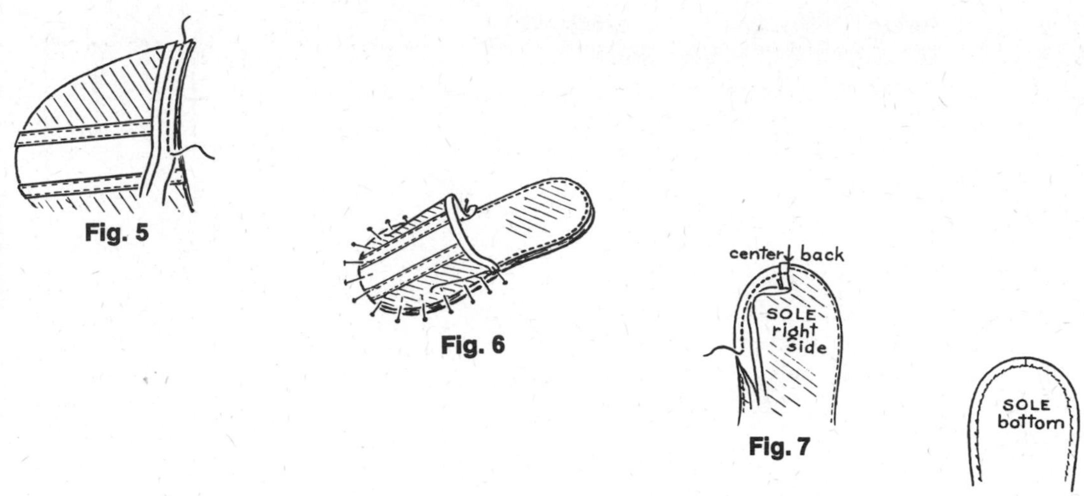

Fig. 5

Fig. 6

Fig. 7

Fig. 8

Women's Slippers

Materials. 1 yd. Gingham. 1 package White baby Rickrack. 1/4 yd. heaviest-weight nonwoven Interfacing. White Mercerized Sewing Thread. 12″ square Cotton Batting. 2 small bunches Artificial Field Flowers. Tissue Paper.

Pattern. Enlarge pattern in desired size from Figs. 1 and 2 (one square = 1″). Cut out.

Cutting. Cut out pieces as marked, following cutting chart for gingham in Fig. 3. From remaining fabric, cut 1″ strips of bias, as shown; total of 4 yds. of strips will be needed for each slipper.

To Make. 1. Place sole pieces together as follows: one gingham, two interfacing, one cotton batting, one gingham. Baste together, edges even. Quilt with stitching lines 1″ apart, as in Fig. 4. **2.** Join bias strips to make 5-yd. length (reserve remainder of bias). Turn in 1/8″ along one edge and apply rickrack, as in Fig. 5. Using ruffler, gather raw edge of strip; you will need about 1 1/2 yds. of ruffling for each slipper. **3.** 1″ in from edge, stitch a row of ruffling around front edge of top (gathered edge is simply stitched down, without being turned under). In applying rows of ruffling, try to use lengths between seam joinings. Apply 2 more rows, each 3/4″ above previous row, as in Fig. 6. **4.** Pin 2nd top piece (lining) to wrong side of 1st piece, with edges even. Run a line of

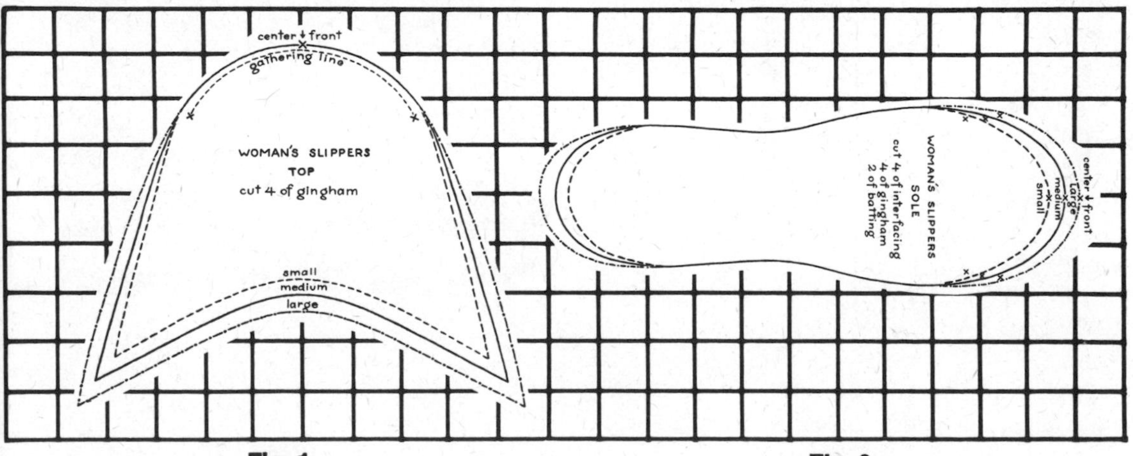

Fig. 1

Fig. 2

gathering st through both layers between x's. **5.** Cut a 20″ long piece of ruffling. Stitch center part along instep edge of top, letting ends extend, as in Fig. 7. Bind this edge with strip of bias (see step 4 in men's slippers, page 520, for application). Stitch a row of rickrack along inside edge of bias. **6.** Pin center front of top to center front of sole (padded side up), raw edges even. Draw up gathers to match x's on sole. Pin around (leaving edges raw, as on men's slippers). Stitch around, taking in ends of bound edge. **7.** Baste ruffle ends around back part of sole, raw edges even, as in Fig. 8. Stitch ends tog at back. Stitch around entire sole. **8.** Bind edges with bias as for men's slippers (see step 6, page 520). Turn ruffle to outside around sole. Stitch rickrack along base of ruffle. **9.** Tack on flowers lightly, for easy removal for laundering.

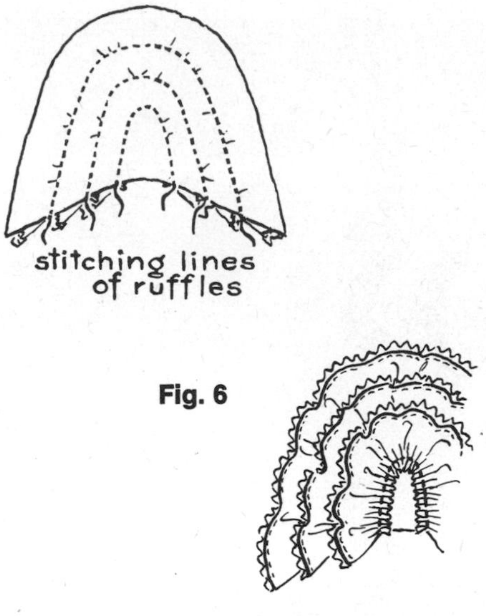

stitching lines of ruffles

Fig. 6

CUTTING CHART ~ GINGHAM

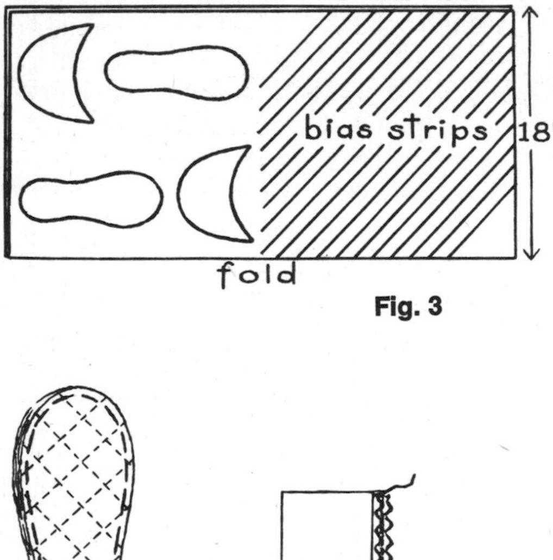

bias strips

18"

fold

Fig. 3

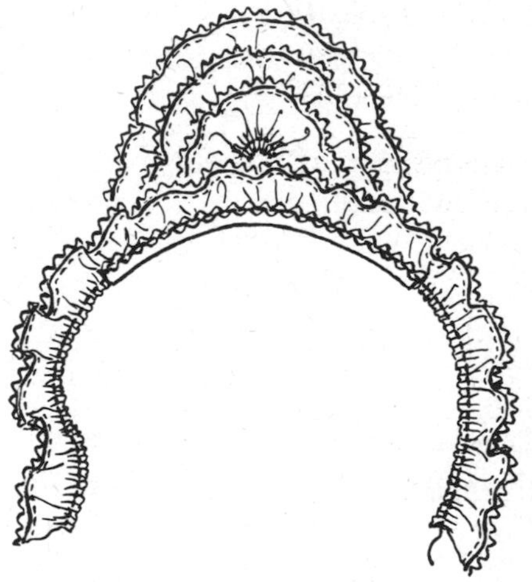

Fig. 7

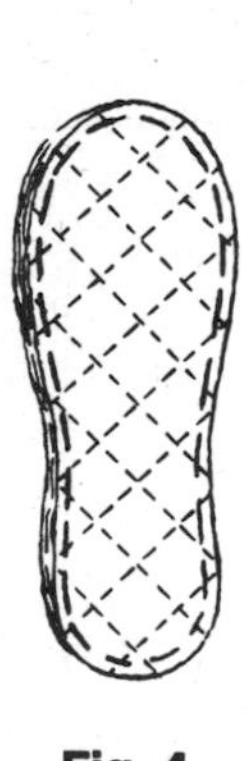

Fig. 4

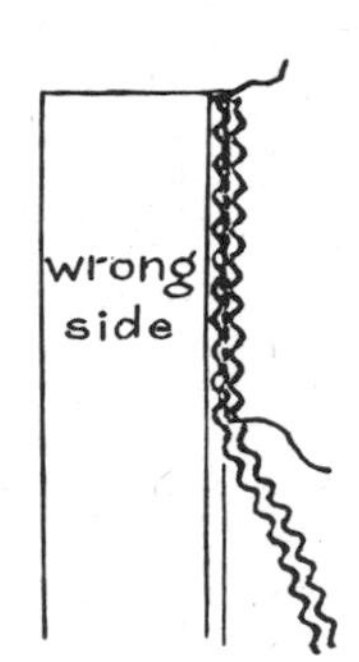

Fig. 5

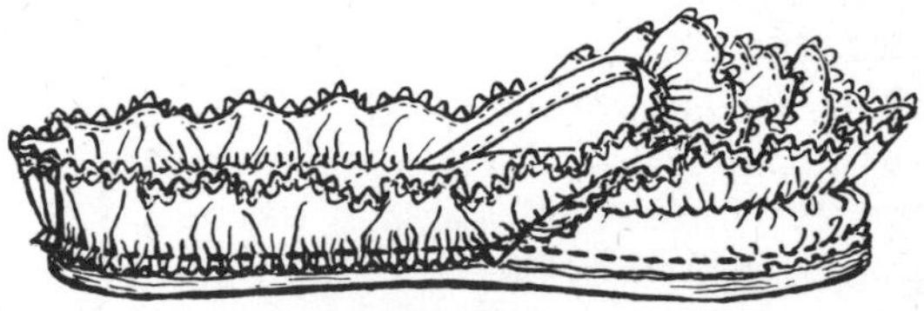

Fig. 8

Tot's Slippers

Materials. ½ yd. Gingham. ¼ yd. nonwoven Interfacing. 9″ square Cotton Batting. 1 package White Rickrack. 1¼ yds. White Bias Tape. White Mercerized Sewing Thread. ½ yd ¼″ wide White Elastic. 2 small bunches Artificial Flowers. Tracing Paper.

Pattern and Cutting. Enlarge pattern, following Figs. 1 and 2 in size desired (one square = 1″). Cut out. From pattern, cut out pieces as marked. From remaining gingham, cut two 1¾″ x 14″ strips for straps and four 1½ x 10″ bias strips for trimming.

To Make. 1. Prepare sole as directed for woman's slippers (page 521), making quilting lines ¾″ apart. **2.** To prepare straps, fold straight gingham strips in half lengthwise; fold edges in ¼″, and topstitch together. Insert a 6″ length of elastic, letting fabric gather. Stitch ends. **3.** Pin ends of strap to instep edge of slipper top, ½″ in from side edges, as in Fig. 3. With strap between, pin second top piece over first. Stitch ¼″ seam. **4.** Turn right side out; fold on seamed edge, and topstitch. Stitch rickrack over topstitching, as in Fig. 4. **5.** Pin top piece to sole, matching x's at center front. Stitch and bind with bias tape as for men's slippers, step 6, page 520. **6.** Turn under ¼″ along one edge of bias strip; stitch on rickrack, as in Fig. 5. Repeat for all strips. **7.** Seam together ends of bias strips, forming 2 rings for each slipper. Gather raw edge of bias strips to form rosettes; pull up gathers so that 2 rosettes are slightly smaller than other 2. Place smaller rosette on top of larger, as in Fig. 6; attach to slipper top. **8.** Tack on flowers lightly, for easy removal for laundering.

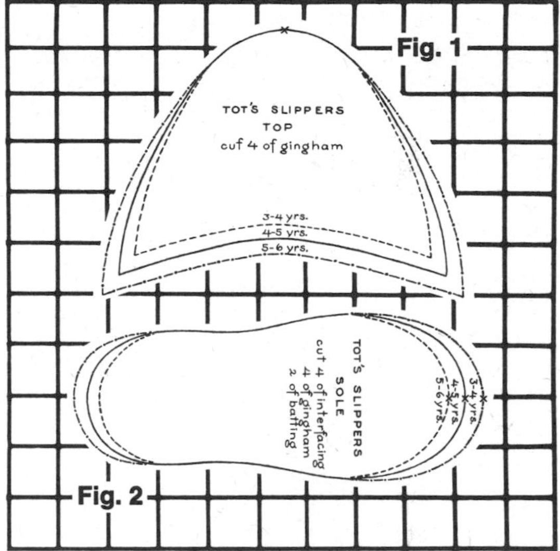

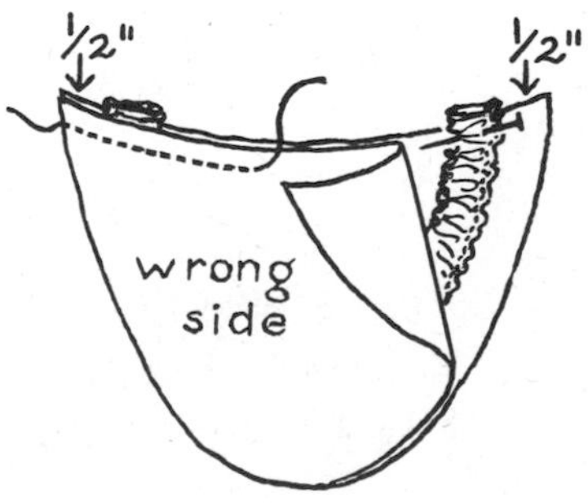

Fig. 3

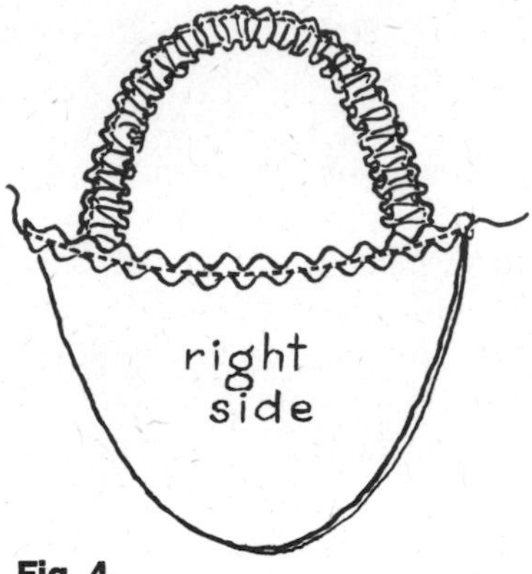

Fig. 4

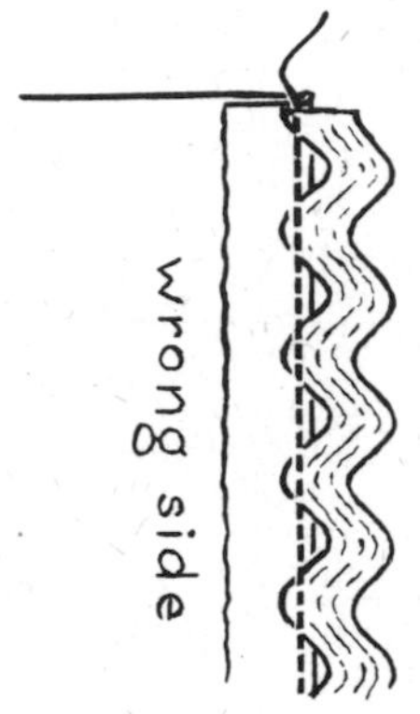

Fig. 5

Fig. 6

Baby's Slippers

Materials. 8″ x 11″ piece of Red-and-White Dotted Cotton. 8″ x 11″ piece of White Cotton. 6″ square Cotton Batting. 1 package White Bias Tape. Mercerized Sewing Thread, 1 spool Red, 1 spool White. 3″ piece ¾″ wide White Elastic. Tissue Paper.

Quilting. Cut out one 6″ square each from dotted and white cottons. Place batting between, as in Fig. 1. Quilt diagonally in ½″ squares.

Pattern and Cutting. Pattern is given in 2 sizes (Figs. 2 and 3). Enlarge the desired one on tissue paper (one square = 1″). Cut out. Cut fabric as marked (be sure to cut soles facing each other—left and right) on Fig. 4.

To Make. SOLES: Bind soles with bias tape, as in Fig. 4. TOPS (make ¼″ seams): **1.** Cut elastic into two 1½″ pieces. Cut two 1½″ x 2″ pieces of White fabric. Fold fabric over elastic, as in Fig. 5; stretching elastic while stitching, topstitch by machine. Make 2 more lines of stitching, as shown. **2.** Attach elastic to top fabric as follows: Clip corners of inside edge of top, as shown (inset), not quite through seam allowance. Baste and stitch raw edges of elastic piece to top, following shape of top, as in Fig. 6. **3.** Right sides facing, place top fabric and lining together. Stitch inside edges together, stopping short of elastic (see Fig. 7). Press seams open. **4.** Open section flat; pin and stitch back seam, as in Fig. 8. Press seam open. **5.** Fold lining to inside on stitching line. Clip corners of lining; turn raw edges in, and hem to elastic piece as in Fig. 9. Press. **6.** Beginning at center back seam, bind together bottom edges with bias tape, same as for sole.

To Assemble: 1. With top section and sole wrong sides out, pin together edges all around, matching center back and front. Whip bias tapes together securely by hand (Fig. 10). Turn to right side. **2.** Cut two 15″ lengths of bias tape. Fold and stitch edges together. Tack to back seam of slipper (see Fig. 11).

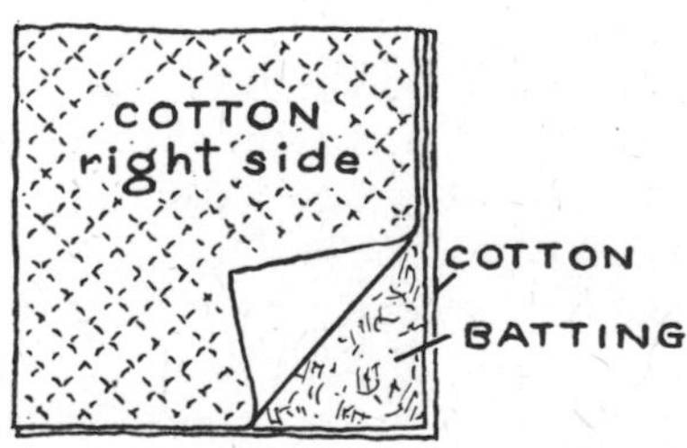

Fig. 1

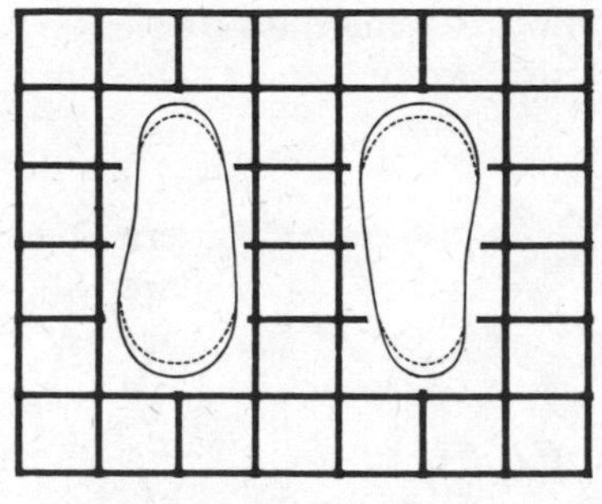
Fig. 2

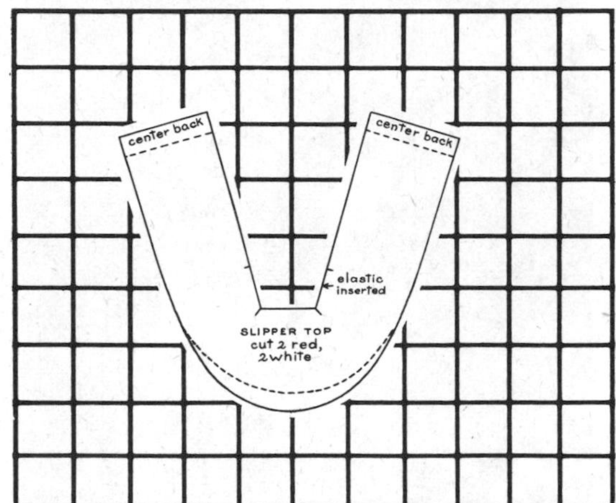

Fig. 3

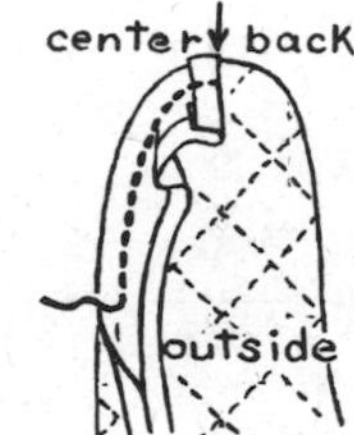

Fig. 4

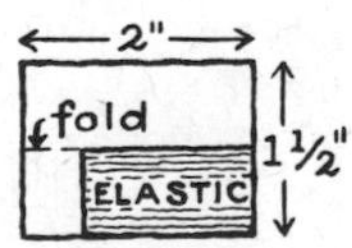

Fig. 5

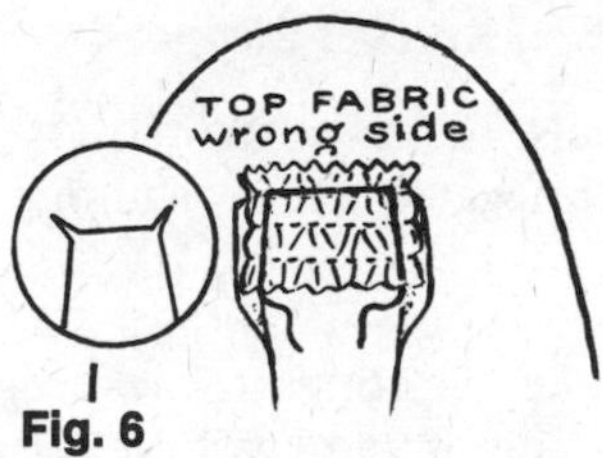

Fig. 6

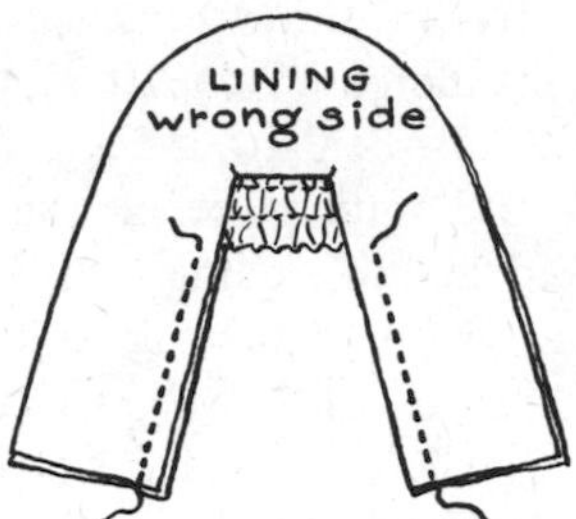

Fig. 7

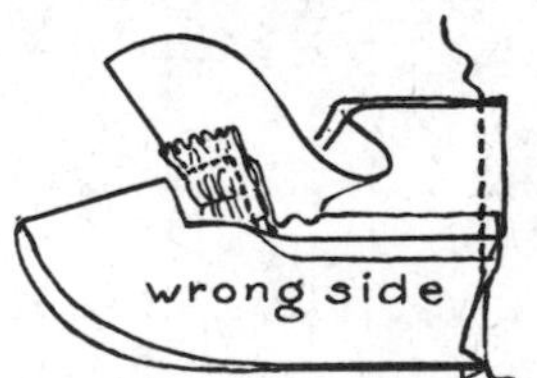

Fig. 8

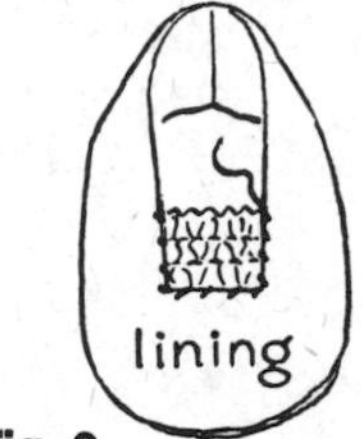

Fig. 9

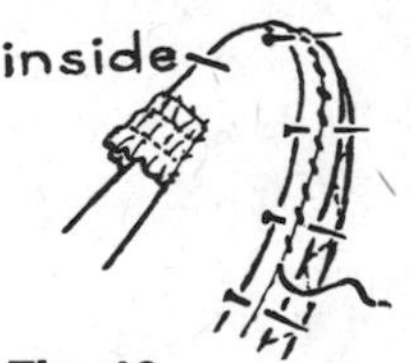

Fig. 10

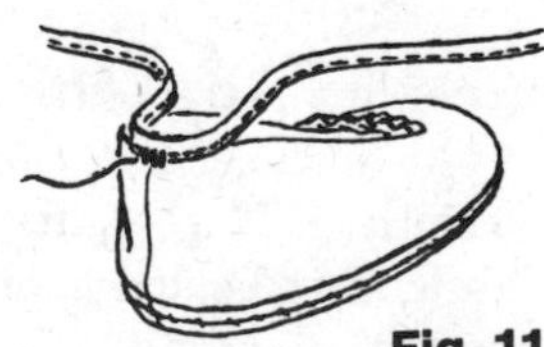
Fig. 11

Knitted Slippers

Materials. Knitting Worsted—two 2-oz. skeins Variegated Rose. Knitting Needles, No. 10½.

Gauge. 3½ sts—1″. 4 rows—1″.

To Make. Starting at back edge with a double strand of yarn, cast on 22 sts. **Row 1** (wrong side): P 10; * k 5 in next st working alternately from front and back; repeat from * once (8 sts increased); p 10. **Row 2:** K 10, p 10, k 10. **Row 3:** P 10, k 10, p 10. Repeat Rows 2 and 3 until piece measures 2″ less than desired length, ending with Row 3. TO SHAPE TOE: **Row 1:** K 2 tog, p 2, k 2, p 2, k 2; p 10; k 2, p 2, k 2, p 2, k 2 tog. **Row 2:** P 2 tog, k 1, p 2, k 2, p 2; k 10, p 2, k 2, p 2, k 1, p 2 tog. **Row 3:** K 2 tog, k 2, p 2, k 2, p 10, k 2, p 2, k 2, k 2 tog. **Row 4:** P 2 tog, p 1, k 2, p 2, k 10, p 2, k 2, p 1, p 2 tog. **Row 5:** K 2 tog, p 2, k 2, p 10, k 2, p 2, k 2 tog. **Row 6:** P 2 tog, k 1, p 2, k 10, p 2, k 1, p 2 tog. **Row 7:** K 2 tog, k 2, p 10, k 2, k 2 tog. **Row 8:** P 2 tog, p 1, k 10, p 1, p 2 tog. **Row 9:** K 2 tog, p 10, k 2 tog. **Row 10:** P 2 tog, k 8, p 2 tog. Slip remaining sts on a strand of yarn. FINISHING: Draw up the strand at end tightly and fasten securely. Sew back seam. Sew dec edges of toe and next 2″ of sides together. Wind double strand 50 times over 5″ cardboard. Cut strands at each edge and tie together at center. Sew pompon to center of vamp.

Log Carrier

Materials. Two 1¼ yd. pieces of heavy Cotton Fabric—one for the outside, one for the lining (ours is striped outside, solid inside). Heavy-duty Thread to match. Two Dowel Sticks, 23″ long and ¾″ thick. Carpet Tacks.

Pattern. Make your own of heavy paper to the measurements given on our diagram at right.

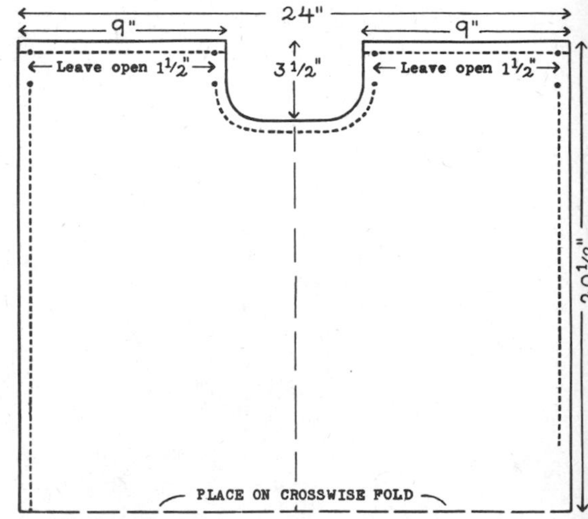

Log Carrier Pattern

Cutting. Place pattern on crosswise fold of fabric as indicated in diagram; cut pieces for outside and lining.

To Make. (½″ seam allowance throughout): With right sides together, place lining to outer fabric and stitch all sides as indicated on pattern. Be sure to leave openings at top sides for dowel sticks and on one edge for turning right side out. Press seam allowance at topside openings and slip-stitch in place. Trim seams, clip curves and corners, turn right side out and press. Close side opening with slip stitching. Insert dowels through tops. Using carpet tacks, secure tops to dowel sticks on lining side.

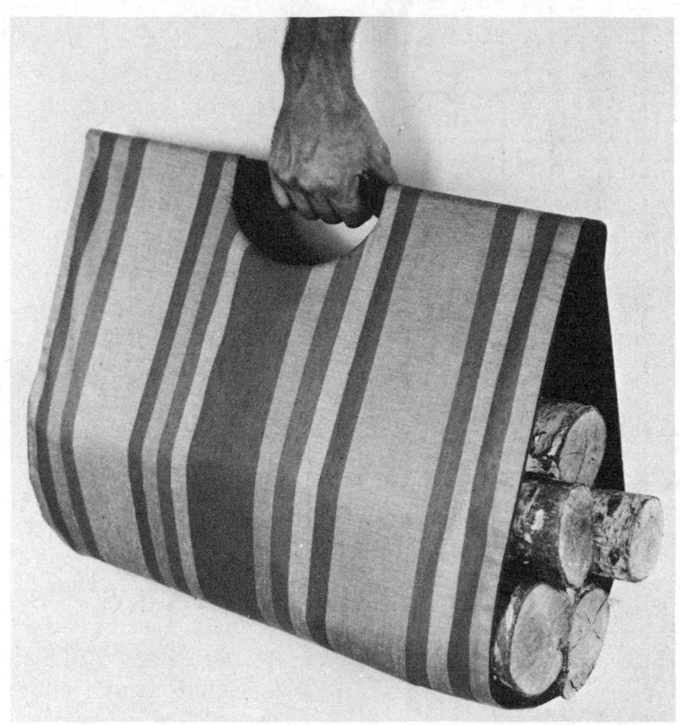

Hand Puppets

Chipmunk

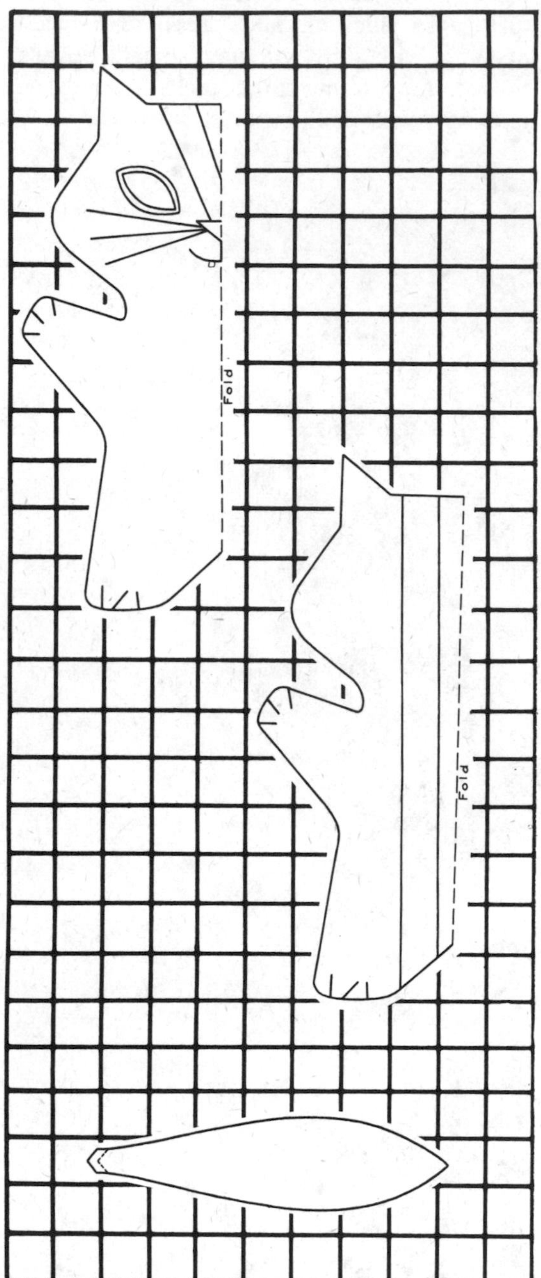

Materials. 12″ x 18″ piece of Golden-Brown Felt. Brown, White, and Black Plastic Tape.

Pattern. FRONT: Fold a piece of paper, and enlarge outline, face, and claws (one square = 1″). BACK: With another piece of paper, following same procedure, enlarge outline, tail, and claws.

Cutting. Using patterns, cut front, back, and tail out of felt.

To Make. Sew tail to lower back, overlapping ¼″. Lay front of puppet on back. Leaving lower edge open, pin and stitch around by hand or machine ¼″ from edge.

Make patterns for nose, entire eye and inside (pupil), and forehead stripes; cut plastic tape—BROWN: whiskers (very narrow strips), inside of eye, and forehead stripes. BLACK: nose, mouth, claws (narrow strips). WHITE: teeth and outside eye (cut large eye of white, and stick brown inside eye on top). Stick tape pieces on the felt, following diagram. On back of chipmunk, stick two stripes of brown tape the full length (see diagram).

Space-Man Puppet I

Materials. 12½″ x 20″ piece of Red Felt. 6″ x 2½″ piece of Gold Felt. 3″ x 4½″ piece of Gray Felt. Scraps of Pink, White, and Black Felt. 7″ Blue by-the-yard Sequins. 2 Blue Glass Buttons, ¼″ diameter. 1 large Gold oval or round Sequin. Tracing Paper.

Pattern. (9 pieces) BACK: Fold a piece of paper and enlarge outline of body and head of spaceman (one square = 1″), omitting scalloped hair. Then turn paper over, and complete body outline. FRONT: With another piece of paper, follow same procedure as above and enlarge the face, mouth, scalloped hair, collar, medallion in middle front, and body outline, only as far up as top of collar (indicated by dotted line). Make a pattern of large oval for eye and the larger circle for pupil. Smaller circle indicates location of glass button.

Cutting. Use scalloping and pinking shears where indicated. Cut back, front body, and face out of Red felt. Cut mouth and medallion out of Pink felt. Cut hair out of Gold felt. Cut eyes out of White felt and pupils out of Black felt. Cut collar out of Gray felt.

To Make. Pin collar in place over front body piece; pin face to top of collar, as in diagram, and stitch. Pin together, matching ears of front and back pieces. Slip scalloped hairpiece between front and back at top, as

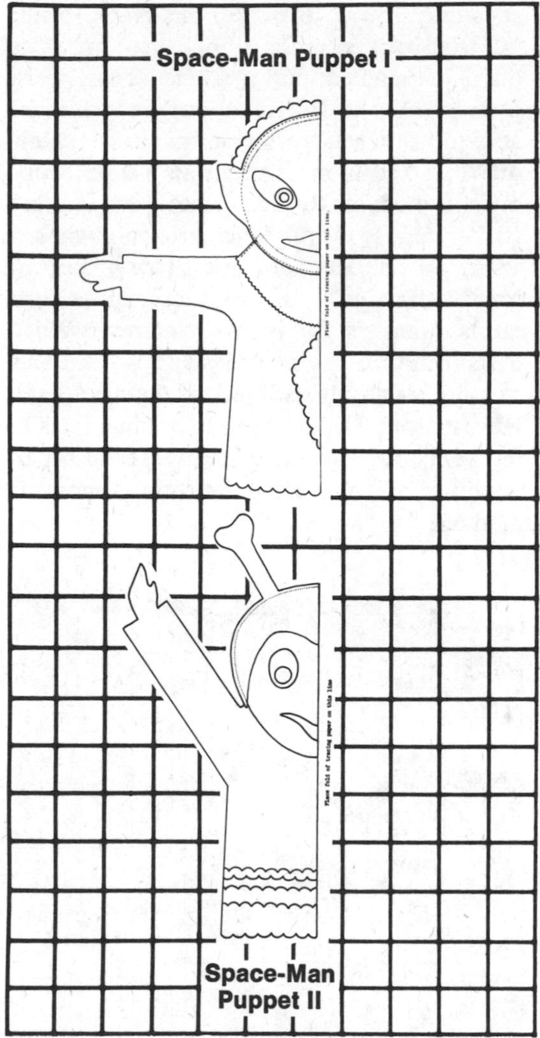

in diagram. Stitch all around edge, leaving scalloped bottom open. With fabric adhesive, glue features in place; glue medallion on front. Stitch or glue string of sequins near pinked edge of collar. Sew glass buttons on eyes. Sew or glue gold sequin in middle of forehead.

Space-Man Puppet II

Materials. 21″ x 23″ piece of Dark-Green Felt. 5″ x 6″ piece of Chartreuse Felt. 1″ x 5″ piece of Blue Felt. Scraps of White and Fuchsia Felt. 2 Blue Glass Buttons, ½″ diameter. Tracing Paper.

Pattern. Fold a piece of paper and enlarge outline of body (one square = 1″). Remove paper, turn paper over, and complete body outline.

In same manner, make patterns for face (top indicated by dotted line), helmet, mouth, and oval for eyes (circle in center of eyes may be of felt or glass buttons).

Cutting. Use scalloping shears where indicated and cut 2 body pieces and helmet out of Dark-Green felt. Cut face and two ½″ x 5″ scalloped strips out of Chartreuse felt (use scalloping shears for strips). Cut large ovals of White felt for eyes. Cut mouth out of Fuchsia felt. Cut 2 ¼″ x 5″ scalloped strips out of Blue felt.

To Make. Glue face to head. Pin helmet in place over face. Pin front body piece to back body piece; stitch all around edge, leaving scalloped bottom open. Glue features and trimmings in place.

Dog Coat

Measurements are based on length of dog from base of neck to base of tail. Directions are for 13″ length. Changes for 15″ and 17″ lengths are in parentheses.

Materials. Knitting Worsted—1-oz. skeins: 4 (5–5) skeins of Main Color (MC). One ⅓-oz. skein of Contrasting Color (CC). Knitting Needles, No. 5 (or size required to obtain the specified gauge). 4 Buttons.

Gauge. 5 sts—1″. 7 rows—1″.

Back Section. Starting at back edge with MC, cast on 25 (27, 29) sts. Work in moss st as follows: **Row 1:** K 1; * p 1, k 1; repeat from * across. **Row 2:** P and k in first st; * p 1, k 1; repeat from * to last st, k and p in last st. **Row 3:** P 1; * k 1, p 1; repeat from * across. **Row 4:** K and p in first st; * k 1, p 1; repeat from * to last st, p and k in last st. **Rows 5 through 8:** Repeat rows 1 through 4; there are 33 (35, 37) sts. **Row 9:** Work in moss st across first 6 sts; to last 6 sts; work moss st to end of row. **Row 10:** Work 6 sts in moss st, inc 1 st in next st, p to last 7 sts, inc 1 st in next st, work 6 sts in moss st. Repeat rows 9 and 10 for 17 (18, 19) more times. Keeping 6 sts at each edge in moss st and remaining sts in stockinette st as before, work even on 69 (73, 77) sts until total length is 8″ (9″, 10″), ending with a p row. Draw dog's name on graph paper; count the number of sts in each letter and 1 st for each space between letters; mark off this number of sts at center of last row. Following chart, work sts of letters in CC; always carry strands *very* loosely across wrong side of work when not in use and pick up new strand from underneath dropped strand to avoid leaving a hole between colors. When name has been completed, work even as before until total length is 12″ (14″, 16″), ending with a row on wrong side.

Neck. Row 1: Work 6 sts in moss st; k 14 (15, 16); work center 29 (31, 33) sts in moss st; k 14 (15, 16); work 6 sts in moss st. **Row 2:** Work 6 sts in moss st, p 14 (15, 16); work 29 (31, 33) sts in moss st, p. 14 (15, 16); work 6 sts in moss st. **Rows 3 through 8:** Repeat rows 1 and 2. **Row 9:** Work 6 sts in moss st; p 14 (15, 16); work 6 sts in moss st; bind off center 17 (19, 21) sts; complete row. Work the last set of sts as follows: **Row 1:** Work 6 sts in moss st; p to last 6 sts; work 6 sts in moss st. **Row 2:** Work 6 sts in moss st; k 2 tog; k to last 6 sts; work 6 sts in moss st. Repeat these 2 rows until 13 sts remain. Dec 1 st at center of every row 6 times. Bind off remaining 7 sts. Starting at opposite neck edge, work other side to correspond, making dec at neck side.

Chest Section. Starting at back edge, cast on 75 (81, 87) sts. Work in moss st for 8 rows. Now work as follows: **Row 1:** Bind off 10 (11, 12) sts; work in moss st until there are 6 sts on right hand needle; k 2 tog, k to last 18 (19, 20) sts, k 2 tog; work in moss st to end of row. **Row 2:** Bind off 10 ((11, 12) sts; work in moss st until there are 6 sts on right hand needle; p to last 6 sts, work 6 sts in moss st. **Row 3:** Work 6 sts in moss st; k to last 6 sts; work 6 sts in moss st. **Row 4:** Work 6 sts in moss st; p to last 6 sts; work 6 sts in moss st. **Row 5:** Work 6 sts in moss st; k 2 tog; k to last 8 sts, k 2 tog; work 6 sts in moss st. **Row 6:** Repeat row 4. Repeat rows 3 through 6 until 21 sts remain. Work all sts in moss st for 4 rows. **Next row:** Work 3 sts, bind off the next 3 sts; * work 3 sts beyond bound-off sts; bind off the next 3 sts. Repeat from * once; work remaining sts. On the next row, cast on 3 sts over each set of bound-off sts. Work 3 more rows in moss st; bind off.

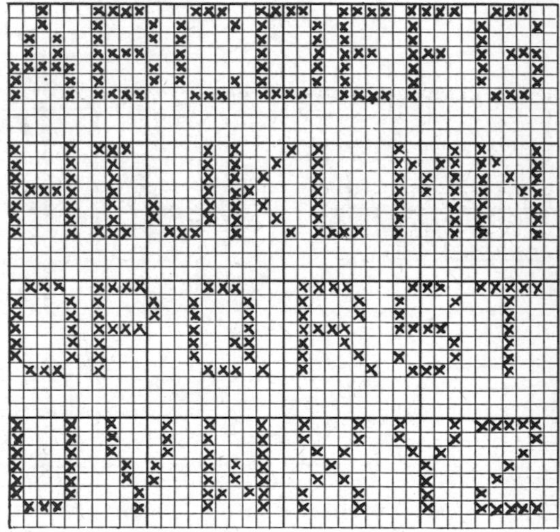

Finishing. Block pieces. Sew a button to end of one tab on chest section; make buttonloop on end of other tab. Sew a button to one point of shoulder on back section; make buttonloop on opposite point. Sew remaining 2 buttons 1″ from neck button on each side. Button chest section to these 3 buttons.

Easy-to-Make Scarf

Directions are for Man's Scarf. Changes for Woman's Scarf are in parentheses.

Materials. Mohair—4 balls. Knitting Needles, No. 7.

Measurements:

Man's .... Approximately 6″ x 42″ without fringe

Woman's ..... Approximately 7″ x 46″ without fringe

Gauge. 7 sts—1″.

Pattern. Cast on 37 (43) sts. **Row 1:** Wrong side. P 1, * k 1 inserting needles into back of st, p 1. Repeat from * to end. **Row 2:** K 1 inserting needle into back of st, * p 1, k 1 as before. Repeat from * to end. Repeat these 2 rows for pattern until 42 (46)″ from beginning. Bind off. Steam lightly.

Fringe. Wind yarn 114 (132) times around 2 (2¾)″ cardboard. Cut at one side. Beginning at cast-on end, knot 3 strands of yarn in 1st stitch and every 2nd stitch to end. Knot fringe in same way at other end. Trim evenly. Steam lightly.

Ski Headband

Materials. Fingering Yarn—1 oz. Knitting Needles, 1 pair each Nos. 1 and 3.

Gauge. 9 sts—1″ (with No. 1 needles).

To Make. With No. 1 needles, cast on 35 sts. **Row 1** (right side): K 1; * p 1, k 1; repeat from * across row. **Row 2:** P 1; * k 1, p 1; repeat from * across row. Repeat these two rows until work measures 2¾″. Change to No. 3 needles, and continue in ribbing for 3½″. Change to No. 1 needles, and work even for 4½″. Change to No. 3 needles, and work even for 3½″. Change to No. 1 needles, and work even for 2¾″; bind off in ribbing. STRAPS: (make 2—optional): With No. 1 needles, cast on 13 sts. Work in k 1, p 1 ribbing for 7½″. Bind off in ribbing. Sew headband tog. Sew straps to inside of top edge as pictured.

Index